The Sporting News

COMPLETE BASEBALL RECORD BOOK

1995 EDITION

Editor / Complete Baseball Record Book
CRAIG CARTER

The Sporting News

— PUBLISHING CO. —

Francis P. Pandolfi, Chairman and Chief Executive Officer; **Nicholas H. Niles,** President; **John D. Rawlings,** Editorial Director; **Kathy Kinkeade,** Vice President/Production; **Mike Nahrstedt,** Managing Editor; **Mike Huguenin,** Assistant Managing Editor; **Joe Hoppel,** Senior Editor; **Tom Dienhart and Dave Sloan,** Associate Editors; **Craig Carter,** Statistical Editor; **George Puro and Kyle Veltrop,** Assistant Editors; **Fred Barnes,** Director of Graphics; **Steve Levin,** Photo Editor; **Gary Brinker,** Director/Information Systems; **Bob Parajon,** Prepress Director; **Marilyn Kasal,** Production Manager; **Michael Bruner,** Graphics Network Manager; **Patrick Kolieboi,** Network Manager; **Vern Kasal,** Composing Room Supervisor; **Gary Levy,** Special Projects Editor.

A Times Mirror
Company

ISBN: 0-89204-515-9 (perfect-bound)
      0-89204-518-3 (comb-bound)

10 9 8 7 6 5 4 3 2 1

CONTENTS

ON THE COVER: First baseman Jeff Bagwell of the Houston Astros tied a major league record on June 24, 1994, by hitting two home runs in one inning. (Photo by Tom DiPace)

NOTES ON MAJOR LEAGUE RECORDS

Records noted in this book refer to the following leagues: M.L.—major leagues, 1876 to date; N.L.—National League, 1876 to date; A.A.—American Association, 1882 to 1891; U.A.—Union Association, 1884; P.L.—Players League, 1890; A.L.—American League, 1901 to date. This book does not include the Federal League of 1914 and 1915 as a major league.

Fewest-for-leader records are for seasons when 154 games or 162 games were scheduled, except for pitchers.

Two games in one day (a.m. and p.m.) are included with doubleheader records.

American League and National League records are based on a 154-game schedule, but if the feat was surpassed since the adoption of a 162-game schedule, records for both lengths of schedules are listed. For example, Roger Maris' 61 home runs in a 162-game season and Babe Ruth's 60 home runs in a 154-game season are both included as A.L. entries under the category, "Most home runs, season." Hack Wilson's 56 home runs in a 154-game season is the lone N.L. entry in this category because Willie Mays' and George Foster's 52-homer seasons (the best N.L. efforts in 162-game seasons) represent lower totals in longer seasons.

References to 154- and 162-game seasons refer to the following years:

	National League	American League
154-game season	1901-1961	1901-1960
162-game season	1962-present	1961-present

Similarly, league records are listed for 8-, 10-, 12- and 14-club leagues unless the number achieved with a larger number of clubs is lower than that of the record for a smaller number of clubs.

References to 8-, 10-, 12- and 14-club leagues refer to the following years:

	National League	American League
8-club league	1901-1961	1901-1960
10-club league	1962-1968	1961-1968
12-club league	1969-1992	1969-1976
14-club league	1993-present	1977-present

In years when many games were canceled because of player strikes (1972, 1981 and 1994), club and league records for fewest are omitted.

REGULAR SEASON

Service (Individual, Club, League)

Batting (Individual, Club, League)

Baserunning (Individual, Club, League)

Pitching (Individual, Club, League)

Fielding (Individual, Club, League)

Miscellaneous (Individual, Club, League)

Non-Playing Personnel

Yearly Leaders

Career Milestones

General Reference

American League Team Records

National League Team Records

INDIVIDUAL SERVICE

ALL PLAYERS

YEARS

Most years played

M.L.—27—Nolan Ryan, New York, Houston N.L.; California, Texas A.L.; 1966 through 1993, except 1967 (14 in N.L., 13 in A.L.), 807 games.

A.L.—25—Eddie Collins, Philadelphia, Chicago, 1906 through 1930, 2,826 games.

N.L.—24—Pete Rose, Cincinnati, Philadelphia, Montreal, 1963 through 1986, 3,562 games.

Most consecutive years played

M.L.—26—Nolan Ryan, New York, Houston N.L.; California, Texas A.L.; 1968 through 1993 (13 in N.L., 13 in A.L.), 805 games.

A.L.—25—Eddie Collins, Philadelphia, Chicago, 1906 through 1930, 2,826 games.

N.L.—24—Pete Rose, Cincinnati, Philadelphia, Montreal, 1963 through 1986, 3,562 games.

Most years with one club

A.L.—23

Brooks Robinson, Baltimore, 1955 through 1977, 2,896 games.

Carl Yastrzemski, Boston, 1961 through 1983, 3,308 games.

N.L.—22

Cap Anson, Chicago, 1876 through 1897, 2,253 games.

Mel Ott, New York, 1926 through 1947, 2,730 games.

Stan Musial, St. Louis, 1941 through 1963, except 1945 in military service, 3,026 games.

Most consecutive years with one club

A.L.—23

Brooks Robinson, Baltimore, 1955 through 1977, 2,896 games.

Carl Yastrzemski, Boston, 1961 through 1983, 3,308 games.

N.L.—22

Cap Anson, Chicago, 1876 through 1897, 2,253 games.

Mel Ott, New York, 1926 through 1947, 2,730 games.

(Military service in 1945 interrupted a 22-year streak by Stan Musial, who played for St. Louis from 1941 through 1963, 3,026 games.)

BY POSITION (EXCEPT PITCHERS)

Most years by first baseman

N.L.—22—Willie McCovey, San Francisco, San Diego, 1959 through 1980, 2,045 games.

A.L.—20—Joe Judge, Washington, Boston, 1915 through 1934, 2,084 games.

Most years by second baseman

M.L.—22—Joe Morgan, Houston N.L., Cincinnati N.L., San Francisco N.L., Philadelphia N.L., Oakland A.L., 1963 through 1984, 2,527 games.

A.L.—21—Eddie Collins, Philadelphia, Chicago, 1908 through 1928, 2,651 games.

N.L.—21—Joe Morgan, Houston, Cincinnati, San Francisco, Philadelphia, 1963 through 1983, 2,427 games.

Most years by third baseman

A.L.—23—Brooks Robinson, Baltimore, 1955 through 1977, 2,870 games.

N.L.—18—Mike Schmidt, Philadelphia, 1972 through 1989, 2,212 games.

Most years by shortstop

M.L.—20

Bill Dahlen, Chicago N.L., Brooklyn N.L., New York N.L., Boston N.L., 1891 through 1911, except 1910, 2,139 games.

Bobby Wallace, St. Louis N.L., St. Louis A.L., 1899 through 1918, 1,828 games.

Luke Appling, Chicago A.L., 1930 through 1950, except 1944 in military service, 2,218 games.

A.L.—20—Luke Appling, Chicago, 1930 through 1950, except 1944 in military service, 2,219 games.

N.L.—20—Bill Dahlen, Chicago, Brooklyn, New York, Boston, 1891 through 1911, except 1910, 2,139 games.

N.L. since 1900—19

Rabbit Maranville, Boston, Pittsburgh, Chicago, Brooklyn, St. Louis, 1912 through 1931, except 1924, 2,153 games.

Dave Concepcion, Cincinnati, 1970 through 1988, 2,178 games.

Chris Speier, San Francisco, Montreal, St. Louis, Chicago, 1971 through 1989, 1,888 games.

Most years by outfielder

A.L.—24—Ty Cobb, Detroit, Philadelphia, 1905 through 1928, 2,938 games.

N.L.—22—Willie Mays, original New York club, San Francisco, present New York club, 1951 through 1973, except 1953 in military service, 2,843 games.

Most years by catcher

M.L.—25—Deacon McGuire, Toledo, Cleveland, Rochester, Washington A.A.; Detroit, Philadelphia, Washington, Brooklyn N.L.; Detroit, New York, Boston, Cleveland A.L., 1884 through 1912, except 1889, 1908, 1909, 1911, 1,608 games.

A.L.—24—Carlton Fisk, Boston, Chicago, 1969 through 1993, except 1970, 2,226 games.

N.L.—21—Bob O'Farrell, Chicago, St. Louis, New York, Cincinnati, 1915 through 1935, 1,338 games.

YOUNGEST AND OLDEST PLAYERS

Youngest player, game

N.L.—15 years, 10 months, 11 days—Joe Nuxhall, Cincinnati, June 10, 1944 (pitcher).

A.L.—16 years, 8 months, 5 days—Carl Scheib, Philadelphia, September 6, 1943, second game (pitcher).

Oldest player, game

A.L.—59 years, 2 months, 18 days—Satchel Paige, Kansas City, September 25, 1965 (pitcher).

N.L.—52 years, 29 days—Jim O'Rourke, New York, September 22, 1904 (catcher).

LEAGUES AND CLUBS

Most leagues played for, career

4—Held by 20 players. Last time—Lave Cross, A.A., P.L., N.L., A.L., 1887 through 1907, 21 years, 2,259 games.

Most leagues played for, season

3—Willie Murphy, 1884, N.L., A.A., U.A.

Walter Prince, 1884, N.L., A.A., U.A.

George Strief, 1884, A.A., U.A., N.L.

Most clubs played for, career

M.L.—12

Pop Smith, Cincinnati, Cleveland, Worcester, Buffalo, Pittsburgh, Boston N.L.; Philadelphia, Baltimore, Louisville, Columbus, Pittsburgh, Washington, A.A., 1880 through 1891, 12 years.

Deacon McGuire, Toledo, Cleveland, Rochester, Washington, A.A.; Detroit, Philadelphia, Washington, Brooklyn N.L.; Detroit, New York, Boston, Cleveland A.L.; 1884 to 1912, except 1889, 1909, 1911.

M.L. since 1900—10

Bob L. Miller, St. Louis N.L., New York N.L., Los Angeles N.L., Minnesota A.L., Cleveland A.L., Chicago A.L., Chicago N.L., San Diego N.L., Pittsburgh N.L., Detroit A.L., 1957, 1959 through 1974, 17 years.

Tommy Davis, Los Angeles N.L., New York N.L., Chicago A.L., Seattle A.L., Houston N.L., Chicago N.L., Oakland A.L., Baltimore A.L., California A.L., Kansas City A.L., 1959 through 1976, 18 years.

Ken Brett, Boston A.L., Milwaukee A.L., Philadelphia N.L., Pittsburgh N.L., New York A.L., Chicago A.L., California A.L., Minnesota A.L., Los Angeles N.L., Kansas City A.L., 1967, 1969 through 1981, 14 years.

N.L.—9—Dan Brouthers, Troy, Buffalo, Detroit, Boston, Brooklyn, Baltimore, Louisville, Philadelphia, New York, 1879 through 1889, 1892 through 1896, 1904, 17 years.

N.L. since 1899—7

Jack Barry, Washington, Boston, Philadelphia, Chicago, Cincinnati, St. Louis, New York, 1899 through 1908, 10 years.

Joe Schultz Sr., Boston, Brooklyn, Chicago, Pittsburgh, St. Louis, Philadelphia, Cincinnati, 1912 through 1925, except 1914, 1917 and 1918, 11 years.

Frank J. Thomas, Pittsburgh, Cincinnati, Chicago, Milwaukee, New York, Philadelphia, Houston, 1951 through 1966, 16 years.

A.L.—8—Juan Beniquez, Boston, Texas, New York, Seattle, California, Baltimore, Kansas City, Toronto, 1971 through 1988, except 1973, 17 years.

Most clubs played for, season

M.L.—4—Held by many players. Last player—Dave Kingman, New York N.L., San Diego N.L., California A.L., New York A.L., 132 games, 1977.

N.L.—4—Tom Dowse, Louisville, Cincinnati, Philadelphia, Washington, 63 games, 1892.

A.L.—4

Frank Huelsman, Chicago, Detroit, St. Louis, Washington, 112 games, 1904.

Paul Lehner, Philadelphia, Chicago, St. Louis, Cleveland, 65 games, 1951.

Ted Gray, Chicago, Cleveland, New York, Baltimore, 14 games, 1955.

Most clubs played for, one day

N.L.—2

Max Flack, Chicago, St. Louis, May 30 a.m., p.m., 1922.

Cliff Heathcote, St. Louis, Chicago, May 30 a.m., p.m., 1922.

Joel Youngblood, New York, Montreal, August 4, 1982.

| POSITIONS |

Most positions played, season

N.L.—9

Sport McAllister, Cleveland, 110 games, 1899.

Jimmy M.T. Walsh, Philadelphia, 84 games, 1911.

Gene Paulette, St. Louis, 125 games, 1918.

Jose Oquendo, St. Louis, 148 games, 1988.

A.L.—9

Sam Mertes, Chicago, 129 games, 1902.

Jack Rothrock, Boston, 117 games, 1928.

Bert Campaneris, Kansas City, 144 games, 1965.

Cesar Tovar, Minnesota, 157 games, 1968.

Most positions played, game

A.L.—9

Bert Campaneris, Kansas City, September 8, 1965; played 8⅔ innings of 13-inning game.

Cesar Tovar, Minnesota, September 22, 1968.

PITCHERS

| YEARS |

Most years pitched

M.L.—27—Nolan Ryan, New York N.L., California A.L., Houston N.L., Texas A.L., 1966 through 1993, except 1967, 807 games.

A.L.—23—Early Wynn, Washington, Cleveland, Chicago, 1939, 1941 through 1963, except 1945, in military service, 691 games.

N.L.—22—Steve Carlton, St. Louis, Philadelphia, San Francisco, 1965 through 1986, 695 games.

Most consecutive years pitched

M.L.—26—Nolan Ryan, New York N.L., California A.L., Houston N.L., Texas A.L., 1968 through 1993.

A.L.—22

Samuel P. Jones, Cleveland, Boston, New York, St. Louis, Washington, Chicago, 1914 through 1935.

(Military service in 1918 interrupted a 22-year streak by Herb Pennock, who pitched for Philadelphia, Boston and New York from 1912 through 1934; military service in 1945 interrupted a 22-year streak by Early Wynn, who pitched for Washington, Cleveland and Chicago from 1941 through 1963; military service in 1943 and 1944 interrupted a 22-year streak by Red Ruffing, who pitched For Boston, New York and Chicago from 1924 through 1947.)

N.L.—22—Steve Carlton, St. Louis, Philadelphia, San Francisco, 1965 through 1986.

Most years pitched with one club

A.L.—21

Walter Johnson, Washington, 1907 through 1927, 802 games.

Ted Lyons, Chicago, 1923 through 1946, except 1943, 1944, 1945, in military service, 594 games.

N.L.—21—Phil Niekro, Milwaukee, Atlanta, 1964 through 1983, 1987, 740 games.

Most consecutive years pitched with one club

A.L.—21

Walter Johnson, Washington, 1907 through 1927, 802 games.

(Military service from 1943 through 1945 interrupted a 21-year streak by Ted Lyons, who pitched for Chicago from 1923 through 1946, 594 games.)

N.L.—20

Phil Niekro, Milwaukee, Atlanta, 1964 through 1983, 739 games.

(Military service from 1943 through 1945 interrupted a 20-year streak for Warren Spahn, who pitched for Boston and Milwaukee from 1942 through 1964, 714 games.)

| YOUNGEST AND OLDEST PITCHERS |

Youngest pitcher, game

N.L.—15 years, 10 months, 11 days—Joe Nuxhall, Cincinnati, June 10, 1944.

A.L.—16 years, 8 months, 5 days—Carl Scheib, Philadelphia, September 6, 1943, second game.

Oldest pitcher, game

A.L.—59 years, 2 months, 18 days—Satchel Paige, Kansas City, September 25, 1965.

N.L.—50 years, 2 days—Jack Quinn, Cincinnati, July 7, 1933.

| LEAGUES AND CLUBS |

Most leagues pitched in

4—Jersey Bakely, A.A., U.A., N.L., P.L.

Ed Crane, U.A., N.L., P.L., A.A.

Frank Foreman, U.A., A.A., N.L., A.L.

Con Murphy, U.A., N.L., P.L., A.A.

Most clubs pitched on

M.L.—10

Bob L. Miller, St. Louis N.L., New York N.L., Los Angeles N.L., Minnesota A.L., Cleveland A.L., Chicago A.L., Chicago N.L., San Diego N.L., Pittsburgh N.L., Detroit A.L., 1957, 1959 through 1974, 17 years, 694 games.

Ken Brett, Boston A.L., Milwaukee A.L., Philadelphia N.L., Pittsburgh N.L., New York A.L., Chicago A.L., California A.L., Minnesota A.L., Los Angeles N.L., Kansas City A.L., 1967, 1969 through 1981, 14 years, 349 games.

A.L. (12-club league)—7

Ken Sanders, Kansas City No. 1, 1964, Boston, Kansas City No. 1, 1966, Oakland, 1968, Milwaukee 1970, 1971, 1972, Minnesota, 1973, Cleveland, 1973, 1974, California, 1974, Kansas City No. 2, 1976, 9 years, 348 games. (Note: Oakland considered part of Kansas City No. 1

franchise and is not considered as separate club).
Ken Brett, Boston, Milwaukee, New York, Chicago, California, Minnesota, Kansas City, 1967, 1969 through 1972, 1976 through 1981, 11 years, 238 games.

A.L. (8-club league) — 6

Sam P. Jones, Cleveland, Boston, New York, St. Louis, Washington, Chicago, 1914 through 1935, 22 years, 647 games.

Pete Appleton, Cleveland, Boston, New York, Washington, Chicago, St. Louis, 1930 through 1945, except 1934, 1935, 1943, 1944, 12 years, 304 games.

Bobo Newsom, St. Louis, Washington, Boston, Detroit, Philadelphia, New York, 1934 through 1947, also Washington, 1952, Philadelphia, 1952, 1953, 16 years, 555 games.

Bill Wight, New York, Chicago, Boston, Detroit Cleveland, Baltimore, 1946 through 1957, except 1954, 11 years, 312 games.

N.L. — 6

Burleigh Grimes, Pittsburgh, Brooklyn, New York, Boston, St. Louis, Chicago, 1916 through 1934, 19 years, 605 games.

Bob L. Miller, St. Louis, New York, Los Angeles, Chicago, San Diego, Pittsburgh, 1957 through 1974 except 1958, 1968, 1969, 15 years, 549 games.

Elias Sosa, San Francisco, St. Louis, Atlanta, Los Angeles, Montreal, San Diego, 1972 through 1983, except 1978, 1982, 10 years, 495 games.

Most clubs pitched on, season

M.L. — 4

Willis Hudlin, Cleveland A.L., Washington A.L., St. Louis A.L., New York N.L., 19 games, 1940.

Ted Gray, Chicago A.L., Cleveland A.L., New York A.L., Baltimore A.L., 14 games, 1955.

Mike Kilkenny, Detroit A.L., Oakland A.L., San Diego N.L., Cleveland A.L., 29 games, 1972.

A.L. — 4 — Ted Gray, Chicago, Cleveland, New York, Baltimore, 14 games, 1955.

N.L. — 3 — Held by many pitchers. Last pitcher — Bob L. Miller, Chicago, San Diego, Pittsburgh, 56 games, 1971.

CLUB SERVICE

PLAYERS USED

Most players used, season
A.L.—56—Philadelphia, 1915.
N.L. (162-game season)—54—New York, 1967.
N.L. (154-game season)—53—Brooklyn, 1944.

Fewest players used, season
A.L. (154-game season)—18—Boston, 1905.
A.L. (154-game season)—30—New York, 1963; Boston, 1965; Baltimore, 1969.
N.L. (154-game season)—20—Chicago, 1905.
N.L. (162-game season)—29—Cincinnati, 1975.

Most players used, nine-inning game
A.L.—27—Kansas City vs. California, September 10, 1969.
N.L.—25
  St. Louis vs. Los Angeles, April 16, 1959.
  Milwaukee vs. Philadelphia, September 26, 1964.
  Philadelphia vs. Chicago, September 27, 1981, second game.

Most players used, extra-inning game
A.L.—30—Oakland vs. Chicago, September 19, 1972, 15 innings.
N.L.—27
  Philadelphia vs. St. Louis, September 13, 1974, 17 innings.
  Chicago vs. Pittsburgh, September 21, 1978, 14 innings.
  Chicago vs. Houston, September 2, finished September 3, 1986, 18 innings.
  Los Angeles vs. San Francisco, September 28, 1986, 16 innings.

Most players used by both clubs, nine-inning game
N.L.—45—Chicago 24, Montreal 21, September 5, 1978.
A.L.—42—Oakland 24, Kansas City 18, September 20, 1975.

Most players used by both clubs, extra-inning game
A.L.—54—Seattle 29, Texas 25, September 25, 1992, 16 innings.
N.L.—53—Chicago 27, Houston 26, September 2, finished September 3, 1986, 18 innings.

Most players used, doubleheader (18 innings)
A.L.—41—Chicago vs. Oakland, September 7, 1970.
N.L.—41—San Diego vs. San Francisco, May 30, 1977.

Most players used, doubleheader (more than 18 innings)
N.L.—42
  St. Louis vs. Brooklyn, August 29, 1948, 19 innings.
  Montreal vs. Pittsburgh, September 5, 1975, 19 innings.
A.L.—Less than nine-inning record.

Most players used by both clubs, doubleheader (18 innings)
N.L.—74—San Diego 41, San Francisco 33, May 30, 1977.
A.L.—70—Oakland 36, Texas 34, September 7, 1975.

Most players used by both clubs, doubleheader (more than 18 innings)
N.L.—74—Montreal 42, Pittsburgh 32, September 5, 1975, 19 innings.
A.L.—73—Washington 37, Cleveland 36, September 14, finished September 20, 1971, 29 innings.

PINCH-HITTERS

Most pinch-hitters used, nine-inning game
N.L.—9
  Los Angeles vs. St. Louis, September 22, 1959.
  Montreal vs. Pittsburgh, September 5, 1975, second game.
A.L.—8—Baltimore vs. Chicago, May 28, 1954, first game.

Most pinch-hitters used, extra-inning game
A.L.—10—Oakland vs. Chicago, September 17, 1972, 15 innings.

N.L.—9—San Francisco vs. Los Angeles, September 28, 1986, 16 innings.

Most pinch-hitters used by both clubs, nine-inning game
N.L.—13—Atlanta 9, Montreal 4, September 21, 1993.
A.L.—10—Baltimore 6, New York 4, April 26, 1959, second game.

Most pinch-hitters used by both clubs, extra-inning game
N.L.—14
  New York 7, Chicago 7, May 2, 1956, 17 innings.
  San Francisco 9, Los Angeles 5, September 28, 1986, 16 innings.
A.L.—14—Oakland 10, Chicago 4, September 17, 1972, 15 innings.

Most pinch-hitters used, doubleheader (18 innings)
A.L.—10
  New York vs. Boston, September 6, 1954.
  Baltimore vs. Washington, April 19, 1959.
N.L.—10
  St. Louis vs. Chicago, May 11, 1958.
  St. Louis vs. Pittsburgh, July 13, 1958.

Most pinch-hitters used, doubleheader (more than 18 innings)
N.L.—15—Montreal vs. Pittsburgh, September 5, 1975, 19 innings.
A.L.—9—New York vs. Washington, August 14, 1960, 24 innings.

Most pinch-hitters used by both clubs, doubleheader (18 innings)
N.L.—15—Milwaukee 8, San Francisco 7, August 30, 1964.
A.L.—14—New York 10, Boston 4, September 6, 1954.

Most pinch-hitters used by both clubs, doubleheader (more than 18 innings)
N.L.—19—Montreal 15, Pittsburgh 4, September 5, 1975, 19 innings.
A.L.—17—New York 9, Washington 8, August 14, 1960, 24 innings.

Most pinch-hitters used, inning
N.L.—6
  San Francisco vs. Pittsburgh, May 5, 1958, ninth inning.
  San Diego vs. San Francisco, September 16, 1986, ninth inning.
A.L.—6—Detroit vs. New York, September 5, 1971, seventh inning.

Most consecutive pinch-hitters used, inning
N.L.-A.L.—5—Made in many innings.
N.L.—Last time—New York vs. San Francisco, September 16, 1966, ninth inning.
A.L.—Last time—New York vs. Milwaukee, September 22, 1987, first game, eighth inning.

Most pinch-hitters used by both clubs, inning
A.L.—8—Chicago 5, Baltimore 3, May 18, 1957, seventh inning.
N.L.—8
  Philadelphia 5, St. Louis 3, April 30, 1961, eighth inning.
  New York 5, San Francisco 3, September 16, 1966, ninth inning.

PINCH-RUNNERS

Most pinch-runners used, inning
A.L.—4
  Chicago vs. Minnesota, September 16, 1967, ninth inning.
  Texas vs. California, September 10, 1987, ninth inning.
N.L.—3—Held by many clubs.

Most pinch-runners used by both clubs, inning
N.L.—5—Pittsburgh 3, New York 2, September 21, 1981, ninth inning.
A.L.—4—Occurred in many innings.

INFIELDERS

Most first basemen used, nine-inning game
A.L.—5—Chicago vs. New York, June 25, 1953.
N.L.—3—Made in many games.

Most first basemen used, extra-inning game
N.L.—4—Philadelphia vs. Milwaukee, July 23, 1964, 10 innings.
A.L.—4—Detroit vs. Philadelphia, September 30, 1907, 17 innings.

Most first basemen used by both clubs, game
A.L.—6—Chicago 5, New York 1, June 25, 1953.
N.L.—5
Los Angeles 3, Houston 2, June 8, 1962, 13 innings.
Philadelphia 3, Houston 2, July 17, 1963, 10 innings.
Philadelphia 4, Milwaukee 1, July 23, 1964, 10 innings.
Los Angeles 3, New York 2, September 12, 1966.
Cincinnati 3, New York 2, August 24, 1968.

Most second basemen used, nine-inning game
A.L.-N.L.—4—Made in many games.

Most second basemen used, extra-inning game
A.L.—6—Oakland vs. Chicago, September 19, 1972, 15 innings.
N.L.—5—New York vs. Cincinnati, July 20, 1954, 13 innings.

Most second basemen used by both clubs, nine-inning game
A.L.—6
Oakland 4, Cleveland 2, May 5, 1973.
Oakland 4, Cleveland 2, May 6, 1973, first game.
Oakland 4, Cleveland 2, May 6, 1973, second game.
N.L.—5
Brooklyn 4, New York 1, April 21, 1948.
Chicago 4, New York 1, August 21, 1952, second game.

Most second basemen used by both clubs, extra-inning game
A.L.—8—Oakland 6, Chicago 2, September 19, 1972, 15 innings.
N.L.—7—New York 5, Cincinnati 2, July 20, 1954, 13 innings.

Most third basemen used, game
N.L.—5
Atlanta vs. Philadelphia, April 21, 1966.
Philadelphia vs. Pittsburgh, August 6, 1971.
A.L.—4—Held by many clubs.

Most third basemen used by both clubs, game
N.L.—7—Philadelphia 5, Pittsburgh 2, August 6, 1971.
A.L.—6
Detroit 3, Cleveland 3, July 10, 1969, 11 innings.
Minnesota 3, Cleveland 3, July 27, 1969.

Most shortstops used, nine-inning game
A.L.—4
New York vs. Washington, September 5, 1954.
Minnesota vs. Oakland, September 22, 1968.
N.L.—4—San Francisco vs. Cincinnati, September 4, 1989.

Most shortstops used, extra-inning game
N.L.—5
Philadelphia vs. Cincinnati, May 8, 1949, 12 innings.
San Francisco vs. Los Angeles, September 28, 1986, 16 innings.
A.L.—4
Detroit vs. New York, July 28, 1957, second game, 15 innings.
Baltimore vs. New York, September 26, 1958, 12 innings.

Most shortstops used by both clubs, nine-inning game
A.L.—6—Detroit 3, Washington 3, September 21, 1968.
N.L.—5
Cincinnati 3, Houston 2, July 13, 1969.
Montreal 3, Pittsburgh 2, October 1, 1969.
San Francisco 4, Cincinnati 1, September 4, 1989.

Most right fielders used, nine-inning game
N.L.—4
Philadelphia vs. St. Louis, June 2, 1928.
Los Angeles vs. Houston, June 10, 1962, first game.
A.L.—4—Baltimore vs. Washington, September 25, 1955.

Most right fielders used, extra-inning game
A.L.—6—Kansas City vs. California, September 8, 1965, 13 innings.
N.L.—5—New York vs. Cincinnati, July 22, 1986, 14 innings.

Most right fielders used by both clubs, nine-inning game
N.L.—6—Los Angeles 4, Houston 2, June 10, 1962, first game.
A.L.—5
Chicago 3, St. Louis 2, May 6, 1917, first game.
Baltimore 4, Washington 1, September 25, 1955.
Cleveland 3, Detroit 2, June 2, 1962.
Cleveland 3, Kansas City 2, June 26, 1966, second game.
Boston 3, California 2, August 20, 1967, second game.
California 3, Chicago 2, July 20, 1968.
California 3, Chicago 2, April 14, 1969.
Oakland 3, Chicago 2, September 7, 1970, second game.
Boston 3, Oakland 2, May 20, 1975.

Most right fielders used by both clubs, extra-inning game
N.L.—8—San Francisco 4, Los Angeles 4, September 28, 1986, 16 innings.
A.L.—7—Kansas City 6, California 1, September 8, 1965, 13 innings.

Most center fielders used, game
A.L.—5—Minnesota vs. Oakland, September 22, 1968.
N.L.—4
Boston vs. Brooklyn, April 25, 1917, 12 innings.
Cincinnati vs. St. Louis, May 30, 1942, second game.
Philadelphia vs. St. Louis, September 25, 1966, 13 innings.
Houston vs. Chicago, September 2, finished September 3, 1986, 18 innings.
Philadelphia vs. Cincinnati, July 20, 1987, 11 innings.

Most center fielders used by both clubs, nine-inning game
A.L.—7—Minnesota 5, Oakland 2, September 22, 1968.
N.L.—6—Cincinnati 4, St. Louis 2, May 30, 1942, second game.

Most center fielders used by both clubs, extra-inning game
N.L.—7—Houston 4, Chicago 3, September 2, finished September 3, 1986, 18 innings.
A.L.—Less than nine-inning record.

Most left fielders used, nine-inning game
A.L.—5—Seattle vs. Oakland, September 11, 1992.
N.L.—4
Brooklyn vs. Philadelphia, September 26, 1946.
Los Angeles vs. New York, June 4, 1966.

Most left fielders used, extra-inning game
N.L.—5—Philadelphia vs. Milwaukee, July 23, 1964, 10 innings.
A.L.—4
Boston vs. Chicago, August 16, 1916, first game, 16 innings.
New York vs. Boston, September 26, 1953, 11 innings.

Most left fielders used by both clubs, nine-inning game
N.L.—6—New York 3, San Francisco 3, September 22, 1963.
A.L.—6
Oakland 4, Cleveland 2, July 20, 1974.
Seattle 5, Oakland 1, September 11, 1992.

Most left fielders used by both clubs, extra-inning game
N.L.—7—Los Angeles 4, St. Louis 3, May 12, 1962, 15 innings.
A.L.—6
Minnesota 3, Baltimore 3, April 16, 1961, second game, 11 innings.
Minnesota 3, Oakland 3, September 6, 1969, 18 innings.

BATTERY

Most catchers used, game

N.L.—4
  Boston vs. New York, October 6, 1929.
  Brooklyn vs. St. Louis, May 5, 1940.
  New York vs. St. Louis, September 12, 1962.
A.L.—4
  Minnesota vs. California, September 27, 1967.
  Kansas City vs. Chicago, September 21, 1973, 12 innings.

Most catchers used by both clubs, game

A.L.—6
  Chicago 3, Philadelphia 3, July 10, 1926.
  Chicago 3, New York 3, September 10, 1955, 10 innings.
  California 3, Oakland 3, September 28, 1969, 11 innings.
  Kansas City 4, Chicago 2, September 21, 1972, 12 innings.
N.L.—6
  Boston 4, New York 2, October 6, 1929.
  Brooklyn 4, St. Louis 2, May 5, 1940.
  New York 4, St. Louis 2, September 2, 1962.

Most pitchers used, season

A.L.—27—Philadelphia, 1915; Kansas City, 1955.
N.L. (162-game season)—27—New York, 1967.
N.L. (154-game season)—24—Cincinnati, 1912; Philadelphia, 1946.

Fewest pitchers used, season

A.L. (154-game season)—5—Boston, 1904.
A.L. (162-game season)—11—Baltimore, 1972, 1974; Oakland, 1974; Boston, 1976.
N.L. (154-game season)—5—Boston, 1901.
N.L. (162-game season)—11—Philadelphia, 1976; Atlanta, 1980.

Most relief appearances, season

N.L.—453—Colorado, 1993.
A.L.—424—Oakland, 1993.

Most pitchers used, nine-inning game

A.L.—9—St. Louis vs. Chicago, October 2, 1949, first game.
N.L.—8—Held by many clubs.

Most pitchers used, extra-inning game

A.L.—11—Seattle vs. Texas, September 25, 1992, 16 innings.
N.L.—10—Chicago vs. Pittsburgh, April 20, finished August 11, 1986, 17 innings.

Most pitchers used by both clubs, nine-inning game

N.L.—15—St. Louis 8, Cincinnati 7, September 7, 1993, first game.
A.L.—14—Kansas City 7, Cleveland 7, April 23, 1961.

Most pitchers used by both clubs, extra-inning game

A.L.—18—Washington 9, Cleveland 9, September 14, finished September 20, 1971, 20 innings.
N.L.—17
  Chicago 10, Pittsburgh 7, April 20, finished August 11, 1986, 17 innings.

Houston 9, Chicago 8, September 2, finished September 3, 1986, 18 innings.

Most pitchers used by winning club, shutout game

A.L.—7—Kansas City vs. Cleveland, September 15, 1966, 11 innings (won 1-0).
N.L.—6
  Los Angeles vs. Milwaukee, October 3, 1965 (won 3-0).
  Florida vs. Chicago, May 15, 1994 (won 3-0).
  St. Louis vs. Pittsburgh, May 17, 1994 (won 2-0).

Most pitchers used by winning club, no-hit game

A.L.—4
  Oakland vs. California, September 28, 1975 (won 5-0).
  Baltimore vs. Oakland, July 13, 1991 (won 2-0).
N.L.—3—Atlanta vs. San Diego, September 11, 1991 (won 1-0).

Most pitchers used, doubleheader (18 innings)

N.L.—13—San Diego vs. San Francisco, May 30, 1977.
A.L.—12
  Cleveland vs. Detroit, September 7, 1959.
  California vs. Detroit, September 30, 1967.

Most pitchers used, doubleheader (more than 18 innings)

N.L.—13—Milwaukee vs. Philadelphia, May 12, 1963, 23 innings.
A.L.—13—Baltimore vs. Texas, August 13, 1991, 21 innings.

Most pitchers used by both clubs, doubleheader (18 innings)

N.L.—22—Milwaukee 11, New York 11, July 26, 1964.
A.L.—21—Detroit 11, Kansas City 10, July 23, 1961.

Most pitchers used by both clubs, doubleheader (more than 18 innings)

A.L.—22—Washington 12, Cleveland 10, September 14, finished September 20, 1971, 29 innings.
N.L.—20—St. Louis 12, Cincinnati 8, July 1, 1956, 19 innings.

Most pitchers used, inning

A.L.—6—Oakland vs. Cleveland, September 3, 1983, ninth inning.
N.L.—5—Occurred in many innings. Last times—Los Angeles vs. New York, August 26, 1987, eighth inning; Chicago vs. Philadelphia, September 16, 1987, seventh inning.

Most pitchers used by both clubs, inning

N.L.—8—Los Angeles 5, New York 3, August 26, 1987, eighth inning.
A.L.—7—Chicago 4, Baltimore 3, July 16, 1955, ninth inning.

FRANCHISE LONGEVITY

Most years in same city by a franchise

N.L.—119—Chicago, 1876 through 1994 (consecutive).
A.L.—94—Boston, Chicago, Cleveland, Detroit, 1901 through 1994 (consecutive).

LEAGUE SERVICE

Most players, season (since 1900)

A.L. (14-club league) —582 in 1993.
A.L. (12-club league) —440 in 1969.
A.L. (10-club league) —369 in 1962.
A.L. (8-club league) —323 in 1955.
N.L. (14-club league) —565 in 1993.
N.L. (12-club league) —491 in 1990.
N.L. (10-club league) —373 in 1967.
N.L. (8-club league) —333 in 1946.

Most players in 150 or more games, season (since 1900)

A.L. (14-club league) —44 in 1985.
A.L. (12-club league) —32 in 1976.
A.L. (10-club league) —30 in 1962.
A.L. (8-club league) — 19 in 1921, 1936.
N.L. (12-club league) —40 in 1978, 1979.
N.L. (10-club league) —34 in 1965.
N.L. (8-club league) —23 in 1953.

Fewest players, season (since 1900)

A.L. (12-club league) —412 in 1976.
A.L. (8-club league) — 166 in 1904.
N.L. (12-club league) —420 in 1979.
N.L. (8-club league) — 188 in 1905.

Most players playing in all games, season (since 1900)

N.L. — 10 in 1932.
A.L. — 10 in 1933.

Fewest players playing in all games, season

A.L. —0— 1910, 1963.
N.L. —0— 1914.

Most players with two or more clubs, season (since 1900)

A.L. —47 in 1952.
N.L. —31 in 1919.

Fewest players with two or more clubs, season (since 1900)

A.L. —2 in 1940.
N.L. —5 in 1935.

Most players with three or more clubs, season (since 1900)

A.L. —4 in 1952.
N.L. —3 in 1919.

Most pitchers in league, season

A.L. (14-club league) —277 in 1993.
A.L. (12-club league) — 189 in 1970.
A.L. (10-club league) — 170 in 1962.
A.L. (8-club league) — 141 in 1946, 1955.
N.L. (14-club league) —256 in 1993.
N.L. (12-club league) —228 in 1990.
N.L. (10-club league) — 167 in 1967.
N.L. (8-club league) — 152 in 1946.

Most pitchers in league, one day

N.L. —72—September 7, 1964.
A.L. —62—August 9, 1970.

Most pitchers in both leagues, one day

121—September 7, 1964, 72 in N.L. (10 games), 49 in A.L. (eight games).

INDIVIDUAL BATTING

GAMES

Most games, career

N.L.—3,562—Pete Rose, Cincinnati, Philadelphia, Montreal, 24 years, 1963 through 1986.

A.L.—3,308—Carl Yastrzemski, Boston, 23 years, 1961 through 1983.

Most consecutive games, career

A.L.—2,130—Lou Gehrig, New York, June 1, 1925, through April 30, 1939.

N.L.—1,207—Steve Garvey, Los Angeles, San Diego, September 3, 1975, through July 29, 1983, first game.

Most consecutive games from start of career

N.L.—424—Ernie Banks, Chicago, September 17, 1953, through August 10, 1957.

A.L.—394—Al Simmons, Philadelphia, April 15, 1924, through July 20, 1926.

Most games played, season

N.L. (162-game season)—165—Maury Wills, Los Angeles, 1962.

N.L. (154-game season)—160
Heinie Groh, Cincinnati, 1915.
Tommy Griffith, Cincinnati, 1915.

A.L. (162-game season)—164—Cesar Tovar, Minnesota, 1967.

A.L. (154-game season)—162—Jimmy Barrett, Detroit, 1904.

Most games played with two clubs, season

N.L. (162-game season)—164—Frank Taveras, Pittsburgh, New York, 1979.

N.L. (154-game season)—158—Ralph Kiner, Pittsburgh, Chicago, 1953.

A.L. (162-game season)—160—Julio Cruz, Seattle, Chicago, 1983.

A.L. (154-game season)—155
Patsy Dougherty, Boston, New York, 1904.
Eddie Robinson, Washington, Chicago, 1950.

Most games by rookie, season

A.L. (162-game season)—162
Jake Wood, Detroit, 1961.
Bobby Knoop, Los Angeles, 1964.
George Scott, Boston, 1966.

A.L. (154-game season)—155
Topper Rigney, Detroit, 1922.
Tony Lazzeri, New York, 1926.
Dale Alexander, Detroit, 1929.
Billy Johnson, New York, 1943.
Dick Wakefield, Detroit, 1943.
Al Rosen, Cleveland, 1950.
Harvey Kuenn, Detroit, 1953.

N.L. (162-game season)—162
Dick Allen, Philadelphia, 1964.
Johnny Ray, Pittsburgh, 1982.
Jeff Conine, Florida, 1993.

N.L. (154-game season)—157—Ray Jablonski, St. Louis, 1953.

Most games by righthander, season

N.L. (162-game season)—164
Jose Pagan, San Francisco, 1962.
Ron Santo, Chicago, 1965.
Frank Taveras, Pittsburgh, New York, 1979.

N.L. (154-game season)—160—Heinie Groh, Cincinnati, 1915.

A.L. (162-game season)—164—Cesar Tovar, Minnesota, 1967.

A.L. (154-game season)—159
Nap Lajoie, Cleveland, 1910.
Del Pratt, St. Louis, 1915.

Most games by lefthander, season

N.L. (162-game season)—164—Billy Williams, Chicago, 1965.

N.L. (154-game season)—160—Tommy Griffith, Cincinnati, 1915.

A.L. (162-game season)—163
Leon Wagner, Cleveland, 1964.
Al Oliver, Texas, 1980.
Greg Walker, Chicago, 1985.

A.L. (154-game season)—162—Jimmy Barrett, Detroit, 1904.

Most games by switch-hitter, season

N.L.—165—Maury Wills, Los Angeles, 1962.

A.L.—163
Don Buford, Chicago, 1966.
Tony Fernandez, Toronto, 1986.

Most games by pinch-hitter, season

N.L. (162-game season)—94—Rusty Staub, New York, 1983.

N.L. (154-game season)—76—Gerry Lynch, Cincinnati, 1960.

A.L.—81—Elmer Valo, New York, Washington, 1960.

Most years leading league in games

A.L.—7
Lou Gehrig, New York, 1927, 1930 (tied), 1932, 1934 (tied), 1936 (tied), 1937, 1938 (tied).
Cal Ripken Jr., Baltimore, 1983 (tied), 1984 (tied), 1987, 1989 (tied), 1991 (tied), 1992, 1993.

N.L.—6
Ernie Banks, Chicago, 1954 (tied), 1955 (tied), 1957 (tied), 1958, 1959 (tied), 1960.
Steve Garvey, Los Angeles, 1977 (tied), 1978 (tied), 1980, 1981 (tied), 1982 (tied), San Diego, 1985 (tied).

Most years played all clubs' games

A.L.—13—Lou Gehrig, New York, 1926 through 1938 (consecutive).

N.L.—10—Pete Rose, Cincinnati, 1965, 1972, 1974, 1975, 1976, 1977, Philadelphia, 1979, 1980, 1981, 1982.

Most consecutive years played all clubs' games

A.L.—13—Lou Gehrig, New York, 1926 through 1938.

N.L.—7—Steve Garvey, Los Angeles, 1976 through 1982.

Most years playing 150 or more games

N.L.—17—Pete Rose, Cincinnati, Philadelphia, 1963 through 1983, except 1964, 1967, 1968, 1981.

A.L.—14—Brooks Robinson, Baltimore, 1960 through 1974, except 1965.

Most consecutive years playing 150 or more games

N.L.—13—Willie Mays, New York, San Francisco, 1954 through 1966.

A.L.—12—Cal Ripken, Baltimore, 1982 through 1993.

Most years playing 100 or more games

N.L.—23—Pete Rose, Cincinnati, Philadelphia, Montreal, 1963 through 1985.

A.L.—22—Carl Yastrzemski, Boston, 1961 through 1983, except 1981.

Most consecutive years playing 100 or more games

N.L.—23—Pete Rose, Cincinnati, Philadelphia, Montreal, 1963 through 1985.

A.L.—20—Carl Yastrzemski, Boston, 1961 through 1980.

Fewest games for leader, season

N.L.—152
Stan Hack, Chicago, 1938.
Billy Herman, Chicago, 1938.

A.L.—154—Held by many players.

BATTING AVERAGE

Highest average, career (15 or more seasons)

A.L.—.367—Ty Cobb, Detroit, Philadelphia, 24 years, 1905 through 1928 (11,429 at-bats, 4,191 hits).

N.L.—.359—Rogers Hornsby, St. Louis, New York, Boston,

Chicago, 19 years, 1915 through 1933 (8,058 at-bats, 2,895 hits).

Highest average, season (100 or more games)
N.L.—.438—Hugh Duffy, Boston, 124 games, 1894.
N.L. since 1900—.424—Rogers Hornsby, St. Louis, 143 games, 1924.
A.L.—.422—Nap Lajoie, Philadelphia, 131 games, 1901.

Highest average for non-leader, season (100 or more games)
A.L.—.408—Joe Jackson, Cleveland, 147 games, 1911.
N.L.—.406—Fred Clarke, Louisville, 129 games, 1897.
N.L. since 1900—.393—Babe Herman, Brooklyn, 153 games, 1930.

Highest average by rookie, season (100 or more games)
N.L.—.373—George Watkins, St. Louis, 119 games, 1930.
A.L.—.349—Wade Boggs, Boston, 104 games, 1982.
(Boggs did not have enough plate appearances to qualify for batting championship. Highest qualifying average was .343 by Dale Alexander, Detroit, 155 games, 1929. Watkins qualified for N.L. title in 1930 under different regulations than presently used.)

Leading rookie batsmen, season
N.L.—.356—Abner Dalrymple, Milwaukee, 60 games, 1878.
A.L.—.323—Tony Oliva, Minnesota, 161 games, 1964.

Highest average by righthander, season (100 or more games)
N.L.—.438—Hugh Duffy, Boston, 124 games, 1894.
N.L. since 1900—.424—Rogers Hornsby, St. Louis, 143 games, 1924.
A.L.—.422—Nap Lajoie, Philadelphia, 131 games, 1910.

Highest average by lefthander, season (100 or more games)
N.L.—.432—Willie Keeler, Baltimore, 128 games, 1897.
A.L.—.41979—George Sisler, St. Louis, 142 games, 1922.
N.L. since 1900—.401—Bill Terry, New York, 154 games, 1930.

Highest average by switch-hitter, season (100 or more games)
N.L.—.373—George Davis, New York, 133 games, 1893.
A.L.—.365—Mickey Mantle, New York, 144 games, 1957.
N.L. since 1900—.353—Willie McGee, St. Louis 152 games, 1985.

Highest average by first baseman, season (100 or more games)
A.L.—.420—George Sisler, St. Louis, 142 games, 1922; 141 games at first base.
N.L.—.401—Bill Terry, New York, 154 games, 1930; 154 games at first base.

Highest average by second baseman, season (100 or more games)
N.L.—.424—Rogers Hornsby, St. Louis, 143 games, 1924; 143 games at second base.
A.L.—.422—Nap Lajoie, Philadelphia, 131 games, 1901; 130 games at second base.

Highest average by third baseman, season (100 or more games)
A.L.—.390—George Brett, Kansas City, 117 games, 1980; 112 games at third base.
N.L.—.390—John McGraw, Baltimore, 118 games, 1899; 118 games at third base.
N.L. since 1900—.379—Fred Lindstrom, New York, 148 games, 1930; 148 games at third base.

Highest average by shortstop, season (100 or more games)
N.L.—.397—Hughey Jennings, Baltimore, 129 games, 1896; 129 games at shortstop.
A.L.—.388—Luke Appling, Chicago, 138 games, 1936; 137 games at shortstop.
N.L. since 1900—.385—Arky Vaughan, Pittsburgh, 137 games, 1935; 137 games at shortstop.

Highest average by outfielder, season (100 or more games)
N.L.—.438—Hugh Duffy, Boston, 124 games, 1894; 123 games in outfield.
A.L.—.420—Ty Cobb, Detroit, 146 games, 1911; 146 games in outfield.
N.L. since 1900—.398—Lefty O'Doul, Philadelphia, 154 games, 1929; 154 games in outfield.

Highest average by catcher, season (100 or more games)
A.L.—.362—Bill Dickey, New York, 112 games, 1936; caught in 107 games.
N.L.—.358—Chief Meyers, New York, 126 games, 1912; caught in 122 games.

Highest average by pitcher, season (only for games as a pitcher)
A.L.—.440—Walter Johnson, Washington, 36 games, 1925; pitched 30 games.
N.L.—.406—Jack Bentley, New York, 52 games, 1923; pitched 31 games.

Most years leading league in batting average
A.L.—12—Ty Cobb, Detroit, 1907, 1908, 1909, 1910, 1911, 1912, 1913, 1914, 1915, 1917, 1918, 1919.
N.L.—8—Honus Wagner, Pittsburgh, 1900, 1903, 1904, 1906, 1907, 1908, 1909, 1911.

Most consecutive years leading league in batting average
A.L.—9—Ty Cobb, Detroit, 1907 through 1915.
N.L.—6—Rogers Hornsby, St. Louis, 1920 through 1925.

Most years batting .400 or over (50 or more games)
N.L.—3
Jesse Burkett, Cleveland, St. Louis, 1895, 1896, 1899.
Rogers Hornsby, St. Louis, 1922, 1924, 1925.
A.L.—3—Ty Cobb, Detroit, 1911, 1912, 1922.

Most consecutive years batting .400 or over (50 or more games)
N.L.—2
Jesse Burkett, Cleveland, 1895, 1896.
Rogers Hornsby, St. Louis, 1924, 1925.
A.L.—2—Ty Cobb, Detroit, 1911, 1912.

Most years batting .300 or over (50 or more games)
A.L.—23—Ty Cobb, Detroit, Philadelphia 1906 through 1928.
N.L.—18—Cap Anson, Chicago, 1876 through 1897, except 1877, 1879, 1891 and 1892.
N.L. since 1900—17—Stan Musial, St. Louis, 1942 through 1958, and 1962, except 1945, in military service.

Most consecutive years batting .300 or over (50 or more games)
A.L.—23—Ty Cobb, Detroit, Philadelphia, 1906 through 1928.
N.L.—17—Honus Wagner, Louisville, Pittsburgh, 1897 through 1913.
N.L. since 1900—13—Stan Musial, St. Louis, 1946 through 1958 (military service in 1945 interrupted a 16-year streak by Musial, who batted .300 for St. Louis from 1942 through 1958).

Most consecutive years batting .300 or over from start of career (50 or more games)
N.L.—17—Honus Wagner, Louisville, Pittsburgh, 1897 through 1913.
N.L. since 1900—12
Paul Waner, Pittsburgh, 1926 through 1937.
(Military service in 1945 interrupted a 16-year streak by Stan Musial, who batted .300 for St. Louis from 1942 through 1958.)
A.L.—11
Al Simmons, Philadelphia, Chicago, 1924 through 1934.
(Military service from 1943 through 1945 and most of 1952 and 1953 interrupted a 15-year streak by Ted Williams, who batted .300 for Boston from 1939 through 1958.)

Most years batting .300 or over by pitcher
A.L.—8—Red Ruffing, Boston, New York, 1928, 1929, 1930, 1931, 1932, 1935, 1939, 1941.
N.L.—5—Jack Stivetts, Boston, 1892, 1893, 1894, 1896, 1897.

Highest average over five consecutive seasons (100 or more games)
N.L.—.4024—Rogers Hornsby, St. Louis, 1921 through 1925.
A.L.—.3965—Ty Cobb, Detroit, 1909 through 1913.

Highest average over four consecutive seasons (100 or more games)
N.L.—.4039—Rogers Hornsby, St. Louis, 1922 through 1925.
A.L.—.4019—Ty Cobb, Detroit, 1910 through 1913.

Highest average over three consecutive seasons (100 or more games)
A.L.—.4084—Ty Cobb, Detroit, 1911, 1912, 1913.
N.L.—.40647—Willie Keeler, Baltimore, 1895, 1896, 1897.
N.L. since 1900—.405—Rogers Hornsby, St. Louis, 1923, 1924, 1925.

Highest average over two consecutive seasons (100 or more games)

N.L.—.417—Jesse Burkett, Cleveland, 1895, 1896.
A.L.—.415—Ty Cobb, Detroit, 1911, 1912.
N.L. since 1900—.413—Rogers Hornsby, St. Louis, 1924, 1925.

Lowest average, season (150 or more games)

A.L.—.182—Monte Cross, Philadelphia, 153 games, 1904.
N.L.—.201—Dal Maxvill, St. Louis, 152 games, 1970.

Lowest average for leader, season (100 or more games)

A.L.—.301—Carl Yastrzemski, Boston, 157 games, 1968.
N.L.—.313—Tony Gwynn, San Diego, 133 games, 1988.

SLUGGING AVERAGE

Highest slugging average, career (15 or more years)

M.L.—.690—Babe Ruth, Boston A.L., New York A.L., Boston N.L., 22 years, 1914 through 1935.
A.L.—.692—Babe Ruth, Boston, New York, 21 years, 1914 through 1934.
N.L.—.578—Rogers Hornsby, St. Louis, New York, Boston, Chicago 19 years, 1915 through 1933.

Highest slugging average, season (100 or more games)

A.L.—.847—Babe Ruth, New York, 142 games, 1920.
N.L.—.756—Rogers Hornsby, St. Louis, 138 games, 1925.

Highest slugging average by rookie, season (100 or more games)

N.L.—.621—George Watkins, St. Louis, 119 games, 1930.
A.L.—.618—Mark McGwire, Oakland, 151 games, 1987.

Highest slugging average by righthander, season (100 or more games)

N.L.—.756—Rogers Hornsby, St. Louis, 138 games, 1925.
A.L.—.749—Jimmie Foxx, Philadelphia, 154 games, 1932.

Highest slugging average by lefthander, season (100 or more games)

A.L.—.847—Babe Ruth, New York, 142 games, 1920.
N.L.—.702—Stan Musial, St. Louis, 155 games, 1948.

Highest slugging average by switch-hitter, season

A.L.—.705—Mickey Mantle, New York, 150 games, 1956.
N.L.—.615—Jimmy Collins, St. Louis, 154 games, 1934.

Most years leading league in slugging average (100 or more games)

A.L.—13—Babe Ruth, Boston, New York, 1918 through 1931, except 1925. (Played only 95 games in 1918, short season due to war.)
N.L.—9—Rogers Hornsby, St. Louis, Boston, Chicago, 1917, 1920, 1921, 1922, 1923, 1924, 1925, 1928, 1929.

Lowest slugging average, season (150 or more games)

N.L.—.223—Dal Maxvill, St. Louis, 152 games, 1970.
A.L.—.243—George McBride, Washington, 156 games, 1914.

Lowest leading slugging average, season (100 or more games)

N.L.—.436—Hy Myers, Brooklyn, 133 games, 1919.
A.L.—.466—Elmer Flick, Cleveland, 131 games, 1905.

AT-BATS AND PLATE APPEARANCES

CAREER AND SEASON

Most at-bats, career

N.L.—14,053—Pete Rose, Cincinnati, Philadelphia, Montreal, 24 years, 1963 through 1986.
A.L.—11,988—Carl Yastrzemski, Boston, 23 years, 1961 through 1983.

Most plate appearances, career

N.L.—15,890—Pete Rose, Cincinnati, Philadelphia, Montreal, 24 years, 1963 through 1986.
A.L.—13,990—Carl Yastrzemski, Boston, 23 years, 1961 through 1983.

Most at-bats, season

A.L. (162-game season)—705—Willie Wilson, Kansas City, 161 games, 1980.
A.L. (154-game season)—679—Harvey Kuenn, Detroit, 155 games, 1953.
N.L. (154-game season)—696—Woody Jensen, Pittsburgh, 153 games, 1936.

Most plate appearances, season

N.L. (162-game season)—771—Pete Rose, Cincinnati, 163 games, 1974.
N.L. (154-game season)—755—Woody English, Chicago, 156 games, 1930.
A.L. (162-game season)—758—Wade Boggs, Boston, 161 games, 1985.
A.L. (154-game season)—757—Frankie Crosetti, New York, 157 games, 1938.

Most at-bats by rookie, season

N.L. (162-game season)—701—Juan Samuel, Philadelphia, 160 games, 1984.
N.L. (154-game season)—643—Frankie Baumholtz, Cincinnati, 151 games, 1947.
A.L.—679—Harvey Kuenn, Detroit, 155 games, 1953.

Most at-bats by righthander, season

N.L. (162-game season)—701—Juan Samuel, Philadelphia, 160 games, 1984.
N.L. (154-game season)—672—Rabbit Maranville, Pittsburgh, 155 games, 1922.
A.L. (162-game season)—692—Bobby Richardson, New York, 161 games, 1962.
A.L. (154-game season)—679—Harvey Kuenn, Detroit, 155 games, 1953.

Most at-bats by lefthander, season

N.L. (162-game season)—698—Matty Alou, Pittsburgh, 162 games, 1969.
N.L. (154-game season)—696—Woody Jensen, Pittsburgh, 153 games, 1936.
A.L. (162-game season)—677—Don Mattingly, New York, 162 games, 1986.
A.L. (154-game season)—671—Jack Tobin, St. Louis, 150 games, 1921.

Most at-bats by switch-hitter, season

A.L.—705—Willie Wilson, Kansas City, 161 games, 1980.
N.L.—695—Maury Wills, Los Angeles, 165 games, 1962.

Most at-bats by pinch-hitter, season

N.L. (162-game season)—81—Rusty Staub, New York, 94 games, 1983.
N.L. (154-game season)—72—Sam Leslie, New York, 75 games, 1932.
A.L. (162-game season)—72—Dave Philley, Baltimore 79 games, 1961.
A.L. (154-game season)—66—Julio Becquer, Washington, 70 games, 1957.

Most years leading league in at-bats

A.L.—7—Doc Cramer, Philadelphia, Boston, Washington, Detroit, 1933, 1934, 1935, 1938, 1940, 1941, 1942.
N.L.—4
Abner Dalrymple, Chicago, 1880, 1882, 1884, 1885.
Pete Rose, Cincinnati, 1965, 1972, 1973, 1977.

Most consecutive years leading league in at-bats

N.L.—3
Sparky Adams, Chicago, 1925, 1926, 1927.
Dave Cash, Philadelphia, 1974, 1975, 1976.
A.L.—3
Doc Cramer, Philadelphia, 1933, 1934, 1935.
Doc Cramer, Boston, Washington, Detroit, 1940, 1941, 1942.
Bobby Richardson, New York, 1962, 1963, 1964.

Most years with 600 or more at-bats

N.L.—17—Pete Rose, Cincinnati, 1963 through 1978, except 1964, 1967, Philadelphia, 1979, 1980, 1982.
A.L.—12—Nellie Fox, Chicago, 1951 through 1962.

Most consecutive years with 600 or more at-bats

N.L.—13—Pete Rose, Cincinnati, Philadelphia, 1968 through 1980.
A.L.—12—Nellie Fox, Chicago, 1951 through 1962.

Fewest at-bats, season (150 or more games)
N.L.—362—Jim Eisenreich, Philadelphia, 153 games, 1993.
A.L.—389—Tom McCraw, Chicago, 151 games, 1966.
Fewest at-bats for leader, season
N.L.—585—Spike Shannon, New York, 155 games, 1907.
A.L.—588—Ty Cobb, Detroit, 152 games, 1917.

GAME AND INNING

Most at-bats, nine-inning game
N.L.—8—Held by 18 players. Last player—Barry Mc-Cormick, Chicago, June 29, 1897.
N.L. since 1900—7—Held by many players.
A.L.—7—Held by many players.

Most at-bats, extra-inning game
N.L.—11
  Carson Bigbee, Pittsburgh, August 22, 1917, 22 innings.
  Charlie Pick, Boston, May 1, 1920, 26 innings.
  Tony Boeckel, Boston, May 1, 1920, 26 innings.
  Ralph Garr, Atlanta, May 4, 1973, 20 innings.
  Dave Schneck, New York, September 11, 1974, 25 innings.
  Dave Cash, Montreal, May 21, 1977, 21 innings.
A.L.—11
  Johnny Burnett, Cleveland, July 10, 1932, 18 innings.
  Ed Morgan, Cleveland, July 10, 1932, 18 innings.
  Irv Hall, Philadelphia, July 21, 1945, 24 innings.
  Bobby Richardson, New York, June 24, 1962, 22 innings.
  Cecil Cooper, Milwaukee, May 8, completed May 9, 1984, 25 innings.
  Julio Cruz, Chicago, May 8, completed May 9, 1984, 25 innings.
  Carlton Fisk, Chicago, May 8, completed May 9, 1984, 25 innings.
  Rudy Law, Chicago, May 8, completed May 9, 1984, 25 innings.

Most times faced pitcher as batsman, nine-inning game
N.L. before 1900—8—Held by many players.
N.L. since 1900—8
  Russ Wrightstone, Philadelphia, August 25, 1922.
  Frank Parkinson, Philadelphia, August 25, 1922.
  Taylor Douthit, St. Louis, July 6, 1929, second game.
  Andy High, St. Louis, July 6, 1929, second game.
A.L.—8—Clyde Vollmer, Boston, June 8, 1950.

Most times faced pitcher as batsman, extra-inning game
N.L.—12
  Felix Millan, New York, September 11, 1974, 25 innings.
  John Milner, New York, September 11, 1974, 25 innings.
A.L.—12
  Harold Baines, Chicago, May 8, completed May 9, 1984, 25 innings.
  Carlton Fisk, Chicago, May 8, completed May 9, 1984, 25 innings.
  Rudy Law, Chicago, May 8, completed May 9, 1984, 25 innings.

Most times faced pitcher with no official at-bats, game
N.L.—6
  Pop Smith, Boston, April 17, 1890 (5 bases on balls, 1 hit by pitch).
  Walt Wilmot, Chicago, August 22, 1891 (6 bases on balls).
  Miller Huggins, St. Louis, June 1, 1910 (4 bases on balls, 1 sacrifice hit, 1 sacrifice fly).
  Billy Urbanski, Boston, June 13, 1934 (4 bases on balls, 2 sacrifice hits).
A.L.—6—Jimmie Foxx, Boston, June 16, 1938 (6 bases on balls).

Most at-bats, doubleheader (18 innings)
N.L.—13
  Rabbit Maranville, Pittsburgh, August 8, 1922.
  Billy Herman, Chicago, August 21, 1935.
A.L.—13—Dave Philley, Chicago, May 30, 1950.

Most at-bats, doubleheader (more than 18 innings)
N.L.—14
  Jesus Alou, San Francisco, May 31, 1964, 32 innings.
  Joe Christopher, New York, May 31, 1964, 32 innings.
  Jim Hickman, New York, May 31, 1964, 32 innings.
  Ed Kranepool, New York, May 31, 1964, 32 innings.
  Roy McMillan, New York, May 31, 1964, 32 innings.
  Frank J. Thomas, New York, May 31, 1964, 32 innings.
A.L.—14
  Rick Monday, Kansas City, June 17, 1967, 28 innings.
  Ramon Webster, Kansas City, June 17, 1967, 28 innings.

Most times faced pitcher as batsman, inning
A.A.—3—Larry Murphy, Washington, June 17, 1891, first inning.
N.L. before 1900—3—Held by 10 players.
N.L. since 1900—3
  Marty Callaghan, Chicago, August 25, 1922, fourth inning.
  Billy Cox, Pee Wee Reese and Duke Snider, Brooklyn, May 21, 1952, first inning.
  Gil Hodges, Brooklyn, August 8, 1954, eighth inning.
  Dusty Baker, Atlanta, September 20, 1972, second inning.
  Mariano Duncan and Luis Quinones, Cincinnati, August 3, 1989, first inning.
A.L.—3
  Ted Williams, Boston, July 4, 1948, seventh inning.
  Sammy White, Gene Stephens, Tom Umphlett, Johnny Lipon and George Kell, Boston, June 18, 1953, seventh inning.

RUNS

CAREER AND SEASON

Most runs, career
A.L.—2,245—Ty Cobb, Detroit, Philadelphia, 24 years, 1905 through 1928.
N.L.—2,165—Pete Rose, Cincinnati, Philadelphia, Montreal, 24 years, 1963 through 1986.

Most runs, season
N.L.—196—Billy Hamilton, Philadelphia, 131 games, 1894.
A.L.—177—Babe Ruth, New York, 152 games, 1921.
N.L. since 1900—158—Chuck Klein, Philadelphia, 156 games, 1930.

Most runs by rookie, season
A.A.—152—Mike Griffin, Baltimore, 136 games, 1887.
N.L.—135—Roy Thomas, Philadelphia, 148 games, 1899.
N.L. since 1900—133—Lloyd Waner, Pittsburgh, 150 games, 1927.
A.L.—132—Joe DiMaggio, New York, 138 games, 1936.

Most runs by righthander, season
N.L.—167—Joe Kelley, Baltimore, 129 games, 1894.
N.L. since 1900—156—Rogers Hornsby, Chicago, 156 games, 1929.
A.L.—152—Al Simmons, Philadelphia, 138 games, 1930.

Most runs by lefthander, season
N.L.—196—Billy Hamilton, Philadelphia, 131 games, 1894.
A.L.—177—Babe Ruth, New York, 152 games, 1921.
N.L. since 1900—158—Chuck Klein, Philadelphia, 156 games, 1930.

Most runs by switch-hitter, season
N.L.—140—Max Carey, Pittsburgh, 155 games, 1922.
A.L.—133—Willie Wilson, Kansas City, 161 games, 1980.

Most years leading league in runs
A.L.—8—Babe Ruth, Boston, New York, 1919, 1920, 1921, 1923, 1924, 1926, 1927, 1928.
N.L.—5
  George Burns, New York, 1914, 1916, 1917, 1919, 1920.
  Rogers Hornsby, St. Louis, New York, Chicago, 1921, 1922, 1924 (tied), 1927 (tied), 1929.
  Stan Musial, St. Louis, 1946, 1948, 1951 (tied), 1952 (tied), 1954 (tied).

Most consecutive years leading league in runs
N.L.—3
   King Kelly, Chicago, 1884, 1885, 1886.
   Chuck Klein, Philadelphia, 1930, 1931 (tied), 1932.
   Duke Snider, Brooklyn, 1953, 1954 (tied), 1955.
   Pete Rose, Cincinnati, 1974, 1975, 1976.
A.L.—3
   Ty Cobb, Detroit, 1909, 1910, 1911.
   Eddie Collins, Philadelphia, 1912, 1913, 1914.
   Babe Ruth, Boston, 1919, New York, 1920, 1921 and New
      York, 1926, 1927, 1928.
   Ted Williams, Boston, 1940, 1941, 1942 (military service from
      1943 through 1945 interrupted a five-year streak by Wil-
      liams of Boston, who led in runs from 1940 through 1947).
   Mickey Mantle, New York, 1956, 1957, 1958.

Most years with 150 or more runs
A.L.—6—Babe Ruth, New York, 1920, 1921, 1923, 1927,
      1928, 1930.
N.L.—4—Billy Hamilton, Philadelphia, Boston, 1894, 1895,
      1896, 1897.
N.L. since 1900—2—Chuck Klein, Philadelphia, 1930, 1932.

Most years scoring 100 or more runs
N.L.—15—Hank Aaron, Milwaukee, Atlanta, 1955 through
      1970, except 1968.
A.L.—13—Lou Gehrig, New York, 1926 through 1938.

Most consecutive years scoring 100 or more runs
A.L.—13—Lou Gehrig, New York, 1926 through 1938.
N.L.—13—Hank Aaron, Milwaukee, Atlanta, 1955 through
      1967.

Fewest runs for leader, season
N.L.—89—Gavvy Cravath, Philadelphia, 150 games, 1915.
A.L.—92—Harry H. Davis, Philadelphia, 149 games, 1905.

Fewest runs, season (150 or more games)
A.L.—25—Leo Cardenas, California, 150 games, 1972.
N.L.—32—Mike Doolan, Philadelphia, 151 games, 1913.

GAME AND INNING

Most runs, game
A.A.—7—Guy Hecker, Louisville, August 15, 1886, second
      game.
N.L.—6
   Jim Whitney, Boston, June 9, 1883.
   Cap Anson, Chicago, August 24, 1886.
   Mike Tiernan, New York, June 15, 1887.
   King Kelly, Boston, August 27, 1887.
   Ezra Sutton, Boston, August 27, 1887.
   Jimmy Ryan, Chicago, July 25, 1894.
   Bobby Lowe, Boston, May 3, 1895.
   Ginger Beaumont, Pittsburgh, July 22, 1899.
   Mel Ott, New York, August 4, 1934, second game; April 30,
      1944, first game.
   Frank Torre, Milwaukee, September 2, 1957, first game.
A.L.—6
   Johnny Pesky, Boston, May 8, 1946.
   Spike Owen, Boston, August 21, 1986.

Most runs by pitcher, game
A.A.—7—Guy Hecker, Louisville, August 15, 1886, second
      game.
N.L.—5—Nig Cuppy, Cleveland, August 9, 1895.
N.L. since 1900—4—Held by many pitchers. Last pitch-
      er—Jim Tobin, Boston, September 12, 1940, first game.
A.L.—4—Held by many pitchers. Last pitcher—Billy Hoeft,
      Detroit, May 5, 1956.

Most runs, two consecutive games (18 innings)
A.A.—11—Guy Hecker, Louisville, August 12, August 15,
      second game, 1886.
A.L.—9
   Mel Almada, Washington, July 25, 25, 1937.
   Mark McGwire, Oakland, June 27, 28, 1987.
N.L.—9
   Herman Long, Boston, May 30, 30, 1894.
   Jimmy Ryan, Chicago, July 24, 25, 1894.

   Bill Dahlen, Chicago, September 20, 21, 1894.
N.L. since 1900—8
   Kiki Cuyler, Pittsburgh, June 20, 22, 1925.
   Johnny Frederick, Brooklyn, May 17, 18, 1929.
   Mel Ott, New York, August 4, second game, August 5, 1934.
   Chuck Klein, Chicago, August 21, 21, 1935.
   Stan Musial, St. Louis, May 19, 20, 1948.

Most runs, doubleheader (18 innings)
N.L.—9—Herman Long, Boston, May 30, 1894.
A.L.—9—Mel Almada, Washington, July 25, 1937.
N.L. since 1900—8—Chuck Klein, Chicago, August 21, 1935.

Most consecutive games scoring one or more runs, season
N.L.—24—Billy Hamilton, Philadelphia, July 6 through Au-
      gust 2, 1894 (35 runs).
A.L.—18—Red Rolfe, New York, August 9 through August
      25, second game, 1939 (30 runs).
N.L. since 1900—17—Ted Kluszewski, Cincinnati, August 27
      through September 13, 1954 (24 runs).

Most times five or more runs in one game, career
M.L.—6
   George Gore, Chicago N.L., 1880, 1881, 1882 (2), 1883,
      New York P. L. 1890.
   Jimmy Ryan, Chicago N. L., 1887, 1889, 1891, 1894 (2),
      1897.
   Willie Keeler, Baltimore N. L., 1895 (2), 1897 (2), Brooklyn
      N. L., 1901, 1902.
N.L.—6
   Jimmy Ryan, Chicago, 1887, 1889, 1891, 1894 (2), 1897.
   Willie Keeler, Baltimore, Brooklyn, 1895 (2), 1897 (2),
      1901, 1902.
N.L. since 1900—3
   Mel Ott, New York, 1934, 1944 (2).
   Willie Mays, New York, San Francisco, 1954, 1964 (2).
A.L.—3
   Lou Gehrig, New York, 1928, 1936 (2).
   Jimmie Foxx, Philadelphia, Boston, 1932, 1935, 1939.

Most times with five or more runs in one game, season
N.L.—2—Held by many players.
N.L. since 1900—2
   Kiki Cuyler, Pittsburgh, May 12, second game, June 20,
      1925.
   Mel Ott, New York, April 30, first game, June 12, 1944.
   Phil Weintraub, New York, April 30, first game, June 12,
      1944.
   Willie Mays, San Francisco, April 24, September 19, 1964.
A.L.—2—Lou Gehrig, New York, May 3, July 28, 1936.

Most runs, inning
A.L.—3—Sammy White, Boston, June 18, 1953, seventh inning.
N.L.—3
   Tom Burns, Chicago, September 6, 1883, seventh inning.
   Ned Williamson, Chicago, September 6, 1883, seventh inning.
N.L. since 1900—2—Held by many players.

HITS

CAREER AND SEASON

Most hits, career
N.L.—4,256—Pete Rose, Cincinnati, Philadelphia, Montreal,
      24 years, 1963 through 1986.
A.L.—4,191—Ty Cobb, Detroit, Philadelphia, 24 years, 1905
      through 1928.

Most hits by pinch-hitter, career
N.L.—150—Manny Mota, San Francisco, Pittsburgh, Mont-
      real, Los Angeles, 20 years, 1962 through 1982, except
      1981, 599 games.
A.L.—107—Gates Brown, Detroit, 13 years, 1963 through
      1975, 525 games.

Most hits, season (Except 1887, when bases on balls counted as hits)
A.L.—257—George Sisler, St. Louis, 154 games, 1920.
N.L.—254

— 17 —

Lefty O'Doul, Philadelphia, 154 games, 1929.
Bill Terry, New York, 154 games, 1930.

Most hits by rookie, season

N.L.—223—Lloyd Waner, Pittsburgh, 150 games, 1927.
A.L. (162-game season)—217—Tony Oliva, Minnesota, 161 games, 1964.
A.L. (154-game season)—215—Dale Alexander, Detroit, 155 games, 1929.

Most hits by righthander, season

A.L.—253—Al Simmons, Philadelphia, 153 games, 1925.
N.L.—250—Rogers Hornsby, St. Louis, 154 games, 1922.

Most hits by lefthander, season

A.L.—257—George Sisler, St. Louis, 154 games, 1920.
N.L.—254
Lefty O'Doul, Philadelphia, 154 games, 1929.
Bill Terry, New York, 154 games, 1930.

Most hits by switch-hitter, season

N.L.—230—Pete Rose, Cincinnati, 160 games, 1973.
A.L.—230—Willie Wilson, Kansas City, 161 games, 1980.

Switch-hitters with 100 or more hits from each side of plate, season

N.L.—Garry Templeton, St. Louis, 154 games, 1979 (111 hits lefthanded, 100 righthanded).
A.L.—Willie Wilson, Kansas City, 161 games, 1980 (130 hits lefthanded, 100 righthanded).

Most hits by pinch-hitter, season

N.L. (162-game season)—25—Jose Morales, Montreal, 82 games, 1976.
N.L. (154-game season)—22—Sam Leslie, New York, 75 games, 1932.
A.L. (162-game season)—24—Dave Philley, Baltimore, 79 games, 1961.
A.L. (154-game season)—20—Ed Coleman, St. Louis, 74 games, 1936.

Most years leading league in hits

A.L.—8—Ty Cobb, Detroit, 1907, 1908, 1909, 1911, 1912, 1915, 1917, 1919 (tied).
N.L.—7—Pete Rose, Cincinnati, 1965, 1968 (tied), 1970 (tied), 1972, 1973, 1976, Philadelphia, 1981.

Most consecutive years leading league in hits

N.L.—3
Ginger Beaumont, Pittsburgh, 1902, 1903, 1904.
Rogers Hornsby, St. Louis, 1920, 1921, 1922.
Frank McCormick, Cincinnati, 1938, 1939, 1940 (tied).
A.L.—3
Ty Cobb, Detroit, 1907, 1908, 1909.
Tony Oliva, Minnesota, 1964, 1965, 1966.
Kirby Puckett, Minnesota, 1987 (tied), 1988, 1989.

Most games with one or more hits, season

N.L.—135
Rogers Hornsby, St. Louis, 154 games, 1922.
Chuck Klein, Philadelphia, 156 games, 1930.
A.L.—135—Wade Boggs, Boston, 161 games, 1985.

Most years with 200 or more hits, career

N.L.—10—Pete Rose, Cincinnati, 1965, 1966, 1968, 1969, 1970, 1973, 1975, 1976, 1977, Philadelphia, 1979.
A.L.—9—Ty Cobb, Detroit, 1907, 1909, 1911, 1912, 1915, 1916, 1917, 1922, 1924.

Most consecutive years with 200 or more hits, career

N.L.—8—Willie Keeler, Baltimore, Brooklyn, 1894 through 1901.
A.L.—7—Wade Boggs, Boston, 1983 through 1989.
N.L. since 1900—5—Chuck Klein, Philadelphia, 1929 through 1933.

200 or more hits by rookies, season

N.L.—Lloyd Waner, Pittsburgh, 223 hits in 150 games, 1927.
Jimmy Williams, Pittsburgh, 219 hits in 153 games, 1899.
Johnny Frederick, Brooklyn, 206 hits in 148 games, 1929.
Dick Allen, Philadelphia, 201 hits in 162 games, 1964.
A.L.—Tony Oliva, Minnesota, 217 hits in 161 games, 1964.
Dale Alexander, Detroit, 215 hits in 155 games, 1929.

Harvey Kuenn, Detroit, 209 hits in 155 games, 1953.
Kevin Seitzer, Kansas City, 207 hits in 161 games, 1987.
Joe DiMaggio, New York, 206 hits in 138 games, 1936.
Hal Trosky, Cleveland, 206 hits in 154 games, 1934.
Johnny Pesky, Boston, 205 hits in 147 games, 1942.
Roy Johnson, Detroit, 201 hits in 148 games, 1929.
Dick Wakefield, Detroit, 200 hits in 155 games, 1943.

Most hits, two consecutive seasons

N.L.—485—Rogers Hornsby, St. Louis, 235 in 1921, 250 in 1922.
A.L.—475—Ty Cobb, Detroit, 248 in 1911, 227 in 1912.

Fewest hits, season (150 or more games)

N.L.—80—Dal Maxvill, St. Louis, 152 games, 1970.
A.L.—82—Eddie Brinkman, Washington, 154 games, 1965.

Fewest hits for leader, season

N.L.—171—Sherry Magee, Philadelphia, 146 games, 1914.
A.L.—177—Bert Campaneris, Oakland, 159 games, 1968.

Most at-bats in hitless season

N.L.—70—Bob Buhl, Milwaukee, Chicago, 35 games, 1962.
A.L.—61—Bill Wight, Chicago, 30 games, 1950.

GAME AND DOUBLEHEADER

Most hits, nine-inning game

N.L.—7
Wilbert Robinson, Baltimore, June 10, 1892, first game (6 singles, 1 double; consecutive).
Rennie Stennett, Pittsburgh, September 16, 1975 (4 singles, 2 doubles, 1 triple; consecutive).
A.L.—6—Held by many players.

Most hits, extra-inning game

A.L.—9—Johnny Burnett, Cleveland, July 10, 1932, 18 innings (7 singles, 2 doubles).
N.L.—6—Held by 13 players. Last player—Gene Richards, San Diego, July 26, 1977, second game, 15 innings (5 singles, 1 double).

Most times reached base, nine-inning game (batting 1.000)

N.L.—8—Piggy Ward, Cincinnati, June 18, 1893 (2 singles, 5 bases on balls, 1 hit by pitch).
N.L. since 1900—7
Cliff Heathcote, Chicago, August 25, 1922 (3 singles, 2 doubles, 2 bases on balls).
Cookie Lavagetto, Brooklyn, September 23, 1939, first game (4 singles, 1 double, 1 triple, 1 base on balls).
Mel Ott, New York, April 30, 1944, first game (2 singles, 5 bases on balls).
Rennie Stennett, Pittsburgh, September 16, 1975 (4 singles, 2 doubles, 1 triple).
A.L.—7—Ben Chapman, New York, May 24, 1936 (2 doubles, 5 bases on balls).

Most times reached base, extra-inning game (batting 1.000)

N.L.—9—Max Carey, Pittsburgh, July 7, 1922, 18 innings (5 singles, 1 double, 3 bases on balls).
A.L.—7
Cesar Gutierrez, Detroit, June 21, 1970, second game, 12 innings (6 singles, 1 double).
Tim Raines, Chicago, April 20, 1994, 12 innings (3 singles, 4 bases on balls).

Most clubs with one or more hits, one day

N.L.—2—Joel Youngblood, New York, Montreal, August 4, 1982.

Most hits in first major league game, nine innings

N.L.—5—Fred Clarke, Louisville, June 30, 1894 (4 singles, 1 triple).
N.L. since 1900—4
Casey Stengel, Brooklyn, September 17, 1912 (4 singles).
Ed Freed, Philadelphia, September 11, 1942 (1 single, 2 doubles, 1 triple).
Willie McCovey, San Francisco, July 30, 1959 (2 singles, 2 triples; consecutive).

Mack Jones, Milwaukee, July 13, 1961 (3 singles, 1 double).
Delino DeShields, Montreal, April 9, 1990 (3 singles, 1 double).

A.L.—4
Ray Jansen, St. Louis, September 30, 1910 (4 singles; only game in major league career).
Art Shires, Chicago, August 20, 1928 (3 singles, 1 triple).
Russ Van Atta, New York, April 25, 1933 (4 singles).
Forrest Jacobs, Philadelphia, April 13, 1954 (4 singles).
Ted Cox, Boston, September 18, 1977 (3 singles, 1 double; consecutive).
Kirby Puckett, Minnesota, May 8, 1984 (4 singles).
Billy Bean, Detroit, April 25, 1987 (2 singles, 2 doubles).

Most hits in first major league game, extra innings
A.L.—5—Cecil Travis, Washington, May 16, 1933, 12 innings (5 singles).
N.L.—Less than nine-inning record.

Most hits by pitcher, game
A.A.—6—Guy Hecker, Louisville, August 15, 1886, second game.
N.L.-A.L.—5—Held by many pitchers.
N.L.—Last pitcher—Pete Donohue, Cincinnati, May 22, 1925 (4 singles, 1 home run).
A.L.—Last pitcher—Mel Stottlemyre, New York, September 26, 1964 (4 singles, 1 double).

Most hits, opening day of season
N.L.-A.L.—5—Held by many players.
N.L.—Last player—Billy Herman, Chicago, April 14, 1936 (1 single, 3 doubles, 1 home run).
A.L.—Last player—Nellie Fox, Chicago, April 10, 1959, 14 innings (3 singles, 1 double, 1 home run).

Most hits comprising all of club's hits, game
A.L.—4—Kid Elberfeld, New York, August 1, 1903 (4 singles).
N.L.—4—Billy Williams, Chicago, September 5, 1969 (2 doubles, 2 home runs).

Most at-bats with no hits, extra-inning game
N.L.—11—Charles Pick, Boston, May 1, 1920, 26 innings.
A.L.—10—George Kell, Philadelphia, July 21, 1945, 24 innings.

Most times with six hits in six times at bat in game, career
M.L.—2
Ed Delahanty, Cleveland, P.L., June 2, 1890; Philadelphia, N.L., June 16, 1894.
Jim Bottomley, St. Louis N.L., September 16, 1924; August 5, 1931, second game.
Doc Cramer, Philadelphia A.L., June 20, 1932; July 13, 1935.
N.L.—2—Jim Bottomley, St. Louis, September 16, 1924; August 5, 1931, second game.
A.L.—2—Doc Cramer, Philadelphia, June 20, 1932; July 13, 1935.

Most times with five or more hits in one game, career
A.L.—14—Ty Cobb, Detroit, Philadelphia, 1908 to 1927.
N.L.—10—Pete Rose, Cincinnati, Philadelphia, 1965 to 1986.

Most times with five hits in one game, by pitcher, career
3—Jim Callahan, Chicago N.L., 1897, Chicago A.L., 1902, 1903.

Most times with five or more hits in one game, season
N.L.—4
Willie Keeler, Baltimore, July 17, August 14, September 3, September 6, first game, 1897.
Stan Musial, St. Louis, April 30, May 19, June 22, September 22, 1948.
Tony Gwynn, San Diego, April 18, April 30, July 27, August 4, 1993.
A.L.—4—Ty Cobb, Detroit, May 7, July 7, second game, July 12, July 17, 1922.

Most hits, doubleheader
A.A.—9—Fred Carroll, Pittsburgh, July 5, 1886.
N.L.—9
Wilbert Robinson, Baltimore, June 10, 1892.
Joe Kelley, Baltimore, September 3, 1894 (consecutive).
Fred Lindstrom, New York, June 25, 1928.

Bill Terry, New York, June 18, 1929.
A.L.—9
Ray Morehart, Chicago, August 31, 1926.
George Case, Washington, July 4, 1940.
Pete Runnels, Boston, August 30, 1960, 25 innings.
Lee Thomas, Los Angeles, September 5, 1961.

Most hits by pinch-hitter, doubleheader
N.L.-A.L.—2—Held by many pinch-hitters.

Most hits in first doubleheader in majors
N.L.-A.L.—6—Held by many players.

Most hits, two consecutive doubleheaders
A.L.—14—Ty Cobb, Detroit, July 17 (7), 19 (7), 1912.
N.L.—14—Will White, St. Louis, July 17 (8), 18 (6), 1961.

Most at-bats with no hits, doubleheader (nine-inning games)
A.L.—11—Albie Pearson, Los Angeles, July 1, 1962.
N.L.—10—Held by many players.

Most at-bats with no hits, doubleheader (over 18 innings)
N.L.—12—Red Schoendienst, St. Louis, June 9, 1947, 24 innings.
A.L.—12—Bob Saverine, Washington, June 8, 1966, 23 innings.

HITTING FOR CYCLE
(Single, double, triple and home run in game)

Hitting for cycle, game
N.L.—113 times. Last player—Mark Grace, Chicago, May 9, 1993.
A.L.—95 times. Last player—Scott Cooper, Boston, April 12, 1994.

Most times hitting for cycle, career
M.L.—3
John Reilly, Cincinnati A.A., 1883 (2), Cincinnati N.L., 1890.
Bob Meusel, New York A.L., 1921, 1922, 1928.
Babe Herman, Brooklyn N.L., 1931 (2), Chicago N.L., 1933.
A.L.—3—Bob Meusel, New York, 1921, 1922, 1928.
N.L.—3—Babe Herman, Brooklyn, 1931 (2), Chicago, 1933.

Hitting for cycle in American and National leagues
Bob Watson, Houston N.L., June 24, 1977; Boston A.L., September 15, 1979.

INNING

Most hits, inning
N.L.—3
Tommy Burns, Chicago, September 6, 1883, seventh inning (2 doubles, 1 home run).
Fred Pfeffer, Chicago, September 6, 1883, seventh inning (2 singles, 1 double).
Ned Williamson, Chicago, September 6, 1883, seventh inning (2 singles, 1 double).
A.L.—3—Gene Stephens, Boston, June 18, 1953, seventh inning (2 singles, 1 double).

Most hits in one inning of first major league game
A.L.—2
Billy Martin, New York, April 18, 1950, eighth inning.
Russ Morman, Chicago, August 3, 1986, fourth inning.
Chad Kreuter, Texas, September 14, 1988, fifth inning.
N.L.—1—Held by many players.

Most times with two hits in one inning, game
N.L.—2
Max Carey, Pittsburgh, June 22, 1925, first and eighth innings (2 singles in each inning).
Rennie Stennett, Pittsburgh, September 16, 1975, first inning (single and double); fifth inning (double and single).
A.L.—2
Johnny Hodapp, Cleveland, July 29, 1928, second and sixth innings (2 singles in each inning).
Sherm Lollar, Chicago, April 23, 1955, second inning (single and home run); sixth inning (2 singles).

Most times reached first base safely, inning

N.L.—3
Ned Williamson, Chicago, September 6, 1883, seventh inning.
Tommy Burns, Chicago, September 6, 1883, seventh inning.
Fred Pfeffer, Chicago, September 6, 1883, seventh inning.
Herman Long, Boston, June 18, 1894, a.m. game, first inning.
Bobby Lowe, Boston, June 18, 1894, a.m. game, first inning.
Hugh Duffy, Boston, June 18, 1894, a.m. game, first inning.
Pee Wee Reese, Brooklyn, May 21, 1952, first inning.

A.L.—3
Sammy White, Boston, June 18, 1953, seventh inning.
Gene Stephens, Boston, June 18, 1953, seventh inning.
Tommy Umphlett, Boston, June 18, 1953, seventh inning.

BATTING STREAKS

Most consecutive hits, season (bases on balls shown in streak)

A.L.—12
Pinky Higgins, Boston, June 19, 19, 21, 21, 1938 (2 B.B.).
Walt Dropo, Detroit, July 14, 15, 15, 1952 (0 B.B.).

N.L.—10
Ed Delahanty, Philadelphia, July 13, 13, 14, 1897 (1 B.B.).
Jake Gettman, Washington, September 10, 11, 11, 1897 (0 B.B.).
Ed Konetchy, Brooklyn, June 28, second game, June 29, July 1, 1919 (0 B.B.).
Kiki Cuyler, Pittsburgh, September 18, 19, 21, 1925 (1 B.B.).
Chick Hafey, St. Louis, July 6, second game, July 8, 9, 1929 (2 B.B.).
Joe Medwick, St. Louis, July 19, 19, 21, 1936 (1 B.B.).
Buddy Hassett, Boston, June 9, second game, June 10, 14, 1940 (1 B.B.).
Woody Williams, Cincinnati, September 5, second game, September 6, 6, 1943 (1 B.B.).
Bip Roberts, Cincinnati, September 19, 20, 22, second game, 23 1992 (1 B.B.).

Most consecutive times reached base safely, season

A.L.—16—Ted Williams, Boston, September 17 (1), 18 (1), 20 (1), 21 (4), 22 (4), 23 (5), 1957 (2 singles, 4 home runs, 9 bases on balls, 1 hit by pitch).
N.L.—14—Pedro Guerrero, Los Angeles, July 23 (2), 24 (4), 25 (4), 26 (4), 1985 (2 singles, 3 doubles, 2 home runs, 6 bases on balls, 1 hit by pitch).

Most consecutive hits from start of career

A.L.—6—Ted Cox, Boston, September 18, 19, 1977.

Most consecutive hits by pinch-hitter, career

N.L.—9—Dave Philley, Philadelphia, September 9 through September 28, 1958; April 16, 1959.

Most consecutive hits by pinch-hitter, season

N.L.—8
Dave Philley, Philadelphia, September 9 through September 28, 1958.
Rusty Staub, New York, June 11 through June 26, first game, 1983 (1 hit by pitch during streak).

A.L.—7
Bill Stein, Texas, April 14 through May 25, 1981.
Randy Bush, Minnesota, July 5 through August 19, 1991.

Most consecutive games batted safely during season

A.L.—56—Joe DiMaggio, New York, May 15 through July 16, 1941.
N.L.—44
Willie Keeler, Baltimore, April 22 through June 18, 1897.
Pete Rose, Cincinnati, June 14 through July 31, 1978.

Most consecutive games batted safely by rookie, season

N.L.—34—Benito Santiago, San Diego, August 25 through October 2, 1987.
A.L.—26—Guy Curtright, Chicago, June 6, first game, through July 1, 1943.

Most consecutive games batted safely by righthander, season

A.L.—56—Joe DiMaggio, New York, May 15 through July 16, 1941.
N.L.—42—Bill Dahlen, Chicago, June 20 through August 6, 1894.
N.L. since 1900—34—Benito Santiago, San Diego, August 25 through October 2, 1987.

Most consecutive games batted safely by lefthander, season

N.L.—44—Willie Keeler, Baltimore, April 22 to June 18, 1897.
A.L.—41—George Sisler, St. Louis, July 27 to September 17, 1922.
N.L. since 1900—37—Tommy Holmes, Boston, June 6, first game, to July 8, second game, 1945.

Most consecutive games batted safely by switch-hitter, season

N.L.—44—Pete Rose, Cincinnati, June 14 through July 31, 1978.
A.L.—22—Eddie Murray, Baltimore, August 17 through September 10, 1984.

Most consecutive games batted safely from start of season

N.L.—44—Willie Keeler, Baltimore, April 22 through June 18, 1897.
A.L.—34—George Sisler, St. Louis, April 14 through May 19, 1925.
N.L. since 1900—25—Charlie Grimm, Pittsburgh, April 17 through May 16, 1923.

Most 20-game batting streaks, career

A.L.—8—Ty Cobb, Detroit, Philadelphia, 1906, 1911, 1912, 1917, 1918, 1920, 1926, 1927.
N.L.—8—Willie Keeler, Baltimore, Brooklyn, 1894, 1896, 1897, 1898 (2), 1899, 1900, 1902.
N.L. since 1900—7—Pete Rose, Cincinnati, Philadelphia, 1967, 1968, 1977 (2), 1978, 1979, 1982.

Most 20-game batting streaks, season

A.L.—3—Tris Speaker, Boston, 1912.
N.L.—2—Held by many players. Last player—Steve Garvey, Los Angeles, 1978.

Most hits in two consecutive nine-inning games

N.L.—12—Cal McVey, Chicago, July 22 (6), 25 (6), 1876.
N.L. since 1900—10—Rennie Stennett, Pittsburgh, September 16 (7), 17 (3), 1975.
A.L.—10—Kirby Puckett, Minnesota, August 29 (4), 30 (6), 1987.

Most hits in two consecutive extra-inning games

A.L.—11—Johnny Burnett, Cleveland, July 9, second game (2), 10 (9), 1932, 27 innings.
N.L.—10—Roberto Clemente, Pittsburgh, August 22 (5), 23 (5), 1970, 25 innings.

Most hits by pitcher in two consecutive games

A.A.—10—Guy Hecker, Louisville, August 12, 15, second game, 1886.
A.L.—8—George Earnshaw, Philadelphia, June 9, 12, second game, 1931.
N.L. since 1900—8—Kirby Higbe, Brooklyn, August 11, 17, first game, 1941.

Most hits in three consecutive games

N.L.—15—Cal McVey, Chicago, July 20, 22, 25, 1876.
A.L.—13
Joe Cronin, Washington, June 19, 21, 22, 1933.
Walt Dropo, Detroit, July 14, 15, 15, 1952.
Tim Salmon, California, May 10, 11, 13, 1994.
N.L. since 1900—12
Willie Keeler, Brooklyn, June 19, 20, 21, 1901.
Milt Stock, Brooklyn, June 30, July 1, 2, 1925.
Stan Musial, St. Louis, August 11, 11, 12, 1946.
Rennie Stennett, Pittsburgh, September 16, 17, 18, 1975.

Most hits in four consecutive games

N.L.—17
Cal McVey, Chicago, July 20, 22, 25, 27, 1876.
Willie Keeler, Baltimore, September 2, 3, 4, 6, first game, 1897.

N.L. since 1900—16—Milt Stock, Brooklyn, June 30, July 1, 2, 3, 1925.
A.A.—17—Guy Hecker, Louisville, August 8, 10, 12, 15, second game, 1886.
A.L.—15
  Joe Cronin, Washington, June 18, second game, 19, 21, 22, 1933.
  Joe Cronin, Washington, June 19, 21, 22, 23, 1933.
  John Lewis Jr., Washington, July 25, 27, 28, 1937.
  Walt Dropo, Detroit, July 14, 15, 15, 16, 1952.

Most consecutive games with three or more hits, season
A.L.—6—George Brett, Kansas City, May 8, 9, 10, 11, 12, 13, 1976.

SINGLES

Most singles, career
N.L.—3,215—Pete Rose, Cincinnati, Philadelphia, Montreal, 24 years, 1963 through 1986.
A.L.—3,052—Ty Cobb, Detroit, Philadelphia, 24 years, 1905 through 1928.

Most singles, season
N.L.—202—Willie Keeler, Baltimore, 128 games, 1898.
N.L. since 1900—198—Lloyd Waner, Pittsburgh, 150 games, 1927.
A.L.—187—Wade Boggs, Boston, 161 games, 1985.

Most singles by rookie, season
N.L.—198—Lloyd Waner, Pittsburgh, 150 games, 1927.
A.L.—167—Harvey Kuenn, Detroit, 155 games, 1953.

Most singles by righthander, season
A.L.—174—Al Simmons, Philadelphia, 153 games, 1925.
N.L. (162-game season)—178—Curt Flood, St. Louis, 162 games, 1964.
N.L. (154-game season)—172—Mickey Witek, New York, 153 games, 1943.

Most singles by lefthander, season
N.L.—202—Willie Keeler, Baltimore, 128 games, 1898.
N.L. since 1900—198—Lloyd Waner, Pittsburgh, 150 games, 1927.
A.L.—187—Wade Boggs, Boston, 161 games, 1985.

Most singles by switch-hitter, season
A.L.—184—Willie Wilson, Kansas City, 161 games, 1980.
N.L.—181—Pete Rose, Cincinnati, 160 games, 1973.

Most years leading league in singles
A.L.—8—Nellie Fox, Chicago, 1952, 1954, 1955, 1956, 1957, 1958, 1959, 1960.
N.L.—5—Tony Gwynn, San Diego, 1984, 1986 (tied), 1987, 1989, 1994.

Most consecutive years leading league in singles
A.L.—7—Nellie Fox, Chicago, 1954, 1955, 1956, 1957, 1958, 1959, 1960.
N.L.—4—Brett Butler, San Francisco, 1990, Los Angeles, 1991, 1992, 1993.

Fewest singles, season (150 or more games)
A.L.—53—Mark McGwire, Oakland, 154 games, 1991.
N.L.—63—Mike Schmidt, Philadelphia, 160 games, 1979.

Fewest singles by leader, season
A.L.—129—Don Buford, Chicago, 155 games, 1965.
N.L.—127—Enos Slaughter, St. Louis, 152 games, 1942.

Most singles, nine-inning game
N.L.-A.A.-A.L.—6—Held by many players.
N.L.—Last player—Dave Bancroft, New York, June 28, 1920.
A.L.—Last player—Floyd Robinson, Chicago, July 22, 1962.

Most singles, extra-inning game
A.L.—7—Johnny Burnett, Cleveland, July 10, 1932, 18 innings.
N.L.—6—Held by many players. Last player—Willie Davis, Los Angeles, May 24, 1973, 19 innings.

Most singles in a game, each batting in three runs
N.L.-A.L.—1—Held by many players.
N.L.—Last player—Willie Montanez, Philadelphia, September 8, 1974, eighth inning.
A.L.—Last player—Ernest Riles, Milwaukee, June 5, 1985, third inning.

Most singles, doubleheader
N.L.-A.L.—8—Held by many players.
A.L.—Last player—Earl Averill, Cleveland, May 7, 1933.
N.L.—Last player—Ken Hubbs, Chicago, May 20, 1962.

Most singles, inning
N.L.-A.L.—2—Held by many players.

DOUBLES

CAREER AND SEASON

Most doubles, career
A.L.—793—Tris Speaker, Boston, Cleveland, Washington, Philadelphia, 22 years, 1907 through 1928.
N.L.—746—Pete Rose, Cincinnati, Philadelphia, Montreal, 24 years, 1963 through 1986.

Most doubles, season
A.L.—67—Earl Webb, Boston, 151 games, 1931.
N.L.—64—Joe Medwick, St. Louis, 155 games, 1936.

Most doubles by rookie, season
N.L.—52—Johnny Frederick, Brooklyn, 148 games, 1929.
A.L. (162-game season)—47—Fred Lynn, Boston, 145 games, 1975.
A.L. (154-game season)—45
  Roy Johnson, Detroit, 148 games, 1929.
  Hal Trosky, Cleveland, 154 games, 1934.

Most doubles by righthander, season
A.L.—64—George Burns, Cleveland, 151 games, 1926.
N.L.—64—Joe Medwick, St. Louis, 155 games, 1936.

Most doubles by lefthander, season
A.L.—67—Earl Webb, Boston, 151 games, 1931.
N.L.—62—Paul Waner, Pittsburgh, 154 games, 1932.

Most doubles by switch-hitter, season
N.L.—51—Pete Rose, Cincinnati, 159 games, 1978.
A.L.—47—John Anderson, Milwaukee, 138 games, 1901.

Most doubles by catcher, season
A.L.—42—Mickey Cochrane, Philadelphia, 130 games, 1930; caught 130 games.
N.L.—40
  Johnny Bench, Cincinnati, 154 games, 1968; caught 154 games.
  Terry Kennedy, San Diego, 153 games, 1982; caught 139 games (also had two doubles as first baseman).

Most years leading league in doubles
N.L.—8
  Honus Wagner, Pittsburgh, 1900, 1901 (tied), 1902, 1904, 1906, 1907, 1908, 1909.
  Stan Musial, St. Louis, 1943, 1944, 1946, 1948, 1949, 1952, 1953, 1954.
A.L.—8—Tris Speaker, Boston, 1912, Cleveland, 1914, 1916 (tied), 1918, 1920, 1921, 1922, 1923.

Most consecutive years leading league in doubles
N.L.—4—Honus Wagner, Pittsburgh, 1906, 1907, 1908, 1909.
A.L.—4—Tris Speaker, Cleveland, 1920, 1921, 1922, 1923.

Most years with 50 or more doubles, career
A.L.—5—Tris Speaker, Boston, 1912, Cleveland, 1920, 1921, 1923, 1926.
N.L.—3
  Paul Waner, Pittsburgh, 1928, 1932, 1936.
  Stan Musial, St. Louis, 1944, 1946, 1953.

Fewest doubles, season (150 or more games)
N.L.—5—Dal Maxvill, St. Louis, 152 games, 1970.

A.L.—6—Billy Purtell, Chicago, Boston, 151 games, 1910.

Fewest doubles for leader, season

A.L.—32
Sal Bando, Oakland, 162 games, 1973.
Pedro Garcia, Milwaukee, 160 games, 1973.
N.L.—34—Hank Aaron, Milwaukee, 153 games, 1956.

GAME AND INNING

Most doubles, game

N.L.—4—19 times (held by 19 players). Last player—Billy Hatcher, Cincinnati, August 21, 1990.
A.L.—4—17 times (held by 17 players). Last player—Kirby Puckett, Minnesota, May 13, 1989.
A.A.—4—2 times (held by 2 players).

Most consecutive doubles, nine-inning game

N.L.—4
Frank Bonner, Baltimore, August 4, 1894.
Joe Kelley, Baltimore, September 3, 1894, second game.
Dick Bartell, Philadelphia, April 25, 1933.
Ernie Lombardi, Cincinnati, May 8, 1935, first game.
Bill Werber, Cincinnati, May 13, 1940.
Willie Jones, Philadelphia, April 20, 1949.
Billy Williams, Chicago, April 9, 1969.
A.L.—4
Bill Werber, Boston, July 17, 1935, first game.
Mike Kreevich, Chicago, September 4, 1937.
Johnny Lindell, New York, August 17, 1944.
Lou Boudreau, Cleveland, July 14, 1946, first game.
Vic Wertz, Cleveland, September 26, 1956.
Bill Bruton, Detroit, May 19, 1963.
Dave Duncan, Baltimore, June 30, 1975, second game.

Most doubles, opening game of season

A.L.—4—Frank Dillon, Detroit, April 25, 1901.
N.L.—4—Jim Greengrass, Cincinnati, April 13, 1954.

Most doubles by pitcher, game

N.L.—3
George Hemming, Baltimore, August 1, 1895.
Andy Messersmith, Los Angeles, April 25, 1975.
A.L.—3
George Mullin, Detroit, April 27, 1903.
Walter Johnson, Washington, July 29, 1917.
Babe Ruth, Boston, May 9, 1918, 10 innings.
George Uhle, Cleveland, June 1, 1923.
Red Ruffing, Boston, May 25, 1929, second game.
Don Ferrarese, Cleveland, May 26, 1959.

Most doubles, each batting in three runs, game

N.L.—2
Bob Gilks, Cleveland, August 5, 1890 (1 in second, 1 in eighth).
Harry Davis, New York, June 27, 1896 (1 in fifth, 1 in ninth).
William Douglass, Philadelphia, July 11, 1898 (1 in second, 1 in sixth).
Gavvy Cravath, Philadelphia, August 8, 1915 (1 in fourth, 1 in eighth).
A.L.—1—Held by many players.

Most doubles, doubleheader

A.L.—6—Hank Majeski, Philadelphia, August 27, 1948.
N.L.—5
Chick Hafey, Cincinnati, July 23, 1933.
Joe Medwick, St. Louis, May 30, 1935.
Red Schoendienst, St. Louis, June 6, 1948.
Mike Ivie, San Diego, May 30, 1977.

Most doubles in two consecutive games

N.L.—6
Cap Anson, Chicago, July 3, 4, a.m. game, 1883.
Sam Thompson, Philadelphia, June 29, July 1, 1895, 22 innings.
Red Schoendienst, St. Louis, June 5, 6, first game, 1948.
A.L.—6
Joe Dugan, Philadelphia, September 24, 25, 1920.
Earl Sheely, Chicago, May 20, 21, 1926.

Hank Majeski, Philadelphia, August 27, 28, 1948.
Kirby Puckett, Minnesota, May 13, 14, 1989.

Most doubles in three consecutive games

N.L.—8—Red Schoendienst, St. Louis, June 5, 6, 6, 1948.
A.L.—7
Joe Dugan, Philadelphia, September 23, 24, 25, 1920.
Earl Sheely, Chicago, May 20, 21, 22, 1926.

Most doubles by pinch-hitter, three consecutive games

N.L.—3
Bert Haas, Brooklyn, September 18, 19, 20, 1937.
Doug Clemens, Philadelphia, June 6, 6, 7, 1967.
A.L.—Never accomplished.

Most doubles, inning

N.L.-A.L.—2—Held by many players.
N.L.—Last player—Rick Schu, Philadelphia, October 3, 1985, third inning.
A.L.—Last player—Bernie Williams, New York, June 22, 1994, seventh inning.

Most doubles by pitcher, inning

N.L.—2
Fred Goldsmith, Chicago, September 6, 1883, seventh inning.
Hank Borowy, Chicago, May 5, 1946, first game, seventh inning.
A.L.—2
Joe Wood, Boston, July 4, 1913, a.m. game, fourth inning.
Ted Lyons, Chicago, July 28, 1935, first game, second inning.

TRIPLES

CAREER AND SEASON

Most triples, career

M.L.—312—Sam Crawford, Cincinnati N.L., Detroit A.L., 19 years, 1899 through 1917 (62 in N.L. and 250 in A.L.).
A.L.—298—Ty Cobb, Detroit, Philadelphia, 24 years, 1905 through 1928.
N.L.—252—Honus Wagner, Louisville, Pittsburgh, 21 years, 1897 through 1917.
N.L. since 1900—231—Honus Wagner, Pittsburgh, 18 years, 1900 through 1917.

Most triples with bases filled, career

A.L.—8—Shano Collins, Chicago, Boston, 1910, 1915, 1916, 1918 (3), 1920 (2).
N.L.—7—Stan Musial, St. Louis, 1946, 1947 (2), 1948, 1949, 1951, 1954.

Most triples, season

N.L.—36—Owen Wilson, Pittsburgh, 152 games, 1912.
A.L.—26
Joe Jackson, Cleveland, 152 games, 1912.
Sam Crawford, Detroit, 157 games, 1914.

Most triples by rookie, season

N.L.—27—Jimmy Williams, Pittsburgh, 153 games, 1899.
N.L. since 1900—22—Paul Waner, Pittsburgh, 144 games, 1926.
A.L.—17—Russ Scarritt, Boston, 151 games, 1929.

Most triples by righthander, season

N.L.—33—Perry Werden, St. Louis, 124 games, 1893.
N.L. since 1900—26—Kiki Cuyler, Pittsburgh, 153 games, 1925.
A.L.—23—Jimmy Williams, Baltimore, 125 games, 1902.

Most triples by lefthander, season

N.L.—36—Owen Wilson, Pittsburgh, 152 games, 1912.
A.L.—26
Joe Jackson, Cleveland, 152 games, 1912.
Sam Crawford, Detroit, 157 games, 1914.

Most triples by switch-hitter, season

N.L.—26—George Davis, New York, 133 games, 1893.
A.L.—21—Willie Wilson, Kansas City, 141 games, 1985.
N.L. since 1900—19
Max Carey, 153 games, 1923.
Garry Templeton, St. Louis, 154 games, 1979.

Most triples with bases filled, season

A.L.—3
   Shano Collins, Chicago, 103 games, 1918.
   Elmer Valo, Philadelphia, 150 games, 1949.
   Jackie Jensen, Boston, 151 games, 1956.
N.L.—3
   George J. Burns, New York, 154 games, 1914.
   Ted Sizemore, Los Angeles, 159 games, 1969.
   Manny Sanguillen, Pittsburgh, 138 games, 1971.
   Alfredo Griffin, Los Angeles, 95 games, 1988.

Most years leading league in triples (since 1900)

M.L.—6—Sam Crawford, Cincinnati N.L., 1902; Detroit A.L.,
      1903, 1910, 1913, 1914, 1915.
A.L.—5
   Sam Crawford, Detroit, 1903, 1910, 1913, 1914, 1915.
   Willie Wilson, Kansas City, 1980 (tied), 1982, 1985, 1987,
      1988 (tied).
N.L.—5—Stan Musial, St. Louis, 1943, 1946, 1948, 1949
      (tied), 1951 (tied).

Most consecutive years leading league in triples (since 1900)

A.L.—4—Lance Johnson, Chicago, 1991 (tied), 1992, 1993,
      1994.
N.L.—3—Garry Templeton, St. Louis, 1977, 1978, 1979.

Most years with 20 or more triples

M.L.—5—Sam Crawford, Cincinnati N.L., 1902; Detroit A.L.,
      1903, 1912, 1913, 1914.
A.L.—4
   Sam Crawford, Detroit, 1903, 1912, 1913, 1914.
   Ty Cobb, Detroit, 1908, 1911, 1912, 1917.
N.L.—2—Held by many players. Last player—Stan Musial,
      St. Louis, 1943, 1946.

Most at-bats without a triple, season

A.L.—646—Cal Ripken Jr., Baltimore, 162 games, 1989.
N.L.—621—Cookie Rojas, Philadelphia, 152 games, 1968.

Fewest triples for league leader, season

A.L.—8—Del Unser, Washington, 153 games, 1969.
N.L.—10
   Johnny Callison, Philadelphia, 157 games, 1962.
   Willie Davis, Los Angeles, 157 games, 1962.
   Bill Virdon, Pittsburgh, 156 games, 1962.
   Maury Wills, Los Angeles, 165 games, 1962.
   Dickie Thon, Houston, 136 games, 1982.

GAME AND INNING

Most triples, game

A.A.—4—George Strief, Philadelphia, June 25, 1885.
N.L.—4—Bill Joyce, New York, May 18, 1897.
N.L. since 1900—3—Held by many players. Last player—Shawon Dunston, Chicago, July 28, 1990. Herm
   Winningham, Cincinnati, August 15, 1990, 12 innings.
A.L.—3—Held by many players. Last player—Ken Landreaux, Minnesota, July 3, 1980.

Most triples, first major league game

A.L.—2
   Ed Irvin, Detroit, May 18, 1912 (only major league game).
   Roy Weatherly, Cleveland, June 27, 1936.
N.L.—2
   Willie McCovey, San Francisco, July 30, 1959.
   John Sipin, San Diego, May 24, 1969 (only major league
   triples).

Most triples by pitcher, game

N.L.—3—Jouett Meekin, New York, July 4, 1894, first game.

Most consecutive triples, nine-inning game

N.L.-A.L.—3—Held by many players.
N.L.—Last player—Roberto Clemente, Pittsburgh, September 8, 1958.
A.L.—Last player—Ben Chapman, Cleveland, July 3, 1939.

Most triples with bases filled, game

N.L.—2
   Sam Thompson, Detroit, May 7, 1887.

Heinie Reitz, Baltimore, June 4, 1894, 1 in third inning, 1 in
   seventh inning.
Willie Clark, Pittsburgh, September 17, 1898, second game,
   1 in first inning, 1 in seventh inning.
Bill Bruton, Milwaukee, August 2, 1959, second game, 1 in
   first inning, 1 in sixth inning.
A.L.—2
   Elmer Valo, Philadelphia, May 1, 1949, first game, 1 in third
      inning, 1 in seventh inning.
   Duane Kuiper, Cleveland, July 27, 1978, second game, 1 in
      first inning, 1 in fifth inning.

Most times with three triples in one game, career

N.L.—2
   John Reilly, Cincinnati, 1890, 1891.
   George Davis, Cleveland, New York, 1891, 1894.
   Bill Dahlen, Chicago, 1896, 1898.
   Dave Brain, St. Louis, Pittsburgh, 1905 (2).
A.L.—1—Held by many players.

Most times with three triples in one game, season

N.L.—2—Dave Brain, St. Louis, May 29, 1905; Pittsburgh,
      August 8, 1905.
A.L.—1—Held by many players.

Hitting triple and home run in first major league game

A.L.—Hank Arft, St. Louis, July 27, 1948.
N.L.—Lloyd Merriman, Cincinnati, April 24, 1949, first game.
   Frank Ernaga, Chicago, May 24, 1957.
   Ken Caminiti, Houston, July 16, 1987.

Hitting triple and home run with bases filled, game

N.L.—Dennis Brouthers, Detroit, May 17, 1887.
   Kid Nichols, Boston, September 19, 1892.
   Jake Stenzel, Pittsburgh, July 15, 1893.
   Del Bissonette, Brooklyn, April 21, 1930.
   Eddie Phillips, Pittsburgh, May 28, 1931.
   Luis Olmo, Brooklyn, May 18, 1945.
A.L.—George Sisler, St. Louis, July 11, 1925.
   Harry Heilmann, Detroit, July 26, 1928, second game.

Most triples, doubleheader

A.A.—4—Billy Hamilton, Kansas City, June 28, 1889.
N.L.—4—Mike Donlin, Cincinnati, September 22, 1903.
A.L.—3—Held by many players.

Most triples in five consecutive games

N.L.—6—Owen Wilson, Pittsburgh, June 17, 18, 19, 20, 20
      (2), 1912.

Most triples, inning

N.L.—2
   Joe Hornung, Boston, May 6, 1882, eighth inning.
   Heinie Peitz, St. Louis, July 2, 1895, first inning.
   Frank Shugart, Louisville, July 30, 1895, fifth inning.
   Buck Freeman, Boston, July 25, 1900, first inning.
   Bill Dahlen, Brooklyn, August 30, 1900, eighth inning.
   Curt Walker, Cincinnati, July 22, 1926, second inning.
A.A.—2
   Harry Wheeler, Cincinnati, June 28, 1882, 11th inning.
   Harry Stovey, Philadelphia, August 18, 1884, eighth inning.
A.L.—2
   Al Zarilla, St. Louis, July 13, 1946, fourth inning.
   Gil Coan, Washington, April 21, 1951, sixth inning.

HOME RUNS

CAREER

Most home runs, career

M.L.—755—Hank Aaron, Milwaukee N.L., Atlanta N.L., Milwaukee A.L., 23 years, 1954 through 1976 (733 in N.L.;
      22 in A.L.).
N.L.—733—Hank Aaron, Milwaukee, Atlanta, 21 years, 1954
      through 1974.
A.L.—708—Babe Ruth, Boston, New York, 21 years, 1914
      through 1934.

Most home runs with one club, career

N.L.—733—Hank Aaron, Milwaukee, Atlanta, 21 years, 1954

through 1974.
A.L.—659—Babe Ruth, New York, 15 years, 1920 through 1934.

Most home runs by righthander, career

M.L.—755—Hank Aaron, Milwaukee N.L., Atlanta N.L., Milwaukee A.L., 23 years, 1954 through 1976 (733 in N.L.; 22 in A.L.).

N.L.—733—Hank Aaron, Milwaukee, Atlanta, 21 years, 1954 through 1974.

A.L.—573—Harmon Killebrew, Washington, Minnesota, Kansas City, 22 years, 1954 through 1975.

Most home runs by lefthander, career

M.L.—714—Babe Ruth, Boston A.L., New York A.L., Boston N.L., 22 years, 1914 through 1935 (708 in A.L.; 6 in N.L.).

Most home runs by lefthander, career

A.L.—708—Babe Ruth, Boston, New York, 21 years, 1914 through 1934.

N.L.—521—Willie McCovey, San Francisco, San Diego, 22 years, 1959 through 1980.

Most home runs by switch-hitter, career

A.L.—536—Mickey Mantle, New York, 18 years, 1951 through 1968.

N.L.—202—Howard Johnson, New York, Colorado, 10 years, 1985 through 1994.

Most home runs by pinch-hitter, career

M.L.—20—Cliff Johnson, Houston N.L., New York A.L., Cleveland A.L., Chicago N.L., Oakland A.L., Toronto A.L., 1974 (5), 1975 (1), 1976 (1), 1977 (3), 1978 (2), 1979 (1), 1980 (3), 1981 (1), 1983 (1), 1984 (1), 1986 (1).

N.L.—18—Jerry Lynch, Cincinnati, Pittsburgh, 1957 (3), 1958 (1), 1959 (1), 1961 (5), 1962 (1), 1963 (4), 1964 (1), 1965 (1), 1966 (1).

A.L.—16—Gates Brown, Detroit, 1963 (1), 1964 (1), 1965 (1), 1966 (2), 1968 (3), 1970 (1), 1971 (2), 1972 (1), 1974 (3), 1975 (1).

Most home runs as leadoff batter, career

A.L.—66—Rickey Henderson, Oakland, New York, Toronto, 16 years, 1979 through 1994.

N.L.—30—Bobby Bonds, San Francisco, St. Louis, Chicago, 1968 through 1974, nine years, 1980 through 1981.

Most home runs in extra innings, career

N.L.—22—Willie Mays, original New York club, San Francisco, present New York club, 22 years, 1951 through 1973, except 1953 in military service.

A.L.—16—Babe Ruth, Boston, New York, 21 years, 1914 through 1934.

Most home runs in opening games of season, career

M.L.—8—Frank Robinson, Cincinnati N.L., 1959, 1961, 1963; Baltimore A.L., 1966, 1969, 1970; California A.L., 1973; Cleveland A.L., 1975 (5 in A.L., 3 in N.L.).

N.L.—7
Eddie Mathews, Milwaukee, 1954 (2), 1958 (2), 1959, 1961, 1965.
Willie Mays, New York, 1954; San Francisco, 1962, 1963, 1964 (2), 1966, 1971.

A.L.—6
Babe Ruth, Boston, 1919; New York, 1923, 1929, 1931, 1932 (2).
Brooks Robinson, Baltimore, 1960, 1966, 1967, 1968, 1973 (2).
Carl Yastrzemski, Boston, 1963, 1968 (2), 1973, 1974, 1980.

Most home runs by first baseman, career

A.L.—493—Lou Gehrig, New York, 17 years, 1923 through 1939.

N.L.—439—Willie McCovey, San Francisco, San Diego, 22 years, 1959 through 1980.

Most home runs by second baseman, career

M.L.—266—Joe Morgan, Houston N.L., Cincinnati N.L., San Francisco N.L., Philadelphia N.L., Oakland A.L., 22 years, 1963 through 1984 (260 in N.L., 6 in A.L.).

N.L.—263—Rogers Hornsby, St. Louis, New York, Boston, Chicago, 15 years, 1916, 1919 through 1931, 1933.

A.L.—246—Joe Gordon, New York, Cleveland, 11 years, 1938 through 1950, except 1944, 1945 in military service.

Most home runs by third baseman, career

N.L.—509—Mike Schmidt, Philadelphia, 18 years, 1972 through 1989.

A.L.—319—Graig Nettles, Minnesota, Cleveland, New York, 16 years, 1968 through 1983.

Most home runs by shortstop, career

A.L.—302—Cal Ripken Jr., Baltimore, 14 years, 1981 through 1994.

N.L.—277—Ernie Banks, Chicago, nine years, 1953 through 1961.

Most home runs by outfielder, career

M.L.—692—Babe Ruth, Boston A.L., New York A.L., Boston N.L., 17 years, 1918 through 1935 (686 in A.L.; 6 in N.L.).

A.L.—686—Babe Ruth, Boston, New York, 17 years, 1918 through 1934.

N.L.—661—Hank Aaron, Milwaukee, Atlanta, 21 years, 1954 through 1974.

Most home runs by catcher, career

A.L.—351—Carlton Fisk, Boston, Chicago, 24 years, 1969 through 1993, except 1970.

N.L.—327—Johnny Bench, Cincinnati, 17 years, 1967 through 1983.

Most home runs by pitcher, career

A.L.—36—Wes Ferrell, Cleveland, Boston, Washington, New York, 13 years, 1927 through 1939. (Also one home run as pinch-hitter, 1935; one home run as pitcher, Boston N.L., 1941).

N.L.—35—Warren Spahn, Boston, Milwaukee, New York, San Francisco, 21 years, 1942 through 1965, except 1943, 1944, 1945 in military service.

Hitting home run in all major league parks (15) in use during career

Harry Heilmann, Detroit A.L., 1914, 1916 through 1929, Cincinnati N.L., 1930, 1932.
Jeff Heath, Cleveland A.L., 1936 through 1945, Washington A.L., 1946, St. Louis A.L., 1946, 1947, Boston N.L., 1948, 1949 (League Park and Municipal Stadium, Cleveland).
Johnny Mize, St. Louis N.L., 1936 through 1941, New York N.L., 1942, 1946 through 1949, New York A.L., 1949 through 1953.

Hitting one or more home runs in most parks, career

M.L.—32
Frank Robinson, Cincinnati N.L., Baltimore A.L., Los Angeles N.L., California A.L., Cleveland A.L., 21 years, 1956 through 1976.
Rusty Staub, Houston N.L., Montreal N.L., New York N.L., Detroit A.L., Texas A.L., 23 years, 1963 through 1985.

N.L.—22
Hank Aaron, Milwaukee, Atlanta, 21 years, 1954 through 1974.
Willie Mays, New York, San Francisco, 22 years, 1951 through 1973, except 1953.
Willie McCovey, San Francisco, San Diego, 22 years, 1959 through 1980.

A.L.—19
Carl Yastrzemski, Boston, 23 years, 1961 through 1983.
Reggie Jackson, Kansas City, Oakland, Baltimore, New York, California, 21 years, 1967 through 1987.

Most consecutive at-bats without hitting a home run, career

N.L.—3,347—Tommy Thevenow, St. Louis, Philadelphia, Pittsburgh, Cincinnati, Boston, September 24, 1926 through October 2, 1938 (end of career).

A.L.—3,278—Eddie Foster, Washington, Boston, St. Louis, April 20, 1916 through August 5, 1923 (end of career).

| SEASON |

Most home runs, season

A.L. (162-game season)—61—Roger Maris, New York, 161 games, 1961.

— 24 —

Most home runs for runner-up, season

A.L. (154-game season)—60—Babe Ruth, New York, 151 games, 1927.
N.L.—56—Hack Wilson, Chicago, 155 games, 1930.

Most home runs for runner-up, season

A.L. (162-game season)—54—Mickey Mantle, New York, 153 games, 1961.
A.L. (154-game season)—50—Jimmie Foxx, Boston, 149 games, 1938.
N.L.—47
  Ted Kluszewski, Cincinnati, 153 games, 1955 (154-game season).
  Hank Aaron, Atlanta, 139 games, 1971 (162-game season).

Most years leading league in home runs

A.L.—12—Babe Ruth, Boston, New York, 1918 (tied), 1919, 1920, 1921, 1923, 1924, 1926, 1927, 1928, 1929, 1930, 1931 (tied).
N.L.—8—Mike Schmidt, Philadelphia, 1974, 1975, 1976, 1980, 1981, 1983, 1984 (tied), 1986.

Most consecutive years leading league in home runs

N.L.—7—Ralph Kiner, Pittsburgh, 1946, 1947 (tied), 1948 (tied), 1949, 1950, 1951, 1952 (tied).
A.L.—6—Babe Ruth, New York, 1926 through 1931 (tied in 1931).

Most home runs by rookie, season

A.L.—49—Mark McGwire, Oakland, 151 games, 1987.
N.L.—38
  Wally Berger, Boston, 151 games, 1930.
  Frank Robinson, Cincinnati, 152 games, 1956.

Most home runs by righthander, season

A.L.—58
  Jimmie Foxx, Philadelphia, 154 games, 1932.
  Hank Greenberg, Detroit, 155 games, 1938.
N.L.—56—Hack Wilson, Chicago, 155 games, 1930.

Most home runs by lefthander, season

A.L. (162-game season)—61—Roger Maris, New York, 161 games, 1961.
A.L. (154-game season)—60—Babe Ruth, New York, 151 games, 1927.
N.L.—51—Johnny Mize, New York, 154 games, 1947.

Most home runs by switch-hitter, season

A.L.—54—Mickey Mantle, New York, 153 games, 1961.
N.L.—38—Howard Johnson, New York, 156 games, 1991.

Most home runs by pinch-hitter, season

N.L.—6—Johnny Frederick, Brooklyn, 1932.
A.L.—5—Joe Cronin, Boston, 1943.

Most home runs as leadoff batter, season

N.L.—11—Bobby Bonds, San Francisco, 160 games, 1973 (39 home runs for season).
A.L.—9—Rickey Henderson, New York, 153 games, 1986 (28 home runs for season).

Most home runs by first baseman, season

A.L.—58—Hank Greenberg, Detroit, 155 games, 1938, 154 games at first base.
N.L.—51—Johnny Mize, New York, 154 games, 1947, 154 games at first base.

Most home runs by second baseman, season

N.L.—42
  Rogers Hornsby, St. Louis, 154 games, 1922, 154 games at second base.
  Dave Johnson, Atlanta, 157 games, 1973, 156 games at second base (also had one home run as pinch-hitter).
A.L.—32—Joe Gordon, Cleveland, 144 games, 1948, 144 games at second base.

Most home runs by third baseman, season

N.L.—48—Mike Schmidt, Philadelphia, 150 games, 1980, 149 games at third base.
A.L.—43—Al Rosen, Cleveland, 155 games, 1953, 154 games at third base.

Most home runs by shortstop, season

N.L.—47—Ernie Banks, Chicago, 154 games, 1958, 154 games at shortstop.
A.L.—40—Rico Petrocelli, Boston, 154 games, 1969, 153 games at shortstop.

Most home runs by outfielder, season

A.L.—61—Roger Maris, New York, 161 games, 1961, 160 games in outfield.
N.L.—56—Hack Wilson, Chicago, 155 games, 1930, 155 games in outfield.

Most home runs by catcher, season

N.L.—40
  Roy Campanella, Brooklyn, 144 games, 1953, caught 140 games (also had one home run as pinch-hitter).
  (Johnny Bench, Cincinnati, 1970, had 38 home runs in 139 games as catcher, six home runs in 24 games as outfielder, one home run in 12 games as first baseman.)
A.L.—33—Carlton Fisk, Chicago, 153 games, 1985, caught 130 games (also had four home runs as designated hitter).

Most home runs by pitcher, season (only those hit as pitcher)

A.L.—9—Wes Ferrell, Cleveland, 48 games, 1931, pitched 40 games.
N.L.—7
  Don Newcombe, Brooklyn, 57 games, 1955, pitched 34 games.
  Don Drysdale, Los Angeles, 47 games, 1958, pitched 44 games.
  Don Drysdale, Los Angeles, 58 games, 1965, pitched 44 games.

Most home runs against one club, season

A.L. (8-club league)—14—Lou Gehrig, New York vs. Cleveland, 1936 (6 at New York, 8 at Cleveland).
A.L. (10-club league)—13—Roger Maris, New York vs. Chicago, 1961 (8 at New York, 5 at Chicago).
A.L. (12-club league)—11—Harmon Killebrew, Minnesota vs. Oakland, 1969 (6 at Minnesota, 5 at Oakland).
N.L. (8-club league)—13
  Hank Sauer, Chicago vs. Pittsburgh, 1954 (8 at Chicago, 5 at Pittsburgh).
  Joe Adcock, Milwaukee vs. Brooklyn, 1956 (5 at Milwaukee, 7 at Brooklyn, 1 at Jersey City).
N.L. (10-club league)—11—Frank Robinson, Cincinnati vs. Milwaukee, 1962 (8 at Cincinnati, 3 at Milwaukee).
N.L. (12-club league)—11
  Willie Stargell, Pittsburgh vs. Atlanta, 1971 (6 at Pittsburgh, 5 at Atlanta).
  Dale Murphy, Atlanta vs. San Francisco, 1983 (6 at Atlanta, 5 at San Francisco).

Most at-bats without a home run, season

N.L.—672—Rabbit Maranville, Pittsburgh, 155 games, 1922.
A.L.—658—Doc Cramer, Boston, 148 games, 1938.

Fewest home runs by leader, season (154-game schedule)

A.L.—7
  Sam Crawford, Detroit, 152 games, 1908.
  Bob Roth, Chicago, Cleveland, 109 games, 1915.
N.L.—7—Red Murray, New York, 149 games, 1909.

HOME AND ROAD

Most home runs hit at home, season

A.L.—39—Hank Greenberg, Detroit, 1938.
N.L.—34—Ted Kluszewski, Cincinnati, 1954.

Most home runs hit at home by righthander, season

A.L.—39—Hank Greenberg, Detroit, 1938.
N.L.—33—Hack Wilson, Chicago, 1930.

Most home runs hit at home by lefthander, season

N.L.—34—Ted Kluszewski, Cincinnati, 1954.
A.L.—32
  Babe Ruth, New York, 1921.
  Kenny Williams, St. Louis, 1922.

Most home runs hit at home by switch-hitter, season

A.L.—27—Mickey Mantle, New York, 1956.
N.L.—22—Rip Collins, St. Louis, 1934.

Most home runs hit at home against one club, season
A.L.—10—Gus Zernial, Philadelphia vs. St. Louis, 1951.
N.L.—9—Stan Musial, St. Louis vs. New York, 1954.

Most home runs hit on road, season
A.L.—32—Babe Ruth, New York, 1927.
N.L.—31—George Foster, Cincinnati, 1977.

Most home runs hit on road by righthander, season
N.L.—31—George Foster, Cincinnati, 1977.
A.L.—28
   Harmon Killebrew, Minnesota, 1962.
   George Bell, Toronto, 1987.

Most home runs hit on road by lefthander, season
A.L.—32—Babe Ruth, New York, 1927.
N.L.—30—Eddie Mathews, Milwaukee, 1953.

Most home runs hit on road by switch-hitter, season
A.L.—30—Mickey Mantle, New York, 1961.
N.L.—23—Howard Johnson, New York, 1987.

Most home runs hit on road against one club, season
A.L.—10—Harry Heilmann, Detroit at Philadelphia, 1922.
N.L.—9
   Joe Adcock, Milwaukee at Brooklyn, 1954.
   Willie Mays, New York at Brooklyn, 1955.

Players hitting home runs in all 12 parks in league, season
N.L.—Willie McCovey, San Francisco, 1970.
   Joe Pepitone, Houston, Chicago, 1970.
   Willie Stargell, Pittsburgh, 1970 (13 including both Pittsburgh parks).
   Johnny Bench, Cincinnati, 1972.
   George Foster, Cincinnati, 1977.
   Mike Schmidt, Philadelphia, 1979.
   Matt Williams, San Francisco, 1991.
A.L.—Reggie Jackson, Oakland, 1975.

Most years hitting home runs in all parks, career
A.L.—11—Babe Ruth, Boston, New York, 1919, 1920, 1921, 1923, 1924, 1926, 1927, 1928, 1929, 1930, 1931.
N.L.—9—Hank Aaron, Milwaukee, Atlanta, 1954, 1955, 1956, 1957, 1958, 1959, 1960, 1963, 1966.

☐ 50, 40, 30 AND 20 IN SEASON ☐

Most years with 50 or more home runs
A.L.—4—Babe Ruth, New York, 1920, 1921, 1927, 1928.
N.L.—2
   Ralph Kiner, Pittsburgh, 1947, 1949.
   Willie Mays, New York, 1955, San Francisco, 1965.

Most consecutive years with 50 or more home runs
A.L.—2—Babe Ruth, New York, 1920, 1921 and 1927, 1928.
N.L.—Never accomplished.

Most years with 40 or more home runs
A.L.—11—Babe Ruth, New York, 1920, 1921, 1923, 1924, 1926, 1927, 1928, 1929, 1930, 1931, 1932.
N.L.—8—Hank Aaron, Milwaukee, Atlanta, 1957, 1960, 1962, 1963, 1966, 1969, 1971, 1973.

Most consecutive years with 40 or more home runs
A.L.—7—Babe Ruth, New York, 1926 through 1932.
N.L.—5
   Ralph Kiner, Pittsburgh, 1947 through 1951.
   Duke Snider, Brooklyn, 1953 through 1957.

Most years with 30 or more home runs
N.L.—15—Hank Aaron, Milwaukee, Atlanta, 1957 through 1973, except 1964, 1968.
A.L.—13—Babe Ruth, New York, 1920 through 1933, except 1925.

Most consecutive years with 30 or more home runs
A.L.—12—Jimmie Foxx, Philadelphia, Boston, 1929 through 1940.
N.L.—9
   Eddie Mathews, Milwaukee, 1953 through 1961.
   Mike Schmidt, Philadelphia, 1979 through 1987.

Most years with 20 or more home runs
N.L.—20—Hank Aaron, Milwaukee, Atlanta, 1955 through 1974.
A.L.—16
   Babe Ruth, Boston, New York, 1919 through 1934.
   Ted Williams, Boston, 1939, 1940, 1941, 1942, 1946, 1947, 1948, 1949, 1950, 1951, 1954, 1955, 1956, 1957, 1958, 1960.
   Reggie Jackson, Oakland, Baltimore, New York, California, 1968 through 1980, 1982, 1984, 1985.

Most consecutive years with 20 or more home runs
N.L.—20—Hank Aaron, Milwaukee, Atlanta, 1955 through 1974.
A.L.—16—Babe Ruth, Boston, New York, 1919 through 1934.

☐ TWO CONSECUTIVE SEASONS ☐

Most home runs, two consecutive seasons
A.L.—114—Babe Ruth, New York, 60 in 1927, 54 in 1928.
N.L.—101—Ralph Kiner, Pittsburgh, 54 in 1949, 47 in 1950.

Most home runs by righthander, two consecutive seasons
A.L.—106—Jimmie Foxx, Philadelphia, 58 in 1932, 48 in 1933.
N.L.—101—Ralph Kiner, Pittsburgh, 54 in 1949, 47 in 1950.

Most home runs by lefthander, two consecutive seasons
A.L.—114—Babe Ruth, New York, 60 in 1927, 54 in 1928.
N.L.—96—Ted Kluszewski, Cincinnati, 49 in 1954, 47 in 1955.

Most home runs by switch-hitter, two consecutive seasons
A.L.—94—Mickey Mantle, New York, 40 in 1960, 54 in 1961.
N.L.—61
   Reggie Smith, Los Angeles, 32 in 1977, 29 in 1978.
   Howard Johnson, New York, 23 in 1990, 38 in 1991.

☐ MONTH AND WEEK ☐

Most home runs, one month (from first through last day of month)
A.L.—18—Rudy York, Detroit, August, 1937.
N.L.—17—Willie Mays, San Francisco, August, 1965.

Most home runs by righthander, one month
A.L.—18—Rudy York, Detroit, August, 1937.
N.L.—17—Willie Mays, San Francisco, August, 1965.

Most home runs by lefthander, one month
A.L.—17—Babe Ruth, New York, September 1927.
N.L.—15
   Cy Williams, Philadelphia, May, 1923.
   Duke Snider, Brooklyn, August, 1953.

Most home runs by switch-hitter, one month
A.L.—16—Mickey Mantle, New York, May, 1956.
N.L.—11
   Rip Collins, St. Louis, June, 1935.
   Ken Henderson, San Francisco, August, 1972.

Most home runs in April
N.L.—11
   Willie Stargell, Pittsburgh, April 1971.
   Mike Schmidt, Philadelphia, April 1976.
A.L.—11—Graig Nettles, New York, April 1974.

Most home runs in May
A.L.—16—Mickey Mantle, New York, May 1956.
N.L.—15—Cy Williams, Philadelphia, May 1923.

Most home runs through May 31
A.L.—22—Ken Griffey Jr., Seattle, 1994.
N.L.—19—Eric Davis, Cincinnati, 1987.

Most home runs in June
A.L.—15
   Babe Ruth, New York, June 1930.
   Bob Johnson, Philadelphia, June 1934.
   Roger Maris, New York, June 1961.
N.L.—15—Pedro Guerrero, Los Angeles, June 1985.

Most home runs through June 30
A.L.—32—Ken Griffey Jr., Seattle, 1994.
N.L.—29—Matt Williams, San Francisco, 1994.

Most home runs in July
A.L.—15
  Joe DiMaggio, New York, July 1937.
  Hank Greenberg, Detroit, July 1938.
N.L.—15—Joe Adcock, Milwaukee, July 1956.

Most home runs through July 31
A.L.—41
  Babe Ruth, New York, 1928.
  Jimmie Foxx, Philadelphia, 1932.
N.L.—40—Matt Williams, San Francisco, 1994.

Most home runs in August
A.L.—18—Rudy York, Detroit, August 1937.
N.L.—17—Willie Mays, San Francisco, August 1965.

Most home runs through August 31
A.L.—51—Roger Maris, New York, 1961.
N.L.—46—Hack Wilson, Chicago, 1930.

Most home runs in September
A.L.—17—Babe Ruth, New York, September 1927.
N.L.—16—Ralph Kiner, Pittsburgh, September 1949.

Most home runs through September 30
A.L.—60
  Babe Ruth, New York, 1927.
  Roger Maris, New York, 1961.
N.L.—56—Hack Wilson, Chicago, 1930.

Most home runs in October
A.A.—4—John Milligan, St. Louis, October 1889.
N.L.—4
  Ned Williamson, Chicago, October 1884.
  Mike Schmidt, Philadelphia, October 1980.
  Dave Parker, Cincinnati, October 1985.
A.L.—4
  Gus Zernial, Chicago, October 1950.
  George Brett, Kansas City, October 1985.
  Ron Kittle, Chicago, October 1985.
  Wally Joyner, California, October 1987.

Most home runs in one week (Sunday through Saturday)
A.L.—10—Frank Howard, Washington, May 12 through 18, 1968, six games.
N.L.—8
  Ralph Kiner, Pittsburgh, September 7 through 13, 1947, seven games.
  Ted Kluszewski, Cincinnati, July 1, first game, through 7, 1956, seven games.
  Nate Colbert, San Diego, July 30, first game, through August 5, 1972, nine games.

| GAME, DOUBLEHEADER, INNING |

Most home runs, game
N.L.—4
  Bobby Lowe, Boston, May 30, 1894, p.m. game (consecutive).
  Ed Delahanty, Philadelphia, July 13, 1896.
  Chuck Klein, Philadelphia, July 10, 1936, 10 innings.
  Gil Hodges, Brooklyn, August 31, 1950.
  Joe Adcock, Milwaukee, July 31, 1954.
  Willie Mays, San Francisco, April 30, 1961.
  Mike Schmidt, Philadelphia, April 17, 1976, 10 innings (consecutive).
  Bob Horner, Atlanta, July 6, 1986.
  Mark Whiten, St. Louis, September 7, 1993, second game.
A.L.—4
  Lou Gehrig, New York, June 3, 1932 (consecutive).
  Pat Seerey, Chicago, July 18, 1948, first game, 11 innings.
  Rocky Colavito, Cleveland, June 10, 1959 (consecutive).

Most home runs by pitcher, game
A.A.—3—Guy Hecker, Louisville, August 15, 1886, second game.
N.L.—3—Jim Tobin, Boston, May 13, 1942.

A.L.—2—Held by many pitchers. Last pitcher—Sonny Siebert, Boston, September 2, 1971.

Most home runs, first game in major leagues
A.A.—2—Charlie Reilly, Columbus, October 9, 1889 (on third and fifth times at bat).
A.L.—2
  Bob Nieman, St. Louis, September 14, 1951 (on first 2 times at bat).
  Bert Campaneris, Kansas City, July 23, 1964 (on first and fourth times at bat).
N.L.—1—Held by many players.

Most home runs, opening game of season
A.L.—3—George Bell, Toronto, April 4, 1988.
N.L.—3—Karl Rhodes, Chicago, April 4, 1994.

Most inside-the-park home runs, game
N.L.—3—Tom McCreery, Louisville, July 12, 1897.
N.L.-A.L. since 1900—2—Held by many players.
N.L.—Last player—Hank Thompson, New York at New York, August 16, 1950.
A.L.—Last player—Greg Gagne, Minnesota at Minnesota, October 4, 1986.

Most home runs in extra innings, game
A.L.—2
  Vern Stephens, St. Louis, September 29, 1943, first game, 11th and 13th innings (consecutive).
  Willie Kirkland, Cleveland, June 14, 1963, second game, 11th and 19th innings.
  Mike Young, Baltimore, May 28, 1987, 10th and 12th innings (consecutive).
N.L.—2
  Art Shamsky, Cincinnati, August 12, 1966, 10th and 11th innings (consecutive).
  Ralph Garr, Atlanta, May 17, 1971, 10th and 12th innings (consecutive).

Home run winning longest extra-inning game
A.L.—Harold Baines, Chicago, 25 innings, 0 on base, Chicago won vs. Milwaukee, 7-6, May 8, completed May 9, 1984.
N.L.—Rick Dempsey, Los Angeles, 22 innings, 0 on base, Los Angeles won vs. Montreal, 1-0, August 23, 1989.

Home run winning longest 1-0 game
N.L.—Rick Dempsey, Los Angeles, August 23, 1989, 22 innings.
A.L.—Bill Skowron, New York, April 22, 1959, 14 innings.

Home run by pitcher winning 1-0 extra-inning complete game
A.L.—Tom Hughes, Washington, August 3, 1906, 10 innings.
  Red Ruffing, New York, August 13, 1932, 10 innings.
N.L.—Never accomplished—(Johnny Klippstein, Cincinnati, on August 6, 1962, hit home run in 13th inning, after relieving Bob Purkey, who had pitched first 10 innings).

Home run in first major league at-bat
*On first pitch † Not first plate appearance
A.A.—George Tebeau, Cincinnati, April 16, 1887.
  Mike Griffin, Baltimore, April 16, 1887.

Total number of occurrences: (2)

A.L.—Earl Averill, Cleveland, April 16, 1929.
  Ace Parker, Philadelphia, April 30, 1937.
  Gene Hasson, Philadelphia, September 9, 1937, first game.
  Bill Lefebvre, Boston, June 10, 1938.*
  Hack Miller, Detroit, April 23, 1944, second game.
  Eddie Pellagrini, Boston, April 22, 1946.
  George Vico, Detroit, April 20, 1948.*
  Bob Nieman, St. Louis, September 14, 1951.
  Bob Tillman, Boston, May 19, 1962.†
  John Kennedy, Washington, September 5, 1962, first game.
  Buster Narum, Baltimore, May 3, 1963.
  Gates Brown, Detroit, June 19, 1963.
  Bert Campaneris, Kansas City, July 23, 1964.*
  Bill Roman, Detroit, September 30, 1964, second game.
  Brant Alyea, Washington, September 12, 1965.*

John Miller, New York, September 11, 1966.
Rick Renick, Minnesota, July 11, 1968.
Joe Keough, Oakland, August 7, 1968, second game.
Gene Lamont, Detroit, September 2, 1970, second game.
Don Rose, California, May 24, 1972.*
Reggie J. Sanders, Detroit, September 1, 1974.
Dave McKay, Minnesota, August 22, 1975.
Al Woods, Toronto, April 7, 1977.
Dave Machemer, California, June 21, 1978.
Gary Gaetti, Minnesota, September 20, 1981.
Andre David, Minnesota, June 29, 1984, first game.
Terry Steinbach, Oakland, September 12, 1986.
Jay Bell, Cleveland, September 29, 1986.*
Junior Felix, Toronto, May 4, 1989.*

Total number of occurrences: (29)

N.L.—Joe Harrington, Boston, September 10, 1895.
Bill Duggleby, Philadelphia, April 21, 1898.
Johnny Bates, Boston, April 12, 1906.
Walter Mueller, Pittsburgh, May 7, 1922.
Clise Dudley, Brooklyn, April 27, 1929.*
Gordon Slade, Brooklyn, May 24, 1930.
Eddie Morgan, St. Louis, April 14, 1936.*
Ernie Koy, Brooklyn, April 19, 1938.
Emmett Mueller, Philadelphia, April 19, 1938.
Clyde Vollmer, Cincinnati, May 31, 1942, second game.*
Paul Gillespie, Chicago, September 11, 1942.
Buddy Kerr, New York, September 8, 1943.
Whitey Lockman, New York, July 5, 1945.
Dan Bankhead, Brooklyn, August 26, 1947.
Les Layton, New York, May 21, 1948.
Ed Sanicki, Philadelphia, September 14, 1949.
Ted Tappe, Cincinnati, September 14, 1950, first game.
Hoyt Wilhelm, New York, April 23, 1952.
Wally Moon, St. Louis, April 13, 1954.
Chuck Tanner, Milwaukee, April 12, 1955.*
Bill White, New York, May 7, 1956.
Frank Ernaga, Chicago, May 24, 1957.
Don Leppert, Pittsburgh, June 18, 1961, first game.
Cuno Barragan, Chicago, September 1, 1961.
Benny Ayala, New York, August 27, 1974.
John Montefusco, San Francisco, September 3, 1974.†
Jose Sosa, Houston, July 30, 1975.
Johnnie LeMaster, San Francisco, September 2, 1975.
Tim Wallach, Montreal, September 6, 1980.†
Carmelo Martinez, Chicago, August 22, 1983.†
Mike Fitzgerald, New York, September 13, 1983.
Will Clark, San Francisco, April 8, 1986.
Ricky Jordan, Philadelphia, July 17, 1988.†
Jose Offerman, Los Angeles, August 19, 1990.
Dave Eiland, San Diego, April 10, 1992.
Jim Bullinger, Chicago, June 8, 1992, first game.*
Jay Gainer, Colorado, May 14, 1993.*
Mitch Lyden, Florida, June 16, 1993.

Total number of occurrences: (38)

Players hitting a pinch home run in first major league at-bat

N.L.—Eddie Morgan, St. Louis, April 14, 1936, seventh inning.
Les Layton, New York, May 21, 1948, ninth inning.
Ted Tappe, Cincinnati, September 14, 1950, first game, eighth inning.
Chuck Tanner, Milwaukee, April 12, 1955, eighth inning.
A.L.—Ace Parker, Philadelphia, April 30, 1937, ninth inning.
John Kennedy, Washington, September 5, 1962, first game, sixth inning.
Gates Brown, Detroit, June 19, 1963, fifth inning.
Bill Roman, Detroit, September 30, 1964, second game, seventh inning.
Brant Alyea, Washington, September 12, 1965, sixth inning.
Joe Keough, Oakland, August 7, 1968, second game, eighth inning.
Al Woods, Toronto, April 7, 1977, fifth inning.

Most home runs, doubleheader (homering in each game)

N.L.—5
Stan Musial, St. Louis, May 2, 1954.
Nate Colbert, San Diego, August 1, 1972.
A.L.—4
Earl Averill, Cleveland, September 17, 1930.
Jimmie Foxx, Philadelphia, July 2, 1933, 19 innings.
Jim Tabor, Boston, July 4, 1939.
Gus Zernial, Chicago, October 1, 1950.
Charlie Maxwell, Detroit, May 3, 1959 (consecutive).
Roger Maris, New York, July 25, 1961.
Rocky Colavito, Detroit, August 27, 1961.
Harmon Killebrew, Minnesota, September 21, 1963.
Bobby Murcer, New York, June 24, 1970 (consecutive).
Graig Nettles, New York, April 14, 1974.
Otto Velez, Toronto, May 4, 1980, 19 innings.
Al Oliver, Texas, August 17, 1980.

Most home runs by pinch-hitter, doubleheader

A.L.—2—Joe Cronin, Boston, June 17, 1943.
N.L.—2—Hal Breeden, Montreal, July 13, 1973.

Most home runs, inning

A.A.—2—Ed Cartwright, St. Louis, September 23, 1890, third inning.
P.L.—2—Lou Bierbauer, Brooklyn, July 12, 1890, third inning.
A.L.—2
Kenny Williams, St. Louis, August 7, 1922, sixth inning.
Bill Regan, Boston, June 16, 1928, fourth inning.
Joe DiMaggio, New York, June 24, 1936, fifth inning.
Al Kaline, Detroit, April 17, 1955, sixth inning.
Jim Lemon, Washington, September 5, 1959, third inning.
Joe Pepitone, New York, May 23, 1962, eighth inning.
Rick Reichardt, California, April 30, 1966, eighth inning.
Cliff Johnson, New York, June 30, 1977, eighth inning.
Ellis Burks, Boston, August 27, 1990, fourth inning.
Carlos Baerga, Cleveland, April 8, 1993, seventh inning.
Joe Carter, Toronto, October 3, 1993, second inning.
N.L.—2
Charley Jones, Boston, June 10, 1880, eighth inning.
Bobby Lowe, Boston, May 30, 1894, p.m. game, third inning.
Jake Stenzel, Pittsburgh, June 6, 1894, third inning.
Hack Wilson, New York, July 1, 1925, second game, third inning.
Hank Leiber, New York, August 24, 1935, second inning.
Andy Seminick, Philadelphia, June 2, 1949, eighth inning.
Sid Gordon, New York, July 31, 1949, second game, second inning.
Willie McCovey, San Francisco, April 12, 1973, fourth inning and June 27, 1977, sixth inning.
John Boccabella, Montreal, July 6, 1973, first game, sixth inning.
Lee May, Houston, April 29, 1974, sixth inning.
Andre Dawson, Montreal, July 30, 1978, third inning and September 24, 1985, fifth inning.
Ray Knight, Cincinnati, May 13, 1980, fifth inning.
Von Hayes, Philadelphia, June 11, 1985, first inning.
Dale Murphy, Atlanta, July 27, 1989, sixth inning.
Jeff Bagwell, Houston, June 24, 1994, sixth inning.

THREE AND TWO IN GAME

Most times hitting three or more home runs in a game, career

M.L.—6—Johnny Mize, St. Louis N.L., 1938 (2), 1940 (2), New York N.L., 1947, New York A.L., 1950.
N.L.—5—Johnny Mize, St. Louis, 1938 (2), 1940 (2); New York, 1947.
A.L.—5—Joe Carter, Cleveland, 1986, 1987, 1989 (2); Toronto, 1993.

Most times hitting three or more home runs in a game, season

N.L.—2
Johnny Mize, St. Louis, twice, July 13, July 20, second game, 1938; May 13, September 8, first game, 1940.
Ralph Kiner, Pittsburgh, August 16, September 11, second game, 1947.
Willie Mays, San Francisco, April 30, 4 home runs, June 29, first game, 1961.

Willie Stargell, Pittsburgh, April 10, April 21, 1971.
Dave Kingman, Chicago, May 17, July 28, 1979.
A.L.—2
Ted Williams, Boston, May 8, June 13, 1957.
Doug DeCinces, California, August 3, August 8, 1982.
Joe Carter, Cleveland, June 24, July 19, 1989.
Cecil Fielder, Detroit, May 6, June 6, 1990.

Most times hitting three home runs in a doubleheader, career (homering in both games)
A.L.—7—Babe Ruth, New York, 1920, 1922, 1926, 1927, 1930, 1933 (2).
N.L.—5—Mel Ott, New York, 1929, 1931, 1932, 1933, 1944.

Most times hitting three consecutive home runs in a game, career
4—Johnny Mize, St. Louis, N.L., 1938, 1940, New York, N.L., 1947, New York A.L., 1950.

Most times hitting three or more consecutive home runs in a game, career
N.L.—3—Johnny Mize, St. Louis, 1938, 1940, New York, 1947.
A.L.—2
Joe DiMaggio, New York, 1937, 1948.
Rocky Colavito, Cleveland, 1959, Detroit, 1962.

Most times hitting two or more home runs in a game, career
M.L.—72—Babe Ruth, Boston A.L., New York A.L., Boston N.L., 22 years, 1914 through 1935 (71 in A.L., 1 in N.L.).
A.L.—71—Babe Ruth, Boston, New York, 21 years, 1914 through 1934.
N.L.—63—Willie Mays, original New York club, San Francisco, present New York club, 22 years, 1951 through 1973, except 1953 in military service.

Most times hitting two or more home runs in a game, season
A.L.—11—Hank Greenberg, Detroit, 1938.
N.L.—10—Ralph Kiner, Pittsburgh, 1947.

Most times pitcher hitting two home runs in a game, career
A.L.—5—Wes Ferrell, Cleveland, Boston, 1931, 1934 (2), 1935, 1936.
N.L.—3—Don Newcombe, Brooklyn, 1955 (2), 1956.

Most times pitcher hitting two home runs in a game, season
A.L.—2
Wes Ferrell, Boston, 1934.
Jack Harshman, Baltimore, 1958.
Dick Donovan, Cleveland, 1962.
N.L.—2
Don Newcombe, Brooklyn, 1955.
Tony Cloninger, Atlanta, 1966.
Rick Wise, Philadelphia, 1971.

Most games hitting home runs from both sides of plate, career
M.L.—11—Eddie Murray, Baltimore A.L., 1977, 1979, 1981, 1982 (2), 1985, 1987 (2); Los Angeles N.L., 1990 (2); Cleveland A.L., 1994.
A.L.—10—Mickey Mantle, New York, 1955 (2), 1956 (2), 1957, 1958, 1959, 1961, 1962, 1964.
N.L.—5—Bobby Bonilla, Pittsburgh, 1987, 1988; New York, 1993 (2), 1994.

Most games hitting home runs from both sides of plate, season
A.L.—2
Mickey Mantle, New York, 1955, 1956.
Eddie Murray, Baltimore, 1982, 1987.
Chili Davis, California, 1994.
N.L.—2
Kevin Bass, Houston, 1987.
Chili Davis, San Francisco, 1987.
Eddie Murray, Los Angeles, 1990.
Bobby Bonilla, New York, 1993.

Hitting home runs from both sides of plate, game
A.L.—Wally Schang, Philadelphia, September 8, 1916.
Johnny Lucadello, St. Louis, September 16, 1940.
Mickey Mantle, New York, May 13, 1955 (1 righthanded, 2 lefthanded).
Mickey Mantle, New York, August 15, 1955, second game.
Mickey Mantle, New York, May 18, 1956.

Mickey Mantle, New York, July 1, 1956, second game.
Mickey Mantle, New York, June 12, 1957.
Mickey Mantle, New York, July 28, 1958.
Mickey Mantle, New York, September 15, 1959.
Mickey Mantle, New York, April 26, 1961.
Mickey Mantle, New York, May 6, 1962, second game.
Tom Tresh, New York, September 1, 1963.
Tom Tresh, New York, July 13, 1964.
Mickey Mantle, New York, August 12, 1964.
Tom Tresh, New York, June 6, 1965, second game (1 righthanded, 2 lefthanded).
Reggie Smith, Boston, August 20, 1967, first game.
Reggie Smith, Boston, August 11, 1968, second game.
Don Buford, Baltimore, April 9, 1970.
Roy White, New York, May 7, 1970.
Reggie Smith, Boston, July 2, 1972, first game.
Reggie Smith, Boston, April 16, 1973.
Roy White, New York, August 13, 1973.
Roy White, New York, April 23, 1975.
Ken Henderson, Chicago, August 29, 1975.
Roy White, New York, August 18, 1976.
Eddie Murray, Baltimore, August 3, 1977.
Roy White, New York, June 13, 1978.
Larry Milbourne, Seattle, July 15, 1978.
Willie Wilson, Kansas City, June 15, 1979.
Eddie Murray, Baltimore, August 29, 1979, second game (2 righthanded, 1 lefthanded).
U.L. Washington, Kansas City, September 21, 1979.
Eddie Murray, Baltimore, August 16, 1981.
Eddie Murray, Baltimore, April 24, 1982.
Ted Simmons, Milwaukee, May 2, 1982.
Eddie Murray, Baltimore, August 26, 1982.
Roy Smalley, New York, September 5, 1982.
Donnie Scott, Seattle, April 29, 1985.
Mike Young, Baltimore, August 13, 1985.
Eddie Murray, Baltimore, August 26, 1985 (1 righthanded, 2 lefthanded).
Nelson Simmons, Detroit, September 16, 1985.
Roy Smalley, Minnesota, May 30, 1986.
Tony Bernazard, Cleveland, July 1, 1986.
Ruben Sierra, Texas, September 13, 1986.
Eddie Murray, Baltimore, May 8, 1987.
Eddie Murray, Baltimore, May 9, 1987.
Devon White, California, June 23, 1987.
Dale Sveum, Milwaukee, July 17, 1987 (1 righthanded, 2 lefthanded).
Dale Sveum, Milwaukee, June 12, 1988.
Mickey Tettleton, Baltimore, June 13, 1988.
Chili Davis, California, July 30, 1988.
Ruben Sierra, Texas, August 27, 1988.
Ruben Sierra, Texas, June 8, 1989.
Chili Davis, California, July 1, 1989.
Devon White, California, June 29, 1990.
Roberto Alomar, Toronto, May 10, 1991.
Devon White, Toronto, June 1, 1992.
Chili Davis, Minnesota, October 2, 1992.
Carlos Baerga, Cleveland, April 8, 1993.
Mickey Tettleton, Detroit, May 7, 1993, 12 innings.
Tim Raines, Chicago, August 31, 1993.
Chad Kreuter, Detroit, September 7, 1993.
Eddie Murray, Cleveland, April 21, 1994.
Chili Davis, California, May 11, 1994.
Bernie Williams, New York, June 6, 1994.
Ruben Sierra, Oakland, June 7, 1994.
Chili Davis, California, July 30, 1994.

Total number of occurrences: (66)

N.L.—Augie Galan, Chicago, June 25, 1937.
Jim Russell, Boston, June 7, 1948.
Jim Russell, Brooklyn, July 26, 1950.
Red Schoendienst, St. Louis, July 8, 1951, second game.
Maury Wills, Los Angeles, May 30, 1962, first game.
Ellis Burton, Chicago, August 1, 1963.
Ellis Burton, Chicago, September 7, 1964, first game.
Jim Lefebvre, Los Angeles, May 7, 1966.

Wes Parker, Los Angeles, June 5, 1966, first game.
Pete Rose, Cincinnati, August 30, 1966.
Pete Rose, Cincinnati, August 2, 1967.
Ted Simmons, St. Louis, April 17, 1975.
Reggie Smith, St. Louis, May 4, 1975.
Reggie Smith, St. Louis, May 22, 1976 (2 righthanded, 1 lefthanded).
Lee Mazzilli, New York, September 3, 1978.
Ted Simmons, St. Louis, June 11, 1979.
Alan Ashby, Houston, September 27, 1982.
Chili Davis, San Francisco, June 5, 1983.
Mark Bailey, Houston, September 16, 1984.
Chili Davis, San Francisco, June 27, 1987.
Bobby Bonilla, Pittsburgh, July 3, 1987.
Kevin Bass, Houston, August 3, 1987, 13 innings.
Kevin Bass, Houston, September 2, 1987.
Chili Davis, San Francisco, September 15, 1987.
Bobby Bonilla, Pittsburgh, April 6, 1988, 14 innings.
Tim Raines, Montreal, July 16, 1988.
Steve Jeltz, Philadelphia, June 8, 1989.
Kevin Bass, Houston, August 20, 1989.
Eddie Murray, Los Angeles, April 18, 1990.
Eddie Murray, Los Angeles, June 9, 1990.
Bret Barberie, Montreal, August 2, 1991.
Howard Johnson, New York, August 31, 1991.
Kevin Bass, San Francisco, August 2, 1992, second game.
Bobby Bonilla, New York, April 23, 1993.
Bobby Bonilla, New York, June 10, 1993.
Todd Benzinger, San Francisco, August 30, 1993.
Mark Whiten, St. Louis, September 14, 1993.
Geronimo Pena, St. Louis, April 17, 1994.
Bobby Bonilla, New York, May 4, 1994.
Todd Hundley, New York, June 18, 1994.
Ken Caminiti, Houston, July 3, 1994.

Total number of occurrences: (41)

Hitting home runs from both sides of plate, inning
A.L.—Carlos Baerga, Cleveland, April 8, 1993, seventh inning.
N.L.—Never accomplished.

CONSECUTIVE AND IN CONSECUTIVE GAMES

Most consecutive home runs, game
N.L.—4
Bobby Lowe, Boston, May 30, 1894, p.m. game.
Mike Schmidt, Philadelphia, April 17, 1976, 10 innings.
A.L.—4
Lou Gehrig, New York, June 3, 1932.
Rocky Colavito, Cleveland, June 10, 1959.

Most consecutive home runs, two games (*also base on balls)
A.L.—4
Jimmie Foxx, Philadelphia, June 7 (1), 8 (3), 1933.
Hank Greenberg, Detroit, July 26 (2), 27 (2), 1938.
Charlie Maxwell, Detroit, May 3, first game (1), 3, second game (3), 1959.
Willie Kirkland, Cleveland, July 9, second game (3), 13 (1), 1961 (also two bases on balls and one sacrifice hit).
Mickey Mantle, New York, July 4, second game (2), 6 (2), 1962.
*Bobby Murcer, New York, June 24, first game (1), 24, second game (3), 1970.
Mike Epstein, Oakland, June 15 (2), 16 (2), 1971.
*Don Baylor, Baltimore, July 1 (1), 2 (3), 1975.
Larry Herndon, Detroit, May 16 (1), 18 (3), 1982.
Bo Jackson, Kansas City, July 17 (3), August 26 (1), 1990.
N.L.—4
*Bill Nicholson, Chicago, July 22 (1), 23, first game (3), 1944.
*Ralph Kiner, Pittsburgh, August 15 (1), 16 (3), 1947.
Ralph Kiner, Pittsburgh, September 11 (2), 13 (2), 1949.
*Stan Musial, St. Louis, July 7, second game (1), 8 (3), 1962.
Art Shamsky, Cincinnati, August 12 (3), 14 (1), 1966.

Deron Johnson, Philadelphia, July 10, second game (1), 11 (3), 1971.
Mike Schmidt, Philadelphia, July 6 (1), 7 (3), 1979.

Most consecutive home runs, three games
A.L.—4—Johnny Blanchard, New York, July 21 (1), 22 (1), 26 (2), 1961.
N.L.—Never accomplished.

Most consecutive home runs, four games
A.L.—4—Ted Williams, Boston, September 17, 20, 21, 22, 1957 (four bases on balls in streak).
N.L.—Never accomplished.

Most home runs in consecutive at-bats as a pinch-hitter
N.L.—3
Lee Lacy, Los Angeles, May 2, 6, 17, 1978 (includes one base on balls during streak).
Del Unser, Philadelphia, June 30, July 5, 10, 1979.
A.L.—2
Ray Caldwell, New York, June 10, 11, 1915.
Joe Cronin, Boston, June 17, first game, 17, second game, 1943.
Charlie Keller, New York, September 12, 14, 1948.
Del Wilber, Boston, May 6, 10, 1953.
Ted Williams, Boston, September 17, 20, 1957 (includes one base on balls during streak).
Johnny Blanchard, New York, July 21, 22, 1961.
Chuck Schilling, Boston, April 30, May 1, 1965.
Ray Barker, New York, June 20, 22, first game, 1965.
Curt Motton, Baltimore, May 15, 17, 1968.
Gates Brown, Detroit, August 9, 11, first game, 1968.
Gary Alexander, Cleveland, July 5, 6, 1980.
Daryl Sconiers, California, April 30, May 7, 1983.
Alex Sanchez, Detroit, July 20, 23, 1985.
Randy Bush, Minnesota, June 20, 23, 1986.

Most consecutive games hitting home run in each game
N.L.—8—Dale Long, Pittsburgh, May 19, 20, first game, 20, second game, 22, 23, 25, 26, 28, 1956 (eight home runs).
A.L.—8
Don Mattingly, New York, July 8 (2), 9, 10, 11, 12, 16 (2), 17, 18, 1987 (10 home runs).
Ken Griffey Jr., Seattle, July 20, 21, 22, 23, 24, 25, 27, 28, 1993 (eight home runs).

Most consecutive games hitting home run by pitcher
N.L.—4—Ken Brett, Philadelphia, June 9, 13, 18, 23, 1973.
A.L.—2—Held by many pitchers.

Most home runs, two consecutive days
A.L.—6
Babe Ruth, New York, May 21 (3), 21 (0), 22 (2), 22 (1), 1930, four games.
Tony Lazzeri, New York, May 23 (1), 23 (2), 24 (3), 1936, three games.
N.L.—6—Ralph Kiner, Pittsburgh, September 11 (1), 11 (3), 12 (2), 1947, three games.

Most hits, all home runs, consecutive games
N.L.—6
Frank Hurst, Philadelphia, July 28 through August 2, 1929, six games.
Moises Alou, Montreal, July 6 (2), 7, 8, 9 (2), 1993, four games.
A.L.—5—Kenny Williams, St. Louis, July 28 through August 1, 1922, five games.

Most home runs, first two major league games
A.A.—3—Charlie Reilly, Columbus, October 9 (2), 10 (1), 1889.
N.L.—2—Joe Cunningham, St. Louis, June 30 (1), July 1 (2), 1954.
A.L.—2
Earl Averill, Cleveland, April 16 (1), 17 (1), 1929.
Bob Nieman, St. Louis, September 14 (2), 15 (0), 1951.
Bert Campaneris, Kansas City, July 23 (2), 24 (0), 1964.
Curt Blefary, Baltimore, April 14 (0), 17 (2), 1965.
Joe Lefebvre, New York, May 22 (1), 23 (1), 1980.
Dave Stapleton, Boston, May 30 (0), 31 (2), 1980.
Tim Laudner, Minnesota, August 28 (1), 29 (1), 1981.

Alvin Davis, Seattle, April 11 (1), 13 (1), 1984.
Sam Horn, Boston, July 25 (1), 26 (1), 1987.

Most home runs in two straight games (homering in each game)
N.L.—5
Cap Anson, Chicago, August 5 (2), 6 (3), 1884.
Ralph Kiner, Pittsburgh, August 15 (2), 16 (3), 1947, also September 11 (3), 12 (2), 1947.
Don Mueller, New York, September 1 (3), 2 (2), 1951.
Stan Musial, St. Louis, May 2, first game (3), 2, second game (2), 1954.
Joe Adcock, Milwaukee, July 30 (1), 31 (4), 1954.
Billy Williams, Chicago, September 8 (2), 10 (3), 1968.
Nate Colbert, San Diego, August 1, first game (2), second game (3), 1972.
Mike Schmidt, Philadelphia, April 17 (4), 18 (1), 1976.
Dave Kingman, Chicago, July 27 (2), 28 (3), 1979.
Gary Carter, New York, September 3 (3), 4 (2), 1985.
Barry Larkin, Cincinnati, June 27 (2), 28 (3), 1991.
A.L.—5
Ty Cobb, Detroit, May 5 (3), 6 (2), 1925.
Tony Lazzeri, New York, May 23, second game (2), 24 (3), 1936.
Carl Yastrzemski, Boston, May 19 (3), 20 (2), 1976.
Mark McGwire, Oakland, June 27 (3), 28 (2), 1987.
Joe Carter, Cleveland, July 18 (2), 19 (3), 1989.

Most home runs in three straight games (homering in each game)
A.L.—6
Tony Lazzeri, New York, May 23 (1), 23 (2), 24 (3), 1936.
Gus Zernial, Philadelphia, May 13, second game (2), 15 (2), 16 (2), 1951.
N.L.—6
Ralph Kiner, Pittsburgh, August 14 (1), 15 (2), 16 (3), 1947, also September 10 (2), 11 (1), 11 (3), 1947.
Frank Thomas, New York, August 1 (2), 2 (2), 3 (2), 1962.
Lee May, Cincinnati, May 24 (2), 25 (2), 28 (2), 1969.
Mike Schmidt, Philadelphia, April 17 (4), 18 (1), 20 (1), 1976.

Most home runs in four straight games (homering in each game)
N.L.—8—Ralph Kiner, Pittsburgh, September 10 (2), 11 (1), 11 (3), 12 (2), 1947.
A.L.—7
Tony Lazzeri, New York, May 21 (1), 23 (1), 23 (2), 24 (3), 1936.
Gus Zernial, Philadelphia, May 13, second game (2), 15 (2), 16 (2), 17 (1), 1951.
Frank Howard, Washington, May 12 (2), 14 (2), 15 (1), 16 (2), 1968.

Players hitting home runs in first four games of season
N.L.—4—Willie Mays, San Francisco, April 6 (1), 7 (1), 8 (1), 10 (1), 1971.

Most home runs in five straight games (homering in each game)
A.L.—8
Frank Howard, Washington, May 12 (2), 14 (2), 15 (1), 16 (2), 17 (1), 1968.
Frank Howard, Washington, May 14 (2), 15 (1), 16 (2), 17 (1), 18 (2), 1968.
N.L.—7
Jim Bottomley, St. Louis, July 5 (1), 6 (2), 6 (1), 8 (1), 9 (2), 1929.
Johnny Bench, Cincinnati, May 30 (2), 31 (1), June 1 (1), 2 (2), 3 (1), 1972.
Mike Schmidt, Philadelphia, July 6 (1), 7 (3), 8 (1), 9 (1), 10 (1), 1979.

Most home runs in six straight games (homering in each game)
A.L.—10—Frank Howard, Washington, May 12 (2), 14 (2), 15, 16 (2), 17, 18 (2), 1968.
N.L.—7
George Kelly, New York, July 11, 12 (2), 13, 14, 15, 16, 1924.
Walker Cooper, New York, June 22 (2), 23, 24, 25, 27, 28, 1947.
Willie Mays, New York, September 14 (2), 16, 17, 18, 20, 1955.

Graig Nettles, San Diego, August 11 (1), 12 (1), 16 (1), 17 (2), 21 (1), 22 (1), 1984.

Most home runs in seven straight games (homering in each game)
A.L.—9—Don Mattingly, New York, July 8 (2), 9, 10, 11, 12, 16 (2), 17, 1987.
N.L.—7—Dale Long, Pittsburgh, May 19, 20, 20, 22, 23, 25, 26, 1956.

Most homers in eight straight games (homering in each game)
A.L.—10—Don Mattingly, New York, July 8 (2), 9, 10, 11, 12, 16 (2), 17, 18, 1987.
N.L.—8—Dale Long, Pittsburgh, May 19, 20, 20, 22, 23, 25, 26, 28, 1956.

GRAND SLAMS

Most grand slams, career
A.L.—23—Lou Gehrig, New York, 17 years, 1923 through 1939.
N.L.—18—Willie McCovey, San Francisco, San Diego, 22 years, 1959 through 1980.

Most grand slams by pinch-hitter, career
N.L.—3
Ron Northey, St. Louis, September 3, 1947; May 30, 1948, second game; Chicago, September 18, 1950.
Willie McCovey, San Francisco, June 12, 1960; September 10, 1965; San Diego, May 30, 1975.
A.L.—3—Rich Reese, Minnesota, August 3, 1969, June 7, 1970, July 9, 1972.

Most grand slams, season
A.L. (162-game season)—6—Don Mattingly, New York, 141 games, 1987.
A.L. (154-game season)—4
Babe Ruth, Boston, 130 games, 1919.
Lou Gehrig, New York, 154 games, 1934.
Rudy York, Detroit, 135 games, 1938.
Tommy Henrich, New York, 146 games, 1948.
Al Rosen, Cleveland, 154 games, 1951.
Ray Boone, Cleveland, Detroit, 135 games, 1953.
N.L.—5—Ernie Banks, Chicago, 154 games, 1955.

Most grand slams by pinch-hitter, season
N.L.—2
Dave Johnson, Philadelphia, April 30, June 3, 1978.
Mike Ivie, San Francisco, May 28, June 30, first game, 1978.
A.L.—1—Held by many pinch-hitters.

Most grand slams in one month
A.L.—3
Rudy York, Detroit, May 16, 22, 30, first game, 1938.
Jim Northrup, Detroit, June 24 (2), 29, 1968.
Larry Parrish, Texas, July 4, 7, 10, first game, 1982.
N.L.—3—Eric Davis, Cincinnati, May 1, 3, 30, 1987.

Most grand slams in one week (Sunday through Saturday)
A.L.—3
Jim Northrup, Detroit, June 24 (2), 29, 1968. (Lou Gehrig, New York, hit grand slams on Saturday, August 29, Monday, August 31, Tuesday, September 1, 1931, second game.)
Larry Parrish, Texas, July 4, 7, 10, first game, 1982.
N.L.—2—Held by many players. Last player—Fred McGriff, San Diego, August 13, 14, 1991.

Most grand slams in one game
A.L.—2
Tony Lazzeri, New York, May 24, 1936, second and fifth innings.
Jim Tabor, Boston, July 4, 1939, second game, third and sixth innings.
Rudy York, Boston July 27, 1946, second and fifth innings.
Jim Gentile, Baltimore, May 9, 1961, first and second innings.
Jim Northrup, Detroit, June 24, 1968, fifth and sixth innings.
Frank Robinson, Baltimore, June 26, 1970, fifth and sixth innings.

N.L.—2—Tony Cloninger, Atlanta, July 3, 1966, first and fourth innings.

Most grand slams in first major league game

N.L.—1

Bill Duggleby, Philadelphia, April 21, 1898, second inning (on first at-bat).

Bobby Bonds, San Francisco, June 25, 1968, sixth inning (on third at-bat).

A.L.—Never accomplished.

Most grand slams, two straight games (homering in each game)

N.L.—2

Jimmy Bannon, Boston, August 6, 7, 1894.

Jim Sheckard, Brooklyn, September 23, 24, 1901.

Phil Garner, Pittsburgh, September 14, 15, 1978.

Fred McGriff, San Diego, August 13, 14, 1991.

A.L.—2

Babe Ruth, New York, September 27, 29, 1927; also August 6, second game, August 7, first game, 1929.

Bill Dickey, New York, August 3, second game, 4, 1937.

Jimmie Foxx, Boston, May 20, 21, 1940.

Jim Busby, Cleveland, July 5, 6, 1956.

Brooks Robinson, Baltimore, May 6, 9, 1962.

Willie Aikens, California, June 13, second game, 14, 1979.

Greg Luzinski, Chicago, June 8, 9, 1984.

Rob Deer, Milwaukee, August 19, 20, 1987.

Mike Blowers, Seattle, May 16, 17, 1993.

Dan Gladden, Detroit, August 10, 11, 1993.

TOTAL BASES

CAREER AND SEASON

Most total bases, career

M.L.—6,856—Hank Aaron, Milwaukee N.L., Atlanta N.L., Milwaukee A.L., 23 years, 1954 through 1976 (6,591 in N.L., 265 in A.L.).

N.L.—6,591—Hank Aaron, Milwaukee, Atlanta, 21 years, 1954 through 1974.

A.L.—5,862—Ty Cobb, Detroit, Philadelphia, 24 years, 1905 through 1928.

Most total bases, season

A.L.—457—Babe Ruth, New York, 152 games 1921.

N.L.—450—Rogers Hornsby, St. Louis, 154 games, 1922.

Most total bases by rookie, season

A.L.—374

Hal Trosky, Cleveland, 154 games, 1934 (154-game season).

Tony Oliva, Minnesota, 161 games, 1964 (162-game season).

N.L. (162-game season)—352—Dick Allen, Philadelphia, 162 games, 1964.

N.L. (154-game season)—342—Johnny Frederick, Brooklyn, 148 games, 1929.

Most total bases by righthander, season

N.L.—450—Rogers Hornsby, St. Louis, 154 games, 1922.

A.L.—438—Jimmie Foxx, Philadelphia, 154 games, 1932.

Most total bases by lefthander, season

A.L.—457—Babe Ruth, New York, 152 games, 1921.

N.L.—445—Chuck Klein, Philadelphia, 156 games, 1930.

Most total bases by switch-hitter, season

A.L.—376—Mickey Mantle, New York, 150 games, 1956.

N.L.—369—Rip Collins, St. Louis, 154 games, 1934.

Most years leading league in total bases

N.L.—8—Hank Aaron, Milwaukee, 1956, 1957, 1959, 1960, 1961, 1963, Atlanta, 1967, 1969.

A.L.—6

Ty Cobb, Detroit, 1907, 1908, 1909, 1911, 1915, 1917.

Babe Ruth, Boston, 1919, New York, 1921, 1923, 1924, 1926, 1928.

Ted Williams, Boston, 1939, 1942, 1946, 1947, 1949, 1951.

Most consecutive years leading league in total bases

N.L.—4

Honus Wagner, Pittsburgh, 1906, 1907, 1908, 1909.

Chuck Klein, Philadelphia, 1930, 1931, 1932, 1933.

A.L.—3

Ty Cobb, Detroit, 1907, 1908, 1909.

Jim Rice, Boston, 1977, 1978, 1979.

(Military service from 1943 through 1945 interrupted a three-year streak by Ted Williams of Boston, who led in total bases from 1942 through 1947.)

Most years with 400 or more total bases

A.L.—5—Lou Gehrig, New York, 1927, 1930, 1931, 1934, 1936.

N.L.—3—Chuck Klein, Philadelphia, 1929, 1930, 1932.

Most consecutive years with 400 or more total bases

A.L.—2

Lou Gehrig, New York, 1930, 1931.

Jimmie Foxx, Philadelphia, 1932, 1933.

N.L.—2—Chuck Klein, Philadelphia, 1929, 1930.

Most years with 300 or more total bases

N.L.—15—Hank Aaron, Milwaukee, Atlanta, 1955 through 1971, except 1964, 1970.

A.L.—13—Lou Gehrig, New York, 1926 through 1938.

Most consecutive years with 300 or more total bases

A.L.—13—Lou Gehrig, New York, 1926 through 1938.

N.L.—13—Willie Mays, New York, San Francisco, 1954 through 1966.

Fewest total bases, season (150 or more games)

N.L.—89—Dal Maxvill, St. Louis, 152 games, 1970.

A.L.—114—Eddie Brinkman, Washington, 154 games, 1965.

Fewest total bases for leader

N.L.—237—Honus Wagner, Pittsburgh, 140 games, 1906.

A.L.—260—George Stone, St. Louis, 154 games, 1905.

GAME AND INNING

Most total bases, game

N.L.—18—Joe Adcock, Milwaukee, July 31, 1954 (4 home runs, 1 double).

A.L.—16

Ty Cobb, Detroit, May 5, 1925 (3 home runs, 1 double, 2 singles).

Lou Gehrig, New York, June 3, 1932 (4 home runs).

Jimmie Foxx, Philadelphia, July 10, 1932, 18 innings (3 home runs, 1 double, 2 singles).

Jim Seerey, Chicago, July 18, 1948, first game, 11 innings (4 home runs).

Rocky Colavito, Cleveland, June 10, 1959 (4 home runs).

Fred Lynn, Boston, June 18, 1975 (3 home runs, 1 triple, 1 single).

Most total bases by pitcher, nine-inning game

A.A.—15—Guy Hecker, Louisville, August 15, 1886, second game (3 home runs, 3 singles).

N.L.—12—Jim Tobin, Boston, May 13, 1942 (3 home runs).

A.L.—10

Hooks Wiltse, Philadelphia, August 10, 1901, second game (2 triples, 2 doubles).

Babe Ruth, Boston, May 9, 1918, 10 innings (1 single, 3 doubles, 1 triple).

Red Ruffing, New York, June 17, 1936, first game (2 singles, 2 home runs).

Jack Harshman, Baltimore, September 23, 1958 (2 home runs, 1 double).

Most total bases, doubleheader

N.L.—22—Nate Colbert, San Diego, August 1, 1972.

A.L.—21

Jimmie Foxx, Philadelphia, July 2, 1933, 19 innings.

Al Oliver, Texas, August 17, 1980.

Most total bases, two consecutive games

A.L.—25—Ty Cobb, Detroit, May 5, 6, 1925.

N.L.—25—Joe Adcock, Milwaukee, July 30, 31, 1954.

Most total bases, inning

N.L.-A.L.—8—Held by many players.

CAREER AND SEASON

Most long hits, career

M.L.—1,477—Hank Aaron, Milwaukee N.L., Atlanta N.L., Milwaukee A.L., 1954 through 1976 (1,429 in N.L., 48 in A.L.; 624 doubles, 98 triples, 755 home runs).

N.L.—1,429—Hank Aaron, Milwaukee, Atlanta, 21 years, 1954 through 1974 (600 doubles, 96 triples, 733 home runs).

A.L.—1,350—Babe Ruth, Boston, New York, 21 years, 1914 through 1934 (506 doubles, 136 triples, 708 home runs).

Most long hits, season

A.L.—119—Babe Ruth, New York, 152 games, 1921 (44 doubles, 16 triples, 59 home runs).

N.L.—107—Chuck Klein, Philadelphia, 156 games, 1930 (59 doubles, 8 triples, 40 home runs).

Most long hits by rookie, season

A.L.—89—Hal Trosky, Cleveland, 154 games, 1934 (45 doubles, 9 triples, 35 home runs).

N.L.—82—Johnny Frederick, Brooklyn, 148 games, 1929 (52 doubles, 6 triples, 24 home runs).

Most long hits by righthander, season

A.L.—103—Hank Greenberg, Detroit, 154 games, 1937 (49 doubles, 14 triples, 40 home runs).

N.L.—102—Rogers Hornsby, St. Louis, 154 games, 1922 (46 doubles, 14 triples, 42 home runs).

Most long hits by lefthander, season

A.L.—119—Babe Ruth, New York, 152 games, 1921 (44 doubles, 16 triples, 59 home runs).

N.L.—107—Chuck Klein, Philadelphia, 156 games, 1930 (59 doubles, 8 triples, 40 home runs).

Most long hits by switch-hitter, season

N.L.—87—Rip Collins, St. Louis, 154 games, 1934.

A.L.—79—Mickey Mantle, New York, 150 games, 1956.

Most years leading league in doubles, triples and home runs in same season

A.A.—1—Tip O'Neill, St. Louis, 123 games, 1887 (46 doubles, 24 triples, 13 home runs. Also led in batting, .492).

N.L.-A.L.—Never accomplished.

Twenty or more doubles, triples and homers in one season

N.L.—Buck Freeman, Washington, 155 games, 1899 (20 doubles, 26 triples, 25 home runs).
Frank Schulte, Chicago, 154 games, 1911 (30 doubles, 21 triples, 21 homers).
Jim Bottomley, St. Louis, 149 games, 1928 (42 doubles, 20 triples, 31 homers).
Willie Mays, New York, 152 games, 1957 (26 doubles, 20 triples, 35 homers).

A.L.—Jeff Heath, Cleveland, 151 games, 1941 (32 doubles, 20 triples, 24 homers).
George Brett, Kansas City, 154 games, 1979 (42 doubles, 20 triples, 23 homers).

Most years leading league in long hits

N.L.—7
Honus Wagner, Pittsburgh, 1900, 1902, 1903, 1904, 1907, 1908, 1909.
Stan Musial, St. Louis, 1943, 1944, 1946, 1948, 1949, 1950, 1953.

A.L.—7—Babe Ruth, Boston, New York, 1918, 1919, 1920, 1921, 1923, 1924, 1928.

Most consecutive years leading league in long hits

A.L.—4—Babe Ruth, Boston, New York, 1918, 1919, 1920, 1921.

N.L.—3—Held by many players. Last player—Duke Snider, Brooklyn, 1954, 1955 (tied), 1956.

Fewest long hits, season (150 or more games)

N.L.—7—Dal Maxvill, St. Louis, 152 games, 1970 (5 doubles, 2 triples).

A.L.—10
Luis Gomez, Toronto, 153 games, 1978 (7 doubles, 3 triples).
Felix Fermin, Cleveland, 156 games, 1989 (9 doubles, 1 triple).

Fewest long hits for leader (154-game season)

N.L.—50—Sherry Magee, Philadelphia, 154 games, 1906 (36 doubles, 8 triples, 6 home runs).

A.L.—54—Sam Crawford, Detroit, 156 games, 1915 (31 doubles, 19 triples, 4 home runs).

Most consecutive long hits, season

A.L.—7
Elmer Smith, Cleveland, September 4, 5, 5, 1921 (3 doubles, 4 home runs; 2 bases on balls in streak).
Earl Sheely, Chicago, May 20, 21, 1926 (6 doubles, 1 home run; 1 sacrifice hit in streak).

N.L.—5—Held by many players.

Most consecutive games with one or more long hits, season

N.L.—14—Paul Waner, Pittsburgh, June 3 through 19, 1927 (12 doubles, 4 triples, 4 home runs).

A.L.—11—Jesse Barfield, Toronto, August 17 through 27, 1985 (8 doubles, 3 triples, 1 home run).

GAME AND INNING

Most long hits, game

A.A.—5—George Strief, Philadelphia, June 25, 1885 (4 triples, 1 double; consecutive).

N.L.—5
George Gore, Chicago, July 9, 1885 (2 triples, 3 doubles; consecutive).
Larry Twitchell, Cleveland, August 15, 1889 (1 double, 3 triples, 1 home run).
Joe Adcock, Milwaukee, July 31, 1954 (4 home runs, 1 double; consecutive).
Willie Stargell, Pittsburgh, August 1, 1970 (3 doubles, 2 home runs).
Steve Garvey, Los Angeles, August 28, 1977 (3 doubles, 2 home runs; consecutive).

A.L.—5—Lou Boudreau, Cleveland, July 14, 1946, first game (4 doubles, 1 home run).

Most long hits, opening game of season

N.L.—4
George Myers, Indianapolis, April 20, 1888 (3 doubles, 1 home run).
Billy Herman, Chicago, April 14, 1936 (3 doubles, 1 home run).
Jim Greengrass, Cincinnati, April 13, 1954 (4 doubles).

A.L.—4
Frank Dillon, Detroit, April 25, 1901 (4 doubles).
Don Baylor, Baltimore, April 6, 1973 (2 doubles, 1 triple, 1 home run).

Most long hits by pitcher, nine-inning game

A.A.—4—Bob Caruthers, St. Louis, August 16, 1886 (2 home runs, 1 triple, 1 double).

A.L.—4—Lewis Wiltse, Philadelphia, August 10, 1901, second game (2 triples, 2 doubles).

N.L.—3—Held by many players—Last pitcher—Andy Messersmith, Los Angeles, April 25, 1975 (3 doubles).

Most long hits by pitcher, extra-inning game

A.L.—4—Babe Ruth, Boston, May 9, 1918, 10 innings (3 doubles, 1 triple).

Most games with four or more long hits, career

A.L.—5
Lou Gehrig, New York, 1926, 1928, 1930, 1932, 1934.
Joe DiMaggio, New York, 1936, 1937, 1941, 1948, 1950.

N.L.—4—Willie Stargell, Pittsburgh, 1965, 1968, 1970, 1973.

Most games with four long hits, season

A.A.—2—Henry Larkin, Philadelphia, June 16, July 29, 1885.

A.L.—2
George H. Burns, Cleveland, June 19, first game, July 23, 1924.

— 33 —

Jimmie Foxx, Philadelphia, April 24, July 2, second game, 1933.

N.L.—2
Joe Medwick, St. Louis, May 12, August 4, 1937.
Billy Williams, Chicago, April 9, September 5, 1969.

Most long hits, doubleheader (nine-inning games)

N.L.—6
Joe Medwick, St. Louis, May 30, 1935 (5 doubles, 1 triple).
Red Schoendienst, St. Louis, June 6, 1948 (5 doubles, 1 home run).

A.L.—6
John Stone, Detroit, April 30, 1933 (4 doubles, 2 home runs).
Hank Majeski, Philadelphia, August 27, 1948 (6 doubles).
Hal McRae, Kansas City, August 27, 1974 (5 doubles, 1 home run).
Al Oliver, Texas, August 17, 1980 (1 double, 1 triple, 4 home runs).

Most long hits, doubleheader (more than 18 innings)

N.L.—6
Chick Hafey, St. Louis, July 28, 1928, 21 innings (4 doubles, 2 home runs).
Mel Ott, New York, June 19, 1929, 20 innings (4 doubles, 2 home runs).
Dusty Rhodes, New York, 20 innings, August 29, 1954 (2 doubles, 2 triples, 2 home runs).

A.L.—6—Jimmie Foxx, Philadelphia, July 2, 1933, 19 innings (1 double, 1 triple, 4 home runs).

Most long hits in two consecutive games

N.L.—7
Ed Delahanty, Philadelphia, July 13, 14, 1896 (2 doubles, 1 triple, 4 home runs).
Red Schoendienst, St. Louis, June 5, 6, first game, 1948 (6 doubles, 1 home run).
Joe Adcock, Milwaukee, July 30, 31, 1954 (2 doubles, 5 home runs).

A.L.—7—Earl Sheely, Chicago, May 20, 21, 1926 (6 doubles, 1 home run).

Most long hits in three consecutive games

N.L.—9—Red Schoendienst, St. Louis, June 5, 6, 6, 1948 (8 doubles, 1 home run).

A.L.—8—Earl Sheely, Chicago, May 20, 21, 22, 1926 (7 doubles, 1 home run).

Most long hits, inning

N.L.—3—Tommy Burns, Chicago, September 6, 1883, seventh inning (2 doubles, 1 home run).

A.L.-N.L. since 1900—2—Held by many players.

Most long hits by pitcher, inning

N.L.—2
Fred Goldsmith, Chicago, September 6, 1883, seventh inning (2 doubles).
William Terry, Chicago, May 19, 1895, third inning (1 home run, 1 double).
Hank Borowy, Chicago, May 5, 1946, first game, seventh inning (2 doubles).

A.L.—2
Joe Wood, Boston, July 4, 1913, a.m. game, fourth inning (2 doubles).
Bob Shawkey, New York, July 12, 1923, third inning (1 triple, 1 double).
Ted Lyons, Chicago, July 28, 1935, first game, second inning (2 doubles).

EXTRA BASES ON LONG HITS

Most extra bases on long hits, career

M.L.—3,085—Hank Aaron, Milwaukee N.L., Atlanta N.L., Milwaukee A.L., 23 years, 1954 through 1976 (2,991 in A.L., 94 in A.L.).

N.L.—2,991—Hank Aaron, Milwaukee, Atlanta, 21 years, 1954 through 1974.

A.L.—2,902—Babe Ruth, Boston, New York, 21 years, 1914 through 1934.

Most extra bases on long hits, season

A.L.—253—Babe Ruth, New York, 152 games, 1921.
N.L.—215—Hack Wilson, Chicago, 155 games, 1930.

Most extra bases on long hits by rookie, season

A.L.—183—Mark McGwire, Oakland, 151 games, 1987.
N.L.—169—Wally Berger, Boston, 151 games, 1930.

Most extra bases on long hits by righthander, season

A.L.—225—Jimmie Foxx, Philadelphia, 154 games, 1932.
N.L.—215—Hack Wilson, Chicago, 155 games, 1930.

Most extra bases on long hits by lefthander, season

A.L.—253—Babe Ruth, New York, 152 games, 1921.
N.L.—199—Stan Musial, St. Louis, 155 games, 1948.

Most extra bases on long hits by switch-hitter, season

A.L.—190—Mickey Mantle, New York, 153 games, 1961.
N.L.—169—Rip Collins, St. Louis, 154 games, 1934.

Most years leading league in extra bases on long hits

A.L.—9—Babe Ruth, Boston, New York, 1918, 1919, 1920, 1921, 1923, 1924, 1926, 1928, 1929.
N.L.—7—Mike Schmidt, Philadelphia, 1974, 1975, 1976, 1980, 1981, 1982, 1986.

Most consecutive years leading league in extra bases on long hits

A.L.—4—Babe Ruth, Boston, New York, 1918, 1919, 1920, 1921.
N.L.—3—Held by many players. Last player—Mike Schmidt, Philadelphia, 1980, 1981, 1982.

Most years with 200 or more extra bases on long hits

A.L.—4—Babe Ruth, New York, 1920, 1921, 1927, 1928.
N.L.—1
Rogers Hornsby, St. Louis, 1922.
Hack Wilson, Chicago, 1930.

Most consecutive years with 200 or more extra bases on long hits

A.L.—2—Babe Ruth, New York, 1920, 1921, also 1927, 1928.
N.L.—No player with two consecutive years.

Most years with 100 or more extra bases on long hits

N.L.—19—Hank Aaron, Milwaukee, Atlanta, 1955 through 1973.
A.L.—16—Ted Williams, Boston, 1939, 1940, 1941, 1942, 1946, 1947, 1948, 1949, 1950, 1951, 1954, 1955, 1956, 1957, 1958, 1960.

Most consecutive years with 100 or more extra bases on long hits

N.L.—19—Hank Aaron, Milwaukee, Atlanta, 1955 through 1973.
A.L.—14—Lou Gehrig, New York, 1925 through 1938. (Military service from 1943 through 1945 and most of 1952 and 1953 interrupted a 15-year streak by Ted Williams of Boston, who compiled 100 extra bases on long hits from 1939 through 1958.)

Fewest extra bases on long hits, season (150 or more games)

N.L.—9—Dal Maxvill, St. Louis, 152 games, 1970.
A.L.—11—Mike Tresh, Chicago, 150 games, 1945.

Fewest extra bases on long hits by leader

N.L.—74
Harry Lumley, Brooklyn, 131 games, 1906.
Honus Wagner, Pittsburgh, 137 games, 1909.
A.L.—80—Sam Crawford, Detroit, 144 games, 1907.

Most extra bases on long hits, game

N.L.—13—Joe Adcock, Milwaukee, July 31, 1954 (4 home runs, 1 double).
A.L.—12
Lou Gehrig, New York, June 3, 1932 (4 home runs).
Pat Seerey, Chicago, July 18, 1948, first game, 11 innings (4 home runs).
Rocky Colavito, Cleveland, June 10, 1959 (4 home runs).

Most extra bases on long hits, doubleheader (each game nine innings)

N.L.—15
Stan Musial, St. Louis, May 2, 1954.
Nate Colbert, San Diego, August 1, 1972.
A.L.—15—Al Oliver, Texas, August 17, 1980.

Most extra bases on long hits, doubleheader (more than 18 innings)
A.L.— 15—Jimmie Foxx, Philadelphia, July 2, 1933, 19 innings.
N.L.— 13—Ralph Kiner, Pittsburgh, September 11, 1947, 22 innings.

Most extra bases on long hits, two consecutive games
A.L.— 17—Tony Lazzeri, New York, May 23, second game, May 24, 1936 (5 home runs, 1 triple).
N.L.— 17—Joe Adcock, Milwaukee, July 30, July 31, 1954 (5 home runs, 2 doubles).

Most extra bases on long hits, inning
N.L.-A.L.—6—Held by many players.

RUNS BATTED IN

CAREER AND SEASON

Most runs batted in, career
M.L.—2,297—Hank Aaron, Milwaukee N.L., Atlanta N.L., Milwaukee A.L., 23 years, 1954 through 1976 (2,202 in N.L., 95 in A.L.).
N.L.—2,202—Hank Aaron, Milwaukee, Atlanta, 21 years, 1954 through 1974.
A.L.—2,192—Babe Ruth, Boston, New York, 21 years, 1914 through 1934.

Most runs batted in, season
N.L.— 190—Hack Wilson, Chicago, 155 games, 1930.
A.L.— 184—Lou Gehrig, New York, 155 games, 1931.

Most runs batted in by rookie, season
A.L.— 145—Ted Williams, Boston, 149 games, 1939.
N.L.— 119—Wally Berger, Boston, 151 games, 1930.

Most runs batted in by righthander, season
N.L.— 190—Hack Wilson, Chicago, 155 games, 1930.
A.L.— 183—Hank Greenberg, Detroit, 154 games, 1937.

Most runs batted in by lefthander, season
A.L.— 184—Lou Gehrig, New York, 155 games, 1931.
N.L.— 170—Chuck Klein, Philadelphia, 156 games, 1930.

Most runs batted in by switch-hitter, season
A.L.— 130—Mickey Mantle, New York, 150 games, 1956.
N.L.— 128—Rip Collins, St. Louis, 154 games, 1934.

Most runs batted in by catcher, season
N.L.— 142—Roy Campanella, Brooklyn, 144 games, 1953; caught 140 games.
A.L.— 133—Bill Dickey, New York, 140 games, 1937; caught 137 games.

Most years leading league in runs batted in
A.L.—6—Babe Ruth, Boston, New York, 1919, 1920, 1921, 1923, 1926, 1928 (tied).
N.L.—4
Rogers Hornsby, St. Louis, 1920 (tied), 1921, 1922, 1925.
Hank Aaron, Milwaukee, Atlanta, 1957, 1960, 1963, 1966.
Mike Schmidt, Philadelphia, 1980, 1981, 1984 (tied), 1986.

Most consecutive years leading league in runs batted in
A.L.—3
Ty Cobb, Detroit, 1907, 1908, 1909.
Babe Ruth, Boston, New York, 1919, 1920, 1921.
Cecil Fielder, Detroit, 1990, 1991, 1992.
N.L.—3
Honus Wagner, Pittsburgh, 1907, 1908, 1909.
Rogers Hornsby, St. Louis, 1920 (tied), 1921, 1922.
Joe Medwick, St. Louis, 1936, 1937, 1938.
George Foster, Cincinnati, 1976, 1977, 1978.

Most years with 100 or more runs batted in
A.L.— 13
Babe Ruth, Boston, New York, 1919 through 1933, except 1922 and 1925.
Lou Gehrig, New York, 1926 through 1938.
Jimmie Foxx, Philadelphia, Boston, 1929 through 1941.
N.L.— 11—Hank Aaron, Milwaukee, Atlanta, 1955, 1957, 1959, 1960, 1961, 1962, 1963, 1966, 1967, 1970, 1971.

Most consecutive years with 100 or more runs batted in
A.L.— 13
Lou Gehrig, New York, 1926 through 1938.
Jimmie Foxx, Philadelphia, Boston, 1929 through 1941.
N.L.—8
Mel Ott, New York, 1929 through 1936.
Willie Mays, San Francisco, 1959 through 1966.

Most years with 150 or more runs batted in
A.L.—7—Lou Gehrig, New York, 1927, 1930, 1931, 1932, 1934, 1936, 1937.
N.L.—2—Hack Wilson, Chicago, 1929, 1930.

Most consecutive years with 150 or more runs batted in
A.L.—3
Babe Ruth, New York, 1929, 1930, 1931.
Lou Gehrig, New York, 1930, 1931, 1932.
N.L.—2—Hack Wilson, Chicago, 1929, 1930.

Fewest runs batted in, season (150 or more games)
N.L.—20—Richie Ashburn, Philadelphia, 153 games, 1959.
A.L.—20—Alvaro Espinoza, New York, 150 games, 1990.

Fewest runs batted in by leader, season (since 1920)
N.L.—94
George Kelly, New York, 155 games, 1920.
Rogers Hornsby, St. Louis, 149 games, 1920.
A.L.— 105—Al Rosen, Cleveland, 148 games, 1952.

Most consecutive games with one or more runs batted in, season
N.L.— 17—Oscar Grimes, Chicago, June 27 through July 23, 1922 (27 runs batted in).
A.L.— 13—Taffy Wright, Chicago, May 4 through May 20, 1941 (22 runs batted in).

GAME AND INNING

Most runs batted in, game
N.L.— 12
Jim Bottomley, St. Louis, September 16, 1924.
Mark Whiten, St. Louis, September 7, 1993, second game.
A.L.— 11—Tony Lazzeri, New York, May 24, 1936.

Most runs batted in by pitcher, game
N.L.—9
Henry Staley, Boston, June 1, 1893*
Tony Cloninger, Atlanta, July 3, 1966.
A.L.—7—Vic Raschi, New York, August 4, 1953.
*RBIs not officially adopted until 1920.

Most runs batted in accounting for all club's runs, game
N.L.—8—George Kelly, New York vs. Cincinnati, June 14, 1924 (New York won, 8-6).
A.L.—8—Bob Johnson, Philadelphia vs. St. Louis, June 12, 1938 (Philadelphia won, 8-3).

Most runs batted in, two consecutive games
A.L.— 15—Tony Lazzeri, New York, May 23, second game (4), May 24 (11), 1936.
N.L.— 13
Nate Colbert, San Diego, August 1, first game (5), August 1, second game (8), 1972.
Mark Whiten, St. Louis, September 7, first game (1), September 7, second game (12), 1993.

Most runs batted in, doubleheader
N.L.— 13
Nate Colbert, San Diego, August 1, 1972.
Mark Whiten, St. Louis, September 7, 1993.
A.L.— 11
Earl Averill, Cleveland, September 17, 1930, 17 innings.
Jim Tabor, Boston, July 4, 1939, 18 innings.
Boog Powell, Baltimore, July 6, 1966, 20 innings.

Most runs batted in, inning
A.A.—7—Ed Cartwright, St. Louis, September 23, 1890, third inning.*
N.L.—6
Fred Merkle, New York, May 13, 1911, first inning.*
Jim Ray Hart, San Francisco, July 8, 1970, fifth inning.
Andre Dawson, Montreal, September 24, 1985, fifth inning.

Dale Murphy, Atlanta, July 27, 1989, sixth inning.

A.L.—6
Bob Johnson, Philadelphia, August 29, 1937, first game, first inning.
Tom McBride, Boston, August 4, 1945, second game, fourth inning.
Joe Astroth, Philadelphia, September 23, 1950, sixth inning.
Gil McDougald, New York, May 3, 1951, ninth inning.
Sam Mele, Chicago, June 10, 1952, fourth inning.
Jim Lemon, Washington, September 5, 1959, third inning.
Carlos Quintana, Boston, July 30, 1991, third inning.
*RBIs not officially adopted until 1920.

Most runs batted in, two consecutive innings

A.L.—8
Jim Gentile, Baltimore, May 9, 1961, first and second innings.
Jim Northrup, Detroit, June 24, 1968, fifth and sixth innings.
Frank Robinson, Baltimore, June 26, 1970, fifth and sixth innings.

N.L.—7
Kid Nichols, Boston, September 19, 1892, fifth and sixth innings.
Tony Piet, Pittsburgh, July 28, 1932, second game, second and third innings.
Johnny Rucker, New York, September 29, 1940, second and third innings.
Del Ennis, Philadelphia, July 27, 1950, seventh and eighth innings.
Earl Torgeson, Boston, June 30, 1951, seventh and eighth innings.
Ralph Kiner, Pittsburgh, July 4, 1951, second game, third and fourth innings.
Joe Morgan, Cincinnati, August 19, 1974, second and third innings.

Most runners left on base, game

N.L.—12—Glenn Beckert, Chicago, September 16, 1972.
A.L.—11
Frank Isbell, Chicago, August 10, 1901.
John Donahue, Chicago, June 23, 1907, 12 innings.
George Wright, Texas, August 12, 1984, 11 innings.

GAME-WINNING RBIS (1980-1988)

Most game-winning RBIs, career

N.L.—129—Keith Hernandez, St. Louis, New York, 1980 through 1988.
A.L.—117—Eddie Murray, Baltimore, 1980 through 1988.

Most game-winning RBIs, season

N.L.—24—Keith Hernandez, New York, 158 games, 1985.
A.L.—23—Mike Greenwell, Boston, 158 games, 1988.

Most game-winning RBIs by pitcher, season

N.L.—3
Rick Mahler, Atlanta, 39 games, 1985.
Rick Rhoden, Pittsburgh, 35 games, 1985.
(Tim Leary of Los Angeles had 3 in 1988, but 1 came as a pinch-hitter.)
A.L.—Never accomplished.

Most game-winning RBIs by rookie, season

A.L.—14
Jose Canseco, Oakland, 157 games, 1986.
Wally Joyner, California, 154 games, 1986.
Mark McGwire, Oakland, 151 games, 1987.
N.L.—13
Juan Samuel, Philadelphia, 160 games, 1984.
Darryl Strawberry, New York, 122 games, 1983.

Fewest game-winning RBIs in a season (150 or more games)

N.L.—0
Alan Wiggins, San Diego, 158 games, 1984.
Rafael Palmeiro, Chicago, 152 games, 1988.
A.L.—1
Jackie Gutierrez, Boston, 151 games, 1984.
Tony Phillips, Oakland, 154 games, 1984.
Steve Lombardozzi, Minnesota, 156 games, 1986.

Dick Schofield, California, 155 games, 1988.

Most game-winning RBIs, doubleheader

N.L.-A.L.—2—Held by many players.

Most consecutive games with game-winning RBI, season

A.L.—5—Kirk Gibson, Detroit, July 13 through 20, 1986.
N.L.—4
Johnny Ray, Pittsburgh, September 18 through 21, 1984.
Milt Thompson, Philadelphia, August 19 through 21, second game, 1987.
Ozzie Smith, St. Louis, September 8 through 11, 1988.

Most consecutive victories with game-winning RBI, season

N.L.—6—Johnny Ray, Pittsburgh, September 13 through 21, 1984 (two losses in streak).
A.L.—5—Kirk Gibson, Detroit, July 13 through 20, 1986 (no losses in streak).

BASES ON BALLS

Most bases on balls, career

M.L.—2,056—Babe Ruth, Boston A.L., New York A.L., Boston N.L., 22 years, 1914 through 1935 (2,036 in A.L., 20 in N.L.).
A.L.—2,036—Babe Ruth, Boston, New York, 21 years, 1914 through 1934.
N.L.—1,799—Joe Morgan, Houston, Cincinnati, San Francisco, Philadelphia, 21 years, 1963 through 1983.

Most bases on balls, season

A.L.—170—Babe Ruth, New York, 152 games, 1923.
N.L.—148
Eddie Stanky, Brooklyn, 153 games, 1945.
Jim Wynn, Houston, 149 games, 1969.

Most bases on balls by rookie, season

A.L.—107—Ted Williams, Boston, 149 games, 1939.
N.L.—100—Jim Gilliam, Brooklyn, 151 games, 1953.

Most bases on balls by righthander, season

A.L.—151—Eddie Yost, Washington, 152 games, 1956.
N.L.—148
Eddie Stanky, Brooklyn, 153 games, 1945.
Jim Wynn, Houston, 149 games, 1969.

Most bases on balls by lefthander, season

A.L.—170—Babe Ruth, New York, 152 games, 1923.
N.L.—147—Jim Sheckard, Chicago, 156 games, 1911.

Most bases on balls by switch-hitter, season

A.L.—146—Mickey Mantle, New York, 144 games, 1957.
N.L.—116—Miller Huggins, St. Louis, 151 games, 1910.

Most bases on balls by pinch-hitter, season

A.L.—18—Elmer Valo, New York, Washington, 81 games, 1960.
N.L.—16
Harry McCurdy, Philadelphia, 71 games, 1933.
Merv Rettenmund, San Diego, 86 games, 1977.

Most years leading league in bases on balls

A.L.—11—Babe Ruth, New York, 1920, 1921, 1923, 1924, 1926, 1927, 1928, 1930, 1931, 1932, 1933.
N.L.—6—Mel Ott, New York, 1929, 1931, 1932, 1933, 1937, 1942.

Most consecutive years leading league in bases on balls

A.L.—4
Babe Ruth, New York, 1930 through 1933.
Ted Williams, Boston, 1946 through 1949 (military service from 1943 through 1945 interrupted a six-year streak by Williams of Boston, who led in bases on balls from 1941 through 1949).
N.L.—3
George J. Burns, New York, 1919 through 1921.
Mel Ott, New York, 1931 through 1933.
Arky Vaughan, Pittsburgh, 1934 through 1936.
Eddie Mathews, Milwaukee, 1961 through 1963.
Ron Santo, Chicago, 1966 through 1968.
Mike Schmidt, Philadelphia, 1981 through 1983.

Most years with 100 or more bases on balls
A.L.— 13—Babe Ruth, Boston, New York, 1919, 1920, 1921, 1923, 1924, 1926, 1927, 1928, 1930, 1931, 1932, 1933, 1934.
N.L.— 10—Mel Ott, New York, 1929, 1930, 1932, 1936, 1937, 1938, 1939, 1940, 1941, 1942.

Most consecutive years with 100 or more bases on balls
N.L.— 7—Mel Ott, New York, 1936 through 1942.
A.L.— 6—Eddie Joost, Philadelphia, 1947 through 1952. (Military service from 1943 through 1945 interrupted a six-year streak by Ted Williams of Boston, who collected 100 bases on balls from 1941 through 1949.)

Fewest bases on balls, season (150 or more games)
N.L.— 12—Hal Lanier, San Francisco, 151 games, 1968.
A.L.— 12
　Ozzie Guillen, Chicago, 150 games, 1985.
　Ozzie Guillen, Chicago, 159 games, 1986.

Fewest bases on balls by leader, season
N.L.— 69—Hack Wilson, Chicago, 142 games, 1926.
A.L.— 89—Whitey Witt, New York, 140 games, 1922.

Most consecutive bases on balls
A.L.— 7
　Billy Rogell, Detroit, August 17, second game, August 18, August 19, first game, 1938.
　Jose Canseco, Oakland, August 4, 5, 1992.
N.L.— 7
　Mel Ott, New York, June 16, 17, 18, 1943.
　Eddie Stanky, New York, August 29, 30, 1950.

Most consecutive games with one or more bases on balls
A.L.— 22—Roy Cullenbine, Detroit, July 2 through July 22, 1947 (34 bases on balls).
N.L.— 16—Jack Clark, St. Louis, July 18 through August 10, 1987 (28 bases on balls).
A.A.— 16—Yank Robinson, St. Louis, September 15 through October 2, 1888 (23 bases on balls).

Most bases on balls, game
N.L.— 6—Walt Wilmot, Chicago, August 22, 1891 (consecutive).
A.L.— 6
　Jimmie Foxx, Boston, June 16, 1938 (consecutive).
　Andre Thornton, Cleveland, May 2, 1984, 16 innings.
　N.L. since 1900—5—Held by many players. Last player—Vince Coleman, New York, August 10, 1992.

Most bases on balls by pitcher, game
A.A.— 4—Joe Miller, Philadelphia, September 13, 1886.
A.L.— 4
　Urban Faber, Chicago, June 18, 1915 (consecutive).
　Chuck Stobbs, Boston, June 8, 1950 (consecutive).
N.L.— 3—Held by many pitchers.

Most bases on balls, first major league game
A.L.— 4
　Otto Saltzgaver, New York, April 12, 1932.
　Milt Galatzer, Cleveland, June 25, 1933, first game.
N.L.— 3—Held by many players.

Most times receiving five bases on balls in one game, career
N.L.— 4—Mel Ott, New York, 1929, 1933, 1943, 1944.
A.L.— 2—Max Bishop, Philadelphia, 1929, 1930.

Most bases on balls, doubleheader
A.L.— 8—Max Bishop, Philadelphia, May 21, 1930; Boston, July 8, 1934.
N.L.— 6
　Mel Ott, New York, October 5, 1929.
　Johnny Mize, St. Louis, August 26, 1939.
　Mel Ott, New York, April 30, 1944.
　Clay Dalrymple, Philadelphia, July 4, 1967, 19 innings.
　Cleon Jones, New York, June 25, 1971.
　Jack Clark, St. Louis, July 8, 1987, 19 innings.

Most bases on balls, inning
N.L.-A.L.— 2—Held by many players.

Most times receiving two bases on balls in one inning, career
A.L.— 4—George Selkirk, New York, 1936 (2), 1938, 1940.

N.L.— 2—Eddie Stanky, New York, 1950 (2).

Most times receiving two bases on balls in one inning, season
A.L.— 2
　George Selkirk, New York, June 24, August 28, second game, 1936.
　Skeeter Webb, Chicago, July 30, September 3, 1940.
N.L.— 2—Eddie Stanky, New York, June 27, August 22, 1950.

INTENTIONAL (SINCE 1955)

Most intentional bases on balls, career
M.L.— 293—Hank Aaron (Milwaukee N.L., Atlanta N.L., Milwaukee A.L., 22 years, 1955 through 1976 (289 in N.L., 4 in N.L.).
N.L.— 289—Hank Aaron, Milwaukee, Atlanta, 20 years, 1955 through 1974.
A.L.— 229—George Brett, Kansas City, 21 years, 1973 through 1993.

Most intentional bases on balls, season
N.L.— 45—Willie McCovey, San Francisco, 149 games, 1969.
A.L.— 33
　Ted Williams, Boston, 132 games, 1957.
　John Olerud, Toronto, 158 games, 1993.

Most intentional bases on balls by rookie, season
A.L.— 16—Alvin Davis, Seattle, 152 games, 1984.
N.L.— 14—Willie Montanez, Philadelphia, 158 games, 1971.

Most intentional bases on balls by righthander, season
N.L.— 32—Kevin Mitchell, San Francisco, 154 games, 1989.
A.L.— 29—Frank Howard, Washington, 161 games, 1970.

Most intentional bases on balls by lefthander, season
N.L.— 45—Willie McCovey, San Francisco, 149 games, 1969.
A.L.— 33
　Ted Williams, Boston, 132 games, 1957.
　John Olerud, Toronto, 158 games, 1993.

Most intentional bases on balls by switch-hitter, season
N.L.— 26—Tim Raines, Montreal, 139 games, 1987.
A.L.— 25—Eddie Murray, Baltimore, 162 games, 1984.

Most years leading league in intentional bases on balls
A.L.— 6—Wade Boggs, Boston, 1987, 1988 (tied), 1989, 1990, 1991, 1992.
N.L.— 4
　Frank Robinson, Cincinnati, 1961, 1962 (tied), 1963, 1964.
　Willie McCovey, San Francisco, 1969, 1970, 1971 (tied), 1973.

Most consecutive years leading league in intentional bases on balls
A.L.— 6—Wade Boggs, Boston, 1987, 1988 (tied), 1989, 1990, 1991, 1992.
N.L.— 4—Frank Robinson, Cincinnati, 1961, 1962 (tied), 1963, 1964.

Most years with 10 or more intentional bases on balls
N.L.— 16—Hank Aaron, Milwaukee, Atlanta, 1957 through 1973, except 1964.
A.L.— 11—George Brett, Kansas City, 1979 through 1991, except 1981, 1984.

Most at-bats with no intentional bases on balls, season
A.L.— 691—Kirby Puckett, Minnesota, 161 games, 1985.
N.L.— 669—Larry Bowa, Philadelphia, 162 games, 1974.

Most intentional bases on balls, nine-inning game
A.L.-N.L.— 3—Held by many players.

Most intentional bases on balls, extra-inning game
N.L.— 5—Andre Dawson, Chicago, May 22, 1990, 16 innings.
A.L.— 4—Roger Maris, New York, May 22, 1962, 12 innings.

STRIKEOUTS

CAREER AND SEASON

Most strikeouts, career
A.L.— 2,597—Reggie Jackson, Kansas City, Oakland, Balti-

more, New York, California, 21 years, 1967 through 1987.

N.L.—1,936—Willie Stargell, Pittsburgh, 21 years, 1962 through 1982.

Fewest strikeouts, career (14 or more seasons; excludes pitchers)

A.L.—113—Joe Sewell, Cleveland, New York, 14 years, 1920 through 1933, 1,903 games.

N.L.—173—Lloyd Waner, Pittsburgh, Boston, Cincinnati, Philadelphia, Brooklyn, 18 years, 1927 through 1945, except 1943, 1,993 games.

Most strikeouts, season

N.L. (162-game season)—189—Bobby Bonds, San Francisco, 157 games, 1970.

N.L. (154-game season)—136—Francisco Herrera, Philadelphia, 145 games, 1960.

A.L. (162-game season)—186—Rob Deer, Milwaukee, 134 games, 1987.

A.L. (154-game season)—138—Jim Lemon, Washington, 146 games, 1956.

Most strikeouts by rookie, season

A.L. (162-game season)—185—Pete Incaviglia, Texas, 153 games, 1986.

A.L. (154-game season)—101—Joe Hoover, Detroit, 144 games, 1943.

N.L. (162-game season)—168—Juan Samuel, Philadelphia, 160 games, 1984.

N.L. (154-game season)—115—Eddie Mathews, Boston, 145 games, 1952.

Most strikeouts by righthander, season

N.L. (162-game season)—189—Bobby Bonds, San Francisco, 157 games, 1970.

N.L. (154-game season)—136—Francisco Herrera, Philadelphia, 145 games, 1960.

A.L. (162-game season)—186—Rob Deer, Milwaukee, 134 games, 1987.

A.L. (154-game season)—138—Jim Lemon, Washington, 146 games, 1956.

Most strikeouts by lefthander, season

A.L. (162-game season)—171—Reggie Jackson, Oakland, 154 games, 1968.

A.L. (154-game season)—121—Larry Doby, Cleveland, 149 games, 1953.

N.L. (162-game season)—154—Willie Stargell, Pittsburgh, 141 games, 1971.

N.L. (154-game season)—115—Eddie Mathews, Boston, 145 games, 1952.

Most strikeouts by switch-hitter, season

A.L. (162-game season)—160—Mickey Tettleton, Baltimore, 135 games, 1990.

A.L. (154-game season)—126—Mickey Mantle, New York, 144 games, 1959.

N.L. (162-game season)—130—Orestes Destrade, Florida, 153 games, 1993.

N.L. (154-game season)—112—Sam Jethroe, Boston, 151 games, 1952.

Most strikeouts by pitcher, season (since 1900)

A.L.—65—Wilbur Wood, Chicago, 49 games, 1972.

N.L.—62—Jerry Koosman, New York, 35 games, 1968.

Most years leading league in strikeouts

A.L.—7—Jimmie Foxx, Philadelphia, Boston, 1929, 1930 (tied), 1931, 1933, 1935, 1936, 1941.

N.L.—6—Vince DiMaggio, Boston, Pittsburgh, Philadelphia, 1937, 1938, 1942, 1943, 1944, 1945.

Most consecutive years leading league in strikeouts

N.L.—4

Hack Wilson, Chicago, 1927 through 1930.

Vince DiMaggio, Pittsburgh, Philadelphia, 1942 through 1945.

Juan Samuel, Philadelphia, 1984 through 1987.

A.L.—4—Reggie Jackson, Oakland, 1968 through 1971.

Most years with 100 or more strikeouts

A.L.—18—Reggie Jackson, Oakland, Baltimore, New York, California, 1968 through 1980, 1982 through 1986.

N.L.—13—Willie Stargell, Pittsburgh, 1965 through 1976, 1979.

Most consecutive years with 100 or more strikeouts

A.L.—13—Reggie Jackson, Oakland, Baltimore, New York, 1968 through 1980.

N.L.—12—Willie Stargell, Pittsburgh, 1965 through 1976.

Fewest strikeouts, season (150 or more games)

A.L.—4

Joe Sewell, Cleveland, 155 games, 1925.

Joe Sewell, Cleveland, 152 games, 1929.

N.L.—5—Charlie Hollocher, Chicago, 152 games, 1922.

Fewest strikeouts by rookie, season (150 or more games)

N.L.—17—Buddy Hassett, Brooklyn, 156 games, 1936.

A.L.—25—Tom Oliver, Boston, 154 games, 1930.

Fewest strikeouts by righthander, season (150 or more games)

N.L.—8—Emil Verban, Philadelphia, 155 games, 1947.

A.L.—9

Stuffy McInnis, Boston, 152 games, 1921.

Lou Boudreau, Cleveland, 152 games, 1948.

Fewest strikeouts by lefthander, season (150 or more games)

A.L.—4

Joe Sewell, Cleveland, 155 games, 1925.

Joe Sewell, Cleveland, 152 games, 1929.

N.L.—5—Charlie Hollocher, Chicago, 152 games, 1922.

Fewest strikeouts by switch-hitter, season (150 or more games)

N.L.—10—Frankie Frisch, St. Louis, 153 games, 1927.

A.L.—23—Buck Weaver, Chicago, 151 games, 1920.

Fewest strikeouts by leader, season

N.L.—63—George Grantham, Chicago, 127 games, 1924.

A.L.—66

Jimmie Foxx, Philadelphia, 153 games, 1930.

Ed Morgan, Cleveland, 150 games, 1930.

Most years leading league in fewest strikeouts (150 or more games)

A.L.—11—Nellie Fox, Chicago, 1952 through 1962.

N.L.—4

Stan Musial, St. Louis, 1943, 1948, 1952, 1956 (tied).

Dick Groat, Pittsburgh, St. Louis, 1955, 1958, 1964, 1965 (tied).

Most consecutive games with no strikeouts, season

A.L.—115—Joe Sewell, Cleveland, May 17 through September 19, 1929 (437 at-bats).

N.L.—77—Lloyd Waner, Pittsburgh, Boston, Cincinnati, April 24 through September 16, 1941 (219 at-bats).

GAME AND INNING

Most strikeouts, nine-inning game (*consecutive)

N.L.—5

Oscar Walker, Buffalo, June 20, 1879*.

Pete Dowling, Louisville, August 15, 1899*.

Floyd Young, Pittsburgh, September 29, 1935, second game*.

Bob Sadowski, Milwaukee, April 20, 1964*.

Dick Allen, Philadelphia, June 28, 1964, first game*.

Ron Swoboda, New York, June 22, 1969, first game*.

Steve Whitaker, San Francisco, April 14, 1970*.

Dick Allen, St. Louis, May 24, 1970*.

Bill Russell, Los Angeles, June 9, 1971*.

Jose Mangual, Montreal, August 11, 1975*.

Frank Taveras, New York, May 1, 1979*.

Dave Kingman, New York, May 28, 1982*.

Darryl Strawberry, Los Angeles, May 1, 1991*.

Delino DeShields, Montreal, Sept. 17, 1991, second game*.

A.L.—5

Lefty Grove, Philadelphia, June 10, 1933, first game*.

Johnny Broaca, New York, June 25, 1934*.

Chet Laabs, Detroit, October 2, 1938, first game*.

Larry Doby, Cleveland, April 25, 1948*.

Jim Landis, Chicago, July 28, 1957*.

Bob Allison, Minnesota, September 2, 1965*.

Reggie Jackson, Oakland, September 27, 1968*.

— 38 —

Ray Jarvis, Boston, April 20, 1969*.
Rick Monday, Oakland, April 29, 1970*.
Frank Howard, Washington, September 19, 1970, first game*.
Don Buford, Baltimore, August 26, 1971*.
Rick Manning, Cleveland, May 15, 1977*.
Bo Jackson, Kansas City, April 18, 1987*.
Rob Deer, Milwaukee, August 8, 1987, first game*.
Joey Meyer, Milwaukee, September 20, 1988*.
Phil Bradley, Baltimore, September 7, 1989, first game.
Bernie Williams, New York, August 21, 1991*.
Phil Plantier, Boston, October 1, 1991*.

Most strikeouts, extra-inning game
A.L.—6
Carl Weilman, St. Louis, July 25, 1913, 15 innings (consecutive).
Rick Reichardt, California, May 31, 1966, 17 innings.
Billy Cowan, California, July 9, 1971, 20 innings.
Cecil Cooper, Boston, June 14, 1974, 15 innings.
Sam Horn, Baltimore, July 17, 1991, 15 innings.
N.L.—6—Don Hoak, Chicago, May 2, 1956, 17 innings.

Most times with four or more strikeouts in a game, career
M.L.—15—Dick Allen, Philadelphia N.L., 1964 (2), 1966 (1), 1968 (7), 1969 (2); St. Louis N.L., 1970 (1); Chicago A.L., 1974 (2).
N.L.—13—Dick Allen, Philadelphia, 1964 (2), 1966, 1968 (7), 1969 (2), St. Louis, 1970.
A.L.—10—Mickey Mantle, New York, 1952, 1954, 1959, 1964, 1965, 1966, 1967, 1968 (3).

Most times with four or more strikeouts in a game, season
N.L.—7—Dick Allen, Philadelphia, April 13, May 1, 9, June 29, July 16, 21, August 19, 1968.
A.L.—5
Reggie Jackson, Oakland, April 7, second game, April 21, May 18, June 4, September 21, first game, 1971.
Bobby Darwin, Minnesota, May 12, 13, June 23, July 14, August 6, first game, August 10, 1972.

Most strikeouts, first major league game
N.L.—4
Billy Sunday, Chicago, May 22, 1883.
Wes Bales, Atlanta, August 7, 1966.
A.A.—4—Hercules Burnett, Louisville, June 26, 1888.
A.L.—4
Rollie Naylor, Philadelphia, September 14, 1917.
Sam Ewing, Chicago, September 11, 1973.

Most strikeouts, doubleheader
A.L.—7
Pat Seerey, Chicago, July 24, 1948, 19 innings.
Dave Nicholson, Chicago, June 12, 1963, 17 innings.
Frank Howard, Washington, July 9, 1965, 18 innings.
Bill Melton, Chicago, July 24, 1970, 18 innings.
N.L.—7—Mike Vail, New York, September 26, 1975, 24 innings.

Most strikeouts, two consecutive games (18 innings)
A.L.—8
Rick Monday, Oakland, April 28 (3), 29 (5), 1970.
Gorman Thomas, Milwaukee, July 27, second game (4), 28 (4), 1975.
Jay Buhner, Seattle, August 23 (4), 24 (4), 1990.
N.L.—8
Wayne Twitchell, Philadelphia, May 16 (4), 22 (4), 1973.
Ruppert Jones, San Diego, July 16 (4), 17 (4), 1982.

Most strikeouts, two consecutive games (more than 18 innings)
N.L.—9
Eric Davis, Cincinnati, April 24 (4), 25 (5), 1987 (21 innings).
Jack Clark, San Diego, June 11 (5), 13 (4), 1989 (21 innings).
A.L.—8
Pedro Ramos, Cleveland, August 19, 23, 1963 (22 innings).
Roy Smalley, Minnesota, August 28, 29, 1976 (26 innings).

Most strikeouts, three consecutive games
N.L.—10
Adolfo Phillips, Chicago, June 8 (2), 10 (5), 11 (3), 1966.
Wayne Twitchell, Philadelphia, May 16 (4), 22 (4), 27 (2), 1973.
A.L.—10
Bill Melton, Chicago, July 24 (4), 24 (3), 28 (3), 1970.
Dick Drago, Kansas City, September 5 (3), 10, second game (4), 17 (3), 1970.
Jim Fuller, Baltimore, September 5 (3), 27 (4), 28, first game (3), 1973.
Gorman Thomas, Milwaukee, July 27, second game (4), 28 (4), 29 (2), 1975.
Jay Buhner, Seattle, August 23 (4), 24 (4), 25 (2), 1990.

Most strikeouts, four consecutive games
N.L.—12—Adolfo Phillips, Chicago, June 7 (2), 8 (2), 10 (5), 11 (3), 1966.
A.L.—12
Jim Hannan, Washington, July 24 (4), 29 (2), August 3 (3), 8 (3), 1968.
Bill Melton, Chicago, July 23 (2), 24 (4), 24 (3), 28 (3), 1970.

Ten or more consecutive strikeouts, season (consecutive plate appearances)
N.L.—12—Sandy Koufax, Brooklyn, June 24 to September 24, second game, 1955 (12 at-bats for season, 12 strikeouts).
10—Tommie Sisk, Pittsburgh, July 27 (2), August 1 (3), 6 (4), 12 (1), 1966.
A.L.—11—Dean Chance, Los Angeles, July 24 (1), 30 (2), August 4, first game (3), 9 (4), 13 (1), 1965.
10—Joe Grzenda, Washington, April 7 (2), 22 (1), May 26 (4), June 13 (1), 16 (1), August 3 (1), 1970.

Most consecutive strikeouts, season (not consecutive plate appearances)
N.L.—14
Bill Hands, Chicago, June 9, second game through July 11, 1968, second game (also one base on balls and two sacrifice hits).
Juan Eichelberger, San Diego, June 30 through August 15, 1980 (also one sacrifice hit).
A.L.—13—Jim Hannan, Washington, July 24 through August 13, 1968 (also two bases on balls).

Most strikeouts, inning
A.L.-N.L.—2—Held by many players.

SACRIFICE HITS

Most sacrifices, career
A.L.—511—Eddie Collins, Philadelphia, Chicago, 25 years, 1906 through 1930.
N.L.—392—Jake Daubert, Brooklyn, Cincinnati, 15 years, 1910 through 1924.

Most sacrifices, season (including sacrifice scoring flies)
A.L.—67—Ray Chapman, Cleveland, 156 games, 1917.
N.L.—46—Jim Sheckard, Chicago, 148 games, 1909.

Most sacrifices, season (excludes sacrifice flies)
A.L.—46—Bill Bradley, Cleveland, 139 games, 1907.
N.L.—43—Kid Gleason, Philadelphia, 155 games, 1905.

Most sacrifices by rookie, season (includes sacrifice scoring flies)
A.L.—39—Emory Rigney, Detroit, 155 games, 1922.
N.L.—31—Ozzie Smith, San Diego, 159 games, 1978.

Most sacrifices by rookie, season (since 1931; excludes sacrifice flies)
A.L.—28—Joe Hoover, Detroit, 144 games, 1943.
N.L.—28
Jackie Robinson, Brooklyn, 151 games, 1947.
Ozzie Smith, San Diego, 159 games, 1978.

Most sacrifices by righthander, season
A.L.—67—Ray Chapman, Cleveland, 156 games, 1917 (in-

cludes a few sacrifice scoring flies).

N.L.—43—Kid Gleason, Philadelphia, 155 games, 1905 (does not include sacrifice flies).

Most sacrifices by lefthander, season

A.L.—52—Bob Ganley, Washington, 150 games, 1908 (includes a few sacrifice scoring flies).

N.L.—46—Jim Sheckard, Chicago, 148 games, 1909 (includes a few sacrifice scoring flies).

Most sacrifices by switch-hitter, season

A.L.—52—Donie Bush, Detroit, 157 games, 1909 (includes a few sacrifice scoring flies).

N.L.—35—Leo Magee, St. Louis, 142 games, 1914 (includes sacrifice flies).

Most years leading league in sacrifices

A.L.—6—Mule Haas, Philadelphia, Chicago, 1930, 1931, 1932, 1933, 1934, 1936.

N.L.—4—Otto Knabe, Philadelphia, 1907, 1908, 1910, 1913.

Most consecutive years leading league in sacrifices

A.L.—5—Mule Haas, Philadelphia, Chicago, 1930 through 1934.

N.L.—2—Held by many players. Last player—Jay Bell, Pittsburgh, 1990, 1991.

Most at-bats with no sacrifice hits, season

N.L.—701—Juan Samuel, Philadelphia, 160 games, 1984.

A.L.—670—Al Simmons, Philadelphia, 154 games, 1932.

Fewest sacrifices for leader, season (excludes sacrifice flies)

A.L.—13

Billy Martin, Detroit, 131 games, 1958.
Tony Kubek, New York, 132 games, 1959.
Jim Landis, Chicago, 149 games, 1959.
Al Pilarcik, Baltimore, 130 games, 1959.
Vic Power, Minnesota, 138 games, 1963.
Paul Blair, Baltimore, 150 games, 1969.
Denny McLain, Detroit, 42 games, 1969.

N.L.—13—Maury Wills, Los Angeles, 148 games, 1961.

Most sacrifice hits, game

A.L.—4

Red Killefer, Washington, August 27, 1910, first game.
Jack Barry, Boston, August 21, 1916.
Ray Chapman, Cleveland, August 31, 1919.
Felix Fermin, Cleveland, August 22, 1989, 10 innings.

N.L.—4

Jake Daubert, Brooklyn, August 15, 1914, second game.
Cy Seymour, Cincinnati, July 25, 1902.

Most sacrifice hits, doubleheader

N.L.—6—Jake Daubert, Brooklyn, August 15, 1914.

A.L.—5—Red Killefer, Washington, August 27, 1910.

Most sacrifice hits, inning

A.L.—2—Al Benton, Detroit, August 6, 1941, third inning.

N.L.—1—Held by many players.

SACRIFICE FLIES

Most sacrifice flies, career

A.L.—123—Robin Yount, Milwaukee, 20 years, 1974 through 1993.

N.L.—113—Hank Aaron, Milwaukee, Atlanta, 21 years, 1954 through 1974.

Most sacrifice flies, season

N.L.—19—Gil Hodges, Brooklyn, 154 games, 1954. (Pie Traynor, Pittsburgh, N.L., 144 games, 1928, had 31 sacrifice flies, advancing runners to second base, third base and home.)

A.L.—17—Roy White, New York, 147 games, 1971.

Most sacrifice flies by rookie, season

N.L.—13—Willie Montanez, Philadelphia, 158 games, 1971.

A.L.—13—Gary Gaetti, Minnesota, 145 games, 1982.

Most sacrifice flies by righthander, season

N.L.—19—Gil Hodges, Brooklyn, 154 games, 1954.

A.L.—16—Chick Gandil, Washington, 145 games, 1914.

Most sacrifice flies by lefthander, season

A.L.—16—Sam Crawford, Detroit, 157 games, 1914.

N.L.—13

Willie Montanez, Philadelphia, 158 games, 1971.
Andy Van Slyke, Pittsburgh, 154 games, 1988.
Will Clark, San Francisco, 154 games, 1990.
Barry Bonds, Pittsburgh, 153 games, 1991.

Most sacrifice flies by switch-hitter, season

A.L.—17—Roy White, New York, 147 games, 1971.

N.L.—15

Bobby Bonilla, Pittsburgh, 160 games, 1990.
Howard Johnson, New York, 153 games, 1991.

Most years leading league in sacrifice flies

A.L.—4—Brooks Robinson, Baltimore, 1962 (tied), 1964, 1967 (tied), 1968 (tied).

N.L.—3

Ron Santo, Chicago, 1963, 1967, 1969.
Johnny Bench, Cincinnati, 1970, 1972, 1973 (tied).

Most at-bats with no sacrifice flies, season

N.L.—680

Pete Rose, Cincinnati, 160 games, 1973.
Frank Taveras, Pittsburgh, New York, 164 games, 1979.

A.L.—680—Kirby Puckett, Minnesota, 161 games, 1986.

Most sacrifice flies, game

N.L.—3

Harry Steinfeldt, Chicago, May 5, 1909.
Ernie Banks, Chicago, June 2, 1961.
Vince Coleman, St. Louis, May 1, 1986.
Candy Maldonado, San Francisco, August 29, 1987.

A.L.—3

Bob Meusel, New York, September 15, 1926.
Russ Nixon, Boston, August 31, 1965, second game.
Don Mattingly, New York, May 3, 1986.
George Bell, Toronto, August 14, 1990.
Chad Kreuter, Detroit, July 30, 1994.

HIT BY PITCH

Most hit by pitch, career

A.L.—267—Don Baylor, Baltimore, Oakland, California, New York, Boston, Minnesota, 19 years, 1970 through 1988.

N.L.—243—Ron Hunt, New York, Los Angeles, San Francisco, Montreal, St. Louis, 12 years, 1963 through 1974.

Most hit by pitch, season

N.L.—50—Ron Hunt, Montreal, 152 games, 1971.

A.L.—35—Don Baylor, Boston, 160 games, 1986.

Most hit by pitch by rookie, season

A.A.—29—Tommy Tucker, Baltimore, 136 games, 1887.

N.L.—20—Frank Robinson, Cincinnati, 152 games, 1956.

A.L.—17—Heinie Manush, Detroit, 109 games, 1923.

Most hit by pitch by righthander, season

N.L.—50—Ron Hunt, Montreal, 152 games, 1971.

A.L.—35—Don Baylor, Boston, 160 games, 1986.

Most hit by pitch by lefthander, season

N.L.—31—Steve Evans, St. Louis, 151 games, 1910.

A.L.—17—Harry Gessler, Washington, 128 games, 1911.

Most hit by pitch for switch-hitter, season

N.L.—19—Dave Hollins, Philadelphia, 156 games, 1992.

A.L.—15—Gene Larkin, Minnesota, 149 games, 1988.

Most years leading league in hit by pitch

A.L.—10—Minnie Minoso, Cleveland, Chicago, 1951, 1952, 1953, 1954, 1956, 1957, 1958, 1959, 1960, 1961.

N.L.—7—Ron Hunt, San Francisco, Montreal, St. Louis, 1968, 1969, 1970, 1971, 1972, 1973, 1974.

Most consecutive years leading league in hit by pitch

N.L.—7—Ron Hunt, San Francisco, Montreal, St. Louis, 1968 through 1974.

A.L.—6—Minnie Minoso, Chicago, Cleveland, 1956 through 1961.

Most at-bats with no hit by pitch, season

A.L.—689—Sandy Alomar Sr., California, 162 games, 1971.
N.L.—662
　Hugh Critz, Cincinnati, New York, 152 games, 1930.
　Granny Hamner, Philadelphia, 154 games, 1949.

Fewest hit by pitch for leader, season

A.L.—5
　Frank Crosetti, New York, 138 games, 1934.
　Frank Pytlak, Cleveland, 91 games, 1934.
N.L.—6
　Buddy Blattner, New York, 126 games, 1946.
　Andre Dawson, Montreal, 151 games, 1980.
　Dan Driessen, Cincinnati, 154 games, 1980.
　Tim Foli, Pittsburgh, 127 games, 1980.
　Greg Luzinski, Philadelphia, 106 games, 1980.
　Elliott Maddox, New York, 130 games, 1980.
　Pete Rose, Philadelphia, 162 games, 1980.

Most hit by pitch, nine-inning game

N.L.—3—14 times (held by 11 players). Last player—Glenn Davis, Houston, April 9, 1990.
A.A.—3—5 times (held by 5 players).
A.L.—3—4 times (held by 4 players). Last player—Bill Freehan, Detroit, August 16, 1968 (consecutive).

Most hit by pitch, extra-inning game

N.L.—3—Ron Hunt, San Francisco, April 29, 1969, 13 innings.
A.L.—3
　Jake Stahl, Washington, April 15, 1904, 10 innings.
　Craig Kusick, Minnesota, August 27, 1975, 11 innings.

Most times hit by pitch three times in a game, career

N.L.—3—Hughie Jennings, Baltimore, 1894, 1896, 1898.
N.L. since 1900—2—Frank Chance, Chicago, 1902, 1904.
A.L.—1—Held by 5 players.

Most hit by pitch, doubleheader

N.L.—5—Frank Chance, Chicago, May 30, 1904.
A.L.—3
　Bert Daniels, New York, June 20, 1913.
　Al Smith, Chicago, June 21, 1961.

Most hit by pitch, inning

N.L.—2
　Willard Schmidt, Cincinnati, April 26, 1959, third inning.
　Frank Thomas, New York, April 29, 1962, first game, fourth inning.
A.L.—1—Held by many players.

GROUNDING INTO DOUBLE PLAYS

Most grounding into double plays, career

M.L.—328—Hank Aaron, Milwaukee N.L., Atlanta N.L., Milwaukee A.L., 23 years, 1954 through 1976 (305 in N.L., 23 in A.L.).
A.L.—323—Carl Yastrzemski, Boston, 23 years, 1961 through 1983.
N.L.—305—Hank Aaron, Milwaukee, Atlanta, 21 years, 1954 through 1974.

Most grounding into double plays, season

A.L.—36—Jim Rice, Boston, 159 games, 1984.
N.L.—30—Ernie Lombardi, Cincinnati, 129 games, 1938.

Most grounding into double plays by rookie, season

A.L.—27
　Billy Johnson, New York, 155 games, 1943.
　Al Rosen, Cleveland, 155 games, 1950.
N.L. (162-game season)—20
　Ken Hubbs, Chicago, 160 games, 1962.
　George Foster, San Francisco, Cincinnati, 140 games, 1971.
N.L. (154-game season)—19—Bob Schmidt, San Francisco, 127 games, 1958.

Most grounding into double plays by righthander, season

A.L.—36—Jim Rice, Boston, 159 games, 1984.
N.L.—30—Ernie Lombardi, Cincinnati, 129 games, 1938.

Most grounding into double plays by lefthander, season

A.L. (162-game season)—30—Carl Yastrzemski, Boston, 151 games, 1964.
A.L. (154-game season)—23
　Dick Wakefield, Detroit, 155 games, 1943.
　George Vico, Detroit, 144 games, 1948.
N.L. (162-game season)—26
　Willie Montanez, Philadelphia, San Francisco, 156 games, 1975.
　Dave Parker, Cincinnati, 160 games, 1985.
N.L. (154-game season)—23—Duke Snider, Brooklyn, 150 games, 1951.

Most grounding into double plays by switch-hitter, season

A.L.—29—Dave Philley, Philadelphia, 151 games, 1952.
N.L.—29—Ted Simmons, St. Louis, 161 games, 1973.

Most years leading league in grounding into double plays

N.L.—4—Ernie Lombardi, Cincinnati, New York, 1933, 1934, 1938, 1944.
A.L.—4—Jim Rice, Boston, 1982, 1983 (tied), 1984, 1985.

Fewest grounding into double plays, season (150 or more games)

N.L.—0—Augie Galan, Chicago, 154 games, 1935.
A.L.—0—Dick McAuliffe, Detroit, 151 games, 1968.

Fewest grounding into double plays by rookie, season (150 or more games)

N.L.—3—Vince Coleman, St. Louis, 151 games, 1985.
A.L.—4—Jim Rivera, St. Louis/Chicago, 150 games, 1952.

Fewest grounding into double plays by righthander, season (150 or more games)

N.L.—1—Ron Hunt, Montreal, 152 games, 1971.
A.L.—2
　Cesar Tovar, Minnesota, 157 games, 1968.
　Mark Belanger, Baltimore, 152 games, 1975.

Fewest grounding into double plays by lefthander, season (150 or more games)

A.L.—0—Dick McAuliffe, Detroit, 151 games, 1968.
N.L.—2
　Lou Brock, St. Louis, 155 games, 1965.
　Lou Brock, St. Louis, 157 games, 1969.
　Will Clark, San Francisco, 150 games, 1987.
　Brett Butler, San Francisco, 157 games, 1988.

Fewest grounding into double plays by switch-hitter, season (150 or more games)

N.L.—0—Augie Galan, Chicago, 154 games, 1935.
A.L.—1—Willie Wilson, Kansas City, 154 games, 1979.

Fewest grounding into double plays for leader, season

N.L.—19
　Andy Seminick, Philadelphia, 124 games, 1946.
　George Kurowski, St. Louis, 146 games, 1947.
　Andy Pafko, Chicago, 129 games, 1947.
A.L.—21—Brooks Robinson, Baltimore, 158 games, 1967.

Most years leading league in fewest grounding into double plays (150 or more games)

N.L.—6—Richie Ashburn, Philadelphia, Chicago, 1951, 1952, 1953, 1954, 1958, 1960 (tied).
A.L.—2—Held by 10 players. Last player—Willie Wilson, Kansas City, 1979, 1980.

Most grounding into double plays, nine-inning game

A.L.—4—Goose Goslin, Detroit, April 28, 1934 (consecutive).
N.L.—4—Joe Torre, New York, July 21, 1975 (consecutive).

Most grounding into double plays, two consecutive games

N.L.—5—Hank Bonura, New York, July 8 (3), second game, July 9 (2), 1939.
A.L.—4—Held by many players.

Most grounding into infield triple plays, game or season

N.L.-A.L.—1—Held by many players.

REACHING ON ERRORS OR INTERFERENCE

Most times reaching base on error, game (fair - hit balls)

P.L.—4—Mike Griffin, Philadelphia, June 23, 1890.
N.L.—3
  George Gore, New York, August 15, 1887.
  Al Lopez, Boston, July 16, 1936.
  Jerry Grote, New York, September 5, 1975.
A.L.—2—Held by many players.

Most times reaching base on error, inning (fair - hit balls)

A.L.—2
  Emory Rigney, Detroit, August 21, 1922, sixth inning.
  Fred Spurgeon, Cleveland, April 14, 1925, eighth inning.

  Johnny Bassler, Detroit, June 17, 1925, sixth inning.
  Sam Rice, Washington, July 10, 1926, eighth inning.
N.L.—2—Stu Martin, St. Louis, June 22, 1940, sixth inning.

Most times reaching base on catcher's interference, season

A.L.—8—Roberto Kelly, New York, 152 games, 1992.
N.L.—7—Dale Berra, Pittsburgh, 161 games, 1983.

Most times reaching base on catcher's interference, game

N.L.—2
  Ben Geraghty, Brooklyn, April 26, 1936.
  Pat Corrales, Philadelphia, September 29, 1965.
A.L.—2
  Dan Meyer, Seattle, May 3, 1977.
  Bob Stinson, Seattle, July 24, 1979.

CLUB BATTING

GAMES

Most games, league

N.L.—17,510—Chicago, 119 years, 1876 to date.
A.L.—14,603—Detroit, 94 years, 1901 to date.

Most games, season

N.L. (162-game season) — 165
  Los Angeles, 1962 (3 playoffs).
  San Francisco, 1962 (3 playoffs).
N.L. (154-game season) — 160—Cincinnati, 1915 (6 tied).
A.L. (162-game season) — 164
  Cleveland, 1964 (2 tied).
  New York, 1964, 1968 (2 tied).
  Minnesota, 1967 (2 tied).
  Detroit, 1968 (2 tied).
A.L. (154-game season) — 162—Detroit, 1904 (10 tied, 2 unplayed).

Fewest games, season

A.L. (154-game season) — 147—Cleveland, 1945 (2 tied, 9 unplayed).
A.L. (162-game season) — 158—Baltimore, 1971 (4 unplayed).
N.L. (154-game season) — 149—Philadelphia, 1907 (2 tied, 7 unplayed), 1934 (5 unplayed).
N.L. (162-game season) — 160
  Cincinnati, 1966 (2 unplayed).
  Atlanta, 1979 (2 unplayed).
  Montreal, 1979 (2 unplayed).
  Atlanta, 1988 (2 unplayed).
  New York, 1988 (2 unplayed).
  Pittsburgh, 1988 (2 unplayed).
  Los Angeles, 1989 (2 unplayed).
  Chicago, 1991 (2 unplayed).

Most games, one day

N.L.—3
  Brooklyn and Pittsburgh, September 1, 1890 (Brooklyn won 3).
  Baltimore and Louisville, September 7, 1896 (Baltimore won 3).
  Pittsburgh and Cincinnati, October 2, 1920 (Cincinnati won 2).
A.L.—2—Made on many days.

Most doubleheaders, season

A.L. (154-game season) —44—Chicago, 1943. (Won 11, lost 10, split 23).
A.L. (162-game season) —29
  Chicago, 1967. (Won 9, lost 5, split 15).
  Kansas City, 1967. (Won 3, lost 9, split 17).
N.L. (154-game season) —43—Philadelphia, 1943. (Won 11, lost 14, split 18).
N.L. (162-game season) —30—New York, 1962. (Won 3, lost 17, split 10).

Fewest doubleheaders, season

A.L.—0
  Seattle, 1983, 1993.
  California, 1987, 1990.
  Toronto, 1988, 1990, 1991, 1993.
  Oakland, 1992.
N.L.—0
  Chicago, 1985.
  St. Louis, 1988.
  Montreal, 1989.
  Houston, 1991.
  San Diego, 1991.
  San Francisco, 1991.
  Pittsburgh, 1992.
  Atlanta, 1993.

Most consecutive doubleheaders played, season

N.L.—9—Boston, September 4 through September 15, 1928.

A.L.—8—Washington, July 27 through August 5, 1909.

Most consecutive games between same clubs, season

A.L.—11—Detroit vs. St. Louis, September 8 through 14, 1904.
N.L.—10—Chicago vs. Philadelphia, August 7 through 16, 1907.

Most consecutive doubleheaders between same clubs, season

A.L.—5—Philadelphia vs. Washington, August 5, 7, 8, 9, 10, 1901.
N.L.—4—New York vs. Boston, September 10, 11, 13, 14, 1928.

BATTING AVERAGE

Highest batting average, season

N.L.—.343—Philadelphia, 132 games, 1894.
N.L. since 1900—.319—New York, 154 games, 1930.
A.L.—.316—Detroit, 154 games, 1921.

Highest batting average for pennant winner, season

N.L.—.328—Baltimore, 129 games, 1894.
N.L. since 1900—.314—St. Louis, 154 games, 1930.
A.L.—.307—New York, 155 games, 1927.

Highest batting average for an outfield, season

N.L.—.405—Philadelphia, 132 games, 1894.
A.L.—.367—Detroit, 156 games, 1925.
N.L. since 1900—.350—Chicago, 156 games, 1929.

Most years leading league in batting average (since 1900)

N.L.—22—St. Louis, 1915, 1920, 1921, 1934, 1938, 1939, 1942, 1943, 1944, 1946, 1949, 1952, 1954, 1956, 1957, 1963, 1971, 1975, 1979, 1980, 1985, 1992.
A.L.—20—Boston, 1903, 1938, 1939, 1941, 1942, 1944, 1946, 1949, 1950, 1964, 1967, 1975, 1979, 1981, 1984, 1985, 1987, 1988, 1989, 1990.

Most consecutive years leading league in batting average

A.L.—5—Philadelphia, 1910, 1911, 1912, 1913, 1914.
N.L.—4—New York, 1910, 1911, 1912, 1913.

Most players batting .300 or over, season (50 or more games)

A.L.—10—Philadelphia, 1927.
N.L.—10—St. Louis, 1930.

Most players batting .400 or over, season (50 or more games)

N.L.—3—Philadelphia, 1894.
N.L. since 1900—1—St. Louis, 1922, 1924, 1925; New York, 1930.
A.L.—1—Philadelphia, 1901; Detroit, 1911, 1912, 1922, 1923; Cleveland, 1911; St. Louis, 1920, 1922; Boston, 1941.

Lowest batting average, season

N.L.—.207—Washington, 136 games, 1888.
A.L.—.212—Chicago, 156 games, 1910.
N.L. since 1900—.213—Brooklyn, 154 games, 1908.

Lowest batting average for a pennant winner, season

A.L.—.228—Chicago, 154 games, 1906; last in batting.
N.L.—.242—New York, 162 games, 1969; tied for seventh in batting.

Lowest batting average for club leader, season

A.L.—.240—Oakland, 163 games, 1968.
N.L.—.254—Pittsburgh, 157 games, 1907; St. Louis, 157 games, 1915.

SLUGGING AVERAGE

Highest slugging average, season

A.L.—.489—New York, 155 games, 1927.
N.L.—.481—Chicago, 156 games, 1930.

Most years leading league in slugging average (since 1900)

A.L.—30—New York, 1901 (franchise in Baltimore), 1920, 1921, 1923, 1924, 1926, 1927, 1928, 1930, 1931, 1936, 1937, 1938, 1939, 1943, 1944, 1945, 1947, 1948, 1951, 1953, 1954, 1955, 1956, 1957, 1958, 1960, 1961, 1962, 1986.

N.L.—20—New York/San Francisco, 1904, 1905, 1908, 1910, 1911, 1919, 1923, 1924, 1927, 1928, 1935, 1945, 1947, 1948, 1952, 1961, 1962, 1963, 1989, 1993.

Most consecutive years leading in slugging (since 1900)

A.L.—6—New York, 1953, 1954, 1955, 1956, 1957, 1958.

N.L.—3
St. Louis, 1920, 1921, 1922 and 1938, 1939, 1940 and 1942, 1943, 1944.
Brooklyn, 1949, 1950, 1951 and 1953, 1954, 1955.
San Francisco, 1961, 1962, 1963.
Cincinnati, 1968, 1969, 1970.
New York, 1986, 1987, 1988.

Lowest slugging average, season (150 or more games)

A.L.—.261—Chicago, 156 games, 1910.
N.L.—.274—Boston, 155 games, 1909.

AT-BATS AND PLATE APPEARANCES

Most at-bats, season

N.L.—5,767—Cincinnati, 163 games, 1968.
A.L.—5,733—Milwaukee, 163 games, 1982.

Fewest at-bats, season

N.L.—4,725—Philadelphia, 149 games, 1907.
A.L.—4,827—Chicago, 153 games, 1913.

Most at-bats, nine-inning game

N.L.—66—Chicago vs. Buffalo, July 3, 1883.
N.L. since 1900—58
New York vs. Philadelphia, September 2, 1925, second game.
New York vs. Philadelphia, July 11, 1931, first game.
A.L.—57—Milwaukee vs. Toronto, August 28, 1992.

Most at-bats, extra-inning game

A.L.—95—Chicago vs. Milwaukee, May 8, finished May 9, 1984, 25 innings.
N.L.—89—New York vs. St. Louis, September 11, 1974, 25 innings.

Most plate appearances, nine-inning game

N.L.—71—Chicago vs. Louisville, June 29, 1897.
N.L. since 1900—66
Philadelphia vs. Chicago, August 25, 1922.
St. Louis vs. Philadelphia, July 6, 1929, second game.
A.L.—65—Milwaukee vs. Toronto, August 28, 1992.

Most plate appearances, extra-inning game

A.L.—104—Chicago vs. Milwaukee, May 8, finished May 9, 1984, 25 innings.
N.L.—103—New York vs. St. Louis, September 11, 1974, 25 innings.

Fewest at-bats, nine-inning game

A.L.—23
Chicago vs. St. Louis, May 6, 1917.
Cleveland vs. Chicago, May 9, 1961.
Detroit vs. Baltimore, May 6, 1968.
N.L.—24
Cincinnati vs. Brooklyn, July 22, 1911.
Boston vs. Cincinnati, May 15, 1951.
Pittsburgh vs. Chicago, May 12, 1955.

Fewest at-bats, eight-inning game

A.L.—19—Baltimore vs. Kansas City, September 12, 1964.
N.L.—21—Pittsburgh vs. St. Louis, September 8, 1908.

Most at-bats both clubs, nine-inning game

N.L.—106—Chicago 64, Louisville 42, July 22, 1876.
N.L. since 1900—99
New York 56, Cincinnati 43, June 9, 1901.
New York 58, Philadelphia 41, July 11, 1931, first game.

A.L.—96—Cleveland 51, Philadelphia 45, April 29, 1952.

Most at-bats both clubs, extra-inning game

N.L.—175—New York 89, St. Louis 86, September 11, 1974, 25 innings.
A.L.—175—Chicago 95, Milwaukee 80, May 8, finished May 9, 1984, 25 innings.

Most plate appearances both clubs, nine-inning game

N.L.—125—Philadelphia 66, Chicago 59, August 25, 1922.
A.L.—108—Cleveland 58, Philadelphia 50, April 29, 1952.

Most plate appearances both clubs, extra-inning game

N.L.—202—New York 103, St. Louis 99, September 11, 1974, 25 innings.
A.L.—198—Chicago 104, Milwaukee 94, May 8, finished May 9, 1984, 25 innings.

Fewest at-bats both clubs, nine-inning game

N.L.—48
Boston 25, Philadelphia 23, April 22, 1910.
Brooklyn 24, Cincinnati 24, July 22, 1911.
A.L.—46—Kansas City 27, Baltimore 19, September 12, 1964.

Most at-bats, doubleheader (18 innings)

A.L.—99—New York vs. Philadelphia, June 28, 1939.
N.L.—98—Pittsburgh vs. Philadelphia, August 8, 1922.

Fewest at-bats, doubleheader

A.L.—50—Boston vs. Chicago, August 28, 1912.
N.L.—52—Brooklyn vs. St. Louis, July 24, 1909.

Most at-bats both clubs, doubleheader (18 innings)

N.L.—176—Pittsburgh 98, Philadelphia 78, August 8, 1922.
A.L.—172—Boston 89, Philadelphia 83, July 4, 1939.

Most at-bats both clubs, doubleheader (more than 18 innings)

N.L.—234—New York 119, San Francisco 115, May 31, 1964, 32 innings.
A.L.—215—Kansas City 112, Detroit 103, June 17, 1967, 28 innings.

Fewest at-bats both clubs, doubleheader

N.L.—109—St. Louis 57, Brooklyn 52, July 24, 1909.
A.L.—111—Cleveland 56, Chicago 55, May 28, 1916.

Most plate appearances, inning

A.L.—23—Boston vs. Detroit, June 18, 1953, seventh inning.
N.L.—23—Chicago vs. Detroit, September 6, 1883, seventh inning.
N.L. since 1900—21—Brooklyn vs. Cincinnati, May 21, 1952, first inning.

Most batters facing pitcher three times, inning (club)

N.L.—5—Chicago vs. Detroit, September 6, 1883, seventh inning.
A.L.—5—Boston vs. Detroit, June 18, 1953, seventh inning.
N.L. since 1900—3—Brooklyn vs. Cincinnati, May 21, 1952, first inning.

RUNS

SEASON AND MONTH

Most runs, season

N.L.—1,220—Boston, 133 games, 1894.
A.L.—1,067—New York, 155 games, 1931.
N.L. since 1900—1,004—St. Louis, 154 games, 1930.

Most runs by pennant winner, season

N.L.—1,170—Baltimore, 129 games, 1894.
A.L.—1,065—New York, 155 games, 1936.
N.L. since 1900—1,004—St. Louis, 154 games, 1930.

Most runs at home, season (since 1900)

A.L.—625—Boston, 77 games, 1950.
N.L.—543—Philadelphia, 77 games, 1930.

Most runs on road, season (since 1900)

A.L.—591—New York, 78 games, 1930.
N.L.—492—Chicago, 78 games, 1929.

Most runs against one club, season (since 1900)
N.L.—218—Chicago vs. Philadelphia, 24 games, 1930 (117 at home, 101 at Philadelphia).
A.L.—216—Boston vs. St. Louis, 22 games, 1950 (118 at home, 98 at St. Louis).

Most players scoring 100 or more runs, season
N.L.—7—Boston, 1894.
A.L.—6—New York, 1931.
N.L. since 1900—6—Brooklyn, 1953.

Fewest runs, season
N.L.—372—St. Louis, 154 games, 1908.
A.L.—380—Washington, 156 games, 1909.

Fewest runs scored by leader, season
N.L.—590—St. Louis, 157 games, 1915.
A.L.—622—Philadelphia, 152 games, 1905.

Fewest runs by pennant winner, season
A.L.—550—Boston, 156 games, 1916.
N.L.—571—Chicago, 155 games, 1907.

Most runs scored, month (since 1900)
A.L.—275—New York, August 1938, 36 games.
N.L.—260—New York, June 1929, 33 games.

▮ GAME AND DOUBLEHEADER—ONE CLUB ▯

Most runs, game
N.L.—36—Chicago vs. Louisville (7), June 29, 1897.
A.L.—29
  Boston vs. St. Louis (4), June 8, 1950.
  Chicago vs. Kansas City (6), April 23, 1955.
N.L. since 1900—28—St. Louis vs. Philadelphia (7), July 6, 1929, second game.

Most runs, opening game of season
P.L.—23—Buffalo vs. Cleveland, April 19, 1890 (23-2).
A.L.—21—Cleveland vs. St. Louis, April 14, 1925 (21-14).
N.L.—19—Philadelphia vs. Boston, April 19, 1900, 10 innings (19-17).

Most runs scored by infielders, game
N.L.—16
  Chicago vs. Philadelphia, June 29, 1897.
  Chicago vs. Boston, July 3, 1945.
A.L.—16—Boston vs. St. Louis, June 8, 1950.

Most runs scored by outfielders, game
A.A.—14—Kansas City vs. Philadelphia, September 30, 1888.
N.L.—14
  New York vs. Cincinnati, June 9, 1901.
  New York vs. Brooklyn, April 30, 1944, first game.
A.L.—11
  Chicago vs. Philadelphia, September 11, 1936.
  New York vs. Washington, August 12, 1953.

Biggest run deficit overcome to win game
A.L.—12
  Detroit vs. Chicago, June 18, 1911, at Detroit.
  Chicago .... 7 0 0 3 3 0 2 0 0—15
  Detroit.................... 0 1 0 0 4 3 0 5 3—16
  Philadelphia vs. Cleveland, June 15, 1925, at Philadelphia.
  Cleveland............... 0 4 2 2 4 2 1 0 0—15
  Philadelphia .... 0 1 1 0 0 1 1 13 x—17
N.L.—11
  St. Louis vs. New York, June 15, 1952, first game, at New York.
  St. Louis .... 0 0 0 0 7 0 3 2 2—14
  New York .... 0 5 6 0 0 0 0 0 1—12
  Philadelphia vs. Chicago, April 17, 1976, at Chicago, 10 innings.
  Philadelphia .... 0 1 0 1 2 0 3 5 3 3—18
  Chicago .... 0 7 5 1 0 0 0 0 2 1—16
  Houston vs. St. Louis, July 18, 1994, at Houston.
  St. Louis .... 3 4 4 0 0 0 0 0 1—12
  Houston.................. 0 0 0 2 2 11 0 0 x—15

Most runs scored by two players, game
N.L.—12—Boston vs. Pittsburgh, August 27, 1887 (King Kelly 6, Ezra Sutton 6).
N.L. since 1900—11—New York vs. Brooklyn, April 30, 1944, first game (Mel Ott 6, Joe Medwick 5).
A.L.—10
  Cleveland vs. Baltimore, September 2, 1902 (Harry Bay 5, Bill Bradley 5).
  Chicago vs. Kansas City, April 23, 1955 (Chico Carrasquel 5, Minnie Minoso 5).

Longest extra-inning game without a run
N.L.—24 innings—New York vs. Houston, April 15, 1968.
A.L.—20 innings—California vs. Oakland, July 9, 1971.

Most players scoring six runs, game
N.L.—2—Boston vs. Pittsburgh, August 27, 1887 (Mike Kelly, Ezra Sutton).
N.L. since 1900—1
  New York vs. Philadelphia, August 4, 1934, second game (Mel Ott).
  New York vs. Brooklyn, April 30, 1944, first game (Mel Ott).
  Milwaukee vs. Chicago, September 2, 1957, first game (Frank Torre).
A.L.—1
  Boston vs. Chicago, May 8, 1946 (Johnny Pesky).
  Boston vs. Cleveland, August 21, 1986 (Spike Owen).

Most players scoring five or more runs, game
N.L.—3
  Chicago vs. Cleveland, July 24, 1882.
  Boston vs. Philadelphia, June 20, 1883.
  Boston vs. Pittsburgh, August 27, 1887.
  New York vs. Brooklyn, April 30, 1944, first game.
  Chicago vs. Boston, July 3, 1945.
A.L.—2
  Cleveland vs. Baltimore, September 2, 1902.
  Chicago vs. Kansas City, April 23, 1955.

Most players scoring four or more runs, game
N.L.—6
  Chicago vs. Cleveland, July 24, 1882.
  Chicago vs. Louisville, June 29, 1897.
N.L. since 1900—4—St. Louis vs. Philadelphia, July 6, 1929, second game.
A.L.—4—Boston vs. St. Louis, June 8, 1950.

Most players scoring three or more runs, game
N.L.—9—Chicago vs. Buffalo, July 3, 1883.
A.L.—7—Boston vs. St. Louis, June 8, 1950.
N.L. since 1900—6—New York vs. Philadelphia, September 2, 1925, second game.

Most players scoring two or more runs, game
N.L.—10—Chicago vs. Louisville, June 29, 1897.
A.L.—9
  New York vs. Cleveland, July 14, 1904.
  Cleveland vs. Boston, July 7, 1923, first game.
  New York vs. Chicago, July 26, 1931, second game.
  New York vs. Philadelphia, May 24, 1936.
  Boston vs. Philadelphia, June 29, 1950.
N.L. since 1900—9
  St. Louis vs. Chicago, April 16, 1912.
  Chicago vs. Philadelphia, August 25, 1922.
  St. Louis vs. Philadelphia, July 6, 1929, second game.

Most players scoring one or more runs, game
N.L.—13
  Cincinnati vs. Boston, June 4, 1911.
  New York vs. Boston, June 20, 1912.
  Philadelphia vs. Chicago, August 25, 1922.
  San Francisco vs. San Diego, June 23, 1986.
A.L.—13
  Washington vs. St. Louis, July 10, 1926.
  New York vs. St. Louis, August 7, 1949, first game.
  Oakland vs. Kansas City, September 20, 1975.

Clubs scoring 20 or more runs (most times)
N.L.—38—Chicago, 1876 to date.

A.L.— 19—New York, 1903 to date.
N.L. since 1900— 15—Brooklyn, 1900 through 1957.

Clubs scoring 20 or more runs (most times), season
N.L.—8—Boston, 1894.
N.L. since 1900—3—Philadelphia, 1900.
A.L.—3
  New York, 1939.
  Boston, 1950.

Most runs, doubleheader
N.L.—43—Boston vs. Cincinnati, August 21, 1894.
A.L.—36—Detroit vs. St. Louis, August 14, 1937.
N.L. since 1900—34—St. Louis vs. Philadelphia, July 6, 1929.

Longest doubleheader without scoring a run
N.L.—27 innings
  St. Louis vs. New York, July 2, 1933.
  New York vs. Philadelphia, October 2, 1965.
A.L.— 18 innings—Held by many clubs. Last double-
  header—Cleveland vs. Boston, September 26, 1975.

Most runs, two consecutive games
N.L.—53—Chicago, July 22, 25, 1876.
A.L.—49—Boston vs. St. Louis, June 7, 8, 1950.
N.L. since 1900—45—Pittsburgh, June 20, 22, 1925.

Most runs, three consecutive games
N.L.—71—Chicago, July 20, 22, 25, 1876.
A.L.—56—Boston vs. St. Louis, June 7, 8, 9, 1950.

Most runs, four consecutive games
N.L.—88—Chicago, July 20, 22, 25, 27, 1876.
A.L.—65—Boston, June 5, 6, 7, 8, 1950.

☐ GAME AND DOUBLEHEADER—BOTH CLUBS ☐

Most runs, game
N.L.—49—Chicago 26, Philadelphia 23, August 25, 1922.
A.L.—36—Boston 22, Philadelphia 14, June 29, 1950.

Most runs, opening game of season
N.L.—36—Philadelphia 19, Boston 17, April 19, 1900, 10 in-
  nings.
A.L.—35—Cleveland 21, St. Louis 14, April 14, 1925.

Most players scoring six or more runs, game
N.L.—2—Boston 2 (Mike Kelly, Ezra Sutton), Pittsburgh 0,
  August 27, 1887.
A.L.—1
  Boston 1 (Johnny Pesky), Chicago 0, May 8, 1946.
  Boston 1 (Spike Owen), Cleveland 0, August 21, 1986.

Most players scoring five or more runs, game
N.L.—3
  Chicago 3, Cleveland 0, July 24, 1882.
  Boston 3, Philadelphia 0, June 20, 1883.
  Boston 3, Pittsburgh 0, August 27, 1887.
  New York 3, Brooklyn 0, April 30, 1944, first game.
  Chicago 3, Boston 0, July 3, 1945.
A.L.—2
  Cleveland 2, Baltimore 0, September 2, 1902.
  Chicago 2, Kansas City 0, April 23, 1955.

Most players scoring four or more runs, game
N.L.—6
  Chicago 6, Cleveland 0, July 24, 1882.
  Chicago 6, Louisville 0, June 29, 1897.
N.L. since 1900—4—St. Louis, Philadelphia 0, July 6, 1929,
  second game.
A.L.—4—Boston 4, St. Louis 0, June 8, 1950.

Most players scoring three or more runs, game
N.L.—9—Chicago 9, Buffalo 0, July 3, 1883.
A.L.—7—Boston 7, St. Louis 0, June 8, 1950.
N.L. since 1900—6—New York 6, Philadelphia 0, September
  2, 1925, second game.

Most players scoring two or more runs, game
N.L.— 16—Chicago 9, Philadelphia 7, August 25, 1922.
A.L.— 13—Boston 9, Philadelphia 4, June 29, 1950.

Most players scoring one or more runs, game
N.L.—22—Philadelphia 13, Chicago 9, August 25, 1922.
A.L.— 18—Boston 10, Philadelphia 8, June 29, 1950.

Most runs, doubleheader
N.L.—54—Boston 43, Cincinnati 11, August 21, 1894.
A.L.—54—Boston 35, Philadelphia 19, July 4, 1939.
N.L. since 1900—50
  Brooklyn 26, Philadelphia 24, May 18, 1929.
  St. Louis 34, Philadelphia 16, July 6, 1929.

Fewest runs, doubleheader
N.L.— 1
  Boston 1, Pittsburgh 0, September 4, 1902.
  Philadelphia 1, Boston 0, September 5, 1913.
A.L.—2
  Washington 1, St. Louis 1, September 25, 1904.
  Philadelphia 1, Boston 1, June 1, 1909.
  Philadelphia 1, Boston 1, September 11, 1909.
  Los Angeles 1, Detroit 1, August 18, 1964.
  Washington 1, Kansas City 1, May 2, 1967.
  Baltimore 2, Boston 0, September 2, 1974.

☐ INNING ☐

Most runs, inning
N.L.— 18—Chicago vs. Detroit, September 6, 1883, seventh
  inning.
A.L.— 17—Boston vs. Detroit, June 18, 1953, seventh inning.
N.L. since 1900— 15—Brooklyn vs. Cincinnati, May 21, 1952,
  first inning.

Most runs by both clubs, inning
A.L.— 19—Cleveland 13, Boston 6, April 10, 1977, eighth inning.
A.A.— 19—Washington 14, Baltimore 5, June 17, 1891, first
  inning.
N.L.— 18—Chicago 18, Detroit 0, September 6, 1883, seventh
  inning.
N.L. since 1900— 17—Boston 10, New York 7, June 20, 1912,
  ninth inning.

Most runs, two consecutive innings
N.L.—21—Pittsburgh vs. Boston, June 6, 1894; 12 in third
  inning, 9 in fourth inning.
A.L.— 19
  Boston vs. Philadelphia, May 2, 1901; 9 in second inning,
  10 in third inning.
  Boston vs. Detroit, June 18, 1953; 2 in sixth inning, 17 in
  seventh inning.
N.L. since 1900— 17—New York vs. Boston, September 3,
  1926; 5 in fourth inning, 12 in fifth inning.

Most runs, extra inning
A.L.— 12—Texas vs. Oakland, July 3, 1983, 15th inning.
N.L.— 10
  Kansas City vs. Detroit, July 21, 1886, 11th inning.
  Boston vs. New York, June 17, 1887, a.m. game, 10th in-
  ning.
  Cincinnati vs. Brooklyn, May 15, 1919, 13th inning.

Most runs by both clubs, extra inning
A.L.— 12
  Minnesota 11, Oakland 1, June 21, 1969, 10th inning.
  Texas 12, Oakland 0, July 3, 1983, 15th inning.
N.L.— 11
  New York 8, Pittsburgh 3, June 15, 1929, 14th inning.
  New York 6, Brooklyn 5, April 24, 1955, 10th inning.
  New York 6, Chicago 5, June 30, 1979, 11th inning.

Most runs scored at start of game with none out
A.L.—8
  Cleveland vs. Baltimore, July 6, 1954.
  New York vs. Baltimore, April 24, 1960.
N.L.—7—New York vs. St. Louis, May 13, 1911.

Most runs scored at start of inning with none out
N.L.— 13—Chicago vs. Detroit, September 6, 1883, seventh
  inning.
A.L.— 11—Detroit vs. New York, June 17, 1925, sixth inning.

N.L. since 1900—12—Brooklyn vs. Philadelphia, May 24, 1953, eighth inning.

Most runs scored in inning with two out

A.L.—13
Cleveland vs. Boston, July 7, 1923, first game, sixth inning.
Kansas City vs. Chicago, April 21, 1956, second inning.
N.L.—12
Brooklyn vs. Cincinnati, May 21, 1952, first inning.
Brooklyn vs. Cincinnati, August 8, 1954, eighth inning.

Most runs scored in inning with none on base and two out

N.L.—12—Brooklyn vs. Cincinnati, August 8, 1954, eighth inning.
A.L.—10—Chicago vs. Detroit, September 2, 1959, second game, fifth inning.

Most runs scored by pinch-hitters, inning

N.L.—3
Boston vs. Philadelphia, April 19, 1900, ninth inning.
Brooklyn vs. Philadelphia, September 9, 1926, ninth inning.
San Francisco vs. Pittsburgh, May 5, 1958, ninth inning.
A.L.—3
Chicago vs. Philadelphia, September 19, 1916, ninth inning.
Philadelphia vs. Detroit, September 18, 1940, second game, ninth inning.
Cleveland vs. Detroit, August 7, 1941, ninth inning.

Most runs scored by pinch-runners, inning

A.L.—3
Chicago vs. Minnesota, September 16, 1967, ninth inning.
Chicago vs. Oakland, May 19, 1968, second game, fifth inning.
Oakland vs. California, May 7, 1975, seventh inning.
N.L.—2—Made in many innings.

Most players scoring two or more runs in one inning

N.L.—7—Chicago vs. Detroit, September 6, 1883, seventh inning.
N.L. since 1900—6
Brooklyn vs. Cincinnati, May 21, 1952, first inning.
Cincinnati vs. Houston, August 3, 1989, first inning.
A.L.—5
New York vs. Washington, July 6, 1920, fifth inning.
New York vs. Boston, June 21, 1945, fifth inning.
Boston vs. Philadelphia, July 4, 1948, seventh inning.
Cleveland vs. Philadelphia, June 18, 1950, second game, first inning.
Boston vs. Detroit, June 18, 1953, seventh inning.

Clubs scoring in every inning of nine-inning game

A.A.—9
Columbus vs. Pittsburgh, June 14, 1883.
Kansas City vs. Brooklyn, May 20, 1889.
N.L.—9
Cleveland vs. Boston, August 15, 1889.
Washington vs. Boston, June 22, 1894.
Cleveland vs. Philadelphia, July 12, 1894.
Chicago vs. Louisville, June 29, 1897.
New York vs. Philadelphia, June 1, 1923.
St. Louis vs. Chicago, September 13, 1964.
A.L.—8
Boston vs. Cleveland, September 16, 1903, did not bat in ninth.
Cleveland vs. Boston, July 7, 1923, first game, did not bat in ninth.
New York vs. St. Louis, July 26, 1939 did not bat in ninth.
Chicago vs. Boston, May 11, 1949, did not bat in ninth.

Most innings scored in by both clubs, nine-inning game

N.L.—15
Philadelphia 8, Detroit 7, July 1, 1887.
Washington 9, Boston 6, June 22, 1894.
A.A.—15—Kansas City 9, Brooklyn 6, May 20, 1889.
P.L.—15—New York 8, Chicago 7, May 23, 1890.
A.L.—14
Baltimore 8, Philadelphia 6, May 7, 1901.
St. Louis 7, Detroit 7, April 23, 1927.
Detroit 7, Chicago 7, July 2, 1940.
N.L. since 1900—14

New York 9, Philadelphia 5, June 1, 1923.
Pittsburgh 8, Chicago 6, July 6, 1975.
Los Angeles 8, Chicago 8, May 25, 1976.

Most consecutive innings scoring runs

A.L.—17—Boston, September 15 (last 3 innings), September 16 (8 innings), September 17 (first 6 innings), 1903, 3 games.
N.L.—14
Pittsburgh, July 31 (last 5 innings), August 1 (8 innings), August 2 (first inning), 1894, 3 games.
New York, July 18 (last 3 innings), July 19 (8 innings), July 20 (first 3 innings), 1949, 3 games.

Most times scoring 10 or more runs in one inning

N.L.—30—Chicago, 1876 to date.
A.L.—24—Boston, 1901 to date.
N.L. since 1900—19—Brooklyn-Los Angeles, 1900 through 1957 in Brooklyn, 1958 to date in Los Angeles.

Most innings scoring 10 or more runs, season

N.L.—5—Boston, 1894.
A.L.—3—Washington, 1930.
N.L. since 1900—3—Brooklyn, 1943.

Most innings scoring 10 or more runs in same game

N.L.—2
Chicago vs. Philadelphia, August 25, 1922; 10 in second, 14 in fourth inning.
St. Louis vs. Philadelphia, July 6, 1929, second game; 10 in first, 10 in fifth inning.
Brooklyn vs. Pittsburgh, July 10, 1943; 10 in first, 10 in fourth inning.
A.L.—1—Made in many games.

Most innings with both clubs scoring 10 or more runs in same game (each club scoring)

A.L.—2—Philadelphia, 11 in third; New York, 10 in fifth; June 3, 1933.
N.L.—Never accomplished.

FIRST THROUGH 26TH INNINGS

Most runs, first inning

N.L.—16—Boston vs. Baltimore, June 18, 1894, a.m. game.
N.L. since 1900—15—Brooklyn vs. Cincinnati, May 21, 1952.
A.L.—14—Cleveland vs. Philadelphia, June 18, 1950, second game.

Most runs by both clubs, first inning

A.A.—19—Washington 14, Baltimore 5, June 17, 1891.
N.L.—16—Boston 16, Baltimore 0, June 18, 1894, a.m. game.
N.L. since 1900—15—Brooklyn 15, Cincinnati 0, May 21, 1952.
A.L.—14
Cleveland 14, Philadelphia 0, June 18, 1950, second game.
Chicago 11, Baltimore 3, August 3, 1956.

Most runs, second inning

N.L.—13
New York vs. Cleveland, July 19, 1890, first game.
Atlanta vs. Houston, September 20, 1972.
A.L.—13—Kansas City vs. Chicago, April 21, 1956.

Most runs by both clubs, second inning

A.L.—14
Philadelphia 10, Detroit 4, September 23, 1913.
New York 11, Detroit 3, August 28, 1936, second game.
N.L.—13
New York 13, Cleveland 0, July 19, 1890, first game.
Chicago 10, Philadelphia 3, August 25, 1922.
Brooklyn 11, New York 2, April 29, 1930.
Atlanta 13, Houston 0, September 20, 1972.

Most runs, third inning

N.L.—14—Cleveland vs. Washington, August 7, 1889.
N.L. since 1900—13—San Francisco vs. St. Louis, May 7, 1966.
A.L.—12—New York vs. Washington, September 11, 1949, first game.

Most runs by both clubs, third inning
N.L.—14—Cleveland 14, Washington 0, August 7, 1889.
N.L. since 1900—13
San Francisco 13, St. Louis 0, May 7, 1966.
St. Louis 7, Atlanta 6, August 21, 1973.
A.L.—12
Boston 8, Washington 4, August 12, 1949, second game.
New York 12, Washington 0, September 11, 1949, first game.

Most runs, fourth inning
N.L.—15—Hartford vs. New York, May 13, 1876.
N.L. since 1900—14—Chicago vs. Philadelphia, August 25, 1922.
A.L.—13—Chicago vs. Washington, September 26, 1943, first game.

Most runs by both clubs, fourth inning
N.L.—15
Hartford 15, New York 0, May 13, 1876.
Chicago 14, Philadelphia 1, August 25, 1922.
A.L.—13—Chicago 13, Washington 0, September 26, 1943, first game.

Most runs, fifth inning
A.L.—14—New York vs. Washington, July 6, 1920.
N.L.—13—Chicago vs. Pittsburgh, August 16, 1890.
N.L. since 1900—12
New York vs. Boston, September 3, 1926.
Cincinnati vs. Atlanta, April 25, 1977.
Montreal vs. Chicago, September 24, 1985.

Most runs by both clubs, fifth inning
N.L.—16—Brooklyn 11, New York 5, June 3, 1890.
N.L. since 1900—15
Brooklyn 10, Cincinnati 5, June 12, 1949.
Philadelphia 9, Pittsburgh 6, April 16, 1953.
A.L.—14—New York 14, Washington 0, July 6, 1920.

Most runs, sixth inning
P.L.—14—Philadelphia vs. Buffalo, June 26, 1890.
A.L.—13
Cleveland vs. Boston, July 7, 1923, first game.
Detroit vs. New York, June 17, 1925.
N.L.—12
Chicago vs. Cincinnati, May 8, 1890.
Philadelphia vs. Chicago, July 21, 1923, first game.
Chicago vs. Philadelphia, August 21, 1935, second game.

Most runs by both clubs, sixth inning
A.L.—15
Philadelphia 10, New York 5, September 5, 1912, first game.
Detroit 10, Minnesota 5, June 13, 1967.
N.L.—15—New York 10, Cincinnati 5, June 12, 1979.

Most runs, seventh inning
N.L.—18—Chicago vs. Detroit, September 6, 1883.
A.L.—17—Boston vs. Detroit, June 18, 1953.
N.L. since 1900—12
Chicago vs. Cincinnati, May 28, 1925.
Brooklyn vs. St. Louis, August 30, 1953.

Most runs by both clubs, seventh inning
N.L.—18—Chicago 18, Detroit 0, September 6, 1883.
A.L.—17—Boston 17, Detroit 0, June 18, 1953.

Most runs, eighth inning
A.L.—13
Philadelphia vs. Cleveland, June 15, 1925.
Cleveland vs. Boston, April 10, 1977.
N.L.—13—Brooklyn vs. Cincinnati, August 8, 1954.

Most runs by both clubs, eighth inning
A.L.—19—Cleveland 13, Boston 6, April 10, 1977.
N.L.—14
New York 11, Pittsburgh 3, May 25, 1954.
Brooklyn 13, Cincinnati 1, August 8, 1954.

Most runs, ninth inning
N.L.—14—Baltimore vs. Boston, April 24, 1894.
N.L. since 1900—12—San Francisco vs. Cincinnati, August 23, 1961.

Most runs by both clubs, ninth inning
A.L.—13—California vs. Texas, September 14, 1978.

Most runs by both clubs, ninth inning
N.L.—17—Boston 10, New York 7, June 20, 1912.
A.L.—15—Toronto 11, Seattle 4, July 20, 1984.

Most runs scored in ninth inning with two out
A.L.—9
Cleveland vs. Washington, May 23, 1901 (won 14-13).
Boston vs. Milwaukee, June 2, 1901 (won 13-2).
Cleveland vs. New York, August 4, 1929, second game (won 14-6).
N.L.—7
Chicago vs. Cincinnati, June 29, 1952, first game (won 9-8).
San Francisco vs. Pittsburgh, May 1, 1973 (won 8-7).

Most runs scored in ninth inning with two out and none on base
A.L.—9
Cleveland vs. Washington, May 23, 1901 (won 14-13).
Boston vs. Milwaukee, June 2, 1901 (won 13-2).
N.L.—7—Chicago vs. Cincinnati, June 29, 1952, first game (won 9-8).

Most runs, 10th inning
A.L.—11—Minnesota vs. Oakland, June 21, 1969.
N.L.—10—Boston vs. New York, June 17, 1887, a.m. game.
N.L. since 1900—9—Cincinnati vs. Philadelphia, August 24, 1947, first game.

Most runs by both clubs, 10th inning
A.L.—12—Minnesota 11, Oakland 1, June 21, 1969.
N.L.—11—New York 6, Brooklyn 5, April 24, 1955.

Most runs, 11th inning
N.L.—10—Kansas City vs. Detroit, July 21, 1886.
A.L.—8
Philadelphia vs. Detroit, May 1, 1951.
Texas vs. Seattle, September 23, 1991.
N.L. since 1900—8
Brooklyn vs. Milwaukee, August 29, 1954, first game.
Pittsburgh vs. Montreal, July 24, 1984.

Most runs by both clubs, 11th inning
A.L.—11—Seattle 6, Boston 5, May 16, 1969.
N.L.—11
New York 6, Chicago 5, June 30, 1979.
Pittsburgh 6, Chicago 5, April 21, 1991.

Most runs, 12th inning
A.L.—11—New York vs. Detroit, July 26, 1928, first game.
N.L.—9—Chicago vs. Pittsburgh, July 23, 1923.

Most runs by both clubs, 12th inning
A.L.—11—New York 11, Detroit 0, July 26, 1928, first game.
N.L.—9
Chicago 9, Pittsburgh 0, July 23, 1923.
New York 8, Brooklyn 1, May 30, 1940, second game.
Houston 8, Cincinnati 1, June 2, 1966.
San Diego 5, Houston 4, July 5, 1969.

Most runs, 13th inning
N.L.—10—Cincinnati vs. Brooklyn, May 15, 1919.
A.L.—9—Cleveland vs. Detroit, August 5, 1933, first game.

Most runs, 14th inning
N.L.—8—New York vs. Pittsburgh, June 15, 1929.
A.L.—7
Cleveland vs. St. Louis, June 3, 1935.
Detroit vs. Milwaukee, May 27, 1991.

Most runs, 15th inning
A.L.—12—Texas vs. Oakland, July 3, 1983.
N.L.—7—St. Louis vs. Boston, September 28, 1928.

Most runs, 16th inning
A.L.—8—Chicago vs. Washington, May 20, 1920.
N.L.—5
Cincinnati vs. New York, August 20, 1973.
Houston vs. Cincinnati, April 8, 1988.

Most runs, 17th inning
N.L.—7—New York vs. Pittsburgh, July 16, 1920.
A.L.—6—New York vs. Detroit, July 20, 1941.

Most runs, 18th inning
N.L.—5—Chicago vs. Boston, May 14, 1927.
A.L.—4—Minnesota vs. Seattle, July 19, 1969.

Most runs, 19th inning
N.L.—5—New York vs. Atlanta, July 4, 1985.
A.L.—4—Cleveland vs. Detroit, April 27, 1984.

Most runs by both clubs, 19th inning
N.L.—7—New York 5, Atlanta 2, July 4, 1985.
A.L.—5—Chicago 3, Boston 2, July 13, 1951.

Most runs, 20th inning
N.L.—4—Brooklyn vs. Boston, July 5, 1940.
A.L.—3
  Boston vs. Seattle, July 27, 1969.
  Washington vs. Cleveland, September 14, second game, finished September 20, 1971.

Most runs by both clubs, 20th inning
N.L.—4—Brooklyn 4, Boston 0, July 5, 1940.
A.L.—4
  Boston 3, Seattle 1, July 27, 1969.
  Washington 3, Cleveland 1, September 14, second game, finished September 20, 1971.

Most runs, 21st inning
A.L.—4—Chicago vs. Cleveland, May 26, finished May 28, 1973.
N.L.—3—San Diego vs. Montreal, May 21, 1977.

Most runs by both clubs, 21st inning
A.L.—6—Milwaukee 3, Chicago 3, May 8, finished May 9, 1984.
N.L.—3—San Diego 3, Montreal 0, May 21, 1977.

Most runs, 22nd inning
A.L.—2—New York vs. Detroit, June 24, 1962.
N.L.—1
  Brooklyn vs. Pittsburgh, August 22, 1917.
  Chicago vs. Boston, May 17, 1927.

Most runs, 23rd inning
N.L.—2—San Francisco vs. New York, May 31, 1964, second game.
A.L.—0
  Boston vs. Philadelphia, September 1, 1906.
  Philadelphia vs. Boston, September 1, 1906.
  Detroit vs. Philadelphia, July 21, 1945.
  Philadelphia vs. Detroit, July 21, 1945.

Most runs, 24th inning
A.L.—3—Philadelphia vs. Boston, September 1, 1906.
N.L.—1—Houston vs. New York, April 15, 1968.

Most runs, 25th inning
N.L.—1—St. Louis vs. New York, September 11, 1974.
A.L.—1—Chicago vs. Milwaukee, May 8, finished May 9, 1984.

Most runs, 26th inning
N.L.—0
  Boston vs. Brooklyn, May 1, 1920.
  Brooklyn vs. Boston, May 1, 1920.
A.L.—No twenty-six inning game.

GAMES BEING SHUT OUT

Most games shut out, season
N.L.—33—St. Louis, 1908.
A.L.—30—Washington, 1909 (includes 1 tie).

Most consecutive games shut out, season
N.L.—4
  Boston, May 19 through 23, 1906.
  Cincinnati, July 30 through August 3, 1908.
  Cincinnati, July 31 through August 3, 1931.
  Houston, June 20, 21, 22, 23, first game, 1963.
  Houston, September 9, 10, 11, 11, 1966.
  Chicago, June 16, 16, 19, 20, 1968.
A.L.—4
  Boston, August 2 through 6, 1906.

Philadelphia, September 23 through 25, 1906.
St. Louis, August 25 through 30, 1913.
Washington, September 19, 20, 21, 22, 1958.
Washington, September 1, 2, 4, 5, 1964.

Most games shut out, season (league champion)
N.L. (162-game season)—17—Los Angeles, 1966.
N.L. (154-game season)—16—New York, 1913 (includes one tie).
A.L.—16—Chicago, 1906 (includes two ties; 154-game season).

Most consecutive innings shut out by opponent, season
A.L.—48—Philadelphia, September 22 (last seven innings) through September 26 (first five innings), 1906.
N.L.—48—Chicago, June 15 (last eight innings) through June 21 (first two innings), 1968.

Most consecutive games without being shut out, league
A.L.—308—New York, August 3, 1931 through August 2, 1933.
N.L.—182—Philadelphia, August 17, 1893 through May 10, 1895.
N.L. since 1900—174—Philadelphia, September 20, 1992 through September 29, 1993.

Fewest games shut out, season (150 or more games)
A.L.—0—New York, 156 games, 1932.
N.L.—1
  Brooklyn, 155 games, 1953.
  Cincinnati, 162 games, 1970.

HITS

SEASON

Most hits, season
N.L.—1,783—Philadelphia, 156 games, 1930.
A.L.—1,724—Detroit, 154 games, 1921.

Fewest hits, season
N.L.—1,044—Brooklyn, 154 games, 1908.
A.L.—1,061—Chicago, 156 games, 1910.

Most players with 200 or more hits, season
N.L.—4—Philadelphia, 1929.
A.L.—4—Detroit, 1937.

Most players with 100 or more hits, season
N.L.—9—Pittsburgh, 1921, 1972, 1976; Philadelphia, 1923; New York, 1928; St. Louis, 1979.
A.L.—9—Philadelphia, 1925; Detroit, 1934, 1980; Baltimore, 1973; Kansas City, 1974, 1977, 1980, 1982, 1989; Oakland, 1975; Texas, 1976, 1978; Chicago, 1977; New York, 1977, 1993; California, 1978, 1982, 1988; Milwaukee, 1978, 1991, 1992; Toronto, 1983, 1988, 1992; Boston, 1984, 1991; Minnesota, 1989, 1991.

Fewest players with 100 or more hits, season
N.L.—0—New York, 1972.
A.L.—2—Washington, 1965.

GAME

Most hits, nine-inning game
N.L.—36—Philadelphia vs. Louisville, August 17, 1894.
N.L. since 1900—31—New York vs. Cincinnati, June 9, 1901.
A.L.—31—Milwaukee vs. Toronto, August 28, 1992.

Most hits by both clubs, nine-inning game
N.L.—51—Philadelphia 26, Chicago 25, August 25, 1922.
A.L.—45
  Philadelphia 27, Boston 18, July 8, 1902.
  Detroit 28, New York 17, September 29, 1928.

Most hits, extra-inning game
A.L.—33—Cleveland vs. Philadelphia, July 10, 1932, 18 innings.
N.L.—Less than nine-inning record.

Most hits by both clubs, extra-inning game
A.L.—58—Cleveland 33, Philadelphia 25, July 10, 1932, 18 innings.
N.L.—52—New York 28, Pittsburgh 24, June 15, 1929, 14 innings.

Most hits by pinch-hitters, nine-inning game
N.L.—6—Brooklyn vs. Philadelphia, September 9, 1926.
A.L.—4
Cleveland vs. Chicago, April 22, 1930.
Philadelphia vs. Detroit, September 18, 1940, second game.
Detroit vs. Chicago, April 22, 1953.
Kansas City vs. Detroit, September 1, 1958, a.m. game.
Cleveland vs. Boston, September 21, 1967.
Oakland vs. Detroit, August 30, 1970.
Chicago vs. Oakland, September 7, 1970, second game.

Most hits by infield, game
N.L.—18—Boston vs. St. Louis, May 31, 1897.
A.L.—16—Boston vs. St. Louis, June 8, 1950.
N.L. since 1900—16—Pittsburgh vs. Chicago, September 16, 1975.

Most hits by outfield, game
N.L.—16—New York vs. Cincinnati, June 9, 1901.
A.L.—12
Baltimore vs. Detroit, June 24, 1901.
Detroit vs. Washington, July 30, 1917.
Cleveland vs. Philadelphia, April 29, 1952.
Boston vs. Baltimore, July 11, 1969, second game.

Most hits in shutout loss
N.L.—14—New York vs. Chicago, September 14, 1913 (15 total bases; lost 7-0).
A.L.—14—Cleveland vs. Washington, July 10, 1928, second game (16 total bases; lost 9-0).

Most hits in extra-inning shutout loss
N.L.—15
Boston vs. Pittsburgh, July 10, 1901, 12 innings (16 total bases; lost 1-0).
Boston vs. Pittsburgh, August 1, 1918, 21 innings (15 total bases; lost 2-0).
A.L.—15—Boston vs. Washington, July 3, 1913, 15 innings (19 total bases; lost 1-0).

Most consecutive hits, game
N.L.—12
St. Louis vs. Boston, September 17, 1920, fourth and fifth innings.
Brooklyn vs. Pittsburgh, June 23, 1930, sixth and seventh innings.
A.L.—10
Boston vs. Milwaukee, June 2, 1901, ninth inning.
Detroit vs. Baltimore, September 20, 1983, first inning (one walk during streak).
Toronto vs. Minnesota, September 4, 1992, second inning.

Fewest hits, game
N.L., U.A., A.A., A.L.—0—Made in many games.

Fewest hits, extra-inning game
A.A.—0—Toledo vs. Brooklyn, October 4, 1884, 10 innings.
N.L.—0
Philadelphia vs. New York, July 4, 1908, a.m. game, 10 innings.
Chicago vs. Cincinnati, May 2, 1917, 10 innings.
Chicago vs. Cincinnati, August 19, 1965, first game, 10 innings.
N.L.—1—Milwaukee vs. Pittsburgh, May 26, 1959, 13 innings.
A.L.—1
Cleveland vs. Chicago, September 6, 1903, 10 innings.
Boston vs. St. Louis, September 18, 1934, 10 innings.
Los Angeles vs. New York, May 22, 1962, 12 innings.

Fewest hits by both clubs, nine-inning game
N.L.—1—Los Angeles 1, Chicago 0, September 9, 1965.
A.A.—2—Philadelphia 1, Baltimore 1, August 20, 1886.
A.L.—2
Cleveland 1, Washington 1, July 27, 1915.

Cleveland 1, St. Louis 1, April 23, 1952.
Chicago 1, Baltimore 1, June 21, 1956.
Baltimore 1, Kansas City 1, September 12, 1964.
Baltimore 2, Detroit 0, April 30, 1967, first game.

Most games held hitless, season
A.A.—2—Pittsburgh 1884.
N.L.—2—Providence 1885; Boston 1898; Philadelphia 1960; Chicago 1965; Cincinnati 1971.
A.L.—2—Cleveland 1910; Chicago 1917; Philadelphia 1923; Detroit 1967, 1973; California 1977.

Most consecutive years without being held hitless in a game
N.L.—40—St. Louis, 1920 through 1959.
A.L.—31—New York, 1959 through 1989.

Most games held to one hit, season
A.L.—5
St. Louis, 1910.
Cleveland, 1915.
N.L.—4—New York, 1965.

Most players with six hits in a nine-inning game
A.A.—2—Cincinnati vs. Pittsburgh, September 12, 1883.
N.L.—2—Baltimore vs. St. Louis, September 3, 1897.
A.L.—1—Made in many games.

Most players with five or more hits in a game
N.L.—4—Philadelphia vs. Louisville, August 17, 1894.
N.L. since 1900—3
New York vs. Cincinnati, June 9, 1901.
New York vs. Philadelphia, June 1, 1923.
A.L.—3
Detroit vs. Washington, July 30, 1917.
Cleveland vs. Philadelphia, July 10, 1932, 18 innings.
Washington vs. Cleveland, May 16, 1933, 12 innings.
Chicago vs. Philadelphia, September 11, 1936.

Most players for both clubs with five or more hits, nine-inning game
N.L.—4—Philadelphia 4, Louisville 0, August 17, 1894.
N.L. since 1900—3
New York 3, Cincinnati 0, June 9, 1901.
New York 3, Philadelphia 0, June 1, 1923.
A.L.—3
Detroit 3, Washington 0, July 30, 1917.
Washington 3, Cleveland 0, May 16, 1933, 12 innings.
Chicago 3, Philadelphia 0, September 11, 1936.

Most players for both clubs with five or more hits, extra-inning game
A.L.—5—Cleveland 3, Philadelphia 2, July 10, 1932, 18 innings.

Most players with four or more hits, nine-inning game
N.L.—7—Chicago vs. Cleveland, July 24, 1882.
N.L. since 1900—5—San Francisco vs. Los Angeles, May 13, 1958.
A.L.—4
Detroit vs. New York, September 29, 1928.
Chicago vs. Philadelphia, September 11, 1936.
Boston vs. St. Louis, June 8, 1950.
Milwaukee vs. Toronto, August 28, 1992.

Most players for both clubs with four or more hits, nine-inning game
N.L.—7—Chicago 7, Cleveland 0, July 24, 1882.
N.L. since 1900—5
St. Louis 4, Philadelphia 1, July 6, 1929, second game.
San Francisco 5, Los Angeles 0, May 14, 1958.
A.L.—4
Detroit 4, New York 0, September 29, 1928.
Chicago 4, Philadelphia 0, September 11, 1936.
Boston 4, St. Louis 0, June 8, 1950.
Milwaukee 4, Toronto 0, August 28, 1992.

Most players with three or more hits, nine-inning game
N.L.—8—Chicago vs. Detroit, September 6, 1883.
N.L. since 1900—7
Pittsburgh vs. Philadelphia, June 12, 1928.
Cincinnati vs. Houston, August 3, 1989.
A.L.—7
New York vs. Philadelphia, June 28, 1939, first game.
Chicago vs. Kansas City, April 23, 1955.

Most players with two or more hits, nine-inning game
A.A.— 10—Brooklyn vs. Philadelphia, June 25, 1885.
N.L.— 10
  Pittsburgh vs. Philadelphia, August 7, 1922.
  New York vs. Philadelphia, September 2, 1925, second
  game.
A.L.—9—Held by many clubs.

Most players with one or more hits, nine-inning game
A.L.— 14—Cleveland vs. St. Louis, August 12, 1948, second
  game.
N.L.— 14—San Francisco vs. San Diego, June 23, 1986.

Most players for both clubs with one or more hits, nine-inning game
N.L.— 23—St. Louis 13, Philadelphia 10, May 11, 1923.
A.L.— 22—New York 12, Cleveland 10, July 18, 1934.

Most consecutive games with each player collecting one or more hits
N.L.—5—Pittsburgh, August 5, 7, 8, 9, 10, 1922.

☐ DOUBLEHEADER AND CONSECUTIVE GAMES ☐

Most hits, doubleheader
N.L.— 46—Pittsburgh vs. Philadelphia, August 8, 1922.
A.L.— 43—New York vs. Philadelphia, June 28, 1939.

Most hits by both clubs, doubleheader
N.L.—73
  Washington 41, Philadelphia 32, July 4, 1896.
  St. Louis 43, Philadelphia 30, July 6, 1929.
A.L.—65—Boston 35, Philadelphia 30, July 4, 1939.

Most hits by pitchers, doubleheader
A.L.—8—New York vs. Cleveland, June 17, 1936.

Fewest hits, doubleheader
A.L.—2—Cleveland vs. Boston, April 12, 1992.
N.L.—3
  Brooklyn vs. St. Louis, September 21, 1934.
  New York vs. Philadelphia, June 21, 1964.

Fewest hits by both clubs, doubleheader
A.L.— 11—Detroit 7, St. Louis 4, May 30, 1914.
N.L.— 12
  Chicago 6, Pittsburgh 6, September 3, 1905.
  St. Louis 6, Brooklyn 6, July 24, 1909.

Most hits, two consecutive games
N.L.—55—Philadelphia vs. Louisville, August 16, 17, 1894.
A.L.—51—Boston vs. St. Louis, June 7, 8, 1950.
N.L. since 1900—49—Pittsburgh vs. Philadelphia, August 7,
  8, first game, 1922.

Most hits by pitchers, two consecutive games
N.L.—9—Chicago, May 19, 20, 1895.

Fewest hits, two consecutive nine-inning games
A.A.—2—Baltimore vs. St. Louis/Louisville, July 28 (1),
  July 29 (1), 1886.
N.L.—2
  New York vs. Providence, June 17 (1), June 18 (1), 1884.
  Cincinnati vs. Brooklyn, July 5 (1), July 6 (1), 1900.
  Boston vs. New York, September 28, second game (1);
  September 30, first game (1), 1916.
  New York vs. Milwaukee, September 10 (1), September 11
  (1), 1965.
  Los Angeles vs. Houston, September 26 (0), September 27
  (2), 1981.
A.L.—2
  New York vs. Cleveland, September 25 (1), September 26
  (1), 1907.
  St. Louis vs. Washington, September 25, second game (1),
  vs. Philadelphia, September 27, (1), first game, 1910.
  Chicago vs. Washington, August 10 (1), August 11 (1),
  1917.
  Milwaukee vs. Kansas City, June 18 (2), June 19 (0),
  1974.
  Cleveland vs. Boston, April 12, first game (0), April 12,
  second game (2), 1992.

☐ INNING ☐

Most hits, inning
N.L.— 18—Chicago vs. Detroit, September 6, 1883, seventh
  inning.
N.L. since 1900— 16—Cincinnati vs. Houston, August 3,
  1989, first inning.
A.L.— 14—Boston vs. Detroit, June 18, 1953, seventh inning.

Most hits by pinch-hitters, inning
N.L.—4
  Chicago vs. Brooklyn, May 21, 1927, second game, ninth
  inning.
  Philadelphia vs. Pittsburgh, September 12, 1974, eighth in-
  ning.
A.L.—4—Philadelphia vs. Detroit, September 18, 1940, sec-
  ond game, ninth inning.

Most consecutive hits, inning
N.L.— 10
  St. Louis vs. Boston, September 17, 1920, fourth inning.
  St. Louis vs. Philadelphia, June 12, 1922, sixth inning.
  Chicago vs. Boston, September 7, 1929, first game, fourth
  inning.
  Brooklyn vs. Pittsburgh, June 23, 1930, sixth inning.
A.L.— 10
  Boston vs. Milwaukee, June 2, 1901, ninth inning.
  Detroit vs. Baltimore, September 20, 1983, first inning (one
  walk during streak).
  Toronto vs. Minnesota, September 4, 1992, second inning.

Most consecutive hits by pinch-hitters, inning
N.L.-A.L.—3—Made in many innings.
N.L.—Last time—Pittsburgh vs. San Francisco, July 2, 1961,
  first game, eighth inning.
A.L.—Last time—Boston vs. Chicago, June 4, 1975, ninth in-
  ning.

Most consecutive hits before first out of game
N.L.—8
  Philadelphia vs. Chicago, August 5, 1975 (4 singles, 2 dou-
  bles, 2 home runs).
  Pittsburgh vs. Atlanta, August 26, 1975 (7 singles, 1 tri-
  ple).
A.L.—8
  Oakland vs. Chicago, September 27, 1981, first game (8
  singles).
  New York vs. Baltimore, September 25, 1990 (6 singles, 2
  home runs).

Most batters reaching first base safely, inning
A.L.— 20—Boston vs. Detroit, June 18, 1953, seventh inning.
N.L.— 20—Chicago vs. Detroit, September 6, 1883, seventh
  inning.
N.L. since 1900— 19—Brooklyn vs. Cincinnati, May 21, 1952,
  first inning.

Most consecutive batters reaching base safely, inning
N.L.— 19—Brooklyn vs. Cincinnati, May 21, 1952, first inning.
A.L.— 13—Kansas City vs. Chicago, April 21, 1956, second
  inning.

Most batters reaching base safely three times, inning
N.L.—3
  Chicago vs. Detroit, September 6, 1883, seventh inning.
  Boston vs. Baltimore, June 18, 1894, a.m. game, first inning.
N.L. since 1900— 1—Brooklyn vs. Cincinnati, May 21, 1952,
  first inning.
A.L.—3—Boston vs. Detroit, June 18, 1953, seventh inning.

Most players making two or more hits, inning
N.L.—7—Cincinnati vs. Houston, August 3, 1989, first inning.
A.L.—5
  Philadelphia vs. Boston, July 8, 1902, sixth inning.
  New York vs. Philadelphia, September 10, 1921, ninth inning.

SINGLES

Most singles, season
N.L.—1,338—Philadelphia, 132 games, 1894.
A.L.—1,298—Detroit, 154 games, 1921.
N.L. since 1900—1,297—Pittsburgh, 155 games, 1922.

Fewest singles, season
A.L.—811—Baltimore, 162 games, 1968.
N.L.—843—New York, 156 games, 1972.

Most singles, game
N.L.—28
 Philadelphia vs. Louisville, August 17, 1894.
 Boston vs. Baltimore, April 20, 1896.
A.L.—26—Milwaukee vs. Toronto, August 28, 1992.
N.L. since 1900—23
 New York vs. Chicago, September 21, 1931.
 New York vs. Atlanta, July 4, 1985, 19 innings.

Most singles by both clubs, game
N.L.—37—Baltimore 21, Washington 16, August 8, 1896.
N.L. since 1900—36—New York 22, Cincinnati 14, June 9, 1901.
A.L.—36—Chicago 21, Boston 15, August 15, 1922.

Most singles, inning
N.L.—12—Cincinnati vs. Houston, August 3, 1989, first inning.
A.L.—11—Boston vs. Detroit, June 18, 1953, seventh inning.

Most consecutive singles, inning
N.L.—10—St. Louis vs. Boston, September 17, 1920, fourth inning.
A.L.—8
 Washington vs. Cleveland, May 7, 1951, fourth inning.
 Oakland vs. Chicago, September 27, 1981, first game, first inning.
 Baltimore vs. Texas, May 18, 1990, first inning.

DOUBLES

Most doubles, season
N.L.—373—St. Louis, 154 games, 1930.
A.L.—358—Cleveland, 154 games, 1930.

Fewest doubles, season
N.L.—110—Brooklyn, 154 games, 1908.
A.L.—116—Chicago, 156 games, 1910.

Most consecutive years leading league in doubles
A.L.—8—Cleveland, 1916 through 1923.
N.L.—5—St. Louis, 1920 through 1924.

Most doubles, game
N.L.—14—Chicago vs. Buffalo, July 3, 1883.
N.L. since 1900—13—St. Louis vs. Chicago, July 12, 1931, second game.
A.L.—12—Boston vs. Detroit, July 29, 1990.

Most doubles by pinch-hitters, game
A.L.—3
 Cleveland vs. Washington, June 27, 1948, first game.
 Chicago vs. New York, May 7, 1971.
N.L.—3—San Francisco vs. Pittsburgh, May 5, 1958.

Most doubles by both clubs, game
N.L.—23—St. Louis 13, Chicago 10, July 12, 1931, second game.
A.L.—16—Cleveland 9, New York 7, July 21, 1921.

Most doubles, doubleheader
N.L.—17—St. Louis vs. Chicago, July 12, 1931.
A.L.—14—Philadelphia vs. Boston, July 8, 1905.

Most doubles by both clubs, doubleheader
N.L.—32—St. Louis 17, Chicago 15, July 12, 1931.
A.L.—26—Philadelphia 14, Boston 12, July 8, 1905.

Most doubles with bases filled, game
N.L.-A.L.—Made in many games.

Most doubles with bases filled by both clubs, game
N.L.-A.L.—Made in many games.

Most doubles, inning
N.L.—7—Boston vs. St. Louis, August 25, 1936, first game, first inning.
A.L.—6—Washington vs. Boston, June 9, 1934, eighth inning.

Most consecutive doubles, inning
A.L.—5—Washington vs. Boston, June 9, 1934, eighth inning.
N.L.—4—Held by many clubs. Last time—New York vs. Los Angeles, July 21, 1991, third inning.

Most players with two doubles, inning
N.L.—3—Boston vs. St. Louis, August 25, 1936, first game, first inning.
A.L.—2
 New York vs. Boston, July 3, 1932, sixth inning.
 Toronto vs. Baltimore, June 26, 1978, second inning.

TRIPLES

Most triples, season
N.L.—153—Baltimore, 129 games, 1894.
N.L. since 1900—129—Pittsburgh, 152 games, 1912.
A.L.—112
 Baltimore, 134 games, 1901.
 Boston, 141 games, 1903.

Fewest triples, season
A.L.—12—New York, 161 games, 1988.
N.L.—14—Los Angeles, 162 games, 1986.

Most consecutive years leading league in triples
A.L.—7—Washington, 1931 through 1937 (tied 1934).
N.L.—6—Pittsburgh, 1932 through 1937.

Most triples, game
N.L.—9—Baltimore vs. Cleveland, September 3, 1894, first game.
N.L. since 1900—8—Pittsburgh vs. St. Louis, May 30, 1925, second game.
A.L.—6
 Chicago vs. Milwaukee, September 15, 1901; second game.
 Chicago vs. New York, September 17, 1920.
 Detroit vs. New York, June 17, 1922.

Most triples by both clubs, game
N.L.—11—Baltimore 9, Cleveland 2, September 3, 1894, first game.
N.L. since 1900—9
 Pittsburgh 6, Chicago 3, July 4, 1904, p.m. game.
 Pittsburgh 8, St. Louis 1, May 30, 1925, second game.
A.L.—9—Detroit 6, New York 3, June 17, 1922.

Most triples with bases filled, game
N.L.—2
 Detroit vs. Indianapolis, May 7, 1887.
 Pittsburgh vs. Brooklyn, September 17, 1898.
 Chicago vs. Philadelphia, May 14, 1904.
 Brooklyn vs. St. Louis, August 25, 1917, first game.
 Cincinnati vs. Brooklyn, September 25, 1925.
 Pittsburgh vs. St. Louis, September 10, 1938.
 Chicago vs. Boston, June 12, 1936.
 Brooklyn vs. Philadelphia, May 24, 1953, both in eighth inning.
 Milwaukee vs. St. Louis, August 2, 1959, second game.
 Montreal vs. Cincinnati, September 1, 1979.
 New York vs. Colorado, June 6, 1994.
A.A.—2—Kansas City vs. Philadelphia, August 22, 1889.
A.L.—2
 Boston vs. St. Louis, August 16, 1926, second game.
 Philadelphia vs. Washington, April 26, 1928.
 Philadelphia vs. Washington, May 1, 1949, first game.
 Detroit vs. New York, June 9, 1950.
 Cleveland vs. New York, July 27, 1978, second game.

Most bases-filled triples by both clubs, game (each club connecting)

N.L.—2—Made in many games. Last time—Chicago 1, St. Louis 1, April 22, 1938.

A.L.—2—Made in many games. Last time—Washington 1, New York 1, July 4, 1950, first game.

Longest extra-inning game without a triple

N.L.—26 innings—Brooklyn vs. Boston, May 1, 1920.

A.L.—25 innings
Milwaukee vs. Chicago, May 8, finished May 9, 1984.
Chicago vs. Milwaukee, May 8, finished May 9, 1984.

Longest extra-inning game without a triple by either club

N.L.—25 innings—New York 0, St. Louis 0, September 11, 1974.

A.L.—25 innings—Milwaukee 0, Chicago 0, May 8, finished May 9, 1984.

Most triples, doubleheader

N.L.—9
Baltimore vs. Cleveland, September 3, 1894.
Cincinnati vs. Chicago, May 27, 1922.

A.L.—9—Chicago vs. Milwaukee, September 15, 1901.

Most triples by both clubs, doubleheader

N.L.—11—Baltimore 9, Cleveland 2, September 3, 1894.
N.L. since 1900—10
Cincinnati 9, Chicago 1, May 27, 1922.
New York 7, Pittsburgh 3, July 30, 1923.

A.L.—10—Chicago 9, Milwaukee 1, September 15, 1901.

Most triples, inning

A.L.—5—Chicago vs. Milwaukee, September 15, 1901, second game, eighth inning.

N.L.—4
Boston vs. Troy, May 6, 1882, eighth inning.
Baltimore vs. St. Louis, July 27, 1892, seventh inning.
St. Louis vs. Chicago, July 2, 1895, first inning.
Chicago vs. St. Louis, April 17, 1899, fourth inning.
Brooklyn vs. Pittsburgh, August 23, 1902, third inning.
Cincinnati vs. Boston, July 22, 1926, second inning.
New York vs. Pittsburgh, July 17, 1936, first inning.

Most consecutive triples, inning

A.L.—4—Boston vs. Detroit, May 6, 1934, fourth inning.

N.L.—3—Made in many innings. Last times—Chicago vs. Philadelphia, April 25, 1981, fourth inning; Montreal vs. San Diego, May 6, 1981, ninth inning.

HOME RUNS

SEASON AND MONTH

Most home runs, season

A.L. (162-game season)—240—New York, 163 games, 1961 (112 at home, 128 on road).

A.L. (154-game season)—193—New York, 155 games, 1960 (92 at home, 101 on road).

N.L.—221
New York, 155 games, 1947 (131 at home, 90 on road; 154-game season).
Cincinnati, 155 games, 1956 (128 at home, 93 on road; 154-game season).

Fewest home runs, season

N.L.—9—Pittsburgh, 157 games, 1917.
A.L.—3—Chicago, 156 games, 1908.

Most home runs by pinch-hitters, season

N.L.—12
Cincinnati, 1957.
New York, 1983.

A.L.—11—Baltimore, 1982.

Most home runs at home, season

A.L.—133—Cleveland, 1970, 81 games.
N.L.—131—New York, 1947, 76 games.

Most home runs on road, season

A.L.—128—New York, 1961, 82 games.

N.L.—124—Milwaukee, 1957, 77 games.

Most home runs against one club, season

A.L.—48—New York vs. Kansas City, 1956.
N.L.—44—Cincinnati vs. Brooklyn, 1956.

Most years leading league in home runs (since 1900)

A.L.—34—New York.
N.L.—27—New York/San Francisco (24 by N.Y., 3 by S.F.).

Most consecutive years leading league or tied in home runs

A.L.—12—New York, 1936 through 1947.
N.L.—7—Brooklyn, 1949 through 1955 (1954 tied).

Most years with 200 or more home runs

A.L.—4—Detroit, 209 in 1962; 202 in 1985; 225 in 1987; 209 in 1991.

N.L.—2
Brooklyn, 208 in 1953; 201 in 1955.
Atlanta, 207 in 1966; 206 in 1973.
San Francisco, 204 in 1962; 205 in 1987 (Giants also had 221 representing New York in 1947).

Most years with 100 or more home runs (since 1900)

A.L.—69—New York.
N.L.—58—New York/San Francisco (26 by N.Y., 32 by S.F.).

Most consecutive years with 100 or more home runs

A.L.—35—Boston, 1946 through 1980.
N.L.—29
New York/San Francisco, 1945 through 1957 in New York, 1958 through 1973 in San Francisco.
Cincinnati, 1952 through 1980.

Most home runs by two players, season

A.L. (162-game season)—115—New York, 1961 (Maris 61, Mantle 54).

A.L. (154-game season)—107—New York, 1927 (Ruth 60, Gehrig 47).

N.L.—93—Chicago, 1930 (Wilson 56, Hartnett 37).

Most home runs by three players, season

A.L. (162-game season)—143—New York, 1961 (Maris 61, Mantle, 54, Skowron, 28).

A.L. (154-game season)—125—New York, 1927 (Ruth 60, Gehrig 47, Lazzeri 18).

N.L. (162-game season)—124—Atlanta, 1973 (Johnson 43, Evans 41, Aaron 40).

N.L. (154-game season)—122—New York, 1947 (Mize 51, Marshall 36, Cooper 35).

Most players with 50 or more home runs, season

A.L.—2—New York, 1961 (Maris 61, Mantle 54).
N.L.—1—Held by many clubs.

Most players with 40 or more home runs, season

N.L.—3—Atlanta, 1973 (Johnson 43, Evans 41, Aaron 40).
A.L.—2
New York, 1927 (Ruth 60, Gehrig 47), 1930 (Ruth 49, Gehrig 41), 1931 (Ruth 46, Gehrig 46), 1961 (Maris 61, Mantle 54).
Detroit, 1961 (Colavito 45, Cash 41).
Boston, 1969 (Petrocelli 40, Yastrzemski 40).

Most players with 30 or more home runs, season

N.L.—4—Los Angeles, 1977.
A.L.—3—New York, 1941; Washington, 1959; Minnesota, 1963, 1964, 1987; Boston, 1977; Milwaukee, 1982; Cleveland, 1987; Detroit, 1992, Texas, 1993.

Most players with 20 or more home runs, season

A.L.—6—New York, 1961; Minnesota, 1964; Detroit, 1986.
N.L.—6—Milwaukee, 1965.

Most home runs, one month

A.L.—58—Baltimore, May, 1987.
N.L.—55—New York, July, 1947.

GAME

Most home runs, game

A.L.—10—Toronto vs. Baltimore, September 14, 1987.
N.L.—8

Milwaukee vs. Pittsburgh, August 30, 1953, first game.
Cincinnati vs. Milwaukee, August 18, 1956.
San Francisco vs. Milwaukee, April 30, 1961.
Montreal vs. Atlanta, July 30, 1978.

Most home runs by both clubs, game
A.L.—11
New York 6, Detroit 5, June 23, 1950.
Boston 6, Milwaukee 5, May 22, 1977, first game.
Toronto 10, Baltimore 1, September 14, 1987.
Baltimore 6, California 5, July 1, 1994.
N.L.—11
Pittsburgh 6, Cincinnati 5, August 12, 1966, 13 innings.
Chicago 7, New York 4, June 11, 1967, second game.
Chicago 6, Cincinnati 5, July 28, 1977, 13 innings.
Chicago 6, Philadelphia 5, May 17, 1979, 10 innings.

Most home runs, night game
A.L.—10—Toronto vs. Baltimore, September 14, 1987.
N.L.—8—Cincinnati vs. Milwaukee, August 18, 1956.

Most home runs by both clubs, nine-inning night game
A.L.—11
New York 6, Detroit 5, June 23, 1950.
Toronto 10, Baltimore 1, September 14, 1987.
N.L.—10
Cincinnati 8, Milwaukee 2, August 18, 1956.
Cincinnati 7, Atlanta 3, April 21, 1970.

Most home runs by pinch-hitters, game
A.L.-N.L.—Held by many clubs.

Most home runs by pinch-hitters for both clubs, game
N.L.—3
Philadelphia 2, St. Louis 1, June 2, 1928.
St. Louis 2, Brooklyn 1, July 21, 1930, first game.
A.L.—2—Made in many games. Last times—Cleveland 1, Minnesota 1, May 7, 1989, first game; New York 1, Chicago 1, June 22, 1989.

Most home runs, opening game of season
N.L.—6—New York vs. Montreal, April 4, 1988.
A.L.—5
New York vs. Philadelphia, April 12, 1932.
Boston vs. Washington, April 12, 1965.
Milwaukee vs. Boston, April 10, 1980.

Most home runs by both clubs, opening game of season
A.L.—7
New York 5, Philadelphia 2, April 12, 1932.
Boston 5, Washington 2, April 12, 1965.
Milwaukee 5, Boston 2, April 10, 1980.
N.L.—7
New York 6, Montreal 1, April 4, 1988.
Atlanta 4, Chicago 3, April 5, 1988.

Most home runs by first-game players for both clubs, game
N.L.—2—Brooklyn 1 (Ernie Koy), Philadelphia 1 (Emmett Mueller), April 19, 1938 (each in first inning).

Most home runs, game (no other runs)
A.L.—6—Oakland vs. Minnesota, August 3, 1991.
N.L.—5
New York vs. Chicago, June 16, 1930.
St. Louis vs. Brooklyn, September 1, 1953.
Cincinnati vs. Milwaukee, April 16, 1955.
Chicago vs. Pittsburgh, April 21, 1964.
Pittsburgh vs. Los Angeles, May 7, 1973.
Colorado vs. San Francisco, May 9, 1994.

Most home runs by both clubs, game (no other runs)
N.L.—5
San Francisco 3, Milwaukee 2, August 30, 1962.
Montreal 3, San Diego 2, May 16, 1986.
A.L.—4
Cleveland 4, New York 0, August 2, 1956.
New York 4, Baltimore 0, May 13, 1973, first game.

Most home runs, shutout game (no other runs)
A.L.—4
Cleveland vs. New York, August 2, 1956.
New York vs. Baltimore, May 13, 1973, first game.

N.L.—3
St. Louis vs. New York, July 19, 1923.
Philadelphia vs. Cincinnati, August 27, 1951, second game.
San Francisco vs. Milwaukee, August 14, 1964.
Cincinnati vs. Pittsburgh, September 25, 1968.
New York vs. Philadelphia, June 29, 1971.
New York vs. Pittsburgh, September 17, 1971.
New York vs. Cincinnati, August 29, 1972.

Most home runs with none on bases, nine-inning game
A.L.—7—Boston vs. Toronto, July 4, 1977 (8 home runs in game by Boston).
N.L.—6
New York vs. Philadelphia, August 13, 1939, first game (7 home runs in game by New York).
New York vs. Cincinnati, June 24, 1950 (7 home runs in game by New York).
Atlanta vs. Chicago, August 3, 1967 (7 home runs in game by Atlanta).
Chicago vs. San Diego, August 19, 1970 (7 home runs in game by Chicago).

Most home runs by both clubs, nine-inning game (none on bases)
A.L.—7
Minnesota 6, Cleveland 1, April 29, 1962, second game.
Chicago 5, Cleveland 2, June 18, 1974.
Boston 7, Toronto 0, July 4, 1977.
California 6, Oakland 1, April 23, 1985.
Minnesota 4, Chicago 3, June 21, 1987.
Toronto 6, Baltimore 1, September 14, 1987.
Cleveland 5, Texas 2, June 24, 1989.
Oakland 6, Minnesota 1, August 3, 1991.
N.L.—7
Chicago 6, San Diego 1, August 19, 1970.
Pittsburgh 4, Chicago 3, June 7, 1976.

Most home runs by infield, game
N.L.—6
Milwaukee vs. Brooklyn, July 31, 1954.
Montreal vs. Atlanta, July 30, 1978.
A.L.—5
New York vs. Philadelphia, June 3, 1932.
New York vs. Philadelphia, May 24, 1936.
Cleveland vs. Philadelphia, June 18, 1941.
Boston vs. St. Louis, June 8, 1950.

Most home runs by outfield, game
N.L.—6
Cincinnati vs. Milwaukee, August 18, 1956.
San Francisco vs. Milwaukee, April 30, 1961.
A.L.—5
New York vs. Chicago, July 28, 1940, first game.
Cleveland vs. New York, July 13, 1945.
Cleveland vs. Baltimore, June 10, 1959.
New York vs. Boston, May 30, 1961.

Most times with five or more home runs in game, season
A.L.—8—Boston, 1977.
N.L.—6—New York, 1947.

Most players with three or more home runs in game, season
N.L.—4
Brooklyn, 1950 (Snider, Campanella, Hodges, Brown).
Cincinnati, 1956 (Bell, Bailey, Kluszewski, Thurman).
A.L.—3—Cleveland, 1987 (Snyder, Carter, Jacoby).

Most times with two or more homers by one player in a game, season
A.L.—24—New York, 1961.
N.L.—16—Atlanta, 1966.

Most players with two or more home runs, game
N.L.—3
Pittsburgh vs. St. Louis, August 16, 1947.
Chicago vs. St. Louis, April 16, 1955, 14 innings.
New York vs. Pittsburgh, July 8, 1956, first game.
Cincinnati vs. Milwaukee, August 18, 1956.
A.L.—3
Boston vs. St. Louis, June 8, 1950.
New York vs. Boston, May 30, 1961.
Toronto vs. Baltimore, September 14, 1987.

— 54 —

Most players with two or more homers by both clubs, nine-inning game
N.L.—4—Pittsburgh 3, St. Louis 1, August 16, 1947.
A.L.—3
Boston 3, St. Louis 0, June 8, 1950.
New York 2, Kansas City 1, July 28, 1958.
New York 3, Boston 0, May 30, 1961.
Detroit 2, California 1, July 4, 1968.
Chicago 2, Cleveland 1, June 18, 1974.
Seattle 2, Oakland 1, August 2, 1983.
Toronto 3, Baltimore 0, September 14, 1987.

Most players with one or more home runs, game
A.L.—7—Baltimore vs. Boston, May 17, 1967 (7 home runs in game by Baltimore).
N.L.—7—Los Angeles vs. Cincinnati, May 25, 1979 (7 home runs in game by Los Angeles).

Most players with one or more home runs by both clubs, game
N.L.—9
New York 5, Brooklyn 4, September 2, 1939, first game.
New York 6, Pittsburgh 3, July 11, 1954, first game.
Chicago 5, Pittsburgh 4, April 21, 1964.
Cincinnati 6, Atlanta 3, April 21, 1970.
Los Angeles 5, Atlanta 4, April 24, 1977.
Cincinnati 5, Chicago 4, July 28, 1977, 13 innings.
A.L.—9
New York 5, Detroit 4, June 23, 1950.
Minnesota 5, Boston 4, May 25, 1965.
Baltimore 7, Boston 2, May 17, 1967.
California 5, Cleveland 4, August 30, 1970.
Boston 5, Milwaukee 4, May 22, 1977, first game.
California 5, Oakland 4, April 23, 1985.

Longest extra-inning game without a home run by either club
N.L.—26 innings—Boston 0, Brooklyn 0, May 1, 1920.
A.L.—24 innings
Boston 0, Philadelphia 0, September 1, 1906.
Detroit 0, Philadelphia 0, July 21, 1945.

☐ DOUBLEHEADER AND CONSECUTIVE GAMES ☐

Most home runs, doubleheader
A.L.—13—New York vs. Philadelphia, June 28, 1939.
N.L.—12—Milwaukee vs. Pittsburgh, August 30, 1953.

Most home runs both clubs, doubleheader
N.L.—15—Milwaukee 9, Chicago 6, May 30, 1956.
A.L.—14—New York 9, Philadelphia 5, May 22, 1930.

Most home runs by pinch-hitters, doubleheader
N.L.—3—Montreal vs. Atlanta, July 13, 1973.
A.L.—2—Made in many doubleheaders.

Most home runs by pinch-hitters for both clubs, doubleheader
N.L.—4—St. Louis 2, Brooklyn 2, July 21, 1930.
A.L.—2—Made in many doubleheaders.

Most consecutive games with one or more home runs
A.L.—25
New York, June 1, second game, through June 29, second game, 1941 (40 home runs).
Detroit, May 25 through June 19, 1994 (46 home runs).
N.L.—24—Brooklyn, June 18 through July 10, 1953 (39 home runs).

Most home runs in consecutive games in which homers were hit
N.L.—41—Cincinnati, August 4 through August 24, 1956 (21 games).
A.L.—40—New York, June 1, second game, through June 29, second game, 1941 (25 games).

Most consecutive games with one or more homers, start of season
N.L.—13—Chicago, April 13 through May 2, second game, 1954 (19 home runs).
A.L.—8—New York, April 12 through April 23, 1932 (20 home runs).

Most consecutive games with two or more home runs, season
A.L.—9
Cleveland, May 13, first game, through May 21, 1962 (28 home runs).

Baltimore, May 8 through May 16, 1987 (29 home runs).
N.L.—8—Milwaukee, July 19 through July 26, 1956 (20 home runs).

Most home runs, two consecutive games (connecting each game)
N.L.—13—San Francisco, April 29, 30, 1961.
A.L.—13—New York, June 28, 28, 1939.

Most home runs, three consecutive games
A.L.—16—Boston, June 17 through June 19, 1977.
N.L.—14
Milwaukee, August 30, 30, September 2, 1953.
Milwaukee, May 30, 30, 31, 1956.
San Francisco, April 29, 30, May 2, 1961.
Milwaukee, June 8, 9, 10, 1961.

Most home runs, four consecutive games
A.L.—18—Boston, June 16 through June 19, 1977.
N.L.—16
Milwaukee, August 30, 30, September 2, 3, 1953.
Milwaukee, May 28, 30, 30, 31, 1956.
Milwaukee, June 8, 9, 10, 11, first game, 1961.

Most home runs, five consecutive games
A.L.—21—Boston, June 14 through June 19, 1977.
N.L.—19—New York, July 7 through July 11, first game, 1954.

Most home runs, six consecutive games
A.L.—24—Boston, June 17 through June 22, 1977.
N.L.—22—New York, July 6 through July 11, first game, 1954.

Most home runs, seven consecutive games
A.L.—26—Boston, June 16 through June 22, 1977.
N.L.—24—New York, July 5, second game through July 11, first game, 1954.

Most home runs, eight consecutive games
A.L.—29—Boston, June 14 through June 22, 1977.
N.L.—26—New York, July 5, first game through July 11, first game, 1954.

Most home runs, nine consecutive games
A.L.—30
Boston June 14 through June 23, 1977.
Boston, June 16 through June 24, 1977.
N.L.—27—New York, July 4, second game through July 11, first game, 1954.

Most home runs, 10 consecutive games
A.L.—33—Boston, June 14 through June 24, 1977.
N.L.—28—New York, July 4, first game through July 11, first game, 1954.

☐ INNING ☐

Most home runs, inning
N.L.—5
New York vs. Cincinnati, June 6, 1939, fourth inning.
Philadelphia vs. Cincinnati, June 2, 1949, eighth inning.
San Francisco vs. Cincinnati, August 23, 1961, ninth inning.
A.L.—5—Minnesota vs. Kansas City, June 9, 1966, seventh inning.

Most home runs by pinch-hitters, inning
N.L.—2
New York vs. St. Louis, June 20, 1954, sixth inning (Hofman, Rhodes).
San Francisco vs. Milwaukee, June 4, 1958, 10th inning, (Sauer, Schmidt; consecutive).
Los Angeles vs. Chicago, August 8, 1963, fifth inning (Howard, Skowron; consecutive).
Los Angeles vs. St. Louis, July 23, 1975, ninth inning (Crawford, Lacy; consecutive).
New York vs. San Francisco, May 4, 1991, ninth inning (Sasser, Carreon; consecutive).
A.L.—2
New York vs. Kansas City, July 23, 1955, ninth inning (Cerv, Howard).
Baltimore vs. Boston, August 26, 1966, ninth inning (Roznovsky, Powell; consecutive).

Seattle vs. New York, April 27, 1979, eighth inning (Stinson, Meyer).

Minnesota vs. Oakland, May 16, 1983, ninth inning (Engle, Hatcher).

Baltimore vs. Cleveland, August 12, 1985, ninth inning (Gross, Sheets; consecutive).

Texas vs. Boston, September 1, 1986, ninth inning (McDowell, Porter; consecutive).

Most home runs by both clubs, inning

A.L.—5
St. Louis 3, Philadelphia 2, June 8, 1928, ninth inning.
Detroit 4, New York 1, June 23, 1950, fourth inning.
Minnesota 5, Kansas City 0, June 9, 1966, seventh inning.
Baltimore 4, Boston 1, May 17, 1967, seventh inning.
Minnesota 4, Oakland 1, May 16, 1983, ninth inning.

N.L.—5
New York 5, Cincinnati 0, June 6, 1939, fourth inning.
Philadelphia 5, Cincinnati 0, June 2, 1949, eighth inning.
New York 3, Boston 2, July 6, 1951, third inning.
Cincinnati 3, Brooklyn 2, June 11, 1954, seventh inning.
San Francisco 5, Cincinnati 0, August 23, 1961, ninth inning.
Philadelphia 3, Chicago 2, April 17, 1964, fifth inning.
Chicago 3, Atlanta 2, July 3, 1967, first inning.
Pittsburgh 3, Atlanta 2, August 1, 1970, seventh inning.
Cincinnati 3, Chicago 2, July 28, 1977, first inning.
San Francisco 3, Atlanta 2, May 25, 1979, fourth inning.

Most consecutive home runs, inning

N.L.—4—Milwaukee vs. Cincinnati, June 8, 1961, seventh inning.

A.L.—4
Cleveland vs. Los Angeles, July 31, 1963, second game, sixth inning.
Minnesota vs. Kansas City, May 2, 1964, 11th inning.

Most home runs with two out, inning

N.L.—5—New York vs. Cincinnati, June 6, 1939, fourth inning.

A.L.—3
Cleveland vs. Philadelphia, June 25, 1939, first game, seventh inning.
New York vs. Philadelphia, June 28, 1939, first game, third inning.
Minnesota vs. Kansas City, June 9, 1966, seventh inning.
Washington vs. New York, July 2, 1966, sixth inning.
Oakland vs. Minnesota, June 22, 1969, first game, third inning.

Most home runs with none on base, inning

N.L.—4—New York vs. Philadelphia, August 13, 1939, first game, fourth inning.

A.L.—4
Cleveland vs. Los Angeles, July 31, 1963, second game, sixth inning (consecutive).
Minnesota vs. Kansas City, May 2, 1964, 11th inning (consecutive).
Minnesota vs. Kansas City, June 9, 1966, seventh inning (also one home run with one on base).
Boston vs. New York, June 17, 1977, first inning.
Boston vs. Toronto, July 4, 1977, eighth inning.
Boston vs. Milwaukee, May 31, 1980, fourth inning.
Minnesota vs. New York, May 2, 1992, fifth inning.

Most home runs, start of game

N.L.—3—San Diego vs. San Francisco, April 13, 1987 (Wynne, Gwynn, Kruk).

A.A.—2
Boston vs. Baltimore, June 25, 1891 (Brown, Joyce).
Philadelphia vs. Boston, August 21, 1891 (McTamany, Larkin).

A.L.—2
Chicago vs. Boston, September 2, 1937, first game (Berger, Kreevich).
Detroit vs. Philadelphia, June 22, 1939 (McCosky, Averill).
New York vs. Chicago, April 27, 1955 (Bauer, Carey).
Kansas City vs. Boston, September 18, 1958 (Tuttle, Maris).
Minnesota vs. Cleveland, May 10, 1962 (Green, Power).
Boston vs. Minnesota, May 1, 1971 (Aparicio, Smith).

Cleveland vs. Detroit, June 19, 1971 (Nettles, Pinson).
Boston vs. Milwaukee, June 20, 1973 (Miller, Smith).
Milwaukee vs. Boston, July 29, 1975 (Money, Porter).
Boston vs. New York, June 17, 1977 (Burleson, Lynn).
Oakland vs. Toronto, September 9, 1983 (Henderson, Davis).
Kansas City vs. Milwaukee, May 3, 1984 (Motley, Sheridan).
Boston vs. Cleveland, September 5, 1985, first game (Evans, Boggs).
Minnesota vs. Baltimore, July 18, 1986 (Puckett, Gaetti).
Detroit vs. Cleveland, August 5, 1986, second game (Whitaker, Trammell).
Baltimore vs. Toronto, June 23, 1988 (Gerhart, Lynn).
Toronto vs. Detroit, August 18, 1991 (White, Alomar).
Baltimore vs. Minnesota, July 9, 1992 (Anderson, Devereaux).
Oakland vs. Minnesota, June 12, 1993 (R. Henderson, Paquette).

Most times with three or more home runs in an inning (league)

N.L.—40—New York/San Francisco, 1883 to date.
A.L.—40—New York, 1903 to date.

Most times with three consecutive home runs in an inning (league)

N.L.—11—New York/San Francisco, 1932, 1939 (2), 1948, 1949, 1953, 1954, 1956 in New York, 1963, 1969, 1982 in San Francisco.
A.L.—7—Cleveland, 1902, 1939, 1950, 1951, 1962, 1963, 1970.

Most times with three or more home runs in an inning, season

N.L.—5
New York, 1954.
Chicago, 1955.

A.L.—4
Minnesota, 1964.
Oakland, 1990.

Most times hitting two or more consecutive home runs, season

A.L.—16
Boston, 161 games, 1977.
Milwaukee, 163 games, 1982.

N.L.—12—Cincinnati, 155 games, 1956.

GRAND SLAMS

Most grand slams, season

A.L.—10
Detroit, 1938.
New York, 1987.

N.L.—9—Chicago, 1929.

Most grand slams by pinch-hitters, season

N.L.—3
San Francisco, 1973 (Arnold, Bonds, Goodson).
Chicago, 1975 (Summers, LaCock, Hosley).
San Francisco, 1978 (Ivie 2, Clark).
Philadelphia, 1978 (Johnson 2, McBride).

A.L.—3—Baltimore, 1982 (Ayala, Ford, Crowley).

Most grand slams, game

A.L.—2
Chicago vs. Detroit, May 1, 1901 (Hoy, MacFarland).
Boston vs. Chicago, May 13, 1934 (Walters, Morgan).
New York vs. Philadelphia, May 24, 1936 (Lazzeri 2).
Boston vs. Philadelphia, July 4, 1939, second game (Tabor 2).
Boston vs. St. Louis, July 27, 1946 (York 2).
Detroit vs. Philadelphia, June 11, 1954, first game (Boone, Kaline).
Baltimore vs. New York, April 24, 1960 (Pearson, Klaus).
Boston vs. Chicago, May 10, 1960 (Wertz, Repulski).
Baltimore vs. Minnesota, May 9, 1961 (Gentile 2).
Minnesota vs. Cleveland, July 18, 1962 (Allison, Killebrew).
Detroit vs. Cleveland, June 24, 1968 (Northrup 2).
Baltimore vs. Washington, June 26, 1970 (Frank Robinson 2).
Milwaukee vs. Chicago, June 17, 1973 (Porter, Lahoud).
Milwaukee vs. Boston, April 12, 1980 (Cooper, Money).

California vs. Detroit, April 27, 1983 (Lynn, Sconiers).

Boston vs. Detroit, August 7, 1984, first game (Buckner, Armas).

California vs. Oakland, July 31, 1986 (Downing, Boone).

Baltimore vs. Texas, August 6, 1986 (Sheets, Dwyer).

Boston vs. Baltimore, June 10, 1987 (Burks, Barrett).

New York vs. Toronto, June 29, 1987 (Mattingly, Winfield).

Cleveland vs. Minnesota, April 22, 1988 (Snyder, Carter).

N.L.—2

Chicago vs. Pittsburgh, August 16, 1890, (Burns, Kittredge).

Brooklyn vs. Cincinnati, September 23, 1901 (Kelley, Sheckard).

Boston vs. Chicago, August 12, 1903, second game (Stanley, Moran).

Philadelphia vs. Boston, April 28, 1921 (Miller, Meadows).

New York vs. Philadelphia, September 5, 1924, second game (Kelly, Jackson).

Pittsburgh vs. St. Louis, June 22, 1925 (Grantham, Traynor).

St. Louis vs. Philadelphia, July 6, 1929, second game (Bottomley, Hafey).

Pittsburgh vs. Philadelphia, May 1, 1933 (Vaughan, Grace).

Boston vs. Philadelphia, April 30, 1938 (Moore, Maggert).

New York vs. Brooklyn, July 4, 1938, second game (Bartell, Mancuso).

New York vs. St. Louis, July 13, 1951 (Westrum, Williams).

Cincinnati vs. Pittsburgh, July 29, 1955 (Thurman, Burgess).

Atlanta vs. San Francisco, July 3, 1966 (Cloninger 2).

Houston vs. New York, July 30, 1969, first game (Menke, Wynn).

San Francisco vs. Montreal, April 26, 1970, first game (McCovey, Dietz).

Pittsburgh vs. Chicago, September 14, 1982 (Hebner, Madlock).

Los Angeles vs. Montreal, August 23, 1985 (Guerrero, Duncan).

Atlanta vs. Houston, May 2, 1987 (Nettles, James).

Chicago vs. Houston, June 3, 1987 (Dayett, Moreland).

Cincinnati vs. Chicago, April 24, 1993 (Sabo, Oliver).

Most grand slams by both clubs, game (each club connecting)

A.L.—3—Baltimore 2 (Sheets, Dwyer), Texas 1 (Harrah), August 6, 1986.

N.L.—3—Chicago 2 (Dayett, Moreland), Houston 1 (Hatcher), June 3, 1987.

Most grand slams by pinch-hitters for both clubs, game

N.L.—2—New York 1 (Crawford), Boston 1 (Bell), May 26, 1929.

A.L.—1—Held by many clubs.

Most grand slams, doubleheader

N.L.-A.L.—2—Made in many doubleheaders.

N.L.—Last time—Cincinnati vs. Atlanta, September 12, 1974.

A.L.—Last time—Baltimore vs. Chicago, August 14, 1976.

Most grand slams by both clubs, doubleheader

N.L.—3—Cincinnati 2, Atlanta 1, September 12, 1974.

A.L.—2—Last time—Baltimore 2, Chicago 0, August 14, 1976.

Most grand slams, two consecutive games (connecting each game)

N.L.—3

Brooklyn, September 23 (2), September 24 (1), 1901.

Pittsburgh, June 20 (1), June 22 (2), 1925.

A.L.—3—Milwaukee, April 10 (1), April 12 (2), 1980.

Most consecutive games, one or more grand slams

A.L.—3

Milwaukee, April 7, 8, 9, 1978. (first three games of season.)

Detroit, August 10, 11, 12, 1993.

N.L.—2—Held by many clubs.

Most grand slams, inning

A.L.—2

Minnesota vs. Cleveland, July 18, 1962, first inning (Allison, Killebrew).

Milwaukee vs. Boston, April 12, 1980, second inning (Cooper, Money).

Baltimore vs. Texas, August 6, 1986, fourth inning (Sheets, Dwyer).

N.L.—2

Chicago vs. Pittsburgh, August 16, 1890, fifth inning (Burns, Kittredge).

Houston vs. New York, July 30, 1969, first game, ninth inning (Menke, Wynn).

Most grand slams by both clubs, inning

N.L.—2

Chicago 2 (Burns, Kittredge), Pittsburgh 0, August 16, 1890, fifth inning.

New York 1 (Irvin), Chicago 1 (Walker), May 18, 1950, sixth inning.

Houston 2 (Menke, Wynn), New York 0, July 30, 1969, first game, ninth inning.

Atlanta 1 (Evans), Cincinnati 1, (Geronimo), September 12, 1974, first game, second inning.

A.L.—2

Washington 1 (Tasby), Boston 1 (Pagliaroni), June 18, 1961, first game, ninth inning.

Minnesota 2 (Allison, Killebrew), Cleveland 0, July 18, 1962, first inning.

Milwaukee 2 (Cooper, Money), Boston 0, April 12, 1980, second inning.

Cleveland 1 (Orta), Texas 1 (Sundberg), April 14, 1980, first inning.

Baltimore 2 (Sheets, Dwyer), Texas 0, August 6, 1986, fourth inning.

TOTAL BASES

Most total bases, season

A.L.—2,703—New York, 155 games, 1936.

N.L.—2,684—Chicago, 156 games, 1930.

Fewest total bases, season

N.L.—1,358—Brooklyn, 154 games, 1908.

A.L.—1,310—Chicago, 156 games, 1910.

Most total bases, game

A.L.—60—Boston vs. St. Louis, June 8, 1950.

N.L.—58—Montreal vs. Atlanta, July 30, 1978.

Most total bases by both clubs, nine-inning game

N.L.—79—St. Louis 41, Philadelphia 38, May 11, 1923.

A.L.—77—New York 50, Philadelphia 27, June 3, 1932.

Most total bases by both clubs, extra-inning game

N.L.—97—Chicago 49, Philadelphia 48, May 17, 1979, 10 innings.

A.L.—85—Cleveland 45, Philadelphia 40, July 10, 1932, 18 innings.

Most total bases, doubleheader

A.L.—87—New York vs. Philadelphia, June 28, 1939.

N.L.—73—Milwaukee vs. Pittsburgh, August 30, 1953.

Most total bases by both clubs, doubleheader

A.L.—114—New York 73, Philadelphia 41, May 22, 1930.

N.L.—108—St. Louis 62, Philadelphia 46, July 6, 1929.

Most total bases, two consecutive games

A.L.—102—Boston vs. St. Louis, June 7 (42), June 8 (60), 1950.

N.L.—89—Pittsburgh, June 20 (46), June 22 (43), 1925.

Most total bases, inning

N.L.—29—Chicago vs. Detroit, September 6, 1883, seventh inning.

N.L. since 1900—27—San Francisco vs. Cincinnati, August 23, 1961, ninth inning.

A.L.—25—Boston vs. Philadelphia, September 24, 1940, first game, sixth inning.

LONG HITS

Most long hits, season
A.L.—580—New York, 155 games, 1936 (315 doubles, 83 triples, 182 home runs).
N.L.—566—St. Louis, 154 games, 1930 (373 doubles, 89 triples, 104 home runs).

Fewest long hits, season
A.L.—179—Chicago, 156 games, 1910 (116 doubles, 56 triples, 104 home runs).
N.L.—182—Boston, 155 games, 1909 (124 doubles, 43 triples, 15 home runs).

Most long hits, game
A.L.—17—Boston vs. St. Louis, June 8, 1950.
N.L.—16—Chicago vs. Buffalo, July 3, 1883.
N.L. since 1900—15—Philadelphia vs. Chicago, June 23, 1986.

Most long hits both clubs, game
N.L.—24—St. Louis 13, Chicago 11, July 12, 1931, second game.
A.L.—19—Minnesota 12, Toronto 7, May 8, 1979.

Longest game without a long hit
N.L.—26 innings—Brooklyn vs. Boston, May 1, 1920.
A.L.—19 innings—Detroit vs. New York, August 23, 1968, second game.

Longest game without a long hit by either club
A.L.—18 innings—Chicago 0, New York 0, August 21, 1933.
N.L.—17 innings—Boston 0, Chicago 0, September 21, 1901.

Most long hits, doubleheader
N.L.—21—Baltimore vs. Cleveland, September 3, 1894.
N.L. since 1900—18—Chicago vs. St. Louis, July 12, 1931.
A.L.—18
New York vs. Washington, July 4, 1927.
New York vs. Philadelphia, June 28, 1939.

Most long hits by both clubs, doubleheader
N.L.—35—Chicago 18, St. Louis 17, July 12, 1931.
A.L.—28—Boston 16, Detroit 12, May 14, 1967.

Longest doubleheader without a long hit
A.L.—26—Cleveland vs. Detroit, August 6, 1968.

Most long hits, inning
N.L.—8—Chicago vs. Detroit, September 6, 1883, seventh inning.
N.L. since 1900—7
Boston vs. St. Louis, August 25, 1936, first game, first inning.
Philadelphia vs. Cincinnati, June 2, 1949, eighth inning.
Philadelphia vs. Cincinnati, July 6, 1986, third inning.
A.L.—7
St. Louis vs. Washington, August 7, 1922, sixth inning.
Boston vs. Philadelphia, September 24, 1940, first game, sixth inning.
New York vs. St. Louis, May 3, 1951, ninth inning.

EXTRA BASES ON LONG HITS

Most extra bases on long hits, season
A.L.—1,027—New York, 155 games, 1936.
N.L.—1,016—Brooklyn, 155 games, 1953.

Fewest extra bases on long hits, season
A.L.—249—Chicago, 156 games, 1910.
N.L.—255—Boston, 155 games, 1909.

Most extra bases on long hits, game
A.L.—32—Boston vs. St. Louis, June 8, 1950.
N.L.—30—Montreal vs. Atlanta, July 30, 1978.

Most extra bases on long hits by both clubs, nine-inning game
A.L.—41—New York 27, Philadelphia 14, June 3, 1932.
N.L.—40
Milwaukee 27, Brooklyn 13, July 31, 1954.
Chicago 26, New York 14, June 11, 1967, second game.

Most extra bases on long hits by both clubs, extra-inning game
N.L.—47—Philadelphia 24, Chicago 23, May 17, 1979, 10 innings.
A.L.—Less than nine-inning record.

Most extra bases on long hits, doubleheader
A.L.—44—New York vs. Philadelphia, June 28, 1939.
N.L.—41—Milwaukee vs. Pittsburgh, August 30, 1953.

Most extra bases on long hits, two consecutive games
A.L.—51—Boston vs. St. Louis, June 7 (19), 8 (32), 1950.
N.L.—44—Milwaukee vs. Brooklyn, July 31 (27), August 1 (17), 1954.

Most extra bases on long hits, inning
N.L.—18—Philadelphia vs. Cincinnati, June 2, 1949, eighth inning.
A.L.—17—Boston vs. Philadelphia, September 24, 1940, first game, sixth inning.

RUNS BATTED IN

Most runs batted in, season
A.L.—995—New York, 155 games, 1936.
N.L.—942—St. Louis, 154 games, 1930.

Fewest runs batted in, season (since 1920)
N.L.—354—Philadelphia, 151 games, 1942.
A.L.—424—Texas, 154 games, 1972.

Most players with 100 or more runs batted in, season
A.L.—5—New York, 1936.
N.L.—4—Pittsburgh, 1925; Chicago, 1929; Philadelphia, 1929.

Most runs batted in, game
A.L.—29—Boston vs. St. Louis, June 8, 1950.
N.L.—26—New York vs. Brooklyn, April 30, 1944, first game.

Most runs batted in by both clubs, nine-inning game
N.L.—43—Chicago 24, Philadelphia 19, August 25, 1922.
A.L.—35—Boston 21, Philadelphia 14, June 29, 1950.

Most runs batted in by both clubs, extra-inning game
N.L.—45—Philadelphia 23, Chicago 22, May 17, 1979, 10 innings.
A.L.—Less than nine-inning record.

Longest game without a run batted in by either club
N.L.—19 innings—Cincinnati 0, Brooklyn 0, September 11, 1946.
A.L.—18 innings
Washington 0, Detroit 0, July 16, 1909.
Washington 0, Chicago 0, May 15, 1918.

Most runs batted in, doubleheader
A.L.—34—Boston vs. Philadelphia, July 4, 1939.
N.L.—31—St. Louis vs. Philadelphia, July 6, 1929.

Most runs batted in by both clubs, doubleheader
A.L.—49—Boston 34, Philadelphia 15, July 4, 1939.
N.L.—45—St. Louis 31, Philadelphia 14, July 6, 1929.

Most runs batted in, two consecutive games
A.L.—49—Boston vs. St. Louis, June 7 (20), 8 (29), 1950.
N.L.—39—Pittsburgh, June 20 (19), June 22 (20), 1925.

Most runs batted in, inning
A.L.—17—Boston vs. Detroit, June 18, 1953, seventh inning.
N.L.—15
Chicago vs. Detroit, September 6, 1883, seventh inning.
Brooklyn vs. Cincinnati, May 21, 1952, first inning.

GAME-WINNING RBIS (1980-1988)

Most game-winning RBIs, season
N.L.—102—New York, 1986 (108 games won).
A.L.—99—Oakland, 1988 (104 games won).

Fewest game-winning RBIs, season
A.L.—48—Baltimore, 1988 (54 games won).

N.L.—51—Atlanta, 1988 (54 games won).

Most games won without game-winning RBIs, season
A.L.—12—Detroit, 1980 (84 games won).
N.L.—12—Houston, 1980 (93 games won).

Fewest games won without game-winning RBIs, season
A.L.—0—New York, 1982 (79 games won).
N.L.—1
Pittsburgh, 1985 (57 games won).
Chicago, 1987 (76 games won).

BASES ON BALLS

Most bases on balls, season
A.L.—835—Boston, 155 games, 1949.
N.L.—732—Brooklyn, 155 games, 1947.

Fewest bases on balls, season
N.L.—283—Philadelphia, 153 games, 1920.
A.L.—356—Philadelphia, 156 games, 1920.

Most bases on balls, nine-inning game
A.A.—19—Louisville vs. Cleveland, September 21, 1887.
A.L.—18
Detroit vs. Philadelphia, May 9, 1916.
Cleveland vs. Boston, May 20, 1948.
N.L.—17
Chicago vs. New York, May 30, 1887, a.m. game.
Brooklyn vs. Philadelphia, August 27, 1903.
New York vs. Brooklyn, April 30, 1944, first game.

Most bases on balls by both clubs, nine-inning game
A.L.—30—Detroit 18, Philadelphia 12, May 9, 1916.
N.L.—26—Houston 13, San Francisco 13, May 4, 1975, second game.

Most bases on balls, extra-inning game
A.L.—20—Boston vs. Detroit, September 17, 1920, 12 innings.
N.L.—16—Cincinnati vs. Atlanta, October 1, 1978, 14 innings.

Most bases on balls by both clubs, extra-inning game
A.L.—28—Boston 20, Detroit 8, September 17, 1920, 12 innings.
N.L.—25
Chicago 15, Cincinnati 10, August 9, 1942, first game, 18 innings.
San Diego 13, Chicago 12, June 17, 1974, 13 innings.

Most bases on balls, nine-inning shutout game
A.L.—11—St. Louis vs. New York, August 1, 1941.
N.L.—9—Cincinnati vs. St. Louis, September 1, 1958, first game.

Most bases on balls, extra-inning shutout game
N.L.—10—Chicago vs. Cincinnati, August 19, 1965, first game, 10 innings.
A.L.—Less than nine-inning record.

Longest game without a base on balls
N.L.—22 innings—Los Angeles vs. Montreal, August 23, 1989.
A.L.—20 innings—Philadelphia vs. Boston, July 4, 1905, p.m. game.

Longest game without a base on balls by either club
A.L.—13 innings
Washington 0, Detroit 0, July 22, 1904.
Boston 0, Philadelphia 0, September 9, 1907.
N.L.—12 innings—Chicago 0, Los Angeles 0, July 27, 1980.

Most bases on balls, doubleheader
N.L.—25—New York vs. Brooklyn, April 30, 1944.
A.L.—23—Cleveland vs. Philadelphia, June 18, 1950.

Most bases on balls by both clubs, doubleheader
N.L.—42—Houston 21, San Francisco 21, May 4, 1975.
A.L.—32
Baltimore 18, Chicago 14, May 28, 1954.
Detroit 20, Kansas City 12, August 1, 1962.

Fewest bases on balls by both clubs, doubleheader
N.L.—1
Cincinnati 1, Brooklyn 0, August 6, 1905.
Cincinnati 1, Pittsburgh 0, September 7, 1924.
Brooklyn 1, St. Louis 0, September 22, 1929.
A.L.—2
Philadelphia 2, Detroit 0, August 28, 1908, 20 innings.
Philadelphia 1, Chicago 1, July 12, 1912.
Cleveland 2, Chicago 0, September 6, 1930.

Longest doubleheader without a base on balls
N.L.—27 innings—St. Louis vs. New York, July 2, 1933.
A.L.—20 innings—Detroit vs. Philadelphia, August 28, 1908.

Most bases on balls, two consecutive games
A.L.—29—Detroit vs. Philadelphia, May 9, 10, 1916.
N.L.—25—New York vs. Brooklyn, April 30, 30, 1944.

Most bases on balls by both clubs, two consecutive games
A.L.—48—Detroit 29, Philadelphia 19, May 9, 10, 1916.

Most bases on balls, inning
A.L.—11—New York vs. Washington, September 11, 1949, first game, third inning.
N.L.—9—Cincinnati vs. Chicago, April 24, 1957, fifth inning.

Most consecutive bases on balls, inning
A.L.—7—Chicago vs. Washington, August 28, 1909, first game, second inning.
N.L.—7—Atlanta vs. Pittsburgh, May 25, 1983, third inning.

Most bases on balls by pinch-hitters, inning
N.L.—3
Pittsburgh vs. Philadelphia, June 3, 1911, ninth inning.
Brooklyn vs. New York, April 22, 1922, seventh inning.
Boston vs. Brooklyn, June 2, 1932, first game, ninth inning.
Chicago vs. Philadelphia, July 29, 1947, seventh inning.
A.L.—3
Baltimore vs. Washington, April 22, 1955, seventh inning.
Washington vs. Boston, May 14, 1961, second game, ninth inning (consecutive).

Most consecutive bases on balls by pinch-hitters, inning
N.L.—3
Brooklyn vs. New York, April 22, 1922, seventh inning.
Boston vs. Brooklyn, June 2, 1932, first game, ninth inning.
A.L.—3—Washington vs. Boston, May 14, 1961, second game, ninth inning.

Most players with two bases on balls, inning
A.L.—4—New York vs. Washington, September 11, 1949, first game, third inning.
N.L.—2—Made in many innings.

Most consecutive bases on balls at start of game
N.L.—5—New York vs. Cincinnati, June 16, 1941.
A.L.—3—Made in many games.

INTENTIONAL (SINCE 1955)

Most intentional bases on balls, season
N.L. (162-game season)—102—Pittsburgh, 163 games, 1979.
N.L. (154-game season)—91—Brooklyn, 154 games, 1956.
A.L. (162-game season)—79—Minnesota, 162 games, 1965.
A.L. (154-game season)—66—New York, 154 games, 1957.

Fewest intentional bases on balls, season
A.L.—10—Kansas City, 162 games, 1961.
N.L. (154-game season)—22—Los Angeles, 154 games, 1958.
N.L. (162-game season)—34—New York, 163 games, 1964.

Most intentional bases on balls, nine-inning game
N.L.—6—San Francisco vs. St. Louis, July 19, 1975.
A.L.—5
California vs. New York, May 10, 1967.
Washington vs. Cleveland, September 2, 1970.
New York vs. California, August 29, 1978.
Oakland vs. Cleveland, July 16, 1991.

Most intentional bases on balls, extra-inning game
N.L.—7
Houston vs. Philadelphia, July 15, 1984, 16 innings.

Chicago vs. Cincinnati, May 22, 1990, 16 innings.
A.L.—5
Chicago vs. Washington, June 29, 1958, second game, 11 innings.
Minnesota vs. Milwaukee, May 12, 1972, 22-inning suspended game; completed May 13.

Most intentional bases on balls by both clubs, nine-inning game
A.L.—6—California 5, New York 1, May 10, 1967.
N.L.—6—San Francisco 6, St. Louis 0, July 19, 1975.

Most intentional bases on balls by both clubs, extra-inning game
N.L.—10—New York 6, San Diego 4, August 26, 1980, 18 innings.
A.L.—7—Minnesota 5, Milwaukee 2, May 12, 1972, 22-inning suspended game; completed May 13.

Most intentional bases on balls, inning
N.L.-A.L.—3—Made in many innings.

STRIKEOUTS

Most strikeouts, season
N.L.—1,203—New York, 163 games, 1968.
A.L.—1,185—Detroit, 162 games, 1991.

Fewest strikeouts, season
N.L.—308—Cincinnati, 153 games, 1921.
A.L.—326—Philadelphia, 155 games, 1927.

Most strikeouts, nine-inning game
A.L.—20—Seattle vs. Boston, April 29, 1986.
N.L.—19
Boston vs. Providence, June 7, 1884.
New York vs. St. Louis, September 15, 1969.
San Diego vs. New York, April 22, 1970.
Philadelphia vs. New York, October 6, 1991.
U.A.—19—Boston vs. Chicago, July 7, 1884.

Most strikeouts by both clubs, nine-inning game
A.L.—30—Seattle 18, Oakland 12, April 19, 1986.
U.A.—29
Boston 19, Chicago 10, July 7, 1884.
St. Louis 18, Boston 11, July 19, 1884.
N.L.—29—Boston 19, Providence 10, June 7, 1884.
N.L. since 1900—28—Cincinnati 15, San Diego 13, September 15, 1972.

Most strikeouts, extra-inning game
A.L.—26—California vs. Oakland, July 9, 1971, 20 innings.
N.L.—22
New York vs. San Francisco, May 31, 1964, second game, 23 innings.
Cincinnati vs. Los Angeles, August 8, 1972, 19 innings.
A.L.—21
Baltimore vs. Washington, September 12, 1962, 16 innings.
Detroit vs. Cleveland, September 18, 1966, 10 innings.
Washington vs. Baltimore, June 4, 1967, 19 innings.

Most strikeouts by both clubs, extra-inning game
A.L.—43—California 26, Oakland 17, July 9, 1971, 20 innings.
N.L.—36
New York 22, San Francisco 14, May 31, 1964, second game, 23 innings.
Pittsburgh 19, Cincinnati 17, September 30, 1964, 16 innings.

Most strikeouts by pinch-hitters, nine-inning game
A.L.—5—Detroit vs. New York, September 8, 1979.
N.L.—4
Brooklyn vs. Philadelphia, April 27, 1950.
Philadelphia vs. Milwaukee, September 16, 1960.
Chicago vs. New York, September 21, 1962.
Chicago vs. New York, May 3, 1969.
Cincinnati vs. Houston, September 27, 1969.
Montreal vs. Philadelphia, June 24, 1972.

Most strikeouts by pinch-hitters from both clubs, nine-inning game
A.L.—5
New York 4, Boston 1, July 4, 1955, first game.
Washington 4, Cleveland 1, May 1, 1957.

Detroit 4, Cleveland 1, August 4, 1967.
N.L.—4—Made in many games. Last time—Montreal 4, Philadelphia 0, June 24, 1972.

Most consecutive strikeouts, game
N.L.—10—San Diego vs. New York, April 22, 1970; 1 in sixth inning, 3 in seventh, eighth and ninth innings.
A.L.—8
Boston vs. California, July 9, 1972; 2 in first inning, 3 in second and third innings.
Milwaukee vs. California, August 7, 1973; 1 in first inning, 3 in second and third innings, 1 in fourth inning.
Seattle vs. Boston, April 29, 1986; 3 in fourth and fifth innings, 2 in sixth inning.

Most consecutive strikeouts at start of game
N.L.—9—Cleveland vs. New York, August 28, 1884.
N.L. since 1900—8—Los Angeles vs. Houston, September 23, 1986.
A.L.—7—Texas vs. Chicago, May 28, 1986.

Longest extra-inning game without a strikeout
N.L.—17
New York vs. Cincinnati, June 26, 1893.
Cincinnati vs. New York, August 27, 1920, first game.
A.L.—16—Cleveland vs. New York, June 7, 1936.

Longest extra-inning game without a strikeout, both clubs
A.L.—12—Chicago 0, St. Louis 0, July 7, 1931.
N.L.—10—Boston 0, New York 0, April 19, 1928.

Most strikeouts, inning (*consecutive)
A.A.—4—Pittsburgh vs. Philadelphia, September 30, 1885, seventh inning.
N.L.—4
Chicago vs. New York, October 4, 1888, fifth inning*.
Cincinnati vs. New York, May 15, 1906, fifth inning*.
St. Louis vs. Chicago, May 27, 1956, first game, sixth inning*.
Milwaukee vs. Cincinnati, August 11, 1959, first game, sixth inning.
Cincinnati vs. Los Angeles, April 12, 1962, third inning*.
Philadelphia vs. Los Angeles, April 17, 1965, second inning*.
Pittsburgh vs. St. Louis, June 7, 1966, fourth inning.
Montreal vs. Chicago, July 31, 1974, first game, second inning*.
Pittsburgh vs. Atlanta, July 29, 1977, sixth inning.
Chicago vs. Cincinnati, May 17, 1984, fifth inning*.
Chicago vs. Houston, September 3, 1986, fifth inning.
St. Louis vs. Atlanta, August 22, 1989, fifth inning.
San Francisco vs. Cincinnati, June 4, 1990, seventh inning*.
A.L.—4
Boston vs. Washington, April 15, 1911, fifth inning*.
Philadelphia vs. Cleveland, June 11, 1916, sixth inning*.
Chicago vs. Los Angeles, May 18, 1961, seventh inning.
Washington vs. Cleveland, September 2, 1964, seventh inning.
California vs. Baltimore, May 29, 1970, fourth inning*.
Seattle vs. Cleveland, July 21, 1978, first inning*.
Baltimore vs. Texas, August 2, 1987, second inning*.
New York vs. Texas, July 4, 1988, first inning.
Boston vs. Seattle, September 9, 1990, first inning.

Most strikeouts by pinch-hitters, inning (*consecutive)
A.L.—3
Philadelphia vs. Washington, September 3, 1910, eighth inning*.
Chicago vs. Boston, June 5, 1911, ninth inning*.
Detroit vs. Cleveland, September 19, 1945, eighth inning*.
Philadelphia vs. Cleveland, September 9, 1952, ninth inning.
Cleveland vs. New York, May 12, 1953, eighth inning*.
New York vs. Philadelphia, September 24, 1954, ninth inning*.
Detroit vs. Cleveland, August 4, 1967, eighth inning.
California vs. Minnesota, May 17, 1971, ninth inning*.
N.L.—3
Pittsburgh vs. Cincinnati, June 5, 1953, ninth inning*.
Cincinnati vs. Brooklyn, August 8, 1953, ninth inning.
St. Louis vs. Cincinnati, May 10, 1961, ninth inning.
Cincinnati vs. Houston, June 2, 1966, eighth inning*.
Atlanta vs. Houston, June 18, 1967, eighth inning*.
Cincinnati vs. Houston, September 27, 1969, eighth inning.
St. Louis vs. Montreal, July 4, 1970, eighth inning.

Philadelphia vs. Pittsburgh, July 6, 1970, ninth inning.

Most strikeouts, doubleheader (18 innings)

N.L.—26
 Philadelphia vs. New York, September 9, 1970.
 San Diego vs. New York, May 29, 1971.
 San Francisco vs. Houston, September 5, 1971.
A.L.—25—Los Angeles vs. Cleveland, July 31, 1963.

Most strikeouts, doubleheader (more than 18 innings)

N.L.—31
 Pittsburgh vs. Philadelphia, September 22, 1958, 23 innings.
 New York vs. Philadelphia, October 2, 1965, 27 innings.
A.L.—27—Cleveland vs. Boston, August 25, 1963, 24 innings.

Most strikeouts by both clubs, doubleheader (18 innings)

N.L.—41
 Philadelphia 26, New York 15, September 9, 1970.
 San Diego 26, New York 15, May 29, 1971.
 Chicago 21, New York 20, September 15, 1971.
A.L.—40—Cleveland 23, Los Angeles 17, September 29, 1962.

Most strikeouts by both clubs, doubleheader (more than 18 innings)

N.L.—51—New York 30, Philadelphia 21, September 26, 1975, 24 innings.
A.L.—44—Cleveland 27, Boston 17, August 25, 1963, 24 innings.

Longest doubleheader without a strikeout

N.L.—21—Pittsburgh vs. Philadelphia, July 12, 1924.
A.L.—20—Boston vs. St. Louis, July 28, 1917.

Fewest strikeouts by both clubs, doubleheader

A.L.—1—Cleveland 1, Boston 0, August 28, 1926.
N.L.—2
 Brooklyn 2, New York 0, August 13, 1932.
 Pittsburgh 2, St. Louis 0, September 6, 1948.

Most strikeouts, two consecutive nine-inning games

A.L.—36—Seattle vs. Boston, April 29 (20), April 30 (16), 1986.
N.L.—29—San Diego vs. New York, April 21 (10), April 22 (19), 1970.

Most strikeouts, two consecutive games (more than 18 innings)

N.L.—31
 Pittsburgh vs. Philadelphia, September 22, first game, 14 innings (21), September 22, second game, nine innings (10), 1958, 23 innings.
 New York vs. Philadelphia, October 2, first game, nine innings (10), October 2, second game, 18 innings (21), 1965, 27 innings.
A.L.—Less than nine-inning record.

SACRIFICE HITS

Most sacrifice hits, season (includes sacrifice scoring flies)

A.L.—310—Boston, 157 games, 1917.
N.L.—270—Chicago, 158 games, 1908.

Most sacrifice hits, season (no sacrifice flies)

N.L.—231—Chicago, 154 games, 1906.
A.L.—207—Chicago, 154 games, 1906.

Fewest sacrifice hits, season (no sacrifice flies)

A.L.—18—Toronto, 162 games, 1990.
N.L.—32—New York, 154 games, 1957.

Most sacrifices, game (includes sacrifice flies)

A.L.—8
 New York vs. Boston, May 4, 1918 (two sacrifice scoring flies).
 Chicago vs. Detroit, July 11, 1927.
 St. Louis vs. Cleveland, July 23, 1928.
 Texas vs. Chicago, August 1, 1977.
N.L.—8—Cincinnati vs. Philadelphia, May 6, 1926.

Most sacrifices by both clubs, game (includes sacrifice flies)

A.L.—11—Washington 7, Boston 4, September 1, 1926.

N.L.—9
 New York 5, Chicago 4, August 29, 1921.
 Cincinnati 8, Philadelphia 1, May 6, 1926.
 San Francisco 6, San Diego 3, May 23, 1970, 15 innings (no sacrifice flies in game).

Longest extra-inning game without a sacrifice

A.L.—24 innings—Detroit vs. Philadelphia, July 21, 1945.
N.L.—23 innings—Brooklyn vs. Boston, June 27, 1939.

Longest extra-inning game without a sacrifice by either club

N.L.—19 innings—Philadelphia 0, Cincinnati 0, September 15, 1950, second game.
A.L.—18 innings—Washington 0, St. Louis 0, June 20, 1952.

Most sacrifices, doubleheader (includes sacrifice flies)

A.L.—10—Detroit vs. Chicago, July 7, 1921.
N.L.—9—Held by many clubs.

Most sacrifices by both clubs, doubleheader (includes sacrifice flies)

A.L.—13—Boston 9, Chicago 4, July 17, 1926.

Fewest sacrifices, doubleheader

N.L.-A.L.—0—Made in many doubleheaders.

Longest doubleheader without a sacrifice by either club

N.L.—28 innings—Cincinnati 0, Philadelphia 0, September 15, 1950.
A.L.—18 innings—Made in many doubleheaders.

Most sacrifice hits, inning (no sacrifice flies)

A.L.—3
 Cleveland vs. St. Louis, July 10, 1949, fifth inning.
 Detroit vs. Baltimore, July 12, 1970, first game, second inning (consecutive).
 Cleveland vs. Chicago, June 8, 1980, sixth inning (consecutive).
N.L.—3
 Chicago vs. Milwaukee, August 26, 1962, sixth inning (consecutive).
 Philadelphia vs. Los Angeles, September 23, 1967, seventh inning (consecutive).
 Los Angeles vs. San Francisco, May 23, 1972, sixth inning.
 Houston vs. San Diego, April 29, 1975, seventh inning.
 Houston vs. Atlanta, July 6, 1975, ninth inning.

SACRIFICE FLIES

Most run-scoring sacrifice flies, season

A.L. (162-game season)—77—Oakland, 162 games, 1984.
A.L. (154-game season)—63—Boston, 155 games, 1915.
N.L. (162-game season)—74—Philadelphia, 162 games, 1977.
N.L. (154-game season)—66
 New York, 154 games, 1912.
 St. Louis, 153 games, 1954.

Fewest sacrifice flies, season

N.L.—19—San Diego, 161 games, 1971.
A.L.—23—California, 161 games, 1967.

Most run-scoring sacrifice flies, game

A.L.—5—Seattle vs. Oakland, August 7, 1988.
N.L.—4
 New York vs. San Francisco, July 26, 1967.
 New York vs. Philadelphia, September 23, 1972.
 St. Louis vs. Cincinnati, September 2, 1980.
 Cincinnati vs. Houston, May 5, 1982.
 San Francisco vs. New York, August 29, 1987.
 Pittsburgh vs. Philadelphia, September 9, 1988.
 San Francisco vs. San Diego, September 14, 1988.
 Montreal vs. Florida, May 24, 1994.

Most run-scoring sacrifice flies by both clubs, game

A.L.—5
 Boston 3, Washington 2, August 31, 1965, second game.
 Cleveland 4, Seattle 1, June 1, 1980.
 Cleveland 4, Texas 1, August 13, 1980.
 Seattle 4, Oakland 0, August 7, 1988.
 Toronto 4, Chicago 1, August 14, 1990.
 New York 3, Milwaukee 2, August 1, 1994.

N.L.—5
St. Louis 4, Cincinnati 1, September 2, 1980.
Los Angeles 3, San Francisco 2, April 15, 1984, 11 innings.
San Francisco 3, Atlanta 2, June 28, 1988.
San Francisco 4, San Diego 1, September 14, 1988.

Most run-scoring sacrifice flies, inning

A.L.—3—Chicago vs. Cleveland, July 1, 1962, second game, fifth inning.
N.L.—2—Made in many innings.

HIT BY PITCH

Most hit by pitch, season

N.L.—148—Baltimore, 154 games, 1898.
A.L.—80—Washington, 154 games, 1911.
N.L. since 1900—78
St. Louis, 153 games, 1910.
Montreal, 162 games, 1971.

Fewest hit by pitch, season

A.L.—5—Philadelphia, 154 games, 1937.
N.L.—9
Philadelphia, 152 games, 1939.
San Diego, 162 games, 1969.

Most hit by pitch, nine-inning game

A.A.—6—Brooklyn vs. Baltimore, April 25, 1887.
A.L.—6—New York vs. Washington, June 20, 1913, second game.
N.L.—6—Louisville vs. St. Louis, July 31, 1897, first game.
N.L. since 1900—5—Atlanta vs. Cincinnati, July 2, 1969.

Most hit by pitch, extra-inning game

N.L.—6—New York vs. Chicago, June 16, 1893, 11 innings.

Most hit by pitch by both clubs, nine-inning game

N.L.—8
Washington 5, Pittsburgh 3, May 9, 1896.
Louisville 6, St. Louis 2, July 31, 1897, first game.
N.L. since 1900—7—New York 4, Boston 3, August 1, 1903, second game.
A.L.—7
Detroit 4, Washington 3, August 24, 1914, second game.
Minnesota 4, Kansas City 3, April 13, 1971.
Kansas City 5, Texas 2, September 3, 1989.

Most hit by pitch, doubleheader

N.L.—8—New York vs. Boston, August 1, 1903.
A.L.—6—New York vs. Washington, June 20, 1913.

Most hit by pitch by both clubs, doubleheader

N.L.—11—New York 8, Boston 3, August 1, 1903.
A.L.—8—Detroit 5, Washington 3, August 24, 1914.

Most hit by pitch, inning

N.L.—4—Boston vs. Pittsburgh, August 19, 1893, first game, second inning.
N.L. since 1900—3
New York vs. Pittsburgh, September 25, 1905, first inning.
Chicago vs. Boston, September 17, 1928, ninth inning.
Philadelphia vs. Cincinnati, May 15, 1960, first game, eighth inning.

Atlanta vs. Cincinnati, July 2, 1969, second inning.
Cincinnati vs. Pittsburgh, May 1, 1974, first inning, consecutive.
A.L.—3
New York vs. Washington, June 20, 1913, second game, first inning.
Cleveland vs. New York, August 25, 1921, eighth inning.
Boston vs. New York, June 30, 1954, third inning.
Baltimore vs. California, August 9, 1968, seventh inning.
California vs. Chicago, September 10, 1977, first inning (consecutive).

GROUNDING INTO DOUBLE PLAYS

Most grounding into double plays, season

A.L.—174—Boston, 162 games, 1990.
N.L.—166—St. Louis, 154 games, 1958.

Fewest grounding into double plays, season

N.L.—75—St. Louis, 155 games, 1945.
A.L.—79—Kansas City, 161 games, 1967.

Most grounding into double plays, game

N.L.—7—San Francisco vs. Houston, May 4, 1969.
A.L.—6
Washington vs. Cleveland, August 5, 1948.
Boston vs. California, May 1, 1966, first game.
Baltimore vs. Kansas City, May 6, 1972.
Cleveland vs. New York, April 29, 1975.
Toronto vs. Minnesota, August 29, 1977, first game, 10 innings.
Milwaukee vs. Chicago, May 8, finished May 9, 1984, 25 innings.
Boston vs. Minnesota, July 18, 1990.

Most grounding into double plays by both clubs, nine-inning game

A.L.—9
Boston 6, California 3, May 1, 1966, first game.
Boston 6, Minnesota 3, July 18, 1990.
N.L.—8—Boston 5, Chicago 3, September 18, 1928.

Most grounding into double plays by both clubs, extra-inning game

N.L.—9—Los Angeles 5, New York 4, May 24, 1973, 19 innings.
A.L.—Less than nine-inning record.

REACHING BASE ON ERRORS

Most times reaching first base on error, game

N.L.—10—Chicago vs. Cleveland, July 24, 1882.
A.L.—8—Detroit vs. Chicago, May 6, 1903.

Most times reaching first base on error by both clubs, game

N.L.—16—Chicago 10, Cleveland 6, July 24, 1882.
A.L.—12—Detroit 8, Chicago 4, May 6, 1903.

Most times reaching first base on error, inning

N.L.—4—St. Louis vs. Pittsburgh, August 5, 1901, eighth inning.
A.L.—4—St. Louis vs. Boston, June 8, 1911, fourth inning.

LEAGUE BATTING

GAMES

Most games, season (since 1900)
A.L. (14-club league) — 1,135 in 1982, 1983.
A.L. (12-club league) — 973 in 1969, 1970, 1974.
A.L. (10-club league) — 814 in 1964.
A.L. (8-club league) — 631 in 1914.
N.L. (14-club league) — 1,135 in 1993.
N.L. (12-club league) — 974 in 1983.
N.L. (10-club league) — 813 in 1965, 1968.
N.L. (8-club league) — 625 in 1914, 1917.

Fewest games, season (since 1900, except 1918)
A.L. — 608 in 1933.
N.L. — 608 in 1934.

Most times two games in one day, season
A.L. — 153 in 1943.
N.L. — 146 in 1943.

BATTING AVERAGE

Highest batting average, season (since 1900)
N.L. — .303 in 1930.
A.L. — .29244 in 1921.

Lowest batting average, season (since 1900)
A.L. — .23011 in 1968.
N.L. — .23895 in 1908.

Most .400 batsmen, season (qualifiers for batting championship)
N.L. — 3 in 1894.
A.L. — 2 in 1911, 1922.
N.L. since 1900 — 1 in 1922, 1924, 1925, 1930.

Most clubs batting .300 or over, season (since 1900)
N.L. — 6 in 1930.
A.L. — 4 in 1921.

Most .300 batsmen, season (qualifiers for batting championship)
N.L. — 33 in 1930.
A.L. — 26 in 1924.

Fewest .300 batsmen, season (qualifiers for batting title)
A.L. — 1 in 1968.
N.L. — 4 in 1907.

SLUGGING AVERAGE

Highest slugging average, season (since 1900)
N.L. — .448 in 1930.
A.L. — .425 in 1987.

Lowest slugging average, season (since 1900)
N.L. — .306 in 1908.
A.L. — .312 in 1910.

AT-BATS

Most at-bats, season (since 1900)
A.L. (14-club league) — 77,910 in 1984.
A.L. (12-club league) — 66,276 in 1973.
A.L. (10-club league) — 55,239 in 1962.
A.L. (8-club league) — 43,747 in 1930.
N.L. (14-club league) — 77,489 in 1993.
N.L. (12-club league) — 66,700 in 1977.
N.L. (10-club league) — 55,449 in 1962.
N.L. (8-club league) — 43,891 in 1936.

Most players with 600 or more at-bats, season (since 1900)
A.L. — 20 in 1985.
N.L. — 19 in 1962.

RUNS

Most runs, season (since 1900)
A.L. (14-club league) — 11,112 in 1987.
A.L. (12-club league) — 8,314 in 1973.
A.L. (10-club league) — 7,342 in 1961.
A.L. (8-club league) — 7,009 in 1936.
N.L. (14-club league) — 10,190 in 1993.
N.L. (12-club league) — 8,771 in 1970, 1987.
N.L. (10-club league) — 7,278 in 1962.
N.L. (8-club league) — 7,025 in 1930.

Fewest runs, season (since 1900)
N.L. — 4,136 in 1908.
A.L. — 4,272 in 1909.

Most players with 100 or more runs, season (since 1900)
A.L. — 24 in 1936.
N.L. — 19 in 1929.

Most runs in league, one day
N.L. — 159 — August 7, 1894.
A.L. — 128 — May 30, 1932.
N.L. since 1900 — 118 — July 21, 1923.

Most runs by both leagues, one day
198 on May 30, 1932; 128 in A.L. (8 games); 70 in N.L. (8 games).

Most players scoring five or more runs in a game, season (since 1900)
N.L. — 7 in 1930.
A.L. — 5 in 1939.

Most games with 20 or more runs, league
N.L. — 1876 to date — 252.
N.L. since 1900 to date — 88.
A.L. — 1901 to date — 92.

Most games with 20 or more runs, season
N.L. — 32 in 1894.
N.L. since 1900 — 5 in 1900, 1925.
A.L. — 5 in 1923.

Most innings with 10 or more runs, season
N.L. — 12 in 1894.
N.L. since 1900 — 6 in 1922.
A.L. — 6 in 1936, 1950, 1979.

HITS

Most hits, season (since 1900)
A.L. (14-club league) — 20,958 in 1980.
A.L. (12-club league) — 17,193 in 1973.
A.L. (10-club league) — 14,068 in 1962.
A.L. (8-club league) — 12,657 in 1962.
N.L. (14-club league) — 20,427 in 1993.
N.L. (12-club league) — 17,465 in 1977.
N.L. (10-club league) — 14,453 in 1962.
N.L. (8-club league) — 13,260 in 1930.

Fewest hits, season (since 1900)
N.L. — 9,566 in 1907.
A.L. — 9,719 in 1908.

Most players with 200 or more hits, season
N.L. — 12 in 1929 and 1930.
A.L. — 9 in 1936 and 1937.

Most players with five or more hits in a game, season (since 1900)
N.L. — 27 in 1930.
A.L. — 22 in 1936.

Fewest players with five or more hits in a game, season (since 1900)
N.L. — 1 in 1914.

— 63 —

A.L.—2 in 1913, 1914, 1963.

Most hits in league, one day
A.L.— 190, July 10, 1932.
N.L.— 183, July 21, 1963.

Most hits by both leagues, one day
337 on July 16, 1950; 175 in N.L. (7 games); 162 in A.L. (8 games).

SINGLES

Most singles, season (since 1900)
A.L. (14-club league) — 15,072 in 1980.
A.L. (12-club league) — 12,729 in 1974.
A.L. (10-club league) — 9,878 in 1962.
A.L. (8-club league) — 9,214 in 1921.
N.L. (14-club league) — 14,370 in 1993.
N.L. (12-club league) — 12,564 in 1980.
N.L. (10-club league) — 10,476 in 1922.
N.L. (8-club league) — 9,476 in 1962.

Fewest singles, season (since 1900)
N.L.—7,466 in 1956.
A.L.—7,573 in 1959.

DOUBLES

Most doubles, season (since 1900)
A.L. (14-club league) — 3,861 in 1993.
A.L. (12-club league) — 2,624 in 1973.
A.L. (8-club league) — 2,400 in 1936.
N.L. (14-club league) — 3,588 in 1993.
N.L. (12-club league) — 3,126 in 1987.
N.L. (8-club league) — 2,386 in 1930.

Fewest doubles, season (since 1900)
N.L.— 1,148 in 1907.
A.L.— 1,348 in 1910.

Most players with 40 or more doubles, season (since 1900)
N.L.— 12 in 1920.
A.L.— 12 in 1937.

TRIPLES

Most triples, season (since 1900)
A.L.—694 in 1921.
N.L.—685 in 1912.

Fewest triples, season (since 1900)
A.L.—267 in 1959.
N.L.—323 in 1942.

Most players with 20 or more triples (since 1900)
A.L.—4 in 1912.
N.L.—3 in 1911, 1912.

HOME RUNS

SEASON

Most home runs, season
A.L.— (14-club league) — 2,634 in 1987.
A.L.— (12-club league) — 1,746 in 1970.
A.L.— (10-club league) — 1,552 in 1962.
A.L.— (8-club league) — 1,091 in 1959.
N.L.— (14-club league) — 1,956 in 1993.
N.L.— (12-club league) — 1,824 in 1987.
N.L.— (10-club league) — 1,449 in 1962.
N.L.— (8-club league) — 1,263 in 1955.

Most home runs by both leagues, season
4,458 in 1987 (14-club A.L., 12-club N.L.) — 2,634 in A.L., 1,824 in N.L.
4,030 in 1993 (14-club leagues) — 2,074 in A.L., 1,956 in N.L.

3,429 in 1970 (12-club leagues) — 1,746 in A.L., 1,683 in N.L.
3,001 in 1962 (10-club leagues) — 1,552 in A.L., 1,449 in N.L.

Fewest home runs, season (since 1900)
A.L.— 101 in 1907.
N.L.— 126 in 1906.

Most home runs by pinch-hitters, season
N.L. (12-club league) — 57 in 1986.
N.L. (10-club league) — 45 in 1962.
N.L. (8-club league) — 42 in 1958.
A.L. (14-club league) — 53 in 1980.
A.L. (10-club league) — 50 in 1961.
A.L. (8-club league) — 29 in 1953.

Most home runs by pinch-hitters in both leagues, season
103 in 1987 (14-club A.L., 12-club N.L.) — 53 in N.L., 50 in A.L.
95 in 1970 (12-club leagues) — 49 in A.L., 46 in N.L.
84 in 1962 (10-club leagues) — 45 in N.L., 39 in A.L.
79 in 1993 (14-club leagues) — 53 in N.L., 26 in A.L.

Most clubs with 100 or more home runs, season
A.L. (14-club league) — 14 in 1977, 1982, 1985, 1986, 1987, 1988, 1990, 1993.
A.L. (12-club league) — 11 in 1970, 1973.
A.L. (10-club league) — 10 in 1964.
A.L. (8-club league) — 8 in 1958, 1960.
N.L. (14-club league) — 13 in 1993.
N.L. (12-club league) — 11 in 1970, 1986, 1987.
N.L. (10-club league) — 10 in 1962.
N.L. (8-club league) — 8 in 1956, 1958, 1959, 1961.

Most players with 50 or more home runs, season
A.L.—2 in 1938, 1961.
N.L.—2 in 1947.

Most players with 40 or more home runs, season
N.L.—6 in 1954, 1955.
A.L. (10-club league) — 6 in 1961.
A.L. (8-club league) — 3 in 1936.

Most players with 30 or more home runs, season
A.L. (14-club league) — 20 in 1987.
A.L. (12-club league) — 10 in 1969.
A.L. (10-club league) — 9 in 1964.
N.L. (12-club league) — 12 in 1970.
N.L. (10-club league) — 10 in 1965.

Most players with 20 or more home runs, season
A.L. (14-club league) — 51 in 1987.
A.L.—25
in 1970 (12-club league).
in 1964 (10-club league).
A.L. (8-club league) — 18 in 1959.
N.L. (12-club league) — 29 in 1970.
N.L. (10-club league) — 25 in 1962.
N.L. (8-club league) — 23 in 1956.

Most players hitting homers in all parks, season (eight-club league)
N.L.— 11 in 1956 (8 parks, excluding Jersey City; 5 of 11 connected there).
A.L.—7 in 1953 (8 parks).

Most players hitting homers in all parks, season (10-club league)
A.L.—4 in 1962.
N.L.—3 in 1963.

Most players hitting homers in all parks, season (12-club league)
N.L.—3 in 1970.
A.L.—1 in 1975.

ONE DAY

Most players with two or more home runs in a game, season
A.L. (14-club league) — 156 in 1987.
A.L. (10-club-league) — 98 in 1964.
A.L. (8-club league) — 62 in 1960.
N.L. (12-club league) — 110 in 1987.
N.L. (8-club league) — 84 in 1955.

Fewest players with two or more home runs in a game, season
N.L.—0 in 1907, 1918.

A.L.—0 in 1908, 1915.

Most players with two or more home runs in a game, one day
A.L. (14-club league) —6—August 2, 1983; May 8, 1987.
A.L. (10-club league) —5—June 11, 1961; May 20, 1962.
A.L. (8-club league) —4—April 30, 1933; May 30, 1956.
N.L.—5
August 16, 1947 (8-club league).
April 16, 1955 (8-club league).
June 5, 1966 (10-club league).
May 8, 1970 (12-club league).

Most players with two home runs in a game both leagues, one day
7 on May 8, 1987; 6 in A.L., 1 in N.L.

Most players with three or more home runs in a game, season
A.L.—9 in 1987.
N.L.—7 in 1950.

Most players from both leagues with three homers in a game, season
15 in 1987; 9 in A.L., 6 in N.L.

Most times with five or more home runs in a game, season (club)
A.L. (14-club league) —25 in 1987.
A.L.—8
in 1950 (8-club league).
in 1969 (12-club league).
N.L.— 15 in 1954.

Most times with three or more home runs in an inning, season (club)
N.L. (8-club league) — 13 in 1954, 1955.
A.L. (14-club league) — 12 in 1987.
A.L. (10-club league) — 10 in 1961, 1962.
A.L. (8-club league) —5 in 1936, 1947, 1953, 1954, 1956, 1957, 1959.

Most home runs by pitchers, one day
A.L.—4—July 31, 1935.
N.L.—3—June 3, 1892; May 13, 1942; July 2, 1961; June 23, 1971.

Most home runs by pinch-hitters, one day
N.L.—4—June 2, 1928; July 21, 1930.
A.L.—4—June 28, 1987.

Most home runs in league, one day
N.L.—30—May 8, 1970 (7 games).
A.L.—30
June 10, 1962 (10 games).
June 14, 1964 (10 games).

Most home runs by both leagues, one day
54—June 10, 1962; 30 in A.L. (10 games), 24 in N.L. (10 games).

GRAND SLAMS

Most grand slams, season
A.L. (14-club league) —57 in 1993.
A.L. (10-club league) —48 in 1961.
A.L. (8-club league) —37 in 1938.
N.L. (12-club league) —49 in 1970.
N.L. (10-club league) —37 in 1962.
N.L. (8-club league) —35 in 1950.

Most grand slams by both leagues, season
100 in 1987 (14-club A.L., 12-club N.L.) —55 in A.L.; 45 in N.L.
98 in 1993 (14-club leagues) —57 in A.L.; 41 in N.L.
88 in 1970 (12-club leagues) —49 in N.L.; 39 in A.L.
77 in 1961 (10-club A.L., 8-club N.L.) —48 in A.L.; 29 in N.L.

Fewest grand slams, season
A.L.—0 in 1918 (Short season due to war).
N.L.—1 in 1920.
A.L.—1 in 1907, 1909, 1915.

Fewest grand slams by both leagues, season
3—1907 (2 in N.L., 1 in A.L.).

Most grand slams by pinch-hitters, season
A.L. (14-club league) —5 in 1982, 1988.

A.L. (10-club league) —7 in 1961.
A.L. (8-club league) —5 in 1953.
N.L. (12-club league) —9 in 1978.
N.L. (8-club league) —4 in 1959.

Most grand slams by pinch-hitters in both leagues, season
(14-club A.L.; 12-club N.L.) —13 in 1978 (9 in N.L.; 4 in A.L.).
(12-club leagues) —9 in 1973 (6 in N.L.; 3 in A.L.).
(8-club leagues) —8 in 1953 (5 in A.L.; 3 in N.L.).

Most grand slams, one day
N.L.—3—Performed many times. Last times—May 16, 1993.
A.L.—3—Performed many times. Last times—July 23, 1991; July 31, 1991.

Most grand slams by both leagues, one day
4—September 18, 1949 (3 in N.L.; 1 in A.L.).
April 24, 1960 (3 in A.L.; 1 in N.L.).
August 22, 1963 (2 in A.L.; 2 in N.L.).
May 10, 1969 (2 in N.L.; 2 in A.L.).
August 3, 1969 (3 in A.L.; 1 in N.L.).
June 20, 1971 (3 in N.L.; 1 in A.L.).
June 24, 1974 (3 in N.L.; 1 in A.L.).
September 8, 1974 (2 in A.L.; 2 in N.L.).
August 10, 1986 (3 in A.L.; 1 in N.L.).
June 10, 1987 (3 in A.L.; 1 in N.L.).
September 13, 1988 (2 in A.L.; 2 in N.L.).
July 23, 1991 (3 in A.L.; 1 in N.L.).

TOTAL BASES

Most total bases, season (since 1900)
A.L. (14-club league) —33,111 in 1987.
A.L. (12-club league) —25,281 in 1973.
A.L. (10-club league) —21,762 in 1962.
A.L. (8-club league) — 18,427 in 1936.
N.L. (14-club league) —30,909 in 1993.
N.L. (12-club league) —26,743 in 1987.
N.L. (10-club league) —21,781 in 1962.
N.L. (8-club league) — 19,572 in 1930.

Most players with 300 or more total bases, season (since 1900)
N.L.— 14 in 1930.
A.L.— 12 in 1930, 1937.

Most players with 400 or more total bases, season
N.L.—3 in 1930.
A.L.—2 in 1927, 1936.

LONG HITS AND EXTRA BASES ON LONG HITS

Most long hits, season (since 1900)
A.L. (14-club league) —6,762 in 1987.
A.L. (12-club league) —4,611 in 1970.
A.L. (10-club league —4,190 in 1962.
A.L. (8-club league) —3,706 in 1936.
N.L. (14-club league) —6,057 in 1993.
N.L. (12-club league) —5,385 in 1987.
N.L. (10-club league) —3,977 in 1962.
N.L. (8-club league) —3,903 in 1930.

Most extra bases on long hits, season (since 1900)
A.L. (14-club league) —12,491 in 1987.
A.L. (12-club league) —8,476 in 1970.
A.L. (10-club league) —7,694 in 1962.
A.L. (8-club league) —5,842 in 1940.
N.L. (14-club league) — 10,482 in 1993.
N.L. (12-club league) —9,468 in 1987.
N.L. (10-club league) —7,328 in 1962.
N.L. (8-club league) —6,312 in 1930.

RUNS BATTED IN

Most runs batted in, season
A.L. (14-club league) — 10,480 in 1987.

A.L. (12-club league) —7,769 in 1973.
A.L. (10-club league) —6,842 in 1961.
A.L. (8-club league) —6,520 in 1936.
N.L. (14-club league) —9,533 in 1993.
N.L. (12-club league) —8,233 in 1987.
N.L. (10-club league) —6,760 in 1962.
N.L. (8-club league) —6,582 in 1930.

Most players with 100 or more runs batted in, season

A.L.— 18 in 1936.
N.L.— 17 in 1930.

BASES ON BALLS

Most bases on balls, season (since 1900)

A.L. (14-club league) —8,006 in 1993.
A.L. (12-club league) —7,032 in 1969.
A.L. (10-club league) —5,902 in 1961.
A.L. (8-club league) —5,627 in 1949.
N.L. (14-club league) —7,104 in 1993.
N.L. (12-club league) —6,919 in 1970.
N.L. (10-club league) —5,265 in 1962.
N.L. (8-club league) —4,537 in 1950.

Fewest bases on balls, season (since 1900)

A.L. (12-club league) —6,128 in 1976.
A.L. (8-club league) —3,797 in 1922.
N.L. (12-club league) —5,793 in 1988.
N.L. (8-club league) —2,906 in 1921.

Most players with 100 or more bases on balls, season

A.L.—8 in 1949.
N.L. (12-club league) —5 in 1970.
N.L. (8-club league) —4 in 1949, 1951.

INTENTIONAL (SINCE 1955)

Most intentional bases on balls, season

N.L.—862 in 1973 (12-club league).
A.L.—743 in 1993 (14-club league).

Fewest intentional bases on balls, season

A.L.—471 in 1976 (12-club league).
N.L.—626 in 1991 (12-club league).

STRIKEOUTS

Most strikeouts, season (since 1900)

A.L. (14-club league) — 13,442 in 1987.
A.L. (12-club league) — 10,957 in 1970.
A.L. (10-club league) —9,956 in 1964.
A.L. (8-club league) —6,081 in 1959.
N.L. (14-club league) — 13,358 in 1993.
N.L. (12-club league) — 11,657 in 1987.
N.L. (10-club league) —9,649 in 1965.
N.L. (8-club league) —6,824 in 1960.

Fewest strikeouts, season (since 1900)

A.L. (8-club league) —3,245 in 1924.
A.L. (12-club league) —9,143 in 1976.
N.L. (8-club league) —3,359 in 1926.
N.L. (12-club league) —9,602 in 1976.

Most players with 100 or more strikeouts, season

A.L.— 27 in 1986, 1987 (14-club league).
N.L.— 18 in 1989 (12-club league).

SACRIFICE HITS AND FLIES

Most sacrifices including scoring flies, season (since 1900)

A.L.—1,731 in 1917.
N.L.—1,655 in 1908.

Most sacrifices with no sacrifice flies, season

A.L.—1,349 in 1906.
N.L.—1,349 in 1907.

Fewest sacrifices with no sacrifice flies, season

N.L.—510 in 1957.
A.L.—531 in 1958.

Most sacrifice flies, season

A.L. (14-club league) —765 in 1979.
A.L. (12-club league) —624 in 1976.
A.L. (10-club league) —448 in 1961.
A.L. (8-club league) —370 in 1954.
N.L. (14-club league) —701 in 1993.
N.L. (12-club league) —589 in 1988.
N.L. (8-club league) —425 in 1954.

Fewest sacrifice flies, season

N.L. (14-club league) —701 in 1993.
N.L. (12-club league) —430 in 1969.
N.L. (10-club league) —363 in 1966.
N.L. (8-club league) —304 in 1959.
A.L. (14-club league) —629 in 1987.
A.L. (12-club league) —484 in 1969.
A.L. (10-club league) —348 in 1967.
A.L. (8-club league) —312 in 1959.

HIT BY PITCH

Most hit by pitch, season

A.L. (14-club league) —633 in 1993.
A.L. (8-club league) —464 in 1911.
N.L. (14-club league) —567 in 1993.
N.L. (12-club league) —443 in 1969.
N.L. (8-club league) —415 in 1903.

Fewest hits by pitch, season

A.L. (8-club league) — 132 in 1947.
A.L. (14-club league) —372 in 1982.
N.L. (8-club league) — 157 in 1943.
N.L. (12-club league) —249 in 1984.
N.L. (14-club league) —567 in 1993.

GROUNDING INTO DOUBLE PLAYS

Most grounding into double plays, season

A.L. (14-club league) — 1,968 in 1980.
A.L. (12-club league) — 1,608 in 1973.
A.L. (10-club league) — 1,256 in 1961.
A.L. (8-club league) — 1,181 in 1950.
N.L. (14-club league) — 1,638 in 1993.
N.L. (12-club league) — 1,547 in 1971.
N.L. (10-club league) — 1,251 in 1962.
N.L. (8-club league) — 1,047 in 1958.

Fewest grounding into double plays, season

N.L. (8-club league) —820 in 1945.
N.L. (12-club league) — 1,198 in 1991.
A.L. (8-club league) —890 in 1945.
A.L. (12-club league) — 1,440 in 1976.

INDIVIDUAL BASERUNNING

STOLEN BASES

Most stolen bases, career
A.L.—1,117—Rickey Henderson, Oakland, New York, Toronto, 16 years, 1979 through 1994.
N.L.—938—Lou Brock, Chicago, St. Louis, 19 years, 1961 through 1979.

Highest stolen base percentage, league (minimum 300 attempts)
M.L.—.872—Eric Davis, Cincinnati N.L., Los Angeles N.L., Detroit A.L., 1984 through 1994.
N.L.—.874—Eric Davis, Cincinnati, Los Angeles, 1984 through 1993.
A.L.—.833—Willie Wilson, Kansas City, Oakland, 1976 through 1992.

Most consecutive stolen bases with no caught stealing, career
N.L.—50—Vince Coleman, St. Louis, September 18, 1988 through July 26, 1989.
A.L.—32
Willie Wilson, Kansas City, July 23 through September 23, 1980.
Julio Cruz, Seattle, September 22, 1980 through June 11, 1981.

Most stolen bases, season
A.A.—156—Harry Stovey, Philadelphia, 130 games, 1888.
A.L.—130—Rickey Henderson, Oakland, 149 games, 1982 (42 caught stealing).
N.L.—118—Lou Brock, St. Louis, 153 games, 1974 (33 caught stealing).

Most stolen bases by rookie, season
N.L.—110—Vince Coleman, St. Louis, 151 games, 1985.
A.A.—98—Mike Griffin, Baltimore, 136 games, 1887.
A.L.—66—Kenny Lofton, Cleveland, 148 games, 1992.

Most stolen bases with no caught stealing, season
N.L.—21—Kevin McReynolds, New York, 147 games, 1988.
A.L.—20—Paul Molitor, Toronto, 115 games, 1994.

Most years leading league in stolen bases
A.L.—11—Rickey Henderson, Oakland, New York, 1980 through 1991, except 1987.
N.L.—10—Max Carey, Pittsburgh, 1913, 1915, 1916, 1917, 1918, 1920, 1922, 1923, 1924, 1925.

Most consecutive years leading league in stolen bases
A.L.—9—Luis Aparicio, Chicago, Baltimore, 1956 through 1964.
N.L.—6
Maury Wills, Los Angeles, 1960 through 1965.
Vince Coleman, St. Louis, 1985 through 1990.

Most years with 50 or more stolen bases
N.L.—12—Lou Brock, St. Louis, 1965 through 1976.
A.L.—11—Rickey Henderson, Oakland, New York, Toronto, 1980 through 1993, except 1987 and 1992.

Most consecutive years with 50 or more stolen bases
N.L.—12—Lou Brock, St. Louis, 1965 through 1976.
A.L.—7—Rickey Henderson, Oakland, New York, 1980 through 1986.

Fewest stolen bases for leader, season
A.L.—15—Dom DiMaggio, Boston, 141 games, 1950.
N.L.—16—Stan Hack, Chicago, 152 games, 1938.

Most at-bats with no stolen bases, season
A.L.—677—Don Mattingly, New York, 162 games, 1986 (0 caught stealing).
N.L.—662—Pete Rose, Cincinnati, 162 games, 1975 (1 caught stealing).

Most years with no stolen bases (150 or more games)
M.L.—4
Deron Johnson, Cincinnati N.L., Philadelphia N.L., Chicago A.L.,
Boston A.L., 1965, 1970, 1971, 1975 (3 in N.L., 1 in A.L.).
Ken Singleton, Baltimore A.L., 1977, 1980, 1982, 1983.
Cecil Fielder, Detroit A.L., 1990, 1991, 1992, 1993.
A.L.—4
Ken Singleton, Baltimore, 1977, 1980, 1982, 1983.
Cecil Fielder, Detroit A.L., 1990, 1991, 1992, 1993.
N.L.—3
Dal Maxvill, St. Louis, 1967, 1968, 1970.
Deron Johnson, Cincinnati, Philadelphia, 1965, 1970, 1971.

Most stolen bases, game
N.L.—7
George Gore, Chicago, June 25, 1881.*
Billy Hamilton, Philadelphia, August 31, 1894, second game.
A.L.—6—Eddie Collins, Philadelphia, September 11, 1912; also September 22, 1912, first game.
N.L. since 1900—6—Otis Nixon, Atlanta, June 16, 1991.
*Stolen bases not officially compiled until 1886.

Most stolen bases, two consecutive games
N.L.—8—Walt Wilmot, Chicago, August 6 (4), August 7 (4), 1894.
A.L.—7
Eddie Collins, Philadelphia, September 10 (1), September 11 (6), 1912.
Amos Otis, Kansas City, April 30 (3), May 1 (4), 1975, 13 innings.
Rickey Henderson, Oakland, July 3 (4), 15 innings, July 4 (3), 1983.

Most stolen bases, inning
N.L.—3—Held by many players. Last player—Dusty Baker, San Francisco, June 27, 1984, third inning.
A.L.—3—Held by many players. Last player—Devon White, California, September 9, 1989, sixth inning.

Most stolen bases by pinch-runner, inning
N.L.—2
Bill O'Hara, New York, September 1, 1909, sixth inning.
Bill O'Hara, New York, September 2, 1909, ninth inning.
Sandy Piez, New York, July 6, 1914, second game, ninth inning.
Jake Pitler, Pittsburgh, May 24, 1918, ninth inning.
Dave Concepcion, Cincinnati, July 7, 1974, first game, seventh inning.
Ron LeFlore, Montreal, October 5, 1980, eighth inning.
A.L.—2
Ray Dowd, Philadelphia, July 9, 1919, second game, ninth inning.
Allan Lewis, Kansas City, July 15, 1967, seventh inning.
Bert Campaneris, Oakland, October 4, 1972, fourth inning.
Don Hopkins, Oakland, April 20, 1975, second game, seventh inning.

Appearing as a pinch-runner and pinch-hitter in the same game (different innings)
A.L.—Pat Collins, St. Louis, June 8, 1923 (pinch-runner in third inning, pinch-hitter in ninth inning).

STEALS OF HOME

Most times stole home, career
A.L.—50—Ty Cobb, Detroit, Philadelphia, 24 years, 1905 through 1928.
N.L.—33—Max Carey, Pittsburgh, Brooklyn, 20 years, 1910 through 1929.

Most times stole home, season
A.L.—8—Ty Cobb, Detroit, 140 games, 1912 (61 stolen bases).
N.L.—7—Pete Reiser, Brooklyn, 122 games, 1946 (34 stolen bases).

Most times stole way from first to home in an inning, career

A.L.—4—Ty Cobb, Detroit, 1909, 1911, 1912 (2).
N.L.—3—Honus Wagner, Pittsburgh, 1902, 1907, 1909.
N.L.—Last player—Dusty Baker, San Francisco, June 27, 1984, third inning.
A.L.—Last player—Devon White, California, September 9, 1989, sixth inning.

Most times stole home, game

N.L.—2
  Honus Wagner, Pittsburgh, June 20, 1901.
  Ed Konetchy, St. Louis, September 30, 1907.
  Joe Tinker, Chicago, June 28, 1910.
  Larry Doyle, New York, September 18, 1911.
  Sherry Magee, Philadelphia, July 20, 1912.
  Doc Gautreau, Boston, September 3, 1927, first game.
A.L.—2
  Joe Jackson, Cleveland, August 11, 1912.
  Guy Zinn, New York, August 15, 1912.
  Eddie Collins, Philadelphia, September 6, 1913.
  Bill Barrett, Chicago, May 1, 1924.
  Vic Power, Cleveland, August 14, 1958, 10 innings.

CAUGHT STEALING AND CAUGHT OFF BASE

Most caught stealing, career

N.L.—307—Lou Brock, Chicago, St. Louis, 19 years, 1961 through 1979.
A.L.—255—Rickey Henderson, Oakland, New York, Toronto, 16 years, 1979 through 1994.

Most caught stealing, season

A.L.—42—Rickey Henderson, Oakland, 149 games, 1982 (130 stolen bases).
N.L.—36—Miller Huggins, St. Louis, 148 games, 1914 (32 stolen bases).

Most caught stealing by rookie, season

N.L. (162-game season)—25—Vince Coleman, St. Louis, 151 games, 1985.
N.L. (154-game season)—18—Joe Rapp, New York, Philadelphia, 110 games, 1921.
A.L. (162-game season)—21—Mike Edwards, Oakland, 142 games, 1978.
A.L. (154-game season)—17—Lu Blue, Detroit, 153 games, 1921.

Most years leading league in caught stealing

N.L.—7
  Maury Wills, Los Angeles, Pittsburgh, Montreal, 1961, 1962 (tied), 1963, 1965, 1966, 1968, 1969.
  Lou Brock, Chicago, St. Louis, 1964, 1967, 1971, 1973, 1974, 1976, 1977 (tied).

A.L.—6—Minnie Minoso, Chicago, Cleveland, 1952, 1953, 1954, 1957, 1958, 1960.

Fewest caught stealing with 50 or more stolen bases, season

N.L.—2—Max Carey, Pittsburgh, 155 games, 1922, 51 stolen bases.
A.L.—8
  Luis Aparicio, Chicago, 153 games, 1960, 51 stolen bases.
  Bert Campaneris, Oakland, 135 games, 1969, 62 stolen bases.
  Amos Otis, Kansas City, 147 games, 1971, 52 stolen bases.
  Willie Wilson, Kansas City, 137 games, 1983, 59 stolen bases.
  Rickey Henderson, Oakland, Toronto, 134 games, 1993, 53 stolen bases.
  Vince Coleman, Kansas City, 104 games, 1994, 50 stolen bases.

Fewest caught stealing, season (150 or more games)

N.L.-A.L.—0—Held by many players.

Fewest caught stealing for leader, season

A.L.—9
  Hoot Evers, Detroit, 143 games, 1950.
  Jim Rivera, Chicago, 139 games, 1956.
N.L.—10—Willie Mays, New York, 152 games, 1956.

Most consecutive games with no caught stealing, career

M.L.—1,206—Gus Triandos, New York A.L., Baltimore A.L., Detroit A.L., Philadelphia N.L., Houston N.L., August 3, 1953 through August 15, 1965 (1 stolen base).
A.L.—1,079—Gus Triandos, New York, Baltimore, Detroit, August 3, 1953 through September 28, 1963 (1 stolen base).
N.L.—592—Frank Torre, Milwaukee, Philadelphia, April 20, 1956 through August 10, 1962 (4 stolen bases).

Most caught stealing, nine-inning game

N.L.-A.L.—3—Held by many players.

Most caught stealing, extra-inning game

N.L.—4—Robby Thompson, San Francisco, June 27, 1986, 12 innings.

Most caught off base, game

A.A.—3—John Stricker, Philadelphia, August 29, 1883.
N.L.—3—Ben Kauff, New York, May 26, 1916.

Most times out for being hit by batted ball, game

N.L.—2—Walt Wilmot, Chicago, September 30, 1890.
A.L.—2—Ernie Shore, Boston, July 28, 1917, second game.

Most caught stealing, inning

A.L.—2—Don Baylor, Baltimore, June 15, 1974, ninth inning.
N.L.—2
  Jim Morrison, Pittsburgh, June 15, 1987, eighth inning.
  Paul Noce, Chicago, June 26, 1987, third inning.
  Donell Nixon, San Francisco, July 6, 1988, sixth inning.
  Tony Fernandez, San Diego, June 26, 1992, fifth inning.

CLUB BASERUNNING

Most stolen bases, season

A.A.—638—Philadelphia, 137 games, 1887.
N.L.—426—New York, 136 games, 1893.
N.L. since 1900—347—New York, 154 games, 1911.
A.L.—341—Oakland, 161 games, 1976.

Most players with 50 or more stolen bases, season

A.L.—3—Oakland, 161 games, 1976. Bill North (75), Bert Campaneris (54), Don Baylor (52).
N.L.—3—San Diego, 163 games, 1980. Gene Richards (61), Ozzie Smith (57), Jerry Mumphrey (52).

Most years leading league in stolen bases (since 1900)

A.L.—30—Chicago.
N.L.—21
  Brooklyn-Los Angeles (12-Brooklyn, 9-Los Angeles).
  St. Louis.

Fewest stolen bases, season

A.L. (154-game season)—13—Washington, 154 games, 1957.
A.L. (162-game season)—18—Boston, 162 games, 1964.
N.L. (154-game season)—17—St. Louis, 157 games, 1949.
N.L. (162-game season)—22—San Francisco, 162 games, 1967.

Most stolen bases, game

A.A.—19—Philadelphia vs. Syracuse, April 22, 1890.
N.L.—17—New York vs. Pittsburgh, May 23, 1890.
A.L.—15—New York vs. St. Louis, September 28, 1911.
N.L. since 1900—11
  New York vs. Boston, June 20, 1912.
  St. Louis vs. Pittsburgh, August 13, 1916, second game, five innings.

Most stolen bases by both clubs, game

A.A.—21—Philadelphia 19, Syracuse 2, April 22, 1890.
N.L.—20—New York 17, Pittsburgh 3, May 23, 1890.
N.L. since 1900—16—New York 11, Boston 5, June 20, 1912.
A.L.—15
  New York 15, St. Louis 0, September 28, 1911.
  St. Louis 8, Detroit 7, October 1, 1916.

Most triple steals, game

A.L.—2—Philadelphia vs. Cleveland, July 25, 1930, first and fourth innings.
N.L.—1—Made in many games.

Most triples steals by both clubs, game

A.L.—2—Philadelphia 2, Cleveland 0, July 25, 1930.
N.L.—1—Made in many games.

Longest game without a stolen base

N.L.—26 innings—Boston vs. Brooklyn, May 1, 1920.
A.L.—24 innings
  Detroit vs. Philadelphia, July 21, 1945.
  Philadelphia vs. Detroit, July 21, 1945.

Longest game without a stolen base by either club

A.L.—24 innings—Detroit 0, Philadelphia 0, July 21, 1945.
N.L.—23 innings—San Francisco 0, New York 0, May 31, 1964, second game.

Most stolen bases, inning

A.L.—8—Washington vs. Cleveland, July 19, 1915, first inning.
N.L.—8—Philadelphia vs. New York, July 7, 1919, first game, ninth inning.

Most times stole home, season

A.L.—18—New York, 153 games, 1912 (245 stolen bases).
N.L.—17
  Chicago, 157 games, 1911 (214 stolen bases).
  New York, 154 games, 1912 (319 stolen bases).

Most times stole home, game

A.L.—3
  Chicago vs. St. Louis, July 2, 1909.
  New York vs. Philadelphia, April 17, 1915.
N.L.—3
  St. Louis vs. Boston, September 30, 1907.
  Chicago vs. Boston, August 23, 1909.
  New York vs. Pittsburgh, September 18, 1911.

Most times stole home by both clubs, game

A.L.—3
  Chicago 3, St. Louis 0, July 2, 1909.
  New York 3, Philadelphia 0, April 17, 1915.
  Detroit 2, St. Louis 1, April 22, 1924.
N.L.—3
  St. Louis 3, Boston 0, September 30, 1907.
  Chicago 3, Boston 0, August 23, 1909.
  New York 3, Pittsburgh 0, September 18, 1911.

Most times stole home, inning

N.L.—2—Made in many innings. Last time—St. Louis vs. Brooklyn, September 19, 1925, seventh inning.
A.L.—2—Made in many innings. Last time—Oakland vs. Kansas City, May 28, 1980, first inning.

Most caught stealing, season (since 1920)

N.L.—149—Chicago, 154 games, 1924.
A.L.—123—Oakland, 161 games, 1976.

Fewest caught stealing, season

N.L.—8—Milwaukee, 154 games, 1958 (26 stolen bases).
A.L.—11
  Kansas City, 155 games, 1960 (16 stolen bases).
  Cleveland, 161 games, 1961 (34 stolen bases).

Most caught stealing, game

N.L.—8—Baltimore vs. Washington, May 11, 1897.
N.L. since 1900—7—St. Louis vs. Brooklyn, August 23, 1909, second game.
A.L.—6
  St. Louis vs. Philadelphia, May 12, 1915.
  Chicago vs. Philadelphia, June 18, 1915.

Most caught stealing, inning

A.A.—3—Cincinnati vs. Philadelphia, July 26, 1887, third inning.
A.L.—3—Detroit vs. New York, August 3, 1914, second inning.
N.L.—2—Made in many innings.

Most players caught off base, game

N.L.—5—Chicago vs. Brooklyn, June 24, 1901.
A.A.—3—Philadelphia vs. Louisville, August 29, 1883.
A.L.—3
  New York vs. Washington, June 29, 1910.
  Toronto vs. Baltimore, August 24, 1983.

Most left on base, season

A.L.—1,334—St. Louis, 157 games, 1941.
N.L. (162-game season)—1,328—Cincinnati, 162 games, 1976.
N.L. (154-game season)—1,278—Brooklyn, 155 games, 1947.

Fewest left on base, season

A.L. (154-game season)—925—Kansas City, 154 games, 1957.
A.L. (162-game season)—995—Kansas City, 160 games, 1966.
N.L. (154-game season)—964—Chicago, 154 games, 1924.

N.L. (162-game season)—978—Colorado, 162 games, 1993.

Most left on base, nine-inning game

A.L.—20—New York vs. Boston, September 21, 1956.
A.A.—18—Baltimore vs. Cincinnati, July 7, 1891.
N.L.—18
  Boston vs. Baltimore, August 15, 1897.
  Pittsburgh vs. Cincinnati, September 8, 1905.
  Boston vs. St. Louis, July 11, 1923.
  St. Louis vs. Philadelphia, September 15, 1928, second
    game.
  New York vs. Philadelphia, August 7, 1943.
  St. Louis vs. Cincinnati, June 10, 1944.
  St. Louis vs. Philadelphia, September 14, 1950.
  Pittsburgh vs. Boston, June 5, 1951.
  Atlanta vs. Los Angeles, June 23, 1986.

Most left on base, nine-inning shutout defeat

N.L.—16—St. Louis vs. Philadelphia, May 24, 1994.
A.L.—15
  New York vs. St. Louis, May 22, 1913.
  Washington vs. Cleveland, July 29, 1931.
  St. Louis vs. New York, August 1, 1941.
  Kansas City vs. Detroit, May 12, 1975.

Most left on base, extra-inning shutout defeat

N.L.—16—St. Louis vs. Cincinnati, August 30, 1989, 13 innings.
A.L.—Less than nine-inning record.

Most left on base by both clubs, nine-inning game

N.L.—30
  Brooklyn 16, Pittsburgh 14, June 30, 1893.
  New York 17, Philadelphia 13, July 18, 1943, first game.
A.L.—30
  New York 15, Chicago 15, August 27, 1935, first game.
  Los Angeles 15, Washington 15, July 21, 1961.

Most left on base, extra-inning game

N.L.—27—Atlanta vs. Philadelphia, May 4, 1973, 20 innings.
A.L.—25—Kansas City vs. Texas, June 6, 1991, 18 innings.

Most left on base by both clubs, extra-inning game

N.L.—45—New York 25, St. Louis 20, September 11, 1974, 25
  innings.
A.L.—45—Kansas City 25, Texas 20, June 6, 1991, 18 innings.

Fewest left on base, nine-inning game

A.L.-N.L.—0—Made in many games.

Fewest left on base, extra-inning game

A.L.—0—Philadelphia vs. New York, June 22, 1929, second
  game, 14 innings.
N.L.—No game over nine innings with none left on base.

Fewest left on base by both clubs, extra-inning game

N.L.—3—Chicago 2, Cincinnati 1, May 2, 1917, 10 innings.
A.L.—4—Made in many games.

Fewest left on base by both clubs, nine-inning game

N.L.—1—Los Angeles 1, Chicago 0, September 9, 1965.
A.L.—2—Made in many games. Last time—Cleveland 1,
  Oakland 1, July 19, 1974.

Fewest left on base, two consecutive games

A.L.—2
  Washington, May 27 (2), May 29 (0), 1952, 18 innings.
  Chicago vs. California, September 18 (1), September 19
    (1), 1971, 17 innings.
N.L.—2
  San Francisco, May 6 (2), May 7 (0), 1960, 16 innings.
  San Francisco, June 13 (1), 10 innings, June 14 (1), 8 in-
    nings, 1963, 18 innings.

Most left on base, doubleheader (18 innings)

A.L.—30—Philadelphia vs. St. Louis, June 12, 1949.
N.L.—29
  St. Louis vs. Philadelphia, September 15, 1928.
  Philadelphia vs. Milwaukee, May 15, 1955.

Most left on base, doubleheader (more than 18 innings)

A.L.—34—Cleveland vs. New York, August 18, 1943, 21⅓
  innings.
N.L.—30
  Pittsburgh vs. Brooklyn, June 4, 1946, 20 innings.
  Philadelphia vs. Brooklyn, May 30, 1950, 19 innings.

Most left on base by both clubs, doubleheader (18 innings)

N.L.—49—Brooklyn 25, Pittsburgh 24, July 24, 1926.
A.L.—49—New York 27, Chicago 22, August 27, 1935.

Fewest left on base, doubleheader

A.L.—3—Washington vs. New York, August 6, 1963, 17 innings.
N.L.—3—San Francisco vs. Houston, September 24, 1978, 16
  innings.

Fewest left on base by both clubs, doubleheader

N.L.—10—St. Louis 6, Boston 4, July 19, 1924.
A.L.—13—Chicago 9, Philadelphia 4, July 18, 1918.

LEAGUE BASERUNNING

STOLEN BASES

Most stolen bases, season (since 1900)

N.L. (12-club league) — 1,851 in 1987.
N.L. (14-club league) — 1,714 in 1993.
N.L. (8-club league) — 1,691 in 1911.
A.L. — 1,810 in 1912.

Fewest stolen bases, season (since 1900)

A.L. (8-club league) — 278 in 1950.
A.L. (12-club league) — 863 in 1970.
N.L. (8-club league) — 337 in 1954.
N.L. (12-club league) — 817 in 1969.

CAUGHT STEALING

Most caught stealing, season

A.L. (14-club league) — 936 in 1977.
A.L. (12-club league) — 867 in 1976.
A.L. (8-club league) — 707 in 1920.
N.L. (12-club league) — 870 in 1983.
N.L. (8-club league) — 517 in 1925.

Fewest caught stealing, season

N.L. (8-club league) — 218 in 1953.

N.L. (10-club league) — 409 in 1962.
N.L. (12-club league) — 492 in 1971.
A.L. (8-club league) — 231 in 1950.
A.L. (10-club league) — 270 in 1963.
A.L. (12-club league) — 539 in 1972.

LEFT ON BASE

Most left on base, season (since 1900)

A.L. (14-club league) — 16,238 in 1993.
A.L. (12-club league) — 13,925 in 1973.
A.L. (10-club league) — 11,680 in 1961.
A.L. (8-club league) — 9,628 in 1936.
N.L. (14-club league) — 15,941 in 1993.
N.L. (12-club league) — 14,468 in 1975.
N.L. (10-club league) — 11,416 in 1962.
N.L. (8-club league) — 9,424 in 1945.

Fewest left on base, season (since 1900)

N.L. (8-club league) — 8,254 in 1920.
N.L. (10-club league) — 10,994 in 1966.
N.L. (12-club league) — 13,295 in 1988.
A.L. (8-club league) — 8,619 in 1958.
A.L. (10-club league) — 10,668 in 1966.
A.L. (12-club league) — 13,494 in 1976.

INDIVIDUAL PITCHING

Most games pitched, career

M.L.—1,070—Hoyt Wilhelm, New York N.L., St. Louis N.L., Cleveland A.L., Baltimore A.L., Chicago A.L., California A.L., Atlanta N.L., Chicago N.L., Los Angeles N.L., 21 years, 1952 through 1972 (448 in N.L., 622 in A.L.).

N.L.—1,050—Kent Tekulve, Pittsburgh, Philadelphia, Cincinnati, 16 years, 1974 through 1989.

A.L.—807—Sparky Lyle, Boston, New York, Texas, Chicago, 15 years, 1967 through 1982, except 1981.

Most games pitched with one club

A.L.—802—Walter Johnson, Washington, 21 years, 1907 through 1927.

N.L.—802—Roy Face, Pittsburgh, 15 years, 1953 through 1968, except 1954.

Most complete doubleheaders pitched, career

M.L.—5—Joe McGinnity, Baltimore A.L., 1901 (2); New York N.L., 1903 (3).

N.L.—3—Joe McGinnity, New York, 1903.

A.L.—2—Held by many pitchers.

Most games pitched, season

N.L.—106—Mike G. Marshall, Los Angeles, 1974 (208 innings).

A.L.—90—Mike G. Marshall, Minnesota, 1979 (143 innings).

Most games pitched by rookie, season

A.L.—80—Mitch Williams, Texas, 1986 (0 complete, 98 innings).

N.L.—78—Tim Burke, Montreal, 1985 (0 complete, 120 ⅓ innings).

Most years leading league in games

M.L.—7—Joe McGinnity, Brooklyn N.L., Baltimore A.L., New York N.L., 1900, 1901, 1903, 1904, 1905, 1906, 1907.

N.L.—6—Joe McGinnity, Brooklyn, New York, 1900, 1903, 1904, 1905, 1906, 1907.

A.L.—6—Fred Marberry, Washington, 1924, 1925, 1926, 1928, 1929, 1932.

Fewest games pitched by leader, season

A.L.—40—Joe Haynes, Chicago, 1942 (103 innings).

N.L.—41

Ray Kremer, Pittsburgh, 1924 (259 innings).
Johnny Morrison, Pittsburgh, 1924 (238 innings).

Most complete doubleheaders pitched, season

N.L.—3—Joe McGinnity, New York, August 1, 8, 31, 1903 (won 3).

A.L.—2

Joe McGinnity, Baltimore, 1901 (split 2).
Mule Watson, Philadelphia, 1918 (split 1, lost 1 game and tied 1 in other doubleheader).

Most times pitched opening game of season

M.L.—16—Tom Seaver, New York N.L., Cincinnati N.L., Chicago A.L., 1968 through 1979, 1981 1983, 1985, 1986 (14 in N.L., 2 in A.L.; won seven, lost two).

N.L.—15—Steve Carlton, St. Louis, Philadelphia, 1965, 1972 through 1986, except 1976, 1978 to 1979, 1981 (won three, lost nine).

A.L.—14—Walter Johnson, Washington, 1910 through 1926, except 1911, 1922, 1925 (won nine, lost five).

Most games started, career

M.L.—818—Cy Young, Cleveland N.L., St. Louis N.L., Boston A.L., Cleveland A.L., Boston N.L., 22 years, 1890 through 1911 (460 in N.L., 358 in A.L.).

N.L.—677—Steve Carlton, St. Louis, Philadelphia, San Francisco, 22 years, 1965 through 1986.

A.L.—666—Walter Johnson, Washington, 21 years, 1907 through 1927.

Most season-opening games started

M.L.—16—Tom Seaver, New York N.L., Cincinnati N.L., Chicago A.L., 1968 through 1979, 1981, 1983, 1985, 1986 (14 in N.L., 2 in A.L.).

A.L.—14—Walter Johnson, Washington, 1910 through 1926, except 1911, 1922, 1925.

N.L.—14

Tom Seaver, New York, Cincinnati, 1968 through 1979, 1981, 1983.

Steve Carlton, Philadelphia, 1972 through 1986, except 1976.

Most consecutive starting assignments, career (since 1900)

M.L.—595—Nolan Ryan, California A.L., Houston N.L., Texas A.L., July 30, 1974 through 1993 (313 in A.L., 282 in N.L.).

N.L.—534—Steve Carlton, St. Louis, Philadelphia, San Francisco, May 15, 1971 through 1986.

A.L.—515—Jack Morris, Detroit, Minnesota, Toronto, Cleveland, September 30, 1978 through 1994.

Most games started, season

N.L.—74—Will White, Cincinnati, 1879 (pitched 75 games).

A.L.—51—Jack Chesbro, New York, 1904 (pitched 55 games).

N.L. since 1900—48—Joe McGinnity, New York, 1903 (pitched 55 games).

Most years leading league in games started

N.L.—6—Robin Roberts, Philadelphia, 1950 (tied), 1951, 1952, 1953, 1954, 1955.

A.L.—5

Bob Feller, Cleveland, 1940, 1941, 1946, 1947, 1948.
Early Wynn, Washington, Cleveland, Chicago, 1943 (tied), 1951 (tied), 1954, 1957, 1959 (tied).

Most games started with none complete, season

N.L.—37—Steve Bedrosian, Atlanta, 1985.

A.L.—34—Kirk McCaskill, Chicago, 1992.

Most games taken out as starting pitcher, season

N.L.—37—Steve Bedrosian, Atlanta, 1985 (started 37).

A.L.—36—Stan Bahnsen, Chicago, 1972 (started 41).

Most games as relief pitcher, career

N.L.—1,050—Kent Tekulve, Pittsburgh, Philadelphia, Cincinnati, 16 years, 1974 through 1989.

A.L.—807—Sparky Lyle, Boston, New York, Texas, Chicago, 15 years, 1967 through 1982, except 1981.

Most consecutive appearances as relief pitcher, career

N.L.—1,050—Kent Tekulve, Pittsburgh, Philadelphia, Cincinnati, May 20, 1974 through July 16, 1989.

A.L.—807—Sparky Lyle, Boston, New York, Texas, Chicago, July 4, 1967 through September 9, 1980; August 23, 1982 through September 27, second game, 1982.

Most games pitched, none of which were starts, career

N.L.—1,050—Kent Tekulve, Pittsburgh, Philadelphia, Cincinnati, May 20, 1974 through July 16, 1989.

A.L.—807—Sparky Lyle, Boston, New York, Texas, Chicago, July 4, 1967 through September 9, 1980; August 23, 1982 through September 27, second game, 1982.

Most games as relief pitcher, season

N.L.—106—Mike G. Marshall, Los Angeles, 1974 (started none, 208 innings).

A.L.—89

Mike G. Marshall, Minnesota, 1979 (141 innings; also started one game—two innings).

Mark Eichhorn, Toronto, 1987, started none (127 ⅔ innings).

Most games pitched, none of which were starts, season

N.L.—106—Mike G. Marshall, Los Angeles, 1974 (finished 83, 208 innings).

A.L.—89—Mark Eichhorn, Toronto, 1987 (finished 27, 127⅔ innings).

Most consecutive games pitched as relief pitcher

N.L.—13—Mike G. Marshall, Los Angeles, June 18 through July 3, first game, 1974 (26 ⅔ innings).

A.L.—13—Dale Mohorcic, Texas, August 6 through 20, 1986 (14 innings).

GAMES FINISHED

Most games finished, career

M.L.—709—Rollie Fingers, Oakland A.L., San Diego N.L., Milwaukee A.L., 17 years, 1968 through 1985, except 1983 (491 in A.L., 218 in N.L.).

N.L.—638—Kent Tekulve, Pittsburgh, Philadelphia, Cincinnati, 16 years, 1974 through 1989.

A.L.—599—Sparky Lyle, Boston, New York, Texas, Chicago, 15 years, 1967 through 1982, except 1981.

Most games finished, season

A.L.—84—Mike G. Marshall, Minnesota, 1979 (90 games).

N.L.—83—Mike G. Marshall, Los Angeles 1974 (106 games).

Most years leading league in games finished

M.L.—5
Fred Marberry, Washington, 1924, 1925, 1926, 1928, 1929.
Mike G. Marshall, Montreal N.L., Los Angeles N.L., 1971, 1972, 1973, 1974, Minnesota A.L., 1979.

A.L.—5—Fred Marberry, Washington, 1924, 1925, 1926, 1928, 1929.

N.L.—4
Ace Adams, New York, 1942, 1943, 1944, 1945.
Roy Face, Pittsburgh, 1958, 1960, 1961, 1962.
Mike G. Marshall, Montreal, Los Angeles, 1971, 1972, 1973, 1974.

COMPLETE GAMES

Most complete games, career

M.L.—751—Cy Young, Cleveland N.L., St. Louis N.L., Boston A.L., Cleveland A.L., Boston N.L., 22 years, 1890 through 1911 (428 in N.L., 323 in A.L.).

N.L.—557—Pud Galvin, Buffalo, Pittsburgh, St. Louis 12 years, 1879 through 1892, except 1886, 1890.

A.L.—531—Walter Johnson, Washington, 21 years, 1907 through 1927.

N.L. since 1900—436—Grover Alexander, Philadelphia, Chicago, St. Louis, 20 years, 1911 through 1930.

Most complete games by righthander, career

N.L.—557—Pud Galvin, Buffalo, Pittsburgh, St. Louis 12 years, 1879 through 1892, except 1886, 1890.

A.L.—531—Walter Johnson, Washington, 21 years, 1907 through 1927.

N.L. since 1900—436—Grover Alexander, Philadelphia, Chicago, St. Louis, 20 years, 1911 through 1930.

Most complete games by lefthander, career

A.L.—387—Eddie Plank, Philadelphia, St. Louis, 16 years, 1901 through 1917, except 1915.

N.L.—382—Warren Spahn, Boston, Milwaukee, New York, San Francisco, 21 years, 1942 through 1965, except 1943, 1944, 1945 in military service.

Most complete games, season

N.L.—74—Will White, Cincinnati, 1879; pitched in 75 games.

A.L.—48—Jack Chesbro, New York, 1904; pitched in 55 games.

N.L. since 1900—45—Vic Willis, Boston, 1902; pitched in 51 games.

Most consecutive complete games pitched, season (since 1900)

N.L.—39—Jack W. Taylor, St. Louis, April 15 through Octo-

ber 6, first game, 1904 (352 innings, including two games finished in relief).

A.L.—37—Bill Dinneen, Boston, April 16 through October 10, first game, 1904 (337 innings).

Most years leading league in complete games

N.L.—9—Warren Spahn, Boston, Milwaukee, 1949, 1951, 1957, 1958, 1959, 1960 (tied), 1961, 1962, 1963.

A.L.—6—Walter Johnson, Washington, 1910, 1911, 1913, 1914, 1915, 1916.

Most complete games by rookie, season

N.L.—67—Jim Devlin, Louisville, 1876 (67 games).

N.L. since 1900—41—Irv Young, Boston, 1905 (43 games).

A.L.—36—Roscoe Miller, Detroit, 1901 (38 games).

Fewest complete games for leader, season

N.L.—8—Greg Maddux, Atlanta, 1993.

A.L.—11
Jack Morris, Detroit, 1990.
Dave Stewart, Oakland, 1990.

Most games pitched, none of which were complete, season

N.L.—106—Mike G. Marshall, Los Angeles, 1974, started none (208 innings).

A.L.—90—Mike G. Marshall, Minnesota, 1979, started one (143 innings).

INNINGS

Most innings pitched, career

M.L.—7,377—Cy Young, Cleveland N.L., St. Louis N.L., Boston A.L., Cleveland A.L., Boston N.L., 22 years, 1890 through 1911 (4,143 in N.L., 3,234 in A.L.).

A.L.—5,924—Walter Johnson, Washington, 21 years, 1907 through 1927.

N.L.—5,246—Warren Spahn, Boston, Milwaukee, New York, San Francisco, 21 years, 1942 through 1965, except 1943, 1944, 1945 in military service.

Most consecutive innings without relief, career (since 1900)

N.L.—1,727—Jack W. Taylor, Chicago, St. Louis, June 20, 1901, second game, through August 9, 1906 (203 games, 188 complete games, 15 finished).

Most innings as relief pitcher, career

M.L.—1,870—Hoyt Wilhelm, New York N.L., St. Louis N.L., Cleveland A.L., Baltimore A.L., Chicago A.L., California A.L., Atlanta N.L., Chicago N.L., Los Angeles N.L., 21 years, 1952 through 1972 (916 in N.L., 954 in A.L.).

N.L.—1,436⅓—Kent Tekulve, Pittsburgh, Philadelphia, Cincinnati, 16 years, 1974 through 1989.

A.L.—1,265—Sparky Lyle, Boston, New York, Texas, Chicago, 15 years, 1967 through 1982, except 1981.

Most years leading league in innings pitched

N.L.—7—Grover Alexander, Philadelphia, Chicago, 1911, 1912 (tied), 1914, 1915, 1916, 1917, 1920.

A.L.—5
Walter Johnson, Washington, 1910, 1913, 1914, 1915, 1916.
Bob Feller, Cleveland, 1939, 1940, 1941, 1946, 1947.

Most innings pitched, season

N.L.—683—Will White, Cincinnati, 75 games, 1879.

A.L.—464—Ed Walsh, Chicago, 66 games, 1908.

N.L. since 1900—434—Joe McGinnity, New York, 55 games, 1903.

Most innings pitched by rookie, season (since 1900)

N.L.—378—Irv Young, Boston, 43 games, 1905.

A.L.—316—Reb Russell, Chicago, 43 games, 1913.

Most innings pitched as relief pitcher, season

N.L.—208—Mike G. Marshall, Los Angeles, 1974, pitched 106 games as relief pitcher.

A.L.—168 ⅓—Bob Stanley, Boston, 1982, pitched 48 games as relief pitcher. (Bill Campbell, Minnesota, hurled 167⅔ innings, rounded to 168, as a relief pitcher in 1976.)

Fewest innings pitched by leader, season
N.L.—249 ⅔—Frank Viola, New York, 35 games, 1990.
A.L.—256—Early Wynn, Chicago, 37 games, 1959.

Most consecutive innings without relief, season (since 1900)
N.L.—352—Jack W. Taylor, St. Louis, April 15 through October 6, first game, 1904 (complete season, 39 complete games and two games finished).
A.L.—337—Bill Dinneen, Boston, April 16 through October 10, first game, 1904 (complete season, 37 complete games).

Most years with 200 or more innings pitched
M.L.—19
Cy Young, Cleveland N.L., St. Louis N.L., Boston A.L., Cleveland A.L., 1891 through 1909 (10 in N.L., 9 in A.L.).
Phil Niekro, Milwaukee, N.L., Atlanta N.L., New York A.L., Cleveland A.L., 1967 through 1986, except 1981 (16 in N.L., 3 in A.L.).
A.L.—18—Walter Johnson, Washington, 1908 through 1926, except 1920.
N.L.—17—Warren Spahn, Boston, Milwaukee, 1947 through 1963.

Most years with 300 or more innings pitched
M.L.—16—Cy Young, Cleveland N.L., St. Louis N.L., Boston A.L., 1891 through 1907, except 1906 (10 in N.L., 6 in A.L.).
N.L.—12—Kid Nichols, Boston, 1890 through 1899, 1901, 1904.
N.L. since 1900—11—Christy Mathewson, New York, 1901, 1903, 1904, 1905, 1907, 1908, 1910, 1911, 1912, 1913, 1914.
A.L.—9—Walter Johnson, Washington, 1910 through 1918.

Most consecutive years with 300 or more innings (since 1900)
A.L.—9—Walter Johnson, Washington, 1910 through 1918.
N.L.—7—Grover Alexander, Philadelphia, 1911 through 1917.

Most years with 400 or more innings pitched (since 1900)
N.L.—2—Joe McGinnity, New York, 1903 (434), 1904 (408).
A.L.—2—Ed Walsh, Chicago, 1907 (419), 1908 (464).

Most innings pitched, game
N.L.—26
Leon Cadore, Brooklyn, May 1, 1920 (1-1 tie).
Joe Oeschger, Boston, May 1, 1920 (1-1 tie).
A.L.—24
Jack Coombs, Philadelphia, September 1, 1906 (won 4-1).
Joe Harris, Boston, September 1, 1906 (lost 4-1).

Most innings pitched as relief pitcher finishing game
N.L.—18 ⅓—George Zabel, Chicago, June 17, 1915 (Chicago 4, Brooklyn 3, 19 innings).
A.L.—17—Eddie Rommel, Philadelphia, July 10, 1932 (Philadelphia 18, Cleveland 17, 18 innings).

WINNING PERCENTAGE

Highest percentage of games won, career (200 or more decisions)
A.L.—.690—Whitey Ford, New York, 16 years, 1950 through 1967, except 1951, 1952 in military service (won 236 lost 106).
N.L.—.665—Christy Mathewson, New York, Cincinnati, 17 years, 1900 through 1916 (won 373, lost 188).

Highest percentage of games won, season (70 or more decisions)
N.L.—.833—Hoss Radbourn, Providence, 1884 (won 60, lost 12).

Highest percentage of games won, season (34 or more decisions)
A.L.—.886—Lefty Grove, Philadelphia, 1931 (won 31, lost 4).
N.L.—.842
Jack Chesbro, Pittsburgh, 1902 (won 28, lost 6).
Dazzy Vance, Brooklyn, 1924 (won 28, lost 6).

Highest percentage of games won, season (20 or more victories)
A.L.—.893—Ron Guidry, New York, 1978 (won 25, lost 3).
N.L.—.880
Fred Goldsmith, Chicago, 1880 (won 22, lost 3).
Preacher Roe, Brooklyn, 1951 (won 22 lost 3).

Highest percentage of games won, season (16 or more decisions)
N.L.—.947—Roy Face, Pittsburgh, 1959 (won 18, lost 1).
A.L.—.938—Johnny Allen, Cleveland, 1937 (won 15, lost 1).

Most years leading league in winning percentage (15 or more victories)
A.L.—5—Lefty Grove, Philadelphia, Boston, 1929, 1930, 1931, 1933, 1939.
N.L.—3—Ed Reulbach, Chicago, 1906, 1907, 1908.

GAMES WON

CAREER

Most games won, career
M.L.—511—Cy Young, Cleveland N.L., St. Louis N.L., Boston A.L., Cleveland A.L., Boston N.L., 22 years, 1890 through 1911 (289 in N.L., 222 in A.L.).

Most games won by righthander, career
A.L.—416—Walter Johnson, Washington, 21 years, 1907 through 1927.
N.L.—373
Christy Mathewson, New York, Cincinnati, 17 years, 1900 through 1916.
Grover Alexander, Philadelphia, Chicago, St. Louis, 20 years, 1911 through 1930.

Most games won by lefthander, career
N.L.—363—Warren Spahn, Boston, Milwaukee, New York, San Francisco, 21 years, 1942 through 1965, except 1943, 1944, 1945 in military service.
A.L.—305—Eddie Plank, Philadelphia, St. Louis 16 years, 1901 through 1971, except 1915.

Most games won as relief pitcher, career
M.L.—124—Hoyt Wilhelm, New York N.L., St. Louis N.L., Cleveland A.L., California A.L., Atlanta N.L., Baltimore A.L., Chicago A.L., Chicago N.L., Los Angeles N.L., 21 years, 1952 through 1972 (73 in A.L., 51 in N.L.).
N.L.—96—Roy Face, Pittsburgh, Montreal, 16 years, 1953 through 1969, except 1954 (lost 82).
A.L.—87—Sparky Lyle, Boston, New York, Texas, Chicago, 15 years, 1967 through 1982, except 1981 (lost 67).

Most games won from one club, career
N.L.—70—Grover Alexander, Philadelphia, Chicago, St. Louis, vs. Cincinnati, 20 years, 1911 through 1930.
A.L.—66—Walter Johnson, Washington, vs. Detroit, 21 years, 1907 through 1927.

Most season-opening games won, career
A.L.—9—Walter Johnson, Washington, 1910, 1913, 1914, 1915, 1916, 1917, 1919, 1924, 1926 (all complete; seven shutouts).
N.L.—8—Grover Alexander, Philadelphia, Chicago, St. Louis, 1914, 1915, 1916, 1917, 1921, 1922, 1925, 1929 (seven complete; one shutout).

SEASON AND MONTH

Most games won by righthander, season
N.L.—60—Hoss Radbourn, Providence, 1884 (lost 12).
A.L.—41—Jack Chesbro, New York, 1904 (lost 13).
N.L. since 1900—37—Christy Mathewson, New York, 1908 (lost 11).

Most games won by lefthander, season
N.L.—42—Charles Baldwin, Detroit, 1886 (lost 14).
A.L.—31—Lefty Grove, Philadelphia, 1931 (lost 4).
N.L. since 1900—27
Sandy Koufax, Los Angeles, 1966 (lost 9).
Steve Carlton, Philadelphia, 1972 (lost 10).

Most games won as relief pitcher, season
N.L.—18—Roy Face, Pittsburgh, 1959 (lost 1).
A.L.—17
John Hiller, Detroit, 1974 (lost 14).
Bill Campbell, Minnesota, 1976 (lost 5).

Fewest games won by leader, season

A.L.—18
Whitey Ford, New York, 1955 (lost 7).
Bob Lemon, Cleveland, 1955 (lost 10).
Frank Sullivan, Boston, 1955 (lost 13).
Chuck Estrada, Baltimore, 1960 (lost 11).
Jim Perry, Cleveland, 1960 (lost 10).
N.L.—18—Rick Sutcliffe, Chicago, 1987 (lost 10).

Most years leading league in games won

N.L.—8—Warren Spahn, Boston, Milwaukee, 1949, 1950, 1953 (tied), 1957, 1958 (tied), 1959 (tied), 1960 (tied), 1961 (tied).
A.L.—6
Walter Johnson, Washington, 1913, 1914, 1915, 1916, 1918, 1924.
Bob Feller, Cleveland, 1939, 1940, 1941, 1946 (tied), 1947, 1951.

Most games won by rookie, season

N.L.—47—Al Spalding, Chicago, 1876 (lost 13).
N.L. since 1900—28—Grover Alexander, Philadelphia, 1911 (lost 13).
A.L.—24—Edgar Summers, Detroit, 1908 (lost 12).

Most games won from one club, season

N.L.—12—Hoss Radbourn, Providence vs. Cleveland, 1884.
N.L. since 1900—9—Ed Reulbach, Chicago vs. Brooklyn, 1908 (lost 0).
A.L.—9—Ed Walsh, Chicago vs. New York 1908 (lost 1), and vs. Boston, 1908 (lost 0).

Most games won, one month

N.L.—15—John Clarkson, Chicago, June 1885 (lost 1).
N.L. since 1900—9
Christy Mathewson, New York, August 1903 (lost 1).
Christy Mathewson, New York, August, 1904 (lost 1).
Grover Alexander, Chicago, May 1920 (lost 0).
A.L.—10—Rube Waddell, Philadelphia, July 1902 (lost 1, tied 1).

20 AND 30-WIN SEASONS

Most years winning 30 or more games

N.L.—7—Kid Nichols, Boston, 1891, 1892, 1893, 1894, 1896, 1897, 1898.
N.L. since 1900—4—Christy Mathewson, New York, 1903, 1904, 1905, 1908.
A.L.—2
Cy Young, Boston, 1901, 1902.
Walter Johnson, Washington, 1912, 1913.

Most years winning 20 or more games

M.L.—16—Cy Young, Cleveland N.L., 1891, 1892, 1893, 1894, 1895, 1896, 1897, 1898; St. Louis, N.L., 1899, 1900; Boston A.L., 1901, 1902, 1903, 1904, 1907, 1908 (10 in N.L., 6 in A.L.).

Most years winning 20 or more games by righthander

N.L.—13—Christy Mathewson, New York, 1901, 1903, 1904, 1905, 1906, 1907, 1908, 1909, 1910, 1911, 1912, 1913, 1914.
A.L.—12—Walter Johnson, Washington, 1910, 1911, 1912, 1913, 1914, 1915, 1916, 1917, 1918, 1919, 1924, 1925.

Most years winning 20 or more games by lefthander

N.L.—13—Warren Spahn, Boston, Milwaukee, 1947, 1949, 1950, 1951, 1953, 1954, 1956, 1957, 1958, 1959, 1960, 1961, 1963.
A.L.—8—Lefty Grove, Philadelphia, Boston, 1927, 1928, 1929, 1930, 1931, 1932, 1933, 1935.

Most consecutive years winning 20 or more games

M.L.—14—Cy Young, Cleveland N.L., St. Louis N.L. Boston A.L., 1891 through 1904 (10 in N.L., 4 in A.L.).
N.L.—12—Christy Mathewson, New York, 1903 through 1914.
A.L.—10—Walter Johnson, Washington, 1910 through 1919.

Most consecutive years winning 20 or more games from start of career

N.L.—10—Kid Nichols, Boston, 1890 through 1899.
A.L.—3—Vean Gregg, Cleveland, 1911, 1912, 1913.

| | DOUBLEHEADER | |

Most complete-game doubleheaders won, career

N.L.—3—Joe McGinnity, New York, 1903 (lost 0).
A.L.—2—Ed Walsh, Chicago, 1905, 1908 (lost 0).

Most complete-game doubleheaders won, season

N.L.—3—Joe McGinnity, New York, 1903.
A.L.—1—Held by many pitchers. Last pitcher—Dutch Levsen, Cleveland vs. Boston, August 28, 1926.

| | CONSECUTIVE | |

Most consecutive games won, career

N.L.—24—Carl Hubbell, New York, July 17, 1936, through May 27, 1937 (16 in 1936, 8 in 1937).
A.L.—17
Johnny Allen, Cleveland, September 10, 1936, through September 30, first game, 1937 (2 in 1936, 15 in 1937).
Dave McNally, September 22, 1968 through July 30, 1969 (2 in 1968, 15 in 1969).

Most consecutive games won from start of career as starting pitcher

N.L.—12—George Wiltse, New York, May 29 through September 15, 1904.
A.L.—9—Whitey Ford, New York, July 17 through September 24, second game, 1950.

Most consecutive games won from start of career as relief pitcher

N.L.—12—Butch Metzger, San Francisco, 1974 (1), San Diego, 1975 (1), 1976 (10), September 21, 1974 through August 8, 1976.
A.L.—9—Joe Pate, Philadelphia, April 15 through August 10, 1926.

Most consecutive games won from one club, career

N.L.—24—Christy Mathewson, New York, vs. St. Louis, June 16, 1904 through September 15, 1908.
A.L.—23—Carl Mays, Boston, New York, vs. Philadelphia, August 30, 1918, to July 24, 1923.

Most consecutive games won, season

N.L.—19
Tim Keefe, New York, June 23 through August 10, 1888.
Rube Marquard, New York, April 11 through July 3, first game, 1912.
A.L.—16
Walter Johnson, Washington, July 3, second game, through August 23, first game, 1912.
Joe Wood, Boston, July 8 through September 15, second game, 1912.
Lefty Grove, Philadelphia, June 8 through August 19, 1931.
Schoolboy Rowe, Detroit, June 15 through August 25, 1934.

Most consecutive games won by relief pitcher, season

N.L.—17—Roy Face, Pittsburgh, April 22, through August 30, second game, 1959.
A.L.—12—Luis Arroyo, New York, July 1 through September 9, 1961.

Most consecutive games won from start of season

N.L.—19—Rube Marquard, New York, April 11 through July 3, 1912, first game.
A.L.—15
Johnny Allen, Cleveland, April 23, 1937, through September 30, 1937, first game.
Dave McNally, Baltimore, April 12 through July 30, 1969.

Most consecutive games won by rookie, season

N.L.—17—Pat Luby, Chicago, August 6, second game, through October 3, 1890.
N.L. since 1900—12—George Wiltse, New York, May 29 through September 15, 1904.
A.L.—12
Atley Donald, New York, May 9 through July 25, 1939.

Russ Ford, New York, August 9 through October 6, 1910.

Most consecutive games won by rookie as starting pitcher, season

N.L.—17—Pat Luby, Chicago, August 6, second game, through October 3, 1890.

N.L. since 1900—12—George Wiltse, New York, May 29 through September 15, 1904.

A.L.—12—Atley Donald, New York, May 9 through July 25, 1939.

Most consecutive games won by rookie as relief pitcher, season

N.L.—10
Eddie Yuhas, St. Louis, June 5 through September 25, 1952 (end of season).
Butch Metzger, San Diego, April 20 through August 8, 1976.
A.L.—9—Joe Pate, Philadelphia, April 15 through August 10, 1926.

Most consecutive games won as relief pitcher, three consecutive games

A.L.—3
Hal White, Detroit, September 26, second game, 27 28, 1950, 5⅓ innings.
Grant Jackson, Baltimore, September 29, 30, October 1, 1974, 5⅓ innings.
Sparky Lyle, New York, August 29, 30, 31, 1977, 7⅔ innings.
N.L.—3
Mike G. Marshall, Los Angeles, June 21, 22, 23, 1974, 7 innings.
Gene Garber, Philadelphia, May 15, second game, 16, 17, 1975, 5⅔ innings.
Al Hrabosky, St. Louis, July 12, 13, 17, 1975, five innings.
Kent Tekulve, Pittsburgh, May 6, 7, 9, 1980, 5⅓ innings.

Most consecutive games won, end of season

N.L.—17—Pat Luby, Chicago, August 6, second game, through October 3, 1890.

N.L. since 1900—16—Carl Hubbell, New York, July 17 through September 23, 1936.

A.L.—15—Alvin Crowder, Washington, August 2 through September 25, 1932.

SAVES (SINCE 1969)

Most saves, career

M.L.—434—Lee Smith, Chicago N.L., Boston A.L., St. Louis N.L., New York A.L., Baltimore A.L., 15 years, 1980 through 1994 (340 in N.L., 94 in A.L.).

N.L.—340—Lee Smith, Chicago, St. Louis, 12 years, 1980 through 1987 and 1990 through 1993.

A.L.—294—Dennis Eckersley, Cleveland, Boston, Oakland, 18 years, 1975 through 1984, 1987 through 1994.

Most saves, season

A.L.—57—Bobby Thigpen, Chicago, 1990.
N.L.—53—Randy Myers, Chicago, 1993.

Most saves by rookie, season

N.L.—36—Todd Worrell, St. Louis, 1986.
A.L.—27—Gregg Olson, Baltimore, 1989.

GAMES LOST

Most games lost, career

M.L.—313—Cy Young, Cleveland, N.L., St. Louis, N.L., Boston, A.L., Cleveland A.L., Boston N.L., 22 years, 1890 through 1911 (172 in N.L., 141 in A.L.).

A.L.—279—Walter Johnson, Washington, 21 years, 1907 through 1927.

N.L.—268—Pud Galvin, Buffalo, Pittsburgh, St. Louis, 12 years, 1879 through 1892, except 1886 and 1890.

N.L. since 1900—251—Eppa Rixey, Philadelphia, Cincinnati, 21 years, 1912 through 1933, except 1918 in military service.

Most games lost by righthander, career

A.L.—279—Walter Johnson, Washington, 21 years, 1907 through 1927.

N.L.—268—Pud Galvin, Buffalo, Pittsburgh, St. Louis, 12 years, 1879 through 1892, except 1886 and 1890.

N.L. since 1900—230—Phil Niekro, Milwaukee, Atlanta, 21 years, 1964 through 1983, 1987.

Most games lost by lefthander, career

N.L.—251—Eppa Rixey, Philadelphia, Cincinnati, 21 years, 1912 through 1933, except 1918 in military service.

A.L.—191—Jim Kaat, Washington, Minnesota, Chicago, New York, 19 years, 1959 through 1975, 1979 through 1980.

Most consecutive games lost, career

N.L.—27—Anthony Young, New York, May 6, 1992 through July 24, 1993 (14 in 1992, 13 in 1993).

A.L.—19—Jack Nabors, Philadelphia, April 28 through September 28, 1916.

Most consecutive games lost to one club, career

N.L.—13—Don Sutton, Los Angeles vs. Chicago, April 23, 1966 through July 24, 1969 (start of career).

A.L.—10—Dave Morehead, Boston vs. Los Angeles, July 28, 1963 through September 28, 1965 (start of career).

Most consecutive games lost from start of career

A.L.—16—Terry Felton, Minnesota, April 18, 1980, second game, through September 12, 1982.

A.A.—10—Charlie Stecher, Philadelphia, September 6 through October 9, 1890.

Most games lost, season

N.L.—48—John F. Coleman, Philadelphia, 1883 (won 11).
N.L. since 1900—29—Vic Willis, Boston, 1905 (won 12).
A.L.—26
Jack Townsend, Washington, 1904 (won five).
Bob Groom, Washington, 1909 (won six).

Most years leading league in games lost

A.L.—4
Bobo Newsom, St. Louis, Washington, Detroit, Philadelphia, 1934, 1935, 1941, 1945.
Pedro Ramos, Washington, Minnesota, 1958, 1959, 1960, 1961.
N.L.—4—Phil Niekro, Atlanta, 1977 (tied), 1978, 1979, 1980.

Fewest games lost for leader, season

A.L.—14
Ted Gray, Detroit, 1951 (won seven).
Alex Kellner, Philadelphia, 1951 (won 11).
Bob Lemon, Cleveland 1951 (won 17).
Billy Pierce, Chicago, 1951 (won 15).
Duane Pillette, St. Louis, 1951 (won six).
Dizzy Trout, Detroit, 1951 (won nine).
N.L.—15
Don Carman, Philadelphia, 1989 (won five).
Orel Hershiser, Los Angeles, 1989 (won 15).
Ken Hill, St. Louis, 1989 (won seven).

Most games lost as relief pitcher, season

N.L.—16—Gene Garber, Atlanta, 1979 (won six).
A.L.—14
Darold Knowles, Washington, 1970 (won two).
John Hiller, Detroit, 1974 (won 17).
Mike G. Marshall, Minnesota, 1979 (won 10, also lost one game as starter).

Most games lost by rookie, season

N.L.—34
Jim Devlin, Louisville, 1876 (won 30).
Bobby Mathews, New York, 1876 (won 21).
N.L. since 1900—25—Harry McIntire, Brooklyn, 1906 (won eight).
A.L.—26—Bob Groom, Washington, 1909 (won six).

Most games lost to one club, season (since 1900)

N.L.—7—Held by seven pitchers. Last time—Cal McLish, Cincinnati vs. Pittsburgh, 1960 (won none).
A.L.—7—Held by 4 pitchers. Last time—Camilo Pascual, Washington vs. New York, 1956 (won none).

Most consecutive games lost, season

A.L.—19—Jack Nabors, Philadelphia, April 28 through September 28, 1916.

N.L.—18
Cliff Curtis, Boston, June 13, first game, through September 20, first game, 1910.
Roger Craig, New York, May 4 through August 4, 1963.

Most consecutive games lost by rookie, season

N.L.—16—Charles Dean, Cincinnati, July 11 through September 12, 1876.
N.L. since 1900—14—Anthony Young, New York, May 6 through September 29, 1992.
A.L.—13
Guy Morton, Cleveland, June 24 through September 20, 1914.
Terry Felton, Minnesota, April 17 through September 12, 1982.

Most consecutive games lost from start of season

A.L.—14
Joe Harris, Boston, May 10 through July 25, 1906.
Matt Keough, Oakland, April 15 through August 8, 1979.
N.L.—13—Anthony Young, New York, April 9 through July 24, 1993.

Most consecutive games lost at end of season

A.L.—19—Jack Nabors, Philadelphia, April 28 through September 28, 1916.
N.L.—18—Cliff Curtis, Boston, June 13, first game, through September 20, 1910, first game.

AT-BATS AND PLATE APPEARANCES

Most at-bats, career

A.L.—21,663—Walter Johnson, Washington, 21 years, 1907 through 1927.
N.L.—19,778—Warren Spahn, Boston, Milwaukee, New York, San Francisco, 21 years, 1942 through 1965, except 1943, 1944, 1945 in military service.

Most at-bats, season

N.L.—2,808—Will White, Cincinnati, 75 games, 683 innings, 1879.
N.L. since 1900—1,658—Joe McGinnity, New York, 55 games, 434 innings, 1903.
A.L.—1,690—Ed Walsh, Chicago, 66 games 464 innings, 1908.

Most years leading league in at-bats

N.L.—6—Grover Alexander, Philadelphia, Chicago, 1911, 1914, 1915, 1916, 1917, 1920.
A.L.—4
Ed Walsh, Chicago, 1908, 1910, 1911, 1912.
Walter Johnson, Washington, 1913, 1914, 1915, 1916.
Bob Lemon, Cleveland, 1948, 1950, 1952, 1953.

Most consecutive years leading league in at-bats

A.L.—4—Walter Johnson, Washington, 1913, 1914, 1915, 1916.
N.L.—4
Grover Alexander, Philadelphia, 1914, 1915, 1916, 1917.
Robin Roberts, Philadelphia, 1952, 1953, 1954, 1955.

Fewest official at-bats for leader, season

A.L.—942—Jim Bunning, Detroit, 250 innings, 1959.
N.L.—1,009—Dave Koslo, New York, 265 innings, 1946.

Most at-bats, game

N.L.—66—George Derby, Buffalo, July 3, 1883.
N.L. since 1900—49
Harley Parker, Cincinnati, June 21, 1901.
Bill Phillips, Cincinnati, June 24, 1901, second game.
A.L.—53—Roy Patterson, Chicago, May 5, 1901.

Most men facing pitcher, nine-inning game

N.L.—67—George Derby, Buffalo, July 3, 1883.
N.L. since 1900—53—Bill Phillips, Cincinnati, June 24, 1901, second game.
A.L.—57—Roy Patterson, Chicago, May 5, 1901.

Most men facing pitcher, inning

N.L.—22—Tony Mullane, Baltimore, June 18, 1894, a.m. game, first inning.

N.L. since 1900—16—Hal Kelleher, Philadelphia, May 5, 1938, eighth inning.
A.L.—16
Merle Adkins, Boston, July 8, 1902, sixth inning.
Lefty O'Doul, Boston, July 7, 1923, first game, sixth inning.
Howard Ehmke, Boston, September 28, 1923, sixth inning.

RUNS

Most runs allowed, career

M.L.—3,303—Pud Galvin, Buffalo N.L., Pittsburgh A.A., Pittsburgh N.L., Pittsburgh P.L., St. Louis N.L., 14 years, 1879 through 1892.
A.L.—2,117—Red Ruffing, Boston, New York, Chicago, 22 years, 1924 through 1947, except 1943, 1944.
N.L.—2,037—Burleigh Grimes, Pittsburgh, Brooklyn, New York, Boston, St. Louis, Chicago, 19 years, 1916 through 1934.

Most runs allowed, season

N.L.—544—John F. Coleman, Philadelphia, 63 games, 538 innings, 1883.
N.L. since 1900—224—Bill Carrick, New York, 45 games, 342 innings, 1900.
A.L.—219—Joe McGinnity, Baltimore, 48 games, 378 innings, 1901.

Most years leading league in runs allowed

N.L.—3
Burleigh Grimes, Brooklyn, Pittsburgh, 1923, 1924, 1928.
Robin Roberts, Philadelphia, 1955, 1956, 1957.
Phil Niekro, Atlanta, 1977, 1978, 1979.
Rick Mahler, Atlanta, Cincinnati, 1986, 1988, 1989.
A.L.—3—Wilbur Wood, Chicago, 1972, 1973, 1975.

Fewest runs allowed for leader, season

N.L.—102—George Smith, New York, Philadelphia, 196 innings, 1919.
A.L.—108—Jim Bagby, Cleveland, 280 innings, 1918.

Most runs allowed, game

N.L.—35—Dave Rowe, Cleveland, July 24, 1882.
N.L. since 1900—21—Harley Parker, Cincinnati, June 21, 1901.
A.L.—24—Allan Travers, Detroit, May 18, 1912 (only major league game).

Fewest runs allowed, doubleheader

N.L.—0—Ed Reulbach, Chicago, September 26, 1908.
A.L.—1
Ed Walsh, Chicago, September 29, 1908.
Carl Mays, Boston, August 30, 1918.

Most runs allowed, inning

N.L.—16—Tony Mullane, Baltimore, June 18, 1894, a.m. game, first inning.
N.L. since 1900—12—Hal Kelleher, Philadelphia, May 5, 1938, eighth inning.
A.L.—13—Lefty O'Doul, Boston, July 7, 1923, first game, sixth inning.

EARNED RUNS

Most earned runs allowed, season (since 1900)

A.L.—186—Bobo Newsom, St. Louis, 330 innings, 1938.
N.L.—155—Guy Bush, Chicago, 225 innings, 1930.

Most years leading league in earned runs allowed

N.L.—3
Burleigh Grimes, Brooklyn, 1922, 1924, 1925.
Murry Dickson, St. Louis, Pittsburgh, 1948, 1951, 1952 (tied).
Robin Roberts, Philadelphia, 1955, 1956, 1957.
Jack Fisher, New York, 1964 (tied), 1965 (tied), 1967.
A.L.—3
Bobo Newsom, St. Louis, Washington, Philadelphia, 1938, 1942, 1945.
Wilbur Wood, Chicago, 1972, 1973, 1975.

Fewest earned runs for leader, season
A.L.—83
  Willie Adams, Philadelphia, 169 innings, 1918.
  George Dauss, Detroit, 250 innings, 1918.
N.L.—85
  Pete Schneider, Cincinnati, 217 innings, 1918.
  Art Nehf, Boston, 284 innings, 1918.
  Wilbur Cooper, Pittsburgh, 287 innings, 1919.

EARNED-RUN AVERAGE

Lowest earned-run average, career (300 or more games won)
A. L.—2.47—Walter Johnson, Washington, 802 games, 21 years, 1907 through 1927. (Johnson's record includes 520 total runs in 1,729 innings from 1907 through 1912, a period in which earned runs were not compiled. Had earned runs been compiled for that period, Johnson's earned-run average would be even lower.)
N.L.—2.61—Grover Alexander, Philadelphia, Chicago, St. Louis, 696 games, 20 years, 1911 through 1930. (Alexander's record includes 133 total runs in 366 innings in 1911, a year in which earned runs were not compiled. Had earned runs been compiled that year, Alexander's earned-run average would be even lower.)

Lowest earned-run average, career (200 or more games won)
A.L.—2.47—Walter Johnson, Washington, 802 games, 21 years, 1907 through 1927. (Johnson's record includes 520 total runs in 1,729 innings from 1907 through 1912, a period in which earned runs were not compiled. Had earned runs been compiled for that period, Johnson's earned-run average would be even lower.)
N.L.—2.61—Grover Alexander, Philadelphia, Chicago, St. Louis, 696 games, 20 years, 1911 through 1930. (Alexander's record includes 133 total runs in 366 innings in 1911, a year in which earned runs were not compiled. Had earned runs been compiled that year, Alexander's earned-run average would be even lower).

Lowest earned-run average, career (2,000 or more innings)
N.L.—2.33—Hippo Vaughn, Chicago, 2,217 innings, 305 games, nine years, 1913 through 1921.
A.L.—2.47—Walter Johnson, Washington, 5,924 innings, 802 games, 21 years, 1907 through 1927. (Johnson's record includes 520 total runs in 1,729 innings from 1907 through 1912, a period in which earned runs were not compiled. Had earned runs been compiled for that period, Johnson's earned-run average would be even lower.)

Lowest earned-run average, season (300 or more innings)
N.L.—1.12—Bob Gibson, St. Louis, 305 innings, 1968.
A.L.—1.14—Walter Johnson, Washington, 346 innings, 1913.

Lowest earned-run average by righthander, season (300 or more innings)
N.L.—1.12—Bob Gibson, St. Louis, 305 innings, 1968.
A.L.—1.14—Walter Johnson, Washington, 346 innings, 1913.

Lowest earned-run average by lefthander, season (300 or more innings)
N.L.—1.66—Carl Hubbell, New York, 309 innings, 1933.
A.L.—1.75—Babe Ruth, Boston, 324 innings, 1916.

Lowest earned-run average, season (200 or more innings)
A.L.—1.00—Dutch H. Leonard, Boston, 225 innings, 1914.
N.L.—1.12—Bob Gibson, St. Louis, 305 innings, 1968.

Most years leading league in lowest earned-run average
A.L.—9—Lefty Grove, Philadelphia, Boston, 1926, 1929, 1930, 1931, 1932, 1935, 1936, 1938, 1939.
N.L.—5
  Grover Alexander, Philadelphia, Chicago, 1915, 1916, 1917, 1919, 1920.
  Sandy Koufax, Los Angeles, 1962, 1963, 1964, 1965, 1966.

Most consecutive years leading league in lowest earned-run average
N.L.—5—Sandy Koufax, Los Angeles, 1962, 1963, 1964, 1965, 1966.
A.L.—4—Lefty Grove, Philadelphia, 1929, 1930, 1931, 1932.

Highest earned-run average for leader, season
A.L.—3.20—Early Wynn, Cleveland, 214 innings, 1950.
N.L.—3.08—Bill Walker, New York, 178 innings, 1929.

SHUTOUTS

Most shutouts won or tied by righthander, career
A.L.—110—Walter Johnson, Washington, 21 years, 1907 through 1927.
N.L.—90—Grover Alexander, Philadelphia, Chicago, St. Louis, 20 years, 1911 through 1930.

Most shutouts won or tied by lefthander, career
A.L.—64—Eddie Plank, Philadelphia, St. Louis, 16 years, 1901 through 1917, except 1915.
N.L.—63—Warren Spahn, Boston, Milwaukee, New York, San Francisco, 21 years, 1942 through 1965, except 1943, 1944, 1945 in military service.

Most shutouts won from one club, career
A.L.—23—Walter Johnson, Washington, vs. Philadelphia, 21 years, 1907 through 1927.
N.L.—20—Grover Alexander, Philadelphia, Chicago, St. Louis vs. Cincinnati, 20 years, 1911 through 1930.

Most shutouts lost, career
A.L.—65—Walter Johnson, Washington, 21 years, 1907 through 1927 (won 109, tied 1).
N.L.—40—Christy Mathewson, New York, Cincinnati, 17 years, 1900 through 1916 (won 83).

Most shutouts won or tied in season openers
A.L.—7—Walter Johnson, Washington, 1910 to 1926.
N.L.—3
  Rip Sewell, Pittsburgh, 1943, 1947, 1949.
  Chris Short, Philadelphia, 1965, 1968, 1970.
  Rick Mahler, Atlanta, 1982, 1986, 1987.

Most shutouts won or tied by righthander, season
N.L.—16
  George Bradley, St. Louis, 1876.
  Grover Alexander, Philadelphia, 1916.
A.L.—13—Jack Coombs, Philadelphia, 1910.

Most shutouts won or tied by lefthander, season
A.A.—12—Ed Morris, Pittsburgh, 1886.
N.L.—11—Sandy Koufax, Los Angeles, 1963.
A.L.—9
  Babe Ruth, Boston, 1916.
  Ron Guidry, New York, 1978.

Most shutouts participated in, season
N.L.—20—Grover Alexander, Philadelphia, 1916 (won 16, lost 4).
A.L.—18—Ed Walsh, Chicago, 1908 (won 12, lost 6).

Most shutouts lost, season
N.L.—14—Jim Devlin, Louisville, 1876 (won 5).
N.L. since 1900—11—Art Raymond, St. Louis, 1908 (won 5).
A.L.—10—Walter Johnson, Washington, 1909 (won 4).

Most years leading league in shutouts won or tied
N.L.—7—Grover Alexander, Philadelphia Chicago, 1911 (tied), 1913, 1915, 1916, 1917, 1919, 1921 (tied).
A.L.—7—Walter Johnson, Washington, 1911 (tied), 1913, 1914, 1915, 1918 (tied), 1919, 1924.

Most shutouts won or tied by rookie, season
N.L.—16—George Bradley, St. Louis, 1876.
N.L. since 1900—8—Fernando Valenzuela, Los Angeles, 1981.
A.L.—8
  Russ Ford, New York, 1910.
  Reb Russell, Chicago, 1913.

Most years with 10 or more shutouts won or tied
A.L.—2—Ed Walsh, Chicago, 1906, 1908.
N.L.—2—Grover Alexander, Philadelphia, 1915, 1916.

Most clubs shut out (won or tied), season
N.L. (10-club league)—8—Bob Gibson, St. Louis, 1968.
N.L. (8-club league)—7
  Pud Galvin, Buffalo, 1884.
  Christy Mathewson, New York, 1907.
  Grover Alexander, Philadelphia, 1913 and 1916; also with
    Chicago, 1919.
A.L. (12-club league)—8—Nolan Ryan, California, 1972.
A.L. (8-club league)—7
  Cy Young, Boston, 1904.
  Jack Coombs, Philadelphia, 1910.

Most shutouts won from one club, season
N.L.—5
  Charles Baldwin, Detroit vs. Philadelphia, 1886.
  Grover Alexander, Philadelphia vs. Cincinnati, 1916.
  Larry Jaster, St. Louis vs. Los Angeles, 1966, consecutive.
A.L.—5—Tom Hughes, Washington vs. Cleveland, 1905.
A.A.—5—Tony Mullane, Cincinnati vs. New York, 1887.

Most shutouts lost to one club, season
N.L.—5—Jim Devlin, Louisville vs. Hartford, 1876.
A.L.—5—Walter Johnson, Washington vs. Chicago, 1909.
N.L. since 1900—4—Irv Young, Boston vs. Pittsburgh, 1906.

Most shutouts won or tied, one month
A.L.—6
  Doc White, Chicago, September, 1904.
  Ed Walsh, Chicago, August, 1906; September, 1908.
N.L.—5
  George Bradley, St. Louis, May, 1876.
  Tommy Bond, Hartford, June, 1876.
  Pud Galvin, Buffalo, August, 1884.
  Ben Sanders, Philadelphia, September, 1888.
  Don Drysdale, Los Angeles, May, 1968.
  Bob Gibson, St. Louis, June, 1968.
  Orel Hershiser, Los Angeles, September, 1988.

Most shutouts lost, one month
A.L.—5—Walter Johnson, Washington, July, 1909.
N.L.—4
  Jim Devlin, Louisville, June, 1876.
  Fred Fitzsimmons, New York, September, 1934.
  Jim McAndrew, New York, August, 1968.

Fewest shutouts pitched by leader, season
N.L.—3—Held by eight pitchers in 1921.
A.L.—3—Held by three pitchers in 1930.

Pitching shutout in first major league game (nine innings)
N.L.—Held by 37 pitchers. Last pitcher—Mike Remlinger,
  San Francisco, June 15, 1991.
A.L.—Held by 35 pitchers. Last pitcher—Mike Norris, Oak-
  land, April 10, 1975.

Most shutouts, first two major league games
N.L.—2
  Al Spalding, Chicago, April 25, 27, 1876.
  Monte Ward, Providence, July 18, 20, 1878.
  Jim Hughes, Baltimore, April 18, 22, 1898.
  Al Worthington, New York, July 6, 11, 1953.
  Karl Spooner, Brooklyn, September 22, 26, 1954.
A.L.—2
  Joe Doyle, New York, August 25, first game, August 30,
    first game, 1906.
  John Marcum, Philadelphia, September 7, September 11,
    second game, 1933.
  Dave Ferriss, Boston, April 29, first game, May 6, first
    game, 1945.
  Tom Phoebus, Baltimore, September 15, first game, Sep-
    tember 20, 1966.

Most shutouts won or tied, four consecutive days
A.L.—3
  Jimmy Dygert, Philadelphia, October 1, 3, 4, second game,
    1907.

  Walter Johnson, Washington, September 4, 5, 7, first game,
    1908.
N.L.—2—held by many pitchers.

Most shutouts won or tied, five consecutive days
N.L.—3
  George Bradley, St. Louis, July 11, 13, 15, 1876.
  John Clarkson, Chicago, May 21, 22, 25, 1885.

Most consecutive shutouts won or tied, season
N.L.—6—Don Drysdale, Los Angeles, May 14, 18, 22, 26, 31,
  June 4, 1968.
A.L.—5—Doc White, Chicago, September 12, 16, 19, 25, 30,
  1904.

Most consecutive shutouts lost, season
N.L.—4—Jim McAndrew, New York, July 21, first game, August 4, second game, August 10, second game, August
  17, 1968.
A.L.—2—Held by many pitchers.

Most doubleheader shutouts
N.L.—1—Ed Reulbach, Chicago vs. Brooklyn, September 26,
  1908 (won 5-0, 3-0).
A.L.—None.

Longest shutout game
N.L.—18 innings
  Monte Ward, Providence, August 17, 1882 (won 1-0).
  Carl Hubbell, New York, July 2, 1933, first game (won 1-0).
A.L.—18
  Ed Summers, Detroit, July 16, 1909 (0-0 tie).
  Walter Johnson, Washington, May 15, 1918 (won 1-0).

CONSECUTIVE SCORELESS INNINGS

Most consecutive scoreless innings by righthander, season
N.L.—59—Orel Hershiser, Los Angeles, from sixth inning,
  August 30 through 10th inning, September 28, 1988.
A.L.—55⅔—Walter Johnson, Washington, from second in-
  ning, April 10 through third inning, May 14, 1913 (in-
  cludes two relief appearances).

Most consecutive scoreless innings by lefthander, season
N.L.—45⅓—Carl Hubbell, New York, from seventh inning,
  July 13 through fifth inning, August 1, 1933 (includes
  two relief appearances).
A.L.—45—Doc White, Chicago, September 12 through Sep-
  tember 30, 1904.

Most consecutive scoreless innings from start of career
N.L.—25—George McQuillan, Philadelphia, from first inning,
  May 8, through ninth inning, September 29, first game,
  1907.
A.L.—22—Dave Ferriss, Boston, from first inning, April 29,
  through fourth inning, May 13, 1945.

Most consecutive scoreless innings, game
N.L.—21—Joe Oeschger, Boston, May 1, 1920; sixth through
  26th innings.
A.L.—20—Joe Harris, Boston, September 1, 1906; fourth
  through 23rd innings.

1-0 GAMES

Most 1-0 games won, career
A.L.—38—Walter Johnson, Washington, 21 years, 1907
  through 1927.
N.L.—17—Grover Alexander, Philadelphia, Chicago, St.
  Louis, 20 years, 1911 through 1930.

Most 1-0 complete games won, season
A.L.—5
  Reb Russell, Chicago, 1913.
  Walter Johnson, Washington, 1913, 1919.
  Joe Bush, Boston, 1918.
  Dean Chance, Los Angeles, 1964 (also one incomplete
    game).
N.L.—5—Carl Hubbell, New York, 1933.

Most years leading league in 1-0 games won

A.L.—8—Walter Johnson, Washington, 1913 (tied), 1914, 1915 (tied), 1919, 1920 (tied), 1922, 1923 (tied), 1926 (tied).

N.L.—4

Grover Alexander, Philadelphia, Chicago, 1913 (tied), 1916 (tied), 1917 (tied), 1922 (tied).

Bill C. Lee, Chicago, Philadelphia, Boston, 1934 (tied), 1936, 1944 (tied), 1945 (tied).

Most 1-0 games won from one club, season

A.L.—3

Stan Coveleski, Cleveland vs. Detroit, 1917.

Walter Johnson, Washington vs. Philadelphia, 1919.

Jim Bagby Jr., Cleveland vs. Detroit, 1943.

N.L.—2—Held by many pitchers.

Most 1-0 games lost, career

A.L.—26—Walter Johnson, Washington, 21 years, 1907 through 1927 (won 38).

N.L.—13—Lee Meadows, St. Louis, Philadelphia, Pittsburgh, 15 years, 1915 through 1929 (won 7).

Most 1-0 games lost, season

A.L.—5

Bill Donovan, Detroit, 1903 (won 1).

Jack Warhop, New York, 1914 (won 0).

N.L.—5

George McQuillan, Philadelphia, 1908 (won 2).

Roger Craig, New York, 1963 (won 0).

Jim Bunning, Philadelphia, 1967 (won 1).

Ferguson Jenkins, Chicago, 1968. (won 0).

Most 1-0 games lost to one club, season

A.L.—3—Jack Warhop, New York vs. Washington, 1914.

N.L.—2—Held by many pitchers.

HITS

Most hits allowed, career

M.L.—7,078—Cy Young, Cleveland N.L., St. Louis N.L., Boston A.L., Cleveland A.L., Boston N.L., 22 years, 1890 through 1911 (4,282 in N.L., 2,796 in A.L.).

N.L.—5,490—Pud Galvin, Buffalo, Pittsburgh, St. Louis 12 years, 1879 through 1892, except 1886, 1890.

N.L. since 1900—4,868—Grover Alexander, Philadelphia, Chicago, St. Louis, 20 years, 1911 through 1930.

A.L.—4,920—Walter Johnson, Washington, 21 years, 1907 through 1927.

Most hits allowed, season

N.L.—809—John F. Coleman, Philadelphia, 63 games, 548 innings, 1883.

N.L. since 1900—415—Bill Carrick, New York, 45 games, 342 innings, 1900.

A.L.—401—Joe McGinnity, Baltimore, 48 games, 378 innings, 1901.

Fewest hits allowed for leader, season

N.L.—230—Andy Benes, San Diego, 231⅓ innings, 1992.

A.L.—243—Mel Stottlemyre, New York, 279 innings, 1968.

Most years leading league in hits allowed

N.L.—5—Robin Roberts, Philadelphia, 1952, 1953, 1954, 1955, 1956.

A.L.—4—Jim Kaat, Minnesota, Chicago, 1965, 1966, 1967, 1975.

Most consecutive hitless innings, season

A.L.—23—Cy Young, Boston, from seventh inning, April 25 through sixth inning, May 11, 1904. (Note: On April 30 Young relieved in third inning after another pitcher had given up hits in that inning.)

N.L.—21—Johnny Vander Meer, Cincinnati, from first inning, June 11 through third inning, June 19, first game, 1938.

Most consecutive batsmen retired, season

N.L.—41—Jim Barr, San Francisco, August 23 (last 21), August 29 (first 20), 1972.

A.L.—33

Steve Busby, Kansas City, June 19 (last 24), June 24 (first 9), 1974.

John Montague, Seattle, July 22 (last 13), July 24 (first 20), first game, 1977.

Most hits allowed, game

N.L.—36—John Wadsworth, Louisville, August 17, 1894.

N.L. since 1900—26—Harley Parker, Cincinnati, June 21, 1901.

A.L.—26

Hod Lisenbee, Philadelphia, September 11, 1936.

Allan Travers, Detroit, May 18, 1912 (only major league game).

Most hits allowed, extra-inning game

A.L.—29—Eddie Rommel, Philadelphia, July 10, 1932, pitched last 17 innings of 18-inning game.

N.L.—23—Jeff Pfeffer, Brooklyn, June 1, 1919, 18 innings.

Most hits allowed, two consecutive games

N.L.—48—Jim Callahan, Chicago, September 6 (25), September 11, first game (23), 1900.

Most hits allowed, nine-inning shutout game

N.L.—14—Larry Cheney, Chicago vs. New York, September 14, 1913 (won 7-0).

A.L.—14—Milt Gaston, Washington vs. Cleveland, July 10, 1928, second game (won 9-0).

Fewest hits allowed, first major league game (nine innings)

N.L.—0—Charles L. Jones, Cincinnati, October 15, 1892.

N.L. since 1900—1

Juan Marichal, San Francisco, July 19, 1960 (single in eighth inning).

Jimmy Jones, San Diego, September 21, 1986 (triple in third inning).

A.L.—1

Addie Joss, Cleveland, April 26, 1902 (single in seventh inning).

Mike Fornieles, Washington, September 2, 1952, second game (single in second inning).

Billy Rohr, Boston, April 14, 1967 (single with two out in ninth inning).

Fewest hits allowed, opening game of season (nine innings)

A.L.—0—Bob Feller, Cleveland, April 16, 1940.

N.L.—1—Held by many pitchers. Last pitcher—Lon Warneke, Chicago, April 15, 1909. (Leon Ames, New York, allowed no hits in 9⅓ innings on April 15, 1909, but lost on seven hits in 13 innings.)

Fewest hits allowed, doubleheader (18 innings)

A.A.—3—Tim Keefe, New York, July 4, 1883.

N.L.—6

Fred Toney, Cincinnati, July 1, 1917.

Herman Bell, St. Louis, July 19, 1924.

A.L.—7

Frank Owen, Chicago, July 1, 1905.

Ed Walsh, Chicago, September 29, 1908.

Fewest hits allowed, two consecutive games (18 innings)

N.L.—0—Johnny Vander Meer, Cincinnati, June 11, 15, 1938.

A.L.—1—Howard Ehmke, Boston, September 7 (0), September 11 (1), 1923.

U.A.—1—Ed Cushman, Milwaukee, September 28 (0), October 4 (1), 1884.

A.A.—2—Tom Ramsey, Louisville, July 29 (1), July 31 (1), 12 innings, 1886.

Fewest hits allowed, three consecutive games

N.L.—3—Johnny Vander Meer, Cincinnati, June 5 (3), June 11 (0), June 15 (0), 1938.

A.L.—5—Held by many pitchers.

Most hits allowed, inning

N.L.—13—George Weidman, Detroit, September 6, 1883, seventh inning.

A.L.—12—Merle Adkins, Boston, July 8, 1902, sixth inning.

N.L. since 1900—11—Reggie Grabowski, Philadelphia, August 4, 1934, second game, ninth inning.

Most consecutive hits allowed from start of game

N.L.—7—Bill Bonham, Chicago, August 5, 1975 (3 singles, 2 doubles, 2 homers).

A.L.—5

Frank Tanana, California, May 18, 1980 (1 single, 2 doubles, 2 triples).

Luis Leal, Toronto, June 2, 1980 (2 singles, 3 doubles).

Ross Baumgarten, Chicago, September 27, 1981, first game (5 singles).

Most consecutive hits allowed, game

A.L.—10—Bill Reidy, Milwaukee, June 2, 1901, ninth inning.

N.L.—10—Heinie Meine, Pittsburgh, June 23, 1930, sixth inning.

NO-HIT AND ONE-HIT GAMES

Most no-hitters pitched, career (nine or more innings)

M.L.—7—Nolan Ryan, California, A.L., 1973 (2), 1974, 1975; Houston, N.L., 1981; Texas, A.L., 1990, 1991.

A.L.—6—Nolan Ryan, California, 1973 (2), 1974, 1975; Texas, 1990, 1991.

N.L.—4—Sandy Koufax, Los Angeles, 1962, 1963, 1964, 1965.

Most no-hit games, season

N.L.—2

Johnny Vander Meer, Cincinnati, June 11, 15, 1938 (consecutive).

Jim Maloney, Cincinnati, June 14, first 10 innings of 11-inning game, August 19, 1965, first game, 10 innings.

A.L.—2

Allie Reynolds, New York, July 12, September 28, first game, 1951.

Virgil Trucks, Detroit, May 15, August 25, 1952.

Nolan Ryan, California, May 15, July 15, 1973.

Most consecutive no-hit games

N.L.—2—Johnny Vander Meer, Cincinnati, June 11, 15, 1938.

A.L.—Never accomplished.

Longest no-hit complete game

A.A.—10 innings—Sam Kimber, Brooklyn, vs. Toledo, October 4, 1884.

N.L.—10 innings

George Wiltse, New York vs. Philadelphia, July 4, 1908, a.m. game.

Fred Toney, Cincinnati vs. Chicago, May 2, 1917.

Jim Maloney, Cincinnati vs. Chicago, August 19, 1965, first game.

A.L.—9—Held by many pitchers.

Longest one-hit complete game

N.L.—12⅔ innings—Harvey Haddix, Pittsburgh vs. Milwaukee, May 26, 1959 (one double).

A.L.—10

Doc White, Chicago vs. Cleveland, September 6, 1903 (one double).

Bobo Newsom, St. Louis vs. Boston, September 18, 1934 (one single).

Bert Blyleven, Texas vs. Oakland, June 21, 1976 (one single).

Most low-hit (no-hit and one-hit) games, career (nine or more innings)

M.L.—19—Nolan Ryan, New York N.L., California A.L., Houston N.L., Texas A.L., 1966, 1968 through 1992 (6 no-hit, 9 one-hit in A.L.; 1 no-hit, 3 one-hit in N.L.).

A.L.—15—Nolan Ryan, California, Texas, 1972 through 1979, 1989 through 1992 (6 no-hit, 9 one-hit).

N.L.—8

Hoss Radbourn, Buffalo, Providence, Boston, Cincinnati, 1880 through 1889, 1891 (1 no-hit, 7 one-hit).

Jim Maloney, Cincinnati, 1960 through 1970 (3 no-hit, 5 one-hit).

Most low-hit (no-hit and one-hit) games, season (nine or more innings)

U.A.—4—Hugh Daily, Chicago, 1884.

N.L.—4—Grover Alexander, Philadelphia, 1915.

A.L.—3

Addie Joss, Cleveland, 1907.

Bob Feller, Cleveland, 1946.

Virgil Trucks, Detroit, 1952.

Nolan Ryan, California, 1973.

Dave Stieb, Toronto, 1988.

Most consecutive one-hit games

U.A.—2—Hugh Daily, Chicago, July 7, 10, 1884.

N.L.—2

Charlie Buffinton, Philadelphia, August 6, 9, 1887.

Rube Marquard, New York, August 28, September 1, second game, 1911.

Lon Warneke, Chicago, April 17, 22, 1934 (his first two games of season).

Morton Cooper, St. Louis, May 31, first game, June 4, 1943.

A.A.—2—Tom Ramsey, Louisville, July 29, 31, 12 innings, 1886.

A.L.—2

Whitey Ford, New York, September 2, 7, 1955.

Sam McDowell, Cleveland, April 25, May 1, 1966.

Dave Stieb, Toronto, September 24, 30, 1988.

SINGLES, DOUBLES AND TRIPLES

Most singles allowed, game

N.L.—28—John Wadsworth, Louisville, August 17, 1894.

A.L.—23—Charles Baker, Cleveland, April 28, 1901.

Most singles allowed, inning

N.L.—10—Reggie Grabowski, Philadelphia, August 4, 1934, second game, ninth inning.

A.L.—10—Eldon Auker, Detroit, September 29, 1935, second game, second inning.

Most doubles allowed, game

N.L.—14—George Derby, Buffalo, July 3, 1883.

A.L.—8—Ed LaFitte, Detroit, October 8, 1911, first game.

Most doubles allowed, inning

A.L.—6—Lefty Grove, Boston, June 9, 1934, eighth inning.

N.L.—5—Duke Esper, Washington, April 21, 1894, second inning.

Most triples allowed, game

N.L.—9—Mike Sullivan, Cleveland, September 3, 1894, first game.

A.L.—5

Barney Pelty, St. Louis, April 27, 1907.

Allan Travers, Detroit, May 18, 1912.

Most triples allowed, inning

A.L.—4

Fred Marberry, Detroit, May 6, 1934, fourth inning.

Allan Travers, Detroit, May 18, 1912, fifth inning.

HOME RUNS

Most home runs allowed, career

M.L.—505—Robin Roberts, Philadelphia N.L., Baltimore A.L., Houston N.L., Chicago N.L., 19 years, 1948 through 1966 (418 in N.L., 87 in A.L.).

N.L.—434—Warren Spahn, Boston, Milwaukee, New York, San Francisco, 21 years, 1942 through 1965, except 1943, 1944, 1945 in military service.

A.L.—422—Frank Tanana, California, Boston, Texas, Detroit, New York, 21 years, 1973 through 1993.

Most grand slams allowed, career

M.L.—10—Nolan Ryan, New York N.L., California A.L., Houston N.L., Texas A.L., 1970, 1972, 1973, 1977, 1984, 1985, 1988, 1990, 1992 (2) (6 in A.L., 4 in N.L.).

A.L.—9—Ned Garver, St. Louis, Detroit, Kansas City, 1949, 1950 (2), 1951, 1952, 1954, 1955 (2), 1959.

N.L.—9—Jerry Reuss, St. Louis, Houston, Pittsburgh, Los Angeles, 1971 (2), 1972, 1973, 1974, 1976 (2), 1979, 1980.

Most home runs allowed, season

A.L.—50—Bert Blyleven, Minnesota, 36 games, 271⅔ innings, 1986.
N.L.—46—Robin Roberts, Philadelphia, 43 games, 297 innings, 1956.

Most home runs allowed, season (vs. one club)

A.L.— 15—Jim Perry, Cleveland vs. New York, 1960.
N.L.—13
  Warren Hacker, Chicago vs. Brooklyn, 1956.
  Warren Spahn, Milwaukee vs. Chicago, 1958.

Most grand slams allowed, season

A.L.—4
  Ray Narleski, Detroit, 1959.
  Mike Schooler, Seattle, 1992.
N.L.—4—Tug McGraw, Philadelphia, 1979.

Fewest home runs allowed, season (most innings)

A.L.—0—Allen Sothoron, St. Louis, Boston, Cleveland, 29 games, 178 innings, 1921.
N.L.—1—Eppa Rixey, Cincinnati, 40 games, 301 innings, 1921.

Fewest home runs allowed, season (since 1950; 250 or more innings)

N.L.—5
  Bob Veale, Pittsburgh, 39 games, 266 innings, 1965.
  Ron Reed, Atlanta, St. Louis, 34 games, 250 innings, 1975.
A.L.—6—Mike Garcia, Cleveland, 45 games, 259 innings, 1954.

Most years leading league in home runs allowed

M.L.—7—Ferguson Jenkins, Chicago N.L., Texas A.L., 1967, 1968 (tied), 1971, 1972, 1973, 1975, 1979 (5 in N.L., 2 in A.L.).
N.L.—5
  Robin Roberts, Philadelphia, 1954, 1955, 1956, 1957, 1960.
  Ferguson Jenkins, Chicago, 1967, 1968 (tied), 1971, 1972, 1973.
A.L.—3
  Pedro Ramos, Washington, Minnesota, 1957, 1958, 1961.
  Denny McLain, Detroit, 1966, 1967, 1968.

Most years allowing 30 or more home runs

M.L.—9—Robin Roberts, Philadelphia N.L., Baltimore A.L., 1953, 1954, 1955, 1956, 1957, 1958, 1959, 1960, 1963.
N.L.—8—Robin Roberts, Philadelphia, 1953, 1954, 1955, 1956, 1957, 1958, 1959, 1960.
A.L.—4
  Mudcat Grant, Cleveland, Minnesota, 1961, 1963, 1964, 1965.
  Denny McLain, Detroit, Washington, 1966, 1967, 1968, 1971.
  Jack Morris, Detroit, 1982, 1983, 1986, 1987.

Most home runs allowed, game

N.L.—7—Charlie Sweeney, St. Louis, June 12, 1886.
N.L. since 1900—6
  Larry Benton, New York, May 12, 1930.
  Hollis Thurston, Brooklyn, August 13, 1932, first game.
  Wayman Kerksieck, Philadelphia, August 13, 1939, first game.
A.L.—6
  Al Thomas, St. Louis, June 27, 1936.
  George Caster, Philadelphia, September 24, 1940, first game.

Most home runs allowed, inning

N.L.—4
  Bill Lampe, Boston, June 6, 1894, third inning.
  Larry Benton, New York, May 12, 1930, seventh inning.
  Wayman Kerksieck, Philadelphia, August 13, 1939, first game, fourth inning.
  Charlie Bicknell, Philadelphia, June 6, 1948, first game, sixth inning.
  Ben Wade, Brooklyn, May 28, 1954, eighth inning.

Mario Soto, Cincinnati, April 29, 1986, fourth inning.
John Smoltz, Atlanta, June 19, 1994, first inning.
A.L.—4
  George Caster, Philadelphia, September 24, 1940, first game, sixth inning.
  Cal McLish, Cleveland, May 22, 1957, sixth inning.
  Paul Foytack, Los Angeles, July 31, 1963, second game, sixth inning (consecutive).
  Catfish Hunter, New York, June 17, 1977, first inning.
  Mike Caldwell, Milwaukee May 31, 1980, fourth inning.
  Scott Sanderson, New York, May 2, 1992, fifth inning.

Most consecutive home runs allowed, inning

A.L.—4—Paul Foytack, Los Angeles, July 31, 1963, second game, sixth inning.
N.L.—3—held by many pitchers. Last pitchers—Anthony Young, Chicago, April 15, 1994, first inning; Rick Sutcliffe, St. Louis, April 18, 1994, first inning.

LONG HITS AND TOTAL BASES

Most long hits allowed, game

N.L.— 16—George Derby, Buffalo, July 3, 1883.
A.L.— 10—Dale Gear, Washington, August 10, 1901, second game.

Most total bases allowed, game

N.L.—55—Bill Rhodes, Louisville, June 18, 1893.
N.L. since 1900—39—Dummy Taylor, New York, September 23, 1903.
A.L.—41—Dale Gear, Washington, August 10, 1901, second game.

Most total bases allowed, inning

N.L.—23—Bill Rhodes, Louisville, June 18, 1893, first inning.
N.L. since 1900—18—Charlie Bicknell, Philadelphia, June 6, 1948, first game, sixth inning.
A.L.—22—George Caster, Philadelphia, September 24, 1940, first game, sixth inning.

BASES ON BALLS

Most bases on balls, career

M.L.—2,795—Nolan Ryan, New York N.L., California A.L., Houston N.L., Texas A.L., 27 years, 1966, 1968 through 1993 (1,655 in A.L., 1,140 in N.L.).
A.L.— 1,775—Early Wynn, Washington, Cleveland, Chicago, 23 years, 1939, 1941, through 1963, except 1945 in military service.
N.L.— 1,717—Steve Carlton, St. Louis, Philadelphia, San Francisco, 22 years, 1965 through 1986.

Most bases on balls, season

N.L.—276—Amos Rusie, New York, 64 games, 1890.
N.L. since 1900— 185—Sam Jones, Chicago, 242 innings, 1955.
A.L.—208—Bob Feller, Cleveland, 278 innings, 1938.

Most intentional bases on balls, season

N.L.—23
  Mike Garman, St. Louis, 66 games, 79 innings, 1975.
  Dale Murray, Cincinnati, New York, 68 games, 119 innings, 1978.
  Kent Tekulve, Pittsburgh, 85 games, 128⅔ innings, 1982.
A.L.— 19—John Hiller, Detroit, 59 games, 150 innings, 1974.

Most years leading league in bases on balls

M.L.—8—Nolan Ryan, California A.L., 1972 through 1978, except 1975; Houston N.L., 1980, 1982.
A.L.—6—Nolan Ryan, California, 1972, 1973, 1974, 1976, 1977, 1978.
N.L.—5—Amos Rusie, New York, 1890, 1891, 1892, 1893, 1894.
N.L. since 1900—4
  Jimmy Ring, Philadelphia, 1922, 1923, 1924, 1925.
  Kirby Higbe, Chicago, Philadelphia, Pittsburgh, Brooklyn, 1939, 1940, 1941, 1947.

Sam Jones, Chicago, St. Louis, San Francisco, 1955, 1956, 1958, 1959.
Bob Veale, Pittsburgh, 1964, 1965 (tied), 1967, 1968.

Fewest bases on balls, season (250 or more innings)
N.L.—18—Babe Adams, Pittsburgh, 263 innings, 1920.
A.L.—28—Cy Young, Boston, 380 innings, 1904.

Most consecutive innings with no bases on balls, season
A.L.—84⅓—Bill Fischer, Kansas City, August 3 through September 30, 1962.
N.L.—68
Christy Mathewson, New York, June 19 through July 18, 1913.
Randy Jones, San Diego, May 17, eighth inning, through June 22, 1976, seventh inning.

Most consecutive innings with no bases on balls from start of season
N.L.—52—Grover Alexander, Chicago, April 18 through May 17, 1923.

Most bases on balls, nine-inning game
N.L.—16
Bill George, New York, May 30, 1887, first game.
George Van Haltren, Chicago, June 27, 1887.
N.L. since 1900—14—Henry Mathewson, New York, October 5, 1906.
P.L.—16—Henry Gruber, Cleveland, April 19, 1890.
A.L.—16—Bruno Haas, Philadelphia, June 23, 1915 (his first major league game).

Most bases on balls, extra-inning game
A.L.—16—Tommy Byrne, St. Louis, August 22, 1951, 13 innings.
N.L.—13
Cy Seymour, New York, May 24, 1899, 10 innings.
Bud Podbielan, Cincinnati, May 18, 1953, 10 innings.

Most bases on balls, shutout game
A.L.—11
Lefty Gomez, New York, August 1, 1941.
Mel Stottlemyre, New York, May 21, 1970; pitched first 8⅓ innings.
N.L.—9—Vinegar Bend Mizell, St. Louis, September 1, 1958, first game.

Most bases on balls, shutout game (more than nine innings)
N.L.—10
Jim Maloney, Cincinnati, August 19, 1965, first game, 10 innings.
J.R. Richard, Houston, July 6, 1976, 10 innings.
A.L.—Less than nine-inning game.

Longest game without a base on balls
N.L.—21 innings—Babe Adams, Pittsburgh, July 17, 1914.
A.L.—20 innings—Cy Young, Boston, July 4, 1905, p.m. game.

Fewest bases on balls, doubleheader (18 innings)
A.A.—0—Guy Hecker, Louisville, July 4, 1884.
A.L.—1—Ed Walsh, Chicago, September 29, 1908.
N.L.—1—Grover Alexander, Philadelphia, September 23, 1916, September 3, 1917.

Most bases on balls, inning
A.L.—8—Bill Gray, Washington, August 28, 1909, first game, second inning.
N.L.—7
Tony Mullane, Baltimore, June 18, 1894, a.m. game, first inning.
Bob Ewing, Cincinnati, April 19, 1902, fourth inning. (His first major league game).

Most consecutive bases on balls, inning
A.L.—7—Bill Gray, Washington, August 28, 1909, first game, second inning.
N.L.—6—Bill Kennedy, Brooklyn, August 31, 1900, second inning.

CAREER

Most strikeouts, career
M.L.—5,714—Nolan Ryan, New York N.L., California A.L., Houston N.L., Texas A.L., 27 years, 1966, 1968 through 1993 (3,355 in A.L., 2,359 in N.L.).
N.L.—4,000—Steve Carlton, St. Louis, Philadelphia, San Francisco, 22 years, 1965 through 1986.
A.L.—3,508—Walter Johnson, Washington, 21 years, 1907 through 1927.

Most strikeouts by righthanded pitcher, career
A.L.—3,508—Walter Johnson, Washington, 21 years, 1907 through 1927.
N.L.—3,272—Tom Seaver, New York, Cincinnati, 17 years, 1967 through 1983.

Most strikeouts by lefthanded pitcher, career
N.L.—4,000—Steve Carlton, St. Louis, Philadelphia, San Francisco, 22 years, 1965 through 1986.
A.L.—2,679—Mickey Lolich, Detroit, 13 years, 1963 through 1975.

SEASON

Most strikeouts, season
A.A.—505—Matt Kilroy, Baltimore, 65 games, 570 innings, 1886.
N.L.—411—Hoss Radbourn, Providence, 72 games, 679 innings, 1884.
N.L. since 1900—382—Sandy Koufax, Los Angeles, 43 games, 336 innings, 1965.
A.L.—383—Nolan Ryan, California, 41 games, 326 innings, 1973.

Most strikeouts by righthanded pitcher, season
U.A.—483—Hugh Daily, Chicago, Pittsburgh, Washington, 58 games, 501 innings, 1884.
N.L.—411—Hoss Radbourn, Providence, 72 games, 679 innings, 1884.
N.L. since 1900—313—J.R. Richard, Houston, 38 games, 292 innings, 1979.
A.L.—383—Nolan Ryan, California, 41 games, 326 innings, 1973.

Most strikeouts by lefthanded pitcher, season
A.A.—505—Matt Kilroy, Baltimore, 65 games, 570 innings, 1886.
N.L.—382—Sandy Koufax, Los Angeles, 43 games, 336 innings, 1965.
A.L.—349—Rube Waddell, Philadelphia, 46 games, 384 innings, 1904.

Most strikeouts by relief pitcher, season
A.L.—181—Dick Radatz, Boston, 1964, 79 games, 157 innings.
N.L.—151—Rich Gossage, Pittsburgh, 1977, 72 games, 133 innings.

Most strikeouts by rookie, season (since 1900)
N.L.—276—Dwight Gooden, New York, 218 innings, 1984.
A.L.—245—Herb Score, Cleveland, 227 innings, 1955.

Fewest strikeouts for leader, season
A.L.—113
Cecil Hughson, Boston, 281 innings, 1942.
Bobo Newsom, Washington, 214 innings, 1942.
N.L.—133—Rube Waddell, Pittsburgh, 213 innings, 1900.

Most years leading league in strikeouts
A.L.—12—Walter Johnson, Washington, 1910, 1912, 1913, 1914, 1915, 1916, 1917, 1918, 1919, 1921, 1923, 1924.
N.L.—7—Dazzy Vance, Brooklyn, 1922 through 1928.

Most consecutive years leading league in strikeouts
A.L.—8—Walter Johnson, Washington, 1912 through 1919.
N.L.—7—Dazzy Vance, Brooklyn, 1922 through 1928.

Most years with 100 or more strikeouts

M.L.—24—Nolan Ryan, New York N.L., California A.L., Houston N.L., Texas A.L., 1968 through 1992, except 1969 (12 in N.L., 12 in A.L.).

A.L.—18—Walter Johnson, Washington, 1908 through 1926, except 1920.

N.L.—18—Steve Carlton, St. Louis, Philadelphia, 1967 through 1984.

Most consecutive years with 100 or more strikeouts

M.L.—23—Nolan Ryan, New York N.L., California A.L., Houston N.L., Texas A.L., 1970 through 1992 (11 in N.L., 12 in A.L.).

N.L.—18—Steve Carlton, St. Louis, Philadelphia, 1967 through 1984.

A.L.—13
Eddie Plank, Philadelphia, 1902 through 1914.
Mickey Lolich, Detroit, 1963 through 1975.

Most years with 200 or more strikeouts

M.L.—15—Nolan Ryan, California A.L., Houston N.L., Texas A.L., 1972 through 1974, 1976 through 1980, 1982, 1985, 1987 through 1991.

N.L.—10—Tom Seaver, New York, Cincinnati, 1968 through 1976, 1978.

A.L.—10—Nolan Ryan, California, Texas, 1972 through 1974, 1976 through 1979, 1989 through 1991.

Most consecutive years with 200 or more strikeouts

N.L.—9—Tom Seaver, New York, 1968 through 1976.

A.L.—7
Rube Waddell, Philadelphia, St. Louis, 1902 through 1908.
Walter Johnson, Washington, 1910 through 1916.
Roger Clemens, Boston, 1986 through 1992.

Most years with 300 or more strikeouts

A.L.—6—Nolan Ryan, California, 1972 (329), 1973 (383), 1974 (367), 1976 (327), 1977 (341), Texas, 1989 (301).

N.L.—3
Amos Rusie, New York, 1890 (345), 1891 (321), 1892 (303).
Sandy Koufax, Los Angeles, 1963 (303), 1965 (382), 1966 (317).

Most years with 400 or more strikeouts

M.L.—1
Fred Shaw, Detroit N.L., Boston U.A., 1884.
Hugh Daily, Chicago U.A., Pittsburgh U.A., Washington U.A., 1884.
Hoss Radbourn, Providence N.L., 1884.
Charlie Buffinton, Boston N.L., 1884.
Matt Kilroy, Baltimore A.A., 1886.
Tom Ramsey, Louisville A.A., 1886.

A.A.—1
Matt Kilroy, Baltimore, 1886.
Tom Ramsey, Louisville, 1886.

U.A.—1—Hugh Daily, Chicago, Pittsburgh, Washington, 1884.

N.L.—1
Hoss Radbourn, Providence, 1884.
Charlie Buffinton, Boston, 1884.

GAME AND INNING

Most strikeouts, nine-inning game

A.L.—20—Roger Clemens, Boston, April 29, 1986.

N.L.—19
Charlie Sweeney, Providence, June 7, 1884.
Steve Carlton, St. Louis, September 15, 1969.
Tom Seaver, New York, April 22, 1970.
David Cone, New York, October 6, 1991.

U.A.—19—Hugh Daily, Chicago, July 7, 1884.

Most strikeouts, extra-inning game

A.L.—21—Tom Cheney, Washington vs. Baltimore, September 12, 1962, 16 innings.

N.L.—Less than nine-inning record.

Most strikeouts by righthanded pitcher, nine-inning game

A.L.—20—Roger Clemens, Boston, April 29, 1986.

N.L.—19
Charlie Sweeney, Providence, June 7, 1884.
Tom Seaver, New York, April 22, 1970.
David Cone, New York, October 6, 1991.

Most strikeouts by lefthanded pitcher, game

N.L.—19—Steve Carlton, St. Louis, September 15, 1969.

A.L.—18
Ron Guidry, New York, June 17, 1978.
Randy Johnson, Seattle, September 27, 1992.

Most strikeouts by righthanded pitcher, extra-inning game

A.L.—21—Tom Cheney, Washington, September 12, 1962, 16 innings.

N.L.—Less than nine-inning record.

Most strikeouts, nine-inning night game

A.L.—20—Roger Clemens, Boston, April 29, 1986.

N.L.—19—Steve Carlton, St. Louis, September 15, 1969.

Most strikeouts by losing pitcher, nine-inning game

N.L.—19—Steve Carlton, St. Louis, September 15, 1969 (lost 4-3).

U.A.—18
Fred Shaw, Boston, July 19, 1884 (lost 1-0).
Henry Porter, Milwaukee, October 3, 1884 (lost 5-4).

A.L.—18—Bob Feller, Cleveland, October 2, 1938, first game (lost 4-1).

A.A.—17—Guy Hecker, Louisville, August 26, 1884 (lost 4-3).

Most strikeouts by losing pitcher, extra-inning game

A.L.—19—Nolan Ryan, California, August 20, 1974, 11 innings (lost 1-0).

N.L.—18
Warren Spahn, Boston, June 14, 1952, 15 innings (lost 3-1).
Jim Maloney, Cincinnati, June 14, 1965, 11 innings (lost 1-0).

Most strikeouts, first major league game (since 1900)

N.L.—15
Karl Spooner, Brooklyn, September 22, 1954.
J.R. Richard, Houston, September 5, 1971, second game.

A.L.—12—Elmer Myers, Philadelphia, October 6, 1915, second game.

Most strikeouts by relief pitcher, game

N.L.—14—Rube Marquard, New York, May 13, 1911, last eight innings of nine-inning game.

A.L.—15—Walter Johnson, Washington, July 25, 1913, last 11⅓ innings of 15-inning game.
14—Denny McLain, Detroit, June 15, 1965, 6⅔ innings of nine-inning game.

Most times with 15 or more strikeouts in game, career

M.L.—26—Nolan Ryan, New York N.L., California A.L., Houston N.L., Texas A.L., 27 years, 1966 through 1993, except 1967 (23 in A.L., 3 in N.L.).

A.L.—23—Nolan Ryan, California, 1972 (4), 1973 (2), 1974 (6), 1976 (3), 1977 (2), 1978 (1), 1979 (1), Texas, 1989 (1), 1990 (2), 1991 (1).

N.L.—8—Sandy Koufax, Brooklyn, Los Angeles, 1959 (2), 1960 (2), 1961 (1), 1962 (2), 1966 (1).

Most times with 10 or more strikeouts in game, career

M.L.—215—Nolan Ryan, New York N.L., California A.L., Houston N.L., Texas A.L., 27 years, 1966 through 1993, except 1967 (148 in A.L., 67 in N.L.).

A.L.—148—Nolan Ryan, California, Texas, 13 years, 1972 through 1979, 1989 through 1993.

N.L.—97—Sandy Koufax, Brooklyn, Los Angeles, 12 years, 1955 through 1966.

Most times with 10 or more strikeouts in game, season

A.L.—23—Nolan Ryan, California, 1973.

N.L.—21—Sandy Koufax, Los Angeles, 1965.

Most strikeouts, inning (*consecutive)

A.A.—4—Bobby Mathews, Philadelphia, September 30, 1885, seventh inning.

N.L.—4
Ed Crane, New York, October 4, 1888, *fifth inning.
George Wiltse, New York, May 15, 1906, *fifth inning.

Jim Davis, Chicago, May 27, 1956, first game, *sixth inning.
Joe Nuxhall, Cincinnati, August 11, 1959, first game, sixth inning.
Pete Richert, Los Angeles, April 12, 1962, *third inning.
Don Drysdale, Los Angeles, April 17, 1965, *second inning.
Bob Gibson, St. Louis, June 7, 1966, fourth inning.
Bill Bonham, Chicago, July 31, 1974, first game, *second inning.
Phil Niekro, Atlanta, July 29, 1977, sixth inning.
Mario Soto, Cincinnati, May 17, 1984, Atlanta, August 22, 1989, fifth inning.
Mike Scott, Houston, September 3, 1986, fifth inning.
Paul Assenmacher, Atlanta, August 22, 1989, fifth inning.
Tim Birtsas, Cincinnati, June 4, 1990, seventh inning.
A.L.—4
Walter Johnson, Washington, April 15, 1911, fifth inning.
Guy Morton, Cleveland, June 11, 1916, seventh inning.
Ryne Duren, Los Angeles, May 18, 1961, seventh inning.
Lee Stange, Cleveland, September 2, 1964, seventh inning.
Mike Cuellar, Baltimore, May 29, 1970, *fourth inning.
Mike Paxton, Cleveland, July 21, 1978, *fifth inning.
Bobby Witt, Texas, August 2, 1987, *second inning.
Charlie Hough, Texas, July 4, 1988, first inning.
Matt Young, Seattle, September 9, 1990, first inning.
Paul Shuey, Cleveland, May 14, 1994, ninth inning.

Three strikeouts on nine pitched balls, inning

A.L.—
Rube Waddell, Philadelphia, July 1, 1902, third inning.
Hollis Thurston, Chicago, August 22, 1923, 12th inning.
Lefty Grove, Philadelphia, August 23, 1928, second inning.
Lefty Grove, Philadelphia, September 27, 1928, seventh inning.
Jim Bunning, Detroit, August 2, 1959, ninth inning.
Al Downing, New York, August 11, 1967, first game, second inning.
Nolan Ryan, California, July 9, 1972, second inning.
Ron Guidry, New York, August 7, 1984, second game, ninth inning.
Jeff Montgomery, Kansas City, April 29, 1990, eighth inning.
N.L.—
Pat Ragan, Brooklyn, October 5, 1914, second game, eighth inning.
Hod Eller, Cincinnati, August 21, 1917, ninth inning.
Joe Oeschger, Boston, September 8, 1921, first game, fourth inning.
Dazzy Vance, Brooklyn, September 14, 1924, third inning.
Sandy Koufax, Los Angeles, June 30, 1962, first inning.
Sandy Koufax, Los Angeles, April 18, 1964, third inning.
Bob Bruce, Houston, April 19, 1964, eighth inning.
Nolan Ryan, New York, April 19, 1968, third inning.
Bob Gibson, St. Louis, May 12, 1969, seventh inning.
Lynn McGlothen, St. Louis, August 19, 1975, second inning.
Bruce Sutter, Chicago, September 8, 1977, ninth inning.
Jeff Robinson, Pittsburgh, September 7, 1987, eighth inning.
Rob Dibble, Cincinnati, June 4, 1989, eighth inning.
Andy Ashby, Philadelphia, June 15, 1991, fourth inning.
David Cone, New York, August 30, 1991, fifth inning.
Pete Harnisch, Houston, September 6, 1991, seventh inning.
Trevor Wilson, San Francisco, June 7, 1992, ninth inning.

CONSECUTIVE AND IN CONSECUTIVE GAMES

Most consecutive strikeouts, game

N.L.—10—Tom Seaver, New York, April 22, 1970, 1 in sixth inning, 3 in seventh inning, 3 in eighth inning, 3 in ninth inning.
A.L.—8
Nolan Ryan, California, July 9, 1972, 2 in first inning, 3 in second inning, 3 in third inning.
Nolan Ryan, California, July 15, 1973, 1 in first inning, 3 in second inning, 3 in third inning, 1 in fourth inning.
Ron Davis, New York, May 4, 1981, 2 in seventh inning, 3 in eighth inning, 3 in ninth inning.
Roger Clemens, Boston, April 29, 1986, 3 in fourth inning, 3

in fifth inning, 2 in sixth inning.

Most consecutive strikeouts, first major league game

A.L.—7—Sammy Stewart, Baltimore, September 1, 1978, second game, 3 in second inning, 3 in third inning, 1 in fourth inning.
N.L.—6
Karl Spooner, Brooklyn, September 22, 1954, 3 in seventh inning, 3 in eighth inning.
Pete Richert, Los Angeles, April 12, 1962, 1 in second inning, 4 in third inning, 1 in fourth inning (first six batters he faced in majors).

Most consecutive strikeouts by relief pitcher, game

A.L.—8—Ron Davis, New York, May 4, 1981, 2 in seventh inning, 3 in eighth inning, 3 in ninth inning.
N.L.—6
Jack Meyer, Philadelphia, September 22, 1958, first game, 3 in 12th inning, 3 in 13th inning (first six batters he faced).
Pete Richert, Los Angeles, April 12, 1962, 1 in second inning, 4 in third inning, 1 in fourth inning (first six batters he faced in majors).
Ron Perranoski, Los Angeles, September 12, 1966, 3 in fifth inning, 3 in sixth inning (first six batters he faced).
Dick Kelley, Atlanta, September 8, 1967, 2 in sixth inning, 3 in seventh inning, 1 in eighth inning.
Joe Hoerner, St. Louis, June 1, 1968, 3 in ninth inning, 3 in 10th inning.
Don Gullett, Cincinnati, August 23, 1970, second game, 3 in sixth inning, 3 in seventh inning (first 6 batters he faced).
Bruce Sutter, Chicago, September 8, 1977, 3 in eighth inning, 3 in ninth inning (first 6 batters he faced).
Willie Hernandez, Philadelphia, July 3, 1983, 3 in eighth inning, 3 in ninth inning (all 6 batters he faced).
Joe Price, Cincinnati, May 8, 1985, 3 in eighth inning, 3 in ninth inning.
Randy Myers, Cincinnati, September 8, 1990, 2 in seventh inning, 3 in eighth inning, 1 in ninth inning (first 6 batters he faced).
Rob Dibble, Cincinnati, April 23, 1991, 3 in eighth inning, 3 in ninth inning.

Most consecutive strikeouts from start of game

N.L.—9—Mickey Welch, New York, August 28, 1884.
N.L. since 1900—8—Jim Deshaies, Houston, September 23, 1986.
A.L.—7—Joe Cowley, Chicago, May 28, 1986.

Most strikeouts, two consecutive games

U.A.—34—Fred Shaw, Boston, July 19 (18), July 21 (16), 1884, 19 innings.
A.L.—32
Luis Tiant, Cleveland, June 29, first game (13), July 3 (19), 1968, 19 innings.
Nolan Ryan, California, August 7 (13), August 12 (19), 1974, 17 innings.
N.L.—32—Dwight Gooden, New York, September 12 (16), September 17 (16), 1984, 17 innings.

Most strikeouts, three consecutive games

U.A.—48—Fred Shaw, Boston, July 16, 19, 21, 1884, 28 innings.
A.L.—47—Nolan Ryan, California, August 12 (19), 16 (9), 20 (19), 1974, 27⅓ innings.
N.L.—43—Dwight Gooden, New York, September 7 (11), 12 (16), 17 (16), 1984, 26 innings.

HIT BATSMEN

Most hit batsmen, career

A.L.—206—Walter Johnson, Washington, 21 years, 1907 through 1927.
N.L.—195—Emerson Hawley, St. Louis, Pittsburgh, Cincinnati, New York, 9 years, 1892 through 1900.
N.L. since 1900—154—Don Drysdale, Brooklyn, Los Angeles, 14 years, 1956 through 1969.

Most hit batsmen, season
A.A.—54—Phil Knell, Columbus, 58 games, 1891.
N.L.—41—Joe McGinnity, Brooklyn, 45 games, 1900.
A.L.—31—Chick Fraser, Philadelphia, 39 games, 1901.

Fewest hit batsmen for leader, season
A.L.—6—Held by five pitchers. Last pitchers—Spud Chandler, New York, 1940; Al Smith, Cleveland, 1940.
N.L.—6—Held by five pitchers. Last pitchers—Rex Barney, Brooklyn, 1948; Sheldon Jones, New York, 1948; Kent Peterson, Cincinnati, 1948.

Most years leading league in hit batsmen
A.L.—6—Howard Ehmke, Detroit, Boston, Philadelphia, 1920, 1921, (tied), 1922, 1923 (tied), 1925, 1927.
N.L.—5—Don Drysdale, Los Angeles, 1958, 1959, 1960, 1961, 1965 (tied).

Most innings with no hit batsmen, season
A.L.—327—Alvin Crowder, Washington, 50 games, 1932.
N.L.—323—Sandy Koufax, Los Angeles, 41 games, 1966.

Most innings allowing no hit batsmen over three consecutive seasons
N.L.—755—Larry Benton, New York, Cincinnati, 1928, 1929, 1930.
A.L.—569—Bill Wight, Chicago, Boston, 1949, 1950, 1951.

Most hit batsmen, nine-inning game
A.A.—6—Ed Knouff, Baltimore, April 25, 1887.
N.L.—6—John Grimes, St. Louis, July 31, 1897, first game.
N.L. since 1900—4—Held by five pitchers. Last time—Moe Drabowsky, Chicago, June 2, 1957, first game.
A.L.—4—Held by 10 pitchers. Last time—Bert Blyleven, Minnesota, April 22, 1988.

Most hit batsmen, two consecutive games
N.L.—9—Sam Shaw, Chicago, June 13 (5), June 16 (4), 1893.

Longest game without a hit batsman
N.L.—26 innings
Leon Cadore, Brooklyn, May 1, 1920.
Joe Oeschger, Boston, May 1, 1920.
A.L.—21 innings—Ted Lyons, Chicago, May 24, 1929.

Most hit batsmen, inning (*consecutive)
N.L.—3
Pat Luby, Chicago, September 5, 1890, sixth inning.
Emerson Hawley, St. Louis, July 4, 1894, first game, *first inning.
Emerson Hawley, Pittsburgh, May 9, 1896, seventh inning.
Walter Thornton, Chicago, May 18, 1898, *fourth inning.
Deacon Phillippe, Pittsburgh, September 25, 1905, first inning.
Ray Boggs, Boston, September 17, 1928, ninth inning.
Raul Sanchez, Cincinnati, May 15, 1960, first game, eighth inning.
Dock Ellis, Pittsburgh, May 1, 1974, *first inning.
Mark Gardner, Montreal, August 15, 1992, first inning.
A.L.—3
Bert Gallia, Washington, June 20, 1913, second game, first inning.
Harry Harper, New York, August 25, 1921, eighth inning.
Tom Morgan, New York, June 30, 1954, third inning.
Wilbur Wood, Chicago, September 10, 1977, *first inning.
Bud Black, Cleveland, July 8, 1988, fourth inning.
Bert Blyleven, Minnesota, September 28, 1988, second inning.

WILD PITCHES

Most wild pitches, career
M.L.—277—Nolan Ryan, New York N.L., California A.L., Houston N.L., Texas A.L., 27 years, 1966, 1968 through 1993.
A.L.—206—Jack Morris, Detroit, Minnesota, Toronto, Cleveland, 18 years, 1977 through 1994.
N.L.—200—Phil Niekro, Milwaukee, Atlanta, 21 years, 1964 through 1983, 1987.

Most wild pitches, season
N.L.—64—Bill Stemmyer, Boston, 41 games, 1886.

N.L. since 1900—30—Leon Ames, New York, 263 innings, 1905.
A.L.—26—Juan Guzman, Toronto, 221 innings, 1993.

Fewest wild pitches by leader, season
N.L.—6
Kirby Higbe, Brooklyn, 211 innings, 1946.
Charley Schanz, Philadelphia, 116 innings, 1946.
A.L.—7—Held by eight pitchers. Last two pitchers—George Earnshaw, Philadelphia, 1928. Joe Shaute, Cleveland, 1928.

Most years leading league in wild pitches
M.L.—6
Nolan Ryan, California A.L., Houston N.L., Texas A.L., 1972, 1977, 1978, 1981, 1986, 1989.
Larry Cheney, Chicago N.L., Brooklyn N.L., 1912, 1913, 1914, 1916, 1917 (tied), 1918.
Jack Morris, Detroit A.L., Minnesota A.L., Cleveland A.L., 1983, 1984, 1985, 1987, 1991, 1994 (tied).
N.L.—6—Larry Cheney, Chicago, Brooklyn, 1912, 1913, 1914, 1916, 1917 (tied), 1918.
A.L..—6—Jack Morris, Detroit, Minnesota, Cleveland, 1983, 1984, 1985, 1987, 1991, 1994 (tied).

Most innings with no wild pitches, season
N.L.—340—Joe McGinnity, New York, 1906.
A.L.—327—Alvin Crowder, Washington, 1932.

Most innings with no wild pitches or hit batsmen, season
A.L.—327—Alvin Crowder, Washington, 1932.
N.L.—268—Jesse Barnes, Boston, 1924.

Most wild pitches, game
N.L.—10—Johnny Ryan, Louisville, July 22, 1876.
N.L. since 1900—6
J.R. Richard, Houston, April 10, 1979.
Phil Niekro, Atlanta, August 14, 1979, second game.
Bill Gullickson, Montreal, April 10, 1982.
A.L.—5
Charlie Wheatley, Detroit, September 27, 1912.
Jack Morris, Detroit, August 3, 1987, 10 innings.

Most wild pitches, first major league game
A.A.—5—Tom Seymour, Pittsburgh, September 23, 1882 (his only game in majors).
N.L.—5
Mike Corcoran, Chicago, July 15, 1884 (his only game in majors).
George Winkelman, Washington, August 2, 1886.

Most wild pitches, opening game of season
N.L.—4—Larry Cheney, Chicago, April 14, 1914.

Longest game without a wild pitch
N.L.—26 innings—Leon Cadore, Brooklyn, May 1, 1920.
A.L.—24 innings
Jack Coombs, Philadelphia, September 1, 1906.
Joe Harris, Boston, September 1, 1906.

Most wild pitches, inning
P.L.—5—Bert Cunningham, Buffalo, September 15, 1890, second game, first inning.
A.L.—4—Walter Johnson, Washington, September 21, 1914, fourth inning.
N.L.—4—Phil Niekro, Atlanta, August 4, 1979, second game, fifth inning.

SACRIFICE HITS

Most sacrifices allowed, season (sacrifice hits and sacrifice flies)
A.L.—54
Stan Coveleski, Cleveland, 316 innings, 1921.
Eddie Rommel, Philadelphia, 298 innings, 1923.
N.L.—49
Eppa Rixey, Philadelphia, 284 innings, 1920.
Jack Scott, Philadelphia, 233 innings, 1927.

Most sacrifice hits allowed, season (no sacrifice flies)
N.L.—35—Ed Brandt, Boston, 283 innings, 1933.
A.L.—28—Earl Whitehill, Detroit, 272 innings, 1931.

Fewest sacrifice hits allowed by leader, season (no sacrifice flies)

N.L.— 13
  Johnny Antonelli, San Francisco, 242 innings, 1958.
  Dick Farrell, Philadelphia, 94 innings, 1958.
  Ron Kline, Pittsburgh, 237 innings, 1958.
A.L.— 11
  Gaylord Perry, Seattle, Kansas City, 186⅓ innings, 1983.
  Bob Stanley, Boston, 145⅓ innings, 1983.

Most innings by pitcher allowing no sacrifice hits, season

N.L.— 183—Carl Willey, New York, 30 games, 1963.

Most years leading league in most sacrifices allowed

N.L.—3—Eppa Rixey, Philadelphia, Cincinnati, 1920, 1921, 1928.
A.L.—3—Earl Whitehill, Detroit, Washington, 1931, 1934, 1935.

SACRIFICE FLIES

Most sacrifice flies allowed, career

M.L.— 141—Jim Kaat, Washington A.L., Minnesota A.L., Chicago A.L., Philadelphia N.L., New York A.L., St. Louis N.L., 25 years, 1959 through 1983 (108 in A.L., 33 in N.L.).
A.L.— 108—Jim Kaat, Washington, Minnesota, Chicago, New York, 19 years, 1959 through 1975, 1979 through 1980.
N.L.—95—Bob Gibson, St. Louis, 17 years, 1959 through 1975.

Most sacrifice flies allowed, season

A.L.— 17
  Larry Gura, Kansas City, 200⅓ innings, 1983.
  Jaime Navarro, Milwaukee, 214⅓ innings, 1993.
N.L.— 15—Randy Lerch, Philadelphia, 214 innings, 1979.

Most innings by pitcher allowing no sacrifice flies, season

N.L.—284—Phil Niekro, Atlanta, 40 games, 1969.

BALKS

Most balks, season

A.L.— 16—Dave Stewart, Oakland, 275⅔ innings, 1988.
N.L.— 11—Steve Carlton, Philadelphia, 251 innings, 1979.

Most balks, game

N.L.—5—Bob Shaw, Milwaukee, May 4, 1963.
A.L.—4
  Vic Raschi, New York, May 3, 1950.
  Bobby Witt, Texas, April 12, 1988.
  Rick Honeycutt, Oakland, April 13, 1988.
  Gene Walter, Seattle, July 18, 1988.
  John Dopson, Boston, June 13, 1989.

Most balks, inning

A.L.—3
  Milt Shoffner, Cleveland, May 12, 1930, third inning.
  Don Heinkel, Detroit, May 3, 1988, sixth inning.
N.L.—3
  Jim Owens, Cincinnati, April 24, 1963, second inning.
  Bob Shaw, Milwaukee, May 4, 1963, third inning.
  Jim Gott, Pittsburgh, August 6, 1988, eighth inning.

CLUB PITCHING

COMPLETE GAMES

Most complete games, season
A.L.—148—Boston, 157 games, 1904.
N.L.—146—St. Louis, 155 games, 1904.
Fewest complete games, season
A.L.—3—New York, 162 games, 1991.
N.L.—4
Florida, 162 games, 1993.
San Francisco, 162 games, 1993.
Most consecutive games, none complete
A.L.—83—New York, July 12 through October 6, 1991.
N.L.—74—San Diego, May 5 through July 25, 1977.

INNINGS

Most innings, season
A.L. (162-game season)—1,507—New York, 164 games, 1964.
A.L. (154-game season)—1,465—Cleveland, 161 games, 1910.
N.L. (162-game season)—1,493—Pittsburgh, 163 games, 1979.
N.L. (154-game season)—1,453—Philadelphia, 159 games, 1913.
Most pitchers with 300 or more innings, season
N.L. (154-game season)—3—Boston, 1905, 1906.
A.L. (154-game season)—3—Detroit, 1904.

GAMES WON

Most games won by two pitchers on same club, season
N.L.—77—Providence 1884 (Hoss Radbourn, 60, Charlie Sweeney, 17).
N.L. since 1900—68—New York, 1904 (Joe McGinnity, 35, Christy Mathewson, 33).
A.L.—64—New York, 1904 (Jack Chesbro, 41, Jack Powell, 23).
Most pitchers winning 20 or more games, season (since 1900)
A.L.—4
Chicago, 1920.
Baltimore, 1971.
N.L.—3
Pittsburgh, 1902.
Chicago, 1903.
New York, 1904, 1905, 1913, 1920.
Cincinnati, 1923.
Most consecutive years with pitchers winning 20 or more games
A.L.—13—Baltimore, 1968 through 1980.
N.L.—12—New York, 1903 through 1914.
Most consecutive years without pitchers winning 20 or more games
N.L.—32—Philadelphia, 1918 through 1949.
A.L.—20
California, 1975 through 1994.
Cleveland, 1975 through 1994.

SAVES

Most saves, season
A.L.—68—Chicago, 162 games, 1990.
N.L.—61—Montreal, 163 games, 1993.
Fewest saves, season
A.L.—11—Toronto, 162 games, 1979.
N.L.—13
Chicago, 162 games, 1971.
St. Louis, 156 games, 1972.

GAMES LOST

Most pitchers losing 20 or more games, season (since 1900)
N.L.—4—Boston, 1905, 1906.
A.L.—3
Washington, 1904.
St. Louis, 1905.
Philadelphia, 1916.

AT-BATS AND PLATE APPEARANCES

Most at-bats allowed, season
N.L.—5,763—Philadelphia, 156 games, 1930.
A.L.—5,671—Boston, 163 games, 1978.
Fewest at-bats allowed, season
A.L.—4,933—Cleveland, 147 games, 1945.
N.L.—5,062—Philadelphia, 155 games, 1947.
Most opponents' men facing pitcher, season
N.L.—6,549—Philadelphia, 156 games, 1930.
A.L.—6,439—Cleveland, 163 games, 1986.
Fewest opponents' men facing pitcher, season
A.L.—5,653—St. Louis, 155 games, 1936.
N.L.—5,684—Brooklyn, 154 games, 1956.

RUNS, EARNED RUNS AND ERA

Most runs allowed, season
N.L.—1,199—Philadelphia, 156 games, 1930.
A.L.—1,064—St. Louis, 155 games, 1936.
Fewest runs allowed, season
A.L. (154-game season)—408—Philadelphia, 153 games, 1909.
A.L. (162-game season)—491—Chicago, 162 games, 1967.
N.L. (154-game season)—379—Chicago, 154 games, 1906.
N.L. (162-game season)—472—St. Louis, 162 games, 1968.
Most earned runs allowed, season
N.L.—1,024—Philadelphia, 156 games, 1930.
A.L.—935—St. Louis, 155 games, 1936.
Fewest earned runs allowed, season
N.L.—332—Philadelphia, 153 games, 1915.
A.L.—343—Chicago, 156 games, 1917.
Lowest earned-run average, season
A.L.—2.16—Chicago, 156 games, 1917.
N.L.—2.18—Philadelphia, 153 games, 1915.
Highest earned-run average, season
N.L.—6.70—Philadelphia, 156 games, 1930.
A.L.—6.24—St. Louis, 155 games, 1936.

SHUTOUTS

Most shutout games participated in, season
A.L.—47—Chicago, 1910 (won 22, lost 24, tied 1).
N.L. (162-game season)—47—New York, 1968 (won 25, lost 22).
N.L. (154-game season)—46—St. Louis, 1908 (won 13, lost 33).
Fewest shutout games participated in, season
A.L.—5—Chicago, 1977 (won 3, lost 2).
N.L.—6—Philadelphia, 1930 (won 3, lost 3).
Most shutout games won or tied, season
N.L.—32—Chicago, 1907, 1909.
A.L.—32—Chicago, 1906 (including 2 ties).

Fewest shutout games won or tied, season (150 or more games)

N.L.—0
  Brooklyn, 1898.
  Washington, 1898.
  St. Louis, 1898.
  Cleveland, 1899.
  Colorado, 1993.
A.L.—1
  Chicago, 1924.
  Washington, 1956.
  Seattle, 1977.

Most shutouts won from one club, season

N.L. (162-game season)—7—New York vs. Philadelphia, 1969 (lost 1).
N.L. (154-game season) — 10—Pittsburgh vs. Boston, 1906 (lost 1).
A.L. (162-game season)—8—Oakland vs. Cleveland 1968 (lost 1).
A.L. (154-game season)—8
  Chicago vs. Boston, 1906 (lost 1).
  Cleveland vs. Washington, 1956 (lost 0).

Most consecutive shutout games won, season

N.L.—6—Pittsburgh, June 2 through June 6, 1903 (51 innings).
A.L.—5—Baltimore, September 2, 2, 4, 6, 6, 1974 (45 innings).

Largest score, shutout day game

N.L.—28-0—Providence vs. Philadelphia, August 21, 1883.
N.L. since 1900—22-0—Pittsburgh vs. Chicago, September 16, 1975.
A.L.—21-0
  Detroit vs. Cleveland, September 15, 1901, eight innings.
  New York vs. Philadelphia, August 13, 1939, second game, eight innings.

Largest score, shutout night game

N.L.—19-0
  Pittsburgh vs. St. Louis, August 3, 1961, at St. Louis.
  Los Angeles vs. San Diego, June 28, 1969, at San Diego.
A.L.—17-0—Los Angeles vs. Washington, August 23, 1963, at Washington.

Most runs, doubleheader shutout

A.L.—26—Detroit vs. St. Louis, September 22, 1936 (12-0, 14-0).
N.L.—19—New York vs. Cincinnati, July 31, 1949 (10-0, 9-0).

Doubleheader shutouts since 1900

N.L.—Occurred 101 times. Last time—September 29, 1987, St. Louis vs. Montreal (St. Louis won, 1-0 and 3-0).
A.L.—Occurred 89 times. Last time—June 26, 1988, Minnesota vs. Oakland (Minnesota won, 11-0 and 5-0).

Most consecutive innings shut out opponent, season

N.L.—56—Pittsburgh, June 1 (last two innings) through June 9 (first three innings), 1903.
A.L.—54—Baltimore, September 1, (last inning) through September 7 (first eight innings), 1974.

1-0 GAMES

Most 1-0 games won, season

A.L.—11—Washington, 1914 (lost 4).
N.L.—10—Pittsburgh, 1908 (lost 1).

Fewest 1-0 games won, season

N.L.-A.L.—0—Held by many clubs.
N.L.—Last clubs—Cincinnati, Colorado, Philadelphia, San Diego, 1993.
A.L.—Last clubs—California, Detroit, Milwaukee, Minnesota, Oakland, Seattle, 1993.

Most 1-0 games lost, season

N.L.—10—Pittsburgh, 1914; Chicago, 1916; Philadelphia, 1967.
A.L.—9—New York, 1914; Chicago, 1968.

Fewest 1-0 games lost, season

N.L.-A.L.—0—Held by many clubs.

N.L.—Last clubs—New York, Philadelphia, San Francisco, 1993.
A.L.—Last clubs—Boston, Cleveland, Detroit, New York, Texas, Toronto, 1993.

Most consecutive 1-0 games won, season

A.L.—3—Chicago, April 25, 26, 27, 1909.
N.L.—3—St. Louis, August 31, second game (five innings), September 1, 1, 1917.

Most consecutive 1-0 games lost, season

A.L.—3
  St. Louis, April 25, 26, 27, 1909.
  Washington, May 7, 8, 10 (11 innings), 1909.
N.L.—3
  Brooklyn, September 7, 7, 8 (11 innings), 1908.
  Pittsburgh, August 31, second game (five innings), September 1, 1, 1917.
  Philadelphia, May 11, 12, 13, 1960.

Most 1-0 games won from one club, season

N.L.—4—Held by four clubs. Last club—Cincinnati vs. Brooklyn, 1910.
A.L.—4—Held by four clubs. Last club—Detroit vs. Boston, 1917.

Winning two 1-0 games in one day

N.L.—12 times. Last time—Pittsburgh vs. St. Louis, October 3, 1976.
A.L.—1 time—Baltimore vs. Boston, September 2, 1974.

HITS AND HOME RUNS

Most hits allowed, season

N.L.—1,993—Philadelphia, 156 games, 1930.
A.L.—1,776—St. Louis, 155 games, 1936.

Fewest hits allowed, season

A.L.—1,087—Cleveland, 162 games, 1968.
N.L.—1,174—Pittsburgh, 153 games, 1909.

Most home runs allowed, season

A.L. (162-game season)—226—Baltimore, 162 games, 1987.
A.L. (154-game season)—187—Kansas City, 154 games, 1956.
N.L. (162-game season)—192—New York, 161 games, 1962.
N.L. (154-game season)—185—St. Louis, 154 games, 1955.

Most home runs allowed at home, season

A.L.—132—at Kansas City, 1964, 81 games.
N.L.—120—at New York, 1962, 80 games.

Most grand slams allowed, season

A.L.—10—Seattle, 162 games, 1992.
N.L.—9—Houston, 162 games, 1987.

Fewest grand slams allowed, season

N.L.-A.L.—0—Held by many clubs.
N.L.—Last club—Los Angeles, 1993.
A.L.—Last club—Cleveland, 1990.

NO-HIT AND ONE-HIT GAMES

Most no-hit games, season

A.A.—2—Louisville 1882; Columbus 1884; Philadelphia 1888.
A.L.—2—Boston 1904; Cleveland 1908; Chicago 1914; Boston 1916; St. Louis 1917; New York 1951; Detroit 1952; Boston 1962; California 1973.
N.L.—2—Brooklyn 1906; Cincinnati 1938; Brooklyn 1956; Milwaukee 1960; Cincinnati 1965; Chicago 1972.

Most consecutive years with no-hit games by pitchers

N.L.—4—Los Angeles, 1962, 1963, 1964, 1965.
A.L.—3
  Boston, 1916, 1917, 1918.
  Cleveland, 1946, 1947, 1948.
  Baltimore, 1967, 1968, 1969.
  California, 1973, 1974, 1975.

Most consecutive years without no-hit games by pitchers

N.L.—57—Philadelphia, 1907 through 1963.

A.L.—39—Detroit, 1913 through 1951.

Most one-hit games, season

A.L. (162-game season)—5—Baltimore, 1964.
A.L. (154-game season)—4
  Cleveland, 1907.
  New York, 1934.
N.L.—4
  Chicago, 1906, 1909 (154-game seasons).
  Philadelphia, 1907, 1911, 1915 (154-game seasons).
  Philadelphia, 1979 (162-game season).

Most consecutive one-hit nine-inning games

N.L.—2
  Providence vs. New York, June 17, 18, 1884.
  Brooklyn vs. Cincinnati, July 5, 6, 1900.
  New York vs. Boston, September 28, second game, 30, first
    game, 1916.
  Milwaukee vs. New York, September 10, 11, 1965.
  New York vs. Chicago, Philadelphia, May 13, 15, 1970.
  Houston vs. Philadelphia, New York, June 18, 19, 1972.
A.L.—2
  Cleveland vs. New York, September 25, 26, 1907.
  Washington vs. Chicago, August 10, 11, 1917.

BASES ON BALLS

Most bases on balls, season

A.L.—827—Philadelphia, 154 games, 1915.
N.L. (162-game season)—716—Montreal, 162 games, 1970.
N.L. (154-game season)—671—Brooklyn, 157 games, 1946.

Fewest bases on balls, season

N.L.—295—New York, 153 games, 1921.
A.L.—359—Detroit, 158 games, 1909.

Most intentional bases on balls, season

N.L.—116—San Diego, 162 games, 1974.
A.L.—94—Seattle, 163 games, 1980.

Fewest intentional bases on balls, season

N.L.—9—Los Angeles, 162 games, 1974.
A.L.—16
  Minnesota, 162 games, 1973.
  New York, 159 games, 1976.

STRIKEOUTS

Most strikeouts, season

N.L. (162-game season)—1,221—Houston, 162 games, 1969.
N.L. (154-game season)—1,122—Los Angeles, 154 games,
  1960.
A.L. (162-game season)—1,189—Cleveland, 162 games, 1967.
A.L. (154-game season)—896—Detroit, 155 games, 1946.

Fewest strikeouts, season

A.L.—356—Boston, 154 games, 1930.
N.L.—357—New York, 153 games, 1921.

HIT BATSMEN AND WILD PITCHES

Most hit batsmen, season

N.L.—85—Pittsburgh, 134 games, 1895.
A.L.—81—Philadelphia, 152 games, 1911.

N.L. since 1900—68—Brooklyn, 139 games, 1903.

Fewest hit batsmen, season

A.L. (154-game season)—5—St. Louis, 154 games, 1945.
A.L. (162-game season)—10—Baltimore, 162 games, 1983.
N.L. (154-game season)—10—St. Louis, 155 games, 1948.
N.L. (162-game season)—11—Pittsburgh, 162 games, 1984.

Most wild pitches, season

A.L. (162-game season)—94—Texas, 162 games, 1986.
A.L. (154-game season)—67—Philadelphia, 154 games, 1936.
N.L. (162-game season)—91
  Houston, 162 games, 1970.
  Philadelphia, 163 games, 1989.
N.L. (154-game season)—70—Los Angeles, 154 games, 1958.

Fewest wild pitches, season

N.L.—9—Cincinnati, 155 games, 1944.
A.L.—10
  St. Louis, 154 games, 1930.
  Cleveland, 153 games, 1943.

SACRIFICE HITS AND FLIES

Most sacrifice hits allowed, season

N.L. (162-game season)—112—San Diego, 162 games, 1975.
N.L. (154-game season)—106—New York, 154 games, 1956.
A.L.—110—Kansas City, 158 games, 1960.

Fewest sacrifice hits allowed, season

A.L.—31—Minnesota, 162 games, 1984.
N.L.—44—Montreal, 156 games, 1972.

Most sacrifice flies allowed, season

N.L.—79—Pittsburgh, 154 games, 1954.
A.L.—73—Cleveland, 163 games, 1984.

Fewest sacrifice flies allowed, season

N.L.—17—San Francisco, 162 games, 1963.
A.L.—17—Detroit, 164 games, 1968.

BALKS

Most balks, season

A.L.—76—Oakland, 162 games, 1988.
N.L.—41—Montreal, 163 games, 1988.

Fewest balks season

A.L.-N.L.—0—Held by many clubs.

Most balks, nine-inning game

N.L.—6—Milwaukee vs. Chicago, May 4, 1963.
A.L.—5
  Milwaukee vs. New York, April 10, 1988.
  Oakland vs. Seattle, April 13, 1988.

Most balks by both clubs, nine-inning game

N.L.—7
  Pittsburgh 4, Cincinnati 3, April 13, 1963.
  Milwaukee 6, Chicago 1, May 4, 1963.
A.L.—6
  Milwaukee 5, New York 1, April 10, 1988.
  Chicago 4, California 2, April 12, 1988.

LEAGUE PITCHING

COMPLETE GAMES AND INNINGS

Most complete games, season
A.L.—1,100 in 1904.
N.L.—1,089 in 1904.

Fewest complete games, season
N.L.—150 in 1991.
A.L.—209 in 1993.

Most pitchers with 300 or more innings, season
A.L.—12 in 1904.
N.L.—10 in 1905.

GAMES WON AND LOST

Most pitchers winning 20 or more games, season (since 1900)
A.L. (12-club league) — 12 in 1973.
A.L. (8-club league) — 10 in 1907, 1920.
N.L.—9
in 1903 (8-club league).
in 1969 (12-club league).

Fewest pitchers winning 20 or more games, season (since 1900)
N.L.—0 in 1931, 1983, 1987.
A.L.—0 in 1955, 1960, 1982.

Most pitchers losing 20 or more games, season
N.L.—8 in 1905.
A.L.—7 in 1904.

RUNS, EARNED RUNS AND ERA

Most runs, season
A.L. (14-club league) — 11,112 in 1987.
A.L. (12-club league) — 8,314 in 1973.
A.L. (10-club league) — 7,342 in 1961.
A.L. (8-club league) — 7,009 in 1936.
N.L. (14-club league) — 10,190 in 1993.
N.L. (12-club league) — 8,771 in 1970, 1987.
N.L. (10-club league) — 7,278 in 1962.
N.L. (8-club league) — 7,025 in 1930.

Fewest runs, season
N.L.—4,136 in 1908.
A.L.—4,272 in 1909.

Most earned runs, season
A.L. (14-club league) — 9,999 in 1987.
A.L. (12-club league) — 7,376 in 1973.
A.L. (10-club league) — 6,451 in 1961.
A.L. (8-club league) — 6,120 in 1936.
N.L. (14-club league) — 9,105 in 1993.
N.L. (12-club league) — 7,878 in 1987.
N.L. (10-club league) — 6,345 in 1962.
N.L. (8-club league) — 6,046 in 1930.

Fewest earned runs, season
N.L.—3,258 in 1916.
A.L.—3,414 in 1914.

Lowest earned-run average, season
N.L.—2.62 in 1916.
A.L.—2.73 in 1914.

Highest earned-run average, season
A.L.—5.04 in 1936.
N.L.—4.97 in 1930.

SHUTOUTS

Most shutouts, season
A.L. (12-club league) — 193 in 1972.
A.L. (10-club league) — 154 in 1968.

A.L. (8-club league) — 146 in 1909.
N.L. (10-club league) — 185 in 1968.
N.L. (8-club league) — 164 in 1908.

Most extra-inning shutouts, season
A.L.—12
in 1918 (8-club league).
in 1976 (12-club league).
N.L. (12-club league) — 12 in 1976.
N.L. (10-club league) — 11 in 1965.
N.L. (8-club league) — 8 in 1908, 1909, 1910.

Fewest shutouts, season
A.L. (8-club league) — 41 in 1930.
A.L. (10-club league) — 100 in 1961.
A.L. (14-club league) — 108 in 1985.
N.L. (8-club league) — 48 in 1925.
N.L. (10-club league) — 95 in 1962.
N.L. (12-club league) — 98 in 1987.
N.L. (14-club league) — 110 in 1993.

Most shutouts, one day
N.L.—5
July 13, 1888 (six games).
June 24, 1892 (eight games).
July 21, 1896 (seven games).
July 8, 1907 (five games).
September 7, 1908 (eight games).
September 9, 1916 (seven games).
May 31, 1943 (eight games).
June 17, 1969 (nine games).
August 9, 1984 (six games).
A.L.—5
September 7, 1903 (eight games).
August 5, 1909 (six games).
May 6, 1945 (eight games).
June 4, 1972 (nine games).

Most shutouts in both leagues, one day
8—June 4, 1972, 5 in A.L. (nine games), 3 in N.L. (seven games).

1-0 GAMES

Most 1-0 games, season
N.L. (10-club league) — 44 in 1968.
N.L. (8-club league) — 43 in 1907.
A.L. (12-club league) — 42 in 1971.
A.L. (8-club league) — 41 in 1908.

Fewest 1-0 games, season
A.L. (8-club league) — 4 in 1930, 1936.
A.L. (14-club league) — 11 in 1985.
N.L. (8-club league) — 5 in 1932, 1956.
N.L. (10-club league) — 13 in 1962.
N.L. (12-club league) — 13 in 1983, 1990.
N.L. (14-club league) — 22 in 1993.

Most 1-0 games, one day
A.L.—3—May 14, 1914; July 17, 1962.
N.L.—3—July 4, 1918; September 12, 1969; September 1, 1976.

NO-HIT AND ONE-HIT GAMES

Most no-hit games of nine or more innings, season
M.L.—8
in 1884 (4 in A.A., 2 in N.L., 2 in U.A.).
in 1990 (6 in A.L., 2 in N.L.).
A.L. (14-club league) — 6 in 1990.
A.L. (8-club league) — 5 in 1917.
N.L. (12-club league) — 5 in 1969.
N.L. (8-club league) — 4 in 1880.

Fewest no-hit games, season

N.L.—0—Made in many seasons. Last season—1989.
A.L.—0—Made in many seasons. Last season—1989.

Most no-hit games, one day

N.L.—2 on April 22, 1898.
A.L.—1—Made on many days.

Most one-hit games of nine or more innings, season

A.L. (14-club league) — 13 in 1979, 1988.
A.L. (8-club league) — 12 in 1910, 1915.
N.L. (10-club league) — 13 in 1965.
N.L. (8-club league) — 12 in 1906, 1910.

Fewest one-hit games of nine or more innings, season

A.L. (12-club league) —4— 1971.
A.L. (8-club league) —0— 1922, 1926, 1927, 1930.
N.L. (12-club league) —4— 1980, 1987.
N.L. (8-club league) —0— 1924, 1929, 1932, 1952.

HOME RUNS

Most pitchers allowing 30 or more home runs, season

A.L. (14-club league) —18 in 1987.
N.L. (12-club league) —5 in 1970.

BASES ON BALLS

Most bases on balls, season

A.L. (14-club season) —8,006 in 1993.
A.L. (12-club league) —7,032 in 1969.
A.L. (10-club league) —5,902 in 1961.
A.L. (8-club league) —5,627 in 1949.
N.L. (14-club league) —7,104 in 1993.
N.L. (12-club league) —6,919 in 1970.
N.L. (10-club league) —5,265 in 1962.
N.L. (8-club league) —4,537 in 1950.

Fewest bases on balls, season

N.L.—2,906 in 1921.
A.L.—3,797 in 1922.

Most intentional bases on balls, season (since 1955)

N.L. (12-club league) —862 in 1973.
N.L. (10-club league) —804 in 1967.
N.L. (8-club league) —504 in 1956.
A.L. (12-club league) —668 in 1969.
A.L. (10-club league) —534 in 1965.
A.L. (8-club league) —353 in 1957.

STRIKEOUTS

Most strikeouts, season

A.L. (14-club league) —13,442 in 1987.
A.L. (12-club league) —10,957 in 1970.
A.L. (10-club league) —9,956 in 1964.
A.L. (8-club league) —6,081 in 1959.
N.L. (14-club league) —13,358 in 1993.
N.L. (12-club league) —11,657 in 1987.

N.L. (10-club league) —9,649 in 1965.
N.L. (8-club league) —6,824 in 1960.

Most pitchers with 300 or more strikeouts, season

A.A.—6 in 1884.
N.L.—4 in 1884.
N.L. since 1900—1 in 1963, 1965, 1966, 1972, 1978, 1979.
U.A.—3 in 1884.
A.L.—2 in 1971.

Most pitchers with 200 or more strikeouts, season

N.L.— 12 in 1969.
A.L.—7 in 1967, 1973, 1986.

Most pitchers with 100 or more strikeouts, season

N.L.—45 in 1970.
A.L.—41 in 1986, 1987.

Fewest strikeouts, season

A.L.—3,245 in 1924.
N.L.—3,359 in 1926.

HIT BATSMEN

Most hit batsmen, season

A.L. (14-club league) —633 in 1993.
A.L. (12-club league) —439 in 1969.
A.L. (8-club league) —435 in 1909.
N.L. (14-club league) —567 in 1993.
N.L. (12-club league) —443 in 1969.
N.L. (8-club league) —415 in 1903.

Fewest hit batsmen, season

A.L.— 132 in 1947.
N.L.— 157 in 1943.

WILD PITCHES AND BALKS

Most wild pitches, season

A.L. (14-club league) —775 in 1990.
A.L. (12-club league) —636 in 1969.
A.L. (10-club league) —513 in 1966.
A.L. (8-club league) —325 in 1936.
N.L. (14-club league) —747 in 1993.
N.L. (12-club league) —648 in 1969.
N.L. (10-club league) —550 in 1965.
N.L. (8-club league) —356 in 1961.

Fewest wild pitches, season

A.L.— 166 in 1931.
N.L.— 174 in 1943.

Most balks, season

A.L. (14-club league) —558 in 1988.
A.L. (12-club league) —60 in 1976.
A.L. (10-club league) —51 in 1966.
N.L. (12-club league) —366 in 1988.
N.L. (10-club league) — 147 in 1963.

Fewest balks, season

N.L. — 13 in 1936, 1946, 1956.
A.L. — 18 in 1933, 1941.

INDIVIDUAL FIELDING

FIRST BASEMEN

GAMES AND INNINGS

Most games, career

M.L.—2,394—Eddie Murray, Baltimore A.L., Los Angeles N.L., New York N.L., Cleveland A.L., 1977 through 1994, 18 years.

N.L.—2,247—Jake Beckley, Pittsburgh, New York, Cincinnati, St. Louis, 1888 through 1907, except 1890, 19 years.

N.L. since 1900—2,132—Charlie Grimm, St. Louis, Pittsburgh, Chicago, 1918 through 1936, 19 years.

A.L.—2,227—Mickey Vernon, Washington, Cleveland, Boston, 1939 through 1958, except 1944, 1945 in military service, 18 years.

Most consecutive games, career

A.L.—885—Lou Gehrig, New York, June 2, 1925, through September 27, 1930.

N.L.—652—Frank McCormick, Cincinnati, April 19, 1938, through May 24, 1942, second game.

Most games, season

A.L. (162-game season)—162
Norm Siebern, Kansas City, 1962.
Bill Buckner, Boston, 1985.

A.L. (154-game season)—157
George LaChance, Boston, 1904.
Jiggs Donahue, Chicago, 1907.
Lou Gehrig, New York, 1937, 1938.

N.L. (162-game season)—162
Bill White, St. Louis, 1963.
Ernie Banks, Chicago, 1965.
Steve Garvey, Los Angeles, 1976, 1979, 1980.
Steve Garvey, San Diego, 1985.
Pete Rose, Philadelphia, 1980, 1982.

N.L. (154-game season)—158
Ed Konetchy, St. Louis, 1911; Boston, 1916.
Dick Hoblitzel, Cincinnati, 1911.
Babe Dahlgren, Pittsburgh, 1944.
Gil Hodges, Brooklyn, 1951.

Most years leading league in most games

N.L.—9—Steve Garvey, Los Angeles, 1975, 1976, 1977, 1978, 1979, 1980 (tied), 1981; San Diego, 1984, 1985.

A.L.—7—Lou Gehrig, New York, 1926, 1927, 1928 (tied), 1932, 1936, 1937, 1938.

Fewest games for leader, season

A.L.—121—Vic Power, Cleveland, 1959.

N.L.—134—Ed Bouchee, Philadelphia, 1959.

Most innings played, game

N.L.—26
Walter Holke, Boston, May 1, 1920.
Ed Konetchy, Brooklyn, May 1, 1920.

A.L.—25—Ted Simmons, Milwaukee, May 8, finished May 9, 1984 (fielded 24⅓ innings).

AVERAGE

Highest fielding average, career (1,000 or more games)

N.L.—.996
Wes Parker, Los Angeles, 1964 through 1972, nine years, 1,108 games.
Steve Garvey, Los Angeles, San Diego, 1972 through 1987, 16 years, 2,059 games.

A.L.—.996—Don Mattingly, New York, 1983 through 1994, 12 years, 1,509 games.

Highest fielding average, season (150 or more games)

N.L.—1.000—Steve Garvey, San Diego, 159 games, 1984.

A.L.—.999—Stuffy McInnis, Boston, 152 games, 1921.

Highest fielding average, season (100 or more games)

N.L.—1.000—Steve Garvey, San Diego, 159 games, 1984.

A.L.—.999.
Stuffy McInnis, Boston, 152 games, 1921.
Jim Spencer, California, Texas, 125 games, 1973.

Most years leading league in fielding (100 or more games)

N.L.—9—Charlie Grimm, Pittsburgh, Chicago, 1920, 1922 (tied), 1923, 1924, 1928 (tied), 1930, 1931, 1932 (tied), 1933.

A.L.—6
Joe Judge, Washington, 1923, 1924 (tied), 1925, 1927, 1929, 1930.
Don Mattingly, New York, 1984 (tied), 1985, 1986 (tied), 1987, 1992, 1993.

Most consecutive years leading league in fielding (100 or more games)

N.L.—5—Ted Kluszewski, Cincinnati, 1951, 1952, 1953, 1954, 1955.

A.L.—4—Chick Gandil, Cleveland, Chicago, 1916, 1917, 1918, 1919.

Lowest fielding average for leader, season (100 or more games)

N.L.—.978—Alex McKinnon, St. Louis, 100 games, 1885.

A.L.—.981—John Anderson, Milwaukee, 125 games, 1901.

N.L. since 1900—.986
Dan McGann, St. Louis, 113 games, 1901.
Kitty Bransfield, Pittsburgh, 100 games, 1902.

Lowest fielding average, season (100 or more games)

N.L.—.954—Alex McKinnon, New York, 112 games, 1884.

N.L. since 1900—.970—Jack Doyle, New York, 130 games, 1900.

A.L.—.972
Harry Davis, Philadelphia, 100 games, 1903.
Pat Newnam, St. Louis, 103 games, 1910.

PUTOUTS

Most putouts, career

M.L.—23,696—Jake Beckley, Pittsburgh N.L., Pittsburgh P.L., New York N.L., Cincinnati N.L., St. Louis N.L., 1888 through 1907, 20 years.

N.L.—22,438—Jake Beckley, New York, Pittsburgh, Cincinnati, St. Louis, 1888 through 1907, except 1890, 19 years.

N.L. since 1900—20,700—Charlie Grimm, St. Louis, Pittsburgh, Chicago, 1918 through 1936, 19 years.

A.L.—19,754—Mickey Vernon, Washington, Cleveland, Boston, 1939 through 1958, except 1944, 1945 in military service, 18 years.

Most putouts, season

A.L.—1,846—Jiggs Donahue, Chicago, 157 games, 1907.

N.L.—1,759—George Kelly, New York, 155 games, 1920.

Most years leading league in putouts

N.L.—6
Jake Beckley, Pittsburgh, Cincinnati, St. Louis, 1892, 1894, 1895, 1900, 1902, 1904.
Frank McCormick, Cincinnati, 1939, 1940, 1941, 1942, 1944, 1945.
Steve Garvey, Los Angeles, San Diego, 1974, 1975, 1976, 1977, 1978, 1985.

A.L.—4—Wally Pipp, New York, 1915, 1919, 1920, 1922.

Fewest putouts, season (150 or more games)

A.L.—1,159—Dick Stuart, Boston, 155 games, 1964.

N.L.—1,162—Gordy Coleman, Cincinnati, 150 games, 1961.

Fewest putouts for leader, season

A.L.—971—Vic Wertz, Cleveland, 133 games, 1956.

N.L.—1,127—Ed Bouchee, Philadelphia, 134 games, 1959.

Most putouts, nine-inning game

A.L.—22
Tom Jones, St. Louis, May 11, 1906.

Hal Chase, New York, September 21, 1906, first game.
Don Mattingly, New York, July 20, 1987.
Alvin Davis, Seattle, May 28, 1988.
N.L.—22—Ernie Banks, Chicago, May 9, 1963.

Most putouts, extra-inning game

N.L.—42—Walter Holke, Boston, May 1, 1920, 26 innings.
A.L.—32
    Mike Epstein, Washington, June 12, 1967, 22 innings.
    Rod Carew, California, April 13, finished April 14, 1982, 20
        innings.

Fewest putouts, nine-inning game

A.A.—0—Al McCauley, Washington, August 6, 1891.
A.L.—0
    Bud Clancy, Chicago, April 27, 1930.
    Rudy York, Detroit, June 18, 1943.
    Frank Robinson, Baltimore, July 1, 1971.
    Gene Tenace, Oakland, September 1, 1974.
N.L.—0
    Rip Collins, St. Louis, August 21, 1935.
    Rip Collins, Chicago, June 29, 1937.
    Dolph Camilli, Philadelphia, July 30, 1937.
    Earl Torgeson, Boston, May 30, 1947, first game.
    Gary Thomasson, San Francisco, July 31, 1977.
    Len Matuszek, Philadelphia, June 1, 1984.
    Franklin Stubbs, Houston, July 25, 1990.

ASSISTS

Most assists, career

M.L.—1,842—Eddie Murray, Baltimore A.L., Los Angeles
    N.L., New York N.L., Cleveland A.L., 1977 through 1994,
    18 years.
N.L.—1,662—Keith Hernandez, St. Louis, New York, 1974
    through 1989, 16 years.
A.L.—1,444—Mickey Vernon, Washington, Cleveland,
    Washington, Boston, 1939 through 1958, except 1944,
    1945 in military service, 18 years.

Most assists, season

A.L.—184—Bill Buckner, Boston, 162 games, 1985.
N.L.—180—Mark Grace, Chicago, 153 games, 1990.

Most years leading league in assists

N.L.—8—Fred Tenney, Boston, 1899, 1901, 1902, 1903,
    1904, 1905, 1906, 1907.
A.L.—6
    George Sisler, St. Louis, 1919, 1920, 1922, 1924, 1925,
        1927.
    Vic Power, Kansas City, Cleveland, Minnesota, 1955, 1957,
        1959, 1960, 1961, 1962.

Fewest assists, season (150 or more games)

N.L.—54—Jim Bottomley, St. Louis, 154 games, 1926.
A.L.—58—Lou Gehrig, New York, 154 games, 1931.

Fewest assists for leader, season

N.L.—83—Herm Reich, Chicago, 85 games, 1949.
A.L.—85—Wally Pipp, New York, 134 games, 1915.

Most assists, nine-inning game

N.L.—8—Bob Robertson, Pittsburgh, June 21, 1971.
A.L.—7—George Stovall, St. Louis, August 7, 1912.

Most assists, extra-inning game

N.L.—8—Bob Skinner, Pittsburgh, July 22, 1954, 14 innings.
A.L.—7—Ferris Fain, Philadelphia, June 9, 1949, 12 innings.

Most assists, doubleheader

A.L.—8
    Charlie Carr, Detroit, June 26, 1904.
    George Sisler, St. Louis, September 12, 1926.
    Rudy York, Chicago, September 27, 1947.
    Jim Spencer, California, August 25, 1970, 21 innings.
N.L.—8
    Gil Hodges, Brooklyn, July 24, 1952, 20 innings.
    Dale Long, Pittsburgh, May 1, 1955.

Most consecutive games with one or more assists, season

A.L.—16—Vic Power, Cleveland, June 9 through June 25,
    1960 (29 assists).

N.L.—14—Bill Terry, New York, May 13, through May 27,
    1930 (16 assists).

Most assists, inning

A.L.—3
    Dick Stuart, Boston, June 28, 1963, first inning.
    Jim Maler, Seattle, April 29, 1982, third inning.
N.L.—3
    Andre Thornton, Chicago, August 22, 1975, fifth inning.
    Leon Durham, Chicago, July 22, 1986, first inning.
    Mark Grace, Chicago, May 23, 1990, fourth inning.
    Phil Stephenson, San Diego, August 23, 1992, fourth inning.

CHANCES ACCEPTED AND OFFERED

Most chances accepted, career

M.L.—25,000—Jake Beckley, Pittsburgh N.L., Pittsburgh
    P.L., New York N.L., Cincinnati N.L., St. Louis N.L., 1888
    through 1907, 20 years.
N.L.—23,687—Jake Beckley, Pittsburgh, New York, Cincin-
    nati, St. Louis, 1888 through 1907, except 1890, 19 years.
N.L. since 1900—21,914—Charlie Grimm, St. Louis, Pitts-
    burgh, Chicago, 1918 through 1936, 19 years.
A.L.—21,198—Mickey Vernon, Washington, Cleveland, Bos-
    ton, 1939 through 1958, except 1944, 1945 in military
    service, 18 years.

Most chances accepted, season

A.L.—1,986—Jiggs Donahue, Chicago, 157 games, 1907.
N.L.—1,862—George Kelly, New York, 155 games, 1920.

Most years leading league in chances accepted

N.L.—6
    Jake Beckley, Pittsburgh, Cincinnati, St. Louis, 1892, 1894,
        1895, 1900, 1902, 1904.
    Bill Terry, New York, 1927 (tied), 1928, 1929, 1930, 1932,
        1934.
A.L.—4—Wally Pipp, New York, 1915, 1919, 1920, 1922.

Fewest chances accepted, season (150 or more games)

N.L.—1,251—Deron Johnson, Philadelphia, 154 games,
    1970.
A.L.—1,263—Dick Stuart, Boston, 155 games, 1964.

Fewest chances accepted by leader, season

A.L.—1,048
    Bill Skowron, New York, 120 games, 1956.
    Vic Wertz, Cleveland, 133 games, 1956.
N.L.—1,222—Ed Bouchee, Philadelphia, 134 games, 1959.

Most chances accepted, nine-inning game

A.L.-N.L.—22—Held by many first basemen.
A.L.—Last first baseman—Alvin Davis, Seattle, May 28,
    1988 (22 putouts).
N.L.—Last first baseman—Ernie Banks, Chicago, May 9,
    1963 (22 putouts).

Most chances accepted, extra-inning game

N.L.—43—Walter Holke, Boston, May 1, 1920, 26 innings.
A.L.—34
    Rudy York, Detroit, July 21, 1945, 24 innings.
    Mike Epstein, Washington, June 12, 1967, 22 innings.
    Rod Carew, California, April 13, finished April 14, 1982, 20
        innings.

Most chances accepted, doubleheader (18 innings)

A.L.—38—Hal Chase, New York, August 5, 1905.
N.L.—35—Hal Chase, New York, August 26, 1919.

Most chances accepted, two consecutive games

N.L.—39—Harvey Cotter, Chicago, July 10, 1924, second
    game; July 11, 1924.
A.L.—38—Hal Chase, New York, August 5, 5, 1905.

Fewest chances offered, game

A.A.—0
    Guy Hecker, Louisville, October 9, 1887, fielded eight in-
        nings.
    Al McCauley, Washington, August 6, 1891.
A.L.—0
    Bud Clancy, Chicago, April 27, 1930.
    Norm Cash, Detroit, June 27, 1963, fielded eight innings.

Gene Tenace, Oakland, September 1, 1974.
N.L.—0—Rip Collins, Chicago, June 29, 1937.

Fewest chances offered, doubleheader (18 innings)
N.L.—7
Cap Anson, Chicago, July 19, 1896.
Frank Bowerman, Pittsburgh, August 19, 1899.
N.L. since 1900—8
Eddie Waitkus, Chicago, May 31, 1948.
George Crowe, Cincinnati, June 2, 1957.
A.L.—9—Hank Greenberg, Detroit, August 26, 1935.

Fewest chances offered, two consecutive games (18 innings)
A.L.—6—Dick Kryhoski, New York, April 29 (3), 30 (3), 1949.
N.L.—7
Cap Anson, Chicago, July 19 (5), 19 (2), 1896.
Frank Bowerman, Pittsburgh, August 19 (5), 19 (2), 1899.
Phil Cavarretta, Chicago, April 25 (6), 26 (1), 1935.

Fewest chances offered, two consecutive games (17 innings)
A.L.—5—Gene Tenace, Oakland, August 31 (5), September 1 (0), 1974.

ERRORS

Most errors, league
N.L.—568—Cap Anson, Chicago, 1879 through 1897, 19 years.
A.L.—285—Hal Chase, New York, Chicago, 1905 through 1914, 10 years, 1,175 games.
N.L. since 1900—252—Fred Tenney, Boston, New York, 1900 through 1911, except 1910, 11 years.

Most errors, season
U.A.—62—Joe Quinn, St. Louis, 100 games, 1884.
N.L.—58—Cap Anson, Chicago, 108 games, 1884.
N.L. since 1900—43—Jack Doyle, New York, 130 games, 1900.
A.L.—41—Jerry Freeman, Washington, 154 games, 1908.

Most years leading league in errors
M.L.—7—Dick Stuart, Pittsburgh N.L. 1958 (tied), 1959, 1960 (tied), 1961, 1962 (tied); Boston, A.L., 1963, 1964.
N.L.—5
Cap Anson, Chicago, 1882, 1884, 1885, 1886, 1892.
Dick Stuart, Pittsburgh, 1958 (tied), 1959, 1960 (tied), 1961, 1962 (tied).
Willie McCovey, San Francisco, 1967 (tied), 1968, 1970, 1971, 1977.
A.L.—5
Hal Chase, New York, Chicago, 1905, 1909, 1911, 1912 (tied), 1913.
George Sisler, St. Louis, 1916, 1917, 1924, 1925, 1927.
Ferris Fain, Philadelphia, 1947 (tied), 1948, 1949, 1950, 1952.

Fewest errors, season (150 or more games)
N.L.—0—Steve Garvey, San Diego, 159 games, 1984.
A.L.—1—Stuffy McInnis, Boston, 152 games, 1921.

Fewest errors for leader, season
A.L.—10
Vic Power, Kansas City, 144 games, 1955.
Gus Triandos, Baltimore, 103 games, 1955.
N.L.—12
Fred McGriff, San Diego, 151 games, 1992.
Eddie Murray, New York, 154 games, 1992.

Most consecutive errorless games, career
N.L.—193—Steve Garvey, San Diego, June 26, second game, 1983 through April 14, 1985 (1,623 chances accepted).
A.L.—178—Mike Hegan, Milwaukee, Oakland, September 24, 1970, through May 20, 1973 (758 chances accepted).

Most consecutive errorless games, season
N.L.—159—Steve Garvey, San Diego, April 3 through September 29, 1984 (entire season; 1,319 chances accepted).
A.L.—119—Stuffy McInnis, Boston, May 21, first game, through October 2, 1921 (1,300 chances accepted).

Most consecutive chances accepted without an error, career
A.L.—1,700—Stuffy McInnis, Boston, Cleveland, May 31, 1921, first game, through June 2, 1922, 163 games (1,300 in 1921, 400 in 1922).
N.L.—1,633—Steve Garvey, San Diego, June 26, first game, 1983 through April 15, 1985 (255 in 1983, 1,319 in 1984, 59 in 1985).

Most consecutive chances accepted without an error, season
N.L.—1,319—Steve Garvey, San Diego, April 3 through September 29, 1984 (entire season; 159 games).
A.L.—1,300—Stuffy McInnis, Boston, May 31, first game, through October 2, 1921, 119 games.

Most errors, nine-inning game
A.A.—5—Lew Brown, Louisville, September 10, 1883.
U.A.—5
John Gorman, Kansas City, June 28, 1884.
Joe Quinn, St. Louis, July 4, 1884.
N.L.—5
John Carbine, Louisville, April 29, 1876.
George Zettlein, Philadelphia, June 22, 1876.
Everett Mills, Hartford, October 7, 1876.
Tom Esterbrook, Buffalo, July 27, 1880.
Roger Connor, Troy City, May 27, 1882.
N.L. since 1900—4
John Menefee, Chicago, October 6, 1901.
Johnny Lush, Philadelphia, June 11, 1904, and September 15, 1904, second game.
Fred Tenney, Boston, July 12, 1905, first game.
A.L.—4
Hal Chase, Chicago, July 23, 1913.
George Sisler, St. Louis, April 14, 1925.
Jimmy Wasdell, Washington, May 3, 1939.
Glenn Davis, Baltimore, April 18, 1991.

Most errors, two consecutive games
A.A.—8—Lew Brown, Louisville, September 9, 10, 1883.

Longest errorless game
N.L.—26 innings
Walter Holke, Boston, May 1, 1920.
Ed Konetchy, Brooklyn, May 1, 1920.
A.L.—25 innings—Ted Simmons, Milwaukee, May 8, finished May 9, 1984 (fielded 24⅓ innings).

Most errors, inning
N.L.—3
Dolph Camilli, Philadelphia, August 2, 1935, first inning.
Al Oliver, Pittsburgh, May 23, 1969, fourth inning.
Jack Clark, St. Louis, May 25, 1987, second inning.
A.L.—3
George Metkovich, Boston, April 17, 1945, seventh inning.
Tom McCraw, Chicago, May 3, 1968, third inning.
Willie Upshaw, Toronto, July 1, 1986, fifth inning.

DOUBLE PLAYS

Most double plays, career
M.L.—2,044—Mickey Vernon, Washington A.L., Cleveland A.L., Boston A.L., Milwaukee N.L., 1939 through 1959, except 1944, 1945 in military service, 19 years, 2,237 games (2,041 in A.L., 3 in N.L.).
A.L.—2,041—Mickey Vernon, Washington, Cleveland, Boston, 1939 through 1958, except 1944, 1945 in military service, 18 years, 2,227 games.
N.L.—1,708—Charlie Grimm, St. Louis, Pittsburgh, Chicago, 1918 through 1936, 19 years, 2,132 games.

Most double plays, season
A.L.—194—Ferris Fain, Philadelphia, 150 games, 1949.
N.L.—182—Donn Clendenon, Pittsburgh, 152 games, 1966.

Most unassisted double plays, season
A.L.—8—Jim Bottomley, St. Louis, 140 games, 1936.
N.L.—8—Bill White, St. Louis, 151 games, 1961.

Most years leading league in double plays
N.L.—6—Keith Hernandez, St. Louis, New York, 1977, 1979, 1980, 1981, 1983, 1984.

A.L.—4
Stuffy McInnis, Philadelphia, Boston, 1912, 1914, 1919, 1920 (tied).
Wally Pipp, New York, 1915, 1916, 1917 (tied), 1920 (tied).
Cecil Cooper, Milwaukee, 1980, 1981, 1982, 1983.

Fewest double plays, season (150 or more games)
A.L.—87—Lou Gehrig, New York, 155 games, 1926.
N.L.—88—Eddie Murray, Los Angeles, 150 games, 1990.

Fewest double plays for leader, season
A.L.—98—Vic Power, Cleveland, 121 games, 1959.
N.L.—109—Bill White, St. Louis, 123 games, 1960.

Most double plays, game
N.L.—7—Curt Blefary, Houston, May 4, 1969.
A.L.—6
Jimmie Foxx, Philadelphia, August 24, 1935, 15 innings.
Ferris Fain, Philadelphia, September 1, 1947, second game.
George Vico, Detroit, May 19, 1948.
Eddie Robinson, Cleveland, August 5, 1948.
Lee Thomas, Los Angeles, August 23, 1963.
Bob Oliver, Kansas City, May 14, 1971.
John Mayberry, Kansas City, May 6, 1972.
Bob Oliver, New York, April 29, 1975.
Rod Carew, Minnesota, August 29, 1977, first game, 10 innings.

Most double plays started, nine-inning game
A.L.—3
Lu Blue, Detroit, September 8, 1922.
Walt Judnich, St. Louis, September 6, 1947.
Vic Power, Philadelphia, September 26, 1954.
Pete O'Brien, Texas, May 22, 1984.
N.L.—3
Frank Hurst, Philadelphia, September 17, 1930.
Tommie Aaron, Milwaukee, May 27, 1962.

Most unassisted double plays, game
N.L.—2—Held by 15 first basemen. Last first baseman— Dave Kingman, New York, July 25, 1982.
A.L.—2—Held by 12 first basemen. Last first baseman—Dan Briggs, California, April 16, 1977.

Most double plays, doubleheader (18 innings)
N.L.—8—Ray Sanders, St. Louis, June 11, 1944.
A.L.—8
Walt Judnich, St. Louis, September 16, 1947.
Walt Dropo, Boston, June 25, 1950.

Most double plays, doubleheader (more than 18 innings)
A.L.—10—Mickey Vernon, Washington, August 18, 1943, 23 innings.

SECOND BASEMEN

GAMES AND INNINGS

Most games, career
A.L.—2,651—Eddie Collins, Philadelphia, Chicago, 21 years, 1908 through 1928.
N.L.—2,427—Joe Morgan, Houston, Cincinnati, San Francisco, Philadelphia, 1963 through 1983, 21 years.

Most consecutive games, career
A.L.—798—Nellie Fox, Chicago, August 7, 1955 through September 3, 1960.
N.L.—443—Dave Cash, Pittsburgh, Philadelphia, September 20, 1973 through August 5, 1976.

Most games, season
A.L. (162-game season)—162
Jake Wood, Detroit, 1961.
Bobby Grich, Baltimore, 1973.
A.L. (154-game season)—158—Del Pratt, St. Louis, 1915; also in 1916.
N.L. (162-game season)—163—Bill Mazeroski, Pittsburgh, 1967.
N.L. (154-game season)—156
Claude Ritchey, Pittsburgh, 1904.

Miller Huggins, Cincinnati, 1907.
Rogers Hornsby, Chicago, 1929.
Billy Herman, Chicago, 1939.
Jackie Robinson, Brooklyn, 1949.

Most years leading league in games
A.L.—8—Nellie Fox, Chicago, 1952, 1953, 1954, 1955, 1956, 1957, 1958, 1959.
N.L.—7—Billy Herman, Chicago, Brooklyn, 1932 (tied), 1933, 1935, 1936 (tied), 1938, 1939, 1942.

Fewest games for leader, season
A.L.—133—Frank LaPorte, St. Louis, 1911.
N.L.—134—George Cutshaw, Pittsburgh, 1917.

Most innings played, game
N.L.—26
Charlie Pick, Boston, May 1, 1920.
Ivy Olson, Brooklyn, May 1, 1920.
A.L.—25
Julio Cruz, Chicago, May 8, finished May 9, 1984.
Jim Gantner, Milwaukee, May 8, finished May 9, 1984 (fielded 24⅓ innings).

AVERAGE

Highest fielding average, career (1,000 or more games)
N.L.—.990—Ryne Sandberg, Philadelphia, Chicago, 1981 through 1994, 14 years, 1,723 games.
A.L.—.985—Jim Gantner, Milwaukee, 1978 through 1992, 15 years, 1,449 games.

Highest fielding average, season (150 or more games)
N.L.—.996—Jose Oquendo, St. Louis, 150 games, 1990.
A.L.—.995—Bobby Grich, Baltimore, 162 games, 1973.

Highest fielding average, season (100 or more games)
N.L.—.9956
Ken Boswell, New York, 101 games, 1970.
Jose Oquendo, St. Louis, 150 games, 1990.
A.L.—.9967—Bobby Grich, California, 116 games, 1985.

Most years leading league in fielding (100 or more games)
A.L.—9—Eddie Collins, Philadelphia, Chicago, 1909, 1910, 1914, 1915, 1916, 1920, 1921, 1922, 1924.
N.L.—7—Red Schoendienst, St. Louis, New York, Milwaukee, 1946, 1949, 1953, 1955, 1956, 1957 (tied), 1958.

Most consecutive years leading league in fielding (100 or more games)
N.L.—6—Claude Ritchey, Pittsburgh, 1902, 1903, 1904 (tied), 1905, 1906, 1907.
A.L.—4—Charlie Gehringer, Detroit, 1934 (tied), 1935, 1936, 1937.

Lowest fielding average for leader, season (100 or more games)
N.L.—.928—Charley Bassett, Indianapolis, 119 games, 1887.
N.L. since 1900—.953—John Miller, Pittsburgh, 150 games, 1909.
A.L.—.960—Jimmy Williams, New York, 132 games, 1903.

Lowest fielding average, season (100 or more games)
N.L.—.893—Fred Pfeffer, Chicago, 109 games, 1885.
A.L.—.914—Frank Truesdale, St. Louis, 122 games, 1910.
N.L. since 1900—.927—John Farrell, St. Louis, 118 games, 1903.

PUTOUTS

Most putouts, career
A.L.—6,526—Eddie Collins, Philadelphia, Chicago, 1908 through 1928, 21 years.
N.L.—5,541—Joe Morgan, Houston, Cincinnati, San Francisco, Philadelphia, 1963 through 1983, 21 years.

Most putouts, season
A.A.—525—John McPhee, Cincinnati, 140 games, 1886.
A.L. (162-game season)—484—Bobby Grich, Baltimore 160 games, 1974.
A.L. (154-game season)—479—Bucky Harris, Washington, 154 games, 1922.

N.L. (154-game season)—466—Billy Herman, Chicago, 153 games, 1933.

Most years leading league in putouts

A.L.—10—Nellie Fox, Chicago, 1952, 1953, 1954, 1955, 1956, 1957, 1958, 1959, 1960, 1961.

N.L.—7

Fred Pfeffer, Chicago, 1884, 1885, 1886, 1887, 1888, 1889, 1891.

Billy Herman, Chicago, Brooklyn, 1933, 1935, 1936, 1938, 1939, 1940 (tied), 1942.

Fewest putouts, season (150 or more games)

A.L.—254—Roberto Alomar, Toronto, 150 games, 1993.

N.L.—260—John Miller, Pittsburgh, 150 games, 1909.

Fewest putouts for leader, season

N.L.—292—Larry Doyle, New York, 144 games, 1909.

A.L.—304—Charlie Gehringer, Detroit, 121 games, 1927.

Most putouts, nine-inning game

A.A.—12—Lou Bierbauer, Philadelphia, June 22, 1888.

A.L.—12—Bobby Knoop, California, August 30, 1966.

N.L.—11

Sam Wise, Washington, May 9, 1893.
John McPhee, Cincinnati, April 21, 1894.
Nap Lajoie, Philadelphia, April 25, 1899.
Billy Herman, Chicago, June 28, 1933, first game.
Gene Baker, Chicago, May 27, 1955.
Charlie Neal, Los Angeles, July 2, 1959.
Julian Javier, St. Louis, June 27, 1964.

Most putouts, extra-inning game

N.L.—15—Jake Pitler, Pittsburgh, August 22, 1917, 22 innings.

A.L.—12

Billy Gardner, Baltimore, May 21, 1957, 16 innings.
Vern Fuller, Cleveland, April 11, 1969, 16 innings.

Longest game with no putouts

A.L.—15 innings

Steve Yerkes, Boston, June 11, 1913.
Denny Doyle, California, June 14, 1974.

N.L.—12 innings—Ken Boswell, New York, August 7, 1972 (none out in 13th inning).

Most putouts, two consecutive nine-inning games

A.A.—19—Bill Greenwood, Rochester, July 15, 16, 1890.

Most putouts, doubleheader (18 innings)

N.L.—16

Fred Pfeffer, Chicago, May 31, 1897.
Billy Herman, Chicago, June 28, 1933.

A.L.—15—Cass Michaels, Washington, July 30, 1950.

Longest game with no putouts

A.L.—21⅓ innings—Eddie Foster, Washington, July 5, 1917.

N.L.—18 innings

Claude Ritchey, Pittsburgh, September 2, 1901.
Gene DeMontreville, Boston, September 20, 1901.
Johnny Evers, Boston, August 3, 1916.
John Rawlings, Boston, September 10, 1917.
Lee Magee, Cincinnati, August 18, 1918.
Buck Herzog, Boston, June 2, 1919.
Milt Stock, Brooklyn, August 10, 1925.
Rogers Hornsby, Boston, September 10, 1928.
Bama Rowell, Boston, July 4, 1941.
Bill Rigney, New York, September 1, 1947.
Connie Ryan, Philadelphia, June 14, 1953.
Tony Taylor, Philadelphia, August 9, 1960.
Jerry Buchek, New York, May 28, 1967.

ASSISTS

Most assists, career

A.L.—7,630—Eddie Collins, Philadelphia, Chicago, 21 years, 1908 through 1928.

N.L.—6,738—Joe Morgan, Houston, Cincinnati, San Francisco, Philadelphia, 1963 through 1983, 21 years.

Most assists, season

N.L.—641—Frankie Frisch, St. Louis, 153 games, 1927.

A.L.—572—Oscar Melillo, St. Louis, 148 games, 1930.

Most years leading league in assists

N.L.—9—Bill Mazeroski, Pittsburgh, 1958, 1960, 1961, 1962, 1963, 1964, 1966, 1967, 1968.

A.L.—7—Charlie Gehringer, Detroit, 1927, 1928, 1933, 1934, 1935, 1936, 1938.

Most consecutive years leading league in assists

A.L.—6—Horace Clarke, New York, 1967 through 1972.

N.L.—5—Bill Mazeroski, Pittsburgh, 1960 through 1964.

Fewest assists, season (150 or more games)

A.L.—350—Billy Gardner, Baltimore, 151 games, 1958.

N.L.—358—Tony Taylor, Philadelphia, 150 games, 1964.

Fewest assists for leader, season

N.L.—381—Emil Verban, Philadelphia, 138 games, 1946.

A.L.—396—Nellie Fox, Chicago, 154 games, 1956.

Most years with 500 or more assists

A.L.—6—Charlie Gehringer, Detroit, 1928, 1929, 1930, 1933, 1934, 1936.

N.L.—6—Ryne Sandberg, Chicago, 1983, 1984, 1985, 1988, 1991, 1992.

Most assists, nine-inning game

N.L.—12

Monte Ward, Brooklyn, June 10, 1892, first game.
Jim Gilliam, Brooklyn, July 21, 1956.
Ryne Sandberg, Chicago, June 12, 1983.
Glenn Hubbard, Atlanta, April 14, 1985.
Juan Samuel, Philadelphia, April 20, 1985.

A.L.—12

Don Money, Milwaukee, June 24, 1977.
Tony Phillips, Oakland, July 6, 1986.
Harold Reynolds, Seattle, August 27, 1986.

Most assists, extra-inning game

N.L.—15—Lave Cross, Philadelphia, August 5, 1897, 12 innings.

N.L. since 1900—13—Morrie Rath, Cincinnati, August 26, 1919, 15 innings.

A.L.—13

Bobby Avila, Cleveland, July 1, 1952, 19 innings.
Willie Randolph, New York, August 25, 1976, 19 innings.

CHANCES ACCEPTED AND OFFERED

Most chances accepted, career

A.L.—14,156—Eddie Collins, Philadelphia, Chicago, 1908 through 1928, 21 years.

N.L.—12,279—Joe Morgan, Houston, Cincinnati, San Francisco, Philadelphia, 1963 through 1983, 21 years.

Most chances accepted, season

N.L.—1,037—Frankie Frisch, St. Louis, 153 games, 1927.

A.L.—988—Nap Lajoie, Cleveland, 156 games, 1908.

Most years leading league in chances accepted

A.L.—9—Nellie Fox, Chicago, 1952, 1953, 1954, 1955, 1956, 1957, 1958, 1959, 1960.

N.L.—8—Bill Mazeroski, Pittsburgh, 1958, 1960, 1961, 1962, 1963, 1964, 1966, 1967.

Fewest chances accepted, season (150 or more games)

A.L.—674—Danny Murphy, Philadelphia, 150 games, 1905.

N.L.—678—Jose Oquendo, St. Louis, 150 games, 1990.

Fewest chances accepted by leader, season

N.L.—686—John Miller, Pittsburgh, 150 games, 1909.

A.L.—697—Eddie Collins, Philadelphia, 132 games, 1911.

Most years with 900 or more chances accepted

N.L.—5—Billy Herman, Chicago, 1932, 1933, 1935, 1936, 1938.

A.L.—4—Charlie Gehringer, Detroit, 1929, 1930, 1933, 1936.

Most chances accepted, nine-inning game

A.A.—18—Clarence Childs, Syracuse, June 1, 1890.

N.L.—18—Terry Harmon, Philadelphia, June 12, 1971.

A.L.—17

Jimmie Dykes, Philadelphia, August 28, 1921.

Nellie Fox, Chicago, June 12, 1952.

Most chances accepted, extra-inning game

N.L.—21—Eddie Moore, Boston vs. Chicago, May 17, 1927, 22 innings.

A.L.—20—Willie Randolph, New York, August 25, 1976, 19 innings.

Most chances accepted, doubleheader

N.L.—26—Frank Parkinson, Philadelphia, September 5, 1922.

A.L.—24

Cass Michaels, Washington, July 30, 1950.
Billy Martin, New York, September 24, 1952, 19 innings.

Longest game with no chances offered

A.L.—15 innings—Steve Yerkes, Boston, June 11, 1919.

N.L.—12 innings—Ken Boswell, New York, August 7, 1972 (none out in 13th inning).

Most chances accepted, two consecutive games

A.A.—31—Bill Greenwood, Rochester, July 15, 16, 1890.

N.L.—28

Fred Pfeffer, Chicago, August 13, 14, 1884.
Monte Ward, New York, July 18, 19, first game, 1893.

A.L.—28—Bobby Doerr, Boston, May 30, second game, June 3, first game, 1946.

N.L. since 1900—26

Frank Parkinson, Philadelphia, September 5, 5, 1922.
Emil Verban, Philadelphia, August 1, 2, 1947.

Most chances accepted, two consecutive games (extra innings)

A.L.—34—Jackie Hayes, Chicago, July 14, 15, 1932, 22 innings.

N.L.—Less than nine-inning-games record.

Fewest chances offered, doubleheader

N.L.—1—Buck Herzog, Boston, June 2, 1919.

A.L.—1—Eddie Foster, Washington, July 5, 1917, 21⅓ innings.

Fewest chances offered, two consecutive games

N.L.—1

Buck Herzog, Boston, April 28, 30, 1919, 19 innings, also June 2, 2, 1919, 18 innings.
Jerry Buchek, New York, May 28, second game, 29, 1967, 17 innings.

A.L.—1

Bobby Young, St. Louis, April 19, 20, 1951, 17 innings.
Bobby Avila, Cleveland, April 19, 20, first game, 1952, 18 innings.
Eddie Foster, Washington, July 5, 5, 1917, 21⅓ innings.

Fewest chances offered, three consecutive games

N.L.—3—Eddie Stanky, Boston, April 25, 26, 27, 1949, 26 innings.

A.L.—4—Held by many second basemen.

Fewest chances offered, four consecutive games

N.L.—5—Buck Herzog, Boston, June 2, 2, 3, 3, 1919, 37 innings.

A.L.—6—Held by many second basemen.

| | **ERRORS** | |

Most errors, career

M.L.—828—Fred Pfeffer, Troy N.L., Chicago N.L., Chicago P.L., Louisville N.L., New York N.L., 16 years, 1882 through 1897 (654 in N.L., 74 in P.L.)

N.L.—754—Fred Pfeffer, Troy, Chicago, Louisville, New York, 1882 through 1897, except 1890, 15 years.

N.L. since 1900—443—Larry Doyle, New York, Chicago, 1907 through 1920, 14 years.

A.L.—435—Eddie Collins, Philadelphia, Chicago, 1908 through 1928, 21 years.

Most errors, season

N.L.—88

Charles Smith, Cincinnati, 80 games, 1880.
Bob Ferguson, Philadelphia, 85 games, 1883.

N.L. since 1900—55—George Grantham, Chicago, 150 games, 1923.

A.A.—87

Yank Robinson, St. Louis, 129 games, 1886.
Bill McClellan, Brooklyn, 136 games, 1887.

A.L.—61

Kid Gleason, Detroit, 136 games, 1901.
Hobe Ferris, Boston, 138 games, 1901.

Most years leading league in errors

N.L.—5—Fred Pfeffer, Chicago, 1884, 1885, 1886, 1887, 1888.

N.L. since 1900—4

Billy Herman, Chicago, 1932, 1933, 1937, 1939.
Glenn Beckert, Chicago, 1966, 1967, 1969, 1970 (tied).

M.L. since 1900—4—Tito Fuentes, San Francisco N.L., 1971, 1972; San Diego N.L., 1976; Detroit A.L., 1977.

A.L.—4

Bill Wambsganss, Cleveland, Boston, 1917, 1919, 1920, 1924.
Joe Gordon, New York, 1938, 1941, 1942, 1943 (tied).
Harold Reynolds, Seattle, 1987, 1988, 1989, 1990 (tied).

Fewest errors, season (150 or more games)

N.L.—3—Jose Oquendo, St. Louis, 150 games, 1990.

A.L.—5

Jerry Adair, Baltimore, 153 games, 1964.
Bobby Grich, Baltimore, 162 games, 1973.
Roberto Alomar, Toronto, 150 games, 1992.

Fewest errors for leader, season

A.L.—14—Hector Lopez, Kansas City, 96 games, 1958.

N.L.—15

Ted Sizemore, Chicago, 96 games, 1979.
Glenn Hubbard, Atlanta, 91 games, 1979.

Most consecutive errorless games, career

N.L.—123—Ryne Sandberg, Chicago, June 21, 1989 through May 17, 1990 (577 chances accepted).

A.L.—89—Jerry Adair, Baltimore, July 22, 1964 through May 6, 1965 (458 chances accepted).

Most consecutive errorless games, season

N.L.—90—Ryne Sandberg, Chicago, June 21 through October 1, 1989 (430 chances accepted).

A.L.—86—Rich Dauer, Baltimore, April 10 through September 29, 1978 (418 chances accepted).

Most consecutive chances accepted without an error, season

N.L.—479—Manny Trillo, Philadelphia, April 8 (part) through July 31 (part), 1982, 91 games.

A.L.—425—Rich Dauer, Baltimore, April 10 through September 30 (part), 1978, 87 games.

Most errors, nine-inning game

N.L.—9—Andy Leonard, Boston, June 14, 1876.

N.L. since 1900—4—Held by six second basemen. Last player—Casey Wise, Chicago, May 3, 1957.

A.L.—5

Charles Hickman, Washington, September 29, 1905.
Nap Lajoie, Philadelphia, April 22, 1915.

Longest errorless game

N.L.—25 innings

Felix Millan, New York, September 11, 1974.
Ted Sizemore, St. Louis, September 11, 1974.

A.L.—25 innings

Julio Cruz, Chicago, May 8, finished May 9, 1984.
Jim Gantner, Milwaukee, May 8, finished May 9, 1984 (fielded 24⅓ innings).

Most errors, two consecutive games

N.L.—11—Andy Leonard, Boston, June 10, 14, 1876.

Most errors, three consecutive games

N.L.—13—Andy Leonard, Boston, June 10, 14, 15, 1876.

Most errors, inning

N.L.—3

John McPhee, Cincinnati, September 23, 1894; first game, second inning.
Claude Ritchey, Pittsburgh, September 22, 1900, sixth inning.
Bama Rowell, Boston, September 25, 1941, third inning.

Eddie Stanky, Chicago, June 20, 1943, first game, eighth inning.
George Hausmann, New York, August 13, 1944, second game, fourth inning.
Kermit Wahl, Cincinnati, September 18, 1945, first game, 11th inning.
Davey Lopes, Los Angeles, June 2, 1973, first inning.
Ted Sizemore, St. Louis, April 17, 1975, sixth inning.
A.L.—2
Del Pratt, St. Louis, September 1, 1914, second game, fourth inning.
Bill Wambsganss, Cleveland, May 15, 1923, fourth inning.
Tim Cullen, Washington, August 30, 1969, eighth inning (consecutive).

DOUBLE PLAYS

Most double plays, career
N.L.—1,706—Bill Mazeroski, Pittsburgh, 17 years, 1956 through 1972.
A.L.—1,568—Nellie Fox, Philadelphia, Chicago, 17 years, 1947 through 1963.
Most double plays, season
N.L.—161—Bill Mazeroski, Pittsburgh, 162 games, 1966.
A.L.—150—Gerry Priddy, Detroit, 157 games, 1950.
Most years leading league in double plays
N.L.—8—Bill Mazeroski, Pittsburgh, 1960, 1961, 1962, 1963, 1964, 1965, 1966, 1967.
A.L.—5
Nap Lajoie, Cleveland, 1903, 1906, 1907, 1908, 1909 (tied).
Eddie Collins, Philadelphia, Chicago, 1909 (tied), 1910, 1912, 1916, 1919.
Bucky Harris, Washington, 1921, 1922, 1923, 1924 (tied), 1925.
Bobby Doerr, Boston, 1938, 1940, 1943, 1946, 1947.
Nellie Fox, Chicago, 1954, 1956, 1957, 1958, 1960.
Fewest double plays, season (150 or more games)
N.L.—65
George Hausmann, New York, 154 games, 1945.
Jose Oquendo, St. Louis, 150 games, 1990.
A.L.—66—Roberto Alomar, Toronto, 150 games, 1992.
Fewest double plays for leader, season
N.L.—81—Rogers Hornsby, St. Louis, 154 games, 1922.
A.L.—84—Charlie Gehringer, Detroit, 121 games, 1927.
Most double plays, nine-inning game
A.L.—6—Bobby Knoop, California, May 1, 1966, first game.
N.L.—5—Held by many second basemen. Last player—Teddy Martinez, Los Angeles, August 21, 1977.
Most double plays, extra-inning game
A.L.—6—Joe Gordon, Cleveland, August 31, 1949, first game, 14 innings.
N.L.—6—Felix Millan, Atlanta, August 5, 1971, 17 innings.
Most double plays started, game
A.L.—5—Gerry Priddy, Detroit, May 20, 1950.
N.L.—4
Fred Dunlap, Detroit, June 11, 1887.
Frank Gustine, Pittsburgh, August 22, 1940, second game.
Emil Verban, Philadelphia, July 18, 1947.
Red Schoendienst, St. Louis, August 20, 1954.
Felix Millan, Atlanta, August 5, 1971, 17 innings.
Most unassisted double plays, game
N.L.—2
Dave Force, Buffalo, September 15, 1881.
Claude Ritchey, Louisville, July 9, 1899, first game.
A.L.—2—Mike Edwards, Oakland, August 10, 1978.
Most doubles plays, doubleheader
A.L.—8
Bobby Doerr, Boston, June 25, 1950.
Bobby Knoop, California, May 1, 1966.
N.L.—6—Held by many second basemen.

GAMES AND INNINGS

Most games, career
A.L.—2,870—Brooks Robinson, Baltimore, 23 years, 1955 through 1977.
N.L.—2,212—Mike Schmidt, Philadelphia, 18 years, 1972 through 1989.
Most consecutive games, career
A.L.—576—Eddie Yost, Washington, July 3, 1951, to May 11, 1955.
N.L.—364—Ron Santo, Chicago, April 19, 1964 through May 31, 1966.
Most games, season
N.L. (162-game season)—164—Ron Santo, Chicago, 1965.
N.L. (154-game season)—157
Art Devlin, New York, 1908.
Red Smith, Boston, 1915.
Willie Jones, Philadelphia, 1950.
Eddie Mathews, Milwaukee, 1953.
Ray Jablonski, St. Louis, 1953.
A.L. (162-game season)—163—Brooks Robinson, Baltimore, 1961, 1964.
A.L. (154-game season)—157
George Kell, Detroit, 1950.
Eddie Yost, Washington, 1952.
Most years leading league in most games
A.L.—8—Brooks Robinson, Baltimore, 1960, 1961, 1962, 1963, 1964, 1966 (tied), 1968 (tied), 1970.
N.L.—7—Ron Santo, Chicago, 1961 (tied), 1963, 1965, 1966, 1967, 1968, 1969 (tied).
Fewest games for leader, season
N.L.—111—Art Whitney, Boston, 1934.
A.L.—131—George Kell, Philadelphia, Detroit, 1946.
Most innings played, game
N.L.—26
Tony Boeckel, Boston, May 1, 1920.
Jimmy Johnston, Brooklyn, May 1, 1920.
A.L.—25
Vance Law, Chicago, May 8, finished May 9, 1984.
Randy Ready, Milwaukee, May 8, finished May 9, 1984 (fielded 24 1/3 innings).

AVERAGE

Highest fielding average, career (1,000 or more games)
A.L.—.971—Brooks Robinson, Baltimore, 23 years, 1955 through 1977, 2,870 games.
N.L.—.970—Ken Reitz, St. Louis, San Francisco, Chicago, Pittsburgh, 11 years, 1972 through 1982, 1,321 games.
Highest fielding average, season (100 or more games)
A.L.—.991—Steve Buechele, Texas, 111 games, 1991.
N.L.—.983—Heinie Groh, New York, 145 games, 1924.
Highest fielding average, season (150 or more games)
A.L.—.989—Don Money, Milwaukee, 157 games, 1974.
N.L.—.980—Ken Reitz, St. Louis, 157 games, 1977.
Most years leading league in fielding (100 or more games)
A.L.—11—Brooks Robinson, Baltimore, 1960, 1961, 1962, 1963, 1964, 1966, 1967, 1968, 1969 (tied), 1972, 1975.
N.L.—6
Heinie Groh, Cincinnati, New York, 1915 (tied), 1917, 1918, 1922, 1923, 1924.
Ken Reitz, St. Louis, Chicago, 1973, 1974, 1977, 1978, 1980, 1981.
Most consecutive years leading in fielding (100 or more games)
A.L.—6—Willie Kamm, Chicago, 1924 through 1929.
N.L.—4—Willie Jones, Philadelphia, 1953 through 1956.
Lowest fielding average for leader, season (100 or more games)
N.L.—.891—Ned Williamson, Chicago, 111 games, 1885.

N.L. since 1900—.917
  Bobby Lowe, Boston, 111 games, 1901.
  Charlie Irwin, Cincinnati, Brooklyn, 131 games, 1901.
A.L.—.936—Bill Bradley, Cleveland, 133 games, 1901.

Lowest fielding average, season (100 or more games)
N.L.—.836—Charles Hickman, New York, 118 games, 1900.
A.L.—.860—Hunter Hill, Washington, 135 games, 1904.

PUTOUTS

Most putouts, career
A.L.—2,697—Brooks Robinson, Baltimore, 23 years, 1955 through 1977.
N.L.—2,288—Pie Traynor, Pittsburgh, 16 years, 1921 through 1937, except 1936.

Most putouts, season
A.A.—252—Denny Lyons, Philadelphia, 137 games, 1887.
N.L.—252—Jimmy Collins, Boston, 142 games, 1900.
A.L.—243—Willie Kamm, Chicago, 155 games, 1928.

Most years leading league in putouts
A.L.—8—Eddie Yost, Washington, Detroit, 1948, 1950, 1951, 1952, 1953, 1954 (tied), 1956, 1959.
N.L.—7
  Pie Traynor, Pittsburgh, 1923, 1925, 1926, 1927, 1931, 1933, 1934.
  Willie Jones, Philadelphia, 1949, 1950, 1952, 1953, 1954, 1955, 1956.
  Ron Santo, Chicago, 1962, 1963, 1964, 1965, 1966, 1967, 1969.

Fewest putouts for leader, season
N.L.—116—Pie Traynor, Pittsburgh, 110 games, 1934.
A.L.—121—Wade Boggs, Boston, 149 games, 1986.

Fewest putouts, season (150 or more games)
A.L.—82—Jim Presley, Seattle, 154 games, 1985.
N.L.—83—Todd Zeile, St. Louis, 153 games, 1993.

Most putouts, nine-inning game
N.L.—10—Willie Kuehne, Pittsburgh, May 24, 1889.
N.L. since 1900—9—Pat Dillard, St. Louis, June 18, 1900.
A.L.—7
  Bill Bradley, Cleveland, September 21, 1901, first game; also May 13, 1909.
  Harry Riconda, Philadelphia, July 5, 1924, second game.
  Ossie Bluege, Washington, June 18, 1927.
  Ray Boone, Detroit, April 24, 1954.

Longest game with no putouts
N.L.—20 innings—Lew Malone, Brooklyn, April 30, 1919.
A.L.—18⅓ innings—Vern Stephens, Boston, July 13, 1951.

Most consecutive games with no putouts
A.L.—10—Felix Torres, Los Angeles, June 14 through June 23, 1963.
N.L.—8—Ken Boyer, St. Louis, August 4, first game through August 11, 1963.

ASSISTS

Most assists, career
A.L.—6,205—Brooks Robinson, Baltimore, 23 years, 1955 through 1977.
N.L.—5,045—Mike Schmidt, Philadelphia, 18 years, 1972 through 1989.

Most assists, season
A.L. (162-game season)—412—Graig Nettles, Cleveland, 158 games, 1971.
A.L. (154-game season)—405—Harlond Clift, St. Louis, 155 games, 1937.
N.L. before 1900—384—Bill Shindle, Baltimore, 134 games, 1892.
N.L. since 1900
  (162-game season)—404—Mike Schmidt, Philadelphia, 162 games, 1974.
  (154-game season)—371—Tommy Leach, Pittsburgh, 146 games, 1904.

Most years leading league in assists
A.L.—8—Brooks Robinson, Baltimore, 1960, 1963, 1964, 1966, 1967, 1968, 1969, 1974.
N.L.—7
  Ron Santo, Chicago, 1962, 1963, 1964, 1965, 1966, 1967, 1968.
  Mike Schmidt, Philadelphia, 1974, 1976, 1977, 1980, 1981, 1982, 1983.

Fewest assists, season (150 or more games)
A.L.—221—Harry Lord, Chicago, 150 games, 1913.
N.L.—247—Stan Hack, Chicago, 150 games, 1937.

Fewest assists for leader, season
N.L.—227—Art Whitney, Boston, 111 games, 1934.
A.L.—258—Ossie Bluege, Washington, 134 games, 1930.

Most assists, nine-inning game
N.L.—11
  Deacon White, Buffalo, May 16, 1884.
  Jerry Denny, New York, May 29, 1890.
  Damon Phillips, Boston, August 29, 1944.
  Chris Sabo, Cincinnati, April 7, 1988.
A.L.—11
  Ken McMullen, Washington, September 26, 1966, first game.
  Mike Ferraro, New York, September 14, 1968.

Most assists, extra-inning game
N.L.—12—Bobby Byrne, Pittsburgh, June 8, 1910, second game, 11 innings.
A.L.—11
  Home Run Baker, New York, May 24, 1918, 19 innings.
  Doug DeCinces, California, May 7, 1983, 12 innings.

Most innings with no assists, extra-inning game
A.L.—17—Toby Harrah, Texas, September 17, 1977.

CHANCES ACCEPTED AND OFFERED

Most chances accepted, career
A.L.—8,902—Brooks Robinson, Baltimore, 23 years, 1955 through 1977.
N.L.—6,636—Mike Schmidt, Philadelphia, 18 years, 1972 through 1989.

Most chances accepted, season
A.L.—603—Harlond Clift, St. Louis, 155 games, 1937.
N.L.—601—Jimmy Collins, Boston, 151 games, 1899.
N.L. since 1900—583—Tommy Leach, Pittsburgh, 146 games, 1904.

Most years leading league in chances accepted
N.L.—9—Ron Santo, Chicago, 1961, 1962, 1963, 1964, 1965, 1966, 1967, 1968, 1969 (tied).
A.L.—8
  Home Run Baker, Philadelphia, New York, 1909, 1910, 1912, 1913, 1914, 1917, 1918, 1919.
  Brooks Robinson, Baltimore, 1960, 1963, 1964, 1966, 1967, 1968, 1969, 1974.

Fewest chances accepted, season (150 or more games)
N.L.—349—Jim Morrison, Pittsburgh, 151 games, 1986.
A.L.—349—Wade Boggs, Boston, 152 games, 1990.

Fewest chances accepted for leader, season
N.L.—332—Art Whitney, Boston, 111 games, 1934.
A.L.—396—Ossie Bluege, Washington, 134 games, 1930.

Most chances accepted, nine-inning game
N.L.—13
  Bill Kuehne, Pittsburgh, May 24, 1889.
  Jerry Denny, New York, May 19, 1890.
  Bill Shindle, Baltimore, September 28, 1893.
  Bill Joyce, Washington, May 26, 1894.
  Art Devlin, New York, May 23, 1908, first game.
  Tony Cuccinello, Brooklyn, July 12, 1934, first game.
  Roy Hughes, Chicago, August 29, 1944, second game.
A.L.—13—Wid Conroy, Washington, September 25, 1911.

Most chances accepted, extra-inning game

N.L.—16—Jerry Denny, Providence, August 17, 1882, 18 innings.

N.L. since 1900—14—Don Hoak, Cincinnati, May 4, 1958, second game, 14 innings.

A.L.—14

Jimmy Collins, Boston, June 21, 1902, 15 innings.
Ben Dyer, Detroit, July 16, 1919, 14 innings.

Most chances accepted, two consecutive games

N.L.—23—Joe Farrell, Detroit, June 30, July 1, 1884.

N.L. since 1900—18

Harry Steinfeldt, Cincinnati, June 14, 16, 1902.
Bobby Byrne, Pittsburgh, June 15, 17, 1910.
Eddie Zimmerman, Brooklyn, July 4, 4, 1911.
Babe Pinelli, Cincinnati, July 11, second game, July 13, 1925.
Lee Handley, Pittsburgh, June 15, 16, first game, 1946.

A.L.—18

Hobe Ferris, St. Louis, July 12, 13, 1909, first game.
Terry Turner, Cleveland, May 21, June 1, 1916, first game.
Aaron Ward, New York, April 20, 21, 1921.

Most chances accepted, doubleheader

N.L.—18—Eddie Zimmerman, Brooklyn, July 4, 1911.
A.L.—16—Billy Purtell, Chicago, July 14, 1909.

Longest game with no chances offered

N.L.—15 innings

Harry Steinfeldt, Chicago, August 22, 1908.
Heinie Groh, Cincinnati, August 26, 1919, second game.
Tony Boeckel, Boston, June 16, 1921; also September 12, 1921, first game.

A.L.—12⅔ innings—Jim Tabor, Boston, July 7, 1943.

Longest doubleheader with no chances offered

A.L.—21⅔ innings—Billy Gardner, Cleveland, August 23, 1920.
N.L.—19 innings—Tony Boeckel, Boston, July 26, 1922.

ERRORS

Most errors, career

M.L.—780—Arlie Latham, St. Louis A.A., Chicago P.L., Cincinnati N.L., St. Louis N.L., 14 years, 1883 through 1896.

N.L.—533—Jerry Denny, Providence, St. Louis, Indianapolis, New York, Cleveland, Philadelphia, Louisville, 1881 through 1894, except 1892, 13 years.

N.L. since 1900—324—Pie Traynor, Pittsburgh, 1921 through 1935, 1937, 16 years, 1,864 games.

A.L.—359—Jimmy Austin, New York, St. Louis, 1909 through 1922, 1925, 1926, 1929, 17 years, 1,433 games.

Most errors, season

N.L.—91—Charles Hickman, New York, 118 games, 1900.
A.L.—64—Sammy Strang, Chicago, 137 games, 1902.

Most years leading league in errors

N.L.—5—Pie Traynor, Pittsburgh, 1926, 1928 (tied), 1931, 1932, 1933.

A.L.—5—Jim Tabor, Boston, 1939, 1940 (tied), 1941, 1942, 1943 (tied).

Fewest errors, season (150 or more games)

A.L.—5—Don Money, Milwaukee, 157 games, 1974.
N.L.—8—Ken Reitz, St. Louis, 150 games, 1980.

Fewest errors for leader, season

N.L.—16

Eddie Mathews, Milwaukee, 147 games, 1957.
Gene Freese, Pittsburgh, 74 games, 1957.

A.L.—17—Cecil Travis, Washington, 56 games, 1946.

Most errors, game

U.A.—6—Jim Donnelly, Kansas City, July 16, 1884.

A.A.—6

Joe Moffett, Toledo, August 2, 1884.
Joe Werrick, Louisville, July 28, 1888.
Billy Alvord, Toledo, May 22, 1890.

N.L.—6—Joe Mulvey, Philadelphia, July 30, 1884.

N.L. since 1900—5—Dave Brain, Boston, June 11, 1906.

A.L.—4—Held by 22 third basemen. Last third basemen—Mike Blowers, New York, May 3, 1990; Edgar Martinez, Seattle, May 6, 1990.

Most consecutive errorless games, career

N.L.—97—Jim Davenport, San Francisco, July 29, 1966 through April 28, 1968 (209 chances accepted; played other positions during streak).

A.L.—88—Don Money, Milwaukee, September 28, 1973, second game, through July 16, 1974 (261 chances accepted).

Most consecutive errorless games, season

A.L.—86—Don Money, Milwaukee, April 5 through July 16, 1974 (257 chances accepted).

N.L.—64—Jim Davenport, San Francisco, May 22 through September 30, 1967, first game (137 chances accepted; played other positions during streak).

N.L.—57—Bob Aspromonte, Houston, July 14 through September 18, 1962, second game (145 chances accepted).

Most consecutive chances accepted without an error, career

A.L.—261—Don Money, Milwaukee, September 28, 1973, first game, through July 16, 1974, 88 games.

Most consecutive chances accepted without an error, season

A.L.—257—Don Money, Milwaukee, April 5 through July 16, 1974, 88 games.

N.L.—163—Don Money, Philadelphia, July 27, first game, through September 11, 1972, 48 games.

Longest errorless game

N.L.—26 innings

Tony Boeckel, Boston, May 1, 1920.
Jimmy Johnston, Brooklyn, May 1, 1920.

A.L.—25 innings—Vance Law, Chicago, May 8, finished May 9, 1984.

Most errors, doubleheader (since 1900)

N.L.—5

Bill Bradley, Chicago, May 30, 1900.
Tommy Leach, Pittsburgh, August 20, 1903.

A.L.—4—Held by many third basemen. Last third baseman—Herb Plews, Washington, June 3, 1958.

Most errors, two consecutive games

A.A.—9—Tom Esterbrook, New York, July 15, 26, 1883.

Most errors, inning

N.L.—4

Lew Whistler, New York, June 19, 1891, fourth inning.
Bob Brenly, San Francisco, September 14, 1986, fourth inning.

A.L.—4—Jimmy Burke, Milwaukee, May 27, 1901, fourth inning.

DOUBLE PLAYS

Most double plays, career

A.L.—618—Brooks Robinson, Baltimore, 23 years, 1955 through 1977.

N.L.—450—Mike Schmidt, Philadelphia, 18 years, 1972 through 1989.

Most double plays, season

A.L. (162-game season)—54—Graig Nettles, Cleveland, 158 games, 1971.

A.L. (154-game season)—50—Harlond Clift, St. Louis, 155 games, 1937.

N.L. (162-game season)—45—Darrell Evans, Atlanta, 160 games, 1974.

N.L. (154-game season)—43—Hank Thompson, New York, 138 games, 1950.

Most years leading league in double plays

N.L.—6

Heinie Groh, Cincinnati, New York, 1915, 1916, 1918, 1919, 1920 (tied), 1922.

Ron Santo, Chicago, 1961, 1964, 1966, 1967, 1968 (tied), 1971.

Mike Schmidt, Philadelphia, 1978, 1979, 1980, 1982 (tied), 1983, 1987.
A.L.—5
Jimmy Austin, New York, St. Louis, 1909, 1911, 1913, 1915, 1917.
Ken Keltner, Cleveland, 1939, 1941, 1942, 1944, 1947.
Frank Malzone, Boston, 1957, 1958, 1959, 1960, 1961.

Fewest double plays, season (150 or more games)
N.L.—10—Bob Aspromonte, Houston, 155 games, 1964.
A.L.—17
Max Alvis, Cleveland, 156 games, 1965.
Wade Boggs, Boston, 151 games, 1988.

Fewest double plays for leader, season
N.L.—17
Joe Stripp, Brooklyn, 140 games, 1933.
Johnny Vergez, New York, 123 games, 1933.
Whitey Kurowski, St. Louis, 138 games, 1946.
Jim Tabor, Philadelphia, 124 games, 1946.
A.L.—23—Marty McManus, Detroit, 130 games, 1930.

Most unassisted double plays, season
A.L.—4—Joe Dugan, New York, 148 games, 1924.
N.L.—2—Held by many third basemen. Last third baseman—Mike Shannon, St. Louis, 156 games, 1968.

Most double plays, game
N.L.—4
Pie Traynor, Pittsburgh, July 9, 1925, first game.
Johnny Vergez, Philadelphia, August 15, 1935.
A.L.—4
Andy Carey, New York, July 31, 1955, second game.
Felix Torres, Los Angeles, August 23, 1963.
Ken McMullen, Washington, August 13, 1965.

Most double plays started, nine-inning game
N.L.—4
Pie Traynor, Pittsburgh, July 9, 1925, first game.
Johnny Vergez, Philadelphia, August 15, 1935.
A.L.—4
Felix Torres, Los Angeles, August 23, 1963.
Ken McMullen, Washington, August 13, 1965.

Most unassisted double plays, game
N.L.-A.L.—1—Held by many third basemen.

Most unassisted double plays, two consecutive games
A.L.—2
Jim Delahanty, Detroit, August 28, 29, 1911.
Marv Owen, Detroit, April 28, 29, 1934.
N.L.—Never accomplished.

SHORTSTOPS

GAMES AND INNINGS

Most games, career
A.L.—2,581—Luis Aparicio, Chicago, Baltimore, Boston, 18 years, 1956 through 1973.
N.L.—2,418—Ozzie Smith, San Diego, St. Louis, 17 years, 1978 through 1994.

Most consecutive games, career
A.L.—1,982—Cal Ripken, Baltimore, July 1, 1982 through August 10, 1994.
N.L.—584—Roy McMillan, Cincinnati, September 16, 1951, first game, through August 6, 1955.

Most games, season
N.L. (162-game season)—165—Maury Wills, Los Angeles, 1962.
N.L. (154-game season)—157
Joe Tinker, Chicago, 1908.
Granny Hamner, Philadelphia, 1950.
A.L. (162-game season)—163—Tony Fernandez, Toronto, 1986.
A.L. (154-game season)—158—Eddie Lake, Detroit, 1947.

Most games by lefthanded shortstop, season
N.L.—73—Billy Hulen, Philadelphia, 1896.

Most years leading league in games
A.L.—10—Cal Ripken, Baltimore, 1983, 1984, 1987, 1988, 1989, 1990, 1991, 1992, 1993, 1994.
N.L.—6
Mickey Doolan, Philadelphia, 1906, 1909, 1910, 1911, 1912, 1913.
Arky Vaughan, Pittsburgh, 1933 (tied), 1934, 1936, 1938, 1939, 1940.
Roy McMillan, Cincinnati, Milwaukee, 1952, 1953, 1954 (tied), 1956, 1957, 1961.

Fewest games for leader, season
N.L.—141—Rabbit Maranville, Pittsburgh, 1923.
A.L.—142—Luis Aparicio, Chicago, 1957.

Most innings played, game
N.L.—26
Chuck Ward, Brooklyn, May 1, 1920.
Rabbit Maranville, Boston, May 1, 1920.
A.L.—25—Robin Yount, Milwaukee, May 8, finished May 9, 1984, fielded 24 1/3 innings.

AVERAGE

Highest fielding average, career (1,000 or more games)
M.L.—.980
Larry Bowa, Philadelphia N.L., Chicago N.L., 16 years, 1970 through 1985, 2,222 games.
Tony Fernandez, Toronto A.L., San Diego N.L., New York N.L., Cincinnati N.L., 12 years, 1983 through 1994, 1,460 games.
A.L.—.982—Tony Fernandez, Toronto, 9 years, 1983 through 1990, 1993, 1,104 games.
N.L.—.980—Larry Bowa, Philadelphia, Chicago, 16 years, 1970 through 1985, 2,222 games.

Highest fielding average, season (150 or more games)
A.L.—.996—Cal Ripken, Baltimore, 161 games, 1990.
N.L.—.987
Larry Bowa, Philadelphia, 157 games, 1971.
Larry Bowa, Philadelphia, 150 games, 1972.
Ozzie Smith, St. Louis, 158 games, 1987.
Ozzie Smith, St. Louis, 150 games, 1991.

Highest fielding average, season (100 or more games)
A.L.—.996—Cal Ripken, Baltimore, 161 games, 1990.
N.L.—.991—Larry Bowa, Philadelphia, 146 games, 1979.

Most years leading league in fielding (100 or more games)
A.L.—8
Everett Scott, Boston, New York, 1916, 1917, 1918, 1919, 1920, 1921, 1922, 1923, consecutive.
Lou Boudreau, Cleveland, 1940, 1941, 1942, 1943, 1944, 1946, 1947, 1948.
Luis Aparicio, Chicago, Baltimore, 1959, 1960, 1961, 1962, 1963, 1964, 1965, 1966, consecutive.
N.L.—7—Ozzie Smith, San Diego, St. Louis, 1981, 1982, 1984, 1985, 1986, 1987, 1991. (Note: Smith also led N.L. shortstops in fielding in the strike-shortened 1994 season, when he played in 96 games.)

Most consecutive years leading league in fielding (100 or more games)
A.L.—8
Everett Scott, Boston, New York, 1916 through 1923.
Luis Aparicio, Chicago, Baltimore, 1959 through 1966.
N.L.—5—Hughie Jennings, Baltimore, 1894 through 1898.
N.L. since 1900—4
Eddie R. Miller, Boston, Cincinnati, 1940 through 1943.
Ozzie Smith, St. Louis, 1984 through 1987.

Lowest fielding average for leader (100 or more games)
N.L.—.900
Jack Glasscock, Indianapolis, 109 games, 1888.
Arthur Irwin, Philadelphia, 121 games, 1888.
N.L. since 1900—.936—Tommy Corcoran, Cincinnati, 150 games, 1904.
A.L.—.934
Freddy Parent, Boston, 139 games, 1903.
Monte Cross, Philadelphia, 138 games, 1903.

Lowest fielding average, season (100 or more games)
A.L.—.861—Bill Keister, Baltimore, 114 games, 1901.
N.L.—.884—Tom Burns, Chicago, 111 games, 1885.
N.L. since 1900—.891—Otto Krueger, St. Louis, 107 games, 1902.

PUTOUTS

Most putouts, career
N.L.—5,133—Rabbit Maranville, Boston, Pittsburgh, Chicago, Brooklyn, St. Louis, 1912 through 1931, except 1924, 19 years.
A.L.—4,548—Luis Aparicio, Chicago, Baltimore, Boston, 1956 through 1973, 18 years.

Most putouts, season
N.L.—425—Hughie Jennings, Baltimore, 131 games, 1895.
A.L.—425—Donie Bush, Detroit, 157 games, 1914.
N.L. since 1900—407—Rabbit Maranville, Boston, 156 games, 1914.

Most years leading league in putouts
N.L.—6—Rabbit Maranville, Boston, Pittsburgh, 1914, 1915 (tied), 1916, 1917, 1919, 1923.
A.L.—6—Cal Ripken, Baltimore, 1984, 1985, 1988, 1989, 1991, 1992.

Fewest putouts, season (150 or more games)
N.L.—180—Larry Bowa, Philadelphia, 156 games, 1976.
A.L.—220—Ozzie Guillen, Chicago, 150 games, 1985.

Fewest putouts for leader, season
N.L.—235—Kevin Elster, New York, 150 games, 1989.
A.L.—248—Joe DeMaestri, Kansas City, 134 games, 1957.

Most putouts, nine-inning game
N.L.—11
  Shorty Fuller, New York, August 20, 1895.
  Hod Ford, Cincinnati, September 18, 1929.
A.L.—11—John Cassidy, Washington, August 30, 1904, first game.

Most putouts, opening game of season (nine innings)
N.L.—9—Bill Dahlen, Brooklyn, April 19, 1900.

Most putouts in extra-inning game
N.L.—14—Monte Cross, Philadelphia, July 7, 1899, 11 innings.
A.L.—Less than nine-inning game.

Most putouts with no assists, game
N.L.—9—Buck Herzog, Cincinnati, May 26, 1916.

ASSISTS

Most assists, career
N.L.—8,084—Ozzie Smith, San Diego, St. Louis, 17 years, 1978 through 1994.
A.L.—8,016—Luis Aparicio, Chicago, Baltimore, Boston, 18 years, 1956 through 1973.

Most assists, season
N.L. (162-game season) —621—Ozzie Smith, San Diego, 158 games, 1980.
N.L. (154-game season) —601—Glenn Wright, Pittsburgh, 153 games, 1924.
A.L. (162-game season) —583—Cal Ripken, Baltimore, 162 games, 1984.
A.L. (154-game season) —570—Terry Turner, Cleveland, 147 games, 1906.

Most years leading league in assists
N.L.—8—Ozzie Smith, San Diego, 1979, 1980, 1981, St. Louis, 1982, 1985, 1987, 1988, 1989.
A.L.—7
  Luke Appling, Chicago, 1933, 1935, 1937, 1939, 1941, 1943, 1946.
  Luis Aparicio, Chicago, 1956, 1957, 1958, 1959, 1960, 1961, 1968.
  Cal Ripken Jr., Baltimore, 1983, 1984, 1986, 1987, 1989, 1991, 1993.

Most consecutive years leading league in assists
A.L.—6—Luis Aparicio, Chicago, 1956 through 1961.
N.L.—4
  Germany Smith, Cincinnati, 1891 through 1894.
  Ozzie Smith, San Diego, St. Louis, 1979 through 1982.

Fewest assists, season (150 or more games)
A.L.—347—Jackie Gutierrez, Boston, 150 games, 1984.
N.L.—374—Kevin Elster, New York, 150 games, 1989.

Most years with 500 or more assists
N.L.—8—Ozzie Smith, San Diego, 1978, 1979, 1980, St. Louis, 1982, 1983, 1985, 1987, 1988.
A.L.—6—Donie Bush, Detroit, 1909, 1912, 1913, 1914, 1915.

Fewest assists for leader, season
A.L.—438—Joe Sewell, Cleveland, 137 games, 1928.
N.L.—440—Johnny Logan, Milwaukee, 129 games, 1957.

Most assists, nine-inning game
N.L.—14—Tommy Corcoran, Cincinnati, August 7, 1903.
A.L.—13—Bobby Reeves, Washington, August 7, 1927.

Most assists, extra-inning game
A.L.—15—Rick Burleson, California, April 13, finished April 14, 1982, 20 innings.
N.L.—14
  Herman Long, Boston, May 6, 1892, 14 innings.
  Bud Harrelson, New York, May 24, 1973, 19 innings.

Fewest assists in longest extra-inning game
N.L.—0—Jack Coffey, Boston, July 26, 1909, 17 innings.
A.L.—0—John Gochnaur, Cleveland, July 14, 1903, 12 innings.

CHANCES ACCEPTED AND OFFERED

Most chances accepted, career
A.L.—12,564—Luis Aparicio, Chicago, Baltimore, Boston, 1956 through 1973, 18 years.
N.L.—12,471—Rabbit Maranville, Boston, Pittsburgh, Chicago, Brooklyn, St. Louis, 1912 through 1931, except 1924, 19 years.

Most chances accepted, season
N.L.—984—Dave Bancroft, New York, 156 games, 1922.
A.L.—969—Donie Bush, Detroit, 157 games, 1914.

Most years leading league in chances accepted
N.L.—8—Ozzie Smith, San Diego, St. Louis, 1978, 1980, 1981, 1983, 1985, 1987, 1988, 1989.
A.L.—7—Luis Aparicio, Chicago, 1956, 1957, 1958, 1959, 1960, 1961, 1968.

Fewest chances accepted, season, 150 or more games
A.L.—575—Jackie Gutierrez, Boston, 150 games, 1984.
N.L.—609—Kevin Elster, New York, 150 games, 1989.

Fewest chances accepted by leader in chances accepted, season
N.L.—692—Ozzie Smith, St. Louis, 153 games, 1989.
A.L.—695—Luis Aparicio, Chicago, 142 games, 1957.

Most chances accepted in nine-inning game
N.L.—19
  Danny Richardson, Washington, June 20, 1892, first game.
  Eddie Joost, Cincinnati, May 7, 1941.
A.L.—17—Bobby Wallace, St. Louis, June 10, 1902.

Most chances accepted in extra-inning game
N.L.—21—Eddie R. Miller, Boston, June 27, 1939, 23 innings.
A.L.—18
  Freddy Parent, Boston, July 9, 1902, 17 innings.
  Chico Carrasquel, Chicago, July 13, 1951, 19 innings.
  Skeeter Webb, Detroit, July 21, 1945, 24 innings.
  Pete Runnels, Washington, June 3, 1952, 17 innings.
  Ron Hansen, Chicago, August 29, 1965, first game, 14 innings.

Most chances accepted in doubleheader
N.L.—25—Danny Richardson, Washington, June 20, 1892.
N.L. since 1900—24
  Heinie Sand, Philadelphia, July 4, 1924.
  Dave Bancroft, Boston, July 31, 1926.

A.L.—24
George McBride, Washington, August 19, 1908.
Roger Peckinpaugh, New York, September 8, 1919.
Topper Rigney, Boston, July 15, 1926.

Most chances accepted in doubleheader, more than 18 innings

A.L.—28—Ron Hansen, Chicago, August 29, 1965, 23 innings.
N.L.—26—Arky Vaughan, Pittsburgh, August 22, 1940, 21 innings.

Most chances accepted in three consecutive games

A.L.—37—Wally Gerber, St. Louis, May 27, 29, 30, first game, 1923.
N.L.—35
George Davis, New York, May 23, 24, 25, 1899.
George Davis, New York, July 19, 20, 21, 1900.

Most chances accepted in four consecutive games

A.L.—48—Wally Gerber, St. Louis, May 27, 29, 30, 30, 1923.
N.L.—45—George Davis, New York, May 23, 24, 25, 26, 1899.
N.L. since 1900—44—George Davis, New York, July 18, 19, 20, 21, 1900.

Longest game with no chances offered

A.L.—12 innings
John Gochnaur, Cleveland, July 14, 1903.
Billy Rogell, Detroit, June 16, 1937, fielded 11⅔ innings.
N.L.—12 innings—Irv Ray, Boston, August 15, 1888.
N.L. since 1900—11⅔ innings—Eddie Feinberg, Philadelphia, May 19, 1939.

Fewest chances offered, opening game of season

A.L.—0—Frankie Crosetti, New York, April 16, 1940, 9⅔ innings.
N.L.—0—Honus Wagner, Pittsburgh, April 14, 1910, nine innings.

Fewest chances offered, doubleheader

A.L.—0—Toby Harrah, Texas, June 25, 1976, 18 innings.
N.L.—1—Travis Jackson, New York, May 30, 1934, 18 innings.

Fewest chances offered, two consecutive games

A.L.—0
Tom Tresh, New York, July 31, August 1, 1968, 18 innings.
Toby Harrah, Texas, June 25, 25, 1976, 18 innings.
N.L.—1
Travis Jackson, New York, May 30, 1934, 18 innings.
Chico Fernandez, Philadelphia, May 7, 8, 1957, 18 innings.
Mike Fischlin, Houston, June 18, 20, 1978, 18 innings.

Fewest chances offered, three consecutive games

A.L.—0—Tom Tresh, New York, July 30, 31, August 1, 1968, 26 innings.
N.L.—3—Chico Fernandez, Philadelphia, May 5, second game, 7, 8, 1957, 27 innings.

| ERRORS |

Most errors, career

M.L.—1,037—Herman Long, Kansas City A.A., Boston N.L., New York A.L., Detroit A.L., 15 years, 1889 through 1903.
N.L.—972—Bill Dahlen, Chicago, Brooklyn, New York, Boston, 1891 through 1911, except 1910, 20 years, 2,139 games.
N.L. since 1900—676—Honus Wagner, Pittsburgh, 1901 through 1917, 17 years, 1,887 games.
A.L.—689—Donie Bush, Detroit, Washington, 1908 through 1921, 14 years, 1,866 games.

Most errors, season

P.L.—115—Bill Shindle, Philadelphia, 132 games, 1890.
N.L.—106—Joe Sullivan, Washington, 127 games, 1893.
N.L. since 1900—81—Rudy Hulswitt, Philadelphia, 138 games, 1903.
A.L.—95—John Gochnaur, Cleveland, 128 games, 1903.

Fewest errors, season (150 or more games)

A.L.—3—Cal Ripken, Baltimore, 161 games, 1990.
N.L.—8—Ozzie Smith, St. Louis, 150 games, 1991.

Fewest errors for leader, season

N.L.—21—Mariano Duncan, Los Angeles, 67 games, 1987.

A.L.—23—Felix Fermin, Cleveland, 140 games, 1993.

Most years leading league in errors

N.L.—6
Dick Groat, Pittsburgh, St. Louis, 1955, 1956, 1959, 1961, 1962, 1964.
Rafael Ramirez, Atlanta, 1981, 1982, 1983, 1984 (tied), 1985, Houston, 1989.
A.L.—5—Luke Appling, Chicago, 1933, 1935, 1937, 1939, 1946.

Most errors, nine-inning game

N.L.—7—Jimmy Hallinan, New York, July 29, 1876.
N.L. since 1900—5
Charlie Babb, New York, August 24, 1903, first game; also with Brooklyn, June 20, 1904.
Phil Lewis, Brooklyn, July 20, 1905.
A.A.—7—Germany Smith, Brooklyn, June 17, 1885.
A.L.—5—Donie Bush, Detroit, August 25, 1911, first game.

Most errors, extra-inning game

A.L.—6—Bill O'Neill, Boston, May 21, 1904, 13 innings.
N.L.—5—Held by many shortstops.

Most errors, opening game of season (nine innings)

N.L.—5—Dasher Troy, New York, May 1, 1883.
N.L. since 1900—4—Lou Stringer, Chicago, April 15, 1941.
A.L.—3—Held by many shortstops.

Most errors, first major league game

N.L.—4—Lou Stringer, Chicago, April 15, 1941.
A.L.—3—Held by many shortstops.

Most errors, two consecutive nine-inning games

A.A.—10—Germany Smith, Brooklyn, June 16, 17, 1885.
N.L.—9—Fred Pfeffer, Troy, September 7, 9, 1882.
A.L.—6—Juan Beniquez, Boston, July 13, 14, 1972.

Most errors, doubleheader (18 innings)

P.L.—9—Ed Delahanty, Cleveland, July 4, 1890.
N.L.—7—Bill Shindle, Baltimore, April 23, 1892.
N.L. since 1900—6—Sammy Strang, Chicago, October 8, 1900.
A.L.—5
John Gochnaur, Cleveland, September 10, 1902.
Al Brancato, Philadelphia, September 13, 1940.
Zoilo Versalles, Minnesota, July 5, 1963.

Longest errorless game

N.L.—26 innings—Rabbit Maranville, Boston, May 1, 1920.
A.L.—25 innings—Robin Yount, Milwaukee, May 8, finished May 9, 1984, fielded 24⅓ innings.

Most consecutive errorless games, career

A.L.—95—Cal Ripken, Baltimore, April 14 through July 27, 1990 (429 chances accepted).
N.L.—88—Kevin Elster, New York, July 20, 1988 through May 8, 1989 (287 chances accepted).

Most consecutive errorless games, season

A.L.—95—Cal Ripken, Baltimore, April 14 through July 27, 1990 (429 chances accepted).
N.L.—63—Spike Owen, Montreal, April 9 through June 22, 1990 (252 chances accepted).

Most consecutive chances accepted without an error, career

A.L.—431—Cal Ripken, Baltimore, April 14 to July 28, first game, 1990.
N.L.—383—Buddy Kerr, New York, July 28, first game (part), 1946 through May 25, 1947 (part) (286 in 1946; 97 in 1947).

Most consecutive chances accepted without an error, season

A.L.—431—Cal Ripken, Baltimore, April 14 to July 28, first game, 1990.
N.L.—286—Buddy Kerr, New York, July 28, first game (part), through September 29, 1946.

Most errors, inning

N.L.—4
Shorty Fuller, Washington, August 17, 1888, second inning.
Lennie Merullo, Chicago, September 13, 1942, second game, second inning.

A.L.—4—Ray Chapman, Cleveland, June 20, 1914, fifth inning.

| | DOUBLE PLAYS | |

Most double plays, career
A.L.—1,553—Luis Aparicio, Chicago, Baltimore, Boston, 18 years, 1956 through 1973.
N.L.—1,526—Ozzie Smith, San Diego, St. Louis, 17 years, 1978 through 1994.

Most double plays, season
A.L.—147—Rick Burleson, Boston, 155 games, 1980.
N.L.—137—Bobby Wine, Montreal, 159 games, 1970.

Most years leading league in double plays
A.L.—7—Cal Ripken, Baltimore, 1983, 1984, 1985, 1989, 1991, 1992, 1994.
N.L.—5
Mickey Doolan, Philadelphia, 1907, 1909 (tied), 1910, 1911, 1913.
Dick Groat, Pittsburgh, St. Louis, 1958, 1959, 1961, 1962, 1964.
Ozzie Smith, San Diego, St. Louis, 1980, 1984 (tied), 1986 (tied), 1987, 1991.

Fewest double plays, season (150 or more games)
A.L.—60—Jackie Gutierrez, Boston, 150 games, 1984.
N.L.—63—Kevin Elster, New York, 150 games, 1989.

Fewest double plays for leader, season
N.L.—79—Ozzie Smith, St. Louis, 150 games, 1991.
A.L.—81—Roger Peckinpaugh, Washington, 155 games, 1924.

Most double plays, nine-inning game
A.L.—5—29 times. Held by 25 shortstops. Last shortstop—Nelson Norman, Texas, April 23, 1979.
N.L.—5—18 times. Held by 18 shortstops. Last shortstop—Dave Concepcion, Cincinnati, June 25, 1975.

Most double plays, extra-inning game
A.L.—6—Bert Campaneris, Oakland, September 13, 1970, first game, 11 innings.
N.L.—6
Ozzie Smith, San Diego, August 25, 1979, 19 innings.
Rafael Ramirez, Atlanta, June 27, 1982, 14 innings.

Most double plays started, game
A.L.—5
Charley O'Leary, Detroit, July 23, 1905.
John P. Sullivan, Washington, August 13, 1944, second game.
Jim Fregosi, California, May 1, 1966, first game.
N.L.—4
Larry Kopf, Boston, April 28, 1922.
Jimmy E. Cooney, Chicago, June 13, 1926.
Billy Myers, Cincinnati, June 4, 1939.
Alvin Dark, New York, July 21, 1955.
Don Kessinger, July 21, 1971.

Most unassisted double plays, game
A.L.—2—Lee Tannehill, Chicago, August 4, 1911, first game.
N.L.—1—Held by many shortstops.

| | OUTFIELDERS | |

| | GAMES AND INNINGS | |

Most games, career
A.L.—2,938—Ty Cobb, Detroit, Philadelphia, 1905 through 1928, 24 years.
N.L.—2,843—Willie Mays, original New York club, San Francisco, present New York club, 1951 through 1973, 22 years, except 1953 in military service.

Most consecutive games played, career
N.L.—897—Billy Williams, Chicago, September 22, 1963 through June 13, 1969.
A.L.—511—Clyde Milan, Washington, August 12, 1910, through October 3, 1913, second game.

Most games, season
A.L. (162-game season)—163—Leon Wagner, Cleveland, 1964.
A.L. (154-game season)—162—Jimmy Barrett, Detroit, 1904.
N.L. (162-game season)—164—Billy Williams, Chicago, 1965.
N.L. (154-game season)—160—Tommy Griffith, Cincinnati, 1915.

Most years leading league in games played
N.L.—6
George J. Burns, New York, Cincinnati, 1914 (tied), 1916 (tied), 1919, 1920 (tied), 1922, 1923 (tied).
Billy Williams, Chicago, 1964 (tied), 1965, 1966, 1967, 1968, 1970 (tied).
Dale Murphy, Atlanta, 1982 (tied), 1983 (tied), 1984 (tied), 1985, 1987, 1988.
A.L.—5—Rocky Colavito, Cleveland, Detroit, 1959, 1961, 1962, 1963, 1965.

Fewest games for leader, season
A.L.—147—Ted Williams, Boston, 1951.
N.L.—149
Max Carey, Pittsburgh, 1924.
Chet Ross, Boston, 1940.

Most innings played, game
N.L.—26
Walt Cruise, Boston, May 1, 1920.
Les Mann, Boston, May 1, 1920.
Bernie Neis, Brooklyn, May 1, 1920.
Ray Powell, Boston, May 1, 1920.
Zack Wheat, Brooklyn, May 1, 1920.
A.L.—25
Harold Baines, Chicago, May 8, finished May 9, 1984.
Rudy Law, Chicago, May 8, finished May 9, 1984.
Ben Oglivie, Milwaukee, May 8, finished May 9, 1984 (fielded 24 ⅓ innings).

| | AVERAGE | |

Highest fielding average, career (1,000 or more games)
M.L.—.9932—Terry Puhl, Houston N.L., Kansas City A.L., 15 years, 1977 through 1991, 1,300 games.
N.L.—.9932—Terry Puhl, Houston, 14 years, 1977 through 1990, 1,299 games.
A.L.—.9910—Amos Otis, Kansas City, 14 years, 1970 through 1983, 1,845 games.

Highest fielding average, season (150 or more games)
N.L.—1.000
Danny Litwhiler, Philadelphia, 151 games, 1942.
Curt Flood, St. Louis, 159 games, 1966.
Terry Puhl, Houston, 152 games, 1979.
Brett Butler, Los Angeles, 161 games, 1991.
Brett Butler, Los Angeles, 155 games, 1993.
A.L.—1.000
Rocky Colavito, Cleveland, 162 games, 1965.
Brian Downing, California, 158 games, 1982.

Most years leading league in fielding (100 or more games; 162-game season, 108 or more games)
A.L.—5—Amos Strunk, Philadelphia, Boston, Chicago, 1912, 1914, 1917 (tied), 1918, 1920.
N.L.—4
Joe Hornung, Boston, 1881, 1882, 1883, 1887.
Steve Brodie, Boston, Pittsburgh, Baltimore, 1890, 1891, 1897, 1899.
N.L. since 1900—3
Stan Musial, St. Louis, 1949, 1954, 1961.
Tony Gonzalez, Philadelphia, 1962, 1964, 1967.
Pete Rose, Cincinnati 1970, 1971 (tied), 1974.

Most consecutive years leading league in fielding (100 or more games)
A.L.—3—Gene Woodling, New York, 1951 (tied), 1952, 1953 (tied).
N.L.—3—Joe Hornung, Boston, 1881, 1882, 1883.
N.L. since 1900—2—Held by many outfielders. Last outfielder—Pete Rose, Cincinnati, 1970, 1971 (tied).

Lowest fielding average for leader (100 or more games)
N.L.—.941—Pete Gillespie, New York, 102 games, 1885.
N.L. since 1900—.968
  Red Murray, New York, 143 games, 1912.
  Max Carey, Pittsburgh, 150 games, 1912.
  Zack Wheat, Brooklyn, 120 games, 1912.
A.L.—.959—Chick Stahl, Boston, 130 games, 1901.

Lowest fielding average, season (100 or more games)
N.L.—.843—Jack Manning, Philadelphia, 103 games, 1884.
N.L. since 1900—.900—Mike Donlin, Cincinnati, 118 games, 1903.
A.L.—.872—Bill O'Neill, Washington, 112 games, 1904.

PUTOUTS

Most putouts, career
N.L.—7,095—Willie Mays, original New York club, San Francisco, present New York club, 22 years, 1951 through 1973, except 1953 in military service.
A.L.—6,794—Tris Speaker, Boston, Cleveland, Washington, Philadelphia, 1907 through 1928, 22 years.

Most putouts, season
N.L.—547—Taylor Douthit, St. Louis, 154 games, 1928.
A.L.—512—Chet Lemon, Chicago, 149 games, 1977.

Most years leading league in putouts
N.L.—9
  Max Carey, Pittsburgh, 1912, 1913, 1916, 1917, 1918, 1921, 1922, 1923, 1924.
  Richie Ashburn, Philadelphia, 1949, 1950, 1951, 1952, 1953, 1954, 1956, 1957, 1958.
A.L.—7—Tris Speaker, Boston, Cleveland, 1909, 1910, 1913, 1914, 1915, 1918, 1919.

Fewest putouts, season (150 or more games)
A.L.—182—Ed Hahn, Chicago, 156 games, 1907.
N.L.—210—Sam Thompson, Philadelphia, 151 games, 1892.
N.L. since 1900—221—Wildfire Schulte, Chicago, 150 games, 1910.

Fewest putouts for leader, season
A.L.—319—Tris Speaker, Boston, 142 games, 1909.
N.L.—321—Roy Thomas, Philadelphia, 139 games, 1904.

Most years with 500 or more putouts
N.L.—4—Richie Ashburn, Philadelphia, 1949, 1951, 1956, 1957.
A.L.—1
  Dom DiMaggio, Boston, 1948.
  Chet Lemon, Chicago, 1977.
  Dwayne Murphy, Oakland, 1980.

Most years with 400 or more putouts
N.L.—9—Richie Ashburn, Philadelphia, 1949, 1950, 1951, 1952, 1953, 1954, 1956, 1957, 1958.
A.L.—5
  Chet Lemon, Chicago, Detroit, 1977, 1979, 1983, 1984, 1985.
  Kirby Puckett, Minnesota, 1984, 1985, 1986, 1988, 1989.

Most putouts by center fielder, nine-inning game
N.L.—12—Earl Clark, Boston, May 10, 1929.
A.L.—12—Lyman Bostock, Minnesota, May 25, 1977, second game.

Most putouts by center fielder, extra-inning game
A.L.—12
  Harry Bay, Cleveland, July 19, 1904, 12 innings.
  Ruppert Jones, Seattle, May 16, 1978, 16 innings.
  Rick Manning, Milwaukee, July 11, 1983, 15 innings.
  Gary Pettis, California, June 4, 1985, 15 innings.
  Oddibe McDowell, Texas, July 20, 1985, 15 innings.
N.L.—12
  Carden Gillenwater, Boston, September 11, 1946, 17 innings.
  Lloyd Merriman, Cincinnati, September 7, 1951, 18 innings.
  Garry Maddox, Philadelphia, June 10, 1984, 12 innings.

Most putouts by left fielder, nine-inning game
N.L.—11

Dick Harley, St. Louis, June 30, 1898.
Topsy Hartsel, Chicago, September 10, 1901.
A.L.—11
  Paul Lehner, Philadelphia, June 25, 1950, second game.
  Willie Horton, Detroit, July 18, 1969.

Most putouts by left fielder, extra-inning game
A.L.—12—Tom McBride, Washington, July 2, 1948, 12 innings.
N.L.—Less than nine-inning record.

Most putouts by right fielder, nine-inning game
A.L.—11—Tony Armas, Oakland, June 12, 1982.
N.L.—10—Bill Nicholson, Chicago, September 17, 1945.

Most putouts by right fielder, extra-inning game
N.L.—12—Rolando Roomes, Cincinnati, July 28, 1989, 17 innings.
A.L.—Less than nine-inning record.

Most putouts by center fielder, doubleheader (18 innings)
N.L.—18—Lloyd Waner, Pittsburgh, June 26, 1935.
A.L.—17—Lyman Bostock, Minnesota, May 25, 1977.

Most consecutive putouts, game
A.L.—7—Ben Chapman, Boston, June 25, 1937 (right field).
N.L.—6—Edd Roush, Cincinnati, July 4, 1919, a.m. game (center field).

ASSISTS

Most assists, career
A.L.—450—Tris Speaker, Boston, Cleveland, Washington, Philadelphia, 1907 through 1928, 22 years.
N.L.—356—Jimmy Ryan, Chicago, 1885 through 1900, except 1890, 15 years.
N.L. since 1900—339—Max Carey, Pittsburgh, Brooklyn, 1910 through 1929, 20 years.

Most assists, season
N.L.—45—Hardy Richardson, Buffalo, 78 games, 1881.
N.L. since 1900—44—Chuck Klein, Philadelphia, 156 games, 1930.
A.L.—35
  Sam Mertes, Chicago, 123 games, 1902.
  Tris Speaker, Boston, 142 games, 1909, also 153 games, 1912.

Most years leading league in assists
A.L.—7—Carl Yastrzemski, Boston, 1962, 1963, 1964 (tied), 1966, 1969, 1971, 1977.
N.L.—5—Roberto Clemente, Pittsburgh, 1958, 1960, 1961, 1966, 1967.

Fewest assists, season (150 or more games)
A.L.—1—Harmon Killebrew, Minnesota, 157 games, 1964.
N.L.—2—Lenny Dykstra, Philadelphia, 160 games, 1993.

Fewest assists for leader, season
A.L.—13
  Ken Berry, California, 116 games, 1972.
  Carlos May, Chicago, 145 games, 1972.
N.L.—14
  Bill Bruton, Milwaukee, 141 games, 1954.
  Don Mueller, New York, 153 games, 1954.
  Frank Thomas, Pittsburgh, 153 games, 1954.
  Barry Bonds, Pittsburgh, 150 games, 1990.
  Kevin McReynolds, New York, 144 games, 1990.

Most assists, nine-inning game
N.L.—4
  Harry Schafer, Boston, September 26, 1877.
  Bill Crowley, Buffalo, May 24, 1880.
  Bill Crowley, Buffalo, August 27, 1880.
  Fred Clarke, Pittsburgh, August 23, 1910.
A.L.—4
  James W. Holmes, Chicago, August 21, 1903.
  Lee Magee, New York, June 28, 1916.
  Happy Felsch, Chicago, August 14, 1919.
  Bob Meusel, New York, September 5, 1921, second game.
  Sam Langford, Cleveland, May 1, 1928.

Most assists, extra-inning game

N.L.—4—Dusty Miller, May 30, 1895, second game, 11 innings.
A.L.—3—Held by many outfielders.

Most assists by outfielder to catcher, game

N.L.—3
　Dummy Hoy, Washington, June 19, 1899.
　Jim Jones, New York, June 30, 1902.
　Jack McCarthy, Chicago, April 26, 1905.
A.L.—2—Held by many outfielders.

Most assists, inning

A.L.-N.L.—2—Held by many outfielders.

CHANCES ACCEPTED AND OFFERED

Most chances accepted, career

N.L.—7,290—Willie Mays, original New York club, San Francisco, present New York club, 22 years, 1951 through 1973, except 1953 in military service.
A.L.—7,244—Tris Speaker, Boston, Cleveland, Washington, Philadelphia, 22 years, 1907 through 1928.

Most chances accepted, season

N.L.—557—Taylor Douthit, St. Louis, 154 games, 1928.
A.L.—524—Chet Lemon, Chicago, 149 games, 1977.

Most years leading league in chances accepted

N.L.—9
　Max Carey, Pittsburgh, 1912, 1913, 1916, 1917, 1918, 1921, 1922, 1923, 1924.
　Richie Ashburn, Philadelphia, 1949, 1950, 1951, 1952, 1953, 1954, 1956, 1957, 1958.
A.L.—8—Tris Speaker, Boston, Cleveland, 1909, 1910, 1912, 1913, 1914, 1915, 1918, 1919.

Fewest chances accepted, season (150 or more games)

A.L.—206—Ed Hahn, Chicago, 156 games, 1907.
N.L.—235—Dusty Baker, Los Angeles, 152 games, 1977.

Fewest chances accepted for leader, season

A.L.—333—Sam Crawford, Detroit, 144 games, 1907.
N.L.—342—Roy Thomas, Philadelphia, 139 games, 1904.

Most chances accepted by center fielder, nine-inning game

N.L.—13—Earl Clark, Boston, May 10, 1929.
A.L.—12
　Happy Felsch, Chicago, June 23, 1919.
　Johnny Mostil, Chicago, May 22, 1928.
　Lyman Bostock, Minnesota, May 25, 1977, second game.

Most chances accepted by center fielder, extra-inning game

A.L.—12
　Harry Bay, Cleveland, July 19, 1904, 12 innings.
　Ruppert Jones, Seattle, May 16, 1978, 16 innings.
　Rick Manning, Milwaukee, July 11, 1983, 15 innings.
　Gary Pettis, California, June 4, 1985, 15 innings.
　Oddibe McDowell, Texas, July 20, 1985, 15 innings.
N.L.—12
　Carden Gillenwater, Boston, September 11, 1946, 17 innings.
　Lloyd Merriman, Cincinnati, September 7, 1951, 18 innings.
　Garry Maddox, Philadelphia, June 10, 1984, 12 innings.

Most chances accepted by left fielder, nine-inning game

N.L.—11
　Joe Hornung, Boston, September 23, 1881.
　Dick Harley, St. Louis, June 30, 1898.
　Topsy Hartsel, Chicago, September 10, 1901.
A.L.—11
　Paul Lehner, Philadelphia, June 25, 1950, second game.
　Willie Horton, Detroit, July 18, 1969.

Most chances accepted by left fielder, extra-inning game

A.L.—12—Tom McBride, Washington, July 2, 1948, 12 innings.
N.L.—Less than nine-inning record.

Most chances accepted by right fielder, nine-inning game

A.L.—12—Tony Armas, Oakland, June 12, 1982.
N.L.—11—Harry Schafer, Boston, September 26, 1877.
N.L. since 1900—10
　Greasy Neale, Cincinnati, July 13, 1920.
　Casey Stengel, Philadelphia, July 30, 1920.

Bill Nicholson, Chicago, September 17, 1945.
Bake McBride, Philadelphia, September 8, 1978, second game.

Most chances accepted by center fielder, doubleheader

N.L.—18—Lloyd Waner, Pittsburgh, June 26, 1935.
A.L.—17—Lyman Bostock, Minnesota, May 25, 1977.

Most chances accepted by center fielder, two consecutive games

A.L.—21—Happy Felsch, Chicago, June 23, 24, 1919.
N.L.—20—Earl Clark, Boston, May 10, 11, 1929.

Longest game with no chances offered

A.L.—22 innings
　Bill Bruton, Detroit, June 24, 1962.
　Cap Peterson, Washington, June 12, 1967.
N.L.—18 innings
　Lance Richbourg, Boston, May 14, 1927.
　Art Shamsky, Cincinnati, July 19, 1966.

Longest season-opening game with no chances offered

A.L.—14 innings
　Charlie Hemphill, New York, April 14, 1910.
　Clyde Engle, New York, April 14, 1910.
N.L.—13 innings
　Buck Herzog, New York, April 15, 1909.
　Bill O'Hara, New York, April 15, 1909.

Longest game with no chances offered by center fielder

A.L.—22 innings—Bill Bruton, Detroit, June 24, 1962.
N.L.—17⅓ innings—Ernie Orsatti, St. Louis, July 2, 1933, first game.

Longest game with no chances offered by left fielder

N.L.—16 innings—Joe Delahanty, St. Louis, July 19, 1908.
A.L.—16 innings
　Bob L. Johnson, Philadelphia, June 5, 1942.
　Pat Mullin, Detroit, May 9, 1952.

Longest game with no chances offered by right fielder

A.L.—22 innings—Cap Peterson, Washington, June 12, 1967.
N.L.—18 innings
　Lance Richbourg, Boston, May 14, 1927.
　Art Shamsky, Cincinnati, July 19, 1966.

Longest doubleheader with no chances offered

A.L.—24 innings—Roger Maris, New York, August 6, 1961.
N.L.—21 innings—Dain Clay, Cincinnati, September 21, 1944.

Most consecutive games with no chances offered

A.L.—7—Baby Doll Jacobson, Boston, June 18, 19, 20, 21, 24, 25, 25, 1926, 64⅓ innings (right field).
N.L.—6—Wildfire Schulte, Chicago, June 25, 25, 26, 27, 28, 29, 1912 (right field).

ERRORS

Most errors, career

M.L.—384—Dummy Hoy, Washington N.L., Buffalo P.L., St. Louis A.A., Cincinnati N.L., Louisville N.L., Chicago A.L., 14 years, 1888 through 1902, except 1900.
N.L.—347—George Gore, Chicago, New York, St. Louis, 13 years, 1879 through 1892, except 1890.
N.L. since 1900—235—Max Carey, Pittsburgh, Brooklyn, 20 years, 1910 through 1929.
A.L.—271—Ty Cobb, Detroit, Philadelphia, 24 years, 1905 through 1928.

Most errors, season

P.L.—52—Ed Beecher, Buffalo, 125 games, 1890.
N.L.—47—George Van Haltren, Baltimore, Pittsburgh, 143 games, 1892.
N.L. since 1900—36—Cy Seymour, Cincinnati, 135 games, 1903.
A.L.—31—Roy C. Johnson, Detroit, 146 games, 1929.

Most years leading league in errors

N.L.—7—Lou Brock, Chicago, St. Louis, 1964, 1965, 1966, 1967, 1968 (tied), 1972, 1973 (tied).

A.L.—5
Burt Shotton, St. Louis, Washington, 1912 (tied), 1914, 1915 (tied), 1916, 1918.
Reggie Jackson, Oakland, Baltimore, 1968, 1970, 1972, 1975, 1976 (tied).

Fewest errors, season (150 or more games)
N.L.—0
Danny Litwhiler, Philadelphia, 151 games, 1942.
Curt Flood, St. Louis, 159 games, 1966.
Terry Puhl, Houston, 152 games, 1979.
Brett Butler, Los Angeles, 161 games, 1991.
Brett Butler, Los Angeles, 155 games, 1993.
A.L.—0
Rocky Colavito, Cleveland, 162 games, 1965.
Brian Downing, California, 158 games, 1982.

Fewest errors for leader, season
N.L.—8—David Justice, Atlanta, 140 games, 1992.
A.L.—9
Roger Maris, Cleveland, Kansas City, 146 games, 1958.
Reggie Jackson, Oakland, 135 games, 1972.
Albert Belle, Cleveland, 89 games, 1991.
Jose Canseco, Oakland, 131 games, 1991.
Chad Curtis, California, 151 games, 1993.
Lance Johnson, Chicago, 146 games, 1993.
Kenny Lofton, Cleveland, 146 games, 1993.

Most errors, nine-inning game
A.A.—5—Jim Clinton, Baltimore, May 3, 1884.
U.A.—5—Fred Tenney, Washington, May 29, 1884.
A.L.—5—Kip Selbach, Baltimore, August 19, 1902.
N.L.—5
Jack Manning, Boston, May 1, 1876.
Pop Snyder, Louisville, July 29, 1876.
Jim O'Rourke, Boston, June 21, 1877.
Charlie Bennett, Milwaukee, June 15, 1878.
Mike Dorgan, New York, May 24, 1884.
Mike Tiernan, New York, May 16, 1887.
Marty Sullivan, Chicago, May 18, 1887.
N.L. since 1900—4—Fred Nicholson, Boston, June 16, 1922.

Longest errorless game
N.L.—26 innings
Walt Cruise, Boston, May 1, 1920.
Les Mann, Boston, May 1, 1920.
Bernie Neis, Brooklyn, May 1, 1920.
Ray Powell, Boston, May 1, 1920.
Zack Wheat, Brooklyn, May 1, 1920.
A.L.—25 innings
Harold Baines, Chicago, May 8, finished May 9, 1984.
Rudy Law, Chicago, May 8, finished May 9, 1984.
Ben Oglivie, Milwaukee, May 8, finished May 9, 1984 (fielded 24 1/3 innings).

Most consecutive errorless games, season
A.L.—162—Rocky Colavito, Cleveland, April 13 through October 3, 1965 (274 chances accepted).
N.L.—161—Brett Butler, Los Angeles, April 10 through October 6, 1991 (380 chances accepted).

Most consecutive errorless games, career
M.L.—392—Darren Lewis, Oakland A.L., San Francisco N.L., August 21, 1990 through June 29, 1994 (938 chances accepted).
N.L.—369—Darren Lewis, San Francisco, July 13, 1991 through June 29, 1994 (905 chances accepted).
A.L.—244—Brian Downing, California, May 25, 1981 through July 21, 1983, second game (471 chances accepted).

Most consecutive chances accepted without an error, career
M.L.—938—Darren Lewis, Oakland A.L., San Francisco N.L., August 21, 1990 through June 29, 1994, 392 games.
N.L.—905—Darren Lewis, San Francisco, July 13, 1991 through June 29, 1994, 369 games.
A.L.—573—Ken Griffey Jr., Seattle, April 16, 1992 through August 8, 1993, 236 games.

Most errors, inning
N.L.—3
George Gore, Chicago, August 8, 1883, first inning.

Larry Herndon, San Francisco, September 6, 1980, fourth inning.
A.A.—3—Jim Donahue, Kansas City, July 4, 1889, p.m. game, first inning.
A.L.—3
Kip Selbach, Washington, June 23, 1904, eighth inning.
Harry Bay, Cleveland, June 29, 1905, second game, ninth inning.
Harry Heilmann, Detroit, May 22, 1914, first inning.
Herschel Bennett, St. Louis, April 14, 1925, eighth inning.
Scott Lusader, Detroit, September 9, 1989, first inning.

DOUBLE PLAYS

Most double plays, career
A.L.—135—Tris Speaker, Boston, Cleveland, Washington, Philadelphia, 22 years, 1907 through 1928.
N.L.—86—Max Carey, Pittsburgh, Brooklyn, 20 years, 1910 through 1929.

Most unassisted double plays, career
M.L.—4
Tris Speaker, Boston A.L., Cleveland A.L., 1909 (1), 1914 (1), 1918 (2).
Elmer J. Smith, Cleveland A.L., New York A.L., 1915 (1), 1920 (1), 1923 (1), Cincinnati N.L., 1925 (1) (3 in A.L., 1 in N.L.).
A.L.—4—Tris Speaker, Boston, Cleveland, 1909 (1), 1914 (1), 1918 (2).
N.L.—2—Held by many outfielders.

Most double plays, season
A.L.—15—Happy Felsch, Chicago, 125 games, 1919.
N.L.—12—Mel Ott, New York, 149 games, 1929.

Most unassisted double plays, season
A.L.—2
Socks Seybold, Philadelphia, August 15, September 10, first game, 1907.
Tris Speaker, Cleveland, April 18, April 29, 1918.
Jose Cardenal, Cleveland, June 8, July 16, 1968.
N.L.—2—Adam Comorosky, Pittsburgh, May 31, June 13, 1931.

Most years leading league in double plays
A.L.—5—Tris Speaker, Boston, Cleveland, 1909, 1912, 1914, 1915, 1916.
N.L.—4—Willie Mays, New York, San Francisco, 1954, 1955, 1956, 1965.

Fewest double plays, season (150 or more games)
N.L.-A.L.—0—Held by many outfielders.
N.L.—Last outfielders—Barry Bonds, San Francisco, 157 games, 1993; Brett Butler, Los Angeles, 155 games, 1993; Lenny Dykstra, Philadelphia, 160 games, 1993.
A.L.—Last outfielder—Joe Carter, Toronto, 151 games, 1993.

Fewest double plays for leader, season
N.L.—3
Brett Butler, Los Angeles, 161 games, 1991.
Willie McGee, San Francisco, 128 games, 1991.
A.L.—4—Held by 19 players. Last outfielders—Tony Armas, Oakland, 132 games, 1977; Roy White, New York, 135 games, 1977.

Most double plays started, game
A.A.—3—Candy Nelson, New York, June 9, 1887.
N.L.—3—Jack McCarthy, Chicago, April 26, 1905.
A.L.—3—Ira Flagstead, Boston, April 19, 1926, p.m. game.

Most unassisted double plays, game
N.L.-A.L.—1—Held by many outfielders.
N.L.—Last outfielder—Andy Van Slyke, Pittsburgh, July 7, 1992, sixth inning.
A.L.—Last outfielder—Brian McRae, Kansas City, August 23, 1992, eighth inning.

Most triple plays started, season
A.L.—2—Charlie Jamieson, Cleveland, May 23, June 9, 1928.
N.L.—1—Held by many outfielders.

GAMES AND INNINGS

Most games, career

A.L.—2,226—Carlton Fisk, Boston, Chicago, 1969 through 1993, except 1970, 24 years.

N.L.—2,056—Gary Carter, Montreal, New York, San Francisco, Los Angeles, 1974 through 1992, 19 years.

Most consecutive games, career

A.L.—312—Frankie Hayes, St. Louis, Philadelphia, Cleveland, October 2, second game, 1943 through April 21, 1946.

N.L.—233—Ray Mueller, Cincinnati, July 31, 1943, through May 5, 1946, except 1945 in military service.

Most games, season

N.L. (162-game season)—160—Randy Hundley, Chicago, 1968.

N.L. (154-game season)—155—Ray Mueller, Cincinnati, 1944.

A.L.—155

Jim Sundberg, Texas, 1975 (162-game season).
Frankie Hayes, Philadelphia, 1944 (154-game season).

Most games by lefthanded catcher, season

N.L.—105—Jack Clements, Philadelphia, 1891.

A.L.—23—Jiggs Donahue, St. Louis, 1902.

Most games catching all club's games, season

N.L.—155—Ray Mueller, Cincinnati, 1944 (135 complete games).

A.L.—155—Frankie Hayes, Philadelphia, 1944 (135 complete games).

Most consecutive games, season

A.L.—155—Frankie Hayes, Philadelphia, April 18 through October 1, second game, 1944 (135 complete).

N.L.—155—Ray Mueller, Cincinnati, April 18 through October 1, 1944 (135 complete).

Most games by rookie, season

N.L.—154—Johnny Bench, Cincinnati, 1968.

A.L.—150—Buck Rodgers, Los Angeles, 1962.

Most years leading league in games

A.L.—8—Yogi Berra, New York, 1950, 1951, 1952, 1953, 1954, 1955, 1956, 1957.

N.L.—6—Gary Carter, Montreal, 1977, 1978, 1979, 1980, 1981, 1982.

Most years with 100 or more games

M.L.—15—Bob Boone, Philadelphia N.L., California A.L., Kansas City A.L., 1973, 1974, 1976 through 1980, 1982 through 1989.

A.L.—13—Bill Dickey, New York, 1929 through 1941.

N.L.—13—Johnny Bench, Cincinnati, 1968 through 1980.

Most consecutive years with 100 or more games

A.L.—13—Bill Dickey, New York, 1929 through 1941.

N.L.—13—Johnny Bench, Cincinnati, 1968 through 1980.

Fewest games for leader, season

N.L.—96—Ernie Lombardi, New York, 1945.

A.L.—98—Jake Early, Washington, 1942.

Most innings caught, game

A.L.—25—Carlton Fisk, Chicago, May 8, finished May 9, 1984.

N.L.—24

Hal King, Houston, April 15, 1968.
Jerry Grote, New York, April 15, 1968 (caught 23⅓ innings).

Most innings caught, doubleheader

A.L.—29—Ossee Schreckengost, Philadelphia, July 4, 1905.

N.L.—27

Bill Fischer, Chicago, June 28, 1916.
Gus Mancuso, New York, July 2, 1933.

AVERAGE

Highest fielding average, career (1,000 or more games)

A.L.—.9933—Bill Freehan, Detroit, 15 years, 1961, 1963 through 1976, 1,483 games.

N.L.—.992—Johnny Edwards, Cincinnati, St. Louis, Houston, 14 years, 1961 through 1974, 1,392 games.

Highest fielding average, season (100 or more games)

A.L.—1.000—Buddy Rosar, Philadelphia, 117 games, 1946.

N.L.—.999

Wes Westrum, New York, 139 games, 1950.
Tom Pagnozzi, St. Louis, 138 games, 1992.

Highest fielding average, season (150 or more games)

N.L.—.996—Randy Hundley, Chicago, 152 games, 1967.

A.L.—.995—Jim Sundberg, Texas, 150 games, 1979.

Most years leading league in fielding (100 or more games)

A.L.—8—Ray Schalk, Chicago, 1913, 1914, 1915, 1916, 1917, 1920, 1921, 1922.

N.L.—7—Gabby Hartnett, Chicago, 1925, 1928, 1930, 1934, 1935, 1936, 1937.

Most consecutive years leading league in fielding (100 or more games)

A.L.—6—Bill Freehan, Detroit, 1965, 1966, 1967 (tied), 1968, 1969 (tied), 1970.

N.L.—4

Johnny Kling, Chicago, 1902 through 1905.
Gabby Hartnett, Chicago, 1934 through 1937.

Lowest average for leader, season (100 or more games, since 1900)

A.L.—.954—Mike Powers, Philadelphia, 111 games, 1901.

N.L.—.958—Gabby Hartnett, Chicago, 110 games, 1925.

Lowest fielding average, season (100 or more games)

A.L.—.934—Sam Agnew, St. Louis, 102 games, 1915.

N.L. since 1900—.947—Red Dooin, Philadelphia, 140 games, 1909.

PUTOUTS

Most putouts, career

N.L.—11,785—Gary Carter, Montreal, New York, San Francisco, Los Angeles, 19 years, 1974 through 1992.

A.L.—11,369—Carlton Fisk, Boston, Chicago, 24 years, 1969 through 1993, except 1970.

Most putouts, season

N.L. (162-game season)—1,135—Johnny Edwards, Houston, 151 games, 1969.

N.L. (154-game season)—877—Johnny Roseboro, Los Angeles, 125 games, 1961.

A.L. (162-game season)—971—Bill Freehan, Detroit, 138 games, 1968.

A.L. (154-game season)—785—Ossee Schreckengost, Philadelphia, 114 games, 1905.

Fewest putouts, season (150 or more games)

N.L.—471—Ray Mueller, Cincinnati, 155 games, 1944.

A.L.—575—Mike Tresh, Chicago, 150 games, 1945.

Most years leading league in putouts

A.L.—9—Ray Schalk, Chicago, 1913, 1914, 1915, 1916, 1917, 1918, 1919, 1920, 1922.

N.L.—8—Gary Carter, Montreal, 1977, 1978, 1979, 1980, 1981, 1982, New York, 1985, 1988.

Fewest putouts for leader, season

N.L.—409—Gabby Hartnett, Chicago, 110 games, 1925.

A.L.—446—Birdie Tebbetts, Detroit, 97 games, 1942.

Most putouts, nine-inning game

N.L.—20—Jerry Grote, New York, April 22, 1970 (19 strikeouts).

A.L.—20—Rich Gedman, Boston, April 29, 1986 (20 strikeouts).

Most putouts, extra-inning game

N.L.—22

Bob Schmidt, San Francisco, June 22, 1958, first game, 14

innings (19 strikeouts).
Tom Haller, San Francisco, May 31, 1964, second game, 23 innings (22 strikeouts).
Steve Yeager, Los Angeles, August 8, 1972, 19 innings (22 strikeouts).
A.L.—21—Ellie Rodriguez, California, June 14, 1974, 15 innings (20 strikeouts).

Longest game with no putouts

A.L.—14 innings
Wally Schang, Boston, September 13, 1920.
Gene Desautels, Cleveland, August 11, 1942, first game.
N.L.—13 innings
Jimmie Wilson, Philadelphia, August 31, 1927, first game.
Hal Finney, Pittsburgh, September 22, 1931.

Most consecutive putouts, game

N.L.—10—Jerry Grote, New York, April 22, 1970; 1 in sixth inning, 3 in seventh inning, 3 in eighth inning, 3 in ninth inning (10 strikeouts).
A.L.—8
Mike Brumley Sr., Washington, September 4, 1965; 3 in first inning, 3 in second inning, 2 in third inning (8 strikeouts).
John Stephenson, California, July 9, 1972; 2 in first inning, 3 in second inning, 3 in third inning (8 strikeouts).
Art Kusnyer, California, July 15, 1973; 1 in first inning, 3 in second inning, 3 in third inning, 1 in fourth inning.

Most consecutive putouts from start of game

N.L.—9
Art Wilson, New York, May 30, 1911, a.m. game (4 strikeouts, 3 fouled out, 1 tagged out, 1 forced out).
John Bateman, Houston, July 14, 1968, second game (9 strikeouts).
A.L.—8—Mike Brumley Sr., Washington, September 4, 1965 (8 strikeouts).

Most putouts, two consecutive games

A.L.—36—Rich Gedman, Boston, April 29 (20), April 30 (16), 1986 (36 strikeouts).
N.L.—31—Jerry Grote, New York, April 21 (11), April 22 (20), 1970 (29 strikeouts).

Most putouts, doubleheader (18 innings)

N.L.—25—John Bateman, Houston, September 10, 1968 (22 strikeouts).
A.L.—25—Hank Severeid, St. Louis, July 13, 1920 (21 strikeouts).

Most fouls caught, game

N.L.—6—Wes Westrum, New York, August 24, 1949.
A.L.—6—Sherm Lollar, Chicago, April 10, 1962.

Most fouls caught, inning

N.L.—3
Mickey Owen, Brooklyn, August 4, 1941, third inning.
Wes Westrum, New York, August 24, 1949, ninth inning.
Wes Westrum, New York, September 23, 1956, fifth inning.
A.L.—3—Matt Batts, Detroit, August 2, 1953, second game, fourth game.

	ASSISTS	

Most assists, career

M.L.—1,835—Deacon McGuire, Toledo, Cleveland, Rochester, Washington A.A., Detroit, Philadelphia, Washington, Brooklyn N.L., Detroit, New York, Boston, Cleveland A.L., 1884 through 1912, except 1889, 1908, 1909, 1911, 25 years.
A.L.—1,810—Ray Schalk, Chicago, 1912 through 1928, 17 years.
N.L.—1,593—Red Dooin, Philadelphia, Cincinnati, New York, 1902 through 1916, 15 years.

Most assists, season

N.L.—214—Pat Moran, Boston, 107 games, 1903.
A.L.—212—Oscar Stanage, Detroit, 141 games, 1911.

Fewest assists, season (150 or more games)

N.L.—59—C. Randy Hundley, Chicago, 152 games, 1967.
A.L.—69—Carlton Fisk, Boston, 151 games, 1977.

Most years leading league in assists

N.L.—6
Gabby Hartnett, Chicago, 1925, 1927, 1928 (tied), 1930, 1934, 1935.
Del Crandall, Milwaukee, 1953, 1954, 1957, 1958, 1959, 1960.
A.L.—6—Jim Sundberg, Texas, 1975, 1976, 1977, 1978, 1980, 1981.

Fewest assists for leader, season

N.L.—52—Phil Masi, Boston, 95 games, 1945.
A.L.—58—Terry Kennedy, Baltimore, 142 games, 1987.

Most assists, nine-inning game

N.L.—9—Mike Hines, Boston, May 1, 1883.
A.L.—8—Wally Schang, Boston, May 12, 1920.
N.L. since 1900—7
Ed McFarland, Philadelphia, May 7, 1901.
Bill Bergen, Brooklyn, August 23, 1909, second game.
Jimmy Archer, Pittsburgh, May 24, 1918.
Bert Adams, Philadelphia, August 21, 1919.

Most assists, inning

A.A.—3—Jocko Milligan, Philadelphia, July 26, 1887, third inning.
A.L.—3
Les Nunamaker, New York, August 3, 1914, second inning.
Ray Schalk, Chicago, September 30, 1921, eighth inning.
Bill Dickey, New York, May 13, 1929, sixth inning.
Jim Sundberg, Texas, September 3, 1976, fifth inning.
N.L.—3
Bruce Edwards, Brooklyn, August 15, 1946, fourth inning.
Jim Campbell, Houston, June 16, 1963, second game, third inning.

	CHANCES ACCEPTED AND OFFERED	

Most chances accepted, career

N.L.—12,988—Gary Carter, Montreal, New York, San Francisco, Los Angeles, 19 years, 1974 through 1992.
A.L.—12,417—Carlton Fisk, Boston, Chicago, 24 years, 1969 through 1993, except 1970.

Most chances accepted, season

N.L. (162-game season)—1,214—Johnny Edwards, Houston, 151 games, 1969.
N.L. (154-game season)—933—Johnny Roseboro, Los Angeles, 125 games, 1961.
A.L. (162-game season)—1,044—Bill Freehan, Detroit, 138 games, 1968.
A.L. (154-game season)—924—Gabby Street, Washington, 137 games, 1909.

Most years leading league in chances accepted

A.L.—8
Ray Schalk, Chicago, 1913, 1914, 1915, 1916, 1917, 1919, 1920, 1922.
Yogi Berra, New York, 1950, 1951, 1952, 1954, 1955, 1956, 1957, 1959.
N.L.—8—Gary Carter, Montreal, 1977, 1978, 1979, 1980, 1981, 1982, New York, 1985, 1988.

Fewest chances accepted, season (150 or more games)

N.L.—536—Ray Mueller, Cincinnati, 155 games, 1944.
A.L.—677—Mike Tresh, Chicago, 150 games, 1945.

Fewest chances accepted by leader, season

N.L.—474—Ernie Lombardi, New York, 96 games, 1945.
A.L.—515—Birdie Tebbetts, Detroit, 97 games, 1942.

Most chances accepted, nine-inning game

U.A.—23—George Bignell, Milwaukee, October 3, 1884 (18 strikeouts).
N.L.—22—Sandy Nava, Providence, June 7, 1884 (19 strikeouts).
N.L. since 1900—20—Jerry Grote, New York, April 22, 1970 (19 strikeouts).
A.L.—20
Ellie Rodriguez, California, August 12, 1974 (19 strikeouts).

Rich Gedman, Boston, April 29, 1986 (20 strikeouts).

Most chances accepted, extra-inning game

A.L.—26—Mike Powers, Philadelphia, September 1, 1906, 24 innings (18 strikeouts).

N.L.—24—Steve Yeager, Los Angeles, August 8, 1972, 19 innings (22 strikeouts).

Most chances accepted, doubleheader (18 innings)

A.L.—27—Hank Severeid, St. Louis, July 13, 1920 (21 strikeouts).

N.L.—26—John Bateman, Houston, September 10, 1968 (22 strikeouts).

Most chances accepted, two consecutive nine-inning games

A.L.—37—Rich Gedman, Boston, April 29, 30, 1986 (36 strikeouts).

N.L.—31—Jerry Grote, New York, April 21, 22, 1970 (29 strikeouts).

Most chances accepted, inning

N.L.—5—Joe Garagiola, St. Louis, June 17, 1949, eighth inning (3 putouts, 2 assists).

A.L.—4—Held by many catchers. Last catcher—Gene Tenace, Oakland, May 24, 1975, fifth inning (3 putouts, 1 assist).

Longest game with no chances offered

A.L.—14 innings—Gene Desautels, Cleveland, August 11, 1942, first game.

N.L.—13 innings—Jimmie Wilson, Philadelphia, August 31, 1927, first game.

Fewest chances offered, doubleheader

N.L.—0—Harry McCurdy, St. Louis, July 10, 1923.

A.L.—2

Yam Yaryan, Chicago, May 26, 1921.
Hank Severeid, St. Louis, September 5, 1921.
Luke Sewell, Cleveland, August 28, 1926.

Fewest chances offered, two consecutive games

A.L.—0—Cy Perkins, Philadelphia, September 16, 17, 1922.

N.L.—0

Harry McCurdy, St. Louis, July 10, 1923.
Andy Seminick, Cincinnati, September 15, 16, 1953.

ERRORS

Most errors, career (since 1900)

N.L.—234—Ivy Wingo, St. Louis, Cincinnati, 17 years, 1911 through 1929, except 1927, 1928.

A.L.—218—Wally Schang, Philadelphia, Boston, New York, St. Louis, Detroit, 19 years, 1913 through 1931.

Most years leading league in errors

N.L.—7—Ivy Wingo, St. Louis, Cincinnati, 1912 (tied), 1913, 1916, 1917, 1918, 1920, 1921.

A.L.—6—Birdie Tebbetts, Detroit, Boston, 1939, 1940 (tied), 1942 (tied), 1947, 1948, 1949.

Most errors, season

N.L.—94—Nat Hicks, New York, 45 games, 1876.

N.L. since 1900—40—Red Dooin, Philadelphia, 140 games, 1909.

A.A.—85—Ed Whiting, Baltimore, 72 games, 1882.

A.L.—41—Oscar Stanage, Detroit, 141 games, 1911.

Fewest errors, season (150 or more games)

N.L.—4—Randy Hundley, Chicago, 152 games, 1967.

A.L.—4—Jim Sundberg, Texas, 150 games, 1979.

Fewest errors, season (100 or more games)

A.L.—0—Buddy Rosar, Philadelphia, 117 games, 1946.

N.L.—1

Earl Grace, Pittsburgh, 114 games, 1932.
Wes Westrum, New York, 139 games, 1950.
Tom Pagnozzi, St. Louis, 138 games, 1992.

Fewest errors for leader, season

A.L.—7—Rick Ferrell, St. Louis, 137 games, 1933.

N.L.—9—Hank Foiles, Pittsburgh, 109 games, 1957.

Most errors, nine-inning game (all fielding errors)

N.L.—7

Jack Rowe, Buffalo, May 16, 1883.
Dickie Lowe, Detroit, June 26, 1884.

N.L. since 1900—4—Gabby Street, Boston, June 7, 1905.

A.A.—7—Billy Taylor, Baltimore, May 29, 1886, a.m. game.

A.L.—4

John Peters, Cleveland, May 16, 1918.
Lena Styles, Philadelphia, July 29, 1921.
Bill Moore, Boston, September 26, 1927, second game.

Most errors, doubleheader

A.A.—8—Jim Donahue, Kansas City, August 31, 1889.

N.L.—8—Lew Graulich, Philadelphia, September 19, 1891.

N.L. since 1900—4—Held by many catchers.

A.L.—4—Held by many catchers.

Most errors, inning

N.L.—4—Doggie Miller, St. Louis, May 24, 1895, second inning.

N.L. since 1900—3—Jeff Reed, Montreal, July 28, 1987, seventh inning.

A.L.—3

Jeff Sweeney, New York, July 10, 1912, first inning.
John Peters, Cleveland, May 16, 1918, first inning.

Longest errorless game

A.L.—24 innings

Mike R. Powers, Philadelphia, September 1, 1906.
Buddy Rosar, Philadelphia, July 21, 1945.
Bob Swift, Detroit, July 21, 1945.

N.L.—24 innings

Hal King, Houston, April 15, 1968.
Jerry Grote, New York, April 15, 1968 (caught 23⅓ innings).

Most consecutive errorless games, career

A.L.—159—Rick Cerone, New York, Boston, July 5, 1987 through May 8, 1989 (896 chances accepted).

N.L.—138—Johnny Edwards, Houston, July 11, 1970, through August 20, 1971 (805 chances accepted).

Most consecutive errorless games, season

A.L.—117—Buddy Rosar, Philadelphia, April 16 through September 29, 1946, first game (605 chances accepted).

N.L.—110—Earl Grace, Pittsburgh, April 12 through September 7, 1932 (400 chances accepted).

Most consecutive errorless games, start of career

A.L.—93—Frankie Pytlak, Cleveland, April 22, 1932, through May 5, 1934.

Most consecutive chances accepted without an error, career

A.L.—950—Yogi Berra, New York, 148 games, July 28, 1957, second game, through May 10, 1959, second game.

N.L.—805—Johnny Edwards, Houston, July 10, 1970 through August 20, 1971.

Most consecutive chances accepted without an error, season

A.L.—605—Buddy Rosar, Philadelphia, 117 games, April 16 through September 29, 1946, first game.

N.L.—476—Mickey Owen, Brooklyn, 100 games, April 15 through August 29, 1941.

PASSED BALLS

Most passed balls, season

N.L.—99

Pop Snyder, Boston, 58 games, 1881.
Michael P. Hines, Boston, 56 games, 1883.

N.L. since 1900—29—Frank Bowerman, New York, 73 games, 1900.

A.L.—35—Geno Petralli, Texas, 63 games, 1987.

Most years leading league in passed balls

N.L.—10—Ernie Lombardi, Cincinnati, Boston, New York, 1932, 1935, 1936 (tied), 1937, 1938, 1939, 1940 (tied), 1941, 1942 1945.

A.L.—5—Rick Ferrell, St. Louis, Washington, 1931 (tied), 1939, 1940, 1944, 1945.

Fewest passed balls, season (150 or more games)
N.L.—1—Gary Carter, Montreal, 152 games, 1978.
A.L.—4
  Jim Hegan, Cleveland, 152 games, 1949.
  Carlton Fisk, Boston, 151 games, 1977.

Fewest passed balls, season (100 or more games)
N.L.—0
  Al Todd, Pittsburgh, 128 games, 1937.
  Al Lopez, Pittsburgh, 114 games, 1941.
  Johnny Bench, Cincinnati, 121 games, 1975.
  Benito Santiago, San Diego, 103 games, 1992.
A.L.—0—Bill Dickey, New York, 125 games, 1931.

Fewest passed balls for leader, season
A.L.—6
  Mickey Cochrane, Philadelphia, 117 games, 1931.
  Charlie F. Berry, Boston, 102 games, 1931.
  Rick Ferrell, St. Louis, 108 games, 1931.
N.L.—7—Held by five catchers.

Most passed balls, game
A.A.—12—Gid Gardner, Washington, May 10, 1884.
N.L.—10—Pat Dealey, Boston, May 1886.
N.L. since 1900—6—Harry Vickers, Cincinnati, October 4, 1902.
A.L.—6—Geno Petralli, Texas, August 30, 1987.

Most passed balls, two consecutive games
N.L.—13—Pete Hotaling, Worcester, September 20, 21, 1881.

Longest game with no passed balls
A.L.—25 innings—Carlton Fisk, Chicago, May 8, finished May 9, 1984.
N.L.—24 innings
  Hal King, Houston, April 15, 1968.
  Jerry Grote, New York, April 15, 1968 (caught 23⅓ innings).

Most passed balls, inning
A.A.—5—Dan Sullivan, St. Louis, August 9, 1885, third inning.
N.L.—4—Ray Katt, New York, September 10, 1954, eighth inning.
A.L.—4—Geno Petralli, Texas, August 22, 1987, seventh inning.

DOUBLE PLAYS

Most double plays, career
A.L.—217—Ray Schalk, Chicago, 17 years, 1912 through 1928.
N.L.—163—Gabby Hartnett, Chicago, New York, 20 years, 1922 through 1941.

Most unassisted double plays, career
A.L.—2
  Boss Schmidt, Detroit, 1906, 1907.
  Frank Crossin, St. Louis, 1914 (2).
  Clint Courtney, Baltimore, 1954, 1960.
  Yogi Berra, New York, 1947, 1962.
  Buck Rodgers, Los Angeles, 1965; California, 1969.
N.L.—2
  Mike Gonzalez, St. Louis, 1915, 1918.
  Chris Cannizzaro, New York, 1964, 1965.
  Ed Bailey, San Francisco, 1963; Chicago, 1965.
  Hawk Taylor, New York, 1964, 1967.

Most double plays, season
A.L.—29—Frankie Hayes, Philadelphia, Cleveland, 151 games, 1945.
N.L.—23—Tom Haller, Los Angeles, 139 games, 1968.

Most unassisted double plays, season
A.L.—2—Frank Crossin, St. Louis, 1914.
N.L.—1—Held by many catchers.

Most years leading league in double plays
N.L.—6—Gabby Hartnett, Chicago, 1925 (tied), 1927, 1930 (tied), 1931, 1934, 1935.
A.L.—6—Yogi Berra, New York, 1949, 1950, 1951, 1952, 1954, 1956.

Fewest double plays for leader, season
N.L.—8
  Phil Masi, Boston/Pittsburgh, 81 games, 1949.
  Clyde McCullough, Pittsburgh, 90 games, 1949.
A.L.—9
  Earl Battey, Minnesota, 131 games, 1961.
  Gus Triandos, Baltimore, 114 games, 1961.

Most double plays, nine-inning game
N.L.—3
  Jack O'Neill, Chicago, April 26, 1905.
  Shanty Hogan, New York, August 19, 1931.
  Ebba St. Claire, Boston, August 9, 1951.
A.L.—3
  Charlie F. Berry, Chicago, May 17, 1932.
  J.C. Martin, Chicago, June 23, 1963, first game.
  Earl Battey, Minnesota, August 11, 1966.
  Ed Herrmann, Chicago, July 4, 1972.
  Rick Dempsey, Baltimore, June 1, 1977.

Most double plays, extra-inning game
N.L.—3
  Bob O'Farrell, Chicago, July 9, 1919, second game, 10⅓ innings.
  Ron Hodges, New York, April 23, 1978, 11⅔ innings.
A.L.—3—Billy Sullivan, Chicago, July 25, 1912, 10 innings.

Most double plays started, game
N.L.—3—J. Shanty Hogan, New York, August 19, 1931.
A.L.—2—Held by many catchers.

Most unassisted double plays, game
A.L.-N.L.—1—Held by many players.

BASERUNNERS VS. CATCHERS

Most stolen bases off catcher, game
A.A.—19—Grant Briggs, Syracuse, April 22, 1890.
N.L.—17—Doggie Miller, Pittsburgh, May 23, 1890.
N.L. since 1900—11—Bill Fischer, St. Louis, August 13, 1916, second game, five innings.
A.L.—13—Branch Rickey, New York, June 28, 1907.

Most stolen bases off catcher, inning
A.L.—8—Steve O'Neill, Cleveland, July 19, 1915, first inning.
N.L.—8—Mike Gonzalez, New York, July 7, 1919, first game, ninth inning.

Most runners caught stealing, nine-inning game
N.L.—8—Duke Farrell, Washington, May 11, 1897.
N.L. since 1900—7—Bill Bergen, Brooklyn, August 23, 1909, second game.
A.L.—6—Wally Schang, Philadelphia, May 12, 1915.

Most runners caught stealing, inning
A.A.—3—Jocko Milligan, Philadelphia, July 26, 1887, third inning.
A.L.—3—Les Nunamaker, New York, August 3, 1914, second inning.
N.L.—2—Held by many catchers.

NO-HITTERS CAUGHT

Most no-hit games caught, career (nine innings)
A.L.—4—Ray Schalk, Chicago, 1914 (2), 1917, 1922. (In one of Schalk's 1914 games, the no-hitter was broken up in the 10th inning.)
N.L.—3
  Roy Campanella, Brooklyn, 1952, 1956 (2).
  Del Crandall, Milwaukee, 1954, 1960 (2).
  Alan Ashby, Houston, 1979, 1981, 1986.

Most no-hit victories caught, career (entire game)
M.L.—3
  Bill Carrigan, Boston A.L., 1911, 1916 (2).
  Ray Schalk, Chicago A.L., 1914, 1917, 1922.
  Val Picinich, Philadelphia A.L., 1916, Washington A.L., 1920, Boston A.L., 1923.
  Luke Sewell, Cleveland A.L., 1931, Chicago A.L., 1935, 1937.

Jim Hegan, Cleveland A.L., 1947, 1948, 1951.
Roy Campanella, Brooklyn N.L., 1952, 1956 (2).
Del Crandall, Milwaukee N.L., 1954, 1960 (2).
Jeff Torborg, Los Angeles N.L., 1965, 1970; California A.L., 1973.
Alan Ashby, Houston N.L., 1979, 1981, 1986.
A.L.—3
Ray Schalk, Chicago, 1914, 1917, 1922.
Bill Carrigan, Boston, 1911, 1916 (2).
Val Picinich, Philadelphia, 1916, Washington, 1920, Boston, 1923.
Luke Sewell, Cleveland, 1931, Chicago, 1935, 1937.
Jim Hegan, Cleveland, 1947, 1948, 1951.
N.L.—3
Roy Campanella, Brooklyn, 1952, 1956 (2).
Del Crandall, Milwaukee, 1954, 1960 (2).
Alan Ashby, Houston, 1979, 1981, 1986.

PITCHERS

GAMES AND INNINGS

Most games pitched, career
M.L.—1,070—Hoyt Wilhelm, New York N.L., St. Louis N.L., Cleveland A.L., Baltimore A.L., Chicago A.L., California A.L., Atlanta N.L., Chicago N.L., Los Angeles N.L., 21 years, 1952 through 1972 (448 in N.L., 622 in A.L.).
N.L.—1,050—Kent Tekulve, Pittsburgh, Philadelphia, Cincinnati, 16 years, 1974 through 1989.
A.L.—807—Sparky Lyle, Boston, New York, Texas, Chicago, 15 years, 1967 through 1982, except 1981.

Most games pitched, season
N.L.—106—Mike Marshall, Los Angeles, 208 innings, 1974.
A.L.—90—Mike Marshall, Minnesota, 143 innings, 1979.

Most years leading league in games pitched
M.L.—7—Joe McGinnity, Brooklyn N.L., Baltimore A.L., New York N.L., 1900, 1901, 1903, 1904, 1905, 1906, 1907.
N.L.—6—Joe McGinnity, Brooklyn, New York, 1900, 1903, 1904, 1905, 1906, 1907.
A.L.—6—Firpo Marberry, Washington, 1924, 1925, 1926, 1928, 1929, 1932.

Fewest games for leader, season
A.L.—40—Joe Haynes, Chicago, 1942 (103 innings).
N.L.—41
Ray Kremer, Pittsburgh, 1924 (259 innings).
Johnny Morrison, Pittsburgh, 1924 (238 innings).

Most innings pitched, game
N.L.—26 innings
Leon Cadore, Brooklyn, May 1, 1920.
Joe Oeschger, Boston, May 1, 1920.
A.L.—24 innings
Jack Coombs, Philadelphia, September 1, 1906.
Joe Harris, Boston, September 1, 1906.

AVERAGE

Highest fielding average with most chances accepted, season
N.L.—1.000—Randy Jones, San Diego, 1976, 40 games (31 putouts, 81 assists, 112 chances accepted).
A.L.—1.000—Walter Johnson, Washington, 1913, 48 games (21 putouts, 82 assists, 103 chances accepted).

Most years with highest average and most chances accepted, season
N.L.—4
Claude Passeau, Philadelphia, Chicago, 1939, 1942, 1943, 1945.
Larry Jackson, St. Louis, Chicago, Philadelphia, 1957, 1964, 1965, 1968.
A.L.—3—Walter Johnson, Washington, 1913, 1917, 1922 (tied).

PUTOUTS

Most putouts, career (since 1900)
A.L.—387—Jack Morris, Detroit, Minnesota, Toronto, Cleve-

land, 18 years, 1977 through 1994.
N.L.—340—Phil Niekro, Milwaukee, Atlanta, 21 years, 1964 through 1983, 1987.

Most putouts, season
N.L.—52—Al Spalding, Chicago, 60 games, 1876.
A.L.—49
Nick Altrock, Chicago, 38 games, 1904.
Mike Boddicker, Baltimore, 34 games, 1984.
N.L. since 1900—39
Vic Willis, Boston, 43 games, 1904.
Greg Maddux, Chicago, 35 games, 1990.
Greg Maddux, Chicago, 37 games, 1991.
Greg Maddux, Atlanta, 36 games, 1993.

Most years leading league in putouts
A.L.—5—Bob Lemon, Cleveland, 1948, 1949, 1952, 1953, 1954.
N.L.—5—Greg Maddux, Chicago, 1989, 1990, 1991, 1992; Atlanta, 1993.

Fewest putouts for leader, season
N.L.—14
Howie Camnitz, Pittsburgh, 38 games, 1910.
Art Nehf, New York, 37 games, 1922.
Tony Kaufmann, Chicago, 37 games, 1922.
A.L.—16—Roxie Lawson, Detroit, 27 games, 1937.

Most putouts, nine-inning game
N.L.—7—Greg Maddux, Chicago, April 29, 1990.
A.L.—6
Bert Blyleven, Cleveland, June 24, 1984.
Eric King, Detroit, July 8, 1986.

Most putouts, extra-inning game
A.L.—7—Dick Fowler, Philadelphia, June 9, 1949, 12 innings.
N.L.—Less than nine-inning record.

Most putouts, inning
A.L.—3
Jim Bagby Jr., Boston, September 26, 1940, fourth inning.
Bob Heffner, Boston, June 28, 1963, first inning.
Jim Beattie, New York, September 13, 1978, second inning.
Roger Clemens, Boston, June 27, 1992, sixth inning.
N.L.—3
Rick Reuschel, Chicago, April 25, 1975, third inning.
Ed Lynch, Chicago, July 22, 1986, first inning.
Mike Harkey, Chicago, May 23, 1990, fourth inning.

ASSISTS

Most assists, career (since 1900)
N.L.—1,489—Christy Mathewson, New York, Cincinnati, 17 years, 1900 through 1916.
A.L.—1,337—Walter Johnson, Washington, 21 years, 1907 through 1927.

Most assists, season
A.L.—227—Ed Walsh, Chicago, 56 games, 1907.
N.L.—168—John Clarkson, Boston, 72 games, 1889.
N.L. since 1900—141—Christy Mathewson, New York, 56 games, 1908.

Most years leading league in assists
A.L.—6—Bob Lemon, Cleveland, 1948, 1949, 1951, 1952, 1953, 1956.
N.L.—5—Christy Mathewson, New York, 1901, 1905, 1908, 1910, 1911.

Fewest assists for leader, season
A.L.—42—Mark Langston, California, 33 games, 1990.
N.L.—47
Ron Darling, New York, 36 games, 1985.
Ron Darling, New York, 34 games, 1986.
Bob Knepper, Houston, 40 games, 1986.
Fernando Valenzuela, Los Angeles, 34 games, 1986.

Most assists, nine-inning game
N.L.—11—Rip Sewell, Pittsburgh, June 6, 1941, second game.
A.L.—11
Al Orth, New York, August 12, 1906.

Ed Walsh, Chicago, April 19, 1907.
Ed Walsh, Chicago, August 12, 1907.
George McConnell, New York, September 2, 1912, second game.
Mellie Wolfgang, Chicago, August 29, 1914.

Most assists, extra-inning game

N.L.—12—Leon Cadore, Brooklyn, May 1, 1920, 26 innings.
A.L.—12
Nick Altrock, Chicago, June 7, 1908, 10 innings.
Ed Walsh, Chicago, July 16, 1907, 13 innings.

Most assists, inning

N.L.-A.L.—3—Held by many pitchers.

CHANCES ACCEPTED AND OFFERED

Most chances accepted, career (since 1900)

N.L.—1,761—Christy Mathewson, New York, Cincinnati, 17 years, 1900 through 1916.
A.L.—1,606—Walter Johnson, Washington, 21 years, 1907 through 1927.

Most chances accepted, season

A.L.—262—Ed Walsh, Chicago, 56 games, 1907.
N.L.—206—John Clarkson, Boston, 72 games, 1889.
N.L. since 1900—168—Christy Mathewson, New York, 56 games, 1908.

Most years leading league in chances accepted

A.L.—8—Bob Lemon, Cleveland, 1948, 1949, 1950, 1951, 1952, 1953, 1954, 1956.
N.L.—7—Burleigh Grimes, Brooklyn, New York, Pittsburgh, 1921, 1922, 1923, 1924, 1925, 1927, 1928.

Fewest chances accepted for leader, season

A.L.—63
Frank Sullivan, Boston, 35 games, 1955.
Ray Herbert, Kansas City, 37 games, 1960.
Jim Perry, Cleveland, 41 games, 1960.
N.L.—67
Paul Minner, Chicago, 31 games, 1953.
Robin Roberts, Philadelphia, 44 games, 1953.
Jim Hearn, New York, 39 games, 1955.

Most chances accepted, nine-inning game

A.L.—13
Nick Altrock, Chicago, August 6, 1904 (3 putouts, 10 assists).
Ed Walsh, Chicago, April 19, 1907 (2 putouts, 11 assists).
N.L.—12—Rip Sewell, Pittsburgh, June 6, 1941, second game (1 putout, 11 assists).

Most chances accepted, extra-inning game

A.L.—15—Ed Walsh, Chicago, July 16, 1907, 13 innings.
N.L.—13—Leon Cadore, Brooklyn, May 1, 1920, 26 innings.

Most chances accepted, two consecutive games

A.L.—20—Ed Walsh, Chicago, April 13, 19, 1907 (2 putouts, 18 assists).

Most chances accepted, inning

N.L.—4—Phil Regan, Chicago, June 6, 1969, sixth inning (1 putout, 3 assists).
A.L.—3—Held by many pitchers.

Longest game with no chances offered

N.L.—20 innings—Milt Watson, Philadelphia, July 17, 1918.
A.L.—15 innings—Red Ruffing, New York, July 23, 1932, first game.

Fewest chances offered, two consecutive games (over 18 innings)

A.A—0—Jack Neagle, Pittsburgh, July 13, 17, 1884, 12 innings each.
N.L.-A.L.—1—Held by many pitchers.

Fewest chances offered, doubleheader

A.A.—1—Toad Ramsey, Louisville, July 5, 1886 (1 putout).
N.L.—3
Joe McGinnity, New York, August 1, 1903 (1 putout, 1 assist, 1 error).
Grover Alexander, Philadelphia, September 3, 1917 (1 putout, 2 assists).

Hi Bell, St. Louis, July 19, 1924 (1 putout, 2 assists).
A.L.—3—Ed Walsh, Chicago, September 29, 1908 (0 putouts, 3 assists).

ERRORS

Most errors, career (since 1900)

N.L.—64—Hippo Vaughn, Chicago, nine years, 1913 through 1921.
A.L.—55—Ed Walsh, Chicago, 13 years, 1904 through 1916.

Most errors, season

A.A.—63—Tim Keefe, New York, 68 games, 1883.
N.L.—28—Jim Whitney, Boston, 63 games, 1881.
N.L. since 1900—17—Doc Newton, Cincinnati, Brooklyn, 33 games, 1901.
A.L.—15
Jack Chesbro, New York, 55 games, 1904.
Rube Waddell, Philadelphia, 46 games, 1905.
Ed Walsh, Chicago, 62 games, 1912.

Most years leading league in errors

N.L.—5
Hippo Vaughn, Chicago, 1914, 1915 (tied), 1917 (tied), 1919, 1920.
Warren Spahn, Boston, Milwaukee, 1949 (tied), 1950, 1952 (tied), 1954 (tied), 1964 (tied).
A.L.—4
Allen Sothoron, St. Louis, 1917, 1918 (tied), 1919, 1920.
Nolan Ryan, California, 1975, 1976, 1977 (tied), 1978.

Fewest errors for leader, season

N.L.-A.L.—4—Held by many pitchers.

Most errors, game

N.L.—5—Ed Doheny, New York, August 15, 1899.
N.L. since 1900—4
Doc Newton, Cincinnati, September 13, 1900, first game.
Lave Winham, Pittsburgh, September 21, 1903, first game.
A.L.—4—Buster Ross, Boston, May 17, 1925.

Most errors, inning

N.L.—3—Cy Seymour, New York, May 21, 1898, sixth inning.
A.L.—3—Tommy John, New York, July 27, 1988, fourth inning.

Longest errorless game

N.L.—26 innings
Leon Cadore, Brooklyn, May 1, 1920.
Joe Oeschger, Boston, May 1, 1920.
A.L.—24 innings
Jack Coombs, Philadelphia, September 1, 1906.
Joe Harris, Boston, September 1, 1906.

Most consecutive errorless games, career

N.L.—546—Lee Smith, Chicago, St. Louis, July 5, 1982 through September 22, 1992 (93 chances accepted).
A.L.—466—Dennis Eckersley, Oakland, May 1, 1987 through August 9, 1994 (75 chances accepted).

Most consecutive chances accepted without an error, career

N.L.—273—Claude Passeau, Chicago, September 21, first game, 1941 through May 20, 1946, 145 games.
A.L.—230—Rick Langford, Oakland, April 13, 1977 to October 2, 1980, 142 games.

Most consecutive errorless games, season

A.L.—88—Wilbur Wood, Chicago, April 10 through September 29, 1968 (32 chances accepted).
N.L.—84—Ted Abernathy, Chicago, April 12, through October 3, 1965 (52 chances accepted).

DOUBLE PLAYS

Most double plays, career

M.L.—83—Phil Niekro, Milwaukee N.L., Atlanta N.L., New York A.L., Cleveland A.L., Toronto A.L., 24 years, 1964 through 1987.
N.L.—82—Warren Spahn, Boston, Milwaukee, New York, San Francisco, 21 years, 1942 through 1965, except

1943, 1944, 1945 in military service.
A.L.—78—Bob Lemon, Cleveland, 13 years, 1946 through 1958.

Most unassisted double plays, career
N.L.—2
  Tex Carleton, Chicago, Brooklyn, 1935, 1940.
  Claude Passeau, Philadelphia, Chicago, 1938, 1945.
A.L.—1—Held by many pitchers.

Most double plays, season
A.L.—15—Bob Lemon, Cleveland, 41 games, 1953.
N.L.—12
  Art Nehf, New York, 40 games, 1920.
  Curt Davis, Philadelphia, 51 games, 1934.
  Randy Jones, San Diego, 40 games, 1976.

Most years leading league in double plays
N.L.—5
  Bucky Walters, Philadelphia, Cincinnati, 1937, 1939, 1941 (tied), 1943 (tied), 1944 (tied).
  Warren Spahn, Milwaukee, 1953 (tied), 1956, 1960 (tied), 1961 (tied), 1963.
A.L.—4—Willis Hudlin, Cleveland, 1929, 1930, 1931, 1934.

Fewest double plays for leader, season
N.L.—4
  Bud Black, San Francisco, 1992.
  Doug Drabek, Pittsburgh, 1992.
  Omar Olivares, St. Louis, 1992.
A.L.—5—Held by many players.

Most double plays started, game
A.L.—4
  Milt Gaston, Chicago, May 17, 1932.
  Hal Newhouser, Detroit, May 19, 1948.
N.L.—3—Held by 5 pitchers. Last pitcher—Gene Conley, Milwaukee, July 19, 1957.

Most unassisted double plays, game
N.L.—1—Held by many pitchers. Last pitcher—Jim McAndrew, New York, August 17, 1968.
A.L.—1—Held by many pitchers. Last pitcher—Clay Parker, Detroit, August 10, 1990.

Most triple plays started, season
N.L.—2—Wilbur Cooper, Pittsburgh, July 7, August 21, 1920.
A.L.—1—Held by many pitchers.

CLUB FIELDING

AVERAGE

Highest fielding average, season
A.L.—.98606—Toronto, 162 games, 1990.
N.L.—.9851—St. Louis, 162 games, 1992.

Lowest fielding average, season (since 1900)
A.L.—.928—Detroit, 136 games, 1901.
N.L.—.936—Philadelphia, 155 games, 1904.

Most consecutive years leading league in fielding
A.L.—6—Boston, 1916 through 1921.
N.L.—6—St. Louis, 1984 through 1989.

PUTOUTS

Most putouts, season
A.L. (162-game season)—4,520—New York, 164 games, 1964.
A.L. (154-game season)—4,396—Cleveland, 161 games, 1910.
N.L. (162-game season)—4,480—Pittsburgh, 163 games, 1979.
N.L. (154-game season)—4,359—Philadelphia, 159 games, 1913.

Fewest putouts, season
N.L. (154-game season)—3,887—Philadelphia, 149 games, 1907.
N.L. (162-game season)—4,223—Atlanta, 160 games, 1979.
A.L. (154-game season)—3,907—Cleveland, 147 games, 1945.
A.L. (162-game season)—4,188—Detroit, 159 games, 1975.

Most players with one or more putouts, nine-inning game
A.L.—14—New York vs. Cleveland, July 17, 1952, first game.
N.L.—13
   St. Louis vs. Los Angeles, April 13, 1960.
   Chicago vs. New York, August 8, 1965, second game.

Most players from both clubs with one or more putouts, nine-inning game
A.L.—22—New York 14, Cleveland 8, July 17, 1952, first game.
N.L.—22—Chicago 13, New York 9, August 8, 1965, second game.

Most putouts by infield, nine-inning game
A.L.—26—Seattle vs. New York, May 28, 1988.
N.L.—25
   Chicago vs. Philadelphia, September 24, 1927.
   Pittsburgh vs. New York, June 6, 1941, second game.
   St. Louis vs. Boston, July 17, 1947.
   Chicago vs. Pittsburgh, May 9, 1963.

Most putouts by infielders from both clubs, nine-inning game
N.L.—46
   Cincinnati 24, New York 22, May 7, 1941.
   St. Louis 25, Boston 21, July 17, 1947.
A.L.—45
   Detroit 24, Washington 21, September 15, 1945, second game.
   Boston 24, Cleveland 21, July 11, 1977.

Fewest putouts by infield, nine-inning game
A.L.—3
   St. Louis vs. New York, July 20, 1945, second game.
   Boston vs. Seattle, April 29, 1986.
N.L.—3—New York vs. San Diego, April 22, 1970.

Most putouts by outfield, nine-inning game
N.L.—19—Pittsburgh vs. Cincinnati, July 5, 1948, second game.
A.L.—18
   Cleveland vs. St. Louis, September 28, 1929.
   New York vs. Boston, October 1, 1933.

Most putouts by outfielders from both clubs, nine-inning game
N.L.—30—Chicago 16, Philadelphia 14, August 7, 1953.
A.L.—29—Washington 17, St. Louis 12, May 3, 1939.

Most putouts by outfield, extra-inning game
N.L.—23
   Brooklyn vs. Boston, May 1, 1920, 26 innings.
   Chicago vs. Boston, May 17, 1927, 22 innings.
A.L.—22—Chicago vs. Washington, May 15, 1918, 18 innings.

Most putouts by outfielders from both clubs, extra-inning game
N.L.—42—New York 21, Pittsburgh 21, July 17, 1914, 21 innings.
A.L.—38—Washington 20, St. Louis 18, July 19, 1924, 16 innings.

Longest game with no putouts by outfield
N.L.—13 innings
   New York vs. Brooklyn, April 15, 1909.
   St. Louis vs. Philadelphia, August 13, 1987.
A.L.—11 innings—St. Louis vs. Cleveland, April 23, 1905.

Fewest putouts by outfielders from both clubs, nine-inning game
A.A.—1—St. Louis 1, New York 0, June 30, 1886.
N.L.—1—Pittsburgh 1, Brooklyn 0, August 26, 1910.
A.L.—2—New York 2, Detroit 0, May 9, 1930.

Most putouts by outfield, doubleheader (more than 18 innings)
N.L.—29—Boston vs. New York, September 3, 1933, 23 innings.
A.L.—Less than for 18 innings.

Most putouts by outfield, doubleheader
N.L.—27—Pittsburgh vs. Cincinnati, July 5, 1948.
A.L.—24—Detroit vs. Philadelphia, June 28, 1931.

Most putouts by outfielders from both clubs, doubleheader
N.L.—47—Pittsburgh 26, Boston 21, June 26, 1935.
A.L.—34—Detroit 24, Philadelphia 19, June 28, 1931.

ASSISTS

Most assists, season
N.L.—2,293—St. Louis, 154 games, 1917.
A.L.—2,446—Chicago, 157 games, 1907.

Fewest assists, season
N.L.—1,437—Philadelphia, 156 games, 1957.
A.L.—1,443—Detroit, 161 games, 1962.

Most consecutive years leading league in assists
A.L.—6—Chicago, 1905 through 1910.
N.L.—6—New York, 1933 through 1938.

Most assists, nine-inning game
N.L.—28—Pittsburgh vs. New York, June 7, 1911.
A.L.—27—St. Louis vs. Philadelphia, August 16, 1919.

Most assists by both clubs, nine-inning game
A.L.—45—New York 23, Chicago 22, August 21, 1905.
N.L.—44
   Brooklyn 23, New York 21, April 21, 1903.
   New York 25, Cincinnati 19, May 15, 1909.

Most assists, extra-inning game
N.L.—41—Boston vs. Brooklyn, May 1, 1920, 26 innings.
A.L.—38
   Detroit vs. Philadelphia, July 21, 1945, 24 innings.
   Washington vs. Chicago, June 12, 1967, 22 innings.

Most assists by both clubs, extra-inning game
N.L.—72—Boston 41, Brooklyn 31, May 1, 1920, 26 innings.
A.L.—72—Detroit 38, Philadelphia 34, July 21, 1945, 24 innings.

Most players with one or more assists, nine-inning game
A.L.—11
   Washington vs. Philadelphia, October 3, 1920.
   Boston vs. Philadelphia, May 1, 1929.
   Washington vs. Baltimore, April 29, 1956, first game.
   Chicago vs. Kansas City, September 22, 1970, second game.
N.L.—11—Brooklyn vs. Philadelphia, April 22, 1953.

Most assists, two consecutive games

N.L.—48—Boston vs. New York, June 24, 25, 1918.
A.L.—43—Washington vs. St. Louis, August 19, 20, 1923.

Fewest assists, game

A.L.—0
St. Louis vs. Cleveland, August 8, 1943, second game (fielded eight innings).
Cleveland vs. New York, July 4, 1945, first game.
N.L.—0—New York vs. Philadelphia, June 25, 1989.

Fewest assists by both clubs, nine-inning game

A.L.—5
Baltimore 3, Cleveland 2, August 31, 1955.
Boston 4, New York 1, August 9, 1992.
N.L.—6
Chicago 5, Philadelphia 1, May 2, 1957.
San Francisco 3, Philadelphia 3, May 13, 1959.

Fewest assists, two consecutive nine-inning games

N.L.—5—Chicago vs. Philadelphia, Brooklyn, August 23 (1), 24 (4), 1932.
A.L.—7
Chicago vs. Boston, June 11 (2), 11 (5), 1960, 17 innings.
Kansas City vs. Milwaukee, California, April 16 (3), April 17 (4), 1970, 18 innings.

Most assists, doubleheader (nine-inning games)

N.L.—42—New York vs. Boston, September 30, 1914.
A.L.—41
Boston vs. Detroit, September 20, 1927.
Boston vs. Washington, September 26, 1927.

Most assists by both clubs, doubleheader (nine-inning games)

N.L.—70—Brooklyn 36, Philadelphia 34, September 5, 1922.
A.L.—68
Detroit 34, Philadelphia 34, September 5, 1901.
Cleveland 35, Boston 33, September 7, 1935.
St. Louis 39, Boston 29, July 23, 1939.

Fewest assists, doubleheader (nine-inning games)

A.L.—8
Philadelphia vs. New York, July 7, 1946.
Minnesota vs. Los Angeles, July 19, 1961, 17⅔ innings.
N.L.—7—New York vs. San Diego, May 29, 1971.

Fewest assists by both clubs, doubleheader

N.L.—22—Milwaukee 14, Philadelphia 8, September 12, 1954.
A.L.—25—Washington 13, New York 12, July 4, 1931.

Most assists by infield, nine-inning game

A.L.—22—Seattle vs. New York, May 28, 1988.
N.L.—21
New York vs. Pittsburgh, July 13, 1919.
Philadelphia vs. Boston, May 30, 1931, p.m. game.
Brooklyn vs. Pittsburgh, August 18, 1935, second game.

Most assists by infielders from both clubs, nine-inning game

N.L.—38—Brooklyn 20, Cincinnati 18, June 10, 1917.
A.L.—35
Detroit 19, Cleveland 16, April 18, 1924.
Chicago 18, Boston 17, September 17, 1945, second game.

Fewest assists by infield, nine-inning game

N.L.—0
Pittsburgh vs. Chicago, July 19, 1902.
New York vs. Philadelphia, July 29, 1934, first game.
Chicago vs. Cincinnati, April 26, 1935.
Cincinnati vs. Brooklyn, August 6, 1938.
Boston vs. Pittsburgh, June 17, 1940, first game.
New York vs. Chicago, May 6, 1953.
Philadelphia, vs. Chicago, May 2, 1957.
Houston vs. Cincinnati, September 10, 1968, first game.
Pittsburgh vs. Montreal, September 17, 1977.
New York vs. Philadelphia, June 25, 1989.
A.L.—0
Boston vs. Chicago, August 13, 1924, first game.
Cleveland vs. New York, July 4, 1945, first game.
St. Louis vs. New York, July 20, 1945, second game.
Washington vs. St. Louis, May 20, 1952.

Fewest assists by infielders from both clubs, nine-inning game

A.L.—2—Philadelphia 2, Washington 0, May 5, 1910, Washington fielded only eight innings.
N.L.—2—Chicago 2, Philadelphia 0, May 2, 1957.

Most assists by outfield, game

N.L.—5—Pittsburgh vs. Philadelphia, August 23, 1910.
A.L.—5
New York vs. Boston, September 5, 1921, second game.
Cleveland vs. St. Louis, May 1, 1928.

Most assists from outfielder to catcher with runner thrown out, game

N.L.—3
Washington vs. Indianapolis, June 19, 1889.
New York vs. Boston, June 30, 1902.
Chicago vs. Pittsburgh, April 26, 1905.
A.L.—2—Made in many games.

Longest game with no outfield assists

N.L.—26 innings—Boston vs. Brooklyn, May 1, 1920.
A.L.—24 innings
Boston vs. Philadelphia, September 1, 1906.
Philadelphia vs. Detroit, July 21, 1945.

Longest game with no outfield assists by either club

N.L.—24 innings—Houston 0, New York 0, April 15, 1968.
A.L.—22 innings—Chicago 0, Washington 0, June 12, 1967.

Most assists, inning

A.L.—10
Cleveland vs. Philadelphia, August 17, 1921, first inning.
Boston vs. New York, May 10, 1952, fifth inning.
N.L.—8—Boston vs. Philadelphia, May 1, 1911, fourth inning.

CHANCES ACCEPTED AND OFFERED

Most chances accepted, season

A.L.—6,655—Chicago, 157 games, 1907.
N.L. (162-game season)—6,508—Chicago, 162 games, 1977.
N.L. (154-game season)—6,472—New York, 155 games, 1920.

Fewest chances accepted, season

A.L.—5,470—Cleveland, 147 games, 1945.
N.L.—5,545—Philadelphia, 154 games, 1955.

Most chances accepted, nine-inning game

N.L.—55—Pittsburgh vs. New York, June 7, 1911.
A.L.—54—St. Louis vs. Philadelphia, August 16, 1919.

Most chances accepted, extra-inning game

N.L.—119—Boston vs. Brooklyn, May 1, 1920, 26 innings.
A.L.—110—Detroit vs. Philadelphia, July 21, 1945, 24 innings.

Most chances accepted by both clubs, nine-inning game

N.L.—98
Brooklyn 50, New York 48, April 21, 1903.
New York 52, Cincinnati 46, May 15, 1909.
A.L.—98—Cleveland 49, St. Louis 49, May 7, 1909.

Most chances accepted by infield, nine-inning game

A.L.—48—Seattle vs. New York, May 28, 1988.
N.L.—45
New York vs. Pittsburgh, July 13, 1919.
Chicago vs. Philadelphia, September 24, 1927.
Chicago vs. Pittsburgh, May 9, 1963.

Most chances accepted by infielders from both clubs, nine-inning game

N.L.—78—Cincinnati 41, New York 37, May 7, 1941.
A.L.—76—Boston 43, Cleveland 33, June 24, 1931.

Fewest chances offered by infield, nine-inning game

A.L.—3—St. Louis vs. New York, July 20, 1945, second game.
N.L.—4—New York vs. San Diego, April 22, 1970.

Fewest chances offered by infielders from both clubs, nine-inning game
A.L.— 18—Cleveland 9, Baltimore 9, August 31, 1955.
N.L.— 19—Chicago 10, Philadelphia 9, May 2, 1957.

Most chances accepted by outfield, game
N.L.—20—Pittsburgh vs. Cincinnati, July 5, 1948, second game.
A.L.— 18
   Cleveland vs. St. Louis, September 28, 1929.
   New York vs. Boston, October 1, 1933.
   Philadelphia vs. Boston, May 27, 1941, second game.
   New York vs. Cleveland, June 26, 1955, second game.

Most chances accepted by outfielders from both clubs, game
A.L.—30—Washington 17, St. Louis 13, May 3, 1939.
N.L.—30—Chicago 16, Philadelphia 14, August 7, 1953.

Most chances accepted by outfield, extra-inning game
N.L.—24
   Brooklyn vs. Boston, May 1, 1920, 26 innings.
   Chicago vs. Boston, May 17, 1927, 22 innings.
A.L.—22—Chicago vs. Washington, May 15, 1918, 18 innings.

Most chances accepted by outfielders from both clubs, extra-inning game
N.L.—43—New York 22, Pittsburgh 21, July 17, 1914, 21 innings.
A.L.—40—Washington 21, St. Louis 19, July 19, 1924, 16 innings.

Fewest chances offered by outfield, nine-inning game
N.L.—0—Made in many games.
A.L.—0—Made in many games.

Longest game with no outfield chances offered
N.L.— 13 innings—St. Louis vs. Philadelphia, August 13, 1987.
A.L.— 11 innings—St. Louis vs. Cleveland, April 23, 1905.

Fewest chances offered by outfielders from both clubs, nine-inning game
A.A.—2—St. Louis 2, New York 0, June 30, 1886.
N.L.—2
   Pittsburgh 1, Brooklyn 1, August 26, 1910.
   Cincinnati 1, New York 1, May 7, 1941.
A.L.—3
   St. Louis 2, Chicago 1, April 24, 1908.
   New York 2, Boston 1, May 4, 1911.
   New York 2, Detroit 1, May 9, 1930.

Fewest chances offered by outfield, two consecutive games
U.A.—0—Milwaukee vs. Boston, October 4, 5, 1884.
A.L.— 1—St. Louis, April 16, 10 innings, April 17, 1908.
N.L.—2—Held by many clubs.

Most chances accepted by outfield, doubleheader
N.L.—28—Pittsburgh vs. Cincinnati, July 5, 1948.
A.L.—24
   Detroit vs. Philadelphia, June 28, 1931.
   Philadelphia vs. Boston, May 27, 1941.

Most chances accepted by outfielders from both clubs, doubleheader
N.L.—48—Pittsburgh 26, Boston 22, June 26, 1935.
A.L.—44—Detroit 24, Philadelphia 20, June 28, 1931.

ERRORS

Most errors, season
N.L.—867—Washington, 122 games, 1886.
N.L. since 1900—408—Brooklyn, 155 games, 1905.
A.L.—425—Detroit, 136 games, 1901.

Fewest errors, season
A.L.—84—Minnesota, 162 games, 1988.
N.L.—94—St. Louis, 162 games, 1992.

Most errorless games, season
A.L. (162-game season)—103—Toronto, 162 games, 1990.
A.L. (154-game season)—84—Detroit, 156 games, 1972.
N.L. (162-game season)—100—St. Louis, 162 games, 1992.
N.L. (154-game season)—82—Cincinnati, 154 games, 1958.

Most consecutive years leading league in errors
N.L.—7—Philadelphia, 1930 through 1936.
A.L.—6
   Philadelphia, 1936 through 1941.
   St. Louis, 1948 through 1953.

Most years leading league with fewest errors
N.L. since 1900—20—Cincinnati.

Most errors, game
N.L.—24—Boston vs. St. Louis, June 14, 1876.
N.L. since 1900— 11
   St. Louis vs. Pittsburgh, April 19, 1902.
   Boston vs. St. Louis, June 11, 1906.
   St. Louis vs. Cincinnati, July 3, 1909, second game.
A.L.— 12
   Detroit vs. Chicago, May 1, 1901.
   Chicago vs. Detroit, May 6, 1903.

Most errors by both clubs, game
N.L.—40—Boston 24, St. Louis 16, June 14, 1876.
N.L. since 1900— 15
   St. Louis 11, Pittsburgh 4, April 19, 1902.
   Boston 10, Chicago 5, October 3, 1904.
A.L.— 18—Chicago 12, Detroit 6, May 6, 1903.

Longest game with no errors
A.L.—22 innings
   Chicago vs. Washington, June 12, 1967.
   Washington vs. Chicago, June 12, 1967.
N.L.—21 innings
   Boston vs. Pittsburgh, August 1, 1918.
   Chicago vs. Philadelphia, July 17, 1918.
   Philadelphia vs. Chicago, July 17, 1918 (fielded 20 innings; Chicago scored winning run with none out in 21st inning).
   San Francisco vs. Cincinnati, September 1, 1967.
   San Diego vs. Montreal, May 21, 1977.

Longest game with no errors by either club
A.L.—22—Chicago 0, Washington 0, June 12, 1967.
N.L.—21—Chicago 0, Philadelphia 0, July 17, 1918 (Philadelphia fielded 20 innings; Chicago scored winning run with none out in 21st inning).

Most consecutive errorless games, season
N.L.— 16—St. Louis, July 30 through August 16, 1992.
A.L.— 14—California, June 14 through 28, 1991.

Most errors, doubleheader (since 1900)
N.L.— 17
   Cincinnati vs. Brooklyn, September 13, 1900.
   Chicago vs. Cincinnati, October 8, 1900.
   St. Louis vs. Cincinnati, July 3, 1909.
A.L.— 16—Cleveland vs. Washington, September 21, 1901.

Most errors by both clubs, doubleheader (since 1900)
N.L.—25—Chicago 17, Cincinnati 8, October 8, 1900.
A.L.—22—Cleveland 16, Washington 6, September 21, 1901.

Longest doubleheader without an error
A.L.—27 innings—Detroit vs. New York, August 23, 1968, (first game, Detroit fielded eight innings; second game 19 innings).
N.L.—25 innings—Philadelphia vs. Cincinnati, July 8, 1924.

Longest doubleheader without an error by either club
A.L.—24 innings
   New York 0, Philadelphia 0, July 4, 1925.
   Washington 0, New York 0, August 14, 1960.
N.L.—20 innings
   Boston 0, Chicago 0, September 18, 1924.
   New York 0, Chicago 0, August 27, 1951.

Most errors by infield, nine-inning game
N.L.— 17—Boston vs. St. Louis, June 14, 1876.
A.L.— 10—Detroit vs. Chicago, May 1, 1901.

Most errors by infielders from both clubs, nine-inning game
N.L.—22—Boston 17, St. Louis 5, June 14, 1876.
A.L.— 13—Chicago 8, Detroit 5, May 6, 1903.

Longest game without an error by infield
A.L.—25—Chicago vs. Milwaukee, May 8, finished May 9, 1984.

N.L.—24—Houston vs. New York, April 15, 1968.

Most errors by outfield, nine-inning game
N.L.—11—Boston vs. Hartford, May 1, 1876.
N.L. since 1900—4—Made in many games. Last time—San Francisco vs. Los Angeles, July 4, 1971.
A.L.—5—Baltimore vs. St. Louis, August 19, 1902.

Most errors, inning (since 1900)
A.L.—7—Cleveland vs. Chicago, September 20, 1905, eighth inning.
N.L.—6—Pittsburgh vs. New York, August 20, 1903, first game, first inning.

PASSED BALLS

Most passed balls, season
N.L.—167—Boston, 98 games, 1883.
N.L. since 1900—42
  Boston, 156 games, 1905 (154-game season).
  Atlanta, 162 games, 1967 (162-game season).
A.L. (162-game season)—73—Texas, 162 games, 1987.
A.L. (154-game season)—49—Baltimore, 155 games, 1959.

Fewest passed balls, season
A.L. (154-game season)—0—New York, 155 games, 1931.
A.L. (162-game season)—3
  Boston, 160 games, 1975.
  Kansas City, 162 games, 1984.
  Toronto, 161 games, 1985.
N.L.—2
  Boston, 153 games, 1943 (154-game season).
  New York, 162 games, 1980 (162-game season).
  San Diego, 162 games, 1992 (162-game season).

Most passed balls, game
A.A.—12—Washington vs. New York, May 10, 1884.
N.L.—10—Boston vs. Washington, May 3, 1886.
N.L. since 1900—6—Cincinnati 6, Pittsburgh 0, October 4, 1902.
A.L.—6—Texas vs. Detroit, August 30, 1987.

Most passed balls by both clubs, game
A.A.—14—Washington 12, New York 2, May 10, 1884.
N.L.—11—Troy 7, Cleveland 4, June 16, 1880.
N.L. since 1900—6—Cincinnati 6, Pittsburgh 0, October 4, 1902.
A.L.—6—Texas 6, Detroit 0, August 30, 1987.

Longest game with no passed balls
N.L.—26 innings
  Boston vs. Brooklyn, May 1, 1920.
  Brooklyn vs. Boston, May 1, 1920.
A.L.—25 innings
  Chicago vs. Milwaukee, May 8, finished May 9, 1984.
  Milwaukee vs. Chicago, May 8, finished May 9, 1984 (fielded 24 ⅓ innings).

Longest game with no passed balls by either club
N.L.—26 innings—Boston 0, Brooklyn 0, May 1, 1920.
A.L.—25 innings—Chicago 0, Milwaukee 0, May 8, finished May 9, 1984 (Milwaukee fielded 24 ⅓ innings).

DOUBLE PLAYS

Most double plays, season
A.L.—217—Philadelphia, 154 games, 1949.
N.L. (162-game season)—215—Pittsburgh, 162 games, 1966.
N.L. (154-game season)—198—Los Angeles, 154 games, 1958.

Most years with 200 or more double plays
A.L.—3—Philadelphia, 1949 (217), 1950 (208), 1951 (204).
N.L.—1—Pittsburgh, 1966 (215).

Fewest double plays, season (A.L.—since 1912; N.L.—since 1919)
A.L.—74—Boston, 151 games, 1913.
N.L.—94—Pittsburgh, 153 games, 1935.

Most times with five or more double plays in a game, season
N.L.—3—New York, 1950.

A.L.—3
  Cleveland, 1970.
  Kansas City, 1971.

Most double plays, game
A.L.—7—New York vs. Philadelphia, August 14, 1942.
N.L.—7
  Houston vs. San Francisco, May 4, 1969.
  Atlanta vs. Cincinnati, June 27, 1982, 14 innings.
  St. Louis vs. Pittsburgh, June 16, 1994, 10 innings.

Most double plays by both clubs, nine-inning game
A.L.—10—Minnesota 6, Boston 4, July 18, 1990.
N.L.—9
  Chicago 5, Cincinnati 4, July 3, 1929.
  Los Angeles 5, Pittsburgh 4, April 15, 1961.

Most double plays by both clubs, extra-inning game
N.L.—10
  Boston 5, Cincinnati 5, June 7, 1925, 12 innings.
  Cincinnati 6, New York 4, May 1, 1955, 16 innings.
A.L.—9—California 5, Baltimore 4, May 19, 1988, first game, 10 innings.

Most unassisted double plays, game
N.L.-A.L.—2—Made in many games.

Most unassisted double plays by both clubs, game
N.L.-A.L.—2—Made in many games.

Most double plays, doubleheader
A.L.—10—Washington vs. Chicago, August 18, 1943, 22 ⅓ innings.
N.L.—9—St. Louis vs. Cincinnati, June 11, 1944, 18 innings.

Most double plays by both clubs, doubleheader
N.L.—13
  New York 7, Philadelphia 6, September 28, 1939.
  Pittsburgh 8, St. Louis 5, September 6, 1948.
A.L.—12
  Philadelphia 9, Cleveland 3, September 14, 1931.
  Boston 7, Chicago 5, September 15, 1947.
  New York 7, Kansas City 5, July 31, 1955.
  California 8, Boston 4, May 1, 1966.
  California 7, Baltimore 5, May 19, 1988, 19 innings.

Most consecutive games with one or more double plays
A.L.—25
  Boston, May 7 through June 4, second game, 1951.
  Cleveland, August 21, second game, through September 12, 1953.
N.L.—23—Brooklyn, August 7, second game, through August 27, 1952.

Most consecutive games with one or more double or triple plays
N.L.—26—New York, August 21 through September 16, second game, 1951 (44 double plays, 1 triple play).
A.L.—25
  Boston, May 7 through June 4, second game, 1951 (38 double plays).
  Cleveland, August 21, second game, through September 12, 1953 (38 double plays).

Most double plays, two consecutive nine-inning games
N.L.—10—New York vs. Brooklyn, August 12, August 13, first game, 1932.
A.L.—10
  Detroit vs. Boston, May 18 (4), 19 (6), 1948.
  Cleveland vs. Kansas City, May 3 (5); vs. Chicago, May 5 (5), 1970.
  Kansas City vs. Baltimore, May 5 (4), May 6 (6), 1972.

Most double plays, three consecutive games (making one each game)
N.L.—13—San Francisco, April 24 through April 26, 1987.
A.L.—12
  Boston, June 25 through June 27, 1950.
  New York, April 19 through April 21, 1952.
  Chicago, September 2 through September 3, second game, 1973.

Most double plays, four consecutive games (making one each game)
N.L.—15—San Francisco, April 24 through April 27, 1987.

A.L.— 14
  Chicago, July 12 through July 14, 1951.
  New York, April 18 through April 21, 1952.

TRIPLE PLAYS

Most triple plays, season
A.A.—3
  Cincinnati, 1882.
  Rochester, 1890.
A.L.—3—Detroit, 1911; Boston, 1924, 1979; Oakland, 1979.
N.L.—3—Philadelphia, 1964; Chicago, 1965.

Most triple plays, game
A.L.—2—Minnesota vs. Boston, July 17, 1990, fourth and
  eighth innings.
N.L.—1—Held by many clubs.

Most triple plays by both clubs, game
A.L.—2—Minnesota 2, Boston 0, July 17, 1990.
N.L.—1—Made in many games.

Most consecutive games with triple play
A.L.—2—Detroit vs. Boston, June 6, 7, 1908.
N.L.—1—Held by many clubs.

LEAGUE FIELDING

GAMES

Most catchers catching 100 or more games, season
A.L. (14-club league) — 12 in 1985, 1990.
A.L. (10-club league) — 9 in 1966.
A.L. (8-club league) — 8 in 1921, 1952.
N.L. (12-club league) — 12 in 1987.
N.L. (10-club league) — 9 in 1965, 1966.
N.L. (8-club league) — 8 in 1931, 1941.

Fewest catchers catching 100 or more games, season (since 1890)
A.L. — 0 in 1902, 1903, 1942.
N.L. — 0 in 1893, 1896, 1900, 1945.

AVERAGE

Highest fielding percentage, season
A.L. — .981 in 1988, 1990, 1991, 1992, 1993.
N.L. — .981 in 1992.

Lowest fielding percentage, season (since 1900)
A.L. — .937 in 1901.
N.L. — .949 in 1903.

PUTOUTS

Most putouts, season (since 1900)
A.L. (14-club league) — 61,146 in 1991.
A.L. (12-club league) — 52,510 in 1969.
A.L. (10-club league) — 43,847 in 1964.
A.L. (8-club league) — 33,830 in 1916.
N.L. (14-club league) — 60,854 in 1993.
N.L. (12-club league) — 52,630 in 1982.
N.L. (10-club league) — 44,042 in 1968.
N.L. (8-club league) — 33,724 in 1917.

Fewest putouts, season (since 1900)
A.L. (8-club league) — 32,235 in 1938.
A.L. (12-club league) — 51,821 in 1975.
A.L. (14-club league) — 60,155 in 1979.
N.L. (8-club league) — 32,296 in 1906.
N.L. (12-club league) — 52,000 in 1978.
N.L. (14-club league) — 60,854 in 1993.

Most outfielders with 400 or more putouts, season
A.L. — 5 in 1979, 1980, 1984, 1985, 1986, 1992.
N.L. — 5 in 1992.

ASSISTS

Most assists, season (since 1900)
A.L. (14-club league) — 25,626 in 1980.
A.L. (12-club league) — 21,786 in 1976.
A.L. (10-club league) — 17,269 in 1961.
A.L. (8-club league) — 17,167 in 1910.
N.L. (14-club league) — 24,442 in 1993.
N.L. (12-club league) — 22,341 in 1980.
N.L. (10-club league) — 18,205 in 1968.
N.L. (8-club league) — 16,759 in 1920.

Fewest assists, season (since 1900)
A.L. (8-club league) — 13,219 in 1958.
A.L. (12-club league) — 21,001 in 1971.
A.L. (14-club league) — 23,398 in 1986.
N.L. (8-club league) — 13,345 in 1956.
N.L. (12-club league) — 20,351 in 1990.
N.L. (14-club league) — 24,442 in 1993.

Most first basemen with 100 or more assists, season
A.L. — 7 in 1985, 1986.
N.L. — 6 in 1982, 1993.

Most second basemen with 500 or more assists, season
N.L. — 4 in 1924.
A.L. — 3 in 1930.

Most shortstops with 500 or more assists, season
N.L. — 5 in 1978.
A.L. — 5 in 1979.

CHANCES ACCEPTED

Most chances accepted, season (since 1900)
A.L. (14-club league) — 86,621 in 1980.
A.L. (12-club league) — 74,191 in 1976.
A.L. (10-club league) — 60,997 in 1964.
A.L. (8-club league) — 50,870 in 1910.
N.L. (14-club league) — 85,296 in 1993.
N.L. (12-club league) — 74,930 in 1980.
N.L. (10-club league) — 62,247 in 1968.
N.L. (8-club league) — 50,419 in 1920.

Fewest chances accepted, season (since 1900)
A.L. (8-club league) — 46,086 in 1938.
A.L. (12-club league) — 72,875 in 1971.
A.L. (14-club league) — 84,008 in 1986.
N.L. (8-club league) — 46,404 in 1955.
N.L. (12-club league) — 73,273 in 1970.
N.L. (14-club league) — 85,296 in 1993.

ERRORS

Most errors, season (since 1900)
A.L. — 2,889 in 1901.
N.L. — 2,590 in 1904.

Fewest errors, season (since 1900)
A.L. (8-club league) — 1,002 in 1958.
A.L. (10-club league) — 1,261 in 1964.
A.L. (12-club league) — 1,512 in 1971.
A.L. (14-club league) — 1,627 in 1991.
N.L. (8-club league) — 1,082 in 1956.
N.L. (10-club league) — 1,389 in 1968.
N.L. (12-club league) — 1,401 in 1992.
N.L. (14-club league) — 1,876 in 1993.

PASSED BALLS

Most passed balls, season (since 1900)
A.L. (14-club league) — 267 in 1987.
A.L. (12-club league) — 247 in 1969.
A.L. (10-club league) — 211 in 1965.
A.L. (8-club league) — 178 in 1914.
N.L. (12-club league) — 217 in 1969.
N.L. (10-club league) — 216 in 1962.
N.L. (8-club league) — 202 in 1905.

Fewest passed balls, season
A.L. (8-club league) — 53 in 1949.
A.L. (12-club league) — 127 in 1976.
A.L. (14-club league) — 128 in 1977.
N.L. (8-club league) — 65 in 1936.
N.L. (12-club league) — 122 in 1980.
N.L. (14-club league) — 199 in 1993.

DOUBLE PLAYS

Most double plays, season
A.L. (14-club league) — 2,368 in 1980.
A.L. (12-club league) — 1,994 in 1973.
A.L. (10-club league) — 1,585 in 1961.
A.L. (8-club league) — 1,487 in 1949.

N.L. (14-club league) —2,028 in 1993.
N.L. (12-club league) — 1,888 in 1971.
N.L. (10-club league) — 1,596 in 1962.
N.L. (8-club league) — 1,337 in 1951.

Fewest double plays, season (A.L. since 1912; N.L. since 1920)

A.L. (8-club league) —818 in 1912.
A.L. (12-club league) — 1,388 in 1967, 1968.
A.L. (14-club league) —2,119 in 1987.
N.L. (8-club league) — 1,007 in 1920.
N.L. (12-club league) — 1,431 in 1963.
N.L. (14-club league) —2,028 in 1993.

Most double plays, one day

N.L.—29—July 23, 1972.
A.L.—28—July 24, 1976.

Most unassisted double plays by first basemen, season

A.L.—38 in 1949.
N.L.—32 in 1953.

Most unassisted double plays by catchers, season

N.L.—5 in 1965.
A.L.—3 in 1914, 1969.

Most unassisted double plays by pitchers, season

N.L.—3 in 1935, 1940.
A.L.—2 in 1908, 1932.

TRIPLE PLAYS

Most triple plays, season

A.L. (14-club league) — 10 in 1979.
A.L. (8-club league) —7 in 1922, 1936.
N.L. —7 in 1891, 1905, 1910, 1929.

Fewest triple plays, season

N.L.—0 in 1928, 1938, 1941, 1943, 1945, 1946, 1959, 1961, 1974, 1984, 1994.
A.L.—0 in 1904, 1933, 1942, 1956, 1961, 1962, 1974, 1975, 1987, 1993.

Fewest triple plays by both leagues, season

0 in 1961, 1974.

Most triple plays, one day

N.L.—2—May 29, 1897; August 30, 1921.
A.L.—2—July 17, 1990.

INDIVIDUAL MISCELLANEOUS

First player with two clubs in one season
N.L.—Neal Phelps, New York, Philadelphia, 1876.
A.L.—Harry Lockhead, Detroit, Philadelphia, 1901.

First player with three clubs in one season
N.L.—Gus Krock, Chicago, Indianapolis, Washington, 1889.
A.L.—Pat Donahue, Boston, Cleveland, Philadelphia, 1910. (See next item: Frank Huelsman played with four clubs in 1904.)

First player with four clubs in one season
N.L.—Tom Dowse, Louisville, Cincinnati, Philadelphia, Washington, 63 games, 1892.
A.L.—Frank Huelsman, Chicago, Detroit, St. Louis, Washington, 112 games, 1904.

First pitcher with two clubs in one season
N.L.—Tom Healey, Providence, Indianapolis, 1878.
A.L.—Charles Baker, Cleveland, Philadelphia, 1901.

First pitcher with three clubs in one season
N.L.—Gus Krock, Chicago, Indianapolis, Washington, 1889.
A.L.—Bill James, Detroit, Boston, Chicago, 1919.

First player to enter military service in World War I
Hank Gowdy, Boston N.L., June 27, 1917.

First player to enter military service in World War II
Hugh Mulcahy, Philadelphia N.L., March 8, 1941.

First player to come to bat three times in one inning
N.L.—Tom Carey, Hartford, May 13, 1876, fourth inning.
A.L.—Ted Williams, Boston, July 4, 1948, seventh inning.

First player with seven at-bats in nine-inning game
N.L.—Jack Burdock, Hartford, May 13, 1876.
A.L.—Billy Gilbert, Milwaukee, May 5, 1901.

First player with eight at-bats in nine-inning game
N.L.—Ross Barnes, Chicago, July 22, 1876.

First player to score five runs in nine-inning game
N.L.—George Hall, Philadelphia, June 17, 1876.
A.L.—Mike Donlin, Baltimore, June 24, 1901.

First player to score six runs in nine-inning game
N.L.—Jim Whitney, Boston, June 9, 1883.
A.L.—Johnny Pesky, Boston, May 8, 1946.

First player with five hits in nine-inning game
N.L.—Joe Battin, St. Louis, May 13, 1876.
　　　Jack Burdock, Hartford, May 13, 1876.
　　　Tom Carey, Hartford, May 13, 1876.
A.L.—Irv Waldron, Milwaukee, April 28, 1901.

First player with six hits in nine-inning game
N.L.—Dave Force, Philadelphia, June 27, 1876 (six at-bats).
A.L.—Mike Donlin, Baltimore, June 24, 1901 (six at-bats).

First player with eight hits in a doubleheader
A.A.—Henry Simon, Syracuse, October 11, 1890. (See next entry: Fred Carroll had nine hits in doubleheader in 1886.)
N.L.—Joe Quinn, St. Louis, September 30, 1893. (See next entry: Wilbert Robinson had nine hits in doubleheader in 1892.)
A.L.—Charles Hickman, Washington, September 7, 1905.

First player with nine hits in a doubleheader
A.A.—Fred Carroll, Pittsburgh, July 5, 1886.
N.L.—Wilbert Robinson, Baltimore, June 10, 1892.
A.L.—Ray Morehart, Chicago, August 31, 1926.

First player with four long hits in nine-inning game
N.L.—George Hall, Philadelphia, June 14, 1876 (3 triples, 1 home run).
A.L.—Frank Dillon, Detroit, April 25, 1901 (4 doubles).

First player with five long hits in nine-inning game
A.A.—George Strief, Philadelphia, June 25, 1885 (4 triples, 1 double).
N.L.—George Gore, Chicago, July 9, 1885 (2 triples, 3 doubles).
A.L.—Lou Boudreau, Cleveland, July 14, 1946, first game (4 doubles, 1 home run).

First player with four doubles in nine-inning game
N.L.—John O'Rourke, Boston, September 15, 1880.
A.L.—Frank Dillon, Detroit, April 25, 1901.

First player with three triples in nine-inning game
N.L.—George Hall, Philadelphia, June 14, 1876.
　　　Ezra Sutton, Philadelphia, June 14, 1876.
A.L.—Elmer Flick, Cleveland, July 6, 1902.

First player with four triples in nine-inning game
A.A.—George Strief, Philadelphia, June 25, 1885.
N.L.—Bill Joyce, New York, May 18, 1897.
A.L.—Never accomplished.

First players to hit home runs
N.L.—Ross Barnes, Chicago, May 2, 1876.
　　　Charley Jones, Cincinnati, May 2, 1876.
A.L.—Erve Beck, Cleveland, April 25, 1901.

First players to hit two homers in nine-inning game
N.L.—George Hall, Philadelphia, June 17, 1876.
A.L.—Buck Freeman, Boston, June 1, 1901.

First players to hit three homers in nine-inning game
N.L.—Ned Williamson, Chicago, May 30, 1884, p.m. game.
A.L.—Kenny Williams, St. Louis, April 22, 1922.

First players to hit four homers in nine-inning game
N.L.—Bobby Lowe, Boston, May 30, 1894, p.m. game.
A.L.—Lou Gehrig, New York, June 3, 1932.

First players to hit two homers in one inning
N.L.—Charley Jones, Boston, June 10, 1880, eighth inning.
A.L.—Kenny Williams, St. Louis, August 7, 1922, sixth inning.

First players to hit grand slams
N.L.—Roger Connor, Troy, September 10, 1881.
A.L.—Herm McFarland, Chicago, May 1, 1901.

First players to hit grand slams as pinch-hitters
N.L.—Mike O'Neill, St. Louis, June 3, 1902, ninth inning.
A.L.—Marty Kavanagh, Cleveland, September 24, 1916, fifth inning.

First players to hit home runs in night game
N.L.—Babe Herman, Cincinnati, July 10, 1935.
A.L.—Frankie Hayes, Philadelphia, May 16, 1939.

First players to hit for cycle
N.L.—Curry Foley, Buffalo, May 25, 1882.
A.L.—Harry Davis, Philadelphia, July 10, 1901.

First players to receive five bases on balls in nine-inning game
A.A.—Henry Larkin, Philadelphia, May 2, 1887.
N.L.—Fred Carroll, Pittsburgh, July 4, 1889, a.m. game.
A.L.—Sammy Strang, Chicago, April 27, 1902.

First players to receive six bases on balls in nine-inning game
N.L.—Walt Wilmot, Chicago, August 22, 1891.
A.L.—Jimmie Foxx, Boston, June 16, 1938.

First players to receive two bases on balls in one inning
N.L.—Elmer Smith, Pittsburgh, April 22, 1892, first inning.
A.L.—Donie Bush, Detroit, August 27, 1909, fourth inning.

First players to strike out four times in nine-inning game
N.L.—George Derby, Detroit, August 6, 1881. (See next item: Oscar Walker had five strikeouts in game in 1879.)
A.L.—Emmet Heidrick, St. Louis, May 16, 1902.

First players to strike out five times in nine-inning game
N.L.—Oscar Walker, Buffalo, June 20, 1879.

A.L.—Lefty Grove, Philadelphia, June 10, 1933, first game.

First players to strike out twice in one inning

A.L.—Billy Purtell, Chicago, May 10, 1910, sixth inning.
N.L.—Edd Roush, Cincinnati, July 22, 1916, sixth inning.

First pinch-hitters

N.L.—Mickey Welch, New York, August 10, 1889 (struck out).
A.L.—Larry McLean, Boston, April 26, 1901 (doubled).

First hit by pinch-hitter

N.L.—Tom Daly, Brooklyn, May 14, 1892 (homered).
A.L.—Larry McLean, Boston, April 26, 1901 (doubled).

First pitcher to lose doubleheader (two complete games)

N.L.—Dave Anderson, Pittsburgh vs. Brooklyn, September 1, 1890; lost 3-2, 8-4 (pitched 2 games of tripleheader).

First player to be intentionally walked with bases filled

A.L.—Nap Lajoie, Philadelphia, May 23, 1901, ninth inning.

First managers ejected from two games in one day by umpires

N.L.—Mel Ott, New York vs. Pittsburgh, June 9, 1946, doubleheader.
A.L.—Billy Martin, Texas vs. Milwaukee, July 14, 1974, doubleheader.

First lefthanded catcher

Bill Harbidge, Hartford N.L., May 6, 1876.

First lefthanded pitcher

Bobby Mitchell, Cincinnati N.L., 1878.

First pitcher to wear glasses

Will White, Boston N.L., 1877.

First infielder to wear glasses

George Toporcer, St. Louis N.L., 1921.

First catcher to wear glasses

Clint Courtney, New York A.L., 1951.

CLUB MISCELLANEOUS

First shutout game
N.L.—April 25, 1876, Chicago 4, Louisville 0.
A.L.—May 15, 1901, Washington 4, Boston 0.

First 1-0 game
N.L.—May 5, 1876, St. Louis 1, Chicago 0.
A.L.—July 27, 1901, Detroit 1, Baltimore 0.

First tie game
N.L.—May 25, 1876, Philadelphia 2, Louisville 2, 14 innings (darkness).
A.L.—May 31, 1901, Washington 3, Milwaukee 3, 7 innings (darkness).

First extra-inning game
N.L.—April 29, 1876, Hartford 3, Boston 2, 10 innings.
A.L.—April 30, 1901, Boston 8, Philadelphia 6, 10 innings.

First extra-inning shutout game
N.L.—May 25, 1876, Boston 4, Cincinnati 0, 10 innings.
A.L.—August 11, 1902, Philadelphia 1, Detroit 0, 13 innings.

First extra-inning 1-0 shutout game
N.L.—June 10, 1876, New York Mutuals 1, Cincinnati 0, 10 innings.
A.L.—August 11, 1902, Philadelphia 1, Detroit 0, 13 innings.

First extra-inning tie game
N.L.—May 25, 1876, Philadelphia 2, Louisville 2, 14 innings (darkness).
A.L.—August 27, 1901, Milwaukee 5, Baltimore 5, 11 innings (darkness):

First time two games played in one day
N.L.—September 9, 1876, Hartford 14, Cincinnati 6; Hartford 8, Cincinnati 3.
A.L.—May 30, 1901, Baltimore 10, Detroit 7; Detroit 4, Baltimore 1.
   Chicago 8, Boston 3; Chicago 5, Boston 3.
   Milwaukee 5, Washington 2; Milwaukee 14, Washington 3.
   Philadelphia 3, Cleveland 1; Philadelphia 8, Cleveland 2, 8 innings.

First doubleheader
N.L.—September 25, 1882, Worcester 4, Providence 3; Providence 8, Worcester 6.
A.L.—July 15, 1901, Washington 3, Baltimore 2; Baltimore 7, Washington 3.

First doubleheader shutout victory
N.L.—July 13, 1888, Pittsburgh 4, Boston 0; Pittsburgh 6, Boston 0.
A.L.—September 3, 1901, Cleveland 1, Boston 0; Cleveland 4, Boston 0.

First forfeited game
N.L.—August 21, 1876, St. Louis 7, Chicago 6; forfeited to St. Louis.
A.L.—May 2, 1901, Detroit 7, Chicago 5; forfeited to Detroit.

Last forfeited game
N.L.—July 18, 1954, second game, Philadelphia 8, St. Louis 1, at St. Louis; forfeited to Philadelphia.
A.L.—July 12, 1979, second game, Detroit 9, Chicago 0, at Chicago; forfeited to Detroit.

First game played by
Boston, N.L.—April 22, 1876—Boston 6, Philadelphia Athletics 5 (A).
Philadelphia Athletics, N.L.—April 22, 1876—Boston 6, Philadelphia 5 (H).
New York Mutuals, N.L.—April 25, 1876—Boston 7, New York Mutuals 6 (H).
Chicago, N.L.—April 25, 1876—Chicago 4, Louisville 0 (A).
Cincinnati, N.L.—April 25, 1876—Cincinnati 2, St. Louis 1 (H).

St. Louis, N.L.—April 25, 1876—Cincinnati 2, St. Louis 1 (A).
Philadelphia, N.L.—May 1, 1883—Providence 4, Philadelphia 3 (H).
New York, N.L. (Original Club)—May 1, 1883—New York 7, Boston 5 (H).
Pittsburgh, N.L.—April 30, 1887—Pittsburgh 6, Chicago 2 (H).
Brooklyn, N.L.—April 19, 1890—Boston 15, Brooklyn 9 (A).
Chicago, A.L.—April 24, 1901—Chicago 8, Cleveland 2 (H).
Cleveland, A.L.—April 24, 1901—Chicago 8, Cleveland 2 (A).
Detroit, A.L.—April 25, 1901—Detroit 14, Milwaukee 13 (H).
Baltimore, A.L.—April 26, 1901—Baltimore 10, Boston 6 (H).
Boston, A.L.—April 26, 1901—Baltimore 10, Boston 6 (A).
Philadelphia, A.L.—April 26, 1901—Washington 5, Philadelphia 1 (H).
Washington, A.L. (Original Club)—April 26, 1901—Washington 5, Philadelphia 1 (A).
Milwaukee, A.L.—April 25, 1901—Detroit 14, Milwaukee 13 (A).
St. Louis, A.L.—April 23, 1902—St. Louis 5, Cleveland 2 (H).
New York, A.L.—April 22, 1903—Washington 3, New York 1 (A).
Milwaukee, N.L. since 1900—April 13, 1953—Milwaukee 2, Cincinnati 0 (A).
Baltimore, A.L. (Present Club)—April 13, 1954—Detroit 3, Baltimore 0 (A).
Kansas City, A.L.—April 12, 1955—Kansas City 6, Detroit 2 (H).
Los Angeles, N.L.—April 15, 1958—San Francisco 8, Los Angeles 0 (A).
San Francisco, N.L.—April 15, 1958—San Francisco 8, Los Angeles 0 (H).
Los Angeles, A.L.—April 11, 1961—Los Angeles 7, Baltimore 2 (A).
Minnesota, A.L.—April 11, 1961—Minnesota 6, New York 0 (A).
Washington, A.L. (Second Club)—April 10, 1961—Chicago 4, Washington 3 (H).
Houston, N.L.—April 10, 1962—Houston 11, Chicago 2 (H).
New York, N.L. (Present Club)—April 11, 1962—St. Louis 11, New York 4 (A).
Atlanta, N.L.—April 12, 1966—Pittsburgh 3, Atlanta 2, 13 innings (H).
Oakland A.L.—April 10, 1968—Baltimore 3, Oakland 1 (A).
San Diego, N.L.—April 8, 1969—San Diego 2, Houston 1 (H).
Seattle, A.L. (Original Club)—April 8, 1969—Seattle 4, California 3 (A).
Montreal, N.L.—April 8, 1969—Montreal 11, New York 10 (A).
Kansas City, A.L. (Present Club)—April 8, 1969—Kansas City 4, Minnesota 3, 12 innings (H).
Milwaukee, A.L. (Present Club)—April 7, 1970—California 12, Milwaukee 0 (H).
Texas, A.L.—April 15, 1972—California 1, Texas 0 (A).
Seattle, A.L. (Present Club)—April 6, 1977—California 7, Seattle 0 (H).
Toronto, A.L.—April 7, 1977—Toronto 9, Chicago 5 (H).
Florida, N.L.—April 5, 1993—Florida 6, Los Angeles 3 (H).
Colorado, N.L.—April 5, 1993—New York 3, Colorado 0 (A).

First game played
At Sportsman's Park (later Busch Stadium), St. Louis—May 5, 1876—St. Louis N.L. 1, Chicago 0.
By St. Louis A.L.—April 23, 1902—St. Louis 5, Cleveland 2.
By St. Louis N.L. since 1900—July 1, 1920—Pittsburgh 6, St. Louis 2, 10 innings.
At Shibe Park (later Connie Mack Stadium), Philadelphia—April 12, 1909—Philadelphia A.L. 8, Boston 1.
At Shibe Park (later Connie Mack Stadium), Philadelphia—May 16, 1927—St. Louis N.L. 2, Philadelphia N.L. 1.
At Forbes Field, Pittsburgh—June 30, 1909—Chicago 3, Pittsburgh 2.
At Comiskey Park (old), Chicago—July 1, 1910—St. Louis A.L. 2, Chicago 0.

— 125 —

At League Park, Cleveland—April 21, 1910—Detroit A.L. 5, Cleveland 0.

At Griffith Stadium, Washington—April 12, 1911—Washington A.L. 8, Boston 5.

At Polo Grounds, New York (first game after fire)—June 28, 1911—New York N.L. 3, Boston 0.

Formal opening—April 19, 1912—New York N.L. 6, Brooklyn 2.

At Redland Field (later Crosley Field), Cincinnati—April 11, 1912—Cincinnati N.L. 10, Chicago 6.

At Navin Field (later Tiger Stadium), Detroit—April 20, 1912—Detroit A.L. 6, Cleveland 5, 11 innings.

At Fenway Park, Boston—April 20, 1912—Boston 7, New York 6 (11 innings).

Formal opening—May 17, 1912—Chicago A.L. 5, Boston 2.

At Ebbets Field, Brooklyn—April 9, 1913—Philadelphia N.L. 1, Brooklyn 0.

At Wrigley Field, Chicago—April 23, 1914—Chicago F.L. 9, Kansas City 1.

By Chicago N.L.—April 20, 1916—Chicago 7, Cincinnati 6, 11 innings.

At Braves Field, Boston—August 18, 1915—Boston N.L. 3, St. Louis 1.

At Yankee Stadium, New York—April 18, 1923, New York A.L. 4, Boston 1.

At Municipal Stadium, Cleveland—July 31, 1932, Philadelphia A.L. 1, Cleveland 0.

At Milwaukee County Stadium, Milwaukee—April 14, 1953, Milwaukee N.L. 3, St. Louis 2, 10 innings.

At Memorial Stadium, Baltimore—April 15, 1954, Baltimore A.L. 3, Chicago 1.

At Municipal Stadium, Kansas City—April 12, 1955, Kansas City A.L. 6, Detroit 2.

At Roosevelt Stadium, Jersey City—April 19, 1956, Brooklyn N.L. 5, Philadelphia 4, 10 innings.

At Seals Stadium, San Francisco—April 15, 1958—San Francisco N.L. 8, Los Angeles 0.

At Memorial Coliseum, Los Angeles—April 18, 1958—Los Angeles N.L. 6, San Francisco 5.

At Candlestick Park, San Francisco—April 12, 1960—San Francisco N.L. 3, St. Louis 1.

At Metropolitan Stadium, Minnesota—April 21, 1961—Washington A.L. 5, Minnesota 3.

At Wrigley Field, Los Angeles—April 27, 1961—Minnesota A.L. 4, Los Angeles 2.

At Dodger Stadium, Los Angeles—April 10, 1962—Cincinnati N.L. 6, Los Angeles 3.

At Colt Stadium, Houston—April 10, 1962—Houston N.L. 11, Chicago 2.

At District of Columbia Stadium, Washington—April 9, 1962, Washington A.L. 4, Detroit 1.

At Shea Stadium, New York—April 17, 1964—Pittsburgh N.L. 4, New York 3.

At Astrodome, Houston—April 12, 1965—Philadelphia N.L. 2, Houston 0.

At Atlanta Stadium, Atlanta—April 12, 1966—Pittsburgh N.L. 3, Atlanta 2, 13 innings.

At Anaheim Stadium, California—April 19, 1966—Chicago A.L. 3, California 1.

At Busch Memorial Stadium, St. Louis—May 12, 1966—St. Louis N.L. 4, Atlanta 3, 12 innings.

At Oakland-Alameda County Coliseum—April 17, 1968—Baltimore A.L. 4, Oakland 1.

At San Diego Stadium, San Diego—April 8, 1969—San Diego N.L. 2, Houston 1.

At Sicks' Stadium, Seattle—April 11, 1969—Seattle A.L. 7, Chicago 0.

At Jarry Park, Montreal—April 14, 1969—Montreal N.L. 8, St. Louis 7.

At Riverfront Stadium, Cincinnati—June 30, 1970—Atlanta N.L. 8, Cincinnati 2.

At Three Rivers Stadium, Pittsburgh—July 16, 1970—Cincinnati N.L. 3, Pittsburgh 2.

At Veterans Stadium, Philadelphia—April 10, 1971—Philadelphia N.L. 4, Montreal 1.

At Arlington Stadium, Texas—April 21, 1972—Texas A.L. 7, California 6.

At Royals Stadium, Kansas City—April 10, 1973—Kansas

City A.L. 12, Texas 1.

At Kingdome, Seattle—April 6, 1977—California A.L. 7, Seattle 0.

At Exhibition Stadium, Toronto—April 7, 1977—Toronto A.L. 9, Chicago 5.

At Olympic Stadium, Montreal—April 15, 1977—Philadelphia N.L. 7, Montreal 2.

At Metrodome, Minnesota—April 6, 1982—Seattle A.L. 11, Minnesota 7.

At SkyDome, Toronto—June 5, 1989—Milwaukee A.L. 5, Toronto 3.

At Comiskey Park (new), Chicago—April 18, 1991—Detroit A.L. 16, Chicago 0.

At Oriole Park at Camden Yards, Baltimore—April 6, 1992—Baltimore A.L. 2, Cleveland 0.

At Joe Robbie Stadium, Florida—April 5, 1993—Florida N.L. 6, Los Angeles 3.

At Mile High Stadium, Colorado—April 9, 1993—Colorado N.L. 11, Montreal 4.

At Jacobs Field, Cleveland—April 4, 1994—Cleveland A.L. 4, Seattle 3 (11 innings).

At The Ballpark in Arlington, Texas—April 11, 1994—Milwaukee A.L. 4, Texas 3.

First Sunday game

N.L.—At St. Louis—April 17, 1892, Cincinnati 5, St. Louis 1.

A.L.—At Detroit—April 28, 1901, Detroit 12, Milwaukee 11.

At Chicago, A.L.—April 28, 1901, Chicago 13, Cleveland 1.

First night game

At Cincinnati—May 24, 1935, Cincinnati 2, Philadelphia 1.

By Pittsburgh—At Cincinnati—May 31, 1935, Pittsburgh 4, Cincinnati 1.

By Chicago, N.L.—At Cincinnati—July 1, 1935, Chicago 8, Cincinnati 4.

By Brooklyn—At Cincinnati—July 10, 1935, Cincinnati 15, Brooklyn 2.

By Boston, N.L.—At Cincinnati—July 24, 1935, Cincinnati 5, Boston 4.

By St. Louis, N.L.—At Cincinnati—July 31, 1935, Cincinnati 4, St. Louis 3, 10 innings.

At Brooklyn—June 15, 1938, Cincinnati 6, Brooklyn 0.

At Philadelphia, A.L.—May 16, 1939, Cleveland 8, Philadelphia 3, 10 innings.

By Chicago, A.L.—At Philadelphia—May 24, 1939, Chicago 4, Philadelphia 1.

At Philadelphia, N.L.—June 1, 1939, Pittsburgh 5, Philadelphia 2.

By St. Louis, A.L.—At Philadelphia—June 14, 1939, St. Louis 6, Philadelphia 0.

By Detroit—At Philadelphia—June 20, 1939, Detroit 5, Philadelphia 0.

By New York, A.L.—At Philadelphia—June 26, 1939, Philadelphia 3, New York 2.

At Cleveland—June 27, 1939, Cleveland 5, Detroit 0.

By Washington—At Philadelphia—July 6, 1939, Philadelphia 9, Washington 3.

At Chicago, A.L.—August 14, 1939, Chicago 5, St. Louis 2.

By Boston, A.L.—At Cleveland—July 13, 1939, Boston 6, Cleveland 5, 10 innings.

At New York, N.L.—May 24, 1940, New York 8, Boston 1.

By New York N.L.—May 24, 1940, New York 8, Boston 1.

At St. Louis, A.L.—May 24, 1940, Cleveland 3, St. Louis 2.

At Pittsburgh—June 4, 1940, Pittsburgh 14, Boston 2.

At St. Louis, N.L.—June 4, 1940, Brooklyn 10, St. Louis 1.

At Washington—May 28, 1941, New York 6, Washington 5.

At Boston, N.L.—May 11, 1946, New York 5, Boston 1.

At New York, A.L.—May 28, 1946, Washington 2, New York 1.

At Boston, A.L.—June 13, 1947, Boston 5, Chicago 3.

At Detroit, A.L.—June 15, 1948, Detroit 4, Philadelphia 1.

By Milwaukee, N.L.—At St. Louis—April 20, 1953, St. Louis 9, Milwaukee 4.

At Milwaukee, N.L.—May 8, 1953, Milwaukee 2, Chicago 0.

At Baltimore, A.L.—April 21, 1954, Cleveland 2, Baltimore 1.

At Kansas City, A.L.—April 18, 1955, Cleveland 11, Kansas City 9.

At San Francisco, N.L.—April 16, 1958, Los Angeles 13, San Francisco 1.
At Los Angeles, N.L.—April 22, 1958, Los Angeles 4, Chicago 2.
By Minnesota, A.L.—April 14, 1961, Minnesota 3, Baltimore 2.
At Minnesota, A.L.—May 18, 1961, Kansas City 4, Minnesota 3.
At Los Angeles, A.L.—April 28, 1961, Los Angeles 6, Minnesota 5, 12 innings.
At Houston, N.L.—April 11, 1962, Houston 2, Chicago 0.
At Atlanta, N.L.—April 12, 1966, Pittsburgh 3, Atlanta 2, 13 innings.
At Oakland, A.L.—April 17, 1968, Baltimore 4, Oakland 1.
At San Diego, N.L.—April 8, 1969, San Diego 2, Houston 1.
By Seattle, A.L.—April 8, 1969, Seattle 4, California 3.
By Montreal, N.L.—April 17, 1969, Montreal 7, Philadelphia 0.
At Seattle, A.L.—April 12, 1969, Seattle 5, Chicago 1.
At Montreal, N.L.—April 30, 1969, New York 2, Montreal 1.
By Milwaukee, A.L.—April 13, 1970, Oakland 2, Milwaukee 1.
At Milwaukee A.L.—May 5, 1970, Boston 6, Milwaukee 0.
At Texas, A.L.—April 21, 1972, Texas 7, California 6.
At Toronto, A.L.—May 2, 1977, Milwaukee 3, Toronto 1.
At Chicago, N.L.—August 9, 1988, Chicago 6, New York 4.
At Florida, N.L.—April 6, 1993, Los Angeles 4, Florida 2.
At Colorado, N.L.—April 13, 1993, New York 8, Colorado 4.

First night opening game
N.L.—At St. Louis—April 18, 1950, St. Louis 4, Pittsburgh 2.
A.L.—At Philadelphia—April 17, 1951, Washington 6, Philadelphia 1.

First ladies day
N.L.—At Cincinnati, 1876 season.
N.L.—At Philadelphia, 1876 season.
N.L.—At Providence, 1882 season.
N.L.—At New York, June 16, 1883, New York 5, Cleveland 2.
A.L.—At St. Louis, 1912 season.
N.L.—At St. Louis, 1917 season.

First ladies night
N.L.—At New York, June 27, 1941, New York 7, Philadelphia 4.
N.L.—At Brooklyn, July 31, 1950, Chicago 8, Brooklyn 5.
A.L.—At Boston, August 17, 1950, Boston 10, Philadelphia 6.

First day games completed with lights
N.L.—At Boston, April 23, 1950, second game, Philadelphia 6, Boston 5.
A.L.—At New York, August 29, 1950, New York 6, Cleveland 5.

First time all games played at night
(8-club leagues)—August 9, 1946 (4 in N.L., 4 in A.L.).
(12-club leagues)—April 25, 1969 (6 in N.L., 6 in A.L.).

First time all games were twi-night doubleheaders
N.L.—On August 25, 1953.

First time uniforms were numbered
N.L.—Cincinnati, 1883 season.
A.L.—New York, 1929 season (complete) (Cleveland vs. Chicago at Cleveland, June 26, 1916 wore numbers on the sleeves of their uniforms.)

NIGHT GAMES AND POSTPONEMENTS

Most night games, season (includes twilight games)
A.L.—135—Texas, 1979 (won 68, lost 67).
N.L.—127—Florida, 1993 (won 49, lost 78).

Most games postponed at start of season
A.L.—5
Chicago, April 6 through 10, 1982.
New York, April 6 through 10, 1982.
N.L.—4—New York, April 12 through 15, 1933.

Most consecutive games postponed, season
N.L.—9—Philadelphia, August 10 through 19, 1903.
A.L.—7
Detroit, May 14 through 18, 1945.
Philadelphia, May 14 through 18, 1945.
Washington, April 23 through 29, 1952.

TIES AND ONE-RUN DECISIONS

Most tie games, season
A.L.—10—Detroit, 1904.
N.L.—9—St. Louis, 1911.

Fewest tie games, season
A.L.-N.L.—0—By all clubs in many seasons. A.L. last season—1993. N.L. last season—1992.

Most games decided by one run, season
A.L. (162-game season)—74—Chicago, 1968 (won 30, lost 44).
A.L. (154-game season)—60—Philadelphia, 1945 (won 22, lost 38).
N.L. (162-game season)—75—Houston, 1971 (won 32, lost 43).
N.L. (154-game season)—69—Cincinnati, 1946 (won 28, lost 41).

Fewest games decided by one run, season
A.L. (154-game season)—27—Cleveland, 1948 (won 9, lost 18).
A.L. (162-game season)—30—Detroit, 1993 (won 14, lost 16).
N.L. (154-game season)—28—Brooklyn, 1949 (won 16, lost 12).
N.L. (162-game season)—38—Chicago, 1970 (won 17, lost 21).

LENGTH OF GAMES

BY INNINGS

Longest game
N.L.—26 innings—Brooklyn 1, Boston 1, May 1, 1920, at Boston.
A.L.—25 innings—Chicago 7, Milwaukee 6, May 8, finished May 9, 1984, at Chicago.

Longest night game
N.L.—25 innings—St. Louis 4, New York 3, September 11, 1974, at New York.
A.L.—25 innings—Chicago 7, Milwaukee 6, May 8, finished May 9, 1984, at Chicago.

Longest opening game
A.L.—15 innings
Washington 1, Philadelphia 0, April 13, 1926 at Washington.
Detroit 4, Cleveland 2, April 19, 1960, at Cleveland.
N.L.—14 innings
Philadelphia 5, Brooklyn 5, April 17, 1923, at Brooklyn.
New York 1, Brooklyn 1, April 16, 1933, at Brooklyn (opener for New York only).
Pittsburgh 4, Milwaukee 3, April 15, 1958, at Milwaukee.
Pittsburgh 6, St. Louis 2, April 8, 1969, at St. Louis.
Cincinnati 2, Los Angeles 1, April 7, 1975, at Cincinnati.

Longest 0-0 game
N.L.—19 innings—Brooklyn vs. Cincinnati, September 11, 1946, at Brooklyn.
A.L.—18 innings—Detroit vs. Washington, July 16, 1909, at Detroit.

Longest 0-0 night game
N.L.—18 innings—Philadelphia vs. New York, October 2, 1965, second game, at New York.
A.L.—None.

Longest 1-0 day game
N.L.—18 innings
Providence 1, Detroit 0, August 17, 1882, at Providence.
New York 1, St. Louis 0, July 2, 1933, first game, at New York.
A.L.—18 innings
Washington 1, Chicago 0, May 15, 1918, at Washington.
Washington 1, Chicago 0, June 8, 1947, first game, at Chicago.

Longest 1-0 night game
N.L.—24 innings—Houston 1, New York 0, April 15, 1968, at Houston.
A.L.—20 innings—Oakland 1, California 0, July 9, 1971, at Oakland.

Longest shutout game

N.L.—24 innings—Houston 1, New York 0, April 15, 1968, at Houston.

A.L.—20 innings—Oakland 1, California 0, July 9, 1971, at Oakland.

Longest tie game

N.L.—26 innings—Boston 1, Brooklyn 1, May 1, 1920, at Boston.

A.L.—24 innings—Detroit 1, Philadelphia 1, July 21, 1945, at Philadelphia.

Most innings, one day

N.L.—32—San Francisco at New York, May 31, 1964.

A.L.—29

Boston at Philadelphia, July 4, 1905.

Boston at New York, August 29, 1967,

Most extra-inning games, season

A.L.—31—Boston, 1943 (won 15, lost 14, tied 2).

N.L.—27

Boston, 1943 (won 14, lost 13).

Los Angeles, 1967 (won 10, lost 17).

Most consecutive extra-inning games, one club

A.L.—5—Detroit, September 9 through 13, 1908 (54 innings).

N.L.—4

Pittsburgh, August 18 through 22, 1917 (59 innings).

San Francisco, July 7 through 10, 1987 (49 innings).

Most consecutive extra-inning games between same clubs

A.L.—4

Chicago and Detroit, September 9 through 12, 1908 (43 innings).

Cleveland and St. Louis, May 1, 2, 4, 5, 1910 (46 innings).

Boston and St. Louis, May 31, first game, to June 2, second game, 1943 (45 innings).

N.L.—4—New York and Pittsburgh, May 24, 25, June 23, 24, 1978 (44 innings; both clubs played other teams between these contests).

N.L.—3

Brooklyn and Pittsburgh, August 20 through 22, 1917 (45 innings).

Chicago and Pittsburgh, August 18, 19, 20, 1961 (33 innings).

Cincinnati and New York, May 5, 6, 7, 1980 (36 innings).

Most innings, two consecutive extra-inning games

N.L.—45—Boston, May 1, 3, 1920.

A.L.—37

Minnesota vs. Milwaukee May 12 (22), May 13 (15), 1972.

Milwaukee vs. Minnesota, May 12 (22), May 13 (15), 1972.

Most innings between same clubs, two consecutive extra-inning games

N.L.—40—Boston and Chicago, May 14 (18), May 17 (22), 1927.

A.L.—37—Minnesota and Milwaukee, May 12 (22), May 13 (15), 1972.

Most innings, three consecutive extra-inning games

N.L.—58—Brooklyn, May 1 to 3, 1920.

A.L.—41

Cleveland, April 16 to 21, 1935.

Boston, April 8, 10, 11, 1969.

Most innings between same clubs, three consecutive extra-inning games

N.L.—45—Brooklyn and Pittsburgh, August 20 through 22, 1917.

A.L.—40

Chicago and Washington, August 24 through 26, 1915.

Detroit and Philadelphia, May 12 through 14, 1943.

Most innings, four consecutive extra-inning games

N.L.—59—Pittsburgh, August 18 through 22, 1917.

A.L.—51

Chicago, August 23 through 26, 1915.

Detroit, May 11, second game, through May 14, 1943.

Most innings between same clubs, four consecutive extra-inning games

A.L.—46—Cleveland and St. Louis, May 1, 2, 4, 5, 1910.

N.L.—No performance.

BY TIME

Longest nine-inning game

N.L.—4 hours, 18 minutes—Los Angeles 8, San Francisco 7, October 2, 1962.

A.L.—4 hours, 16 minutes—Baltimore 18, New York 9, June 8, 1986.

Longest extra-inning game

A.L.—8 hours, 6 minutes—Chicago 7, Milwaukee 6, May 8, finished May 9, 1984, 25 innings.

N.L.—7 hours, 23 minutes—San Francisco 8, New York 6, May 31, 1964, second game, 23 innings.

Longest nine-inning 1-0 game

N.L.—3 hours, 7 minutes—New York 1, San Diego 0, May 17, 1988.

A.L.—3 hours, 2 minutes—Milwaukee 1, Minnesota 0, June 29, 1977.

Longest extra-inning 1-0 game

N.L.—6 hours, 14 minutes—Los Angeles 1, Montreal 0, August 23, 1989, 22 innings.

A.L.—5 hours, 5 minutes—Oakland 1, California 0, July 9, 1971, 20 innings.

Longest extra-inning 1-0 night game

N.L.—6 hours, 14 minutes—Los Angeles 1, Montreal 0, August 23, 1989, 22 innings.

A.L.—5 hours, 5 minutes—Oakland 1, California 0, July 9, 1971, 20 innings.

Longest nine-inning night game

A.L.—4 hours, 12 minutes—Toronto 14, Detroit 8, September 15, 1993.

N.L.—4 hours, 2 minutes—Milwaukee 11, San Francisco 9, June 22, 1962.

Longest extra-inning night game

A.L.—8 hours, 6 minutes—Chicago 7, Milwaukee 6, at Chicago, May 8, finished May 9, 1984, 25 innings.

N.L.—7 hours, 14 minutes—Houston 5, Los Angeles 4, at Houston, June 3, 1989, 22 innings.

Longest doubleheader (18 innings)

A.L.—6 hours, 50 minutes—Detroit at Kansas City, July 23, 1961.

N.L.—6 hours, 46 minutes—Brooklyn at New York, August 7, 1952.

Longest doubleheader (more than 18 innings)

N.L.—9 hours, 52 minutes—San Francisco at New York, May 31, 1964, 32 innings.

A.L.—9 hours, 5 minutes—Kansas City at Detroit, June 17, 1967, 28 innings.

Shortest nine-inning game

N.L.—51 minutes—New York 6, Philadelphia 1, September 28, first game, 1919.

A.L.—55 minutes—St. Louis 6, New York 2, September 26, second game, 1926.

Shortest nine-inning night game

N.L.—1 hour, 15 minutes—Boston 2, Cincinnati 0, August 10, 1944.

A.L.—1 hour, 29 minutes—Chicago 1, Washington 0, May 21, 1943.

Shortest 1-0 game

N.L.—57 minutes—New York 1, Brooklyn 0, August 30, 1918.

A.L.—1 hour, 13 minutes—Detroit 1, New York 0, August 8, 1920.

Shortest doubleheader (18 innings)

A.L.—2 hours, 7 minutes—New York at St. Louis, September 26, 1926.

N.L.—2 hours, 20 minutes—Chicago at Brooklyn, August 14, 1919.

Most games won, league

N.L.—8,985—Chicago, 119 years, 1876 through 1994.
A.L.—8,013—New York, 92 years, 1903 through 1994.

Most games won, season

N.L.—116—Chicago, 1906 (lost 36).
A.L.—111—Cleveland, 1954 (lost 43).

Fewest games won, season

N.L. (154-game season)—20—Cleveland, 1899 (lost 134).
N.L. since 1900 (154-game season)—38—Boston, 1935 (lost 115).
N.L. since 1900 (162-game season)—40—New York, 1962 (lost 120).
A.L. (154-game season)—36—Philadelphia, 1916 (lost 117).
A.L. (162-game season)—53—Toronto, 1979 (lost 109).

Most games won, two consecutive seasons

N.L.—223—Chicago, 1906, 1907 (lost 81).
A.L.—217—Baltimore, 1969, 1970 (lost 107).

Most games won, three consecutive seasons

N.L.—322—Chicago, 1906, 1907, 1908 (lost 130).
A.L. (162-game season)—318—Baltimore, 1969, 1970, 1971 (lost 164).
A.L. (154-game season)—313—Philadelphia, 1929, 1930, 1931 (lost 143).

Most years winning 100 or more games

A.L.—14—New York, 1927, 1928, 1932, 1936, 1937, 1939, 1941, 1942, 1954, 1961, 1963, 1977, 1978, 1980.
N.L.—6—St. Louis, 1931, 1942, 1943, 1944, 1967, 1985.

Most consecutive years winning 100 or more games

A.L.—3
  Philadelphia, 1929, 1930, 1931 (154-game seasons).
  Baltimore, 1969, 1970, 1971 (162-game seasons).
N.L.—3—St. Louis, 1942, 1943, 1944.

Most games won at home, season

A.L. (162-game season)—65—New York, 1961 (lost 16).
A.L. (154-game season)—62—New York, 1932 (lost 15).
N.L. (162-game season)—64—Cincinnati, 1975 (lost 17).
N.L. (154-game season)—62—Boston, 1898 (lost 15).
N.L. since 1900 (154-game season)—60
  St. Louis, 1942 (lost 17).
  Brooklyn, 1953 (lost 17).

Most games won on road, season

N.L.—60—Chicago, 1906 (lost 15).
A.L. (162-game season)—55—Oakland, 1971 (lost 25).
A.L. (154-game season)—54—New York, 1939 (lost 20).

Most games won from one club, season

N.L. (8-club league)—21
  Chicago vs. Boston, 1909 (lost 1).
  Pittsburgh vs. Cincinnati, 1937 (lost 1).
  Chicago vs. Cincinnati, 1945 (lost 1).
N.L. (12-club league)—17
  Atlanta vs. San Diego, 1974 (lost 1).
  New York vs. Pittsburgh, 1986 (lost 1).
A.L. (8-club league)—21—New York vs. St. Louis, 1927 (lost 1).
A.L. (12-club league)—15—Baltimore vs. Milwaukee, 1973 (lost 3).

Most games won from one club at home

N.L.—16
  Brooklyn vs. Pittsburgh, 1890 (lost 2).
  Philadelphia vs. Pittsburgh, 1890 (lost 1).
N.L. since 1900—13—New York vs. Philadelphia, 1904 (lost 2).
A.L.—12—Chicago vs. St. Louis, 1915 (lost 0).

Most games won from one club on road

N.L. (8-club league)—11
  Pittsburgh vs. St. Louis, 1908 (lost 0).
  Chicago vs. Boston, 1909 (lost 0).
  Brooklyn vs. Philadelphia, 1945 (lost 0).

A.L. (8-club league)—11
  Chicago vs. Philadelphia, 1915 (lost 0).
  New York vs. St. Louis, 1927 (lost 0).
  New York vs. St. Louis, 1939 (lost 0).
  Cleveland vs. Boston, 1954 (lost 0).

Most games won by one run, season

N.L. (162-game season)—42—San Francisco, 1978 (lost 26).
N.L. (154-game season)—41—Cincinnati, 1940 (lost 17).
A.L. (162-game season)—40
  Baltimore, 1970 (lost 15).
  Baltimore, 1974 (lost 21).
A.L. (154-game season)—38—New York, 1943 (lost 23).

Fewest games won by one run, season

A.L. (154-game season)—9—Cleveland, 1948 (lost 18).
A.L. (162-game season)—11—Texas, 1985 (lost 27).
N.L. (154-game season)—9—New York, 1953 (lost 24).
N.L. (162-game season)—16
  Montreal, 1969 (lost 29).
  Atlanta, 1973 (lost 30).
  St. Louis, 1978 (lost 32).
  Pittsburgh, 1986 (lost 37).
  Cincinnati, 1993 (lost 25).

Most games won from league champions, season

N.L.—16—St. Louis vs. Chicago, 1945 (lost 6).
A.L.—14
  Philadelphia vs. Detroit, 1909 (lost 8).
  Minnesota vs. Oakland, 1973 (lost 4).

Most games won from one club, two consecutive seasons

N.L. (8-club league)—40—Pittsburgh vs. St. Louis, 1907, 1908.
A.L. (8-club league)—37
  Philadelphia vs. St. Louis, 1910, 1911.
  Chicago vs. Philadelphia, 1915, 1916.
  New York vs. Philadelphia, 1919, 1920.
  New York vs. St. Louis, 1926, 1927.

Fewest games won from one club, season

N.L.—0
  Philadelphia vs. Boston, 1883 (lost 14; 8-club league).
  Buffalo vs. Chicago, 1885 (lost 16; 8-club league).
  Baltimore vs. Boston, 1892 (lost 13; 12-club league).
  Cleveland vs. Brooklyn, 1899 (lost 14; 12-club league).
  Cleveland vs. Cincinnati, 1899 (lost 14; 12-club league).
  Colorado vs. Atlanta, 1993 (lost 13; 14-club league).
  San Diego vs. Montreal, 1994 (lost 12; 14-club league).
    (Note: San Diego and Montreal completed the schedule against each other. Los Angeles was 0-6 against Atlanta in 1994, but seven games were cancelled due to a strike.)
A.L.—0
  Kansas City vs. Baltimore, 1970 (lost 12; 12-club league).
  Oakland vs. Baltimore, 1978 (lost 11; 14-club league).
  Baltimore vs. Kansas City, 1988 (lost 12; 14-club league).
  New York vs. Oakland, 1990 (lost 12; 14-club league).
A.A.—1
  Cleveland vs. St. Louis, 1887 (lost 18; 8-club league).
  Louisville vs. Brooklyn, 1889 (lost 19; 8-club league).

Most times winning two games in one day, season

N.L.—20—Chicago, 1945 (lost 3).
A.L. (162-game season)—15—Chicago, 1961 (lost 7).
A.L. (154-game season)—14
  New York, 1943 (lost 7).
  Cleveland, 1943 (lost 8).
  Washington, 1945 (lost 8).
  Boston, 1946 (lost 9).

Most times winning two games in one day, from one club, season

A.L.—7—Chicago vs. Philadelphia, 1943 (lost 0).
N.L.—7—Chicago vs. Cincinnati, 1945 (lost 0).

Fewest times winning two games in one day, season

A.L.-N.L.—0—Held by many clubs.

Most games won, one month

N.L.—29—New York, September, 1916 (lost 5).
A.L.—28—New York, August, 1938 (lost 8).

Most games won, two consecutive days
N.L.—5—Baltimore, September 7 (3), September 8 (2), 1896.
A.L.—4—Made on many days.

```
┌────────────  CONSECUTIVE  ┌────────────┐
```

Most consecutive games won, season
N.L.—26—New York, September 7 through 30, first game, 1916 (1 tie).
A.L.—19
  Chicago, August 2 through 23, 1906 (1 tie).
  New York, June 29, second game, through July 17, second game, 1947.

Most consecutive games won with no tie games, season
N.L.—21
  Chicago, June 2 through July 8, 1880.
  Chicago, September 4 through 27, second game, 1935.
A.L.—19—New York, June 29, second game, through July 17, second game, 1947.

Most consecutive games won at start of season
U.A.—20—St. Louis, April 20 through May 22, 1884.
N.L.—13—Atlanta, April 6 through 21, 1982.
A.L.—13—Milwaukee, April 6 through 20, 1987.

Most consecutive home games won, season
A.A.—27—St. Louis, April 26 through July 16, 1885.
N.L.—26—New York, September 7 through 30, first game, 1916 (1 tie).
A.L.—24—Boston, June 25 through August 13, 1988.

Most consecutive road games won, season
N.L.—17—New York, May 9 through 29, 1916.
A.L.—17—Detroit, April 3 through May 24, 1984 (start of season).

Most consecutive games won from one club, league
A.L. (12-club league)—23—Baltimore vs. Kansas City, May 10, 1969 through August 2, 1970 (last 11 in 1969, all 12 in 1970).
N.L. (8-club league)—22—Boston vs. Philadelphia, May 4, 1883 through June 3, 1884 (all 14 in 1883, first 8 in 1884).
N.L. since 1900 (8-club league)—20—Pittsburgh vs. Cincinnati, May 31, second game, 1937 through April 24, 1938 (last 17 in 1937, first 3 in 1938).
A.L. (8-club league)—22—Boston vs. Washington, August 31, 1903 through September 6, first game, 1904 (last 6 in 1903, first 16 in 1904).

Most consecutive games won from one club at home, league
A.L.—22—Boston vs. Philadelphia, April 27, 1949 through September 10, 1950 (all 11 in 1949, all 11 in 1950).
N.L.—18—Milwaukee/Atlanta vs. New York, June 27, 1964 through April 24, first game, 1966 (last 6 in 1964, all 9 in 1965, first 3 in 1966).

Most consecutive games won from one club on road, league
N.L.—18
  Brooklyn vs. Philadelphia, May 5, first game, 1945 through August 10, 1946 (all 11 in 1945; first 7 in 1946).
  St. Louis vs. Pittsburgh, May 7, 1964 through April 15, 1966 (last 8 in 1964, all 9 in 1965, first 1 in 1966).
A.L.—18—Boston vs. New York, October 3, first game, 1911 through June 2, second game, 1913 (last 3 in 1911; all 10 in 1912; first 6, excluding one tie, in 1913).

Most consecutive doubleheaders won, season (no other games between)
A.L.—5—New York, August 30 through September 4, 1906.
N.L.—4
  Brooklyn, September 1 through 4, 1924.
  New York, September 10 through 14, 1928.

GAMES LOST

Most games lost, league
N.L.—8,963—Philadelphia, 112 years, 1883 through 1994.

A.L.—7,173—Chicago, 94 years, 1901 through 1994.

Most games lost, season
N.L. (154-game season)—134—Cleveland, 1899 (won 20).
N.L. since 1900 (162-game season)—120—New York, 1962 (won 40).
N.L. since 1900 (154-game season)—115—Boston, 1935 (won 38).
A.L.—117—Philadelphia, 1916 (won 36).

Most games lost, two consecutive seasons
N.L.—231—New York, 1962, 1963 (won 91).
A.L.—226—Philadelphia, 1915, 1916 (won 79).

Most games lost, three consecutive seasons
N.L.—340—New York, 1962 through 1964 (won 144).
A.L.—324—Philadelphia, 1915 through 1917 (won 134).

Most years losing 100 or more games
A.L.—15—Philadelphia/Kansas City, 1915, 1916, 1919, 1920, 1921, 1936, 1940, 1943, 1946, 1950, 1954 in Philadelphia, 1956, 1961, 1964, 1965 in Kansas City.
N.L.—14—Philadelphia, 1904, 1921, 1923, 1927, 1928, 1930, 1936, 1938, 1939, 1940, 1941, 1942, 1945, 1961.

Most consecutive years losing 100 or more games
N.L.—5—Philadelphia, 1938 through 1942.
A.L.—4—Washington, 1961 through 1964.

Most night games lost, season
A.L. (162-game season)—83—Seattle, 1980 (won 44).
A.L. (154-game season)—48—Kansas City, 1956 (won 20).
N.L. (162-game season)—82—Atlanta, 1977 (won 43).
N.L. (154-game season)—67—Philadelphia, 1961 (won 23).

Most games lost at home, season
A.L. (154-game season)—59—St. Louis, 1939 (won 18).
N.L. (162-game season)—58—New York, 1962 (won 22).
N.L. (154-game season)—55
  Philadelphia, 1923 (won 20).
  Boston, 1923 (won 22).
  Philadelphia, 1945 (won 22).

Most games lost on road, season
N.L. (154-game season)—102—Cleveland, 1899 (won 11).
N.L. since 1900 (162-game season)—64—New York, 1963 (won 17).
N.L. since 1900 (154-game season)—65—Boston, 1935 (won 13).
A.L. (154-game season)—64—Philadelphia, 1916 (won 13).

Most games lost by one run, season
A.L.—44—Chicago, 1968 (won 30).
N.L. (162-game season)—43—Houston, 1971 (won 32).
N.L. (154-game season)—41—Cincinnati, 1946 (won 28).

Fewest games lost by one run, season
A.L.—10—Boston, 1986 (won 24).
N.L. (154-game season)—12—Brooklyn, 1949 (won 16).
N.L. (162-game season)—14
  Philadelphia, 1962 (won 26).
  St. Louis, 1975 (won 29).
  Montreal, 1987 (won 28).

Most times losing two games in one day, season
N.L.—19—Chicago, 1950 (won 4).
A.L.—18—Philadelphia, 1943 (won 4).

Fewest times losing two games in one day, season
N.L.-A.L.—0—Held by many clubs.

Most games lost, one month
A.L.—29—Washington, July, 1909 (won 5).
N.L.—27
  Pittsburgh, August, 1890 (won 1).
  Cleveland, September, 1899 (won 1).
  St. Louis, September, 1908 (won 7).
  Brooklyn, September, 1908 (won 6).
  Philadelphia, September, 1939 (won 6).

Most games lost, two consecutive days
N.L.—5—Louisville, September 7 (3), September 8 (2), 1896.
A.L.—4—Made on many days.

Most consecutive games lost, season

A.A.—26—Louisville, May 22 through June 22, second game, 1889.
N.L.—24—Cleveland, August 26 through September 16, 1899.
N.L. since 1900—23—Philadelphia, July 29 through August 20, first game, 1961.
A.L.—21—Baltimore, April 4 through 28, 1988.

Most consecutive games lost at start of season

A.L.—21—Baltimore, April 4 through 28, 1988.
N.L.—11—Detroit, May 1 through 15, 1884.
N.L. since 1900—10—Atlanta, April 5 through 16, 1988.

Most consecutive home games lost, season

A.L.—20—St. Louis, June 3 through July 7, 1953.
N.L.—14—Boston, May 8 through 24, 1911.

Most consecutive road games lost, season

N.L.—22
  Pittsburgh, August 13 through September 2, 1890.
  New York, June 16, first game, through July 28, 1963.
A.L.—19—Philadelphia, July 25 through August 8, 1916.

Most consecutive games lost to one club, league

A.L. (12-club league)—23—Kansas City vs. Baltimore, May 9, 1969 through August 2, 1970; last 11 in 1969, all 12 in 1970.
A.L. (8-club league)—22—Washington vs. Boston, August 31, 1903 through September 6, first game, 1904; last 6 in 1903, first 16 in 1904.
N.L. (8-club league)—22—Philadelphia vs. Boston, May 4, 1883 through June 3, 1884; all 14 in 1883, first 8 in 1884.
N.L. since 1900 (8-club league)—20—Cincinnati vs. Pittsburgh, May 31, second game, 1937 through April 24, 1938; last 17 in 1937, first 3 in 1938.

Most consecutive doubleheaders lost, season (no other games between)

N.L.—5—Boston, September 8 through 14, 1928.
A.L.—4—Boston, June 29 through July 5, 1921.

WINNING PERCENTAGE

HIGHEST

Highest percentage games won, season

U.A.—.850—St. Louis, 1884 (won 91, lost 16).
N.L.—.798—Chicago, 1880 (won 67, lost 17).
N.L. since 1900—.763—Chicago, 1906 (won 116, lost 36).
A.L.—.721—Cleveland, 1954 (won 111, lost 43).

Highest percentage games won, season, for league champions since 1969

A.L.—.673—Baltimore, 1969 (won 109, lost 53).
N.L.—.667
  Cincinnati, 1975 (won 108, lost 54).
  New York, 1986 (won 108, lost 54).

Highest percentage games won, season, for second-place team, through 1968

N.L.—.759—New York, 1885 (won 85, lost 27).
N.L. since 1900—.680—Chicago, 1909 (won 104, lost 49).
A.L.—.669—New York, 1954 (won 103, lost 51).

Highest percentage games won, season, for third-place team, through 1968

N.L.—.691—Hartford, 1876 (won 47, lost 21).
N.L. since 1900—.608—Pittsburgh, 1906 (won 93, lost 60).
A.L.—.617—New York, 1920 (won 95, lost 59).

Highest percentage games won, season, for fourth-place team, through 1968

N.L.—.623—Philadelphia, 1886 (won 71, lost 43).
N.L. since 1900 (10-club league)—.578—Pittsburgh, 1962 (won 93, lost 68).
N.L. since 1900 (8-club league)—.569—Pittsburgh, 1904 (won 87, lost 66).
A.L.—.597—Cleveland, 1950 (won 92, lost 62).

Highest percentage games won, season, for fifth-place team, through 1968

A.L. (10-club league)—.537—Cleveland, 1965 (won 87, lost 75).
A.L. (8-club league)—.536—Philadelphia, 1904 (won 81, lost 70).
N.L.—.571—Boston, 1890 (won 76, lost 57).
N.L. since 1900 (10-club league)—.543—Milwaukee, 1964 (won 88, lost 74).
N.L. since 1900 (8-club league)—.529—Chicago, 1924 (won 81, lost 72).

Highest percentage games won, season, for sixth-place team, through 1968

N.L. (10-club league)—.528—Philadelphia, 1965 (won 85, lost 76).
N.L. (8-club league)—.503—Brooklyn, 1928 (won 77, lost 76).
A.L.—.513—Detroit, 1962 (won 79, lost 75).

Highest percentage games won, season, for seventh-place team, through 1968

A.L.—.497—Washington, 1916 (won 76, lost 77).
N.L. (10-club league)—.506—Chicago, 1963 (won 82, lost 80).
N.L. (8-club league)—.464—Brooklyn, 1917 (won 70, lost 81).

Highest percentage games won, season, for eighth-place team, through 1968

A.L.—.475—Boston, 1962 (won 76, lost 84).
N.L.—.469
  Chicago, 1964 (won 76, lost 86).
  Los Angeles, 1968 (won 76, lost 86) (tied for seventh).

Highest percentage games won, season, for ninth-place team, through 1968

N.L.—.451—New York, 1968 (won 73, lost 89).
A.L.—.444
  Kansas City, 1962 (won 72, lost 90).
  Boston, 1966 (won 72, lost 90).
  New York, 1967 (won 72, lost 90).

Highest percentage games won, season, for last-place team

N.L.—.454—New York, 1915 (won 69, lost 83).
A.L. (8-club league)—.431—Chicago, 1924 (won 66, lost 87).
A.L. (10-club league)—.440—New York, 1966 (won 70, lost 89).

Highest percentage games won, one month (15 or more games)

U.A.—.947—St. Louis, May, (won 18, lost 1).
N.L.—.944—Providence, August 1884 (won 17, lost 1).
N.L. since 1900—.897—Chicago, August 1906 (won 26, lost 3).
A.L.—.900—Detroit, April 1984 (won 18, lost 2).

LOWEST

Lowest percentage games won, season

N.L.—.130—Cleveland, 1899 (won 20, lost 134).
N.L. since 1900—.248—Boston, 1935 (won 38, lost 115).
A.L.—.235—Philadelphia, 1916 (won 36, lost 117).

Lowest percentage games won, pennant winner, through 1968

N.L.—.564—Los Angeles, 1959 (won 88, lost 68).
A.L. (154-game season)—.575—Detroit, 1945 (won 88, lost 65).
A.L. (162-game season)—.568—Boston, 1967 (won 92, lost 70).

Lowest percentage games won, league champion, since 1969

N.L.—.509—New York, 1973 (won 82, lost 79).
A.L.—.525—Minnesota, 1987 (won 85, lost 77).

Lowest percentage games won, second-place team, through 1968

A.L.—.532—Chicago, 1958 (won 82, lost 72).
N.L. (8-club league)—.543—Brooklyn, 1902 (won 75, lost 63).
N.L. (10-club league)—.543—San Francisco, 1968 (won 88, lost 74).

Lowest percentage games won, third-place team, through 1968

A.L.—.500—Chicago, 1941 (won 77, lost 77).
N.L.—.508—Chicago, 1889 (won 67, lost 65).
N.L. since 1900—.519
  New York, 1955 (won 80, lost 74; 8-club league).
  San Francisco, 1958 (won 80, lost 74; 8-club league).
  Chicago, 1968 (won 84, lost 78; 10-club league).

Lowest percentage games won, fourth-place team, through 1968
A.L.—.448—Boston, 1954 (won 69, lost 85).
N.L.—.464—Philadelphia, 1906 (won 71, lost 82).

Lowest percentage games won, fifth-place team, through 1968
A.L.—.409—St. Louis, 1931 (won 63, lost 91).
N.L.—.411—Boston, 1885 (won 46, lost 66).
N.L. since 1900—.434—Brooklyn, 1906 (won 66, lost 86).

Lowest percentage games won, sixth-place team, through 1968
N.L.—.250—Milwaukee, 1878 (won 15, lost 45) (six-club league).
N.L. since 1900—.359—Brooklyn, 1909 (won 55, lost 98).
A.L.—.386—St. Louis, 1948 (won 59, lost 94).

Lowest percentage games won, seventh-place team, through 1968
N.L.—.237—Philadelphia, 1876 (won 14, lost 45).
N.L. since 1900—.327—Boston, 1928 (won 50, lost 103).
A.L.—.325—Chicago, 1932 (won 49, lost 102).

Lowest percentage games won, eighth-place team, through 1968
N.L.—.130—Cleveland, 1899 (won 20, lost 134) (last in 12-club league).
N.L. since 1900 (8-club league)—.248—Boston, 1935 (won 38, lost 115).
N.L. since 1900 (10-club league)—.400—Houston, 1962 (won 64, lost 96).
A.L. (8-club league)—.235—Philadelphia, 1916 (won 36, lost 117).
A.L. (10-club league)—.414
California, 1968 (won 67, lost 95).
Chicago, 1968 (won 67, lost 95).

Lowest percentage games won, ninth-place team, through 1968
N.L.—.364—Chicago, 1962 (won 59, lost 103).
A.L.—.379
Kansas City, 1961 (won 61, lost 100).
Washington, 1961 (won 61, lost 100).

Lowest percentage games won, one month (15 or more games)
N.L.—.036
Pittsburgh, August 1890 (won 1, lost 27).
Cleveland, September 1899 (won 1, lost 27).
N.L. since 1900—.120—Philadelphia, May 1928 (won 3, lost 22).
A.L.—.043—Baltimore, April 1988 (won 1, lost 22).

CHAMPIONSHIPS AND FIRST-DIVISION FINISHES

Most championships won, club
A.L.—33—New York, 1921, 1922, 1923, 1926, 1927, 1928, 1932, 1936, 1937, 1938, 1939, 1941, 1942, 1943, 1947, 1949, 1950, 1951, 1952, 1953, 1955, 1956, 1957, 1958, 1960, 1961, 1962, 1963, 1964, 1976, 1977, 1978.
N.L.—21—Brooklyn/Los Angeles, 1890, 1899, 1900, 1916, 1920, 1941, 1947, 1949, 1952, 1953, 1955, 1956 in Brooklyn, 1959, 1963, 1965, 1966, 1974, 1977, 1978, 1981, 1988 in Los Angeles.
N.L. since 1900—19—Brooklyn/Los Angeles, 1900, 1916, 1920, 1941, 1947, 1949, 1952, 1953, 1955, 1956 in Brooklyn, 1959, 1963, 1965, 1966, 1974, 1977, 1978, 1981, 1988 in Los Angeles.

Most consecutive championships won, club
A.L.—5
New York, 1949, 1950, 1951, 1952, 1953.
New York, 1960, 1961, 1962, 1963, 1964.
A.A.—4—St. Louis, 1885, 1886, 1887, 1888.
N.L.—4—New York, 1921, 1922, 1923, 1924.

Most consecutive years without winning championship, league
N.L.—49—Chicago, 1946 through 1994.
A.L.—42—St. Louis, 1902 through 1943.

Most consecutive years with first-division finishes
A.L.—39—New York, 1926 through 1964.
N.L.—14
Chicago, 1878 through 1891.
Pittsburgh, 1900 through 1913.
Chicago, 1926 through 1939.

LAST PLACE AND SECOND-DIVISION FINISHES

Most times finished in last place, league
A.L.—25—Philadelphia/Kansas City/Oakland, 1915, 1916, 1917, 1918, 1919, 1920, 1921, 1935, 1936, 1938, 1940, 1941, 1942, 1943, 1945, 1946, 1950, 1954 in Philadelphia, 1956, 1960, 1961 (tied), 1964, 1965, 1967 in Kansas City, 1993 in Oakland.
N.L.—24—Philadelphia, 1883, 1904, 1919, 1920, 1921, 1923, 1926, 1927, 1928, 1930, 1936, 1938, 1939, 1940, 1941, 1942, 1944, 1945, 1947 (tied), 1958, 1959, 1960, 1961, 1972 (E).

Most consecutive last-place finishes
A.L.—7—Philadelphia, 1915 through 1921.
N.L.—5—Philadelphia, 1938 through 1942.

Most consecutive times with lowest winning percentage, season
A.L.—7—Philadelphia, 1915 through 1921.
N.L.—5—Philadelphia, 1938 through 1942.

Most consecutive years with second-division finishes, through 1968
N.L.—20—Chicago, 1947 through 1966.
A.L.—16—Philadelphia/Kansas City/Oakland, 1953 through 1968.

Most consecutive years without lowest winning percentage, season
N.L.—86—Brooklyn/Los Angeles, 1906 through 1991.
A.L.—54—Cleveland, 1915 through 1968.

GAMES FINISHED AHEAD AND BEHIND

Best gain in games by pennant winner, one season
A.A.—64 games—Louisville, 1890 (won 88, lost 44, .667—in 1889, won 27, lost 111, .196; in eighth place, last).
N.L.—41½ games—Brooklyn, 1899* (won 88, lost 42, .677—in 1898, won 54, lost 91, .372; in 10th place) (*some sources list 1899 record as 101-47, but N.L. president threw out 18 Brooklyn games from the records for illegally signing a player).
N.L. since 1900 (12-club league)—29 games—Atlanta, 1991 (won 94, lost 68, .580—in 1990, won 65, lost 97, .401; in sixth place).
N.L. since 1900 (8-club league)—27 games—New York, 1954 (won 97, lost 57, .630—in 1953, won 70, lost 84, .455; in fifth place).
A.L. (8-club league)—33 games—Boston, 1946 (won 104, lost 50, .675—in 1945, won 71 lost 83, .461; in seventh place).

Best gain in position from previous year, pennant winner, through 1968
N.L.—10th to first—Brooklyn, 1899 (won 88, lost 42, .677—in 1898 finished tenth in 12-club league, won 54 lost 91, .372.) (41½ games.)
N.L. since 1900 (8-club league)—Seventh to first—Los Angeles, 1959 (won 88, lost 68, .564—in 1958 finished seventh, won 71, lost 83, .461.) (16 games.)
N.L. since 1900 (12-club league)—Ninth to first—New York, 1969 (won 100, lost 62, .617—in 1968, finished ninth in 10-club league, won 73, lost 89, .451.) (27 games.)
A.A.—Eighth (last) to first—Louisville, 1890 (won 88, lost 44, .667—in 1889 finished eighth, won 27, lost 111, .196.) (64 games.)
A.L. (8-club league)—Seventh to first
New York, 1926 (won 91, lost 63, .591—in 1925 finished seventh, won 69, lost 85, .448.) (22 games.)
Boston, 1946, won 104, lost 50, .675—in 1945 finished seventh, won 71, lost 83, .461.) (33 games.)
A.L. (10-club league)—Ninth to first—Boston, 1967 (won 92, lost 70, .568—in 1966 finished ninth in 10-club league, won 72, lost 90, .444.) (20 games.)

Best gain in games by club from previous season
A.A.—64—Louisville, 1890 (won 88, lost 44, .667, first place—in 1889 won 27, lost 111, .196; in eighth place, last).

N.L.—41½—Brooklyn, 1899 (won 88, lost 42, .677, first place—in 1898 won 54, lost 91, .372; in 10th place).
N.L. since 1900 (8-club league)—34½—New York, 1903 (won 84, lost 55, .604, in second place—in 1902, won 48, lost 88, .353, in eighth place).
N.L. since 1900 (10-club league)—27½—Chicago, 1967 (won 87, lost 74, .540, in third place—in 1966, won 59, lost 103, .364, in 10th place).
N.L. since 1900 (12-club league)—29—Atlanta, 1991 (won 94, lost 68, .580, in first place—in 1990, won 65, lost 97, .401, in sixth place).
N.L. since 1900 (14-club league)—31—San Francisco, 1993, won 103, lost 59, .636, in second place—in 1992, won 72, lost 90, .444, in fifth place).
A.L.—33—Boston, 1946 (won 104, lost 50, .675, first place—in 1945, won 71, lost 83, .461; in seventh place).

Most games leading league or division at end of season
N.L.—27½—Pittsburgh, 1902.
A.L.—20—Chicago, 1983.

Fewest games leading league or division at end of season (before playoff)
N.L.—0
St. Louis and Brooklyn, 1946 (8-club league).
New York and Brooklyn, 1951 (8-club league).
Los Angeles and Milwaukee, 1959 (8-club league).
San Francisco and Los Angeles, 1962 (10-club league).
Houston and Los Angeles, 1980 (12-club league).
A.L.—0
Cleveland and Boston, 1948 (8-club league).
New York and Boston, 1978 (14-club league).

Most games behind pennant winner, season, through 1968
N.L. (12-club league)—80—Cleveland, 1899.
N.L. since 1900 (8-club league)—66½—Boston, 1906.
A.L. (8-club league)—64½—St. Louis, 1939.

Fewest games behind pennant winner for last-place club, through 1968
N.L. (8-club league)—21—New York, 1915.
A.L. (8-club league)—25—Washington, 1944. (In shortened season of 1918, Philadelphia was 24 games behind.)

Fewest games behind Western Division leader, last-place club, since 1969
A.L.—10
California, 1987.
Texas, 1987.
N.L.—19½—San Diego, 1980.

Fewest games behind Eastern Division leader, last-place club, since 1969
N.L.—11½—Philadelphia, 1973.
A.L.—17
Toronto, 1982.
Cleveland, 1982.

Most games behind Western Division leader, last-place club, since 1969
N.L.—43½—Houston, 1975.
A.L.—42—Chicago, 1970.

Most games behind Eastern Division leader, last-place club, since 1969
A.L.—50½—Toronto, 1979.
N.L.—48—Montreal, 1969.

Largest lead (in games) for pennant winner on July 4, p.m., through 1968
N.L.—14½—New York, 1912.
A.L.—12—New York, 1928.

Most games behind, eventual pennant winner, on July 4, p.m., through 1968
N.L.—15—Boston, 1914 (8th place).
A.L.—6½—Detroit, 1907 (4th place).

PENNANT CLINCHING DATES

Fewest games played before clinching pennant (154 games)
A.L.—136—New York, September 4, 1941 (won 91, lost 45, .669).
N.L.—137—New York, September 22, 1904 (won 100, lost 37, .730).

Earliest date for pennant clinching (154 games), through 1968
A.L.—September 4, 1941—New York (won 91, lost 45, .669, 136th game).
N.L.—September 8, 1955—Brooklyn (won 92, lost 46, .667, 138th game).

Earliest date for Western Division pennant clinching, since 1969
A.L.—September 15, 1971, first game—Oakland (won 94, lost 55, .631, 148th game).
N.L.—September 7, 1975—Cincinnati (won 95, lost 47, .669, 142nd game).

Earliest date for Eastern Division pennant clinching, since 1969
A.L.—September 13, 1969—Baltimore (won 101, lost 45, .690, 146th game).
N.L.—September 17, 1986—New York (won 95, lost 50, .655, 145th game).

DAYS IN FIRST PLACE

Most days in first place, season
A.L. (162-game season)—181—Detroit, entire season, April 3 through September 30, 1984 (5 days tied, 176 days alone).
A.L. (154-game season)—174—New York, A.L., 1927, entire season, April 12 through October 2, 1927 (8 days tied, 166 days alone).
N.L. (162-game season)—181—Philadelphia, April 5 through October 3, except April 9 (fifth day of season), 1993.
N.L. (154-game season)—174—New York, entire season, April 17 through October 7, 1923 (1 day tied, April 17, 173 days alone).

Fewest days in first place, season, for pennant winner, through 1968
N.L.—3—New York, 1951 (before playoff).
A.L.—20—Boston, 1967 (6 days alone).

ATTENDANCE

Highest home attendance, season
N.L.—4,483,350—Colorado, 1993.
A.L.—4,057,947—Toronto, 1993.

Highest road attendance, season
N.L.—2,944,157—Atlanta, 1993.
A.L.—2,636,157—Oakland, 1991.

Largest crowd, day game
N.L.—80,227—Montreal at Colorado, April 9, 1993 (home opener).
A.L.—74,420—Detroit at Cleveland, April 7, 1973 (home opener).

Largest crowd, night game
A.L.—78,382—Chicago at Cleveland, August 20, 1948.
N.L.—72,208—San Francisco at Colorado, July 31, 1993.

Largest crowd, doubleheader
A.L.—84,587—New York at Cleveland, September 12, 1954.
N.L.—72,140—Cincinnati at Los Angeles, August 16, 1961.

Largest crowd, opening day
N.L.—80,227—Montreal at Colorado, April 9, 1993.
A.L.—74,420—Detroit at Cleveland, April 7, 1973.

LEAGUE MISCELLANEOUS

NIGHT GAMES

Most night games, season

A.L. (14-club league) —822 in 1982.
A.L. (12-club league) —661 in 1976.
A.L. (10-club league) —472 in 1965.
N.L. (12-club league) —799 in 1983.
N.L. (10-club league) —487 in 1968.

Most night games in both leagues, season

1,530 in 1993 (14-club leagues; 765 in A.L., 765 in N.L.).
1,432 in 1983 (14-club A.L.; 12-club N.L.; 633 in A.L., 799 in N.L.).
1,274 in 1975 (12-club leagues; 651 in A.L., 623 in N.L.).
960 in 1968 (10-club leagues; 487 in N.L., 473 in A.L.).

CANCELED AND POSTPONED GAMES

Most unplayed games, season (since 1900, except 1918)

A.L.— 19 in 1901.
N.L.— 14 in 1938.

Fewest unplayed scheduled games, season (since 1900)

N.L.-A.L.—0—Made in many years.

Fewest unplayed games in both leagues, season

0 in 1930, 1947, 1949, 1951, 1954, 1956, 1959, 1960, 1964, 1972, 1982, 1983, 1992, 1993 (14 years).

Most postponed games, season

A.L. (8-club league) —97 in 1935.
N.L.—49
  in 1956 (8-club league).
  in 1967 (10-club league).

Fewest postponed dates, season

A.L.— 15 in 1987.
N.L.— 12 in 1987.

Most postponed doubleheaders, season

A.L.— 14 in 1945.
N.L.—5 in 1959.

Fewest postponed doubleheaders, season

A.L.—0 in 1914, 1957.
N.L.—0 in 1961, 1966, 1970.

TIE GAMES

Most tie games, season

A.L.— 19 in 1910.
N.L.— 16 in 1913.

Most tie games, one day

N.L.—3, April 6, 1897.
A.L.—2, made on many days.

Fewest tie games, season

N.L.—0 in 1925, 1954, 1958, 1970, 1976, 1977, 1978, 1982, 1984, 1986, 1987, 1990, 1991, 1992.
A.L.—0 in 1930, 1963, 1965, 1971, 1972, 1973, 1975, 1976, 1977, 1978, 1979, 1987, 1988, 1989, 1990, 1991, 1992, 1993, 1994.

Most 0-0 games, season

A.L.—6 in 1904.
N.L.—3 in 1917.

EXTRA-INNING GAMES

Most extra-inning games, season

A.L. (14-club league) — 117 in 1991.
A.L. (12-club league) — 116 in 1976.

A.L.—91
  in 1943 (8-club league).
  in 1965 (10-club league).
N.L. (12-club league) — 116 in 1986.
N.L. (10-club league) —93 in 1967.
N.L. (8-club league) —86 in 1916.

Most extra-inning games, one day

N.L.—5—May 30, 1892, May 11, 1988.
A.L.—4—June 11, 1969, June 4, 1976.

Most extra-inning games in both leagues, one day

6 on August 22, 1951; 3 in N.L. (five games), 3 in A.L. (five games).
6 on May 12, 1963; 4 in N.L. (eight games), 2 in A.L. (seven games).
6 on May 11, 1988; 5 in N.L. (six games), 1 in A.L. (six games).

100- AND 90-WIN AND -LOSS SEASONS

Most clubs winning 100 or more games, season

A.L. (14-club league) —2 in 1977, 1980.
A.L. (12-club league) —2 in 1971.
A.L. (10-club league) —2 in 1961.
A.L. (8-club league) —2 in 1915, 1954.
N.L. (14-club league) —2 in 1993.
N.L. (12-club league) —2 in 1976.
N.L. (10-club league) —2 in 1962.
N.L. (8-club league) —2 in 1909, 1942.

Most clubs winning 90 or more games, season

N.L. (14-club league) —4 in 1993.
N.L. (12-club league) —4 in 1969, 1976, 1980, 1987.
N.L. (10-club league) —4 in 1962, 1964.
N.L. (8-club league) —3 in many seasons.
A.L. (14-club league) —6 in 1977.
A.L. (12-club league) —4 in 1975.
A.L. (8-club league) —4 in 1950.

Most clubs losing 100 or more games, season

N.L. (14-club league) —2 in 1993.
N.L. (12-club league) —2 in 1969, 1985.
N.L. (10-club league) —2 in 1962.
N.L. (8-club league) —2 in 1898, 1905, 1908, 1923, 1938.
A.L. (14-club league) —2 in 1978, 1979.
A.L. (10-club league) —2 in 1961, 1964, 1965.
A.L. (8-club league) —2 in 1912, 1932, 1949, 1954.

HOME AND ROAD VICTORIES

Most games won by home clubs, season

A.L. (14-club league) —649 in 1978 (lost 482).
A.L. (12-club league) —540 in 1969 (lost 431).
A.L. (10-club league) —454 in 1961 (lost 353).
A.L. (8-club league) —360 in 1945 (lost 244), 1949 (lost 256).
N.L. (14-club league) —602 in 1993 (lost 532).
N.L. (12-club league) —556 in 1978 (lost 415), 1980 (lost 416).
N.L. (10-club league) —464 in 1967 (lost 345).
N.L. (8-club league) —358 in 1931 (lost 256), 1955 (lost 257).

Most games won by home clubs, one day

N.L.-A.L. (8-club leagues) —8—Made on many days.

Most games won by home clubs in both leagues, one day

14 on May 30, 1903 (A.L. won 8, lost 0; N.L. won 6, lost 2).

Most games won by visiting clubs, season

N.L. (14-club league) —532 in 1993 (lost 602).
N.L. (12-club league) —473 in 1982 (lost 499).
N.L. (10-club league) —400 in 1968 (lost 410).
N.L. (8-club league) —307 in 1948 (lost 308).
A.L. (14-club league) —547 in 1980 (lost 582).

A.L. (12-club league)—469 in 1971 (lost 497).
A.L. (10-club league)—391 in 1968 (lost 418).
A.L. (8-club league)—312 in 1953 (lost 301).

Most games won by visiting clubs, one day

N.L.-A.L. (8-club league)—8—Made on many days.

Most games won by visiting clubs in both leagues, one day

(8-club leagues)—
12 on July 4, 1935 (N.L. won 7, lost 1; A.L. won 5, lost 3).
12 on August 5, 1951 (N.L. won 7, lost 0; A.L. won 5, lost 2).
12 on June 15, 1958 (A.L. won 8, lost 0; N.L. won 4, lost 1).

ONE-RUN DECISIONS

Most games won by one run, season

A.L. (14-club league)—368 in 1978.
A.L. (12-club league)—332 in 1969.
A.L. (10-club league)—281 in 1967, 1968.
A.L. (8-club league)—217 in 1943.
N.L. (14-club league)—356 in 1993.
N.L. (12-club league)—346 in 1980.
N.L. (10-club league)—294 in 1968.
N.L. (8-club league)—223 in 1946.

Fewest games won by one run, season

A.L. (8-club league)—157 in 1938.
A.L. (12-club league)—279 in 1973.

A.L. (14-club league)—302 in 1987.
N.L. (8-club league)—170 in 1949.
N.L. (12-club league)—294 in 1970.
N.L. (14-club league)—356 in 1993.

Most games won by one run, one day

A.L.—6—May 30, 1967 (10 games); August 22, 1967 (nine games).
N.L.—6—June 6, 1967 (seven games); June 8, 1969 (six games).

Most games won by one run both leagues, one day

10 on May 30, 1967, A.L. 6 (10 games), N.L. 4 (seven games).

ATTENDANCE

Highest attendance, season

N.L. (14-club league)—36,923,856 in 1993.
N.L. (12-club league)—25,323,834 in 1989.
N.L. (10-club league)—15,015,471 in 1966.
N.L. (8-club league)—10,684,963 in 1960.
A.L. (14-club league)—33,332,603 in 1993.
A.L. (12-club league)—14,657,802 in 1976.
A.L. (10-club league)—11,336,923 in 1967.
A.L. (8-club league)—11,150,099 in 1948.

NON-PLAYING PERSONNEL

MANAGERS

INDIVIDUAL

Most years as manager

M.L.—53—Connie Mack, Pittsburgh N.L. (1894 through 1896), Philadelphia A.L. (1901 through 1950).

A.L.—50—Connie Mack, Philadelphia, 1901 through 1950.

N.L.—32—John McGraw, Baltimore, 1899; New York, 1902 through 1932.

Most clubs managed, career

M.L.—7—Frank Bancroft, Worcester N.L., Detroit N.L., Cleveland N.L., Providence N.L., Philadelphia A.A., Indianapolis N.L., Cincinnati N.L.

M.L. since 1900—6

Jimmie Dykes, Chicago A.L., Philadelphia A.L., Baltimore A.L., Cincinnati N.L., Detroit A.L., Cleveland A.L.

Dick Williams, Boston A.L., Oakland A.L., California A.L., Montreal N.L., San Diego N.L., Seattle A.L.

Most clubs managed in one season

U.A.—2—Ted Sullivan, St. Louis, Kansas City, 1884.

A.A.—2—Billy Barnie, Baltimore, Philadelphia, 1891.

N.L.—2

Leo Durocher, Brooklyn, New York, 1948.

Leo Durocher, Chicago, Houston, 1972.

A.L.—2

Jimmie Dykes, Detroit, Cleveland, 1960.

Joe Gordon, Cleveland, Detroit, 1960.

Billy Martin, Detroit, Texas, 1973.

Billy Martin, Texas, New York, 1975.

Bob Lemon, Chicago, New York, 1978.

Tony La Russa, Chicago, Oakland, 1986.

Most clubs managed in different major leagues, season

2—Joe Battin, 1884 (Pittsburgh A.A., Pittsburgh U.A.).

Bill Watkins, 1888 (Detroit N.L., Kansas City A.A.).

Gus Schmelz, 1890 (Cleveland N.L., Columbus A.A.).

John McGraw, 1902 (Baltimore A.L., New York N.L.).

Rogers Hornsby, 1952 (St. Louis A.L., Cincinnati N.L.).

Bill Virdon, 1975 (New York A.L., Houston N.L.).

Pat Corrales, 1983 (Philadelphia N.L., Cleveland A.L.).

Buck Rodgers, 1991 (Montreal N.L., California A.L.).

Most different times as manager for one major league club

A.L.—5—Billy Martin, New York, 1975 (part) through 1978 (part), 1979 (part), 1983 (complete), 1985 (part), 1988 (part).

N.L.—4—Danny Murtaugh, Pittsburgh, 1957 (part) through 1964; 1967 (part), 1970 through 1971, 1973 (part) through 1976.

Most clubs managed, career

N.L.—6—Frank Bancroft, Worcester, Detroit, Cleveland, Providence, Indianapolis, Cincinnati.

N.L. since 1900—4

Bill McKechnie, Pittsburgh, St. Louis, Boston, Cincinnati.

Rogers Hornsby, St. Louis, Chicago, Boston, Cincinnati.

Leo Durocher, Brooklyn, New York, Chicago, Houston.

A.L.—5

Jimmie Dykes, Chicago, Philadelphia, Baltimore, Detroit, Cleveland.

Billy Martin, Minnesota, Detroit, Texas, New York, Oakland.

Most years managing championship club, league

N.L.—10—John McGraw, New York, 1904, 1905, 1911, 1912, 1913, 1917, 1921, 1922, 1923, 1924.

A.L.—10—Casey Stengel, New York, 1949, 1950, 1951, 1952, 1953, 1955, 1956, 1957, 1958, 1960.

Most consecutive years as championship manager

A.L.—5—Casey Stengel, New York, 1949 through 1953 (first five years as New York manager).

A.A.—4—Charlie Comiskey, St. Louis, 1885 through 1888.

N.L.—4—John McGraw, New York, 1921 through 1924.

Most years managed without winning championship, career

M.L.—26—Gene Mauch, Philadelphia N.L., 1960 to 1968; Montreal N.L., 1969 through 1975; Minnesota A.L., 1976 to 1980; California A.L., 1981 through 1982, 1985 through 1987.

A.L.—20—Jimmie Dykes, Chicago, 1934 through 1946, Philadelphia, 1951 through 1953, Baltimore, 1954, Detroit, 1959, 1960, Cleveland, 1960, 1961.

N.L.—16—Gene Mauch, Philadelphia, 1960 to 1968; Montreal, 1969 through 1975.

Most consecutive years managed without winning championship

M.L.—23—Gene Mauch, Philadelphia N.L., 1960 to 1968; Montreal N.L., 1969 through 1975; Minnesota A.L., 1976 to 1980; California A.L., 1981 through 1982.

A.L.—19—Connie Mack, Philadelphia, 1932 through 1950.

N.L.—16—Gene Mauch, Philadelphia, 1960 to 1968; Montreal, 1969 through 1975.

Youngest Manager to start season

Lou Boudreau, Cleveland A.L., appointed November 25, 1941; 24 years, 4 months, 8 days when appointed.

Youngest manager to finish season

Roger Peckinpaugh, New York A.L., appointed September 16, 1914; 23 years, 7 months, 11 days.

Oldest to make debut as manager

Tom Sheehan, San Francisco N.L., appointed June 18, 1960; 66 years, 2 months, 18 days.

CLUB

Most managers on one club, season

A.A.—7—Louisville, 1889.

N.L.—4

Washington, 1892, 1898.

St. Louis, 1885, 1896, 1897.

N.L. since 1900—3

Cincinnati, 1902.

New York, 1902.

St. Louis, 1905, 1940, 1980.

Pittsburgh, 1917.

Chicago, 1925.

Philadelphia, 1948.

A.L.—4—Texas, 1977.

LEAGUE

Most managers, season (since 1900)

A.L. (14-club league)—19 in 1977, 1981, 1986 (Tony La Russa, Chicago, Oakland, counted as one), 1988.

A.L. (12-club league)—16 in 1969, 1975.

A.L. (10-club league)—15 in 1966.

A.L. (8-club league)—12 in 1933, 1946.

N.L.—16

in 1972, 1991 (Leo Durocher, Chicago, Houston, counted as one in 1991; 12-club leagues).

in 1993 (14-club league).

N.L.—12

in 1902, 1948 (Leo Durocher, Brooklyn, New York, counted as one in 1948; 8-club leagues).

in 1965, 1966, 1967, 1968 (10-club leagues).

Most player/managers in both leagues, season

10 in 1934 (8-club leagues)—6 in N.L., 4 in A.L.

Most managerial changes, start of season

A.L.—6 in 1955.

N.L.—4 in 1909, 1913.

Most years umpired

N.L.—37—Bill Klem, 1905 through 1941.
A.L.—31—Tommy Connolly, 1901 through 1931 (also umpired three years in the National League, 1898 through 1900).

Longest game, plate umpire by time

A.L.—8 hours, 6 minutes—Jim Evans, Milwaukee at Chicago, May 8, 1984, finished May 9 (Chicago won 7-6.)
N.L.—7 hours, 23 minutes—Ed Sudol, San Francisco at New York, May 31, 1964, second game, 23 innings (San Francisco won 8-6).

YEARLY LEADERS

AMERICAN LEAGUE

Year — Club	Manager	W	L	Pct.	*GA
1901—Chicago	Clark Griffith	83	53	.610	4
1902—Philadelphia	Connie Mack	83	53	.610	5
1903—Boston	Jimmy Collins	91	47	.659	14½
1904—Boston	Jimmy Collins	95	59	.617	1½
1905—Philadelphia	Connie Mack	92	56	.622	2
1906—Chicago	Fielder Jones	93	58	.616	3
1907—Detroit	Hughey Jennings	92	58	.613	1½
1908—Detroit	Hughey Jennings	90	63	.588	½
1909—Detroit	Hughey Jennings	98	54	.645	3½
1910—Philadelphia	Connie Mack	102	48	.680	14½
1911—Philadelphia	Connie Mack	101	50	.669	13½
1912—Boston	Jake Stahl	105	47	.691	14
1913—Philadelphia	Connie Mack	96	57	.627	6½
1914—Philadelphia	Connie Mack	99	53	.651	8½
1915—Boston	Bill Carrigan	101	50	.669	2½
1916—Boston	Bill Carrigan	91	63	.591	2
1917—Chicago	Pants Rowland	100	54	.649	9
1918—Boston	Ed Barrow	75	51	.595	2½
1919—Chicago	Kid Gleason	88	52	.629	3½
1920—Cleveland	Tris Speaker	98	56	.636	2
1921—New York	Miller Huggins	98	55	.641	4½
1922—New York	Miller Huggins	94	60	.610	1
1923—New York	Miller Huggins	98	54	.645	16
1924—Washington	Bucky Harris	92	62	.597	2
1925—Washington	Bucky Harris	96	55	.636	8½
1926—New York	Miller Huggins	91	63	.591	3
1927—New York	Miller Huggins	110	44	.714	19
1928—New York	Miller Huggins	101	53	.656	2½
1929—Philadelphia	Connie Mack	104	46	.693	18
1930—Philadelphia	Connie Mack	102	52	.662	8
1931—Philadelphia	Connie Mack	107	45	.704	13½
1932—New York	Joe McCarthy	107	47	.695	13
1933—Washington	Joe Cronin	99	53	.651	7
1934—Detroit	Mickey Cochrane	101	53	.656	7
1935—Detroit	Mickey Cochrane	93	58	.616	3
1936—New York	Joe McCarthy	102	51	.667	19½
1937—New York	Joe McCarthy	102	52	.662	13
1938—New York	Joe McCarthy	99	53	.651	9½
1939—New York	Joe McCarthy	106	45	.702	17
1940—Detroit	Del Baker	90	64	.584	1
1941—New York	Joe McCarthy	101	53	.656	17
1942—New York	Joe McCarthy	103	51	.669	9
1943—New York	Joe McCarthy	98	56	.636	13½
1944—St. Louis	Luke Sewell	89	65	.578	1
1945—Detroit	Steve O'Neill	88	65	.575	1½
1946—Boston	Joe Cronin	104	50	.675	12
1947—New York	Bucky Harris	97	57	.630	12
1948—Cleveland†	Lou Boudreau	97	58	.626	1
1949—New York	Casey Stengel	97	57	.630	1
1950—New York	Casey Stengel	98	56	.636	3
1951—New York	Casey Stengel	98	56	.636	5
1952—New York	Casey Stengel	95	59	.617	2
1953—New York	Casey Stengel	99	52	.656	8½
1954—Cleveland	Al Lopez	111	43	.721	8
1955—New York	Casey Stengel	96	58	.623	3
1956—New York	Casey Stengel	97	57	.630	9
1957—New York	Casey Stengel	98	56	.636	8
1958—New York	Casey Stengel	92	62	.597	10
1959—Chicago	Al Lopez	94	60	.610	5
1960—New York	Casey Stengel	97	57	.630	8
1961—New York	Ralph Houk	109	53	.673	8
1962—New York	Ralph Houk	96	66	.593	5
1963—New York	Ralph Houk	104	57	.646	10½
1964—New York	Yogi Berra	99	63	.611	1
1965—Minnesota	Sam Mele	102	60	.630	7
1966—Baltimore	Hank Bauer	97	63	.606	9
1967—Boston	Dick Williams	92	70	.568	1
1968—Detroit	Mayo Smith	103	59	.636	12

Year	Club	Manager	W	L	Pct.	*GA
1969—Baltimore (E)	Earl Weaver		109	53	.673	19
1970—Baltimore (E)	Earl Weaver		108	54	.667	15
1971—Baltimore (E)	Earl Weaver		101	57	.639	12
1972—Oakland (W)	Dick Williams		93	62	.600	5½
1973—Oakland (W)	Dick Williams		94	68	.580	6
1974—Oakland (W)	Alvin Dark		90	72	.556	5
1975—Boston (E)	Darrell Johnson		95	65	.594	4½
1976—New York (E)	Billy Martin		97	62	.610	10½
1977—New York (E)	Billy Martin		100	62	.617	2½
1978—New York (E) ‡	Billy Martin, Bob Lemon		100	63	.613	1
1979—Baltimore (E)	Earl Weaver		102	57	.642	8
1980—Kansas City (W)	Jim Frey		97	65	.599	14
1981—New York (E)	Gene Michael, Bob Lemon		59	48	.551	§
1982—Milwaukee (E)	Buck Rodgers, Harvey Kuenn		95	67	.586	1
1983—Baltimore (E)	Joe Altobelli		98	64	.605	6
1984—Detroit (E)	Sparky Anderson		104	58	.642	15
1985—Kansas City (W)	Dick Howser		91	71	.562	1
1986—Boston (E)	John McNamara		95	66	.590	5½
1987—Minnesota (W)	Tom Kelly		85	77	.525	2
1988—Oakland (W)	Tony La Russa		104	58	.642	13
1989—Oakland (W)	Tony La Russa		99	63	.611	7
1990—Oakland (W)	Tony La Russa		103	59	.636	9
1991—Minnesota (W)	Tom Kelly		95	67	.586	8
1992—Toronto (E)	Cito Gaston		96	66	.593	4
1993—Toronto (E)	Cito Gaston		95	67	.586	7

1994—No pennant winner.★

*Games ahead of second-place club. †Defeated Boston in one-game playoff. ‡Defeated Boston in one-game playoff to win division. §first half 34-22; second 25-26. ★New York finished the strike-shortened season with the league's best record (70-43; .619).

NATIONAL LEAGUE

Year	Club	Manager	W	L	Pct.	*GA
1876—Chicago	Al Spalding		52	14	.788	6
1877—Boston	Harry Wright		31	17	.646	3
1878—Boston	Harry Wright		41	19	.683	4
1879—Providence	George Wright		55	23	.705	6
1880—Chicago	Cap Anson		67	17	.798	15
1881—Chicago	Cap Anson		56	28	.667	9
1882—Chicago	Cap Anson		55	29	.655	3
1883—Boston	John Morrill		63	35	.643	4
1884—Providence	Frank Bancroft		84	28	.750	10½
1885—Chicago	Cap Anson		87	25	.777	2
1886—Chicago	Cap Anson		90	34	.726	2½
1887—Detroit	Bill Watkins		79	45	.637	3½
1888—New York	Jim Mutrie		84	47	.641	9
1889—New York	Jim Mutrie		83	43	.659	1
1890—Brooklyn	Bill McGunnigle		86	43	.667	6½
1891—Boston	Frank Selee		87	51	.630	3½
1892—Boston	Frank Selee		102	48	.680	8½
1893—Boston	Frank Selee		86	43	.667	5
1894—Baltimore	Ned Hanlon		89	39	.695	3
1895—Baltimore	Ned Hanlon		87	43	.669	3
1896—Baltimore	Ned Hanlon		90	39	.698	9½
1897—Boston	Frank Selee		93	39	.705	2
1898—Boston	Frank Selee		102	47	.685	6
1899—Brooklyn	Ned Hanlon		88	42	.677	4
1900—Brooklyn	Ned Hanlon		82	54	.603	4½
1901—Pittsburgh	Fred Clarke		90	49	.647	7½
1902—Pittsburgh	Fred Clarke		103	36	.741	27½
1903—Pittsburgh	Fred Clarke		91	49	.650	6½
1904—New York	John McGraw		106	47	.693	13
1905—New York	John McGraw		105	48	.686	9
1906—Chicago	Frank Chance		116	36	.763	20
1907—Chicago	Frank Chance		107	45	.704	17
1908—Chicago	Frank Chance		99	55	.643	1
1909—Pittsburgh	Fred Clarke		110	42	.724	6½
1910—Chicago	Frank Chance		104	50	.675	13
1911—New York	John McGraw		99	54	.647	7½
1912—New York	John McGraw		103	48	.682	10
1913—New York	John McGraw		101	51	.664	12½
1914—Boston	George Stallings		94	59	.614	10½
1915—Philadelphia	Pat Moran		90	62	.592	7
1916—Brooklyn	Wilbert Robinson		94	60	.610	2½
1917—New York	John McGraw		98	56	.636	10
1918—Chicago	Fred Mitchell		84	45	.651	10½

Year—Club	Manager	W	L	Pct.	*GA
1919—Cincinnati	Pat Moran	96	44	.686	9
1920—Brooklyn	Wilbert Robinson	93	61	.604	7
1921—New York	John McGraw	94	59	.614	4
1922—New York	John McGraw	93	61	.604	7
1923—New York	John McGraw	95	58	.621	4½
1924—New York	John McGraw	93	60	.608	1½
1925—Pittsburgh	Bill McKechnie	95	58	.621	8½
1926—St. Louis	Rogers Hornsby	89	65	.578	2
1927—Pittsburgh	Donie Bush	94	60	.610	1½
1928—St. Louis	Bill McKechnie	95	59	.617	2
1929—Chicago	Joe McCarthy	98	54	.645	10½
1930—St. Louis	Gabby Street	92	62	.597	2
1931—St. Louis	Gabby Street	101	53	.656	13
1932—Chicago	Charlie Grimm	90	64	.584	4
1933—New York	Bill Terry	91	61	.599	5
1934—St. Louis	Frankie Frisch	95	58	.621	2
1935—Chicago	Charlie Grimm	100	54	.649	4
1936—New York	Bill Terry	92	62	.597	5
1937—New York	Bill Terry	95	57	.625	3
1938—Chicago	Gabby Hartnett	89	63	.586	2
1939—Cincinnati	Bill McKechnie	97	57	.630	4½
1940—Cincinnati	Bill McKechnie	100	53	.654	12
1941—Brooklyn	Leo Durocher	100	54	.649	2½
1942—St. Louis	Billy Southworth	106	48	.688	2
1943—St. Louis	Billy Southworth	105	49	.682	18
1944—St. Louis	Billy Southworth	105	49	.682	14½
1945—Chicago	Charlie Grimm	98	56	.636	3
1946—St. Louis†	Eddie Dyer	98	58	.628	2
1947—Brooklyn	Burt Shotton	94	60	.610	5
1948—Boston	Billy Southworth	91	62	.595	6½
1949—Brooklyn	Burt Shotton	97	57	.630	1
1950—Philadelphia	Eddie Sawyer	91	63	.591	2
1951—New York‡	Leo Durocher	98	59	.624	1
1952—Brooklyn	Charlie Dressen	96	57	.627	4½
1953—Brooklyn	Charlie Dressen	105	49	.682	13
1954—New York	Leo Durocher	97	57	.630	5
1955—Brooklyn	Walter Alston	98	55	.641	13½
1956—Brooklyn	Walter Alston	93	61	.604	1
1957—Milwaukee	Fred Haney	95	59	.617	8
1958—Milwaukee	Fred Haney	92	62	.597	8
1959—Los Angeles§	Walter Alston	88	68	.564	2
1960—Pittsburgh	Danny Murtaugh	95	59	.617	7
1961—Cincinnati	Fred Hutchinson	93	61	.604	4
1962—San Francisco*	Alvin Dark	103	62	.624	1
1963—Los Angeles	Walter Alston	99	63	.611	6
1964—St. Louis	Johnny Keane	93	69	.574	1
1965—Los Angeles	Walter Alston	97	65	.599	2
1966—Los Angeles	Walter Alston	95	67	.586	1½
1967—St. Louis	Red Schoendienst	101	60	.627	10½
1968—St. Louis	Red Schoendienst	97	65	.599	9
1969—New York (E)	Gil Hodges	100	62	.617	8
1970—Cincinnati (W)	Sparky Anderson	102	60	.630	14½
1971—Pittsburgh (E)	Danny Murtaugh	97	65	.599	7
1972—Cincinnati (W)	Sparky Anderson	95	59	.617	10½
1973—New York (E)	Yogi Berra	82	79	.509	1½
1974—Los Angeles (W)	Walter Alston	102	60	.630	4
1975—Cincinnati (W)	Sparky Anderson	108	54	.667	20
1976—Cincinnati (W)	Sparky Anderson	102	60	.630	10
1977—Los Angeles (W)	Tommy Lasorda	98	64	.605	10
1978—Los Angeles (W)	Tommy Lasorda	95	67	.586	2½
1979—Pittsburgh (E)	Chuck Tanner	98	64	.605	2
1980—Philadelphia (E)	Dallas Green	91	71	.562	1
1981—Los Angeles (W)	Tommy Lasorda	63	47	.573	•
1982—St. Louis (E)	Whitey Herzog	92	70	.568	3
1983—Philadelphia (E)	Pat Corrales, Paul Owens	90	72	.556	6
1984—San Diego (W)	Dick Williams	92	70	.568	12
1985—St. Louis (E)	Whitey Herzog	101	61	.623	3
1986—New York (E)	Dave Johnson	108	54	.667	21½
1987—St. Louis (E)	Whitey Herzog	95	67	.586	3
1988—Los Angeles (W)	Tommy Lasorda	94	67	.584	7
1989—San Francisco (W)	Roger Craig	92	70	.568	3
1990—Cincinnati (W)	Lou Piniella	91	71	.562	5
1991—Atlanta (W)	Bobby Cox	94	68	.580	1
1992—Atlanta (W)	Bobby Cox	98	64	.605	8
1993—Philadelphia (E)	Jim Fregosi	97	65	.599	3
1994—No pennant winner. ◆					

*Games ahead of second-place club. †Defeated Brooklyn, two games to none, in playoff for pennant. ‡Defeated Brooklyn, two games to one, in playoff for pennant. §Defeated Milwaukee, two games to none, in playoff for pennant. ★Defeated Los Angeles, two games to one, in playoff for pennant. •First half 36-21; second half 27-26. ◆Montreal finished the strike-shortened season with the league's best record (74-40; .649).

BATTING

BATTING AVERAGE
AMERICAN LEAGUE

Year	Player, Club	Avg.
1901	Nap Lajoie, Philadelphia	.422
1902	Ed Delahanty, Washington	.376
1903	Nap Lajoie, Cleveland	.355
1904	Nap Lajoie, Cleveland	.381
1905	Elmer Flick, Cleveland	.308
1906	George Stone, St. Louis	.358
1907	Ty Cobb, Detroit	.350
1908	Ty Cobb, Detroit	.324
1909	Ty Cobb, Detroit	.377
1910	Ty Cobb, Detroit	.385
1911	Ty Cobb, Detroit	.420
1912	Ty Cobb, Detroit	.410
1913	Ty Cobb, Detroit	.390
1914	Ty Cobb, Detroit	.368
1915	Ty Cobb, Detroit	.369
1916	Tris Speaker, Cleveland	.386
1917	Ty Cobb, Detroit	.383
1918	Ty Cobb, Detroit	.382
1919	Ty Cobb, Detroit	.384
1920	George Sisler, St. Louis	.407
1921	Harry Heilmann, Detroit	.394
1922	George Sisler, St. Louis	.420
1923	Harry Heilmann, Detroit	.403
1924	Babe Ruth, New York	.378
1925	Harry Heilmann, Detroit	.393
1926	Heinie Manush, Detroit	.378
1927	Harry Heilmann, Detroit	.398
1928	Goose Goslin, Washington	.379
1929	Lew Fonseca, Cleveland	.369
1930	Al Simmons, Philadelphia	.381
1931	Al Simmons, Philadelphia	.390
1932	Dale Alexander, Detroit/Boston	.367
1933	Jimmie Foxx, Philadelphia	.356
1934	Lou Gehrig, New York	.363
1935	Buddy Myer, Washington	.349
1936	Luke Appling, Chicago	.388
1937	Charlie Gehringer, Detroit	.371
1938	Jimmie Foxx, Boston	.349
1939	Joe DiMaggio, New York	.381
1940	Joe DiMaggio, New York	.352
1941	Ted Williams, Boston	.406
1942	Ted Williams, Boston	.356
1943	Luke Appling, Chicago	.328
1944	Lou Boudreau, Cleveland	.327
1945	George Stirnweiss, New York	.309
1946	Mickey Vernon, Washington	.353
1947	Ted Williams, Boston	.343
1948	Ted Williams, Boston	.369
1949	George Kell, Detroit	.343
1950	Billy Goodman, Boston	.354
1951	Ferris Fain, Philadelphia	.344
1952	Ferris Fain, Philadelphia	.327
1953	Mickey Vernon, Washington	.337
1954	Bobby Avila, Cleveland	.341
1955	Al Kaline, Detroit	.340
1956	Mickey Mantle, New York	.353
1957	Ted Williams, Boston	.388
1958	Ted Williams, Boston	.328
1959	Harvey Kuenn, Detroit	.353
1960	Pete Runnels, Boston	.320
1961	Norm Cash, Detroit	.361
1962	Pete Runnels, Boston	.326
1963	Carl Yastrzemski, Boston	.321
1964	Tony Oliva, Minnesota	.323
1965	Tony Oliva, Minnesota	.321

Year	Player, Club	Avg.
1966	Frank Robinson, Baltimore	.316
1967	Carl Yastrzemski, Boston	.326
1968	Carl Yastrzemski, Boston	.301
1969	Rod Carew, Minnesota	.332
1970	Alex Johnson, California	.329
1971	Tony Oliva, Minnesota	.337
1972	Rod Carew, Minnesota	.318
1973	Rod Carew, Minnesota	.350
1974	Rod Carew, Minnesota	.364
1975	Rod Carew, Minnesota	.359
1976	George Brett, Kansas City	.333
1977	Rod Carew, Minnesota	.388
1978	Rod Carew, Minnesota	.333
1979	Fred Lynn, Boston	.333
1980	George Brett, Kansas City	.390
1981	Carney Lansford, Boston	.336
1982	Willie Wilson, Kansas City	.332
1983	Wade Boggs, Boston	.361
1984	Don Mattingly, New York	.343
1985	Wade Boggs, Boston	.368
1986	Wade Boggs, Boston	.357
1987	Wade Boggs, Boston	.363
1988	Wade Boggs, Boston	.366
1989	Kirby Puckett, Minnesota	.339
1990	George Brett, Kansas City	.329
1991	Julio Franco, Texas	.341
1992	Edgar Martinez, Seattle	.343
1993	John Olerud, Toronto	.363
1994	Paul O'Neill, New York	.359

NATIONAL LEAGUE

Year	Player, Club	Avg.
1876	Ross Barnes, Chicago	.404
1877	Deacon White, Boston	.385
1878	Abner Dalrymple, Milwaukee	.356
1879	Cap Anson, Chicago	.407
1880	George Gore, Chicago	.365
1881	Cap Anson, Chicago	.399
1882	Dan Brouthers, Buffalo	.367
1883	Dan Brouthers, Buffalo	.371
1884	Jim O'Rourke, Buffalo	.350
1885	Roger Connor, New York	.371
1886	King Kelly, Chicago	.388
1887	Cap Anson, Chicago	.421
1888	Cap Anson, Chicago	.343
1889	Dan Brouthers, Boston	.373
1890	Jack Glasscock, New York	.336
1891	Billy Hamilton, Philadelphia	.338
1892	Dan Brouthers, Brooklyn	.335
	Cupid Childs, Cleveland	.335
1893	Hugh Duffy, Boston	.378
1894	Hugh Duffy, Boston	.438
1895	Jesse Burkett, Cleveland	.423
1896	Jesse Burkett, Cleveland	.410
1897	Willie Keeler, Baltimore	.432
1898	Willie Keeler, Baltimore	.379
1899	Ed Delahanty, Philadelphia	.408
1900	Honus Wagner, Pittsburgh	.381
1901	Jesse Burkett, St. Louis	.382
1902	Ginger Beaumont, Pittsburgh	.357
1903	Honus Wagner, Pittsburgh	.355
1904	Honus Wagner, Pittsburgh	.349
1905	Cy Seymour, Cincinnati	.377
1906	Honus Wagner, Pittsburgh	.339
1907	Honus Wagner, Pittsburgh	.350
1908	Honus Wagner, Pittsburgh	.354
1909	Honus Wagner, Pittsburgh	.339
1910	Sherry Magee, Philadelphia	.331
1911	Honus Wagner, Pittsburgh	.334
1912	Heinie Zimmerman, Chicago	.372

Year	Player, Club	Avg.
1913	Jake Daubert, Brooklyn	.350
1914	Jake Daubert, Brooklyn	.329
1915	Larry Doyle, New York	.320
1916	Hal Chase, Cincinnati	.339
1917	Edd Roush, Cincinnati	.341
1918	Zack Wheat, Brooklyn	.335
1919	Edd Roush, Cincinnati	.321
1920	Rogers Hornsby, St. Louis	.370
1921	Rogers Hornsby, St. Louis	.397
1922	Rogers Hornsby, St. Louis	.401
1923	Rogers Hornsby, St. Louis	.384
1924	Rogers Hornsby, St. Louis	.424
1925	Rogers Hornsby, St. Louis	.403
1926	Bubbles Hargrave, Cincinnati	.353
1927	Paul Waner, Pittsburgh	.380
1928	Rogers Hornsby, Boston	.387
1929	Lefty O'Doul, Philadelphia	.398
1930	Bill Terry, New York	.401
1931	Chick Hafey, St. Louis	.349
1932	Lefty O'Doul, Brooklyn	.368
1933	Chuck Klein, Philadelphia	.368
1934	Paul Waner, Pittsburgh	.362
1935	Arky Vaughan, Pittsburgh	.385
1936	Paul Waner, Pittsburgh	.373
1937	Joe Medwick, St. Louis	.374
1938	Ernie Lombardi, Cincinnati	.342
1939	Johnny Mize, St. Louis	.349
1940	Debs Garms, Pittsburgh	.355
1941	Pete Reiser, Brooklyn	.343
1942	Ernie Lombardi, Boston	.330
1943	Stan Musial, St. Louis	.357
1944	Dixie Walker, Brooklyn	.357
1945	Phil Cavarretta, Chicago	.355
1946	Stan Musial, St. Louis	.365
1947	Harry Walker, St. Louis/Philadelphia	.363
1948	Stan Musial, St. Louis	.376
1949	Jackie Robinson, Brooklyn	.342
1950	Stan Musial, St. Louis	.346
1951	Stan Musial, St. Louis	.355
1952	Stan Musial, St. Louis	.336
1953	Carl Furillo, Brooklyn	.344
1954	Willie Mays, New York	.345
1955	Richie Ashburn, Philadelphia	.338
1956	Hank Aaron, Milwaukee	.328
1957	Stan Musial, St. Louis	.351
1958	Richie Ashburn, Philadelphia	.350
1959	Hank Aaron, Milwaukee	.355
1960	Dick Groat, Pittsburgh	.325
1961	Roberto Clemente, Pittsburgh	.351
1962	Tommy Davis, Los Angeles	.346
1963	Tommy Davis, Los Angeles	.326
1964	Roberto Clemente, Pittsburgh	.339
1965	Roberto Clemente, Pittsburgh	.329
1966	Matty Alou, Pittsburgh	.342
1967	Roberto Clemente, Pittsburgh	.357
1968	Pete Rose, Cincinnati	.335
1969	Pete Rose, Cincinnati	.348
1970	Rico Carty, Atlanta	.366
1971	Joe Torre, St. Louis	.363
1972	Billy Williams, Chicago	.333
1973	Pete Rose, Cincinnati	.338
1974	Ralph Garr, Atlanta	.353
1975	Bill Madlock, Chicago	.354
1976	Bill Madlock, Chicago	.339
1977	Dave Parker, Pittsburgh	.338
1978	Dave Parker, Pittsburgh	.334
1979	Keith Hernandez, St. Louis	.344
1980	Bill Buckner, Chicago	.324
1981	Bill Madlock, Pittsburgh	.341
1982	Al Oliver, Montreal	.331
1983	Bill Madlock, Pittsburgh	.323
1984	Tony Gwynn, San Diego	.351
1985	Willie McGee, St. Louis	.353
1986	Tim Raines, Montreal	.334
1987	Tony Gwynn, San Diego	.370
1988	Tony Gwynn, San Diego	.313

Year	Player, Club	Avg.
1989	Tony Gwynn, San Diego	.336
1990	Willie McGee, St. Louis	.335
1991	Terry Pendleton, Atlanta	.319
1992	Gary Sheffield, San Diego	.330
1993	Andres Galarraga, Colorado	.370
1994	Tony Gwynn, San Diego	.394

Note—Bases on balls counted as hits in 1887.

SLUGGING AVERAGE

AMERICAN LEAGUE

Year	Player, Club	Slug. Avg.
1901	Nap Lajoie, Philadelphia	.635
1902	Ed Delahanty, Washington	.589
1903	Nap Lajoie, Cleveland	.533
1904	Nap Lajoie, Cleveland	.549
1905	Elmer Flick, Cleveland	.466
1906	George Stone, St. Louis	.496
1907	Ty Cobb, Detroit	.473
1908	Ty Cobb, Detroit	.475
1909	Ty Cobb, Detroit	.517
1910	Ty Cobb, Detroit	.554
1911	Ty Cobb, Detroit	.621
1912	Ty Cobb, Detroit	.586
1913	Joe Jackson, Cleveland	.551
1914	Ty Cobb, Detroit	.513
1915	Jack Fournier, Chicago	.491
1916	Tris Speaker, Cleveland	.502
1917	Ty Cobb, Detroit	.571
1918	Babe Ruth, Boston	.555
1919	Babe Ruth, Boston	.657
1920	Babe Ruth, New York	.847
1921	Babe Ruth, New York	.846
1922	Babe Ruth, New York	.672
1923	Babe Ruth, New York	.764
1924	Babe Ruth, New York	.739
1925	Ken Williams, St. Louis	.613
1926	Babe Ruth, New York	.737
1927	Babe Ruth, New York	.772
1928	Babe Ruth, New York	.709
1929	Babe Ruth, New York	.697
1930	Babe Ruth, New York	.732
1931	Babe Ruth, New York	.700
1932	Jimmie Foxx, Philadelphia	.749
1933	Jimmie Foxx, Philadelphia	.703
1934	Lou Gehrig, New York	.706
1935	Jimmie Foxx, Philadelphia	.636
1936	Lou Gehrig, New York	.696
1937	Joe DiMaggio, New York	.673
1938	Jimmie Foxx, Boston	.704
1939	Jimmie Foxx, Boston	.694
1940	Hank Greenberg, Detroit	.670
1941	Ted Williams, Boston	.735
1942	Ted Williams, Boston	.648
1943	Rudy York, Detroit	.527
1944	Bobby Doerr, Boston	.528
1945	George Stirnweiss, New York	.476
1946	Ted Williams, Boston	.667
1947	Ted Williams, Boston	.634
1948	Ted Williams, Boston	.615
1949	Ted Williams, Boston	.650
1950	Joe DiMaggio, New York	.585
1951	Ted Williams, Boston	.556
1952	Larry Doby, Cleveland	.541
1953	Al Rosen, Cleveland	.613
1954	Ted Williams, Boston	.635
1955	Mickey Mantle, New York	.611
1956	Mickey Mantle, New York	.705
1957	Ted Williams, Boston	.731
1958	Rocky Colavito, Cleveland	.620
1959	Al Kaline, Detroit	.530
1960	Roger Maris, New York	.581
1961	Mickey Mantle, New York	.687
1962	Mickey Mantle, New York	.605

Year	Player, Club	Slug. Avg.
1963	Harmon Killebrew, Minnesota	.555
1964	Boog Powell, Baltimore	.606
1965	Carl Yastrzemski, Boston	.536
1966	Frank Robinson, Baltimore	.637
1967	Carl Yastrzemski, Boston	.622
1968	Frank Howard, Washington	.552
1969	Reggie Jackson, Oakland	.608
1970	Carl Yastrzemski, Boston	.592
1971	Tony Oliva, Minnesota	.546
1972	Dick Allen, Chicago	.603
1973	Reggie Jackson, Oakland	.531
1974	Dick Allen, Chicago	.563
1975	Fred Lynn, Boston	.566
1976	Reggie Jackson, Baltimore	.502
1977	Jim Rice, Boston	.593
1978	Jim Rice, Boston	.600
1979	Fred Lynn, Boston	.637
1980	George Brett, Kansas City	.664
1981	Bobby Grich, California	.543
1982	Robin Yount, Milwaukee	.578
1983	George Brett, Kansas City	.563
1984	Harold Baines, Chicago	.541
1985	George Brett, Kansas City	.585
1986	Don Mattingly, New York	.573
1987	Mark McGwire, Oakland	.618
1988	Jose Canseco, Oakland	.569
1989	Ruben Sierra, Texas	.543
1990	Cecil Fielder, Detroit	.592
1991	Danny Tartabull, Kansas City	.593
1992	Mark McGwire, Oakland	.585
1993	Juan Gonzalez, Texas	.632
1994	Frank Thomas, Chicago	.729

NATIONAL LEAGUE

Year	Player, Club	Slug. Avg.
1900	Honus Wagner, Pittsburgh	.572
1901	Jimmy Sheckard, Brooklyn	.541
1902	Honus Wagner, Pittsburgh	.467
1903	Fred Clarke, Pittsburgh	.532
1904	Honus Wagner, Pittsburgh	.520
1905	Cy Seymour, Cincinnati	.559
1906	Harry Lumley, Brooklyn	.477
1907	Honus Wagner, Pittsburgh	.513
1908	Honus Wagner, Pittsburgh	.542
1909	Honus Wagner, Pittsburgh	.489
1910	Sherry Magee, Philadelphia	.507
1911	Frank Schulte, Chicago	.534
1912	Heinie Zimmerman, Chicago	.571
1913	Gavvy Cravath, Philadelphia	.568
1914	Sherry Magee, Philadelphia	.509
1915	Gavvy Cravath, Philadelphia	.510
1916	Zack Wheat, Brooklyn	.461
1917	Rogers Hornsby, St. Louis	.484
1918	Edd Roush, Cincinnati	.455
1919	Hy Myers, Brooklyn	.436
1920	Rogers Hornsby, St. Louis	.559
1921	Rogers Hornsby, St. Louis	.659
1922	Rogers Hornsby, St. Louis	.722
1923	Rogers Hornsby, St. Louis	.627
1924	Rogers Hornsby, St. Louis	.696
1925	Rogers Hornsby, St. Louis	.756
1926	Cy Williams, Philadelphia	.569
1927	Chick Hafey, St. Louis	.590
1928	Rogers Hornsby, Boston	.632
1929	Rogers Hornsby, Chicago	.679
1930	Hack Wilson, Chicago	.723
1931	Chuck Klein, Philadelphia	.584
1932	Chuck Klein, Philadelphia	.646
1933	Chuck Klein, Philadelphia	.602
1934	Rip Collins, St. Louis	.615
1935	Arky Vaughan, Pittsburgh	.607
1936	Mel Ott, New York	.588
1937	Joe Medwick, St. Louis	.641

Year	Player, Club	Slug. Avg.
1938	Johnny Mize, St. Louis	.614
1939	Johnny Mize, St. Louis	.626
1940	Johnny Mize, St. Louis	.636
1941	Pete Reiser, Brooklyn	.558
1942	Johnny Mize, New York	.521
1943	Stan Musial, St. Louis	.562
1944	Stan Musial, St. Louis	.549
1945	Tommy Holmes, Boston	.577
1946	Stan Musial, St. Louis	.587
1947	Ralph Kiner, Pittsburgh	.639
1948	Stan Musial, St. Louis	.702
1949	Ralph Kiner, Pittsburgh	.658
1950	Stan Musial, St. Louis	.596
1951	Ralph Kiner, Pittsburgh	.627
1952	Stan Musial, St. Louis	.538
1953	Duke Snider, Brooklyn	.627
1954	Willie Mays, New York	.667
1955	Willie Mays, New York	.659
1956	Duke Snider, Brooklyn	.598
1957	Willie Mays, New York	.626
1958	Ernie Banks, Chicago	.614
1959	Hank Aaron, Milwaukee	.636
1960	Frank Robinson, Cincinnati	.595
1961	Frank Robinson, Cincinnati	.611
1962	Frank Robinson, Cincinnati	.624
1963	Hank Aaron, Milwaukee	.586
1964	Willie Mays, San Francisco	.607
1965	Willie Mays, San Francisco	.645
1966	Dick Allen, Philadelphia	.632
1967	Hank Aaron, Atlanta	.573
1968	Willie McCovey, San Francisco	.545
1969	Willie McCovey, San Francisco	.656
1970	Willie McCovey, San Francisco	.612
1971	Hank Aaron, Atlanta	.669
1972	Billy Williams, Chicago	.606
1973	Willie Stargell, Pittsburgh	.646
1974	Mike Schmidt, Philadelphia	.546
1975	Dave Parker, Pittsburgh	.541
1976	Joe Morgan, Cincinnati	.576
1977	George Foster, Cincinnati	.631
1978	Dave Parker, Pittsburgh	.585
1979	Dave Kingman, Chicago	.613
1980	Mike Schmidt, Philadelphia	.624
1981	Mike Schmidt, Philadelphia	.644
1982	Mike Schmidt, Philadelphia	.547
1983	Dale Murphy, Atlanta	.540
1984	Dale Murphy, Atlanta	.547
1985	Pedro Guerrero, Los Angeles	.577
1986	Mike Schmidt, Philadelphia	.547
1987	Jack Clark, St. Louis	.597
1988	Darryl Strawberry, New York	.545
1989	Kevin Mitchell, San Francisco	.635
1990	Barry Bonds, Pittsburgh	.565
1991	Will Clark, San Francisco	.536
1992	Barry Bonds, Pittsburgh	.624
1993	Barry Bonds, San Francisco	.677
1994	Jeff Bagwell, Houston	.750

RUNS

AMERICAN LEAGUE

Year	Player, Club	No.
1901	Nap Lajoie, Philadelphia	145
1902	Dave Fultz, Philadelphia	110
1903	Patsy Dougherty, Boston	108
1904	Patsy Dougherty, Boston/New York	113
1905	Harry Davis, Philadelphia	92
1906	Elmer Flick, Cleveland	98
1907	Sam Crawford, Detroit	102
1908	Matty McIntyre, Detroit	105
1909	Ty Cobb, Detroit	116
1910	Ty Cobb, Detroit	106
1911	Ty Cobb, Detroit	147
1912	Eddie Collins, Philadelphia	137

Year	Player, Club	No.
1913	Eddie Collins, Philadelphia	125
1914	Eddie Collins, Philadelphia	122
1915	Ty Cobb, Detroit	144
1916	Ty Cobb, Detroit	113
1917	Donie Bush, Detroit	112
1918	Ray Chapman, Cleveland	84
1919	Babe Ruth, Boston	103
1920	Babe Ruth, New York	158
1921	Babe Ruth, New York	177
1922	George Sisler, St. Louis	134
1923	Babe Ruth, New York	151
1924	Babe Ruth, New York	143
1925	Johnny Mostil, Chicago	135
1926	Babe Ruth, New York	139
1927	Babe Ruth, New York	158
1928	Babe Ruth, New York	163
1929	Charlie Gehringer, Detroit	131
1930	Al Simmons, Philadelphia	152
1931	Lou Gehrig, New York	163
1932	Jimmie Foxx, Philadelphia	151
1933	Lou Gehrig, New York	138
1934	Charlie Gehringer, Detroit	134
1935	Lou Gehrig, New York	125
1936	Lou Gehrig, New York	167
1937	Joe DiMaggio, New York	151
1938	Hank Greenberg, Detroit	144
1939	Red Rolfe, New York	139
1940	Ted Williams, Boston	134
1941	Ted Williams, Boston	135
1942	Ted Williams, Boston	141
1943	George Case, Washington	102
1944	George Stirnweiss, New York	125
1945	George Stirnweiss, New York	107
1946	Ted Williams, Boston	142
1947	Ted Williams, Boston	125
1948	Tommy Henrich, New York	138
1949	Ted Williams, Boston	150
1950	Dom DiMaggio, Boston	131
1951	Dom DiMaggio, Boston	113
1952	Larry Doby, Cleveland	104
1953	Al Rosen, Cleveland	115
1954	Mickey Mantle, New York	129
1955	Al Smith, Cleveland	123
1956	Mickey Mantle, New York	132
1957	Mickey Mantle, New York	121
1958	Mickey Mantle, New York	127
1959	Eddie Yost, Detroit	115
1960	Mickey Mantle, New York	119
1961	Mickey Mantle, New York	132
	Roger Maris, New York	132
1962	Albie Pearson, Los Angeles	115
1963	Bob Allison, Minnesota	99
1964	Tony Oliva, Minnesota	109
1965	Zoilo Versalles, Minnesota	126
1966	Frank Robinson, Baltimore	122
1967	Carl Yastrzemski, Boston	112
1968	Dick McAuliffe, Detroit	95
1969	Reggie Jackson, Oakland	123
1970	Carl Yastrzemski, Boston	125
1971	Don Buford, Baltimore	99
1972	Bobby Murcer, New York	102
1973	Reggie Jackson, Oakland	99
1974	Carl Yastrzemski, Boston	93
1975	Fred Lynn, Boston	103
1976	Roy White, New York	104
1977	Rod Carew, Minnesota	128
1978	Ron LeFlore, Detroit	126
1979	Don Baylor, California	120
1980	Willie Wilson, Kansas City	133
1981	Rickey Henderson, Oakland	89
1982	Paul Molitor, Milwaukee	136
1983	Cal Ripken, Baltimore	121
1984	Dwight Evans, Boston	121
1985	Rickey Henderson, New York	146
1986	Rickey Henderson, New York	130
1987	Paul Molitor, Milwaukee	114

Year	Player, Club	No.
1988	Wade Boggs, Boston	128
1989	Wade Boggs, Boston	113
	Rickey Henderson, New York/Oakland	113
1990	Rickey Henderson, Oakland	119
1991	Paul Molitor, Milwaukee	133
1992	Tony Phillips, Detroit	114
1993	Rafael Palmeiro, Texas	124
1994	Frank Thomas, Chicago	106

NATIONAL LEAGUE

Year	Player, Club	No.
1900	Roy Thomas, Philadelphia	131
1901	Jesse Burkett, St. Louis	139
1902	Honus Wagner, Pittsburgh	105
1903	Ginger Beaumont, Pittsburgh	137
1904	George Browne, New York	99
1905	Mike Donlin, New York	124
1906	Honus Wagner, Pittsburgh	103
	Frank Chance, Chicago	103
1907	Spike Shannon, New York	104
1908	Fred Tenney, New York	101
1909	Tommy Leach, Pittsburgh	126
1910	Sherry Magee, Philadelphia	110
1911	Jimmy Sheckard, Chicago	121
1912	Bob Bescher, Cincinnati	120
1913	Tommy Leach, Chicago	99
	Max Carey, Pittsburgh	99
1914	George J. Burns, New York	100
1915	Gavvy Cravath, Philadelphia	89
1916	George J. Burns, New York	105
1917	George J. Burns, New York	103
1918	Heinie Groh, Cincinnati	88
1919	George J. Burns, New York	86
1920	George J. Burns, New York	115
1921	Rogers Hornsby, St. Louis	131
1922	Rogers Hornsby, St. Louis	141
1923	Ross Youngs, New York	121
1924	Frankie Frisch, New York	121
	Rogers Hornsby, St. Louis	121
1925	Kiki Cuyler, Pittsburgh	144
1926	Kiki Cuyler, Pittsburgh	113
1927	Lloyd Waner, Pittsburgh	133
	Rogers Hornsby, New York	133
1928	Paul Waner, Pittsburgh	142
1929	Rogers Hornsby, Chicago	156
1930	Chuck Klein, Philadelphia	158
1931	Bill Terry, New York	121
	Chuck Klein, Philadelphia	121
1932	Chuck Klein, Philadelphia	152
1933	Pepper Martin, St. Louis	122
1934	Paul Waner, Pittsburgh	122
1935	Augie Galan, Chicago	133
1936	Arky Vaughan, Pittsburgh	122
1937	Joe Medwick, St. Louis	111
1938	Mel Ott, New York	116
1939	Bill Werber, Cincinnati	115
1940	Arky Vaughan, Pittsburgh	113
1941	Pete Reiser, Brooklyn	117
1942	Mel Ott, New York	118
1943	Arky Vaughan, Brooklyn	112
1944	Bill Nicholson, Chicago	116
1945	Eddie Stanky, Brooklyn	128
1946	Stan Musial, St. Louis	124
1947	Johnny Mize, New York	137
1948	Stan Musial, St. Louis	135
1949	Pee Wee Reese, Brooklyn	132
1950	Earl Torgeson, Boston	120
1951	Stan Musial, St. Louis	124
	Ralph Kiner, Pittsburgh	124
1952	Stan Musial, St. Louis	105
	Solly Hemus, St. Louis	105
1953	Duke Snider, Brooklyn	132
1954	Stan Musial, St. Louis	120
	Duke Snider, Brooklyn	120
1955	Duke Snider, Brooklyn	126

Year	Player, Club	No.
1956	Frank Robinson, Cincinnati	122
1957	Hank Aaron, Milwaukee	118
1958	Willie Mays, San Francisco	121
1959	Vada Pinson, Cincinnati	131
1960	Billy Bruton, Milwaukee	112
1961	Willie Mays, San Francisco	129
1962	Frank Robinson, Cincinnati	134
1963	Hank Aaron, Milwaukee	121
1964	Dick Allen, Philadelphia	125
1965	Tommy Harper, Cincinnati	126
1966	Felipe Alou, Atlanta	122
1967	Hank Aaron, Atlanta	113
	Lou Brock, St. Louis	113
1968	Glenn Beckert, Chicago	98
1969	Bobby Bonds, San Francisco	120
	Pete Rose, Cincinnati	120
1970	Billy Williams, Chicago	137
1971	Lou Brock, St. Louis	126
1972	Joe Morgan, Cincinnati	122
1973	Bobby Bonds, San Francisco	131
1974	Pete Rose, Cincinnati	110
1975	Pete Rose, Cincinnati	112
1976	Pete Rose, Cincinnati	130
1977	George Foster, Cincinnati	124
1978	Ivan DeJesus, Chicago	104
1979	Keith Hernandez, St. Louis	116
1980	Keith Hernandez, St. Louis	111
1981	Mike Schmidt, Philadelphia	78
1982	Lonnie Smith, St. Louis	120
1983	Tim Raines, Montreal	133
1984	Ryne Sandberg, Chicago	114
1985	Dale Murphy, Atlanta	118
1986	Tony Gwynn, San Diego	107
	Von Hayes, Philadelphia	107
1987	Tim Raines, Montreal	123
1988	Brett Butler, San Francisco	109
1989	Will Clark, San Francisco	104
	Howard Johnson, New York	104
	Ryne Sandberg, Chicago	104
1990	Ryne Sandberg, Chicago	116
1991	Brett Butler, Los Angeles	112
1992	Barry Bonds, Pittsburgh	109
1993	Lenny Dykstra, Philadelphia	143
1994	Jeff Bagwell, Houston	104

HITS

AMERICAN LEAGUE

Year	Player, Club	No.
1901	Nap Lajoie, Philadelphia	229
1902	Charles Hickman, Boston/Cleveland	194
1903	Patsy Dougherty, Boston	195
1904	Nap Lajoie, Cleveland	211
1905	George Stone, St. Louis	187
1906	Nap Lajoie, Cleveland	214
1907	Ty Cobb, Detroit	212
1908	Ty Cobb, Detroit	188
1909	Ty Cobb, Detroit	216
1910	Nap Lajoie, Cleveland	227
1911	Ty Cobb, Detroit	248
1912	Ty Cobb, Detroit	227
1913	Joe Jackson, Cleveland	197
1914	Tris Speaker, Boston	193
1915	Ty Cobb, Detroit	208
1916	Tris Speaker, Cleveland	211
1917	Ty Cobb, Detroit	225
1918	George H. Burns, Philadelphia	178
1919	Ty Cobb, Detroit	191
	Bobby Veach, Detroit	191
1920	George Sisler, St. Louis	257
1921	Harry Heilmann, Detroit	237
1922	George Sisler, St. Louis	246
1923	Charlie Jamieson, Cleveland	222
1924	Sam Rice, Washington	216

Year	Player, Club	No.
1925	Al Simmons, Philadelphia	253
1926	George H. Burns, Cleveland	216
	Sam Rice, Washington	216
1927	Earle Combs, New York	231
1928	Heinie Manush, St. Louis	241
1929	Dale Alexander, Detroit	215
	Charlie Gehringer, Detroit	215
1930	Johnny Hodapp, Cleveland	225
1931	Lou Gehrig, New York	211
1932	Al Simmons, Philadelphia	216
1933	Heinie Manush, Washington	221
1934	Charlie Gehringer, Detroit	214
1935	Joe Vosmik, Cleveland	216
1936	Earl Averill Sr., Cleveland	232
1937	Beau Bell, St. Louis	218
1938	Joe Vosmik, Boston	201
1939	Red Rolfe, New York	213
1940	Rip Radcliff, St. Louis	200
	Barney McCosky, Detroit	200
	Doc Cramer, Boston	200
1941	Cecil Travis, Washington	218
1942	Johnny Pesky, Boston	205
1943	Dick Wakefield, Detroit	200
1944	George Stirnweiss, New York	205
1945	George Stirnweiss, New York	195
1946	Johnny Pesky, Boston	208
1947	Johnny Pesky, Boston	207
1948	Bob Dillinger, St. Louis	207
1949	Dale Mitchell, Cleveland	203
1950	George Kell, Detroit	218
1951	George Kell, Detroit	191
1952	Nellie Fox, Chicago	192
1953	Harvey Kuenn, Detroit	209
1954	Nellie Fox, Chicago	201
	Harvey Kuenn, Detroit	201
1955	Al Kaline, Detroit	200
1956	Harvey Kuenn, Detroit	196
1957	Nellie Fox, Chicago	196
1958	Nellie Fox, Chicago	187
1959	Harvey Kuenn, Detroit	198
1960	Minnie Minoso, Chicago	184
1961	Norm Cash, Detroit	193
1962	Bobby Richardson, New York	209
1963	Carl Yastrzemski, Boston	183
1964	Tony Oliva, Minnesota	217
1965	Tony Oliva, Minnesota	185
1966	Tony Oliva, Minnesota	191
1967	Carl Yastrzemski, Boston	189
1968	Bert Campaneris, Oakland	177
1969	Tony Oliva, Minnesota	197
1970	Tony Oliva, Minnesota	204
1971	Cesar Tovar, Minnesota	204
1972	Joe Rudi, Oakland	181
1973	Rod Carew, Minnesota	203
1974	Rod Carew, Minnesota	218
1975	George Brett, Kansas City	195
1976	George Brett, Kansas City	215
1977	Rod Carew, Minnesota	239
1978	Jim Rice, Boston	213
1979	George Brett, Kansas City	212
1980	Willie Wilson, Kansas City	230
1981	Rickey Henderson, Oakland	135
1982	Robin Yount, Milwaukee	210
1983	Cal Ripken, Baltimore	211
1984	Don Mattingly, New York	207
1985	Wade Boggs, Boston	240
1986	Don Mattingly, New York	238
1987	Kirby Puckett, Minnesota	207
	Kevin Seitzer, Kansas City	207
1988	Kirby Puckett, Minnesota	234
1989	Kirby Puckett, Minnesota	215
1990	Rafael Palmeiro, Texas	191
1991	Paul Molitor, Milwaukee	216
1992	Kirby Puckett, Minnesota	210
1993	Paul Molitor, Toronto	211
1994	Kenny Lofton, Cleveland	160

NATIONAL LEAGUE

Year	Player, Club	No.
1900	Willie Keeler, Brooklyn	208
1901	Jesse Burkett, St. Louis	228
1902	Ginger Beaumont, Pittsburgh	194
1903	Ginger Beaumont, Pittsburgh	209
1904	Ginger Beaumont, Pittsburgh	185
1905	Cy Seymour, Cincinnati	219
1906	Harry Steinfeldt, Chicago	176
1907	Ginger Beaumont, Boston	187
1908	Honus Wagner, Pittsburgh	201
1909	Larry Doyle, New York	172
1910	Honus Wagner, Pittsburgh	178
	Bobby Byrne, Pittsburgh	178
1911	Doc Miller, Boston	192
1912	Heinie Zimmerman, Chicago	207
1913	Gavvy Cravath, Philadelphia	179
1914	Sherry Magee, Philadelphia	171
1915	Larry Doyle, New York	189
1916	Hal Chase, Cincinnati	184
1917	Heinie Groh, Cincinnati	182
1918	Charlie Hollocher, Chicago	161
1919	Ivy Olson, Brooklyn	164
1920	Rogers Hornsby, St. Louis	218
1921	Rogers Hornsby, St. Louis	235
1922	Rogers Hornsby, St. Louis	250
1923	Frankie Frisch, New York	223
1924	Rogers Hornsby, St. Louis	227
1925	Jim Bottomley, St. Louis	227
1926	Eddie Brown, Boston	201
1927	Paul Waner, Pittsburgh	237
1928	Fred Lindstrom, New York	231
1929	Lefty O'Doul, Philadelphia	254
1930	Bill Terry, New York	254
1931	Lloyd Waner, Pittsburgh	214
1932	Chuck Klein, Philadelphia	226
1933	Chuck Klein, Philadelphia	223
1934	Paul Waner, Pittsburgh	217
1935	Billy Herman, Chicago	227
1936	Joe Medwick, St. Louis	223
1937	Joe Medwick, St. Louis	237
1938	Frank McCormick, Cincinnati	209
1939	Frank McCormick, Cincinnati	209
1940	Stan Hack, Chicago	191
	Frank McCormick, Cincinnati	191
1941	Stan Hack, Chicago	186
1942	Enos Slaughter, St. Louis	188
1943	Stan Musial, St. Louis	220
1944	Stan Musial, St. Louis	197
	Phil Cavarretta, Chicago	197
1945	Tommy Holmes, Boston	224
1946	Stan Musial, St. Louis	228
1947	Tommy Holmes, Boston	191
1948	Stan Musial, St. Louis	230
1949	Stan Musial, St. Louis	207
1950	Duke Snider, Brooklyn	199
1951	Richie Ashburn, Philadelphia	221
1952	Stan Musial, St. Louis	194
1953	Richie Ashburn, Philadelphia	205
1954	Don Mueller, New York	212
1955	Ted Kluszewski, Cincinnati	192
1956	Hank Aaron, Milwaukee	200
1957	Red Schoendienst, New York/Milwaukee	200
1958	Richie Ashburn, Philadelphia	215
1959	Hank Aaron, Milwaukee	223
1960	Willie Mays, San Francisco	190
1961	Vada Pinson, Cincinnati	208
1962	Tommy Davis, Los Angeles	230
1963	Vada Pinson, Cincinnati	204
1964	Roberto Clemente, Pittsburgh	211
	Curt Flood, St. Louis	211
1965	Pete Rose, Cincinnati	209
1966	Felipe Alou, Atlanta	218
1967	Roberto Clemente, Pittsburgh	209
1968	Felipe Alou, Atlanta	210
	Pete Rose, Cincinnati	210

Year	Player, Club	No.
1969	Matty Alou, Pittsburgh	231
1970	Pete Rose, Cincinnati	205
	Billy Williams, Chicago	205
1971	Joe Torre, St. Louis	230
1972	Pete Rose, Cincinnati	198
1973	Pete Rose, Cincinnati	230
1974	Ralph Garr, Atlanta	214
1975	Dave Cash, Philadelphia	213
1976	Pete Rose, Cincinnati	215
1977	Dave Parker, Pittsburgh	215
1978	Steve Garvey, Los Angeles	202
1979	Garry Templeton, St. Louis	211
1980	Steve Garvey, Los Angeles	200
1981	Pete Rose, Philadelphia	140
1982	Al Oliver, Montreal	204
1983	Jose Cruz, Houston	189
	Andre Dawson, Montreal	189
1984	Tony Gwynn, San Diego	213
1985	Willie McGee, St. Louis	216
1986	Tony Gwynn, San Diego	211
1987	Tony Gwynn, San Diego	218
1988	Andres Galarraga, Montreal	184
1989	Tony Gwynn, San Diego	203
1990	Brett Butler, San Francisco	192
	Lenny Dykstra, Philadelphia	192
1991	Terry Pendleton, Atlanta	187
1992	Terry Pendleton, Atlanta	199
	Andy Van Slyke, Pittsburgh	199
1993	Lenny Dykstra, Philadelphia	194
1994	Tony Gwynn, San Diego	165

SINGLES

AMERICAN LEAGUE

Year	Player, Club	No.
1901	Nap Lajoie, Philadelphia	154
1902	Fielder Jones, Chicago	148
1903	Patsy Dougherty, Boston	161
1904	Willie Keeler, New York	164
1905	Willie Keeler, New York	147
1906	Willie Keeler, New York	166
1907	Ty Cobb, Detroit	163
1908	Matty McIntyre, Detroit	131
	George Stone, St. Louis	131
1909	Ty Cobb, Detroit	164
1910	Nap Lajoie, Cleveland	165
1911	Ty Cobb, Detroit	169
1912	Ty Cobb, Detroit	167
1913	Eddie Collins, Philadelphia	145
1914	Stuffy McInnis, Philadelphia	160
1915	Ty Cobb, Detroit	161
1916	Tris Speaker, Cleveland	160
1917	Ty Cobb, Detroit	151
	Clyde Milan, Washington	151
1918	George H. Burns, Philadelphia	141
1919	Sam Rice, Washington	144
1920	George Sisler, St. Louis	171
1921	Jack Tobin, St. Louis	179
1922	George Sisler, St. Louis	178
1923	Charlie Jamieson, Cleveland	172
1924	Charlie Jamieson, Cleveland	168
1925	Sam Rice, Washington	182
1926	Sam Rice, Washington	167
1927	Earle Combs, New York	166
1928	Heinie Manush, St. Louis	161
1929	Earle Combs, New York	151
1930	Sam Rice, Washington	158
1931	Oscar Melillo, St. Louis	142
	John Stone, Detroit	142
1932	Heinie Manush, Washington	145
1933	Heinie Manush, Washington	167
1934	Doc Cramer, Philadelphia	158
1935	Doc Cramer, Philadelphia	170
1936	Rip Radcliff, Chicago	161

Year	Player, Club	No.
1937	Buddy Lewis, Washington	162
1938	Mel Almada, Washington/St. Louis	158
1939	Doc Cramer, Boston	147
1940	Doc Cramer, Boston	160
1941	Cecil Travis, Washington	153
1942	Johnny Pesky, Boston	165
1943	Doc Cramer, Detroit	159
1944	George Stirnweiss, New York	146
1945	Irv Hall, Philadelphia	139
1946	Johnny Pesky, Boston	159
1947	Johnny Pesky, Boston	172
1948	Dale Mitchell, Cleveland	162
1949	Dale Mitchell, Cleveland	161
1950	Phil Rizzuto, New York	150
1951	George Kell, Detroit	150
1952	Nellie Fox, Chicago	157
1953	Harvey Kuenn, Detroit	167
1954	Nellie Fox, Chicago	167
1955	Nellie Fox, Chicago	157
1956	Nellie Fox, Chicago	158
1957	Nellie Fox, Chicago	155
1958	Nellie Fox, Chicago	160
1959	Nellie Fox, Chicago	149
1960	Nellie Fox, Chicago	139
1961	Bobby Richardson, New York	148
1962	Bobby Richardson, New York	158
1963	Albie Pearson, Los Angeles	139
1964	Bobby Richardson, New York	148
1965	Don Buford, Chicago	129
1966	Luis Aparicio, Baltimore	143
1967	Horace Clarke, New York	140
1968	Bert Campaneris, Oakland	139
1969	Horace Clarke, New York	146
1970	Alex Johnson, California	156
1971	Cesar Tovar, Minnesota	171
1972	Rod Carew, Minnesota	143
1973	Rod Carew, Minnesota	156
1974	Rod Carew, Minnesota	180
1975	Thurman Munson, New York	151
1976	George Brett, Kansas City	160
1977	Rod Carew, Minnesota	171
1978	Ron LeFlore, Detroit	153
1979	Willie Wilson, Kansas City	148
1980	Willie Wilson, Kansas City	184
1981	Willie Wilson, Kansas City	115
1982	Willie Wilson, Kansas City	157
1983	Wade Boggs, Boston	154
1984	Wade Boggs, Boston	162
1985	Wade Boggs, Boston	187
1986	Tony Fernandez, Toronto	161
1987	Kevin Seitzer, Kansas City	151
1988	Kirby Puckett, Minnesota	163
1989	Steve Sax, New York	171
1990	Rafael Palmeiro, Texas	136
1991	Julio Franco, Texas	156
1992	Carlos Baerga, Cleveland	152
1993	Kenny Lofton, Cleveland	148
1994	Kenny Lofton, Cleveland	107
	Paul Molitor, Toronto	107

NATIONAL LEAGUE

Year	Player, Club	No.
1900	Willie Keeler, Brooklyn	179
1901	Jesse Burkett, St. Louis	180
1902	Ginger Beaumont, Pittsburgh	167
1903	Ginger Beaumont, Pittsburgh	166
1904	Ginger Beaumont, Pittsburgh	158
1905	Mike Donlin, New York	162
1906	Miller Huggins, Cincinnati	141
	Spike Shannon, St. Louis/New York	141
1907	Ginger Beaumont, Pittsburgh	150
1908	Mike Donlin, New York	153
1909	Eddie Grant, Philadelphia	147
1910	Eddie Grant, Philadelphia	134
1911	Jake Daubert, Brooklyn	146

Year	Player, Club	No.
	Doc Miller, Boston	146
1912	Bill Sweeney, Boston	159
1913	Jake Daubert, Brooklyn	152
1914	Beals Becker, Philadelphia	128
1915	Larry Doyle, New York	135
1916	Dave Robertson, New York	142
1917	Benny Kauff, New York	141
	Edd Roush, Cincinnati	141
1918	Charlie Hollocher, Chicago	130
1919	Ivy Olson, Brooklyn	140
1920	Milt Stock, St. Louis	170
1921	Carson Bigbee, Pittsburgh	161
1922	Carson Bigbee, Pittsburgh	166
1923	Frankie Frisch, New York	169
1924	Zack Wheat, Brooklyn	149
1925	Milt Stock, Brooklyn	164
1926	Eddie Brown, Boston	160
1927	Lloyd Waner, Pittsburgh	198
1928	Lloyd Waner, Pittsburgh	180
1929	Lefty O'Doul, Philadelphia	181
	Lloyd Waner, Pittsburgh	181
1930	Bill Terry, New York	177
1931	Lloyd Waner, Pittsburgh	172
1932	Lefty O'Doul, Brooklyn	158
1933	Chick Fullis, Philadelphia	162
1934	Bill Terry, New York	169
1935	Woody Jensen, Pittsburgh	160
1936	Joe Moore, New York	160
1937	Paul Waner, Pittsburgh	178
1938	Frank McCormick, Cincinnati	160
1939	Buddy Hassett, Boston	162
1940	Burgess Whitehead, New York	141
1941	Stan Hack, Chicago	141
1942	Enos Slaughter, St. Louis	127
1943	Mickey Witek, New York	172
1944	Phil Cavarretta, Chicago	142
1945	Stan Hack, Chicago	155
1946	Stan Musial, St. Louis	142
1947	Tommy Holmes, Boston	146
1948	Stan Rojek, Pittsburgh	150
1949	Red Schoendienst, St. Louis	160
1950	Eddie Waitkus, Philadelphia	143
1951	Richie Ashburn, Philadelphia	181
1952	Bobby Adams, Cincinnati	145
1953	Richie Ashburn, Philadelphia	169
1954	Don Mueller, New York	165
1955	Don Mueller, New York	152
1956	Johnny Temple, Cincinnati	157
1957	Richie Ashburn, Philadelphia	152
1958	Richie Ashburn, Philadelphia	176
1959	Don Blasingame, St. Louis	144
1960	Dick Groat, Pittsburgh	154
1961	Vada Pinson, Cincinnati	150
	Maury Wills, Los Angeles	150
1962	Maury Wills, Los Angeles	179
1963	Curt Flood, St. Louis	152
1964	Curt Flood, St. Louis	178
1965	Maury Wills, Los Angeles	165
1966	Sonny Jackson, Houston	160
1967	Maury Wills, Pittsburgh	162
1968	Curt Flood, St. Louis	160
1969	Matty Alou, Pittsburgh	183
1970	Matty Alou, Pittsburgh	171
1971	Ralph Garr, Atlanta	180
1972	Lou Brock, St. Louis	156
1973	Pete Rose, Cincinnati	181
1974	Dave Cash, Philadelphia	167
1975	Dave Cash, Philadelphia	166
1976	Willie Montanez, San Francisco/Atlanta	164
1977	Garry Templeton, St. Louis	155
1978	Larry Bowa, Philadelphia	153
1979	Pete Rose, Philadelphia	159
1980	Gene Richards, San Diego	155
1981	Pete Rose, Philadelphia	117
1982	Bill Buckner, Chicago	147
1983	Rafael Ramirez, Atlanta	160

Year	Player, Club	No.
1984—Tony Gwynn, San Diego		177
1985—Willie McGee, St. Louis		162
1986—Tony Gwynn, San Diego		157
—Steve Sax, Los Angeles		157
1987—Tony Gwynn, San Diego		162
1988—Steve Sax, Los Angeles		147
1989—Tony Gwynn, San Diego		165
1990—Brett Butler, San Francisco		160
1991—Brett Butler, Los Angeles		162
1992—Brett Butler, Los Angeles		143
1993—Brett Butler, Los Angeles		149
1994—Tony Gwynn, San Diego		117

DOUBLES

AMERICAN LEAGUE

Year	Player, Club	No.
1901—Nap Lajoie, Philadelphia		48
1902—Harry Davis, Philadelphia		43
1903—Socks Seybold, Philadelphia		43
1904—Nap Lajoie, Cleveland		50
1905—Harry Davis, Philadelphia		47
1906—Nap Lajoie, Cleveland		49
1907—Harry Davis, Philadelphia		37
1908—Ty Cobb, Detroit		36
1909—Sam Crawford, Detroit		35
1910—Nap Lajoie, Cleveland		53
1911—Ty Cobb, Detroit		47
1912—Tris Speaker, Boston		53
1913—Joe Jackson, Cleveland		39
1914—Tris Speaker, Boston		46
1915—Bobby Veach, Detroit		40
1916—Jack Graney, Cleveland		41
—Tris Speaker, Cleveland		41
1917—Ty Cobb, Detroit		44
1918—Tris Speaker, Cleveland		33
1919—Bobby Veach, Detroit		45
1920—Tris Speaker, Cleveland		50
1921—Tris Speaker, Cleveland		52
1922—Tris Speaker, Cleveland		48
1923—Tris Speaker, Cleveland		59
1924—Joe Sewell, Cleveland		45
—Harry Heilmann, Detroit		45
1925—Marty McManus, St. Louis		44
1926—George H. Burns, Cleveland		64
1927—Lou Gehrig, New York		52
1928—Heinie Manush, St. Louis		47
—Lou Gehrig, New York		47
1929—Heinie Manush, St. Louis		45
—Roy Johnson, Detroit		45
—Charlie Gehringer, Detroit		45
1930—Johnny Hodapp, Cleveland		51
1931—Earl Webb, Boston		67
1932—Eric McNair, Philadelphia		47
1933—Joe Cronin, Washington		45
1934—Hank Greenberg, Detroit		63
1935—Joe Vosmik, Cleveland		47
1936—Charlie Gehringer, Detroit		60
1937—Beau Bell, St. Louis		51
1938—Joe Cronin, Boston		51
1939—Red Rolfe, New York		46
1940—Hank Greenberg, Detroit		50
1941—Lou Boudreau, Cleveland		45
1942—Don Kolloway, Chicago		40
1943—Dick Wakefield, Detroit		38
1944—Lou Boudreau, Cleveland		45
1945—Wally Moses, Chicago		35
1946—Mickey Vernon, Wash.		51
1947—Lou Boudreau, Cleveland		45
1948—Ted Williams, Boston		44
1949—Ted Williams, Boston		39
1950—George Kell, Detroit		56
1951—George Kell, Detroit		36
—Eddie Yost, Washington		36
—Sam Mele, Washington		36

Year	Player, Club	No.
1952—Ferris Fain, Philadelphia		43
1953—Mickey Vernon, Washington		43
1954—Mickey Vernon, Washington		33
1955—Harvey Kuenn, Detroit		38
1956—Jimmy Piersall, Boston		40
1957—Minnie Minoso, Chicago		36
—Billy Gardner, Baltimore		36
1958—Harvey Kuenn, Detroit		39
1959—Harvey Kuenn, Detroit		42
1960—Tito Francona, Cleveland		36
1961—Al Kaline, Detroit		41
1962—Floyd Robinson, Chicago		45
1963—Carl Yastrzemski, Boston		40
1964—Tony Oliva, Minnesota		43
1965—Zoilo Versalles, Minnesota		45
—Carl Yastrzemski, Boston		45
1966—Carl Yastrzemski, Boston		39
1967—Tony Oliva, Minnesota		34
1968—Reggie Smith, Boston		37
1969—Tony Oliva, Minnesota		39
1970—Tony Oliva, Minnesota		36
—Amos Otis, Kansas City		36
—Cesar Tovar, Minnesota		36
1971—Reggie Smith, Boston		33
1972—Lou Piniella, Kansas City		33
1973—Sal Bando, Oakland		32
—Pedro Garcia, Milwaukee		32
1974—Joe Rudi, Oakland		39
1975—Fred Lynn, Boston		47
1976—Amos Otis, Kansas City		40
1977—Hal McRae, Kansas City		54
1978—George Brett, Kansas City		45
1979—Chet Lemon, Chicago		44
—Cecil Cooper, Milwaukee		44
1980—Robin Yount, Milwaukee		49
1981—Cecil Cooper, Milwaukee		35
1982—Hal McRae, Kansas City		46
—Robin Yount, Milwaukee		46
1983—Cal Ripken, Baltimore		47
1984—Don Mattingly, New York		44
1985—Don Mattingly, New York		48
1986—Don Mattingly, New York		53
1987—Paul Molitor, Milwaukee		41
1988—Wade Boggs, Boston		45
1989—Wade Boggs, Boston		51
1990—George Brett, Kansas City		45
—Jody Reed, Boston		45
1991—Rafael Palmeiro, Texas		49
1992—Edgar Martinez, Seattle		46
—Frank Thomas, Chicago		46
1993—John Olerud, Toronto		54
1994—Chuck Knoblauch, Minnesota		45

NATIONAL LEAGUE

Year	Player, Club	No.
1876—Ross Barnes, Chicago		23
1877—Cap Anson, Chicago		20
1878—Lew Brown, Providence		18
1879—Charlie Eden, Cleveland		31
1880—Fred Dunlap, Cleveland		27
1881—King Kelly, Chicago		28
1882—King Kelly, Chicago		36
1883—Ned Williamson, Chicago		50
1884—Paul Hines, Providence		34
1885—Cap Anson, Chicago		35
1886—Dan Brouthers, Detroit		41
1887—Dan Brouthers, Detroit		35
1888—Jimmy Ryan, Chicago		37
1889—Jack Glasscock, Indianapolis		39
1890—Sam Thompson, Philadelphia		38
1891—Mike Griffin, Brooklyn		36
1892—Dan Brouthers, Brooklyn		33
—Ed Delahanty, Philadelphia		33
1893—Patsy Tebeau, Cleveland		35
1894—Hugh Duffy, Boston		50

Year	Player, Club	No.
1895—	Ed Delahanty, Philadelphia	47
1896—	Ed Delahanty, Philadelphia	42
1897—	Jake Stenzel, Baltimore	40
1898—	Nap Lajoie, Philadelphia	40
1899—	Ed Delahanty, Philadelphia	56
1900—	Honus Wagner, Pittsburgh	45
1901—	Honus Wagner, Pittsburgh	39
	—Jake Beckley, Cincinnati	39
1902—	Honus Wagner, Pittsburgh	33
1903—	Fred Clarke, Pittsburgh	32
	—Sam Mertes, New York	32
	—Harry Steinfeldt, Cincinnati	32
1904—	Honus Wagner, Pittsburgh	44
1905—	Cy Seymour, Cincinnati	40
1906—	Honus Wagner, Pittsburgh	38
1907—	Honus Wagner, Pittsburgh	38
1908—	Honus Wagner, Pittsburgh	39
1909—	Honus Wagner, Pittsburgh	39
1910—	Bobby Byrne, Pittsburgh	43
1911—	Ed Konetchy, St. Louis	38
1912—	Heinie Zimmerman, Chicago	41
1913—	Red Smith, Brooklyn	40
1914—	Sherry Magee, Philadelphia	39
1915—	Larry Doyle, New York	40
1916—	Bert Niehoff, Philadelphia	42
1917—	Heinie Groh, Cincinnati	39
1918—	Heinie Groh, Cincinnati	28
1919—	Ross Youngs, New York	31
1920—	Rogers Hornsby, St. Louis	44
1921—	Rogers Hornsby, St. Louis	44
1922—	Rogers Hornsby, St. Louis	46
1923—	Edd Roush, Cincinnati	41
1924—	Rogers Hornsby, St. Louis	43
1925—	Jim Bottomley, St. Louis	44
1926—	Jim Bottomley, St. Louis	40
1927—	Riggs Stephenson, Chicago	46
1928—	Paul Waner, Pittsburgh	50
1929—	Johnny Frederick, Brooklyn	52
1930—	Chuck Klein, Philadelphia	59
1931—	Sparky Adams, St. Louis	46
1932—	Paul Waner, Pittsburgh	62
1933—	Chuck Klein, Philadelphia	44
1934—	Kiki Cuyler, Chicago	42
	—Ethan Allen, Philadelphia	42
1935—	Billy Herman, Chicago	57
1936—	Joe Medwick, St. Louis	64
1937—	Joe Medwick, St. Louis	56
1938—	Joe Medwick, St. Louis	47
1939—	Enos Slaughter, St. Louis	52
1940—	Frank McCormick, Cincinnati	44
1941—	Pete Reiser, Brooklyn	39
	—Johnny Mize, St. Louis	39
1942—	Marty Marion, St. Louis	38
1943—	Stan Musial, St. Louis	48
1944—	Stan Musial, St. Louis	51
1945—	Tommy Holmes, Boston	47
1946—	Stan Musial, St. Louis	50
1947—	Eddie Miller, Cincinnati	38
1948—	Stan Musial, St. Louis	46
1949—	Stan Musial, St. Louis	41
1950—	Red Schoendienst, St. Louis	43
1951—	Alvin Dark, New York	41
1952—	Stan Musial, St. Louis	42
1953—	Stan Musial, St. Louis	53
1954—	Stan Musial, St. Louis	41
1955—	Johnny Logan, Milwaukee	37
	—Hank Aaron, Milwaukee	37
1956—	Hank Aaron, Milwaukee	34
1957—	Don Hoak, Cincinnati	39
1958—	Orlando Cepeda, San Francisco	38
1959—	Vada Pinson, Cincinnati	47
1960—	Vada Pinson, Cincinnati	37
1961—	Hank Aaron, Milwaukee	39
1962—	Frank Robinson, Cincinnati	51
1963—	Dick Groat, St. Louis	43
1964—	Lee Maye, Milwaukee	44
1965—	Hank Aaron, Milwaukee	40
1966—	Johnny Callison, Philadelphia	40
1967—	Rusty Staub, Houston	44
1968—	Lou Brock, St. Louis	46
1969—	Matty Alou, Pittsburgh	41
1970—	Wes Parker, Los Angeles	47
1971—	Cesar Cedeno, Houston	40
1972—	Cesar Cedeno, Houston	39
	—Willie Montanez, Philadelphia	39
1973—	Willie Stargell, Pittsburgh	43
1974—	Pete Rose, Cincinnati	45
1975—	Pete Rose, Cincinnati	47
1976—	Pete Rose, Cincinnati	42
1977—	Dave Parker, Pittsburgh	44
1978—	Pete Rose, Cincinnati	51
1979—	Keith Hernandez, St. Louis	48
1980—	Pete Rose, Philadelphia	42
1981—	Bill Buckner, Chicago	35
1982—	Al Oliver, Montreal	43
1983—	Bill Buckner, Chicago	38
	—Al Oliver, Montreal	38
	—Johnny Ray, Pittsburgh	38
1984—	Tim Raines, Montreal	38
	—Johnny Ray, Pittsburgh	38
1985—	Dave Parker, Cincinnati	42
1986—	Von Hayes, Philadelphia	46
1987—	Tim Wallach, Montreal	42
1988—	Andres Galarraga, Montreal	42
1989—	Pedro Guerrero, St. Louis	42
	—Tim Wallach, Montreal	42
1990—	Gregg Jefferies, New York	40
1991—	Bobby Bonilla, Pittsburgh	44
1992—	Andy Van Slyke, Pittsburgh	45
1993—	Charlie Hayes, Colorado	45
1994—	Craig Biggio, Houston	44
	—Larry Walker, Montreal	44

TRIPLES

AMERICAN LEAGUE

Year	Player, Club	No.
1901—	Jimmy Williams, Baltimore	22
1902—	Jimmy Williams, Baltimore	23
1903—	Sam Crawford, Detroit	25
1904—	Chick Stahl, Boston	22
1905—	Elmer Flick, Cleveland	19
1906—	Elmer Flick, Cleveland	22
1907—	Elmer Flick, Cleveland	18
1908—	Ty Cobb, Detroit	20
1909—	Home Run Baker, Philadelphia	19
1910—	Sam Crawford, Detroit	19
1911—	Ty Cobb, Detroit	24
1912—	Joe Jackson, Cleveland	26
1913—	Sam Crawford, Detroit	23
1914—	Sam Crawford, Detroit	26
1915—	Sam Crawford, Detroit	19
1916—	Joe Jackson, Chicago	21
1917—	Ty Cobb, Detroit	24
1918—	Ty Cobb, Detroit	14
1919—	Bobby Veach, Detroit	17
1920—	Joe Jackson, Chicago	20
1921—	Howard Shanks, Washington	19
1922—	George Sisler, St. Louis	18
1923—	Sam Rice, Washington	18
	—Goose Goslin, Washington	18
1924—	Wally Pipp, New York	19
1925—	Goose Goslin, Washington	20
1926—	Lou Gehrig, New York	20
1927—	Earle Combs, New York	23
1928—	Earle Combs, New York	21
1929—	Charlie Gehringer, Detroit	19
1930—	Earle Combs, New York	22
1931—	Roy Johnson, Detroit	19
1932—	Joe Cronin, Washington	18
1933—	Heinie Manush, Washington	17

Year	Player, Club	No.
1934—	Ben Chapman, New York	13
1935—	Joe Vosmik, Cleveland	20
1936—	Earl Averill Sr., Cleveland	15
—	Joe DiMaggio, New York	15
—	Red Rolfe, New York	15
1937—	Dixie Walker, Chicago	16
—	Mike Kreevich, Chicago	16
1938—	Jeff Heath, Cleveland	18
1939—	Buddy Lewis, Washington	16
1940—	Barney McCosky, Detroit	19
1941—	Jeff Heath, Cleveland	20
1942—	Stan Spence, Washington	15
1943—	Johnny Lindell, New York	12
—	Wally Moses, Chicago	12
1944—	Johnny Lindell, New York	16
—	George Stirnweiss, New York	16
1945—	George Stirnweiss, New York	22
1946—	Hank Edwards, Cleveland	16
1947—	Tommy Henrich, New York	13
1948—	Tommy Henrich, New York	14
1949—	Dale Mitchell, Cleveland	23
1950—	Dom DiMaggio, Boston	11
—	Bobby Doerr, Boston	11
—	Hoot Evers, Detroit	11
1951—	Minnie Minoso, Cleveland/Chicago	14
1952—	Bobby Avila, Cleveland	11
1953—	Jim Rivera, Chicago	16
1954—	Minnie Minoso, Chicago	18
1955—	Mickey Mantle, New York	11
—	Andy Carey, New York	11
1956—	Minnie Minoso, Chicago	11
—	Jackie Jensen, Boston	11
—	Harry Simpson, Kansas City	11
—	Jim Lemon, Washington	11
1957—	Gil McDougald, New York	9
—	Hank Bauer, New York	9
—	Harry Simpson, New York	9
1958—	Vic Power, Kansas City/Cleveland	10
1959—	Bob Allison, Washington	9
1960—	Nellie Fox, Chicago	10
1961—	Jake Wood, Detroit	14
1962—	Gino Cimoli, Kansas City	15
1963—	Zoilo Versalles, Minnesota	13
1964—	Rich Rollins, Minnesota	10
—	Zoilo Versalles, Minnesota	10
1965—	Bert Campaneris, Kansas City	12
—	Zoilo Versalles, Minnesota	12
1966—	Bobby Knoop, California	11
1967—	Paul Blair, Baltimore	12
1968—	Jim Fregosi, California	13
1969—	Del Unser, Washington	8
1970—	Cesar Tovar, Minnesota	13
1971—	Fred Patek, Kansas City	11
1972—	Carlton Fisk, Boston	9
—	Joe Rudi, Oakland	9
1973—	Al Bumbry, Baltimore	11
—	Rod Carew, Minnesota	11
1974—	Mickey Rivers, California	11
1975—	George Brett, Kansas City	13
—	Mickey Rivers, California	13
1976—	George Brett, Kansas City	14
1977—	Rod Carew, Minnesota	16
1978—	Jim Rice, Boston	15
1979—	George Brett, Kansas City	20
1980—	Alfredo Griffin, Toronto	15
—	Willie Wilson, Kansas City	15
1981—	John Castino, Minnesota	9
1982—	Willie Wilson, Kansas City	15
1983—	Robin Yount, Milwaukee	10
1984—	Dave Collins, Toronto	15
—	Lloyd Moseby, Toronto	15
1985—	Willie Wilson, Kansas City	21
1986—	Brett Butler, Cleveland	14
1987—	Willie Wilson, Kansas City	15
1988—	Harold Reynolds, Seattle	11
—	Willie Wilson, Kansas City	11

Year	Player, Club	No.
—	Robin Yount, Milwaukee	11
1989—	Ruben Sierra, Texas	14
1990—	Tony Fernandez, Toronto	17
1991—	Lance Johnson, Chicago	13
—	Paul Molitor, Milwaukee	13
1992—	Lance Johnson, Chicago	12
1993—	Lance Johnson, Chicago	14
1994—	Lance Johnson, Chicago	14

NATIONAL LEAGUE

Year	Player, Club	No.
1876—	Ross Barnes, Chicago	14
1877—	Deacon White, Boston	11
1878—	Tom York, Providence	10
1879—	Buttercup Dickerson, Cincinnati	14
1880—	Harry Stovey, Worcester	14
1881—	Jack Rowe, Buffalo	11
1882—	Roger Connor, Troy	17
1883—	Dan Brouthers, Buffalo	17
1884—	Buck Ewing, New York	18
1885—	Roger Connor, New York	15
—	Jim O'Rourke, New York	15
1886—	Roger Connor, New York	19
1887—	Sam Thompson, Detroit	23
1888—	Roger Connor, New York	17
—	Dick Johnston, Boston	17
1889—	Roger Connor, New York	17
—	Jim Fogarty, Philadelphia	17
—	Walt Wilmot, Washington	17
1890—	Bid McPhee, Cincinnati	25
1891—	Jake Beckley, Pittsburgh	20
1892—	Dan Brouthers, Brooklyn	20
1893—	Perry Werden, St. Louis	33
1894—	Heinie Reitz, Baltimore	29
1895—	Kip Selbach, Washington	22
—	Sam Thompson, Philadelphia	22
1896—	Tom McCreery, Louisville	21
—	George Van Haltren, New York	21
1897—	Harry Davis, Pittsburgh	28
1898—	John Anderson, Brooklyn/Washington	19
1899—	Jimmy Williams, Pittsburgh	27
1900—	Honus Wagner, Pittsburgh	22
1901—	Jimmy Sheckard, Brooklyn	21
1902—	Sam Crawford, Cincinnati	23
1903—	Honus Wagner, Pittsburgh	19
1904—	Harry Lumley, Brooklyn	18
1905—	Cy Seymour, Cincinnati	21
1906—	Fred Clarke, Pittsburgh	13
—	Frank Schulte, Chicago	13
1907—	John Ganzel, Cincinnati	16
—	Whitey Alperman, Brooklyn	16
1908—	Honus Wagner, Pittsburgh	19
1909—	Mike Mitchell, Cincinnati	17
1910—	Mike Mitchell, Cincinnati	18
1911—	Larry Doyle, New York	25
1912—	Chief Wilson, Pittsburgh	36
1913—	Vic Saier, Chicago	21
1914—	Max Carey, Pittsburgh	17
1915—	Tommy Long, St. Louis	25
1916—	Bill Hinchman, Pittsburgh	16
1917—	Rogers Hornsby, St. Louis	17
1918—	Jake Daubert, Brooklyn	15
1919—	Hy Myers, Brooklyn	14
—	Billy Southworth, Pittsburgh	14
1920—	Hy Myers, Brooklyn	22
1921—	Rogers Hornsby, St. Louis	18
—	Ray Powell, Boston	18
1922—	Jake Daubert, Cincinnati	22
1923—	Max Carey, Pittsburgh	19
—	Pie Traynor, Pittsburgh	19
1924—	Edd Roush, Cincinnati	21
1925—	Kiki Cuyler, Pittsburgh	26
1926—	Paul Waner, Pittsburgh	22
1927—	Paul Waner, Pittsburgh	18
1928—	Jim Bottomley, St. Louis	20

Year	Player, Club	No.
1929	Lloyd Waner, Pittsburgh	20
1930	Adam Comorosky, Pittsburgh	23
1931	Bill Terry, New York	20
1932	Babe Herman, Cincinnati	19
1933	Arky Vaughan, Pittsburgh	19
1934	Joe Medwick, St. Louis	18
1935	Ival Goodman, Cincinnati	18
1936	Ival Goodman, Cincinnati	14
1937	Arky Vaughan, Pittsburgh	17
1938	Johnny Mize, St. Louis	16
1939	Billy Herman, Chicago	18
1940	Arky Vaughan, Pittsburgh	15
1941	Pete Reiser, Brooklyn	17
1942	Enos Slaughter, St. Louis	17
1943	Stan Musial, St. Louis	20
1944	Johnny Barrett, Pittsburgh	19
1945	Luis Olmo, Brooklyn	13
1946	Stan Musial, St. Louis	20
1947	Harry Walker, St. Louis/Philadelphia	16
1948	Stan Musial, St. Louis	18
1949	Stan Musial, St. Louis	13
	Enos Slaughter, St. Louis	13
1950	Richie Ashburn, Philadelphia	14
1951	Stan Musial, St. Louis	12
	Gus Bell, Pittsburgh	12
1952	Bobby Thomson, New York	14
1953	Jim Gilliam, Brooklyn	17
1954	Willie Mays, New York	13
1955	Willie Mays, New York	13
	Dale Long, Pittsburgh	13
1956	Billy Bruton, Milwaukee	15
1957	Willie Mays, New York	20
1958	Richie Ashburn, Philadelphia	13
1959	Wally Moon, Los Angeles	11
	Charlie Neal, Los Angeles	11
1960	Billy Bruton, Milwaukee	13
1961	George Altman, Chicago	12
1962	Johnny Callison, Philadelphia	10
	Bill Virdon, Pittsburgh	10
	Willie Davis, Los Angeles	10
	Maury Wills, Los Angeles	10
1963	Vada Pinson, Cincinnati	14
1964	Dick Allen, Philadelphia	13
	Ron Santo, Chicago	13
1965	Johnny Callison, Philadelphia	16
1966	Tim McCarver, St. Louis	13
1967	Vada Pinson, Cincinnati	13
1968	Lou Brock, St. Louis	14
1969	Roberto Clemente, Pittsburgh	12
1970	Willie Davis, Los Angeles	16
1971	Joe Morgan, Houston	11
	Roger Metzger, Houston	11
1972	Larry Bowa, Philadelphia	13
1973	Roger Metzger, Houston	14
1974	Ralph Garr, Atlanta	17
1975	Ralph Garr, Atlanta	11
1976	Dave Cash, Philadelphia	12
1977	Garry Templeton, St. Louis	18
1978	Garry Templeton, St. Louis	13
1979	Garry Templeton, St. Louis	19
1980	Omar Moreno, Pittsburgh	13
	Rodney Scott, Montreal	13
1981	Craig Reynolds, Houston	12
	Gene Richards, San Diego	12
1982	Dickie Thon, Houston	10
1983	Brett Butler, Atlanta	13
1984	Juan Samuel, Philadelphia	19
	Ryne Sandberg, Chicago	19
1985	Willie McGee, St. Louis	18
1986	Mitch Webster, Montreal	13
1987	Juan Samuel, Philadelphia	15
1988	Andy Van Slyke, Pittsburgh	15
1989	Robby Thompson, San Francisco	11
1990	Mariano Duncan, Cincinnati	11
1991	Ray Lankford, St. Louis	15
1992	Deion Sanders, Atlanta	14

Year	Player, Club	No.
1993	Steve Finley, Houston	13
1994	Brett Butler, Los Angeles	9
	Darren Lewis, San Francisco	9

HOME RUNS

AMERICAN LEAGUE

Year	Player, Club	No.
1901	Nap Lajoie, Philadelphia	14
1902	Socks Seybold, Philadelphia	16
1903	Buck Freeman, Boston	13
1904	Harry Davis, Philadelphia	10
1905	Harry Davis, Philadelphia	8
1906	Harry Davis, Philadelphia	12
1907	Harry Davis, Philadelphia	8
1908	Sam Crawford, Detroit	7
1909	Ty Cobb, Detroit	9
1910	Jake Stahl, Boston	10
1911	Home Run Baker, Philadelphia	11
1912	Home Run Baker, Philadelphia	10
	Tris Speaker, Boston	10
1913	Home Run Baker, Philadelphia	12
1914	Home Run Baker, Philadelphia	9
1915	Braggo Roth, Chicago/Cleveland	7
1916	Wally Pipp, New York	12
1917	Wally Pipp, New York	9
1918	Babe Ruth, Boston	11
	Tilly Walker, Philadelphia	11
1919	Babe Ruth, Boston	29
1920	Babe Ruth, New York	54
1921	Babe Ruth, New York	59
1922	Ken Williams, St. Louis	39
1923	Babe Ruth, New York	41
1924	Babe Ruth, New York	46
1925	Bob Meusel, New York	33
1926	Babe Ruth, New York	47
1927	Babe Ruth, New York	60
1928	Babe Ruth, New York	54
1929	Babe Ruth, New York	46
1930	Babe Ruth, New York	49
1931	Babe Ruth, New York	46
	Lou Gehrig, New York	46
1932	Jimmie Foxx, Philadelphia	58
1933	Jimmie Foxx, Philadelphia	48
1934	Lou Gehrig, New York	49
1935	Jimmie Foxx, Philadelphia	36
	Hank Greenberg, Detroit	36
1936	Lou Gehrig, New York	49
1937	Joe DiMaggio, New York	46
1938	Hank Greenberg, Detroit	58
1939	Jimmie Foxx, Boston	35
1940	Hank Greenberg, Detroit	41
1941	Ted Williams, Boston	37
1942	Ted Williams, Boston	36
1943	Rudy York, Detroit	34
1944	Nick Etten, New York	22
1945	Vern Stephens, St. Louis	24
1946	Hank Greenberg, Detroit	44
1947	Ted Williams, Boston	32
1948	Joe DiMaggio, New York	39
1949	Ted Williams, Boston	43
1950	Al Rosen, Cleveland	37
1951	Gus Zernial, Chicago/Philadelphia	33
1952	Larry Doby, Cleveland	32
1953	Al Rosen, Cleveland	43
1954	Larry Doby, Cleveland	32
1955	Mickey Mantle, New York	37
1956	Mickey Mantle, New York	52
1957	Roy Sievers, Washington	42
1958	Mickey Mantle, New York	42
1959	Rocky Colavito, Cleveland	42
	Harmon Killebrew, Washington	42
1960	Mickey Mantle, New York	40
1961	Roger Maris, New York	61
1962	Harmon Killebrew, Minnesota	48

Year	Player, Club	No.
1963—	Harmon Killebrew, Minnesota	45
1964—	Harmon Killebrew, Minnesota	49
1965—	Tony Conigilaro, Boston	32
1966—	Frank Robinson, Baltimore	49
1967—	Harmon Killebrew, Minnesota	44
	—Carl Yastrzemski, Boston	44
1968—	Frank Howard, Washington	44
1969—	Harmon Killebrew, Minnesota	49
1970—	Frank Howard, Washington	44
1971—	Bill Melton, Chicago	33
1972—	Dick Allen, Chicago	37
1973—	Reggie Jackson, Oakland	32
1974—	Dick Allen, Chicago	32
1975—	Reggie Jackson, Oakland	36
	—George Scott, Milwaukee	36
1976—	Graig Nettles, New York	32
1977—	Jim Rice, Boston	39
1978—	Jim Rice, Boston	46
1979—	Gorman Thomas, Milwaukee	45
1980—	Reggie Jackson, New York	41
	—Ben Oglivie, Milwaukee	41
1981—	Tony Armas, Oakland	22
	—Dwight Evans, Boston	22
	—Bobby Grich, California	22
	—Eddie Murray, Baltimore	22
1982—	Reggie Jackson, California	39
	—Gorman Thomas, Milwaukee	39
1983—	Jim Rice, Boston	39
1984—	Tony Armas, Boston	43
1985—	Darrell Evans, Detroit	40
1986—	Jesse Barfield, Toronto	40
1987—	Mark McGwire, Oakland	49
1988—	Jose Canseco, Oakland	42
1989—	Fred McGriff, Toronto	36
1990—	Cecil Fielder, Detroit	51
1991—	Jose Canseco, Oakland	44
	—Cecil Fielder, Detroit	44
1992—	Juan Gonzalez, Texas	43
1993—	Juan Gonzalez, Texas	46
1994—	Ken Griffey Jr., Seattle	40

NATIONAL LEAGUE

Year	Player, Club	No.
1876—	George Hall, Philadelphia	5
1877—	George Shaffer, Louisville	3
1878—	Paul Hines, Providence	4
1879—	Charley Jones, Boston	9
1880—	Jim O'Rourke, Boston	6
	—Harry Stovey, Worcester	6
1881—	Dan Brouthers, Buffalo	8
1882—	George Wood, Detroit	7
1883—	Buck Ewing, New York	10
1884—	Ned Williamson, Chicago	27
1885—	Abner Dalrymple, Chicago	11
1886—	Hardy Richardson, Detroit	11
1887—	Roger Connor, New York	17
	—Billy O'Brien, Washington	17
1888—	Roger Connor, New York	14
1889—	Sam Thompson, Philadelphia	20
1890—	Walt Wilmot, Chicago	14
1891—	Harry Stovey, Boston	16
	—Mike Tiernan, New York	16
1892—	Bug Holliday, Cincinnati	13
1893—	Ed Delahanty, Philadelphia	19
1894—	Hugh Duffy, Boston	18
	—Bobby Lowe, Boston	18
1895—	Bill Joyce, Washington	17
1896—	Ed Delahanty, Philadelphia	13
	—Sam Thompson, Philadelphia	13
1897—	Nap Lajoie, Philadelphia	10
1898—	Jimmy Collins, Boston	14
1899—	Buck Freeman, Washington	25
1900—	Herman Long, Boston	12
1901—	Sam Crawford, Cincinnati	16
1902—	Tommy Leach, Pittsburgh	6

Year	Player, Club	No.
1903—	Jimmy Sheckard, Brooklyn	9
1904—	Harry Lumley, Brooklyn	9
1905—	Fred Odwell, Cincinnati	9
1906—	Tim Jordan, Brooklyn	12
1907—	Dave Brain, Boston	10
1908—	Tim Jordan, Brooklyn	12
1909—	Red Murray, New York	7
1910—	Fred Beck, Boston	10
	—Frank Schulte, Chicago	10
1911—	Frank Schulte, Chicago	21
1912—	Heinie Zimmerman, Chicago	14
1913—	Gavvy Cravath, Philadelphia	19
1914—	Gavvy Cravath, Philadelphia	19
1915—	Gavvy Cravath, Philadelphia	24
1916—	Dave Robertson, New York	12
	—Cy Williams, Chicago	12
1917—	Dave Robertson, New York	12
	—Gavvy Cravath, Philadelphia	12
1918—	Gavvy Cravath, Philadelphia	8
1919—	Gavvy Cravath, Philadelphia	12
1920—	Cy Williams, Philadelphia	15
1921—	George Kelly, New York	23
1922—	Rogers Hornsby, St. Louis	42
1923—	Cy Williams, Philadelphia	41
1924—	Jack Fournier, Brooklyn	27
1925—	Rogers Hornsby, St. Louis	39
1926—	Hack Wilson, Chicago	21
1927—	Hack Wilson, Chicago	30
	—Cy Williams, Philadelphia	30
1928—	Hack Wilson, Chicago	31
	—Jim Bottomley, St. Louis	31
1929—	Chuck Klein, Philadelphia	43
1930—	Hack Wilson, Chicago	56
1931—	Chuck Klein, Philadelphia	31
1932—	Chuck Klein, Philadelphia	38
	—Mel Ott, New York	38
1933—	Chuck Klein, Philadelphia	28
1934—	Rip Collins, St. Louis	35
	—Mel Ott, New York	35
1935—	Wally Berger, Boston	34
1936—	Mel Ott, New York	33
1937—	Mel Ott, New York	31
	—Joe Medwick, St. Louis	31
1938—	Mel Ott, New York	36
1939—	Johnny Mize, St. Louis	28
1940—	Johnny Mize, St. Louis	43
1941—	Dolf Camilli, Brooklyn	34
1942—	Mel Ott, New York	30
1943—	Bill Nicholson, Chicago	29
1944—	Bill Nicholson, Chicago	33
1945—	Tommy Holmes, Boston	28
1946—	Ralph Kiner, Pittsburgh	23
1947—	Ralph Kiner, Pittsburgh	51
	—Johnny Mize, New York	51
1948—	Ralph Kiner, Pittsburgh	40
	—Johnny Mize, New York	40
1949—	Ralph Kiner, Pittsburgh	54
1950—	Ralph Kiner, Pittsburgh	47
1951—	Ralph Kiner, Pittsburgh	42
1952—	Ralph Kiner, Pittsburgh	37
	—Hank Sauer, Chicago	37
1953—	Eddie Mathews, Milwaukee	47
1954—	Ted Kluszewski, Cincinnati	49
1955—	Willie Mays, New York	51
1956—	Duke Snider, Brooklyn	43
1957—	Hank Aaron, Milwaukee	44
1958—	Ernie Banks, Chicago	47
1959—	Eddie Mathews, Milwaukee	46
1960—	Ernie Banks, Chicago	41
1961—	Orlando Cepeda, San Francisco	46
1962—	Willie Mays, San Francisco	49
1963—	Hank Aaron, Milwaukee	44
	—Willie McCovey, San Francisco	44
1964—	Willie Mays, San Francisco	47
1965—	Willie Mays, San Francisco	52
1966—	Hank Aaron, Atlanta	44

Year	Player, Club	No.
1967	Hank Aaron, Atlanta	39
1968	Willie McCovey, San Francisco	36
1969	Willie McCovey, San Francisco	45
1970	Johnny Bench, Cincinnati	45
1971	Willie Stargell, Pittsburgh	48
1972	Johnny Bench, Cincinnati	40
1973	Willie Stargell, Pittsburgh	44
1974	Mike Schmidt, Philadelphia	36
1975	Mike Schmidt, Philadelphia	38
1976	Mike Schmidt, Philadelphia	38
1977	George Foster, Cincinnati	52
1978	George Foster, Cincinnati	40
1979	Dave Kingman, Chicago	48
1980	Mike Schmidt, Philadelphia	48
1981	Mike Schmidt, Philadelphia	31
1982	Dave Kingman, New York	37
1983	Mike Schmidt, Philadelphia	40
1984	Dale Murphy, Atlanta	36
	Mike Schmidt, Philadelphia	36
1985	Dale Murphy, Atlanta	37
1986	Mike Schmidt, Philadelphia	37
1987	Andre Dawson, Chicago	49
1988	Darryl Strawberry, New York	39
1989	Kevin Mitchell, San Francisco	47
1990	Ryne Sandberg, Chicago	40
1991	Howard Johnson, New York	38
1992	Fred McGriff, San Diego	35
1993	Barry Bonds, San Francisco	46
1994	Matt Williams, San Francisco	43

TOTAL BASES

AMERICAN LEAGUE

Year	Player, Club	No.
1901	Nap Lajoie, Philadelphia	345
1902	Buck Freeman, Boston	287
1903	Buck Freeman, Boston	281
1904	Nap Lajoie, Cleveland	304
1905	George Stone, St. Louis	260
1906	George Stone, St. Louis	288
1907	Ty Cobb, Detroit	286
1908	Ty Cobb, Detroit	276
1909	Ty Cobb, Detroit	296
1910	Nap Lajoie, Cleveland	304
1911	Ty Cobb, Detroit	367
1912	Joe Jackson, Cleveland	331
1913	Sam Crawford, Detroit	298
1914	Tris Speaker, Boston	287
1915	Ty Cobb, Detroit	274
1916	Joe Jackson, Chicago	293
1917	Ty Cobb, Detroit	336
1918	George H. Burns, Philadelphia	236
1919	Babe Ruth, Boston	284
1920	George Sisler, St. Louis	399
1921	Babe Ruth, New York	457
1922	Ken Williams, St. Louis	367
1923	Babe Ruth, New York	399
1924	Babe Ruth, New York	391
1925	Al Simmons, Philadelphia	392
1926	Babe Ruth, New York	365
1927	Lou Gehrig, New York	447
1928	Babe Ruth, New York	380
1929	Al Simmons, Philadelphia	373
1930	Lou Gehrig, New York	419
1931	Lou Gehrig, New York	410
1932	Jimmie Foxx, Philadelphia	438
1933	Jimmie Foxx, Philadelphia	403
1934	Lou Gehrig, New York	409
1935	Hank Greenberg, Detroit	389
1936	Hal Trosky, Cleveland	405
1937	Joe DiMaggio, New York	418
1938	Jimmie Foxx, Philadelphia	398
1939	Ted Williams, Boston	344
1940	Hank Greenberg, Detroit	384
1941	Joe DiMaggio, New York	348

Year	Player, Club	No.
1942	Ted Williams, Boston	338
1943	Rudy York, Detroit	301
1944	Johnny Lindell, New York	297
1945	George Stirnweiss, New York	301
1946	Ted Williams, Boston	343
1947	Ted Williams, Boston	335
1948	Joe DiMaggio, New York	355
1949	Ted Williams, Boston	368
1950	Walt Dropo, Boston	326
1951	Ted Williams, Boston	295
1952	Al Rosen, Cleveland	297
1953	Al Rosen, Cleveland	367
1954	Minnie Minoso, Chicago	304
1955	Al Kaline, Detroit	321
1956	Mickey Mantle, New York	376
1957	Roy Sievers, Washington	331
1958	Mickey Mantle, New York	307
1959	Rocky Colavito, Cleveland	301
1960	Mickey Mantle, New York	294
1961	Roger Maris, New York	366
1962	Rocky Colavito, Detroit	309
1963	Dick Stuart, Boston	319
1964	Tony Oliva, Minnesota	374
1965	Zoilo Versalles, Minnesota	308
1966	Frank Robinson, Baltimore	367
1967	Carl Yastrzemski, Boston	360
1968	Frank Howard, Washington	330
1969	Frank Howard, Washington	340
1970	Carl Yastrzemski, Boston	335
1971	Reggie Smith, Boston	302
1972	Bobby Murcer, New York	314
1973	Dave May, Milwaukee	295
	George Scott, Milwaukee	295
	Sal Bando, Oakland	295
1974	Joe Rudi, Oakland	287
1975	George Scott, Milwaukee	318
1976	George Brett, Kansas City	298
1977	Jim Rice, Boston	382
1978	Jim Rice, Boston	406
1979	Jim Rice, Boston	369
1980	Cecil Cooper, Milwaukee	335
1981	Dwight Evans, Boston	215
1982	Robin Yount, Milwaukee	367
1983	Jim Rice, Boston	344
1984	Tony Armas, Boston	339
1985	Don Mattingly, New York	370
1986	Don Mattingly, New York	388
1987	George Bell, Toronto	369
1988	Kirby Puckett, Minnesota	358
1989	Ruben Sierra, Texas	344
1990	Cecil Fielder, Detroit	339
1991	Cal Ripken, Baltimore	368
1992	Kirby Puckett, Minnesota	313
1993	Ken Griffey Jr., Seattle	359
1994	Albert Belle, Cleveland	294

NATIONAL LEAGUE

Year	Player, Club	No.
1900	Elmer Flick, Philadelphia	305
1901	Jesse Burkett, St. Louis	313
1902	Sam Crawford, Cincinnati	256
1903	Ginger Beaumont, Pittsburgh	272
1904	Honus Wagner, Pittsburgh	255
1905	Cy Seymour, Cincinnati	325
1906	Honus Wagner, Pittsburgh	237
1907	Honus Wagner, Pittsburgh	264
1908	Honus Wagner, Pittsburgh	308
1909	Honus Wagner, Pittsburgh	242
1910	Sherry Magee, Philadelphia	263
1911	Frank Schulte, Chicago	308
1912	Heinie Zimmerman, Chicago	318
1913	Gavvy Cravath, Philadelphia	298
1914	Sherry Magee, Philadelphia	277
1915	Gavvy Cravath, Philadelphia	266
1916	Zack Wheat, Brooklyn	262

Year	Player, Club	No.
1917	Rogers Hornsby, St. Louis	253
1918	Charlie Hollocher, Chicago	202
1919	Hy Myers, Brooklyn	223
1920	Rogers Hornsby, St. Louis	329
1921	Rogers Hornsby, St. Louis	378
1922	Rogers Hornsby, St. Louis	450
1923	Frankie Frisch, New York	311
1924	Rogers Hornsby, St. Louis	373
1925	Rogers Hornsby, St. Louis	381
1926	Jim Bottomley, St. Louis	305
1927	Paul Waner, Pittsburgh	342
1928	Jim Bottomley, St. Louis	362
1929	Rogers Hornsby, Chicago	409
1930	Chuck Klein, Philadelphia	445
1931	Chuck Klein, Philadelphia	347
1932	Chuck Klein, Philadelphia	420
1933	Chuck Klein, Philadelphia	365
1934	Rip Collins, St. Louis	369
1935	Joe Medwick, St. Louis	365
1936	Joe Medwick, St. Louis	367
1937	Joe Medwick, St. Louis	406
1938	Johnny Mize, St. Louis	326
1939	Johnny Mize, St. Louis	353
1940	Johnny Mize, St. Louis	368
1941	Pete Reiser, Brooklyn	299
1942	Enos Slaughter, St. Louis	292
1943	Stan Musial, St. Louis	347
1944	Bill Nicholson, Chicago	317
1945	Tommy Holmes, Boston	367
1946	Stan Musial, St. Louis	366
1947	Ralph Kiner, Pittsburgh	361
1948	Stan Musial, St. Louis	429
1949	Stan Musial, St. Louis	382
1950	Duke Snider, Brooklyn	343
1951	Stan Musial, St. Louis	355
1952	Stan Musial, St. Louis	311
1953	Duke Snider, Brooklyn	370
1954	Duke Snider, Brooklyn	378
1955	Willie Mays, New York	382
1956	Hank Aaron, Milwaukee	340
1957	Hank Aaron, Milwaukee	369
1958	Ernie Banks, Chicago	379
1959	Hank Aaron, Milwaukee	400
1960	Hank Aaron, Milwaukee	334
1961	Hank Aaron, Milwaukee	358
1962	Willie Mays, San Francisco	382
1963	Hank Aaron, Milwaukee	370
1964	Dick Allen, Philadelphia	352
1965	Willie Mays, San Francisco	360
1966	Felipe Alou, Atlanta	355
1967	Hank Aaron, Atlanta	344
1968	Billy Williams, Chicago	321
1969	Hank Aaron, Atlanta	332
1970	Billy Williams, Chicago	373
1971	Joe Torre, St. Louis	352
1972	Billy Williams, Chicago	348
1973	Bobby Bonds, San Francisco	341
1974	Johnny Bench, Cincinnati	315
1975	Greg Luzinski, Philadelphia	322
1976	Mike Schmidt, Philadelphia	306
1977	George Foster, Cincinnati	388
1978	Dave Parker, Pittsburgh	340
1979	Dave Winfield, San Diego	333
1980	Mike Schmidt, Philadelphia	342
1981	Mike Schmidt, Philadelphia	228
1982	Al Oliver, Montreal	317
1983	Andre Dawson, Montreal	341
1984	Dale Murphy, Atlanta	332
1985	Dave Parker, Cincinnati	350
1986	Dave Parker, Cincinnati	304
1987	Andre Dawson, Chicago	353
1988	Andres Galarraga, Montreal	329
1989	Kevin Mitchell, San Francisco	345
1990	Ryne Sandberg, Chicago	344
1991	Will Clark, San Francisco	303
	Terry Pendleton, Atlanta	303

Year	Player, Club	No.
1992	Gary Sheffield, San Diego	323
1993	Barry Bonds, San Francisco	365
1994	Jeff Bagwell, Houston	300

RUNS BATTED IN

AMERICAN LEAGUE

Year	Player, Club	No.
1907	Ty Cobb, Detroit	116
1908	Ty Cobb, Detroit	101
1909	Ty Cobb, Detroit	115
1910	Sam Crawford, Detroit	115
1911	Ty Cobb, Detroit	144
1912	Home Run Baker, Philadelphia	133
1913	Home Run Baker, Philadelphia	126
1914	Sam Crawford, Detroit	112
1915	Sam Crawford, Detroit	116
1916	Wally Pipp, New York	99
1917	Bobby Veach, Detroit	115
1918	George H. Burns, Philadelphia	74
	Bobby Veach, Detroit	74
1919	Babe Ruth, Boston	112
1920	Babe Ruth, New York	137
1921	Babe Ruth, New York	171
1922	Ken Williams, St. Louis	155
1923	Babe Ruth, New York	131
1924	Goose Goslin, Washington	129
1925	Bob Meusel, New York	138
1926	Babe Ruth, New York	145
1927	Lou Gehrig, New York	175
1928	Babe Ruth, New York	142
	Lou Gehrig, New York	142
1929	Al Simmons, Philadelphia	157
1930	Lou Gehrig, New York	174
1931	Lou Gehrig, New York	184
1932	Jimmie Foxx, Philadelphia	169
1933	Jimmie Foxx, Philadelphia	163
1934	Lou Gehrig, New York	165
1935	Hank Greenberg, Detroit	170
1936	Hal Trosky, Cleveland	162
1937	Hank Greenberg, Detroit	183
1938	Jimmie Foxx, Boston	175
1939	Ted Williams, Boston	145
1940	Hank Greenberg, Detroit	150
1941	Joe DiMaggio, New York	125
1942	Ted Williams, Boston	137
1943	Rudy York, Detroit	118
1944	Vern Stephens, St. Louis	109
1945	Nick Etten, New York	111
1946	Hank Greenberg, Detroit	127
1947	Ted Williams, Boston	114
1948	Joe DiMaggio, New York	155
1949	Ted Williams, Boston	159
	Vern Stephens, Boston	159
1950	Walt Dropo, Boston	144
	Vern Stephens, Boston	144
1951	Gus Zernial, Chicago-Philadelphia	129
1952	Al Rosen, Cleveland	105
1953	Al Rosen, Cleveland	145
1954	Larry Doby, Cleveland	126
1955	Ray Boone, Detroit	116
	Jackie Jensen, Boston	116
1956	Mickey Mantle, New York	130
1957	Roy Sievers, Washington	114
1958	Jackie Jensen, Boston	122
1959	Jackie Jensen, Boston	112
1960	Roger Maris, New York	112
1961	Roger Maris, New York	142
1962	Harmon Killebrew, Minnesota	126
1963	Dick Stuart, Boston	118
1964	Brooks Robinson, Baltimore	118
1965	Rocky Colavito, Cleveland	108
1966	Frank Robinson, Baltimore	122
1967	Carl Yastrzemski, Boston	121
1968	Ken Harrelson, Boston	109

Year	Player, Club	No.
1969—Harmon Killebrew, Minnesota		140
1970—Frank Howard, Washington		126
1971—Harmon Killebrew, Minnesota		119
1972—Dick Allen, Chicago		113
1973—Reggie Jackson, Oakland		117
1974—Jeff Burroughs, Texas		118
1975—George Scott, Milwaukee		109
1976—Lee May, Baltimore		109
1977—Larry Hisle, Minnesota		119
1978—Jim Rice, Boston		139
1979—Don Baylor, California		139
1980—Cecil Cooper, Milwaukee		122
1981—Eddie Murray, Baltimore		78
1982—Hal McRae, Kansas City		133
1983—Cecil Cooper, Milwaukee		126
—Jim Rice, Boston		126
1984—Tony Armas, Boston		123
1985—Don Mattingly, New York		145
1986—Joe Carter, Cleveland		121
1987—George Bell, Toronto		134
1988—Jose Canseco, Oakland		124
1989—Ruben Sierra, Texas		119
1990—Cecil Fielder, Detroit		132
1991—Cecil Fielder, Detroit		133
1992—Cecil Fielder, Detroit		124
1993—Albert Belle, Cleveland		129
1994—Kirby Puckett, Minnesota		112

NATIONAL LEAGUE

Year	Player, Club	No.
1907—Honus Wagner, Pittsburgh		91
1908—Honus Wagner, Pittsburgh		106
1909—Honus Wagner, Pittsburgh		102
1910—Sherry Magee, Philadelphia		116
1911—Frank Schulte, Chicago		121
1912—Heinie Zimmerman, Chicago		98
1913—Gavvy Cravath, Philadelphia		118
1914—Sherry Magee, Philadelphia		101
1915—Gavvy Cravath, Philadelphia		118
1916—Hal Chase, Cincinnati		84
1917—Heinie Zimmerman, New York		100
1918—Fred Merkle, Chicago		71
1919—Hy Myers, Brooklyn		72
1920—George Kelly, New York		94
—Rogers Hornsby, St. Louis		94
1921—Rogers Hornsby, St. Louis		126
1922—Rogers Hornsby, St. Louis		152
1923—Irish Meusel, New York		125
1924—George Kelly, New York		136
1925—Rogers Hornsby, St. Louis		143
1926—Jim Bottomley, St. Louis		120
1927—Paul Waner, Pittsburgh		131
1928—Jim Bottomley, St. Louis		136
1929—Hack Wilson, Chicago		159
1930—Hack Wilson, Chicago		190
1931—Chuck Klein, Philadelphia		121
1932—Don Hurst, Philadelphia		143
1933—Chuck Klein, Philadelphia		120
1934—Mel Ott, New York		135
1935—Wally Berger, Boston		130
1936—Joe Medwick, St. Louis		138
1937—Joe Medwick, St. Louis		154
1938—Joe Medwick, St. Louis		122
1939—Frank McCormick, Cincinnati		128
1940—Johnny Mize, St. Louis		137
1941—Dolf Camilli, Brooklyn		120
1942—Johnny Mize, New York		110
1943—Bill Nicholson, Chicago		128
1944—Bill Nicholson, Chicago		122
1945—Dixie Walker, Brooklyn		124
1946—Enos Slaughter, St. Louis		130
1947—Johnny Mize, New York		138
1948—Stan Musial, St. Louis		131
1949—Ralph Kiner, Pittsburgh		127
1950—Del Ennis, Philadelphia		126

Year	Player, Club	No.
1951—Monte Irvin, New York		121
1952—Hank Sauer, Chicago		121
1953—Roy Campanella, Brooklyn		142
1954—Ted Kluszewski, Cincinnati		141
1955—Duke Snider, Brooklyn		136
1956—Stan Musial, St. Louis		109
1957—Hank Aaron, Milwaukee		132
1958—Ernie Banks, Chicago		129
1959—Ernie Banks, Chicago		143
1960—Hank Aaron, Milwaukee		126
1961—Orlando Cepeda, San Francisco		142
1962—Tommy Davis, Los Angeles		153
1963—Hank Aaron, Milwaukee		130
1964—Ken Boyer, St. Louis		119
1965—Deron Johnson, Cincinnati		130
1966—Hank Aaron, Atlanta		127
1967—Orlando Cepeda, St. Louis		111
1968—Willie McCovey, San Francisco		105
1969—Willie McCovey, San Francisco		126
1970—Johnny Bench, Cincinnati		148
1971—Joe Torre, St. Louis		137
1972—Johnny Bench, Cincinnati		125
1973—Willie Stargell, Pittsburgh		119
1974—Johnny Bench, Cincinnati		129
1975—Greg Luzinski, Philadelphia		120
1976—George Foster, Cincinnati		121
1977—George Foster, Cincinnati		149
1978—George Foster, Cincinnati		120
1979—Dave Winfield, San Diego		118
1980—Mike Schmidt, Philadelphia		121
1981—Mike Schmidt, Philadelphia		91
1982—Dale Murphy, Atlanta		109
—Al Oliver, Montreal		109
1983—Dale Murphy, Atlanta		121
1984—Gary Carter, Montreal		106
—Mike Schmidt, Philadelphia		106
1985—Dave Parker, Cincinnati		125
1986—Mike Schmidt, Philadelphia		119
1987—Andre Dawson, Chicago		137
1988—Will Clark, San Francisco		109
1989—Kevin Mitchell, San Francisco		125
1990—Matt Williams, San Francisco		122
1991—Howard Johnson, New York		117
1992—Darren Daulton, Philadelphia		109
1993—Barry Bonds, San Francisco		123
1994—Jeff Bagwell, Houston		116

Note—Not compiled prior to 1907; officially adopted in 1920.

BASES ON BALLS

AMERICAN LEAGUE

Year	Player, Club	No.
1913—Burt Shotton, St. Louis		102
1914—Donie Bush, Detroit		112
1915—Eddie Collins, Chicago		119
1916—Burt Shotton, St. Louis		111
1917—Jack Graney, Cleveland		94
1918—Ray Chapman, Cleveland		84
1919—Jack Graney, Cleveland		105
1920—Babe Ruth, New York		148
1921—Babe Ruth, New York		144
1922—Whitey Witt, New York		89
1923—Babe Ruth, New York		170
1924—Babe Ruth, New York		142
1925—Willie Kamm, Chicago		90
—Johnny Mostil, Chicago		90
1926—Babe Ruth, New York		144
1927—Babe Ruth, New York		138
1928—Babe Ruth, New York		135
1929—Max Bishop, Philadelphia		128
1930—Babe Ruth, New York		136
1931—Babe Ruth, New York		128
1932—Babe Ruth, New York		130

Year	Player, Club	No.
1933	Babe Ruth, New York	114
1934	Jimmie Foxx, Philadelphia	111
1935	Lou Gehrig, New York	132
1936	Lou Gehrig, New York	130
1937	Lou Gehrig, New York	127
1938	Jimmie Foxx, Boston	119
	Hank Greenberg, Detroit	119
1939	Harlond Clift, St. Louis	111
1940	Charlie Keller, New York	106
1941	Ted Williams, Boston	145
1942	Ted Williams, Boston	145
1943	Charlie Keller, New York	106
1944	Nick Etten, New York	97
1945	Roy Cullenbine, Cleveland/Detroit	112
1946	Ted Williams, Boston	156
1947	Ted Williams, Boston	162
1948	Ted Williams, Boston	126
1949	Ted Williams, Boston	162
1950	Eddie Yost, Washington	141
1951	Ted Williams, Boston	144
1952	Eddie Yost, Washington	129
1953	Eddie Yost, Washington	123
1954	Ted Williams, Boston	136
1955	Mickey Mantle, New York	113
1956	Eddie Yost, Washington	151
1957	Mickey Mantle, New York	146
1958	Mickey Mantle, New York	129
1959	Eddie Yost, Detroit	135
1960	Eddie Yost, Detroit	125
1961	Mickey Mantle, New York	126
1962	Mickey Mantle, New York	122
1963	Carl Yastrzemski, Boston	95
1964	Norm Siebern, Baltimore	106
1965	Rocky Colavito, Cleveland	93
1966	Harmon Killebrew, Minnesota	103
1967	Harmon Killebrew, Minnesota	131
1968	Carl Yastrzemski, Boston	119
1969	Harmon Killebrew, Minnesota	145
1970	Frank Howard, Washington	132
1971	Harmon Killebrew, Minnesota	114
1972	Dick Allen, Chicago	99
	Roy White, New York	99
1973	John Mayberry, Kansas City	122
1974	Gene Tenace, Oakland	110
1975	John Mayberry, Kansas City	119
1976	Mike Hargrove, Texas	97
1977	Toby Harrah, Texas	109
1978	Mike Hargrove, Texas	107
1979	Darrell Porter, Kansas City	121
1980	Willie Randolph, New York	119
1981	Dwight Evans, Boston	85
1982	Rickey Henderson, Oakland	116
1983	Rickey Henderson, Oakland	103
1984	Eddie Murray, Baltimore	107
1985	Dwight Evans, Boston	114
1986	Wade Boggs, Boston	105
1987	Brian Downing, California	106
	Dwight Evans, Boston	106
1988	Wade Boggs, Boston	125
1989	Rickey Henderson, New York/Oakland	126
1990	Mark McGwire, Oakland	110
1991	Frank Thomas, Chicago	138
1992	Mickey Tettleton, Detroit	122
	Frank Thomas, Chicago	122
1993	Tony Phillips, Detroit	132
1994	Frank Thomas, Chicago	109

NATIONAL LEAGUE

Year	Player, Club	No.
1910	Miller Huggins, St. Louis	116
1911	Jimmy Sheckard, Chicago	147
1912	Jimmy Sheckard, Chicago	122
1913	Bob Bescher, Cincinnati	94
1914	Miller Huggins, St. Louis	105
1915	Gavvy Cravath, Philadelphia	86
1916	Heinie Groh, Cincinnati	84
1917	George J. Burns, New York	75
1918	Max Carey, Pittsburgh	62
1919	George J. Burns, New York	82
1920	George J. Burns, New York	76
1921	George J. Burns, New York	80
1922	Max Carey, Pittsburgh	80
1923	George J. Burns, New York	101
1924	Rogers Hornsby, St. Louis	89
1925	Jack Fournier, Brooklyn	86
1926	Hack Wilson, Chicago	69
1927	Rogers Hornsby, New York	86
1928	Rogers Hornsby, Boston	107
1929	Mel Ott, New York	113
1930	Hack Wilson, Chicago	105
1931	Mel Ott, New York	80
1932	Mel Ott, New York	100
1933	Mel Ott, New York	75
1934	Arky Vaughan, Pittsburgh	94
1935	Arky Vaughan, Pittsburgh	97
1936	Arky Vaughan, Pittsburgh	118
1937	Mel Ott, New York	102
1938	Dolf Camilli, Brooklyn	119
1939	Dolf Camilli, Brooklyn	110
1940	Elbie Fletcher, Pittsburgh	119
1941	Elbie Fletcher, Pittsburgh	118
1942	Mel Ott, New York	109
1943	Augie Galan, Brooklyn	103
1944	Augie Galan, Brooklyn	101
1945	Eddie Stanky, Brooklyn	148
1946	Eddie Stanky, Brooklyn	137
1947	Hank Greenberg, Pittsburgh	104
	Pee Wee Reese, Brooklyn	104
1948	Bob Elliott, Boston	131
1949	Ralph Kiner, Pittsburgh	117
1950	Eddie Stanky, New York	144
1951	Ralph Kiner, Pittsburgh	137
1952	Ralph Kiner, Pittsburgh	110
1953	Stan Musial, St. Louis	105
1954	Richie Ashburn, Philadelphia	125
1955	Eddie Mathews, Milwaukee	109
1956	Duke Snider, Brooklyn	99
1957	Richie Ashburn, Philadelphia	94
	Johnny Temple, Cincinnati	94
1958	Richie Ashburn, Philadelphia	97
1959	Jim Gilliam, Los Angeles	96
1960	Richie Ashburn, Chicago	116
1961	Eddie Mathews, Milwaukee	93
1962	Eddie Mathews, Milwaukee	101
1963	Eddie Mathews, Milwaukee	124
1964	Ron Santo, Chicago	86
1965	Joe Morgan, Houston	97
1966	Ron Santo, Chicago	95
1967	Ron Santo, Chicago	96
1968	Ron Santo, Chicago	96
1969	Jim Wynn, Houston	148
1970	Willie McCovey, San Francisco	137
1971	Willie Mays, San Francisco	112
1972	Joe Morgan, Cincinnati	115
1973	Darrell Evans, Atlanta	124
1974	Darrell Evans, Atlanta	126
1975	Joe Morgan, Cincinnati	132
1976	Jim Wynn, Atlanta	127
1977	Gene Tenace, San Diego	125
1978	Jeff Burroughs, Atlanta	117
1979	Mike Schmidt, Philadelphia	120
1980	Dan Driessen, Cincinnati	93
	Joe Morgan, Houston	93
1981	Mike Schmidt, Philadelphia	73
1982	Mike Schmidt, Philadelphia	107
1983	Mike Schmidt, Philadelphia	128
1984	Gary Matthews, Chicago	103
1985	Dale Murphy, Atlanta	90
1986	Keith Hernandez, New York	94
1987	Jack Clark, St. Louis	136
1988	Will Clark, San Francisco	100

Year	Player, Club	No.
1989	Jack Clark, San Diego	132
1990	Jack Clark, San Diego	104
1991	Brett Butler, Los Angeles	108
1992	Barry Bonds, Pittsburgh	127
1993	Lenny Dykstra, Philadelphia	129
1994	Barry Bonds, San Francisco	74

Note—Not included in batting records in A.L. prior to 1913 and N.L. prior to 1910.

STRIKEOUTS

AMERICAN LEAGUE

Year	Player, Club	No.
1913	Danny Moeller, Washington	106
1914	Gus Williams, St. Louis	120
1915	Doc Lavan, St. Louis	83
1916	Wally Pipp, New York	82
1917	Braggo Roth, Cleveland	73
1918	Babe Ruth, Boston	58
1919	Red Shannon, Philadelphia/Boston	70
1920	Aaron Ward, New York	84
1921	Bob Meusel, New York	88
1922	Jimmie Dykes, Philadelphia	98
1923	Babe Ruth, New York	93
1924	Babe Ruth, New York	81
1925	Marty McManus, St. Louis	69
1926	Tony Lazzeri, New York	96
1927	Babe Ruth, New York	89
1928	Babe Ruth, New York	87
1929	Jimmie Foxx, Philadelphia	70
1930	Jimmie Foxx, Philadelphia	66
	Ed Morgan, Cleveland	66
1931	Jimmie Foxx, Philadelphia	84
1932	Bruce Campbell, Chicago/St. Louis	104
1933	Jimmie Foxx, Philadelphia	93
1934	Harlond Clift, St. Louis	100
1935	Jimmie Foxx, Philadelphia	99
1936	Jimmie Foxx, Boston	119
1937	Frank Crosetti, New York	105
1938	Frank Crosetti, New York	97
1939	Hank Greenberg, Detroit	95
1940	Sam Chapman, Philadelphia	96
1941	Jimmie Foxx, Boston	103
1942	Joe Gordon, New York	95
1943	Chet Laabs, St. Louis	105
1944	Pat Seerey, Cleveland	99
1945	Pat Seerey, Cleveland	97
1946	Charlie Keller, New York	101
	Pat Seerey, Cleveland	101
1947	Eddie Joost, Philadelphia	110
1948	Pat Seerey, Cleveland/Chicago	102
1949	Dick Kokos, St. Louis	91
1950	Gus Zernial, Chicago	110
1951	Gus Zernial, Chicago/Philadelphia	101
1952	Larry Doby, Cleveland	111
	Mickey Mantle, New York	111
1953	Larry Doby, Cleveland	121
1954	Mickey Mantle, New York	107
1955	Norm Zauchin, Boston	105
1956	Jim Lemon, Washington	138
1957	Jim Lemon, Washington	94
1958	Jim Lemon, Washington	120
	Mickey Mantle, New York	120
1959	Mickey Mantle, New York	126
1960	Mickey Mantle, New York	125
1961	Jake Wood, Detroit	141
1962	Harmon Killebrew, Minnesota	142
1963	Dave Nicholson, Chicago	175
1964	Nelson Mathews, Kansas City	143
1965	Zoilo Versalles, Minnesota	122
1966	George Scott, Boston	152
1967	Frank Howard, Washington	155
1968	Reggie Jackson, Oakland	171
1969	Reggie Jackson, Oakland	142
1970	Reggie Jackson, Oakland	135

Year	Player, Club	No.
1971	Reggie Jackson, Oakland	161
1972	Bobby Darwin, Minnesota	145
1973	Bobby Darwin, Minnesota	137
1974	Bobby Darwin, Minnesota	127
1975	Jeff Burroughs, Texas	155
1976	Jim Rice, Boston	123
1977	Butch Hobson, Boston	162
1978	Gary Alexander, Oakland/Cleveland	166
1979	Gorman Thomas, Milwaukee	175
1980	Gorman Thomas, Milwaukee	170
1981	Tony Armas, Oakland	115
1982	Reggie Jackson, California	156
1983	Ron Kittle, Chicago	150
1984	Tony Armas, Boston	156
1985	Steve Balboni, Kansas City	166
1986	Pete Incaviglia, Texas	185
1987	Rob Deer, Milwaukee	186
1988	Rob Deer, Milwaukee	153
	Pete Incaviglia, Texas	153
1989	Bo Jackson, Kansas City	172
1990	Cecil Fielder, Detroit	182
1991	Rob Deer, Detroit	175
1992	Dean Palmer, Texas	154
1993	Rob Deer, Detroit/Boston	169
1994	Travis Fryman, Detroit	128

NATIONAL LEAGUE

Year	Player, Club	No.
1910	John Hummel, Brooklyn	81
1911	Bob Coulson, Brooklyn	78
	Bob Bescher, Cincinnati	78
1912	Ed McDonald, Boston	91
1913	George J. Burns, New York	74
1914	Fred Merkle, New York	80
1915	Doug Baird, Pittsburgh	88
1916	Gavvy Cravath, Philadelphia	89
1917	Cy Williams, Chicago	78
1918	Ross Youngs, New York	49
	Dode Paskert, Chicago	49
1919	Ray Powell, Boston	79
1920	George Kelly, New York	92
1921	Ray Powell, Boston	85
1922	Frank Parkinson, Philadelphia	93
1923	George Grantham, Chicago	92
1924	George Grantham, Chicago	63
1925	Gabby Hartnett, Chicago	77
1926	Barney Friberg, Philadelphia	77
1927	Hack Wilson, Chicago	70
1928	Hack Wilson, Chicago	94
1929	Hack Wilson, Chicago	83
1930	Hack Wilson, Chicago	84
1931	Nick Cullop, Cincinnati	86
1932	Hack Wilson, Brooklyn	85
1933	Wally Berger, Boston	77
1934	Dolf Camilli, Chicago/Philadelphia	94
1935	Dolf Camilli, Philadelphia	113
1936	Bill Brubaker, Pittsburgh	96
1937	Vince DiMaggio, Boston	111
1938	Vince DiMaggio, Boston	134
1939	Dolf Camilli, Brooklyn	107
1940	Chet Ross, Boston	128
1941	Dolf Camilli, Brooklyn	115
1942	Vince DiMaggio, Pittsburgh	87
1943	Vince DiMaggio, Pittsburgh	126
1944	Vince DiMaggio, Pittsburgh	83
1945	Vince DiMaggio, Philadelphia	91
1946	Ralph Kiner, Pittsburgh	109
1947	Bill Nicholson, Chicago	83
1948	Hank Sauer, Cincinnati	85
1949	Duke Snider, Brooklyn	92
1950	Roy Smalley, Chicago	114
1951	Gil Hodges, Brooklyn	99
1952	Eddie Mathews, Boston	115
1953	Steve Bilko, St. Louis	125
1954	Duke Snider, Brooklyn	96

Year	Player, Club	No.
1955	Wally Post, Cincinnati	102
1956	Wally Post, Cincinnati	124
1957	Duke Snider, Brooklyn	104
1958	Harry Anderson, Philadelphia	95
1959	Wally Post, Philadelphia	101
1960	Frank Herrera, Philadelphia	136
1961	Dick Stuart, Pittsburgh	121
1962	Ken Hubbs, Chicago	129
1963	Donn Clendenon, Pittsburgh	136
1964	Dick Allen, Philadelphia	138
1965	Dick Allen, Philadelphia	150
1966	Byron Browne, Chicago	143
1967	Jim Wynn, Houston	137
1968	Donn Clendenon, Pittsburgh	163
1969	Bobby Bonds, San Francisco	187
1970	Bobby Bonds, San Francisco	189
1971	Willie Stargell, Pittsburgh	154
1972	Lee May, Houston	145
1973	Bobby Bonds, San Francisco	148
1974	Mike Schmidt, Philadelphia	138
1975	Mike Schmidt, Philadelphia	180
1976	Mike Schmidt, Philadelphia	149
1977	Greg Luzinski, Philadelphia	140
1978	Dale Murphy, Atlanta	145
1979	Dave Kingman, Chicago	131
1980	Dale Murphy, Atlanta	133
1981	Dave Kingman, New York	105
1982	Dave Kingman, New York	156
1983	Mike Schmidt, Philadelphia	148
1984	Juan Samuel, Philadelphia	168
1985	Dale Murphy, Atlanta	141
	Juan Samuel, Philadelphia	141
1986	Juan Samuel, Philadelphia	142
1987	Juan Samuel, Philadelphia	162
1988	Andres Galarraga, Montreal	153
1989	Andres Galarraga, Montreal	158
1990	Andres Galarraga, Montreal	169
1991	Delino DeShields, Montreal	151
1992	Ray Lankford, St. Louis	147
1993	Cory Snyder, Los Angeles	147
1994	Reggie Sanders, Cincinnati	114

Note—Not included in batting records in A.L. prior to 1913 and N.L. prior to 1910.

BASERUNNING

STOLEN BASES

AMERICAN LEAGUE

Year	Player, Club	No.
1901	Frank Isbell, Chicago	48
1902	Topsy Hartsel, Philadelphia	54
1903	Harry Bay, Cleveland	46
1904	Elmer Flick, Cleveland	42
	Harry Bay, Cleveland	42
1905	Danny Hoffman, Philadelphia	46
1906	Elmer Flick, Cleveland	39
	John Anderson, Washington	39
1907	Ty Cobb, Detroit	49
1908	Patsy Dougherty, Chicago	47
1909	Ty Cobb, Detroit	76
1910	Eddie Collins, Philadelphia	81
1911	Ty Cobb, Detroit	83
1912	Clyde Milan, Washington	88
1913	Clyde Milan, Washington	75
1914	Fritz Maisel, New York	74
1915	Ty Cobb, Detroit	96
1916	Ty Cobb, Detroit	68
1917	Ty Cobb, Detroit	55
1918	George Sisler, St. Louis	45
1919	Eddie Collins, Chicago	33
1920	Sam Rice, Washington	63
1921	George Sisler, St. Louis	35
1922	George Sisler, St. Louis	51
1923	Eddie Collins, Chicago	49

Year	Player, Club	No.
1924	Eddie Collins, Chicago	42
1925	Johnny Mostil, Chicago	43
1926	Johnny Mostil, Chicago	35
1927	George Sisler, St. Louis	27
1928	Buddy Myer, Boston	30
1929	Charlie Gehringer, Detroit	27
1930	Marty McManus, Detroit	23
1931	Ben Chapman, New York	61
1932	Ben Chapman, New York	38
1933	Ben Chapman, New York	27
1934	Bill Werber, Boston	40
1935	Bill Werber, Boston	29
1936	Lyn Lary, St. Louis	37
1937	Bill Werber, Philadelphia	35
	Ben Chapman, Washington/Boston	35
1938	Frank Crosetti, New York	27
1939	George Case, Washington	51
1940	George Case, Washington	35
1941	George Case, Washington	33
1942	George Case, Washington	44
1943	George Case, Washington	61
1944	George Stirnweiss, New York	55
1945	George Stirnweiss, New York	33
1946	George Case, Cleveland	28
1947	Bob Dillinger, St. Louis	34
1948	Bob Dillinger, St. Louis	28
1949	Bob Dillinger, St. Louis	20
1950	Dom DiMaggio, Boston	15
1951	Minnie Minoso, Cleveland/Chicago	31
1952	Minnie Minoso, Chicago	22
1953	Minnie Minoso, Chicago	25
1954	Jackie Jensen, Boston	22
1955	Jim Rivera, Chicago	25
1956	Luis Aparicio, Chicago	21
1957	Luis Aparicio, Chicago	28
1958	Luis Aparicio, Chicago	29
1959	Luis Aparicio, Chicago	56
1960	Luis Aparicio, Chicago	51
1961	Luis Aparicio, Chicago	53
1962	Luis Aparicio, Chicago	31
1963	Luis Aparicio, Baltimore	40
1964	Luis Aparicio, Baltimore	57
1965	Bert Campaneris, Kansas City	51
1966	Bert Campaneris, Kansas City	52
1967	Bert Campaneris, Kansas City	55
1968	Bert Campaneris, Oakland	62
1969	Tommy Harper, Seattle	73
1970	Bert Campaneris, Oakland	42
1971	Amos Otis, Kansas City	52
1972	Bert Campaneris, Oakland	52
1973	Tommy Harper, Boston	54
1974	Billy North, Oakland	54
1975	Mickey Rivers, California	70
1976	Billy North, Oakland	75
1977	Fred Patek, Kansas City	53
1978	Ron LeFlore, Detroit	68
1979	Willie Wilson, Kansas City	83
1980	Rickey Henderson, Oakland	100
1981	Rickey Henderson, Oakland	56
1982	Rickey Henderson, Oakland	130
1983	Rickey Henderson, Oakland	108
1984	Rickey Henderson, Oakland	66
1985	Rickey Henderson, New York	80
1986	Rickey Henderson, New York	87
1987	Harold Reynolds, Seattle	60
1988	Rickey Henderson, New York	93
1989	Rickey Henderson, New York/Oakland	77
1990	Rickey Henderson, Oakland	65
1991	Rickey Henderson, Oakland	58
1992	Kenny Lofton, Cleveland	66
1993	Kenny Lofton, Cleveland	70
1994	Kenny Lofton, Cleveland	60

NATIONAL LEAGUE

Year	Player, Club	No.
1886	Ed Andrews, Philadelphia	56

Year	Player, Club	No.
1887	Monte Ward, New York	111
1888	Dummy Hoy, Washington	82
1889	Jim Fogarty, Philadelphia	99
1890	Billy Hamilton, Philadelphia	102
1891	Billy Hamilton, Philadelphia	115
1892	Monte Ward, Brooklyn	94
1893	Monte Ward, New York	72
1894	Billy Hamilton, Philadelphia	99
1895	Billy Hamilton, Philadelphia	95
1896	Bill Lange, Chicago	100
1897	Bill Lange, Chicago	83
1898	Fred Clarke, Louisville	66
1899	Jimmy Sheckard, Baltimore	78
1900	Jimmy Barrett, Cincinnati	46
1901	Honus Wagner, Pittsburgh	48
1902	Honus Wagner, Pittsburgh	43
1903	Jimmy Sheckard, Brooklyn	67
	Frank Chance, Chicago	67
1904	Honus Wagner, Pittsburgh	53
1905	Billy Maloney, Chicago	59
	Art Devlin, New York	59
1906	Frank Chance, Chicago	57
1907	Honus Wagner, Pittsburgh	61
1908	Honus Wagner, Pittsburgh	53
1909	Bob Bescher, Cincinnati	54
1910	Bob Bescher, Cincinnati	70
1911	Bob Bescher, Cincinnati	81
1912	Bob Bescher, Cincinnati	67
1913	Max Carey, Pittsburgh	61
1914	George J. Burns, New York	62
1915	Max Carey, Pittsburgh	36
1916	Max Carey, Pittsburgh	63
1917	Max Carey, Pittsburgh	46
1918	Max Carey, Pittsburgh	58
1919	George J. Burns, New York	40
1920	Max Carey, Pittsburgh	52
1921	Frankie Frisch, New York	49
1922	Max Carey, Pittsburgh	51
1923	Max Carey, Pittsburgh	51
1924	Max Carey, Pittsburgh	49
1925	Max Carey, Pittsburgh	46
1926	Kiki Cuyler, Pittsburgh	35
1927	Frankie Frisch, St. Louis	48
1928	Kiki Cuyler, Chicago	37
1929	Kiki Cuyler, Chicago	43
1930	Kiki Cuyler, Chicago	37
1931	Frankie Frisch, St. Louis	28
1932	Chuck Klein, Philadelphia	20
1933	Pepper Martin, St. Louis	26
1934	Pepper Martin, St. Louis	23
1935	Augie Galan, Chicago	22
1936	Pepper Martin, St. Louis	23
1937	Augie Galan, Chicago	23
1938	Stan Hack, Chicago	16
1939	Stan Hack, Chicago	17
	Lee Handley, Pittsburgh	17
1940	Lonny Frey, Cincinnati	22
1941	Danny Murtaugh, Philadelphia	18
1942	Pete Reiser, Brooklyn	20
1943	Arky Vaughan, Brooklyn	20
1944	Johnny Barrett, Pittsburgh	28
1945	Red Schoendienst, St. Louis	26
1946	Pete Reiser, Brooklyn	34
1947	Jackie Robinson, Brooklyn	29
1948	Richie Ashburn, Philadelphia	32
1949	Jackie Robinson, Brooklyn	37
1950	Sam Jethroe, Boston	35
1951	Sam Jethroe, Boston	35
1952	Pee Wee Reese, Brooklyn	30
1953	Billy Bruton, Milwaukee	26
1954	Billy Bruton, Milwaukee	34
1955	Billy Bruton, Milwaukee	35
1956	Willie Mays, New York	40
1957	Willie Mays, New York	38
1958	Willie Mays, San Francisco	31
1959	Willie Mays, San Francisco	27

Year	Player, Club	No.
1960	Maury Wills, Los Angeles	50
1961	Maury Wills, Los Angeles	35
1962	Maury Wills, Los Angeles	104
1963	Maury Wills, Los Angeles	40
1964	Maury Wills, Los Angeles	53
1965	Maury Wills, Los Angeles	94
1966	Lou Brock, St. Louis	74
1967	Lou Brock, St. Louis	52
1968	Lou Brock, St. Louis	62
1969	Lou Brock, St. Louis	53
1970	Bobby Tolan, Cincinnati	57
1971	Lou Brock, St. Louis	64
1972	Lou Brock, St. Louis	63
1973	Lou Brock, St. Louis	70
1974	Lou Brock, St. Louis	118
1975	Dave Lopes, Los Angeles	77
1976	Dave Lopes, Los Angeles	63
1977	Frank Taveras, Pittsburgh	70
1978	Omar Moreno, Pittsburgh	71
1979	Omar Moreno, Pittsburgh	77
1980	Ron LeFlore, Montreal	97
1981	Tim Raines, Montreal	71
1982	Tim Raines, Montreal	78
1983	Tim Raines, Montreal	90
1984	Tim Raines, Montreal	75
1985	Vince Coleman, St. Louis	110
1986	Vince Coleman, St. Louis	107
1987	Vince Coleman, St. Louis	109
1988	Vince Coleman, St. Louis	81
1989	Vince Coleman, St. Louis	65
1990	Vince Coleman, St. Louis	77
1991	Marquis Grissom, Montreal	76
1992	Marquis Grissom, Montreal	78
1993	Chuck Carr, Florida	58
1994	Craig Biggio, Houston	39

PITCHING

WINNING PERCENTAGE

AMERICAN LEAGUE

Year	Pitcher, Club	W	L	Pct.
1901	Clark Griffith, Chicago	24	7	.774
1902	Bill Bernhard, Phi./Cle.	18	5	.783
1903	Cy Young, Boston	28	9	.757
1904	Jack Chesbro, New York	41	13	.759
1905	Jesse Tannehill, Boston	22	9	.710
1906	Eddie Plank, Philadelphia	19	6	.760
1907	Bill Donovan, Detroit	25	4	.862
1908	Ed Walsh Sr., Chicago	40	15	.727
1909	George Mullin, Detroit	29	8	.784
1910	Chief Bender, Philadelphia	23	5	.821
1911	Chief Bender, Philadelphia	17	5	.773
1912	Joe Wood, Boston	34	5	.872
1913	Walter Johnson, Washington	36	7	.837
1914	Chief Bender, Philadelphia	17	3	.850
1915	Joe Wood, Boston	15	5	.750
1916	Ed Cicotte, Chicago	15	7	.682
1917	Reb Russell, Chicago	15	5	.750
1918	Sam Jones, Boston	16	5	.762
1919	Ed Cicotte, Chicago	29	7	.806
1920	Jim Bagby Sr., Cleveland	31	12	.721
1921	Carl Mays, New York	27	9	.750
1922	Joe Bush, New York	26	7	.788
1923	Herb Pennock, New York	19	6	.760
1924	Walter Johnson, Washington	23	7	.767
1925	Stan Coveleski, Washington	20	5	.800
1926	George Uhle, Cleveland	27	11	.711
1927	Waite Hoyt, New York	22	7	.759
1928	Alvin Crowder, St. Louis	21	5	.808
1929	Lefty Grove, Philadelphia	20	6	.769
1930	Lefty Grove, Philadelphia	28	5	.848
1931	Lefty Grove, Philadelphia	31	4	.886
1932	Johnny Allen, New York	17	4	.810
1933	Lefty Grove, Philadelphia	24	8	.750

Year	Pitcher, Club	W	L	Pct.
1934—Lefty Gomez, New York		26	5	.839
1935—Eldon Auker, Detroit		18	7	.720
1936—Monte Pearson, New York		19	7	.731
1937—Johnny Allen, Cleveland		15	1	.938
1938—Red Ruffing, New York		21	7	.750
1939—Lefty Grove, Boston		15	4	.789
1940—Schoolboy Rowe, Detroit		16	3	.842
1941—Lefty Gomez, New York		15	5	.750
1942—Tiny Bonham, New York		21	5	.808
1943—Spud Chandler, New York		20	4	.833
1944—Tex Hughson, Boston		18	5	.783
1945—Hal Newhouser, Detroit		25	9	.735
1946—Boo Ferriss, Boston		25	6	.806
1947—Allie Reynolds, New York		19	8	.704
1948—Jack Kramer, Boston		18	5	.783
1949—Ellis Kinder, Boston		23	6	.793
1950—Vic Raschi, New York		21	8	.724
1951—Bob Feller, Cleveland		22	8	.733
1952—Bobby Shantz, Philadelphia		24	7	.774
1953—Eddie Lopat, New York		16	4	.800
1954—Sandy Consuegra, Chicago		16	3	.842
1955—Tommy Byrne, New York		16	5	.762
1956—Whitey Ford, New York		19	6	.760
1957—Dick Donovan, Chicago		16	6	.727
—Tom Sturdivant, New York		16	6	.727
1958—Bob Turley, New York		21	7	.750
1959—Bob Shaw, Chicago		18	6	.750
1960—Jim Perry, Cleveland		18	10	.643
1961—Whitey Ford, New York		25	4	.862
1962—Ray Herbert, Chicago		20	9	.690
1963—Whitey Ford, New York		24	7	.774
1964—Wally Bunker, Baltimore		19	5	.792
1965—Mudcat Grant, Minnesota		21	7	.750
1966—Sonny Siebert, Cleveland		16	8	.667
1967—Joe Horlen, Chicago		19	7	.731
1968—Denny McLain, Detroit		31	6	.838
1969—Jim Palmer, Baltimore		16	4	.800
1970—Mike Cuellar, Baltimore		24	8	.750
1971—Dave McNally, Baltimore		21	5	.808
1972—Catfish Hunter, Oakland		21	7	.750
1973—Catfish Hunter, Oakland		21	5	.808
1974—Mike Cuellar, Baltimore		22	10	.688
1975—Mike Torrez, Baltimore		20	9	.690
1976—Bill Campbell, Minnesota		17	5	.773
1977—Paul Splittorff, Kansas City		16	6	.727
1978—Ron Guidry, New York		25	3	.893
1979—Mike Caldwell, Milwaukee		16	6	.727
1980—Steve Stone, Baltimore		25	7	.781
1981—Pete Vuckovich, Milwaukee		14	4	.778
1982—Pete Vuckovich, Milwaukee		18	6	.750
1983—Rich Dotson, Chicago		22	7	.759
1984—Doyle Alexander, Toronto		17	6	.739
1985—Ron Guidry, New York		22	6	.786
1986—Roger Clemens, Boston		24	4	.857
1987—Roger Clemens, Boston		20	9	.690
1988—Frank Viola, Minnesota		24	7	.774
1989—Bret Saberhagen, Kansas City		23	6	.793
1990—Bob Welch, Oakland		27	6	.818
1991—Scott Erickson, Minnesota		20	8	.714
1992—Mike Mussina, Baltimore		18	5	.783
1993—Jimmy Key, New York		18	6	.750
1994—Jason Bere, Chicago		12	2	.857

NATIONAL LEAGUE

Year	Pitcher, Club	W	L	Pct.
1876—Al Spalding, Chicago		47	13	.783
1877—Tommy Bond, Boston		31	17	.646
1878—Tommy Bond, Boston		40	19	.678
1879—Monte Ward, Providence		44	18	.710
1880—Fred Goldsmith, Chicago		22	3	.880
1881—Hoss Radbourn, Providence		25	11	.694
1882—Larry Corcoran, Chicago		27	13	.675
1883—Jim McCormick, Cleveland		27	13	.675
1884—Hoss Radbourn, Providence		60	12	.833
1885—Mickey Welch, New York		44	11	.800
1886—Jocko Flynn, Chicago		24	6	.800
1887—Charlie Getzien, Detroit		29	13	.690
1888—Tim Keefe, New York		35	12	.745
1889—John Clarkson, Boston		49	19	.721
1890—Tom Lovett, Brooklyn		32	11	.744
1891—John Ewing, New York		22	8	.733
1892—Cy Young, Cleveland		36	11	.766
1893—Frank Killen, Pittsburgh		34	10	.773
1894—Jouett Meekin, New York		34	9	.791
1895—Bill Hoffer, Baltimore		30	7	.811
1896—Bill Hoffer, Baltimore		26	7	.788
1897—Fred Klobedanz, Boston		26	7	.788
1898—Ted Lewis, Boston		26	8	.765
1899—Jim Hughes, Brooklyn		28	6	.824
1900—Joe McGinnity, Brooklyn		29	9	.763
1901—Jack Chesbro, Pittsburgh		21	9	.700
1902—Jack Chesbro, Pittsburgh		28	6	.824
1903—Sam Leever, Pittsburgh		25	7	.781
1904—Joe McGinnity, New York		35	8	.814
1905—Sam Leever, Pittsburgh		20	5	.800
1906—Ed Reulbach, Chicago		19	4	.826
1907—Ed Reulbach, Chicago		17	4	.810
1908—Ed Reulbach, Chicago		24	7	.774
1909—Christy Mathewson, New York		25	6	.806
—Howie Camnitz, Pittsburgh		25	6	.806
1910—King Cole, Chicago		20	4	.833
1911—Rube Marquard, New York		24	7	.774
1912—Claude Hendrix, Pittsburgh		24	9	.727
1913—Bert Humphries, Chicago		16	4	.800
1914—Bill James, Boston		26	7	.788
1915—Grover Alexander, Philadelphia		31	10	.756
1916—Tom Hughes, Boston		16	3	.842
1917—Ferdie Schupp, New York		21	7	.750
1918—Claude Hendrix, Chicago		20	7	.741
1919—Dutch Ruether, Cincinnati		19	6	.760
1920—Burleigh Grimes, Brooklyn		23	11	.676
1921—Bill Doak, St. Louis		15	6	.714
1922—Pete Donohue, Cincinnati		18	9	.667
1923—Dolf Luque, Cincinnati		27	8	.771
1924—Emil Yde, Pittsburgh		16	3	.842
1925—Willie Sherdel, St. Louis		15	6	.714
1926—Ray Kremer, Pittsburgh		20	6	.769
1927—Larry Benton, Boston/New York		17	7	.708
1928—Larry Benton, New York		25	9	.735
1929—Charlie Root, Chicago		19	6	.760
1930—Freddie Fitzsimmons, New York		19	7	.731
1931—Paul Derringer, St. Louis		18	8	.692
1932—Lon Warneke, Chicago		22	6	.786
1933—Ben Cantwell, Boston		20	10	.667
1934—Dizzy Dean, St. Louis		30	7	.811
1935—Bill Lee, Chicago		20	6	.769
1936—Carl Hubbell, New York		26	6	.813
1937—Carl Hubbell, New York		22	8	.733
1938—Bill Lee, Chicago		22	9	.710
1939—Paul Derringer, Cincinnati		25	7	.781
1940—Freddie Fitzsimmons, Brooklyn		16	2	.889
1941—Elmer Riddle, Cincinnati		19	4	.826
1942—Larry French, Brooklyn		15	4	.789
1943—Mort Cooper, St. Louis		21	8	.724
1944—Ted Wilks, St. Louis		17	4	.810
1945—Harry Brecheen, St. Louis		15	4	.789
1946—Murry Dickson, St. Louis		15	6	.714
1947—Larry Jansen, New York		21	5	.808
1948—Harry Brecheen, St. Louis		20	7	.741
1949—Preacher Roe, Brooklyn		15	6	.714
1950—Sal Maglie, New York		18	4	.818
1951—Preacher Roe, Brooklyn		22	3	.880
1952—Hoyt Wilhelm, New York		15	3	.833
1953—Carl Erskine, Brooklyn		20	6	.769
1954—Johnny Antonelli, New York		21	7	.750
1955—Don Newcombe, Brooklyn		20	5	.800
1956—Don Newcombe, Brooklyn		27	7	.794
1957—Bob Buhl, Milwaukee		18	7	.720
1958—Warren Spahn, Milwaukee		22	11	.667
—Lew Burdette, Milwaukee		20	10	.667
1959—Roy Face, Pittsburgh		18	1	.947

Year	Pitcher, Club	W	L	Pct.
1960	Ernie Broglio, St. Louis	21	9	.700
1961	Johnny Podres, Los Angeles	18	5	.783
1962	Bob Purkey, Cincinnati	23	5	.821
1963	Ron Perranoski, Los Angeles	16	3	.842
1964	Sandy Koufax, Los Angeles	19	5	.792
1965	Sandy Koufax, Los Angeles	26	8	.765
1966	Juan Marichal, San Francisco	25	6	.806
1967	Dick Hughes, St. Louis	16	6	.727
1968	Steve Blass, Pittsburgh	18	6	.750
1969	Tom Seaver, New York	25	7	.781
1970	Bob Gibson, St. Louis	23	7	.767
1971	Don Gullett, Cincinnati	16	6	.727
1972	Gary Nolan, Cincinnati	15	5	.750
1973	Tommy John, Los Angeles	16	7	.696
1974	Andy Messersmith, Los Angeles	20	6	.769
1975	Don Gullett, Cincinnati	15	4	.789
1976	Steve Carlton, Philadelphia	20	7	.741
1977	John Candelaria, Pittsburgh	20	5	.800
1978	Gaylord Perry, San Diego	21	6	.778
1979	Tom Seaver, Cincinnati	16	6	.727
1980	Jim Bibby, Pittsburgh	19	6	.760
1981	Tom Seaver, Cincinnati	14	2	.875
1982	Phil Niekro, Atlanta	17	4	.810
1983	John Denny, Philadelphia	19	6	.760
1984	Rick Sutcliffe, Chicago	16	1	.941
1985	Orel Hershiser, Los Angeles	19	3	.864
1986	Bob Ojeda, New York	18	5	.783
1987	Dwight Gooden, New York	15	7	.682
1988	David Cone, New York	20	3	.870
1989	Mike Bielecki, Chicago	18	7	.720
1990	Doug Drabek, Pittsburgh	22	6	.786
1991	John Smiley, Pittsburgh	20	8	.714
	Jose Rijo, Cincinnati	15	6	.714
1992	Bob Tewksbury, St. Louis	16	5	.762
1993	Mark Portugal, Houston	18	4	.818
1994	Marvin Freeman, Colorado	10	2	.833

Note— Based on 15 or more victories.
Note— 1981 and 1994 percentages based on 10 or more victories.

EARNED-RUN AVERAGE

AMERICAN LEAGUE

Year	Pitcher, Club	G	IP	ERA
1913	Walter Johnson, Washington	48	346	1.14
1914	Dutch H. Leonard, Boston	35	225	1.00
1915	Joe Wood, Boston	25	157	1.49
1916	Babe Ruth, Boston	44	324	1.75
1917	Ed Cicotte, Chicago	49	346	1.53
1918	Walter Johnson, Washington	39	325	1.27
1919	Walter Johnson, Washington	39	290	1.49
1920	Bob Shawkey, New York	38	267	2.45
1921	Red Faber, Chicago	43	331	2.47
1922	Red Faber, Chicago	43	353	2.80
1923	Stan Coveleski, Cleveland	33	228	2.76
1924	Walter Johnson, Washington	38	278	2.72
1925	Stan Coveleski, Washington	32	241	2.84
1926	Lefty Grove, Philadelphia	45	258	2.51
1927	Wilcy Moore, New York	50	213	2.28
1928	Garland Braxton, Washington	38	218	2.52
1929	Lefty Grove, Philadelphia	42	275	2.81
1930	Lefty Grove, Philadelphia	50	291	2.54
1931	Lefty Grove, Philadelphia	41	289	2.06
1932	Lefty Grove, Philadelphia	44	292	2.84
1933	Monte Pearson, Cleveland	19	135	2.33
1934	Lefty Gomez, New York	38	282	2.33
1935	Lefty Grove, Boston	35	273	2.70
1936	Lefty Grove, Boston	35	253	2.81
1937	Lefty Gomez, New York	34	278	2.33
1938	Lefty Grove, Boston	24	164	3.07
1939	Lefty Grove, Boston	23	191	2.54
1940	Bob Feller, Cleveland	43	320	2.62
1941	Thornton Lee, Chicago	35	300	2.37
1942	Ted Lyons, Chicago	20	180	2.10
1943	Spud Chandler, New York	30	253	1.64

Year	Pitcher, Club	G	IP	ERA
1944	Dizzy Trout, Detroit	49	352	2.12
1945	Hal Newhouser, Detroit	40	313	1.81
1946	Hal Newhouser, Detroit	37	293	1.94
1947	Spud Chandler, New York	17	128	2.46
1948	Gene Bearden, Cleveland	37	230	2.43
1949	Mel Parnell, Boston	39	295	2.78
1950	Early Wynn, Cleveland	32	214	3.20
1951	Saul Rogovin, Detroit/Chicago	27	217	2.78
1952	Allie Reynolds, New York	35	244	2.07
1953	Eddie Lopat, New York	25	178	2.43
1954	Mike Garcia, Cleveland	45	259	2.64
1955	Billy Pierce, Chicago	33	206	1.97
1956	Whitey Ford, New York	31	226	2.47
1957	Bobby Shantz, New York	30	173	2.45
1958	Whitey Ford, New York	30	219	2.01
1959	Hoyt Wilhelm, Baltimore	32	226	2.19
1960	Frank Baumann, Chicago	47	185	2.68
1961	Dick Donovan, Washington	23	169	2.40
1962	Hank Aguirre, Detroit	42	216	2.21
1963	Gary Peters, Chicago	41	243	2.33
1964	Dean Chance, Los Angeles	46	278	1.65
1965	Sam McDowell, Cleveland	42	273	2.18
1966	Gary Peters, Chicago	30	205	1.98
1967	Joe Horlen, Chicago	35	258	2.06
1968	Luis Tiant, Cleveland	34	258	1.60
1969	Dick Bosman, Washington	31	193	2.19
1970	Diego Segui, Oakland	47	162	2.56
1971	Vida Blue, Oakland	39	312	1.82
1972	Luis Tiant, Boston	43	179	1.91
1973	Jim Palmer, Baltimore	38	296	2.40
1974	Catfish Hunter, Oakland	41	318	2.49
1975	Jim Palmer, Baltimore	39	323	2.09
1976	Mark Fidrych, Detroit	31	250	2.34
1977	Frank Tanana, California	31	241	2.54
1978	Ron Guidry, New York	35	274	1.74
1979	Ron Guidry, New York	33	236	2.78
1980	Rudy May, New York	41	175	2.47
1981	Steve McCatty, Oakland	22	186	2.32
1982	Rick Sutcliffe, Cleveland	34	216	2.96
1983	Rick Honeycutt, Texas	25	174.2	2.42
1984	Mike Boddicker, Baltimore	34	261.1	2.79
1985	Dave Stieb, Toronto	36	265	2.48
1986	Roger Clemens, Boston	33	254	2.48
1987	Jimmy Key, Toronto	36	261	2.76
1988	Allan Anderson, Minnesota	30	202.1	2.45
1989	Bret Saberhagen, Kansas City	36	262.1	2.16
1990	Roger Clemens, Boston	31	228.1	1.93
1991	Roger Clemens, Boston	35	271.1	2.62
1992	Roger Clemens, Boston	32	246.2	2.41
1993	Kevin Appier, Kansas City	34	238.2	2.56
1994	Steve Ontiveros, Oakland	27	115.1	2.65

NATIONAL LEAGUE

Year	Pitcher, Club	G	IP	ERA
1912	Jeff Tesreau, New York	36	243	1.96
1913	Christy Mathewson, New York	40	306	2.06
1914	Bill Doak, St. Louis	36	256	1.72
1915	Grover Alexander, Philadelphia	49	376	1.22
1916	Grover Alexander, Philadelphia	48	390	1.55
1917	Grover Alexander, Philadelphia	45	388	1.83
1918	Hippo Vaughn, Chicago	35	290	1.74
1919	Grover Alexander, Chicago	30	235	1.72
1920	Grover Alexander, Chicago	46	363	1.91
1921	Bill Doak, St. Louis	32	209	2.58
1922	Rosy Ryan, New York	46	192	3.00
1923	Dolf Luque, Cincinnati	41	322	1.93
1924	Dazzy Vance, Brooklyn	35	309	2.16
1925	Dolf Luque, Cincinnati	36	291	2.63
1926	Ray Kremer, Pittsburgh	37	231	2.61
1927	Ray Kremer, Pittsburgh	35	226	2.47
1928	Dazzy Vance, Brooklyn	38	280	2.09
1929	Bill Walker, New York	29	178	3.08
1930	Dazzy Vance, Brooklyn	35	259	2.61
1931	Bill Walker, New York	37	239	2.26

Year	Pitcher, Club	G	IP	ERA
1932—Lon Warneke, Chicago		35	277	2.37
1933—Carl Hubbell, New York		45	309	1.66
1934—Carl Hubbell, New York		49	313	2.30
1935—Cy Blanton, Pittsburgh		35	254	2.59
1936—Carl Hubbell, New York		42	304	2.31
1937—Jim Turner, Boston		33	257	2.38
1938—Bill Lee, Chicago		44	291	2.66
1939—Bucky Walters, Cincinnati		39	319	2.29
1940—Bucky Walters, Cincinnati		36	305	2.48
1941—Elmer Riddle, Cincinnati		33	217	2.24
1942—Mort Cooper, St. Louis		37	279	1.77
1943—Howie Pollet, St. Louis		16	118	1.75
1944—Ed Heusser, Cincinnati		30	193	2.38
1945—Hank Borowy, Chicago		15	122	2.14
1946—Howie Pollet, St. Louis		40	266	2.10
1947—Warren Spahn, Boston		40	290	2.33
1948—Harry Brecheen, St. Louis		33	233	2.24
1949—Dave Koslo, New York		38	212	2.50
1950—Jim Hearn, St. Louis/New York		22	134	2.49
1951—Chet Nichols, Boston		33	156	2.88
1952—Hoyt Wilhelm, New York		71	159	2.43
1953—Warren Spahn, Milwaukee		35	266	2.10
1954—Johnny Antonelli, New York		39	259	2.29
1955—Bob Friend, Pittsburgh		44	200	2.84
1956—Lew Burdette, Milwaukee		39	256	2.71
1957—Johnny Podres, Brooklyn		31	196	2.66
1958—Stu Miller, San Francisco		41	182	2.47
1959—Sam Jones, San Francisco		50	271	2.82
1960—Mike McCormick, San Francisco		40	253	2.70
1961—Warren Spahn, Milwaukee		38	263	3.01
1962—Sandy Koufax, Los Angeles		28	184	2.54
1963—Sandy Koufax, Los Angeles		40	311	1.88
1964—Sandy Koufax, Los Angeles		29	223	1.74
1965—Sandy Koufax, Los Angeles		43	336	2.04
1966—Sandy Koufax, Los Angeles		41	323	1.73
1967—Phil Niekro, Atlanta		46	207	1.87
1968—Bob Gibson, St. Louis		34	305	1.12
1969—Juan Marichal, San Francisco		37	300	2.10
1970—Tom Seaver, New York		37	291	2.81
1971—Tom Seaver, New York		36	286	1.76
1972—Steve Carlton, Philadelphia		41	346	1.98
1973—Tom Seaver, New York		36	290	2.08
1974—Buzz Capra, Atlanta		39	217	2.28
1975—Randy Jones, San Diego		37	285	2.24
1976—John Denny, St. Louis		30	207	2.52
1977—John Candelaria, Pittsburgh		33	231	2.34
1978—Craig Swan, New York		29	207	2.43
1979—J.R. Richard, Houston		38	292	2.71
1980—Don Sutton, Los Angeles		32	212	2.21
1981—Nolan Ryan, Houston		21	149	1.69
1982—Steve Rogers, Montreal		35	277	2.40
1983—Atlee Hammaker, San Francisco		23	172.1	2.25
1984—Alejandro Pena, Los Angeles		28	199.1	2.48
1985—Dwight Gooden, New York		35	276.2	1.53
1986—Mike Scott, Houston		37	275.1	2.22
1987—Nolan Ryan, Houston		34	211.2	2.76
1988—Joe Magrane, St. Louis		24	165.1	2.18
1989—Scott Garrelts, San Francisco		30	193.1	2.28
1990—Danny Darwin, Houston		48	162.2	2.21
1991—Dennis Martinez, Montreal		31	222	2.39
1992—Bill Swift, San Francisco		30	164.2	2.08
1993—Greg Maddux, Atlanta		36	267.0	2.36
1994—Greg Maddux, Atlanta		25	202.0	1.56

Note—Based on 10 complete games through 1950, then 154 innings until 1961 in A.L. and 1962 in N.L., when it became 162 innings.

Note—ERA records not tabulated in N.L. prior to 1912 and A.L. prior to 1913.

Note—1981 ERA champion determined by taking leader who pitched as many innings as his team's total number of games played.

Note—Wilcy Moore pitched only six complete games—he started 12—in 1927, but was recognized as A.L. leader because of 213 innings pitched; Tiny Bonham, New York, had 1.91 ERA and 10 complete games in 1940, but appeared in only 12 games and 99 innings, and Bob Feller was recognized as the leader.

	SHUTOUTS	

AMERICAN LEAGUE

Year	Pitcher, Club	No.
1901—Clark Griffith, Chicago		5
—Cy Young, Boston		5
1902—Addie Joss, Cleveland		5
1903—Cy Young, Boston		7
1904—Cy Young, Boston		10
1905—Ed Killian, Detroit		8
1906—Ed Walsh Sr., Chicago		10
1907—Eddie Plank, Philadelphia		8
1908—Ed Walsh Sr., Chicago		12
1909—Ed Walsh Sr., Chicago		8
1910—Jack Coombs, Philadelphia		13
1911—Walter Johnson, Washington		6
—Eddie Plank, Philadelphia		6
1912—Joe Wood, Boston		10
1913—Walter Johnson, Washington		11
1914—Walter Johnson, Washington		9
1915—Walter Johnson, Washington		7
1916—Babe Ruth, Boston		9
1917—Stan Coveleski, Cleveland		9
1918—Walter Johnson, Washington		8
—Carl Mays, Boston		8
1919—Walter Johnson, Washington		7
1920—Carl Mays, New York		6
1921—Sam P. Jones, Boston		5
1922—George Uhle, Cleveland		5
1923—Stan Coveleski, Cleveland		5
1924—Walter Johnson, Washington		6
1925—Ted Lyons, Chicago		5
1926—Ed Wells, Detroit		4
1927—Hod Lisenbee, Washington		4
1928—Herb Pennock, New York		5
1929—George Blaeholder, St. Louis		4
—Alvin Crowder, St. Louis		4
—Sam Gray, St. Louis		4
—Danny MacFayden, Boston		4
1930—Clint Brown, Cleveland		3
—George Earnshaw, Philadelphia		3
—George Pipgras, New York		3
1931—Lefty Grove, Philadelphia		4
—Vic Sorrell, Detroit		4
1932—Tommy Bridges, Detroit		4
—Lefty Grove, Philadelphia		4
1933—Oral Hildebrand, Cleveland		6
1934—Lefty Gomez, New York		6
—Mel Harder, Cleveland		6
1935—Schoolboy Rowe, Detroit		6
1936—Lefty Grove, Boston		6
1937—Lefty Gomez, New York		6
1938—Lefty Gomez, New York		4
1939—Red Ruffing, New York		5
1940—Bob Feller, Cleveland		4
—Ted Lyons, Chicago		4
—Al Milnar, Cleveland		4
1941—Bob Feller, Cleveland		6
1942—Tiny Bonham, New York		6
1943—Spud Chandler, New York		5
—Dizzy Trout, Detroit		5
1944—Dizzy Trout, Detroit		7
1945—Hal Newhouser, Detroit		8
1946—Bob Feller, Cleveland		10
1947—Bob Feller, Cleveland		5
1948—Bob Lemon, Cleveland		10
1949—Mike Garcia, Cleveland		6
—Ellis Kinder, Boston		6
—Virgil Trucks, Detroit		6
1950—Art Houtteman, Detroit		4
1951—Allie Reynolds, New York		7
1952—Mike Garcia, Cleveland		6
—Allie Reynolds, New York		6

Year	Pitcher, Club	No.
1953	Bob Porterfield, Washington	9
1954	Mike Garcia, Cleveland	5
	Virgil Trucks, Chicago	5
1955	Billy Hoeft, Detroit	7
1956	Herb Score, Cleveland	5
1957	Jim Wilson, Chicago	5
1958	Whitey Ford, New York	7
1959	Camilo Pascual, Washington	6
1960	Whitey Ford, New York	4
	Jim Perry, Cleveland	4
	Early Wynn, Chicago	4
1961	Steve Barber, Baltimore	8
	Camilo Pascual, Minnesota	8
1962	Dick Donovan, Cleveland	5
	Jim Kaat, Minnesota	5
	Camilo Pascual, Minnesota	5
1963	Ray Herbert, Chicago	7
1964	Dean Chance, Los Angeles	11
1965	Mudcat Grant, Minnesota	6
1966	Tommy John, Chicago	5
	Sam McDowell, Cleveland	5
	Luis Tiant, Cleveland	5
1967	Steve Hargan, Cleveland	6
	Joe Horlen, Chicago	6
	Tommy John, Chicago	6
	Mickey Lolich, Detroit	6
	Jim McGlothlin, California	6
1968	Luis Tiant, Cleveland	9
1969	Denny McLain, Detroit	9
1970	Chuck Dobson, Oakland	5
	Jim Palmer, Baltimore	5
1971	Vida Blue, Oakland	8
1972	Nolan Ryan, California	9
1973	Bert Blyleven, Minnesota	9
1974	Luis Tiant, Boston	7
1975	Jim Palmer, Baltimore	10
1976	Nolan Ryan, California	7
1977	Frank Tanana, California	7
1978	Ron Guidry, New York	9
1979	Nolan Ryan, California	5
	Mike Flanagan, Baltimore	5
	Dennis Leonard, Kansas City	5
1980	Tommy John, New York	6
1981	Rich Dotson, Chicago	4
	Ken Forsch, California	4
	Steve McCatty, Oakland	4
	Doc Medich, Texas	4
1982	Dave Stieb, Toronto	5
1983	Mike Boddicker, Baltimore	5
1984	Bob Ojeda, Boston	5
	Geoff Zahn, California	5
1985	Bert Blyleven, Cleveland/Minnesota	5
1986	Jack Morris, Detroit	6
1987	Roger Clemens, Boston	7
1988	Roger Clemens, Boston	8
1989	Bert Blyleven, California	5
1990	Roger Clemens, Boston	4
	Dave Stewart, Oakland	4
1991	Roger Clemens, Boston	4
1992	Roger Clemens, Boston	5
1993	Jack McDowell, Chicago	4
1994	Randy Johnson, Seattle	4

NATIONAL LEAGUE

Year	Pitcher, Club	No.
1900	Clark Griffith, Chicago	4
	Noodles Hahn, Cincinnati	4
	Kid Nichols, Boston	4
	Cy Young, St. Louis	4
1901	Jack Chesbro, Pittsburgh	6
	Al Orth, Philadelphia	6
	Vic Willis, Boston	6
1902	Jack Chesbro, Pittsburgh	8
	Christy Mathewson, New York	8
1903	Sam Leever, Pittsburgh	7
1904	Joe McGinnity, New York	9
1905	Christy Mathewson, New York	9
1906	Mordecai Brown, Chicago	9
1907	Orval Overall, Chicago	9
	Christy Mathewson, New York	9
1908	Christy Mathewson, New York	12
1909	Orval Overall, Chicago	9
1910	Earl Moore, Philadelphia	7
1911	Grover Alexander, Philadelphia	7
1912	Nap Rucker, Brooklyn	6
1913	Grover Alexander, Philadelphia	9
1914	Jeff Tesreau, New York	8
1915	Grover Alexander, Philadelphia	12
1916	Grover Alexander, Philadelphia	16
1917	Grover Alexander, Philadelphia	8
1918	Lefty Tyler, Chicago	8
	Hippo Vaughn, Chicago	8
1919	Grover Alexander, Chicago	9
1920	Babe Adams, Pittsburgh	8
1921	Grover Alexander, Chicago	3
	Phil Douglas, New York	3
	Dana Fillingim, Boston	3
	Dolf Luque, Cincinnati	3
	Clarence Mitchell, Brooklyn	3
	Johnny Morrison, Pittsburgh	3
	Joe Oeschger, Boston	3
	Jesse Haines, St. Louis	3
1922	Dazzy Vance, Brooklyn	6
1923	Dolf Luque, Cincinnati	6
1924	Jesse Barnes, Boston	4
	Wilbur Cooper, Pittsburgh	4
	Ray Kremer, Pittsburgh	4
	Eppa Rixey, Cincinnati	4
	Allen Sothoron, St. Louis	4
	Emil Yde, Pittsburgh	4
1925	Hal Carlson, Philadelphia	4
	Dolf Luque, Cincinnati	4
	Dazzy Vance, Brooklyn	4
1926	Pete Donohue, Cincinnati	5
1927	Jesse Haines, St. Louis	6
1928	Sheriff Blake, Chicago	4
	Burleigh Grimes, Pittsburgh	4
	Red Lucas, Cincinnati	4
	Doug McWeeny, Brooklyn	4
	Dazzy Vance, Brooklyn	4
1929	Pat Malone, Chicago	5
1930	Charlie Root, Chicago	4
	Dazzy Vance, Brooklyn	4
1931	Bill Walker, New York	6
1932	Lon Warneke, Chicago	4
	Dizzy Dean, St. Louis	4
	Steve Swetonic, Pittsburgh	4
1933	Carl Hubbell, New York	10
1934	Dizzy Dean, St. Louis	7
1935	Cy Blanton, Pittsburgh	4
	Freddie Fitzsimmons, New York	4
	Larry French, Chicago	4
	Van Lingle Mungo, Brooklyn	4
	Jim Weaver, Pittsburgh	4
1936	Cy Blanton, Pittsburgh	4
	Tex Carleton, Chicago	4
	Larry French, Chicago	4
	Bill Lee, Chicago	4
	Al Smith, New York	4
	Bucky Walters, Philadelphia	4
	Lon Warneke, Chicago	4
1937	Lou Fette, Boston	5
	Lee Grissom, Cincinnati	5
	Jim Turner, Boston	5
1938	Bill Lee, Chicago	9
1939	Lou Fette, Boston	6
1940	Bill Lohrman, New York	5
	Manny Salvo, Boston	5
	Whitlow Wyatt, Brooklyn	5
1941	Whitlow Wyatt, Brooklyn	7
1942	Mort Cooper, St. Louis	10

Year	Pitcher, Club	No.
1943—Hi Bithorn, Chicago		7
1944—Mort Cooper, St. Louis		7
1945—Claude Passeau, Chicago		5
1946—Ewell Blackwell, Cincinnati		6
1947—Warren Spahn, Boston		7
1948—Harry Brecheen, St. Louis		7
1949—Ken Heintzelman, Philadelphia		5
—Don Newcombe, Brooklyn		5
—Howie Pollet, St. Louis		5
—Ken Raffensberger, Cincinnati		5
1950—Jim Hearn, New York		5
—Larry Jansen, New York		5
—Sal Maglie, New York		5
—Robin Roberts, Philadelphia		5
1951—Warren Spahn, Boston		7
1952—Ken Raffensberger, Cincinnati		6
—Curt Simmons, Philadelphia		6
1953—Harvey Haddix, St. Louis		6
1954—Johnny Antonelli, New York		6
1955—Joe Nuxhall, Cincinnati		5
1956—Johnny Antonelli, New York		6
—Lew Burdette, Milwaukee		6
1957—Johnny Podres, Brooklyn		6
1958—Carl Willey, Milwaukee		4
1959—Johnny Antonelli, San Francisco		4
—Bob Buhl, Milwaukee		4
—Lew Burdette, Milwaukee		4
—Roger Craig, Los Angeles		4
—Don Drysdale, Los Angeles		4
—Sam Jones, San Francisco		4
—Warren Spahn, Milwaukee		4
1960—Jack Sanford, San Francisco		6
1961—Joey Jay, Cincinnati		4
—Warren Spahn, Milwaukee		4
1962—Bob Friend, Pittsburgh		5
—Bob Gibson, St. Louis		5
1963—Sandy Koufax, Los Angeles		11
1964—Sandy Koufax, Los Angeles		7
1965—Juan Marichal, San Francisco		10
1966—Jim Bunning, Philadelphia		5
—Bob Gibson, St. Louis		5
—Larry Jackson, Philadelphia		5
—Larry Jaster, St. Louis		5
—Sandy Koufax, Los Angeles		5
—Jim Maloney, Cincinnati		5
1967—Jim Bunning, Philadelphia		6
1968—Bob Gibson, St. Louis		13
1969—Juan Marichal, San Francisco		8
1970—Gaylord Perry, San Francisco		5
1971—Steve Blass, Pittsburgh		5
—Al Downing, Los Angeles		5
—Bob Gibson, St. Louis		5
—Milt Pappas, Chicago		5
1972—Don Sutton, Los Angeles		9
1973—Jack Billingham, Cincinnati		7
1974—Jon Matlack, New York		7
1975—Andy Messersmith, Los Angeles		7
1976—Jon Matlack, New York		6
—John Montefusco, San Francisco		6
1977—Tom Seaver, New York/Cincinnati		7
1978—Bob Knepper, San Francisco		6
1979—Tom Seaver, Cincinnati		5
—Joe Niekro, Houston		5
—Steve Rogers, Montreal		5
1980—Jerry Reuss, Los Angeles		6
1981—Fernando Valenzuela, Los Angeles		8
1982—Steve Carlton, Philadelphia		6
1983—Steve Rogers, Montreal		5
1984—Joaquin Andujar, St. Louis		4
—Orel Hershiser, Los Angeles		4
—Alejandro Pena, Los Angeles		4
1985—John Tudor, St. Louis		10
1986—Bob Knepper, Houston		5
—Mike Scott, Houston		5
1987—Rick Reuschel, Pittsburgh/San Francisco		4
—Bob Welch, Los Angeles		4
1988—Orel Hershiser, Los Angeles		8
1989—Tim Belcher, Los Angeles		8
1990—Bruce Hurst, San Diego		4
—Mike Morgan, Los Angeles		4
1991—Dennis Martinez, Montreal		5
1992—David Cone, New York		5
—Tom Glavine, Atlanta		5
1993—Pete Harnisch, Houston		4
1994—Greg Maddux, Atlanta		3
—Ramon Martinez, Los Angeles		3

STRIKEOUTS

AMERICAN LEAGUE

Year	Pitcher, Club	No.
1901—Cy Young, Boston		159
1902—Rube Waddell, Philadelphia		210
1903—Rube Waddell, Philadelphia		301
1904—Rube Waddell, Philadelphia		349
1905—Rube Waddell, Philadelphia		286
1906—Rube Waddell, Philadelphia		203
1907—Rube Waddell, Philadelphia		226
1908—Ed Walsh, Chicago		269
1909—Frank Smith, Chicago		177
1910—Walter Johnson, Washington		313
1911—Ed Walsh, Chicago		255
1912—Walter Johnson, Washington		303
1913—Walter Johnson, Washington		243
1914—Walter Johnson, Washington		225
1915—Walter Johnson, Washington		203
1916—Walter Johnson, Washington		228
1917—Walter Johnson, Washington		188
1918—Walter Johnson, Washington		162
1919—Walter Johnson, Washington		147
1920—Stan Coveleski, Cleveland		133
1921—Walter Johnson, Washington		143
1922—Urban Shocker, St. Louis		149
1923—Walter Johnson, Washington		130
1924—Walter Johnson, Washington		158
1925—Lefty Grove, Philadelphia		116
1926—Lefty Grove, Philadelphia		194
1927—Lefty Grove, Philadelphia		174
1928—Lefty Grove, Philadelphia		183
1929—Lefty Grove, Philadelphia		170
1930—Lefty Grove, Philadelphia		209
1931—Lefty Grove, Philadelphia		175
1932—Red Ruffing, New York		190
1933—Lefty Gomez, New York		163
1934—Lefty Gomez, New York		158
1935—Tommy Bridges, Detroit		163
1936—Tommy Bridges, Detroit		175
1937—Lefty Gomez, New York		194
1938—Bob Feller, Cleveland		240
1939—Bob Feller, Cleveland		246
1940—Bob Feller, Cleveland		261
1941—Bob Feller, Cleveland		260
1942—Bobo Newsom, Washington		113
—Tex Hughson, Boston		113
1943—Allie Reynolds, Cleveland		151
1944—Hal Newhouser, Detroit		187
1945—Hal Newhouser, Detroit		212
1946—Bob Feller, Cleveland		348
1947—Bob Feller, Cleveland		196
1948—Bob Feller, Cleveland		164
1949—Virgil Trucks, Detroit		153
1950—Bob Lemon, Cleveland		170
1951—Vic Raschi, New York		164
1952—Allie Reynolds, New York		160
1953—Billy Pierce, Chicago		186
1954—Bob Turley, Baltimore		185
1955—Herb Score, Cleveland		245
1956—Herb Score, Cleveland		263
1957—Early Wynn, Cleveland		184
1958—Early Wynn, Chicago		179
1959—Jim Bunning, Detroit		201

Year	Pitcher, Club	No.
1960	Jim Bunning, Detroit	201
1961	Camilo Pascual, Minnesota	221
1962	Camilo Pascual, Minnesota	206
1963	Camilo Pascual, Minnesota	202
1964	Al Downing, New York	217
1965	Sam McDowell, Cleveland	325
1966	Sam McDowell, Cleveland	225
1967	Jim Lonborg, Boston	246
1968	Sam McDowell, Cleveland	283
1969	Sam McDowell, Cleveland	279
1970	Sam McDowell, Cleveland	304
1971	Mickey Lolich, Detroit	308
1972	Nolan Ryan, California	329
1973	Nolan Ryan, California	383
1974	Nolan Ryan, California	367
1975	Frank Tanana, California	269
1976	Nolan Ryan, California	327
1977	Nolan Ryan, California	341
1978	Nolan Ryan, California	260
1979	Nolan Ryan, California	223
1980	Len Barker, Cleveland	187
1981	Len Barker, Cleveland	127
1982	Floyd Bannister, Seattle	209
1983	Jack Morris, Detroit	232
1984	Mark Langston, Seattle	204
1985	Bert Blyleven, Cleveland/Minnesota	206
1986	Mark Langston, Seattle	245
1987	Mark Langston, Seattle	262
1988	Roger Clemens, Boston	291
1989	Nolan Ryan, Texas	301
1990	Nolan Ryan, Texas	232
1991	Roger Clemens, Boston	241
1992	Randy Johnson, Seattle	241
1993	Randy Johnson, Seattle	308
1994	Randy Johnson, Seattle	204

NATIONAL LEAGUE

Year	Pitcher, Club	No.
1900	Rube Waddell, Pittsburgh	133
1901	Noodles Hahn, Cincinnati	233
1902	Vic Willis, Boston	226
1903	Christy Mathewson, New York	267
1904	Christy Mathewson, New York	212
1905	Christy Mathewson, New York	206
1906	Fred Beebe, Chicago/St. Louis	171
1907	Christy Mathewson, New York	178
1908	Christy Mathewson, New York	259
1909	Orval Overall, Chicago	205
1910	Christy Mathewson, New York	190
1911	Rube Marquard, New York	237
1912	Grover Alexander, Philadelphia	195
1913	Tom Seaton, Philadelphia	168
1914	Grover Alexander, Philadelphia	214
1915	Grover Alexander, Philadelphia	241
1916	Grover Alexander, Philadelphia	167
1917	Grover Alexander, Philadelphia	200
1918	Hippo Vaughn, Chicago	148
1919	Hippo Vaughn, Chicago	141
1920	Grover Alexander, Chicago	173
1921	Burleigh Grimes, Brooklyn	136
1922	Dazzy Vance, Brooklyn	134
1923	Dazzy Vance, Brooklyn	197
1924	Dazzy Vance, Brooklyn	262
1925	Dazzy Vance, Brooklyn	221
1925	Dazzy Vance, Brooklyn	140
1927	Dazzy Vance, Brooklyn	184
1928	Dazzy Vance, Brooklyn	200

Year	Pitcher, Club	No.
1929	Pat Malone, Chicago	166
1930	Bill Hallahan, St. Louis	177
1931	Bill Hallahan, St. Louis	159
1932	Dizzy Dean, St. Louis	191
1933	Dizzy Dean, St. Louis	199
1934	Dizzy Dean, St. Louis	195
1935	Dizzy Dean, St. Louis	182
1936	Van Lingle Mungo, Brooklyn	238
1937	Carl Hubbell, New York	159
1938	Clay Bryant, Chicago	135
1939	Claude Passeau, Philadelphia/Chicago	137
	Bucky Walters, Cincinnati	137
1940	Kirby Higbe, Philadelphia	137
1941	Johnny Vander Meer, Cincinnati	202
1942	Johnny Vander Meer, Cincinnati	186
1943	Johnny Vander Meer, Cincinnati	174
1944	Bill Voiselle, New York	161
1945	Preacher Roe, Pittsburgh	148
1946	Johnny Schmitz, Chicago	135
1947	Ewell Blackwell, Cincinnati	193
1948	Harry Brecheen, St. Louis	149
1949	Warren Spahn, Boston	151
1950	Warren Spahn, Boston	191
1951	Warren Spahn, Boston	164
	Don Newcombe, Brooklyn	164
1952	Warren Spahn, Boston	183
1953	Robin Roberts, Philadelphia	198
1954	Robin Roberts, Philadelphia	185
1955	Sam Jones, Chicago	198
1956	Sam Jones, Chicago	176
1957	Jack Sanford, Philadelphia	188
1958	Sam Jones, St. Louis	225
1959	Don Drysdale, Los Angeles	242
1960	Don Drysdale, Los Angeles	246
1961	Sandy Koufax, Los Angeles	269
1962	Don Drysdale, Los Angeles	232
1963	Sandy Koufax, Los Angeles	306
1964	Bob Veale, Pittsburgh	250
1965	Sandy Koufax, Los Angeles	382
1966	Sandy Koufax, Los Angeles	317
1967	Jim Bunning, Philadelphia	253
1968	Bob Gibson, St. Louis	268
1969	Ferguson Jenkins, Chicago	273
1970	Tom Seaver, New York	283
1971	Tom Seaver, New York	289
1972	Steve Carlton, Philadelphia	310
1973	Tom Seaver, New York	251
1974	Steve Carlton, Philadelphia	240
1975	Tom Seaver, New York	243
1976	Tom Seaver, New York	235
1977	Phil Niekro, Atlanta	262
1978	J.R. Richard, Houston	303
1979	J.R. Richard, Houston	313
1980	Steve Carlton, Philadelphia	286
1981	Fernando Valenzuela, Los Angeles	180
1982	Steve Carlton, Philadelphia	286
1983	Steve Carlton, Philadelphia	275
1984	Dwight Gooden, New York	276
1985	Dwight Gooden, New York	268
1986	Mike Scott, Houston	306
1987	Nolan Ryan, Houston	270
1988	Nolan Ryan, Houston	228
1989	Jose DeLeon, St. Louis	201
1990	David Cone, New York	233
1991	David Cone, New York	241
1992	John Smoltz, Atlanta	215
1993	Jose Rijo, Cincinnati	227
1994	Andy Benes, San Diego	189

CAREER MILESTONES

SERVICE

20-YEAR PLAYERS

(Does not include pitchers)

Rk.	Player	Yrs.	Games
1.	Deacon McGuire	26	1,781
2.	Eddie Collins	25	2,826
	Bobby Wallace	25	2,369
4.	Pete Rose	24	3,562
	Ty Cobb	24	3,033
	Carlton Fisk	24	2,499
	Rick Dempsey	24	1,766
8.	Carl Yastrzemski	23	3,308
	Rabbit Maranville	23	2,670
	Rogers Hornsby	23	2,259
	Hank Aaron	23	3,298
	Rusty Staub	23	2,951
	Brooks Robinson	23	2,896
	Tony Perez	23	2,777
15.	Stan Musial	22	3,026
	Willie Mays	22	2,992
	Al Kaline	22	2,834
	Tris Speaker	22	2,789
	Mel Ott	22	2,730
	Graig Nettles	22	2,700
	Joe Morgan	22	2,649
	Willie McCovey	22	2,588
	Bill Buckner	22	2,517
	Babe Ruth	22	2,503
	Harmon Killebrew	22	2,435
	Bill Dahlen	22	2,431
	Jimmie Dykes	22	2,282
	Cap Anson	22	2,253
	Phil Cavarretta	22	2,030
	Kid Gleason	22	1,942
	Harry H. Davis	22	1,746
32.	**Dave Winfield**	21	**2,927**
	Reggie Jackson	21	2,820
	Frank Robinson	21	2,808
	Honus Wagner	21	2,785
	George Brett	21	2,707
	Darrell Evans	21	2,687
	Nap Lajoie	21	2,475
	Ted Simmons	21	2,456
	Ron Fairly	21	2,442
	Willie Stargell	21	2,360
	Lave Cross	21	2,259
	Fred Clarke	21	2,204
	Bob O'Farrell	21	1,492
	Tim McCarver	21	1,909
	Jack O'Connor	21	1,404
47.	Robin Yount	20	2,856
	Dwight Evans	20	2,606
	Paul Waner	20	2,549
	Max Carey	20	2,469
	Luke Appling	20	2,422
	Mickey Vernon	20	2,409
	Sam Rice	20	2,404
	Jake Beckley	20	2,373
	George Davis	20	2,370
	Brian Downing	20	2,344
	Jimmie Foxx	20	2,317
	Doc Cramer	20	2,239
	Al Simmons	20	2,215
	Joe Judge	20	2,170
	Charlie Grimm	20	2,166
	Joe Cronin	20	2,124
	Gabby Hartnett	20	1,990
	Elmer Valo	20	1,806

Rk.	Player	Yrs.	Games
	Jay Johnstone	20	1,748
	Luke Sewell	20	1,630
	Manny Mota	20	1,536
	Johnny Cooney	20	1,172

Total number of players: (68)

20-YEAR PITCHERS

Rk.	Pitcher	Yrs.	Games
1.	Nolan Ryan	27	807
2.	Tommy John	26	760
3.	Jim Kaat	25	898
	Charlie Hough	25	**858**
5.	Phil Niekro	24	864
	Steve Carlton	24	741
7.	Don Sutton	23	774
	Early Wynn	23	691
9.	**Rich Gossage**	22	**1,002**
	Cy Young	22	906
	Gaylord Perry	22	777
	Joe Niekro	22	702
	Bert Blyleven	22	692
	Sam Jones	22	647
	Jerry Reuss	22	628
	Red Ruffing	22	624
	Herb Pennock	22	617
18.	Hoyt Wilhelm	21	1,070
	Lindy McDaniel	21	987
	Walter Johnson	21	802
	Warren Spahn	21	750
	Eppa Rixey	21	692
	Waite Hoyt	21	675
	Jack Quinn	21	665
	Frank Tanana	21	638
	Ted Lyons	21	594
27.	**Dennis Eckersley**	20	**849**
	Grover Alexander	20	696
	Red Faber	20	669
	Tom Seaver	20	656
	Dutch Leonard	20	640
	Bobo Newsom	20	600
	Mel Harder	20	582
	Curt Simmons	20	569
	Dolf Luque	20	550
	Clark Griffith	20	416

Total number of pitchers: (36)

BATTING

2,400 GAMES

(Does not include pitchers)

Rk.	Player	No.
1.	Pete Rose	3,562
2.	Carl Yastrzemski	3,308
3.	Hank Aaron	3,298
4.	Ty Cobb	3,033
5.	Stan Musial	3,026
6.	Willie Mays	2,992
7.	Rusty Staub	2,951
8.	**Dave Winfield**	**2,927**
9.	Brooks Robinson	2,896
10.	Robin Yount	2,856
11.	Al Kaline	2,834
12.	Eddie Collins	2,826
13.	Reggie Jackson	2,820

Rk.	Player	No.
14.	Frank Robinson	2,808
15.	Tris Speaker	2,790
16.	Honus Wagner	2,785
17.	Tony Perez	2,777
18.	Mel Ott	2,730
19.	George Brett	2,707
20.	**Eddie Murray**	**2,706**
21.	Graig Nettles	2,700
22.	Darrell Evans	2,687
23.	Rabbit Maranville	2,670
24.	Joe Morgan	2,649
25.	Lou Brock	2,616
26.	Dwight Evans	2,606
27.	Luis Aparicio	2,599
28.	Willie McCovey	2,588
29.	Paul Waner	2,549
30.	Ernie Banks	2,528
31.	Bill Buckner	2,517
32.	**Andre Dawson**	**2,506**
33.	Sam Crawford	2,505
34.	Babe Ruth	2,503
35.	Carlton Fisk	2,499
36.	Billy Williams	2,488
	Dave Concepcion	2,488
38.	Nap Lajoie	2,475
39.	Max Carey	2,469
	Vada Pinson	2,469
	Rod Carew	2,469
42.	Dave Parker	2,466
43.	Ted Simmons	2,456
44.	**Ozzie Smith**	**2,447**
45.	Ron Fairly	2,442
46.	Harmon Killebrew	2,435
47.	Roberto Clemente	2,433
48.	Bill Dahlen	2,431
49.	Willie Davis	2,429
50.	Luke Appling	2,422
51.	Mickey Vernon	2,409
52.	Zack Wheat	2,406
53.	Buddy Bell	2,405
54.	Sam Rice	2,404
	Mike Schmidt	2,404
56.	Mickey Mantle	2,401

Total number of players: (55)

500 CONSECUTIVE GAMES

Rk.	Player	No.
1.	Lou Gehrig	2,130
2.	**Cal Ripken Jr.**	**2,009**
3.	Everett Scott	1,307
4.	Steve Garvey	1,207
5.	Billy Williams	1,117
6.	Joe Sewell	1,103
7.	Stan Musial	895
8.	Eddie Yost	829
9.	Gus Suhr	822
10.	Nellie Fox	798
11.	Pete Rose*	745
12.	Dale Murphy	740
13.	Richie Ashburn	730
14.	Ernie Banks	717
15.	Pete Rose*	678
16.	Earl Averill	673
17.	Frank McCormick	652
18.	Sandy Alomar Sr.	648
19.	Eddie Brown	618
20.	Roy McMillan	585

Rk.	Player	No.
21.	George Pinckney	577
22.	Steve Brodie	574
23.	Aaron Ward	565
24.	Candy LaChance	540
25.	Buck Freeman	535
26.	Fred Luderus	533
27.	Charlie Gehringer*	511
	Clyde Milan	511
29.	Vada Pinson	508
30.	Joe Carter	507
31.	Tony Cuccinello	504
32.	Charlie Gehringer*	504
33.	Omar Moreno	503

*Only players with two streaks.

Total number of players: (33)

☐ BATTING .300, 10 TIMES ☐
(50 or more games, season)

Rk.	Player	Yrs.	Cons.
1.	Ty Cobb	23	23
2.	Cap Anson	18	*11
	Tris Speaker	18	10
4.	Honus Wagner	17	*17
	Stan Musial	17	†*16
	Eddie Collins	17	9
	Babe Ruth	17	8
8.	Ted Williams	16	†*15
9.	Rod Carew	15	15
	Dennis Brouthers	15	14
	Nap Lajoie	15	10
	Pete Rose	15	9
13.	Rogers Hornsby	14	12
	Paul Waner	14	*12
	Luke Appling	14	9
	Hank Aaron	14	5
17.	Willie Keeler	13	13
	Frankie Frisch	13	11
	Al Simmons	13	*11
	George Sisler	13	9
	George Van Haltren	13	9
	Roberto Clemente	13	8
	Charlie Gehringer	13	8
	Jim Ryan	13	7
	Jake Beckley	13	6
	Zack Wheat	13	6
	Jim O'Rourke	13	5
	Sam Rice	13	5
29.	Ed Delahanty	12	12
	Lou Gehrig	12	12
31.	Tony Gwynn	12	12
	Billy Hamilton	12	12
	Harry Heilmann	12	12
	Edd Roush	12	11
	Wade Boggs	12	*10
	Joe Medwick	12	*10
	Arky Vaughan	12	*10
	Riggs Stephenson	12	8
	Roger Connor	12	6
	Jimmie Foxx	12	5
	Joe Kelley	11	11
	Jesse Burkett	11	10
	Hugh Duffy	11	10
	Bill Terry	11	10
	Al Oliver	11	9
	Joe DiMaggio	11	7
	Goose Goslin	11	7
	Heinie Manush	11	7
	Bill Dickey	11	6
	George Brett	11	5
	Fred Clarke	11	5
	Stuffy McInnis	11	5
53.	Buck Ewing	10	8
	Pete Browning	10	7
	Spud Davis	10	7
	Willie Mays	10	7
	Kenny Williams	10	7
	Jake Daubert	10	6
	Patsy Donovan	10	6
	Pie Traynor	10	6
	Dixie Walker	10	6
	Lloyd Waner	10	6
	Ernie Lombardi	10	5
	Mickey Mantle	10	5
	Enos Slaughter	10	5
	Sam Crawford	10	4
	Kiki Cuyler	10	4
	Paul Molitor	10	4
	Mel Ott	10	3

*From start of career.
†Streak interrupted by military service.

Total number of players: (69)

☐ .300 LIFETIME AVERAGE ☐
(1,500 or more hits)

Rk.	Player	Hits	Avg.
1.	Ty Cobb	4,191	.367
2.	Rogers Hornsby	2,930	.358
3.	Joe Jackson	1,772	.356
4.	Pete Browning	1,719	.354
5.	Dennis Brouthers	2,349	.349
6.	Ed Delahanty	2,593	.346
7.	Tris Speaker	3,515	.345
	Willie Keeler	2,955	.345
9.	Ted Williams	2,654	.344
	Billy Hamilton	2,157	.344
11.	Babe Ruth	2,873	.342
	Jesse Burkett	2,872	.342
	Harry Heilmann	2,660	.342
14.	Bill Terry	2,193	.341
15.	George Sisler	2,812	.340
	Lou Gehrig	2,721	.340
17.	Nap Lajoie	3,252	.339
	Cap Anson	3,081	.339
19.	Sam Thompson	2,016	.336
	Riggs Stephenson	1,515	.336
21.	Wade Boggs	2,392	.335
22.	Al Simmons	2,927	.334
23.	Eddie Collins	3,309	.333
	Paul Waner	3,152	.333
	Tony Gwynn	2,204	.333
26.	Stan Musial	3,630	.331
27.	Heinie Manush	2,524	.330
	Hugh Duffy	2,307	.330
29.	Honus Wagner	3,430	.329
30.	Rod Carew	3,053	.328
31.	Jimmie Foxx	2,646	.325
	Roger Connor	2,535	.325
	Joe DiMaggio	2,214	.325
	Edd Roush	2,158	.325
	Earle Combs	1,866	.325
36.	Joe Medwick	2,471	.324
	Babe Herman	1,818	.324
38.	Sam Rice	2,987	.322
39.	George Van Haltren	2,573	.321
	Kiki Cuyler	2,299	.321
	Joe Kelley	2,245	.321
	Harry Stovey	1,925	.321
43.	Charlie Gehringer	2,839	.320
	Pie Traynor	2,416	.320
	Chuck Klein	2,076	.320
	Mickey Cochrane	1,652	.320
47.	Kenny Williams	1,552	.319
48.	Kirby Puckett	2,135	.318
	Arky Vaughan	2,103	.318
	Earl Averill	2,019	.318
51.	Roberto Clemente	3,000	.317
	Zack Wheat	2,884	.317
	Mike Tiernan	1,875	.317
54.	Lloyd Waner	2,459	.316
	Frankie Frisch	2,880	.316
	Goose Goslin	2,735	.316
57.	Fred Clarke	2,703	.315
	Elmer Flick	1,767	.315
	Jack Tobin	1,579	.315
60.	Jim Ryan	2,577	.314
	Jim O'Rourke	2,314	.314
	Cecil Travis	1,544	.314
	Hughey Jennings	1,520	.314
64.	Bill Dickey	1,969	.313
	King Kelly	1,853	.313
	Jack Fournier	1,631	.313
	Hank Greenberg	1,628	.313
68.	Joe Sewell	2,226	.312
	Johnny Mize	2,011	.312
	Ed Miller	1,937	.312
	Cupid Childs	1,757	.312
72.	Ginger Beaumont	1,754	.311
	Fred Lindstrom	1,747	.311
	Bill Jacobson	1,714	.311
	Buck Ewing	1,663	.311
	Jackie Robinson	1,518	.311
77.	Luke Appling	2,749	.310
	Jim Bottomley	2,313	.310
	Ed McKean	2,139	.310
	Bobby Veach	2,064	.310
	Emil Meusel	1,521	.310
82.	Sam Crawford	2,964	.309
	Jake Beckley	2,930	.309
	Don Mattingly	2,021	.309
	Bob Meusel	1,693	.309
86.	Richie Ashburn	2,574	.308
	Stuffy McInnis	2,406	.308
	Steve Brodie	1,749	.308
	George Gore	1,653	.308
90.	Paul Molitor	2,647	.307
	George Burns	2,018	.307
	Home Run Baker	1,838	.307
	Mike Griffin	1,830	.307
	Joe Vosmik	1,682	.307
	Chick Stahl	1,552	.307
	Matty Alou	1,777	.307
97.	Dixie Walker	2,064	.306
	George Kell	2,054	.306
	Ernie Lombardi	1,792	.306
	Deacon White	1,612	.306
	Ralph Garr	1,562	.306
102.	Hank Aaron	3,771	.305
	George Brett	3,154	.305
	Bill Madlock	2,008	.305
105.	Mel Ott	2,876	.304
	Billy Herman	2,345	.304
	Patsy Donovan	2,254	.304
	Paul Hines	1,884	.304
	Cy Seymour	1,720	.304
	Hardy Richardson	1,705	.304
	Tony Oliva	1,917	.304
112.	Pete Rose	4,256	.303
	Al Oliver	2,743	.303
	Jake Daubert	2,326	.303
	Buddy Myer	2,131	.303
	Harvey Kuenn	2,092	.303
	Charlie Jamieson	1,990	.303
118.	Ben Chapman	1,958	.302
	Hal Trosky	1,561	.302
	George Grantham	1,508	.302
	Tommy Holmes	1,507	.302
	Jack Doyle	1,814	.302
	Willie Mays	3,283	.302
124.	Joe Cronin	2,285	.301
	Stan Hack	2,193	.301

Rk.	Player	Hits	Avg.
	Julio Franco	1,922	.301
127.	Wally Berger	1,550	.300
	Billy Goodman	1,691	.300
	Pedro Guerrero	1,618	.300
	Enos Slaughter	2,383	.300

Total number of players: (130)

SLUGGING AVERAGE

(Players with 4,000 total bases)

Rk.	Player	TB	Slug Avg.
1.	Babe Ruth	5,793	.690
2.	Ted Williams	4,884	.634
3.	Lou Gehrig	5,060	.632
4.	Jimmie Foxx	4,956	.609
5.	Rogers Hornsby	4,712	.577
6.	Stan Musial	6,134	.559
7.	Willie Mays	6,066	.557
	Mickey Mantle	4,511	.557
9.	Hank Aaron	6,856	.555
10.	Frank Robinson	5,373	.537
11.	Al Simmons	4,685	.535
12.	Mel Ott	5,041	.533
13.	Willie Stargell	4,190	.529
14.	Mike Schmidt	4,404	.527
15.	Harry Heilmann	4,053	.520
16.	Willie McCovey	4,219	.515
17.	Ty Cobb	5,862	.513
18.	Eddie Mathews	4,349	.509
	Harmon Killebrew	4,143	.509
20.	Jim Rice	4,129	.502
21.	Goose Goslin	4,325	.500
	Tris Speaker	5,103	.500
	Ernie Banks	4,706	.500
24.	Billy Williams	4,599	.492
25.	Reggie Jackson	4,834	.490
26.	George Brett	5,044	.487
27.	Andre Dawson	4,665	.484
28.	Charlie Gehringer	4,257	.481
29.	Eddie Murray	4,883	.480
30.	Al Kaline	4,852	.480
31.	Dave Winfield	5,188	.476
32.	Roberto Clemente	4,492	.475
33.	Paul Waner	4,478	.473
34.	Dave Parker	4,405	.471
35.	Dwight Evans	4,230	.470
36.	Honus Wagner	4,888	.469
37.	Nap Lajoie	4,478	.467
38.	Tony Perez	4,532	.463
39.	Carl Yastrzemski	5,539	.462
40.	Cap Anson	4,145	.456
41.	Sam Crawford	4,328	.452
42.	Al Oliver	4,083	.451
43.	Zack Wheat	4,100	.450
44.	Vada Pinson	4,264	.442
45.	Jake Beckley	4,138	.437
46.	Rusty Staub	4,185	.431
47.	Robin Yount	4,730	.430
48.	Eddie Collins	4,259	.428
49.	Lou Brock	4,238	.410
50.	Pete Rose	5,752	.409
51.	Brooks Robinson	4,270	.401

Total number of players: (51)

9,000 AT-BATS

Rk.	Player	No.
1.	Pete Rose	14,053
2.	Hank Aaron	12,364
3.	Carl Yastrzemski	11,988
4.	Ty Cobb	11,429
5.	Robin Yount	11,008
6.	Stan Musial	10,972
7.	Dave Winfield	10,888
8.	Willie Mays	10,881
9.	Brooks Robinson	10,654
10.	Honus Wagner	10,427
11.	George Brett	10,349
12.	Lou Brock	10,332
13.	Luis Aparicio	10,230
14.	Tris Speaker	10,196
15.	Eddie Murray	10,167
16.	Al Kaline	10,116
17.	Rabbit Maranville	10,078
18.	Frank Robinson	10,006
19.	Eddie Collins	9,946
20.	Reggie Jackson	9,864
21.	Tony Perez	9,778
22.	Rusty Staub	9,720
23.	Vada Pinson	9,645
24.	Andre Dawson	9,643
25.	Nap Lajoie	9,589
26.	Sam Crawford	9,579
27.	Jake Beckley	9,476
28.	Paul Waner	9,459
29.	Mel Ott	9,456
30.	Roberto Clemente	9,454
31.	Ernie Banks	9,421
32.	Bill Buckner	9,397
33.	Max Carey	9,363
34.	Dave Parker	9,358
35.	Billy Williams	9,350
36.	Rod Carew	9,315
37.	Joe Morgan	9,277
38.	Sam Rice	9,269
39.	Nellie Fox	9,232
40.	Willie Davis	9,174
41.	Roger Cramer	9,140
42.	Frankie Frisch	9,112
43.	Zack Wheat	9,106
44.	Cap Anson	9,084
45.	Lave Cross	9,065
46.	Al Oliver	9,049
47.	George Davis	9,027
48.	Bill Dahlen	9,019
49.	Ozzie Smith	9,013

Total number of players: (49)

1,500 RUNS

Rk.	Player	No.
1.	Ty Cobb	2,245
2.	Hank Aaron	2,174
	Babe Ruth	2,174
4.	Pete Rose	2,165
5.	Willie Mays	2,062
6.	Stan Musial	1,949
7.	Lou Gehrig	1,888
8.	Tris Speaker	1,881
9.	Mel Ott	1,859
10.	Frank Robinson	1,829
11.	Eddie Collins	1,816
	Carl Yastrzemski	1,816
13.	Ted Williams	1,798
14.	Charlie Gehringer	1,774
15.	Jimmie Foxx	1,751
16.	Honus Wagner	1,740
17.	Willie Keeler	1,720
18.	Cap Anson	1,712
19.	Jesse Burkett	1,708
20.	Billy Hamilton	1,690
21.	Mickey Mantle	1,677
22.	Bid McPhee	1,674
23.	Dave Winfield	1,658
24.	Rickey Henderson	1,652
25.	Joe Morgan	1,650
	George Van Haltren	1,650
27.	Jim Ryan	1,640
28.	Robin Yount	1,632
29.	Paul Waner	1,627
30.	Al Kaline	1,622
31.	Fred Clarke	1,620
32.	Lou Brock	1,610
33.	Roger Connor	1,607
34.	Jake Beckley	1,601
35.	Ed Delahanty	1,596
36.	Bill Dahlen	1,594
37.	George Brett	1,583
38.	Rogers Hornsby	1,579
39.	Reggie Jackson	1,551
40.	George Davis	1,546
41.	Max Carey	1,545
	Hugh Duffy	1,545
43.	Frankie Frisch	1,532
44.	Sam Rice	1,514
45.	Eddie Mathews	1,509
46.	Dennis Brouthers	1,507
	Tom Brown	1,507
	Al Simmons	1,507
49.	Nap Lajoie	1,506
	Mike Schmidt	1,506

Total number of players: (50)

2,500 HITS

Rk.	Player	No.
1.	Pete Rose	4,256
2.	Ty Cobb	4,191
3.	Hank Aaron	3,771
4.	Stan Musial	3,630
5.	Tris Speaker	3,515
6.	Honus Wagner	3,430
7.	Carl Yastrzemski	3,419
8.	Eddie Collins	3,309
9.	Willie Mays	3,283
10.	Nap Lajoie	3,252
11.	George Brett	3,154
12.	Paul Waner	3,152
13.	Robin Yount	3,142
14.	Dave Winfield	3,088
15.	Cap Anson	3,081
16.	Rod Carew	3,053
17.	Lou Brock	3,023
18.	Al Kaline	3,007
19.	Roberto Clemente	3,000
20.	Sam Rice	2,987
21.	Sam Crawford	2,964
22.	Willie Keeler	2,955
23.	Frank Robinson	2,943
24.	Jake Beckley	2,930
	Rogers Hornsby	2,930
	Eddie Murray	2,930
27.	Al Simmons	2,927
28.	Zack Wheat	2,884
29.	Frankie Frisch	2,880
30.	Mel Ott	2,876
31.	Babe Ruth	2,873
32.	Jesse Burkett	2,872
33.	Brooks Robinson	2,848
34.	Charlie Gehringer	2,839
35.	George Sisler	2,812
36.	Vada Pinson	2,757
37.	Luke Appling	2,749
38.	Al Oliver	2,743
39.	Goose Goslin	2,735
40.	Tony Perez	2,732
41.	Lou Gehrig	2,721
42.	Rusty Staub	2,716
43.	Bill Buckner	2,715

Rk.	Player	No.
44.	Dave Parker	2,712
45.	Billy Williams	2,711
46.	Roger Cramer	2,705
47.	Fred Clarke	2,703
48.	**Andre Dawson**	**2,700**
49.	George Davis	2,683
50.	Luis Aparicio	2,677
51.	Max Carey	2,665
52.	Nellie Fox	2,663
53.	Harry Heilmann	2,660
54.	Lave Cross	2,654
	Ted Williams	2,654
56.	**Paul Molitor**	**2,647**
57.	Jimmie Foxx	2,646
58.	Rabbit Maranville	2,605
59.	Steve Garvey	2,599
60.	Ed Delahanty	2,593
61.	Reggie Jackson	2,584
62.	Ernie Banks	2,583
63.	Jim Ryan	2,577
64.	Richie Ashburn	2,574
65.	George Van Haltren	2,573
66.	Willie Davis	2,561
67.	Roger Connor	2,535
68.	Heinie Manush	2,524
69.	Joe Morgan	2,517
70.	Buddy Bell	2,514

Total number of players: (70)

[] 200-HIT SEASONS, 4 TIMES []

Rk.	Player	Yrs.
1.	Pete Rose	10
2.	Ty Cobb	9
3.	Lou Gehrig	8
	Willie Keeler	8
	Paul Waner	8
6.	**Wade Boggs**	**7**
	Charlie Gehringer	7
	Rogers Hornsby	7
9.	Jesse Burkett	6
	Steve Garvey	6
	Stan Musial	6
	Sam Rice	6
	Al Simmons	6
	George Sisler	6
	Bill Terry	6
16.	Chuck Klein	5
	Nap Lajoie	5
	Kirby Puckett	**5**
19.	Lou Brock	4
	Rod Carew	4
	Roberto Clemente	4
	Tony Gwynn	**4**
	Harry Heilmann	4
	Joe Jackson	4
	Heinie Manush	4
	Joe Medwick	4
	Vada Pinson	4
	Jim Rice	4
	Tris Speaker	4
	Jack Tobin	4
	Lloyd Waner	4

Total number of players: (31)

[] 2,000 SINGLES []

Rk.	Player	No.
1.	Pete Rose	3,215
2.	Ty Cobb	3,052
3.	Eddie Collins	2,639
4.	Willie Keeler	2,534
5.	Honus Wagner	2,426
6.	Rod Carew	2,404
7.	Tris Speaker	2,383
8.	Nap Lajoie	2,354
9.	Cap Anson	2,330
10.	Jesse Burkett	2,301
11.	Hank Aaron	2,294
12.	Sam Rice	2,272
13.	Carl Yastrzemski	2,262
14.	Stan Musial	2,253
15.	Lou Brock	2,247
16.	Paul Waner	2,243
17.	Robin Yount	2,182
18.	Frankie Frisch	2,171
19.	Roger Cramer	2,163
20.	Luke Appling	2,162
21.	Nellie Fox	2,161
22.	Roberto Clemente	2,154
23.	Jake Beckley	2,142
24.	George Sisler	2,122
25.	Richie Ashburn	2,119
26.	Luis Aparicio	2,108
27.	Zack Wheat	2,104
28.	Sam Crawford	2,102
29.	Lave Cross	2,077
30.	Fred Clarke	2,061
31.	George Brett	2,035
32.	Al Kaline	2,035
33.	Lloyd Waner	2,032
34.	Brooks Robinson	2,030
35.	Rabbit Maranville	2,020
36.	Max Carey	2,018
37.	George Van Haltren	2,008
38.	George Davis	2,007
39.	**Dave Winfield**	**2,002**

Total number of players: (39)

[] 450 DOUBLES []

Rk.	Player	No.
1.	Tris Speaker	793
2.	Pete Rose	746
3.	Stan Musial	725
4.	Ty Cobb	724
5.	George Brett	665
6.	Nap Lajoie	652
7.	Honus Wagner	651
8.	Carl Yastrzemski	646
9.	Hank Aaron	624
10.	Paul Waner	605
11.	Robin Yount	583
12.	Charlie Gehringer	574
13.	Harry Heilmann	542
14.	Rogers Hornsby	541
15.	Joe Medwick	540
16.	Al Simmons	539
17.	**Dave Winfield**	**535**
18.	Lou Gehrig	534
19.	Cap Anson	530
20.	Al Oliver	529
21.	Frank Robinson	528
22.	Dave Parker	526
23.	Ted Williams	525
24.	Willie Mays	523
25.	Joe Cronin	516
26.	**Eddie Murray**	**511**
27.	Ed Delahanty	508
28.	Babe Ruth	506
29.	Tony Perez	505
30.	Goose Goslin	500
31.	Rusty Staub	499
32.	Bill Buckner	498
	Al Kaline	498
	Sam Rice	498

Rk.	Player	No.
35.	**Andre Dawson**	**491**
36.	Heinie Manush	491
37.	Mickey Vernon	490
38.	Mel Ott	488
39.	Lou Brock	486
	Billy Herman	486
41.	Vada Pinson	485
42.	Hal McRae	484
43.	Dwight Evans	483
	Ted Simmons	483
45.	Brooks Robinson	482
46.	Zack Wheat	476
47.	**Paul Molitor**	**472**
48.	**Wade Boggs**	**467**
49.	Frankie Frisch	466
50.	Jim Bottomley	465
51.	Reggie Jackson	463
52.	Jimmie Foxx	458
53.	Jake Beckley	455
	Sam Crawford	455
55.	Jimmie Dykes	453

Total number of players: (55)

[] 150 TRIPLES []

Rk.	Player	No.
1.	Sam Crawford	312
2.	Ty Cobb	298
3.	Honus Wagner	252
4.	Jake Beckley	246
5.	Roger Connor	227
6.	Tris Speaker	222
7.	Fred Clarke	219
8.	Dennis Brouthers	212
9.	Paul Waner	191
10.	Joe Kelley	189
11.	Eddie Collins	186
12.	Jesse Burkett	185
	Harry Stovey	185
14.	Sam Rice	184
15.	Ed Delahanty	182
16.	Bid McPhee	180
17.	Bill Ewing	179
18.	Rabbit Maranville	177
	Stan Musial	177
20.	Goose Goslin	173
21.	Zack Wheat	172
22.	Elmer Flick	170
	Tommy Leach	170
24.	Rogers Hornsby	169
25.	Joe Jackson	168
	Edd Roush	168
27.	George Davis	167
28.	Roberto Clemente	166
	Bill Dahlen	166
	Sherry Magee	166
31.	Jake Daubert	165
32.	Nap Lajoie	164
	George Sisler	164
	Pie Traynor	164
35.	Lou Gehrig	163
	Ed Konetchy	163
37.	Harry Hooper	160
	Heinie Manush	160
39.	Max Carey	159
	Joe Judge	159
	Mike Tiernan	159
	George Van Haltren	159
43.	Kiki Cuyler	157
44.	Willie Keeler	155
45.	Earle Combs	154
46.	Jim Ryan	153
47.	Ed McKean	152

Rk.	Player	No.
48.	Jim Bottomley	151
	Tommy Corcoran	151
	Harry Heilmann	151

Total number of players: (50)

250 HOME RUNS

Rk.	Player	No.
1.	Hank Aaron	755
2.	Babe Ruth	714
3.	Willie Mays	660
4.	Frank Robinson	586
5.	Harmon Killebrew	573
6.	Reggie Jackson	563
7.	Mike Schmidt	548
8.	Mickey Mantle	536
9.	Jimmie Foxx	534
10.	Willie McCovey	521
	Ted Williams	521
12.	Ernie Banks	512
	Eddie Mathews	512
14.	Mel Ott	511
15.	Lou Gehrig	493
16.	Stan Musial	475
	Willie Stargell	475
18.	Dave Winfield	463
19.	Eddie Murray	458
20.	Carl Yastrzemski	452
21.	Dave Kingman	442
22.	Andre Dawson	428
23.	Billy Williams	426
24.	Darrell Evans	414
25.	Duke Snider	407
26.	Al Kaline	399
27.	Dale Murphy	398
28.	Graig Nettles	390
29.	Johnny Bench	389
30.	Dwight Evans	385
31.	Frank Howard	382
	Jim Rice	382
33.	Orlando Cepeda	379
	Tony Perez	379
35.	Norm Cash	377
36.	Carlton Fisk	376
37.	Rocky Colavito	374
38.	Gil Hodges	370
39.	Ralph Kiner	369
40.	Joe DiMaggio	361
41.	Johnny Mize	359
42.	Yogi Berra	358
43.	Lee May	354
44.	Dick Allen	351
45.	George Foster	348
46.	Ron Santo	342
47.	Jack Clark	340
48.	Dave Parker	339
	Boog Powell	339
50.	Don Baylor	338
51.	Joe Adcock	336
52.	Bobby Bonds	332
53.	Hank Greenberg	331
54.	Willie Horton	325
55.	Gary Carter	324
56.	Roy Sievers	318
57.	George Brett	317
	Lance Parrish	317
59.	Ron Cey	316
60.	Reggie Smith	314
61.	Cal Ripken Jr.	310
62.	Greg Luzinski	307
	Al Simmons	307
64.	Fred Lynn	306
65.	Joe Carter	302
66.	Rogers Hornsby	301
67.	Chuck Klein	300

Rk.	Player	No.
68.	Darryl Strawberry	294
69.	Kent Hrbek	293
70.	Rusty Staub	292
71.	Jim Wynn	291
72.	Del Ennis	288
	Bob Johnson	288
	Hank Sauer	288
75.	Frank J. Thomas	286
76.	Ken Boyer	282
77.	Ted Kluszewski	279
78.	Harold Baines	277
	Rudy York	277
80.	Jose Canseco	276
81.	Brian Downing	275
	Roger Maris	275
83.	Steve Garvey	272
84.	Tom Brunansky	271
	George Scott	271
86.	Joe Morgan	268
	Brooks Robinson	268
	Gorman Thomas	268
89.	George Hendrick	267
90.	Vic Wertz	266
91.	George Bell	265
92.	Bobby Thomson	264
93.	Fred McGriff	262
94.	Barry Bonds	259
95.	Gary Gaetti	257
96.	Bob Allison	256
	Larry Parrish	256
	Vada Pinson	256
99.	John Mayberry	255
100.	Larry Doby	253
	Joe Gordon	253
	Andre Thornton	253
103.	Bobby Murcer	252
	Joe Torre	252
105.	Tony Armas	251
	Cy Williams	251
	Robin Yount	251
108.	Chili Davis	250

Total number of players: (108)

10 PINCH HOME RUNS

Rk.	Player	No.
1.	Cliff Johnson	20
2.	Jerry Lynch	18
3.	Gates Brown	16
	Smoky Burgess	16
	Willie McCovey	16
6.	George Crowe	14
7.	Joe Adcock	12
	Bob Cerv	12
	Jose Morales	12
	Graig Nettles	12
11.	Jeff Burroughs	11
	Jay Johnstone	11
	Fred Whitfield	11
	Cy Williams	11
15.	Jim Dwyer	10
	Mike Lum	10
	Ken McMullen	10
	Don Mincher	10
	Wally Post	10
	Champ Summers	10
	Jerry Turner	10
	Gus Zernial	10

Total number of players: (22)

25 MULTIPLE-HR GAMES

Rk.	Player	No.
1.	Babe Ruth	72

Rk.	Player	No.
2.	Willie Mays	63
3.	Hank Aaron	62
4.	Jimmie Foxx	55
5.	Frank Robinson	54
6.	Eddie Mathews	49
	Mel Ott	49
8.	Harmon Killebrew	46
	Mickey Mantle	46
10.	Willie McCovey	44
	Mike Schmidt	44
12.	Lou Gehrig	43
	Dave Kingman	43
14.	Ernie Banks	42
	Reggie Jackson	42
16.	Ralph Kiner	40
17.	Andre Dawson	38
18.	Stan Musial	37
	Ted Williams	37
20.	Willie Stargell	36
21.	Joe DiMaggio	35
	Hank Greenberg	35
	Lee May	35
	Jim Rice	35
25.	Duke Snider	34
26.	Dick Allen	32
	Rocky Colavito	32
	Dale Murphy	32
	Gus Zernial	32
30.	Hank Sauer	31
	Billy Williams	31
32.	Joe Carter	30
	Gil Hodges	30
	Willie Horton	30
	Johnny Mize	30
	Dave Winfield	30
37.	Joe Adcock	28
	Chuck Klein	28
	Eddie Murray	28
40.	Graig Nettles	27
	Roy Sievers	27
	Hack Wilson	27
	Carl Yastrzemski	27
44.	Gary Carter	26
	Bob Horner	26
	Frank Howard	26
	Mark McGwire	26
	Ron Santo	26
49.	Norm Cash	25
	Carlton Fisk	25
	Roger Maris	25
	Darryl Strawberry	25
	Hal Trosky	25

Total number of players: (53)

8 GRAND SLAMS

Rk.	Player	No.
1.	Lou Gehrig	23
2.	Willie McCovey	18
3.	Jimmie Foxx	17
	Eddie Murray	17
	Ted Williams	17
6.	Hank Aaron	16
	Dave Kingman	16
	Babe Ruth	16
9.	Gil Hodges	14
10.	Joe DiMaggio	13
	George Foster	13
	Ralph Kiner	13
13.	Ernie Banks	12
	Don Baylor	12
	Rogers Hornsby	12
	Joe Rudi	12
	Rudy York	12

Rk.	Player	No.
18.	Johnny Bench	11
	Gary Carter	11
	Hank Greenberg	11
	Reggie Jackson	11
	Harmon Killebrew	11
	Lee May	11
	Willie Stargell	11
	Dave Winfield	11
26.	Joe Adcock	10
	George Bell	10
	Jeff Burroughs	10
	Darrell Evans	10
	John Milner	10
	Roy Sievers	10
	Al Simmons	10
	Vern Stephens	10
	Danny Tartabull	10
	Vic Wertz	10
36.	Yogi Berra	9
	Orlando Cepeda	9
	Sam Chapman	9
	Jack Clark	9
	Walker Cooper	9
	Alvin Davis	9
	Willie Horton	9
	Mickey Mantle	9
	Stan Musial	9
	Rico Petrocelli	9
	Al Rosen	9
	Ted Simmons	9
	Rusty Staub	9
	Dick Stuart	9
	Gus Zernial	9
51.	Dick Allen	8
	Harold Baines	8
	Buddy Bell	8
	Ray Boone	8
	Hubie Brooks	8
	Ellis Burks	8
	Norm Cash	8
	Bill Dickey	8
	Bobby Doerr	8
	Carl Furillo	8
	Kent Hrbek	8
	Jackie Jensen	8
	Bob Johnson	8
	George Kelly	8
	Tony Lazzeri	8
	Eddie Mathews	8
	Willie Mays	8
	Dick McAuliffe	8
	Bill Nicholson	8
	Ron Northey	8
	Jim Northrup	8
	Dave Parker	8
	Vada Pinson	8
	Jim Rice	8
	Andy Seminick	8
	Bobby Thomson	8
	Billy Williams	8

Total number of players: (77)

4,000 TOTAL BASES

Rk.	Player	No.
1.	Hank Aaron	6,856
2.	Stan Musial	6,134
3.	Willie Mays	6,066
4.	Ty Cobb	5,862
5.	Babe Ruth	5,793
6.	Pete Rose	5,752
7.	Carl Yastrzemski	5,539
8.	Frank Robinson	5,373
9.	**Dave Winfield**	5,188
10.	Tris Speaker	5,103
11.	Lou Gehrig	5,060
12.	George Brett	5,044
13.	Mel Ott	5,041
14.	Jimmie Foxx	4,956
15.	Honus Wagner	4,888
16.	Ted Williams	4,884
17.	**Eddie Murray**	4,883
18.	Al Kaline	4,852
19.	Reggie Jackson	4,834
20.	Robin Yount	4,730
21.	Rogers Hornsby	4,712
22.	Ernie Banks	4,706
23.	Al Simmons	4,685
24.	**Andre Dawson**	4,665
25.	Billy Williams	4,599
26.	Tony Perez	4,532
27.	Mickey Mantle	4,511
28.	Roberto Clemente	4,492
29.	Nap Lajoie	4,478
	Paul Waner	4,478
31.	Dave Parker	4,405
32.	Mike Schmidt	4,404
33.	Eddie Mathews	4,349
34.	Sam Crawford	4,328
35.	Goose Goslin	4,325
36.	Brooks Robinson	4,270
37.	Vada Pinson	4,264
38.	Eddie Collins	4,259
39.	Charlie Gehringer	4,257
40.	Lou Brock	4,238
41.	Dwight Evans	4,230
42.	Willie McCovey	4,219
43.	Willie Stargell	4,190
44.	Rusty Staub	4,185
45.	Cap Anson	4,145
46.	Harmon Killebrew	4,143
47.	Jake Beckley	4,138
48.	Jim Rice	4,129
49.	Zack Wheat	4,100
50.	Al Oliver	4,083
51.	Harry Heilmann	4,053

Total number of players: (51)

800 LONG HITS

Rk.	Player	No.
1.	Hank Aaron	1,477
2.	Stan Musial	1,377
3.	Babe Ruth	1,356
4.	Willie Mays	1,323
5.	Lou Gehrig	1,190
6.	Frank Robinson	1,186
7.	Carl Yastrzemski	1,157
8.	Ty Cobb	1,139
9.	Tris Speaker	1,132
10.	George Brett	1,119
11.	Jimmie Foxx	1,117
	Ted Williams	1,117
13.	**Dave Winfield**	1,086
14.	Reggie Jackson	1,075
15.	Mel Ott	1,071
16.	Pete Rose	1,041
17.	Mike Schmidt	1,015
18.	**Andre Dawson**	1,014
19.	Rogers Hornsby	1,011
20.	Ernie Banks	1,009
21.	Honus Wagner	1,004
22.	**Eddie Murray**	1,003
23.	Al Simmons	995
24.	Al Kaline	972
25.	Tony Perez	963
26.	Robin Yount	960
27.	Willie Stargell	953
28.	Mickey Mantle	952
29.	Billy Williams	948
30.	Dwight Evans	941
31.	Dave Parker	940
32.	Eddie Mathews	938
33.	Goose Goslin	921
34.	Willie McCovey	920
35.	Paul Waner	909
36.	Charlie Gehringer	904
37.	Nap Lajoie	898
38.	Harmon Killebrew	887
39.	Joe DiMaggio	881
40.	Harry Heilmann	876
41.	Vada Pinson	868
42.	Sam Crawford	862
43.	Joe Medwick	858
44.	Duke Snider	850
45.	Roberto Clemente	846
46.	Carlton Fisk	844
47.	Rusty Staub	838
48.	Jim Bottomley	835
49.	Jim Rice	834
50.	Al Oliver	825
51.	Orlando Cepeda	823
52.	Brooks Robinson	818
53.	Joe Morgan	813
54.	Johnny Mize	809
55.	Joe Cronin	803

Total number of players: (55)

1,500 EXTRA BASES

Rk.	Player	No.
1.	Hank Aaron	3,085
2.	Babe Ruth	2,920
3.	Willie Mays	2,783
4.	Stan Musial	2,504
5.	Frank Robinson	2,430
6.	Lou Gehrig	2,339
7.	Jimmie Foxx	2,310
8.	Reggie Jackson	2,250
9.	Ted Williams	2,230
10.	Mike Schmidt	2,170
11.	Mel Ott	2,165
12.	Ernie Banks	2,123
13.	Carl Yastrzemski	2,120
14.	**Dave Winfield**	2,100
15.	Mickey Mantle	2,096
16.	Harmon Killebrew	2,057
17.	Eddie Mathews	2,034
18.	Willie McCovey	2,008
19.	**Andre Dawson**	1,965
20.	**Eddie Murray**	1,953
21.	Willie Stargell	1,951
22.	Billy Williams	1,888
23.	Al Kaline	1,845
24.	George Brett	1,890
25.	Tony Perez	1,800
26.	Dwight Evans	1,784
27.	Rogers Hornsby	1,782
28.	Al Simmons	1,758
29.	Duke Snider	1,749
30.	Joe DiMaggio	1,734
31.	Dave Parker	1,693
32.	Jim Rice	1,677
33.	Ty Cobb	1,671
34.	Darrell Evans	1,643
	Carlton Fisk	1,643
36.	Dale Murphy	1,622
37.	Dave Kingman	1,616
38.	Johnny Mize	1,610
39.	Orlando Cepeda	1,608
40.	Johnny Bench	1,596
41.	Goose Goslin	1,590

Rk.	Player	No.
42.	Tris Speaker	1,588
	Robin Yount	1,588
44.	Graig Nettles	1,554
45.	Dick Allen	1,531
46.	Ron Santo	1,525
47.	Hank Greenberg	1,514
48.	Vada Pinson	1,507
49.	Gil Hodges	1,501

Total number of players: (49)

☐ 1,200 RUNS BATTED IN ☐

Rk.	Player	No.
1.	Hank Aaron	2,297
2.	Babe Ruth	2,204
3.	Lou Gehrig	1,990
4.	Ty Cobb	1,960
5.	Stan Musial	1,951
6.	Jimmie Foxx	1,921
7.	Willie Mays	1,903
8.	Mel Ott	1,861
9.	Carl Yastrzemski	1,844
10.	Ted Williams	1,839
11.	**Dave Winfield**	**1,829**
12.	Al Simmons	1,827
13.	Frank Robinson	1,812
14.	**Eddie Murray**	**1,738**
15.	Reggie Jackson	1,702
16.	Tony Perez	1,652
17.	Ernie Banks	1,636
18.	Goose Goslin	1,609
19.	George Brett	1,595
	Mike Schmidt	1,595
21.	Harmon Killebrew	1,584
22.	Al Kaline	1,583
23.	Rogers Hornsby	1,578
24.	Tris Speaker	1,562
25.	Willie McCovey	1,555
26.	Harry Heilmann	1,551
27.	**Andre Dawson**	**1,540**
	Willie Stargell	1,540
29.	Joe DiMaggio	1,537
30.	Mickey Mantle	1,509
31.	Dave Parker	1,493
32.	Billy Williams	1,476
33.	Rusty Staub	1,466
34.	Eddie Mathews	1,453
35.	Jim Rice	1,451
36.	Yogi Berra	1,430
37.	Charlie Gehringer	1,427
38.	Joe Cronin	1,423
39.	Jim Bottomley	1,422
40.	Robin Yount	1,406
41.	Ted Simmons	1,389
42.	Dwight Evans	1,384
43.	Joe Medwick	1,383
44.	Johnny Bench	1,376
45.	Orlando Cepeda	1,365
46.	Brooks Robinson	1,357
47.	Darrell Evans	1,354
48.	Johnny Mize	1,337
49.	Duke Snider	1,333
50.	Ron Santo	1,331
51.	Carlton Fisk	1,330
52.	Al Oliver	1,326
53.	Graig Nettles	1,314
	Pete Rose	1,314
55.	Mickey Vernon	1,311
56.	Paul Waner	1,309
57.	Steve Garvey	1,308
58.	Eddie Collins	1,307
59.	Roberto Clemente	1,305
60.	Enos Slaughter	1,304
61.	Del Ennis	1,284

Rk.	Player	No.
62.	Bob Johnson	1,283
63.	Don Baylor	1,276
	Hank Greenberg	1,276
65.	Gil Hodges	1,274
66.	Pie Traynor	1,273
67.	Dale Murphy	1,266
68.	Zack Wheat	1,265
69.	Bobby Doerr	1,247
70.	Lee May	1,244
71.	Frankie Frisch	1,242
72.	George Foster	1,239
73.	Gary Carter	1,225
74.	Dave Kingman	1,210
75.	Bill Dickey	1,209
76.	Bill Buckner	1,208
77.	Chuck Klein	1,202

Total number of players: (77)

☐ 1,000 BASES ON BALLS ☐

Rk.	Player	No.
1.	Babe Ruth	2,056
2.	Ted Williams	2,019
3.	Joe Morgan	1,865
4.	Carl Yastrzemski	1,845
5.	Mickey Mantle	1,734
6.	Mel Ott	1,708
7.	Eddie Yost	1,614
8.	Darrell Evans	1,605
9.	Stan Musial	1,599
10.	Pete Rose	1,566
11.	Harmon Killebrew	1,559
12.	Lou Gehrig	1,508
13.	Mike Schmidt	1,507
14.	**Rickey Henderson**	**1,478**
15.	Willie Mays	1,464
16.	Jimmie Foxx	1,452
17.	Eddie Mathews	1,444
18.	Frank Robinson	1,420
19.	Hank Aaron	1,402
20.	Dwight Evans	1,391
21.	Reggie Jackson	1,375
22.	Willie McCovey	1,345
23.	Luke Appling	1,302
24.	Al Kaline	1,277
25.	Jack Clark	1,262
	Ken Singleton	1,262
27.	Rusty Staub	1,255
28.	Willie Randolph	1,243
29.	Jim Wynn	1,224
30.	**Eddie Murray**	**1,218**
31.	Eddie Collins	1,213
32.	Pee Wee Reese	1,210
33.	**Dave Winfield**	**1,202**
34.	Richie Ashburn	1,198
35.	Brian Downing	1,197
36.	Charlie Gehringer	1,185
37.	**Lou Whitaker**	**1,166**
38.	Max Bishop	1,153
	Toby Harrah	1,153
40.	Tris Speaker	1,146
41.	**Wade Boggs**	**1,139**
42.	Ron Santo	1,108
43.	George Brett	1,096
44.	Lu Blue	1,092
	Stan Hack	1,092
46.	Paul Waner	1,091
47.	Graig Nettles	1,088
48.	Bobby Grich	1,087
49.	Bob Johnson	1,073
50.	Harlond Clift	1,070
	Keith Hernandez	1,070
52.	**Tim Raines**	**1,064**
53.	Joe Cronin	1,059

Rk.	Player	No.
54.	Ron Fairly	1,052
55.	Billy Williams	1,045
56.	Norm Cash	1,043
57.	Eddie Joost	1,041
58.	Max Carey	1,040
59.	Rogers Hornsby	1,038
60.	Junior Gilliam	1,036
61.	Sal Bando	1,031
62.	**Ozzie Smith**	**1,030**
63.	Rod Carew	1,018
	Enos Slaughter	1,018
65.	Ron Cey	1,012
66.	**Brett Butler**	**1,011**
67.	Ralph Kiner	1,011
68.	Boog Powell	1,001

Total number of players: (68)

Note—Does not include seasons in N.L. before 1910 and in A.L. prior to 1913.

☐ 1,200 STRIKEOUTS ☐

Rk.	Player	No.
1.	Reggie Jackson	2,597
2.	Willie Stargell	1,936
3.	Mike Schmidt	1,883
4.	Tony Perez	1,867
5.	Dave Kingman	1,816
6.	Bobby Bonds	1,757
7.	Dale Murphy	1,748
8.	Lou Brock	1,730
9.	Mickey Mantle	1,710
10.	Harmon Killebrew	1,699
11.	Dwight Evans	1,697
12.	**Dave Winfield**	**1,660**
13.	Lee May	1,570
14.	Dick Allen	1,556
15.	Willie McCovey	1,550
16.	Dave Parker	1,537
17.	Frank Robinson	1,532
18.	Willie Mays	1,526
19.	Rick Monday	1,513
20.	Greg Luzinski	1,495
21.	Eddie Mathews	1,487
22.	**Lance Parrish**	**1,475**
23.	Frank Howard	1,460
24.	**Andre Dawson**	**1,451**
25.	Jack Clark	1,441
26.	Jim Wynn	1,427
27.	Jim Rice	1,423
28.	George Foster	1,419
29.	George Scott	1,418
30.	Darrell Evans	1,410
31.	Carl Yastrzemski	1,393
32.	Carlton Fisk	1,386
33.	Hank Aaron	1,383
34.	Rob Deer	1,379
35.	Larry Parrish	1,359
36.	Robin Yount	1,350
37.	Ron Santo	1,343
38.	Gorman Thomas	1,339
39.	**Eddie Murray**	**1,338**
40.	Babe Ruth	1,330
41.	Deron Johnson	1,318
42.	Willie Horton	1,313
43.	Jimmie Foxx	1,311
44.	**Chili Davis**	**1,306**
45.	**Juan Samuel**	**1,287**
46.	Johnny Bench	1,278
	Bobby Grich	1,278
48.	Claudell Washington	1,266
49.	Ken Singleton	1,246
50.	Duke Snider	1,237
51.	Ernie Banks	1,236
52.	Ron Cey	1,235

Rk.	Player	No.
53.	Jesse Barfield	1,234
54.	Roberto Clemente	1,230
55.	Boog Powell	1,226
56.	Kirk Gibson	1,224
57.	Gary Gaetti	1,210
58.	Graig Nettles	1,209
59.	Tony Armas	1,201

Total number of players: (59)

BASERUNNING

400 STOLEN BASES

Rk.	Player	No.
1.	Rickey Henderson	1,117
2.	Lou Brock	938
3.	Billy Hamilton	937
4.	Ty Cobb	892
5.	Arlie Latham	791
6.	Tim Raines	764
7.	Harry Stovey	744
8.	Eddie Collins	743
9.	Max Carey	738
10.	Honus Wagner	720
11.	Vince Coleman	698
12.	Tom Brown	697
13.	Joe Morgan	689
14.	Willie Wilson	668
15.	Bert Campaneris	649
16.	George Davis	632
17.	Dummy Hoy	605
	Monte Ward	605
19.	Bid McPhee	602
20.	Hugh Duffy	597
21.	Bill Dahlen	587
22.	Maury Wills	586
23.	Ozzie Smith	569
24.	Jack Doyle	560
25.	Dave Lopes	557
26.	Herman Long	554
27.	Cesar Cedeno	550
28.	Mike Griffin	549
29.	George Van Haltren	537
30.	Pat Donovan	531
31.	Fred Clarke	527
32.	Curt Welch	526
33.	Willie Keeler	519
34.	Luis Aparicio	506
	Tom McCarthy	506
36.	Brett Butler	503
37.	Clyde Milan	495
38.	Omar Moreno	487
39.	Ed Delahanty	478
40.	Jim Sheckard	475
41.	Bobby Bonds	461
42.	Joe Kelley	458
43.	Ron LeFlore	455
44.	Paul Molitor	454
45.	Bill Lange	453
46.	Mike Tiernan	449
47.	John McGraw	444
	Steve Sax	444
49.	Sherry Magee	441
50.	Charlie Comiskey	440
	Jim Ryan	434
52.	Tris Speaker	433
53.	Bob Bescher	428
54.	Tommy Corcoran	420
55.	Frankie Frisch	419
56.	Tommy Harper	408
57.	Tom Daly	407
58.	Donie Bush	405
	Frank Chance	405

Total number of players: (59)

10 STEALS OF HOME

Rk.	Player	No.
1.	Ty Cobb	50
2.	Max Carey	33
3.	George Burns	28
4.	Honus Wagner	27
5.	Sherry Magee	23
	Frank Schulte	23
7.	John Evers	21
8.	George Sisler	20
9.	Frankie Frisch	19
	Jackie Robinson	19
11.	Jim Sheckard	18
	Tris Speaker	18
	Joe Tinker	18
14.	Rod Carew	17
	Eddie Collins	17
	Larry Doyle	17
17.	Tommy Leach	16
18.	Ben Chapman	15
	Fred Clarke	15
	Lou Gehrig	15
21.	Bob Byrne	14
	Fred Maisel	14
	Fred Merkle	14
	Vic Saier	14
25.	Heinie Zimmerman	13
26.	Donie Bush	12
	Sam Rice	12
28.	Shano Collins	11
	Harry Hooper	11
	George Moriarty	11
	Bob Roth	11
32.	Buck Herzog	10
	Jim Johnston	10
	Rabbit Maranville	10
	Paul Molitor	10
	Babe Ruth	10
	Bill Werber	10
	Ross Youngs	10

Total number of players: (38)

Note—Steals of home are not recorded as official statistics and most are uncovered in newspaper accounts. Researchers are constantly finding additional steals of home for many players, which explains the changes in this list each year.

PITCHING

700 GAMES

Rk.	Pitcher	Yrs.	Games
1.	Hoyt Wilhelm	21	1,070
2.	Kent Tekulve	16	1,050
3.	Rich Gossage	22	1,002
4.	Lindy McDaniel	21	987
5.	Rollie Fingers	17	944
6.	Gene Garber	19	931
7.	Cy Young	22	906
8.	Sparky Lyle	16	899
9.	Jim Kaat	25	898
10.	Lee Smith	15	891
11.	Jeff Reardon	16	880
12.	Don McMahon	18	874
13.	Phil Niekro	24	864
14.	Charlie Hough	25	858
15.	Dennis Eckersley	20	849
16.	Roy Face	16	848
17.	Tug McGraw	19	824
18.	Nolan Ryan	27	807
19.	Walter Johnson	21	802
20.	Gaylord Perry	22	777

Rk.	Pitcher	Yrs.	Games
21.	Don Sutton	23	774
22.	Darold Knowles	16	765
23.	Tommy John	26	760
24.	Jesse Orosco	15	754
25.	Ron Reed	19	751
26.	Warren Spahn	21	750
27.	Tom Burgmeier	17	745
	Gary Lavelle	13	745
29.	Willie Hernandez	13	744
30.	Steve Carlton	24	741
31.	Ron Perranoski	13	737
32.	Ron Kline	17	736
33.	Clay Carroll	15	731
34.	Mike G. Marshall	14	723
35.	Johnny Klippstein	18	711
36.	Greg Minton	16	710
37.	Dave Righetti	15	708
38.	Stu Miller	16	704
39.	Steve Bedrosian	13	703
40.	Joe Niekro	22	702
41.	Bill Campbell	15	700

Total number of pitchers: (41)

500 GAMES STARTED

Rk.	Pitcher	No.
1.	Cy Young	818
2.	Nolan Ryan	773
3.	Don Sutton	756
4.	Phil Niekro	716
5.	Steve Carlton	709
6.	Tommy John	700
7.	Gaylord Perry	690
8.	Bert Blyleven	685
9.	Pud Galvin	682
10.	Walter Johnson	666
11.	Warren Spahn	665
12.	Tom Seaver	647
13.	Jim Kaat	625
14.	Frank Tanana	616
15.	Early Wynn	612
16.	Robin Roberts	609
17.	Grover Alexander	598
18.	Ferguson Jenkins	594
19.	Tim Keefe	593
20.	Kid Nichols	561
21.	Eppa Rixey	552
22.	Christy Mathewson	551
23.	Mickey Welch	549
24.	Jerry Reuss	547
25.	Red Ruffing	536
26.	Rick Reuschel	529
27.	Jerry Koosman	527
	Jack Morris	527
29.	Jim Palmer	521
30.	Jim Bunning	519
31.	John Clarkson	518
32.	Jack Powell	517
33.	Tony Mullane	505
34.	Hoss Radbourn	503
	Gus Weyhing	503

Total number of pitchers: (35)

300 COMPLETE GAMES

Rk.	Pitcher	No.
1.	Cy Young	751
2.	Pud Galvin	641
3.	Tim Keefe	554
4.	Walter Johnson	531
	Kid Nichols	531
6.	Mickey Welch	525
7.	John Clarkson	487

Rk.	Pitcher	No.
8.	Hoss Radbourn	479
9.	Tony Mullane	464
10.	Jim McCormick	462
11.	Gus Weyhing	447
12.	Grover Alexander	436
13.	Christy Mathewson	434
14.	Jack Powell	422
15.	Will White	394
16.	Amos Rusie	391
17.	Vic Willis	388
18.	Eddie Plank	387
19.	Warren Spahn	382
20.	Jim Whitney	373
21.	William Terry	368
22.	Ted Lyons	356
23.	Charlie Buffinton	350
24.	Chick Fraser	342
25.	George Mullin	339
26.	Clark Griffith	337
27.	Red Ruffing	335
28.	Charles King	327
29.	Al Orth	323
30.	Bill Hutchinson	321
31.	Burleigh Grimes	314
	Joe McGinnity	314
33.	Red Donahue	312
34.	Guy Hecker	310
35.	Bill Dinneen	305
	Robin Roberts	305
37.	Gaylord Perry	303
38.	Ted Breitenstein	300
	Lefty Grove	300

Total number of pitchers: (39)

3,500 INNINGS

Rk.	Pitcher	No.
1.	Cy Young	7,377
2.	Pud Galvin	5,959
3.	Walter Johnson	5,923
4.	Phil Niekro	5,403⅔
5.	Nolan Ryan	5,387
6.	Gaylord Perry	5,352
7.	Don Sutton	5,281⅔
8.	Warren Spahn	5,246
9.	Steve Carlton	5,216⅓
10.	Grover Alexander	5,188
11.	Kid Nichols	5,067
12.	Tim Keefe	5,043
13.	Bert Blyleven	4,970⅓
14.	Mickey Welch	4,784
15.	Tom Seaver	4,782
16.	Christy Mathewson	4,781
17.	Tommy John	4,707⅓
18.	Robin Roberts	4,689
19.	Early Wynn	4,566
20.	Hoss Radbourn	4,543
21.	John Clarkson	4,534
22.	Jim Kaat	4,527⅔
23.	Tony Mullane	4,506
24.	Ferguson Jenkins	4,498⅔
25.	Eppa Rixey	4,494
26.	Jack Powell	4,390
27.	Red Ruffing	4,342
28.	Gus Weyhing	4,335
29.	Jim McCormick	4,264
30.	Eddie Plank	4,234
31.	Frank Tanana	4,186⅔
32.	Burleigh Grimes	4,178
33.	Ted Lyons	4,162
34.	Urban Faber	4,087
35.	Vic Willis	3,994
36.	Jim Palmer	3,947⅓
37.	Lefty Grove	3,940

Rk.	Pitcher	No.
38.	Bob Gibson	3,885
39.	Sam Jones	3,884
40.	Jerry Koosman	3,839⅓
41.	Bob Feller	3,828
42.	**Jack Morris**	**3,824⅔**
43.	**Charlie Hough**	**3,800⅓**
44.	Waite Hoyt	3,762
45.	Jim Bunning	3,759
46.	Bobo Newsom	3,758
47.	Amos Rusie	3,750
48.	Jerry Reuss	3,668⅔
49.	Paul Derringer	3,646
50.	Mickey Lolich	3,640
51.	Bob Friend	3,612
52.	Carl Hubbell	3,591
53.	Joe Niekro	3,584⅔
54.	Herb Pennock	3,572
55.	Earl Whitehill	3,563
56.	**Dennis Martinez**	**3,561**
56.	Rick Reuschel	3,549⅔
57.	Will White	3,543
58.	William Terry	3,523
59.	Juan Marichal	3,506

Total number of pitchers: (60)

1,800 RUNS

Rk.	Pitcher	No.
1.	Pud Galvin	3,303
2.	Cy Young	3,168
3.	Gus Weyhing	2,770
4.	Mickey Welch	2,555
5.	Tony Mullane	2,520
6.	Kid Nichols	2,477
7.	Tim Keefe	2,461
8.	John Clarkson	2,396
9.	Phil Niekro	2,337
10.	Hoss Radbourn	2,300
11.	Nolan Ryan	2,178
12.	Steve Carlton	2,130
13.	Jim McCormick	2,129
14.	Gaylord Perry	2,128
15.	Red Ruffing	2,117
16.	Don Sutton	2,104
17.	Jim Whitney	2,060
18.	Ted Lyons	2,056
19.	Burleigh Grimes	2,048
20.	Jim Kaat	2,038
21.	Early Wynn	2,037
22.	Bert Blyleven	2,029
23.	Earl Whitehill	2,018
24.	Tommy John	2,017
25.	Warren Spahn	2,016
26.	Sam Jones	2,008
27.	Eppa Rixey	1,986
28.	Chick Fraser	1,984
29.	Jack Powell	1,976
30.	Robin Roberts	1,962
31.	Frank Tanana	1,910
32.	Bobo Newsom	1,908
	Amos Rusie	1,908
34.	Walter Johnson	1,902
35.	Ferguson Jenkins	1,853
36.	Grover Alexander	1,851
37.	Charles King	1,834
38.	**Jack Morris**	**1,815**
39.	Urban Faber	1,813
40.	Jack Stivetts	1,809
41.	**Charlie Hough**	**1,807**

Total number of pitchers: (41)

3.50 OR UNDER ERA

(Pitchers with 3,000 or more innings; does not include any seasons in N.L. before 1912 and in A.L. prior to 1913)

Rk.	Pitcher	IP	ERA
1.	Walter Johnson (a)	4,195	2.37
2.	Gro. Alexander (b) ..	4,822	2.56
3.	Whitey Ford	3,171	2.74
4.	Tom Seaver	4,782	2.86
	Jim Palmer	3,947⅓	2.86
6.	Stan Coveleski	3,071	2.88
7.	Juan Marichal	3,506	2.89
	Wilbur Cooper	3,482	2.89
9.	Bob Gibson	3,885	2.91
10.	Carl Mays	3,022	2.92
11.	Don Drysdale	3,432	2.95
12.	Carl Hubbell	3,591	2.98
13.	Lefty Grove	3,940	3.06
14.	Warren Spahn	5,246	3.08
15.	Gaylord Perry	5,352	3.10
16.	Eppa Rixey	4,494	3.15
	Urban Faber	4,087	3.15
18.	Nolan Ryan	5,321	3.19
19.	Steve Carlton	5,216⅓	3.22
20.	Dolf Luque	3,221	3.24
21.	Bob Feller	3,828	3.25
	Dutch J. Leonard	3,220	3.25
23.	Don Sutton	5,281⅔	3.26
	Catfish Hunter	3,449	3.26
	Vida Blue	3,344	3.26
26.	Jim Bunning	3,759	3.27
	Billy Pierce	3,305	3.27
28.	Luis Tiant	3,485⅔	3.30
	Bucky Walters	3,104	3.30
	Claude Osteen	3,459	3.30
31.	Bert Blyleven	4,970⅓	3.31
32.	George Dauss	3,374	3.32
33.	Tommy John	4,707⅓	3.34
	Ferguson Jenkins	4,498⅔	3.34
35.	Phil Niekro	5,403⅔	3.35
36.	Jerry Koosman	3,839⅓	3.36
37.	Rick Reuschel	3,549⅔	3.37
38.	Lee Meadows	3,151	3.38
39.	Robin Roberts	4,689	3.40
	Larry Jackson	3,262	3.40
	Milt Pappas	3,186	3.40
42.	Mickey Lolich	3,640	3.44
	Larry French	3,152	3.44
	Jim Perry	3,287	3.44
45.	Jim Kaat	4,527⅔	3.46
	Paul Derringer	3,646	3.46
	Dennis Eckersley	**3,082⅔**	**3.46**
48.	**Bob Welch**	**3,091⅓**	**3.47**
49.	Joe Bush	3,088	3.49

Total number of pitchers: (49)

(a) Does not include 1,729 innings pitched 1907 through 1912; allowed 520 total runs in that period; earned-run total not available and if all the 520 runs were included in Johnson's earned-run total, his career earned-run average would be 2.47.

(b) Does not include 367 innings pitched in 1911; allowed 133 total runs in that year; earned-run total not available. If all the 133 runs were included in Alexander's earned-run total, his career ERA would be 2.61.

4,000 HITS

Rk.	Pitcher	No.
1.	Cy Young	7,078
2.	Pud Galvin	*6,334
3.	Phil Niekro	5,044
4.	Gaylord Perry	4,938
5.	Walter Johnson	4,920

Rk.	Pitcher	No.
6.	Grover Alexander	4,868
7.	Kid Nichols	4,854
8.	Warren Spahn	4,830
9.	Tommy John	4,783
10.	Don Sutton	4,692
11.	Steve Carlton	4,672
12.	Gus Weyhing	*4,669
13.	Mickey Welch	*4,646
14.	Eppa Rixey	4,633
15.	Bert Blyleven	4,632
16.	Jim Kaat	4,620
17.	Robin Roberts	4,582
18.	Tim Keefe	*4,524
19.	Hoss Radbourn	*4,500
20.	Ted Lyons	4,489
21.	Burleigh Grimes	4,406
22.	John Clarkson	*4,376
23.	Jack Powell	4,323
24.	Red Ruffing	4,294
25.	Early Wynn	4,291
26.	Tony Mullane	*4,238
27.	Christy Mathewson	4,203
28.	Jim McCormick	*4,166
29.	Ferguson Jenkins	4,142
30.	Urban Faber	4,104
31.	Sam Jones	4,084
32.	Frank Tanana	4,063
33.	Waite Hoyt	4,037

Total number of pitchers: (33)

*Includes 1887 bases on balls, scored as hits under rules in effect for that year.

7 GRAND SLAMS

Rk.	Pitcher	No.
1.	Nolan Ryan	10
2.	Ned Garver	9
	Milt Pappas	9
	Jerry Reuss	9
	Frank Viola	**9**
6.	Bert Blyleven	8
	Jim Brewer	8
	Roy Face	8
	Bob Feller	8
	Jim Kaat	8
	Johnny Klippstein	8
	Lindy McDaniel	8
	Tug McGraw	8
	Frank Tanana	8
	Early Wynn	8
16.	Doug Bair	7
	Larry French	7
	Jim Hearn	7
	Phil Niekro	7
	Gaylord Perry	7
	Ray Sadecki	7
	Jack Sanford	7
	Willie Sherdel	7
	Don Sutton	7
	Mike Torrez	7
	Lon Warneke	7
	Matt Young	7

Total number of pitchers: (27)

200 VICTORIES

Rk.	Pitcher	W	L
1.	Cy Young	511	313
2.	Walter Johnson	416	279
3.	Christy Mathewson	373	188
	Grover Alexander	373	208
5.	Warren Spahn	363	245
6.	Kid Nichols	361	208
	Pud Galvin	361	309
8.	Tim Keefe	342	225
9.	Steve Carlton	329	244
10.	John Clarkson	327	176
11.	Don Sutton	324	256
	Nolan Ryan	324	292
13.	Phil Niekro	318	274
14.	Gaylord Perry	314	265
15.	Tom Seaver	311	205
16.	Hoss Radbourn	308	191
17.	Mickey Welch	307	209
18.	Eddie Plank	305	181
19.	Lefty Grove	300	141
	Early Wynn	300	244
21.	Tommy John	288	231
22.	Bert Blyleven	287	250
23.	Robin Roberts	286	245
24.	Tony Mullane	285	213
25.	Ferguson Jenkins	284	226
26.	Jim Kaat	283	237
27.	Red Ruffing	273	225
28.	Burleigh Grimes	270	212
29.	Jim Palmer	268	152
30.	Bob Feller	266	162
	Eppa Rixey	266	251
32.	Jim McCormick	265	215
33.	Gus Weyhing	262	226
34.	Ted Lyons	260	230
35.	**Jack Morris**	**254**	**186**
	Urban Faber	254	212
37.	Carl Hubbell	253	154
38.	Bob Gibson	251	174
39.	Vic Willis	249	205
40.	Joe McGinnity	247	145
	Jack Powell	247	254
42.	Juan Marichal	243	142
43.	Amos Rusie	241	158
44.	Clark Griffith	240	140
	Herb Pennock	240	162
	Frank Tanana	240	236
47.	Waite Hoyt	237	182
48.	Whitey Ford	236	106
49.	Charlie Buffinton	231	153
50.	Luis Tiant	229	172
	Sam Jones	229	217
52.	Will White	227	167
53.	Catfish Hunter	224	166
	Jim Bunning	224	184
55.	Mel Harder	223	186
	Paul Derringer	223	212
57.	George Dauss	222	182
	Jerry Koosman	222	209
59.	Joe Niekro	221	204
60.	Jerry Reuss	220	191
61.	**Dennis Martinez**	**219**	**171**
62.	Earl Whitehill	218	186
63.	Bob Caruthers	217	101
	Fred Fitzsimmons	217	146
	Mickey Lolich	217	191
66.	Wilbur Cooper	216	178
	Charlie Hough	**216**	**216**
68.	Stan Coveleski	215	141
	Jim Perry	215	174
70.	Rick Reuschel	214	191
71.	George Mullin	212	181
	Jack Quinn	212	181
73.	**Bob Welch**	**211**	**146**
	Billy Pierce	211	169
	Bobo Newsom	211	222
76.	Ed Cicotte	210	149
	Jesse Haines	210	158
78.	Vida Blue	209	161

Rk.	Pitcher	W	L
	Milt Pappas	209	164
	Don Drysdale	209	166
81.	Mordecai Brown	208	111
	Chief Bender	208	112
	Carl Mays	208	126
84.	Bob Lemon	207	128
	Hal Newhouser	207	150
86.	William Terry	205	197
87.	Charles King	204	152
88.	Jack Stivetts	203	132
	Lew Burdette	203	144
90.	Al Orth	202	188
91.	Charlie Root	201	160
	Rube Marquard	201	177
93.	George Uhle	200	166

Total number of pitchers: (93)

20 VICTORIES, 5 TIMES

Rk.	Pitcher	Yrs.
1.	Cy Young	16
2.	Christy Mathewson	13
	Warren Spahn	13
4.	Walter Johnson	12
5.	Kid Nichols	11
6.	Pud Galvin	10
7.	Grover Alexander	9
	Hoss Radbourn	9
	Mickey Welch	9
10.	John Clarkson	8
	Lefty Grove	8
	Jim McCormick	8
	Joe McGinnity	8
	Tony Mullane	8
	Jim Palmer	8
	Amos Rusie	8
17.	Charlie Buffinton	7
	Clark Griffith	7
	Ferguson Jenkins	7
	Tim Keefe	7
	Bob Lemon	7
	Eddie Plank	7
	Gus Weyhing	7
	Vic Willis	7
25.	Mordecai Brown	6
	Steve Carlton	6
	Bob Caruthers	6
	Bob Feller	6
	Wes Ferrell	6
	Juan Marichal	6
	Robin Roberts	6
	Jack Stivetts	6
	Jesse Tannehill	6
34.	Tommy Bond	5
	Jack Chesbro	5
	Larry Corcoran	5
	Stan Coveleski	5
	Bob Gibson	5
	Burleigh Grimes	5
	Carl Hubbell	5
	Catfish Hunter	5
	Charles King	5
	Carl Mays	5
	John McMahon	5
	George Mullin	5
	Gaylord Perry	5
	Deacon Phillippe	5
	Tom Seaver	5
	Hippo Vaughn	5
	Will White	5
	Jim Whitney	5
	Early Wynn	5

Total number of pitchers: (52)

30 VICTORIES, 2 TIMES

Rk.	Pitcher	Yrs.
1.	Kid Nichols	7
2.	John Clarkson	6
	Tim Keefe	6
4.	Tony Mullane	5
	Cy Young	5
6.	Tommy Bond	4
	Larry Corcoran	4
	Charles King	4
	Christy Mathewson	4
	Jim McCormick	4
	Mickey Welch	4
	Will White	4
13.	Grover Alexander	3
	Bob Caruthers	3
	Pud Galvin	3
	Bill Hutchison	3
	Bobby Mathews	3
	Ed Morris	3
	Hoss Radbourn	3
	Amos Rusie	3
21.	Dave Foutz	2
	George Haddock	2
	Guy Hecker	2
	Walter Johnson	2
	Frank Killen	2
	Joe McGinnity	2
	John McMahon	2
	Tom Ramsey	2
	Jack Stivetts	2
	Monte Ward	2
	Gus Weyhing	2
	Jim Whitney	2

Total number of pitchers: (32)

100 SAVES
(Since 1969)

Rk.	Pitcher	No.
1.	Lee Smith	434
2.	Jeff Reardon	367
3.	Rollie Fingers	341
4.	Rich Gossage	310
5.	Bruce Sutter	300
6.	Dennis Eckersley	294
7.	Tom Henke	275
8.	John Franco	266
9.	Dave Righetti	252
10.	Dan Quisenberry	244
11.	Sparky Lyle	222
12.	Gene Garber	218
13.	Doug Jones	217
14.	Dave Smith	216
15.	Randy Myers	205
16.	Bobby Thigpen	201
17.	Mitch Williams	192
18.	Jeff Montgomery	187
19.	Steve Bedrosian	184
	Kent Tekulve	184
21.	Rich Aguilera	179
	Tug McGraw	179
23.	Mike Marshall	178
24.	Bryan Harvey	177
25.	Jeff Russell	163
26.	Gregg Olson	161
27.	Jay Howell	155
28.	Roger McDowell	151
29.	Greg Minton	150
30.	Willie Hernandez	147
31.	Todd Worrell	145
32.	Dave Giusti	140
33.	Mike Henneman	136
	Gary Lavelle	136

Rk.	Pitcher	No.
35.	Dan Plesac	134
36.	Steve Farr	132
	Bob Stanley	132
38.	Ron Davis	130
	Jesse Orosco	130
40.	Terry Forster	127
41.	Bill Campbell	126
	Dave LaRoche	126
43.	Duane Ward	121
44.	John Hiller	119
45.	Tippy Martinez	115
46.	Clay Carroll	113
47.	Jim Brewer	112
	Darold Knowles	112
49.	Bill Caudill	106
	John Wetteland	106
51.	Wayne Granger	104
52.	Ron Reed	103
53.	Tim Burke	102
54.	Craig Lefferts	101

Total number of pitchers: (54)

40 SHUTOUTS

Rk.	Pitcher	No.
1.	Walter Johnson	110
2.	Grover Alexander	90
3.	Christy Mathewson	83
4.	Cy Young	76
5.	Eddie Plank	64
6.	Warren Spahn	63
7.	Nolan Ryan	61
	Tom Seaver	61
9.	Bert Blyleven	60
10.	Ed Walsh	58
	Don Sutton	58
12.	Pud Galvin	57
13.	Bob Gibson	56
14.	Steve Carlton	55
15.	Jim Palmer	53
	Gaylord Perry	53
17.	Juan Marichal	52
18.	Mordecai Brown	50
	Rube Waddell	50
	Vic Willis	50
21.	Early Wynn	49
	Don Drysdale	49
	Luis Tiant	49
	Ferguson Jenkins	49
25.	Kid Nichols	48
26.	Jack Powell	46
	Guy White	46
	Tommy John	46
29.	Babe Adams	45
	Addie Joss	45
	Red Ruffing	45
	Robin Roberts	45
	Whitey Ford	45
	Phil Niekro	45
35.	Bob Feller	44
36.	Milt Pappas	43
37.	Bucky Walters	42
	Catfish Hunter	42
39.	Chief Bender	41
	Mickey Lolich	41
	Hippo Vaughn	41
	Mickey Welch	41
43.	Larry French	40
	Sandy Koufax	40
	Jim Bunning	40
	Mel Stottlemyre	40
	Claude Osteen	40
	Tim Keefe	40

Total number of pitchers: (48)

10, 1 - 0 VICTORIES
(Complete Games)

Rk.	Pitcher	No.
1.	Walter Johnson	38
2.	Grover Alexander	17
3.	Bert Blyleven	15
4.	Christy Mathewson	14
5.	Eddie Plank	13
	Ed Walsh	13
	Doc White	13
	Cy Young	13
	Dean Chance	13
10.	Stan Coveleski	12
	Gaylord Perry	12
	Steve Carlton	12
13.	Nap Rucker	11
	Kid Nichols	11
	Ferguson Jenkins	11
	Nolan Ryan	11
17.	Joe Bush	10
	Paul Derringer	10
	Bill Doak	10
	Addie Joss	10
	Dick Rudolph	10
	Hippo Vaughn	10
	Lefty Tyler	10
	Warren Spahn	10
	Sandy Koufax	10

Total number of pitchers: (25)

1,200 BASES ON BALLS

Rk.	Pitcher	No.
1.	Nolan Ryan	2,795
2.	Steve Carlton	1,833
3.	Phil Niekro	1,809
4.	Early Wynn	1,775
5.	Bob Feller	1,764
6.	Bobo Newsom	1,732
7.	Charlie Hough	1,665
8.	Amos Rusie	1,637
9.	Gus Weyhing	1,569
10.	Red Ruffing	1,541
11.	Bump Hadley	1,442
12.	Warren Spahn	1,434
13.	Earl Whitehill	1,431
14.	Sam Jones	1,396
15.	Jack Morris	1,390
	Tom Seaver	1,390
17.	Tony Mullane	1,379
	Gaylord Perry	1,379
19.	Mike Torrez	1,371
20.	Walter Johnson	1,353
21.	Don Sutton	1,343
22.	Bob Gibson	1,336
23.	Chick Fraser	1,332
24.	Bert Blyleven	1,322
25.	Sam McDowell	1,312
26.	Jim Palmer	1,311
27.	Mickey Welch	1,305
28.	Burleigh Grimes	1,295
29.	Mark Baldwin	1,285
30.	Joe Niekro	1,262
31.	Allie Reynolds	1,261
32.	Joe Bush	1,260
33.	Tommy John	1,259
34.	Frank Tanana	1,255
35.	Bob Lemon	1,251
36.	Hal Newhouser	1,249
37.	Kid Nichols	1,245
38.	Bill Terry	1,244

Rk.	Pitcher	No.
39.	Tim Keefe	1,225
40.	Urban Faber	1,213
41.	Cy Young	1,209

Total number of pitchers: (41)

2,000 STRIKEOUTS

Rk.	Pitcher	No.
1.	Nolan Ryan	5,714
2.	Steve Carlton	4,136
3.	Bert Blyleven	3,701
4.	Tom Seaver	3,640
5.	Don Sutton	3,574
6.	Gaylord Perry	3,534
7.	Walter Johnson	3,508
8.	Phil Niekro	3,342
9.	Ferguson Jenkins	3,192
10.	Bob Gibson	3,117
11.	Jim Bunning	2,855
12.	Mickey Lolich	2,832
13.	Cy Young	2,819
14.	Frank Tanana	2,773
15.	Warren Spahn	2,583
16.	Bob Feller	2,581
17.	Jerry Koosman	2,556
18.	Tim Keefe	2,538
19.	Christy Mathewson	2,505
20.	Don Drysdale	2,486
21.	**Jack Morris**	**2,478**
22.	Jim Kaat	2,461
23.	Sam McDowell	2,453
24.	Luis Tiant	2,416
25.	Sandy Koufax	2,396
26.	**Charlie Hough**	**2,362**
27.	Robin Roberts	2,357
28.	Early Wynn	2,334
29.	Rube Waddell	2,310
30.	Juan Marichal	2,303
31.	Lefty Grove	2,266
32.	**Dennis Eckersley**	**2,245**
	Tommy John	2,245
34.	Jim Palmer	2,212
35.	Grover Alexander	2,198
36.	Vida Blue	2,175
37.	Camilo Pascual	2,167
38.	Eddie Plank	2,112
39.	**Mark Langston**	**2,110**
40.	Bobo Newsom	2,082
41.	Dazzy Vance	2,045
42.	**Roger Clemens**	**2,201**
43.	Rick Reuschel	2,015
44.	Catfish Hunter	2,012

Total number of pitchers: (44)

GENERAL REFERENCE

BATTING

TRIPLE CROWN HITTERS

AMERICAN LEAGUE

Year	Player, Club	Avg.	HR	RBI
1909	Ty Cobb, Detroit	.377	9	*115
1933	Jimmie Foxx, Philadelphia	.356	48	163
1934	Lou Gehrig, New York	.363	49	165
1942	Ted Williams, Boston	.356	36	137
1947	Ted Williams, Boston	.343	32	114
1956	Mickey Mantle, New York	.353	52	130
1966	Frank Robinson, Baltimore	.316	49	122
1967	Carl Yastrzemski, Boston	.326	44	121

Total number of occurrences: (8)

NATIONAL LEAGUE

Year	Player, Club	Avg.	HR	RBI
1912	Heinie Zimmerman, Chicago	.372	14	*98
1922	Rogers Hornsby, St. Louis	.401	42	152
1925	Rogers Hornsby, St. Louis	.403	39	143
1933	Chuck Klein, Philadelphia	.368	28	120
1937	Joe Medwick, St. Louis	.374	31	154

*RBIs not officially adopted until 1920.

Total number of occurrences: (5)

.400 HITTERS

Year	Player, Club	Avg.
1887	Tip O'Neill, St. Louis A.A.*†	.492
1887	Pete Browning, Louisville A.A.*†	.471
1887	Denny Lyons, Philadelphia A.A.†	.469
1887	Bob Caruthers, St. Louis A.A.†	.459
1894	Hugh Duffy, Boston N.L.*	.438
1897	Willie Keeler, Baltimore N.L.*	.432
1887	Yank Robinson, St. Louis A.A.†	.426
1924	Rogers Hornsby, St. Louis N.L.*	.424
1894	George Turner, Philadelphia N.L.	.423
1895	Jesse Burkett, Cleveland N.L.*	.423
1901	Nap Lajoie, Philadelphia A.L.*	.422
1887	Cap Anson, Chicago N.L.†	.421
1884	Fred Dunlap, St. Louis U.A.	.420
1911	Ty Cobb, Detroit A.L.*	.420
1922	George Sisler, St. Louis A.L.*	.420
1887	Dennis Brouthers, Detroit N.L.†	.419
1887	Reddy Mack, Louisville A.A.†	.410
1896	Jesse Burkett, Cleveland N.L.*	.410
1912	Ty Cobb, Detroit A.L.*	.410
1893	Jacob Stenzel, Pittsburgh N.L.	.409
1884	Tom Esterbrook, New York A.A.*	.408
1899	Ed Delahanty, Philadelphia N.L.*	.408
1911	Joe Jackson, Cleveland A.L.*	.408
1879	Cap Anson, Chicago N.L.	.407
1920	George Sisler, St. Louis A.L.*	.407
1887	Sam Thompson, Detroit N.L.†	.406
1897	Fred Clarke, Louisville N.L.*	.406
1941	Ted Williams, Boston A.L.*	.406
1876	Ross Barnes, Chicago N.L.*	.404
1884	Harry Stovey, Philadelphia A.A.*	.404
1894	Sam Thompson, Philadelphia N.L.*	.404
1887	Paul Radford, New York A.A.†	.404
1887	Dave Orr, New York A.A.†	.403
1923	Harry Heilmann, Detroit A.L.*	.403
1925	Rogers Hornsby, St. Louis N.L.*	.403
1887	Harry Stovey, Philadelphia A.A.†	.402
1899	Jesse Burkett, St. Louis N.L.*	.402
1887	Tom Burns, Baltimore A.A.†	.401
1922	Ty Cobb, Detroit A.L.*	.401
1922	Rogers Hornsby, St. Louis N.L.*	.401
1930	Bill Terry, New York N.L.*	.401
1894	Ed Delahanty, Philadelphia N.L.*	.400

*Qualify as .400 hitters under present rule 10.23 of Official Baseball Rules.

†Bases on balls counted as hits in 1887.

Total number of occurrences: (42)

30-GAME BATTING STREAKS

Year	Player, Club	G
1941	Joe DiMaggio, New York A.L.	56
1897	Willie Keeler, Baltimore N.L.*	44
1978	Pete Rose, Cincinnati N.L.	44
1894	Bill Dahlen, Chicago N.L.	42
1922	George Sisler, St. Louis A.L.	41
1911	Ty Cobb, Detroit A.L.	40
1987	Paul Molitor, Milwaukee A.L.	39
1945	Tommy Holmes, Boston N.L.	37
1894	Billy Hamilton, Philadelphia N.L.	36
1895	Fred Clarke, Louisville N.L.	35
1917	Ty Cobb, Detroit A.L.	35
1912	Ty Cobb, Detroit A.L.	34
1925	George Sisler, St. Louis A.L.*	34
1938	George McQuinn, St. Louis A.L.	34
1949	Dom DiMaggio, Boston A.L.	34
1987	Benito Santiago, San Diego N.L.	34
1893	George Davis, New York N.L.	33
1907	Hal Chase, New York A.L.	33
1922	Rogers Hornsby, St. Louis N.L.	33
1933	Heinie Manush, Washington A.L.	33
1899	Ed Delahanty, Philadelphia N.L.	31
1906	Nap Lajoie, Cleveland A.L.	31
1924	Sam Rice, Washington A.L.	31
1969	Willie Davis, Los Angeles N.L.	31
1970	Rico Carty, Atlanta N.L.	31
1980	Ken Landreaux, Minnesota A.L.	31
1898	Elmer E. Smith, Cincinnati N.L.	30
1912	Tris Speaker, Boston A.L.	30
1934	Goose Goslin, Detroit A.L.	30
1950	Stan Musial, St. Louis N.L.	30
1976	Ron LeFlore, Detroit A.L.*	30
1980	George Brett, Kansas City A.L.	30
1989	Jerome Walton, Chicago N.L.	30

*From start of season.

Total number of occurrences: (33)

40 HOME RUNS IN SEASON

AMERICAN LEAGUE

Year	Player, Club	No.
1961	Roger Maris, New York	61
1927	Babe Ruth, New York	60
1921	Babe Ruth, New York	59
1932	Jimmie Foxx, Philadelphia	58
1938	Hank Greenberg, Detroit	58
1920	Babe Ruth, New York	54
1928	Babe Ruth, New York	54
1961	Mickey Mantle, New York	54
1956	Mickey Mantle, New York	52
1990	Cecil Fielder, Detroit	51
1938	Jimmie Foxx, Boston	50
1930	Babe Ruth, New York	49
1934	Lou Gehrig, New York	49
1936	Lou Gehrig, New York	49
1964	Harmon Killebrew, Minnesota	49
1966	Frank Robinson, Baltimore	49

— 178 —

Year	Player, Club	No.
1969	Harmon Killebrew, Minnesota	49
1987	Mark McGwire, Oakland	49
1933	Jimmie Foxx, Philadelphia	48
1962	Harmon Killebrew, Minnesota	48
1969	Frank Howard, Washington	48
1926	Babe Ruth, New York	47
1927	Lou Gehrig, New York	47
1969	Reggie Jackson, Oakland	47
1987	George Bell, Toronto	47
1924	Babe Ruth, New York	46
1929	Babe Ruth, New York	46
1931	Lou Gehrig, New York	46
1931	Babe Ruth, New York	46
1937	Joe DiMaggio, New York	46
1961	Jim Gentile, Baltimore	46
1961	Harmon Killebrew, Minnesota	46
1978	Jim Rice, Boston	46
1993	Juan Gonzalez, Texas	46
1961	Rocky Colavito, Detroit	45
1963	Harmon Killebrew, Minnesota	45
1979	Gorman Thomas, Milwaukee	45
1993	Ken Griffey Jr., Seattle	45
1934	Jimmie Foxx, Philadelphia	44
1946	Hank Greenberg, Detroit	44
1967	Harmon Killebrew, Minnesota	44
1967	Carl Yastrzemski, Boston	44
1968	Frank Howard, Washington	44
1970	Frank Howard, Washington	44
1991	Jose Canseco, Oakland	44
1991	Cecil Fielder, Detroit	44
1949	Ted Williams, Boston	43
1953	Al Rosen, Cleveland	43
1984	Tony Armas, Boston	43
1992	Juan Gonzalez, Texas	43
1936	Hal Trosky, Cleveland	42
1953	Gus Zernial, Philadelphia	42
1957	Roy Sievers, Washington	42
1958	Mickey Mantle, New York	42
1959	Rocky Colavito, Cleveland	42
1959	Harmon Killebrew, Washington	42
1963	Dick Stuart, Boston	42
1988	Jose Canseco, Oakland	42
1992	Mark McGwire, Oakland	42
1923	Babe Ruth, New York	41
1930	Lou Gehrig, New York	41
1932	Babe Ruth, New York	41
1936	Jimmie Foxx, Boston	41
1940	Hank Greenberg, Detroit	41
1958	Rocky Colavito, Cleveland	41
1961	Norm Cash, Detroit	41
1970	Harmon Killebrew, Minnesota	41
1980	Reggie Jackson, New York	41
1980	Ben Oglivie, Milwaukee	41
1993	Frank E. Thomas, Chicago	41
1937	Hank Greenberg, Detroit	40
1960	Mickey Mantle, New York	40
1969	Rico Petrocelli, Boston	40
1969	Carl Yastrzemski, Boston	40
1970	Carl Yastrzemski, Boston	40
1985	Darrell Evans, Detroit	40
1986	Jesse Barfield, Toronto	40
1994	Ken Griffey Jr., Seattle	40

Total number of occurrences: (78)

NATIONAL LEAGUE

Year	Player, Club	No.
1930	Hack Wilson, Chicago	56
1949	Ralph Kiner, Pittsburgh	54
1965	Willie Mays, San Francisco	52
1977	George Foster, Cincinnati	52
1947	Ralph Kiner, Pittsburgh	51
1947	Johnny Mize, New York	51
1955	Willie Mays, New York	51
1954	Ted Kluszewski, Cincinnati	49
1962	Willie Mays, San Francisco	49

Year	Player, Club	No.
1987	Andre Dawson, Chicago	49
1971	Willie Stargell, Pittsburgh	48
1979	Dave Kingman, Chicago	48
1980	Mike Schmidt, Philadelphia	48
1950	Ralph Kiner, Pittsburgh	47
1953	Eddie Mathews, Milwaukee	47
1955	Ted Kluszewski, Cincinnati	47
1958	Ernie Banks, Chicago	47
1964	Willie Mays, San Francisco	47
1971	Hank Aaron, Atlanta	47
1989	Kevin Mitchell, San Francisco	47
1959	Eddie Mathews, Milwaukee	46
1961	Orlando Cepeda, San Francisco	46
1993	Barry Bonds, San Francisco	46
1959	Ernie Banks, Chicago	45
1962	Hank Aaron, Milwaukee	45
1969	Willie McCovey, San Francisco	45
1970	Johnny Bench, Cincinnati	45
1979	Mike Schmidt, Philadelphia	45
1955	Ernie Banks, Chicago	44
1957	Hank Aaron, Milwaukee	44
1963	Hank Aaron, Milwaukee	44
1963	Willie McCovey, San Francisco	44
1966	Hank Aaron, Atlanta	44
1969	Hank Aaron, Atlanta	44
1973	Willie Stargell, Pittsburgh	44
1987	Dale Murphy, Atlanta	44
1929	Chuck Klein, Philadelphia	43
1940	Johnny Mize, St. Louis	43
1956	Duke Snider, Brooklyn	43
1957	Ernie Banks, Chicago	43
1973	Dave Johnson, Atlanta	43
1994	Matt Williams, San Francisco	43
1922	Rogers Hornsby, St. Louis	42
1929	Mel Ott, New York	42
1951	Ralph Kiner, Pittsburgh	42
1953	Duke Snider, Brooklyn	42
1954	Gil Hodges, Brooklyn	42
1955	Duke Snider, Brooklyn	42
1970	Billy Williams, Chicago	42
1923	Fred Williams, Philadelphia	41
1953	Roy Campanella, Brooklyn	41
1954	Hank Sauer, Chicago	41
1954	Willie Mays, New York	41
1955	Eddie Mathews, Milwaukee	41
1960	Ernie Banks, Chicago	41
1973	Darrell Evans, Atlanta	41
1977	Jeff Burroughs, Atlanta	41
1930	Chuck Klein, Philadelphia	40
1948	Ralph Kiner, Pittsburgh	40
1948	Johnny Mize, New York	40
1951	Gil Hodges, Brooklyn	40
1953	Ted Kluszewski, Cincinnati	40
1954	Duke Snider, Brooklyn	40
1954	Eddie Mathews, Milwaukee	40
1955	Wally Post, Cincinnati	40
1957	Duke Snider, Brooklyn	40
1960	Hank Aaron, Milwaukee	40
1961	Willie Mays, San Francisco	40
1966	Dick Allen, Philadelphia	40
1970	Tony Perez, Cincinnati	40
1972	Johnny Bench, Cincinnati	40
1973	Hank Aaron, Atlanta	40
1978	George Foster, Cincinnati	40
1983	Mike Schmidt, Philadelphia	40
1990	Ryne Sandberg, Chicago	40
1993	David Justice, Atlanta	40

Total number of occurrences: (76)

☐ PLAYERS WITH FOUR HOMERS IN GAME ☐
NATIONAL LEAGUE

BOBBY LOWE, Boston, May 30, 1894, second game (H).
Ed Delahanty, Philadelphia, July 13, 1896 (A) (three consecutive).

Chuck Klein, Philadelphia, July 10, 1936, 10 innings (A) (three consecutive).
Gil Hodges, Brooklyn, August 31, 1950 (H).
Joe Adcock, Milwaukee, July 31, 1954 (A) (three consecutive).
Willie Mays, San Francisco, April 30, 1961 (A).
MIKE SCHMIDT, Philadelphia, April 17, 1976, 10 innings (A).
Bob Horner, Atlanta, July 6, 1986 (H).
Mark Whiten, St. Louis, September 7, 1993 (A) (three consecutive).

Total number of occurrences: (9)

AMERICAN LEAGUE

LOU GEHRIG, New York, June 3, 1932 (A).
Pat Seerey, Chicago, July 18, 1948, first game, 11 innings (A) (three consecutive).
ROCKY COLAVITO, Cleveland, June 10, 1959 (A).

Note—Capitalized name denotes four consecutive homers (bases on balls excluded); parentheses denotes home or away games.

Total number of occurrences: (3)

☐ PLAYERS WITH THREE HOMERS IN GAME ☐
AMERICAN ASSOCIATION

Guy Hecker, Louisville, August 15, 1886, second game (H).

Total number of occurrences: (1)

AMERICAN LEAGUE

Kenny Williams, St. Louis, April 22, 1922 (H).
Joe Hauser, Philadelphia, August 2, 1924 (A).
Goose Goslin, Washington, June 19, 1925, 12 innings (A).
Ty Cobb, Detroit, May 5, 1925 (A).
Mickey Cochrane, Philadelphia, May 21, 1925 (A).
Tony Lazzeri, New York, June 8, 1927 (H).
Lou Gehrig, New York, June 23, 1927 (A).
Lou Gehrig, New York, May 4, 1929 (A).
Babe Ruth, New York, May 21, 1930, first game (A).
Lou Gehrig, New York, May 22, 1930, second game (A).
CARL REYNOLDS, Chicago, July 2, 1930, second game (A).
GOOSE GOSLIN, St. Louis, August 19, 1930 (A).
EARL AVERILL, Cleveland, September 17, 1930, first game (H).
Goose Goslin, St. Louis, June 23, 1932 (A).
Ben Chapman, New York, July 9, 1932, second game (H).
Jimmie Foxx, Philadelphia, July 10, 1932, 18 innings (A).
Al Simmons, Philadelphia, July 15, 1932 (A).
JIMMIE FOXX, Philadelphia, June 8, 1933 (H).
HAL TROSKY, Cleveland, May 30, 1934, second game (H).
ED COLEMAN, Philadelphia, August 17, 1934, first game (H).
FRANK HIGGINS, Philadelphia, June 27, 1935 (H).
MOOSE SOLTERS, St. Louis, July 7, 1935 (A).
Tony Lazzeri, New York, May 24, 1936 (A).
JOE DiMAGGIO, New York, June 13, 1937, second game, 11 innings (A).
Hal Trosky, Cleveland, July 5, 1937, first game (A).
MERV CONNORS, Chicago, September 17, 1938, second game (H).
KEN KELTNER, Cleveland, May 25, 1939 (A).
Jim Tabor, Boston, July 4, 1939, second game (A).
BILL DICKEY, New York, July 26, 1939 (H).
FRANK HIGGINS, Detroit, May 20, 1940 (H).
Charlie Keller, New York, July 28, 1940, first game (A).
Rudy York, Detroit, September 1, 1941, first game (H).
Pat Seerey, Cleveland, July 13, 1945 (A).
Ted Williams, Boston, July 14, 1946, first game (H).
Sam Chapman, Philadelphia, August 15, 1946 (H).
JOE DiMAGGIO, New York, May 23, 1948, first game (H).
Pat Mullin, Detroit, June 26, 1949, second game (A).
Bobby Doerr, Boston, June 8, 1950 (H).
LARRY DOBY, Cleveland, August 2, 1950 (H).

Joe DiMaggio, New York, September 10, 1950 (A).
JOHNNY MIZE, New York, September 15, 1950 (A).
Gus Zernial, Chicago, October 1, 1950, second game (H).
Bobby Avila, Cleveland, June 20, 1951 (A).
Clyde Vollmer, Boston, July 26, 1951 (H).
Al Rosen, Cleveland, April 29, 1952 (A).
BILL GLYNN, Cleveland, July 5, 1954, first game (A).
Al Kaline, Detroit, April 17, 1955 (H).
Mickey Mantle, New York, May 13, 1955 (H).
Norm Zauchin, Boston, May 27, 1955 (H).
JIM LEMON, Washington, August 31, 1956 (H).
Ted Williams, Boston, May 8, 1957 (A).
Ted Williams, Boston, June 13, 1957 (A).
Hector Lopez, Kansas City, June 26, 1958 (H).
PRESTON WARD, Kansas City, September 9, 1958 (H).
CHARLIE MAXWELL, Detroit, May 3, 1959, second game (H).
Bob Cerv, Kansas City, August 20, 1959 (H).
WILLIE KIRKLAND, Cleveland, July 9, 1961, second game (H).
Rocky Colavito, Detroit, August 27, 1961, second game (A).
Lee Thomas, Los Angeles, September 5, 1961, second game (A).
ROCKY COLAVITO, Detroit, July 5, 1962 (A).
Steve Boros, Detroit, August 6, 1962 (A).
DON LEPPERT, Washington, April 11, 1963 (H).
BOB ALLISON, Minnesota, May 17, 1963 (A).
BOOG POWELL, Baltimore, August 10, 1963 (A).
Harmon Killebrew, Minnesota, September 21, 1963, first game (A).
Jim King, Washington, June 8, 1964 (H).
Boog Powell, Baltimore, June 27, 1964 (A).
MANNY JIMENEZ, Kansas City, July 4, 1964 (A).
TOM TRESH, New York, June 6, 1965, second game (H).
Boog Powell, Baltimore, August 15, 1966 (A).
Tom McGraw, Chicago, May 24, 1967 (A).
Curt Blefary, Baltimore, June 6, 1967, first game (A).
KEN HARRELSON, Boston, June 14, 1968 (A).
Mike Epstein, Washington, May 16, 1969 (H).
Joe Lahoud, Boston, June 11, 1969 (A).
BILL MELTON, Chicago, June 24, 1969, second game (A).
Reggie Jackson, Oakland, July 2, 1969 (H).
Paul Blair, Baltimore, April 29, 1970 (A).
Tony Horton, Cleveland, May 24, 1970, second game (H).
Willie Horton, Detroit, June 9, 1970 (H).
BOBBY MURCER, New York, June 24, 1970, second game (H).
Bill Freehan, Detroit, August 9, 1971 (A).
GEORGE HENDRICK, Cleveland, June 19, 1973 (H).
Tony Oliva, Minnesota, July 3, 1973 (A).
Leroy Stanton, California, July 10, 1973, 10 innings (A).
Bobby Murcer, New York, July 13, 1973 (H).
BOBBY GRICH, Baltimore, June 18, 1974 (A).
Fred Lynn, Boston, June 18, 1975 (A).
John Mayberry, Kansas City, July 1, 1975 (A).
DON BAYLOR, Baltimore, July 2, 1975 (A).
TONY SOLAITA, Kansas City, September 7, 1975, 11 innings (A).
Carl Yastrzemski, Boston, May 19, 1976 (A).
Willie Horton, Texas, May 15, 1977 (A).
JOHN MAYBERRY, Kansas City, June 1, 1977 (A).
CLIFF JOHNSON, New York, June 30, 1977 (A).
JIM RICE, Boston, August 29, 1977 (H).
Al Oliver, Texas, May 23, 1979 (H).
Ben Oglivie, Milwaukee, July 8, 1979, first game (H).
Claudell Washington, Chicago, July 14, 1979 (H).
George Brett, Kansas City, July 22, 1979 (A).
Cecil Cooper, Milwaukee, July 27, 1979 (H).
EDDIE MURRAY, Baltimore, August 29, 1979, second game (A).
CARNEY LANSFORD, California, September 1, 1979 (A).
Otto Velez, Toronto, May 4, 1980, first game, 10 innings (H).
Fred Patek, California, June 20, 1980 (A).
AL OLIVER, Texas, August 17, 1980, second game (A).
Eddie Murray, Baltimore, September 14, 1980, 13 innings (A).
Jeff Burroughs, Seattle, August 14, 1981, second game (A).
Paul Molitor, Milwaukee, May 12, 1982 (A).
LARRY HERNDON, Detroit, May 18, 1982 (H).
BEN OGLIVIE, Milwaukee, July 9, 1982 (A).
HAROLD BAINES, Chicago, July 7, 1982 (H).
DOUG DeCINCES, California, August 3, 1982 (H).
Doug DeCinces, California, August 8, 1982 (A).
George Brett, Kansas City, April 20, 1983 (A).

Ben Oglivie, Milwaukee, May 14, 1983 (H).
Dan Ford, Baltimore, July 20, 1983 (A).
Jim Rice, Boston, August 29, 1983, second game (A).
DAVE KINGMAN, Oakland, April 16, 1984 (A).
Harold Baines, Chicago, September 17, 1984 (A).
GORMAN THOMAS, Seattle, April 11, 1985 (H).
LARRY PARRISH, Texas, April 29, 1985 (H).
Eddie Murray, Baltimore, August 26, 1985 (A).
Leon Lacy, Baltimore, June 8, 1986 (A).
JUAN BENIQUEZ, Baltimore, June 12, 1986 (H).
Joe Carter, Cleveland, August 29, 1986 (A).
Jim Presley, Seattle, September 1, 1986 (H).
Reggie Jackson, California, September 18, 1986 (H).
Cory Snyder, Cleveland, May 21, 1987 (H).
Joe Carter, Cleveland, May 28, 1987 (A).
Mark McGwire, Oakland, June 27, 1987 (A).
Bill Madlock, Detroit, June 28, 1987, 11 innings (H).
BROOK JACOBY, Cleveland, July 3, 1987 (H).
Dale Sveum, Milwaukee, July 17, 1987 (H).
Mike Brantley, Seattle, September 14, 1987 (H).
Ernie Whitt, Toronto, September 14, 1987 (H).
Wally Joyner, California, October 3, 1987 (H).
George Bell, Toronto, April 4, 1988 (A).
Jose Canseco, Oakland, July 3, 1988 (A).
JOE CARTER, Cleveland, June 24, 1989 (A).
Joe Carter, Cleveland, July 19, 1989 (A).
CECIL FIELDER, Detroit, May 6, 1990 (A).
CECIL FIELDER, Detroit, June 6, 1990 (A).
RANDY MILLIGAN, Baltimore, June 9, 1990 (H).
BO JACKSON, Kansas City, July 17, 1990 (A).
TOM BRUNANSKY, Boston, September 29, 1990 (H).
DAVE WINFIELD, California, April 13, 1991 (A).
Harold Baines, Oakland, May 7, 1991 (A).
Danny Tartabull, Kansas City, July 6, 1991 (H).
Jack Clark, Boston, July 31, 1991 (H).
DAVE HENDERSON, Oakland, August 3, 1991 (H).
Juan Gonzalez, Texas, June 7, 1992 (H).
Albert Belle, Cleveland, September 6, 1992 (H).
Carlos Baerga, Cleveland, June 17, 1993 (A).
Joe Carter, Toronto, August 23, 1993 (H).
Juan Gonzalez, Texas, August 28, 1993 (H).
Tim Raines, Chicago, April 18, 1994 (A).
Jose Canseco, Texas, June 13, 1994 (A).
Darnell Coles, Toronto, July 5, 1994 (A).
JIM THOME, Cleveland, July 22, 1994 (H).

Note—Capitalized name denotes three consecutive homers (bases on balls excluded); parentheses denotes home or away games.

Total number of occurrences: (160)

NATIONAL LEAGUE

Ned Williamson, Chicago, May 30, 1884, second game (H).
CAP ANSON, Chicago, August 6, 1884 (H).
JACK MANNING, Philadelphia, October 9, 1884 (A).
Dennis Brouthers, Detroit, September 10, 1886 (A).
Roger Connor, New York, May 9, 1888 (A).
Frank Shugart, St. Louis, May 10, 1894 (A).
BILL JOYCE, Washington, August 20, 1894 (A).
Tom McCreery, Louisville, July 12, 1897 (A).
Jake Beckley, Cincinnati, September 26, 1897, first game (A).
Butch Henline, Philadelphia, September 15, 1922 (H).
Fred Williams, Philadelphia, May 11, 1923 (H).
GEORGE KELLY, New York, September 17, 1923 (H).
George Kelly, New York, June 14, 1924 (H).
Jack Fournier, Brooklyn, July 13, 1926 (A).
Les Bell, Boston, June 2, 1928 (H).
GEORGE HARPER, St. Louis, September 20, 1928, first game (A).
Hack Wilson, Chicago, July 26, 1930 (H).
MEL OTT, New York, August 31, 1930, second game (H).
ROGERS HORNSBY, Chicago, April 24, 1931 (A).
GEORGE WATKINS, St. Louis, June 24, 1931, second game (A).
Bill Terry, New York, August 13, 1932, first game (H).
Babe Herman, Chicago, July 20, 1933 (H).
Hal Lee, Boston, July 6, 1934 (A).
Babe Ruth, Boston, May 25, 1935 (A).

JOHNNY MOORE, Philadelphia, July 22, 1936 (H).
Alex Kampouris, Cincinnati, May 9, 1937 (A).
JOHNNY MIZE, St. Louis, July 13, 1938 (H).
Johnny Mize, St. Louis, July 20, 1938, second game (H).
HANK LEIBER, Chicago, July 4, 1939, first game (H).
Johnny Mize, St. Louis, May 13, 1940, 14 innings (A).
JOHNNY MIZE, St. Louis, September 8, 1940, first game (H).
JIM TOBIN, Boston, May 13, 1942 (H).
CLYDE McCULLOUGH, Chicago, July 26, 1942, first game (A).
BILL NICHOLSON, Chicago, July 23, 1944, first game (A).
JOHNNY MIZE, New York, April 24, 1947 (A).
WILLARD MARSHALL, New York, July 18, 1947 (H).
RALPH KINER, Pittsburgh, August 16, 1947 (H).
RALPH KINER, Pittsburgh, September 11, 1947, second game (H).
Ralph Kiner, Pittsburgh, July 5, 1948, first game (H).
GENE HERMANSKI, Brooklyn, August 5, 1948 (H).
Andy Seminick, Philadelphia, June 2, 1949 (H).
Walker Cooper, Cincinnati, July 6, 1949 (H).
BOB ELLIOTT, Boston, September 24, 1949 (A).
DUKE SNIDER, Brooklyn, May 30, 1950, second game (H).
Wes Westrum, New York, June 24, 1950 (H).
ANDY PAFKO, Chicago, August 2, 1950, second game (A).
ROY CAMPANELLA, Brooklyn, August 26, 1950 (A).
HANK SAUER, Chicago, August 28, 1950, first game (H).
TOMMY BROWN, Brooklyn, September 18, 1950 (H).
Ralph Kiner, Pittsburgh, July 18, 1951 (A).
DEL WILBER, Philadelphia, August 27, 1951, second game (H).
Don Mueller, New York, September 1, 1951 (H).
Hank Sauer, Chicago, June 11, 1952 (H).
EDDIE MATHEWS, Boston, September 27, 1952 (A).
DUSTY RHODES, New York, August 26, 1953 (H).
Jim Pendleton, Milwaukee, August 30, 1953, first game (A).
Stan Musial, St. Louis, May 2, 1954, first game (H).
HANK THOMPSON, New York, June 3, 1954 (A).
DUSTY RHODES, New York, July 28, 1954 (H).
Duke Snider, Brooklyn, June 1, 1955 (H).
GUS BELL, Cincinnati, July 21, 1955 (A).
Del Ennis, Philadelphia, July 23, 1955 (H).
Smoky Burgess, Cincinnati, July 29, 1955 (H).
Ernie Banks, Chicago, August 4, 1955 (H).
GUS BELL, Cincinnati, May 29, 1956 (A).
Ed Bailey, Cincinnati, June 24, 1956, first game (A).
Ted Kluszewski, Cincinnati, July 1, 1956, first game, 10 innings (A).
BOB THURMAN, Cincinnati, August 18, 1956 (H).
ERNIE BANKS, Chicago, September 14, 1957, second game (H).
Lee Walls, Chicago, April 24, 1958 (A).
Roman Mejias, Pittsburgh, May 4, 1958, first game (A).
Walt Moryn, Chicago, May 30, 1958, second game (H).
FRANK THOMAS, Pittsburgh, August 16, 1958 (A).
Don Demeter, Los Angeles, April 21, 1959, 11 innings (H).
Hank Aaron, Milwaukee, June 21, 1959 (A).
FRANK ROBINSON, Cincinnati, August 22, 1959 (A).
DICK STUART, Pittsburgh, June 30, 1960, second game (H).
Willie Mays, San Francisco, June 29, 1961, 10 innings (A).
BILL WHITE, St. Louis, July 5, 1961 (A).
Don Demeter, Philadelphia, September 12, 1961 (A).
ERNIE BANKS, Chicago, May 29, 1962 (H).
STAN MUSIAL, St. Louis, July 8, 1962 (A).
Willie Mays, San Francisco, June 2, 1963 (A).
Ernie Banks, Chicago, June 9, 1963 (H).
WILLIE McCOVEY, San Francisco, September 22, 1963, (H).
WILLIE McCOVEY, San Francisco, April 22, 1964 (A).
JOHNNY CALLISON, Philadelphia, September 27, 1964 (H).
Johnny Callison, Philadelphia, June 6, 1965, second game (A).
Willie Stargell, Pittsburgh, June 24, 1965 (A).
JIM HICKMAN, New York, September 3, 1965 (A).
Gene Oliver, Atlanta, July 30, 1966, second game (H).
ART SHAMSKY, Cincinnati, August 12, 1966, 13 innings (H).
Willie McCovey, San Francisco, September 17, 1966, 10 innings (H).
Roberto Clemente, Pittsburgh, May 15, 1967, 10 innings (A).
ADOLFO PHILLIPS, Chicago, June 11, 1967, second game (H).
JIM WYNN, Houston, June 15, 1967 (A).
Willie Stargell, Pittsburgh, May 22, 1968 (A).
Billy Williams, Chicago, September 10, 1968 (H).

DICK ALLEN, Philadelphia, September 29, 1968 (A).
BOB TILLMAN, Atlanta, July 30, 1969, first game (A).
ROBERTO CLEMENTE, Pittsburgh, August 13, 1969 (A).
Rico Carty, Atlanta, May 31, 1970 (H).
Mike Lum, Atlanta, July 3, 1970, first game (H).
JOHNNY BENCH, Cincinnati, July 26, 1970 (H).
ORLANDO CEPEDA, Atlanta, July 26, 1970, first game (A).
Willie Stargell, Pittsburgh, April 10, 1971, 12 innings (A).
WILLIE STARGELL, Pittsburgh, April 21, 1971 (H).
DERON JOHNSON, Philadelphia, July 11, 1971 (H).
RICK MONDAY, Chicago, May 16, 1972 (A).
Nate Colbert, San Diego, August 1, 1972, second game (A).
Johnny Bench, Cincinnati, May 9, 1973 (A).
Lee May, Houston, June 21, 1973 (A).
George Mitterwald, Chicago, April 17, 1974 (H).
Jim Wynn, Los Angeles, May 11, 1974 (A).
Dave Lopes, Los Angeles, August 20, 1974 (A).
Reggie Smith, St. Louis, May 22, 1976 (A).
Dave Kingman, New York, June 4, 1976 (A).
Bill Robinson, Pittsburgh, June 5, 1976, 15 innings (H).
Gary Matthews, San Francisco, September 25, 1976 (H).
GARY CARTER, Montreal, April 20, 1977 (H).
LARRY PARRISH, Montreal, May 29, 1977 (A).
GEORGE FOSTER, Cincinnati, July 14, 1977 (H).
Pete Rose, Cincinnati, April 29, 1978 (A).
Dave Kingman, Chicago, May 14, 1978 (A).
LARRY PARRISH, Montreal, July 30, 1978 (A).
Dave Kingman, Chicago, May 17, 1979 (H).
Dale Murphy, Altanta, May 18, 1979 (H).
MIKE SCHMIDT, Philadelphia, July 7, 1979 (H).
DAVE KINGMAN, Chicago, July 28, 1979 (A).
Larry Parrish, Montreal, April 25, 1980 (A).
Johnny Bench, Cincinnati, May 29, 1980 (A).
Claudell Washington, New York, June 22, 1980 (A).
Darrell Evans, San Francisco, June 15, 1983 (H).
DARRYL STRAWBERRY, New York, August 5, 1985 (A).
GARY CARTER, New York, September 3, 1985 (A).
Andre Dawson, Montreal, September 24, 1985 (A).
Ken Griffey Sr., Atlanta, July 22, 1986, 11 innings (H).
Eric Davis, Cincinnati, September 10, 1986 (A).
ERIC DAVIS, Cincinnati, May 3, 1987 (A).
Tim Wallach, Montreal, May 4, 1987 (A).
MIKE SCHMIDT, Philadelphia, June 14, 1987 (A).
Andre Dawson, Chicago, August 1, 1987 (H).
GLENN DAVIS, Houston, September 10, 1987 (A).
Darnell Coles, Pittsburgh, September 30, 1987, second game (H).
Von Hayes, Philadelphia, August 29, 1989 (A).
KEVIN MITCHELL, San Francisco, May 25, 1990 (A).
Jeff Treadway, Atlanta, May 26, 1990 (A).
GLENN DAVIS, Houston, June 1, 1990 (A).
BARRY LARKIN, Cincinnati, June 28, 1991 (H).
Jeff Blauser, Atlanta, July 12, 1992, 10 innings (A).
KARL RHODES, Chicago, April 4, 1994 (H).
Cory Snyder, Los Angeles, April 17, 1994 (A).
JEFF BAGWELL, Houston, June 24, 1994 (H).
Barry Bonds, San Francisco, August 2, 1994 (H).

Total number of occurrences: (154)

40 STOLEN BASES AND 40 HOMERS IN SEASON
AMERICAN LEAGUE

Player, Club	Year	G	SB	HR
Jose Canseco, Oakland	1988	158	40	42

Total number of occurrences: (1)

30 STOLEN BASES AND 30 HOMERS IN SEASON
AMERICAN LEAGUE

Player, Club	Year	G	SB	HR
Kenny Williams, St. Louis	1922	153	37	39
Tommy Harper, Milwaukee	1970	154	38	31
Bobby Bonds, New York	1975	145	30	32
Bobby Bonds, California	1977	158	41	37
Bobby Bonds, Chicago/Texas	1978	156	43	31

| Joe Carter, Cleveland | 1987 | 149 | 31 | 32 |
| Jose Canseco, Oakland | 1988 | 158 | 40 | 42 |

Total number of occurrences: (7)

NATIONAL LEAGUE

Player, Club	Year	G	SB	HR
Willie Mays, New York	1956	152	40	36
Willie Mays, New York	1957	152	38	35
Hank Aaron, Milwaukee	1963	161	31	44
Bobby Bonds, San Francisco	1969	158	45	32
Bobby Bonds, San Francisco	1973	160	43	39
Dale Murphy, Atlanta	1983	162	30	36
Eric Davis, Cincinnati	1987	129	50	37
Howard Johnson, New York	1987	157	32	36
Darryl Strawberry, New York	1987	154	36	39
Howard Johnson, New York	1989	153	41	36
Ron Gant, Atlanta	1990	152	33	32
Barry Bonds, Pittsburgh	1990	151	52	33
Ron Gant, Atlanta	1991	154	34	32
Howard Johnson, New York	1991	156	30	38
Barry Bonds, Pittsburgh	1992	140	39	34
Sammy Sosa, Chicago	1993	159	36	33

Total number of occurrences: (16)

50 STOLEN BASES AND 20 HOMERS IN SEASON
AMERICAN LEAGUE

Player, Club	Year	G	SB	HR
Rickey Henderson, New York	1985	143	80	24
Rickey Henderson, New York	1986	153	87	28
Rickey Henderson, Oakland	1990	136	65	28
Brady Anderson, Baltimore	1992	159	53	21

Total number of occurrences: (4)

NATIONAL LEAGUE

Player, Club	Year	G	SB	HR
Lou Brock, St. Louis	1967	159	52	21
Cesar Cedeno, Houston	1972	139	55	22
Cesar Cedeno, Houston	1973	139	56	25
Joe Morgan, Cincinnati	1973	157	67	26
Cesar Cedeno, Houston	1974	160	57	26
Joe Morgan, Cincinnati	1974	149	58	22
Joe Morgan, Cincinnati	1976	141	60	27
Ryne Sandberg, Chicago	1985	153	54	26
Eric Davis, Cincinnati	1986	132	80	27
Eric Davis, Cincinnati	1987	129	50	37
Barry Bonds, Pittsburgh	1990	151	52	33

Total number of occurrences: (11)

400 TOTAL BASES IN SEASON
AMERICAN LEAGUE

Year	Player, Club	No.
1921—Babe Ruth, New York		457
1927—Lou Gehrig, New York		447
1932—Jimmie Foxx, Philadelphia		438
1930—Lou Gehrig, New York		419
1937—Joe DiMaggio, New York		418
1927—Babe Ruth, New York		417
1931—Lou Gehrig, New York		410
1934—Lou Gehrig, New York		409
1978—Jim Rice, Boston		406
1936—Hal Trosky, Cleveland		405
1936—Lou Gehrig, New York		403
1933—Jimmie Foxx, Philadelphia		403

Total number of occurrences: (12)

NATIONAL LEAGUE

Year — Player, Club	No.
1922 — Rogers Hornsby, St. Louis	450
1930 — Chuck Klein, Philadelphia	445
1948 — Stan Musial, St. Louis	429
1930 — Hack Wilson, Chicago	423
1932 — Chuck Klein, Philadelphia	420

Year — Player, Club	No.
1930 — Babe Herman, Brooklyn	416
1929 — Rogers Hornsby, Chicago	409
1937 — Joe Medwick, St. Louis	406
1929 — Chuck Klein, Philadelphia	405
1959 — Hank Aaron, Milwaukee	400

Total number of occurrences: (10)

SIX HITS IN ONE GAME

AMERICAN ASSOCIATION

Player	Club, Date	Place	AB	R	H	2B	3B	HR
Hick Carpenter	Cincinnati, September 12, 1883	H	7	5	6	0	0	0
John Reilly	Cincinnati, September 12, 1883	H	7	6	6	1	1	1
Oscar Walker	Brooklyn, May 31, 1884	H	6	2	6	1	1	0
Lon Knight	Philadelphia, July 30, 1884	H	6	5	6	0	1	0
Dave Orr	New York, June 12, 1885	H	6	4	6	2	1	1
Henry Larkin	Philadelphia, June 16, 1885	H	6	4	6	2	1	1
George Pinckney	Brooklyn, June 25, 1885	H	6	5	6	0	0	0
Arlie Latham	St. Louis, April 24, 1886	H	6	5	6	0	1	0
Guy Hecker	Louisville, August 15, 1886†	H	7	7	6	0	0	3
Denny Lyons	Philadelphia, April 26, 1887	H	6	4	6	2	1	0
Pete Hotaling	Cleveland, June 6, 1888	H	7	5	6	0	1	0
Jim McTamany	Kansas City, June 15, 1888	H	6	3	6	0	0	1
Darby O'Brien	Brooklyn, August 8, 1889	A	6	1	6	3	0	0
Farmer Weaver	Louisville, August 12, 1890	H	6	3	6	1	2	1
Frank Sheibeck	Toledo, September 27, 1890	H	6	4	6	1	1	0
Reddy Mack	Louisville, May 26, 1887	H	6	5	6	0	0	0

Total number of occurrences: (16)

PLAYERS LEAGUE

Player	Club, Date	Place	AB	R	H	2B	3B	HR
Ed Delahanty	Cleveland, June 2, 1890	H	6	4	6	1	1	0
Bill Shindle	Philadelphia, August 26, 1890	H	6	3	6	2	1	0

Total number of occurrences: (2)

AMERICAN LEAGUE

Player	Club, Date	Place	AB	R	H	2B	3B	HR
Mike Donlin	Baltimore, June 24, 1901	H	6	5	6	2	2	0
Doc Nance	Detroit, July 13, 1901	H	6	3	6	1	0	0
Erwin Harvey	Cleveland, April 25, 1902	A	6	3	6	0	0	0
Danny Murphy	Philadelphia, July 8, 1902	A	6	3	6	0	0	1
Jimmy Williams	Baltimore, August 25, 1902	H	6	1	6	1	1	0
Bobby Veach	Detroit, September 17, 1920, 12 innings	H	6	2	6	1	1	1
George Sisler	St. Louis, August 9, 1921, 19 innings	A	9	2	6	0	1	0
Frank Brower	Cleveland, August 7, 1923	A	6	3	6	1	0	0
George Burns	Cleveland, June 19, 1924, first game	A	6	2	6	3	1	0
Ty Cobb	Detroit, May 5, 1925	A	6	4	6	1	0	3
Jimmie Foxx	Philadelphia, May 30, 1930, first game, 13 innings	H	7	0	6	2	1	0
Roger Cramer	Philadelphia, June 20, 1932	A	6	3	6	0	0	0
Jimmie Foxx	Philadelphia, July 10, 1932, 18 innings	A	9	4	6	1	0	3
Johnny Burnett	Cleveland, July 10, 1932, 18 innings	H	11	4	9	2	0	0
Sam West	St. Louis, April 13, 1933, 11 innings	H	6	2	6	1	0	0
Myril Hoag	New York, June 6, 1934, first game	A	6	3	6	0	0	0
Bob Johnson	Philadelphia, June 16, 1934, second game, 11 innings	H	6	3	6	1	0	2
Roger Cramer	Philadelphia, July 13, 1935, first game	A	6	3	6	1	0	0
Bruce Campbell	Cleveland, July 2, 1936, first game	A	6	1	6	1	0	0
Ray Radcliff	Chicago, July 18, 1936, second game	A	7	4	6	2	0	0
Henry Steinbacher	Chicago, June 22, 1938	H	6	3	6	1	0	0
George Myatt	Washington, May 1, 1944	A	6	3	6	1	0	0
Stan Spence	Washington, June 1, 1944	A	6	2	6	0	0	1
George Kell	Detroit, September 20, 1946	A	7	4	6	1	0	0
Jim Fridley	Cleveland, April 29, 1952	A	6	4	6	0	0	0
Jimmy Piersall	Boston, June 10, 1953, first game	A	6	2	6	1	0	0
Joe DeMaestri	Kansas City, July 8, 1955, 11 innings	A	6	2	6	0	0	0
Jim Runnels	Boston, August 30, 1960, first game, 15 innings	H	7	1	6	1	0	0
Rocky Colavito	Detroit, June 24, 1962, 22 innings	H	10	1	7	0	1	0
Floyd Robinson	Chicago, July 22, 1962	A	6	1	6	0	0	0
Bob Oliver	Kansas City, May 4, 1969	A	6	2	6	1	0	1
Jim Northrup	Detroit, August 28, 1969, 13 innings	H	6	2	6	0	0	2
Cesar Gutierrez	Detroit, June 21, 1970, second game, 12 innings	A	7	3	7	1	0	0
John Briggs	Milwaukee, August 4, 1973	A	6	2	6	2	0	0

Player	Club, Date	Place	AB	R	H	2B	3B	HR
Jorge Orta	Cleveland, June 15, 1980	H	6	4	6	1	0	0
Jerry Remy	Boston, September 3, 1981, 20 innings	H	10	2	6	0	0	0
Kevin Seitzer	Kansas City, August 2, 1987	H	6	4	6	1	0	2
Kirby Puckett	Minnesota, August 30, 1987	A	6	4	6	2	0	2
Kirby Puckett	Minnesota, May 23, 1991, 11 innings	H	7	2	6	0	1	0
Carlos Baerga	Cleveland, April 11, 1992, 18 innings	H	9	1	6	0	0	0
Kevin Reimer	Milwaukee, August 24, 1993, second game	H	6	4	6	2	0	0

Total number of occurrences: (41)

NATIONAL LEAGUE

Player	Club, Date	Place	AB	R	H	2B	3B	HR
David Force	Philadelphia, June 27, 1876	H	6	3	6	1	0	0
Cal McVey	Chicago, July 22, 1876	H	7	4	6	1	0	0
Cal McVey	Chicago, July 25, 1876	H	7	4	6	1	0	0
Ross Barnes	Chicago, July 27, 1876	H	6	3	6	1	1	0
Paul Hines	Providence, August 26, 1879, 10 innings	H	6	1	6	0	0	0
George Gore	Chicago, May 7, 1880	H	6	5	6	0	0	0
Lew Dickerson	Worcester, June 16, 1881	H	6	3	6	0	1	0
Sam Wise	Boston, June 20, 1883	H	7	5	6	1	1	0
Dennis Brouthers	Buffalo, July 19, 1883	H	6	3	6	2	0	0
Danny Richardson	New York, June 11, 1887	H	7	2	6	0	0	0
King Kelly	Boston, August 27, 1887	H	7	6	6	1	0	1
Jerry Denny	Indianapolis, May 4, 1889	H	6	3	6	1	0	1
Larry Twitchell	Cleveland, August 15, 1889	H	6	5	6	1	3	1
John Glasscock	New York, September 27, 1890	A	6	2	6	0	0	0
Bobby Lowe	Boston, June 11, 1891	H	6	4	6	1	0	1
Henry Larkin	Washington, June 7, 1892	H	7	3	6	0	1	0
Wilbert Robinson	Baltimore, June 10, 1892, first game	H	7	1	7	1	0	0
John Boyle	Philadelphia, July 6, 1893, 11 innings	A	6	1	6	1	0	0
Duff Cooley	St. Louis, September 30, 1893, second game	A	6	1	6	1	1	0
Ed Delahanty	Philadelphia, June 16, 1894	H	6	4	6	1	0	0
Steve Brodie	Baltimore, July 9, 1894	H	6	2	6	2	1	0
Chief Zimmer	Cleveland, July 11, 1894, 10 innings	H	6	3	6	2	0	0
Sam Thompson	Philadelphia, August 17, 1894	H	7	4	6	1	1	0
Roger Connor	St. Louis, June 1, 1895	A	6	4	6	2	1	0
George Davis	New York, August 15, 1895	A	6	3	6	2	1	0
Jacob Stenzel	Pittsburgh, May 14, 1896	H	6	3	6	0	0	0
Fred Tenney	Boston, May 31, 1897	H	8	3	6	1	0	0
Dick Harley	St. Louis, June 24, 1897, 12 innings	A	6	2	6	1	0	0
Barry McCormick	Chicago, June 29, 1897	H	8	5	6	0	1	1
Tommy Tucker	Washington, July 15, 1897	A	6	1	6	1	0	0
Willie Keeler	Baltimore, September 3, 1897	H	6	5	6	0	1	0
Jack Doyle	Baltimore, September 3, 1897	H	6	2	6	2	0	0
Chick Stahl	Boston, May 31, 1899	H	6	4	6	0	0	0
Ginger Beaumont	Pittsburgh, July 22, 1899	H	6	6	6	0	0	0
Kip Selbach	New York, June 9, 1901	A	7	4	6	2	0	0
George Cutshaw	Brooklyn, August 9, 1915	A	6	2	6	0	0	0
Carson Bigbee	Pittsburgh, August 22, 1917, 22 innings	A	11	0	6	0	0	0
Dave Bancroft	New York, June 28, 1920	A	6	2	6	0	0	0
Johnny Gooch	Pittsburgh, July 7, 1922, 18 innings	H	8	1	6	1	0	0
Max Carey	Pittsburgh, July 7, 1922, 18 innings	H	6	3	6	1	0	0
Jack Fournier	Brooklyn, June 29, 1923	A	6	1	6	2	0	1
Kiki Cuyler	Pittsburgh, August 9, 1924, first game	A	6	3	6	3	1	0
Frankie Frisch	New York, September 10, 1924, first game	H	7	3	6	0	0	1
Jim Bottomley	St. Louis, September 16, 1924	A	6	3	6	1	0	2
Paul Waner	Pittsburgh, August 26, 1926	H	6	1	6	2	0	0
Lloyd Waner	Pittsburgh, June 15, 1929, 14 innings	H	8	2	6	1	1	0
Hank DeBerry	Brooklyn, June 23, 1929, 14 innings	H	6	0	6	0	0	0
Wally Gilbert	Brooklyn, May 30, 1931, second game	A	7	3	6	1	0	0
Jim Bottomley	St. Louis, August 5, 1931, second game	A	6	2	6	1	0	0
Tony Cuccinello	Cincinnati, August 13, 1931, first game	A	6	4	6	2	1	0
Terry Moore	St. Louis, September 5, 1935	H	6	2	6	1	0	0
Ernie Lombardi	Cincinnati, May 9, 1937	A	6	3	6	1	0	0
Frank Demaree	Chicago, July 5, 1937, first game, 14 innings	H	7	2	6	3	0	0
Cookie Lavagetto	Brooklyn, September 23, 1939, first game	A	6	4	6	1	1	0
Walker Cooper	Cincinnati, July 6, 1949	H	7	5	6	0	0	3
Johnny Hopp	Pittsburgh, May 14, 1950, second game	A	6	3	6	0	0	2
Connie Ryan	Philadelphia, April 16, 1953	A	6	3	6	2	0	0
Dick Groat	Pittsburgh, May 13, 1960	A	6	2	6	3	0	0
Jesus Alou	San Francisco, July 10, 1964	A	6	1	6	0	0	1
Joe Morgan	Houston, July 8, 1965, 12 innings	A	6	4	6	0	1	2
Felix Millan	Atlanta, July 6, 1970	H	6	2	6	1	1	0
Don Kessinger	Chicago, July 17, 1971, 10 innings	H	6	3	6	1	0	0
Willie Davis	Los Angeles, May 24, 1973, 19 innings	H	9	1	6	0	0	0
Bill Madlock	Chicago, July 26, 1975, 10 innings	H	6	1	6	0	1	0

Player	Club, Date	Place	AB	R	H	2B	3B	HR
Rennie Stennett	Pittsburgh, September 16, 1975	A	7	5	7	2	1	0
Jose Cardenal	Chicago, May 2, 1976, first game, 14 innings	A	7	2	6	1	0	1
Gene Richards	San Diego, July 26, 1977, second game, 15 innings	H	7	1	6	1	0	1
Joe Lefebvre	San Diego, September 13, 1982, 16 innings	A	8	1	6	1	0	1
Wally Backman	Pittsburgh, April 27, 1990	A	6	1	6	1	0	0
Sammy Sosa	Chicago, July 2, 1993	A	6	2	6	1	0	0
Tony Gwynn	San Diego, August 4, 1993, 12 innings	H	7	2	6	2	0	0

Total number of occurrences: (71)

ROGER MARIS' 61 HOME RUNS—1961

HR No.	Team game No.	Date		Opposing pitcher, Club	Place	Innings	On base
1	11	April	26	Paul Foytack (righthander), Detroit	A	5	0
2	17	May	3	Pedro Ramos (righthander), Minnesota	A	7	2
3	20	May	6	Eli Grba (righthander), Los Angeles	A	5	0
4	29	May	17	Pete Burnside (lefthander), Washington	H	8	1
5	30	May	19	Jim Perry (righthander), Cleveland	A	1	1
6	31	May	20	Gary Bell (righthander), Cleveland	A	3	0
7	32	May	21	Chuck Estrada (righthander), Baltimore	H	1	0
8	35	May	24	Gene Conley (righthander), Boston	H	4	1
9	38	May	28	Cal McLish (righthander), Chicago	H	2	1
10	40	May	30	Gene Conley (righthander), Boston	A	3	0
11	40	May	30	Mike Fornieles (righthander), Boston	A	8	2
12	41	May	31	Billy Muffett (righthander), Boston	A	3	0
13	43	June	2	Cal McLish (righthander), Chicago	A	3	2
14	44	June	3	Bob Shaw (righthander), Chicago	A	8	2
15	45	June	4	Russ Kemmerer (righthander), Chicago	A	3	0
16	48	June	6	Ed Palmquist (righthander), Minnesota	H	6	2
17	49	June	7	Pedro Ramos (righthander), Minnesota	H	3	2
18	52	June	9	Ray Herbert (righthander), Kansas City	H	7	1
19	55	June	11†	Eli Grba (righthander), Los Angeles	H	3	0
20	55	June	11†	Johnny James (righthander), Los Angeles	H	7	0
21	57	June	13	Jim Perry (righthander), Cleveland	A	6	0
22	58	June	14	Gary Bell (righthander), Cleveland	A	4	1
23	61	June	17	Don Mossi (lefthander), Detroit	A	4	0
24	62	June	18	Jerry Casale (righthander), Detroit	A	8	1
25	63	June	19	Jim Archer (lefthander), Kansas City	A	9	0
26	64	June	20	Joe Nuxhall (lefthander), Kansas City	A	1	0
27	66	June	22	Norm Bass (righthander), Kansas City	A	2	1
28	74	July	1	Dave Sisler (righthander), Washington	H	9	1
29	75	July	2	Pete Burnside (lefthander), Washington	H	3	2
30	75	July	2	Johnny Klippstein (righthander), Washington	H	7	1
31	77	July	4†	Frank Lary (righthander), Detroit	H	8	1
32	78	July	5	Frank Funk (righthander), Cleveland	H	7	0
33	82	July	9*	Bill Monbouquette (righthander), Boston	H	7	0
34	84	July	13	Early Wynn (righthander), Chicago	A	1	1
35	86	July	15	Ray Herbert (righthander), Chicago	A	3	0
36	92	July	21	Bill Monbouquette (righthander), Boston	A	1	0
37	95	July	25*	Frank Baumann (lefthander), Chicago	H	4	1
38	95	July	25*	Don Larsen (righthander), Chicago	H	8	0
39	96	July	25†	Russ Kemmerer (righthander), Chicago	H	4	0
40	96	July	25†	Warren Hacker (righthander), Chicago	H	6	2
41	106	Aug.	4	Camilo Pascual (righthander), Minnesota	H	1	2
42	114	Aug.	11	Pete Burnside (lefthander), Washington	A	5	0
43	115	Aug.	12	Dick Donovan (righthander), Washington	A	4	0
44	116	Aug.	13*	Bennie Daniels (righthander), Washington	A	4	0
45	117	Aug.	13†	Marty Kutyna (righthander), Washington	A	1	1
46	118	Aug.	15	Juan Pizarro (lefthander), Chicago	H	4	0
47	119	Aug.	16	Billy Pierce (lefthander), Chicago	H	1	1
48	119	Aug.	16	Billy Pierce (lefthander), Chicago	H	3	1
49	124	Aug.	20	Jim Perry (righthander), Cleveland	A	3	1
50	125	Aug.	22	Ken McBride (righthander), Los Angeles	A	6	1
51	129	Aug.	26	Jerry Walker (righthander), Kansas City	A	6	0
52	135	Sept.	2	Frank Lary (righthander), Detroit	H	6	0
53	135	Sept.	2	Hank Aguirre (lefthander), Detroit	H	8	1
54	140	Sept.	6	Tom Cheney (righthander), Washington	H	4	0
55	141	Sept.	7	Dick Stigman (lefthander), Cleveland	H	3	0
56	143	Sept.	9	Mudcat Grant (righthander), Cleveland	H	7	0
57	151	Sept.	16	Frank Lary (righthander), Detroit	A	3	1
58	152	Sept.	17	Terry Fox (righthander), Detroit	A	12	1
59	155	Sept.	20	Milt Pappas (righthander), Baltimore	A	3	0
60	159	Sept.	26	Jack Fisher (righthander), Baltimore	H	3	0
61	163	Oct.	1	Tracy Stallard (righthander), Boston	H	4	0

New York played 163 games in 1961 (one tie on April 22). Maris did not hit a home run in this game. Maris played in 161 games.

BABE RUTH'S 60 HOME RUNS—1927

HR No.	Team game No.	Date		Opposing pitcher, Club	Place	Innings	On base
1	4	April	15	Howard Ehmke (righthander), Philadelphia	H	1	0
2	11	April	23	Rube Walberg (lefthander), Philadelphia	A	1	0
3	12	April	24	Sloppy Thurston (righthander), Washington	A	6	0
4	14	April	29	Slim Harriss (righthander), Boston	A	5	0
5	16	May	1	Jack Quinn (righthander), Philadelphia	H	1	1
6	16	May	1	Rube Walberg (lefthander), Philadelphia	H	8	0
7	24	May	10	Milt Gaston (righthander), St. Louis	A	1	2
8	25	May	11	Ernie Nevers (righthander), St. Louis	A	1	1
9	29	May	17	Rip H. Collins (righthander), Detroit	A	8	0
10	33	May	22	Benn Karr (righthander), Cleveland	A	6	1
11	34	May	23	Sloppy Thurston (righthander), Washington	A	1	0
12	37	May	28*	Sloppy Thurston (righthander), Washington	H	7	2
13	39	May	29	Danny MacFayden (righthander), Boston	H	8	0
14	41	May	30‡	Rube Walberg (lefthander), Philadelphia	A	11	0
15	42	May	31*	Jack Quinn (righthander), Philadelphia	A	1	1
16	43	May	31†	Howard Ehmke (righthander), Philadelphia	A	5	1
17	47	June	5	Earl Whitehill (lefthander), Detroit	H	6	0
18	48	June	7	Tommy Thomas (righthander), Chicago	H	4	0
19	52	June	11	Garland Buckeye (lefthander), Cleveland	H	3	1
20	52	June	11	Garland Buckeye (lefthander), Cleveland	H	5	0
21	53	June	12	George Uhle (righthander), Cleveland	H	7	0
22	55	June	16	Tom Zachary (lefthander), St. Louis	H	1	1
23	60	June	22*	Hal Wiltse (lefthander), Boston	A	5	0
24	60	June	22*	Hal Wiltse (lefthander), Boston	A	7	1
25	70	June	30	Slim Harriss (righthander), Boston	H	4	1
26	73	July	3	Hod Lisenbee (righthander), Washington	A	1	0
27	78	July	8†	Don Hankins (righthander), Detroit	A	2	2
28	79	July	9*	Ken Holloway (righthander), Detroit	A	1	1
29	79	July	9*	Ken Holloway (righthander), Detroit	A	4	2
30	83	July	12	Joe Shaute (lefthander), Cleveland	A	9	1
31	94	July	24	Tommy Thomas (righthander), Chicago	A	3	0
32	95	July	26*	Milt Gaston (righthander), St. Louis	H	1	1
33	95	July	26*	Milt Gaston (righthander), St. Louis	H	6	0
34	98	July	28	Lefty Stewart (lefthander), St. Louis	H	8	1
35	106	Aug.	5	George S. Smith (righthander), Detroit	H	8	0
36	110	Aug.	10	Tom Zachary (lefthander), Washington	A	3	2
37	114	Aug.	16	Tommy Thomas (righthander), Chicago	A	5	0
38	115	Aug.	17	Sarge Connally (righthander), Chicago	A	11	0
39	118	Aug.	20	Jake Miller (lefthander), Cleveland	A	1	1
40	120	Aug.	22	Joe Shaute (lefthander), Cleveland	A	6	0
41	124	Aug.	27	Ernie Nevers (righthander), St. Louis	A	8	1
42	125	Aug.	28	Ernie Wingard (lefthander), St. Louis	A	1	1
43	127	Aug.	31	Tony Welzer (righthander), Boston	H	8	0
44	128	Sept.	2	Rube Walberg (lefthander), Philadelphia	A	1	0
45	132	Sept.	6*	Tony Welzer (righthander), Boston	A	6	2
46	132	Sept.	6*	Tony Welzer (righthander), Boston	A	7	1
47	133	Sept.	6†	Jack Russell (righthander), Boston	A	9	0
48	134	Sept.	7	Danny MacFayden (righthander), Boston	A	1	0
49	134	Sept.	7	Slim Harriss (righthander), Boston	A	8	1
50	138	Sept.	11	Milt Gaston (righthander), St. Louis	H	4	0
51	139	Sept.	13*	Willis Hudlin (righthander), Cleveland	H	7	1
52	140	Sept.	13†	Joe Shaute (lefthander), Cleveland	H	4	0
53	143	Sept.	16	Ted Blankenship (righthander), Chicago	H	3	0
54	147	Sept.	18†	Ted Lyons (righthander), Chicago	H	5	1
55	148	Sept.	21	Sam Gibson (righthander), Detroit	H	9	0
56	149	Sept.	22	Ken Holloway (righthander), Detroit	H	9	1
57	152	Sept.	27	Lefty Grove (lefthander), Philadelphia	H	6	3
58	153	Sept.	29	Hod Lisenbee (righthander), Washington	H	1	0
59	153	Sept.	29	Paul Hopkins (righthander), Washington	H	5	3
60	154	Sept.	30	Tom Zachary (lefthander), Washington	H	8	1

*First game of doubleheader. †Second game of doubleheader. ‡Afternoon game of split doubleheader.
New York A.L. played 155 games in 1927 (one tie on April 14), with Ruth participating in 151 games. (No home run for Ruth in game No. 155 on October 1.)

— 186 —

Date	Opposing pitcher, Club	AB	R	H	2B	3B	HR	RBI
May	15 — Eddie Smith, Chicago	4	0	1	0	0	0	1
	16 — Thornton Lee, Chicago	4	2	2	0	1	1	1
	17 — Johnny Rigney, Chicago	3	1	1	0	0	0	0
	18 — Bob Harris (2), Johnny Niggeling (1), St. Louis	3	3	3	1	0	0	1
	19 — Denny Galehouse, St. Louis	3	0	1	1	0	0	0
	20 — Eldon Auker, St. Louis	5	1	1	0	0	0	1
	21 — Schoolboy Rowe (1), Al Benton (1), Detroit	5	0	2	0	0	0	1
	22 — Archie McKain, Detroit	4	0	1	0	0	0	1
	23 — Dick Newsome, Boston	5	0	1	0	0	0	2
	24 — Earl Johnson, Boston	4	2	1	0	0	0	2
	25 — Lefty Grove, Boston	4	0	1	0	0	0	0
	27 — Ken Chase (1), Red Anderson (2), — Alex Carrasquel (1), Washington	5	3	4	0	0	1	3
	28 — Sid Hudson, Washington	4	1	1	0	1	0	0
	29 — Steve Sundra, Washington	3	1	1	0	0	0	0
	30 — Earl Johnson, Boston	2	1	1	0	0	0	0
	30 — Mickey Harris, Boston	3	0	1	1	0	0	0
June	1 — Al Milnar, Cleveland	4	1	1	0	0	0	0
	1 — Mel Harder, Cleveland	4	0	1	0	0	0	0
	2 — Bob Feller, Cleveland	4	2	2	1	0	0	0
	3 — Dizzy Trout, Detroit	4	1	1	0	0	1	1
	5 — Hal Newhouser, Detroit	5	1	1	0	1	0	1
	7 — Bob Muncrief (1), Johnny Allen (1), — George Caster (1), St. Louis	5	2	3	0	0	0	1
	8 — Eldon Auker, St. Louis	4	3	2	0	0	2	4
	8 — George Caster (1), Jack Kramer (1), St. Louis	4	1	2	1	0	1	3
	10 — Johnny Rigney, Chicago	5	1	1	0	0	0	0
	12 — Thornton Lee, Chicago	4	1	2	0	0	1	1
	14 — Bob Feller, Cleveland	2	0	1	1	0	0	1
	15 — Jim Bagby, Cleveland	3	1	1	0	0	1	1
	16 — Al Milnar, Cleveland	5	0	1	1	0	0	0
	17 — Johnny Rigney, Chicago	4	1	1	0	0	0	0
	18 — Thornton Lee, Chicago	3	0	1	0	0	0	0
	19 — Eddie Smith (1), Buck Ross (2), Chicago	3	2	3	0	0	1	2
	20 — Bobo Newsom (2), Archie McKain (2), Detroit	5	3	4	1	0	0	1
	21 — Dizzy Trout, Detroit	4	0	1	0	0	0	1
	22 — Hal Newhouser (1), Bobo Newsom (1), Detroit	5	1	2	1	0	1	2
	24 — Bob Muncrief, St. Louis	4	1	1	0	0	0	0
	25 — Denny Galehouse, St. Louis	4	1	1	0	0	1	3
	26 — Eldon Auker, St. Louis	4	0	1	1	0	0	1
	27 — Chubby Dean, Philadelphia	3	1	2	0	0	1	2
	28 — Johnny Babich (1), Lum Harris (1), Philadelphia	5	1	2	1	0	0	0
	29 — Dutch E. Leonard, Washington	4	1	1	1	0	0	0
	29 — Red Anderson, Washington	5	1	1	0	0	0	1
July	1 — Mickey Harris (1), Mike Ryba (1), Boston	4	0	2	0	0	0	1
	1 — Jack Wilson, Boston	3	1	1	0	0	0	1
	2 — Dick Newsome, Boston	5	1	1	0	0	1	3
	5 — Phil Marchildon, Philadelphia	4	2	1	0	0	1	2
	6 — Johnny Babich (1), Bump Hadley (3), Phi.	5	2	4	1	0	0	2
	6 — Jack Knott, Philadelphia	4	0	2	0	1	0	2
	10 — Johnny Niggeling, St. Louis	2	0	1	0	0	0	0
	11 — Bob Harris (3), Jack Kramer (1), St. Louis	5	1	4	0	0	1	2
	12 — Eldon Auker (1), Bob Muncrief (1), St. Louis	5	1	2	1	0	0	1
	13 — Ted Lyons (2), Jack Hallett (1), Chicago	4	2	3	0	0	0	0
	13 — Thornton Lee, Chicago	4	0	1	0	0	0	0
	14 — Johnny Rigney, Chicago	3	0	1	0	0	0	0
	15 — Eddie Smith, Chicago	4	1	2	1	0	0	2
	16 — Al Milnar (2), Joe Krakauskas (1), Cleveland	4	3	3	1	0	0	0
	Totals for 56 games	223	56	91	16	4	15	55

Stopped July 17 at Cleveland, New York won, 4-3. First inning, Al Smith pitching, thrown out by Ken Keltner; fourth inning, Smith pitching, received base on balls; seventh inning, Smith pitching, thrown out by Keltner; eighth inning, Jim Bagby Jr., pitching, grounded into double play.

HOME RUNS BY CLUBS, EACH YEAR

AMERICAN LEAGUE (1901-1994)

*Denotes leader or tie.

Year	Bal.	Bos.	Cal.	Chi.	Cle.	Det.	K.C.	Mil.	Min.	N.Y.	Oak.	Sea.	Tex.	Tor.	Total
1901	..	*36	..	31	11	29	..	..	34	..	34	..	..	..	226
1902	29	43	..	14	32	21	..	..	*47	..	38	..	..	..	256
1903	11	*48	..	14	30	12	..	..	17	18	32	..	..	..	182
1904	10	26	..	14	22	14	..	..	9	27	*31	..	..	..	153

Year	Bal.	Bos.	Cal.	Chi.	Cle.	Det.	K.C.	Mil.	Min.	N.Y.	Oak.	Sea.	Tex.	Tor.	Total
1905	16	*29	..	11	22	10	..	..	25	23	23	..	..	..	159
1906	20	13	..	7	12	9	..	..	26	17	*31	..	..	..	135
1907	19	14	..	7	11	11	..	..	11	15	*22	..	..	..	101
1908	*21	13	..	3	18	19	..	..	8	13	20	..	..	..	115
1909	10	*21	..	4	10	20	..	..	8	16	20	..	..	..	109
1910	12	*44	..	7	8	28	..	..	8	20	18	..	..	..	145
1911	16	*35	..	20	19	28	..	..	15	25	*35	..	..	..	193
1912	19	*28	..	17	10	18	..	..	17	18	22	..	..	..	149
1913	18	17	..	23	16	24	..	..	19	8	*33	..	..	..	158
1914	17	18	..	19	11	25	..	..	18	12	*28	..	..	..	148
1915	19	13	..	25	20	23	..	..	12	*31	16	..	..	..	159
1916	14	14	..	17	16	17	..	..	12	*35	19	..	..	..	144
1917	15	14	..	19	13	25	..	..	4	*27	16	..	..	..	133
1918	5	16	..	8	9	13	..	..	4	20	*22	..	..	..	97
1919	32	33	..	25	24	23	..	..	24	*45	35	..	..	..	241
1920	50	22	..	36	35	30	..	..	36	*115	46	..	..	..	370
1921	66	17	..	35	42	58	..	..	42	*134	83	..	..	..	477
1922	97	45	..	45	32	54	..	..	45	95	*111	..	..	..	524
1923	82	34	..	42	59	41	..	..	26	*105	52	..	..	..	441
1924	67	30	..	41	40	35	..	..	22	*98	63	..	..	..	396
1925	*110	41	..	38	52	50	..	..	56	*110	76	..	..	..	533
1926	72	32	..	32	27	36	..	..	43	*121	61	..	..	..	424
1927	55	28	..	36	26	51	..	..	29	*158	56	..	..	..	439
1928	63	38	..	24	34	62	..	..	40	*133	89	..	..	..	483
1929	47	28	..	37	62	110	..	..	48	*142	122	..	..	..	596
1930	75	47	..	63	72	82	..	..	57	*152	125	..	..	..	673
1931	76	37	..	27	71	43	..	..	49	*155	118	..	..	..	576
1932	67	53	..	36	78	80	..	..	61	160	*173	..	..	..	708
1933	64	50	..	43	50	57	..	..	60	*144	140	..	..	..	608
1934	62	51	..	71	100	74	..	..	51	135	*144	..	..	..	688
1935	73	69	..	74	93	106	..	..	32	104	*112	..	..	..	663
1936	79	86	..	60	123	94	..	..	62	*182	72	..	..	..	758
1937	71	100	..	67	103	150	..	..	47	*174	94	..	..	..	806
1938	92	98	..	67	113	137	..	..	85	*174	98	..	..	..	864
1939	91	124	..	64	85	124	..	..	44	*166	98	..	..	..	796
1940	118	145	..	73	101	134	..	..	52	*155	105	..	..	..	883
1941	91	124	..	47	103	81	..	..	52	*151	85	..	..	..	734
1942	98	103	..	25	50	76	..	..	40	*108	33	..	..	..	533
1943	78	57	..	33	55	77	..	..	47	*100	26	..	..	..	473
1944	72	69	..	23	70	60	..	..	33	*96	36	..	..	..	459
1945	63	50	..	22	65	77	..	..	27	*93	33	..	..	..	430
1946	84	109	..	37	79	108	..	..	60	*136	40	..	..	..	653
1947	90	103	..	53	112	103	..	..	42	*115	61	..	..	..	679
1948	63	121	..	55	*155	78	..	..	31	139	68	..	..	..	710
1949	117	*131	..	43	112	88	..	..	81	115	82	..	..	..	769
1950	106	161	..	93	*164	114	..	..	76	159	100	..	..	..	973
1951	86	127	..	86	*140	104	..	..	54	*140	102	..	..	..	839
1952	82	113	..	80	*148	103	..	..	50	129	89	..	..	..	794
1953	112	101	..	74	*160	108	..	..	69	139	116	..	..	..	879
1954	52	132	..	94	*156	90	..	..	81	133	94	..	..	..	823
1955	54	137	..	116	148	130	..	..	80	*175	121	..	..	..	961
1956	91	139	..	128	153	150	..	..	112	*190	112	..	..	..	1,075
1957	87	153	..	106	140	116	..	..	111	145	*166	..	..	..	1,024
1958	108	155	..	101	161	109	..	..	121	*164	138	..	..	..	1,057
1959	109	125	..	97	*167	160	..	..	163	153	117	..	..	..	1,091
1960	123	124	..	112	127	150	..	..	147	*193	110	..	..	..	1,086
1961	149	112	189	138	150	180	..	..	167	*240	90	..	119	..	1,534
1962	156	146	137	92	180	*209	..	..	185	199	116	..	132	..	1,552
1963	146	171	95	114	169	148	..	..	*225	188	95	..	138	..	1,489
1964	162	186	102	106	164	157	..	..	*221	162	166	..	125	..	1,551
1965	125	*165	92	125	156	162	..	..	150	149	110	..	136	..	1,370
1966	175	145	122	87	155	*179	..	..	144	162	70	..	126	..	1,365
1967	138	*158	114	89	131	152	..	..	131	100	69	..	115	..	1,197
1968	133	125	83	71	75	*185	..	..	105	109	94	..	124	..	1,104
1969	175	*197	88	112	119	182	98	y125	163	94	148	..	148	..	1,649
1970	179	*203	114	123	183	148	97	126	153	111	171	..	138	..	1,746
1971	158	161	96	138	109	*179	80	104	116	97	160	..	86	..	1,484
1972	100	124	78	108	91	122	78	88	93	103	*134	..	56	..	1,175
1973	119	147	93	111	*158	157	114	145	120	131	147	..	110	..	1,552
1974	116	109	95	*135	131	131	89	120	111	101	132	..	99	..	1,369
1975	124	134	55	94	*153	125	118	146	121	110	151	..	134	..	1,465
1976	119	*134	63	73	85	101	65	88	81	120	113	..	80	..	1,122
1977	148	*213	131	192	100	166	146	125	123	184	117	133	135	100	2,013
1978	154	172	108	106	106	129	98	*173	82	125	100	97	132	98	1,680

Year	Bal.	Bos.	Cal.	Chi.	Cle.	Det.	K.C.	Mil.	Min.	N.Y.	Oak.	Sea.	Tex.	Tor.	Total
1979	181	*194	164	127	138	164	116	185	112	150	108	132	140	95	2,006
1980	156	162	106	91	89	143	115	*203	99	189	137	104	124	126	1,844
1981	88	90	97	76	39	65	61	96	47	100	*104	89	49	61	1,062
1982	179	136	186	136	109	177	132	*216	148	161	149	130	115	106	2,080
1983	*168	142	154	157	86	156	109	132	141	153	121	111	106	167	1,903
1984	160	181	150	172	123	*187	117	96	114	130	158	129	120	143	1,980
1985	*214	162	153	146	116	202	154	101	141	176	155	171	129	158	2,178
1986	169	144	167	121	157	*198	137	127	196	188	163	158	184	181	2,290
1987	211	174	172	173	187	*225	168	163	196	196	199	161	194	215	2,634
1988	137	124	124	132	134	143	121	113	151	148	156	148	112	*158	1,901
1989	129	108	*145	94	127	116	101	126	117	130	127	134	122	142	1,718
1990	132	106	147	106	110	*172	100	128	100	147	164	107	110	167	1,796
1991	170	126	115	139	79	*209	117	116	140	147	159	126	177	133	1,953
1992	148	84	88	110	127	*182	75	82	104	163	142	149	159	163	1,776
1993	157	114	114	162	141	178	125	125	121	178	158	161	*181	159	2,074
1994	139	120	120	121	*167	161	100	99	103	139	113	153	124	115	1,774
Totals	8,750	8,945	4,057	6,798	8,521	9,549	2,831	3,348	7,303	11,035	8,758	2,393	4,279	2,487	89,137

Note: Figures in Baltimore column 1902-1953 are for St. Louis (3,012); in Oakland column 1901-54 are for Philadelphia (3,498), Kansas City, 1955-67 (1,480); Minnesota column 1901-1960 are for old Washington club (2,782). Texas column represents second Washington club, 1961 through 1971. Figures in Totals column are all inclusive. (Baltimore had 24 in 1901 and 32 in 1902 and Milwaukee had 27 in 1901); these are included in League Totals but not in Club Totals. yPredecessor Seattle club. California column represents the Los Angeles Angels for 1961 through September 1, 1965.

NATIONAL LEAGUE (1900-1994)

*Denotes leader or tie.

Year	Atl.	Chi.	Cin.	Col.	Fla.	Hou.	L.A.	Mon.	N.Y.	Phi.	Pit.	St.L.	S.D.	S.F.	Total
1900	*47	33	30	..	..	..	27	..	..	28	26	37	..	23	251
1901	28	18	38	..	..	..	32	..	..	23	28	*39	..	19	225
1902	13	7	18	..	..	..	*19	..	..	5	18	10	..	6	96
1903	25	10	28	..	..	..	14	..	..	12	*33	5	..	20	147
1904	24	22	21	..	..	..	15	..	..	23	15	24	..	*31	175
1905	17	12	27	..	..	..	29	..	..	16	22	20	..	*39	182
1906	16	20	16	..	..	..	*25	..	..	12	12	10	..	15	126
1907	22	13	15	..	..	..	18	..	..	12	19	10	..	*23	141
1908	17	19	14	..	..	..	*28	..	..	11	25	17	..	20	151
1909	15	20	22	..	..	..	16	..	..	12	25	15	..	*26	151
1910	31	*34	23	..	..	..	25	..	..	22	33	15	..	31	214
1911	37	54	21	..	..	..	28	..	..	*60	48	27	..	39	314
1912	35	42	19	..	..	..	32	..	..	42	39	27	..	*48	284
1913	32	59	27	..	..	..	39	..	..	*73	35	15	..	31	311
1914	35	41	16	..	..	..	31	..	..	*62	18	33	..	30	266
1915	17	53	15	..	..	..	14	..	..	*58	24	20	..	24	225
1916	22	*46	14	..	..	..	28	..	..	42	20	25	..	42	239
1917	22	17	26	..	..	..	25	..	..	38	9	26	..	*39	202
1918	13	20	15	..	..	..	10	..	..	25	15	*27	..	13	138
1919	24	21	19	..	..	..	25	..	..	*42	17	18	..	40	206
1920	23	34	18	..	..	..	28	..	..	*64	16	32	..	46	261
1921	61	37	20	..	..	..	59	..	..	*88	37	83	..	75	460
1922	32	42	45	..	..	..	56	..	..	*116	52	107	..	80	530
1923	32	90	45	..	..	..	62	..	..	*112	49	63	..	85	538
1924	25	66	36	..	..	..	72	..	..	94	43	67	..	*95	498
1925	41	85	44	..	..	..	64	..	..	100	77	109	..	*114	634
1926	16	66	35	..	..	..	40	..	..	75	44	*90	..	73	439
1927	37	74	29	..	..	..	39	..	..	57	54	84	..	*109	483
1928	52	92	32	..	..	..	66	..	..	85	52	113	..	*118	610
1929	32	139	34	..	..	..	99	..	..	*153	60	100	..	136	753
1930	66	*171	74	..	..	..	122	..	..	126	86	104	..	143	892
1931	34	83	21	..	..	..	71	..	..	81	41	60	..	*101	492
1932	63	69	47	..	..	..	109	..	..	*122	47	76	..	116	549
1933	54	72	34	..	..	..	62	..	..	60	39	57	..	*82	460
1934	83	101	55	..	..	..	79	..	..	56	52	104	..	*126	656
1935	75	88	73	..	..	..	59	..	..	92	66	86	..	*123	662
1936	68	76	82	..	..	..	33	..	..	*103	60	88	..	97	607
1937	63	96	73	..	..	..	37	..	..	103	47	94	..	*111	624
1938	54	65	110	..	..	..	61	..	..	40	65	91	..	*125	611
1939	56	91	98	..	..	..	78	..	..	49	63	98	..	*116	649
1940	59	86	89	..	..	..	93	..	..	75	76	*119	..	91	688
1941	48	99	64	..	..	..	*101	..	..	64	56	70	..	95	597
1942	68	75	66	..	..	..	62	..	..	44	54	60	..	*109	538
1943	39	52	43	..	..	..	39	..	..	66	42	70	..	*81	432
1944	79	71	51	..	..	..	56	..	..	55	70	*100	..	93	575
1945	101	57	56	..	..	..	57	..	..	56	72	64	..	*114	577
1946	44	56	65	..	..	..	55	..	..	80	60	81	..	*121	562

Year	Atl.	Chi.	Cin.	Col.	Fla.	Hou.	L.A.	Mon.	N.Y.	Phi.	Pit.	St.L.	S.D.	S.F.	Total
1947	85	71	95	..	..	..	83	..	..	60	156	115	..	*221	886
1948	95	87	104	..	..	..	91	..	..	91	108	105	..	*164	845
1949	103	97	86	..	..	..	*152	..	..	122	126	102	..	147	935
1950	148	161	99	..	..	..	*194	..	..	125	138	102	..	133	1,100
1951	130	103	88	..	..	..	*184	..	..	108	137	95	..	179	1,024
1952	110	107	104	..	..	..	*153	..	..	93	92	97	..	151	907
1953	156	137	166	..	..	..	*208	..	..	115	99	140	..	176	1,197
1954	139	159	147	..	..	..	*186	..	..	102	76	119	..	*186	1,114
1955	182	164	181	..	..	..	*201	..	..	132	91	143	..	169	1,263
1956	177	142	*221	..	..	..	179	..	..	121	110	124	..	145	1,219
1957	*199	147	187	..	..	..	147	..	..	117	92	132	..	157	1,178
1958	167	*182	123	..	..	..	172	..	..	124	134	111	..	170	1,183
1959	*177	163	161	..	..	..	148	..	..	113	112	118	..	167	1,159
1960	*170	119	140	..	..	..	126	..	..	99	120	138	..	130	1,042
1961	*188	176	158	..	..	..	157	..	..	103	128	103	..	183	1,196
1962	181	126	167	..	..	105	140	..	139	142	108	137	..	*204	1,449
1963	139	127	122	..	..	62	110	..	96	126	108	128	..	*197	1,215
1964	159	145	130	..	..	70	79	..	103	130	121	109	..	*165	1,211
1965	*196	134	183	..	..	97	78	..	107	144	111	109	..	159	1,318
1966	*207	140	149	..	..	112	108	..	98	117	158	108	..	181	1,378
1967	*158	128	109	..	..	93	82	..	83	103	91	115	..	140	1,102
1968	80	*130	106	..	..	66	67	..	81	100	80	73	..	108	891
1969	141	142	*171	..	..	104	97	125	109	137	119	90	99	136	1,470
1970	160	179	*191	..	..	129	87	136	120	101	130	113	172	165	1,683
1971	153	128	138	..	..	71	95	88	98	123	*154	95	96	140	1,379
1972	144	133	124	..	..	134	98	91	105	98	110	70	102	*150	1,359
1973	*206	117	137	..	..	134	110	125	85	134	154	75	112	161	1,550
1974	120	110	135	..	..	110	*139	86	96	95	114	83	99	93	1,280
1975	107	95	124	..	..	84	118	98	101	125	*138	81	78	84	1,233
1976	82	105	*141	..	..	66	91	94	102	110	110	63	64	85	1,113
1977	139	111	181	..	..	114	*191	138	88	186	133	96	120	134	1,631
1978	123	72	136	..	..	70	*149	121	86	133	115	79	75	117	1,276
1979	126	135	132	..	..	49	*183	143	74	119	148	100	93	125	1,427
1980	144	107	113	..	..	75	*148	114	61	117	116	101	67	80	1,243
1981	64	57	64	..	..	45	*82	81	57	69	55	50	32	63	719
1982	*146	102	82	..	..	74	138	133	97	112	134	67	81	133	1,299
1983	130	140	107	..	..	97	*146	102	112	125	121	83	93	142	1,398
1984	111	136	106	..	..	79	102	96	107	*147	98	75	109	112	1,278
1985	126	*150	114	..	..	121	129	118	134	141	80	87	109	115	1,424
1986	138	*155	144	..	..	125	130	110	148	154	111	58	136	114	1,523
1987	152	*209	192	..	..	122	125	120	192	169	131	94	113	205	1,824
1988	96	113	122	..	..	96	99	107	*152	106	110	71	94	113	1,279
1989	128	124	128	..	..	97	89	100	*147	123	95	73	120	141	1,365
1990	162	136	125	..	..	94	129	114	*172	103	138	73	123	152	1,521
1991	141	159	*164	..	..	79	108	95	117	111	126	68	121	141	1,430
1992	*138	104	99	..	..	96	72	102	93	118	106	94	135	105	1,262
1993	*169	161	137	142	94	138	130	122	158	156	110	118	153	168	1,956
1994	*137	109	124	125	94	120	115	108	117	80	80	108	92	123	1,532
Totals	8,726	8,928	8,320	267	188	3,120	8,384	2,867	3,635	8,513	7,493	7,387	2,688	10,263	80,787

Note: Figures in Atlanta column 1900-1952 are for Boston (2,588) and 1953-1965 for Milwaukee (2,230); in Los Angeles column 1900-1957 are for Brooklyn (4,017); San Francisco column 1900-1957 are for New York Giants (5,162); New York column represents the present Met franchise. Figures in Totals columns are all inclusive.

CLUBS WITH FIVE HOME RUNS IN INNING

AMERICAN LEAGUE

Date	Inn.	Club (Players)
June 9, 1966	7	Minnesota (Rollins, Versalles, OLIVA, MINCHER, KILLEBREW).

Total number of clubs: (1)

NATIONAL LEAGUE

Date	Inn.	Club (Players)
June 6, 1939	4	New York (Danning, Demaree, WHITEHEAD, SALVO, MOORE).
June 2, 1949	8	Philadelphia (Ennis, Seminick, Jones, Rowe, Seminick).
Aug. 23, 1961	9	San Francisco (Cepeda, F. Alou, Davenport, Mays, Orsino).

Note—Capitalized letters denote three or more homers were consecutive.

Total number of clubs: (3)

CLUBS WITH FOUR HOME RUNS IN INNING

AMERICAN LEAGUE

Date	Inn.	Club (Players)
Sept. 24, 1940*	6	Boston (WILLIAMS, FOXX, CRONIN, Tabor).
June 23, 1950	4	Detroit (Trout, Priddy, Wertz, Evers).
May 22, 1957	6	Boston (Mauch, Williams, Gernert, Malzone).
Aug. 26, 1957	7	Boston (Zauchin, Lepcio, Piersall, Malzone).
July 31, 1963†	6	Cleveland (HELD, RAMOS, FRANCONA, BROWN).
May 2, 1964	11	Minnesota (OLIVA, ALLISON, HALL, KILLEBREW).
May 17, 1967	7	Baltimore (Etchebarren, Bowens, Powell, D. Johnson).
July 29, 1974	1	Detroit (KALINE, FREEHAN, STANLEY, Brinkman).
June 17, 1977	1	Boston (Burleson, Lynn, Fisk, Scott).
July 4, 1977	8	Boston (LYNN, RICE, YASTRZEMSKI, Scott).
May 31, 1980	4	Boston (Stapleton, PEREZ, FISK, HOBSON).
May 16, 1983	9	Minnesota (Engle, Mitchell, Gaetti, Hatcher).
Sept. 10, 1986	4	Detroit (Lemon, Heath, Gibson, Coles).
May 2, 1992	5	Minnesota (Mack, Puckett, Hrbek, Bush).

Total number of clubs: (14)

NATIONAL LEAGUE

Date	Inn.	Club (Players)
June 6, 1894	3	Pittsburgh (Stenzel, Lyons, Bierbauer, Stenzel).
May 12, 1930	7	Chicago (Heathcote, Wilson, Grimm, Beck).
Aug. 13, 1939*	4	New York (Bonura, KAMPOURIS, LOHRMAN, MOORE).
June 6, 1948*	6	St. Louis (Dusak, Schoendienst, Slaughter, Jones).
May 28, 1954	8	New York (Williams, Dark, Irvin, Gardner).
July 8, 1956*	4	New York (Mays, THOMPSON, SPENCER, WESTRUM).
June 8, 1961	7	Milwaukee (MATHEWS, AARON, ADCOCK, THOMAS).
June 8, 1965	10	Milwaukee (Torre, Mathews, Aaron, Oliver).
July 10, 1970	9	San Diego (Murrell, Spiezio, Campbell, Gaston).
June 21, 1971*	8	Atlanta (Lum, King, H. Aaron, Evans).
July 30, 1978	3	Montreal (Dawson, Parrish, Cash, Dawson).
Aug. 17, 1985	7	Philadelphia (SAMUEL, WILSON, SCHMIDT, Daulton).
Apr. 29, 1986	4	Montreal (Dawson, Brooks, Wallach, Fitzgerald).
Sept. 20, 1992	6	Atlanta (JUSTICE, HUNTER, GANT, Lemke).
June 19, 1994	1	Cincinnati (Morris, Mitchell, Branson, Taubensee).

Note—Capitalized letters denote three or more homers were consecutive.
*First game. †Second game.

Total number of clubs: (15)

CLUBS WITH THREE CONSECUTIVE HOME RUNS IN INNING

PLAYERS LEAGUE

Date	Inn.	Club (Players)
May 31, 1890	8	New York (GORE, EWING, CONNOR).

Total number of clubs: (1)

AMERICAN LEAGUE

Date	Inn.	Club (Players)
June 30, 1902*	6	Cleveland (LAJOIE, HICKMAN, BRADLEY).
May 2, 1922	4	Philadelphia (WALKER, PERKINS, MILLER).
Sept. 10, 1925*	4	New York (MEUSEL, RUTH, GEHRIG).
May 4, 1929	7	New York (RUTH, GEHRIG, MEUSEL).
June 18, 1930	5	Philadelphia (SIMMONS, FOXX, MILLER).
July 17, 1934	4	Philadelphia (JOHNSON, FOXX, HIGGINS).
June 25, 1939*	7	Cleveland (CHAPMAN, TROSKY, HEATH).
Sept. 24, 1940*‡	6	Boston (WILLIAMS, FOXX, CRONIN).
May 23, 1946	5	New York (DiMAGGIO, ETTEN, GORDON).
April 23, 1947	8	Detroit (CULLENBINE, WAKEFIELD, EVERS).
May 13, 1947	6	New York (KELLER, DiMAGGIO, LINDELL).
April 19, 1948*	2	Boston (SPENCE, STEPHENS, DOERR).
June 6, 1948†	6	Boston (WILLIAMS, SPENCE, STEPHENS).
July 28, 1950	3	Cleveland (DOBY, ROSEN, EASTER).
Sept. 2, 1951	1	Cleveland (SIMPSON, ROSEN, EASTER).
July 16, 1953†	5	St. Louis (COURTNEY, KRYHOSKI, DYCK).
July 7, 1956	7	Detroit (KUENN, TORGESON, MAXWELL).
Sept. 7, 1959	2	Boston (BUDDIN, CASALE, GREEN).
April 30, 1961†	7	Baltimore (GENTILE, TRIANDOS, HANSEN).
May 23, 1961	9	Detroit (CASH, BOROS, BROWN).
June 27, 1961	1	Washington (GREEN, TASBY, LONG).
June 17, 1962*	2	Cleveland (KINDALL, PHILLIPS, MAHONEY).

Date		Inn.	Club (Players)
Aug.	19, 1962	7	Kansas City (CIMOLI, CAUSEY, BRYAN).
Aug.	28, 1962	4	Los Angeles (J. L. THOMAS, WAGNER, RODGERS).
July	31, 1963†‡	6	Cleveland (HELD, RAMOS, FRANCONA, BROWN).
May	2 1964‡	11	Minnesota (OLIVA, ALLISON, HALL, KILLEBREW).
Sept.	10, 1965	8	Baltimore (ROBINSON, BLEFARY, ADAIR).
June	9, 1966‡	7	Minnesota (OLIVA, MINCHER, KILLEBREW).
June	29, 1966	3	New York (RICHARDSON, MANTLE, PEPITONE).
July	2, 1966	6	Washington (HOWARD, LOCK, McMULLEN).
June	22, 1969*	3	Oakland (KUBIAK, JACKSON, BANDO).
Aug.	10, 1969	6	New York (MURCER, MUNSON, MICHAEL).
Sept.	4, 1969	9	Baltimore (F. ROBINSON, POWELL, B. C. ROBINSON).
Aug.	22, 1970	6	Cleveland (SIMS, NETTLES, LEON).
April	17, 1971	7	Detroit (NORTHRUP, CASH, HORTON).
June	27, 1972	1	Detroit (RODRIGUEZ, KALINE, HORTON).
July	15, 1973	8	Minnesota (MITTERWALD, LIS, HOLT).
July	29, 1974‡	1	Detroit (KALINE, FREEHAN, STANLEY).
May	11, 1977	2	California (BONDS, BAYLOR, JACKSON).
July	4, 1977	8	Boston (LYNN, RICE, YASTRZEMSKI).
Aug.	13, 1977	6	Boston (SCOTT, HOBSON, EVANS).
May	8, 1979	6	Baltimore (MURRAY, MAY, ROENICKE).
June	19, 1979	4	Oakland (GROSS, REVERING, HEATH).
May	31, 1980‡	4	Boston (PEREZ, FISK, HOBSON).
June	3, 1980	3	Oakland (REVERING, PAGE, ARMAS).
May	28, 1982	6	Milwaukee (COOPER, MONEY, THOMAS).
June	5, 1982	7	Milwaukee (YOUNT, COOPER, OGLIVIE).
June	7, 1982	8	Minnesota (WASHINGTON, BRUNANSKY, HRBEK).
Sept.	12, 1982	3	Milwaukee (COOPER, SIMMONS, OGLIVIE).
Aug.	2, 1983	3	Seattle (S. HENDERSON, D. HENDERSON, RAMOS).
Sept.	9, 1983	1	Chicago (FISK, PACIOREK, LUZINSKI).
April	24, 1984	4	California (R.M. JACKSON, DOWNING, GRICH).
April	26, 1984	6	Toronto (UPSHAW, BELL, BARFIELD).
May	29, 1984	6	New York (MATTINGLY, BAYLOR, WINFIELD).
June	3, 1984	4	New York (GAMBLE, KEMP, HARRAH).
June	29, 1984	5	Cleveland (THORNTON, HALL, WILLARD).
Aug.	19, 1984	7	Kansas City (MOTLEY, WHITE, BALBONI).
Aug.	24, 1985	9	Chicago (LAW, LITTLE, BAINES).
Sept.	16, 1985	8	Baltimore (RIPKEN, MURRAY, LYNN).
July	8, 1986	4	Detroit (GIBSON, PARRISH, EVANS).
July	31, 1986	5	Detroit (TRAMMELL, GIBSON, GRUBB).
Sept.	28, 1986	4	Kansas City (BRETT, WHITE, QUIRK).
June	28, 1987	9	Detroit (GRUBB, NOKES, MADLOCK).
Sept.	12, 1987	8	Toronto (WHITT, BARFIELD, GRUBER).
July	9, 1988*	4	Chicago (PASQUA, WALKER, BOSTON).
May	16, 1990	4	Oakland (CANSECO, McGWIRE, HASSEY).
June	17, 1990	7	Cleveland (MALDONADO, JACOBY, SNYDER).
July	6, 1990†	3	Oakland (R. HENDERSON, LANSFORD, CANSECO).
Aug.	7, 1990	9	Detroit (TRAMMELL, FIELDER, WARD).
April	20, 1992	3	Detroit (TRAMMELL, FIELDER, TETTLETON).
May	8, 1994	6	New York (TARTABULL, STANLEY, G. WILLIAMS).

Total number of clubs: (71)

NATIONAL LEAGUE

Date		Inn.	Club (Players)
May	10, 1894	7	St. Louis (SHUGART, MILLER, PEITZ).
Aug.	13, 1932*	4	New York (TERRY, OTT, LINDSTROM).
June	10, 1935	8	Pittsburgh (P. WANER, VAUGHAN, YOUNG).
July	9, 1938	3	Boston (CUCCINELLO, WEST, FLETCHER).
June	6, 1939‡	4	New York (WHITEHEAD, SALVO, MOORE).
Aug.	13, 1939*‡	4	New York (KAMPOURIS, LOHRMAN, MOORE).
Aug.	11, 1941	5	Chicago (CAVARRETTA, HACK, NICHOLSON).
June	11, 1944†	8	St. Louis (W. COOPER, KUROWSKI, LITWHILER).
Aug.	11, 1946*	8	Cincinnati (HATTON, WEST, MUELLER).
June	20, 1948†	8	New York (MIZE, MARSHALL, GORDON).
June	4, 1949	6	New York (LOCKMAN, GORDON, MARSHALL).
April	19, 1952	7	Brooklyn (CAMPANELLA, PAFKO, SNIDER).
Sept.	27, 1952	7	Pittsburgh (KINER, GARAGIOLA, BELL).
Sept.	4, 1953	4	New York (WESTRUM, CORWIN, LOCKMAN).
June	20, 1954	6	New York (HOFMAN, WESTRUM, RHODES).
Aug.	15, 1954	9	Cincinnati (BELL, KLUSZEWSKI, GREENGRASS).
April	16, 1955	2	Chicago (JACKSON, BANKS, FONDY).
July	6, 1955*	6	Pittsburgh (LYNCH, THOMAS, LONG).
May	30, 1956*	1	Milwaukee (MATHEWS, AARON, THOMSON).
May	31, 1956	9	Cincinnati (BELL, KLUSZEWSKI, ROBINSON).
June	29, 1956	9	Brooklyn (SNIDER, JACKSON, HODGES).
July	8, 1956*‡	4	New York (THOMPSON, SPENCER, WESTRUM).

Date	Inn.	Club (Players)
April 21, 1957*	3	Pittsburgh (THOMAS, SMITH, GROAT).
June 26, 1957	5	Milwaukee (AARON, MATHEWS, COVINGTON).
May 7, 1958	5	Pittsburgh (SKINNER, KLUSZEWSKI, THOMAS).
May 31, 1958	1	Milwaukee (AARON, MATHEWS, COVINGTON).
June 8, 1961‡	7	Milwaukee (MATHEWS, AARON, ADCOCK, THOMAS).
June 18, 1961	3	Milwaukee (AARON, ADCOCK, THOMAS).
April 28, 1962	6	New York (THOMAS, NEAL, HODGES).
Aug. 27, 1963	3	San Francisco (MAYS, CEPEDA, F. ALOU).
July 18, 1964	8	St. Louis (BOYER, WHITE, McCARVER).
Aug. 5, 1969*	5	San Francisco (MARSHALL, HUNT, BONDS).
May 18, 1970	8	New York (MARSHALL, FOY, GROTE).
Aug. 1, 1970	7	Pittsburgh (ROBERTSON, STARGELL, PAGAN).
July 16, 1974	9	San Diego (COLBERT, McCOVEY, WINFIELD).
July 20, 1974	5	New York (THEODORE, STAUB, JONES).
May 17, 1977	5	Chicago (BIITTNER, MURCER, MORALES).
Sept. 30, 1977	2	Philadelphia (LUZINSKI, HEBNER, MADDOX).
Aug. 14, 1978	3	Atlanta (MATTHEWS, BURROUGHS, HORNER).
June 17, 1979	4	Montreal (PEREZ, CARTER, VALENTINE).
July 11, 1979	1	San Diego (TURNER, WINFIELD, TENACE).
May 27, 1980	3	Cincinnati (GRIFFEY, FOSTER, DRIESSEN).
Aug. 31, 1980†	2	Los Angeles (CEY, MONDAY, FERGUSON).
July 11, 1982	2	San Francisco (SMITH, MAY, SUMMERS).
June 24, 1984	5	Houston (CABELL, GARNER, CRUZ).
Aug. 17, 1985‡	7	Philadelphia (SAMUEL, WILSON, SCHMIDT).
July 27, 1986	3	New York (CARTER, STRAWBERRY, MITCHELL).
April 13, 1987	1	San Diego (WYNNE, GWYNN, KRUK).
July 26, 1987	8	Philadelphia (THOMPSON, HAYES, SCHMIDT).
May 1, 1988	5	New York (TEUFEL, HERNANDEZ, STRAWBERRY).
April 17, 1989	3	New York (STRAWBERRY, McREYNOLDS, HERNANDEZ).
June 16, 1990	5	Cincinnati (SABO, LARKIN, DAVIS).
Sept. 14, 1991	4	Cincinnati (DUNCAN, MORRIS, O'NEILL).
Sept. 20, 1992	6	Atlanta (JUSTICE, HUNTER, GANT).
Sept. 6, 1993	6	Chicago (BUECHELE, WILSON, LAKE).
April 15, 1994	1	Atlanta (McGRIFF, PENDLETON, TARASCO).
April 18, 1994	1	Atlanta (KLESKO, McGRIFF, JUSTICE).

*First game. †Second game. ‡Club had more than three homers in inning.

Total number of clubs: (57)

PITCHING

NO-HIT GAMES

PERFECT GAMES OF NINE OR MORE INNINGS
AMERICAN LEAGUE

Year	Score
1904 —Cy Young, Boston vs. Philadelphia, May 5	3-0
1908 —Addie Joss, Cleveland vs. Chicago, October 2	1-0
1922 —Charlie Robertson, Chicago at Detroit, April 30	2-0
1968 —Catfish Hunter, Oakland vs. Minnesota, May 8	4-0
1981 —Len Barker, Cleveland vs. Toronto, May 15	3-0
1984 —Mike Witt, California at Texas, September 30	1-0
1994 —Kenny Rogers, Texas vs. California, July 28	4-0

Note: Ernie Shore of Boston is often included in the list of perfect game pitchers. In the first game of a June 23, 1917 double-header at Boston, Babe Ruth, the starting Red Sox pitcher, was removed for arguing with umpire Brick Owens after giving a base on balls to Washington's Ray Morgan, the first batter. Shore, without warming up, took Ruth's place. Morgan was retired trying to steal second. From then on, Shore faced 26 batters, with none reaching base. Shore won the game, 4-0. He and Ruth are listed under the category "No-hit games of nine or more innings."

Note: Don Larsen of the New York Yankees pitched a perfect game in the World Series, defeating the Brooklyn Dodgers, 2-0, at Yankee Stadium on October 8, 1956.

Total number of games (excluding Shore's and Larsen's): (7)

NATIONAL LEAGUE

Year	Score
1880 —Lee Richmond, Worcester vs. Cleveland, June 12	1-0
—Monte Ward, Providence vs. Buffalo, June 17	5-0
1964 —Jim Bunning, Philadelphia at New York, June 21, first game	6-0
1965 —Sandy Koufax, Los Angeles vs. Chicago, September 9	1-0
1988 —Tom Browning, Cincinnati vs. Los Angeles, September 16	1-0
1991 —Dennis Martinez, Montreal at Los Angeles, July 28	2-0

Total number of games: (6)

PERFECT GAMES FOR NINE INNINGS THAT WERE BROKEN UP IN EXTRA INNINGS
NATIONAL LEAGUE

Year	Score
1959 —Harvey Haddix, Pittsburgh at Milwaukee, May 26 (Haddix pitched 12 perfect innings before Felix Mantilla, leading off the 13th, reached base on third baseman Don Hoak's throwing error. After Eddie Mathews sacrificed and Hank Aaron was walked intentionally, Joe Adcock doubled to score Mantilla, ending the game.)	0-1

Total number of games: (1)

PERFECT GAMES OF LESS THAN NINE INNINGS
AMERICAN LEAGUE

Year	Score
1907 —Rube Vickers, Philadelphia at Washington, October 5, second game, five innings	4-0
1967 —Dean Chance, Minnesota vs. Boston, August 6, five innings	2-0

Total number of games: (2)

NATIONAL LEAGUE

Year	Score
1907 —Ed Karger, St. Louis vs. Boston, August 11, second game, seven innings	4-0
1984 —David Palmer, Montreal at St. Louis, April 21, second game, five innings	4-0

Total number of games: (2)

NO-HIT GAMES OF NINE OR MORE INNINGS
AMERICAN ASSOCIATION

Year	Score
1882 —Tony Mullane, Louisville at Cincinnati, September 11 (first no-hitter at 50-foot distance)	2-0
—Guy Hecker, Louisville at Pittsburgh, September 19	3-1
1884 —Al Atkisson, Philadelphia vs. Pittsburgh, May 24	10-1
—Ed Morris, Columbus at Pittsburgh, May 29	5-0
—Frank Mountain, Columbus at Washington, June 5	12-0
—Sam Kimber, Brooklyn vs. Toledo, October 4, 10 innings	0-0
1886 —Al Atkisson, Philadelphia vs. New York, May 1	3-2
—Adonis Terry, Brooklyn vs. St. Louis, July 24	1-0
—Matt Kilroy, Baltimore at Pittsburgh, October 6	6-0
1888 —Adonis Terry, Brooklyn vs. Louisville, May 27	4-0
—Henry Porter, Kansas City at Baltimore, June 6	4-0
—Ed Seward, Philadelphia vs. Cincinnati, July 26	12-2
—Gus Weyhing, Philadelphia vs. Kansas City, July 31	4-0
1890 —Cannonball Titcomb, Rochester vs. Syracuse, September 15	7-0
1891 —Ted Breitenstein, St. Louis vs. Louisville, October 4, first game (first major league start)	8-0

Total number of games: (15)

UNION ASSOCIATION

Year	Score
1884 —Dick Burns, Cincinnati at Kansas City, August 26	3-1
1884 —Ed Cushman, Milwaukee vs. Washington, September 28	5-0

Total number of games: (2)

AMERICAN LEAGUE

Year	Score
1902 —Nixey Callahan, Chicago vs. Detroit, September 20, first game	3-0
1904 —Jesse Tannehill, Boston at Chicago, August 17	6-0
1905 —Weldon Henley, Philadelphia at St. Louis, July 22, first game	6-0
—Frank E. Smith, Chicago at Detroit, September 6, second game	15-0
—Bill Dinneen, Boston vs. Chicago, September 27, first game	2-0
1908 —Cy Young, Boston at New York, June 30	8-0
—Bob Rhoads, Cleveland vs. Boston, September 18	2-1
—Frank Smith, Chicago vs. Philadelphia, September 20	1-0
1910 —Addie Joss, Cleveland at Chicago, April 20	1-0
—Chief Bender, Philadelphia vs. Cleveland, May 12	4-0
1911 —Joe Wood, Boston vs. St. Louis, July 29, first game	5-0
—Ed Walsh Sr., Chicago vs. Boston, August 27	5-0
1912 —George Mullin, Detroit vs. St. Louis, July 4, second game	7-0
—Earl Hamilton, St. Louis at Detroit, August 30	5-1
1914 —Joe Benz, Chicago vs. Cleveland, May 31	6-1
1916 —Rube Foster, Boston vs. New York, June 21	2-0
—Bullet Joe Bush, Philadelphia vs. Cleveland, August 26	5-0
—Dutch H. Leonard, Boston vs. St. Louis, August 30	4-0
1917 —Eddie Cicotte, Chicago at St. Louis, April 14	11-0
—George Mogridge, New York at Boston, April 24	2-1
—Ernie Koob, St. Louis vs. Chicago, May 5	1-0

—Bob Groom, St. Louis vs. Chicago, May 6, second game 3-0
—Babe Ruth (0 innings) and Ernie Shore (9 innings), Boston vs. Washington, June 23, first game (see note under
   American League "perfect games of nine or more innings") 4-0
1918 —Dutch H. Leonard, Boston at Detroit, June 3 5-0
1919 —Ray Caldwell, Cleveland at New York, September 10, first game 3-0
1920 —Walter Johnson, Washington at Boston, July 1 1-0
1923 —Sad Sam Jones, New York at Philadelphia, September 4 2-0
   —Howard Ehmke, Boston at Philadelphia, September 7 4-0
1926 —Ted Lyons, Chicago at Boston, August 21 6-0
1931 —Wes Ferrell, Cleveland vs. St. Louis, April 29 9-0
   —Bobby Burke, Washington vs. Boston, August 8 5-0
1935 —Vern Kennedy, Chicago vs. Cleveland, August 31 5-0
1937 —Bill Dietrich, Chicago vs. St. Louis, June 1 8-0
1938 —Monte Pearson, New York vs. Cleveland, August 27, second game 13-0
1940 —Bob Feller, Cleveland at Chicago, April 16 (season opener for both clubs) 1-0
1945 —Dick Fowler, Philadelphia vs. St. Louis, September 9, second game 1-0
1946 —Bob Feller, Cleveland at New York, April 30 1-0
1947 —Don Black, Cleveland vs. Philadelphia, July 10, first game 3-0
   —Bill McCahan, Philadelphia vs. Washington, September 3 3-0
1948 —Bob Lemon, Cleveland at Detroit, June 30 2-0
1951 —Bob Feller, Cleveland vs. Detroit, July 1, first game 2-1
   —Allie Reynolds, New York at Cleveland, July 12 1-0
   —Allie Reynolds, New York vs. Boston, September 28, first game 8-0
1952 —Virgil Trucks, Detroit vs. Washington, May 15 1-0
   —Virgil Trucks, Detroit at New York, August 25 1-0
1953 —Bobo Holloman, St. Louis vs. Philadelphia, May 6 (first major league start) 6-0
1956 —Mel Parnell, Boston vs. Chicago, July 14 4-0
1957 —Bob Keegan, Chicago vs. Washington, August 20, second game 6-0
1958 —Jim Bunning, Detroit at Boston, July 20, first game 3-0
   —Hoyt Wilhelm, Baltimore vs. New York, September 20 1-0
1962 —Bo Belinsky, Los Angeles vs. Baltimore, May 5 2-0
   —Earl Wilson, Boston vs. Los Angeles, June 26 2-0
   —Bill Monbouquette, Boston at Chicago, August 1 1-0
   —Jack Kralick, Minnesota vs. Kansas City, August 26 1-0
1965 —Dave Morehead, Boston vs. Cleveland, September 16 2-0
1966 —Sonny Siebert, Cleveland vs. Washington, June 10 2-0
1967 —Steve Barber (8⅔ innings) and Stu Miller (⅓ inning), Baltimore vs. Detroit, April 30, first game 1-2
   —Dean Chance, Minnesota at Cleveland, August 25, second game 2-1
   —Joel Horlen, Chicago vs. Detroit, September 10, first game 6-0
1968 —Tom Phoebus, Baltimore vs. Boston, April 27 6-0
1969 —Jim Palmer, Baltimore vs. Oakland, August 13 8-0
1970 —Clyde Wright, California vs. Oakland, July 3 4-0
   —Vida Blue, Oakland vs. Minnesota, September 21 6-0
1973 —Steve Busby, Kansas City at Detroit, April 27 3-0
   —Nolan Ryan, California at Kansas City, May 15 3-0
   —Nolan Ryan, California at Detroit, July 15 6-0
   —Jim Bibby, Texas at Oakland, July 30 6-0
1974 —Steve Busby, Kansas City at Milwaukee, June 19 2-0
   —Dick Bosman, Cleveland vs. Oakland, July 19 4-0
   —Nolan Ryan, California vs. Minnesota, September 28 4-0
1975 —Nolan Ryan, California vs. Baltimore, June 1 1-0
   —Vida Blue (five innings), Glenn Abbott (one inning), Paul Lindblad (one inning) and Rollie Fingers (two innings),
     Oakland vs. California, September 28 5-0
1976 —Blue Moon Odom (five innings) and Francisco Barrios (four innings), Chicago at Oakland, July 28 2-1
1977 —Jim Colborn, Kansas City vs. Texas, May 14 6-0
   —Dennis Eckersley, Cleveland vs. California, May 30 1-0
   —Bert Blyleven, Texas at California, September 22 6-0
1983 —Dave Righetti, New York vs. Boston, July 4 4-0
   —Mike Warren, Oakland vs. Chicago, September 29 3-0
1984 —Jack Morris, Detroit at Chicago, April 7 4-0
1986 —Joe Cowley, Chicago at California, September 19 7-1
1987 —Juan Nieves, Milwaukee at Baltimore, April 15 7-0
1990 —Mark Langston (seven innings) and Mike Witt (two innings), California vs. Seattle, April 11 1-0
   —Randy Johnson, Seattle vs. Detroit, June 2 2-0
   —Nolan Ryan, Texas at Oakland, June 11 5-0
   —Dave Stewart, Oakland at Toronto, June 29 5-0
   —Dave Stieb, Toronto at Cleveland, September 2 3-0
1991 —Nolan Ryan, Texas vs. Toronto, May 1 3-0
   —Bob Milacki (six innings), Mike Flanagan (one inning), Mark Williamson (one inning) and Gregg Olson (one in-
     ning), Baltimore at Oakland, July 13 2-0
   —Wilson Alvarez, Chicago at Baltimore, August 11 7-0
   —Bret Saberhagen, Kansas City vs. Chicago, August 26 7-0
1993 —Chris Bosio, Seattle vs. Boston, April 22 2-0
   —Jim Abbott, New York vs. Cleveland, September 4 4-0
1994 —Scott Erickson, Minnesota vs. Milwaukee, April 27 6-0

Note: Andy Hawkins (1990) and Matt Young (1992), as visiting teams' pitchers, pitched all eight innings of nine-inning, no-hit losses. Both are listed under the category "No-hit games of less than nine innings."

Total number of games (excluding Hawkins' and M. Young's): (93)

NATIONAL LEAGUE

Year	Score
1876 — George Bradley, St. Louis vs. Hartford, July 15	2-0
1880 — Larry Corcoran, Chicago vs. Boston, August 19	6-0
— Pud Galvin, Buffalo at Worcester, August 20	1-0
1882 — Larry Corcoran, Chicago vs. Worcester, September 20	5-0
1883 — Hoss Radbourn, Providence at Cleveland, July 25	8-0
— Hugh Daily, Cleveland at Philadelphia, September 13	1-0
1884 — Larry Corcoran, Chicago vs. Providence, June 27	6-0
— Pud Galvin, Buffalo at Detroit, August 4	18-0
1885 — John Clarkson, Chicago at Providence, July 27	4-0
— Charlie J. Ferguson, Philadelphia vs. Providence, August 29	1-0
1891 — Tom Lovett, Brooklyn vs. New York, June 22	4-0
— Amos Rusie, New York vs. Brooklyn, July 31	6-0
1892 — Jack Stivetts, Boston vs. Brooklyn, August 6	11-0
— Ben Sanders, Louisville vs. Baltimore, August 22	6-2
— Bumpus Jones, Cincinnati vs. Pittsburgh, October 15 (first major league game)	7-1
1893 — Bill Hawke, Baltimore vs. Washington, August 16 (first no-hitter at 60-foot, 6-inch distance)	5-0
1897 — Cy Young, Cleveland vs. Cincinnati, September 18, first game	6-0
1898 — Ted Breitenstein, Cincinnati vs. Pittsburgh, April 22	11-0
— Jim J. Hughes, Baltimore vs. Boston, April 22	8-0
— Frank Donahue, Philadelphia vs. Boston, July 8	5-0
— Walter Thornton, Chicago vs. Brooklyn, August 21, second game	2-0
1899 — Deacon Phillippe, Louisville vs. New York, May 25	7-0
— Vic Willis, Boston vs. Washington, August 7	7-1
1900 — Noodles Hahn, Cincinnati vs. Philadelphia, July 12	4-0
1901 — Christy Mathewson, New York at St. Louis, July 15	5-0
1903 — Chick Fraser, Philadelphia at Chicago, September 18, second game	10-0
1905 — Christy Mathewson, New York at Chicago, June 13	1-0
1906 — Johnny Lush, Philadelphia at Brooklyn, May 1	6-0
— Mal Eason, Brooklyn at St. Louis, July 20	2-0
1907 — Frank Pfeffer, Boston vs. Cincinnati, May 8	6-0
— Nick Maddox, Pittsburgh vs. Brooklyn, September 20	2-1
1908 — Hooks Wiltse, New York vs. Philadelphia, July 4, first game, 10 innings	1-0
— Nap Rucker, Brooklyn vs. Boston, September 5, second game	6-0
1912 — Jeff Tesreau, New York at Philadelphia, September 6, first game	3-0
1914 — George A. Davis, Boston vs. Philadelphia, September 9, second game	7-0
1915 — Rube Marquard, New York vs. Brooklyn, April 15	2-0
— Jimmy Lavender, Chicago at New York, August 31, first game	2-0
1916 — Tom L. Hughes, Boston vs. Pittsburgh, June 16	2-0
1917 — Fred Toney, Cincinnati at Chicago, May 2, 10 innings (Hippo Vaughn of Chicago pitched 9 ⅓ hitless innings in the same game before his no-hitter was spoiled.)	1-0
1919 — Hod Eller, Cincinnati vs. St. Louis, May 11	6-0
1922 — Jesse Barnes, New York vs. Philadelphia, May 7	6-0
1924 — Jesse Haines, St. Louis vs. Boston, July 17	5-0
1925 — Dazzy Vance, Brooklyn vs. Philadelphia, September 13, first game	10-1
1929 — Carl Hubbell, New York vs. Pittsburgh, May 8	11-0
1934 — Paul Dean, St. Louis at Brooklyn, September 21, second game	3-0
1938 — Johnny Vander Meer, Cincinnati vs. Boston, June 11	3-0
— Johnny Vander Meer, Cincinnati at Brooklyn, June 15 (His two no-hitters were consecutive.)	6-0
1940 — Tex Carleton, Brooklyn at Cincinnati, April 30	3-0
1941 — Lon Warneke, St. Louis at Cincinnati, August 30	2-0
1944 — Jim Tobin, Boston vs. Brooklyn, April 27	2-0
— Clyde Shoun, Cincinnati vs. Boston, May 15	1-0
1946 — Ed Head, Brooklyn vs. Boston, April 23	5-0
1947 — Ewell Blackwell, Cincinnati vs. Boston, June 18	6-0
1948 — Rex Barney, Brooklyn at New York, September 9	2-0
1950 — Vern Bickford, Boston vs. Brooklyn, August 11	7-0
1951 — Cliff Chambers, Pittsburgh at Boston, May 6, second game	3-0
1952 — Carl Erskine, Brooklyn vs. Chicago, June 19	5-0
1954 — Jim Wilson, Milwaukee vs. Philadelphia, June 12	2-0
1955 — Sam Jones, Chicago vs. Pittsburgh, May 12	4-0
— Carl Erskine, Brooklyn vs. New York, May 12	3-0
1956 — Sal Maglie, Brooklyn vs. Philadelphia, September 25	5-0
1960 — Don Cardwell, Chicago vs. St. Louis, May 15, second game	4-0
— Lew Burdette, Milwaukee vs. Philadelphia, August 18	1-0
— Warren Spahn, Milwaukee vs. Philadelphia, September 16	4-0
1961 — Warren Spahn, Milwaukee vs. San Francisco, April 28	1-0
1962 — Sandy Koufax, Los Angeles vs. New York, June 30	5-0
1963 — Sandy Koufax, Los Angeles vs. San Francisco, May 11	8-0
— Don Nottebart, Houston vs. Philadelphia, May 17	4-1
— Juan Marichal, San Francisco vs. Houston, June 15	1-0

Year	Score
1964 —Ken Johnson, Houston vs. Cincinnati, April 23	0-1
—Sandy Koufax, Los Angeles at Philadelphia, June 4	3-0
1965 —Jim Maloney, Cincinnati at Chicago, August 19, first game, 10 innings	1-0
1967 —Don Wilson, Houston vs. Atlanta, June 18	2-0
1968 —George Culver, Cincinnati at Philadelphia, July 29, second game	6-1
—Gaylord Perry, San Francisco vs. St. Louis, September 17	1-0
—Ray Washburn, St. Louis at San Francisco, September 18	2-0
1969 —Bill Stoneman, Montreal at Philadelphia, April 17	7-0
—Jim Maloney, Cincinnati vs. Houston, April 30	10-0
—Don Wilson, Houston at Cincinnati, May 1	4-0
—Ken Holtzman, Chicago vs. Atlanta, August 19	3-0
—Bob Moose, Pittsburgh at New York, September 20	4-0
1970 —Dock Ellis, Pittsburgh at San Diego, June 12, first game	2-0
—Bill Singer, Los Angeles vs. Philadelphia, July 20	5-0
1971 —Ken Holtzman, Chicago at Cincinnati, June 3	1-0
—Rick Wise, Philadelphia at Cincinnati, June 23	4-0
—Bob Gibson, St. Louis at Pittsburgh, August 14	11-0
1972 —Burt Hooton, Chicago vs. Philadelphia, April 16	4-0
—Milt Pappas, Chicago vs. San Diego, September 2	8-0
—Bill Stoneman, Montreal vs. New York, October 2, first game	7-0
1973 —Phil Niekro, Atlanta vs. San Diego, August 5	9-0
1975 —Ed Halicki, San Francisco vs. New York, August 24, second game	6-0
1976 —Larry Dierker, Houston vs. Montreal, July 9	6-0
—John Candelaria, Pittsburgh vs. Los Angeles, August 9	2-0
—John Montefusco, San Francisco at Atlanta, September 29	9-0
1978 —Bob Forsch, St. Louis vs. Philadelphia, April 16	5-0
—Tom Seaver, Cincinnati vs. St. Louis, June 16	4-0
1979 —Ken Forsch, Houston vs. Atlanta, April 7	6-0
1980 —Jerry Reuss, Los Angeles at San Francisco, June 27	8-0
1981 —Charlie Lea, Montreal vs. San Francisco, May 10, second game	4-0
—Nolan Ryan, Houston vs. Los Angeles, September 26	5-0
1983 —Bob Forsch, St. Louis vs. Montreal, September 26	3-0
1986 —Mike Scott, Houston vs. San Francisco, September 25	2-0
1990 —Fernando Valenzuela, Los Angeles vs. St. Louis, June 29	6-0
—Terry Mulholland, Philadelphia vs. San Francisco, August 15	6-0
1991 —Tommy Greene, Philadelphia at Montreal, May 23	2-0
—Kent Mercker (six innings), Mark Wohlers (two innings) and Alejandro Pena (one inning), Atlanta vs. San Diego, September 11	1-0
1992 —Kevin Gross, Los Angeles vs. San Francisco, August 17	2-0
1993 —Darryl Kile, Houston vs. New York, September 8	7-1
1994 —Kent Mercker, Atlanta vs. Los Angeles, April 8	6-0

Total number of games: (109)

NO-HIT GAMES FOR NINE OR MORE INNINGS THAT WERE BROKEN UP IN EXTRA INNINGS
AMERICAN LEAGUE

Year	Score
1901 —Earl Moore, Cleveland vs. Chicago, May 9 (Moore pitched nine hitless innings before Sam Mertes singled; lost on two hits in 10 innings.)	2-4
1910 —Tom L. Hughes, New York vs. Cleveland, August 30, second game (Hughes pitched 9⅓ hitless innings before Harry Niles singled; lost on seven hits in 11 innings.)	0-5
1914 —Jim Scott, Chicago at Washington, May 14 (Scott pitched nine hitless innings before Chick Gandil singled; lost on two hits in 10 innings)	0-1
1934 —Bobo Newsom, St. Louis vs. Boston, September 18 (Newsom pitched 9⅔ hitless innings before Roy Johnson singled; lost on one hit in 10 innings.)	1-2

Total number of games: (4)

NATIONAL LEAGUE

Year	Score
1904 —Bob Wicker, Chicago at New York, June 11 (pitched 9⅓ hitless innings before Sam Mertes singled; won on one hit in 12 innings.)	1-0
1906 —Harry McIntire, Brooklyn vs. Pittsburgh, August 1. (pitched 10⅔ hitless innings before Claude Ritchey singled; lost on four hits in 13 innings.)	0-1
1909 —Red Ames, New York vs. Brooklyn, April 15 (pitched 9⅓ hitless innings before Whitey Alperman singled; lost on seven hits in 13 innings. The game was both teams' season opener.)	0-3
1917 —Hippo Vaughn, Chicago vs. Cincinnati, May 2 (pitched 9⅓ hitless innings before Larry Kopf singled; lost on two hits in 10 innings. Fred Toney of Cincinnati pitched 10 no-hit innings in the same game.)	0-1
1956 —Johnny Klippstein (seven innings), Hershell Freeman (one inning) and Joe Black (three innings), Cincinnati at Milwaukee, May 26 (Jack Dittmer doubled for the first hit with two outs in the 10th inning and Black lost on three hits in 11 innings.)	1-2
1965 —Jim Maloney, Cincinnati vs. New York, June 14 (pitched 10 hitless innings before Johnny Lewis homered; lost on two hits in 11 innings.)	0-1

Year	Score
1991 — Mark Gardner (nine innings) and Jeff Fassero (no innings), Montreal at Los Angeles, July 26 (Lenny Harris singled off Gardner in the 10th inning; Gardner allowed another hit and Fassero allowed one hit; Gardner lost the game in the 10th inning.)	0-1

Total number of games: (7)

NO-HIT GAMES OF LESS THAN NINE INNINGS
AMERICAN ASSOCIATION

Year	Score
1884 — Larry McKeon, Indianapolis at Cincinnati, May 6, six innings	0-0
1889 — Matt Kilroy, Baltimore vs. St. Louis, July 29, second game, seven innings	0-0
1890 — George Nicol, St. Louis vs. Philadelphia, September 23, seven innings	21-2
— Hank Gastright, Columbus vs. Toledo, October 12, eight innings	6-0

Total number of games: (4)

PLAYERS LEAGUE

Year	Score
1890 — Charles King, Chicago vs. Brooklyn, June 21, eight innings	0-1

Total number of games: (1)

UNION ASSOCIATION

Year	Score
1884 — Charlie Geggus, Washington vs. Wilmington, August 21, eight innings	12-1
— Charlie Sweeney (two innings) and Henry Boyle (three innings), St. Louis vs. St. Paul, October 5, five innings	0-1

Total number of games: (2)

AMERICAN LEAGUE

Year	Score
1905 — Rube Waddell, Philadelphia vs. St. Louis, August 15, five innings	2-0
1907 — Ed Walsh Sr., Chicago vs. New York, May 26, five innings	8-1
1912 — Jay Cashion, Washington vs. Cleveland, August 20, second game, six innings	2-0
1924 — Walter Johnson, Washington vs. St. Louis, August 25, seven innings	2-0
1940 — John Whitehead, St. Louis vs. Detroit, August 5, second game, six innings	4-0
1990 — Andy Hawkins, New York at Chicago, July 1 (As a visiting team's pitcher, he pitched all eight innings of a nine-inning, no-hit loss.)	0-4
— Melido Perez, Chicago at New York, July 12, six innings	8-0
1992 — Matt Young, Boston at Cleveland, April 12 (As a visiting team's pitcher, he pitched all eight innings of a nine-inning, no-hit loss.)	1-2

Total number of games: (8)

NATIONAL LEAGUE

Year	Score
1884 — Charlie Getzien, Detroit vs. Philadelphia, October 1, six innings	1-0
1885 — Fred Shaw, Providence at Buffalo, October 7, first game, five innings	4-0
1888 — George Van Haltren, Chicago vs. Pittsburgh, June 21, six innings	1-0
— Cannonball Crane, New York vs. Washington, September 27, seven innings	3-0
1892 — Jack Stivetts, Boston at Washington, October 15, second game, five innings	4-0
1893 — Elton Chamberlain, Cincinnati vs. Boston, September 23, second game, seven innings	6-0
1894 — Ed Stein, Brooklyn vs. Chicago, June 2, six innings	1-0
1903 — Red Ames, New York at St. Louis, September 14, second game, five innings (first major league game)	5-0
1906 — Jake Weimer, Cincinnati vs. Brooklyn, August 24, second game, seven innings	1-0
— Stoney McGlynn, St. Louis at Brooklyn, September 24, second game, seven innings	1-1
— Lefty Leifield, Pittsburgh at Philadelphia, September 26, second game, six innings	8-0
1907 — Howie Camnitz, Pittsburgh at New York, August 23, second game, five innings	1-0
1908 — Johnny Lush, St. Louis at Brooklyn, August 6, six innings	2-0
1910 — King Cole, Chicago at St. Louis, July 31, second game, seven innings	4-0
1937 — Fred Frankhouse, Brooklyn vs. Cincinnati, August 27, eight innings	5-0
1944 — Jim Tobin, Boston vs. Philadelphia, June 22, second game, five innings	7-0
1959 — Mike McCormick, San Francisco at Philadelphia, June 12, five innings (McCormick allowed a single to Richie Ashburn in the sixth inning, but the game was halted because of rain before completion of the inning. The hit was erased because, under existing rules, records reverted to the last completed inning.)	3-0
— Sam Jones, San Francisco at St. Louis, September 26, seven innings	4-0
1988 — Pascual Perez, Montreal at Philadelphia, September 24, five innings	1-0

Total number of games: (19)

☐ TWO COMPLETE-GAME VICTORIES IN ONE DAY ☐
AMERICAN ASSOCIATION

	Scores	
July 4, 1883 ...... Tim Keefe, New York	9-1	3-0
July 4, 1884 ...... Guy Hecker, Louisville	5-4	8-2

		Scores	
July 26, 1887 .... Matt Kilroy, Baltimore	‡8-0	9-1
Oct. 1, 1887 ...... Matt Kilroy, Baltimore	5-2	‡8-0
Sept. 20, 1888 .. Tony Mullane, Cincinnati	1-0	2-1

Total number of occurrences: (5)

PLAYERS LEAGUE

	Scores	
July 26, 1890 .... Henry Gruber, Cleveland	6-1	8-7
Aug. 20, 1890 .. Bert Cunningham, Buffalo	6-2	7-0
Sept. 27, 1890 .. Ed Crane, New York	9-8	8-3

Total number of occurrences: (3)

AMERICAN LEAGUE

	Scores	
July 1, 1905 ...... Frank Owen, Chicago	3-2	2-0
Sept. 26, 1905 ... Ed Walsh, Chicago	10-5	§3-1
Sept. 22, 1906 .. George Mullin, Detroit	5-3	4-3
Sept. 25, 1908 .. Ed Summers, Detroit	7-2	x1-0
Sept. 29, 1908 .. Ed Walsh, Chicago	5-1	2-0
Sept. 22, 1914 .. Ray Collins, Boston	5-3	§5-0
July 29, 1916 .... Dave Davenport, St. Louis	3-1	3-2
Aug. 30, 1918 .... Carl Mays, Boston	12-0	4-1
Sept. 6, 1924 ..... Urban Shocker, St. Louis	6-2	6-2
Aug. 28, 1926 .... Dutch Levsen, Cleveland	6-1	5-1

Total number of occurrences: (10)

NATIONAL LEAGUE

	Scores	
Sept. 19, 1876 .. Candy Cummings, Hartford	14-4	8-4
Aug. 9, 1878 ..... Monte Ward, Providence	12-6	8-5
July 12, 1879 ..... Pud Galvin, Buffalo	4-3	z5-4
July 4, 1881 ...... Mickey Welch, Troy	8-0	12-3
July 4, 1882 ...... Pud Galvin, Buffalo	9-5	18-8
May 30, 1884 .... Hoss Radbourn, Providence ...	12-9	9-2
Oct. 7, 1885 ...... Fred Shaw, Providence	*4-0	*6-1
Oct. 10, 1885 .... Fred Shaw, Providence	†3-0	*7-3
Oct. 9, 1886 ...... Charlie Ferguson, Philadelphia	5-1	†6-1
Aug. 20, 1887 .... Jim Whitney, Washington	3-1	4-3
Sept. 12, 1889 .. John Clarkson, Boston	3-2	5-0
May 30, 1890 .... Bill Hutchinson, Chicago	6-4	11-7
Oct. 4, 1890 ...... Cy Young, Cleveland	5-1	7-3
Sept. 12, 1891 .. Mark Baldwin, Pittsburgh	13-3	8-4
Sept. 28, 1891 .. Amos Rusie, New York	10-4	†13-5
May 30, 1892 .... Mark Baldwin, Pittsburgh	11-1	4-3
Sept. 5, 1892 ... Jack Stivetts, Boston	y2-1	5-2
Oct. 4, 1892 ...... Amos Rusie, New York	6-4	9-5
May 30, 1893 .... William Kennedy, Brooklyn	3-0	6-2
June 3, 1897 ..... Cy Seymour, New York	6-1	‡10-6
Oct. 13, 1898 .... Al Orth, Philadelphia	5-1	*9-6
Aug. 1, 1903 ..... Joe McGinnity, New York	4-1	5-2
Aug. 8, 1903 ..... Joe McGinnity, New York	6-1	4-3
Aug. 31, 1903 ... Joe McGinnity, New York	4-1	9-2
Oct. 3, 1905 ...... Doc Scanlan, Brooklyn	4-0	3-2
Sept. 26, 1908 .. Ed Reulbach, Chicago	5-0	3-0
Sept. 9, 1916 .... Pol Perritt, New York	3-1	3-0
Sept. 20, 1916 .. Al Demaree, Philadelphia	7-0	3-2
Sept. 23, 1916 .. Grover Alexander, Philadelphia	7-3	4-0
July 1, 1917 ...... Fred Toney, Cincinnati	4-1	5-1
Sept. 3, 1917 .... Grover Alexander, Philadelphia	5-0	9-3
Sept. 18, 1917 .. Bill Doak, St. Louis	2-0	12-4
Aug. 13, 1921 ... Mule Watson, Boston	4-3	8-0
July 10, 1923 ... Johnny Stuart, St. Louis	11-1	6-3
July 19, 1924 .... Herman Bell, St. Louis	6-1	2-1

*5 innings. †6 innings. ‡7 innings. §8 innings. x10 innings. y11 innings. z12 innings.

Total number of occurrences: (35)

[] PITCHERS WITH 12 STRAIGHT VICTORIES IN SEASON []
AMERICAN ASSOCIATION

Year	Pitcher	Won
1890—Scott Stratton, St. Louis		15
1884—John Lynch, New York		14
1882—Will White, Cincinnati		12

Total number of occurrences: (3)

UNION ASSOCIATION

Year	Pitcher	Won
1884—Jim McCormick, Cincinnati		14

Total number of occurrences: (1)

AMERICAN LEAGUE

Year	Pitcher	Won
1912—Walter Johnson, Washington	16
1912—Joe Wood, Boston	16
1931—Lefty Grove, Philadelphia	16
1934—Schoolboy Rowe, Detroit	16
1932—Alvin Crowder, Washington	15
1937—Johnny Allen, Cleveland	15
1969—Dave McNally, Baltimore	15
1974—Gaylord Perry, Cleveland	15
1904—Jack Chesbro, New York	14
1913—Walter Johnson, Washington	14
1914—Chief Bender, Philadelphia	14
1928—Lefty Grove, Philadelphia	14
1961—Whitey Ford, New York	14
1980—Steve Stone, Baltimore	14
1986—Roger Clemens, Boston	14
1924—Walter Johnson, Washington	13
1925—Stan Coveleski, Washington	13
1930—Wes Ferrell, Cleveland	13
1940—Bobo Newsom, Detroit	13
1949—Ellis Kinder, Boston	13
1971—Dave McNally, Baltimore	13
1973—Catfish Hunter, Oakland	13
1978—Ron Guidry, New York	13
1983—LaMarr Hoyt, Chicago	13
1901—Cy Young, Boston	12
1910—Russ Ford, New York	12
1914—Dutch H. Leonard, Boston	12
1929—Tom Zachary, New York	12
1931—George Earnshaw, Philadelphia	12
1938—Johnny Allen, Cleveland	12
1939—Atley Donald, New York	12
1946—Dave Ferriss, Boston	12
1961—Luis Arroyo, New York	12
1963—Whitey Ford, New York	12
1968—Dave McNally, Baltimore	12
1971—Pat Dobson, Baltimore	12
1985—Ron Guidry, New York	12
1990—Bobby Witt, Texas	12
1991—Scott Erickson, Minnesota	12

Total number of occurrences: (39)

NATIONAL LEAGUE

Year	Pitcher	Won
1888—Tim Keefe, New York	19
1912—Rube Marquard, New York	19
1884—Hoss Radbourn, Providence	18
1885—Mickey Welch, New York	17
1890—Pat Luby, Chicago	17
1959—Elroy Face, Pittsburgh	17
1886—Jim McCormick, Chicago	16
1936—Carl Hubbell, New York	16
1947—Ewell Blackwell, Cincinnati	16
1962—Jack Sanford, San Francisco	16
1924—Dazzy Vance, Brooklyn	15
1968—Bob Gibson, St. Louis	15
1972—Steve Carlton, Philadelphia	15
1885—Jim McCormick, Chicago	14
1886—John Flynn, Chicago	14
1904—Joe McGinnity, New York	14
1909—Ed Reulbach, Chicago	14
1984—Rick Sutcliffe, Chicago	14
1985—Dwight Gooden, New York	14
1880—Larry Corcoran, Chicago	13
1884—Charlie Buffinton, Boston	13
1885—John Clarkson, Chicago	13
1892—Cy Young, Cleveland	13
1893—Frank Killen, Pittsburgh	13
1896—Frank Dwyer, Cincinnati	13
1897—Fred Klobedanz, Boston	13
1898—Ed Lewis, Boston	13
1909—Christy Mathewson, New York	13
1910—Deacon Phillippe, Pittsburgh	13
1927—Burleigh Grimes, New York	13
1956—Brooks Lawrence, Cincinnati	13

Year	Pitcher	Won
1966—Phil Regan, Los Angeles		13
1971—Dock Ellis, Pittsburgh		13
1992—Tom Glavine, Atlanta		13
1886—Charlie Ferguson, Philadelphia		12
1902—Jack Chesbro, Pittsburgh		12
1904—George Wiltse, New York		12
1906—Ed Reulbach, Chicago		12
1914—Dick Rudolph, Boston		12
1975—Burt Hooton, Los Angeles		12
1993—Mark Portugal, Houston		12

Total number of occurrences: (41)

☐ PITCHERS WITH 12 STRAIGHT LOSSES IN SEASON ☐
AMERICAN ASSOCIATION

Year	Pitcher	Lost
1882—Fred Nichols, Baltimore		12
1887—Billy Crowell, Cleveland		12

Total number of occurrences: (2)

AMERICAN LEAGUE

Year	Pitcher	Lost
1916—John Nabors, Philadelphia		19
1980—Mike Parrott, Seattle		16
1909—Bob Groom, Washington		15
1906—Joe Harris, Boston		14
1949—Howard Judson, Chicago		14
1949—Paul Calvert, Washington		14
1979—Matt Keough, Oakland		14
1914—Guy Morton, Cleveland		13
1920—Roy Moore, Philadelphia		13
1930—Frank Henry, Chicago		13
1943—Luman Harris, Philadelphia		13
1982—Terry Felton, Minnesota		13
1929—Red Ruffing, Boston		12
1940—Walt Masterson, Washington		12
1945—Bobo Newsom, Philadelphia		12
1945—Steve Gerkin, Philadelphia		12
1953—Charlie Bishop, Philadelphia		12

Total number of occurrences: (17)

NATIONAL LEAGUE

Year	Pitcher	Lost
1910—Cliff Curtis, Boston		18
1963—Roger Craig, New York		18
1876—Dory Dean, Cincinnati		16
1899—Jim Hughey, Cleveland		16
1962—Craig Anderson, New York		16
1887—Frank Gilmore, Washington		14
1899—Fred Bates, Cleveland		14
1908—Jim Pastorius, Brooklyn		14
1911—Buster Brown, Boston		14
1992—Anthony Young, New York		14
1884—Sam Moffett, Cleveland		13
1917—Burleigh Grimes, Pittsburgh		13
1922—Joe Oeschger, Boston		13
1935—Ben Cantwell, Boston		13
1948—Bob McCall, Chicago		13
1993—Anthony Young, New York		13
1880—William Purcell, Cincinnati		12
1883—John Coleman, Philadelphia		12
1902—Henry Thielman, Cincinnati		12
1905—Mal Eason, Brooklyn		12
1914—Rube Marquard, New York		12
1914—Pete Schneider, Cincinnati		12
1928—Russ Miller, Philadelphia		12
1933—Silas Johnson, Cincinnati		12
1939—Max Butcher, Philadelphia-Pittsburgh		12
1940—Hugh Mulcahy, Philadelphia		12
1962—Bob Miller, New York		12
1972—Ken Reynolds, Philadelphia		12

Total number of occurrences: (28)

☐ 20-GAME WINNERS ☐

(Numbers in parentheses after club denotes
position of team at close of season)

AMERICAN ASSOCIATION

1882 (5)	W	L
Will White, Cincinnati (1)	40	12
Tony Mullane, Louisville (2)	30	24
Sam Weaver, Philadelphia (3)	26	15
George McGinnis, St. Louis (5)	25	21
Harry Salisbury, Pittsburgh (5)	20	19

1883 (8)	W	L
Will White, Cincinnati (3)	43	22
Tim Keefe, New York (4)	41	27
Tony Mullane, St. Louis (2)	35	15
Bobby Mathews, Philadelphia (1)	30	14
George McGinnis, St. Louis (2)	29	15
Guy Hecker, Louisville (5)	28	25
Frank Mountain, Columbus (6)	26	33
Sam Weaver, Louisville (5)	24	20

1884 (12)	W	L
Guy Hecker, Louisville (3)	52	20
Jack Lynch, New York (1)	37	15
Ed Morris, Columbus (2)	35	13
Tim Keefe, New York (1)	37	17
Tony Mullane, Toledo (8)	35	25
Will White, Cincinnati (5)	34	18
Bob Emslie, Baltimore (6)	32	18
Bobby Mathews, Philadelphia (7)	30	18
Hardie Henderson, Baltimore (6)	27	22
George McGinnis, St. Louis (4)	24	16
Frank Mountain, Columbus (2)	24	17
Billy Mountjoy, Cincinnati (5)	20	12

1885 (9)	W	L
Bob Caruthers, St. Louis (1)	40	13
Ed Morris, Pittsburgh (3)	39	24
Dave Foutz, St. Louis (1)	33	14
Henry Porter, Brooklyn (5T)	33	21
Bobby Mathews, Philadelphia (4)	30	17
Guy Hecker, Louisville (5T)	30	24
Hardie Henderson, Baltimore (8)	26	35
Jack Lynch, New York (7)	23	21
Larry McKeon, Cincinnati (2)	20	15

1886 (11)	W	L
Dave Foutz, St. Louis (1)	41	16
Ed Morris, Pittsburgh (2)	41	20
Tom Ramsey, Louisville (4)	37	27
Tony Mullane, Cincinnati (5)	31	27
Bob Caruthers, St. Louis (1)	30	14
Pud Galvin, Pittsburgh (2)	29	21
Matt Kilroy, Baltimore (8)	29	34
Henry Porter, Brooklyn (3)	28	20
Guy Hecker, Louisville (4)	27	23
Al Atkisson, Philadelphia (6)	25	17
Jack Lynch, New York (7)	20	20

1887 (10)	W	L
Matt Kilroy, Baltimore (3)	46	20
Tom Ramsey, Louisville (4)	39	27
Charles King, St. Louis (1)	34	11
Elmer Smith, Cincinnati (2)	33	18
Tony Mullane, Cincinnati (2)	31	17
Bob Caruthers, St. Louis (1)	29	9
John Smith, Baltimore (3)	29	29
Gus Weyhing, Philadelphia (5)	26	25
Ed Seward, Philadelphia (5)	25	24
Dave Foutz, St. Louis (1)	24	12

1888 (12)	W	L
Charles King, St. Louis (1)	45	21
Ed Seward, Philadelphia (3)	34	19
Bob Caruthers, Brooklyn (2)	29	15
Gus Weyhing, Philadelphia (3)	29	19

	W	L
Elton Chamberlain, 9-8 Louisville (7), 16-4 St. Louis (1)	25	12
Lee Viau, Cincinnati (4)	27	14
Tony Mullane, Cincinnati (4)	26	16
Nat Hudson, St. Louis (1)	25	11
Mickey Hughes, Brooklyn (2)	25	13
Ed Bakely, Cleveland (6)	25	33
Elmer Smith, Cincinnati (4)	22	17
Bert Cunningham, Baltimore (5)	22	29

1889 (11)
	W	L
Bob Caruthers, Brooklyn (1)	40	12
Elton Chamberlain, St. Louis (2)	35	15
Charles King, St. Louis (2)	33	17
Jesse Duryea, Cincinnati (4)	32	21
Gus Weyhing, Philadelphia (3)	28	19
Matt Kilroy, Baltimore (5)	28	25
Mark Baldwin, Columbus (6)	26	24
Frank Foreman, Baltimore (5)	25	21
William Terry, Brooklyn (1)	21	16
Ed Seward, Philadelphia (3)	21	16
Lee Viau, Cincinnati (4)	21	19

1890 (8)
	W	L
John McMahon, 29-19 Philadelphia (8), 7-2 Baltimore (6)	36	21
Scott Stratton, Louisville (1)	34	13
Hank Gastright, Columbus (2)	29	13
Bob Barr, Rochester (5)	28	25
John Stivetts, St. Louis (3)	27	21
Tom Ramsey, St. Louis (3)	26	16
Red Ehret, Louisville (1)	25	14
John Healy, Toledo (4)	22	23

1891 (8)
	W	L
George Haddock, Boston (1)	34	11
John McMahon, Baltimore (3)	34	24
John Stivetts, St. Louis (2)	33	22
Gus Weyhing, Philadelphia (4)	31	20
Charlie Buffinton, Boston (1)	29	9
Phil Knell, Columbus (5)	27	26
Elton Chamberlain, Philadelphia (4)	23	23
Willie McGill, 2-5 Cincinnati (5), 19-10 St. Louis (2)	21	15

PLAYERS LEAGUE

1890 (9)
	W	L
Mark Baldwin, Chicago (4)	32	24
Gus Weyhing, Brooklyn (2)	30	16
Charles King, Chicago (4)	30	22
Charles Radbourn, Boston (1)	27	12
Addison Gumbert, Boston (1)	23	12
Hank O'Day, New York (3)	22	13
Henry Gruber, Cleveland (7)	22	23
Phil Knell, Philadelphia (5)	21	10
Harry Staley, Pittsburgh (6)	21	23

UNION ASSOCIATION

1884 (9)
	W	L
Bill Sweeney, Baltimore (3)	40	21
Hugh Daily, 22-25 Chicago (6), 1-1 Washington (5), 5-4 Pittsburgh (8)	28	30
Billy Taylor, St. Louis (1)	25	4
Dick Burns, Cincinnati (2)	25	15
Charlie Sweeney, St. Louis (1)	24	8
Bill Wise, Washington (5)	23	20
Jim McCormick, Cincinnati (2)	22	4
Fred Shaw, Boston (4)	22	15
George Bradley, Cincinnati (2)	21	13

AMERICAN LEAGUE

1901 (5)
	W	L
Cy Young, Boston (2)	33	10
Joe McGinnity, Baltimore (5)	26	21
Clark Griffith, Chicago (1)	24	7
Roscoe Miller, Detroit (3)	23	13
Chick Fraser, Philadelphia (4)	20	15

1902 (7)
	W	L
Cy Young, Boston (3)	32	11
Rube Waddell, Philadelphia (1)	23	7
Frank Donahue, St. Louis (2)	22	11
Jack Powell, St. Louis (2)	22	17
Bill Dinneen, Boston (3)	21	21
Roy Patterson, Chicago (4)	20	12
Eddie Plank, Philadelphia (1)	20	15

1903 (7)
	W	L
Cy Young, Boston (1)	28	9
Eddie Plank, Philadelphia (2)	23	16
Bill Dinneen, Boston (1)	21	13
Willie Sudhoff, St. Louis (6)	21	15
Jack Chesbro, New York (4)	21	15
Rube Waddell, Philadelphia (2)	21	16
Tom Hughes, Boston (1)	20	7

1904 (9)
	W	L
Jack Chesbro, New York (2)	41	13
Cy Young, Boston (1)	26	16
Eddie Plank, Philadelphia (5)	26	17
Rube Waddell, Philadelphia (5)	25	19
Bill Bernhard, Cleveland (4)	23	13
Bill Dinneen, Boston (1)	23	14
Jack Powell, New York (2)	23	19
Jesse Tannehill, Boston (1)	21	11
Frank Owen, Chicago (3)	21	15

1905 (9)
	W	L
Rube Waddell, Philadelphia (1)	26	11
Eddie Plank, Philadelphia (1)	25	12
Nick Altrock, Chicago (2)	24	12
Ed Killian, Detroit (3)	23	13
Jesse Tannehill, Boston (4)	22	9
Frank Owen, Chicago (2)	21	13
George Mullin, Detroit (3)	21	20
Addie Joss, Cleveland (5)	20	11
Frank Smith, Chicago (2)	20	14

1906 (8)
	W	L
Al Orth, New York (2)	27	17
Jack Chesbro, New York (2)	24	16
Bob Rhoades, Cleveland (3)	22	10
Frank Owen, Chicago (1)	22	13
Addie Joss, Cleveland (3)	21	9
George Mullin, Detroit (6)	21	18
Nick Altrock, Chicago (1)	20	13
Otto Hess, Cleveland (3)	20	17

1907 (10)
	W	L
Addie Joss, Cleveland (4)	27	10
Guy White, Chicago (3)	27	13
Bill Donovan, Detroit (1)	25	4
Ed Killian, Detroit (1)	25	13
Eddie Plank, Philadelphia (2)	24	16
Ed Walsh, Chicago (3)	24	18
Frank Smith, Chicago (3)	22	11
Cy Young, Boston (7)	22	15
Jimmy Dygert, Philadelphia (2)	20	9
George Mullin, Detroit (1)	20	20

1908 (4)
	W	L
Ed Walsh, Chicago (3)	40	15
Addie Joss, Cleveland (2)	24	11
Ed Summers, Detroit (1)	24	12
Cy Young, Boston (5)	21	11

1909 (3)
	W	L
George Mullin, Detroit (1)	29	8
Frank Smith, Chicago (4)	25	17
Ed Willett, Detroit (1)	22	9

1910 (5)
	W	L
Jack Coombs, Philadelphia (1)	31	9
Russ Ford, New York (2)	26	6
Walter Johnson, Washington (7)	25	17

	W	L
Chief Bender, Philadelphia (1)	23	5
George Mullin, Detroit (3)	21	12

1911 (7)

	W	L
Jack Coombs, Philadelphia (1)	28	12
Ed Walsh, Chicago (4)	27	18
Walter Johnson, Washington (7)	25	13
Vean Gregg, Cleveland (3)	23	7
Joe Wood, Boston (5)	23	17
Eddie Plank, Philadelphia (1)	22	8
Russ Ford, New York (6)	22	11

1912 (9)

	W	L
Joe Wood, Boston (1)	34	5
Walter Johnson, Washington (2)	32	12
Ed Walsh, Chicago (4)	27	17
Eddie Plank, Philadelphia (3)	26	6
Bob Groom, Washington (2)	24	13
Jack Coombs, Philadelphia (3)	21	10
Hugh Bedient, Boston (1)	20	9
Vean Gregg, Cleveland (5)	20	13
Tom O'Brien, Boston (1)	20	13

1913 (6)

	W	L
Walter Johnson, Washington (2)	36	7
Fred Falkenberg, Cleveland (3)	23	10
Ewell Russell, Chicago (5)	22	16
Chief Bender, Philadelphia (1)	21	10
Vean Gregg, Cleveland (3)	20	13
Jim Scott, Chicago (5)	20	20

1914 (3)

	W	L
Walter Johnson, Washington (3)	28	18
Harry Coveleski, Detroit (4)	22	12
Ray Collins, Boston (2)	20	13

1915 (5)

	W	L
Walter Johnson, Washington (4)	27	13
Jim Scott, Chicago (3)	24	11
George Dauss, Detroit (2)	24	13
Urban Faber, Chicago (3)	24	14
Harry Coveleski, Detroit (2)	22	13

1916 (4)

	W	L
Walter Johnson, Washington (7)	25	20
Bob Shawkey, New York (4)	24	14
Babe Ruth, Boston (1)	23	12
Harry Coveleski, Detroit (3)	21	11

1917 (5)

	W	L
Ed Cicotte, Chicago (1)	28	12
Babe Ruth, Boston (2)	24	13
Jim Bagby, Cleveland (3)	23	13
Walter Johnson, Washington (5)	23	16
Carl Mays, Boston (2)	22	9

1918 (4)

	W	L
Walter Johnson, Washington (3)	23	13
Stan Coveleski, Cleveland (2)	22	13
Carl Mays, Boston (1)	21	13
Scott Perry, Philadelphia (8)	20	19

1919 (7)

	W	L
Ed Cicotte, Chicago (1)	29	7
Lefty Williams, Chicago (1)	23	11
Stan Coveleski, Cleveland (2)	23	12
George Dauss, Detroit (4)	21	9
Allen Sothoron, St. Louis (5)	21	11
Bob Shawkey, New York (3)	20	13
Walter Johnson, Washington (7)	20	14

1920 (10)

	W	L
Jim Bagby, Cleveland (1)	31	12
Carl Mays, New York (3)	26	11
Stan Coveleski, Cleveland (1)	24	14
Red Faber, Chicago (2)	23	13
Lefty Williams, Chicago (2)	22	14
Dickie Kerr, Chicago (2)	21	9
Ed Cicotte, Chicago (2)	21	10
Ray Caldwell, Cleveland (1)	20	10

	W	L
Urban Shocker, St. Louis (4)	20	10
Bob Shawkey, New York (3)	20	13

1921 (5)

	W	L
Carl Mays, New York (1)	27	9
Urban Shocker, St. Louis (3)	27	12
Red Faber, Chicago (7)	25	15
Stan Coveleski, Cleveland (2)	23	13
Sam Jones, Boston (5)	23	16

1922 (6)

	W	L
Eddie Rommel, Philadelphia (7)	27	13
Joe Bush, New York (1)	26	7
Urban Shocker, St. Louis (2)	24	17
George Uhle, Cleveland (4)	22	16
Red Faber, Chicago (5)	21	17
Bob Shawkey, New York (1)	20	12

1923 (5)

	W	L
George Uhle, Cleveland (3)	26	16
Sam Jones, New York (1)	21	8
George Dauss, Detroit (2)	21	13
Urban Shocker, St. Louis (5)	20	12
Howard Ehmke, Boston (8)	20	17

1924 (4)

	W	L
Walter Johnson, Washington (1)	23	7
Herb Pennock, New York (2)	21	9
Sloppy Thurston, Chicago (8)	20	14
Joe Shaute, Cleveland (6)	20	17

1925 (4)

	W	L
Eddie Rommel, Philadelphia (2)	21	10
Ted Lyons, Chicago (5)	21	11
Stan Coveleski, Washington (1)	20	5
Walter Johnson, Washington (1)	20	7

1926 (2)

	W	L
George Uhle, Cleveland (2)	27	11
Herb Pennock, New York (1)	23	11

1927 (3)

	W	L
Waite Hoyt, New York (1)	22	7
Ted Lyons, Chicago (5)	22	14
Lefty Grove, Philadelphia (2)	20	13

1928 (5)

	W	L
Lefty Grove, Philadelphia (2)	24	8
George Pipgras, New York (1)	24	13
Waite Hoyt, New York (1)	23	7
Alvin Crowder, St. Louis (3)	21	5
Sam Gray, St. Louis (3)	20	12

1929 (3)

	W	L
George Earnshaw, Philadelphia (1)	24	8
Wes Ferrell, Cleveland (3)	21	10
Lefty Grove, Philadelphia (1)	20	6

1930 (5)

	W	L
Lefty Grove, Philadelphia (1)	28	5
Wes Ferrell, Cleveland (4)	25	13
George Earnshaw, Philadelphia (1)	22	13
Ted Lyons, Chicago (7)	22	15
Walter Stewart, St. Louis (6)	20	12

1931 (5)

	W	L
Lefty Grove, Philadelphia (1)	31	4
Wes Ferrell, Cleveland (4)	22	12
George Earnshaw, Philadelphia (1)	21	7
Lefty Gomez, New York (2)	21	9
Rube Walberg, Philadelphia (1)	20	12

1932 (5)

	W	L
Alvin Crowder, Washington (3)	26	13
Lefty Grove, Philadelphia (2)	25	10
Lefty Gomez, New York (1)	24	7
Wes Ferrell, Cleveland (4)	23	13
Monte Weaver, Washington (3)	22	10

1933 (3)

	W	L
Lefty Grove, Philadelphia (3)	24	8
Alvin Crowder, Washington (1)	24	15

	W	L
Earl Whitehill, Washington (1)	22	8
1934 (4)	**W**	**L**
Lefty Gomez, New York (2)	26	5
Schoolboy Rowe, Detroit (1)	24	8
Tommy Bridges, Detroit (1)	22	11
Mel Harder, Cleveland (3)	20	12
1935 (4)	**W**	**L**
Wes Ferrell, Boston (4)	25	14
Mel Harder, Cleveland (3)	22	11
Tommy Bridges, Detroit (1)	21	10
Lefty Grove, Boston (4)	20	12
1936 (5)	**W**	**L**
Tommy Bridges, Detroit (2)	23	11
Vern Kennedy, Chicago (3)	21	9
Johnny Allen, Cleveland (5)	20	10
Red Ruffing, New York (1)	20	12
Wes Ferrell, Boston (6)	20	15
1937 (2)	**W**	**L**
Lefty Gomez, New York (1)	21	11
Red Ruffing, New York (1)	20	7
1938 (2)	**W**	**L**
Red Ruffing, New York (1)	21	7
Bobo Newsom, St. Louis (7)	20	16
1939 (4)	**W**	**L**
Bob Feller, Cleveland (3)	24	9
Red Ruffing, New York (1)	21	7
Dutch E. Leonard, Washington (6)	20	8
Bobo Newsom, 3- 1 St. Louis (8),		
17- 10 Detroit (5)	20	11
1940 (2)	**W**	**L**
Bob Feller, Cleveland (2)	27	11
Bobo Newsom, Detroit (1)	21	5
1941 (2)	**W**	**L**
Bob Feller, Cleveland (4T)	25	13
Thornton Lee, Chicago (3)	22	11
1942 (2)	**W**	**L**
Cecil Hughson, Boston (2)	22	6
Ernie Bonham, New York (1)	21	5
1943 (2)	**W**	**L**
Spud Chandler, New York (1)	20	4
Dizzy Trout, Detroit (5)	20	12
1944 (2)	**W**	**L**
Hal Newhouser, Detroit (2)	29	9
Dizzy Trout, Detroit (2)	27	14
1945 (3)	**W**	**L**
Hal Newhouser, Detroit (1)	25	9
Dave Ferriss, Boston (7)	21	10
Roger Wolff, Washington (2)	20	10
1946 (5)	**W**	**L**
Hal Newhouser, Detroit (2)	26	9
Bob Feller, Cleveland (6)	26	15
Dave Ferriss, Boston (1)	25	6
Spud Chandler, New York (3)	20	8
Cecil Hughson, Boston (1)	20	11
1947 (1)	**W**	**L**
Bob Feller, Cleveland (4)	20	11
1948 (3)	**W**	**L**
Hal Newhouser, Detroit (5)	21	12
Gene Bearden, Cleveland (1)	20	7
Bob Lemon, Cleveland (1)	20	14
1949 (5)	**W**	**L**
Mel Parnell, Boston (2)	25	7
Ellis Kinder, Boston (2)	23	6
Bob Lemon, Cleveland (3)	22	10
Vic Raschi, New York (1)	21	10
Alex Kellner, Philadelphia (5)	20	12

	W	L
1950 (2)		
Bob Lemon, Cleveland (4)	23	11
Vic Raschi, New York (1)	21	8
1951 (6)	**W**	**L**
Bob Feller, Cleveland (2)	22	8
Eddie Lopat, New York (1)	21	9
Vic Raschi, New York (1)	21	10
Ned Garver, St. Louis (8)	20	12
Mike Garcia, Cleveland (2)	20	13
Early Wynn, Cleveland (2)	20	13
1952 (5)		**L**
Bobby Shantz, Philadelphia (4)	24	7
Early Wynn, Cleveland (2)	23	12
Mike Garcia, Cleveland (2)	22	11
Bob Lemon, Cleveland (2)	22	11
Allie Reynolds, New York (1)	20	8
1953 (4)	**W**	**L**
Bob Porterfield, Washington (5)	22	10
Mel Parnell, Boston (4)	21	8
Bob Lemon, Cleveland (2)	21	15
Virgil Trucks, 5-4 St. Louis (8),		
15-6 Chicago (3)	20	10
1954 (3)	**W**	**L**
Bob Lemon, Cleveland (1)	23	7
Early Wynn, Cleveland (1)	23	11
Bob Grim, New York (2)	20	6
1955 (0)		
1956 (6)	**W**	**L**
Frank Lary, Detroit (5)	21	13
Herb Score, Cleveland (2)	20	9
Early Wynn, Cleveland (2)	20	9
Billy Pierce, Chicago (3)	20	9
Bob Lemon, Cleveland (2)	20	14
Billy Hoeft, Detroit (5)	20	14
1957 (2)	**W**	**L**
Jim Bunning, Detroit (4)	20	8
Billy Pierce, Chicago (2)	20	12
1958 (1)	**W**	**L**
Bob Turley, New York (1)	21	7
1959 (1)	**W**	**L**
Early Wynn, Chicago (1)	22	10
1960 (0)		
1961 (2)	**W**	**L**
Whitey Ford, New York (1)	25	4
Frank Lary, Detroit (2)	23	9
1962 (4)	**W**	**L**
Ralph Terry, New York (1)	23	12
Ray Herbert, Chicago (5)	20	9
Dick Donovan, Cleveland (6)	20	10
Camilo Pascual, Minnesota (2)	20	11
1963 (5)	**W**	**L**
Whitey Ford, New York (1)	24	7
Jim Bouton, New York (1)	21	7
Camilo Pascual, Minnesota (3)	21	9
Bill Monbouquette, Boston (7)	20	10
Steve Barber, Baltimore (4)	20	13
1964 (2)	**W**	**L**
Dean Chance, Los Angeles (5)	20	9
Gary Peters, Chicago (2)	20	8
1965 (2)	**W**	**L**
Mudcat Grant, Minnesota (1)	21	7
Mel Stottlemyre, New York (6)	20	9
1966 (2)	**W**	**L**
Jim Kaat, Minnesota (2)	25	13
Denny McLain, Detroit (3)	20	14

1967 (3)

	W	L
Jim Lonborg, Boston (1)	22	9
Earl Wilson, Detroit (2T)	22	11
Dean Chance, Minnesota (2T)	20	14

1968 (4)

	W	L
Denny McLain, Detroit (1)	31	6
Dave McNally, Baltimore (2)	22	10
Luis Tiant, Cleveland (3)	21	9
Mel Stottlemyre, New York (5)	21	12

1969 (6)

	W	L
Denny McLain, Detroit (2E)	24	9
Mike Cuellar, Baltimore (1E)	23	11
Jim Perry, Minnesota (1W)	20	6
Dave McNally, Baltimore (1E)	20	7
Dave Boswell, Minnesota (1W)	20	12
Mel Stottlemyre, New York (5E)	20	14

1970 (7)

	W	L
Mike Cuellar, Baltimore (1E)	24	8
Dave McNally, Baltimore (1E)	24	9
Jim Perry, Minnesota (1W)	24	12
Clyde Wright, California (3W)	22	12
Jim Palmer, Baltimore (1E)	20	10
Fred Peterson, New York (2E)	20	11
Sam McDowell, Cleveland (5E)	20	12

1971 (10)

	W	L
Mickey Lolich, Detroit (2E)	25	14
Vida Blue, Oakland (1W)	24	8
Wilbur Wood, Chicago (3W)	22	13
Dave McNally, Baltimore (1E)	21	5
Catfish Hunter, Oakland (1W)	21	11
Pat Dobson, Baltimore (1E)	20	8
Jim Palmer, Baltimore (1E)	20	9
Mike Cuellar, Baltimore (1E)	20	9
Joe Coleman, Detroit (2E)	20	9
Andy Messersmith, California (4W)	20	13

1972 (6)

	W	L
Gaylord Perry, Cleveland (5W)	24	16
Wilbur Wood, Chicago (2W)	24	17
Mickey Lolich, Detroit (1E)	22	14
Catfish Hunter, Oakland (1W)	21	7
Jim Palmer, Baltimore (3E)	21	10
Stan Bahnsen, Chicago (2W)	21	16

1973 (12)

	W	L
Wilbur Wood, Chicago (5W)	24	20
Joe Coleman, Detroit (3E)	23	15
Jim Palmer, Baltimore (1E)	22	9
Catfish Hunter, Oakland (1W)	21	5
Ken Holtzman, Oakland (1W)	21	13
Nolan Ryan, California (4W)	21	16
Vida Blue, Oakland (1W)	20	9
Paul Splittorff, Kansas City (2W)	20	11
Jim Colborn, Milwaukee (5E)	20	12
Luis Tiant, Boston (2E)	20	13
Bill Singer, California (4W)	20	14
Bert Blyleven, Minnesota (3W)	20	17

1974 (9)

	W	L
Catfish Hunter, Oakland (1W)	25	12
Ferguson Jenkins, Texas (2W)	25	12
Mike Cuellar, Baltimore (1E)	22	10
Luis Tiant, Boston (3E)	22	13
Steve Busby, Kansas City (5W)	22	14
Nolan Ryan, California (6W)	22	16
Jim Kaat, Chicago (4W)	21	13
Gaylord Perry, Cleveland (4E)	21	13
Wilbur Wood, Chicago (4W)	20	19

1975 (5)

	W	L
Jim Palmer, Baltimore (2E)	23	11
Catfish Hunter, New York (3E)	23	14
Vida Blue, Oakland (1W)	22	11
Mike Torrez, Baltimore (2E)	20	9
Jim Kaat, Chicago (5W)	20	14

1976 (3)

	W	L
Jim Palmer, Baltimore (2E)	22	13
Luis Tiant, Boston (3E)	21	12
Wayne Garland, Baltimore (2E)	20	7

1977 (3)

	W	L
Jim Palmer, Baltimore (2TE)	20	11
Dave Goltz, Minnesota (4W)	20	11
Dennis Leonard, Kansas City (1W)	20	12

1978 (6)

	W	L
Ron Guidry, New York (1E)	25	3
Mike Caldwell, Milwaukee (3E)	22	9
Jim Palmer, Baltimore (4E)	21	12
Dennis Leonard, Kansas City (1W)	21	17
Dennis Eckersley, Boston (2E)	20	8
Ed Figueroa, New York (1E)	20	9

1979 (3)

	W	L
Mike Flanagan, Baltimore (1E)	23	9
Tommy John, New York (4E)	21	9
Jerry Koosman, Minnesota (4W)	20	13

1980 (5)

	W	L
Steve Stone, Baltimore (2E)	25	7
Tommy John, New York (1E)	22	9
Mike Norris, Oakland (2W)	22	9
Scott McGregor, Baltimore (2E)	20	8
Dennis Leonard, Kansas City (1W)	20	11

1981 (0)

1982 (0)

1983 (4)

	W	L
LaMarr Hoyt, Chicago (1W)	24	10
Rich Dotson, Chicago (1W)	22	7
Ron Guidry, New York (3E)	21	9
Jack Morris, Detroit (2E)	20	13

1984 (1)

	W	L
Mike Boddicker, Baltimore (5E)	20	11

1985 (2)

	W	L
Ron Guidry, New York (2E)	22	6
Bret Saberhagen, Kansas City (1W)	20	6

1986 (3)

	W	L
Roger Clemens, Boston (1E)	24	4
Jack Morris, Detroit (3E)	21	8
Ted Higuera, Milwaukee (6E)	20	11

1987 (2)

	W	L
Roger Clemens, Boston (5E)	20	9
Dave Stewart, Oakland (3W)	20	13

1988 (3)

	W	L
Frank Viola, Minnesota (2W)	24	7
Dave Stewart, Oakland (1W)	21	12
Mark Gubicza, Kansas City (3W)	20	8

1989 (2)

	W	L
Bret Saberhagen, Kansas City (2W)	23	6
Dave Stewart, Oakland (1W)	21	9

1990 (3)

	W	L
Bob Welch, Oakland (1W)	27	6
Dave Stewart, Oakland (1W)	22	11
Roger Clemens, Boston (1E)	21	6

1991 (2)

	W	L
Scott Erickson, Minnesota (1W)	20	8
Bill Gullickson, Detroit (2TE)	20	9

1992 (3)

	W	L
Jack Morris, Toronto (1E)	21	6
Kevin Brown, Texas (4W)	21	11
Jack McDowell, Chicago (3W)	20	10

1993 (1)

	W	L
Jack McDowell, Chicago (1W)	22	10

1994 (0)

1876 (5)	W	L
Al Spalding, Chicago (1)	47	13
George Bradley, St. Louis (2)	45	19
Tommy Bond, Hartford (3)	32	13
Jim Devlin, Louisville (5)	30	34
Bobby Mathews, New York (6)	21	34

1877 (3)	W	L
Tommy Bond, Boston (1)	31	17
Jim Devlin, Louisville (2)	28	20
Terry Larkin, Hartford (3)	22	21

1878 (4)	W	L
Tommy Bond, Boston (1)	40	19
Will White, Cincinnati (2)	29	21
Terry Larkin, Chicago (4)	29	26
Monte Ward, Providence (3)	22	13

1879 (6)	W	L
Monte Ward, Providence (1)	44	18
Tommy Bond, Boston (2)	43	19
Will White, Cincinnati (5)	43	31
Pud Galvin, Buffalo (3T)	37	27
Terry Larkin, Chicago (3T)	30	23
Jim McCormick, Cleveland (6)	20	40

1880 (8)	W	L
Jim McCormick, Cleveland (3)	45	28
Larry Corcoran, Chicago (1)	43	14
Monte Ward, Providence (2)	40	23
Mickey Welch, Troy (4)	34	30
Lee Richmond, Worcester (5)	31	33
Tommy Bond, Boston (6)	26	29
Fred Goldsmith, Chicago (1)	22	3
Pud Galvin, Buffalo (7)	20	37

1881 (9)	W	L
Larry Corcoran, Chicago (1)	31	14
Jim Whitney, Boston (6)	31	33
Pud Galvin, Buffalo (3)	29	24
George Derby, Detroit (4)	29	26
Jim McCormick, Cleveland (7)	26	30
Hoss Radbourn, Providence (2)	25	11
Fred Goldsmith, Chicago (1)	25	13
Lee Richmond, Worcester (8)	25	27
Mickey Welch, Troy (5)	21	18

1882 (7)	W	L
Jim McCormick, Cleveland (5)	36	29
Hoss Radbourn, Providence (2)	31	19
Pud Galvin, Buffalo (3T)	28	22
Fred Goldsmith, Chicago (1)	28	16
Larry Corcoran, Chicago (1)	27	13
George Weidman, Detroit (6)	26	20
Jim Whitney, Boston (3T)	24	22

1883 (9)	W	L
Hoss Radbourn, Providence (3)	49	25
Pud Galvin, Buffalo (5)	46	29
Jim Whitney, Boston (1)	37	21
Larry Corcoran, Chicago (2)	31	21
Fred Goldsmith, Chicago (2)	28	18
Jim McCormick, Cleveland (4)	27	13
Charlie Buffinton, Boston (1)	25	14
Mickey Welch, New York (6)	25	23
Hugh Daily, Cleveland (4)	24	18

1884 (7)	W	L
Hoss Radbourn, Providence (1)	60	12
Charlie Buffinton, Boston (2)	48	16
Pud Galvin, Buffalo (3)	46	22
Mickey Welch, New York (4T)	39	21
Larry Corcoran, Chicago (4T)	35	23
Jim Whitney, Boston (2)	23	14
Charlie Ferguson, Philadelphia (6)	21	24

1885 (9)	W	L
John Clarkson, Chicago (1)	53	16
Mickey Welch, New York (2)	44	11
Tim Keefe, New York (2)	32	13
Charlie Ferguson, Philadelphia (3)	26	19
Hoss Radbourn, Providence (4)	26	20
Ed Daily, Philadelphia (3)	26	22
Fred Shaw, Providence (4)	23	26
Charlie Buffinton, Boston (5)	22	27
Jim McCormick, 1-3 Providence (4), 20-4 Chicago (1)	21	7

1886 (11)	W	L
Charles Baldwin, Detroit (2)	42	13
Tim Keefe, New York (3)	42	20
John Clarkson, Chicago (1)	35	17
Mickey Welch, New York (3)	33	22
Charlie Ferguson, Philadelphia (4)	32	9
Charlie Getzien, Detroit (2)	31	11
Jim McCormick, Chicago (1)	31	11
Hoss Radbourn, Boston (5)	27	30
Dan Casey, Philadelphia (4)	25	19
John Flynn, Chicago (1)	24	6
Bill Stemmyer, Boston (5)	22	18

1887 (11)	W	L
John Clarkson, Chicago (3)	38	21
Tim Keefe, New York (4)	35	19
Charlie Getzien, Detroit (1)	29	13
Dan Casey, Philadelphia (2)	28	13
Pud Galvin, Pittsburgh (6)	28	21
Jim Whitney, Washington (7)	24	21
Hoss Radbourn, Boston (5)	24	23
Mickey Welch, New York (4)	22	15
Michael Madden, Boston (5)	22	14
Charlie Ferguson, Philadelphia (2)	21	10
Charlie Buffinton, Philadelphia (2)	21	17

1888 (8)	W	L
Tim Keefe, New York (1)	35	12
John Clarkson, Boston (4)	33	20
Pete Conway, Detroit (5)	30	14
Ed Morris, Pittsburgh (6)	29	23
Charlie Buffinton, Philadelphia (3)	28	17
Mickey Welch, New York (1)	26	19
Gus Krock, Chicago (2)	25	14
Pud Galvin, Pittsburgh (6)	23	25

1889 (10)	W	L
John Clarkson, Boston (2)	49	19
Tim Keefe, New York (1)	28	13
Mickey Welch, New York (1)	27	12
Charlie Buffinton, Philadelphia (4)	26	17
Pud Galvin, Pittsburgh (5)	23	16
John O'Brien, Cleveland (6)	22	17
Henry Staley, Pittsburgh (5)	21	26
Hoss Radbourn, Boston (2)	20	11
Ed Beatin, Cleveland (6)	20	14
Henry Boyle, Indianapolis (7)	20	23

1890 (13)	W	L
Bill Hutchinson, Chicago (2)	42	25
Kid Gleason, Philadelphia (3)	38	16
Tom Lovett, Brooklyn (1)	32	11
Amos Rusie, New York (6)	29	30
Billy Rhines, Cincinnati (4)	28	17
Kid Nichols, Boston (5)	27	19
John Clarkson, Boston (5)	26	18
William Terry, Brooklyn (1)	25	16
Charlie Buffinton, Boston (5)	24	18
Bob Caruthers, Brooklyn (1)	23	11
Tom Vickery, Philadelphia (3)	22	23
Ed Beatin, Cleveland (7)	22	31
Pat Luby, Chicago (2)	21	9

1891 (12)	W	L
Bill Hutchinson, Chicago (2)	43	19
John Clarkson, Boston (1)	33	19
Amos Rusie, New York (3)	32	19
Kid Nichols, Boston (1)	30	17
Cy Young, Cleveland (5)	27	20

	W	L
Henry Staley, 4-5 Pittsburgh (8)		
20-8 Boston (1)	24	13
Kid Gleason, Philadelphia (4)	24	19
Tony Mullane, Cincinnati (7)	24	25
John Ewing, New York (3)	22	8
Tom Lovett, Brooklyn (6)	21	20
Mark Baldwin, Pittsburgh (8)	21	27
Charles Esper, Philadelphia (4)	20	14

1892 (22)

	W	L
Bill Hutchinson, Chicago (7)	37	34
Cy Young, Cleveland (2)	36	11
Kid Nichols, Boston (1)	35	16
Jack Stivetts, Boston (1)	35	16
George Haddock, Brooklyn (3)	31	13
Amos Rusie, New York (8)	31	28
Frank Killen, Washington (10)	30	23
George Cuppy, Cleveland (2)	28	12
Gus Weyhing, Philadelphia (4)	28	18
Mark Baldwin, Pittsburgh (6)	27	20
Ed Stein, Brooklyn (3)	26	16
John Clarkson, 8-6 Boston (1)		
17-10 Cleveland (2)	25	16
Ad Gumbert, Chicago (7)	23	21
Henry Staley, Boston (1)	22	10
Charles King, New York (8)	22	24
Tony Mullane, Cincinnati (5)	21	10
William Terry 2-4, Baltimore (12)		
19-6 Pittsburgh (6)	21	10
Frank Dwyer 3-11, St. Louis (11)		
18-8 Cincinnati (5)	21	19
Scott Stratton, Louisville (9)	21	19
Elton Chamberlain, Cincinnati (5)	20	22
Kid Gleason, St. Louis (11)	20	24
John McMahon, Baltimore (12)	20	25

1893 (8)

	W	L
Frank Killen, Pittsburgh (2)	36	14
Kid Nichols, Boston (1)	34	14
Cy Young, Cleveland (3)	32	16
Amos Rusie, New York (5)	29	18
William Kennedy, Brooklyn (6T)	26	19
John McMahon, Baltimore (8)	24	16
Gus Weyhing, Philadelphia (4)	24	16
Jack Stivetts, Boston (1)	20	12

1894 (13)

	W	L
Amos Rusie, New York (2)	36	13
Jouett Meekin, New York (2)	34	9
Kid Nichols, Boston (3)	32	13
Ted Breitenstein, St. Louis (9)	27	22
Jack Stivetts, Boston (3)	26	14
John McMahon, Baltimore (1)	25	8
Ed Stein, Brooklyn (5)	25	15
Cy Young, Cleveland (6)	25	22
George Cuppy, Cleveland (6)	23	17
John B. Taylor, Philadelphia (4)	22	11
William Kennedy, Brooklyn (5)	22	20
Clark Griffith, Chicago (8)	21	11
Frank Dwyer, Cincinnati (10)	20	18

1895 (13)

	W	L
Cy Young, Cleveland (2)	35	10
Emerson Hawley, Pittsburgh (7)	32	21
Bill Hoffer, Baltimore (1)	30	7
John B. Taylor, Philadelphia (3)	26	13
Kid Carsey, Philadelphia (3)	26	15
Kid Nichols, Boston (5T)	26	16
Clark Griffith, Chicago (4)	25	13
George Cuppy, Cleveland (2)	25	15
William Terry, Chicago (4)	23	13
Amos Rusie, New York (9)	22	21
George Hemming, Baltimore (1)	20	10
Billy Rhines, Cincinnati (8)	20	10
Ted Breitenstein, St. Louis (11)	20	29

1896 (12)

	W	L
Kid Nichols, Boston (4)	30	14
Frank Killen, Pittsburgh (6)	29	15

	W	L
Cy Young, Cleveland (2)	29	16
Bill Hoffer, Baltimore (1)	26	7
Jouett Meekin, New York (7)	26	13
Frank Dwyer, Cincinnati (3)	25	10
George Cuppy, Cleveland (2)	25	15
George Mercer, Washington (9T)	25	19
Clark Griffith, Chicago (5)	22	13
Jack Stivetts, Boston (4)	22	14
John B. Taylor, Philadelphia (8)	21	20
Emerson Hawley, Pittsburgh (6)	21	21

1897 (13)

	W	L
Kid Nichols, Boston (1)	31	11
Amos Rusie, New York (3)	29	8
Fred Klobedanz, Boston (1)	26	7
Joe Corbett, Baltimore (2)	24	8
George Mercer, Washington (6T)	24	21
Ted Breitenstein, Cincinnati (4)	23	12
Bill Hoffer, Baltimore (2)	22	10
Ed Lewis, Boston (1)	21	12
Cy Young, Cleveland (5)	21	18
Clark Griffith, Chicago (9)	21	19
Jerry Nops, Baltimore (2)	20	7
Jouett Meekin, New York (3)	20	11
Cy Seymour, New York (3)	20	14

1898 (17)

	W	L
Kid Nichols, Boston (1)	31	12
Bert Cunningham, Louisville (9)	28	15
James McJames, Baltimore (2)	27	14
Ed Lewis, Boston (1)	26	8
Clark Griffith, Chicago (4)	26	10
Emerson Hawley, Cincinnati (3)	26	12
Vic Willis, Boston (1)	25	13
Cy Young, Cleveland (5)	25	14
Cy Seymour, New York (7)	25	17
Wiley Piatt, Philadelphia (6)	24	14
Jesse Tannehill, Pittsburgh (8)	24	14
Jack Powell, Cleveland (5)	24	15
Jim Hughes, Baltimore (2)	21	11
Ted Breitenstein, Cincinnati (3)	21	14
Al Maul, Baltimore (2)	20	7
Amos Rusie, New York (7)	20	10
Jim Callahan, Chicago (4)	20	11

1899 (17)

	W	L
Jim Hughes, Brooklyn (1)	28	6
Joe McGinnity, Baltimore (4)	28	17
Vic Willis, Boston (2)	27	8
Cy Young, St. Louis (5)	26	15
Frank Hahn, Cincinnati (6)	23	7
Jim Callahan, Chicago (8)	23	12
Jesse Tannehill, Pittsburgh (7)	23	14
Wiley Piatt, Philadelphia (3)	23	15
Jack Powell, St. Louis (5)	23	21
Frank Donahue, Philadelphia (3)	22	7
Clark Griffith, Chicago (8)	22	13
Jack Dunn, Brooklyn (1)	21	12
Charles Fraser, Philadelphia (3)	21	13
Kid Nichols, Boston (2)	21	19
Frank Kitson, Baltimore (4)	20	16
Deacon Phillippe, Louisville (9)	20	17
Sam Leever, Pittsburgh (7)	20	23

1900 (5)

	W	L
Joe McGinnity, Brooklyn (1)	29	9
William Kennedy, Brooklyn (1)	22	15
Bill Dinneen, Boston (4)	21	15
Jesse Tannehill, Pittsburgh (2)	20	7
Cy Young, St. Louis (5T)	20	18

1901 (9)

	W	L
Bill Donovan, Brooklyn (3)	25	15
Deacon Phillippe, Pittsburgh (1)	22	12
Frank Hahn, Cincinnati (8)	22	19
Jack Chesbro, Pittsburgh (1)	21	9
Al Orth, Philadelphia (2)	20	12
Jack Harper, St. Louis (4)	20	12
Frank Donahue, Philadelphia (2)	20	13

	W	L
Christy Mathewson, New York (7)	20	17
Vic Willis, Boston (5)	20	17

1902 (7)

	W	L
Jack Chesbro, Pittsburgh (1)	28	6
Charlie Pittinger, Boston (3)	27	16
Vic Willis, Boston (3)	27	20
John W. Taylor, Chicago (5)	22	10
Frank Hahn, Cincinnati (4)	22	12
Jesse Tannehill, Pittsburgh (1)	20	6
Deacon Phillippe, Pittsburgh (1)	20	9

1903 (9)

	W	L
Joe McGinnity, New York (2)	31	20
Christy Mathewson, New York (2)	30	13
Sam Leever, Pittsburgh (1)	25	7
Deacon Phillippe, Pittsburgh (1)	25	9
Frank Hahn, Cincinnati (4)	22	12
Henry Schmidt, Brooklyn (5)	22	13
John W. Taylor, Chicago (3)	21	14
Jacob Weimer, Chicago (3)	20	8
Bob Wicker, 0-0 St. Louis (8) 20-9 Chicago (3)	20	9

1904 (7)

	W	L
Joe McGinnity, New York (1)	35	8
Christy Mathewson, New York (1)	33	12
Jack Harper, Cincinnati (3)	23	9
Kid Nichols, St. Louis (5)	21	13
Luther Taylor, New York (1)	21	15
Jacob Weimer, Chicago (2)	20	14
John W. Taylor, St. Louis (5)	20	19

1905 (8)

	W	L
Christy Mathewson, New York(1)	31	9
Charlie Pittinger, Philadelphia (4)	23	14
Leon Ames, New York (1)	22	8
Joe McGinnity, New York (1)	21	15
Sam Leever, Pittsburgh (2)	20	5
Bob Ewing, Cincinnati (5)	20	11
Deacon Phillippe, Pittsburgh (2)	20	13
Irv Young, Boston (7)	20	21

1906 (8)

	W	L
Joe McGinnity, New York (2)	27	12
Mordecai Brown, Chicago (1)	26	6
Vic Willis, Pittsburgh (3)	23	13
Sam Leever, Pittsburgh (3)	22	7
Christy Mathewson, New York (2)	22	12
Jack Pfiester, Chicago (1)	20	8
John W. Taylor, 8-9 St. Louis (7), 12-3 Chicago (1)	20	12
Jacob Weimer, Cincinnati (6)	20	14

1907 (6)

	W	L
Christy Mathewson, New York (4)	24	12
Orval Overall, Chicago (1)	23	8
Frank Sparks, Philadelphia (3)	22	8
Vic Willis, Pittsburgh (2)	21	11
Mordecai Brown, Chicago (1)	20	6
Lefty Leifield, Pittsburgh (2)	20	16

1908 (7)

	W	L
Christy Mathewson, New York (2T)	37	11
Mordecai Brown, Chicago (1)	29	9
Ed Reulbach, Chicago (1)	24	7
Nick Maddox, Pittsburgh (2T)	23	8
Vic Willis, Pittsburgh (2T)	23	11
George Wiltse, New York (2T)	23	14
George McQuillan, Philadelphia (4)	23	17

1909 (6)

	W	L
Mordecai Brown, Chicago (2)	27	9
Howie Camnitz, Pittsburgh (1)	25	6
Christy Mathewson, New York (3)	25	6
Vic Willis, Pittsburgh (1)	22	11
George Wiltse, New York (3)	20	11
Orval Overall, Chicago (2)	20	11

1910 (5)

	W	L
Christy Mathewson, New York (2)	27	9
Mordecai Brown, Chicago (1)	25	14
Earl Moore, Philadelphia (4)	22	15
Leonard Cole, Chicago (1)	20	4
George Suggs, Cincinnati (5)	20	12

1911 (8)

	W	L
Grover Alexander, Philadelphia (4)	28	13
Christy Mathewson, New York (1)	26	13
Rube Marquard, New York (1)	24	7
Bob Harmon, St. Louis (5)	23	16
Babe Adams, Pittsburgh (3)	22	12
George Rucker, Brooklyn (7)	22	18
Mordecai Brown, Chicago (2)	21	11
Howie Camnitz, Pittsburgh (3)	20	15

1912 (5)

	W	L
Larry Cheney, Chicago (3)	26	10
Rube Marquard, New York (1)	26	11
Claude Hendrix, Pittsburgh (2)	24	9
Christy Mathewson, New York (1)	23	12
Howie Camnitz, Pittsburgh (2)	22	12

1913 (7)

	W	L
Tom Seaton, Philadelphia (2)	27	12
Christy Mathewson, New York (1)	25	11
Rube Marquard, New York (1)	23	10
Grover Alexander, Philadelphia (2)	22	8
Jeff Tesreau, New York (1)	22	13
Babe Adams, Pittsburgh (4)	21	10
Larry Cheney, Chicago (3)	21	14

1914 (9)

	W	L
Dick Rudolph, Boston (1)	27	10
Grover Alexander, Philadelphia (6)	27	15
Bill James, Boston (1)	26	7
Jeff Tesreau, New York (2)	26	10
Christy Mathewson, New York (2)	24	13
Jeff Pfeffer, Brooklyn (5)	23	12
Hippo Vaughn, Chicago (4)	21	13
Erskine Mayer, Philadelphia (6)	21	19
Larry Cheney, Chicago (4)	20	18

1915 (5)

	W	L
Grover Alexander, Philadelphia (1)	31	10
Dick Rudolph, Boston (2)	22	19
Al Mamaux, Pittsburgh (5)	21	8
Erskine Mayer, Philadelphia (1)	21	15
Hippo Vaughn, Chicago (4)	20	12

1916 (4)

	W	L
Grover Alexander, Philadelphia (2)	33	12
Jeff Pfeffer, Brooklyn (1)	25	11
Eppa Rixey, Philadelphia (2)	22	10
Al Mamaux, Pittsburgh (6)	21	15

1917 (5)

	W	L
Grover Alexander, Philadelphia (2)	30	13
Fred Toney, Cincinnati (4)	24	16
Hippo Vaughn, Chicago (5)	23	13
Ferdie Schupp, New York (1)	21	7
Pete Schneider, Cincinnati (4)	20	19

1918 (2)

	W	L
Hippo Vaughn, Chicago (1)	22	10
Claude Hendrix, Chicago (1)	20	7

1919 (3)

	W	L
Jesse Barnes, New York (2)	25	9
Harry Sallee, Cincinnati (1)	21	7
Hippo Vaughn, Chicago (3)	21	14

1920 (7)

	W	L
Grover Alexander, Chicago (5T)	27	14
Wilbur Cooper, Pittsburgh (4)	24	15
Burleigh Grimes, Brooklyn (1)	23	11
Fred Toney, New York (2)	21	11
Art Nehf, New York (2)	21	12
Bill Doak, St. Louis (5T)	20	12

	W	L
Jesse Barnes, New York (2)	20	15

1921 (4) — W — L

	W	L
Burleigh Grimes, Brooklyn (5)	22	13
Wilbur Cooper, Pittsburgh (2)	22	14
Art Nehf, New York (1)	20	10
Joe Oeschger, Boston (4)	20	14

1922 (3) — W — L

	W	L
Eppa Rixey, Cincinnati (2)	25	13
Wilbur Cooper, Pittsburgh (3T)	23	14
Walt Ruether, Brooklyn (6)	21	12

1923 (7) — W — L

	W	L
Dolf Luque, Cincinnati (2)	27	8
Johnny Morrison, Pittsburgh (3)	25	13
Grover Alexander, Chicago (4)	22	12
Pete Donohue, Cincinnati (2)	21	15
Burleigh Grimes, Brooklyn (6)	21	18
Jesse Haines, St. Louis (5)	20	13
Eppa Rixey, Cincinnati (2)	20	15

1924 (4) — W — L

	W	L
Dazzy Vance, Brooklyn (2)	28	6
Burleigh Grimes, Brooklyn (2)	22	13
Carl Mays, Cincinnati (4)	20	9
Wilbur Cooper, Pittsburgh (3)	20	14

1925 (3) — W — L

	W	L
Dazzy Vance, Brooklyn (6T)	22	9
Eppa Rixey, Cincinnati (3)	21	11
Pete Donohue, Cincinnati (3)	21	14

1926 (4) — W — L

	W	L
Remy Kremer, Pittsburgh (3)	20	6
Flint Rhem, St. Louis (1)	20	7
Lee Meadows, Pittsburgh (3)	20	9
Pete Donohue, Cincinnati (2)	20	14

1927 (4) — W — L

	W	L
Charlie Root, Chicago (4)	26	15
Jesse Haines, St. Louis (2)	24	10
Carmen Hill, Pittsburgh (1)	22	11
Grover Alexander, St. Louis (2)	21	10

1928 (6) — W — L

	W	L
Larry Benton, New York (2)	25	9
Burleigh Grimes, Pittsbrugh (4)	25	14
Dazzy Vance, Brooklyn (6)	22	10
Bill Sherdel, St. Louis (1)	21	10
Jesse Haines, St. Louis (1)	20	8
Fred Fitzsimmons, New York (2)	20	9

1929 (1) — W — L

	W	L
Pat Malone, Chicago (1)	22	10

1930 (2) — W — L

	W	L
Pat Malone, Chicago (2)	20	9
Remy Kremer, Pittsburgh (5)	20	12

1931 (0)

1932 (2) — W — L

	W	L
Lon Warneke, Chicago (1)	22	6
Watty Clark, Brooklyn (3)	20	12

1933 (4) — W — L

	W	L
Carl Hubbell, New York (1)	23	12
Ben Cantwell, Boston (4)	20	10
Guy Bush, Chicago (3)	20	12
Dizzy Dean, St. Louis (5)	20	18

1934 (4) — W — L

	W	L
Dizzy Dean, St. Louis (1)	30	7
Hal Schumacher, New York (2)	23	10
Lon Warneke, Chicago (3)	22	10
Carl Hubbell, New York (2)	21	12

1935 (5) — W — L

	W	L
Dizzy Dean, St. Louis (2)	28	12
Carl Hubbell, New York (3)	23	12
Paul Derringer, Cincinnati (6)	22	13
Bill Lee, Chicago (1)	20	6

	W	L
Lon Warneke, Chicago (1)	20	13

1936 (2) — W — L

	W	L
Carl Hubbell, New York (1)	26	6
Dizzy Dean, St. Louis (2T)	24	13

1937 (4) — W — L

	W	L
Carl Hubbell, New York (1)	22	8
Cliff Melton, New York (1)	20	9
Lou Fette, Boston (5)	20	10
Jim Turner, Boston (5)	20	11

1938 (2) — W — L

	W	L
Bill Lee, Chicago (1)	22	9
Paul Derringer, Cincinnati (4)	21	14

1939 (4) — W — L

	W	L
Bucky Walters, Cincinnati (1)	27	11
Paul Derringer, Cincinnati (1)	25	7
Curt Davis, St. Louis (2)	22	16
Luke Hamlin, Brooklyn (3)	20	13

1940 (3) — W — L

	W	L
Bucky Walters, Cincinnati (1)	22	10
Paul Derringer, Cincinnati (1)	20	12
Claude Passeau, Chicago (5)	20	13

1941 (2) — W — L

	W	L
Kirby Higbe, Brooklyn (1)	22	9
Whit Wyatt, Brooklyn (1)	22	10

1942 (2) — W — L

	W	L
Mort Cooper, St. Louis (1)	22	7
Johnny Beazley, St. Louis (1)	21	6

1943 (3) — W — L

	W	L
Mort Cooper, St. Louis (1)	21	8
Rip Sewell, Pittsburgh (4)	21	9
Elmer Riddle, Cincinnati (2)	21	11

1944 (4) — W — L

	W	L
Bucky Walters, Cincinnati (3)	23	8
Mort Cooper, St. Louis (1)	22	7
Rip Sewell, Pittsburgh (2)	21	12
Bill Voiselle, New York (5)	21	16

1945 (2) — W — L

	W	L
Red Barrett, 2-3 Boston (6), 21-9 St. Louis (2)	23	12
Hank Wyse, Chicago (1)	22	10

1946 (2) — W — L

	W	L
Howie Pollet, St. Louis (1)	21	10
Johnny Sain, Boston (4)	20	14

1947 (5) — W — L

	W	L
Ewell Blackwell, Cincinnati (5)	22	8
Larry Jansen, New York (4)	21	5
Warren Spahn, Boston (3)	21	10
Ralph Branca, Brooklyn (1)	21	12
Johnny Sain, Boston (3)	21	12

1948 (2) — W — L

	W	L
Johnny Sain, Boston (1)	24	15
Harry Brecheen, St. Louis (2)	20	7

1949 (2) — W — L

	W	L
Warren Spahn, Boston (4)	21	14
Howie Pollet, St. Louis (2)	20	9

1950 (3) — W — L

	W	L
Warren Spahn, Boston (4)	21	17
Robin Roberts, Philadelphia (1)	20	11
Johnny Sain, Boston (4)	20	13

1951 (7) — W — L

	W	L
Sal Maglie, New York (1)	23	6
Larry Jansen, New York (1)	23	11
Preacher Roe, Brooklyn (2)	22	3
Warren Spahn, Boston (4)	22	14
Robin Roberts, Philadelphia (5)	21	15
Don Newcombe, Brooklyn (2)	20	9
Murry Dickson, Pittsburgh (7)	20	16

1952 (1)	W	L
Robin Roberts, Philadelphia (4)	28	7
1953 (4)	**W**	**L**
Warren Spahn, Milwaukee (2)	23	7
Robin Roberts, Philadelphia (3T)	23	16
Carl Erskine, Brooklyn (1)	20	6
Harvey Haddix, St. Louis (3T)	20	9
1954 (3)	**W**	**L**
Robin Roberts, Philadelphia (4)	23	15
Johnny Antonelli, New York (1)	21	7
Warren Spahn, Milwaukee (3)	21	12
1955 (2)	**W**	**L**
Robin Roberts, Philadelphia (4)	23	14
Don Newcombe, Brooklyn (1)	20	5
1956 (3)	**W**	**L**
Don Newcombe, Brooklyn (1)	27	7
Warren Spahn, Milwaukee (2)	20	11
Johnny Antonelli, New York (6)	20	13
1957 (1)	**W**	**L**
Warren Spahn, Milwaukee (1)	21	11
1958 (3)	**W**	**L**
Warren Spahn, Milwaukee (1)	22	11
Bob Friend, Pittsburgh (2)	22	14
Lew Burdette, Milwaukee (1)	20	10
1959 (3)	**W**	**L**
Lew Burdette, Milwaukee (2)	21	15
Warren Spahn, Milwaukee (2)	21	15
Sam Jones, San Francisco (3)	21	15
1960 (3)	**W**	**L**
Ernie Broglio, St. Louis (3)	21	9
Warren Spahn, Milwaukee (2)	21	10
Vernon Law, Pittsburgh (1)	20	9
1961 (2)	**W**	**L**
Joey Jay, Cincinnati (1)	21	10
Warren Spahn, Milwaukee (4)	21	13
1962 (4)	**W**	**L**
Don Drysdale, Los Angeles (2)	25	9
Jack Sanford, San Francisco (1)	24	7
Bob Purkey, Cincinnati (3)	23	5
Joey Jay, Cincinnati (3)	21	14
1963 (5)	**W**	**L**
Sandy Koufax, Los Angeles (1)	25	5
Juan Marichal, San Francisco (3)	25	8
Jim Maloney, Cincinnati (5)	23	7
Warren Spahn, Milwaukee (6)	23	7
Dick Ellsworth, Chicago (7)	22	10
1964 (3)	**W**	**L**
Larry Jackson, Chicago (8)	24	11
Juan Marichal, San Francisco (4)	21	8
Ray Sadecki, St. Louis (1)	20	11
1965 (7)	**W**	**L**
Sandy Koufax, Los Angeles (1)	26	8
Tony Cloninger, Milwaukee (5)	24	11
Don Drysdale, Los Angeles (1)	23	12
Sammy Ellis, Cincinnati (4)	22	10
Juan Marichal, San Francisco (2)	22	13
Jim Maloney, Cincinnati (4)	20	9
Bob Gibson, St. Louis (7)	20	12
1966 (5)	**W**	**L**
Sandy Koufax, Los Angeles (1)	27	9
Juan Marichal, San Francisco (2)	25	6
Gaylord Perry, San Francisco (2)	21	8
Bob Gibson, St. Louis (6)	21	12
Chris Short, Philadelphia (4)	20	10
1967 (2)	**W**	**L**
Mike McCormick, San Francisco (2)	22	10
Ferguson Jenkins, Chicago (3)	20	13

1968 (3)	W	L
Juan Marichal, San Francisco (2)	26	9
Bob Gibson, St. Louis (1)	22	9
Ferguson Jenkins, Chicago (3)	20	15
1969 (9)	**W**	**L**
Tom Seaver, New York (1E)	25	7
Phil Niekro, Atlanta (1W)	23	13
Juan Marichal, San Francisco (2W)	21	11
Ferguson Jenkins, Chicago (2E)	21	15
Bill Singer, Los Angeles (4W)	20	12
Larry Dierker, Houston (5W)	20	13
Bob Gibson, St. Louis (4E)	20	13
Bill Hands, Chicago (2E)	20	14
Claude Osteen, Los Angeles (4W)	20	15
1970 (4)	**W**	**L**
Bob Gibson, St. Louis (4E)	23	7
Gaylord Perry, San Francisco (3W)	23	13
Ferguson Jenkins, Chicago (2E)	22	16
Jim Merritt, Cincinnati (1W)	20	12
1971 (4)	**W**	**L**
Ferguson Jenkins, Chicago (3ET)	24	13
Al Downing, Los Angeles (2W)	20	9
Steve Carlton, St. Louis (2E)	20	9
Tom Seaver, New York (3ET)	20	10
1972 (4)	**W**	**L**
Steve Carlton, Philadelphia (6E)	27	10
Tom Seaver, New York (3E)	21	12
Claude Osteen, Los Angeles (3W)	20	11
Ferguson Jenkins, Chicago (2E)	20	12
1973 (1)	**W**	**L**
Ron Bryant, San Francisco (3W)	24	12
1974 (2)	**W**	**L**
Andy Messersmith, Los Angeles (1W)	20	6
Phil Niekro, Atlanta (3W)	20	13
1975 (2)	**W**	**L**
Tom Seaver, New York (3ET)	22	9
Randy Jones, San Diego (4W)	20	12
1976 (5)	**W**	**L**
Randy Jones, San Diego (5W)	22	14
Jerry Koosman, New York (3E)	21	10
Don Sutton, Los Angeles (2W)	21	10
Steve Carlton, Philadelphia (1E)	20	7
J.R. Richard, Houston (3W)	20	15
1977 (6)	**W**	**L**
Steve Carlton, Philadelphia (1E)	23	10
Tom Seaver, New York-Cincinnati (2W)	21	6
John Candelaria, Pittsburgh (2E)	20	5
Bob Forsch, St. Louis (3E)	20	7
Tommy John, Los Angeles (1W)	20	7
Rick Reuschel, Chicago (4E)	20	10
1978 (2)	**W**	**L**
Gaylord Perry, San Diego (3W)	21	6
Ross Grimsley, Montreal (4E)	20	11
1979 (2)	**W**	**L**
Joe Niekro, Houston (2W)	21	11
Phil Niekro, Atlanta (6W)	21	20
1980 (2)	**W**	**L**
Steve Carlton, Philadelphia (1E)	24	9
Joe Niekro, Houston (1W)	20	12
1981 (0)		
1982 (1)	**W**	**L**
Steve Carlton, Philadelphia (2E)	23	11
1983 (0)		
1984 (1)	**W**	**L**
Joaquin Andujar, St. Louis (3E)	20	14
1985 (4)	**W**	**L**
Dwight Gooden, New York (2E)	24	4

	W	L		W	L
John Tudor, St. Louis (1E)	21	8	Bill Swift, San Francisco (2W)	21	8
Joaquin Andujar, St. Louis (1E)	21	12	Greg Maddux, Atlanta (1W)	20	10
Tom Browning, Cincinnati (2W)	20	9	**1994 (0)**		

1986 (2)

	W	L
Fernando Valenzuela, Los Angeles (5W)	21	11
Mike Krukow, San Francisco (3W)	20	9

1987 (0)

1988 (3)

	W	L
Orel Hershiser, Los Angeles (1W)	23	8
Danny Jackson, Cincinnati (2W)	23	8
David Cone, New York (1E)	20	3

1989 (1)

	W	L
Mike Scott, Houston (3W)	20	10

1990 (3)

	W	L
Doug Drabek, Pittsburgh (1E)	22	6
Ramon Martinez, Los Angeles (2W)	20	6
Frank Viola, New York (2E)	20	12

1991 (2)

	W	L
John Smiley, Pittsburgh (1E)	20	8
Tom Glavine, Atlanta (1W)	20	11

1992 (2)

	W	L
Tom Glavine, Atlanta (1W)	20	8
Greg Maddux, Chicago (4E)	20	11

1993 (4)

	W	L
Tom Glavine, Atlanta (1W)	22	6
John Burkett, San Francisco (2W)	22	7

TWO LEAGUES IN SEASON

1884 (4)

	W	L
Billy Taylor, 25-4 St. Louis U.A. (1), 18-12 Philadelphia A.A. (7)	43	16
Charlie Sweeney, 17-7 Providence N.L. (1), 24-8 St. Louis U.A. (1)	41	15
Jim McCormick, 19-22 Cleveland N.L. (7), 22-4 Cincinnati U.A. (2)	41	26
Fred Shaw, 8-18 Detroit N.L. (8), 22-15 Boston U.A. (4)	30	33

1902 (1)

	W	L
Joe McGinnity, 13-10 Baltimore A.L. (8), 8-8 New York N.L. (8)	21	18

1904 (1)

	W	L
Patsy Flaherty, 2-2 Chicago A.L. (3), 19-9 Pittsburgh N.L. (4)	21	11

1945 (1)

	W	L
Hank Borowy, 10-5 New York A.L. (4), 11-2 Chicago N.L. (1)	21	7

1984 (1)

	W	L
Rick Sutcliffe, 4-5 Cleveland A.L. (6E), 16-1 Chicago N.L. (1E)	20	6

FIELDING

UNASSISTED TRIPLE PLAYS

Neal Ball, shortstop, Cleveland A.L. vs. Boston at Cleveland, July 19, 1909, first game, second inning. Ball caught McConnell's liner, touched second, retiring Wagner, who was on his way to third base, and then tagged Stahl as he came up to second.

George H. Burns, first baseman, Boston A.L. vs. Cleveland at Boston, September 14, 1923, second inning. Burns caught Brower's liner, tagged Lutzke off first and then ran to second and reached that bag before Stephenson could return from third base.

Ernie Padgett, shortstop, Boston N.L. vs. Philadelphia at Boston, October 6, 1923, second game, fourth inning. Padgett caught Holke's liner, ran to second to retire Tierney, then tagged Lee before he could return to first.

Glenn Wright, shortstop, Pittsburgh N.L. vs. St. Louis at Pittsburgh, May 7, 1925, ninth inning. Wright caught Bottomley's liner, ran to second to retire Cooney and then tagged Hornsby, who was on his way to second.

Jimmy E. Cooney, shortstop, Chicago N.L. vs. Pittsburgh at Pittsburgh, May 30, 1927, a.m. game, fourth inning. Cooney caught Paul Waner's liner, stepped on second to retire Lloyd Waner, then tagged Barnhart off first.

Johnny Neun, first baseman, Detroit A.L. vs. Cleveland at Detroit, May 31, 1927, ninth inning. Neun caught Summa's liner, ran over and tagged Jamieson between first and second and then touched second base before Myatt could return.

Ron Hansen, shortstop, Washington A.L. vs. Cleveland at Cleveland, July 30, 1968, first inning. With the count 3-and-2 on Azcue, Nelson broke for third base. Hansen caught Azcue's liner, stepped on second to double Nelson and then tagged Snyder going into second base.

Mickey Morandini, second baseman, Philadelphia N.L. vs. Pittsburgh at Pittsburgh, September 20, 1992, sixth inning. Morandini caught King's liner, stepped on second to retire Van Slyke, then tagged Bonds coming from first.

John Valentin, shortstop, Boston A.L. vs. Seattle at Boston, July 8, 1994, sixth inning. Valentin caught Newfield's line drive, stepped on second to retire Blowers, then tagged Mitchell coming from first.

(Note: All above unassisted triple plays made with runners on first and second bases only. In addition to the eight regular-season unassisted triple plays, Bill Wambsganss turned one in the 1920 World Series. For details see World Series General Reference section.)

Total number of occurrences (excluding Wambsganss'): (9)

CLUB MISCELLANEOUS

LIFETIME FRANCHISE WON-LOST RECORDS

CURRENT AMERICAN LEAGUE CLUBS (1901 THROUGH 1994)

Present Franchise	Years	Total Games	Won	Lost	Tied	Pct.
Baltimore	1954-94	6,459	3,439	3,011	9	.533
Boston	1901-94	14,563	7,375	7,104	84	.509
California*	1961-94	5,399	2,600	2,796	3	.482
Chicago	1901-94	14,569	7,295	7,173	101	.504

Present Franchise	Years	Total Games	Won	Lost	Tied	Pct.
Cleveland	1901-94	14,577	7,335	7,151	91	.506
Detroit	1901-94	14,603	7,509	7,000	94	.518
Kansas City	1969-94	4,097	2,123	1,972	2	.518
Milwaukee	1970-94	3,940	1,913	2,025	2	.486
Minnesota	1961-94	5,395	2,717	2,671	7	.504
New York	1903-94	14,275	8,013	6,177	85	.565
Oakland	1968-94	4,264	2,213	2,050	1	.519
Seattle	1977-94	2,812	1,215	1,595	2	.432
Texas	1972-94	3,611	1,717	1,890	4	.476
Toronto	1977-94	2,812	1,406	1,404	2	.500
Present Totals		111,376	56,870	54,019	487	.513

*Known as Los Angeles 1961-65.

EXTINCT AMERICAN LEAGUE CLUBS (1901 THROUGH 1971)

Extinct Franchise	Years	Total Games	Won	Lost	Tied	Pct.
Baltimore	1901-02	276	118	153	5	.437
Kansas City	1955-67	2,060	829	1,224	7	.404
Milwaukee	1901	139	48	89	2	.353
Philadelphia	1901-54	8,213	3,886	4,248	79	.478
St. Louis	1902-53	7,974	3,414	4,465	95	.434
Seattle	1969	163	64	98	1	.396
aWashington	1901-60	9,188	4,223	4,864	101	.465
bWashington	1961-71	1,773	740	1,032	1	.418
Extinct Totals		29,786	13,322	16,173	291	.452
American League Totals		141,162	70,192	70,192	778	.500

aOriginal Washington club.
bSecond Washington club.

CURRENT NATIONAL LEAGUE CLUBS (1876 THROUGH 1994)

Present Franchise	Years	Total Games	Won	Lost	Tied	Pct.
Atlanta	1966-94	4,582	2,202	2,373	7	.481
Chicago	1876-94	17,510	8,985	8,371	154	.518
Cincinnati	1890-94	16,138	8,109	7,905	124	.506
Colorado	1993-94	279	120	159	0	.430
Florida	1993-94	277	115	162	0	.415
Houston	1962-94	5,240	2,539	2,697	4	.485
Los Angeles	1958-94	5,862	3,153	2,703	6	.538
Montreal	1969-94	4,100	2,022	2,074	4	.494
New York	1962-94	5,233	2,427	2,798	8	.464
Philadelphia	1883-94	16,908	7,832	8,963	113	.466
Pittsburgh	1887-94	16,520	8,479	7,913	128	.517
St. Louis	1892-94	15,868	7,945	7,795	128	.505
San Diego	1969-94	4,105	1,830	2,273	2	.446
San Francisco	1958-94	5,862	3,022	2,835	5	.516
Present Totals		118,484	58,780	59,021	683	.499

EXTINCT NATIONAL LEAGUE CLUBS (1876 THROUGH 1965)

Extinct Franchise	Years	Total Games	Won	Lost	Tied	Pct.
Baltimore	1892-99	1,117	644	447	26	.588
Boston	1876-52	10,852	5,118	5,598	136	.478
Brooklyn	1890-57	10,253	5,214	4,926	113	.514
Buffalo	1879-85	656	314	333	9	.486
Cincinnati	1876-80	348	125	217	6	.368
Cleveland	1879-84	549	242	299	8	.448
Cleveland	1889-99	1,534	738	764	32	.492
Detroit	1881-88	879	426	437	16	.494
Hartford	1876-77	129	78	48	3	.619
Indianapolis	1878	63	24	36	3	.405
Indianapolis	1887-89	398	146	249	3	.371
Kansas City	1886	126	30	91	5	.258
Louisville	1876-77	130	65	61	4	.515
Louisville	1892-99	1,121	419	683	19	.382
Milwaukee	1878	61	15	45	1	.254
Milwaukee	1953-65	2,044	1,146	890	8	.563
New York	1876	57	21	35	1	.377
New York	1883-57	11,116	6,067	4,898	151	.553
Philadelphia	1876	60	14	45	1	.242

Extinct Franchise	Years	Total Games	Won	Lost	Tied	Pct.
Providence	1878-85	725	438	278	9	.610
St. Louis	1876-77	124	73	51	0	.589
St. Louis	1885-86	236	79	151	6	.347
Syracuse	1879	71	22	48	1	.317
Troy	1879-82	330	134	191	5	.414
Washington	1886-89	514	163	337	14	.331
Washington	1892-99	1,125	410	697	18	.372
Worcester	1880-82	252	90	159	3	.363
Extinct Totals		44,870	22,255	22,014	601	.503
National League Totals		163,354	81,035	81,035	1,284	.500

AMERICAN ASSOCIATION CLUBS (1882 THROUGH 1891)

Extinct Franchise	Years	Total Games	Won	Lost	Tied	Pct.
Baltimore	1882-89	944	403	519	22	.439
Baltimore	1890-91	174	87	81	6	.517
Boston	1891	139	93	42	4	.684
Brooklyn	1884-89	783	410	354	19	.536
Brooklyn	1890	101	26	74	1	.262
Cincinnati	1882-89	957	549	396	12	.580
Cincinnati	1891	102	43	57	2	.431
Cleveland	1887-88	268	89	174	5	.341
Columbus	1883-84	207	101	104	2	.493
Columbus	1889-91	418	200	209	9	.489
Indianapolis	1884	110	29	78	3	.277
Kansas City	1888-89	271	98	171	2	.365
Louisville	1882-91	1,233	575	638	20	.475
Milwaukee	1891	36	21	15	0	.583
New York	1883-87	592	270	309	13	.467
Philadelphia	1882-91	1,223	633	564	26	.528
Pittsburgh	1882-86	538	236	296	6	.444
Richmond	1884	46	12	30	4	.304
Rochester	1890	133	63	63	7	.500
St. Louis	1882-91	1,235	782	433	20	.641
Syracuse	1890	128	55	72	1	.434
Toledo	1884	110	46	58	6	.446
Toledo	1890	134	68	64	2	.515
Washington	1884	63	12	51	0	.191
Washington	1891	139	43	92	4	.324
American Association Totals		10,084	4,944	4,944	196	.500

☐ CLUBS WITH 13 STRAIGHT VICTORIES IN SEASON ☐

AMERICAN ASSOCIATION

Year Club	G	Home	Away
1887—St. Louis	15	15	0
1885—St. Louis	17	14	3
1889—Philadelphia (1 tie)	14	13	1

UNION ASSOCIATION

Year Club	G	Home	Away
1884—St. Louis	20	16	4
1884—Baltimore	16	7	9

AMERICAN LEAGUE

Year Club	G	Home	Away
1906—Chicago (1 tie)	19	11	8
1947—New York	19	6	13
1953—New York	18	3	15
1912—Washington	17	1	16
1931—Philadelphia	17	5	12
1926—New York	16	12	4
1977—Kansas City	16	9	7
1906—New York	15	12	3
1913—Philadelphia	15	13	2
1946—Boston	15	11	4
1960—New York	15	9	6
1991—Minnesota	15	10	5
1909—Detroit	14	14	0

Year Club	G	Home	Away
1916—St. Louis	14	13	1
1934—Detroit	14	9	5
1941—New York	14	6	8
1951—Chicago	14	3	11
1973—Baltimore	14	10	4
1988—Oakland	14	5	9
1991—Texas	14	7	7
1994—Kansas City	14	12	2
1908—Chicago	13	12	1
1910—Philadelphia (1 tie)	13	12	1
1927—Detroit (1 tie)	13	13	0
1931—Philadelphia	13	13	0
1933—Washington	13	1	12
1942—Cleveland	13	4	9
1948—Boston	13	12	1
1951—Cleveland	13	7	6
1954—New York	13	8	5
1961—New York	13	12	1
1978—Baltimore	13	3	10
1987—Milwaukee	13	6	7

NATIONAL LEAGUE

Year Club	G	Home	Away
1916—New York (1 tie)	26	26	0
1880—Chicago (1 tie)	21	11	10
1935—Chicago	21	18	3
1884—Providence	20	16	4
1885—Chicago	18	14	4
1891—Boston (1 tie)	18	16	2

Year	Club	G	Home	Away
1894—Baltimore		18	13	5
1904—New York		18	13	5
1897—Boston		17	16	1
1907—New York		17	14	3
1916—New York		17	0	17
1887—Philadelphia (1 tie)		16	5	11
1890—Philadelphia		16	14	2
1892—Philadelphia		16	11	5
1909—Pittsburgh		16	12	4
1912—New York		16	11	5
1951—New York		16	13	3
1886—Detroit		15	12	3
1903—Pittsburgh		15	11	4
1924—Brooklyn		15	3	12
1936—Chicago		15	11	4
1936—New York		15	7	8
1886—Chicago		14	13	1
1895—Baltimore		14	13	1
1899—Cincinnati		14	10	4
1903—Pittsburgh (1 tie)		14	7	7
1906—Chicago		14	14	0
1909—Pittsburgh		14	12	2
1913—New York		14	6	8
1932—Chicago		14	14	0
1935—St. Louis		14	12	2
1965—San Francisco		14	6	8
1880—Chicago		13	9	4
1890—Cincinnati		13	13	0
1892—Chicago		13	11	2
1905—New York		13	8	5
1911—Pittsburgh		13	9	4
1922—Pittsburgh		13	2	11
1928—Chicago		13	13	0
1938—Pittsburgh		13	5	8
1947—Brooklyn		13	2	11
1953—Brooklyn		13	7	6
1962—Los Angeles		13	8	5
1965—Los Angeles		13	7	6
1977—Philadelphia		13	8	5
1982—Atlanta		13	5	8
1991—Philadelphia		13	9	4
1992—Atlanta		13	3	10

☐ CLUBS WITH 13 STRAIGHT LOSSES IN SEASON ☐

AMERICAN ASSOCIATION

Year	Club	G	Home	Away
1889—Louisville		26	5	21
1890—Philadelphia		22	6	16
1882—Baltimore		15	0	15
1884—Washington		15	0	15

UNION ASSOCIATION

Year	Club	G	Home	Away
1884—Kansas City (1 tie)		15	3	12
1884—Kansas City		14	0	14

AMERICAN LEAGUE

Year	Club	G	Home	Away
1988—Baltimore		21	8	13
1906—Boston		20	19	1
1916—Philadelphia		20	1	19
1943—Philadelphia		20	3	17
1975—Detroit		19	9	10
1920—Philadelphia		18	0	18
1948—Washington		18	8	10
1959—Washington		18	3	15
1926—Boston		17	14	3
1907—Boston (2 ties)		16	9	7
1927—Boston		15	10	5
1937—Philadelphia		15	10	5
1972—Texas		15	5	10
1911—St. Louis		14	6	8

Year	Club	G	Home	Away
1930—Boston		14	3	11
1940—St. Louis		14	0	14
1945—Philadelphia		14	0	14
1953—St. Louis		14	14	0
1954—Baltimore		14	7	7
1961—Washington		14	11	3
1970—Washington		14	4	10
1977—Oakland		14	9	5
1982—Minnesota		14	6	8
1992—Seattle		14	4	10
1994—Milwaukee		14	6	8
1904—Washington (1 tie)		13	7	6
1913—New York		13	7	6
1920—Detroit		13	5	8
1924—Chicago		13	2	11
1935—Philadelphia		13	10	3
1936—St. Louis		13	2	11
1953—Detroit (2 ties)		13	12	1
1958—Washington		13	4	9
1959—Kansas City		13	4	9
1961—Minnesota		13	0	13
1962—Washington		13	7	6

NATIONAL LEAGUE

Year	Club	G	Home	Away
1899—Cleveland		24	3	21
1890—Pittsburgh		23	1	22
1961—Philadelphia		23	6	17
1894—Louisville		20	0	20
1969—Montreal		20	12	8
1906—Boston		19	3	16
1914—Cincinnati		19	6	13
1876—Cincinnati		18	9	9
1894—Louisville		18	0	18
1894—Washington		17	7	10
1962—New York		17	7	10
1977—Atlanta		17	8	9
1882—Troy		16	5	11
1884—Detroit		16	5	11
1885—Buffalo		16	12	4
1899—Cleveland		16	0	16
1907—Boston		16	5	11
1911—Boston		16	8	8
1944—Brooklyn		16	0	16
1909—Boston		15	0	15
1909—St. Louis		15	11	4
1927—Boston		15	0	15
1935—Boston		15	0	15
1963—New York		15	8	7
1982—New York		15	6	9
1878—Milwaukee		14	7	7
1882—Worcester		14	2	12
1883—Philadelphia		14	4	10
1896—St. Louis		14	5	9
1899—Cleveland		14	0	14
1911—Boston		14	14	0
1916—St. Louis		14	0	14
1935—Boston		14	4	10
1936—Philadelphia		14	10	4
1937—Brooklyn		14	0	14
1937—Cincinnati		14	10	4
1885—Providence		13	2	11
1886—Washington		13	13	0
1902—New York		13	5	8
1909—Boston		13	13	0
1910—St. Louis		13	5	8
1919—Philadelphia		13	0	13
1919—Philadelphia		13	7	6
1930—Cincinnati		13	1	12
1942—Philadelphia		13	4	9
1944—Chicago		13	7	6
1944—New York		13	0	13
1945—Cincinnati		13	2	11
1955—Philadelphia		13	9	4
1962—New York		13	9	4

Year	Club	G	Home	Away
1976—Atlanta		13	6	7
1980—New York		13	3	10
1982—Chicago		13	7	6
1985—Chicago		13	4	9
1993—Colorado		13	7	6
1994—San Diego		13	4	9

GAMES OF 18 OR MORE INNINGS
AMERICAN LEAGUE

25 Innings—(1)

Chicago 7 vs. Milwaukee 6, May 8, finished May 9, 1984.

24 Innings—(2)

Philadelphia 4 at Boston 1, September 1, 1906.
Detroit 1 at Philadelphia 1 (tie), July 21, 1945.

22 Innings—(4)

New York 9 at Detroit 7, June 24, 1962.
Washington 6 vs. Chicago 5, June 12, 1967.
Milwaukee 4 at Minnesota 3, May 12, finished May 13, 1972.
Minnesota 5 vs. Cleveland 4, August 31, 1993.

21 Innings—(3)

Detroit 6 at Chicago 5, May 24, 1929.
Oakland 5 at Washington 3, June 4, 1971.
Chicago 6 vs. Cleveland 3, May 26, finished May 28, 1973.

20 Innings—(8)

Philadelphia 4 at Boston 2, July 4, 1905, p.m. game.
Washington 9 at Minnesota 7, August 9, 1967.
New York 4 vs. Boston 3, August 29, 1967, second game.
Boston 5 at Seattle 3, July 27, 1969.
Oakland 1 vs. California 0, July 9, 1971.
Washington 8 at Cleveland 6, September 14, second game, finished September 20, 1971 (game completed at Washington).
Seattle 8 at Boston 7, September 3, finished September 4, 1981.
California 4 vs. Seattle 3, April 13, finished April 14, 1982.

19 Innings—(15)

Washington 5 at Philadelphia 4, September 27, 1912.
Chicago 5 at Cleveland 4, June 24, 1915.
Cleveland 3 at New York 2, May 24, 1918.
St. Louis 8 at Washington 6, August 9, 1921.
Chicago 5 vs. Boston 4, July 13, 1951.
Cleveland 4 vs. St. Louis 3, July 1, 1952.
Cleveland 3 vs. Washington 2, June 14, 1963, second game.
Baltimore 7 vs. Washington 5, June 4, 1967.
Kansas City 6 at Detroit 5, June 17, 1967, second game.
Detroit 3 at New York 3 (tie), August 23, 1968, second game.
Oakland 5 vs. Chicago 3, August 10, finished August 11, 1972.
New York 5 vs. Minnesota 4, August 25, 1976.
Cleveland 8 at Detroit 4, April 27, 1984.
Milwaukee 10 vs. Chicago 9, May 1, 1991.
Boston 7 at Cleveland 5, April 11, 1992.

18 Innings—(21)

Chicago 6 vs. New York 6 (tie), June 25, 1903.
Washington 0 at Detroit 0 (tie), July 16, 1909.
Washington 1 vs. Chicago 0, May 15, 1918.
Detroit 7 vs. Washington 6, August 4, 1918.
Boston 12 vs. New York 11, September 5, 1927, first game.
Philadelphia 18 at Cleveland 17, July 10, 1932.
New York 3 at Chicago 3 (tie), August 21, 1933.
Washington 1 at Chicago 0, June 8, 1947, first game.
Washington 5 at St. Louis 5 (tie), June 20, 1952.
Chicago 1 at Baltimore 1 (tie), August 6, 1959.
New York 7 vs. Boston 6, April 16, 1967.
Minnesota 3 at New York 2, July 26, 1967, second game.
Baltimore 3 vs. Boston 2, August 25, 1968.
Minnesota 11 at Seattle 7, July 19, finished July 20, 1969.
Oakland 9 vs. Baltimore 8, August 24, 1969, second game.

Minnesota 8 at Oakland 6, September 6, 1969.
Washington 2 vs. New York 1, April 22, 1970.
Texas 4 at Kansas City 3, May 17, 1972.
Detroit 4 vs. Cleveland 3, June 9, finished September 24, 1982.
New York 5 vs. Detroit 4, September 11, 1988.
Kansas City 4 vs. Texas 3, June 6, 1991.

NATIONAL LEAGUE

26 Innings—(1)

Brooklyn 1 at Boston 1 (tie), May 1, 1920.

25 Innings—(1)

St. Louis 4 at New York 3, September 11, 1974.

24 Innings—(1)

Houston 1 vs. New York 0, April 25, 1968.

23 Innings—(2)

Brooklyn 2 at Boston 2 (tie), June 27, 1939.
San Francisco 8 at New York 6, May 31, 1964, second game.

22 Innings—(4)

Brooklyn 6 vs. Pittsburgh 5, August 22, 1917.
Chicago 4 at Boston 3, May 17, 1927.
Houston 5 vs. Los Angeles 4, June 3, 1989.
Los Angeles 1 at Montreal 0, August 23, 1989.

21 Innings—(7)

New York 3 at Pittsburgh 1, July 17, 1914.
Chicago 2 vs. Philadelphia 1, July 17, 1918.
Pittsburgh 2 at Boston 0, August 1, 1918.
San Francisco 1 at Cincinnati 0, September 1, 1967.
Houston 2 at San Diego 1, September 24, 1971, first game.
San Diego 11 at Montreal 8, May 21, 1977.
Los Angeles 2 at Chicago 1, August 17, finished August 18, 1982.

20 Innings—(9)

Chicago 7 at Cincinnati 7 (tie), June 30, 1892.
Chicago 2 at Philadelphia 1, August 24, 1905.
Brooklyn 9 at Philadelphia 9 (tie), April 30, 1919.
St. Louis 8 at Chicago 7, August 28, 1930.
Brooklyn 6 at Boston 2, July 5, 1940.
Philadelphia 5 vs. Atlanta 4, May 4, 1973.
Pittsburgh 5 vs. Chicago 4, July 6, 1980.
Houston 3 at San Diego 1, August 15, 1980.
Philadelphia 7 vs. Los Angeles 6, July 7, 1993.

19 Innings—(16)

Chicago 3 vs. Pittsburgh 2, June 22, 1902.
Pittsburgh 7 at Boston 6, July 31, 1912.
Chicago 4 vs. Brooklyn 3, June 17, 1915.
St. Louis 8 at Philadelphia 8 (tie), June 13, 1918.
Boston 2 vs. Brooklyn 1, May 3, 1920.
Chicago 3 vs. Boston 2, August 17, 1932.
Brooklyn 9 at Chicago 9 (tie), May 17, 1939.
Cincinnati 0 at Brooklyn 0 (tie), September 11, 1946.
Philadelphia 8 vs. Cincinnati 7, September 15, 1950, second game.
Pittsburgh 4 vs. Milwaukee 3, July 19, 1955.
Cincinnati 2 vs. Los Angeles 1, August 8, 1972.
New York 7 at Los Angeles 3, May 24, 1973.
Pittsburgh 4 at San Diego 3, August 25, 1979.
New York 16 at Atlanta 13, July 4, 1985.
Montreal 6 at Houston 3, July 7, 1985.
Atlanta 7 at St. Louis 5, May 14, 1988.

18 Innings—(31)

Providence 1 vs. Detroit 0, August 17, 1882.
Brooklyn 7 at St. Louis 7 (tie), August 17, 1902.
Chicago 2 at St. Louis 1, June 24, 1905.
Pittsburgh 3 at Chicago 2, June 28, 1916, second game.
Philadelphia 10 at Brooklyn 9, June 1, 1919.
New York 9 at Pittsburgh 8, July 7, 1922.
Chicago 7 at Boston 2, May 14, 1927.
New York 1 vs. St. Louis 0, July 2, 1933, first game.
St. Louis 8 at Cincinnati 6, July 1, 1934, first game.
Chicago 10 at Cincinnati 8, August 9, 1942, first game.

Philadelphia 4 vs. Pittsburgh 3, June 9, 1949.
Cincinnati 7 vs. Chicago 6, September 7, 1951.
Philadelphia 0 at New York 0 (tie), October 2, 1965, second game.
Cincinnati 3 at Chicago 2, July 19, 1966.
Philadelphia 2 vs. Cincinnati 1, May 21, 1967.
Pittsburgh 1 at San Diego 0, June 7, 1972, second game.
New York 3 vs. Philadelphia 2, August 1, 1972, first game.
Montreal 5 at Chicago 4, June 27, 1973, finished June 28, 1973.
Chicago 8 at Montreal 7, June 28, 1974, first game.
New York 4 vs. Montreal 3, September 16, 1975.
Pittsburgh 2 vs. Chicago 1, August 10, 1977.
Chicago 9 vs. Cincinnati 8, May 10, finished July 23.
Houston 3 vs. New York 2, June 18, 1979.
San Diego 8 at New York 6, August 26, 1980.
St. Louis 3 at Houston 1, May 27, 1983.
Pittsburgh 4 vs. San Francisco 3, July 13, 1984, second game.
Atlanta 3 at Los Angeles 2, September 6, 1984.
New York 5 vs. Pittsburgh 4, April 28, 1985.
San Francisco 5 at Atlanta 4, June 11, 1985.
Houston 8 at Chicago 7, September 2, finished September 3, 1986.
Pittsburgh 5 vs. Chicago 4, August 6, 1989.

NON-PLAYING PERSONNEL

COMMISSIONERS

Kenesaw Landis, January 12, 1921 to November 25, 1944.
Happy Chandler, April 24, 1945 to July 15, 1951.
Ford Frick, October 8, 1951 through December 14, 1965.

William Eckert, December 15, 1965 to February 4, 1969.
Bowie Kuhn, February 4, 1969 through September 30, 1984.
Peter Ueberroth, October 1, 1984 through March 31, 1989.
Bart Giamatti, April 1 through September 1, 1989.
Fay Vincent, September 2, 1989 through September 7, 1992.

PRESIDENTS

NATIONAL LEAGUE

Morgan Bulkeley, 1876.
William Hulbert, 1876 to 1882.
Arthur Soden, 1882.
A. G. Mills, 1882 to 1884.
Nicholas Young, 1884 to 1902.
Harry Pullman, 1902 to July 29, 1909.
John Heydler, July 30, 1909 to December 15, 1909.
Thomas Lynch, December 15, 1909 to December 9, 1913.
John Tener, December 9, 1913 to August 6, 1918.
John Heydler, December 10, 1918 to December 11, 1934.
Ford Frick, December 11, 1934 to October 8, 1951.
Warren Giles, October 8, 1951 through December 31, 1969.
Chub Feeney, January 1, 1970 to December 11, 1986.
Bart Giamatti, December 11, 1986 through March 31, 1989.
Bill White, April 1, 1989 through February 28, 1994.
Leonard Coleman Jr., March 1, 1994 to present.

AMERICAN LEAGUE

Byron Bancroft Johnson, 1901 to October 17, 1927.
Ernest Barnard, October 31, 1927 to March 27, 1931.
Will Harridge, May 27, 1931 through January 31, 1959.
Joe Cronin, February 1, 1959 through 1973.
Lee MacPhail Jr., January 1, 1974 through 1983.
Bobby Brown, 1984 through July 31, 1994.
Gene Budig, August 1, 1994 to present.

AMERICAN LEAGUE TEAM RECORDS

BALTIMORE ORIOLES

YEARLY FINISHES

Year	Position	W	L	Pct.	*GB	Manager	Attendance
1954	7th	54	100	.351	57	Jimmie Dykes	1,060,910
1955	5th	57	97	.370	39	Paul Richards	852,039
1956	6th	69	85	.448	28	Paul Richards	901,201
1957	5th	76	76	.500	21	Paul Richards	1,029,581
1958	6th	74	79	.484	17½	Paul Richards	829,991
1959	6th	74	80	.481	20	Paul Richards	891,926
1960	2nd	89	65	.578	8	Paul Richards	1,187,849
1961	3rd	95	67	.586	14	Paul Richards, Luman Harris	951,089
1962	7th	77	85	.475	19	Billy Hitchcock	790,254
1963	4th	86	76	.531	18½	Billy Hitchcock	774,343
1964	3rd	97	65	.599	2	Hank Bauer	1,116,215
1965	3rd	94	68	.580	8	Hank Bauer	781,649
1966	1st	97	63	.606	+ 9	Hank Bauer	1,203,366
1967	6th (tied)	76	85	.472	15½	Hank Bauer	955,053
1968	2nd	91	71	.562	12	Hank Bauer, Earl Weaver	943,977

EAST DIVISION

Year	Position	W	L	Pct.	*GB	Manager	Attendance
1969	1st†	109	53	.673	+19	Earl Weaver	1,058,168
1970	1st†	108	54	.667	+15	Earl Weaver	1,057,069
1971	1st†	101	57	.639	+12	Earl Weaver	1,023,037
1972	3rd	80	74	.519	5	Earl Weaver	899,950
1973	1st‡	97	65	.599	+ 8	Earl Weaver	958,667
1974	1st‡	91	71	.562	+ 2	Earl Weaver	962,572
1975	2nd	90	69	.566	4½	Earl Weaver	1,002,157
1976	2nd	88	74	.543	10½	Earl Weaver	1,058,609
1977	2nd (tied)	97	64	.602	2½	Earl Weaver	1,195,769
1978	4th	90	71	.559	9	Earl Weaver	1,051,724
1979	1st†	102	57	.642	+ 8	Earl Weaver	1,681,009
1980	2nd	100	62	.617	3	Earl Weaver	1,797,438
1981	2nd/4th	59	46	.562	§	Earl Weaver	1,024,652
1982	2nd	94	68	.580	1	Earl Weaver	1,613,031
1983	1st†	98	64	.605	+ 6	Joe Altobelli	2,042,071
1984	5th	85	77	.525	19	Joe Altobelli	2,045,784
1985	4th	83	78	.516	16	Joe Altobelli, Earl Weaver	2,132,387
1986	7th	73	89	.451	22½	Earl Weaver	1,973,176
1987	6th	67	95	.414	31	Cal Ripken Sr.	1,835,692
1988	7th	54	107	.335	34½	Cal Ripken Sr., Frank Robinson	1,660,738
1989	2nd	87	75	.537	2	Frank Robinson	2,535,208
1990	5th	76	85	.472	11½	Frank Robinson	2,415,189
1991	6th	67	95	.414	24	Frank Robinson, Johnny Oates	2,552,753
1992	3rd	89	73	.549	7	Johnny Oates	3,567,819
1993	3rd (tied)	85	77	.525	10	Johnny Oates	3,644,965
1994	2nd	63	49	.563	6½	Johnny Oates	2,535,359

*Games behind winner. †Won Championship Series. ‡Lost Championship Series. §First half 31-23; second 28-23.

INDIVIDUAL RECORDS (1954 TO DATE)

SERVICE

Most years by non-pitcher
23—Brooks Robinson
Most years by pitcher
19—Jim Palmer

BATTING

Most games
163—Brooks Robinson, 1961, 1964
Most games, career
2,896—Brooks Robinson
Most at-bats
668—Brooks Robinson, 163 games, 1961

Most at-bats, career
10,654—Brooks Robinson
Most runs
122—Frank Robinson, 155 games, 1966
Most runs, career
1,232—Brooks Robinson
Most hits
211—Cal Ripken Jr., 162 games, 1983
Most hits, career
2,848—Brooks Robinson
Most singles
158—Al Bumbry, 160 games, 1980
Most singles, career
2,030—Brooks Robinson

Most doubles
47—Cal Ripken Jr., 162 games, 1983
Most doubles, career
482—Brooks Robinson
Most triples
12—Paul Blair, 151 games, 1967
Most triples, career
68—Brooks Robinson
Most homers by lefthander
46—Jim Gentile, 148 games, 1961
Most homers by righthander
49—Frank Robinson, 155 games, 1966
Most homers by switch-hitter
35—Ken Singleton, 159 games, 1979
Most homers by rookie
28—Cal Ripken Jr., 160 games, 1982
Most homers at home
27—Frank Robinson, 1966
Most homers on road
30—Jim Gentile, 1961
Most homers, month
15—Jim Gentile, August, 1961
Most homers by switch-hitter, career
333—Eddie Murray
Most homers by righthander, career
310—Cal Ripken Jr.
Most homers by lefthander, career
303—Boog Powell
Most grand slams
5—Jim Gentile, 148 games, 1961
Most grand slams, career
14—Eddie Murray
Most total bases
368—Cal Ripken Jr., 162 games, 1991
Most total bases, career
4,270—Brooks Robinson
Most long hits
85—Frank Robinson, 155 games, 1966
        Cal Ripken Jr., 162 games, 1991
Most long hits, career
818—Brooks Robinson
Most extra bases on long hits
185—Frank Robinson, 155 games, 1966
Most extra bases on long hits, career
1,422—Brooks Robinson
Most sacrifice hits
23—Mark Belanger, 152 games, 1975
Most sacrifice flies
11—Cal Ripken Jr., 162 games, 1987
Most bases on balls
118—Ken Singleton, 155 games, 1975
Most bases on balls, career
889—Boog Powell
Most strikeouts
160—Mickey Tettleton, 135 games, 1990
Most strikeouts, career
1,102—Boog Powell
Fewest strikeouts
19—Rich Dauer, 152 games, 1980
Most hit by pitch
20—Bobby Grich, 160 games, 1974
Most runs batted in
141—Jim Gentile, 148 games, 1961
Most runs batted in, career
1,357—Brooks Robinson
Most game-winning RBIs
20—Eddie Murray, 151 games, 1982
Highest batting average
.328—Ken Singleton, 152 games, 1977
Highest batting average, career
.303—Bob Nieman
Highest slugging average
.646—Jim Gentile, 148 games, 1961
Highest slugging average, career
.543—Frank Robinson
Longest batting streak
24 games—Rafael Palmeiro, 1994

Most grounded into double play
32—Cal Ripken Jr., 161 games, 1985
Fewest grounded into double play
2—Mark Belanger, 152 games, 1975
        Brady Anderson, 159 games, 1992

BASERUNNING

Most stolen bases
57—Luis Aparicio, 146 games, 1964
Most stolen bases, career
252—Al Bumbry
Most caught stealing
18—Don Buford, 144 games, 1969

PITCHING

Most games
76—Tippy Martinez, 1982
Most games, career
558—Jim Palmer
Most games started
40—Dave McNally, 1969
        Mike Cuellar, 1970
        Dave McNally, 1970
        Jim Palmer, 1976
        Mike Flanagan, 1978
Most games started, career
521—Jim Palmer
Most complete games
25—Jim Palmer, 1975
Most complete games, career
211—Jim Palmer
Most games finished
62—Gregg Olson, 1991
Most innings
323—Jim Palmer, 1975
Most innings, career
3,947 ⅓ —Jim Palmer
Most games won
25—Steve Stone, 1980
Most games won, career
268—Jim Palmer
Most 20-victory seasons
8—Jim Palmer
Most games, lost
21—Don Larsen, 1954
Most games lost, career
152—Jim Palmer
Highest winning percentage
.808—Dave McNally (21-5), 1971
Longest winning streak
15 games—Dave McNally, 1969
Longest winning streak over two seasons
17 games—Dave McNally, 1968 (2), 1969 (15)
Longest losing streak
10—Jay Tibbs, 1988
Longest losing streak over two seasons
13—Mike Boddicker, 1987 (5), 1988 (8)
Most saves
37—Gregg Olson, 1990
Most bases on balls
181—Bob Turley, 1954
Most bases on balls, career
1,311—Jim Palmer
Most strikeouts
202—Dave McNally, 1968
Most strikeouts, career
2,212—Jim Palmer
Most strikeouts, game
14—Bob Turley, April 21, 1954
        Connie Johnson, September 2, 1957, second game
        Mike Mussina, May 16, 1993
Most shutouts
10—Jim Palmer, 1975
Most shutouts, career
53—Jim Palmer

Most 1-0 shutouts won
3—Mike Cuellar, 1974
    Ross Grimsley, 1974
    Jim Palmer, 1975, 1978
Most runs
129—Dennis Martinez, 1979
Most earned runs
126—Mike Flanagan, 1978
Most hits
279—Dennis Martinez, 1979
Most wild pitches
14—Milt Pappas, 1959

Most hits batsmen
15—Chuck Estrada, 1960
Most home runs
35—Robin Roberts, 1963
    Scott McGregor, 1986
Most sacrifice hits
20—Mike Cuellar, 1975
Most sacrifice flies
14—Jim Palmer, 1976
Lowest ERA
1.95—Dave McNally, 273 innings, 1968

CLUB RECORDS

Most players
54 in 1955
Fewest players
30 in 1969
Most games
163 in 1961, 1964, 1982
Most at-bats
5,604 in 1991
Most runs
818 in 1985
Fewest runs
483 in 1954
Most opponents' runs
880 in 1987
Most hits
1,523 in 1980
Fewest hits
1,153 in 1972
Most singles
1,080 in 1980
Most doubles
287 in 1993
Most triples
49 in 1954
Most homers
214 in 1985
Fewest homers
52 in 1954
Most homers at Memorial Stadium, home and opponents
235 in 1987
Most homers at Oriole Park at Camden Yards, home and opponents
168 in 1993
Most grand slams
8 in 1979, 1982, 1983, 1984
Most pinch home runs
11 in 1982
Most long hits
478 in 1983
Most extra bases on long hits
920 in 1985
Most total bases
2,371 in 1985
Most sacrifice hits
110 in 1957
Most sacrifice flies
59 in 1969, 1992
Most stolen bases
150 in 1976
Most caught stealing
64 in 1973
Most bases on balls
717 in 1970
Most strikeouts
1,019 in 1964, 1968
Fewest strikeouts
634 in 1954
Most hit by pitch
58 in 1974
Fewest hit by pitch
19 in 1955, 1985
Most runs batted in
773 in 1985

Most game-winning RBIs
95 in 1980, 1983
Highest batting average
.273 in 1980
Lowest batting average
.225 in 1968
Highest slugging average
.430 in 1985
Lowest slugging average
.320 in 1955
Most grounded into double play
159 in 1986
Fewest grounded into double play
102 in 1968
Most left on bases
1,262 in 1970
Fewest left on bases
1,043 in 1972
Most .300 hitters
3 in 1980
Most putouts
4,436 in 1970
Fewest putouts
4,082 in 1956
Most assists
1,974 in 1975
Fewest assists
1,516 in 1958
Most chances accepted
6,344 in 1974
Fewest chances accepted
5,625 in 1958
Most errors
167 in 1955
Fewest errors
87 in 1989
Most errorless games
93 in 1989
Most consecutive errorless games
13 in 1991
Most double plays
189 in 1977
Fewest double plays
131 in 1968
Most passed balls
49 in 1959
Fewest passed balls
4 in 1985
Highest fielding average
.986 in 1989
Lowest fielding average
.972 in 1955
Highest home attendance
3,644,965 in 1993
Highest road attendance
2,190,759 in 1993
Most games won
109 in 1969
Most games lost
107 in 1988
Most games won, month
25 in June 1966

Most games lost, month
25 in August 1954
Highest percentage games won
.673 in 1969 (won 109, lost 53)
Lowest percentage games won
.335 in 1988 (won 54, lost 107)
Games won, league
3,439 in 41 years
Games lost, league
3,011 in 41 years
Most shutouts won
21 in 1961
Most shutouts lost
22 in 1955
Most 1-0 games won
8 in 1974
Most 1-0 games lost
5 in 1973
Most consecutive games won
14 in 1973
Most consecutive games lost
21 in 1988
Number of times league champions
6
Number of last-place finishes
1
Most runs, game
19 vs. Cleveland, August 28, 1957
Most runs by opponent, game
24 by Toronto, June 26, 1978

Most runs, shutout game
17 vs. Chicago, July 27, 1969
Most runs by opponent, shutout game
16 by New York, April 30, 1960
Most runs doubleheader shutout
13 vs. Washington, July 9, 1959
Most runs, inning
10 vs. New York, July 8, 1969, first game, fourth inning
vs. Oakland, April 29, 1979, seventh inning
vs. Seattle, August 21, 1985, third inning
Longest 1-0 game won
17 innings vs. Milwaukee, September 27, 1974
Longest 1-0 game lost
15 innings vs. Cleveland, May 14, 1961, first game
Most hits, game
26 vs. California, August 28, 1980
Most home runs, game
7 vs. Boston, May 17, 1967
vs. California, August 26, 1985
Most consecutive games with one or more homers
17 (30 homers), 1994
Most total bases, game
40 vs. California, April 27, 1994
Largest crowd, day game
52,395 vs. Milwaukee, April 4, 1988
Largest crowd, doubleheader
51,883 vs. Milwaukee, October 1, 1982
Largest crowd, night game
52,159 vs. Boston, June 27, 1986
Largest crowd, home opener
52,395 vs. Milwaukee, April 4, 1988

BOSTON RED SOX

YEARLY FINISHES

Year	Position	W	L	Pct.	*GB	Manager	Attendance
1901—2nd		79	57	.581	4	Jimmy Collins	289,448
1902—3rd		77	60	.562	6½	Jimmy Collins	348,567
1903—1st		91	47	.659	+14½	Jimmy Collins	379,338
1904—1st		95	59	.617	+ 1½	Jimmy Collins	623,295
1905—4th		78	74	.513	16	Jimmy Collins	468,828
1906—8th		49	105	.318	45½	Jimmy Collins, Chick Stahl	410,209
1907—7th		59	90	.396	32½	George Huff, Bob Unglaub, Deacon McGuire	436,777
1908—5th		75	79	.487	15½	Deacon McGuire, Fred Lake	473,048
1909—3rd		88	63	.583	9½	Fred Lake	668,965
1910—4th		81	72	.529	22½	Patsy Donovan	584,619
1911—5th		78	75	.510	24	Patsy Donovan	503,961
1912—1st		105	47	.691	+14	Jake Stahl	597,096
1913—4th		79	71	.527	15½	Jake Stahl, Bill Carrigan	437,194
1914—2nd		91	62	.595	8½	Bill Carrigan	481,359
1915—1st		101	50	.669	+ 2½	Bill Carrigan	539,885
1916—1st		91	63	.591	+ 2	Bill Carrigan	496,397
1917—2nd		90	62	.592	9	Jack Barry	387,856
1918—1st		75	51	.595	+ 2½	Ed Barrow	249,513
1919—6th		66	71	.482	20½	Ed Barrow	417,291
1920—5th		72	81	.471	25½	Ed Barrow	402,445
1921—5th		75	79	.487	23½	Hugh Duffy	279,273
1922—8th		61	93	.396	33	Hugh Duffy	259,184
1923—8th		61	91	.401	37	Frank Chance	229,668
1924—7th		67	87	.435	25	Lee Fohl	448,556
1925—8th		47	105	.309	49½	Lee Fohl	267,782
1926—8th		46	107	.301	44½	Lee Fohl	285,155
1927—8th		51	103	.331	59	Bill Carrigan	305,275
1928—8th		57	96	.373	43½	Bill Carrigan	396,920
1929—8th		58	96	.377	48	Bill Carrigan	394,620
1930—8th		52	102	.338	50	Heinie Wagner	444,045
1931—6th		62	90	.408	45	Shano Collins	350,975
1932—8th		43	111	.279	64	Shano Collins, Marty McManus	182,150
1933—7th		63	86	.423	34½	Marty McManus	268,715
1934—4th		76	76	.500	24	Bucky Harris	610,640
1935—4th		78	75	.510	16	Joseph Cronin	558,568
1936—6th		74	80	.481	28½	Joe Cronin	626,895
1937—5th		80	72	.526	21	Joe Cronin	559,659
1938—2nd		88	61	.591	9½	Joe Cronin	646,459
1939—2nd		89	62	.589	17	Joe Cronin	573,070

Year	Position	W	L	Pct.	*GB	Manager	Attendance
1940	4th (tied)	82	72	.532	8	Joe Cronin	716,234
1941	2nd	84	70	.545	17	Joe Cronin	718,497
1942	2nd	93	59	.612	9	Joe Cronin	730,340
1943	7th	68	84	.447	29	Joe Cronin	358,275
1944	4th	77	77	.500	12	Joe Cronin	506,975
1945	7th	71	83	.461	17½	Joe Cronin	603,794
1946	1st	104	50	.675	+12	Joe Cronin	1,416,944
1947	3rd	83	71	.539	14	Joe Cronin	1,427,315
1948	2nd†	96	59	.619	1	Joe McCarthy	1,558,798
1949	2nd	96	58	.623	1	Joe McCarthy	1,596,650
1950	3rd	94	60	.610	4	Joe McCarthy, Steve O'Neill	1,344,080
1951	3rd	87	67	.565	11	Steve O'Neill	1,312,282
1952	6th	76	78	.494	19	Lou Boudreau	1,115,750
1953	4th	84	69	.549	16	Lou Boudreau	1,026,133
1954	4th	69	85	.448	42	Lou Boudreau	931,127
1955	4th	84	70	.545	12	Pinky Higgins	1,203,200
1956	4th	84	70	.545	13	Pinky Higgins	1,137,158
1957	3rd	82	72	.532	16	Pinky Higgins	1,181,087
1958	3rd	79	75	.513	13	Pinky Higgins	1,077,047
1959	5th	75	79	.487	19	Pinky Higgins, Billy Jurges	984,102
1960	7th	65	89	.422	32	Billy Jurges, Pinky Higgins	1,129,866
1961	6th	76	86	.469	33	Pinky Higgins	850,589
1962	8th	76	84	.475	19	Pinky Higgins	733,080
1963	7th	76	85	.472	28	Johnny Pesky	942,642
1964	8th	72	90	.444	27	Johnny Pesky, Billy Herman	883,276
1965	9th	62	100	.383	40	Billy Herman	652,201
1966	9th	72	90	.444	26	Billy Herman, Pete Runnels	811,172
1967	1st	92	70	.568	+ 1	Dick Williams	1,727,832
1968	4th	86	76	.531	17	Dick Williams	1,940,788

EAST DIVISION

Year	Position	W	L	Pct.	*GB	Manager	Attendance
1969	3rd	87	75	.537	22	Dick Williams, Eddie Popowski	1,833,246
1970	3rd	87	75	.537	21	Eddie Kasko	1,595,278
1971	3rd	85	77	.525	18	Eddie Kasko	1,678,732
1972	2nd	85	70	.548	½	Eddie Kasko	1,441,718
1973	2nd	89	73	.549	8	Eddie Kasko	1,481,002
1974	3rd	84	78	.519	7	Darrell Johnson	1,556,411
1975	1st‡	95	65	.594	+ 4½	Darrell Johnson	1,748,587
1976	3rd	83	79	.512	15½	Darrell Johnson, Don Zimmer	1,895,846
1977	2nd (tied)	97	64	.602	2½	Don Zimmer	2,074,549
1978	2nd §	99	64	.607	1	Don Zimmer	2,320,643
1979	3rd	91	69	.569	11½	Don Zimmer	2,353,114
1980	4th	83	77	.519	19	Don Zimmer, Johnny Pesky	1,956,092
1981	5th/2nd (tied)	59	49	.546	★	Ralph Houk	1,060,379
1982	3rd	89	73	.549	6	Ralph Houk	1,950,124
1983	6th	78	84	.481	20	Ralph Houk	1,782,285
1984	4th	86	76	.531	18	Ralph Houk	1,661,618
1985	5th	81	81	.500	18½	John McNamara	1,786,633
1986	1st‡	95	66	.590	+ 5½	John McNamara	2,147,641
1987	5th	78	84	.481	20	John McNamara	2,231,551
1988	1st •	89	73	.549	+ 1	John McNamara, Joe Morgan	2,464,851
1989	3rd	83	79	.512	6	Joe Morgan	2,510,012
1990	1st •	88	74	.543	+ 2	Joe Morgan	2,528,986
1991	2nd (tied)	84	78	.519	7	Joe Morgan	2,562,435
1992	7th	73	89	.451	23	Butch Hobson	2,468,574
1993	5th	80	82	.494	15	Butch Hobson	2,422,021
1994	4th	54	61	.470	17	Butch Hobson	1,775,818

*Games behind winner. †Lost pennant playoff. ‡Won Championship Series. §Lost division playoff. ★First half 30-26; second 29-23. •Lost Championship Series.

INDIVIDUAL RECORDS (1901 TO DATE)

SERVICE

Most years by non-pitcher
23—Carl Yastrzemski
Most years by pitcher
13—Bob Stanley

BATTING

Most games
163—Jim Rice, 1978
Most games, career
3,308—Carl Yastrzemski

Most at-bats
677—Jim Rice, 163 games, 1978
Most at-bats, career
11,988—Carl Yastrzemski
Most runs
150—Ted Williams, 155 games, 1949
Most runs, career
1,816—Carl Yastrzemski
Most hits
240—Wade Boggs, 161 games, 1985
Most hits, career
3,419—Carl Yastrzemski

Most singles
187—Wade Boggs, 161 games, 1985
Most singles, career
2,262—Carl Yastrzemski
Most doubles
67—Earl Webb, 151 games, 1931
Most doubles, career
646—Carl Yastrzemski
Most triples
22—Chick Stahl, 157 games, 1904
Tris Speaker, 141 games, 1913
Most triples, career
130—Harry Hooper
Most homers by righthander
50—Jimmie Foxx, 149 games, 1938
Most homers by lefthander
44—Carl Yastrzemski, 161 games, 1967
Most homers by rookie
34—Walt Dropo, 136 games, 1950
Most homers at home
35—Jimmie Foxx, 1938
Most homers on road
26—Ted Williams, 1957
Most homers, month
14—Jackie Jensen, June, 1958
Most homers by righthander, career
382—Jim Rice
Most homers by lefthander, career
521—Ted Williams
Most grand slams
4—Babe Ruth, 130 games, 1919
Most grand slams, career
17—Ted Williams
Most total bases
406—Jim Rice, 163 games, 1978
Most total bases, career
5,539—Carl Yastrzemski
Most long hits
92—Jimmie Foxx, 149 games, 1938
Most long hits, career
1,157—Carl Yastrzemski
Most extra bases on long hits
201—Jimmie Foxx, 149 games, 1938
Most extra bases on long hits, career
2,230—Ted Williams
Most sacrifices (sacrifice hits and sacrifice flies)
54—Jack Barry, 116 games, 1917
Most sacrifice hits
35—Freddy Parent, 153 games, 1905
Most sacrifice flies
12—Jackie Jensen, 152 games, 1955
Jimmy Piersall, 155 games, 1956
Jackie Jensen, 148 games, 1959
Most bases on balls
162—Ted Williams, 156 games, 1947
Ted Williams, 155 games, 1949
Most bases on balls, career
2,019—Ted Williams
Most strikeouts
162—Butch Hobson, 159 games, 1977
Most strikeouts, career
1,423—Jim Rice
Fewest strikeouts
9—Stuffy McInnis, 152 games, 1921
Most hit by pitch
35—Don Baylor, 1986
Most runs batted in
175—Jimmie Foxx, 149 games, 1938
Most runs batted in, career
1,844—Carl Yastrzemski
Most game-winning RBIs
23—Mike Greenwell, 158 games, 1988
Most consecutive games with RBI
12—Ted Williams (18 RBIs), 1942
Joe Cronin (19 RBIs), 1939
Highest batting average
.406—Ted Williams, 143 games, 1941

Highest batting average, career
.344—Ted Williams
Highest slugging average
.735—Ted Williams, 143 games, 1941
Highest slugging average, career
.634—Ted Williams
Longest batting streak
34 games—Dom DiMaggio, 1949
Most grounded into double play
36—Jim Rice, 159 games, 1984
Fewest grounded into double play
3—Tony Lupien, 154 games, 1943

BASERUNNING

Most stolen bases
54—Tommy Harper, 147 games, 1973
Most stolen bases, career
300—Harry Hooper
Most caught stealing
19—Mike Menosky, 141 games, 1920

PITCHING

Most games
80—Greg Harris, 1993
Most games, career
637—Bob Stanley
Most games started
43—Cy Young, 1902
Most games started, career
325—Roger Clemens
Most complete games
41—Cy Young, 1902
Most complete games, career
275—Cy Young
Most games finished
67—Dick Radatz, 1964
Most innings
386—Cy Young, 1902
Most innings, career
2,730—Cy Young
Most games won
34—Smokey Joe Wood, 1912
Most games won, career
193—Cy Young
Most 20-victory seasons
6—Cy Young
Most games lost
25—Red Ruffing, 1928
Most games lost, career
112—Cy Young
Highest winning percentage
.882—Bob Stanley (15-2), 1978
Longest winning streak
16 games—Smokey Joe Wood, 1912
Longest losing streak
14 games—Joe W. Harris, 1906
Most saves
40—Jeff Reardon, 1991
Most bases on balls
134—Mel Parnell, 1949
Most bases on balls, career
758—Mel Parnell
Most strikeouts
291—Roger Clemens, 1988
Most strikeouts, career
2,201—Roger Clemens
Most strikeouts, game
20—Roger Clemens, April 29, 1986
Most shutouts
10—Cy Young, 1904
Smokey Joe Wood, 1912
Most shutouts, career
38—Cy Young
Most 1-0 shutouts won
5—Joe Bush, 1918

Most runs
162—Red Ruffing, 1929
       Jack Russell, 1930
Most earned runs
139—Jack Russell, 1930
Most hits
337—Cy Young, 1902
Most hit batsmen
20—Howard Ehmke, 1923
Most wild pitches
21—Earl Wilson, 1963

Most home runs
37—Earl Wilson, 1964
Most sacrifice hits
24—Tex Hughson, 1943
Most sacrifice flies
14—Dave Morehead, 1964
Lowest ERA
1.00—H. Dutch Leonard, 225 innings, 1914

CLUB RECORDS

Most players
48 in 1952
Fewest players
18 in 1904
Most games
163 in 1961, 1978, 1985
Most at-bats
5,720 in 1985
Most runs
1,027 in 1950
Fewest runs
463 in 1906
Most opponents' runs
922 in 1925
Most hits
1,665 in 1950
Fewest hits
1,175 in 1905
Most singles
1,156 in 1950
Most doubles
326 in 1989
Most triples
112 in 1903
Most homers
213 in 1977
Fewest homers (154 or 162-game schedule)
12 in 1906
Most homers at Fenway Park, home and opponents
219 in 1977
Most grand slams
9 in 1941, 1950, 1987
Most pinch home runs
6 in 1953
Most long hits
538 in 1979
Most extra bases on long hits
1,009 in 1977
Most total bases
2,560 in 1977
Most sacrifices (sacrifice hits and sacrifice flies)
310 in 1917
Most sacrifice hits
142 in 1906
Most sacrifice flies
59 in 1976, 1977, 1979
Most stolen bases
215 in 1909
Most caught stealing
111 in 1920
Most bases on balls
835 in 1949
Most strikeouts
1,020 in 1966, 1967
Fewest strikeouts
329 in 1921
Most hit by pitch
66 in 1986
Fewest hit by pitch
11, in 1934
Most runs batted in
974 in 1950

Most game-winning RBIs
84 in 1982, 1986
Highest batting average
.302 in 1950
Lowest batting average
.234 in 1905, 1907
Highest slugging average
.465 in 1977
Lowest slugging average
.318 in 1916, 1917
Most grounded into double play
174 in 1990
Fewest grounded into double play
94 in 1942
Most left on bases
1,308 in 1989
Fewest left on bases
1,015 in 1929
Most .300 hitters
9 in 1950
Most putouts
4,418 in 1978
Fewest putouts
3,949 in 1938
Most assists
2,195 in 1907
Fewest assists
1,542 in 1988
Most changes accepted
6,425 in 1907
Fewest chances accepted
5,667 in 1938
Most errors
373 in 1901
Fewest errors
93 in 1988
Most errorless games
92 in 1988
Most consecutive errorless games
10 in 1986
Most double plays
207 in 1949
Fewest double plays
74 in 1913
Most passed balls
30 in 1987
Fewest passed balls
3 in 1933, 1975
Highest fielding average
.984 in 1988
Lowest fielding average
.943 in 1901
Highest home attendance
2,562,435 in 1991
Highest road attendance
2,542,249 in 1993
Most games won
105 in 1912
Most games lost
111 in 1932
Most games won, month
25 in July 1948

Most games lost, month
  24 in July 1925, June 1927, July 1928
Highest percentage games won
  .691 in 1912 (won 105, lost 47)
Lowest percentage games won
  .279 in 1932 (won 43, lost 111)
Games won, league
  7,375 in 94 years
Games lost, league
  7,104 in 94 years
Most shutouts won
  26 in 1918
Most shutouts lost
  28 in 1906
Most 1-0 games won
  8 in 1918
Most 1-0 games lost
  7 in 1909, 1914
Most consecutive games won
  15 in 1946
Most consecutive games lost
  20 in 1906
Number of times league champions
  10
Number of last-place finishes
  10
Most runs, game
  29 vs. St. Louis, June 8, 1950
Most runs by opponent, game
  27 by Cleveland, July 7, 1923, first game

Most runs, shutout game
  19 vs. Philadelphia, April 30, 1950, first game
Most runs by opponent, shutout game
  19 by Cleveland, May 18, 1955
Most runs, doubleheader shutout
  16 vs. Cleveland, August 21, 1920
Most runs, inning
  17 vs. Detroit, June 18, 1953, seventh inning
Longest 1-0 game won
  15 innings vs. Detroit, May 11, 1904
Longest 1-0 game lost
  15 innings vs. Washington, July 3, 1915
Most hits, game
  28 vs. St. Louis, June 8, 1950
Most home runs, game
  8 vs. Toronto, July 4, 1977
Most consecutive games with one or more homers
  14 (23 homers), 1985
Most total bases, game
  60 vs. St. Louis, June 8, 1950
Largest crowd, day game
  36,388 vs. Cleveland, April 22, 1978
Largest crowd, doubleheader
  47,627 vs. New York, September 22, 1935
Largest crowd, night game
  36,228 vs. New York, June 28, 1949
Largest crowd, home opener
  35,343 vs. Baltimore, April 14, 1969

CALIFORNIA ANGELS

YEARLY FINISHES

(Known as Los Angeles Angels through September 1, 1965)

Year	Position	W	L	Pct.	*GB	Manager	Attendance
1961 — 8th		70	91	.435	38½	Bill Rigney	603,510
1962 — 3rd		86	76	.531	10	Bill Rigney	1,144,063
1963 — 9th		70	91	.435	34	Bill Rigney	821,015
1964 — 5th		82	80	.506	17	Bill Rigney	760,439
1965 — 7th		75	87	.463	27	Bill Rigney	566,727
1966 — 6th		80	82	.494	18	Bill Rigney	1,400,321
1967 — 5th		84	77	.522	7½	Bill Rigney	1,317,713
1968 — 8th		67	95	.414	36	Bill Rigney	1,025,956

WEST DIVISION

Year	Position	W	L	Pct.	*GB	Manager	Attendance
1969 — 3rd		71	91	.438	26	Bill Rigney, Lefty Phillips	758,388
1970 — 3rd		86	76	.531	12	Lefty Phillips	1,077,741
1971 — 4th		76	86	.469	25½	Lefty Phillips	926,373
1972 — 5th		75	80	.484	18	Del Rice	744,190
1973 — 4th		79	83	.488	15	Bobby Winkles	1,058,206
1974 — 6th		68	94	.420	22	Bobby Winkles, Dick Williams	917,269
1975 — 6th		72	89	.447	25½	Dick Williams	1,058,163
1976 — 4th (tied)		76	86	.469	14	Dick Williams, Norm Sherry	1,006,774
1977 — 5th		74	88	.457	28	Norm Sherry, Dave Garcia	1,432,633
1978 — 2nd (tied)		87	75	.537	5	Dave Garcia, Jim Fregosi	1,755,386
1979 — 1st†		88	74	.543	+ 3	Jim Fregosi	2,523,575
1980 — 6th		65	95	.406	31	Jim Fregosi	2,297,327
1981 — 4th/7th		51	59	.464	‡	Jim Fregosi, Gene Mauch	1,441,545
1982 — 1st†		93	69	.574	+ 3	Gene Mauch	2,807,360
1983 — 5th (tied)		70	92	.432	29	John McNamara	2,555,016
1984 — 2nd (tied)		81	81	.500	3	John McNamara	2,402,997
1985 — 2nd		90	72	.556	1	Gene Mauch	2,567,427
1986 — 1st†		92	70	.568	+ 5	Gene Mauch	2,655,872
1987 — 6th (tied)		75	87	.463	10	Gene Mauch	2,696,299
1988 — 4th		75	87	.463	29	Cookie Rojas	2,340,925
1989 — 3rd		91	71	.562	8	Doug Rader	2,647,291
1990 — 4th		80	82	.494	23	Doug Rader	2,555,688
1991 — 7th		81	81	.500	14	Doug Rader, Buck Rodgers	2,416,236
1992 — 5th (tied)		72	90	.444	24	Buck Rodgers	2,065,444
1993 — 5th (tied)		71	91	.438	23	Buck Rodgers	2,057,460
1994 — 4th		47	68	.409	5½	Buck Rodgers, Marcel Lachemann	1,512,622

*Games behind winner. †Lost Championship Series. ‡First half 31-29; second 20-30.

SERVICE

Most years by non-pitcher
13—Brian Downing
Most years by pitcher
10—Mike Witt

BATTING

Most games
162—Bobby Knoop, 1964
Jim Fregosi, 1966
Sandy Alomar, 1970, 1971
Don Baylor, 1979
Most games, career
1,661—Brian Downing
Most at-bats
689—Sandy Alomar, 162 games, 1971
Most at-bats, career
5,854—Brian Downing
Most runs
120—Don Baylor, 162 games, 1979
Most runs, career
889—Brian Downing
Most hits
202—Alex Johnson, 156 games, 1970
Most hits, career
1,588—Brian Downing
Most singles
156—Alex Johnson, 156 games, 1970
Most singles, career
1,062—Brian Downing
Most doubles
42—Doug DeCinces, 153 games, 1982
Johnny Ray, 153 games, 1988
Most doubles, career
282—Brian Downing
Most triples
13—Jim Fregosi, 159 games, 1968
Mickey Rivers, 155 games, 1975
Devon White, 156 games, 1989
Most triples, career
70—Jim Fregosi
Most homers by righthander
37—Bobby Bonds, 158 games, 1977
Most homers by lefthander
39—Reggie Jackson, 153 games, 1982
Most homers by rookie
31—Tim Salmon, 142 games, 1993
Most homers at home
23—Tim Salmon, 1993
Most homers on road
24—Leon Wagner, 1962, 1963
Most homers, month
12—Bobby Bonds, August, 1977
Most homers by righthander, career
222—Brian Downing
Most homers by lefthander, career
123—Reggie Jackson
Most grand slams
3—Joe Rudi, 133 games, 1978
Joe Rudi, 90 games, 1979
Most grand slams, career
7—Joe Rudi
Most total bases
333—Don Baylor, 162 games, 1979
Most total bases, career
2,580—Brian Downing
Most long hits
77—Doug DeCinces, 153 games, 1982
Most long hits, career
526—Brian Downing
Most extra bases on long hits
152—Bobby Bonds, 158 games, 1977

Most extra bases on long hits, career
992—Brian Downing
Most sacrifice hits
26—Tim Foli, 150 games, 1982
Most sacrifice flies
13—Danny Ford, 142 games, 1979
Most bases on balls
106—Brian Downing, 155 games, 1987
Most bases on balls, career
866—Brian Downing
Most strikeouts
156—Reggie Jackson, 153 games, 1982
Most strikeouts, career
835—Jim Fregosi
Fewest strikeouts
35—Bob Boone, 150 games, 1985
Most hit by pitch
18—Rick Reichardt, 151 games, 1968
Don Baylor, 158 games, 1978
Longest batting streak
25 games—Rod Carew, 1982
Most runs batted in
139—Don Baylor, 162 games, 1979
Most runs batted in, career
846—Brian Downing
Most game-winning RBIs
21—Don Baylor, 157 games, 1982
Highest batting average
.339—Rod Carew, 129 games, 1983
Highest batting average, career
.314—Rod Carew
Highest slugging average
.548—Doug DeCinces, 153 games, 1982
Highest slugging average, career
.490—Leon Wagner
Most grounded into double play
26—Lyman Bostock, 147 games, 1978
Fewest grounded into double play
5—Leon Wagner, 160 games, 1962
Albie Pearson, 154 games, 1963
Dick Schofield, 155 games, 1988

BASERUNNING

Most stolen bases
70—Mickey Rivers, 155 games, 1975
Most stolen bases, career
186—Gary Pettis
Most caught stealing
24—Chad Curtis, 152 games, 1993
Luis Polonia, 152 games, 1993

PITCHING

Most games
72—Minnie Rojas, 1967
Most games, career
314—Mike Witt
Most games started
41—Nolan Ryan, 1974
Most games started, career
288—Nolan Ryan
Most complete games
26—Nolan Ryan, 1973, 1974
Most complete games, career
156—Nolan Ryan
Most games finished
63—Bryan Harvey, 1991
Most innings
333—Nolan Ryan, 1974
Most innings, career
2,182—Nolan Ryan
Most games won
22—Clyde Wright, 1970
Nolan Ryan, 1974

Most games won, career
138—Nolan Ryan
Highest winning percentage
.773—Bert Blyleven (17-5), 1989
Longest winning streak
10 games—Ken McBride, 1962
           Bert Blyleven, 1989
Longest losing streak
11 games—Andy Hassler, 1975
Most saves
46—Bryan Harvey, 1991
Most 20-victory seasons
2—Nolan Ryan
Most games lost
19—George Brunet, 1967
     Clyde Wright, 1973
     Frank Tanana, 1974
     Kirk McCaskill, 1991
Most games lost, career
121—Nolan Ryan
Most bases on balls
204—Nolan Ryan, 1977
Most bases on balls, career
1,302—Nolan Ryan
Most strikeouts
383—Nolan Ryan, 1973
Most strikeouts, career
2,416—Nolan Ryan
Most strikeouts, game
19—Nolan Ryan, August 12, 1974

Nolan Ryan, June 14, 1974, pitched first 13 innings of 15-inning game
Nolan Ryan, August 20, 1974, 11 innings
Nolan Ryan, June 8, 1977, pitched first 10 innings of 13-inning game
Most shutouts
11—Dean Chance, 1964
Most shutouts, career
40—Nolan Ryan
Most 1-0 shutouts won
5—Dean Chance, 1964
Most runs
130—Mike Witt, 1988
Most earned runs
117—Willie Fraser, 1988
Most hits
280—Bill Singer, 1973
Most hit batsmen
21—Tom Murphy, 1969
Most wild pitches
21—Nolan Ryan, 1977
Most home runs
38—Don Sutton, 1987
Most sacrifice hits
22—Nolan Ryan, 1977
Most sacrifice flies
14—Nolan Ryan, 1978
Lowest ERA
1.65—Dean Chance, 278 innings, 1964

CLUB RECORDS

Most players
48 in 1975
Fewest players
33 in 1963
Most games
163 in 1969, 1974
Most at-bats
5,640 in 1983
Most runs
866 in 1979
Fewest runs
454 in 1972
Most opponents' runs
803 in 1987
Most hits
1,563 in 1979
Fewest hits
1,209 in 1968
Most singles
1,114 in 1979
Most doubles
268 in 1982
Most triples
54 in 1966
Most homers
189 in 1961
Fewest homers
55 in 1975
Most homers at Wrigley Field, home and opponents
248 in 1961
Most homers at Chavez Ravine, home and opponents
102 in 1964
Most homers at Anaheim Stadium, home and opponents
204 in 1987
Most grand slams
8 in 1979, 1983
Most pinch home runs
9 in 1987
Most total bases
2,396 in 1982
Most long hits
480 in 1982
Most extra bases on long hits
878 in 1982

Most sacrifice hits
114 in 1982
Most sacrifice flies
61 in 1986
Most stolen bases
220 in 1975
Most caught stealing
108 in 1975
Most bases on balls
681 in 1961
Most strikeouts
1,080 in 1968
Fewest strikeouts
682 in 1978
Most hit by pitch
67 in 1978
Fewest hit by pitch
22 in 1965
Most runs batted in
808 in 1979
Most game-winning RBIs
85 in 1982
Highest batting average
.282 in 1979
Lowest batting average
.227 in 1968
Highest slugging average
.433 in 1982
Lowest slugging average
.318 in 1968, 1976
Most grounded into double play
147 in 1983
Fewest grounded into double play
98 in 1975
Most left on bases
1,202 in 1990
Fewest left on bases
975 in 1992
Most .300 hitters
2 in 1963, 1964, 1979, 1982
Most putouts
4,443 in 1971
Fewest putouts
4,133 in 1972

Most assists
2,077 in 1983
Fewest assists
1,576 in 1980
Most chances accepted
6,499 in 1983
Fewest chances
5,740 in 1972
Most errors
192 in 1961
Fewest errors
96 in 1989
Most errorless games
91 in 1989
Most consecutive errorless games
14 in 1991
Most double plays
202 in 1985
Fewest double plays
135 in 1967, 1972, 1978
Most passed balls
30 in 1969
Fewest passed balls
4 in 1982, 1984
Highest fielding average
.985 in 1989
Lowest fielding average
.969 in 1961
Highest home attendance
2,807,360 in 1982
Highest road attendance
2,336,299 in 1991
Most games won
93 in 1982
Most games lost
95 in 1968, 1980
Most games won, month
20 in June 1967
Most games lost, month
22 in June 1961, May 1964, August 1968
Games won, league
2,600 in 34 years
Games lost, league
2,796 in 34 years
Highest percentage games won
.574 in 1982 (won 93, lost 69)
Lowest percentage games won
.406 in 1980 (won 65, lost 95)
Most shutouts won
28 in 1964
Most shutouts lost
23 in 1971

Most 1-0 games won
10 in 1964
Most 1-0 games lost
5 in 1968
Most consecutive games won
11 in 1964
Most consecutive games lost
12 in 1988
Number of times league champions
0
Number of last-place finishes
2
Most runs, inning
13 vs. Texas, September 14, 1978, ninth inning
Most runs, game
24 vs. Toronto, August 25, 1979
Most runs by opponent, game
20 by Milwaukee, July 8, 1990
Most hits, game
26 vs. Toronto, August 25, 1979
    vs. Boston, June 20, 1980
Most home runs, game
6 vs. Boston, June 20, 1980
    vs. Oakland, April 23, 1985
    vs. Chicago, June 28, 1987
Most runs, shutout game
17 vs. Washington, August 23, 1963
    vs. Minnesota, April 23, 1980
Most runs by opponent, shutout game
14 by Seattle, August 7, 1987
Most runs, doubleheader shutout
7 vs. Kansas City, June 26, 1964
Longest 1-0 game won
15 innings vs. Chicago, April 13, 1963
Longest 1-0 game lost
20 innings vs. Oakland, July 9, 1971
Longest shutout game won
16 innings, 3-0 vs. Chicago, September 22, 1975
Most consecutive games with one or more homers
18 (30 homers), 1982
Most total bases, game
52 vs. Boston, June 20, 1980
Largest crowd, day game
63,132 vs. Kansas City, July 4, 1983
Largest crowd, doubleheader
43,461 vs. Chicago, August 5, 1988
Largest crowd, night game
63,073 vs. Baltimore, April 23, 1983
Largest crowd, home opener
45,586 vs. Oakland, April 8, 1988

CHICAGO WHITE SOX

YEARLY FINISHES

Year	Position	W	L	Pct.	*GB	Manager	Attendance
1901 — 1st	83	53	.610	+ 4	Clark Griffith	354,350
1902 — 4th	74	60	.552	8	Clark Griffith	337,898
1903 — 7th	60	77	.438	30½	Nixey Callahan	286,183
1904 — 3rd	89	65	.578	6	Nixey Callahan, Fielder Jones	557,123
1905 — 2nd	92	60	.605	2	Fielder Jones	687,419
1906 — 1st	93	58	.616	+ 3	Fielder Jones	585,202
1907 — 3rd	87	64	.576	5½	Fielder Jones	666,307
1908 — 3rd	88	64	.579	1½	Fielder Jones	636,096
1909 — 4th	78	74	.513	20	Billy Sullivan	478,400
1910 — 6th	68	85	.444	35½	Hugh Duffy	552,084
1911 — 4th	77	74	.510	24	Hugh Duffy	583,208
1912 — 4th	78	76	.506	28	Nixey Callahan	602,241
1913 — 5th	78	74	.513	17½	Nixey Callahan	644,501
1914 — 6th (tied)	70	84	.455	30	Nixey Callahan	469,290
1915 — 3rd	93	61	.604	9½	Pants Rowland	539,461
1916 — 2nd	89	65	.578	2	Pants Rowland	679,923
1917 — 1st	100	54	.649	+ 9	Pants Rowland	684,521
1918 — 6th	57	67	.460	17	Pants Rowland	195,081

Year	Position	W	L	Pct.	*GB	Manager	Attendance
1919 — 1st	88	52	.629	+ 3½	Kid Gleason	627,186
1920 — 2nd	96	58	.623	2	Kid Gleason	833,492
1921 — 7th	62	92	.403	36½	Kid Gleason	543,650
1922 — 5th	77	77	.500	17	Kid Gleason	602,860
1923 — 7th	69	85	.448	30	Kid Gleason	573,778
1924 — 8th	66	87	.431	25½	Johnny Evers	606,658
1925 — 5th	79	75	.513	18½	Eddie Collins	832,231
1926 — 5th	81	72	.529	9½	Eddie Collins	710,339
1927 — 5th	70	83	.458	29½	Ray Schalk	614,423
1928 — 5th	72	82	.468	29	Ray Schalk, Lena Blackburne	494,152
1929 — 7th	59	93	.388	46	Lena Blackburne	426,795
1930 — 7th	62	92	.403	40	Donie Bush	406,123
1931 — 8th	56	97	.366	51	Donie Bush	403,550
1932 — 7th	49	102	.325	56½	Lew Fonseca	233,198
1933 — 6th	67	83	.447	31	Lew Fonseca	397,789
1934 — 8th	53	99	.349	47	Lew Fonseca, Jimmie Dykes	236,559
1935 — 5th	74	78	.487	19½	Jimmie Dykes	470,281
1936 — 3rd	81	70	.536	20	Jimmie Dykes	440,810
1937 — 3rd	86	68	.558	16	Jimmie Dykes	589,245
1938 — 6th	65	83	.439	32	Jimmie Dykes	338,278
1939 — 4th	85	69	.552	22½	Jimmie Dykes	594,104
1940 — 4th (tied)	82	72	.532	8	Jimmie Dykes	660,336
1941 — 3rd	77	77	.500	24	Jimmie Dykes	677,077
1942 — 6th	66	82	.446	34	Jimmie Dykes	425,734
1943 — 4th	82	72	.532	16	Jimmie Dykes	508,962
1944 — 7th	71	83	.461	18	Jimmie Dykes	563,539
1945 — 6th	71	78	.477	15	Jimmie Dykes	657,981
1946 — 5th	74	80	.481	30	Jimmie Dykes, Ted Lyons	983,403
1947 — 6th	70	84	.455	27	Ted Lyons	876,948
1948 — 8th	51	101	.336	44½	Ted Lyons	777,844
1949 — 6th	63	91	.409	34	Jack Onslow	937,151
1950 — 6th	60	94	.390	38	Jack Onslow, Red Corriden	781,330
1951 — 4th	81	73	.526	17	Paul Richards	1,328,234
1952 — 3rd	81	73	.526	14	Paul Richards	1,231,675
1953 — 3rd	89	65	.578	11½	Paul Richards	1,191,353
1954 — 3rd	94	60	.610	17	Paul Richards, Marty Marion	1,231,629
1955 — 3rd	91	63	.591	5	Marty Marion	1,175,684
1956 — 3rd	85	69	.552	12	Marty Marion	1,000,090
1957 — 2nd	90	64	.584	8	Al Lopez	1,135,668
1958 — 2nd	82	72	.532	10	Al Lopez	797,451
1959 — 1st	94	60	.610	+ 5	Al Lopez	1,423,144
1960 — 3rd	87	67	.565	10	Al Lopez	1,644,460
1961 — 4th	86	76	.531	23	Al Lopez	1,146,019
1962 — 5th	85	77	.525	11	Al Lopez	1,131,562
1963 — 2nd	94	68	.580	10½	Al Lopez	1,158,848
1964 — 2nd	98	64	.605	1	Al Lopez	1,250,053
1965 — 2nd	95	67	.586	7	Al Lopez	1,130,519
1966 — 4th	83	79	.512	15	Eddie Stanky	990,016
1967 — 4th	89	73	.549	3	Eddie Stanky	985,634
1968 — 8th (tied)	67	95	.414	36	Eddie Stanky, Al Lopez	803,775

WEST DIVISION

Year	Position	W	L	Pct.	*GB	Manager	Attendance
1969 — 5th	68	94	.420	29	Al Lopez, Don Gutteridge	589,546
1970 — 6th	56	106	.346	42	Don Gutteridge, Chuck Tanner	495,355
1971 — 3rd	79	83	.488	22½	Chuck Tanner	833,891
1972 — 2nd	87	67	.565	5½	Chuck Tanner	1,177,318
1973 — 5th	77	85	.475	17	Chuck Tanner	1,302,527
1974 — 4th	80	80	.500	9	Chuck Tanner	1,149,596
1975 — 5th	75	86	.466	22½	Chuck Tanner	750,802
1976 — 6th	64	97	.398	25½	Paul Richards	914,945
1977 — 3rd	90	72	.556	12	Bob Lemon	1,657,135
1978 — 5th	71	90	.441	20½	Bob Lemon, Larry Doby	1,491,100
1979 — 5th	73	87	.456	14	Don Kessinger, Tony La Russa	1,280,702
1980 — 5th	70	90	.438	26	Tony La Russa	1,200,365
1981 — 3rd/6th	54	52	.509	†	Tony La Russa	946,651
1982 — 3rd	87	75	.537	6	Tony La Russa	1,567,787
1983 — 1st‡	99	63	.611	+20	Tony La Russa	2,132,821
1984 — 5th (tied)	74	88	.457	10	Tony La Russa	2,136,988
1985 — 3rd	85	77	.525	6	Tony La Russa	1,669,888
1986 — 5th	72	90	.444	20	Tony La Russa, Jim Fregosi	1,424,313
1987 — 5th	77	85	.475	8	Jim Fregosi	1,208,060
1988 — 5th	71	90	.441	32½	Jim Fregosi	1,115,749
1989 — 7th	69	92	.429	29½	Jeff Torborg	1,045,651
1990 — 2nd	94	68	.580	9	Jeff Torborg	2,002,357

Year	Position	W	L	Pct.	*GB	Manager	Attendance
1991 —2nd		87	75	.537	8	Jeff Torborg	2,934,154
1992 —3rd		86	76	.531	10	Gene Lamont	2,681,156
1993 —1st‡		94	68	.580	+ 8	Gene Lamont	2,581,091

CENTRAL DIVISION

Year	Position	W	L	Pct.	*GB	Manager	Attendance
1994 — 1st		67	46	.593	+ 1	Gene Lamont	1,697,398

*Games behind winner. †First half 31-22; second 23-30. ‡Lost Championship Series.

INDIVIDUAL RECORDS (1901 TO DATE)

SERVICE

Most years by non-pitcher
20—Luke Appling
Most years by pitcher
21—Ted Lyons

BATTING

Most games
163—Don Buford, 1966
Greg Walker, 1985
Most games, career
2,422—Luke Appling
Most at-bats
649—Nellie Fox, 154 games, 1956
Most at-bats, career
8,857—Luke Appling
Most runs
135—Johnny Mostil, 153 games, 1925
Most runs, career
1,319—Luke Appling
Most hits
222—Eddie Collins, 153 games, 1920
Most hits, career
2,749—Luke Appling
Most singles
169—Eddie Collins, 153 games, 1920
Most singles, career
2,162—Luke Appling
Most doubles
46—Frank Thomas, 160 games, 1992
Most doubles, career
440—Luke Appling
Most triples
21—Joe Jackson, 153 games, 1916
Most triples, career
104—Shano Collins
Nellie Fox
Most homers by righthander
41—Frank Thomas, 153 games, 1993
Most homers by lefthander
31—Oscar Gamble, 137 games, 1977
Most homers by rookie
35—Ron Kittle, 145 games, 1983
Most homers at home
27—Dick Allen, 1972
Most homers on road
19—Eddie Robinson, 1951
Most homers, month
13—Dick Allen, July, 1972
Most homers by righthander, career
214—Carlton Fisk
Most homers by lefthander, career
186—Harold Baines
Most grand slams
3—Pete Ward, 144 games, 1964
Most grand slams, career
5—Harold Baines
Most total bases
336—Joe Jackson, 146 games, 1920
Most total bases, career
3,528—Luke Appling
Most long hits
77—Frank Thomas, 153 games, 1993

Most long hits, career
587—Luke Appling
Most extra bases on long hits
159—Frank Thomas, 153 games, 1993
Most extra bases on long hits, career
913—Harold Baines
Most sacrifices (sacrifice hits and sacrifice flies)
44—Buck Weaver, 151 games, 1916
Most sacrifice hits
40—George Davis, 151 games, 1905
Most sacrifice flies
13—Frank Thomas, 153 games, 1993
Most bases on balls
138—Frank Thomas, 158 games, 1991
Most bases on balls, career
1,302—Luke Appling
Most strikeouts
175—Dave Nicholson, 126 games, 1963
Most strikeouts, career
798—Carlton Fisk
Fewest strikeouts
11—Nellie Fox, 155 games, 1958
Most hit by pitch
23—Minnie Minoso, 151 games, 1956
Most runs batted in
138—Zeke Bonura, 148 games, 1936
Most runs batted in, career
1,116—Luke Appling
Most game-winning RBIs
22—Harold Baines, 156 games, 1983
Most consecutive games with RBI
13—Taft Wright (22 RBIs), 1941
Highest batting average
.388—Luke Appling, 138 games, 1936
Highest batting average, career
.340—Joe Jackson
Highest slugging average
.607—Frank Thomas, 153 games, 1993
Highest slugging average, career
.590—Frank Thomas
Longest batting streak
27 games—Luke Appling, 1936
Most grounded into double play
29—George Bell, 155 games, 1992
Fewest grounded into double play
3—Tony Lupien, 154 games, 1948
Don Buford, 163 games, 1966
Don Buford, 156 games, 1967

BASERUNNING

Most stolen bases
77—Rudy Law, 141 games, 1983
Most stolen bases, career
368—Eddie Collins
Most caught stealing
29—Eddie Collins, 145 games, 1923

PITCHING

Most games
88—Wilbur Wood, 1968
Most games, career
669—Red Faber
Most games started
49—Ed A. Walsh, 1908
Wilbur Wood, 1972

— 228 —

Most games started, career
484—Red Faber
　　　Ted Lyons
Most complete games
42—Ed A. Walsh, 1908
Most complete games, career
356—Ted Lyons
Most games finished
73—Bobby Thigpen, 1990
Most innings
465—Ed A. Walsh, 1908
Most innings, career
4,162—Ted Lyons
Most games won
40—Ed A. Walsh, 1908
Most games won, career
260—Ted Lyons
Most 20-victory seasons
4—Ed A. Walsh
　　Red Faber
　　Wilbur Wood
Most games lost
25—Patrick Flaherty, 1903
Most games lost, career
230—Ted Lyons
Highest winning percentage
.842—Sandy Consuegra (16-3), 1954
Longest winning streak
13 games—LaMarr Hoyt, 1983
Longest winning streak, two seasons
15 games—Wilson Alvarez, 1993 (7), 1994 (8)
Longest losing streak
14 games—Howard Judson, 1949
Most saves
57—Bobby Thigpen, 1990

Most bases on balls
147—Vern Kennedy, 1936
Most bases on balls, career
1,213—Red Faber
Most strikeouts
269—Ed A. Walsh, 1908
Most strikeouts, career
1,796—Billy Pierce
Most strikeouts, game
16—Jack Harshman, July 25, 1954, first game
Most shutouts
12—Ed A. Walsh, 1908
Most shutouts, career
58—Ed A. Walsh
Most 1-0 shutouts won
5—Reb Russell, 1913
Most runs
182—Dick Kerr, 1921
Most earned runs
162—Dick Kerr, 1921
Most hits
381—Wilbur Wood, 1973
Most hit batsmen
16—Jim Scott, 1909
Most wild pitches
17—Tommy John, 1970
Most home runs
38—Floyd Bannister, 1987
Most sacrifice hits
21—Wilbur Wood, 1972
Most sacrifice flies
16—Charlie Hough, 1991
Lowest ERA
1.53—Ed Cicotte, 346 innings, 1917

CLUB RECORDS

Most players
50 in 1932
Fewest players
19 in 1905
Most games
163 in 1961, 1966, 1974, 1985
Most at-bats
5,633 in 1977
Most runs
920 in 1936
Fewest runs
447 in 1910
Most opponents' runs
946 in 1934
Most hits
1,597 in 1936
Fewest hits
1,061 in 1910
Most singles
1,199 in 1936
Most doubles
314 in 1926
Most triples
102 in 1915
Most homers
192 in 1977
Fewest homers (154 or 162-game schedule)
3 in 1908
Most homers at old Comiskey Park, home and opponents
175 in 1970
Most homers at new Comiskey Park, home and opponents
153 in 1991
Most grand slams
7 in 1961, 1993
Most pinch home runs
9 in 1984
Most total bases
2,502 in 1977

Most long hits
498 in 1977
Most extra bases on long hits
934 in 1977
Most sacrifices (sacrifice hits and sacrifice flies)
270 in 1915
Most sacrifice hits
207 in 1906
Most sacrifice flies
69 in 1992
Most stolen bases
275 in 1901
Most caught stealing
119 in 1923
Most bases on balls
702 in 1949
Most strikeouts
991 in 1972
Fewest strikeouts
355 in 1920
Most hit by pitch
75 in 1956
Fewest hit by pitch
10 in 1940
Highest batting average
.295 in 1920
Lowest batting average
.212 in 1910
Most runs batted in
862 in 1936
Most game-winning RBIs
95 in 1983
Highest slugging average
.444 in 1977
Lowest slugging average
.261 in 1910
Most grounded into double play
156 in 1950, 1974

Fewest grounded into double play
94 in 1966
Most left on bases
1,279 in 1936
Fewest left on bases
1,009 in 1985
Most .300 hitters
8 in 1924
Most putouts
4,471 in 1967
Fewest putouts
3,943 in 1942
Most assists
2,446 in 1907
Fewest assists
1,622 in 1977
Most chances accepted
6,655 in 1907
Fewest chances accepted
5,670 in 1942
Most errors
358 in 1901
Fewest errors
107 in 1957
Most errorless games
89 in 1962
Most consecutive errorless games
9 in 1955, 1964
Most double plays
188 in 1974
Fewest double plays
94 in 1915
Most passed balls
45 in 1965
Fewest passed balls
3 in 1922
Highest fielding average
.982 in 1954, 1957, 1960, 1962, 1985, 1991, 1993
Lowest fielding average
.938 in 1901
Highest home attendance
2,934,154 in 1991
Highest road attendance
2,571,969 in 1993
Most games won
100 in 1917
Most games lost
106 in 1970
Most games won, month
23 in September 1905
Most games lost, month
24 in June 1934, August 1968
Highest percentage games won
.649 in 1917 (won 100, lost 54)
Lowest percentage games won
.325 in 1932 (won 49, lost 102)

Games won, league
7,295 in 94 years
Games lost, league
7,173 in 94 years
Most shutouts won
30 in 1906
Most shutouts lost
24 in 1910
Most 1-0 games won
9 in 1909, 1967
Most 1-0 games lost
9 in 1968
Most consecutive games won
19 in 1906
Most consecutive games lost
13 in 1924
Number of times league champion
5
Number of last-place finishes
6
Most runs, game
29 vs. Kansas City, April 23, 1955
Most runs by opponent, game
22 by New York, July 26, 1931, second game
Most runs, shutout game
17 vs. Washington, September 19, 1925, second game
vs. Cleveland, July 5, 1987
Most runs by opponent, shutout game
17 by Baltimore, July 27, 1969
Most runs, doubleheader shutout
17 vs. Detroit, September 6, 1905
Most runs, inning
13 vs. Washington, September 26, 1943, first game, fourth inning
Most hits, game
29 vs. Kansas City, April 23, 1955
Most home runs, game
7 vs. Kansas City, April 23, 1955
Longest 1-0 game won
17 innings vs. Cleveland, September 13, 1967, night game
Longest 1-0 game lost
18 innings vs. Washington, May 15, 1918
vs. Washington, June 8, 1947, first game
Most consecutive games with one or more homers
16 (32 homers), 1987
Most total bases, game
55 vs. Kansas City, April 23, 1955
Largest crowd, day game
51,560 vs. Milwaukee, April 14, 1981
Largest crowd, doubleheader
55,555 vs. Minnesota, May 20, 1973
Largest crowd, night game
53,940 vs. New York, June 8, 1951
Largest crowd, home opener
51,560 vs. Milwaukee, April 14, 1981

CLEVELAND INDIANS

YEARLY FINISHES

Year	Position	W	L	Pct.	*GB	Manager	Attendance
1901	7th	54	82	.397	29	James McAleer	131,380
1902	5th	69	67	.507	14	Bill Armour	275,395
1903	3rd	77	63	.550	15	Bill Armour	311,280
1904	4th	86	65	.570	7 ½	Bill Armour	264,749
1905	5th	76	78	.494	19	Nap Lajoie	316,306
1906	3rd	89	64	.582	5	Nap Lajoie	325,733
1907	4th	85	67	.559	8	Nap Lajoie	382,046
1908	2nd	90	64	.584	½	Nap Lajoie	422,242
1909	6th	71	82	.464	27 ½	Nap Lajoie, Deacon McGuire	354,627
1910	5th	71	81	.467	32	Deacon McGuire	293,456
1911	3rd	80	73	.523	22	Deacon McGuire, George Stovall	406,296
1912	5th	75	78	.490	30 ½	Harry Davis, J.L. Birmingham	336,844
1913	3rd	86	66	.566	9 ½	J.L. Birmingham	541,000

Year	Position	W	L	Pct.	*GB	Manager	Attendance
1914 —8th		51	102	.333	48 ½	J.L. Birmingham	185,997
1915 —7th		57	95	.375	44 ½	J.L. Birmingham, Lee Fohl	159,285
1916 —6th		77	77	.500	14	Lee Fohl	492,106
1917 —3rd		88	66	.571	12	Lee Fohl	477,298
1918 —2nd		73	54	.575	2 ½	Lee Fohl	295,515
1919 —2nd		84	55	.604	3 ½	Lee Fohl, Tris Speaker	538,135
1920 — 1st		98	56	.636	+ 2	Tris Speaker	912,832
1921 —2nd		94	60	.610	4 ½	Tris Speaker	748,705
1922 —4th		78	76	.507	16	Tris Speaker	528,145
1923 —3rd		82	71	.536	16 ½	Tris Speaker	558,856
1924 —6th		67	86	.438	24 ½	Tris Speaker	481,905
1925 —6th		70	84	.455	27 ½	Tris Speaker	419,005
1926 —2nd		88	66	.571	3	Tris Speaker	627,426
1927 —6th		66	87	.431	43 ½	Jack McAllister	373,138
1928 —7th		62	92	.403	39	Roger Peckinpaugh	375,907
1929 —3rd		81	71	.533	24	Roger Peckinpaugh	536,210
1930 —4th		81	73	.536	21	Roger Peckinpaugh	528,657
1931 —4th		78	76	.506	30	Roger Peckinpaugh	483,027
1932 —4th		87	65	.572	19	Roger Peckinpaugh	468,953
1933 —4th		75	76	.497	23 ½	Roger Peckinpaugh, Walter Johnson	387,936
1934 —3rd		85	69	.552	16	Walter Johnson	391,338
1935 —3rd		82	71	.536	12	Walter Johnson, Steve O'Neill	397,615
1936 —5th		80	74	.519	22 ½	Steve O'Neill	500,391
1937 —4th		83	71	.539	19	Steve O'Neill	564,849
1938 —3rd		86	66	.566	13	Ossie Vitt	652,006
1939 —3rd		87	67	.565	20 ½	Ossie Vitt	563,926
1940 —2nd		89	65	.578	1	Ossie Vitt	902,576
1941 —4th (tied)		75	79	.487	26	Roger Peckinpaugh	745,948
1942 —4th		75	79	.487	28	Lou Boudreau	459,447
1943 —3rd		82	71	.536	15 ½	Lou Boudreau	438,894
1944 —5th (tied)		72	82	.468	17	Lou Boudreau	475,272
1945 —5th		73	72	.503	11	Lou Boudreau	558,182
1946 —6th		68	86	.442	36	Lou Boudreau	1,057,289
1947 —4th		80	74	.519	17	Lou Boudreau	1,521,978
1948 — 1st†		97	58	.626	+ 1	Lou Boudreau	2,620,627
1949 —3rd		89	65	.578	8	Lou Boudreau	2,233,771
1950 —4th		92	62	.597	6	Lou Boudreau	1,727,464
1951 —2nd		93	61	.604	5	Al Lopez	1,704,984
1952 —2nd		93	61	.604	2	Al Lopez	1,444,607
1953 —2nd		92	62	.597	8 ½	Al Lopez	1,069,176
1954 — 1st		111	43	.721	+ 8	Al Lopez	1,335,472
1955 —2nd		93	61	.604	3	Al Lopez	1,221,780
1956 —2nd		88	66	.571	9	Al Lopez	865,467
1957 —6th		76	77	.497	21 ½	Kerby Farrell	722,256
1958 —4th		77	76	.503	14 ½	Bobby Bragan, Joe Gordon	663,805
1959 —2nd		89	65	.578	5	Joe Gordon	1,497,976
1960 —4th		76	78	.494	21	Joe Gordon, Jimmie Dykes	950,985
1961 —5th		78	83	.484	30 ½	Jimmie Dykes	725,547
1962 —6th		80	82	.494	16	Mel McGaha	716,076
1963 —5th (tied)		79	83	.488	25 ½	Birdie Tebbetts	562,507
1964 —6th (tied)		79	83	.488	20	Birdie Tebbetts	653,293
1965 —5th		87	75	.537	15	Birdie Tebbetts	934,786
1966 —5th		81	81	.500	17	Birdie Tebbetts, George Strickland	903,359
1967 —8th		75	87	.463	17	Joe Adcock	662,980
1968 —3rd		86	75	.534	16 ½	Alvin Dark	857,994

EAST DIVISION

Year	Position	W	L	Pct.	*GB	Manager	Attendance
1969 —6th		62	99	.385	46 ½	Alvin Dark	619,970
1970 —5th		76	86	.469	32	Alvin Dark	729,752
1971 —6th		60	102	.370	43	Alvin Dark, John Lipon	591,361
1972 —5th		72	84	.462	14	Ken Aspromonte	626,354
1973 —6th		71	91	.438	26	Ken Aspromonte	615,107
1974 —4th		77	85	.475	14	Ken Aspromonte	1,114,262
1975 —4th		79	80	.497	15 ½	Frank Robinson	977,039
1976 —4th		81	78	.509	16	Frank Robinson	948,776
1977 —5th		71	90	.441	28 ½	Frank Robinson, Jeff Torborg	900,365
1978 —6th		69	90	.434	29	Jeff Torborg	800,584
1979 —6th		81	80	.503	22	Jeff Torborg, Dave Garcia	1,011,644
1980 —6th		79	81	.494	23	Dave Garcia	1,033,827
1981 —6th/5th		52	51	.504	‡	Dave Garcia	661,395
1982 —6th (tied)		78	84	.481	17	Dave Garcia	1,044,021
1983 —7th		70	92	.432	28	Mike Ferraro, Pat Corrales	768,941
1984 —6th		75	87	.463	29	Pat Corrales	734,079
1985 —7th		60	102	.370	39 ½	Pat Corrales	655,181

— 231 —

Year	Position	W	L	Pct.	*GB	Manager	Attendance
1986 —5th		84	78	.519	11½	Pat Corrales	1,471,805
1987 —7th		61	101	.377	37	Pat Corrales, Doc Edwards	1,077,898
1988 —6th		78	84	.481	11	Doc Edwards	1,411,610
1989 —6th		73	89	.451	16	Doc Edwards, John Hart	1,285,542
1990 —4th		77	85	.475	11	John McNamara	1,225,240
1991 —7th		57	105	.352	34	John McNamara, Mike Hargrove	1,051,863
1992 —4th (tied)		76	86	.469	20	Mike Hargrove	1,224,274
1993 —6th		76	86	.469	19	Mike Hargrove	2,177,908

CENTRAL DIVISION

Year	Position	W	L	Pct.	*GB	Manager	Attendance
1994 —2nd		66	47	.584	1	Mike Hargrove	1,995,174

*Games behind winner. †Won pennant playoff. ‡First half 26-24; second 26-27.

INDIVIDUAL RECORDS (1901 TO DATE)

SERVICE

Most years by non-pitcher
15—Terry Turner
Most years by pitcher
20—Mel Harder

BATTING

Most games
163—Leon Wagner, 1964
Most games, career
1,619—Terry Turner
Most at-bats
663—Joe Carter, 162 games, 1986
Most at-bats, career
6,037—Nap Lajoie
Most runs
140—Earl Averill, 155 games, 1931
Most runs, career
1,154—Earl Averill
Most hits
233—Joe Jackson, 147 games, 1911
Most hits league
2,051—Nap Lajoie
Most singles
172—Charles Jamieson, 152 games, 1923
Most singles, career
1,516—Nap Lajoie
Most doubles
64—George Burns, 151 games, 1926
Most doubles, career
486—Tris Speaker
Most triples
26—Joe Jackson, 152 games, 1912
Most triples, career
121—Earl Averill
Most homers by righthander
43—Al Rosen, 155 games, 1953
Most homers by lefthander
42—Hal Trosky, 151 games, 1936
Most homers by rookie
37—Al Rosen, 155 games, 1950
Most homers at home
30—Hal Trosky, 1936
Most homers on road
22—Rocky Colavito, 1959
Most homers, month
13—Hal Trosky, July 1937
Rocky Colavito, August 1958
Most homers by lefthander, career
226—Earl Averill
Most homers by righthander, career
214—Andre Thornton
Most grand slams
4—Al Rosen, 154 games, 1951
Most grand slams, career
9—Al Rosen

Most total bases
405—Hal Trosky, 151 games, 1936
Most total bases, career
3,201—Earl Averill
Most long hits
96—Hal Trosky, 151 games, 1936
Most long hits, career
724—Earl Averill
Most extra bases on long hits
189—Hal Trosky, 151 games, 1936
Most extra bases on long hits, career
1,904—Earl Averill
Most sacrifices (sacrifice hits and sacrifice flies)
67—Ray Chapman, 156 games, 1917
Most sacrifice hits
46—Bill Bradley, 139 games, 1907
Most sacrifice flies
14—Albert Belle, 159 games, 1993
Most bases on balls
111—Mike Hargrove, 160 games, 1980
Most bases on balls, career
726—Earl Averill
Most strikeouts
166—Cory Snyder, 157 games, 1987
Most strikeouts, career
805—Larry Doby
Fewest strikeouts
4—Joe Sewell, 155 games, 1925
Joe Sewell, 152 games, 1929
Most hit by pitch
17—Minnie Minoso, 148 games, 1959
Most runs batted in
162—Hal Trosky, 151 games, 1936
Most runs batted in, career
1,085—Earl Averill
Most game-winning RBIs
15—Andre Thornton, 161 games, 1982
Most consecutive games with RBI
9—Al Rosen (18 RBI), 1954
Highest batting average
.408—Joe Jackson, 147 games, 1911
Highest batting average, career
.375—Joe Jackson
Highest slugging average
.644—Hal Trosky, 151 games, 1936
Highest slugging average, career
.551—Hal Trosky
Longest batting streak
29 games—Bill Bradley, 1902
Most grounded into double play
28—Julio Franco, 149 games, 1986
Fewest grounded into double play
3—Jose Cardenal, 157 games, 1968
Cory Snyder, 157 games, 1987

BASERUNNING

Most stolen bases
70—Kenny Lofton, 148 games, 1993

— 232 —

Most stolen bases, career
254—Terry Turner
Most caught stealing
23—Bobby Bonds, 146 games, 1979

PITCHING

Most games
76—Sid Monge, 1979
Most games, career
582—Mel Harder
Most games started
44—George Uhle, 1923
Most games started, career
484—Bob Feller
Most complete games
36—Bob Feller, 1946
Most complete games, career
279—Bob Feller
Most games finished
64—Doug Jones, 1990
Most innings
371—Bob Feller, 1946
Most innings, career
3,828—Bob Feller
Most games won
31—Jim Bagby Sr., 1920
Most games won, career
266—Bob Feller
Most 20-victory seasons
7—Bob Lemon
Most games lost
22—Peter Dowling, 1901
Most games lost, career
186—Mel Harder
Highest winning precentage
.938—Johnny Allen (15-1), 1937
Longest winning streak
15—Johnny Allen, 1937
     Gaylord Perry, 1974
Longest winning streak over two seasons
17—Johnny Allen, 1936 (2), 1937 (15)
Longest losing streak
13—Guy Morton, 1914

Most saves, season
43—Doug Jones, 1990
Most bases on balls
208—Bob Feller, 1938
Most bases on balls, career
1,764—Bob Feller
Most strikeouts
348—Bob Feller, 1946
Most strikeouts, game
19—Luis Tiant, July 3, 1968, 10 innings
18—Bob Feller, October 2, 1938, first game
Most strikeouts, career
2,581—Bob Feller
Most shutouts
10—Bob Feller, 1946
     Bob Lemon, 1948
Most shutouts, career
45—Adrian Joss
Most 1-0 shutouts won
3—Adrian Joss, 1908
     Stan Coveleski, 1917
     James Bagby Jr., 1943
     Bob Feller, 1946
Most runs
167—George Uhle, 1923
Most earned runs
150—George Uhle, 1923
Most hits
378—George Uhle, 1923
Most hit batsmen
20—Otto Hess, 1906
Most wild pitches
18—Sam McDowell, 1967
Most home runs
37—Luis Tiant, 1969
Most sacrifice hits
20—Early Wynn, 1951
Most sacrifice flies
12—Early Wynn, 1956
     Gaylord Perry, 1974
     Ken Schrom, 1986
Lowest ERA
1.60—Luis Tiant, 258 innings, 1968

CLUB RECORDS

Most players
53 in 1991
Fewest players
24 in 1904
Most games
164 in 1964
Most at-bats
5,702 in 1986
Most runs
925 in 1921
Fewest runs
472 in 1972
Most opponents' runs
957 in 1987
Most hits
1,715 in 1936
Fewest hits
1,210 in 1915
Most singles
1,218 in 1925
Most doubles
358 in 1930
Most triples
95 in 1920
Most homers
187 in 1987
Fewest homers (154 or 162-game schedule)
8 in 1910
Most homers at Municipal Stadium, home and opponents
236 in 1970

Most grand slams
8 in 1979
Most pinch home runs
9 in 1965, 1970
Most total bases
2,605 in 1936
Most long hits
562 in 1936
Most extra bases on long hits
890 in 1936
Most sacrifices (sacrifice hits and sacrifice flies)
262 in 1917
Most sacrifice hits
195 in 1906
Most sacrifice flies
74 in 1980
Most stolen bases
211 in 1917
Most caught stealing
92 in 1920
Most bases on balls
723 in 1955
Most strikeouts
1,063 in 1964
Fewest strikeouts
331 in 1922, 1926
Most hit by pitch
54 in 1962
Fewest hit by pitch
11 in 1943, 1976

Most runs batted in
852 in 1936
Most game-winning RBIs
80 in 1986
Highest batting average
.308 in 1921
Lowest batting average
.234 in 1968, 1972
Highest slugging average
.461 in 1936
Lowest slugging average
.305 in 1910
Most grounded into double play
165 in 1980
Fewest grounded into double play
94 in 1941
Most left on bases
1,258 in 1982
Fewest left on bases
995 in 1959
Most .300 hitters
9 in 1921
Most putouts
4,463 in 1964
Fewest putouts
3,907 in 1945
Most assists
2,206 in 1907
Fewest assists
1,468 in 1968
Most chances accepted
6,563 in 1910
Fewest chances accepted
5,470 in 1945
Most errors
336 in 1901
Fewest errors
103 in 1949
Most errorless games
85 in 1971
Most consecutive errorless games
11 in 1967
Most double plays
197 in 1953
Fewest double plays
77 in 1915
Most passed balls
35 in 1958
Fewest passed balls
3 in 1943
Highest fielding average
.983 in 1947, 1949, 1980
Lowest fielding average
.941 in 1901
Highest home attendance
2,620,627 in 1948
Highest road attendance
2,223,384 in 1992
Most games won
111 in 1954
Most games lost
105 in 1991

Most games won, month
26 in August 1954
Most games lost, month
24 in July 1914
Highest percentage games won
.721 in 1954 (won 111, lost 43)
Lowest percentage games won
.333 in 1914 (won 51, lost 102)
Games won, league
7,335 in 94 years
Games lost, league
7,151 in 94 years
Most shutouts won, season
27 in 1906
Most shutouts lost, season
24 in 1914
Most 1-0 games won
7 in 1989
Most 1-0 games lost
7 in 1918, 1955
Most consecutive games won
13 in 1942, 1951
Most consecutive games lost
12 in 1931
Number of times league champions
3
Number of last-place finishes
6
Most runs, game
27 vs. Boston, July 7, 1923, first game
Most runs by opponent, game
24 by Boston, August 21, 1986
Most runs, shutout game
19 vs. Boston, May 18, 1955
Most runs by opponent, shutout game
21 by Detroit, September 15, 1901, eight innings
Most runs, doubleheader shutout
23 vs. Boston, June 23, 1931
Longest 1-0 game won
15 innings vs. Baltimore, May 14, 1961, first game
Longest 1-0 game lost
17 innings vs. Chicago, September 13, 1967
Most runs, inning
14 vs. Philadelphia, June 18, 1950, second game, first inning
Most hits, game
29 vs. St. Louis, August 12, 1948, second game
Most home runs, game
7 vs. Detroit, July 17, 1966, second game
Most consecutive games with one or more homers
16 (25 homers), 1963
Most total bases, game
45 vs. Philadelphia, July 10, 1932, 18 innings
43 vs. Boston, May 25, 1934
vs. Detroit, July 17, 1966, second game
Largest crowd, day game
74,420 vs. Detroit, April 7, 1973
Largest crowd, doubleheader
84,587 vs. New York, September 12, 1954
Largest crowd, night game
78,382 vs. Chicago, August 20, 1948
Largest crowd, home opener
74,420 vs. Detroit, April 7, 1973

DETROIT TIGERS

YEARLY FINISHES

Year	Position	W	L	Pct.	*GB	Manager	Attendance
1901 — 3rd		74	61	.548	8½	George Stallings	259,430
1902 — 7th		52	83	.385	30½	Frank Dwyer	189,469
1903 — 5th		65	71	.478	25	Ed Barrow	224,523
1904 — 7th		62	90	.408	32	Ed Barrow, Bobby Lowe	177,796
1905 — 3rd		79	74	.516	15½	Bill Armour	193,384
1906 — 6th		71	78	.477	21	Bill Armour	174,043
1907 — 1st		92	58	.613	+1½	Hughey Jennings	297,079
1908 — 1st		90	63	.588	+½	Hughey Jennings	436,199

Year	Position	W	L	Pct.	*GB	Manager	Attendance
1909 — 1st		98	54	.645	+3½	Hughey Jennings	490,490
1910 — 3rd		86	68	.558	18	Hughey Jennings	391,288
1911 — 2nd		89	65	.578	13½	Hughey Jennings	484,988
1912 — 6th		69	84	.451	36½	Hughey Jennings	402,870
1913 — 6th		66	87	.431	30	Hughey Jennings	398,502
1914 — 4th		80	73	.523	19½	Hughey Jennings	416,225
1915 — 2nd		100	54	.649	2½	Hughey Jennings	476,105
1916 — 3rd		87	67	.565	4	Hughey Jennings	616,772
1917 — 4th		78	75	.510	21½	Hughey Jennings	457,289
1918 — 7th		55	71	.437	20	Hughey Jennings	203,719
1919 — 4th		80	60	.571	8	Hughey Jennings	643,805
1920 — 7th		61	93	.396	37	Hughey Jennings	579,650
1921 — 6th		71	82	.464	27	Ty Cobb	661,527
1922 — 3rd		79	75	.513	15	Ty Cobb	861,206
1923 — 2nd		83	71	.539	16	Ty Cobb	911,377
1924 — 3rd		86	68	.558	6	Ty Cobb	1,015,136
1925 — 4th		81	73	.526	16½	Ty Cobb	820,766
1926 — 6th		79	75	.513	12	Ty Cobb	711,914
1927 — 4th		82	71	.536	27½	George Moriarty	773,716
1928 — 6th		68	86	.442	33	George Moriarty	474,323
1929 — 6th		70	84	.455	36	Bucky Harris	869,318
1930 — 5th		75	79	.487	27	Bucky Harris	649,450
1931 — 7th		61	93	.396	47	Bucky Harris	434,056
1932 — 5th		76	75	.503	29½	Bucky Harris	397,157
1933 — 5th		75	79	.487	25	Del Baker	320,972
1934 — 1st		101	53	.656	+7	Mickey Cochrane	919,161
1935 — 1st		93	58	.616	+3	Mickey Cochrane	1,034,929
1936 — 2nd		83	71	.539	19½	Mickey Cochrane	875,948
1937 — 2nd		89	65	.578	13	Mickey Cochrane	1,072,276
1938 — 4th		84	70	.545	16	Mickey Cochrane, Del Baker	799,557
1939 — 5th		81	73	.526	26½	Del Baker	836,279
1940 — 1st		90	64	.584	+1	Del Baker	1,112,693
1941 — 4th (tied)		75	79	.487	26	Del Baker	684,915
1942 — 5th		73	81	.474	30	Del Baker	580,087
1943 — 5th		78	76	.506	20	Steve O'Neill	606,287
1944 — 2nd		88	66	.571	1	Steve O'Neill	923,176
1945 — 1st		88	65	.575	+1½	Steve O'Neill	1,280,341
1946 — 2nd		92	62	.597	12	Steve O'Neill	1,722,590
1947 — 2nd		85	69	.552	12	Steve O'Neill	1,398,093
1948 — 5th		78	76	.506	18½	Steve O'Neill	1,743,035
1949 — 4th		87	67	.565	10	Red Rolfe	1,821,204
1950 — 2nd		95	59	.617	3	Red Rolfe	1,951,474
1951 — 5th		73	81	.474	25	Red Rolfe	1,132,641
1952 — 8th		50	104	.325	45	Red Rolfe, Fred Hutchinson	1,026,846
1953 — 6th		60	94	.390	40½	Fred Hutchinson	884,658
1954 — 5th		68	86	.442	43	Fred Hutchinson	1,079,847
1955 — 5th		79	75	.513	17	Bucky Harris	1,181,838
1956 — 5th		82	72	.532	15	Bucky Harris	1,051,182
1957 — 4th		78	76	.506	20	Jack Tighe	1,272,346
1958 — 5th		77	77	.500	15	Jack Tighe, Bill Norman	1,098,924
1959 — 4th		76	78	.494	18	Bill Norman, Jimmie Dykes	1,221,221
1960 — 6th		71	83	.461	26	Jimmie Dykes, Billy Hitchcock, Joe Gordon	1,167,669
1961 — 2nd		101	61	.623	8	Bob Scheffing	1,600,710
1962 — 4th		85	76	.528	10½	Bob Scheffing	1,207,881
1963 — 5th (tied)		79	83	.488	25½	Bob Scheffing, Charlie Dressen	821,952
1964 — 4th		85	77	.525	14	Charlie Dressen	816,139
1965 — 4th		89	73	.549	13	Charlie Dressen, Bob Swift	1,029,645
1966 — 3rd		88	74	.543	10	Charlie Dressen, Bob Swift, Frank Skaff	1,124,293
1967 — 2nd		91	71	.562	1	Mayo Smith	1,447,143
1968 — 1st		103	59	.636	+12	Mayo Smith	2,031,847

EAST DIVISION

Year	Position	W	L	Pct.	*GB	Manager	Attendance
1969 — 2nd		90	72	.556	19	Mayo Smith	1,577,481
1970 — 4th		79	83	.488	29	Mayo Smith	1,501,293
1971 — 2nd		91	71	.562	12	Billy Martin	1,591,073
1972 — 1st†		86	70	.551	+½	Billy Martin	1,892,386
1973 — 3rd		85	77	.525	12	Billy Martin, Joe Schultz	1,724,146
1974 — 6th		72	90	.444	19	Ralph Houk	1,243,080
1975 — 6th		57	102	.358	37½	Ralph Houk	1,058,836
1976 — 5th		74	87	.460	24	Ralph Houk	1,467,020
1977 — 4th		74	88	.457	26	Ralph Houk	1,359,856
1978 — 5th		86	76	.531	13½	Ralph Houk	1,714,893
1979 — 5th		85	76	.528	18	Les Moss, Dick Tracewski, Sparky Anderson	1,630,929
1980 — 5th		84	78	.519	19	Sparky Anderson	1,785,293

Year	Position	W	L	Pct.	*GB	Manager	Attendance
1981—4th/2nd (tied)		60	49	.550	‡	Sparky Anderson	1,149,144
1982—4th		83	79	.512	12	Sparky Anderson	1,636,058
1983—2nd		92	70	.568	6	Sparky Anderson	1,829,636
1984—1st§		104	58	.642	+15	Sparky Anderson	2,704,794
1985—3rd		84	77	.522	15	Sparky Anderson	2,286,609
1986—3rd		87	75	.537	8½	Sparky Anderson	1,899,437
1987—1st†		98	64	.605	+2	Sparky Anderson	2,061,830
1988—2nd		88	74	.543	1	Sparky Anderson	2,081,162
1989—7th		59	103	.364	30	Sparky Anderson	1,543,656
1990—3rd		79	83	.488	9	Sparky Anderson	1,495,785
1991—2nd		84	78	.519	7	Sparky Anderson	1,641,661
1992—6th		75	87	.463	21	Sparky Anderson	1,423,963
1993—3rd (tied)		85	77	.525	10	Sparky Anderson	1,971,421
1994—5th		53	62	.461	18	Sparky Anderson	1,184,783

*Games behind winner. †Lost Championship Series. ‡First half 31-26; second 29-23. §Won Championship Series.

INDIVIDUAL RECORDS (1901 TO DATE)

SERVICE

Most years by non-pitcher
22—Ty Cobb, Al Kaline
Most years by pitcher
16—Tommy Bridges

BATTING

Most games
163—Rocky Colavito, 1961
Most games, career
2,834—Albert W. Kaline
Most at-bats
679—Harvey Kuenn, 155 games, 1953
Most at-bats, career
10,586—Ty Cobb
Most singles
169—Ty Cobb, 146 games, 1911
Most singles, career
2,839—Ty Cobb
Most runs
147—Ty Cobb, 146 games, 1911
Most runs, career
2,086—Ty Cobb
Most hits
248—Ty Cobb, 146 games, 1911
Most hits, career
3,902—Ty Cobb
Most doubles
63—Hank Greenberg, 153 games, 1934
Most doubles, career
664—Ty Cobb
Most triples
26—Sam Crawford, 157 games, 1914
Most triples, career
287—Ty Cobb
Most homers by righthander
58—Hank Greenberg, 155 games, 1938
Most homers by lefthander
41—Norm Cash, 159 games, 1961
Most homers by rookie
35—Rudy York, 104 games, 1937
Most homers at home
39—Hank Greenberg, 1938
Most homers on road
27—Rocky Colavito, 1961
Most homers, month
18—Rudy York, August, 1937
Most homers by righthander, career
399—Al Kaline
Most homers by lefthander, career
373—Norm Cash
Most grand slams
4—Rudy York, 135 games, 1938
Jim Northrup, 155 games, 1968

Most grand slams, career
10—Rudy York
Hank Greenberg
Most total bases
397—Hank Greenberg, 154 games, 1937
Most total bases, career
5,474—Ty Cobb
Most long hits
103—Hank Greenberg, 154 games, 1937
Most long hits, career
1,063—Ty Cobb
Most extra bases on long hits
205—Hank Greenberg, 155 games, 1938
Most extra bases on long hits, career
1,845—Al Kaline
Most sacrifices (sacrifice hits and sacrifice flies)
52—Donie Bush, 157 games, 1909
Most sacrifice hits
36—Bill Coughlin, 147 games, 1906
Most sacrifice flies
16—Sam Crawford, 157 games, 1914
Most bases on balls
137—Roy Cullenbine, 142 games, 1947
Most bases on balls, career
1,277—Al Kaline
Most strikeouts
182—Cecil Fielder, 159 games, 1990
Most strikeouts, career
1,081—Norm Cash
Fewest strikeouts
13—Charlie Gehringer, 154 games, 1936
Harvey Kuenn, 155 games, 1954
Most hit by pitch
24—Bill Freehan, 155 games, 1968
Most runs batted in
183—Hank Greenberg, 154 games, 1937
Most runs batted in, career
1,826—Ty Cobb
Most game-winning RBIs
17—Kirk Gibson, 149 games, 1984
Most consecutive games with RBI
10—Willie Horton (17 RBIs), 1976
Highest batting average
.420—Ty Cobb, 146 games, 1911
Highest batting average, career
.368—Ty Cobb
Highest slugging average
.683—Hank Greenberg, 155 games, 1938
Highest slugging average, career
.616—Hank Greenberg
Longest batting streak
40 games—Ty Cobb, 1911
Most grounded into double play
29—Jimmy Bloodworth, 129 games, 1943
Fewest grounded into double play
0—Dick McAuliffe, 151 games, 1968

BASERUNNING

Most stolen bases
96—Ty Cobb, 156 games, 1915
Most stolen bases, career
865—Ty Cobb
Most caught stealing
38—Ty Cobb, 156 games, 1915

PITCHING

Most games
80—Willie Hernandez, 1984
Most games, career
545—John Hiller
Most games started
45—Mickey Lolich, 1971
Most games started, career
459—Mickey Lolich
Most complete games
42—George Mullin, 1904
Most complete games, career
336—George Mullin
Most games finished
68—Willie Hernandez, 1984
Most innings
382—George Mullin 1904
Most innings, career
3,398—George Mullin
Most games won
31—Denny McLain, 1968
Most games won, career
222—Hooks Dauss
Most games lost, career
183—Hooks Dauss
Most 20-victory seasons
5—George Mullin
Most games lost
23—George Mullin, 1904
Highest winning percentage
.862—Bill Donovan (25-4), 1907
Longest winning streak
16 games—Schoolboy Rowe, 1934

Longest losing streak
10 games—Mickey Lolich, 1967
Most saves
38—John Hiller, 1973
Most bases on balls
158—Joe Coleman Jr., 1974
Most bases on balls, career
1,227—Hal Newhouser
Most strikeouts
308—Mickey Lolich, 1971
Most strikeouts, career
2,679—Mickey Lolich
Most strikeouts, game
16—Mickey Lolich, May 23, 1969
Mickey Lolich, June 9, 1969, first nine innings of 10-inning game
Most shutouts
9—Denny McLain, 1969
Most shutouts, career
39—Mickey Lolich
Most 1-0 shutouts won
4—Ed Summers, 1908
Most runs
160—Joe Coleman Jr., 1974
Most earned runs
142—Mickey Lolich, 1974
Most hits
336—Mickey Lolich, 1971
Most hit batsmen
23—Howard Ehmke, 1922
Most wild pitches
24—Jack Morris, 1987
Most home runs
42—Denny McLain, 1966
Most sacrifice hits
28—Earl Whitehill, 1931
Most sacrifice flies
13—Jack Morris, 1980
Lowest ERA
1.81—Hal Newhouser, 313 innings, 1945

CLUB RECORDS

Most players
53 in 1912
Fewest players
24 in 1906, 1907
Most games
164 in 1968
Most at-bats
5,649 in 1987
Most runs
958 in 1934
Fewest runs
499 in 1904
Most opponents' runs
928 in 1929
Most hits
1,724 in 1921
Fewest hits
1,204 in 1905
Most singles
1,298 in 1921
Most doubles
349 in 1934
Most triples
102 in 1913
Most homers
225 in 1987
Fewest homers (154 or 162-game schedule)
9 in 1906
Most homers at Tiger Stadium, home and opponents
226 in 1987

Most grand slams
10 in 1938
Most pinch home runs
8 in 1971
Most total bases
2,548 in 1987
Most long hits
546 in 1929
Most extra bases on long hits
1,013 in 1987
Most sacrifices (sacrifice hits and sacrifice flies)
256 in 1923
Most sacrifice hits
182 in 1906
Most sacrifice flies
59 in 1983
Most stolen bases
281 in 1909
Most caught stealing
92 in 1921
Most bases on balls
765 in 1993
Most strikeouts
1,185 in 1991
Fewest strikeouts
376 in 1921
Most hit by pitch
61 in 1968
Fewest hit by pitch
9 in 1945

Most runs batted in
873 in 1937
Most game-winning RBIs
97 in 1984
Highest batting average
.316 in 1921
Lowest batting average
.230 in 1904
Highest slugging average
.453 in 1929
Lowest slugging average
.321 in 1918
Most grounded into double play
164 in 1949
Fewest grounded into double play
81 in 1985
Most left on base
1,312 in 1993
Fewest left on base
1,025 in 1972
Most .300 hitters
8 in 1922, 1924, 1934
Most putouts
4,469 in 1968
Fewest putouts
4,006 in 1906
Most assists
2,272 in 1914
Fewest assists, season
1,443 in 1962
Most chances accepted
6,504 in 1914
Fewest chances accepted
5,594 in 1959
Most errors
425 in 1901
Fewest errors
96 in 1972
Most errorless games
85 in 1988
Most consecutive errorless games
12 in 1963
Most double plays
194 in 1950
Fewest double plays
94 in 1912, 1917
Most passed balls
28 in 1912
Fewest passed balls
4 in 1924
Highest fielding average
.984 in 1972
Lowest fielding average
.922 in 1901
Highest home attendance
2,704,794 in 1984
Highest road attendance
2,396,528 in 1991
Most games won
104 in 1984
Most games lost
104 in 1952
Most games won, month
23 in July 1908, August 1915, August 1934, August 1935
Most games lost, month
24 in June 1975

Highest percentage games won
.656 in 1934 (won 101, lost 53)
Lowest percentage games won
.325 in 1952 (won 50, lost 104)
Games won, league
7,509 in 94 years
Games lost, league
7,000 in 94 years
Most shutouts won
20 in 1917, 1944, 1969
Most shutouts lost
22 in 1904
Most 1-0 games won
9 in 1908
Most 1-0 games lost
7 in 1903, 1943
Most consecutive games won
14 in 1909, 1934
Most consecutive games lost
19 in 1975
Number of times league champions
9
Number of last place finishes
3
Most runs, game
21 vs. Cleveland, September 15, 1901, eight innings
vs. Philadelphia, July 17, 1908
vs. St. Louis, July 25, 1920
vs. Chicago, July 1, 1936
Most runs by opponent, game
24 by Philadelphia, May 18, 1912
Most runs, shutout game
21 vs. Cleveland, September 15, 1901, eight innings
Most runs by opponent, shutout game
16 by St. Louis, September 9, 1922
Most runs, doubleheader shutout
26 vs. St. Louis, September 22, 1936
Most runs, inning
13 vs. New York, June 17, 1925, sixth inning
Longest 1-0 game won
12 innings vs. St. Louis, September 8, 1917
vs. Cleveland, June 26, 1919
vs. Chicago, September 10, 1950, first game
Longest 1-0 game lost
16 innings vs. Chicago, August 14, 1954
Most hits, game
28 vs. New York, September 29, 1928
Most home runs, game
6 vs. St. Louis, August 14, 1937, second game
vs. Philadelphia, June 11, 1954, first game
vs. Kansas City, July 20, 1962
vs. California, July 4, 1968
vs. Oakland, August 17, 1969
vs. Boston, August 9, 1971
vs. Milwaukee, September 10, 1986
Most consecutive games with one or more homers
25 (46 homers), 1994
Most total bases
45 vs. St. Louis, August 14, 1937, second game
Largest crowd, day game
57,888 vs. Cleveland, September 26, 1948
Largest crowd, doubleheader
58,369 vs. New York, July 20, 1947
Largest crowd, night game
56,586 vs. Cleveland, August 9, 1948
Largest crowd, home opener
54,089 vs. Cleveland, April 6, 1971

KANSAS CITY A'S

YEARLY FINISHES

Year	Position	W	L	Pct.	*GB	Manager	Attendance
1955 — 6th		63	91	.409	33	Lou Boudreau	1,393,054
1956 — 8th		52	102	.338	45	Lou Boudreau	1,015,154
1957 — 7th		59	94	.386	38½	Lou Boudreau, Harry Craft	901,067

Year	Position	W	L	Pct.	*GB	Manager	Attendance
1958—7th		73	81	.474	19	Harry Craft	925,090
1959—7th		66	88	.429	28	Harry Craft	963,683
1960—8th		58	96	.377	39	Bob Elliot	774,944
1961—9th†		61	100	.379	47½	Joe Gordon, Hank Bauer	683,817
1962—9th		72	90	.444	24	Hank Bauer	635,675
1963—8th		73	89	.451	31½	Ed Lopat	762,364
1964—10th		57	105	.352	42	Ed Lopat, Mel McGaha	642,478
1965—10th		59	103	.364	43	Mel McGaha, Haywood Sullivan	528,344
1966—7th		74	86	.463	23	Alvin Dark	773,929
1967—10th		62	99	.385	29½	Alvin Dark, Luke Appling	726,639

*Games behind winner.   †Tied for position.

INDIVIDUAL RECORDS (1955 TO 1967)

SERVICE

Most years by non-pitcher
6—Ed Charles
Billy Bryan
Wayne Causey
Most years by pitcher
6—John Wyatt

BATTING

Most games
162—Norm Siebern, 1962
Most games, career
726—Ed Charles
Most at-bats
641—Jerry Lumpe, 156 games, 1962
Most at-bats, career
2,782—Jerry Lumpe
Most runs
114—Norm Siebern, 162 games, 1962
Most runs, career
361—Jerry Lumpe
Most hits
193—Jerry Lumpe, 156 games, 1962
Most hits, career
775—Jerry Lumpe
Most doubles
36—Norm Siebern, 153 games, 1961
Most doubles, career
119—Jerry Lumpe
Most triples
15—Gino Cimoli, 152 games, 1962
Most triples, career
34—Jerry Lumpe
Most homers by righthander
38—Bob Cerv, 141 games, 1958
Most homers by lefthander
28—Jim Gentile, 136 games, 1964
Most homers by rookie
20—Woodie Held, 92 games, 1957
Most homers at home
22—Rocky Colavito, 1964
Most homers on road
17—Bob Cerv, 1958
Most homers, month
10—Rocky Colavito, May, 1964
Most homers, career
78—Norm Siebern
Most grand slams
2—Roger Maris, 99 games, 1958
Marv Throneberry, 104 games, 1960
Most grand slams, career
3—Roger Maris, Marv Throneberry
Most pinch homers, career
4—George Alusik, Bob Cerv
Most total bases
305—Bob Cerv, 141 games, 1958
Most total bases, career
1,065—Ed Charles
Most long hits
67—Rocky Colavito, 160 games, 1964

Most extra bases on long hits
148—Bob Cerv, 141 games, 1958
Most sacrifice hits
11—Dick Williams, 130 games, 1959
Most sacrifice flies
12—Leo Posada, 116 games, 1961
Most bases on balls
110—Norm Siebern, 162 games, 1962
Most bases on balls, career
343—Norm Siebern
Most strikeouts
143—Nelson Mathews, 157 games, 1964
Fewest strikeouts
38—Dick Howser, 158 games, 1961
Jerry Lumpe, 156 games, 1962
Most strikeouts, career
379—Ed Charles
Most hit by pitch
13—Bobby Del Greco, 132 games, 1962
Most runs batted in
117—Norm Siebern, 162 games, 1962
Most runs batted in, career
367—Norm Siebern
Highest batting average
.319—Vic Power, 147 games, 1955
Highest slugging average
.592—Bob Cerv, 148 games, 1958
Longest batting streak
22 games—Hector Lopez, 1957
Vic Power, 1958
Most grounded into double play
23—Hector Lopez, 151 games, 1958
Fewest grounded into double play
4—Norm Siebern, 153 games, 1961

BASERUNNING

Most stolen bases
55—Bert Campaneris, 147 games, 1967
Most stolen bases, career
168—Bert Campaneris
Most caught stealing
19—Bert Campaneris, 144 games, 1965

PITCHING

Most games
81—John Wyatt, 1964
Most games, career
292—John Wyatt
Most games started
35—Bud Daley, 1960
Ed Rakow, 1962
Diego Segui, 1964
Catfish Hunter, 1967
Most games started, career
98—Ray Herbert
Most complete games
14—Art Ditmar, 1956
Ray Herbert, 1960
Most complete games, career
32—Ray Herbert
Most games finished
57—John Wyatt, 1964
Jack Aker, 1966

— 239 —

Most innings
260—Catfish Hunter, 1967
Most innings, career
784—Ray Herbert
Most games won
16—Bud Daley, 1959, 1960
Most games won, career
39—Bud Daley
Most games lost
22—Art Ditmar, 1956
Most games lost, career
48—Ray Herbert
Highest winning percentage
.552—Bud Daley (16-13), 1959
Longest winning streak
9 games—Bud Daley, 1960
Longest losing streak
11 games—Troy Herriage, 1956
Most bases on balls
108—Art Ditmar, 1956
Most bases on balls, career
280—Diego Segui
Most strikeouts
196—Catfish Hunter, 1967
Most strikeouts, game
12—Jim Nash, July 13, 1967

Jim Nash, July 23, 1967, second game
Catfish Hunter, September 12, 1967
Most strikeouts, career
513—Diego Segui
Most shutouts
5—Catfish Hunter, 1967
Most shutouts, career
8—Ned Garver
Most 1-0 shutouts won
2—Alex Kellner, 1955
Catfish Hunter, 1967
Most runs
141—Art Ditmar, 1956
Most earned runs
125—Art Ditmar, 1956
Most hits
256—Ray Herbert, 1960
Most hit batsmen
12—Johnny Kucks, 1959
Most wild pitches
13—John Wyatt, 1965
Most home runs
40—Orlando Pena, 1964
Lowest ERA
2.80—Catfish Hunter, 260 innings, 1967

CLUB RECORDS

Most players
52 in 1955, 1961
Fewest players
38 in 1957
Most games
163 in 1964
Most at-bats
5,576 in 1962
Most runs
745 in 1962
Most opponents' runs
911 in 1955
Most hits
1,467 in 1962
Most singles
1,073 in 1962
Most doubles
231 in 1959
Most triples
59 in 1965
Most homers
166 in 1957, 1964
Fewest homers
69 in 1967
Most homers at Municipal Stadium, home and opponents
239 in 1964
Most grand slams
4 in 1958, 1959, 1960
Most pinch home runs
7 in 1964
Most total bases
2,151 in 1962
Most long hits
411 in 1964
Most extra bases on long hits
773 in 1957
Most sacrifice hits
89 in 1961
Most sacrifice flies
50 in 1962
Fewest sacrifice flies
25 in 1964
Most stolen bases
132 in 1966, 1967
Most caught stealing
59 in 1967

Fewest caught stealing
11 in 1960
Most bases on balls
580 in 1961
Most strikeouts
1,104 in 1964
Most hit by pitch
42 in 1962, 1964, 1967
Fewest hit by pitch
12 in 1960
Most runs batted in
691 in 1962
Highest batting average
.263 in 1959, 1962
Lowest batting average
.233 in 1967
Highest slugging average
.394 in 1957
Lowest slugging average
.330 in 1967
Most grounded into double play
154 in 1960
Fewest grounded into double play
79 in 1967
Most left on bases
1,224 in 1962
Fewest left on bases
925 in 1957
Most .300 hitters
4 in 1955
Most putouts
4,374 in 1963
Most assists
1,782 in 1956
Fewest assists
1,532 in 1967
Most chances accepted
6,103 in 1963
Fewest chances accepted
5,750 in 1959
Most errors
175 in 1961
Most errorless games
78 in 1963
Fewest errors
125 in 1957, 1958
Most consecutive errorless games
8 in 1960, 1964

Most double plays
187 in 1956
Most passed balls
34 in 1958
Highest fielding average
.980 in 1963
Lowest fielding average
.972 in 1961
Highest home attendance
1,393,054 in 1955
Highest road attendance
938,214 in 1967
Most games won
74 in 1966
Most games lost
105 in 1964
Most games won, month
19, July 1959
Most games lost, month
26, August 1961
Highest percentage games won
.474 in 1958 (won 73, lost 81)
Lowest percentage games won
.338 in 1956 (won 52, lost 102)
Games won, league
829 in 13 years
Games lost, league
1,224 in 13 years
Most shutouts won
11 in 1963, 1966
Most shutouts lost
19 in 1967
Most 1-0 games won
4 in 1966
Most 1-0 games lost
5 in 1967
Most consecutive games won
11 in 1959
Most consecutive games lost
13 in 1959
Number of times league champions
0
Number of last-place finishes
6 (tied in 1961)

Most runs, game
20 vs. Minnesota, April 25, 1961
Most runs by opponent, game
29 by Chicago, April 23, 1955
Most runs, shutout game
16 vs. Chicago, May 23, 1959
Most runs by opponent, shutout game
16 by Detroit, April 17, 1955
by Boston, August 26, 1957
Most runs, doubleheader shutout
9 vs. Detroit, July 9, 1959
Most runs, inning
13 vs. Chicago, April 21, 1956, second inning
Longest 1-0 game won
11 innings vs. Cleveland, September 15, 1966
Longest 1-0 game lost
None over nine innings
Most hits, nine-inning game
21 vs. Washington, June 13, 1956
vs. Chicago, May 23, 1959
vs. Cleveland, May 5, 1962, first game
Most hits, extra-inning game
26 vs. New York, July 27, 1956, 14 innings
Most home runs, game
5 vs. Cleveland, April 18, 1955
vs. Cleveland, April 24, 1957
vs. Baltimore, September 9, 1958
Most consecutive games with one or more homer
11 (13 homers), 1964
Most total bases, game
36 vs. New York, July 27, 1956, 14 innings
vs. Washington, June 13, 1956
vs. Chicago, May 23, 1959
vs. Cleveland, May 5, 1962, first game
Largest crowd, day game
34,065 vs. New York, August 27, 1961
Largest crowd, doubleheader
35,147 vs. New York, August 18, 1962
Largest crowd, night game
33,471 vs. New York, April 29, 1955
Largest crowd, home opener
32,147 vs. Detroit, April 12, 1955

KANSAS CITY ROYALS

YEARLY FINISHES

WEST DIVISION

Year	Position	W	L	Pct.	*GB	Manager	Attendance
1969	4th	69	93	.429	28	Joe Gordon	902,414
1970	4th (tied)	65	97	.401	33	Charlie Metro, Bob Lemon	693,047
1971	2nd	85	76	.528	16	Bob Lemon	910,784
1972	4th	76	78	.494	16½	Bob Lemon	707,656
1973	2nd	88	74	.543	6	Jack McKeon	1,345,341
1974	5th	77	85	.475	13	Jack McKeon	1,173,292
1975	2nd	91	71	.562	7	Jack McKeon, Whitey Herzog	1,151,836
1976	1st†	90	72	.556	+ 2½	Whitey Herzog	1,680,265
1977	1st†	102	60	.630	+ 8	Whitey Herzog	1,852,603
1978	1st†	92	70	.568	+ 5	Whitey Herzog	2,255,493
1979	2nd	85	77	.525	3	Whitey Herzog	2,261,845
1980	1st‡	97	65	.599	+14	Jim Frey	2,288,714
1981	5th/1st	50	53	.485	§	Jim Frey, Dick Howser	1,279,403
1982	2nd	90	72	.556	3	Dick Howser	2,284,464
1983	2nd	79	83	.488	20	Dick Howser	1,963,875
1984	1st†	84	78	.519	+ 3	Dick Howser	1,810,018
1985	1st‡	91	71	.562	+ 1	Dick Howser	2,162,717
1986	3rd (tied)	76	86	.469	16	Dick Howser, Mike Ferraro	2,320,794
1987	2nd	83	79	.512	2	Billy Gardner, John Wathan	2,392,471
1988	3rd	84	77	.522	19½	John Wathan	2,350,181
1989	2nd	92	70	.568	7	John Wathan	2,477,700
1990	6th	75	86	.466	27½	John Wathan	2,244,956
1991	6th	82	80	.506	13	John Wathan, Hal McRae	2,161,537
1992	5th (tied)	72	90	.444	24	Hal McRae	1,867,689
1993	3rd	84	78	.519	10	Hal McRae	1,934,578

Year	Position	W	L	Pct.	*GB	Manager	Attendance
1994	—3rd	64	51	.557	4	Hal McRae	1,400,494

*Games behind winner.   †Lost Championship Series.   ‡Won Championship Series.   §First half 20-30; second 30-23.

INDIVIDUAL RECORDS (1969 TO DATE)

SERVICE

Most years by non-pitcher
21—George Brett
Most years by pitcher
15—Paul Splittorff

BATTING

Most games
162—Al Cowens, 1977
    Hal McRae, 1977
Most games, career
2,707—George Brett
Most at-bats
705—Willie Wilson, 161 games, 1980
Most at-bats, career
10,349—George Brett
Most runs
133—Willie Wilson, 161 games, 1980
Most runs, career
1,583—George Brett
Most hits
230—Willie Wilson, 161 games, 1980
Most hits, career
3,154—George Brett
Most singles
184—Willie Wilson, 161 games, 1980
Most singles, career
2,035—George Brett
Most doubles
54—Hal McRae, 162 games, 1977
Most doubles, career
665—George Brett
Most triples
21—Willie Wilson, 141 games, 1985
Most triples, career
137—George Brett
Most homers by lefthander
34—John Mayberry, 156 games, 1975
Most homers by righthander
36—Steve Balboni, 160 games, 1985
Most homers by rookie
24—Bob Hamelin, 101 games, 1994
Most homers, month
12—John Mayberry, July, 1975
Most homers at home
17—Steve Balboni, 1985
Most homers on road
23—John Mayberry, 1975
Most homers by lefthander, career
317—George Brett
Most homers by righthander, career
193—Amos Otis
Most grand slams
3—Danny Tartabull, 1988
Most grand slams, career
6—Frank White
Most total bases
363—George Brett, 154 games, 1979
Most total bases, career
5,044—George Brett
Most long hits
86—Hal McRae, 162 games, 1977
Most long hits, career
1,119—George Brett
Most extra bases on long hits
151—George Brett, 154 games, 1979

Most extra bases on long hits, career
1,890—George Brett
Most sacrifice hits
18—Frank White, 152 games, 1976
Most sacrifice flies
13—Darrell Porter, 157 games, 1979
Most bases on balls
122—John Mayberry, 152 games, 1973
Most bases on balls, career
1,096—George Brett
Most strikeouts
172—Bo Jackson, 135 games, 1989
Most strikeouts, career
1,035—Frank White
Fewest strikeouts
22—George Brett, 117 games, 1980
Most hit by pitch
18—Mike Macfarlane, 92 games, 1994
Most runs batted in
133—Hal McRae, 159 games, 1982
Most runs batted in, career
1,595—George Brett
Most game-winning RBIs
21—Danny Tartabull, 158 games, 1987
Longest batting streak
30 games—George Brett, 1980
Highest batting average
.390—George Brett, 117 games, 1980
Highest batting average, career
.305—George Brett
Highest slugging average
.664—George Brett, 117 games, 1980
Highest slugging average, career
.487—George Brett
Most grounded into double play
26—John Wathan, 121 games, 1982
Fewest grounded into double play
1—Willie Wilson, 154 games, 1979

BASERUNNING

Most stolen bases
83—Willie Wilson, 154 games, 1979
Most stolen bases, career
612—Willie Wilson
Most caught stealing
17—Greg Gagne, 107 games, 1994

PITCHING

Most games
84—Dan Quisenberry, 1985
Most games, career
573—Dan Quisenberry
Most games started
40—Dennis Leonard, 1978
Most games started, career
392—Paul Splittorff
Most complete games
21—Dennis Leonard, 1977
Most complete games, career
103—Dennis Leonard
Most games finished
76—Dan Quisenberry, 1985
Most innings
295—Dennis Leonard, 1978
Most innings, career
2,555—Paul Splittorff
Most games won
23—Bret Saberhagen, 1989

Most games won, career
166—Paul Splittorff
Most games lost
19—Paul Splittorff, 1974
Most games lost, career
143—Paul Splittorff
Most 20-victory seasons
3—Dennis Leonard
Highest winning percentage
.800—Larry Gura (16-4), 1978
Longest winning streak
11 games—Rich Gale, 1980
Longest winning streak, two seasons
11 games—Paul Splittorff, 1977-78
Longest losing streak
8 games—Dick Drago, 1970
Wally Bunker, 1970
Bill Butler, 1970
Most saves
45—Dan Quisenberry, 1983
Jeff Montgomery, 1993
Most bases on balls
120—Mark Gubicza, 1987
Most bases on balls, career
780—Paul Splittorff
Most strikeouts
244—Dennis Leonard, 1977
Most strikeouts, career
1,323—Dennis Leonard
Most strikeouts, game
14—Mark Gubicza, August 27, 1988

Most shutouts won
6—Roger Nelson, 1972
Most 1-0 shutouts won
2—Dick Drago, 1971
Roger Nelson, 1972
Al Fitzmorris, 1974
Dennis Leonard, 1979
Larry Gura, 1982
Most shutouts, career
23—Dennis Leonard
Most runs
137—Larry Gura, 1979
Paul Splittorff, 1979
Most earned runs
118—Dennis Leonard, 1980
Most hits
284—Steve Busby, 1974
Most wild pitches
17—Tom Gordon, 1993
Most hit batsmen
13—Jim Colborn, 1977
Mike Boddicker, 1991
Most home runs
33—Dennis Leonard, 1979
Most sacrifice hits
18—Larry Gura, 1978
Most sacrifice flies
17—Larry Gura, 1983
Lowest ERA
2.08—Roger Nelson, 173 innings, 1972

CLUB RECORDS

Most players
46 in 1990
Fewest players
32 in 1975
Most games
163 in 1969, 1983
Most at-bats
5,714 in 1980
Most runs
851 in 1979
Fewest runs
580 in 1972
Most opponents' runs
816 in 1979
Most hits
1,633 in 1980
Fewest hits
1,311 in 1969
Most singles
1,193 in 1980
Most doubles
316 in 1990
Most triples
79 in 1979
Most homers
168 in 1987
Fewest homers
65 in 1976
Most homers at Municipal Stadium, home and opponents
102 in 1969
Most homers at Royals Stadium, home and opponents
134 in 1979
Most grand slams
7 in 1991
Most pinch home runs
5 in 1991
Most total bases
2,440 in 1977
Most long hits
522 in 1977
Most extra bases on long hits
891 in 1977

Most sacrifice hits
72 in 1972
Most sacrifice flies
76 in 1979
Most stolen bases
218 in 1976
Most caught stealing
87 in 1977
Most bases on balls
644 in 1973
Most strikeouts
1,034 in 1987
Fewest strikeouts
644 in 1978
Most hit by pitch
52 in 1993
Fewest hit by pitch
23 in 1983
Most runs batted in
791 in 1979
Most game-winning RBIs
92 in 1980
Highest batting average
.286 in 1980
Lowest batting average
.240 in 1969
Most .300 hitters
3 in 1980, 1982, 1983
Highest slugging average
.436 in 1977
Lowest slugging average
.338 in 1969
Most grounded into double play
147 in 1980
Fewest grounded into double play
95 in 1978
Most left on bases
1,209 in 1980
Fewest left on bases
1,057 in 1985
Most putouts
4,417 in 1976

Fewest putouts
4,144 in 1972
Most assists
1,912 in 1973
Fewest assists
1,598 in 1990
Most chances accepted
6,290 in 1974. 1985
Fewest chances accepted
5,860 in 1990
Most errors
167 in 1973
Fewest errors
97 in 1993
Most errorless games
95 in 1993
Most consecutive errorless games
9 in 1994
Most double plays
192 in 1973
Fewest double plays
114 in 1969
Most passed balls
29 in 1974
Fewest passed balls
3 in 1984
Highest fielding average
.984 in 1993
Lowest fielding average
.974 in 1973, 1983
Highest home attendance
2,477,700 in 1989
Highest road attendance
2,378,624 in 1993
Most games won
102 in 1977
Most games lost
97 in 1970
Most games won, month
25 in September 1977
Most games lost, month
20 in September 1974
Highest percentage games won
.630 in 1977 (won 102, lost 60)
Lowest percentage games won
.401 in 1970 (won 65, lost 97)
Games won, league
2,123 in 26 years
Games lost, league
1,972 in 26 years

Most shutouts won
16 in 1972
Most shutouts lost
18 in 1971, 1989
Most 1 - 0 shutouts won
5 in 1972
Most 1 - 0 shutouts lost
4 in 1971, 1989, 1992
Most consecutive games won
16 in 1977
Most consecutive games lost
11 in 1986
Number of times league champions
2
Number of last - place finishes
0
Most runs, inning
11 vs. Toronto, August 6, 1979, seventh inning
vs. Boston, August 2, 1986, seventh inning
Most runs, game
23 vs. Minnesota, April 6, 1974
Most runs by opponent, game
22 by Boston, April 12, 1994
Most runs, shutout game
16 vs. Oakland, June 25, 1984
Most runs by opponent, shutout game
17 by Detroit, July 19, 1991
Most runs, doubleheader shutout
No performance
Longest 1 - 0 game won
15 innings vs. Minnesota, May 23, 1981
Longest 1 - 0 game lost
14 innings vs. Cleveland, July 23, 1992
Most hits, game
24 vs. Detroit, June 15, 1976
Most home runs, game
6 vs. Detroit, July 14, 1991
Most consecutive games with one or more homers
12 (19 homers), 1985
Most total bases, game
36 vs. Detroit, June 15, 1976
vs. Chicago, May 13, 1979
vs. Milwaukee, May 11, 1982
Largest crowd, day game
41,329 vs. Oakland, September 21, 1980
Largest crowd. doubleheader
42,039 vs. Milwaukee, August 8, 1983
Largest crowd, night game
41,860 vs. New York, July 26, 1980
Largest crowd, home opener
41,086 vs. Toronto, April 8, 1985

MILWAUKEE BREWERS

YEARLY FINISHES

WEST DIVISION

Year Position	W	L	Pct.	*GB	Manager	Attendance
1970 —4th	65	97	.401	33	Dave Bristol	933,690
1971 —6th	69	92	.429	32	Dave Bristol	731,531

EAST DIVISION

Year Position	W	L	Pct.	*GB	Manager	Attendance
1972 —6th	65	91	.417	21	Dave Bristol, Del Crandall	600,440
1973 —5th	74	88	.457	23	Del Crandall	1,092,158
1974 —5th	76	86	.469	15	Del Crandall	955,741
1975 —5th	68	94	.420	28	Del Crandall	1,213,357
1976 —6th	66	95	.410	32	Alex Grammas	1,012,164
1977 —6th	67	95	.414	33	Alex Grammas	1,114,938
1978 —3rd	93	69	.574	6½	George Bamberger	1,601,406
1979 —2nd	95	66	.590	8	George Bamberger	1,918,343
1980 —3rd	86	76	.531	17	George Bamberger, Buck Rodgers	1,857,408
1981 —3rd/ 1st‡	62	47	.569	†	Buck Rodgers	878,432
1982 — 1st‡	95	67	.586	+ 1	Buck Rodgers, Harvey Kuenn	1,978,896
1983 —5th	87	75	.537	11	Harvey Kuenn	2,397,131

Year	Position	W	L	Pct.	*GB	Manager	Attendance
1984 —7th	67	94	.416	36½	Rene Lachemann	1,608,509
1985 —6th	71	90	.441	28	George Bamberger	1,360,265
1986 —6th	77	84	.478	18	George Bamberger, Tom Trebelhorn	1,265,041
1987 —3rd	91	71	.562	7	Tom Trebelhorn	1,909,244
1988 —3rd (tied)	87	75	.537	2	Tom Trebelhorn	1,923,238
1989 —4th	81	81	.500	8	Tom Trebelhorn	1,970,735
1990 —6th	74	88	.457	14	Tom Trebelhorn	1,752,900
1991 —4th	83	79	.512	8	Tom Trebelhorn	1,478,729
1992 —2nd	92	70	.568	4	Phil Garner	1,857,314
1993 —7th	69	93	.426	26	Phil Garner	1,688,080

CENTRAL DIVISION

Year	Position	W	L	Pct.	*GB	Manager	Attendance
1994 —5th	53	62	.461	15	Phil Garner	1,268,399

*Games behind winner.   †First half 31-25; second 31-22.   ‡Won Championship Series.

INDIVIDUAL RECORDS (1970 TO DATE)

SERVICE

Most years by non-pitcher
20—Robin Yount
Most years by pitcher
12—Jim Slaton

BATTING

Most games
162—Gorman Thomas, 1980
Robin Yount, 1988
Most games, career
2,856—Robin Yount
Most at-bats
666—Paul Molitor, 160 games, 1982
Most at-bats, career
11,008—Robin Yount
Most runs
136—Paul Molitor, 160 games, 1982
Most runs, career
1,632—Robin Yount
Most hits
219—Cecil Cooper, 153 games, 1980
Most hits, career
3,142—Robin Yount
Most singles
157—Cecil Cooper, 153 games, 1980
Most singles, career
2,182—Robin Yount
Most doubles
49—Robin Yount, 143 games, 1980
Most doubles, career
583—Robin Yount
Most triples
16—Paul Molitor, 140 games, 1979
Most triples, career
126—Robin Yount
Most homers by righthander
45—Gorman Thomas, 156 games, 1979
Most homers by lefthander
41—Ben Oglivie, 156 games, 1980
Most homers by rookie
17—Greg Vaughn, 120 games, 1990
Most homers at home
22—Gorman Thomas, 1979
Most homers on road
26—Ben Oglivie, 156 games, 1980
Most homers, month
12—Gorman Thomas, August, 1979
Most homers by righthander, career
251—Robin Yount
Most homers by lefthander, career
201—Cecil Cooper
Most grand slams
2—Davey May, 156 games, 1973

Sixto Lezcano, 132 games, 1978
Robin Yount, 143 games, 1980
Rob Deer, 134 games, 1987
Most grand slams, career
5—Cecil Cooper
Most total bases
367—Robin Yount, 156 games, 1982
Most total bases, career
4,730—Robin Yount
Most long hits
87—Robin Yount, 156 games, 1982
Most long hits, career
960—Robin Yount
Most extra bases on long hits
164—Gorman Thomas, 156 games, 1979
Most extra bases on long hits, career
1,588—Robin Yount
Most sacrifice hits
19—Ron Theobald, 126 games, 1971
Most sacrifice flies
14—Dave Parker, 157 games, 1990
Most bases on balls
98—Gorman Thomas, 156 games, 1979
Most bases on balls, career
966—Robin Yount
Most strikeouts
186—Rob Deer, 134 games, 1987
Most strikeouts, career
1,350—Robin Yount
Fewest strikeouts
42—Cecil Cooper, 153 games, 1980
Most hit by pitch
10—Ellie Rodriguez, 94 games, 1973
Jim Gantner, 116 games, 1989
John Jaha, 84 games, 1994
Longest batting streak
39 games—Paul Molitor, 1987
Most runs batted in
126—Cecil Cooper, 160 games, 1983
Most runs batted in, career
1,406—Robin Yount
Most game-winning RBIs
17—Cecil Cooper, 160 games, 1983
Ted Simmons, 153 games, 1983
Robin Yount, 158 games, 1987
Highest batting average
.353—Paul Molitor, 118 games, 1987
Highest batting average, career
.303—Paul Molitor
Highest slugging average
.578—Robin Yount, 156 games, 1982
Highest slugging average, career
.505—Larry Hisle
Most grounded into double play
26—George Scott, 158 games, 1975
Fewest grounded into double play
3—Tommy Harper, 152 games, 1971

BASERUNNING

Most stolen bases
54—Pat Listach, 149 games, 1992
Most stolen bases, career
412—Paul Molitor
Most caught stealing
18—Pat Listach, 149 games, 1992

PITCHING

Most games
83—Ken Sanders, 1971
Most games, career
365—Dan Plesac
Most games started
38—Jim Slaton, 1973, 1976
Most games started, career
268—Jim Slaton
Most complete games
23—Mike Caldwell, 1978
Most complete games, career
81—Mike Caldwell
Most games finished
77—Ken Sanders, 1971
Most innings
314—Jim Colborn, 1973
Most innings, career
2,025—Jim Slaton
Most games won
22—Mike Caldwell, 1978
Most games won, career
117—Jim Slaton
Most games lost
20—Clyde Wright, 1974
Most games lost, career
121—Jim Slaton
Highest winning percentage
.750—Pete Vuckovich (18-6), 1982
Most 20-victory seasons
1—Jim Colborn, Mike Caldwell, Teddy Higuera

Longest winning streak
10 games—Chris Bosio, 1992
Cal Eldred, 1992
Longest losing streak
10 games—Danny Darwin, 1985
Most saves, season
33—Dan Plesac, 1989
Most bases on balls
106—Pete Broberg, 1975
Most bases on balls, career
760—Jim Slaton
Most strikeouts
240—Teddy Higuera, 1987
Most strikeouts, career
1,081—Teddy Higuera
Most strikeouts, game
14—Moose Haas, April 12, 1978
Most shutouts won
6—Mike Caldwell, 1978
Most shutouts, career
19—Jim Slaton
Most 1-0 shutouts won
1—Held by many pitchers
Most runs
135—Jaime Navarro, 1993
Most earned runs
127—Jaime Navarro, 1993
Most hits
297—Jim Colborn, 1973
Most hit batsmen
16—Pete Broberg, 1975
Most wild pitches
14—Jim Slaton, 1974
Chris Bosio, 1987
Most home runs allowed
35—Mike Caldwell, 1983
Most sacrifice hits
15—Jim Slaton, 1976
Most sacrifice flies
17—Jaime Navarro, 1993
Lowest ERA
2.37—Mike Caldwell, 293 innings, 1978

CLUB RECORDS

Most players
45 in 1970
Fewest players
31 in 1979
Most games
163 in 1970, 1982
Most at-bats
5,733 in 1982
Most runs
891 in 1982
Fewest runs
494 in 1972
Most opponents' runs
817 in 1987
Most hits
1,599 in 1982
Fewest hits
1,188 in 1971
Most singles
1,107 in 1991
Most doubles
298 in 1980
Most triples
57 in 1983
Most homers
216 in 1982
Fewest homers
82 in 1992
Most homers at County Stadium, home and opponents
172 in 1979

Most grand slams
8 in 1980
Most pinch home runs
5 in 1970
Most long hits
537 in 1980
Most extra bases on long hits
1,007 in 1982
Most total bases
2,606 in 1982
Most sacrifice hits
115 in 1970
Most sacrifice flies
72 in 1992
Most stolen bases
256 in 1992
Most caught stealing
115 in 1992
Most bases on balls
598 in 1987
Most strikeouts
1,040 in 1987
Fewest strikeouts
673 in 1984
Most hit by pitch
50 in 1989
Fewest hit by pitch
18 in 1982
Most runs batted in
843 in 1982

Most game-winning RBIs
  87 in 1982
Highest batting average
  .280 in 1979
Lowest batting average
  .229 in 1971
Most .300 batters
  3 in 1979, 1980, 1982, 1983
Highest slugging average
  .455 in 1982
Lowest slugging average
  .328 in 1972
Most grounded into double play
  152 in 1984
Fewest grounded into double play
  94 in 1978
Most left on bases
  1,162 in 1970, 1978
Fewest left on bases
  1,031 in 1972
Most putouts
  4,402 in 1982
Fewest putouts
  4,175 in 1972
Most assists
  1,976 in 1978
Most chances accepted
  6,284 in 1978
Fewest chances accepted
  5,784 in 1972
Most errors
  180 in 1975
Fewest errors
  89 in 1992
Most errorless games
  90 in 1992
Most consecutive errorless games
  10 in 1970, 1979
Most double plays
  189 in 1980
Fewest double plays
  142 in 1970
Most passed balls
  20 in 1975
Fewest passed balls
  4 in 1978
Highest fielding average
  .986 in 1992
Lowest fielding average
  .971 in 1975
Highest home attendance
  2,397,131 in 1983
Highest road attendance
  2,269,151 in 1993
Most games won
  95 in 1979, 1982
Most games lost
  97 in 1970
Most games won, month
  21 in June 1978

Most games lost, month
  23 in August 1977
Games won, league
  1,913 in 25 years
Games lost, league
  2,025 in 25 years
Highest percentage games won
  .590 in 1979 (won 95, lost 66)
Lowest percentage games won
  .401 in 1970 (won 65, lost 97)
Most shutout won
  23 in 1971
Most shutouts lost
  20 in 1972
Most 1-0 games won
  5 in 1971
Most 1-0 games lost
  4 in 1974
Most consecutive games won
  13 in 1987
Most consecutive games lost
  14 in 1994
Number of times league champion
  1
Number of last-place finishes
  1
Most runs, game
  22 vs. Toronto, August 28, 1992
Most runs by opponent, game
  20 by Boston, September 6, 1975
Most runs, shutout game
  18 vs. Boston, April 16, 1990
Most runs by opponent, shutout game
  14 by Chicago, September 4, 1973
Most runs, doubleheader shutout
  No performance
Most runs, inning
  13 vs. California, July 8, 1990, fifth inning
Longest 1-0 game won
  14 innings vs. California, August 24, 1983
Longest 1-0 game lost
  17 innings vs. Baltimore, September 27, 1974
Most hits, game
  31 vs. Toronto, August 28, 1992
Most home runs, game
  7 vs. Cleveland, April 29, 1980
Most consecutive games with one or more homers
  15 (35 homers), 1982
Most total bases, game
  38 vs. Toronto, August 28, 1992
Largest crowd, day game
  55,887 vs. New York, April 15, 1988
Largest crowd doubleheader
  54,630 vs. Detroit, July 6, 1979
Largest crowd, night game
  55,716 vs. Boston, July 3, 1982
Largest crowd, home opener
  55,887 vs. New York, April 15, 1988

MINNESOTA TWINS

YEARLY FINISHES

Year	Position	W	L	Pct.	*GB	Manager	Attendance
1961 —7th		70	90	.438	38	Cookie Lavagetto, Sam Mele	1,256,723
1962 —2nd		91	71	.562	5	Sam Mele	1,433,116
1963 —3rd		91	70	.565	13	Sam Mele	1,406,652
1964 —6th (tied)		79	83	.488	20	Sam Mele	1,207,514
1965 —1st		102	60	.630	+ 7	Sam Mele	1,463,258
1966 —2nd		89	73	.549	9	Sam Mele	1,259,374
1967 —2nd (tied)		91	71	.562	1	Sam Mele, Cal Ermer	1,483,547
1968 —7th		79	83	.488	24	Cal Ermer	1,143,257

WEST DIVISION

Year	Position	W	L	Pct.	*GB	Manager	Attendance
1969 — 1st†	....	97	65	.599	+ 9	Billy Martin	1,349,328
1970 — 1st†	....	98	64	.605	+ 9	Bill Rigney	1,261,887
1971 — 5th	....	74	86	.463	26½	Bill Rigney	940,858
1972 — 3rd	....	77	77	.500	15½	Bill Rigney, Frank Quilici	797,901
1973 — 3rd	....	81	81	.500	13	Frank Quilici	907,499
1974 — 3rd	....	82	80	.506	8	Frank Quilici	662,401
1975 — 4th	....	76	83	.478	20½	Frank Quilici	737,156
1976 — 3rd	....	85	77	.525	5	Gene Mauch	715,394
1977 — 4th	....	84	77	.522	17½	Gene Mauch	1,162,727
1978 — 4th	....	73	89	.451	19	Gene Mauch	787,878
1979 — 4th	....	82	80	.506	6	Gene Mauch	1,070,521
1980 — 3rd	....	77	84	.478	19½	Gene Mauch, Johnny Goryl	769,206
1981 — 7th/4th	....	41	68	.376	‡	Johnny Goryl, Billy Gardner	469,090
1982 — 7th	....	60	102	.370	33	Billy Gardner	921,186
1983 — 5th (tied)	....	70	92	.432	29	Billy Gardner	858,939
1984 — 2nd (tied)	...	81	81	.500	3	Billy Gardner	1,598,422
1985 — 4th (tied)	...	77	85	.475	14	Billy Gardner, Ray Miller	1,651,814
1986 — 6th	....	71	91	.438	21	Ray Miller, Tom Kelly	1,255,453
1987 — 1st §		85	77	.525	+ 2	Tom Kelly	2,081,976
1988 — 2nd	....	91	71	.562	13	Tom Kelly	3,030,672
1989 — 5th	....	80	82	.494	19	Tom Kelly	2,277,438
1990 — 7th	....	74	88	.457	29	Tom Kelly	1,751,584
1991 — 1st §		95	67	.586	+ 8	Tom Kelly	2,293,842
1992 — 2nd	....	90	72	.556	6	Tom Kelly	2,482,428
1993 — 5th (tied)	....	71	91	.438	23	Tom Kelly	2,048,673

CENTRAL DIVISION

Year	Position	W	L	Pct.	*GB	Manager	Attendance
1994 — 4th	....	53	60	.469	14	Tom Kelly	1,398,565

*Games behind winner. †Lost Championship Series. ‡First half 17-39; second 24-29. §Won Championship Series.

INDIVIDUAL RECORDS (1961 TO DATE)

SERVICE

Most years by non-pitcher
15—Tony Oliva
Most years by pitcher
13—Jim Kaat

BATTING

Most games
164—Cesar Tovar, 1967
Most games, career
1,939—Harmon Killebrew
Most at-bats
691—Kirby Puckett, 161 games, 1985
Most at-bats, career
6,706—Kirby Puckett
Most runs
128—Rod Carew, 155 games, 1977
Most runs, career
1,047—Harmon Killebrew
Most hits
239—Rod Carew, 155 games, 1977
Most hits, career
2,135—Kirby Puckett
Most singles
180—Rod Carew, 153 games, 1974
Most singles, career
1,616—Rod Carew
Most doubles
45—Zoilo Versalles, 160 games, 1965
Kirby Puckett, 159 games, 1989
Chuck Knoblauch, 109 games, 1994
Most doubles, career
375—Kirby Puckett
Most triples
16—Rod Carew, 155 games, 1977
Most triples, career
90—Rod Carew
Most homers by righthander
49—Harmon Killebrew, 158 games, 1964
Harmon Killebrew, 162 games, 1969

Most homers by lefthander
34—Kent Hrbek, 143 games, 1987
Most homers by rookie
33—Jimmie Hall, 156 games, 1963
Most homers at home
29—Harmon Killebrew, 1961
Most homers on road
28—Harmon Killebrew, 1962
Most homers, month
14—Harmon Killebrew, June, 1964
Most homers by righthander, career
475—Harmon Killebrew
Most homers by lefthander, career
293—Kent Hrbek
Most grand slams
3—Bob Allison, 159 games, 1961
Rod Carew, 156 games, 1976
Kent Hrbek, 158 games, 1985
Kirby Puckett, 160 games, 1992
Most grand slams, career
10—Harmon Killebrew
Most total bases
374—Tony Oliva, 161 games, 1964
Most total bases, career
3,412—Harmon Killebrew
Most long hits
84—Tony Oliva, 161 games, 1964
Most long hits, career
728—Harmon Killebrew
Most extra bases on long hits
172—Harmon Killebrew, 150 games, 1961
Most extra bases on long hits, career
1,699—Harmon Killebrew
Most sacrifice hits
25—Rob Wilfong, 140 games, 1979
Most sacrifice flies
13—Gary Gaetti, 145 games, 1982
Tom Brunansky, 157 games, 1985
Most bases on balls
145—Harmon Killebrew, 162 games, 1969

Most bases on balls, career
1,321—Harmon Killebrew
Most strikeouts
145—Bob Darwin, 145 games, 1972
Fewest strikeouts
24—Vic Power, 138 games, 1963
Most strikeouts, career
1,314—Harmon Killebrew
Most hit by pitch
17—Cesar Tovar, 157 games, 1968
Most runs batted in
140—Harmon Killebrew, 162 games, 1969
Most runs batted in, career
1,325—Harmon Killebrew
Most game-winning RBIs
15—Tom Brunansky, 151 games, 1983
Most consecutive games with RBI
11—Kirby Puckett (15 RBIs), 1988
Highest batting average
.388—Rod Carew, 155 games, 1977
Highest batting average, career
.334—Rod Carew
Highest slugging percentage
.606—Harmon Killebrew, 150 games, 1961
Highest slugging average, career
.518—Harmon Killebrew
Longest batting streak
31 games—Ken Landreaux, 1980
Most grounded into double play
28—Harmon Killebrew, 157 games, 1970
Fewest grounded into double play
2—Cesar Tovar, 157 games, 1968

BASERUNNING

Most stolen bases
49—Rod Carew, 156 games, 1976
Most stolen bases, career
271—Rod Carew
Most caught stealing
22—Rod Carew, 156 games, 1976

PITCHING

Most games
90—Mike Marshall, 1979
Most games, career
468—Jim Kaat
Most games started
42—Jim Kaat, 1965
Most games started, career
422—Jim Kaat
Most complete games
25—Bert Blyleven, 1973
Most complete games, career
133—Jim Kaat
Most games finished
84—Mike Marshall, 1979
Most innings
325—Bert Blyleven, 1973
Most innings pitched, career
2,958—Jim Kaat

Most games won
25—Jim Kaat, 1966
Most games won, career
189—Jim Kaat
Most games lost, season
20—Pedro Ramos, 1961
Most games lost, career
152—Jim Kaat
Highest winning percentage
.774—Frank Viola (24-7), 1988
Longest winning streak
12 games—Scott Erickson, 1991
Longest losing streak
13 games—Terry Felton, 1982
Most saves
42—Jeff Reardon, 1988
Rick Aguilera, 1991
Most 20-victory seasons
2—Camilo Pascual, Jim Perry
Most bases on balls
127—Jim Hughes, 1975
Most bases on balls, career
694—Jim Kaat
Most strikeouts
258—Bert Blyleven, 1973
Most strikeouts, career
2,035—Bert Blyleven
Most strikeouts, game
15—Camilo Pascual, July 19, 1961, first game
Joe Decker, June 26, 1973
Jerry Koosman, June 23, 1980
Bert Blyleven, August 1, 1986
Most shutouts
9—Bert Blyleven, 1973
Most shutouts, career
29—Bert Blyleven
Most 1-0 shutouts won
3—Bert Blyleven, 1971
Most runs
141—Frank Viola, 1983
Most earned runs
128—Frank Viola, 1983
Most hits
296—Bert Blyleven, 1973
Most hit batsmen
18—Jim Kaat, 1962
Most wild pitches
15—Dave Goltz, 1976
Mike Smithson, 1986
Jack Morris, 1991
Most home runs
50—Bert Blyleven, 1986
Most sacrifice hits
17—Dean Chance, 1968
Jerry Koosman, 1980
Most sacrifice flies
13—Bert Blyleven, 1973
Scott Erickson, 1993
Lowest ERA
2.45—Allan Anderson, 202⅓ innings, 1988

CLUB RECORDS

Most players
44 in 1964
Fewest players
31 in 1976
Most games
164 in 1967
Most at-bats
5,677 in 1969
Most runs
867 in 1977
Most opponents' runs
839 in 1986

Most hits
1,588 in 1977
Fewest hits
1,274 in 1968
Most singles
1,192 in 1974
Most doubles
294 in 1988
Most triples
60 in 1977
Most homers
225 in 1963

Fewest homers
81 in 1976
Most homers at Metropolitan Stadium, home and opponents
211 in 1963
Most homers at Metrodome, home and opponents
223 in 1986
Most grand slams
8 in 1961
Most pinch home runs
7 in 1964, 1967
Most total bases
2,395 in 1964
Most long hits
494 in 1964
Most extra bases on long hits
982 in 1964
Most sacrifice hits
142 in 1979
Most sacrifice flies
59 in 1965, 1992
Most stolen bases
146 in 1976
Most caught stealing
75 in 1976
Most bases on balls
649 in 1962
Most strikeouts
1019 in 1964
Fewest strikeouts
684 in 1978
Most hit by pitch
55 in 1988
Fewest hit by pitch
21 in 1980
Most runs batted in
804 in 1977
Most game-winning RBIs
86 in 1988
Highest batting average
.282 in 1977
Lowest batting average
.237 in 1968
Highest slugging average
.430 in 1963, 1987
Lowest slugging average
.344 in 1972
Most grounded into double play
159 in 1974
Fewest grounded into double play
93 in 1965
Most left on bases
1,263 in 1974
Fewest left on bases
1,041 in 1987
Most .300 hitters
3 in 1969, 1970, 1977, 1988, 1992
Most putouts
4,493 in 1969
Fewest putouts
4,198 in 1972
Most assists
2,007 in 1979
Fewest assists
1,500 in 1988
Most chances accepted
6,349 in 1969
Fewest chances accepted
5,795 in 1988
Most errors
174 in 1961
Fewest errors
84 in 1988
Most errorless games
96 in 1988
Most consecutive errorless games
10 in 1987

Most double plays
203 in 1979
Fewest double plays
117 in 1968
Most passed balls
21 in 1987, 1993
Fewest passed balls
4 in 1984
Highest fielding average
.986 in 1988
Lowest fielding average
.972 in 1961
Highest home attendance
3,030,672 in 1988
Highest road attendance
2,306,583 in 1991
Most games won
102 in 1965
Most games lost
102 in 1982
Most games won, month
23 in July 1969
Most games lost, month
26 in May 1981, May 1982
Highest percentage games won
.630, in 1965 (won 102, lost 60)
Lowest percentage games won
.370, in 1982 (won 60, lost 102)
Games won, league
2,717 in 34 years
Games lost, league
2,671 in 34 years
Most shutouts won
18 in 1967, 1973
Most shutouts lost
14 in 1964, 1972, 1990
Most 1-0 games won
5 in 1966
Most 1-0 games lost
5 in 1974
Most consecutive games won
15 in 1991
Most consecutive games lost
14 in 1982
Number of times league champions
3
Number of last-place finishes
1
Most runs, game
21 vs. Boston, May 20, 1994
   vs. Detroit, June 4, 1994
Most runs by opponent, game
23 by Kansas City, April 6, 1974
Most runs, shutout game
16 vs. Boston, May 25, 1990
Most runs by opponent, shutout game
17 by California, April 23, 1980
Most runs, doubleheader shutout
16 vs. Oakland, June 26, 1988
Most runs, inning
11 vs. Cleveland, July 18, 1962, first inning
   vs. Oakland, June 21, 1969, 10th inning
   vs. Cleveland, August 5, 1977, fourth inning
   vs. Boston, May 20, 1994, fifth inning
Longest 1-0 game won
13 innings vs. Texas, September 22, 1992
Longest 1-0 game lost
15 innings vs. Kansas City, May 23, 1981
Most hits, game
24 vs. Boston, May 25, 1977
   vs. Seattle, September 20, 1989, 11 innings
   vs. Detroit, June 4, 1994
Most home runs, game
8 vs. Washington, August 29, 1963, first game
Most consecutive games with one or more homers
16 (28 homers), 1979

Most total bases, game
47 vs. Washington, August 29, 1963, first game
Largest crowd, day game
53,106 vs. Kansas City, September 27, 1987
Largest crowd, doubleheader
51,017 vs. Oakland, July 28, 1990

Largest crowd, night game
53,067 vs. Toronto, April 8, 1988
Largest crowd, home opener
53,067 vs. Toronto, April 8, 1988

NEW YORK YANKEES

YEARLY FINISHES

(Baltimore Orioles, 1901 to 1902)

Year	Position	W	L	Pct.	*GB	Manager	Attendance
1901	5th	68	65	.511	13½	John McGraw	141,952
1902	8th	50	88	.362	34	John McGraw, Wilbert Robinson	174,606
1903	4th	72	62	.537	17	Clark Griffith	211,808
1904	2nd	92	59	.609	1½	Clark Griffith	438,919
1905	6th	71	78	.477	21½	Clark Griffith	309,100
1906	2nd	90	61	.596	3	Clark Griffith	434,709
1907	5th	70	78	.473	21	Clark Griffith	350,020
1908	8th	51	103	.331	39½	Clark Griffith, Kid Elberfeld	305,500
1909	5th	74	77	.490	23½	George Stallings	501,000
1910	2nd	88	63	.583	14½	George Stallings, Hal Chase	355,857
1911	6th	76	76	.500	25½	Hal Chase	302,444
1912	8th	50	102	.329	55	Harry Wolverton	242,194
1913	7th	57	94	.377	38	Frank Chance	357,551
1914	6th (tied)	70	84	.455	30	Frank Chance, Roger Peckinpaugh	359,477
1915	5th	69	83	.454	32½	Bill Donovan	256,035
1916	4th	80	74	.519	11	Bill Donovan	469,211
1917	6th	71	82	.464	28½	Bill Donovan	330,294
1918	4th	60	63	.488	13½	Miller Huggins	282,047
1919	3rd	80	59	.576	7½	Miller Huggins	619,164
1920	3rd	95	59	.617	3	Miller Huggins	1,289,422
1921	1st	98	55	.641	+ 4½	Miller Huggins	1,230,696
1922	1st	94	60	.610	+ 1	Miller Huggins	1,026,134
1923	1st	98	54	.645	+16	Miller Huggins	1,007,066
1924	2nd	89	63	.586	2	Miller Huggins	1,053,533
1925	7th	69	85	.448	30	Miller Huggins	697,267
1926	1st	91	63	.591	+ 3	Miller Huggins	1,027,095
1927	1st	110	44	.714	+19	Miller Huggins	1,164,015
1928	1st	101	53	.656	+ 2½	Miller Huggins	1,072,132
1929	2nd	88	66	.571	18	Miller Huggins, Art Fletcher	960,148
1930	3rd	86	68	.558	16	Bob Shawkey	1,169,230
1931	2nd	94	59	.614	13½	Joe McCarthy	912,437
1932	1st	107	47	.695	+13	Joe McCarthy	962,320
1933	2nd	91	59	.607	7	Joe McCarthy	728,014
1934	2nd	94	60	.610	7	Joe McCarthy	854,682
1935	2nd	89	60	.597	3	Joe McCarthy	657,508
1936	1st	102	51	.667	+19½	Joe McCarthy	976,913
1937	1st	102	52	.662	+13	Joe McCarthy	998,148
1938	1st	99	53	.651	+ 9½	Joe McCarthy	970,916
1939	1st	106	45	.702	+17	Joe McCarthy	859,785
1940	3rd	88	66	.571	2	Joe McCarthy	988,975
1941	1st	101	53	.656	+17	Joe McCarthy	964,722
1942	1st	103	51	.669	+ 9	Joe McCarthy	988,251
1943	1st	98	56	.636	+13½	Joe McCarthy	645,006
1944	3rd	83	71	.539	6	Joe McCarthy	822,864
1945	4th	81	71	.533	6½	Joe McCarthy	881,846
1946	3rd	87	67	.565	17	Joe McCarthy, Bill Dickey, Johnny Neun	2,265,512
1947	1st	97	57	.630	+12	Bucky Harris	2,178,937
1948	3rd	94	60	.610	2½	Bucky Harris	2,373,901
1949	1st	97	57	.630	+ 1	Casey Stengel	2,281,676
1950	1st	98	56	.636	+ 3	Casey Stengel	2,081,380
1951	1st	98	56	.636	+ 5	Casey Stengel	1,950,107
1952	1st	95	59	.617	+ 2	Casey Stengel	1,629,665
1953	1st	99	52	.656	+ 8½	Casey Stengel	1,537,811
1954	2nd	103	51	.669	8	Casey Stengel	1,475,171
1955	1st	96	58	.623	+ 3	Casey Stengel	1,490,138
1956	1st	97	57	.630	+ 9	Casey Stengel	1,491,784
1957	1st	98	56	.636	+ 8	Casey Stengel	1,497,134
1958	1st	92	62	.597	+10	Casey Stengel	1,428,438
1959	3rd	79	75	.513	15	Casey Stengel	1,552,030
1960	1st	97	57	.630	+ 8	Casey Stengel	1,627,349
1961	1st	109	53	.673	+ 8	Ralph Houk	1,747,725
1962	1st	96	66	.593	+ 5	Ralph Houk	1,493,574
1963	1st	104	57	.646	+10½	Ralph Houk	1,308,920

Year	Position	W	L	Pct.	*GB	Manager	Attendance
1964 — 1st	99	63	.611	+ 1	Yogi Berra	1,305,638
1965 — 6th	77	85	.475	25	Johnny Keane	1,213,552
1966 — 10th	70	89	.440	26½	Johnny Keane, Ralph Houk	1,124,648
1967 — 9th	72	90	.444	20	Ralph Houk	1,259,514
1968 — 5th	83	79	.512	20	Ralph Houk	1,185,666

EAST DIVISION

Year	Position	W	L	Pct.	*GB	Manager	Attendance
1969 — 5th	80	81	.497	28½	Ralph Houk	1,067,996
1970 — 2nd	93	69	.574	15	Ralph Houk	1,136,879
1971 — 4th	82	80	.506	21	Ralph Houk	1,070,771
1972 — 4th	79	76	.510	6½	Ralph Houk	966,328
1973 — 4th	80	82	.494	17	Ralph Houk	1,262,103
1974 — 2nd	89	73	.549	2	Bill Virdon	1,273,075
1975 — 3rd	83	77	.519	12	Bill Virdon, Billy Martin	1,288,048
1976 — 1st†	97	62	.610	+10½	Billy Martin	2,012,434
1977 — 1st†	100	62	.617	+ 2½	Billy Martin	2,103,092
1978 — 1st‡†	100	63	.613	+ 1	Billy Martin, Bob Lemon	2,335,871
1979 — 4th	89	71	.556	13½	Bob Lemon, Billy Martin	2,537,765
1980 — 1st §	103	59	.636	+ 3	Dick Howser	2,627,417
1981 — 1st/6th	59	48	.551	†s	Gene Michael, Bob Lemon	1,614,533
1982 — 5th	79	83	.488	16	Bob Lemon, Gene Michael, Clyde King	2,041,219
1983 — 3rd	91	71	.562	7	Billy Martin	2,257,976
1984 — 3rd	87	75	.537	17	Yogi Berra	1,821,815
1985 — 2nd	97	64	.602	2	Yogi Berra, Billy Martin	2,214,587
1986 — 2nd	90	72	.556	5½	Lou Piniella	2,268,030
1987 — 4th	89	73	.549	9	Lou Piniella	2,427,672
1988 — 5th	85	76	.528	3½	Billy Martin, Lou Piniella	2,633,701
1989 — 5th	74	87	.460	14½	Dallas Green, Bucky Dent	2,170,485
1990 — 7th	67	95	.414	21	Bucky Dent, Stump Merrill	2,006,436
1991 — 5th	71	91	.438	20	Stump Merrill	1,863,733
1992 — 4th (tied)	76	86	.469	20	Buck Showalter	1,748,733
1993 — 2nd	88	74	.543	7	Buck Showalter	2,416,965
1994 — 1st	70	43	.619	+ 6½	Buck Showalter	1,675,556

*Games behind winner. †Won Championship Series. ‡Won pennant playoff. §Lost Championship Series. ★First half 34-22; second 25-26.

INDIVIDUAL RECORDS (1903 TO DATE)

SERVICE

Most years by non-pitcher
18—Yogi Berra
     Mickey Mantle
Most years by pitcher
16—Whitey Ford

BATTING

Most games
162—Bobby Richardson, 1961
     Roy White, 1970
     Chris Chambliss, 1978
     Don Mattingly, 1986
     Roberto Kelly, 1990
Most games, career
2,401—Mickey Mantle
Most at-bats
692—Bobby Richardson, 161 games, 1962
Most at-bats, career
8,102—Mickey Mantle
Most runs
177—Babe Ruth, 152 games, 1921
Most runs, career
1,959—Babe Ruth
Most hits
238—Don Mattingly, 162 games, 1986
Most hits, career
2,721—Lou Gehrig
Most singles
171—Steve Sax, 158 games, 1989
Most singles, career
1,531—Lou Gehrig
Most doubles
53—Don Mattingly, 162 games, 1986

Most doubles, career
535—Lou Gehrig
Most triples
23—Earle Combs, 152 games, 1927
Most triples, career
162—Lou Gehrig
Most homers by righthander
46—Joe DiMaggio, 151 games, 1937
Most homers by lefthander
61—Roger Maris, 161 games, 1961
60—Babe Ruth, 151 games, 1927
Most homers by rookie
29—Joe DiMaggio, 138 games, 1936
Most grand slams
6—Don Mattingly, 141 games, 1987
Most grand slams, career
23—Lou Gehrig
Most homers at home
32—Babe Ruth, 1921 (Polo Grounds)
30—Lou Gehrig, 1934 (Yankee Stadium)
     Roger Maris, 1961 (Yankee Stadium)
Most homers on road
32—Babe Ruth, 1927
Most homers, month
17—Babe Ruth, September, 1927
Most homers by lefthander, career
659—Babe Ruth
Most homers by righthander, career
361—Joe DiMaggio
Most homers by switch-hitter, career
536—Mickey Mantle
Most total bases
457—Babe Ruth, 152 games, 1921
Most total bases, career
5,131—Babe Ruth

Most long hits
119—Babe Ruth, 152 games, 1921
Most long hits, career
1,190—Lou Gehrig
Most extra bases on long hits
253—Babe Ruth, 152 games, 1921
Most extra bases on long hits, career
2,613—Babe Ruth
Most sacrifice hits
42—Willie Keeler, 149 games, 1905
Most sacrifice flies
17—Roy White, 147 games, 1971
Most bases on balls
170—Babe Ruth, 152 games, 1923
Most bases on balls, career
1,847—Babe Ruth
Most strikeouts, season
156—Danny Tartabull, 138 games, 1993
Most strikeouts, career
1,710—Mickey Mantle
Fewest strikeouts
3—Joe Sewell, 124 games, 1932
Most hit by pitch
24—Don Baylor, 142 games, 1985
Most runs batted in
184—Lou Gehrig, 155 games, 1931
Most runs batted in, career
1,990—Lou Gehrig
Most game-winning RBIs
21—Dave Winfield, 152 games, 1983
Don Mattingly, 159 games, 1985
Most consecutive games with RBI
11—Babe Ruth (18 RBIs), 1931
Highest batting average
.393—Babe Ruth, 152 games, 1923
Highest batting average, career
.349—Babe Ruth
Highest slugging average
.847—Babe Ruth, 142 games, 1920
Highest slugging average, career
.711—Babe Ruth
Longest batting streak
56 games—Joe DiMaggio, 1941
Most grounded into double play
30—Dave Winfield, 152 games, 1983
Fewest grounded into double play
2—Mickey Mantle, 153 games, 1961

BASERUNNING

Most stolen bases
93—Rickey Henderson, 140 games, 1988
Most stolen bases, career
326—Rickey Henderson
Most caught stealing
23—Ben Chapman, 149 games, 1931

PITCHING

Most games
74—Dave Righetti, 1985, 1986
Most games, career
522—Dave Righetti
Most games started
51—Jack Chesbro, 1904
Most games started, career
438—Whitey Ford

Most complete games
48—Jack Chesbro, 1904
Most complete games, career
262—Red Ruffing
Most games finished
68—Dave Righetti, 1986
Most innings
454—Jack Chesbro, 1904
Most innings, career
3,171—Whitey Ford
Most games won
41—Jack Chesbro, 1904
Most games won, career
236—Whitey Ford
Most 20-victory seasons
4—Bob Shawkey, Lefty Gomez, Red Ruffing
Most games lost
21—Al Orth, 1907
Sam Jones, 1925
Joe Lake, 1908
Russ Ford, 1912
Most games lost, career
139—Mel Stottlemyre Sr.
Highest winning percentage
.893—Ron Guidry (25-3), 1978
Longest winning streak
14 games—Jack Chesbro, 1904
Whitey Ford, 1961
Longest losing streak
9 games—Bill Hogg, 1908
Thad Tillotson, 1967
Most saves
46—Dave Righetti, 1986
Most bases on balls
179—Tommy Byrne, 1949
Most bases on balls, career
1,090—Lefty Gomez
Most strikeouts
248—Ron Guidry, 1978
Most strikeouts, career
1,956—Whitey Ford
Most strikeouts, game
18—Ron Guidry, June 17, 1978
Most shutouts
9—Ron Guidry, 1978
Most shutouts, career
45—Whitey Ford
Most 1-0 shutouts won
2—Held by many pitchers
Most runs
165—Russ Ford, 1912
Most earned runs
127—Sam Jones, 1925
Most hits
337—Jack Chesbro, 1904
Most hit batsmen
26—Jack Warhop, 1909
Most wild pitches
23—Tim Leary, 1990
Most home runs
40—Ralph Terry, 1962
Most sacrifice hits
22—Lefty Gomez, 1935
Most sacrifice flies
15—Doc Medich, 1975
Lowest ERA
1.64—Spud Chandler, 253 innings, 1943

CLUB RECORDS

Most players
48 in 1987
Fewest players
25 in 1923, 1927
Most games
164 in 1964, 1968

Most at-bats
5,705 in 1964
Most runs
1,067 in 1931
Fewest runs
459 in 1908

Most opponents' runs
898 in 1930

Most hits
1,683 in 1930

Fewest hits
1,137 in 1968

Most singles
1,157 in 1931

Most doubles
315 in 1936

Most triples
110 in 1930

Most homers
240 in 1961

Fewest homers (154 or 162-game schedule)
8 in 1913

Most homers at Yankee Stadium, home and opponents
189 in 1986

Most pinch home runs
10 in 1961

Most grand slams
10 in 1987

Most long hits
580 in 1936

Most extra bases on long hits
1,027 in 1936

Most total bases
2,703 in 1936

Most sacrifices (sacrifice hits and sacrifice flies)
218 in 1922, 1926

Most sacrifice hits
178 in 1906

Most sacrifice flies
72 in 1974

Most stolen bases
289 in 1910

Most caught stealing
82 in 1920

Most bases on balls
766 in 1932

Most strikeouts
1,043 in 1967

Fewest strikeouts
420 in 1924

Most hit by pitch
53 in 1990

Fewest hit by pitch
14 in 1969

Most runs batted in
995 in 1936

Most game-winning RBIs
96 in 1980

Highest batting average
.309 in 1930

Lowest batting average
.214 in 1968

Highest slugging average
.489 in 1927

Lowest slugging average
.287 in 1914

Most grounded into double play
152 in 1982

Fewest grounded into double play
91 in 1963

Most left on bases
1,247 in 1993

Fewest left on bases
1,010 in 1920

Most .300 hitters
9 in 1930

Most putouts
4,520 in 1964

Fewest putouts
3,993 in 1935

Most assists
2,086 in 1904

Fewest assists
1,493 in 1948

Most chances accepted
6,377 in 1968

Fewest chances accepted
5,551 in 1935

Most errors
386 in 1912

Fewest errors
102 in 1987

Most errorless games
91 in 1964

Most consecutive errorless games
10 in 1977, 1993

Most double plays
214 in 1956

Fewest double plays
81 in 1912

Most passed balls
32 in 1913

Fewest passed balls
0 in 1931

Highest fielding average
.983 in 1964, 1987, 1993

Lowest fielding average
.939 in 1912

Highest home attendance
2,633,701 in 1988

Highest road attendance
2,603,338 in 1993

Most games won
110 in 1927

Most games lost
103 in 1908

Most games won, month
28 in August 1938

Most games lost, month
24 in July 1908

Highest percentage games won
.714 in 1927 (won 110, lost 44)

Lowest percentage games won
.329 in 1912 (won 50, lost 102)

Games won, league
8,013 in 92 years

Games lost, league
6,177 in 92 years

Most shutouts won
24 in 1951

Most shutouts lost
27 in 1914

Most 1-0 games won
6 in 1908, 1968

Most 1-0 games lost
9 in 1914

Most consecutive games won
19 in 1947

Most consecutive games lost
13 in 1913

Number of times league champions
33

Number of last-place finishes
5

Most runs, game
25 vs. Philadelphia, May 24, 1936

Most runs by opponent, game
24 by Cleveland, July 29, 1928

Most runs, shutout game
21 vs. Philadelphia, August 13, 1939, second game, eight innings

Most runs by opponent, shutout game
15 by Chicago, July 15, 1907
by Chicago, May 4, 1950

Most runs, doubleheader shutout
24 vs. Philadelphia, September 4, 1944

Most runs, inning
14 vs. Washington, July 6, 1920, fifth inning

Longest 1-0 game won	Most total bases, game
15 innings vs. Philadelphia, July 4, 1925, first game	53 vs. Philadelphia, June 28, 1939, first game

Longest 1-0 game won
15 innings vs. Philadelphia, July 4, 1925, first game
Longest 1-0 game lost
14 innings vs. Boston, September 24, 1969
Most hits, game
30 vs. Boston, September 28, 1923
Most home runs, game
8 vs. Philadelphia, June 28, 1939, first game
Most consecutive games with one or more homers
25 (40 homers), 1941

Most total bases, game
53 vs. Philadelphia, June 28, 1939, first game
Largest crowd, day game
73,205 vs. Philadelphia, April 19, 1931
Largest crowd, doubleheader
81,841 vs. Boston, May 30, 1938
Largest crowd, night game
74,747 vs. Boston, May 26, 1947
Largest crowd, home opener
56,706 vs. Texas, April 4, 1994

OAKLAND A'S

YEARLY FINISHES

Year	Position	W	L	Pct.	*GB	Manager	Attendance
1968	—6th	82	80	.506	21	Bob Kennedy	837,466

WEST DIVISION

Year	Position	W	L	Pct.	*GB	Manager	Attendance
1969	—2nd	88	74	.543	9	Hank Bauer, John McNamara	778,232
1970	—2nd	89	73	.549	9	John McNamara	778,355
1971	—1st†	101	60	.627	+16	Dick Williams	914,993
1972	—1st‡	93	62	.600	+ 5½	Dick Williams	921,323
1973	—1st‡	94	68	.580	+ 6	Dick Williams	1,000,763
1974	—1st‡	90	72	.556	+ 5	Alvin Dark	845,693
1975	—1st†	98	64	.605	+ 7	Alvin Dark	1,075,518
1976	—2nd	87	74	.540	2½	Chuck Tanner	780,593
1977	—7th	63	98	.391	38½	Jack McKeon, Bobby Winkles	495,599
1978	—6th	69	93	.426	23	Bobby Winkles, Jack McKeon	526,999
1979	—7th	54	108	.333	34	Jim Marshall	306,763
1980	—2nd	83	79	.512	14	Billy Martin	842,259
1981	—1st/2nd	64	45	.587	§†	Billy Martin	1,304,054
1982	—5th	68	94	.420	25	Billy Martin	1,735,489
1983	—4th	74	88	.457	25	Steve Boros	1,294,941
1984	—4th	77	85	.475	7	Steve Boros, Jackie Moore	1,353,281
1985	—4th (tied)	77	85	.475	14	Jackie Moore	1,334,599
1986	—3rd (tied)	76	86	.469	16	Jackie Moore, Tony La Russa	1,314,646
1987	—3rd	81	81	.500	4	Tony La Russa	1,678,921
1988	—1st‡	104	58	.642	+13	Tony La Russa	2,287,335
1989	—1st‡	99	63	.611	+ 7	Tony La Russa	2,667,225
1990	—1st‡	103	59	.636	+ 9	Tony La Russa	2,900,217
1991	—4th	84	78	.519	11	Tony La Russa	2,713,493
1992	—1st†	96	66	.593	+ 6	Tony La Russa	2,494,160
1993	—7th	68	94	.420	26	Tony La Russa	2,035,025
1994	—2nd	51	63	.447	1	Tony La Russa	1,242,692

*Games behind winner. †Lost Championship Series. ‡Won Championship Series. §First half 37-23; second 27-22.

INDIVIDUAL RECORDS (1968 TO DATE)

SERVICE

Most years by non-pitcher
12—Rickey Henderson
Most years by pitcher
11—Mike Norris

BATTING

Most games
162—Sal Bando, 1968, 1969, 1973
Alfredo Griffin, 1985, 1986
Most games, career
1,440—Rickey Henderson
Most at-bats
642—Bert Campaneris, 159 games, 1968
Most at-bats, career
5,191—Rickey Henderson
Most runs
123—Reggie Jackson, 152 games, 1969
Most runs, career
1,102—Rickey Henderson
Most hits
187—Jose Canseco, 158 games, 1988
Most hits, career
1,518—Rickey Henderson

Most singles
153—Carney Lansford, 148 games, 1989
Most singles, career
1,093—Rickey Henderson
Most doubles
39—Joe Rudi, 158 games, 1974
Reggie Jackson, 157 games, 1975
Most doubles, career
242—Rickey Henderson
Most triples
12—Phil Garner, 159 games, 1976
Most triples, career
39—Bert Campaneris
Rickey Henderson
Most homers by righthander
49—Mark McGwire, 151 games, 1987
Most homers by lefthander
47—Reggie Jackson, 152 games, 1969
Most homers by rookie
49—Mark McGwire, 151 games, 1987
Most homers at home
26—Reggie Jackson, 1969
Most homers on road
28—Mark McGwire, 1987
Jose Canseco, 1991

Most homers by righthander, career
238—Mark McGwire
Most homers by lefthander, career
268—Reggie Jackson
Most grand slams
3—Gene Tenace, 158 games, 1974
Dave Kingman, 147 games, 1984
Most grand slams, career
7—Sal Bando
Most homers, month
15—Mark McGwire, May 1987
Most total bases
347—Jose Canseco, 158 games, 1988
Most total bases, career
2,287—Reggie Jackson
Most long hits
86—Reggie Jackson, 152 games, 1969
Most long hits, career
521—Reggie Jackson
Most extra bases on long hits
183—Reggie Jackson, 152 games, 1969
Mark McGwire, 151 games, 1987
Most extra bases on long hits, career
1,080—Reggie Jackson
Most sacrifice hits
22—Dwayne Murphy, 159 games, 1980
Most sacrifice flies
14—Dave Kingman, 147 games, 1984
Most bases on balls
118—Sal Bando, 155 games, 1970
Most bases on balls, career
1,037—Rickey Henderson
Most strikeouts
175—Jose Canseco, 157 games, 1986
Most strikeouts, career
1,180—Reggie Jackson
Fewest strikeouts
31—Felipe Alou, 154 games, 1970
Most hit by pitch
20—Don Baylor, 157 games, 1976
Most runs batted in
124—Jose Canseco, 158 games, 1988
Most runs batted in, career
789—Sal Bando
Most game-winning RBIs
20—Mark McGwire, 155 games, 1988
Highest batting average
.336—Carney Lansford, 148 games, 1989
Highest batting average, career
.292—Rickey Henderson
Highest slugging average
.618—Mark McGwire, 151 games, 1987
Highest slugging average, career
.512—Jose Canseco
Most consecutive games with RBI
10—Rick Monday (18 RBIs), 1969
Longest batting streak
24 games—Carney Lansford, 1984
Most grounded into double play
25—Danny Cater, 152 games, 1969
Fewest grounded into double play
3—Reggie Jackson, 154 games, 1968

BASERUNNING

Most stolen bases
130—Rickey Henderson, 149 games, 1982
Most stolen bases, career
769—Rickey Henderson
Most caught stealing
42—Rickey Henderson, 149 games, 1982

PITCHING

Most games, career
502—Rollie Fingers

Most games
76—Rollie Fingers, 1974
Most games started
41—Catfish Hunter, 1974
Most games started, career
270—Catfish Hunter
Most complete games
28—Rick Langford, 1980
Most complete games, career
96—Catfish Hunter
Most games finished
65—Dennis Eckersley, 1992
Most innings
318—Catfish Hunter, 1974
Most innings, career
1,946—Vida Blue
Most games won
27—Bob Welch, 1990
Most games won, career
131—Catfish Hunter
Most 20-victory seasons
4—Catfish Hunter, Dave Stewart
Most games lost
20—Brian Kingman, 1980
Most games lost, career
105—Rick Langford
Longest winning streak
13 games—Catfish Hunter, 1973
Longest losing streak
14 games—Matt Keough, 1979
Highest winning percentage
.818—Bob Welch (27-6), 1990
Most saves
51—Dennis Eckersley, 1992
Most bases on balls
112—John Odom, 1969
Most bases on balls, career
617—Vida Blue
Most strikeouts
301—Vida Blue, 1971
Most strikeouts, career
1,315—Vida Blue
Most strikeouts, game
17—Vida Blue, July 9, 1971, first 11 innings of 20-inning game
16—Jose Rijo, April 19, 1986, first eight innings of nine-inning game
Most shutouts won
8—Vida Blue, 1971
Most shutouts won, career
28—Vida Blue
Most 1-0 shutouts won
2—Vida Blue, 1971
Catfish Hunter, 1971
Most runs
144—Matt Keough, 1982
Most earned runs
133—Matt Keough, 1982
Most hits
284—Vida Blue, 1977
Most hits batsmen
11—Bob Welch, 1991
Most wild pitches
22—Mike Moore, 1992
Most home runs
39—Catfish Hunter, 1973
Most sacrifice hits
17—Bob Lacey, 1977
Most sacrifice flies
15—Dave Stewart, 1991
Lowest ERA
1.82—Vida Blue, 312 innings, 1971

Most players
47 in 1972
Fewest players
34 in 1968, 1980
Most games
163 in 1968
Most at-bats
5,614 in 1969
Most runs
806 in 1987
Fewest runs
532 in 1978
Most opponents' runs
860 in 1979
Most hits
1,475 in 1985
Fewest hits
1,248 in 1972
Most singles
1,061 in 1983
Most doubles
263 in 1987
Most triples
40 in 1968
Most homers
199 in 1987
Fewest homers
94 in 1968
Most homers at Oakland Coliseum, home and opponents
163 in 1987
Most grand slams
7 in 1974, 1991
Most pinch home runs
8 in 1970
Most long hits
495 in 1987
Most extra bases on long hits
926 in 1987
Most total bases
2,358 in 1987
Most sacrifice hits
108 in 1978
Most sacrifice flies
77 in 1984
Most stolen bases
341 in 1976
Most caught stealing
123 in 1976
Most bases on balls
707 in 1992
Most strikeouts
1,056 in 1987
Fewest strikeouts
751 in 1979
Most hit by pitch
63 in 1969
Fewest hit by pitch
16 in 1985
Most runs batted in
761 in 1987
Most game-winning RBIs
99 in 1988
Highest batting average
.264 in 1985
Lowest batting average
.236 in 1982
Highest slugging average
.428 in 1987
Lowest slugging average
.343 in 1968
Most grounded into double play
163 in 1989
Fewest grounded into double play
87 in 1968

Most left on bases
1,244 in 1969
Fewest left on bases
1,030 in 1979
Most putouts
4,468 in 1988
Fewest putouts
4,288 in 1979
Most assists
1,821 in 1976
Fewest assists
1,508 in 1984
Most chances accepted
6,230 in 1969
Fewest chances accepted
5,798 in 1984
Most errors
190 in 1977
Fewest errors
87 in 1990
Most errorless games
95 in 1990
Most consecutive errorless games
9 in 1975, 1985
Most double plays
170 in 1973
Fewest double plays
115 in 1980
Most passed balls
26 in 1969
Fewest passed balls
8 in 1982, 1991, 1992
Highest fielding average
.986 in 1990
Lowest fielding average
.970 in 1977
Highest home attendance
2,900,217 in 1990
Highest road attendance
2,636,157 in 1991
Most games won
104 in 1988
Most games lost
108 in 1979
Most games won, month
23 in August 1971
Most games lost, month
24 in June 1979
Games won, league
2,213 in 27 years
Games lost, league
2,050 in 27 years
Highest percentage games won
.642 in 1988 (won 104, lost 58)
Lowest percentage games won
.333 in 1979 (won 54, lost 108)
Most shutouts won
23 in 1972
Most shutouts lost
19 in 1978
Most 1-0 games won
5 in 1971
Most 1-0 games lost
5 in 1971, 1978
Most consecutive games won
14 in 1988
Most consecutive games lost
14 in 1977
Number of times, league champions
6
Number of last-place finishes
1
Most runs, game
21 vs. Boston, June 14, 1969

Most runs by opponents, game
20 by Minnesota, April 27, 1980
by Cleveland, May 4, 1991
by Detroit, April 13, 1993
Most runs, shutout game
14 vs. Minnesota, April 9, 1994
Most runs by opponents, shutout game
16 by Kansas City, June 25, 1984
Most runs, doubleheader shutout
10 vs. Kansas City, September 9, 1974
Most runs, inning
10 vs. Milwaukee, May 9, 1972, first game, fourth inning
vs. New York, August 29, 1989, fifth inning
vs. Seattle, June 23, 1992, third inning
Longest 1-0 game won
20 innings vs. California, July 9, 1971
Longest 1-0 game lost
13 innings vs. Detroit, May 25, 1973

Most hits, nine-inning game
25 vs. Boston, June 14, 1969
Most hits, extra-inning game
29 vs. Texas, July 1, 1979, 15 innings
Most home runs, game
7 vs. Cleveland, July 6, 1990, second game
Most consecutive games with one or more homers
14 (26 homers), 1987
Most total bases, game
38 vs. Boston, June 14, 1969
Largest crowd, day game
48,758 vs. Detroit, June 6, 1970
Largest crowd, doubleheader
48,592 vs. New York, May 3, 1981
Largest crowd, night game
49,300 vs. New York, August 25, 1980
Largest crowd, home opener
48,348 vs. California, April 6, 1982

PHILADELPHIA A'S

YEARLY FINISHES

Year	Position	W	L	Pct.	*GB	Manager	Attendance
1901 —4th		74	62	.544	9	Connie Mack	206,329
1902 —1st		83	53	.610	+ 5	Connie Mack	442,473
1903 —2nd		75	60	.556	14½	Connie Mack	420,078
1904 —5th		81	70	.536	12½	Connie Mack	512,294
1905 —1st		92	56	.622	+ 2	Connie Mack	554,576
1906 —4th		78	67	.538	12	Connie Mack	489,129
1907 —2nd		88	57	.607	1½	Connie Mack	625,581
1908 —6th		68	85	.444	22	Connie Mack	455,062
1909 —2nd		95	58	.621	3½	Connie Mack	674,915
1910 —1st		102	48	.680	+14½	Connie Mack	588,905
1911 —1st		101	50	.669	+13½	Connie Mack	605,749
1912 —3rd		90	62	.592	15	Connie Mack	517,653
1913 —1st		96	57	.627	+ 6½	Connie Mack	571,896
1914 —1st		99	53	.651	+ 8½	Connie Mack	346,641
1915 —8th		43	109	.283	58½	Connie Mack	146,223
1916 —8th		36	117	.235	54½	Connie Mack	184,471
1917 —8th		55	98	.359	44½	Connie Mack	221,432
1918 —8th		52	76	.406	24	Connie Mack	177,926
1919 —8th		36	104	.257	52	Connie Mack	225,209
1920 —8th		48	106	.312	50	Connie Mack	287,888
1921 —8th		53	100	.346	45	Connie Mack	344,430
1922 —7th		65	89	.422	29	Connie Mack	425,356
1923 —6th		69	83	.454	29	Connie Mack	534,122
1924 —5th		71	81	.467	20	Connie Mack	531,992
1925 —2nd		88	64	.579	8½	Connie Mack	869,703
1926 —3rd		83	67	.553	6	Connie Mack	714,308
1927 —2nd		91	63	.591	19	Connie Mack	605,529
1928 —2nd		98	55	.641	2½	Connie Mack	689,756
1929 —1st		104	46	.693	+18	Connie Mack	839,176
1930 —1st		102	52	.662	+ 8	Connie Mack	721,663
1931 —1st		107	45	.704	+13½	Connie Mack	627,464
1932 —2nd		94	60	.610	13	Connie Mack	405,500
1933 —3rd		79	72	.523	19½	Connie Mack	297,138
1934 —5th		68	82	.453	31	Connie Mack	305,847
1935 —8th		58	91	.389	34	Connie Mack	233,173
1936 —8th		53	100	.346	49	Connie Mack	285,173
1937 —7th		54	97	.358	46½	Connie Mack	430,733
1938 —8th		53	99	.349	46	Connie Mack	385,357
1939 —7th		55	97	.362	51½	Connie Mack	395,022
1940 —8th		54	100	.351	36	Connie Mack	432,145
1941 —8th		64	90	.416	37	Connie Mack	528,894
1942 —8th		55	99	.357	48	Connie Mack	423,487
1943 —8th		49	105	.318	49	Connie Mack	376,735
1944 —5th (tied)		72	82	.468	17	Connie Mack	505,322
1945 —8th		52	98	.347	34½	Connie Mack	462,631
1946 —8th		49	105	.318	55	Connie Mack	621,793
1947 —5th		78	76	.506	19	Connie Mack	911,566
1948 —4th		84	70	.545	12½	Connie Mack	945,076
1949 —5th		81	73	.526	16	Connie Mack	816,514
1950 —8th		52	102	.338	46	Connie Mack	309,805
1951 —6th		70	84	.455	28	Jimmie Dykes	465,469
1952 —4th		79	75	.513	16	Jimmie Dykes	627,100

Year	Position	W	L	Pct.	*GB	Manager	Attendance
1953 —7th		59	95	.383	41½	Jimmie Dykes	362,113
1954 —8th		51	103	.331	60	Ed Joost	304,666

*Games behind winner.

INDIVIDUAL RECORDS (1901 TO 1954)

SERVICE

Most years by non-pitcher
16—Harry Davis
Most years by pitcher
14—Eddie Plank

BATTING

Most games
157—Dave Philley, 1953
Most games, career
1,702—Jimmie Dykes
Most at-bats
670—Al Simmons, 154 games, 1932
Most at-bats, career
6,023—Jimmie Dykes
Most runs
152—Al Simmons, 138 games, 1930
Most runs, career
997—Bob Johnson
Most hits
253—Al Simmons, 153 games, 1925
Most hits, career
1,827—Al Simmons
Most singles
174—Al Simmons, 153 games, 1925
Most doubles
53—Al Simmons, 147 games, 1926
Most doubles, career
365—Jimmie Dykes
Most triples
21—Home Run Baker, 149 games, 1912
Most triples, career
104—Danny Murphy
Most homers by righthander
58—Jimmie Foxx, 154 games, 1932
Most homers by lefthander
27—Joe Hauser, 149 games, 1924
Most homers by rookie
21—Bob Johnson, 142 games, 1933
Most homers at home
31—Jimmie Foxx, 1932
Most homers on road
27—Jimmie Foxx, 1932
Most homers, month
15—Bob Johnson, June, 1934
Most homers, career
302—Jimmie Foxx
Most grand slams
3—Jimmie Foxx, 154 games, 1932
Jimmie Foxx, 150 games, 1934
Bob Johnson, 152 games, 1938
Gus Zernial, 145 games, 1952
Most grand slams, career
9—Jimmie Foxx, Sam Chapman
Most total bases
438—Jimmie Foxx, 154 games, 1932
Most total bases, career
2,998—Al Simmons
Most long hits
100—Jimmie Foxx, 154 games, 1932
Most extra bases on long hits
225—Jimmie Foxx, 154 games, 1932
Most sacrifices (sacrifice hits and sacrifice flies)
43—Roy Grover, 141 games, 1917
Most sacrifice hits
34—Simon Nicholls, 124 games, 1907
Most sacrifice flies
7—Joe DeMaestri, 146 games, 1954

Most bases on balls
149—Ed Joost, 144 games, 1949
Most strikeouts
110—Ed Joost, 151 games, 1947
Fewest strikeouts
17—Dick Siebert, 153 games, 1942
Most hit by pitch
12—Joe Hauser, 146 games, 1923
Most runs batted in
169—Jimmie Foxx, 154 games, 1932
Most runs batted in, career
1,178—Al Simmons
Most consecutive games with RBI
11—Al Simmons (20 RBIs), 1931
Highest batting average
.422—Nap Lajoie, 131 games, 1901
Highest slugging average
.749—Jimmie Foxx, 154 games, 1932
Longest batting streak
29 games—Bill Lamar, 1925
Most grounded into double play
30—Billy Hitchcock, 115 games, 1950
Fewest grounded into double play
5—Ed Joost, 151 games, 1947

BASERUNNING

Most stolen bases
81—Eddie Collins, 153 games, 1910
Most stolen bases, career
375—Eddie Collins
Most caught stealing
15—Whitey Witt, 154 games, 1921
Al Simmons, 152 games, 1924
Bill Werber, 134 games, 1938

PITCHING

Most games
58—Morrie Martin, 1953
Most games, career
524—Eddie Plank
Most games started
46—Rube Waddell, 1904
Most complete games
36—Rube Waddell, 1904
Most games finished
47—Joe Berry, 1944
Most innings
384—Rube Waddell, 1904
Most games won, season
31—Jack Coombs, 1910
Lefty Grove, 1931
Most games won, career
283—Eddie Plank
Most 20-victory seasons
7—Eddie Plank, Lefty Grove
Most games lost
25—Scott Perry, 1920
Most games lost, career
158—Eddie Plank
Highest winning percentage
.886—Lefty Grove (31-4), 1931
Longest winning streak
16 games—Lefty Grove, 1931
Longest losing streak
19 games—Jack Nabors, 1916
Most bases on balls
168—Elmer Myers, 1916
Most bases on balls, career
879—Eddie Plank

— 259 —

Most strikeouts
349—Rube Waddell, 1904
Most strikeouts, career
1,998—Eddie Plank
Most strikeouts, nine-inning game
14—Rube Waddell, July 14, 1903
    Rube Waddell, September 6, 1904, first game
    Rube Waddell, August 2, 1905
Most strikeouts, extra-inning game
18—Jack Coombs, September 1, 1906, 24 innings
    Jack Coombs, August 4, 1910, 16 innings
Most shutouts
13—Jack Coombs, 1910
Most shutouts, career
60—Eddie Plank
Most 1-0 shutouts won
4—Harry Krause, 1909

Most runs
169—Elmer Myers, 1916
Most earned runs
146—George Earnshaw, 1930
Most hits
360—Jack Coombs, 1911
Most hit batsmen
31—Chick Fraser, 1901
Most wild pitches
16—Stu Flythe, 1936
Most home runs
28—Alex Kellner, 1950
Lowest ERA
1.98—Scott Perry, 332 innings, 1918

CLUB RECORDS

Most players
56 in 1915
Fewest players
19 in 1905
Most games
158 in 1914
Most at-bats
5,537 in 1932
Most runs
981 in 1932
Fewest runs
447 in 1916
Most hits
1,659 in 1925
Fewest hits
1,132 in 1908
Most singles
1,206 in 1925
Most doubles
323 in 1928
Most triples
108 in 1912
Most homers
173 in 1932
Fewest homers (154 or 162-game schedule)
16 in 1915, 1917
Most home runs at Shibe Park, home and opponents
189 in 1932
Most pinch home runs
6 in 1952
Most grand slams
8 in 1932
Most long hits
527 in 1932
Most extra bases on long hits
924 in 1932
Most total bases
2,530 in 1932
Most sacrifices (sacrifice hits and sacrifice flies)
239 in 1926
Most sacrifice hits
147 in 1906
Most sacrifice flies
31 in 1954
Most stolen bases
259 in 1912
Most bases on balls
783 in 1949
Most strikeouts
667 in 1954
Fewest strikeouts
326 in 1927
Most hit by pitch
46 in 1920
Fewest hit by pitch
5 in 1937

Most runs batted in
923 in 1932
Highest batting average
.307 in 1925
Lowest batting average
.223 in 1908
Highest slugging average
.457 in 1932
Lowest slugging average
.308 in 1918
Most grounded into double play
170 in 1950
Fewest grounded into double play
105 in 1945
Most left on bases
1,235 in 1949
Fewest left on bases
999 in 1924
Most .300 hitters
11 in 1927
Most putouts
4,231 in 1910
Fewest putouts
3,953 in 1906
Most assists
2,172 in 1920
Fewest assists
1,591 in 1946
Most chances accepted
6,297 in 1920
Fewest chances accepted
5,610 in 1938
Most errors
317 in 1901
Fewest errors
113 in 1948
Most consecutive errorless games
7 in 1951
Most double plays
217 in 1949
Fewest double plays
102 in 1917
Most passed balls
25 in 1914
Fewest passed balls
5 in 1947
Highest fielding average
.981 in 1948
Lowest fielding average
.936 in 1901
Highest home attendance
945,076 in 1948
Highest road attendance
1,562,360 in 1948
Most games won
107 in 1931

Most games lost
117 in 1916
Most games won, month
26—July 1931
Most games lost, month
28—July 1916
Highest percentage games won
.704 in 1931 (won 107, lost 45)
Lowest percentage games won
.235 in 1916 (won 36, lost 117)
Games won, league
3,886 in 54 years
Games lost, league
4,248 in 54 years
Most shutouts won
27 in 1909 (also 1 tie), 26 in 1908
Most shutouts lost
24 in 1943
Most 1-0 games won
9 in 1909
Most 1-0 games lost
7 in 1908, 1909
Most consecutive games won
17 in 1931
Most consecutive games lost
20 in 1916, 1943
Number of times league champions
9
Number of last-place finishes
18
Most runs, game
24 vs. Detroit, May 18, 1912
vs. Boston, May 1, 1929
Most runs by opponent, game
25 by Cleveland, May 11, 1930

by New York, May 24, 1936
Most runs, shutout game
16 vs. Chicago, July 25, 1928, first game
vs. Chicago, August 29, 1937, first game
Most runs by opponent, shutout game
21 by New York, August 13, 1939, second game, eight innings
Most runs, doubleheader shutout
17 vs. Detroit, August 13, 1902
Most runs, inning
13 vs. Cleveland, June 15, 1925, eighth inning
Most hits, game
29 vs. Boston, May 1, 1929
Longest 1-0 game won
13 innings vs. Detroit, August 11, 1902
vs. Boston, September 10, 1904
vs. Chicago, May 16, 1909
vs. Cleveland, May 14, 1914
Longest 1-0 game, lost
16 innings vs. St. Louis, June 5, 1942
Most home runs, game
7 vs. Detroit, June 3, 1921
Most consecutive games with one or more homers
12 (20 homers), 1951
Most total bases, game
44 vs. Boston, May 1, 1929
Largest crowd, day game
37,534 vs. New York, May 16, 1937
Largest crowd, doubleheader
38,800 vs. New York, July 13, 1931
Largest crowd, night game
37,383 vs. New York, June 27, 1947
Largest crowd, home opener
32,825 vs. New York, April 20, 1927

ST. LOUIS BROWNS

YEARLY FINISHES

(Milwaukee Brewers, 1901)

Year	Position	W	L	Pct.	°GB	Manager	Attendance
1901 —8th		48	89	.350	35½	Hugh Duffy	139,034
1902 —2nd		78	58	.574	5	Jimmy McAleer	272,283
1903 —6th		65	74	.468	26½	Jimmy McAleer	380,405
1904 —6th		65	87	.428	29	Jimmy McAleer	318,108
1905 —8th		54	99	.354	40½	Jimmy McAleer	339,112
1906 —5th		76	73	.510	16	Jimmy McAleer	389,157
1907 —6th		69	83	.454	24	Jimmy McAleer	419,025
1908 —4th		83	69	.546	6½	Jimmy McAleer	618,947
1909 —7th		61	89	.407	36	Jimmy McAleer	366,274
1910 —8th		47	107	.305	57	John O'Connor	249,889
1911 —8th		45	107	.296	56½	Bobby Wallace	207,984
1912 —7th		53	101	.344	53	Bobby Wallace, George Stovall	214,070
1913 —8th		57	96	.373	39	George Stovall, Branch Rickey	250,330
1914 —5th		71	82	.464	28½	Branch Rickey	244,714
1915 —6th		63	91	.409	39½	Branch Rickey	150,358
1916 —5th		79	75	.513	12	Fielder Jones	335,740
1917 —7th		57	97	.370	43	Fielder Jones	210,486
1918 —5th		58	64	.475	15	Fielder Jones, Jimmy Austin, Jimmy Burke	122,076
1919 —5th		67	72	.482	20½	Jimmy Burke	349,350
1920 —4th		76	77	.497	21½	Jimmy Burke	419,311
1921 —3rd		81	73	.526	17½	Lee Fohl	355,978
1922 —2nd		93	61	.604	1	Lee Fohl	712,918
1923 —5th		74	78	.487	24	Lee Fohl, Jimmy Austin	430,296
1924 —4th		74	78	.487	17	George Sisler	533,349
1925 —3rd		82	71	.536	15	George Sisler	462,898
1926 —7th		62	92	.403	29	George Sisler	283,986
1927 —7th		59	94	.336	50½	Dan Howley	247,879
1928 —3rd		82	72	.532	19	Dan Howley	339,497
1929 —4th		79	73	.520	26	Dan Howley	280,697
1930 —6th		64	90	.416	38	Bill Killefer	152,088
1931 —5th		63	91	.409	45	Bill Killefer	179,126
1932 —6th		63	91	.409	44	Bill Killefer	112,558
1933 —8th		55	96	.364	43½	Bill Killefer, Allen Sothoron, Rogers Hornsby	88,113
1934 —6th		67	85	.441	33	Rogers Hornsby	115,305

Year	Position	W	L	Pct.	*GB	Manager	Attendance
1935 — 7th		65	87	.428	28½	Rogers Hornsby	80,922
1936 — 7th		57	95	.375	44½	Rogers Hornsby	93,267
1937 — 8th		46	108	.299	56	Rogers Hornsby, Jim Bottomley	123,121
1938 — 7th		55	97	.362	44	Gabby Street	130,417
1939 — 8th		43	111	.279	64½	Fred Haney	109,159
1940 — 6th		67	87	.435	23	Fred Haney	239,591
1941 — 6th (tied)		70	84	.455	31	Fred Haney, Luke Sewell	176,240
1942 — 3rd		82	69	.543	19½	Luke Sewell	255,617
1943 — 6th		72	80	.474	25	Luke Sewell	214,392
1944 — 1st		89	65	.578	+ 1	Luke Sewell	508,644
1945 — 3rd		81	70	.536	6	Luke Sewell	482,986
1946 — 7th		66	88	.429	38	Luke Sewell, Zack Taylor	526,435
1947 — 8th		59	95	.383	38	Muddy Ruel	320,474
1948 — 6th		59	94	.386	37	Zack Taylor	335,546
1949 — 7th		53	101	.344	44	Zack Taylor	270,936
1950 — 7th		58	96	.377	40	Zack Taylor	247,131
1951 — 8th		52	102	.338	46	Zack Taylor	293,790
1952 — 7th		64	90	.416	31	Rogers Hornsby, Marty Marion	518,796
1953 — 8th		54	100	.351	46½	Marty Marion	297,238

*Games behind winner.

INDIVIDUAL RECORDS (1902 TO 1953)

SERVICE

Most years by non-pitcher
16 — Jimmy Austin
Most years by pitcher
10 — George Blaeholder
Barney Pelty
Jack Powell

BATTING

Most games
159 — Del Pratt, 1915
Most games, career
1,647 — George Sisler
Most at-bats
671 — Jack Tobin, 150 games, 1921
Most at-bats, career
6,667 — George Sisler
Most runs
145 — Harlond Clift, 152 games, 1936
Most runs, career
1,091 — George Sisler
Most hits
257 — George Sisler, 154 games, 1920
Most hits, career
2,295 — George Sisler
Most singles
179 — Jack Tobin, 150 games, 1921
Most doubles
51 — Beau Bell, 156 games, 1937
Most doubles, career
343 — George Sisler
Most triples
20 — Heinie Manush, 154 games, 1928
Most triples, career
145 — George Sisler
Most homers by righthander
34 — Harlond Clift, 149 games, 1938
Most homers by lefthander
39 — Ken Williams, 153 games, 1922
Most homers by rookie
24 — Walt Judnich, 137 games, 1940
Most homers at home
32 — Ken Williams, 1922
Most homers, month
15 — Harlond Clift, August, 1938
Most homers, career
185 — Ken Williams
Most grand slams
2 — Held by many players
Most grand slams, career
5 — Ken Williams

Harlond Clift
Vern Stephens
Most total bases
399 — George Sisler, 154 games, 1920
Most total bases, career
3,201 — George Sisler
Most long hits
86 — George Sisler, 154 games, 1920
Most extra bases on long hits
173 — Ken Williams, 153 games, 1922
Most sacrifices (sacrifice hits and sacrifice flies)
48 — Joe Gedeon, 153 games, 1920
Most sacrifice hits
40 — Tom Jones, 144 games, 1906
Most bases on balls
126 — Lu Blue, 151 games, 1929
Most strikeouts
120 — Gus Williams, 143 games, 1914
Fewest strikeouts
13 — Jack Tobin, 151 games, 1923
Most hit by pitch
12 — Frank O'Rourke, 140 games, 1927
Most runs batted in
155 — Ken Williams, 153 games, 1922
Most runs batted in, career
964 — George Sisler
Highest batting average
.420 — George Sisler, 142 games, 1922
Highest batting average, career
.344 — George Sisler
Highest slugging average
.632 — George Sisler, 154 games, 1920
Highest slugging average, career
.558 — Ken Williams
Longest batting streak
41 games — George Sisler, 1922
Most grounding into double play
21 — Glenn McQuillen, 100 games, 1942
Fewest grounding into double play
7 — Vern Stephens, 150 games, 1947

BASERUNNING

Most stolen bases
51 — George Sisler, 142 games, 1922
Most stolen bases, career
351 — George Sisler
Most caught stealing
19 — George Sisler, 142 games, 1922
Ken Williams, 153 games, 1922

PITCHING

Most games
60 — Marlin Stuart, 1953

Most games, career
323—Elam Vangilder
Most games started
40—Bobo Newsom, 1938
Most complete games
36—Jack Powell, 1902
Most games finished
35—Satchel Paige, 1952
Most innings
348—Urban Shocker, 1922
Most games won
27—Urban Shocker, 1922
Most games won, career
126—Urban J. Shocker
Most 20 victory seasons
4—Urban J. Shocker
Most games lost
25—Fred Glade, 1905
Most games lost, career
142—Jack Powell
Highest winning percentage
.808—General Crowder (21-5), 1928
Longest winning streak
Less than 12
Longest losing streak
Less than 12
Most bases on balls
192—Bobo Newsom, 1938
Most bases on balls, career
640—Dixie Davis

Most strikeouts
232—Rube Waddell, 1908
Most strikeouts, career
884—Jack Powell
Most strikeouts, game
17—Rude Waddell, September 20, 1908, 10 innings
16—Rube Waddell, July 29, 1908
Most shutouts
6—Fred Glade, 1904
Harry Howell, 1906
Most shutouts, career
27—Jack Powell
Most 1-0 shutouts won
3—Fred Glade, 1904
Most runs
205—Bobo Newsom, 1938
Most earned runs
186—Bobo Newsom, 1938
Most hits
365—Urban Shocker, 1922
Most hits batsmen
19—Barney Pelty, 1907
Most wild pitches
11—Carl Weilman, 1914
Dave Davenport, 1917
Jack Knott, 1936
Most home runs
21—Urban Shocker, 1921
Lowest ERA
2.12—Carl Weilman, 307 innings, 1914

CLUB RECORDS

Most players
52 in 1951
Fewest players
19 in 1906
Most games
159 in 1914, 1915
Most at-bats
5,510 in 1937
Most runs
897 in 1925
Fewest runs
441 in 1909
Most hits
1,693 in 1922
Fewest hits
1,092 in 1910
Most singles
1,239 in 1920
Most doubles
327 in 1937
Most triples
106 in 1921
Most homers
118 in 1940
Fewest homers (154 or 162-game schedule)
9 in 1906
Most homers at Sportsman's Park, home and opponents
135 in 1940
Most grand slams
5 in 1950
Most home runs by pinch-hitters
4 in 1951
Most total bases
2,463 in 1922
Most long hits
482 in 1922, 1925
Most extra bases on long hits
770 in 1922, 1925
Most sacrifices (sacrifices hits and sacrifice flies)
214 in 1928
Most sacrifices hits
163 in 1906

Most stolen bases
234 in 1916
Most bases on balls
775 in 1941
Most strikeouts
863 in 1914
Fewest strikeouts
339 in 1920
Most hit by pitch
43 in 1927
Fewest hit by pitch
12 in 1931
Most runs batted in
761 in 1936
Highest batting average
.313 in 1922
Lowest batting average
.216 in 1910
Highest slugging average
.455 in 1922
Lowest slugging average
.273 in 1910
Most grounded into double play
151 in 1951
Fewest grounded into double play
93 in 1944
Most left on bases
1,334 in 1941
Fewest left on bases
1,055 in 1951
Most .300 hitters
8 in 1922
Most putouts
4,328 in 1916
Fewest putouts
3,993 in 1911
Most assists
2,189 in 1910
Fewest assists
1,584 in 1938
Most chances accepted
6,516 in 1916

Fewest chances accepted
5,618 in 1938
Most errors
378 in 1910
Fewest errors
134 in 1947
Most consecutive errorless games
8 in 1928
Most double plays
190 in 1948
Fewest double plays
116 in 1914
Most passed balls
30 in 1914, 1915
Fewest passed balls
4 in 1930, 1933
Highest fielding average
.977 in 1947
Lowest fielding average
.943 in 1910
Highest home attendance
712,918 in 1922
Highest road attendance
1,170,349 in 1948
Most games won
93 in 1922
Most games lost
111 in 1939
Most games won, month
23—August 1945
Most games lost, month
24—September 1939
July 1952
Highest percentage games won
.604 in 1922 (won 93, lost 61)
Lowest percentage games won
.279 in 1939 (won 43, lost 111)
Games won, league
3,416 in 52 years
Games lost, league
4,465 in 52 years
Most shutouts won
21 in 1909
Most shutouts lost
25 in 1904, 1906, 1910

Most 1-0 games won
6 in 1909
Most 1-0 games lost
7 in 1907
Most consecutive games won
14 in 1916
Most consecutive games lost
14 in 1911, 1953
Number of times league champions
1
Number of last-place finishes
10
Most runs, game
20 vs. Detroit, August 18, 1951
Most runs by opponent, game
29 by Boston, June 8, 1950
Most runs, shutout game
16 vs. Detroit, September 9, 1922
Most runs by opponent, shutout game
18 by Detroit, April 29, 1935
Most runs, doubleheader shutout
5 vs. Philadelphia, September 23, 1906
Most runs, inning
11 vs. Philadelphia, July 21, 1949, first game, sixth inning
vs. Detroit, August 18, 1951, seventh inning
Longest 1-0 game won
16 innings vs. Philadelphia, June 5, 1942
Longest 1-0 game lost
15 innings vs. Washington, August 14, 1903, first game
vs. Washington, July 25, 1918
Most hits, game
24 vs. Philadelphia, September 17, 1920
vs. Washington, June 14, 1932
Most home runs, game
5 vs. New York, September 16, 1940
Most consecutive games with one or more homers
11 (20 homers), 1922
Most total bases, game
40 vs. Chicago, May 31, 1925
Largest crowd, day game
34,625 vs. New York, October 1, 1944
Largest crowd, night game
22,847 vs. Cleveland, May 24, 1940
Largest crowd, home opener
19,561 vs. Detroit, April 18, 1923

SEATTLE MARINERS

YEARLY FINISHES

WEST DIVISION

Year	Position	W	L	Pct.	*GB	Manager	Attendance
1977	—6th	64	98	.395	38	Darrell Johnson	1,338,511
1978	—7th	56	104	.350	35	Darrell Johnson	877,440
1979	—6th	67	95	.414	21	Darrell Johnson	844,447
1980	—7th	59	103	.364	38	Darrell Johnson, Maury Wills	836,204
1981	—6th/5th	44	65	.404	†	Maury Wills, Rene Lachemann	636,272
1982	—4th	76	86	.469	17	Rene Lachemann	1,070,404
1983	—7th	60	102	.370	39	Rene Lachemann, Del Crandall	813,537
1984	—5th (tied)	74	88	.457	10	Del Crandall, Chuck Cottier	870,372
1985	—6th	74	88	.457	17	Chuck Cottier	1,128,696
1986	—7th	67	95	.414	25	Chuck Cottier, Marty Martinez, Dick Williams	1,029,045
1987	—4th	78	84	.481	7	Dick Williams	1,134,255
1988	—7th	68	93	.422	35½	Dick Williams, Jim Snyder	1,022,398
1989	—6th	73	89	.451	26	Jim Lefebvre	1,298,443
1990	—5th	77	85	.475	26	Jim Lefebvre	1,509,727
1991	—5th	83	79	.512	12	Jim Lefebvre	2,147,905
1992	—7th	64	98	.395	32	Bill Plummer	1,651,398
1993	—4th	82	80	.506	12	Lou Piniella	2,051,853
1994	—3rd	49	63	.438	2	Lou Piniella	1,104,206

*Games behind winner. †First half 21-36; second 23-29.

SERVICE

Most years by non-pitcher
10—Harold Reynolds
    Dave Valle
Most years by pitcher
7—Jim Beattie
   Mike Moore
   Edwin Nunez

BATTING

Most games
162—Ruppert Jones, 1979
     Willie Horton, 1979
Most games, career
1,166—Alvin Davis
Most at-bats
646—Willie Horton, 162 games, 1979
Most at-bats, career
4,136—Alvin Davis
Most runs
113—Ken Griffey Jr., 156 games, 1993
Most runs, career
563—Alvin Davis
Most hits
192—Phil Bradley, 159 games, 1985
Most hits, career
1,163—Alvin Davis
Most singles
152—Jack Perconte, 155 games, 1984
Most singles, career
798—Harold Reynolds
Most doubles
46—Edgar Martinez, 135 games, 1992
Most doubles, career
212—Alvin Davis
Most triples
11—Harold Reynolds, 158 games, 1988
Most triples, career
48—Harold Reynolds
Most homers by righthander
32—Gorman Thomas, 135 games, 1985
Most homers by lefthander
45—Ken Griffey Jr., 156 games, 1993
Most homers by rookie
27—Alvin Davis, 152 games, 1984
Most homers at home
21—Ken Griffey Jr., 1993
Most homers on road
24—Ken Griffey Jr., 1993
Most homers, month
15—Ken Griffey Jr., May 1994
Most homers by righthander, career
115—Jim Presley
Most homers by lefthander, career
172—Ken Griffey Jr.
Most grand slams
3—Alvin Davis, 140 games, 1990
   Ken Griffey Jr., 154 games, 1991
   Mike Blowers, 127 games, 1993
Most grand slams, career
9—Alvin Davis
Most total bases
359—Ken Griffey Jr., 156 games, 1993
Most total bases, career
1,875—Alvin Davis
Most long hits
86—Ken Griffey Jr., 156 games, 1993
Most long hits, career
382—Alvin Davis
Most extra bases on long hits
179—Ken Griffey Jr., 156 games, 1993
Most extra bases on long hits, career
712—Alvin Davis

Most sacrifice hits
15—Craig Reynolds, 135 games, 1977
    Larry Milbourne, 106 games, 1980
Most sacrifice flies
12—Jeffrey Leonard, 150 games, 1989
Most bases on balls
101—Alvin Davis, 142 games, 1989
Most bases on balls—career
672—Alvin Davis
Most strikeouts
172—Jim Presley, 155 games, 1986
Most strikeouts, career
713—Jim Presley
Fewest strikeouts
34—Harold Reynolds, 160 games, 1987
Most hit by pitch
17—Dave Valle, 135 games, 1993
Most runs batted in
116—Alvin Davis, 152 games, 1984
Most runs batted in, career
667—Alvin Davis
Most game-winning RBIs
13—Tom Paciorek, 104 games, 1981
    Alvin Davis, 152 games, 1984
    Jim Presley, 155 games, 1986
Highest batting average
.343—Edgar Martinez, 135 games, 1992
Highest batting average, career
.303—Ken Griffey Jr.
Highest slugging average
.617—Ken Griffey Jr., 156 games, 1993
Highest slugging average, career
.521—Ken Phelps
Longest batting streak
21 games—Dan Meyer, 1979
           Richie Zisk, 1982
Most grounded into double play
29—Jim Presley, 155 games, 1985
Fewest grounded into double play
4—Harold Reynolds, 153 games, 1989

BASERUNNING

Most stolen bases
60—Harold Reynolds, 160 games, 1987
Most stolen bases, career
290—Julio Cruz
Most caught stealing
29—Harold Reynolds, 158 games, 1988

PITCHING

Most games
78—Ed Vande Berg, 1982
Most games, career
272—Ed Vande Berg
Most games started
37—Mike Moore, 1986
Most games started, career
217—Mike Moore
Most complete games
14—Mike Moore, 1985
    Mark Langston, 1987
Most complete games, career
56—Mike Moore
Most games finished
64—Bill Caudill, 1982
Most innings
272—Mark Langston, 1987
Most innings, career
1,457—Mike Moore
Most games won
19—Mark Langston, 1987
    Randy Johnson, 1993
Most games won, career
78—Randy Johnson

Most games lost
19—Matt Young, 1985
Mike Moore, 1987
Most games lost, career
96—Mike Moore
Highest winning percentage
.704—Randy Johnson (19-8), 1993
Longest winning streak
9 games—Scott Bankhead, 1989
Dave Fleming, 1992
Longest losing streak
16 games—Mike Parrott, 1980
Most saves
33—Mike Schooler, 1989
Most bases on balls
152—Randy Johnson, 1991
Most bases on balls, career
657—Randy Johnson
Most strikeouts
308—Randy Johnson, 1993
Most strikeouts, career
1,279—Randy Johnson
Most strikeouts, game
18—Randy Johnson, September 27, 1992
Most shutouts won
4—Dave Fleming, 1992

Randy Johnson, 1994
Most shutouts won, career
12—Randy Johnson
Most 1 - 0 shutouts won
1—Held by many pitchers
Most runs
145—Mike Moore, 1987
Most earned runs
129—Mark Langston, 1986
Most hits
279—Mike Moore, 1986
Most hit batsmen
18—Randy Johnson, 1992
Most wild pitches
16—Matt Young, 1990
Most home runs allowed
35—Scott Bankhead, 1987
Most sacrifice hits
15—Shane Rawley, 1980
Most sacrifice flies
14—Rich DeLucia, 1991
Lowest ERA
3.24—Erik Hanson, 236 innings, 1990
Randy Johnson, 255⅓ innings, 1993

CLUB RECORDS

Most players
48 in 1992, 1993
Fewest players
34 in 1978, 1980
Most games
163 in 1980
Most at-bats
5,626 in 1982
Most runs
760 in 1987
Fewest runs
558 in 1983
Most opponents' runs
855 in 1977
Most hits
1,499 in 1987
Fewest hits
1,280 in 1983
Most singles
1,056 in 1979
Most doubles
282 in 1987
Most triples
52 in 1979
Most homers
171 in 1985
Fewest homers
97 in 1978
Most homers at Kingdome, home and opponents
218 in 1987
Most grand slams
8 in 1993
Most pinch home runs
5 in 1994
Most total bases
2,360 in 1987
Most long hits
491 in 1987
Most extra bases on long hits
866 in 1985
Most sacrifice hits
106 in 1980
Most sacrifice flies
62 in 1991
Most stolen bases
174 in 1987
Most caught stealing
82 in 1982

Most bases on balls
624 in 1993
Most strikeouts
1,148 in 1986
Fewest strikeouts
702 in 1978
Most hit by pitch
56 in 1993
Most runs batted in
717 in 1987
Most game-winning RBIs
73 in 1987
Highest batting average
.272 in 1987
Lowest batting average
.240 in 1983
Highest slugging average
.428 in 1987
Lowest slugging average
.356 in 1980
Most grounded into double play
158 in 1979
Fewest grounded into double play
101 in 1984
Most left on bases
1,227 in 1990
Fewest left on bases
1,034 in 1983
Most .300 hitters
2 in 1989, 1990, 1991, 1992
Most putouts
4,429 in 1982
Fewest putouts
4,255 in 1983
Most assists
1,930 in 1980
Fewest assists
1,612 in 1988
Most chances accepted
6,302 in 1980
Fewest chances accepted
5,896 in 1988
Most errors
156 in 1986
Most errorless games
95 in 1993
Most consecutive errorless games
11 in 1993

Fewest errors
90 in 1993
Most double plays
191 in 1986
Fewest double plays
143 in 1984
Most passed balls
24 in 1991
Fewest passed balls
4 in 1987
Highest fielding average
.985 in 1993
Lowest fielding average
.975 in 1986
Highest home attendance
2,147,905 in 1991
Highest road attendance
2,307,636 in 1993
Most games won
83 in 1991
Most games lost
104 in 1978
Most games won, month
16 in June 1979, June 1986, June 1990
Most games lost, month
22 in August 1977
Games won, league
1,215 in 18 years
Games lost, league
1,595 in 18 years
Highest percentage games won
.512 in 1991 (won 83, lost 79)
Lowest percentage games won
.350 in 1978 (won 56, lost 104)
Most shutouts won
13 in 1991
Most shutouts lost
15 in 1978, 1983, 1990
Most 1-0 games won
3 in 1979
Most 1-0 games lost
4 in 1980, 1989, 1990

Most consecutive games won
8 in 1985, 1991
Most consecutive games lost
14 in 1992
Number of times league champions
0
Number of last-place finishes
5
Most runs, game
19 vs. Texas, May 20, 1994
Most runs by opponent, game
20 by Detroit, April 17, 1993
Most runs, shutout game
14 vs. California, August 7, 1987
Most runs by opponent, shutout game
15 by Minnesota, July 10, 1977
Most runs, inning
10 vs. Milwaukee, July 18, 1991, eighth inning
Longest 1-0 game won
None over nine innings
Longest 1-0 game lost
12 innings vs. Texas, June 29, 1988
Most hits, nine-inning game
23 vs. Texas, May 17, 1993
Most hits, extra-inning game
24 vs. Boston, September 3, 1981, 20 innings
Most home runs, game
7 vs. Oakland, April 11, 1985
Most consecutive games with one or more homers
15 (25 homers), 1994
Most total bases, game
42, vs. Texas, May 20, 1994
Largest crowd, day game
53,287 vs. Detroit, June 16, 1991
Largest crowd, doubleheader
32,597 vs. California, August 12, 1985
Largest crowd, night game
57,806 vs. Minnesota, April 11, 1994
Largest crowd, home opener
57,806 vs. Minnesota, April 11, 1994

SEATTLE PILOTS

YEARLY FINISHES

WEST DIVISION

Year	Position	W	L	Pct.	*GB	Manager	Attendance
1969—6th		64	98	.395	33	Joe Schultz	677,944

*Games behind winner.

INDIVIDUAL RECORDS (1969)

BATTING

Most games
148—Tommy Harper, 1969
Most at-bats
537—Tommy Harper, 148 games, 1969
Most runs
88—Wayne Comer, 147 games, 1969
Most hits
126—Tommy Harper, 148 games, 1969
Most singles
105—Tommy Harper, 148 games, 1969
Most doubles
29—Tommy Davis, 123 games, 1969
Most triples
6—Mike Hegan, 95 games, 1969
Most homers by lefthander
25—Don Mincher, 140 games, 1969
Most homers by righthander
15—Wayne Comer, 147 games, 1969
Most homers by rookie
3—Steve Hovley, 91 games, 1969
Danny Walton, 23 games, 1969

Most homers, month
8—Don Mincher, July 1969
Most homers at home
13—Don Mincher, 1969
Most homers on road
12—Don Mincher, 1969
Most grand slams
1—Don Mincher, 140 games, 1969
Rich Rollins, 58 games, 1969
Fred Talbot, 27 games, 1969
Most total bases
194—Don Mincher, 140 games, 1969
Most long hits
39—Don Mincher, 140 games, 1969
Most extra bases on long hits
89—Don Mincher, 140 games, 1969
Most sacrifice hits
9—Jerry McNertney, 128 games, 1969
Most sacrifice flies
5—Tommy Davis, 123 games, 1969
Most bases on balls
95—Tommy Harper, 148 games, 1969

Most strikeouts
90—Tommy Harper, 148 games, 1969
Fewest strikeouts
46—Tommy Davis, 123 games, 1969
Most hit by pitch
5—Don Mincher, 140 games, 1969
Rich Rollins, 58 games, 1969
Most runs batted in
80—Tommy Davis, 123 games, 1969
Highest batting average
.271—Tommy Davis, 123 games, 1969
Highest slugging average
.454—Don Mincher, 140 games, 1969
Longest batting streak
18 games—Tommy Davis, 1969
Most grounded into double play
17—Tommy Davis, 123 games, 1969
Fewest grounded into double play
8—Tommy Harper, 148 games, 1969

BASERUNNING

Most stolen bases
73—Tommy Harper, 148 games, 1969
Most caught stealing
18—Tommy Harper, 148 games, 1969

PITCHING

Most games
66—Diego Segui, 1969
Most games started
29—Gene Brabender, 1969
Most complete games
7—Gene Brabender, 1969
Most games finished
38—Diego Segui, 1969
Most innings
202—Gene Brabender, 1969
Most games won
13—Gene Brabender, 1969

Most games lost
14—Gene Brabender, 1969
Highest winning percentage
.667—Diego Segui (12-6), 1969
Longest winning streak
5 games—Diego Segui, 1969
Longest losing streak
9 games—John Gelnar, 1969
Most saves
12—Diego Segui, 1969
Most bases on balls
103—Gene Brabender, 1969
Most strikeouts
139—Gene Brabender, 1969
Most strikeouts, game
11—Marty Pattin, April 29, 1969
Most shutouts won
1—held by 5 pitchers
Most 1-0 shutouts won
1—Gene Brabender
Marty Pattin
Most runs
111—Gene Brabender, 1969
Most earned runs
99—Marty Pattin, 1969
Most hits
193—Gene Brabender, 1969
Most wild pitches
8—Jim Bouton, 1969
Most hit batsmen
13—Gene Brabender, 1969
Most home runs
29—Marty Pattin, 1969
Most sacrifice hits
10—Diego Segui, 1969
Most sacrifice flies
6—Gene Brabender, 1969
Lowest ERA
3.36—Diego Segui, 142 innings, 1969

CLUB RECORDS

Most players
53 in 1969
Most games
163 in 1969
Most at-bats
5,444 in 1969
Most runs
639 in 1969
Most opponents' runs
799 in 1969
Most hits
1,276 in 1969
Most singles
945 in 1969
Most doubles
179 in 1969
Most triples
27 in 1969
Most homers
125 in 1969
Fewest homers
125 in 1969
Most homers at Sick's Stadium, home and opponents
167 in 1969
Most grand slams
3 in 1969
Most pinch home runs
3 in 1969
Most total bases
1,884 in 1969
Most long hits
331 in 1969
Most extra bases on long hits
608 in 1969

Most sacrifice hits
72 in 1969
Most sacrifice flies
29 in 1969
Most stolen bases
167 in 1969
Most caught stealing
59 in 1969
Most bases on balls
626 in 1969
Most strikeouts
1,015 in 1969
Most hit by pitch
34 in 1969
Most runs batted in
583 in 1969
Highest batting average
.234 in 1969
Highest slugging average
.346 in 1969
Most grounded into double play
111 in 1969
Most left on bases
1,130 in 1969
Most putouts
4,391 in 1969
Most assists
1,763 in 1969
Most chances accepted
6,154 in 1969
Most errors
167 in 1969
Most errorless games
65 in 1969

Most consecutive errorless games
4 in 1969
Most double plays
149 in 1969
Most passed balls
21 in 1969
Highest fielding average
.974 in 1969
Highest home attendance
677,944 in 1969
Highest road attendance
889,578 in 1969
Most games won
64 in 1969
Most games lost
98 in 1969
Most games won, month
14—June 1969, September 1969
Most games lost, month
22—August 1969
Highest percentage games won
.395 in 1969 (won 64, lost 98)
Most consecutive games won
5 in 1969
Most consecutive games lost
10 in 1969
Most shutouts won
6 in 1969
Most shutouts lost
6 in 1969
Most 1-0 games won
2 in 1969
Most 1-0 games lost
0 in 1969
Number of times league champions
0

Number of last-place finishes
0
Most runs, inning
6 vs. Boston, May 16, 1969, 11th inning
Most runs, game
16 vs. Washington, May 10, 1969
Most runs by opponent, game
15 by Baltimore, August 16, 1969
Most runs, shutout game
8 vs. California, July 9, 1969, first game
Most runs by opponent, shutout game
10 by Baltimore, June 7, 1969
Most runs, doubleheader shutout
No performance
Longest 1-0 game won
None over 9 innings
Longest 1-0 game lost
None
Most hits, game
16 vs. Oakland, September 10, 1969
Most hits, extra-inning game
20 vs. Minnesota, July 19, 1969, 18 innings
Most home runs, game
4 vs. Boston, May 16, 1969, 11 innings
Most consecutive games with one or more homers
5 (8 homers), 1969
Most total bases, game
31 vs. Boston, May 16, 1969, 11 innings
Largest crowd, day game
23,657 vs. New York, August 3, 1969
Largest crowd, doubleheader
18,413 vs. Kansas City, June 20, 1969
Largest crowd, night game
20,490 vs. Baltimore, May 28, 1969
Largest crowd, home opener
14,993 vs. Chicago, April 11, 1969

TEXAS RANGERS

YEARLY FINISHES

WEST DIVISION

Year	Position	W	L	Pct.	*GB	Manager	Attendance
1972	6th	54	100	.351	38½	Ted Williams	662,974
1973	6th	57	105	.352	37	Whitey Herzog, Del Wilber, Billy Martin	686,085
1974	2nd	84	76	.525	5	Billy Martin	1,193,902
1975	3rd	79	83	.488	19	Billy Martin, Frank Lucchesi	1,127,924
1976	4th (tied)	76	86	.469	14	Frank Lucchesi	1,164,982
1977	2nd	94	68	.580	8	Frank Lucchesi, Eddie Stanky, Connie Ryan, Billy Hunter ..	1,250,722
1978	2nd (tied)	87	75	.537	5	Billy Hunter, Pat Corrales	1,447,963
1979	3rd	83	79	.512	5	Pat Corrales	1,519,671
1980	4th	76	85	.472	20½	Pat Corrales	1,198,175
1981	2nd/3rd	57	48	.543	†	Don Zimmer	850,076
1982	6th	64	98	.395	29	Don Zimmer, Darrell Johnson	1,154,432
1983	3rd	77	85	.475	22	Doug Rader	1,363,469
1984	7th	69	92	.429	14½	Doug Rader	1,102,471
1985	7th	62	99	.385	28½	Doug Rader, Bobby Valentine	1,112,497
1986	2nd	87	75	.537	5	Bobby Valentine	1,692,002
1987	6th (tied)	75	87	.463	10	Bobby Valentine	1,763,053
1988	6th	70	91	.435	33½	Bobby Valentine	1,581,901
1989	4th	83	79	.512	16	Bobby Valentine	2,043,993
1990	3rd	83	79	.512	20	Bobby Valentine	2,057,911
1991	3rd	85	77	.525	10	Bobby Valentine	2,297,720
1992	4th	77	85	.475	19	Bobby Valentine, Toby Harrah	2,198,231
1993	2nd	86	76	.531	8	Kevin Kennedy	2,244,616
1994	1st	52	62	.456	+ 1	Kevin Kennedy	2,503,198

*Games behind winner.   †First half 33-22; second 24-26.

INDIVIDUAL RECORDS (1972 TO DATE)

SERVICE

Most years by non-pitcher
12—Jim Sundberg
Most years by pitcher
11—Charlie Hough

BATTING

Most games
163—Al Oliver, 1980
Most games, career
1,512—Jim Sundberg

Most at-bats
670—Buddy Bell, 162 games, 1979
Most at-bats, career
4,684—Jim Sundberg
Most runs
124—Rafael Palmeiro, 160 games, 1993
Most runs, career
588—Ruben Sierra
Most hits
210—Mickey Rivers, 147 games, 1980
Most hits, career
1,180—Jim Sundberg
Most singles
165—Mickey Rivers, 147 games, 1980
Most singles, career
893—Jim Sundberg
Most doubles
49—Rafael Palmeiro, 159 games, 1991
Most doubles, career
230—Ruben Sierra
Most triples
14—Ruben Sierra, 162 games, 1989
Most triples, career
44—Ruben Sierra
Most homers by righthander
46—Juan Gonzalez, 140 games, 1993
Most homers by lefthander
37—Rafael Palmeiro, 160 games, 1993
Most homers by switch-hitter
30—Ruben Sierra, 158 games, 1987
Most homers by rookie
30—Pete Incaviglia, 153 games, 1986
Most homers at home
24—Juan Gonzalez, 1993
Most homers on road
24—Juan Gonzalez, 1992
Most homers, month
12—Juan Gonzalez, August, 1992
Most homers by righthander, career
149—Larry Parrish
Most homers by lefthander, career
114—Pete O'Brien
Most homers by switch-hitter, career
156—Ruben Sierra
Most grand slams
3—Jeff Burroughs, 151 games, 1973
   Larry Parrish, 128 games, 1982
Most grand slams, career
5—Jeff Burroughs
Most total bases
344—Ruben Sierra, 162 games, 1989
Most total bases, career
1,946—Ruben Sierra
Most long hits
80—Juan Gonzalez, 140 games, 1993
Most long hits, career
430—Ruben Sierra
Most extra bases on long hits
173—Juan Gonzalez, 140 games, 1993
Most extra bases on long hits, career
786—Ruben Sierra
Most sacrifice hits
40—Bert Campaneris, 150 games, 1977
Most sacrifice flies
12—Jeff Burroughs, 152 games, 1974
   Ruben Sierra, 158 games, 1987
Most bases on balls
113—Toby Harrah, 126 games, 1985
Most bases on balls, career
668—Toby Harrah
Most strikeouts
185—Pete Incaviglia, 153 games, 1986
Most strikeouts, career
788—Pete Incaviglia
Most hit by pitch
13—Juan Gonzalez, 140 games, 1993

Most runs batted in
119—Ruben Sierra, 162 games, 1989
Most runs batted in, career
673—Ruben Sierra
Most game-winning RBIs
17—Larry Parrish, 145 games, 1983
Most consecutive games with RBI
11—Larry Parrish, 1984 (18 RBIs)
Highest batting average
.341—Julio Franco, 146 games, 1991
Highest batting average, career
.319—Al Oliver
Highest slugging average
.632—Juan Gonzalez, 140 games, 1993
Highest slugging average, career
.470—Ruben Sierra
Longest batting streak
24 games—Mickey Rivers, 1980
Most grounded into double play
27—Julio Franco, 150 games, 1989
Fewest grounded into double play
4—Mickey Rivers, 147 games, 1980

BASERUNNING

Most stolen bases
52—Bump Wills, 157 games, 1978
Most stolen bases, career
161—Bump Wills
Most caught stealing
20—Bert Campaneris, 150 games, 1977
   Bobby Bonds, 130 games, 1978
   Cecil Espy, 142 games, 1989

PITCHING

Most games
85—Mitch Williams, 1987
Most games, career
361—Jeff Russell
Most games started
41—Jim Bibby, 1974
   Ferguson Jenkins, 1974
Most games started, career
313—Charlie Hough
Most complete games
29—Ferguson Jenkins, 1974
Most complete games, career
98—Charlie Hough
Most games finished
66—Jeff Russell, 1989
Most innings
328—Ferguson Jenkins, 1974
Most innings, career
2,307⅔—Charlie Hough
Most games won
25—Ferguson Jenkins, 1974
Most games won, career
139—Charlie Hough
Most games lost
19—Jim Bibby, 1974
Most games lost, career
123—Charlie Hough
Most 20-victory seasons
1—Ferguson Jenkins
   Kevin Brown
Highest winning percentage
.692—Ferguson Jenkins (18-8), 1978
Longest winning streak
12 games—Bobby Witt, 1990
Longest losing streak
9 games—David Clyde, 1974
Most saves
40—Tom Henke, 1993
Most bases on balls
143—Bobby Witt, 1986
Most bases on balls, career
965—Charlie Hough

Most strikeouts
301—Nolan Ryan, 1989
Most strikeouts, career
1,452—Charlie Hough
Most strikeouts, game
16—Nolan Ryan, April 26, 1990
Nolan Ryan, May 1, 1991
Most shutouts
6—Ferguson Jenkins, 1974
Bert Blyleven, 1976
Most shutouts, career
17—Ferguson Jenkins
Most 1-0 shutouts won
4—Ferguson Jenkins, 1974
Bert Blyleven, 1976
Most runs
159—Charlie Hough, 1987

Most earned runs
139—Jim Bibby, 1974
Most hits
286—Ferguson Jenkins, 1974
Most hit batsmen
19—Charlie Hough, 1987
Most wild pitches
22—Bobby Witt, 1986
Most home runs
40—Ferguson Jenkins, 1979
Most sacrifice hits
16—Jim Umbarger, 1976
Most sacrifice flies
14—Charlie Hough, 1987
Lowest ERA
2.17—Mike Paul, 162 innings, 1972

CLUB RECORDS

Most players
52 in 1992
Fewest players
35 in 1984
Most games
163 in 1980, 1983
Most at-bats
5,690 in 1980
Most runs
835 in 1993
Most opponents' runs
849 in 1987
Most hits
1,616 in 1980
Most singles
1,202 in 1980
Most doubles
288 in 1991
Most triples
46 in 1989
Most homers
194 in 1987
Fewest homers
56 in 1972
Most homers at Arlington Stadium, home and opponents
204 in 1987
Most grand slams
5 in 1975, 1980, 1987
Most pinch home runs
7 in 1980
Most long hits
504 in 1993
Most extra bases on long hits
916 in 1987
Most total bases
2,420 in 1991
Most sacrifice hits
116 in 1977
Most sacrifice flies
59 in 1979
Most stolen bases
196 in 1978
Most caught stealing
91 in 1978
Most bases on balls
624 in 1978
Most strikeouts
1,088 in 1986
Most hit by pitch
50 in 1992
Most runs batted in
780 in 1993
Most game-winning RBIs
80 in 1986
Highest batting average
.284 in 1980

Highest slugging average
.431 in 1993
Most grounded into double play
156 in 1980
Most left on bases
1,215 in 1976
Fewest left on bases
1,034 in 1993
Most .300 hitters
3 in 1980, 1989, 1991
Most putouts
4,437 in 1991
Most assists
1,980 in 1975
Fewest assists
1,651 in 1989
Most chances accepted
6,377 in 1975
Most errors
191 in 1975
Fewest errors
113 in 1983
Most errorless games
79 in 1977, 1986, 1993
Most consecutive errorless games
8 in 1993
Most double plays
173 in 1975
Most passed balls
73 in 1987
Fewest passed balls
5 in 1977
Highest fielding average
.982 in 1983
Lowest fielding average
.971 in 1975
Highest home attendance
2,503,198 in 1994
Highest road attendance
2,401,762 in 1993
Most games won
94 in 1977
Most games lost
105 in 1973
Most games won, month
21 in September 1978
Most games lost, month
24 in August 1973
Highest percentage games won
.580 in 1977 (won 94, lost 68)
Lowest percentage games won
.351 in 1972 (won 54, lost 100)
Games won, league
1,717 in 23 years
Games lost, league
1,890 in 23 years

Most shutouts won
17 in 1977
Most shutouts lost
27 in 1972
Most 1-0 games won
5 in 1974, 1975, 1976
Most 1-0 games lost
7 in 1976
Most consecutive games won
14 in 1991
Most consecutive games lost
15 in 1972
Number of times league champions
0
Number of last-place finishes
2
Most runs, game
20 vs. New York, July 19, 1987
Most runs by opponent, game
19 by Minnesota, May 20, 1989
    by Oakland, September 29, 1991
    by Seattle, May 20, 1994
Most runs, inning
12 vs. Oakland, July 3, 1983, fifteenth inning
Most runs, shutout game
14 vs. Oakland, July 26, 1977
Most runs by opponent, shutout game
14 by Chicago, April 18, 1972

by Chicago, September 4, 1973
Most runs, doubleheader shutout
No performance
Longest 1-0 game won
14 innings vs. Boston, April 17, 1983
Longest 1-0 games lost
13 innings vs. Minnesota, September 22, 1992
Most hits, game
22 vs. Cleveland, May 12, 1986
    vs. Baltimore, May 14, 1983, 11 innings
    vs. New York, July 19, 1987
    vs. Seattle, June 13, 1994
    vs. Cleveland, July 20, 1994, 14 innings
Most home runs, game
7 vs. Minnesota, September 13, 1986
Most consecutive games with one or more homers
13 (18 homers), 1987
Most total bases, game
43 vs. Minnesota, September 13, 1986
Largest crowd, day game
46,419 vs. Chicago, May 15, 1994
Largest crowd, doubleheader
42,163 vs. Detroit, July 10, 1982
Largest crowd, night game
46,679 vs. California, July 30, 1994
Largest crowd, home opener
46,056 vs. Milwaukee, April 11, 1994

TORONTO BLUE JAYS

YEARLY FINISHES

EAST DIVISION

Year	Position	W	L	Pct.	*GB	Manager	Attendance
1977	—7th	54	107	.335	45½	Roy Hartsfield	1,701,052
1978	—7th	59	102	.366	40	Roy Hartsfield	1,562,585
1979	—7th	53	109	.327	50½	Roy Hartsfield	1,431,651
1980	—7th	67	95	.414	36	Bobby Mattick	1,400,327
1981	—7th/7th	37	69	.349	†	Bobby Mattick	755,083
1982	—6th (tied)	78	84	.481	17	Bobby Cox	1,275,978
1983	—4th	89	73	.549	9	Bobby Cox	1,930,415
1984	—2nd	89	73	.549	15	Bobby Cox	2,110,009
1985	—1st‡	99	62	.615	+ 2	Bobby Cox	2,468,925
1986	—4th	86	76	.531	9½	Jimy Williams	2,455,477
1987	—2nd	96	66	.593	2	Jimy Williams	2,778,429
1988	—3rd (tied)	87	75	.537	2	Jimy Williams	2,595,175
1989	—1st‡	89	73	.549	+ 2	Jimy Williams, Cito Gaston	3,375,883
1990	—2nd	86	76	.531	2	Cito Gaston	3,885,284
1991	—1st‡	91	71	.562	+ 7	Cito Gaston	4,001,527
1992	—1st§	96	66	.593	+ 4	Cito Gaston	4,028,318
1993	—1st§	95	67	.586	+ 7	Cito Gaston	4,057,947
1994	—3rd	55	60	.478	16	Cito Gaston	2,907,933

*Games behind winner.   †First half 16-42; second 21-27.   ‡Lost Championship Series.   §Won Championship Series.

INDIVIDUAL RECORDS (1977 TO DATE)

SERVICE

Most years by non-pitcher
12—Ernie Whitt
Most years by pitcher
14—Dave Stieb

BATTING

Most games
163—Tony Fernandez, 1986
Most games, career
1,392—Lloyd Moseby
Most at-bats
687—Tony Fernandez, 163 games, 1986
Most at-bats, career
5,124—Lloyd Moseby
Most runs
121—Paul Molitor, 160 games, 1993

Most runs, career
768—Lloyd Moseby
Most hits
213—Tony Fernandez, 163 games, 1986
Most hits, career
1,319—Lloyd Moseby
Most singles
161—Tony Fernandez, 163 games, 1986
Most singles, career
868—Lloyd Moseby
Most doubles
54—John Olerud, 158 games, 1993
Most doubles, career
242—Lloyd Moseby
Most triples
17—Tony Fernandez, 161 games, 1990
Most triples, career
70—Tony Fernandez

Most homers by lefthander
36—Fred McGriff, 161 games, 1989
Most homers by righthander
47—George Bell, 156 games, 1987
Most homers by rookie
20—Fred McGriff, 107 games, 1987
Most homers, month
11—George Bell, May 1987
George Bell, June 1987
Joe Carter, June 1991
Most homers at home
23—Kelly Gruber, 1990
Joe Carter, 1991
Most homers on road
28—George Bell, 1987
Most homers by righthander, career
202—George Bell
Most homers by lefthander, career
149—Lloyd Moseby
Most grand slams
2—Roy Howell, 138 games, 1979
George Bell, 157 games, 1985
George Bell, 156 games, 1987
Jesse Barfield, 136 games, 1988
Most grand slams, career
7—George Bell
Most total bases
369—George Bell, 156 games, 1987
Most total bases, career
2,201—George Bell
Most long hits
83—George Bell, 156 games, 1987
Most long hits, career
471—George Bell
Most extra bases on long hits
181—George Bell, 156 games, 1987
Most extra bases on long hits, career
907—George Bell
Most sacrifice hits
19—Luis Gomez, 153 games, 1978
Most sacrifice flies
14—George Bell, 153 games, 1989
Most bases on balls
119—Fred McGriff, 161 games, 1989
Most bases on balls, career
547—Lloyd Moseby
Most strikeouts
149—Fred McGriff, 154 games, 1988
Most strikeouts, career
1,015—Lloyd Moseby
Fewest strikeouts
21—Bob Bailor, 154 games, 1978
Most hit by pitch
11—Joe Carter, 158 games, 1992
Ed Sprague, 109 games, 1994
Most runs batted in
134—George Bell, 156 games, 1987
Most runs batted in, career
740—George Bell
Most game-winning RBIs
17—George Bell, 156 games, 1988
Highest batting average
.363—John Olerud, 158 games, 1993
Highest batting average, career
.310—Roberto Alomar
Highest slugging average
.605—George Bell, 156 games, 1987
Highest slugging average, career
.530—Fred McGriff
Longest batting streak
26 games—John Olerud, 1993
Most grounded into double play
23—Ed Sprague, 150 games, 1993
Fewest grounded into double play
5—Alfredo Griffin, 162 games, 1983
Willie Upshaw, 155 games, 1986
Roberto Alomar, 161 games, 1991

BASERUNNING

Most stolen bases
60—Dave Collins, 128 games, 1984
Most stolen bases, career
255—Lloyd Moseby
Most caught stealing
23—Alfredo Griffin, 155 games, 1980

PITCHING

Most games
89—Mark Eichhorn, 1987
Most games, career
448—Duane Ward
Most games started
40—Jim Clancy, 1982
Most games started, career
405—Dave Stieb
Most complete games
19—Dave Stieb, 1982
Most complete games, career
103—Dave Stieb
Most games finished
70—Duane Ward, 1993
Most innings
288⅓—Dave Stieb, 1982
Most innings, career
2,823—Dave Stieb
Most games won
21—Jack Morris, 1992
Most games won, career
174—Dave Stieb
Most 20-victory seasons
1—Jack Morris
Most games lost
18—Jerry Garvin, 1977
Phil Huffman, 1979
Most games lost, career
140—Jim Clancy
Longest winning streak
11 games—Dennis Lamp, 1985
Longest losing streak
10 games—Jerry Garvin, 1977, 1978
Paul Mirabella, 1980
Highest winning percentage
.778—Jack Morris (21-6), 1992
Most saves
45—Duane Ward, 1993
Most bases on balls
128—Jim Clancy, 1980
Most bases on balls, career
1,003—Dave Stieb
Most strikeouts
198—Dave Stieb, 1984
Most strikeouts, career
1,631—Dave Stieb
Most strikeouts, game
14—Pat Hentgen, May 3, 1994
Most shutouts
5—Dave Stieb, 1982
Most shutouts, career
30—Dave Stieb
Most 1-0 shutouts won
2—Jim Clancy, 1980
Jimmy Key, 1988
Most runs
143—Dave Lemanczyk, 1977
Most earned runs
125—Jim Clancy, 1984
Most hits
278—Dave Lemanczyk, 1977
Most hit batsmen
15—Dave Stieb, 1986
Most wild pitches
26—Juan Guzman, 1993
Most home runs
33—Jerry Garvin, 1977

Most sacrifice hits
16—Jerry Garvin, 1977
Most sacrifice flies
12—Jim Clancy, 1983

Lowest ERA
2.48—Dave Stieb, 265 innings, 1985

CLUB RECORDS

Most players
45 in 1991
Fewest players
33 in 1983
Most games
163 in 1984, 1986
Most at-bats
5,716 in 1986
Most runs
847 in 1993
Fewest runs
590 in 1978
Most opponent's runs
862 in 1979
Most hits
1,556 in 1993
Fewest hits
1,358 in 1978
Most singles
1,069 in 1984
Most doubles
317 in 1993
Most triples
68 in 1984
Most homers
215 in 1987
Fewest homers
95 in 1979
Most homers at Exhibition Stadium, home and opponents
185 in 1983
Most homers at SkyDome, home and opponents
175 in 1990
Most grand slams
8 in 1989
Most pinch home runs
6 in 1984
Most total bases
2,512 in 1987
Most long hits
530 in 1987
Most extra bases on long hits
998 in 1987
Most sacrifice hits
81 in 1977
Most sacrifice flies
65 in 1991
Most stolen bases
193 in 1984
Most caught stealing
81 in 1982
Most bases on balls
588 in 1993
Most strikeouts
1,043 in 1991
Fewest strikeouts
645 in 1978
Most hit by pitch
58 in 1991
Most runs batted in
796 in 1993
Most game-winning RBIs
90 in 1985, 1987
Highest batting average
.279 in 1993
Lowest batting average
.250 in 1978
Highest slugging average
.446 in 1987

Lowest slugging average
.359 in 1978
Most grounded into double play
156 in 1977
Fewest grounded into double play
91 in 1984
Most left on bases
1,187 in 1993
Fewest left on bases
1,064 in 1979
Most .300 hitters
3 in 1983, 1993
Most putouts
4,428 in 1986
Fewest putouts
4,251 in 1979
Most assists
1,939 in 1980
Fewest assists
1,582 in 1993
Most chances accepted
6,337 in 1980
Fewest chances accepted
5,913 in 1992
Most errors
164 in 1977
Fewest errors
86 in 1990
Most errorless games
103 in 1990
Most consecutive errorless games
11 in 1986
Most double plays
206 in 1980
Fewest double plays
109 in 1992
Most passed balls
21 in 1991
Fewest passed balls
3 in 1985
Highest fielding average
.986 in 1990
Lowest fielding average
.974 in 1977
Highest home attendance
4,057,947 in 1993
Highest road attendance
2,549,898 in 1993
Most games won
99 in 1985
Most games lost
109 in 1979
Most games won, month
20 in September 1988, August 1989
Most games lost, month
23 in May 1979
Highest percentage games won
.615 in 1985 (won 99, lost 62)
Lowest percentage games won
.327 in 1979 (won 53, lost 109)
Games won, league
1,406 in 18 years
Games lost, league
1,404 in 18 years
Most shutouts won
17 in 1988
Most shutouts lost
20 in 1981

Most 1-0 games won
5 in 1980
Most 1-0 games lost
3 in 1979, 1992
Most consecutive games won
11 in 1987
Most consecutive games lost
12 in 1981
Number of times league champions
2
Number of last-place finishes
3
Most runs, game
24 vs. Baltimore, June 26, 1978
Most runs by opponent, game
24 by California, August 25, 1979
Most runs, shutout game
13 vs. Texas, September 18, 1992
Most runs by opponent, shutout game
15 by New York, September 25, 1977, first game
Most runs, inning
11 vs. Seattle, July 20, 1984, ninth inning

Longest 1-0 game won
12 innings vs. Boston, September 26, 1986
Longest 1-0 game lost
15 innings vs. Oakland, July 27, 1986
Most hits, game
24 vs. Baltimore, June 26, 1978
Most home runs, game
10 vs. Baltimore, September 14, 1987
Most consecutive games with one or more home runs
13 (17 homers), 1985
Most total bases, game
53 vs. Baltimore, September 14, 1987
Largest crowd, day game
50,533 vs. Cleveland, April 9, 1993
Largest crowd, doubleheader
48,641 vs. California, July 17, 1989
Largest crowd, night game
50,532 vs. Boston, September 22, 1993
Largest crowd, home opener
50,533 vs. Cleveland, April 9, 1993

WASHINGTON SENATORS (ORIGINAL CLUB)

YEARLY FINISHES

Year	Position	W	L	Pct.	*GB	Manager	Attendance
1901	6th	61	72	.459	20½	Jimmy Manning	161,661
1902	6th	61	75	.449	22	Tom Loftus	188,158
1903	8th	43	94	.314	47½	Tom Loftus	128,878
1904	8th	38	113	.251	55½	Patsy Donovan	131,744
1905	7th	64	87	.421	29½	Jake Stahl	252,027
1906	7th	55	95	.367	37½	Jake Stahl	129,903
1907	8th	49	102	.325	43½	Joe Cantillon	221,929
1908	7th	67	85	.441	22½	Joe Cantillon	264,252
1909	8th	42	110	.276	56	Joe Cantillon	205,199
1910	7th	66	85	.437	36½	Jimmy McAleer	254,591
1911	7th	64	90	.416	38½	Jimmy McAleer	244,884
1912	2nd	91	61	.599	14	Clark Griffith	350,663
1913	2nd	90	64	.584	6½	Clark Griffith	325,831
1914	3rd	81	73	.526	19	Clark Griffith	243,888
1915	4th	85	68	.556	17	Clark Griffith	167,332
1916	7th	76	77	.497	14½	Clark Griffith	177,265
1917	5th	74	79	.484	25½	Clark Griffith	89,682
1918	3rd	72	56	.563	4	Clark Griffith	182,122
1919	7th	56	84	.400	32	Clark Griffith	234,096
1920	6th	68	84	.447	29	Clark Griffith	359,260
1921	4th	80	73	.523	18	George McBride	456,069
1922	6th	69	85	.448	25	Clyde Milan	458,552
1923	4th	75	78	.490	23½	Donie Bush	357,406
1924	1st	92	62	.597	+ 2	Bucky Harris	534,310
1925	1st	96	55	.636	+ 8½	Bucky Harris	817,199
1926	4th	81	69	.540	8	Bucky Harris	551,580
1927	3rd	85	69	.552	25	Bucky Harris	528,976
1928	4th	75	79	.487	26	Bucky Harris	378,501
1929	5th	71	81	.467	34	Walter Johnson	355,506
1930	2nd	94	60	.610	8	Walter Johnson	614,474
1931	3rd	92	62	.597	16	Walter Johnson	492,657
1932	3rd	93	61	.604	14	Walter Johnson	371,396
1933	1st	99	53	.651	+ 7	Joe Cronin	437,533
1934	7th	66	86	.434	34	Joe Cronin	330,074
1935	6th	67	86	.438	27	Bucky Harris	255,011
1936	4th	82	71	.536	20	Bucky Harris	379,525
1937	6th	73	80	.477	28½	Bucky Harris	397,799
1938	5th	75	76	.497	23½	Bucky Harris	522,694
1939	6th	65	87	.428	41½	Bucky Harris	339,257
1940	7th	64	90	.416	26	Bucky Harris	381,241
1941	6th (tied)	70	84	.455	31	Bucky Harris	415,663
1942	7th	62	89	.411	39½	Bucky Harris	403,493
1943	2nd	84	69	.549	13½	Ossie Bluege	574,694
1944	8th	64	90	.416	25	Ossie Bluege	525,235
1945	2nd	87	67	.565	1½	Ossie Bluege	652,660
1946	4th	76	78	.494	28	Ossie Bluege	1,027,216
1947	7th	64	90	.416	33	Ossie Bluege	850,758
1948	7th	56	97	.366	40	Joe Kuhel	795,254

Year	Position	W	L	Pct.	*GB	Manager	Attendance
1949	—8th	50	104	.325	47	Joe Kuhel	770,745
1950	—5th	67	87	.435	31	Bucky Harris	699,697
1951	—7th	62	92	.403	36	Bucky Harris	695,167
1952	—5th	78	76	.506	17	Bucky Harris	699,457
1953	—5th	76	76	.500	23½	Bucky Harris	595,594
1954	—6th	66	88	.429	45	Bucky Harris	503,542
1955	—8th	53	101	.344	43	Chuck Dressen	425,238
1956	—7th	59	95	.383	38	Chuck Dressen	431,647
1957	—8th	55	99	.357	43	Chuck Dressen, Cookie Lavagetto	457,079
1958	—8th	61	93	.396	31	Cookie Lavagetto	475,288
1959	—8th	63	91	.409	31	Cookie Lavagetto	615,372
1960	—5th	73	81	.474	24	Cookie Lavagetto	743,404

*Games behind winner.

INDIVIDUAL RECORDS (1901 TO 1960)

SERVICE

Most years, non-pitcher
19—Sam Rice
Most years played by pitcher
21—Walter Johnson

BATTING

Most games
158—Eddie Foster, 1916
Most games, career
2,307—Sam Rice
Most at-bats
668—Buddy Lewis, 156 games, 1937
Most at-bats, career
8,934—Sam Rice
Most runs
127—Joe Cronin, 154 games, 1930
Most runs, career
1,467—Sam Rice
Most hits
227—Sam Rice, 152 games, 1925
Most hits, career
2,889—Sam Rice
Most singles
182—Sam Rice, 152 games, 1925
Most doubles
51—Mickey Vernon, 148 games, 1946
Most doubles, career
478—Sam Rice
Most triples
20—Goose Goslin, 150 games, 1925
Most triples, career
183—Sam Rice
Most homers by righthander
42—Roy Sievers, 152 games, 1957
Harmon Killebrew, 153 games, 1959
Most homers by lefthander
20—Mickey Vernon, 151 games, 1954
Most homers by rookie
30—Bob Allison, 150 games, 1959
Most homers at home
26—Roy Sievers, 1957
Most homers on road
21—Roy Sievers, 1958
Most homers, month
15—Harmon Killebrew, May, 1959
Most homers, career
180—Roy Sievers
Most grand slams
2—held by many players—last player, Roy Sievers, 152 games, 1957
Most grand slams, career
4—Roy Sievers
Most total bases
331—Roy Sievers, 152 games, 1957
Most total bases, career
3,832—Sam Rice
Most long hits
76—Stan Spence, 152 games, 1946

Most extra bases on long hits
159—Roy Sievers, 152 games, 1957
Most sacrifice (sacrifice hits and sacrifice flies)
52—Bob Ganley, 150 games, 1908
Most sacrifice hits
36—Hunter Hill, 103 games, 1905
Most sacrifice flies
16—Chick Gandil, 145 games, 1914
Most bases on balls
151—Eddie Yost, 152 games, 1956
Most strikeouts
138—Jim Lemon, 146 games, 1956
Fewest strikeouts
9—Sam Rice, 150 games, 1929
Most hit by pitch
24—Kid Elberfeld, 127 games, 1911
Most runs batted in
129—Goose Goslin, 154 games, 1924
Most runs batted in, career
1,044—Sam Rice
Highest batting average
.379—Goose Goslin, 135 games, 1923
Highest batting average, career
.323—Sam Rice, Goose Goslin
Highest slugging average
.614—Goose Goslin, 135 games, 1928
Longest batting streak
33 games—Heinie Manush, 1933
Most grounded into double play
25—Sam Dente, 155 games, 1950
Fewest grounded into double play
5—George Case, 154 games, 1940
George Case, 153 games, 1941
Stan Spence, 153 games, 1944
Eddie Yost, 155 games, 1954

BASERUNNING

Most stolen bases
88—Clyde Milan, 154 games, 1912
Most stolen bases, career
494—Clyde Milan
Most caught stealing
30—Sam Rice, 153 games, 1920

PITCHING

Most games
64—Firpo Marberry, 1926
Most games, career
802—Walter Johnson
Most games started
42—Walter Johnson, 1910
Most games started, career
666—Walter Johnson
Most complete games
38—Walter Johnson, 1910
Most complete games, career
531—Walter Johnson
Most games finished
47—Firpo Marberry, 1926

Most innings
374—Walter Johnson, 1910
Most innings, career
5,923—Walter Johnson
Most games won
36—Walter Johnson, 1913
Most games won, career
416—Walter Johnson
Most 20-victory seasons
12—Walter Johnson
Highest winning percentage
.837—Walter Johnson (36-7), 1913
Longest winning streak
16 games—Walter Johnson, 1912
Longest losing streak
15 games—Bob Groom, 1909
Most games lost
26—Jack Townsend, 1904
Bob Groom, 1909
Most games lost, career
279—Walter Johnson
Most bases on balls
146—Bobo Newsom, 1936
Most bases on balls, career
1,353—Walter Johnson
Most strikeouts
313—Walter Johnson, 1910

Most strikeouts, career
3,508—Walter Johnson
Most strikeouts, game
15—Camilo Pascual, April 18, 1960
Most shutouts
12—Walter Johnson, 1913
Most 1-0 shutouts won
5—Walter Johnson, 1913 and 1919
Most shutouts, career
113—Walter Johnson
Most runs
172—Al Orth, 1903
Most earned runs
144—Jimmie DeShong, 1937
Most hits
328—Dutch Leonard, 1940
Most hit batsmen
20—Walter Johnson, 1923
Most wild pitches
21—Walter Johnson, 1910
Most home runs
43—Pedro Ramos, 1957
Lowest ERA
1.14—Walter Johnson, 346 innings, 1913

CLUB RECORDS

Most players
44 in 1909
Fewest players
25 in 1908, 1917
Most games
159 in 1916
Most at-bats
5,592 in 1935
Most runs
892 in 1930
Fewest runs
380 in 1909
Most hits
1,620 in 1930
Fewest hits
1,112 in 1909
Most singles
1,209 in 1935
Most doubles
308 in 1931
Most triples
100 in 1932
Most homers
163 in 1959
Fewest homers (154 or 162-game schedule)
4 in 1917
Most homers at Griffith Stadium, home and opponents
158 in 1956
Most grand slams
8 in 1938
Most pinch home runs
4 in 1955, 1960
Most total bases
2,287 in 1930
Most long hits
464 in 1932
Most extra bases on long hits
732 in 1960
Most sacrifices (sacrifice hits and sacrifice flies)
232 in 1923, 1924
Most sacrifice hits
135 in 1906
Most sacrifice flies
42 in 1954
Most stolen bases
291 in 1913

Most bases on balls
690 in 1956
Most strikeouts
883 in 1960
Fewest strikeouts
359 in 1927
Most hit by pitch
80 in 1911
Fewest hit by pitch
8 in 1947
Most runs batted in
822 in 1936
Highest batting average
.303 in 1925
Lowest batting average
.223 in 1909
Highest slugging average
.426 in 1930
Lowest slugging average
.287 in 1910
Most grounded into double play
145 in 1951
Fewest grounded into double play
94 in 1943
Most left on bases
1,305 in 1935
Fewest left on bases
998 in 1959
Most .300 hitters
9 in 1925
Most putouts
4,291 in 1916
Fewest putouts
3,944 in 1906
Most assists
2,232 in 1911
Fewest assists
1,587 in 1951
Most chances accepted
6,363 in 1910
Fewest chances accepted
5,672 in 1953
Most errors
325 in 1901
Fewest errors
118 in 1958

Most consecutive errorless games
9 in 1952
Most double plays
186 in 1935
Fewest double plays
93 in 1912
Most passed balls
40 in 1945
Fewest passed balls
3 in 1927
Highest fielding average
.980 in 1958
Lowest fielding average
.936 in 1902
Highest home attendance
1,027,216 in 1946
Highest road attendance
1,055,171 in 1948
Most games won
99 in 1933
Most games lost
113 in 1904
Most games won, month
24—August 1945
Most games lost, month
29—July 1909
Highest percentage games won
.651 in 1933 (won 99, lost 53)
Lowest percentage games won
.252 in 1904 (won 38, lost 113)
Games won, league
4,223 in 60 years
Games lost, league
4,864 in 60 years
Most shutouts won
25 in 1914
Most shutouts lost
29 in 1909
Most 1-0 games won
11 in 1914
Most 1-0 games lost
7 in 1915
Most consecutive games won
17 in 1912
Most consecutive games lost
18 in 1948, 1959

Number of times league champions
3
Number of last-place finishes
10
Most runs, game
21 vs. Detroit, August 5, 1929
Most runs by opponent, game
24 by Boston, September 27, 1940
Most runs, shutout game
14 vs. Boston, September 11, 1905, second game, seven innings
vs. Chicago, September 3, 1942, second game
Most runs by opponent, shutout game
17 by New York, April 24, 1909
by New York, July 6, 1920
by Chicago, September 19, 1925, second game
Most runs, doubleheader shutout
13 vs. Cleveland, August 20, 1945
Most runs, inning
12 vs. St. Louis, July 10, 1926, eighth inning
Longest 1-0 game won
18 innings vs. Chicago, May 15, 1918
vs. Chicago, June 8, 1947, first game
Longest 1-0 game lost
13 innings vs. Boston, August 15, 1916
vs. Chicago, July 29, 1918
Most hits, game
24 vs. Detroit, July 9, 1903
vs. Cleveland, July 18, 1925
Most home runs, nine-inning game
5 vs. Washington vs. Detroit, May 2, 1959
Most home runs, extra-inning game
7 vs. Chicago, May 3, 1949, 10 innings
Most consecutive games with one or more homers
8 (14 homers), 1959
Most total bases, game
41 vs. Detroit, July 9, 1904
Largest crowd, day game
31,728 vs. New York, April 19, 1948
Largest crowd, doubleheader
35,563 vs. New York, July 4, 1936
Largest crowd, night game
30,701 vs. Cleveland, June 17, 1947
Largest crowd, home opener
31,728 vs. New York, April 19, 1948

WASHINGTON SENATORS (SECOND CLUB)

YEARLY FINISHES

Year	Position	W	L	Pct.	*GB	Manager	Attendance
1961	9th (tied)	61	100	.379	47½	Mickey Vernon	597,287
1962	10th	60	101	.373	35½	Mickey Vernon	729,775
1963	10th	56	106	.346	48½	Mickey Vernon, Gil Hodges	535,604
1964	9th	62	100	.383	37	Gil Hodges	600,106
1965	8th	70	92	.432	32	Gil Hodges	560,083
1966	8th	71	88	.447	25½	Gil Hodges	576,260
1967	6th (tied)	76	85	.472	15½	Gil Hodges	770,863
1968	10th	65	96	.404	37½	Jim Lemon	546,661

EAST DIVISION

Year	Position	W	L	Pct.	*GB	Manager	Attendance
1969	4th	86	76	.531	23	Ted Williams	918,106
1970	6th	70	92	.432	38	Ted Williams	824,789
1971	5th	63	96	.396	38½	Ted Williams	655,156

*Games behind winner.

INDIVIDUAL RECORDS (1961 TO 1971)

SERVICE

Most years played by non-pitcher
10—Eddie Brinkman
Most years played by pitcher
9—Jim Hannan

BATTING

Most games
161—Frank Howard, 1969, 1970
Most games, career
1,142—Eddie Brinkman

Most at-bats
635—Del Unser, 156 games, 1968
Most at-bats, career
3,845—Eddie Brinkman
Most runs
111—Frank Howard, 161 games, 1969
Most runs, career
516—Frank Howard
Most hits
175—Frank Howard, 161 games, 1969
Most hits, career
1,071—Frank Howard
Most singles
144—Eddie Brinkman, 158 games, 1970
Most singles, career
685—Eddie Brinkman
Most doubles
31—Aurelio Rodriguez, 142 games, 1970
Most triples
12—Chuck Hinton, 150 games, 1963
Most homers by righthander
48—Frank Howard, 161 games, 1969
Most homers by lefthander
30—Mike Epstein, 131 games, 1969
Most homers by rookie
12—Don Lock, 71 games, 1962
Most homers at home
27—Frank Howard, 1969
Most homers on road
26—Frank Howard, 1968
Most homers, month
15—Frank Howard, May 1968
Most homers, career
237—Frank Howard
Most grand slams
2—Don Zimmer, 121 games, 1964
Most grand slams, career
3—Mike Epstein
Most total bases
340—Frank Howard, 161 games, 1969
Most total bases, career
1,968—Frank Howard
Most long hits
75—Frank Howard, 158 games, 1968
Most long hits, career
403—Frank Howard
Most extra bases on long hits
166—Frank Howard, 158 games, 1968
Most extra bases on long hits, career
897—Frank Howard
Most sacrifice hits
15—Danny O'Connell, 138 games, 1961
Most sacrifice flies
8—Ken McMullen, 158 games, 1959
Most bases on balls
132—Frank Howard, 161 games, 1970
Most strikeouts
155—Frank Howard, 149 games, 1967
Fewest strikeouts
41—Eddie Brinkman, 158 games, 1970
Most hit by pitch
13—Mike Epstein, 123 games, 1968
Most runs batted in
126—Frank Howard, 161 games, 1970
Most runs batted in, career
670—Frank Howard
Highest batting average
.310 Chuck Hinton—151 games, 1962
Highest slugging average
.574—Frank Howard, 161 games, 1969
Longest batting streak
19 games—Ken McMullen, 1967
Most grounding into double play
29—Frank Howard, 161 games, 1969
Frank Howard, 153 games, 1971
Fewest grounding into double play
4—Del Unser, 153 games, 1971

BASERUNNING

Most stolen bases
29—Ed Stroud, 129 games, 1970
Most caught stealing
10—Willie Tasby, 141 games, 1961
Chuck Hinton, 150 games, 1962
Fred Valentine, 146 games, 1966
Del Unser, 153 games, 1969

PITCHING

Most games
74—Ron Kline, 1965
Most games started
36—Claude Osteen, 1964
Joe H. Coleman, 1969
Most complete games
13—Claude Osteen, 1964
Most games finished
58—Ron Kline, 1965
Most innings
257—Claude Osteen, 1964
Most games won
16—Dick Bosman, 1970
Most games won, career
49—Dick Bosman
Most games lost
22—Denny McLain, 1971
Most games lost, career
60—Bennie Daniels
Highest winning percentage
.737—Dick Bosman (14-5), 1969
Longest winning streak
8 games—Dick Bosman, 1969
Longest losing streak
10 games—Bennie Daniels, 1962
Most saves
27—Darold Knowles, 1970
Most bases on balls
100—Joe H. Coleman, 1969
Most strikeouts
195—Pete Richert, 1966
Most strikeouts, nine-inning game
13—Jim Duckworth, September 25, second game, 1965
Most strikeouts, extra-inning game
21—Tom Cheney, September 12, 1962, 16 innings
Most shutouts
4—Tom Cheney, 1963
Frank Bertaina, 1967
Camilo Pascual, 1968
Joe H. Coleman, 1969
Most shutouts, career
7—Tom Cheney
Most 1-0 games won
2—Dick Donovan, 1961
Dave Stenhouse, 1962
Most runs
115—Denny McLain, 1971
Most earned runs
103—Denny McLain, 1971
Most hits
256—Claude Osteen, 1964
Most hit batsmen
12—Joe H. Coleman, 1968
Most wild pitches
17—Frank Bertaina, 1968
Most home runs
36—Pete Richert, 1966
Most sacrifice hits
20—Buster Narum, 1965
Most sacrifice flies
12—Held by four pitchers
Lowest ERA
2.19—Dick Bosman, 193 innings, 1969

Most players
43 in 1963
Fewest players
36 in 1969
Most games
162 in 1962, 1963, 1964, 1966, 1969, 1970
Fewest games
159 in 1966, 1971
Most at-bats
5,484 in 1962
Most runs
694 in 1969
Fewest runs
524 in 1968
Most opponents' runs
812 in 1963
Most hits
1,370 in 1962
Most singles
1,006 in 1969
Most doubles
217 in 1961
Most triples
44 in 1961
Most homers
148 in 1969
Fewest homers
86 in 1971
Most homers at Griffith Stadium, home and opponents
87 in 1961
Most homers at Robert F. Kennedy Memorial Stadium, home and opponents
166 in 1964
Most grand slams
4 in 1961, 1963, 1967
Most pinch home runs
8 in 1965, 1966
Most total bases
2,060 in 1969
Most long hits
380 in 1961
Most extra bases on long hits
695 in 1969
Most sacrifice hits
84 in 1966
Most sacrifice flies
44 in 1961
Most stolen bases
99 in 1962
Most caught stealing
53 in 1962
Most bases on balls
635 in 1970
Most strikeouts
1,125 in 1965
Fewest strikeouts
789 in 1962
Most hit by pitch
46 in 1970
Fewest hit by pitch
15 in 1962
Most runs batted in
640 in 1969
Highest batting average
.251 in 1969
Lowest batting average
.223 in 1967
Highest slugging average
.378 in 1969
Lowest slugging average
.326 in 1967, 1971
Most grounding into double plays
158 in 1969

Fewest grounding into double plays
111 in 1963
Most left on bases
1,196 in 1970
Fewest left on bases
1,054 in 1966
Most .300 hitters
1 in 1961, 1962
Most putouts
4,420 in 1967
Fewest putouts
4,256 in 1971
Most assists
1,946 in 1970
Fewest assists
1,647 in 1965
Most chances accepted
6,319 in 1970
Fewest chances accepted
5,954 in 1965
Most errors
182 in 1963
Fewest errors
116 in 1970
Most errorless games
83 in 1964
Most consecutive errorless games
6 in 1970
Most double plays
173 in 1970
Fewest double plays
139 in 1966
Most passed balls
23 in 1961, 1971
Fewest passed balls
12 in 1970
Highest fielding average
.982 in 1970
Lowest fielding average
.971 in 1963
Highest home attendance
918,106 in 1969
Highest road attendance
1,042,638 in 1968
Most games won
86 in 1969
Most games lost
106 in 1963
Most games won, month
19—July 1967
Most games lost, month
24—August 1961
Games won in franchise history
740 in 11 years
Games lost in franchise history
1,032 in 11 years
Highest percentage games won
.531 in 1969 (won 86, lost 76)
Lowest percentage games won
.346 in 1963 (won 56, lost 106)
Most shutouts won
14 in 1967
Most shutouts lost
22 in 1964
Most 1-0 games won
4 in 1962, 1967, 1968
Most 1-0 games lost
5 in 1963, 1971
Most consecutive games won
8 in 1967
Most consecutive games lost
14 in 1961, 1970
Number of times league champions
0

Number of last-place finishes
4 (tied in 1961)
Most runs, game
15 vs. Detroit, May 18, 1965
    vs. Cleveland, July 5, 1971
Most runs by opponent, game
18 by Baltimore, April 22, 1965
Most runs, shutout game
13 vs. Los Angeles, June 2, first game, 1965
Most runs by opponent, shutout game
17 by Los Angeles, August 23, 1963
Most runs, doubleheader shutout
No performance
Most runs, inning
11 vs. Baltimore, May 11, 1962, sixth inning
Longest 1-0 game won
10 innings vs. Chicago, June 9, first game, 1961
        vs. Chicago, September 19, 1964
Longest 1-0 game lost
10 innings by Washington, September 9, 1966

Most hits, game
20 vs. Boston, July 27, second game, 1962
Most home runs, game
5 vs. Detroit, May 20, 1965
    vs. Chicago, May 16, 1969
    vs. Chicago, June 13, 1970
Most consecutive games with one or more homers
10 (16 homers), 1970
Most total bases, game
32 vs. Boston, July 27, second game, 1962
    vs. Chicago, June 13, 1970
Largest crowd, day game
45,125 vs. New York, April 7, 1969
Largest crowd, doubleheader
40,359 vs. Minnesota, June 14, 1964
Largest crowd, night game
30,421 vs. New York, July 31, 1962
Largest crowd, home opener
45,125 vs. New York, April 7, 1969

NATIONAL LEAGUE TEAM RECORDS

ATLANTA BRAVES

YEARLY FINISHES

Year	Position	W	L	Pct.	*GB	Manager	Attendance
1966 —5th		85	77	.525	10	Bobby Bragan, Billy Hitchcock	1,539,801
1967 —7th		77	85	.475	24½	Billy Hitchcock, Ken Silvestri	1,389,222
1968 —5th		81	81	.500	16	Lum Harris	1,126,540

WEST DIVISION

Year	Position	W	L	Pct.	*GB	Manager	Attendance
1969 —1st†		93	69	.574	+ 3	Lum Harris	1,458,320
1970 —5th		76	86	.469	26	Lum Harris	1,078,848
1971 —3rd		82	80	.506	8	Lum Harris	1,006,320
1972 —4th		70	84	.455	25	Lum Harris, Eddie Mathews	752,973
1973 —5th		76	85	.472	22½	Eddie Mathews	800,655
1974 —3rd		88	74	.543	14	Eddie Mathews, Clyde King	981,085
1975 —5th		67	94	.416	40½	Clyde King, Connie Ryan	534,672
1976 —6th		70	92	.432	32	Dave Bristol	818,179
1977 —6th		61	101	.377	37	Dave Bristol, Ted Turner	872,464
1978 —6th		69	93	.426	26	Bobby Cox	904,494
1979 —6th		66	94	.413	23½	Bobby Cox	769,465
1980 —4th		81	80	.503	11	Bobby Cox	1,048,411
1981 —4th/5th		50	56	.472	‡	Bobby Cox	535,418
1982 —1st†		89	73	.549	+ 1	Joe Torre	1,801,985
1983 —2nd		88	74	.543	3	Joe Torre	2,119,935
1984 —2nd (tied)		80	82	.494	12	Joe Torre	1,724,892
1985 —5th		66	96	.407	29	Eddie Haas, Bobby Wine	1,350,137
1986 —6th		72	89	.447	23½	Chuck Tanner	1,387,181
1987 —5th		69	92	.429	20½	Chuck Tanner	1,217,402
1988 —6th		54	106	.338	39½	Chuck Tanner, Russ Nixon	848,089
1989 —6th		63	97	.394	28	Russ Nixon	984,930
1990 —6th		65	97	.401	26	Russ Nixon, Bobby Cox	980,129
1991 —1st§		94	68	.580	+ 1	Bobby Cox	2,140,217
1992 —1st§		98	64	.605	+ 8	Bobby Cox	3,077,400
1993 —1st†		104	58	.642	+ 1	Bobby Cox	3,884,725
1994 —2nd		68	46	.596	6	Bobby Cox	2,539,240

*Games behind winner.   †Lost Championship Series.   ‡First half 25-29; second 25-27.   §Won Championship Series.

INDIVIDUAL RECORDS (1966 TO DATE)

SERVICE

Most years by non-pitcher
15—Dale Murphy
Most years by pitcher
19—Phil Niekro

BATTING

Most games
162—Felix Millan, 1969
Dale Murphy, 1982, 1983, 1984, 1985
Most games, career
1,926—Dale Murphy
Most at-bats
668—Ralph Garr, 148 games, 1973
Most at-bats, career
7,098—Dale Murphy
Most runs
131—Dale Murphy, 162 games, 1983
Most runs, career
1,103—Dale Murphy
Most hits
219—Ralph Garr, 154 games, 1971
Most hits, career
1,901—Dale Murphy
Most singles
180—Ralph Garr, 154 games, 1971

Most singles, career
1,187—Dale Murphy
Most doubles
39—Terry Pendleton, 160 games, 1992
Most doubles, career
306—Dale Murphy
Most triples
17—Ralph Garr, 143 games, 1974
Most triples, career
40—Ralph Garr
Most homers by righthander
47—Hank Aaron, 139 games, 1971
Most homers by lefthander
41—Darrell Evans, 161 games, 1973
Most homers by rookie
33—Earl Williams, 145 games, 1971
Most homers at home
31—Hank Aaron, 1971
Most homers on road
23—Hank Aaron, 1966, 1969
Most homers, month
14—Bob Horner, July 1980
Most homers by righthander, career
371—Dale Murphy
Most homers by lefthander, career
131—Darrell Evans
Most grand slams
2—held by many players

Most grand slams, career
7—Hank Aaron
Most total bases
355—Felipe Alou, 154 games, 1966
Most total bases, career
3,394—Dale Murphy
Most long hits
79—Hank Aaron, 155 games, 1967
Most long hits, career
714—Dale Murphy
Most extra bases on long hits
169—Hank Aaron, 139 games, 1971
Most extra bases on long hits, career
1,493—Dale Murphy
Most sacrifice hits
20—Rod Gilbreath, 116 games, 1976
    Glenn Hubbard, 145 games, 1982
Most sacrifice flies
10—Bob Horner, 141 games, 1986
    Gerald Perry, 141 games, 1988
Most bases on balls
127—Jimmy Wynn, 148 games, 1976
Most bases on balls, career
912—Dale Murphy
Most strikeouts
145—Dale Murphy, 151 games, 1978
Most strikeouts, career
1,581—Dale Murphy
Fewest strikeouts
35—Felix Millan, 162 games, 1969
Most hit by pitch
16—Jeff Blauser, 161 games, 1993
Most runs batted in
122—Hank Aaron, 158 games, 1966
Most runs batted in, career
1,143—Dale Murphy
Most game-winning RBIs
14—Dale Murphy, 162 games, 1982, 1983, 1985
    Claudell Washington, 150 games, 1982
Highest batting average
.366—Rico Carty, 136 games, 1970
Highest batting average, career
.317—Ralph Garr
Highest slugging average
.669—Hank Aaron, 139 games, 1971
Longest batting streak
31 games—Rico Carty, 1970
Most grounded into double play
24—Dale Murphy, 156 games, 1988
Fewest grounded into double play
5—Brett Butler, 151 games, 1983

BASERUNNING

Most stolen bases
72—Otis Nixon, 124 games, 1991
Most stolen bases, career
174—Jerry Royster
Most caught stealing
23—Brett Butler, 151 games, 1983

PITCHING

Most games
77—Rick Camp, 1980
Most games, career
689—Phil Niekro
Most games started
44—Phil Niekro, 1979

Most games started, career
594—Phil Niekro
Most complete games
23—Phil Niekro, 1979
Most complete games, career
226—Phil Niekro
Most games finished
56—Gene Garber, 1982
Most innings
342—Phil Niekro, 1979
Most innings, career
4,532—Phil Niekro
Most games won
23—Phil Niekro, 1969
Most games won, career
266—Phil Niekro
Most 20-victory seasons
3—Phil Niekro
Most games lost
20—Phil Niekro, 1977, 1979
Most games lost, career
227—Phil Niekro
Highest winning percentage
.810—Phil Niekro (17-4), 1982
Longest winning streak
13 games—Tom Glavine, 1992
Longest losing streak
9 games—Tommy Boggs, 1981
            Marty Clary, 1990
Longest losing streak over two seasons
11 games—Jim Acker, 1986 (6), 1987 (5)
Most saves
30—Gene Garber, 1982
Most bases on balls
164—Phil Niekro, 1977
Most bases on balls, career
1,425—Phil Niekro
Most strikeouts
262—Phil Niekro, 1977
Most strikeouts, career
2,855—Phil Niekro
Most strikeouts, game
15—John Smoltz, May 24, 1992
Most shutouts won
6—Phil Niekro, 1974
Most shutouts, career
43—Phil Niekro
Most 1-0 shutouts won
2—Phil Niekro, 1969
Most runs
166—Phil Niekro, 1977
Most earned runs
148—Phil Niekro, 1977
Most hits
315—Phil Niekro, 1977
Most hit batsmen
13—Phil Niekro, 1978
Most wild pitches
27—Tony Cloninger, 1966
Most home runs
41—Phil Niekro, 1979
Most sacrifice hits
21—Tom Glavine, 1990
Most sacrifice flies
12—Tony Cloninger, 1966
    Carl Morton, 1974
Lowest ERA
1.87—Phil Niekro, 207 innings, 1967

CLUB RECORDS

Most players
46 in 1989, 1990
Fewest players
32 in 1980

Most games
163 in 1966, 1968, 1974
Most at-bats
5,631 in 1973

Most runs
799 in 1973
Fewest runs
514 in 1968
Most opponents' runs
895 in 1977
Most hits
1,497 in 1973
Fewest hits
1,281 in 1989
Most singles
1,109 in 1968
Most doubles
284 in 1987
Most triples
48 in 1992
Most homers
207 in 1966
Fewest homers
80 in 1968
Most homers at Atlanta Stadium, home and opponents
211 in 1970
Most grand slams
7 in 1977
Most pinch home runs
9 in 1992
Most total bases
2,402 in 1973
Most long hits
460 in 1987
Most extra bases on long hits
905 in 1966, 1973
Most sacrifice hits
109 in 1974
Most sacrifice flies
50 in 1992, 1993
Most stolen bases
165 in 1991
Most caught stealing
88 in 1983
Most bases on balls
641 in 1987
Most strikeouts
1,010 in 1990
Fewest strikeouts
665 in 1969
Most hit by pitch
40 in 1966
Fewest hit by pitch
17 in 1977, 1983
Most runs batted in
758 in 1973
Most game-winning RBIs
82 in 1982, 1983
Highest batting average
.272 in 1983
Lowest batting average
.234 in 1989
Highest slugging average
.427 in 1973
Lowest slugging average
.334 in 1976
Most grounded into double play
154 in 1985
Fewest grounded into double play
82 in 1992
Most left on bases
1,213 in 1974
Fewest left on bases
1,038 in 1988
Most .300 hitters
3 in 1966, 1970
Most putouts
4,424 in 1971
Fewest putouts
4,223 in 1979

Most assists
2,028 in 1985
Fewest assists
1,633 in 1972
Most chances accepted
6,400 in 1985
Fewest chances accepted
5,764 in 1972
Most errors
183 in 1979
Fewest errors
108 in 1993
Most errorless games
86 in 1992
Most consecutive errorless games
8 in 1992
Most double plays
197 in 1985
Fewest double plays
114 in 1969
Most passed balls
42 in 1967
Fewest passed balls
6 in 1983
Highest fielding average
.983 in 1993
Lowest fielding average
.970 in 1979
Highest home attendance
3,884,725 in 1993
Highest road attendance
2,944,157 in 1993
Most games won
104 in 1993
Most games lost
106 in 1988
Most games won, month
20 in September 1966
Most games lost, month
21 in May 1976
Games won, league
2,202 in 29 years
Games lost, league
2,373 in 29 years
Highest percentage games won
.642 in 1993 (won 104, lost 58)
Lowest percentage games won
.338 in 1988 (won 54, lost 106)
Most shutouts won
24 in 1992
Most shutouts lost
24 in 1978
Most 1-0 shutouts won
7 in 1974
Most 1-0 shutouts lost
4 in 1988, 1989
Most consecutive games won
13 in 1982, 1992
Most consecutive games lost
17 in 1977
Number of times league champions
2
Number of last-place finishes
5
Most runs, game
19 vs. Chicago, April 15, 1994
Most runs by opponent, game
23 by Cincinnati, April 25, 1977
by San Francisco, June 8, 1990
Most runs, shutout game
15 vs. Pittsburgh, August 14, 1992
Most runs by opponent, shutout game
19 by Montreal, July 30, 1978
Most runs, doubleheader shutout
No performance
Most hits, game
25 vs. Cincinnati, May 1, 1985

Most runs, inning
13 vs. Houston, September 20, 1972, second inning
Longest 1-0 game won
12 innings vs. Los Angeles, September 17, 1976, first game
Longest 1-0 game lost
13 innings vs. Los Angeles, May 18, 1974
vs. St. Louis, May 20, 1989
Most home runs, game
7 vs. Chicago, August 3, 1967
Most consecutive games with one or more homers
20 (36 homers), 1973

Most total bases, game
46 vs. Chicago, April 15, 1994
Largest crowd, day game
51,275 vs. Los Angeles, June 26, 1966
Largest crowd, doubleheader
50,597 vs. Chicago, July 4, 1972
Largest crowd, night game
53,775 vs. Los Angeles, April 8, 1974
Largest crowd, home opener
53,775 vs. Los Angeles, April 8, 1974

BOSTON BRAVES

YEARLY FINISHES

Year	Position	W	L	Pct.	*GB	Manager	Attendance
1901	—5th	69	69	.500	20 ½	Frank Selee	146,502
1902	—3rd	73	64	.533	29	Al Buckenberger	116,960
1903	—6th	58	80	.420	32	Al Buckenberger	143,155
1904	—7th	55	98	.359	51	Al Buckenberger	140,694
1905	—7th	51	103	.331	54 ½	Fred Tenney	150,003
1906	—8th	49	102	.325	66 ½	Fred Tenney	143,280
1907	—7th	58	90	.392	47	Fred Tenney	203,221
1908	—6th	63	91	.409	36	Joe Kelley	253,750
1909	—8th	45	108	.294	65 ½	Frank Bowerman, Harry Smith	195,188
1910	—8th	53	100	.346	50 ½	Fred Lake	149,027
1911	—8th	44	107	.291	54	Fred Tenney	116,000
1912	—8th	52	101	.340	52	Johnny Kling	121,000
1913	—5th	69	82	.457	31 ½	George Stallings	208,000
1914	—1st	94	59	.614	+10 ½	George Stallings	382,913
1915	—2nd	83	69	.546	7	George Stallings	376,283
1916	—3rd	89	63	.586	4	George Stallings	313,495
1917	—6th	72	81	.471	25 ½	George Stallings	174,253
1918	—7th	53	71	.427	28 ½	George Stallings	84,938
1919	—6th	57	82	.410	38 ½	George Stallings	167,401
1920	—7th	62	90	.408	30	George Stallings	162,483
1921	—4th	79	74	.516	15	Fred Mitchell	318,627
1922	—8th	53	100	.346	39 ½	Fred Mitchell	167,965
1923	—7th	54	100	.351	41 ½	Fred Mitchell	227,802
1924	—8th	53	100	.346	40	Dave Bancroft	117,478
1925	—5th	70	83	.458	25	Dave Bancroft	313,528
1926	—7th	66	86	.434	22	Dave Bancroft	303,598
1927	—7th	60	94	.390	34	Dave Bancroft	288,685
1928	—7th	50	103	.327	44 ½	Jack Slattery, Rogers Hornsby	227,001
1929	—8th	56	98	.364	43	Emil Fuchs	372,351
1930	—6th	70	84	.455	22	Bill McKechnie	464,835
1931	—7th	64	90	.416	37	Bill McKechnie	515,005
1932	—5th	77	77	.500	13	Bill McKechnie	507,606
1933	—4th	83	71	.539	9	Bill McKechnie	517,803
1934	—4th	78	73	.517	16	Bill McKechnie	303,205
1935	—8th	38	115	.248	61 ½	Bill McKechnie	232,754
1936	—6th	71	83	.461	21	Bill McKechnie	340,585
1937	—5th	79	73	.520	16	Bill McKechnie	385,339
1938	—5th	77	75	.507	12	Casey Stengel	341,149
1939	—7th	63	88	.417	32 ½	Casey Stengel	285,994
1940	—7th	65	87	.428	34 ½	Casey Stengel	241,616
1941	—7th	62	92	.403	38	Casey Stengel	263,680
1942	—7th	59	89	.399	44	Casey Stengel	285,332
1943	—6th	68	85	.444	36 ½	Casey Stengel	271,289
1944	—6th	65	89	.422	40	Bob Coleman	208,691
1945	—6th	67	85	.441	30	Bob Coleman, Del Bissonette	374,178
1946	—4th	81	72	.529	15 ½	Billy Southworth	969,673
1947	—3rd	86	68	.558	8	Billy Southworth	1,277,361
1948	—1st	91	62	.595	+ 6 ½	Billy Southworth	1,455,439
1949	—4th	75	79	.487	22	Billy Southworth	1,081,795
1950	—4th	83	71	.539	8	Billy Southworth	944,391
1951	—4th	76	78	.494	20 ½	Billy Southworth, Tommy Holmes	487,475
1952	—7th	64	89	.418	32	Tommy Holmes, Charlie Grimm	281,278

INDIVIDUAL RECORDS (1876 TO 1952)

SERVICE

Most years, non-pitcher
15—Fred Tenney

Rabbit Maranville
Johnny Cooney
Most years played by pitcher
12—Kid Nichols

Most years played by pitcher (since 1900)
11—Dick Rudolph

BATTING

Most games
158—Ed Konetchy, 1916
Most games, career
1,795—Rabbit Maranville
Most at-bats
647—Herman Long, 151 games, 1892
Most at-bats, career
6,764—Herman Long
Most at-bats (since 1900)
637—Gene Moore, 151 games, 1936
Most at-bats, career (since 1900)
6,724—Rabbit Maranville
Most runs
160—Hugh Duffy, 124 games, 1894
Most runs (since 1900)
125—Tommy Holmes, 154 games, 1945
Most runs, career
1,294—Herman Long
Most hits
236—Hugh Duffy, 124 games, 1894
Most hits, career
2,002—Fred Tenney
Most hits (since 1900)
224—Tommy Holmes, 154 games, 1945
Most singles
166—Lance Richbourg, 148 games, 1928
Most doubles
50—Hugh Duffy, 124 games, 1894
Most doubles (since 1900)
47—Tommy Holmes, 154 games, 1945
Most doubles, career
291—Tommy Holmes
Most triples
20—Dick Johnston, 124 games, 1887
Most triples (since 1900)
18—Ray Powell, 149 games, 1921
Most triples, career
103—Rabbit Maranville
Most homers by righthander
38—Wally Berger, 151 games, 1930
Most homers by lefthander
28—Tommy Holmes, 154 games, 1945
Most homers, rookie
38—Wally Berger, 151 games, 1930
Most homers at home
19—Chuck Workman, 1945
Most homers on road
22—Sid Gordon, 1950
Most grand slams
4—Sid Gordon, 134 games, 1950
Most grand slams, career
6—Wally Berger
Most home runs, month
11—Wally Berger, May, 1930
Most homers, career
199—Wally Berger
Most total bases
372—Hugh Duffy, 124 games, 1894
Most total bases (since 1900)
367—Tommy Holmes, 154 games, 1945
Most total bases, career
2,629—Herman Long
Most long hits
81—Hugh Duffy, 124 games, 1894
Tommy Holmes, 154 games, 1945
Most extra bases on long hits
169—Wally Berger, 151 games, 1930
Most sacrifices (sacrifice hits and sacrifice flies)
37—Stuffy McInnis, 154 games, 1923
Most sacrifice hits
31—Freddie Maguire, 148 games, 1931
Most bases on balls
131—Bob Elliott, 151 games, 1948

Most strikeouts
134—Vince DiMaggio, 150 games, 1938
Fewest strikeouts
9—Tommy Holmes, 154 games, 1945
Most hit by pitch
11—Sam Jethroe, 148 games, 1951
Most runs batted in
130—Wally Berger, 150 games, 1935
Most runs batted in, career
746—Wally Berger

Highest batting average
.438—Hugh Duffy, 124 games, 1894
Highest batting average (since 1900)
.387—Rogers Hornsby, 140 games, 1928
Highest batting average, career
.338—Billy Hamilton
Highest batting average, career (since 1900)
.304—Wally Berger
Highest slugging average
.632—Rogers Hornsby, 140 games, 1928
Longest batting streak
37 games—Tommy Holmes, 1945
Most grounded into double play
28—Sid Gordon, 150 games, 1951
Fewest grounded into double play
4—Vince DiMaggio, 150 games, 1938

BASERUNNING

Most stolen bases
93—Billy Hamilton, 131 games, 1896
Most stolen bases (since 1900)
57—Hap Myers, 140 games, 1913
Most stolen bases, career
446—Herman Long
Most caught stealing
20—Billy Southworth, 141 games, 1921

PITCHING (SINCE 1900)

Most games
57—Johnny Hutchings, 1945
Most games, career
556—Kid Nichols
Most games started
46—Vic Willis, 1902
Most complete games
45—Vic Willis, 1902
Most games finished
29—Nels Potter, 1949
Most innings
411—Vic Willis, 1902
Most games won
27—Togie Pittinger, 1902
Vic Willis, 1902
Dick Rudolph, 1914
Most games won, career
329—Kid Nichols
Most games won, career
122—Dick Rudolph, Warren Spahn
Most 20-victory seasons
4—Johnny Sain, Warren Spahn
Most games lost
29—Vic Willis, 1905
Highest winning percentage
.842—Tom Hughes (16-3), 1916
Longest winning streak
12 games—Dick Rudolph, 1914
Longest losing streak
18 games—Cliff Curtis, 1910
Most bases on balls
149—Chick Fraser, 1905
Most bases on balls, career
1,118—Kid Nichols
Most bases on balls, career
678—Lefty Tyler
Most strikeouts
226—Vic Willis, 1902

Most strikeouts, career
1,000—Warren Spahn
Most strikeouts, game
18—Warren Spahn, June 14, 1952, 15 innings
13—Vic Willis, May 28, 1902
Warren Spahn, September 13, 1952
Most shutouts
7—Togie Pittinger, 1902
Irv Young, 1905
Warren Spahn, 1947, 1951
Most shutouts league
29—Dick Rudolph
Most 1-0 shutouts won
4—Dick Rudolph, 1916
Joe Oeschger, 1920

Most runs
196—Togie Pittinger, 1903
Most earned runs
130—Johnny Sain, 1949
Most hits
394—Togie Pittinger, 1903
Most hit batsmen
16—Jeff Pfeffer, 1906
Most wild pitches
14—Togie Pittinger, 1903
Most home runs
34—Johnny Sain, 1950
Lowest ERA
1.90—Bill James, 332 innings, 1914

CLUB RECORDS

Most players
48 in 1946
Fewest players
23 in 1905
Most games
158 in 1914, 1916
Most at-bats
5,506 in 1932
Most runs
1,220 in 1894
Most runs (since 1900)
785 in 1950
Fewest runs
408 in 1906
Most hits
1,567 in 1925
Fewest hits
1,115 in 1906
Most singles
196 in 1925
Most doubles
272 in 1948
Most triples
100 in 1921
Most home runs
148 in 1950
Fewest homers (154 or 162-game schedule)
15 in 1909
Most homers at Braves Field, home and opponents
131 in 1945
Most grand slams
7 in 1950
Most total bases
2,173 in 1950
Most long hits
430 in 1950
Most extra bases on long hits
762 in 1950
Most sacrifices (sacrifice hits and sacrifice flies)
221 in 1914
Most sacrifice hits
140 in 1948
Most stolen bases
190 in 1909
Most bases on balls
684 in 1949
Most strikeouts
711 in 1952
Fewest strikeouts
348 in 1926
Most hit by pitch
45 in 1917
Fewest hit by pitch
13 in 1941
Most runs batted in
726 in 1950
Highest batting average
.292 in 1925

Lowest batting average
.223 in 1909
Highest slugging average
.405 in 1950
Lowest slugging average
.274 in 1909
Most grounded into double play
146 in 1936
Fewest grounded into double play
93 in 1944
Most left on bases
1,255 in 1948
Fewest left on bases
1,003 in 1933
Most .300 hitters
8 in 1931
Most putouts
4,262 in 1914
Fewest putouts
3,975 in 1906
Most assists
2,225 in 1908
Fewest assists
1,665 in 1946
Most chances accepted
6,424 in 1914
Fewest chances accepted
5,750 in 1935
Most errors
353 in 1904
Fewest errors
138 in 1933
Most consecutive errorless games
5 in 1933 (twice)
Most double plays
178 in 1939
Fewest double plays
101 in 1935
Most passed balls
167 in 1883
Most passed balls (since 1900)
42 in 1905
Fewest passed balls
2 in 1943
Highest fielding average
.978 in 1933
Lowest fielding average
.945 in 1904
Highest home attendance
1,455,439 in 1948
Highest road attendance
1,308,175 in 1947
Most games won
102 in 1892, 1898
Most games won (since 1900)
94 in 1914
Most games lost
115 in 1935

Most games won, month
26—September 1914
Most games lost, month
25—September 1928
September 1935
Highest percentage games won
.705 in 1897 (won 93, lost 39)
Highest percentage games won (since 1900)
.614 in 1914 (won 94, lost 59)
Lowest percentage games won
.248 in 1935 (won 38, lost 115)
Games won, league
5,118 in 77 years
Games lost, league
5,598 in 77 years
Most shutouts won
21 in 1916
Most shutouts lost
28 in 1906
Most 1-0 games won
9 in 1916
Most 1-0 games lost
6 in 1906, 1933
Most consecutive games won
18 in 1891
Most consecutive games won (since 1900)
9 in 1902, 1914 (twice), 1945
Most consecutive games lost
19 in 1906
Number of times league champions
10
Number of last-place finishes
9
Most runs, game
30 vs. Detroit, June 9, 1883
Most runs, game (since 1900)
20 vs. Philadelphia, June 25, 1900
vs. Philadelphia, October 6, 1910
vs. St. Louis, September 18, 1915, first game
vs. St. Louis, August 25, 1936, first game
Most runs by opponent, game
27 by Pittsburgh, June 6, 1894
Most runs by opponent, game (since 1900)
26 by Cincinnati, June 4, 1911
Most runs, shutout game
18 vs. Buffalo, October 3, 1885
Most runs, shutout game (since 1900)
16 vs. Brooklyn, May 7, 1918

vs. Pittsburgh, September 12, 1952, second game
Most runs by opponent, shutout game
17 by Chicago, September 16, 1884
Most runs by opponent, shutout game (since 1900)
15 by New York, April 15, 1905
by Cincinnati, May 19, 1906
by Philadelphia, July 3, 1928
by New York, May 29, 1936
by New York, July 4, 1934, second game
by St. Louis, August 18, 1934
by St. Louis, May 7, 1950
Most runs, doubleheader shutout
8 vs. Cincinnati, August 7, 1916
vs. Brooklyn, June 30, 1937
vs. Cincinnati, August 3, 1941
Most runs, inning
16 vs. Baltimore, June 18, 1894, a.m. game, first inning
Most runs, inning (since 1900)
13 vs. St. Louis, July 25, 1900, first inning
Longest 1-0 game won
13 innings, 5 times; last time vs. Pittsburgh, May 11, 1921
Longest 1-0 game lost
17 innings vs. Chicago, September 21, 1901
Most hits, game
32 vs. St. Louis, September 3, 1896, first game
Most hits, game (since 1900)
25 vs. St. Louis, August 25, 1936, first game
Most home runs, game
5 vs. Cincinnati, May 30, 1894, p.m. game
vs. Chicago, May 13, 1942
vs. Cincinnati, May 6, 1950
Most total bases, game
46 vs. Detroit, June 9, 1883
vs. Cleveland, July 5, 1894
Most total bases, game (since 1900)
37 vs. Philadelphia, July 6, 1934
vs. Cincinnati, May 6, 1950
Largest crowd, day game
41,527 vs. Chicago, August 8, 1948
Largest crowd, doubleheader
47,123 vs. Philadelphia, May 22, 1932
Largest crowd, night game
39,549 vs. Brooklyn, August 5, 1946
Largest crowd, home opener
25,000 vs. New York, April 16, 1935

BROOKLYN DODGERS

YEARLY FINISHES

Year	Position	W	L	Pct.	*GB	Manager	Attendance
1901	—3rd	79	57	.581	9½	Ned Hanlon	189,200
1902	—2nd	75	63	.543	27½	Ned Hanlon	199,868
1903	—5th	70	66	.515	19	Ned Hanlon	224,670
1904	—6th	56	97	.366	50	Ned Hanlon	214,600
1905	—8th	48	104	.316	56½	Ned Hanlon	227,924
1906	—5th	66	86	.434	50	Patsy Donovan	227,400
1907	—5th	65	83	.439	40	Patsy Donovan	312,500
1908	—7th	53	101	.344	46	Patsy Donovan	275,600
1909	—6th	55	98	.359	55½	Harry Lumley	321,300
1910	—6th	64	90	.416	40	Bill Dahlen	279,321
1911	—7th	64	86	.427	33½	Bill Dahlen	269,000
1912	—7th	58	95	.379	46	Bill Dahlen	243,000
1913	—6th	65	84	.436	34½	Bill Dahlen	347,000
1914	—5th	75	79	.487	19½	Wilbert Robinson	122,671
1915	—3rd	80	72	.526	10	Wilbert Robinson	297,766
1916	—1st	94	60	.610	+ 2½	Wilbert Robinson	447,747
1917	—7th	70	81	.464	26½	Wilbert Robinson	221,619
1918	—5th	57	69	.452	25½	Wilbert Robinson	83,831
1919	—5th	69	71	.493	27	Wilbert Robinson	360,721
1920	—1st	93	61	.604	+ 7	Wilbert Robinson	808,722
1921	—5th	77	75	.507	16½	Wilbert Robinson	613,245
1922	—6th	76	78	.494	17	Wilbert Robinson	498,856

Year	Position	W	L	Pct.	*GB	Manager	Attendance
1923 —6th		76	78	.494	19½	Wilbert Robinson	564,666
1924 —2nd		92	62	.597	1½	Wilbert Robinson	818,883
1925 —6th (tied)		68	85	.444	27	Wilbert Robinson	659,435
1926 —6th		71	82	.464	17½	Wilbert Robinson	650,819
1927 —6th		65	88	.425	28½	Wilbert Robinson	637,230
1928 —6th		77	76	.503	17½	Wilbert Robinson	664,863
1929 —6th		70	83	.458	28½	Wilbert Robinson	731,886
1930 —4th		86	68	.558	6	Wilbert Robinson	1,097,339
1931 —4th		79	73	.520	21	Wilbert Robinson	753,133
1932 —3rd		81	73	.526	9	Max Carey	681,827
1933 —6th		65	88	.425	26½	Max Carey	526,815
1934 —6th		71	81	.467	23½	Casey Stengel	434,188
1935 —5th		70	83	.458	29½	Casey Stengel	470,517
1936 —7th		67	87	.435	25	Casey Stengel	489,618
1937 —6th		62	91	.405	33½	Burleigh Grimes	482,481
1938 —7th		69	80	.463	18½	Burleigh Grimes	663,087
1939 —3rd		84	69	.549	12½	Leo Durocher	955,668
1940 —2nd		88	65	.575	12	Leo Durocher	975,978
1941 —1st		100	54	.649	+ 2½	Leo Durocher	1,214,910
1942 —2nd		104	50	.675	2	Leo Durocher	1,037,765
1943 —3rd		81	72	.529	23½	Leo Durocher	661,739
1944 —7th		63	91	.409	42	Leo Durocher	605,905
1945 —3rd		87	67	.565	11	Leo Durocher	1,059,220
1946 —2nd†		96	60	.615	2	Leo Durocher	1,796,824
1947 —1st		94	60	.610	+ 5	Clyde Sukeforth, Burt Shotton	1,807,526
1948 —3rd		84	70	.545	7½	Leo Durocher, Burt Shotton	1,398,967
1949 —1st		97	57	.630	+ 1	Burt Shotton	1,633,747
1950 —2nd		89	65	.578	2	Burt Shotton	1,185,896
1951 —2nd†		97	60	.618	1	Chuck Dressen	1,282,628
1952 —1st		96	57	.627	+ 4½	Chuck Dressen	1,088,704
1953 —1st		105	49	.682	+13	Chuck Dressen	1,163,419
1954 —2nd		92	62	.597	5	Walter Alston	1,020,531
1955 —1st		98	55	.641	+13½	Walter Alston	1,033,589
1956 —1st		93	61	.604	+ 1	Walter Alston	1,213,562
1957 —3rd		84	70	.545	11	Walter Alston	1,028,258

*Games behind winner.   †Lost pennant playoff.

INDIVIDUAL RECORDS (1890 TO 1957)

SERVICE

Most years by non-pitcher
18—Zack Wheat
Most years by pitcher
12—Dazzy Vance

BATTING

Most games
158—Carl Furillo, 1951
        Gil Hodges, 1951
Most games, career
2,318—Zack Wheat
Most at-bats
667—Carl Furillo, 158 games, 1951
Most at-bats, career
8,859—Zack Wheat
Most runs
143—Hub Collins, 129 games, 1890
        Babe Herman, 153 games, 1930
Most runs, career
1,317—Pee Wee Reese
Most hits
241—Babe Herman, 153 games, 1930
Most hits, career
2,804—Zack Wheat
Most singles
179—Willie Keeler, 137 games, 1900
Most singles, career
2,038—Zack Wheat
Most doubles
52—Johnny Frederick, 148 games, 1929
Most doubles, career
464—Zack Wheat
Most triples
27—George Treadway, 122 games, 1894

Most triples, career
171—Zack Wheat
Most triples (since 1900)
22—Hy Myers, 154 games, 1920
Most homers by righthander
42—Gil Hodges, 154 games, 1954
Most homers by lefthander
43—Duke Snider, 151 games, 1956
Most homers by rookie
25—Del Bissonette, 155 games, 1928
Most homers, month
15—Duke Snider, August, 1953
Most homers at home
25—Duke Snider (includes 2 at Jersey City), 1956
        Gil Hodges, 1954
Most homers on road
24—Gil Hodges, 1951
Most homers by righthander, career
298—Gil Hodges
Most homers by lefthander, career
316—Duke Snider
Most grand slams
2—Held by many players
Most grand slams, career
13—Gil Hodges
Most total bases
416—Babe Herman, 153 games, 1930
Most total bases, career
4,003—Zack Wheat
Most long hits
94—Babe Herman, 153 games, 1930
Most long hits, career
766—Zack Wheat
Most extra bases on long hits
179—Duke Snider, 149 games, 1954
Most extra bases on long hits, career
1,368—Duke Snider

— 289 —

Most sacrifices (sacrifice hits and sacrifice flies)
39—Jake Daubert, 150 games, 1915
Most sacrifice hits
32—Doc Casey, 138 games, 1907
Most sacrifice flies
19—Gil Hodges, 154 games, 1954
Most bases on balls
148—Eddie Stanky, 153 games, 1945
Most strikeouts
115—Dolf Camilli, 149 games, 1941
Fewest strikeouts
15—Jimmy Johnston, 151 games, 1923
Most hit by pitch
14—Jackie Robinson, 149 games, 1952
Most runs batted in
142—Roy Campanella, 144 games, 1953
Most runs batted in, career
1,227—Zack Wheat
Highest batting average
.393—Babe Herman, 153 games, 1930
Highest batting average, career
.339—Babe Herman
Highest slugging average
.678—Babe Herman, 153 games, 1930
Highest slugging average, career
.560—Duke Snider
Longest batting streak
29 games—Zack Wheat, 1916
Most grounded into double play
27—Carl Furillo, 149 games, 1956
Fewest grounded into double play
5—Jackie Robinson, 151 games, 1947
Pee Wee Reese, 155 games, 1949
Jim Gilliam, 153 games, 1956

BASERUNNING

Most stolen bases
94—Monte Ward, 148 games, 1892
Most stolen bases (since 1900)
67—Jimmy Sheckard, 139 games, 1903
Most stolen bases, career
231—Pee Wee Reese
Most caught stealing
16—Jimmy Johnston, 152 games, 1921

PITCHING (SINCE 1900)

Most games
62—Clem Labine, 1956
Most games, career
378—Dazzy Vance
Most games started
41—Oscar Jones, 1904

Most complete games
38—Oscar Jones, 1904
Most games finished
47—Clem Labine, 1956
Most innings
378—Oscar Jones, 1904
Most games won
29—Joe McGinnity, 1900
Most games won, career
190—Dazzy Vance
Most 20 - victory seasons
4—Burleigh Grimes
Most games lost
27—George Bell, 1910
Highest winning percentage
.889—Freddie Fitzsimmons (16-2), 1940
Longest winning streak
15 games—Dazzy Vance, 1924
Longest losing streak
14 games—Jim Pastorius, 1908
Most bases on balls
151—Bill Donovan, 1901
Most bases on balls, career
764—Dazzy Vance
Most strikeouts
262—Dazzy Vance, 1924
Most strikeouts, career
1,915—Dazzy Vance
Most strikeouts, game
17—Dazzy Vance, July 20, 1925, 10 innings
16—Nap Rucker, July 24, 1909
Most shutouts
7—Burleigh Grimes, 1918
Whit Wyatt, 1941
Most shutouts, career
38—Nap Rucker
Most 1 - 0 shutouts won
3—Nap Rucker, 1911
Most runs
188—Harry McIntire, 1905
Most earned runs
138—Burleigh Grimes, 1925
Most hits
364—Joe McGinnity, 1900
Most hit batsmen
41—Joe McGinnity, 1900
Most wild pitches
15—Larry Cheney, 1916
Most home runs
35—Don Newcombe, 1955
Lowest ERA
1.58—Rube Marquard, 205 innings, 1916

CLUB RECORDS

Most players
53 in 1944
Fewest players
23 in 1905
Most games
158 in 1951
Most at - bats
5,574 in 1936
Most runs
955 in 1953
Fewest runs
375 in 1908
Most hits
1,654 in 1930
Fewest hits
1,044 in 1908
Most singles
1,223 in 1925
Most doubles
303 in 1930

Most triples
99 in 1920
Most homers
208 in 1953
Fewest homers (154 or 162 - game schedule)
14 in 1915
Most homers at Ebbets Field, home and opponents
207 in 1950
Most grand slams
8 in 1952
Most pinch home runs
7 in 1932
Most long hits
541 in 1953
Most extra bases on long hits
1,016 in 1953
Most total bases
2,545 in 1953
Most sacrifices (sacrifice hits and sacrifice flies)
203 in 1916

Most sacrifice hits
197 in 1907
Most sacrifice flies
59 in 1954
Most stolen bases
205 in 1904
Most caught stealing
73 in 1921
Most bases on balls
732 in 1947
Most strikeouts
848 in 1957
Fewest strikeouts
318 in 1922
Most hit by pitch
44 in 1951
Fewest hit by pitch
14 in 1942, 1944
Most runs batted in
887 in 1953
Fewest runs batted in
499 in 1927
Highest batting average
.304 in 1930
Lowest batting average
.213 in 1908
Highest slugging average
.474 in 1953
Lowest slugging average
.277 in 1908
Most grounded into double play
151 in 1952
Fewest grounded into double play
86 in 1947
Most left on bases
1,278 in 1947
Fewest left on bases
1,012 in 1921
Most .300 hitters
6 in 1900, 1922, 1925, 1930, 1943, 1953
Most putouts
4,295 in 1940
Fewest putouts
3,911 in 1909
Most assists
2,132 in 1921
Fewest assists
1,574 in 1944
Most chances accepted
6,334 in 1920
Fewest chances accepted
5,672 in 1944
Most errors
408 in 1905
Fewest errors
106 in 1952
Most consecutive errorless games
10 in 1942
Most double plays
192 in 1951
Fewest double plays
95 in 1926
Most passed balls
21 in 1905
Fewest passed balls
4 in 1933, 1951, 1953, 1954
Highest fielding average
.982 in 1952
Lowest fielding average
.937 in 1905
Highest home attendance
1,807,526 in 1947

Highest road attendance
1,863,542 in 1947
Most games won
105 in 1953
Most games lost
104 in 1905
Most games won, month
25—July 1947
August 1953
Most games lost, month
27—September 1908
Highest percentage games won
.682 in 1953 (won 105, lost 49)
Lowest percentage games won
.316 in 1905 (won 48, lost 104)
Games won, league
5,214 in 68 years
Games lost, league
4,926 in 68 years
Most shutouts won
22 in 1906, 1916
Most shutouts lost
26 in 1907
Most 1-0 games won
7 in 1907, 1909
Most 1-0 games lost
9 in 1910, 1913
Most consecutive games won
15 in 1924
Most consecutive games lost
16 in 1944
Number of times league champions
12
Number of last-place finishes
1
Most runs, game
25 vs. Pittsburgh, May 20, 1896
vs. Cincinnati, September 23, 1901
Most runs by opponent, game
28 by Chicago, August 25, 1891
Most runs by opponent, game (since 1900)
26 by New York, April 30, 1944, first game
Most runs, shutout game
15 vs. Philadelphia, August 16, 1952, 6⅓ innings
Most runs by opponent, shutout game
17 by St. Louis, August 24, 1924, second game
Most runs, doubleheader shutout
18 vs. Philadelphia, September 3, 1906
Most runs, inning
15 vs. Cincinnati, May 21, 1952, first inning
Longest 1-0 game won
13 innings vs. St. Louis, August 21, 1909
vs. Boston, May 29, 1938
Longest 1-0 game lost
15 innings vs. Cincinnati, June 11, 1915
Most hits, game
28 vs. Pittsburgh, June 23, 1930
Most home runs, game
6 vs. Milwaukee, June 1, 1955
Most consecutive games with one or more homers
24 (39 homers), 1953
Most total bases, game
46 vs. Philadelphia, September 23, 1939, first game
Largest crowd, day game
37,512 vs. New York, August 30, 1947
Largest crowd, doubleheader
41,209 vs. New York, May 30, 1934
Largest crowd, night game
35,583 vs. Philadelphia, September 24, 1949
Largest crowd, home opener
34,530 vs. New York, April 19, 1949

YEARLY FINISHES

Year	Position	W	L	Pct.	°GB	Manager	Attendance
1901	6th	53	86	.381	37	Tom Loftus	205,071
1902	5th	68	69	.496	34	Frank Selee	263,700
1903	3rd	82	56	.594	8	Frank Selee	386,205
1904	2nd	93	60	.608	13	Frank Selee	439,100
1905	3rd	92	61	.601	13	Frank Selee, Frank Chance	509,900
1906	1st	116	36	.763	+20	Frank Chance	654,300
1907	1st	107	45	.704	+17	Frank Chance	422,550
1908	1st	99	55	.643	+ 1	Frank Chance	665,325
1909	2nd	104	49	.680	6 ½	Frank Chance	633,480
1910	1st	104	50	.675	+13	Frank Chance	526,152
1911	2nd	92	62	.597	7 ½	Frank Chance	576,000
1912	3rd	91	59	.607	11 ½	Frank Chance	514,000
1913	3rd	88	65	.575	13 ½	Johnny Evers	419,000
1914	4th	78	76	.506	16 ½	Hank O'Day	202,516
1915	4th	73	80	.477	17 ½	Roger Bresnahan	217,058
1916	5th	67	86	.438	26 ½	Joe Tinker	453,685
1917	5th	74	80	.481	24	Fred Mitchell	360,218
1918	1st	84	45	.651	+10 ½	Fred Mitchell	337,256
1919	3rd	75	65	.536	21	Fred Mitchell	424,430
1950	5th (tied)	75	79	.487	18	Fred Mitchell	480,783
1921	7th	64	89	.418	30	Johnny Evers, Bill Killefer	410,107
1922	5th	80	74	.519	13	Bill Killefer	542,283
1923	4th	83	71	.539	12 ½	Bill Killefer	703,705
1924	5th	81	72	.529	12	Bill Killefer	716,922
1925	8th	68	86	.442	27 ½	Bill Killefer, Rabbit Maranville, George Gibson	622,610
1926	4th	82	72	.532	7	Joe McCarthy	885,063
1927	4th	85	68	.556	8 ½	Joe McCarthy	1,159,168
1928	3rd	91	63	.591	4	Joe McCarthy	1,143,740
1929	1st	98	54	.645	+10 ½	Joe McCarthy	1,485,166
1930	2nd	90	64	.584	2	Joe McCarthy, Rogers Hornsby	1,463,624
1931	3rd	84	70	.545	17	Rogers Hornsby	1,086,422
1932	1st	90	64	.584	+ 4	Rogers Hornsby, Charlie Grimm	974,688
1933	3rd	86	68	.558	6	Charlie Grimm	594,112
1934	3rd	86	65	.570	8	Charlie Grimm	707,525
1935	1st	100	54	.649	+ 4	Charlie Grimm	692,604
1936	2nd (tied)	87	67	.565	5	Charlie Grimm	699,370
1937	2nd	93	61	.604	3	Charlie Grimm	895,020
1938	1st	89	63	.586	+ 2	Charlie Grimm, Gabby Hartnett	951,640
1939	4th	84	70	.545	13	Gabby Hartnett	726,663
1940	5th	75	79	.487	25 ½	Gabby Hartnett	534,878
1941	6th	70	84	.455	30	Jimmy Wilson	545,159
1942	6th	68	86	.442	38	Jimmy Wilson	590,872
1943	5th	74	79	.484	30 ½	Jimmy Wilson	508,247
1944	4th	75	79	.487	30	Jimmy Wilson, Charlie Grimm	640,110
1945	1st	98	56	.636	+ 3	Charlie Grimm	1,036,386
1946	3rd	82	71	.536	14 ½	Charlie Grimm	1,342,970
1947	6th	69	85	.448	25	Charlie Grimm	1,364,039
1948	8th	64	90	.416	27 ½	Charlie Grimm	1,237,792
1949	8th	61	93	.396	36	Charlie Grimm, Frankie Frisch	1,143,139
1950	7th	64	89	.418	26 ½	Frankie Frisch	1,165,944
1951	8th	62	92	.403	34 ½	Frankie Frisch, Phil Cavarretta	894,415
1952	5th	77	77	.500	19 ½	Phil Cavarretta	1,024,826
1953	7th	65	89	.422	40	Phil Cavarretta	763,658
1954	7th	64	90	.416	33	Stan Hack	748,183
1955	6th	72	81	.471	26	Stan Hack	875,800
1956	8th	60	94	.390	33	Stan Hack	720,118
1957	7th (tied)	62	92	.403	33	Bob Scheffing	670,629
1958	5th (tied)	72	82	.468	20	Bob Scheffing	979,904
1959	5th (tied)	74	80	.481	13	Bob Scheffing	858,255
1960	7th	60	94	.390	35	Charlie Grimm, Lou Boudreau	809,770
1961	7th	64	90	.416	29	Vedie Himsl, Harry Craft, Elvin Tappe, Lou Klein	673,057
1962	9th	59	103	.364	42 ½	Charlie Metro, Elvin Tappe, Lou Klein	609,802
1963	7th	82	80	.506	17	Bob Kennedy	979,551
1964	8th	76	86	.469	17	Bob Kennedy	751,647
1965	8th	72	90	.444	25	Bob Kennedy, Lou Klein	641,361
1966	10th	59	103	.364	36	Leo Durocher	635,891
1967	3rd	87	74	.540	14	Leo Durocher	977,226
1968	3rd	84	78	.519	13	Leo Durocher	1,043,409

EAST DIVISION

Year	Position	W	L	Pct.	*GB	Manager	Attendance
1969	2nd	92	70	.568	8	Leo Durocher	1,674,993
1970	2nd	84	78	.519	5	Leo Durocher	1,642,705
1971	3rd (tied)	83	79	.512	14	Leo Durocher	1,653,007
1972	2nd	85	70	.548	11	Leo Durocher, Whitey Lockman	1,299,163
1973	5th	77	84	.478	5	Whitey Lockman	1,351,705
1974	6th	66	96	.407	22	Whitey Lockman, Jim Marshall	1,015,378
1975	5th (tied)	75	87	.463	17 ½	Jim Marshall	1,034,819
1976	4th	75	87	.463	26	Jim Marshall	1,026,217
1977	4th	81	81	.500	20	Herman Franks	1,439,834
1978	3rd	79	83	.488	11	Herman Franks	1,525,311
1979	5th	80	82	.494	18	Herman Franks, Joe Amalfitano	1,648,587
1980	6th	64	98	.395	27	Preston Gomez, Joe Amalfitano	1,206,776
1981	6th/5th	38	65	.369	†	Joe Amalfitano	565,637
1982	5th	73	89	.451	19	Lee Elia	1,249,278
1983	5th	71	91	.438	19	Lee Elia, Charlie Fox	1,479,717
1984	1st‡	96	65	.596	+ 6 ½	Jim Frey	2,104,219
1985	4th	77	84	.478	23 ½	Jim Frey	2,161,534
1986	5th	70	90	.438	37	Jim Frey, John Vukovich, Gene Michael	1,859,102
1987	6th	76	85	.472	18 ½	Gene Michael, Frank Lucchesi	2,035,130
1988	4th	77	85	.475	24	Don Zimmer	2,089,034
1989	1st‡	93	69	.574	+ 6	Don Zimmer	2,491,942
1990	4th	77	85	.475	18	Don Zimmer	2,243,791
1991	4th	77	83	.481	20	Don Zimmer, Joe Altobelli, Jim Essian	2,314,250
1992	4th	78	84	.481	18	Jim Lefebvre	2,126,720
1993	4th	84	78	.519	13	Jim Lefebvre	2,653,763

CENTRAL DIVISION

Year	Position	W	L	Pct.	*GB	Manager	Attendance
1994	5th	49	64	.434	16 ½	Tom Trebelhorn	1,845,208

*Games behind winner.   †First half 15-37; second 23-28.   ‡Lost Championship Series.

INDIVIDUAL RECORDS (1876 TO DATE)

SERVICE

Most years by non-pitcher
22—Cap Anson
Most years by pitcher
16—Charlie Root

BATTING

Most years (since 1900)
20—Phil Cavarretta
Most games
164—Ron Santo, 1965
Billy Williams, 1965
Most games, career
2,528—Ernie Banks
Most at-bats
666—Billy Herman, 154 games, 1935
Most at-bats, career
9,421—Ernie Banks
Most runs
156—Rogers Hornsby, 156 games, 1929
Most runs, career
1,712—Cap Anson
Most runs, career (since 1900)
1,306—Billy Williams
Most hits
229—Rogers Hornsby, 156 games, 1929
Most hits, career
3,081—Cap Anson
Most hits, career (since 1900)
2,583—Ernie Banks
Most singles
165—Sparky Adams, 146 games, 1927
Most singles, career
2,330—Cap Anson
Most singles, career (since 1900)
1,692—Stan Hack
Most doubles
57—Billy Herman, 154 games, 1935

Billy Herman, 153 games, 1936
Most doubles, career
530—Cap Anson
Most doubles, career (since 1900)
407—Ernie Banks
Most triples
21—Wildfire Schulte, 154 games, 1911
Vic Saier, 149 games, 1913
Most triples, career
137—Jimmy Ryan
Most triples, career (since 1900)
117—Wildfire Schulte
Most homers by lefthander
42—Billy Williams, 161 games, 1970
Most homers by righthander
56—Hack Wilson, 155 games, 1930
Most homers at home
33—Hack Wilson, 1930
Most homers on road
23—Hack Wilson, 1930
Ernie Banks, 1960
Dave Kingman, 1979
Most homers, rookie
25—Billy Williams, 146 games, 1961
Most homers, month
15—Andre Dawson, August, 1987
Most homers by righthander, career
512—Ernie Banks
Most homers by lefthander, career
392—Billy Williams
Most grand slams
5—Ernie Banks, 154 games, 1955
Most grand slams, career
12—Ernie Banks
Most total bases
423—Hack Wilson, 155 games, 1930
Most total bases, career
4,706—Ernie Banks
Most long hits
97—Hack Wilson, 155 games, 1930

Most long hits, career
1,009—Ernie Banks
Most extra bases on long hits
215—Hack Wilson, 155 games, 1930
Most extra bases on long hits, career
2,123—Ernie Banks
Most sacrifices (sacrifice hits and sacrifice flies)
46—Jimmy Sheckard, 148 games, 1909
Most sacrifice hits
40—Jimmy Sheckard, 149 games, 1906
Most sacrifice flies
14—Ron Santo, 1969
Most bases on balls
147—Jimmy Sheckard, 156 games, 1911
Most bases on balls, career
1,092—Stan Hack
Most strikeouts
143—Byron Browne, 120 games, 1966
Most strikeouts, career
1,271—Ron Santo
Fewest strikeouts
5—Charlie Hollocher, 152 games, 1922
Most hit by pitch
12—Adolfo Phillips, 116 games, 1966
Most runs batted in
190—Hack Wilson, 155 games, 1930
Most runs batted in, career
1,636—Ernie Banks
Most game-winning RBIs
19—Gary Matthews, 147 games, 1984
Most consecutive games with RBI
17—Ray Grimes (22 RBIs), 1922
Highest batting average
.388—King Kelly, 118 games, 1886
Bill Lange, 122 games, 1895
Highest batting average (since 1900)
.380—Rogers Hornsby, 156 games, 1929
Highest batting average, career
.339—Cap Anson
Highest batting average, career (since 1900)
.336—Riggs Stephenson
Highest slugging average
.723—Hack Wilson, 155 games, 1930
Longest batting streak
42 games—Bill Dahlen, 1894
Longest batting streak (since 1900)
30 games—Jerome Walton, 1989
Most grounded into double play
27—Ron Santo, 149 games, 1973
Fewest grounded into double play
0—Augie Galan, 154 games, 1935

BASERUNNING

Most stolen bases
100—Bill Lange, 123 games, 1896
Most stolen bases (since 1900)
67—Frank Chance, 123 games, 1903
Most stolen bases, career
404—Frank Chance
Most caught stealing
29—Charlie Hollocher, 152 games, 1922

PITCHING (SINCE 1900)

Most games
84—Ted Abernathy, 1965
Dick Tidrow, 1980
Most games, career
605—Charlie Root
Most games started
42—Ferguson Jenkins, 1969
Most games started, career
347—Ferguson Jenkins
Most complete games
33—Jack Taylor, 1903

Grover Alexander, 1920
Most complete games, career
205—Mordecai Brown
Most games finished
69—Randy Myers, 1993
Most innings
363—Grover Alexander, 1920
Most innings, career
3,138—Charlie Root
Most games won
29—Mordecai Brown, 1908
Most games won, career
201—Charlie Root
Most 20-victory seasons
6—Mordecai Brown, Ferguson Jenkins
Most games lost
22—Tom Hughes, 1901
Dick Ellsworth, 1966
Bill Bonham, 1974
Most games lost, career
156—Charlie Root
Highest winning percentage
.941—Rick Sutcliffe (16-1), 1984
Longest winning streak
14 games—Ed Reulbach, 1909
Rick Sutcliffe, 1984
Longest winning streak, two seasons
16 games—Rick Sutcliffe, 1984-85
Longest losing streak
13 games—Dutch McCall, 1948
Most saves
53—Randy Myers, 1993
Most bases on balls
185—Sam Jones, 1955
Most bases on balls, career
871—Charlie Root
Most strikeouts
274—Ferguson Jenkins, 1970
Most strikeouts, game
17—Jack Pfiester, May 30, 1906, first game, 15 innings
16—John Clarkson, August 18, 1886
15—Dick Drott, May 26, 1957, first game
Burt Hooton, September 15, 1971, second game
Rick Sutcliffe, September 3, 1984, pitched first eight
innings of 12-inning game
Most strikeouts, career
2,036—Ferguson Jenkins
Most shutouts
9—Mordecai Brown, 1906, 1908
Orval Overall, 1907, 1909
Grover Alexander, 1919
Bill Lee, 1938
Most shutouts, career
48—Mordecai Brown
Most 1-0 shutouts won
3—held by many pitchers
Most runs
174—Guy Bush, 1930
Most earned runs
155—Guy Bush, 1930
Most hits
335—Grover Alexander, 1920
Most hit batsmen
20—Nixey Callahan, 1900
Most wild pitches
26—Larry Cheney, 1914
Most home runs
38—Warren Hacker, 1955
Most sacrifice hits
23—Bill Bonham, 1974
Most sacrifice flies
14—Rick Reuschel, 1980
Lowest ERA
1.72—Grover Alexander, 235 innings, 1919

Most players
49 in 1966
Fewest players
20 in 1905
Most games
164 in 1965
Most at-bats
5,675 in 1988
Most runs
998 in 1930
Most opponents' runs
870 in 1930
Fewest runs
530 in 1906
Most hits
1,722 in 1930
Fewest hits
1,224 in 1907
Most singles
1,226 in 1921
Most doubles
340 in 1931
Most triples
101 in 1911
Most homers
209 in 1987
Fewest homers (154 or 162-game schedule)
12 in 1905
Most homers at Wrigley Field, home and opponents
204 in 1987
Most grand slams
9 in 1929
Most pinch home runs
8 in 1958, 1985, 1987, 1993
Most total bases
2,684 in 1930
Most long hits
548 in 1930
Most extra bases on long hits
962 in 1930
Most sacrifices (sacrifice hits and sacrifice flies)
270 in 1908
Most sacrifice hits
231 in 1906
Most sacrifice flies
66 in 1975
Most stolen bases
283 in 1906
Most caught stealing
149 in 1924
Most bases on balls
650 in 1975
Most strikeouts
1,064 in 1987
Fewest strikeouts
374 in 1921
Most hit by pitch
47 in 1966
Fewest hit by pitch
13 in 1956
Most runs batted in
940 in 1930
Most game-winning RBIs
86 in 1984
Highest batting average
.309 in 1930
Lowest batting average
.238 in 1963, 1965
Highest slugging average
.481 in 1930
Lowest slugging average
.311 in 1907
Most grounded into double play
157 in 1938

Fewest grounded into double play
87 in 1991
Most left on bases
1,262 in 1975
Fewest left on bases
964 in 1924
Most .300 hitters
8 in 1921
Most putouts
4,437 in 1980
Fewest putouts
4,024 in 1909
Most assists
2,155 in 1916
Fewest assists
1,607 in 1956
Most chances accepted
6,508 in 1977
Fewest chances accepted
5,706 in 1953
Most errors
310 in 1914
Fewest errors
113 in 1991
Most errorless games
88 in 1992
Most consecutive errorless games
8 in 1978, 1984, 1992, 1994
Most double plays
176 in 1928
Fewest double plays
110 in 1982
Most passed balls
35 in 1961
Fewest passed balls
4 in 1967
Highest fielding average
.982 in 1983, 1991, 1992, 1993
Lowest fielding average
.951 in 1914
Highest home attendance
2,653,763 in 1993
Highest road attendance
2,592,790 in 1993
Most games won
116 in 1906
Most games lost
103 in 1962, 1966
Most games won, month
26 in August 1906, July 1935, July 1945
Most games lost, month
24 in July 1957
Highest percentage games won
.798 in 1880 (won 67, lost 17)
Highest percentage games won (since 1900)
.763 in 1906 (won 116, lost 36)
Lowest percentage games won
.364 in 1962, 1966 (won 59, lost 103)
Games won, league
8,985 in 119 years
Games lost, league
8,371 in 119 years
Most shutouts won
32 in 1907, 1909
Most shutouts lost
22 in 1915, 1968
Most 1-0 games won
9 in 1906
Most 1-0 games lost
10 in 1916
Most consecutive games won
21 in 1880, 1935
Most consecutive games lost
13 in 1944, 1982, 1985

Number of times league champions
16
Number of last-place finishes
12
Most runs, game
36 vs. Louisville, June 29, 1897
Most runs, game (since 1900)
26 vs. Philadelphia, August 25, 1922
Most runs by opponent, game (since 1900)
23 by Philadelphia, August 25, 1922
by Cincinnati, July 6, 1949
by Philadelphia, May 17, 1979, 10 innings
by New York, August 16, 1987
Most runs, shutout game
20 vs. Washington, May 28, 1886
Most runs, shutout game (since 1900)
19 vs. New York, June 7, 1906
vs. San Diego, May 13, 1969
Most runs by opponent, shutout game
22 by Pittsburgh, September 16, 1975
Most runs, doubleheader shutout
12 vs. St. Louis, July 11, 1965
Most runs, inning
18 vs. Detroit, September 6, 1883, seventh inning
Most runs, inning (since 1900)
14 vs. Philadelphia, August 25, 1922, fourth inning
Longest 1-0 game won
17 innings vs. Boston, September 21, 1901
Longest 1-0 game lost
17 innings vs. Houston, August 23, 1980

Most hits, game
32 vs. Buffalo, July 3, 1883
vs. Louisville, June 29, 1897
Most hits, game (since 1900)
28 vs. Boston, July 3, 1945
Most home runs, game
7 vs. New York, June 11, 1967, second game
vs. San Diego, August 19, 1970
vs. San Diego, May 17, 1977
Most consecutive games with one or more homers
14 (29 homers), 1884
(27 homers), 1961
(26 homers), 1987
Most consecutive games with one or more homers, two seasons
15 (3 homers), 1953 (last 2 games); (28 homers), 1954
(first 13 games)
Most total bases, game
54 vs. Brooklyn, August 25, 1891
Most total bases, game (since 1900)
49 vs. Philadelphia, May 17, 1979, 10 innings
45 vs. New York, June 11, 1967, second game
Largest crowd, day game
46,572 vs. Brooklyn, May 18, 1947
Largest crowd, doubleheader
46,965 vs. Pittsburgh, May 31, 1948
Largest crowd, night game
39,002 vs. Montreal, August 7, 1989
Largest crowd, home opener
45,777 vs. Pittsburgh, April 14, 1978

CINCINNATI REDS

YEARLY FINISHES

Year	Position	W	L	Pct.	*GB	Manager	Attendance
1901 — 8th		52	87	.374	38	John McPhee	205,728
1902 — 4th		70	70	.500	33½	John McPhee, Frank Bancroft, Joe Kelley	217,300
1903 — 4th		74	65	.532	16½	Joe Kelley	351,680
1904 — 3rd		88	65	.575	18	Joe Kelley	391,915
1905 — 5th		79	74	.516	26	Joe Kelley	313,927
1906 — 6th		64	87	.424	51½	Ned Hanlon	330,056
1907 — 6th		66	87	.431	41½	Ned Hanlon	317,500
1908 — 5th		73	81	.474	26	John Ganzel	399,200
1909 — 4th		77	76	.503	33½	Clark Griffith	424,643
1910 — 5th		75	79	.487	29	Clark Griffith	380,622
1911 — 6th		70	83	.458	29	Clark Griffith	300,000
1912 — 4th		75	78	.490	29	Hank O'Day	344,000
1913 — 7th		64	89	.418	37½	Joe Tinker	258,000
1914 — 8th		60	94	.390	34½	Buck Herzog	100,791
1915 — 7th		71	83	.461	20	Buck Herzog	218,878
1916 — 7th (tied)		60	93	.392	33½	Buck Herzog, Christy Mathewson	255,846
1917 — 4th		78	76	.506	20	Christy Mathewson	269,056
1918 — 3rd		68	60	.531	15½	Christy Mathewson, Heinie Groh	163,009
1919 — 1st		96	44	.686	+ 9	Pat Moran	532,501
1920 — 3rd		82	71	.536	10½	Pat Moran	568,107
1921 — 6th		70	83	.458	24	Pat Moran	311,227
1922 — 2nd		86	68	.558	7	Pat Moran	493,754
1923 — 2nd		91	63	.591	4½	Pat Moran	575,063
1924 — 4th		83	70	.542	10	Jack Hendricks	437,707
1925 — 3rd		80	73	.523	15	Jack Hendricks	464,920
1926 — 2nd		87	67	.565	2	Jack Hendricks	672,987
1927 — 5th		75	78	.490	18½	Jack Hendricks	442,164
1928 — 5th		78	74	.513	16	Jack Hendricks	490,490
1929 — 7th		66	88	.429	33	Jack Hendricks	295,040
1930 — 7th		59	95	.383	33	Dan Howley	386,727
1931 — 8th		58	96	.377	43	Dan Howley	263,316
1932 — 8th		60	94	.390	30	Dan Howley	356,950
1933 — 8th		58	94	.382	33	Donie Bush	218,281
1934 — 8th		52	99	.344	42	Bob O'Farrell, Chuck Dressen	206,773
1935 — 6th		68	85	.444	31½	Chuck Dressen	448,247
1936 — 5th		74	80	.481	18	Chuck Dressen	466,245
1937 — 8th		56	98	.364	40	Chuck Dressen, Bobby Wallace	411,221
1938 — 4th		82	68	.547	6	Bill McKechnie	706,756
1939 — 1st		97	57	.630	+ 4½	Bill McKechnie	981,443
1940 — 1st		100	53	.654	+12	Bill McKechnie	850,180

Year	Position	W	L	Pct.	*GB	Manager	Attendance
1941	3rd	88	66	.571	12	Bill McKechnie	643,513
1942	4th	76	76	.500	29	Bill McKechnie	427,031
1943	2nd	87	67	.565	18	Bill McKechnie	379,122
1944	3rd	89	65	.578	16	Bill McKechnie	409,567
1945	7th	61	93	.396	37	Bill McKechnie	290,070
1946	6th	67	87	.435	30	Bill McKechnie	715,751
1947	5th	73	81	.474	21	Johnny Neun	899,975
1948	7th	64	89	.418	27	Johnny Neun, Bucky Walters	823,386
1949	7th	62	92	.403	35	Bucky Walters	707,782
1950	6th	66	87	.431	24 ½	Luke Sewell	538,794
1951	6th	68	86	.442	28 ½	Luke Sewell	588,268
1952	6th	69	85	.448	27 ½	Luke Sewell, Rogers Hornsby	604,197
1953	6th	68	86	.442	37	Rogers Hornsby, Buster Mills	548,086
1954	5th	74	80	.481	23	Birdie Tebbetts	704,167
1955	5th	75	79	.487	23 ½	Birdie Tebbetts	693,662
1956	3rd	91	63	.591	2	Birdie Tebbetts	1,125,928
1957	4th	80	74	.519	15	Birdie Tebbetts	1,070,850
1958	4th	76	78	.494	16	Birdie Tebbetts, Jimmie Dykes	788,582
1959	5th (tied)	74	80	.481	13	Mayo Smith, Fred Hutchinson	801,289
1960	6th	67	87	.435	28	Fred Hutchinson	663,486
1961	1st	93	61	.604	+ 4	Fred Hutchinson	1,117,603
1962	3rd	98	64	.605	3 ½	Fred Hutchinson	982,085
1963	5th	86	76	.531	13	Fred Hutchinson	858,805
1964	2nd (tied)	92	70	.549	1	Fred Hutchinson, Dick Sisler	862,466
1965	4th	89	73	.549	8	Dick Sisler	1,047,824
1966	7th	76	84	.475	18	Don Heffner, Dave Bristol	742,958
1967	4th	87	75	.537	14 ½	Dave Bristol	958,300
1968	4th	83	79	.512	14	Dave Bristol	733,354

WEST DIVISION

Year	Position	W	L	Pct.	*GB	Manager	Attendance
1969	3rd	89	73	.549	4	Dave Bristol	987,991
1970	1st†	102	60	.630	+14 ½	Sparky Anderson	1,803,568
1971	4th (tied)	79	83	.488	11	Sparky Anderson	1,501,122
1972	1st†	95	59	.617	+10 ½	Sparky Anderson	1,611,459
1973	1st‡	99	63	.611	+ 3 ½	Sparky Anderson	2,017,601
1974	2nd	98	64	.605	4	Sparky Anderson	2,164,307
1975	1st†	108	54	.667	+20	Sparky Anderson	2,315,603
1976	1st†	102	60	.630	+10	Sparky Anderson	2,629,708
1977	2nd	88	74	.543	10	Sparky Anderson	2,519,670
1978	2nd	92	69	.571	2 ½	Sparky Anderson	2,532,497
1979	1st‡	90	71	.559	+ 1 ½	John McNamara	2,356,933
1980	3rd	89	73	.549	3 ½	John McNamara	2,022,450
1981	2nd/2nd	66	42	.611	§	John McNamara	1,093,730
1982	6th	61	101	.377	28	John McNamara, Russ Nixon	1,326,528
1983	6th	74	88	.457	17	Russ Nixon	1,190,419
1984	5th	70	92	.432	22	Vern Rapp, Pete Rose	1,275,887
1985	2nd	89	72	.553	5 ½	Pete Rose	1,834,619
1986	2nd	86	76	.531	10	Pete Rose	1,692,432
1987	2nd	84	78	.519	6	Pete Rose	2,185,205
1988	2nd	87	74	.540	7	Pete Rose	2,072,528
1989	5th	75	87	.463	17	Pete Rose, Tommy Helms	1,979,320
1990	1st†	91	71	.562	+ 5	Lou Piniella	2,400,892
1991	5th	74	88	.457	20	Lou Piniella	2,372,377
1992	2nd	90	72	.556	8	Lou Piniella	2,315,946
1993	5th	73	89	.451	31	Tony Perez, Dave Johnson	2,453,232

CENTRAL DIVISION

Year	Position	W	L	Pct.	*GB	Manager	Attendance
1994	1st	66	48	.579	+ ½	Dave Johnson	1,897,681

*Games behind winner.   †Won Championship Series.   ‡Lost Championship Series.   §First half 35-21; second 31-21.

INDIVIDUAL RECORDS (1876 to 1889, 1890 TO DATE)

SERVICE

Most years by non-pitcher
19—Pete Rose, Dave Concepcion
Most years by pitcher
15—Joe Nuxhall

BATTING

Most games
163—Leo Cardenas, 1964
Pete Rose, 1974

Most games, career
2,722—Pete Rose
Most at-bats
680—Pete Rose, 160 games, 1973
Most at-bats, career
10,934—Pete Rose
Most runs
134—Frank Robinson, 162 games, 1962
Most runs, career
1,741—Pete Rose

Most hits
230—Pete Rose, 160 games, 1973
Most hits, career
3,358—Pete Rose
Most singles
181—Pete Rose, 160 games, 1973
Most singles, career
2,490—Pete Rose
Most doubles
51—Frank Robinson, 162 games, 1962
Pete Rose, 159 games, 1978
Most doubles, career
601—Pete Rose
Most triples
25—Bid McPhee, 132 games, 1890
Most triples (since 1900)
23—Sam Crawford, 140 games, 1902
Most triples, career
153—Edd Roush
Most homers by righthander
52—George Foster, 158 games, 1977
Most homers by lefthander
49—Ted Kluszewski, 149 games, 1954
Most homers by rookie
38—Frank Robinson, 152 games, 1956
Most homers, month
14—Frank Robinson, August, 1962
Most homers at home
34—Ted Kluszewski, 1954
Most homers on road
31—George Foster, 1977
Most homers by righthander, career
389—Johnny Bench
Most homers by lefthander, career
251—Ted Kluszewski
Most grand slams
3—Frank Robinson, 162 games, 1962
Lee May, 153 games, 1970
Ray Knight, 162 games, 1980
Eric Davis, 129 games, 1987
Chris Sabo, 148 games, 1993
Most grand slams, career
11—Johnny Bench
Most total bases
388—George Foster, 158 games, 1977
Most total bases, career
4,645—Pete Rose
Most long hits
92—Frank Robinson, 162 games, 1962
Most long hits, career
868—Pete Rose
Most extra bases on long hits
191—George Foster, 158 games, 1977
Most extra bases on long hits, career
1,596—Johnny Bench
Most sacrifices (sacrifice hits and sacrifice flies)
39—Jake Daubert, 140 games, 1919
Most sacrifice hits
31—Roy McMillan, 154 games, 1954
Most sacrifice flies
13—Johnny Temple, 149 games, 1959
Most bases on balls
132—Joe Morgan, 146 games, 1975
Most bases on balls, career
1,210—Pete Rose
Most strikeouts
142—Lee May, 158 games, 1969
Most strikeouts, career
1,306—Tony Perez
Fewest strikeouts
13—Frank McCormick, 154 games, 1941
Most hit by pitch
20—Frank Robinson, 152 games, 1956
Most runs batted in
149—George Foster, 158 games, 1977
Most runs batted in, career
1,376—Johnny Bench

Most game-winning RBIs
21—Eric Davis, 135 games, 1988
Highest batting average
.383—Bug Holliday, 122 games, 1894
Highest batting average (since 1900)
.377—Cy Seymour, 149 games, 1905
Highest batting average, career
.331—Edd Roush
Highest slugging average
.642—Ted Kluszewski, 149 games, 1954
Longest batting streak
44 games—Pete Rose, 1978
Most grounded into double play
30—Ernie Lombardi, 129 games, 1938
Fewest grounded into double play
3—Billy Myers, 151 games, 1939

BASERUNNING

Most stolen bases
93—Arlie Latham, 135 games, 1891
Most stolen bases (since 1900)
81—Bob Bescher, 153 games, 1911
Most stolen bases, career
406—Joe Morgan
Most caught stealing
28—Pat Duncan, 151 games, 1922

PITCHING (SINCE 1900)

Most games
90—Wayne Granger, 1969
Most games, career
531—Pedro Borbon
Most games started
42—Noodles Hahn, 1901
Most games started, career
.356—Eppa Rixey
Most complete games
41—Noodles Hahn, 1901
Most complete games, career
195—Bucky Walters
Most games finished
62—Tom Hume, 1980
Most innings
375—Noodles Hahn, 1901
Most innings, career
2,890—Eppa Rixey
Most games won
27—Dolf Luque, 1923
Bucky Walters, 1939
Most games won, career
179—Eppa Rixey
Most 20-victory seasons
4—Paul Derringer
Most games lost
25—Paul Derringer, 1933
Most games lost, career
150—Paul Derringer
Highest winning percentage
.826—Elmer Riddle (19-4), 1941
Longest winning streak
16 games—Ewell Blackwell, 1947
Longest losing streak
12 games—Henry Thielman, 1902
Pete Schneider, 1914
Si Johnson, 1933
Most saves
39—John Franco, 1988
Most bases on balls
162—Johnny Vander Meer, 1943
Most bases on balls, career
1,072—Johnny Vander Meer
Most strikeouts
274—Mario Soto, 1982
Most strikeouts, game
18—Jim Maloney, June 14, 1965, 11 innings
16—Noodles Hahn, May 22, 1901

Jim Maloney, May 21, 1963
Most strikeouts, career
1,592—Jim Maloney
Most shutouts
7—Jake Weimer, 1906
Fred Toney, 1917
Hod Eller, 1919
Jack Billingham, 1973
Most shutouts, career
32—Bucky Walters
Most 1-0 shutouts won
4—Jake Weimer, 1906
Most runs
158—Noodles Hahn, 1901
Most earned runs
145—Herm Wehmeier, 1950

Most hits
368—Noodles Hahn, 1901
Most hits batsmen
23—Jake Weimer, 1907
Most wild pitches
19—Jim Maloney, 1963
Jim Maloney, 1965
Most home runs
36—Tom Browning, 1988
Most sacrifice hits
17—Joey Jay, 1962
Bruce Berenyi, 1982
Most sacrifice flies
13—Bill Gullickson, 1986
Lowest ERA
1.57—Fred Toney, 223 innings, 1915

CLUB RECORDS

Most players
51 in 1993
Fewest players
21 in 1904
Most games
163 in 1964, 1968, 1969, 1974, 1980
Most at-bats
5,767 in 1968
Most runs
857 in 1976
Fewest runs
488 in 1908
Most opponents' runs
857 in 1930
Most hits
1,599 in 1976
Fewest hits
1,108 in 1908
Most singles
1,191 in 1922
Most doubles
284 in 1990
Most triples
120 in 1926
Most homers
221 in 1956
Fewest homers (154 or 162-game schedule)
14 in 1908, 1916
Most homers at Crosley Field, home and opponents
219 in 1957
Most homers at Riverfront Stadium, home and opponents
191 in 1987
Most grand slams
7 in 1974, 1980, 1987
Most pinch home runs
12 in 1957
Most long hits
512 in 1965
Most extra bases on long hits
939 in 1965
Most total bases
2,483 in 1965
Most sacrifices (sacrifice hits and sacrifice flies)
239 in 1926
Most sacrifice hits
195 in 1907
Most sacrifice flies
66 in 1993
Most stolen bases
310 in 1910
Most caught stealing
136 in 1922
Most bases on balls
693 in 1974
Most strikeouts
1,042 in 1969

Fewest strikeouts
308 in 1921
Most hit by pitch
51 in 1956
Fewest hit by pitch
11 in 1951
Most runs batted in
802 in 1976
Most game-winning RBIs
84 in 1980, 1985
Highest batting average
.296 in 1922
Lowest batting average
.227 in 1908
Highest slugging average
.441 in 1956
Lowest slugging average
.304 in 1906
Most grounded into double play
143 in 1982
Fewest grounded into double play
93 in 1935
Most left on bases
1,328 in 1976
Fewest left on bases
997 in 1921
Most .300 hitters
8 in 1926
Most putouts
4,471 in 1968
Fewest putouts
4,006 in 1930
Most assists
2,151 in 1905
Fewest assists
1,534 in 1966
Most chances accepted
6,399 in 1915
Fewest chances accepted
5,655 in 1950
Most errors
314 in 1914
Fewest errors
95 in 1977
Most errorless games
99 in 1992
Most consecutive errorless games
15 in 1975
Most double plays
194 in 1928, 1931, 1954
Fewest double plays
108 in 1989
Most passed balls
39 in 1914
Fewest passed balls
3 in 1975

Highest fielding average
.984 in 1971, 1975, 1976, 1977, 1992
Lowest fielding average
.952 in 1914
Highest home attendance
2,629,708 in 1976
Highest road attendance
2,532,257 in 1993
Most games won
108 in 1975
Most games lost
101 in 1982
Most games won, month
24 in August 1918, July 1973
Most games lost, month
26 in September 1914
Highest percentage games won
.686 in 1919 (won 96, lost 44)
Lowest percentage games won
.138 in 1876 (won 9, lost 56)
Lowest percentage games won (since 1900)
.344 in 1934 (won 52, lost 99)
Games won, league (since 1890)
8,109 in 105 years
Games lost, league (since 1890)
7,905 in 105 years
Most shutouts won
23 in 1919
Most shutouts lost
24 in 1908
Most 1-0 games won
7 in 1910, 1943, 1963
Most 1-0 games lost
7 in 1907, 1916
Most consecutive games won
14 in 1899
Most consecutive games won (since 1900)
12 in 1939, 1957
Most consecutive games lost
19 in 1914
Number of times league champions
9
Number of last-place finishes
11 (tied in 1916)
Most runs, game
30 vs. Louisville, June 18, 1893

Most runs, game (since 1900)
26 vs. Boston, June 4, 1911
Most runs by opponent, game
26 by Philadelphia, July 26, 1892
Most runs by opponent, game (since 1900)
25 by New York, June 9, 1901
by Brooklyn, September 23, 1901
Most runs, shutout game
18 vs. Los Angeles, August 8, 1965
Most runs by opponent, shutout game
18 by Philadelphia, August 10, 1930, first game
by Philadelphia, July 14, 1934, first game
by St. Louis, June 10, 1944
Most runs, doubleheader shutout
14 vs. St. Louis, September 1, 1924
vs. Los Angeles, August 16, 1961
Most runs, inning
14 vs. Louisville, June 18, 1893, first inning
vs. Houston, August 3, 1989, first inning
Longest 1-0 game won
15 innings vs. New York, July 16, 1933, first game
vs. Brooklyn, June 11, 1915
Longest 1-0 game lost
21 innings vs. San Francisco, September 1, 1967
Most hits, game
32 vs. Louisville, June 18, 1893
Most hits, game (since 1900)
28 vs. Philadelphia, May 13, 1902
Most home runs, game
8 vs. Milwaukee, August 18, 1956
Most consecutive games with one or more homers
21 (41 homers), 1956
Most total bases, game
55 vs. Louisville, June 18, 1893
Most total bases, game (since 1900)
48 vs. Chicago, June 1, 1957
Largest crowd, day game
55,438 vs. St. Louis, April 4, 1988
Largest crowd, doubleheader
53,328 vs. Pittsburgh, July 9, 1976
Largest crowd, night game
53,790 vs. Houston, September 17, 1983
Largest crowd, home opener
55,456 vs. Montreal, April 5, 1993

COLORADO ROCKIES

YEARLY FINISHES

WEST DIVISION

Year	Position	W	L	Pct.	*GB	Manager	Attendance
1993 —6th		67	95	.414	37	Don Baylor	4,483,350
1994 —3rd		53	64	.453	6½	Don Baylor	3,281,511

*Games behind winner.

INDIVIDUAL RECORDS (1993 TO DATE)

SERVICE

Most years by non-pitcher
2—Held by many players
Most years by pitcher
2—held by many pitchers

BATTING

Most games
157—Charlie Hayes, 1993
Most games, career
270—Charlie Hayes
Most at-bats
573—Charlie Hayes, 157 games, 1993
Most at-bats, career
1,022—Dante Bichette
Most runs
93—Dante Bichette, 1993, 141 games, 1993

Most runs, career
167—Dante Bichette
Most hits
175—Charlie Hayes, 157 games, 1993
Most hits, career
314—Dante Bichette
Most singles
113—Andres Galarraga, 120 games, 1993
Most singles, career
194—Andres Galarraga
Most doubles
45—Charlie Hayes, 157 games, 1993
Most doubles, career
76—Dante Bichette
Most triples
8—Eric Young, 144 games, 1993
Mike Kingery, 105 games, 1994

— 300 —

Most triples, career
9—Eric Young
Most homers by righthander
31—Andres Galarraga, 103 games, 1994
Most homers by lefthander
14—Daryl Boston, 124 games, 1993
Most homers by rookie
9—Vinny Castilla, 105 games, 1993
Most homers at home
17—Charlie Hayes, 1993
Most homers on road
15—Andres Galarraga, 1994
Most homers, month
9—Dante Bichette, April 1994
Ellis Burks, April 1994
Andres Galarraga, April, May, June, 1994
Most homers by righthander, career
53—Andres Galarraga
Most homers by lefthander, career
14—Daryl Boston
Most grand slams
2—Dante Bichette, 1994
Andres Galarraga, 1994
Most grand slams, career
2—Dante Bichette
Andres Galarraga
Most total bases
299—Charlie Hayes, 157 games, 1993
Most total bases, career
548—Dante Bichette
Most long hits
72—Charlie Hayes, 157 games, 1993
Most long hits, career
131—Dante Bichette
Most extra bases on long hits
124—Charlie Hayes, 157 games, 1993
Most extra bases on long hits, career
234—Dante Bichette
Most sacrifice hits
12—Joe Girardi, 86 games, 1993
Most sacrifice flies
8—Dante Bichette, 141 games, 1993
Charlie Hayes, 157 games, 1993
Mike Kingery, 105 games, 1994
Most bases on balls
63—Eric Young, 144 games, 1993
Most bases on balls, career
101—Eric Young
Most strikeouts
99—Dante Bichette, 141 games, 1993
Most strikeouts, career
169—Dante Bichette
Fewest strikeouts
41—Eric Young, 144 games, 1993
Most hit by pitch
10—Jerald Clark, 140 games, 1993
Most runs batted in
98—Andres Galarraga, 120 games, 1993
Charlie Hayes, 157 games, 1993
Most runs batted in, career
184—Dante Bichette
Highest batting average
.370—Andres Galarraga, 120 games, 1993
Highest slugging average
.602—Andres Galarraga, 120 games, 1993
Longest batting streak
16—Dante Bichette, 1994
Most grounded into double play
25—Charlie Hayes, 157 games, 1993
Fewest grounded into double play
25—Charlie Hayes, 157 games, 1993

BASERUNNING

Most stolen bases
42—Eric Young, 144 games, 1993
Most sacrifice hits
12—Greg Harris, 1994

Armando Reynoso, 1993
Lowest ERA
4.00—Armando Reynoso, 1993
Most sacrifice flies
8—Willie Blair, 1993
Most stolen bases, career
60—Eric Young
Most caught stealing
19—Eric Young, 144 games, 1993

PITCHING

Most games
65—Gary Wayne, 1993
Most games
125—Steve Reed
Most games started
30—Armando Reynoso, 1993
Most games started, career
39—Armando Reynoso
Most complete games
4—Armando Reynoso, 1993
Most complete games, career
5—Armando Reynoso
Most games finished
51—Darren Holmes, 1993
Most innings
189—Armando Reynoso, 1993
Most innings, career
241⅓—Armando Reynoso
Most games won
12—Armando Reynoso, 1993
Most games won, career
15—Armando Reynoso
Most games lost
12—Greg Harris, 1994
Most games lost, career
20—Greg Harris
Highest winning percentage
No pitcher with 15 victories
Longest winning streak
4 games—Steve Reed, 1993
Marvin Freeman, 1994
Longest losing streak
8 games—Greg Harris, 1994
Most saves
25—Darren Holmes, 1993
Most bases on balls
69—Bruce Ruffin, 1993
Most bases on balls, career
99—Bruce Ruffin
Most strikeouts
126—Bruce Ruffin, 1993
Most strikeouts, career
191—Bruce Ruffin
Most strikeouts, game
9—Bruce Ruffin, September 14, 1993
Most shutouts won
1—David Nied, 1994
Most shutouts won, career
1—David Nied
Most 1-0 shutouts won
Never occurred
Most runs
101—Armando Reynoso, 1993
Most earned runs
96—Greg Harris, 1994
Most hits
206—Armando Reynoso, 1993
Most hit batsmen
9—Armando Reynoso, 1993
Most wild pitches
11—Jeff Parrett, 1993
Most home runs allowed
22—Armando Reynoso, 1993
Greg Harris, 1994

Most players
46 in 1993
Fewest players
46 in 1993
Most games
162 in 1993
Most at-bats
5,517 in 1993
Most runs
758 in 1993
Fewest runs
758 in 1993
Most opponents' runs
967 in 1993
Most hits
1,507 in 1993
Fewest hits
1,507 in 1993
Most singles
1,028 in 1993
Most doubles
278 in 1993
Most triples
59 in 1993
Most homers
142 in 1993
Fewest homers
142 in 1993
Most homers at Mile High Stadium, home and opponents
184 in 1993
Most grand slams
5 in 1994
Most pinch home runs
6 in 1994
Most total bases
2,329 in 1993
Most long hits
479 in 1993
Most extra bases on long hits
822 in 1993
Most sacrifice hits
70 in 1993
Most sacrifice flies
52 in 1993
Most stolen bases
146 in 1993
Most caught stealing
90 in 1993
Most bases on balls
388 in 1993
Most strikeouts
944 in 1993
Fewest strikeouts
944 in 1993
Most hit by pitch
46 in 1993
Most runs batted in
704 in 1993
Highest batting average
.273 in 1993
Lowest batting average
.273 in 1993
Highest slugging average
.422 in 1993
Lowest slugging average
.422 in 1993
Most grounded into double play
125 in 1993
Fewest grounded into double play
125 in 1993
Most left on bases
978 in 1993
Fewest left on bases
978 in 1993

Most .300 hitters
3 in 1993
Most putouts
4,294 in 1993
Fewest putouts
4,294 in 1993
Most assists
1,760 in 1993
Fewest assists
1,760 in 1993
Most chances accepted
6,054 in 1993
Fewest chances accepted
6,054 in 1993
Most errors
167 in 1993
Most errorless games
64 in 1993
Most consecutive errorless games
6 in 1994
Fewest errors
167 in 1993
Most double plays
149 in 1993
Fewest double plays
149 in 1993
Most passed balls
11 in 1993
Fewest passed balls
11 in 1993
Highest fielding average
.973 in 1993
Lowest fielding average
.973 in 1993
Highest home attendance
4,483,350 in 1993
Highest road attendance
2,695,071 in 1993
Most games won
67 in 1993
Most games lost
95 in 1993
Most games won, month
17 in September 1993
Most games lost, month
22 in May 1993
Games won, league
120 in 2 years
Games lost, league
159 in 2 years
Highest percentage games won
.414 in 1993 (won 67, lost 95)
Most shutouts won
5 in 1994
Most shutouts lost
13 in 1993
Most 1-0 games won
2 in 1994
Most 1-0 games lost
1 in 1993
Most consecutive games won
6 in 1993
Most consecutive games lost
13 in 1993
Number of times league champions
0
Number of last-place finishes
0
Most runs, game
17 vs. San Diego, June 19, 1993
Most runs by opponent, game
19 by Montreal, April 11, 1993
Most runs, shutout game
8 vs. Houston, June 21, 1994

Most runs by opponent, shutout game
13 by Atlanta, August 11, 1994
Most runs, inning
8 vs. San Diego, June 19, 1993, third inning
vs. Cincinnati, June 23, 1993, seventh inning
Longest 1-0 game won
9 innings vs. San Diego, May 8, 1994
Longest 1-0 game lost
9 innings vs. Chicago, July 15, 1993
Most hits, game
20 vs. Houston, June 12, 1993
vs. Houston, June 22, 1994
Most home runs, game
5 vs. San Francisco, May 9, 1994

Most consecutive games with one or more homers
17 (24 home runs), 1993
Most total bases, game
34 vs. Florida, April 20, 1994
vs. St. Louis, May 3, 1994
vs. Houston, June 22, 1994
Largest crowd, day game
80,227 vs. Montreal, April 9, 1993
Largest crowd, doubleheader
60,613 vs. New York, August 21, 1993
Largest crowd, night game
73,957 vs. San Francisco, June 24, 1994
Largest crowd, home opener
80,227 vs. Montreal, April 9, 1993

FLORIDA MARLINS

YEARLY FINISHES

EAST DIVISION

Year	Position	W	L	Pct.	*GB	Manager	Attendance
1993 —6th	....	64	98	.395	33	Rene Lachemann	3,064,847
1994 —5th	....	51	64	.443	23½	Rene Lachemann	1,937,467

*Games behind winner.

INDIVIDUAL RECORDS (1993 TO DATE)

SERVICE

Most years by non-pitcher
2—held by many players
Most years by pitcher
2—held by many pitchers

BATTING

Most games
162—Jeff Conine, 1993
Most games, career
277—Jeff Conine
Most at-bats
595—Jeff Conine, 162 games, 1993
Most at-bats, career
1,046—Jeff Conine
Most runs
75—Chuck Carr, 142 games, 1993
Jeff Conine, 162 games, 1993
Most runs, career
136—Chuck Carr
Most hits
174—Jeff Conine, 162 games, 1993
Most hits, career
318—Jeff Conine
Most singles
135—Jeff Conine, 162 games, 1993
Most singles, career
228—Jeff Conine
Most doubles
27—Jeff Conine, 115 games, 1994
Most doubles, career
51—Jeff Conine
Most triples
6—Benito Santiago, 139 games, 1993
Jeff Conine, 115 games, 1994
Most triples, career
9—Jeff Conine
Most homers by righthander
27—Gary Sheffield, 87 games, 1994
Most homers by lefthander
4—Dave Magadan, 66 games, 1993
Darrell Whitmore, 76 games, 1993
Most homers by switch-hitter
20—Orestes Destrade, 153 games, 1993
Most homers by rookie
12—Jeff Conine, 162 games, 1993

Most homers at home
15—Gary Sheffield, 1994
Most homers on road
12—Gary Sheffield, 1994
Most homers, month
10—Gary Sheffield, April 1994
Most homers by righthander, career
30—Jeff Conine
Most homers by lefthander, career
4—Dave Magadan
Most homers by switch-hitter, career
25—Orestes Destrade
Most grand slams
2—Jeff Conine, 162 games, 1993
Kurt Abbott, 101 games, 1994
Most grand slams, career
2—Kurt Abbott
Jeff Conine
Most total bases
240—Jeff Conine, 162 games, 1993
Most total bases, career
477—Jeff Conine
Most long hits
51—Jeff Conine, 115 games, 1994
Most long hits, career
90—Jeff Conine
Most extra bases on long hits
99—Gary Sheffield, 87 games, 1994
Most extra bases on long hits, career
159—Jeff Conine
Most sacrifice hits
7—Chuck Carr, 142 games, 1993
Most sacrifice flies
6—Jeff Conine, 162 games, 1993
Orestes Destrade, 153 games, 1993
Most bases on balls
79—Walt Weiss, 158 games, 1993
Most bases on balls, career
92—Jeff Conine
Most strikeouts
135—Jeff Conine, 162 games, 1993
Most strikeouts, career
227—Jeff Conine
Fewest strikeouts
73—Walt Weiss, 158 games, 1993
Most hit by pitch
9—Bret Barberie, 107 games, 1994

Most runs batted in
 87—Orestes Destrade, 153 games, 1993
Most runs batted in, career
 161—Jeff Conine
Highest batting average
 .292—Jeff Conine, 162 games, 1993
Highest slugging average
 .406—Orestes Destrade, 153 games, 1993
Longest batting streak
 15—Chuck Carr, 1993
  Bret Barberie, 1993
Most grounded into double play
 17—Orestes Destrade, 153 games, 1993
Fewest grounded into double play
 5—Walt Weiss, 158 games, 1993

BASERUNNING

Most stolen bases
 58—Chuck Carr, 142 games, 1993
Most stolen bases, career
 90—Chuck Carr
Most caught stealing
 22—Chuck Carr, 142 games, 1993

PITCHING

Most games
 59—Bryan Harvey, 1993
  Joe Klink, 1993
Most games, career
 102—Richie Lewis
Most games started
 34—Charlie Hough, 1993
Most games started
 55—Charlie Hough
Most complete games
 2—Ryan Bowen, 1993
  Pat Rapp, 1994
Most complete games, career
 3—Ryan Bowen
  Pat Rapp
Most games finished
 54—Bryan Harvey, 1993
Most innings
 204⅓—Charlie Hough, 1993
Most innings, career
 318—Charlie Hough
Most games won
 11—Chris Hammond, 1993
Most games won, career
 15—Chris Hammond

Most games lost
 17—Jack Armstrong, 1993
Most games lost, career
 25—Charlie Hough
Highest winning percentage
 No pitcher with 15 victories
Longest winning streak
 8—Chris Hammond, 1993
Longest losing streak
 7—Chris Hammond, 1993
Most saves
 45—Bryan Harvey, 1993
Most bases on balls
 87—Ryan Bowen, 1993
Most bases on balls, career
 123—Ryan Bowen
Most strikeouts
 126—Charlie Hough, 1993
Most strikeouts, career
 191—Charlie Hough
Most strikeouts, game
 10—Jack Armstrong, April 11, 1993
  Mark Gardner, June 26, 1994
Most shutouts won
 1—Ryan Bowen, 1993
  Chris Hammond, 1994
  Charlie Hough, 1994
  Pat Rapp, 1994
Most shutouts won, career
 1—held by many pitchers
Most 1 - 0 shutouts won
 Never occurred
Most runs
 109—Charlie Hough, 1993
Most earned runs
 99—Chris Hammond, 1993
Most hits
 210—Jack Armstrong, 1993
Most hit batsmen
 10—Charlie Hough, 1994
Most wild pitches
 11—Charlie Hough, 1993
Most home runs allowed
 29—Jack Armstrong, 1993
Most sacrifice hits
 14—Charlie Hough, 1994
Most sacrifice flies
 10—Jack Armstrong, 1993
Lowest ERA
 4.27—Charlie Hough, 204⅓ innings, 1993

CLUB RECORDS

Most players
 43 in 1993
Fewest players
 43 in 1993
Most games
 162 in 1993
Most at - bats
 5,475 in 1993
Most runs
 581 in 1993
Fewest runs
 581 in 1993
Most opponents' runs
 724 in 1993
Most hits
 1,356 in 1993
Fewest hits
 1,356 in 1993
Most singles
 1,034 in 1993
Most doubles
 197 in 1993

Most triples
 31 in 1993
Most homers
 94 in 1993, 1994
Fewest homers
 94 in 1993
Most homers at Joe Robbie Stadium, home and opponents
 116 in 1993, 1994
Most grand slams
 4 in 1993
Most pinch home runs
 1 in 1994
Most total bases
 1,897 in 1993
Most long hits
 322 in 1993
Most extra bases on long hits
 541 in 1993
Most sacrifice hits
 58 in 1993
Most sacrifice flies
 43 in 1993

Most stolen bases
117 in 1993
Most caught stealing
56 in 1993
Most bases on balls
498 in 1993
Most strikeouts
1,054 in 1993
Fewest strikeouts
1,054 in 1993
Most hit by pitch
51 in 1993
Most runs batted in
542 in 1993
Highest batting average
.248 in 1993
Lowest batting average
.248 in 1993
Highest slugging average
.346 in 1993
Lowest slugging average
.346 in 1993
Most grounded into double play
122 in 1993
Fewest grounded into double play
122 in 1993
Most left on bases
1,183 in 1993
Fewest left on bases
1,183 in 1993
Most .300 hitters
None
Most putouts
4,321 in 1993
Fewest putouts
4,321 in 1993
Most assists
1,703 in 1993
Fewest assists
1,703 in 1993
Most chances accepted
6,024 in 1993
Fewest chances accepted
6,024 in 1993
Most errors
125 in 1993
Most errorless games
125 in 1993
Most consecutive errorless games
8 in 1994
Fewest errors
125 in 1993
Most double plays
130 in 1993
Fewest double plays
130 in 1993
Most passed balls
29 in 1993
Fewest passed balls
29 in 1993
Highest fielding average
.980 in 1993
Lowest fielding average
.980 in 1993
Highest home attendance
3,064,847 in 1993
Highest road attendance
2,701,068 in 1993

Most games won
64 in 1993
Most games lost
98 in 1993
Most games won, month
13 in June 1993
Most games lost, month
19 in September 1993
Games won, league
115 in 2 years
Games lost, league
162 in 2 years
Highest percentage games won
.395 in 1993 (won 64, lost 98)
Lowest percentage games won
.395 in 1993 (won 64, lost 98)
Most shutouts won
7 in 1994
Most shutouts lost
14 in 1993
Most 1 - 0 games won
2 in 1994
Most 1 - 0 games lost
4 in 1993
Most consecutive games won
5 in 1994
Most consecutive games lost
7 in 1993, 1994
Number of times league champions
0
Number of last - place finishes
0
Most runs, game
15 vs. San Diego, April 9, 1994
Most runs by opponent, game
16 by St. Louis, August 5, 1993
Most runs, shutout game
8 vs. St. Louis, May 15, 1993
Most runs by opponent, shutout game
10 by Pittsburgh, September 16, 1993
Most runs, inning
8 vs. Colorado, April 25, 1993, fourth inning
vs. San Diego, April 9, 1994, seventh inning
Longest 1 - 0 game won
9 innings vs. St. Louis, August 3, 1993
vs. Los Angeles, April 9, 1994
vs. Pittsburgh, May 10, 1994
Longest 1 - 0 game lost
9 innings vs. New York, May 10, 1993
vs. St. Louis, May 16, 1993
vs. Los Angeles, September 12, 1993
Most hits, game
22 vs. St. Louis, June 15, 1994
Most home runs, game
3 many times
Most consecutive games with one or more homers
6 (twice) in 1993 (7 homers each time)
Most total bases, game
36 vs. St. Louis, June 15, 1994
Largest crowd, day game
45,900 vs. New York, October 3, 1993
Largest crowd, doubleheader
35,019 vs. San Francisco, June 1, 1993
Largest crowd, night game
45,796 vs. San Francisco, August 27, 1993
Largest crowd, home opener
43,290 vs. Houston, April 12, 1994

YEARLY FINISHES

(Known as Houston Colt .45s through 1964)

Year	Position	W	L	Pct.	*GB	Manager	Attendance
1962 — 8th		64	96	.400	36 ½	Harry Craft	924,456
1963 — 9th		66	96	.407	33	Harry Craft	719,502
1964 — 9th		66	96	.407	27	Harry Craft, Luman Harris	725,773
1965 — 9th		65	97	.401	32	Luman Harris	2,151,470
1966 — 8th		72	90	.444	23	Grady Hatton	1,872,108
1967 — 9th		69	93	.426	32 ½	Grady Hatton	1,348,303
1968 — 10th		72	90	.444	25	Grady Hatton, Harry Walker	1,312,887

WEST DIVISION

Year	Position	W	L	Pct.	*GB	Manager	Attendance
1969 — 5th		81	81	.500	12	Harry Walker	1,442,995
1970 — 4th		79	83	.488	23	Harry Walker	1,253,444
1971 — 4th (tied)		79	83	.488	11	Harry Walker	1,261,589
1972 — 2nd		84	69	.549	10 ½	Harry Walker, Leo Durocher, Salty Parker	1,469,247
1973 — 4th		82	80	.506	17	Leo Durocher, Preston Gomez	1,394,004
1974 — 4th		81	81	.500	21	Preston Gomez	1,090,728
1975 — 6th		64	97	.398	43 ½	Preston Gomez, Bill Virdon	858,002
1976 — 3rd		80	82	.494	22	Bill Virdon	886,146
1977 — 3rd		81	81	.500	17	Bill Virdon	1,109,560
1978 — 5th		74	88	.457	21	Bill Virdon	1,126,145
1979 — 2nd		89	73	.549	1 ½	Bill Virdon	1,900,312
1980 — 1st†‡		93	70	.571	+ 1	Bill Virdon	2,278,217
1981 — 3rd/1st		61	49	.555	§	Bill Virdon	1,321,282
1982 — 5th		77	85	.475	12	Bill Virdon, Bob Lillis	1,558,555
1983 — 3rd		85	77	.525	6	Bob Lillis	1,351,962
1984 — 2nd (tied)		80	82	.494	12	Bob Lillis	1,229,862
1985 — 3rd (tied)		83	79	.512	12	Bob Lillis	1,184,314
1986 — 1st‡		96	66	.593	+10	Hal Lanier	1,734,276
1987 — 3rd		76	86	.469	14	Hal Lanier	1,909,902
1988 — 5th		82	80	.506	12 ½	Hal Lanier	1,933,505
1989 — 3rd		86	76	.531	6	Art Howe	1,834,908
1990 — 4th (tied)		75	87	.463	16	Art Howe	1,310,927
1991 — 6th		65	97	.401	29	Art Howe	1,196,152
1992 — 4th		81	81	.500	17	Art Howe	1,211,412
1993 — 3rd		85	77	.525	19	Art Howe	2,084,546

CENTRAL DIVISION

Year	Position	W	L	Pct.	*GB	Manager	Attendance
1994 — 2nd		66	49	.574	½	Art Howe	1,561,136

*Games behind winner. †Won division playoff. ‡Lost Championship Series. §First half 28-29; second 33-20.

INDIVIDUAL RECORDS (1962 TO DATE)

SERVICE

Most years by non-pitcher
14—Bob Watson, Terry Puhl
Most years by pitcher
13—Larry Dierker

BATTING

Most games
162—Enos Cabell, 1978
Bill Doran, 1987
Jeff Bagwell, 1992
Craig Biggio, 1992
Steve Finley, 1992
Most games, career
1,870—Jose Cruz
Most at-bats
660—Enos Cabell, 162 games, 1978
Most at-bats, career
6,629—Jose Cruz
Most runs
117—Jimmy Wynn, 145 games, 1972
Most runs, career
890—Cesar Cedeno
Most hits
195—Enos Cabell, 162 games, 1978

Most hits, career
1937—Jose Cruz
Most singles
160—Sonny Jackson, 150 games, 1966
Most singles, career
1,384—Jose Cruz
Most doubles
44—Rusty Staub, 149 games, 1967
Craig Biggio, 114 games, 1994
Most doubles, career
343—Cesar Cedeno
Most triples
14—Roger Metzger, 154 games, 1973
Most triples, career
80—Jose Cruz
Most homers by righthander
39—Jeff Bagwell, 110 games, 1994
Most homers by lefthander
23—Franklin Stubbs, 146 games, 1990
Most homers by switch-hitter
20—Kevin Bass, 1986
Most homers by rookie
20—Glenn Davis, 100 games, 1985
Most homers at home
23—Jeff Bagwell, 1994
Most homers on road
22—Jimmy Wynn, 1967

Most homers, month
13—Jeff Bagwell, June 1994
Most homers by righthander, career
223—Jimmy Wynn
Most homers by lefthander, career
138—Jose Cruz
Most grand slams
2—Held by many players
Most grand slams, career
6—Bob Aspromonte
Most total bases
300—Cesar Cedeno, 139 games, 1972
Jeff Bagwell, 110 games, 1994
Most total bases, career
2,846—Jose Cruz
Most long hits
73—Jeff Bagwell, 110 games, 1994
Most long hits, career
561—Cesar Cedeno
Most extra bases on long hits
153—Jeff Bagwell, 110 games, 1994
Most extra bases on long hits, career
961—Jimmy Wynn
Most sacrifice hits
34—Craig Reynolds, 146 games, 1979
Most sacrifice flies
13—Ray Knight, 158 games, 1982
Jeff Bagwell, 162 games, 1992
Most bases on balls
148—Jimmy Wynn, 149 games, 1969
Most bases on balls, career
847—Jimmy Wynn
Most strikeouts
145—Lee May, 148 games, 1972
Most strikeouts, career
1,088—Jimmy Wynn
Fewest strikeouts
39—Greg Gross, 156 games, 1974
Most hit by pitch
13—Jeff Bagwell, 156 games, 1991
Most runs batted in
116—Jeff Bagwell, 110 games, 1994
Most runs batted in, career
942—Jose Cruz
Most game-winning RBIs
18—Dickie Thon, 154 games, 1983
Highest batting average
.333—Rusty Staub, 149 games, 1967
Highest batting average, career
.297—Bob Watson
Highest slugging average
.537—Cesar Cedeno, 139 games, 1972, 1973
Highest slugging average, career
.454—Cesar Cedeno
Longest batting streak
23 games—Art Howe, 1981
Most grounded into double play
23—Doug Rader, 156 games, 1970
Fewest grounded into double play
4—Joe Morgan, 157 games, 1965
Joe Morgan, 160 games, 1971
Jose Cruz, 160 games, 1983
Phil Garner, 154 games, 1983

BASERUNNING

Most stolen bases
65—Gerald Young, 149 games, 1988
Most stolen bases, career
487—Cesar Cedeno
Most caught stealing
27—Gerald Young, 149 games, 1988

PITCHING

Most games
82—Juan Agosto, 1990

Most games, career
563—Dave Smith
Most games started
40—Jerry Reuss, 1973
Most games started, career
320—Larry Dierker
Most complete games
20—Larry Dierker, 1969
Most complete games, career
106—Larry Dierker
Most games finished
70—Doug Jones, 1992
Most innings
305—Larry Dierker, 1969
Most innings, career
2,296—Larry Dierker
Most games won
21—Joe Niekro, 1979
Most games won, career
144—Joe Niekro
Most 20-victory seasons
2—Joe Niekro
Most games lost, season
20—Dick Farrell, 1962
Most games lost, career
117—Larry Dierker
Highest winning percentage
.818—Mark Portugal (18-4), 1993
Longest winning streak
12—Mark Portugal, 1993
Longest losing streak
11 games—Dick Drott, 1963
Most saves
36—Doug Jones, 1992
Most bases on balls
151—J.R. Richard, 1976
Most bases on balls, career
818—Joe Niekro
Most strikeouts
313—J.R. Richard, 1979
Most strikeouts, career
1,866—Nolan Ryan
Most strikeouts, game
18—Don Wilson, July 14, 1968, second game
Most shutouts
6—Dave A. Roberts, 1973
Most shutouts won, career
25—Larry Dierker
Most 1-0 shutouts won
3—Bob Bruce, 1964
Bob Knepper, 1981
Most runs
124—Larry Dierker, 1970
Most earned runs
116—Larry Dierker, 1970
Jerry Reuss, 1973
Most hits
271—Jerry Reuss, 1973
Most hit batsmen
16—Jack Billingham, 1971
Most wild pitches
21—Joe Niekro, 1985
Most home runs
31—Larry Dierker, 1970
Most sacrifice hits
22—Bob Knepper, 1986
Most sacrifice flies
13—Mark Lemongello, 1978
Jim Deshaies, 1988
Lowest ERA
2.21—Danny Darwin, 162⅔ innings, 1990

CLUB RECORDS

Most players
48 in 1965
Fewest players
32 in 1972
Most games
163 in 1966, 1980
Most at-bats
5,582 in 1985
Most runs
744 in 1970
Fewest runs
464 in 1963
Most opponents' runs
763 in 1970
Most hits
1,465 in 1984
Fewest hits
1,184 in 1963
Most singles
1,097 in 1984
Most doubles
288 in 1993
Most triples
67 in 1980, 1984
Most homers
138 in 1993
Fewest homers
49 in 1979
Most homers at Colt Stadium, home and opponents
85 in 1962
Most homers at Astrodome, home and opponents
118 in 1993
Most grand slams
6 in 1989
Most pinch home runs
7 in 1974, 1986
Most total bases
2,235 in 1993
Most long hits
463 in 1993
Most extra bases on long hits
776 in 1993
Most sacrifice hits
109 in 1979
Most sacrifice flies
55 in 1984
Most stolen bases
198 in 1988
Most caught stealing
95 in 1979, 1983
Most bases on balls
699 in 1969
Most strikeouts
1,027 in 1991
Fewest strikeouts
719 in 1976
Most hit by pitch
49 in 1964
Fewest hit by pitch
13 in 1980
Most runs batted in
694 in 1970
Most game-winning RBIs
90 in 1986
Highest batting average
.267 in 1993
Lowest batting average
.220 in 1963
Most .300 hitters
3 in 1970
Highest slugging average
.409 in 1993
Lowest slugging average
.301 in 1963

Most grounded into double play
144 in 1970
Fewest grounded into double play
76 in 1983
Most left on bases
1,212 in 1969
Fewest left on bases
1,040 in 1964
Most putouts
4,448 in 1980
Fewest putouts
4,284 in 1964
Most assists
1,880 in 1975
Fewest assists
1,565 in 1986
Most chances accepted
6,255 in 1975
Fewest chances accepted
5,827 in 1972
Most errors
174 in 1966
Fewest errors
106 in 1971
Most errorless games
85 in 1973, 1974
Most consecutive errorless games
11 in 1973, 1994
Most double plays
166 in 1975
Fewest double plays
100 in 1963
Most passed balls
38 in 1984
Fewest passed balls
7 in 1993
Highest fielding average
.983 in 1971
Lowest fielding average
.972 in 1966
Highest home attendance
2,278,217 in 1980
Highest road attendance
2,421,566 in 1993
Most games won
96 in 1986
Most games lost
97 in 1965, 1975, 1991
Most games won, month
20 in May 1969, July 1976, June 1979
Most games lost, month
24 in July 1962
Highest percentage games won
.593 in 1986 (won 96, lost 66)
Lowest percentage games won
.398 in 1975 (won 64, lost 97)
Games won, league
2,539 in 33 years
Games lost, league
2,697 in 33 years
Most shutouts won
19 in 1979, 1981, 1986
Most shutouts lost
23 in 1963
Most 1-0 games won
9 in 1976
Most 1-0 games lost
6 in 1964, 1969
Most consecutive games won
10 in 1965, 1969 (twice), 1980, 1989
Most consecutive games lost
10 in 1963, 1967 (twice), 1974
Number of times league champions
0

Number of last-place finishes
3
Longest 1-0 game won
24 innings vs. New York, April 15, 1968
Longest 1-0 game lost
13 innings vs. Cincinnati, August 6, 1962
Most runs, inning
12 vs. Philadelphia, May 31, 1975, eighth inning
Most runs, game
18 vs. San Francisco, July 7, 1971
vs. Chicago, April 29, 1974
Most runs by opponent, game
22 by Chicago, June 3, 1987
Most runs, shutout game
13 vs. Cincinnati, June 4, 1983
Most runs by opponent, shutout game
16 by Philadelphia, September 10, 1963
Most runs, doubleheader shutout
No performance
Most hits, game
25 vs. Atlanta, May 30, 1976, second game

vs. Cincinnati, July 2, 1976, first game, 14 innings
Most home runs, game
5 vs. Atlanta, April 12, 1970
vs. San Diego, June 26, 1972
vs. San Diego, June 21, 1973
vs. Cincinnati, September 12, 1977
Most consecutive games with one or more homers
11 (15 homers), 1988
(12 homers), 1993
Most total bases, game
36 vs. Montreal, August 17, 1972
Largest crowd, day game
49,442 vs. Los Angeles, September 5, 1965
Largest crowd, doubleheader
45,115 vs. Atlanta, August 4, 1979
Largest crowd, night game
50,908 vs. Los Angeles, June 22, 1966
Largest crowd, home opener
44,585 vs. Los Angeles, April 6, 1987

LOS ANGELES DODGERS

YEARLY FINISHES

Year	Position	W	L	Pct.	*GB	Manager	Attendance
1958 — 7th		71	83	.461	21	Walter Alston	1,845,556
1959 — 1st†		88	68	.564	+ 2	Walter Alston	2,071,045
1960 — 4th		82	72	.532	13	Walter Alston	2,253,887
1961 — 2nd		89	65	.578	4	Walter Alston	1,804,250
1962 — 2nd‡		102	63	.618	1	Walter Alston	2,755,184
1963 — 1st		99	63	.611	+ 6	Walter Alston	2,538,602
1964 — 6th (tied)		80	82	.494	13	Walter Alston	2,228,751
1965 — 1st		97	65	.599	+ 2	Walter Alston	2,553,577
1966 — 1st		95	67	.586	+ 1½	Walter Alston	2,617,029
1967 — 8th		73	89	.451	28½	Walter Alston	1,664,362
1968 — 7th		76	86	.469	21	Walter Alston	1,581,093

WEST DIVISION

Year	Position	W	L	Pct.	*GB	Manager	Attendance
1969 — 4th		85	77	.525	8	Walter Alston	1,784,527
1970 — 2nd		87	74	.540	14½	Walter Alston	1,697,142
1971 — 2nd		89	73	.549	1	Walter Alston	2,064,594
1972 — 3rd		85	70	.548	10½	Walter Alston	1,860,858
1973 — 2nd		95	66	.590	3½	Walter Alston	2,136,192
1974 — 1st§		102	60	.630	+ 4	Walter Alston	2,632,474
1975 — 2nd		88	74	.543	20	Walter Alston	2,539,349
1976 — 2nd		92	70	.568	10	Walter Alston, Tommy Lasorda	2,386,301
1977 — 1st§		98	64	.605	+10	Tommy Lasorda	2,955,087
1978 — 1st§		95	67	.586	+ 2½	Tommy Lasorda	3,347,845
1979 — 3rd		79	83	.488	11½	Tommy Lasorda	2,860,954
1980 — 2nd★		92	71	.564	1	Tommy Lasorda	3,249,287
1981 — 1st/4th		63	47	.573	•§	Tommy Lasorda	2,381,292
1982 — 2nd		88	74	.543	1	Tommy Lasorda	3,608,881
1983 — 1st◆		91	71	.652	+ 3	Tommy Lasorda	3,510,313
1984 — 4th		79	83	.488	13	Tommy Lasorda	3,134,824
1985 — 1st◆		95	67	.586	+ 5½	Tommy Lasorda	3,264,593
1986 — 5th		73	89	.451	23	Tommy Lasorda	3,023,208
1987 — 4th		73	89	.451	17	Tommy Lasorda	2,797,409
1988 — 1st§		94	67	.584	+ 7	Tommy Lasorda	2,980,262
1989 — 4th		77	83	.481	14	Tommy Lasorda	2,944,653
1990 — 2nd		86	76	.531	5	Tommy Lasorda	3,002,396
1991 — 2nd		93	69	.574	1	Tommy Lasorda	3,348,170
1992 — 6th		63	99	.389	35	Tommy Lasorda	2,473,266
1993 — 4th		81	81	.500	23	Tommy Lasorda	3,170,392
1994 — 1st		58	56	.509	+ 3½	Tommy Lasorda	2,279,355

*Games behind winner.   †Won pennant playoff.   ‡Lost pennant playoff.   §Won Championship Series.   ★Lost division playoff.   •First half 36-21; second half 27-26.   ◆Lost Championship Series.

SERVICE

Most years by non-pitcher
18—Bill Russell
Most years by pitcher
16—Don Sutton

BATTING

Most games
165—Maury Wills, 1962
Most games, career
2,181—Bill Russell
Most at-bats
695—Maury Wills, 165 games, 1962
Most at-bats, career
7,495—Willie Davis
Most runs
130—Maury Wills, 165 games, 1962
Most runs, career
1,004—Willie Davis
Most hits
230—Tommy Davis, 163 games, 1962
Most hits, career
2,091—Willie Davis
Most singles
179—Maury Wills, 165 games, 1962
Most singles, career
1,530—Bill Russell
Most doubles
47—Wes Parker, 161 games, 1970
Most doubles, career
333—Steve Garvey
Most triples
16—Willie Davis, 146 games, 1970
Most triples, career
110—Willie Davis
Most homers by righthander
35—Mike Piazza, 149 games, 1993
Most homers by lefthander
28—Darryl Strawberry, 139 games, 1991
Most homers by switch-hitter
32—Reggie Smith, 148 games, 1977
Most homers by rookie
35—Mike Piazza, 149 games, 1993
Most homers, month
15—Pedro Guerrero, June, 1985
Most homers by righthander, career
228—Ron Cey
Most homers by lefthander, career
154—Willie Davis
Most homers at home
21—Mike Piazza, 1993
Most homers on road
20—Pedro Guerrero, 1985
Most grand slams
3—Kal Daniels, 130 games, 1990
Most grand slams, career
6—Mike A. Marshall
Most total bases
356—Tommy Davis, 163 games, 1962
Most total bases, career
3,094—Willie Davis
Most long hits
66—Steve Garvey, 162 games, 1978
Pedro Guerrero, 160 games, 1983
Most long hits, career
585—Willie Davis
Most extra bases on long hits
136—Pedro Guerrero, 160 games, 1983
Most extra bases on long hits, career
1,036—Steve Garvey
Most sacrifice hits
25—Jose Offerman, 158 games, 1993

Most sacrifice flies
13—Reggie Smith, 128 games, 1978
Most bases on balls
110—Jimmy Wynn, 130 games, 1975
Most bases on balls, career
765—Ron Cey
Most strikeouts
149—Bill Grabarkewitz, 156 games, 1970
Most strikeouts, career
838—Ron Cey
Fewest strikeouts
28—Jim Gilliam, 151 games, 1960
Most hit by pitch
16—Lou Johnson, 131 games, 1965
Most runs batted in
153—Tommy Davis, 163 games, 1962
Most runs batted in, career
992—Steve Garvey
Most game-winning RBIs
18—Pedro Guerrero, 150 games, 1982
Highest batting average
.346—Tommy Davis, 163 games, 1962
Highest batting average, career
.309—Pedro Guerrero
Longest batting streak
31 games—Willie Davis, 1969
Highest slugging average
.577—Pedro Guerrero, 137 games, 1985
Most grounded into double play
25—Steve Garvey, 162 games, 1979
Fewest grounded into double play
3—Willie Davis, 160 games, 1968
Davey Lopes, 134 games, 1977
Brett Butler, 161 games, 1991

BASERUNNING

Most stolen bases
104—Maury Wills, 165 games, 1962
Most stolen bases, career
490—Maury Wills
Most caught stealing
31—Maury Wills, 158 games, 1965

PITCHING

Most games
106—Mike G. Marshall, 1974
Most games, career
550—Don Sutton
Most games started
42—Don Drysdale, 1963, 1965
Most games started, career
533—Don Sutton
Most complete games
27—Sandy Koufax, 1965, 1966
Most complete games, career
156—Don Drysdale, Don Sutton
Most games finished
83—Mike G. Marshall, 1974
Most innings
336—Sandy Koufax, 1965
Most innings, career
3,815⅓—Don Sutton
Most games won
27—Sandy Koufax, 1966
Most games won, career
233—Don Sutton
Most 20-victory seasons
3—Sandy Koufax
Most games lost
18—Claude Osteen, 1968
Most games lost, career
181—Don Sutton
Highest winning percentage
.864—Orel Hershiser (19-3), 1985

Longest winning streak
13 games—Phil Regan, 1966
Longest losing streak
11 games—Rick Honeycutt, 1987
Most saves
28—Jay Howell, 1989
Most bases on balls
124—Fernando Valenzuela, 1987
Most bases on balls, career
996—Don Sutton
Most strikeouts
382—Sandy Koufax, 1965
Most strikeouts, game
18—Sandy Koufax, August 31, 1959
Sandy Koufax, April 24, 1962
Ramon Martinez, June 4, 1990
Most strikeouts, career
2,696—Don Sutton
Most shutouts
11—Sandy Koufax, 1963
Most shutouts, career
52—Don Sutton

Most 1-0 shutouts won
4—Don Drysdale, 1968
Most hits
298—Claude Osteen, 1967
Most runs
127—Don Sutton, 1970
Most earned runs
118—Don Sutton, 1970
Most home runs
38—Don Sutton, 1970
Most hit batsmen
20—Don Drysdale, 1961
Most wild pitches
17—Sandy Koufax, 1958
Most sacrifice hits
27—Fernando Valenzuela, 1983
Most sacrifice flies
11—Burt Hooton, 1979
Lowest ERA
1.73—Sandy Koufax, 323 innings, 1966

CLUB RECORDS

Most players
48 in 1987
Fewest players
30 in 1962
Most games
165 in 1962
Most at-bats
5,642 in 1982
Most runs
842 in 1962
Fewest runs
470 in 1968
Most opponents' runs
761 in 1958
Most hits
1,515 in 1970
Fewest hits
1,234 in 1968
Most singles
1,128 in 1970
Most doubles
251 in 1978
Most triples
67 in 1970
Most homers
191 in 1977
Fewest homers
67 in 1968
Most homers at Los Angeles Coliseum, home and opponents
193 in 1958
Most homers at Dodger Stadium, home and opponents
161 in 1977, 1979
Most grand slams
6 in 1960, 1977, 1979, 1985
Most pinch home runs
8 in 1983, 1992
Most long hits
442 in 1977
Most extra bases on long hits
852 in 1977
Most total bases
2,336 in 1977
Most sacrifice hits
120 in 1964
Most sacrifice flies
64 in 1974
Most stolen bases
198 in 1962
Most caught stealing
78 in 1992

Most bases on balls
611 in 1975
Most strikeouts
980 in 1968
Fewest strikeouts
744 in 1976
Most hit by pitch
52 in 1965
Fewest hit by pitch
14 in 1984
Most runs batted in
781 in 1962
Most game-winning RBIs
90 in 1988
Highest batting average
.272 in 1974
Lowest batting average
.230 in 1968
Highest slugging average
.418 in 1977
Lowest slugging average
.319 in 1968
Most grounded into double play
145 in 1979
Fewest grounded into double play
79 in 1965
Most left on bases
1,223 in 1982
Fewest left on bases
1,012 in 1958
Most .300 hitters
4 in 1970
Most putouts
4,473 in 1973
Fewest putouts
4,105 in 1958
Most assists
1,946 in 1982
Fewest assists
1,573 in 1961
Most errors
193 in 1962
Fewest errors
114 in 1959
Most errorless games
90 in 1979
Most consecutive errorless games
11 in 1979
Most chances accepted
6,411 in 1982

Fewest chances accepted
5,708 in 1961
Most double plays
198 in 1958
Fewest double plays
106 in 1975
Most passed balls
24 in 1973
Fewest passed balls
6 in 1958
Highest fielding average
.981 in 1959, 1973, 1977, 1979, 1980, 1989
Lowest fielding average
.970 in 1962
Highest home attendance
3,608,881 in 1982
Highest road attendance
2,663,828 in 1993
Most games won
102 in 1962, 1974
Most games lost
99 in 1992
Most games won, month
21 in May 1962, July 1963, June 1973
Most games lost, month
20 in July 1968, June 1979
Highest percentage games won
.630 in 1974 (won 102, lost 60)
Lowest percentage games won
.389 in 1992 (won 63, lost 99)
Games won, league
3,153 in 37 years
Games lost, league
2,703 in 37 years
Most shutouts won
24 in 1963, 1988
Most shutouts lost
23 in 1968
Most 1-0 games won
7 in 1963, 1984
Most 1-0 games lost
7 in 1989
Most consecutive games won
13 in 1962, 1965

Most consecutive games lost
10 in 1961, 1992
Number of times league champions
9
Number of last-place finishes
1
Most runs, game
19 vs. San Diego, June 28, 1969
vs. San Francisco, May 26, 1970
vs. Pittsburgh, April 17, 1994
Most runs by opponent, game
20 by Chicago, May 20, 1967
Most runs, shutout game
19 vs. San Diego, June 28, 1969
Most runs by opponent, shutout game
18 by Cincinnati, August 8, 1965
Most runs, doubleheader shutout
16 vs. Atlanta, September 19, 1971
Most runs, inning
10 vs. San Diego, June 28, 1969, third inning
vs. San Francisco, July 4, 1971, eighth inning
vs. San Diego, September 13, 1977, second innings
Longest 1-0 game won
22 innings vs. Montreal, August 23, 1989
Longest 1-0 game lost
16 innings vs. Houston, April 21, 1976
Most hits, game
24 vs. Chicago, August 20, 1974
Most home runs, game
7 vs. Chicago, May 5, 1976
vs. Cincinnati, May 25, 1979
Most consecutive games with one or more homers
15 (23 homers), 1977
Most total bases, game
48 vs. Chicago, August 20, 1974
Largest crowd, day game
78,672 vs. San Francisco, April 18, 1958
Largest crowd, doubleheader
72,140 vs. Cincinnati, August 16, 1961
Largest crowd, night game
67,550 vs. Chicago, April 12, 1960
Largest crowd, home opener
78,672 vs. San Francisco, April 18, 1958

MILWAUKEE BRAVES

YEARLY FINISHES

Year	Position	W	L	Pct.	*GB	Manager	Attendance
1953	—2nd	92	62	.597	13	Charlie Grimm	1,826,397
1954	—3rd	89	65	.578	8	Charlie Grimm	2,131,388
1955	—2nd	85	69	.552	13½	Charlie Grimm	2,005,836
1956	—2nd	92	62	.597	1	Charlie Grimm, Fred Haney	2,046,331
1957	—1st	95	59	.617	+ 8	Fred Haney	2,215,404
1958	—1st	92	62	.597	+ 8	Fred Haney	1,971,101
1959	—2nd†	86	70	.551	2	Fred Haney	1,749,112
1960	—2nd	88	66	.571	7	Chuck Dressen	1,497,799
1961	—4th	83	71	.539	10	Chuck Dressen, Birdie Tebbetts	1,101,441
1962	—5th	86	76	.531	15½	Birdie Tebbetts	766,921
1963	—6th	84	78	.519	15	Bobby Bragan	773,018
1964	—5th	88	74	.543	5	Bobby Bragan	910,911
1965	—5th	86	76	.531	11	Bobby Bragan	555,584

*Games behind winner. †Lost pennant playoff.

INDIVIDUAL RECORDS (1953 TO 1965)

SERVICE

Most years by non-pitcher
13—Eddie Mathews
Most years by pitcher
12—Warren Spahn

BATTING

Most games
161—Hank Aaron, 1963

Most games, career
1944—Eddie Mathews
Most at-bats
636—Bill Bruton, 149 games, 1955
Most at-bats, career
7,080—Hank Aaron
Most runs
127—Hank Aaron, 156 games, 1962
Most runs, career
1,300—Eddie Mathews

Most hits
223—Hank Aaron, 154 games, 1959
Most hits, career
2,266—Hank Aaron
Most singles
132—Joe Torre, 154 games, 1964
Most doubles
46—Hank Aaron, 154 games, 1959
Most doubles, career
391—Hank Aaron
Most triples
15—Bill Bruton, 147 games, 1956
Most triples, career
80—Hank Aaron
Most homers by lefthander
47—Eddie Mathews, 157 games, 1953
Most homers by righthander
45—Hank Aaron, 156 games, 1962
Most homers by rookie
22—Rico Carty, 133 games, 1964
Most homers, month
15—Joe Adcock, July, 1956
Most homers at home
23—Joe Adcock, 1956
Eddie Mathews, 1960
Most homers on road
30—Eddie Mathews, 1953
Most homers, career
452—Eddie Mathews
Most grand slams
3—Del Crandall, 133 games, 1955
Hank Aaron, 156 games, 1962
Most grand slams, career
9—Hank Aaron
Most total bases
400—Hank Aaron, 154 games, 1959
Most total bases, career
4,011—Hank Aaron
Most long hits
92—Hank Aaron, 154 games, 1959
Most extra bases on long hits
188—Eddie Mathews, 157 games, 1953
Most sacrifice hits
31—Johnny Logan, 148 games, 1956
Most sacrifice flies
12—Hank Aaron, 153 games, 1960
Del Crandall, 142 games, 1960
Most base on balls
124—Eddie Mathews, 158 games, 1963
Most strikeouts
122—Mack Jones, 122 games, 1965
Fewest strikeouts
33—Johnny Logan, 150 games, 1953
Most hit by pitch
9—Frank Torre, 129 games, 1957
Mack Jones, 122 games, 1965
Most runs batted in
135—Eddie Mathews, 157 games, 1953
Most runs batted in, career
1,305—Hank Aaron
Highest batting average
.355—Hank Aaron, 154 games, 1959
Highest batting average, career
.320—Hank Aaron
Highest slugging average
.636—Hank Aaron, 154 games, 1959

Longest batting streak
25 games—Hank Aaron, 1956
Hank Aaron, 1962
Most grounded into double play
26—Joe Torre, 154 games, 1964
Fewest grounded into double play
4—Eddie Mathews, 151 games, 1956
Bill Bruton, 151 games, 1960

BASERUNNING

Most stolen bases
34—Bill Bruton, 142 games, 1954
Most caught stealing
13—Bill Bruton, 142 games, 1954

PITCHING

Most games
62—Billy O'Dell, 1965
Most games, started
39—Lew Burdette, 1959
Most complete games
24—Warren Spahn, 1953
Most games finished
49—Don McMahon, 1959
Most innings
292—Warren Spahn, 1959
Most games won
24—Tony Cloninger, 1965
Most games won, career
234—Warren Spahn
Most 20 victory seasons
9—Warren Spahn
Most games lost
15—Lew Burdette, Warren Spahn, 1959
Most games lost, career
138—Warren Spahn
Highest winning percentage
.767—Warren Spahn (23-7), 1953, 1963
Longest winning streak
11 games—Warren Spahn, 1954
Most bases on balls
121—Bob Buhl, 1957
Most strikeouts
211—Tony Cloninger, 1965
Most strikeouts, game
15—Warren Spahn, September 16, 1960
Most shutouts
7—Warren Spahn, 1963
Most shutouts, career
36—Warren Spahn
Most runs
144—Lew Burdette, 1959
Most earned runs
131—Lew Burdette, 1959
Most hits
312—Lew Burdette, 1959
Most hit batsmen
12—Bob Shaw, 1962
Most wild pitches
22—Tony Cloninger, 1965
Most home runs
38—Lew Burdette, 1959
Lowest ERA
2.10—Warren Spahn, 266 innings, 1953

CLUB RECORDS

Most players
42 in 1964
Fewest players
31 in 1953, 1954
Most games
163 in 1963

Most at-bats
5,591 in 1964
Most runs
803 in 1964
Fewest runs
670 in 1954

Most opponents' runs
744 in 1964
Fewest opponents' runs
541 in 1968
Most hits
1,522 in 1964
Most singles
1,057 in 1964
Most doubles
274 in 1964
Most triples
62 in 1957
Most homers
199 in 1957
Fewest homers
139 in 1954
Most homers at County Stadium, home and opponents
173 in 1965
Most grand slams
8 in 1962
Most pinch home runs
7 in 1965
Most total bases
2,411 in 1957
Most long hits
482 in 1957
Most extra bases on long hits
942 in 1957
Most sacrifice hits
142 in 1956
Most sacrifice flies
60 in 1960
Most stolen bases
75 in 1963
Most caught stealing
52 in 1963
Most bases on balls
581 in 1962
Most strikeouts
976 in 1965
Fewest strikeouts
619 in 1954
Most hit by pitcher
38 in 1964
Most runs batted in
755 in 1964
Highest batting average
.272 in 1964
Highest slugging average
.442 in 1957
Most grounded into double play
134 in 1964
Fewest grounded into double play
99 in 1956
Most left on bases
1,138 in 1962, 1963
Most .300 hitters
5 in 1964
Most putouts
4,416 in 1963
Most assists
1,848 in 1961, 1963
Most chances accepted
6,264 in 1963
Most errors
152 in 1955
Fewest errors
111 in 1961
Most consecutive errorless games
7 in 1954, 1956, 1964
Most double plays
173 in 1957

Most passed balls
28 in 1965
Fewest passed balls
5 in 1956, 1959
Highest fielding average
.982 in 1961
Highest home attendance
2,215,404 in 1957
Highest road attendance
1,633,569 in 1959
Most games won
95 in 1957
Most games lost
78 in 1963
Most games won, month
23 in August 1953, August 1958
Most games lost, month
18 in June 1954
Highest percentage games won
.617 in 1957 (won 95, lost 59)
Lowest percentage games won
.519 in 1963 (won 84, lost 78)
Games won, league
1,146 in 13 years
Games lost, league
890 in 13 years
Most shutouts won
18 in 1959, 1963
Most shutouts lost
13 in 1963
Most 1-0 games won
4 in 1963
Most consecutive games won
11 in 1956
Most consecutive games lost
8 in 1961
Number of times league champions
2
Number of last-place finishes
0
Most runs, game
23 vs. Chicago, September 2, 1957, first game
Most runs, shutout game
15 vs. Cincinnati, May 13, 1956, first game
Most runs by opponent, shutout game
10 by Philadelphia, July 21, 1953, first game
Most runs, doubleheader shutout
No performance
Most runs, inning
10 vs. Pittsburgh, June 12, 1953, second game, first inning
Longest 1-0 game won
13 innings vs. Pittsburgh, May 26, 1959
Longest 1-0 game lost
16 innings vs. San Francisco, July 2, 1963
Most hits, game
26 vs. Chicago, September 2, 1957, first game
Most home runs, game
8 vs. Pittsburgh, August 30, 1953, first game
Most consecutive games with one or more homers
22 (39 homers), 1956
Most total bases, game
47 vs. Pittsburgh, August 30, 1953, first game
Largest crowd, day game
48,642 vs. Philadelphia, September 27, 1959
Largest crowd, doubleheader
47,604 vs. Cincinnati, September 3, 1956
Largest crowd, night game
46,944 vs. New York, August 27, 1954
Largest crowd, home opener
43,640 vs. Cincinnati, April 12, 1955

EAST DIVISION

Year	Position	W	L	Pct.	*GB	Manager	Attendance
1969	—6th	52	110	.321	48	Gene Mauch	1,212,608
1970	—6th	73	89	.451	16	Gene Mauch	1,424,683
1971	—5th	71	90	.441	25½	Gene Mauch	1,290,963
1972	—5th	70	86	.449	26½	Gene Mauch	1,142,145
1973	—4th	79	83	.488	3½	Gene Mauch	1,246,863
1974	—4th	79	82	.491	8½	Gene Mauch	1,019,134
1975	—5th (tied)	75	87	.463	17½	Gene Mauch	908,292
1976	—6th	55	107	.340	46	Karl Kuehl, Charlie Fox	646,704
1977	—5th	75	87	.463	26	Dick Williams	1,433,757
1978	—4th	76	86	.469	14	Dick Williams	1,427,007
1979	—2nd	95	65	.594	2	Dick Williams	2,102,173
1980	—2nd	90	72	.556	1	Dick Williams	2,208,175
1981	—3rd/ 1st	60	48	.556	†‡	Dick Williams, Jim Fanning	1,534,564
1982	—3rd	86	76	.531	6	Jim Fanning	2,318,292
1983	—3rd	82	80	.506	8	Bill Virdon	2,320,651
1984	—5th	78	83	.484	18	Bill Virdon, Jim Fanning	1,606,531
1985	—3rd	84	77	.522	16½	Buck Rodgers	1,502,494
1986	—4th	78	83	.484	29½	Buck Rodgers	1,128,981
1987	—3rd	91	71	.562	4	Buck Rodgers	1,850,324
1988	—3rd	81	81	.500	20	Buck Rodgers	1,478,659
1989	—4th	81	81	.500	12	Buck Rodgers	1,783,533
1990	—3rd	85	77	.525	10	Buck Rodgers	1,373,087
1991	—6th	71	90	.441	26½	Buck Rodgers, Tom Runnells	934,742
1992	—2nd	87	75	.537	9	Tom Runnells, Felipe Alou	1,669,077
1993	—2nd	94	68	.580	3	Felipe Alou	1,641,437
1994	—1st	74	40	.649	+ 6	Felipe Alou	1,276,250

*Games behind winner. †First half 30-25; second 30-23. ‡Lost Championship Series

INDIVIDUAL RECORDS (1969 TO DATE)

SERVICE

Most years by non-pitcher
13—Tim Wallach
Most years by pitcher
13—Steve Rogers

BATTING

Most games
162—Rusty Staub, 1971
    Ken Singleton, 1973
    Warren Cromartie, 1980
Most games, career
1,767—Tim Wallach
Most at-bats
659—Warren Cromartie, 158 games, 1979
Most at-bats, career
6,529—Tim Wallach
Most runs
133—Tim Raines, 156 games, 1983
Most runs, career
934—Tim Raines
Most hits
204—Al Oliver, 160 games, 1982
Most hits, career
1,694—Tim Wallach
Most singles
140—Tim Raines, 151 games, 1986
    Marquis Grissom, 157 games, 1993
Most singles, career
1,148—Tim Raines
Most doubles
46—Warren Cromartie, 158 games, 1979
Most doubles, career
360—Tim Wallach
Most triples
13—Rodney Scott, 154 games, 1980
    Tim Raines, 150 games, 1985
    Mitch Webster, 151 games, 1986

Most triples, career
81—Tim Raines
Most homers by lefthander
30—Rusty Staub, 160 games, 1970
Most homers by righthander
32—Andre Dawson, 159 games, 1983
Most homers by rookie
19—Andre Dawson, 139 games, 1977
    Larry Walker, 133 games, 1990
Most homers, month
12—Rusty Staub, August, 1970
Most homers at home
22—Gary Carter, 1977
Most homers on road
22—Andre Dawson, 1983
Most homers by righthander, career
225—Andre Dawson
Most homers by lefthander, career
86—Ron Fairly
Most homers by switch-hitter, career
96—Tim Raines
Most grand slams
2—Held by many players
Most grand slams, career
7—Gary Carter
Most total bases
341—Andre Dawson, 159 games, 1983
Most total bases, career
2,728—Tim Wallach
Most long hits
79—Andres Galarraga, 157 games, 1988
Most long hits, career
595—Tim Wallach
Most extra bases on long hits
152—Andre Dawson, 159 games, 1983
Most extra bases on long hits, career
1,104—Andre Dawson
Most sacrifice hits
3—Larry Lintz, 113 games, 1974

Most sacrifice flies
18—Andre Dawson, 159 games, 1983
Most bases on balls
123—Ken Singleton, 162 games, 1973
Most bases on balls, career
775—Tim Raines
Most strikeouts
169—Andres Galarraga, 155 games, 1990
Most strikeouts, career
1,009—Tim Wallach
Fewest strikeouts
29—Dave Cash, 159 games, 1978
Most hit by pitch
50—Ron Hunt, 152 games, 1971
Most runs batted in
123—Tim Wallach, 153 games, 1987
Most runs batted in, career
905—Tim Wallach
Most game-winning RBIs
17—Andre Dawson, 151 games, 1980
Highest batting average
.334—Tim Raines, 151 games, 1986
Highest batting average, career
.301—Tim Raines
Highest slugging average
.551—Larry Parrish, 153 games, 1979
Longest batting streak
21 games—Delino DeShields, 1993
Most grounded into double play
27—John Bateman, 139 games, 1971
Ken Singleton, 162 games, 1973
Fewest grounded into double play
1—Ron Hunt, 152 games, 1971

BASERUNNING

Most stolen bases
97—Ron LeFlore, 139 games, 1980
Most stolen bases, career
634—Tim Raines
Most caught stealing
23—Delino DeShields, 151 games, 1991

PITCHING

Most games
92—Mike Marshall, 1973
Most games, career
425—Tim Burke
Most games started
40—Steve Rogers, 1977
Most games started, career
393—Steve Rogers
Most complete games
20—Bill Stoneman, 1971
Most complete games, career
129—Steve Rogers
Most games finished
73—Mike Marshall, 1973
Most innings
302—Steve Rogers, 1977
Most innings, career
2,839 ⅓—Steve Rogers

Most games won
20—Ross Grimsley, 1978
Most games won, career
158—Steve Rogers
Most 20-victory seasons
1—Ross Grimsley
Most games lost
22—Steve Rogers, 1974
Most games lost, career
152—Steve Rogers
Highest winning percentage
.783—Bryn Smith (18-5), 1985
Longest winning streak
11 games—Dennis Martinez, 1989
Longest losing streak
10 games—Steve Renko, 1972
Most saves
43—John Wetteland, 1993
Most bases on balls
146—Bill Stoneman, 1971
Most bases on balls, career
876—Steve Rogers
Most strikeouts
251—Bill Stoneman, 1971
Most strikeouts, career
1,621—Steve Rogers
Most strikeouts, game
18—Bill Gullickson, September 10, 1980
Most shutouts won
5—Bill Stoneman, 1969
Steve Rogers, 1979, 1983
Dennis Martinez, 1991
Most shutouts won, career
37—Steve Rogers
Most 1-0 shutouts won
2—Carl Morton, 1970
Bill Stoneman, 1972
Scott Sanderson, 1980
Pascual Perez, 1988
Most runs
139—Steve Rogers, 1974
Most earned runs
126—Steve Rogers, 1974
Most hits
281—Carl Morton, 1970
Most wild pitches
19—Steve Renko, 1974
Most hit batsmen
14—Bill Stoneman, 1970
Most home runs
27—Carl Morton, 1970
Steve Renko, 1970
Bill Gullickson, 1984
Dennis Martinez, 1993
Most sacrifice hits
21—Steve Rogers, 1979
Most sacrifice flies
11—Woodie Fryman, 1976
Lowest ERA
2.39—Dennis Martinez, 222 innings, 1991

CLUB RECORDS

Most players
48 in 1993
Fewest players
30 in 1972
Most games
163 in 1983, 1988, 1993
Most at-bats
5,675 in 1977
Most runs
741 in 1987
Fewest runs
513 in 1972

Most opponents' runs
807 in 1970
Most hits
1,482 in 1983
Fewest hits
1,205 in 1972
Most singles
1,042 in 1983
Most doubles
310 in 1987
Most triples
61 in 1980

Most homers
143 in 1979
Fewest homers
86 in 1974
Most homers at Jarry Park, home and opponents
168 in 1970
Most homers at Olympic Stadium, home and opponents
136 in 1987
Most grand slams
6 in 1987
Most pinch home runs
9 in 1973
Most total bases
2,282 in 1977
Most long hits
482 in 1977
Most extra bases on long hits
808 in 1977
Most sacrifice hits
115 in 1973
Most sacrifice flies
57 in 1983
Most stolen bases
237 in 1980
Most caught stealing
100 in 1991
Most bases on balls
695 in 1973
Most strikeouts
1,056 in 1991
Fewest strikeouts
733 in 1983
Most hit by pitch
78 in 1971
Fewest hit by pitch
16 in 1976
Most runs batted in
695 in 1987
Most game-winning RBIs
83 in 1980
Highest batting average
.265 in 1987
Lowest batting average
.234 in 1972
Highest slugging average
.408 in 1979
Lowest slugging average
.325 in 1972
Most grounded into double play
144 in 1973
Fewest grounded into double play
95 in 1993
Most left on bases
1,232 in 1973
Fewest left on bases
1,026 in 1979
Most .300 hitters
2 in 1973, 1982, 1987
Most putouts
4,448 in 1988
Fewest putouts
4,204 in 1972
Most assists
1,956 in 1976
Fewest assists
1,630 in 1982
Most chances accepted
6,393 in 1975
Fewest chances accepted
5,956 in 1984
Most errors
184 in 1969
Fewest errors
110 in 1990
Most errorless games
87 in 1990

Most consecutive errorless games
10 in 1977
Most double plays
193 in 1970
Fewest double plays
113 in 1992
Most passed balls
24 in 1973
Fewest passed balls
3 in 1978
Highest fielding average
.982 in 1990
Lowest fielding average
.971 in 1969
Highest home attendance
2,320,651 in 1983
Highest road attendance
2,620,064 in 1993
Most games won
95 in 1979
Most games lost
110 in 1969
Most games won, month
23 in September 1979
Most games lost, month
23 in August 1969, September 1976
Highest percentage games won
.594 in 1979 (won 95, lost 65)
Lowest percentage games won
.321 in 1969 (won 52, lost 110)
Games won, league
2,022 in 26 years
Games lost, league
2,074 in 26 years
Most shutouts won
18 in 1979
Most shutouts lost
20 in 1972
Most 1-0 shutouts won
4 in 1972, 1991
Most 1-0 shutouts lost
5 in 1982, 1986
Most consecutive games won
10 in 1979, 1980
Most consecutive games lost
20 in 1969
Number of times league champions
0
Number of last-place finishes
2 (tied in 1969)
Most runs, inning
12 vs. Chicago, September 24, 1985, fifth inning
Most runs, game
19 vs. New York, July 3, 1973
vs. Chicago, July 4, 1977, first game
vs. Cincinnati, May 7, 1978, first game
vs. Atlanta, July 30, 1978
vs. Houston, June 17, 1979
vs. Colorado, April 11, 1993
Most runs by opponent, game
19 by Cincinnati, May 1, 1989
Most runs, shutout game
19 vs. Atlanta, July 30, 1978
Most runs by opponent, shutout game
16 by St. Louis, August 11, 1980
Most runs, doubleheader shutout
14 vs. New York, August 5, 1975
Longest 1-0 game won
17 innings vs. Philadelphia, September 21, 1981
Longest 1-0 game lost
22 innings vs. Los Angeles, August 23, 1989
Most hits, game
28 vs. Atlanta, July 30, 1978
Most home runs, game
8 vs. Atlanta, July 30, 1978
Most consecutive games with one or more homers
11 (21 homers), 1994

Most total bases, game
58 vs. Atlanta, July 30, 1978
Largest crowd, day game
57,694 vs. Philadelphia, August 15, 1982
Largest crowd, doubleheader
59,282 vs. St. Louis, September 16, 1979

Largest crowd, night game
57,121 vs. Philadelphia, October 3, 1980
Largest crowd, home opener
57,592 vs. Philadelphia, April 15, 1977

NEW YORK GIANTS

YEARLY FINISHES

Year	Position	W	L	Pct.	*GB	Manager	Attendance
1901	7th	52	85	.380	37	George Davis	297,650
1902	8th	48	88	.353	53½	Horace Fogel, Heinie Smith, John McGraw	302,875
1903	2nd	84	55	.604	6½	John McGraw	579,530
1904	1st	106	47	.693	+13	John McGraw	609,826
1905	1st	105	48	.686	+ 9	John McGraw	552,700
1906	2nd	96	56	.632	20	John McGraw	402,850
1907	4th	82	71	.536	25½	John McGraw	538,350
1908	2nd (tied)	98	56	.636	1	John McGraw	910,000
1909	3rd	92	61	.601	18½	John McGraw	783,700
1910	2nd	91	63	.591	13	John McGraw	511,785
1911	1st	99	54	.647	+ 7½	John McGraw	675,000
1912	1st	103	48	.682	+10	John McGraw	638,000
1913	1st	101	51	.664	+12½	John McGraw	630,000
1914	2nd	84	70	.545	10½	John McGraw	364,313
1915	8th	69	83	.454	21	John McGraw	391,850
1916	4th	86	66	.566	7	John McGraw	552,056
1917	1st	98	56	.636	+10	John McGraw	500,264
1918	2nd	71	53	.573	10½	John McGraw	256,618
1919	2nd	87	53	.621	9	John McGraw	708,857
1920	2nd	86	68	.558	7	John McGraw	929,609
1921	1st	94	59	.614	+ 4	John McGraw	773,477
1922	1st	93	61	.604	+ 7	John McGraw	945,809
1923	1st	95	58	.621	+ 4½	John McGraw	820,780
1924	1st	93	60	.608	+ 1½	John McGraw	844,068
1925	2nd	86	66	.566	8½	John McGraw	778,993
1926	5th	74	77	.490	13½	John McGraw	700,362
1927	3rd	92	62	.597	2	John McGraw	858,190
1928	2nd	93	61	.604	2	John McGraw	916,191
1929	3rd	84	67	.556	13½	John McGraw	868,806
1930	3rd	87	67	.565	5	John McGraw	868,714
1931	2nd	87	65	.572	13	John McGraw	812,163
1932	6th (tied)	72	82	.468	18	John McGraw, Bill Terry	484,868
1933	1st	91	61	.599	+ 5	Bill Terry	604,471
1934	2nd	93	60	.608	2	Bill Terry	730,851
1935	3rd	91	62	.595	8½	Bill Terry	748,748
1936	1st	92	62	.597	+ 5	Bill Terry	837,952
1937	1st	95	57	.625	+ 3	Bill Terry	926,887
1938	3rd	83	67	.553	5	Bill Terry	799,633
1939	5th	77	74	.510	18½	Bill Terry	702,457
1940	6th	72	80	.474	27½	Bill Terry	747,852
1941	5th	74	79	.484	25½	Bill Terry	763,098
1942	3rd	85	67	.559	20	Mel Ott	779,621
1943	8th	55	98	.359	49½	Mel Ott	466,095
1944	5th	67	87	.435	38	Mel Ott	674,083
1945	5th	78	74	.513	19	Mel Ott	1,016,468
1946	8th	61	93	.396	36	Mel Ott	1,219,873
1947	4th	81	73	.526	13	Mel Ott	1,600,793
1948	5th	78	76	.506	13½	Mel Ott, Leo Durocher	1,459,269
1949	5th	73	81	.474	24	Leo Durocher	1,218,446
1950	3rd	86	68	.558	5	Leo Durocher	1,008,876
1951	1st (tied)†	98	59	.624	+ 1	Leo Durocher	1,059,539
1952	2nd	92	62	.597	4½	Leo Durocher	984,940
1953	5th	70	84	.455	35	Leo Durocher	811,518
1954	1st	97	57	.630	+ 5	Leo Durocher	1,155,067
1955	3rd	80	74	.519	18½	Leo Durocher	824,112
1956	6th	67	87	.435	26	Bill Rigney	629,179
1957	6th	69	85	.448	26	Bill Rigney	653,923

*Games behind winner.   †Won pennant playoff.

SERVICE

Most years by non-pitcher
 22—Mel Ott
Most years by pitcher
 17—Christy Mathewson

BATTING

Most games
 157—Art Devlin, 1908
Most games, career
 2,730—Mel Ott
Most at-bats
 681—Joe Moore, 155 games, 1935
Most at-bats, career
 9,456—Mel Ott
Most runs
 146—Mike Tiernan, 122 games, 1889
Most runs, career
 1,859—Mel Ott
Most runs (since 1900)
 139—Bill Terry, 154 games, 1930
Most hits
 254—Bill Terry, 154 games, 1930
Most hits, career
 2,876—Mel Ott
Most singles
 177—Bill Terry, 154 games, 1930
Most singles, career
 1,805—Mel Ott
Most doubles
 43—Bill Terry, 153 games, 1931
Most doubles, career
 488—Mel Ott
Most triples
 26—George Davis, 133 games, 1893
Most triples (since 1900)
 25—Larry Doyle, 141 games, 1911
Most triples, career
 159—Mike Tiernan
Most triples, career (since 1900)
 117—Larry Doyle
Most homers by lefthander
 51—Johnny Mize, 154 games, 1947
Most homers by righthander
 51—Willie Mays, 152 games, 1955
Most homers by rookie
 29—Bobby Thomson, 138 games, 1947
Most homers, month
 13—Walker Cooper, June, 1947
   Johnny Mize, August, 1947
   Willie Mays, July, 1955
Most homers at home
 29—Johnny Mize, 1947
Most homers on road
 29—Willie Mays, 1955
Most homers by lefthander, career
 511—Mel Ott
Most homers by righthander, career
 187—Willie Mays
Most grand slams
 3—George Kelly, 149 games, 1921
   Sid Gordon, 142 games, 1948
   Wes Westrum, 124 games, 1951
Most grand slams, career
 7—George Kelly, Mel Ott
Most total bases
 392—Bill Terry, 154 games, 1930
Most total bases, career
 5,041—Mel Ott
Most long hits
 87—Willie Mays, 151 games, 1954
Most long hits, career
 1,071—Mel Ott

Most extra bases on long hits
 197—Willie Mays, 152 games, 1955
Most extra bases on long hits, career
 2,165—Mel Ott
Most sacrifice hits
 36—Art Devlin, 143 games, 1907
Most sacrifice flies
 8—Don Mueller, 153 games, 1954
   Hank Thompson, 135 games, 1955
Most bases on balls
 144—Eddie Stanky, 152 games, 1950
Most strikeouts
 93—Wes Westrum, 124 games, 1951
Fewest strikeouts
 12—Frankie Frisch, 151 games, 1923
Most hit by pitch
 19—Art Fletcher, 151 games, 1917
Most runs batted in
 151—Mel Ott, 150 games, 1929
Most runs batted in, career
 1,860—Mel Ott
Most consecutive games with RBI
 11—Mel Ott (27 RBIs), 1929
Highest batting average
 .401—Bill Terry, 154 games, 1930
Highest batting average, career
 .341—Bill Terry
Highest slugging average
 .667—Willie Mays, 151 games, 1954
Highest slugging average, career
 .593—Willie Mays
Longest batting streak
 33 games—George Davis, 1893
Longest batting streak (since 1900)
 24 games—Freddie Lindstrom, 1930
   Don Mueller, 1955
Most grounded into double play
 26—Bill Jurges, 138 games, 1939
   Sid Gordon, 131 games, 1943
Fewest grounded into double play
 3—Joe Moore, 152 games, 1936

BASERUNNING

Most stolen bases
 111—Monte Ward, 129 games, 1887
Most stolen bases (since 1900)
 62—George J. Burns, 154 games, 1914
Most stolen bases, career
 334—George J. Burns
Most caught stealing
 22—George J. Burns, 154 games, 1920

PITCHING (SINCE 1900)

Most games
 71—Hoyt Wilhelm, 1952
Most games, career
 634—Christy Mathewson
Most games started
 48—Joe McGinnity, 1903
Most complete games
 44—Joe McGinnity, 1903
Most games finished
 52—Ace Adams, 1943
Most innings
 434—Joe McGinnity, 1903
Most games won
 37—Christy Mathewson, 1908
Most games won, career
 372—Christy Mathewson
Most 20-victory seasons
 13—Christy Mathewson
Most games lost
 27—Dummy Taylor, 1901

Most games lost, career
188—Christy Mathewson
Highest winning percentage
.833—Hoyt Wilhelm (15-3), 1952
Longest winning streak
19 games—Rube Marquard, 1912
Longest winning streak over two seasons
24 games—Carl Hubbell, 1936 (16), 1937 (8)
Longest losing streak
12 games—Rube Marquard, 1914
Most bases on balls
128—Jeff Tesreau, 1914
Most bases on balls, career
902—Hal Schumacher
Most strikeouts
267—Christy Mathewson, 1903
Most strikeouts, game
16—Christy Mathewson, October 3, 1904
Most strikeouts, career
2,502—Christy Mathewson

Most shutouts
12—Christy Mathewson, 1908
Most shutouts, career
83—Christy Mathewson
Most 1-0 shutouts won
5—Carl Hubbell, 1933
Most runs
224—Bill Carrick, 1900
Most earned runs
117—Freddie Fitzsimmons, 1932
Most hits
415—Bill Carrick, 1900
Most hit batsmen
36—Ed Doheny, 1899
Most wild pitches
30—Red Ames, 1905
Most home runs
36—Larry Jansen, 1949
Lowest ERA
1.66—Carl Hubbell, 309 innings, 1933

CLUB RECORDS

Most players
49 in 1946
Fewest players
21 in 1905
Most games
158 in 1904, 1909, 1917
Most at-bats
5,623 in 1935
Most runs
959 in 1930
Fewest runs
540 in 1956
Most opponents runs
814 in 1930
Most hits
1,769 in 1930
Fewest hits
1,217 in 1906
Most singles
1,279 in 1930
Most doubles
276 in 1928
Most triples
105 in 1911
Most homers
221 in 1947
Fewest homers (154 or 162-game schedule)
15 in 1906
Most grand slams
7 in 1951, 1954
Most pinch home runs
10 in 1954
Most total bases
2,628 in 1930
Most long hits
490 in 1930
Most extra bases on long hits
979 in 1947
Most sacrifices (sacrifice hits and sacrifice flies)
250 in 1908
Most sacrifice hits
166 in 1904
Most sacrifice flies
52 in 1954
Most stolen bases
347 in 1911
Most caught stealing
114 in 1921
Most bases on balls
671 in 1951
Most strikeouts
672 in 1952

Fewest strikeouts
376 in 1928
Most hit by pitch
52 in 1917
Fewest hit by pitch
15 in 1933
Most runs batted in
880 in 1930
Highest batting average
.319 in 1930
Lowest batting average
.243 in 1909
Highest slugging average
.473 in 1930
Lowest slugging average
.302 in 1906
Most grounded into double play
153 in 1939
Fewest grounded into double play
96 in 1952
Most left on bases
1,214 in 1935
Fewest left on bases
975 in 1926
Most .300 hitters
8 in 1921, 1922, 1924, 1930, 1931
Most putouts
4,306 in 1909
Fewest putouts
3,964 in 1939
Most assists
2,240 in 1920
Fewest assists
1,660 in 1956
Most chances accepted
6,472 in 1920
Fewest chances accepted
5,794 in 1956
Most errors
307 in 1909
Fewest errors
137 in 1950
Most consecutive errorless games
8 in 1950
Most double plays
181 in 1950
Fewest double plays
112 in 1945
Most passed balls
26 in 1906
Fewest passed balls
4 in 1928

Highest fielding average
.977 in 1940, 1942, 1950
Lowest fielding average
.954 in 1909
Highest home attendance
1,600,793 in 1947
Highest road attendance
1,228,330 in 1949
Most games won
106 in 1904
Most games lost
98 in 1943
Most games won, month
29—September 1916
Most games lost, month
25—August 1953
Highest percentage games won
.759 in 1885 (won 85, lost 27)
Highest percentage games won (since 1900)
.693 in 1904 (won 106, lost 47)
Lowest percentage games lost
.353 in 1902 (won 48, lost 88)
Games won, league
6,067 in 75 years
Games lost, league
4,898 in 75 years
Most shutouts won
25 in 1908
Most shutouts lost
20 in 1915
Most 1-0 games won
6 in 1907, 1933
Most 1-0 games lost
8 in 1907
Most consecutive games won
26 in 1916
Most consecutive games lost
13 in 1902, 1944
Number of times league champions
17
Number of last-place finishes
5
Most runs, game
29 vs. Philadelphia, June 15, 1887

Most runs, game (since 1900)
26 vs. Brooklyn, April 30, 1944, first game
Most runs by opponent, game
28 by Hartford, May 13, 1876
Most runs by opponent, game (since 1900)
21 by St. Louis, August 2, 1948
Most runs, shutout game
24 vs. Buffalo, May 27, 1885
Most runs, shutout game (since 1900)
16 vs. Brooklyn, July 3, 1949
Most runs by opponent, shutout game
19 by Chicago, June 7, 1906
Most runs, doubleheader shutout
19 vs. Cincinnati, July 31, 1949
Most runs, inning
13 vs. Philadelphia, September 8, 1883, third inning
vs. Cleveland, July 19, 1890, first game, second inning
vs. St. Louis, May 13, 1911, first inning
Longest 1-0 game won
18 innings vs. St. Louis, July 2, 1933, first game
Longest 1-0 game lost
15 innings vs. Cincinnati, July 16, 1933, first game
Most hits, game
31 vs. Cincinnati, June 9, 1901
Most home runs, game
7 vs. Indianapolis, May 9, 1888
vs. Cincinnati, June 6, 1939
vs. Philadelphia, August 13, 1939, first game
vs. Cincinnati, June 24, 1950
vs. Pittsburgh, July 8, 1956, first game
Most consecutive games with one or more homers
19 (33 homers), 1947
Most total bases, game
47 vs. Philadelphia, July 11, 1931, first game
Largest crowd, day game
54,922 vs. Brooklyn, April 20, 1941
Largest crowd, doubleheader
60,747 vs. Brooklyn, May 31, 1937
Largest crowd, night game
51,790 vs. Brooklyn, May 27, 1947
Largest crowd, home opener
54,392 vs. Brooklyn, April 14, 1936

NEW YORK METS

YEARLY FINISHES

Year	Position	W	L	Pct.	*GB	Manager	Attendance
1962 — 10th		40	120	.250	60½	Casey Stengel	922,530
1963 — 10th		51	111	.315	48	Casey Stengel	1,080,108
1964 — 10th		53	109	.327	40	Casey Stengel	1,732,597
1965 — 10th		50	112	.309	47	Casey Stengel, Wes Westrum	1,768,389
1966 — 9th		66	95	.410	28½	Wes Westrum	1,932,693
1967 — 10th		61	101	.377	40½	Wes Westrum, Salty Parker	1,565,492
1968 — 9th		73	89	.451	24	Gil Hodges	1,781,657

EAST DIVISION

Year	Position	W	L	Pct.	*GB	Manager	Attendance
1969 — 1st†		100	62	.617	+ 8	Gil Hodges	2,175,373
1970 — 3rd		83	79	.512	6	Gil Hodges	2,697,479
1971 — 3rd (tied)		83	79	.512	14	Gil Hodges	2,266,680
1972 — 3rd		83	73	.532	13½	Yogi Berra	2,134,185
1973 — 1st†		82	79	.509	+ 1½	Yogi Berra	1,912,390
1974 — 5th		71	91	.438	17	Yogi Berra	1,722,209
1975 — 3rd (tied)		82	80	.506	10½	Yogi Berra, Roy McMillan	1,730,566
1976 — 3rd		86	76	.531	15	Joe Frazier	1,468,754
1977 — 6th		64	98	.395	37	Joe Frazier, Joe Torre	1,066,825
1978 — 6th		66	96	.407	24	Joe Torre	1,007,328
1979 — 6th		63	99	.389	35	Joe Torre	788,905
1980 — 5th		67	95	.414	24	Joe Torre	1,192,073
1981 — 5th/4th		41	62	.398	‡	Joe Torre	704,244
1982 — 6th		65	97	.401	27	George Bamberger	1,323,036
1983 — 6th		68	94	.420	22	George Bamberger, Frank Howard	1,112,774
1984 — 2nd		90	72	.556	6½	Dave Johnson	1,842,695

Year	Position	W	L	Pct.	*GB	Manager	Attendance
1985 —2nd	....	98	64	.605	3	Dave Johnson	2,761,601
1986 —1st†	....	108	54	.667	+21½	Dave Johnson	2,767,601
1987 —2nd	....	92	70	.568	3	Dave Johnson	3,034,129
1988 —1st§	....	100	60	.625	+15	Dave Johnson	3,055,445
1989 —2nd	....	87	75	.537	6	Dave Johnson	2,918,710
1990 —2nd	....	91	71	.562	4	Dave Johnson, Bud Harrelson	2,732,745
1991 —5th	....	77	84	.478	20½	Bud Harrelson, Mike Cubbage	2,284,484
1992 —5th	....	72	90	.444	24	Jeff Torborg	1,779,534
1993 —7th	....	59	103	.364	38	Jeff Torborg, Dallas Green	1,873,183
1994 —3rd	....	55	58	.487	18½	Dallas Green	1,151,471

*Games behind winner.   †Won Championship Series.   ‡First half 17-34; second 24-28.   §Lost Championship Series.

INDIVIDUAL RECORDS (1962 TO DATE)

SERVICE

Most years by non-pitcher
18—Ed Kranepool
Most years by pitcher
12—Jerry Koosman
Tom Seaver
Craig Swan

BATTING

Most games
162—Felix Millan, 1975
Most games, career
1,853—Ed Kranepool
Most at-bats
676—Felix Millan, 162 games, 1975
Most at-bats, career
5,436—Ed Kranepool
Most runs
108—Darryl Strawberry, 154 games, 1987
Howard Johnson, 156 games, 1991
Most runs, career
662—Darryl Strawberry
Most hits
191—Felix Millan, 162 games, 1975
Most hits, career
1,418—Ed Kranepool
Most singles
155—Felix Millan, 153 games, 1973
Most singles, career
1,050—Ed Kranepool
Most doubles
41—Howard Johnson, 153 games, 1989
Most doubles, career
225—Ed Kranepool
Most triples
10—Mookie Wilson, 154 games, 1984
Most triples, career
62—Mookie Wilson
Most homers by righthander
37—Dave Kingman, 123 games, 1976
Dave Kingman, 149 games, 1982
Most homers by lefthander
39—Darryl Strawberry, 154 games, 1987
Darryl Strawberry, 153 games, 1988
Most homers by switch-hitter
38—Howard Johnson, 156 games, 1991
Most homers by rookie
26—Darryl Strawberry, 122 games, 1983
Most homers, month
13—Dave Kingman, July, 1975
Gary Carter, September, 1985
Most homers at home
24—Darryl Strawberry, 1990
Most homers on road
23—Howard Johnson, 1987
Most homers by lefthander, career
252—Darryl Strawberry
Most homers by righthander, career
154—Dave Kingman

Most homers by switch-hitter, career
185—Howard Johnson
Most grand slams
3—John Milner, 127 games, 1976
Most grand slams, career
5—John Milner, Howard Johnson
Most total bases
319—Howard Johnson, 153 games, 1989
Most total bases, career
2,047—Ed Kranepool
Most long hits
80—Howard Johnson, 153 games, 1989
Most long hits, career
469—Darryl Strawberry
Most extra bases on long hits
159—Darryl Strawberry, 154 games, 1987
Most extra bases on long hits, career
1,003—Darryl Strawberry
Most sacrifice hits
24—Felix Millan, 136 games, 1974
Most sacrifice flies
15—Gary Carter, 132 games, 1986
Howard Johnson, 156 games, 1991
Most bases on balls
97—Keith Hernandez, 154 games, 1984
Darryl Strawberry, 154 games, 1987
Most bases on balls, career
580—Darryl Strawberry
Most strikeouts
156—Tommie Agee, 153 games, 1970
Dave Kingman, 149 games, 1982
Fewest strikeouts
14—Felix Millan, 136 games, 1974
Most strikeouts, career
960—Darryl Strawberry
Most hit by pitch
13—Ron Hunt, 143 games, 1963
Most runs batted in
117—Howard Johnson, 156 games, 1991
Most runs batted in, career
733—Darryl Strawberry
Most game-winning RBIs
24—Keith Hernandez, 158 games, 1985
Most consecutive games with RBI
8—Keith Hernandez (13 RBIs), 1986
Highest batting average
.340—Cleon Jones, 137 games, 1969
Highest batting average, career
.297—Keith Hernandez
Highest slugging average
.583—Darryl Strawberry, 154 games, 1987
Longest batting streak
24 games—Hubie Brooks, 1984
Most grounded into double play
26—Cleon Jones, 134 games, 1970
Fewest grounded into double play
4—Lee Mazzilli, 159 games, 1977
Darryl Strawberry, 154 games, 1987
Howard Johnson, 153 games, 1989
Howard Johnson, 156 games, 1991

BASERUNNING

Most stolen bases
58—Mookie Wilson, 159 games, 1982
Most stolen bases, career
281—Mookie Wilson
Most caught stealing
21—Lenny Randle, 136 games, 1977

PITCHING

Most games
76—Jeff Innis, 1992
Most games, career
401—Tom Seaver
Most complete games
21—Tom Seaver, 1971
Most complete games, career
171—Tom Seaver
Most games started
36—Jack Fisher, 1965
Tom Seaver, 1970, 1973, 1975
Most games started, career
395—Tom Seaver
Most games finished
52—Jesse Orosco, 1984
Roger McDowell, 1986
Most innings
291—Tom Seaver, 1970
Most innings, career
3,045—Tom Seaver
Most games won
25—Tom Seaver, 1969
Most games, won, career
198—Tom Seaver
Most 20-victory seasons
4—Tom Seaver
Most games lost
24—Roger Craig, 1962
Jack Fisher, 1965
Most games lost, career
137—Jerry Koosman
Highest winning percentage
.870—David Cone (20-3), 1988

Most saves
33—John Franco, 1990
Longest winning streak
14 games—Dwight Gooden, 1985
Longest losing streak
18 games—Roger Craig, 1963
Longest losing streak, two seasons
27 games—Anthony Young, 1992 (14), 1993 (13)
Most bases on balls
116—Nolan Ryan, 1971
Most bases on balls, career
847—Tom Seaver
Most strikeouts
289—Tom Seaver, 1971
Most strikeouts, career
2,541—Tom Seaver
Most strikeouts, game
19—Tom Seaver, April 22, 1970
David Cone, October 6, 1991
Most shutouts
8—Dwight Gooden, 1985
Most shutouts, career
44—Tom Seaver
Most 1-0 shutouts won
3—Bob Ojeda, 1988
Most runs
137—Jay Hook, 1962
Most earned runs
117—Roger Craig, 1962
Most hits
261—Roger Craig, 1962
Most hit batsmen
15—Nolan Ryan, 1971
Most wild pitches
18—Jack Hamilton, 1966
Most home runs
35—Roger Craig, 1962
Most sacrifice hits
21—Mike Scott, 1982
Most sacrifice flies
13—Ron Darling, 1989
Lowest ERA
1.53—Dwight Gooden, 276⅔ innings, 1985

CLUB RECORDS

Most players
54 in 1967
Fewest players
32 in 1988
Most games
164 in 1965
Most at-bats
5,601 in 1987
Most runs
823 in 1987
Fewest runs
473 in 1968
Most opponents' runs
948 in 1962
Most hits
1,499 in 1987
Fewest hits
1,154 in 1972
Most singles
1,087 in 1980
Most doubles
287 in 1987
Most triples
47 in 1978
Most homers
192 in 1987
Fewest homers
61 in 1980
Most homers at Polo Grounds, home and opponents
213 in 1962

Most homers at Shea Stadium, home and opponents
156 in 1987
Most grand slams
7 in 1987
Most pinch home runs
12 in 1983
Most total bases
2,430 in 1987
Most long hits
513 in 1987
Most extra bases on long hits
931 in 1987
Most sacrifice hits
108 in 1973
Most sacrifice flies
56 in 1988, 1990
Most stolen bases
159 in 1987
Most caught stealing
99 in 1980
Most bases on balls
684 in 1970
Most strikeouts
1,203 in 1968
Fewest strikeouts
735 in 1974
Most hit by pitch
48 in 1964
Fewest hit by pitch
20 in 1984, 1985

Most runs batted in
771 in 1987
Most game-winning RBIs
102 in 1986
Highest batting average
.268 in 1987
Lowest batting average
.219 in 1963
Highest slugging average
.434 in 1987
Lowest slugging average
.315 in 1963, 1968
Most grounded into double play
148 in 1974
Fewest grounded into double play
87 in 1989
Most left on bases
1,228 in 1974
Fewest left on bases
1,011 in 1993
Most .300 hitters
3 in 1964
Most putouts
4,464 in 1985
Fewest putouts
4,244 in 1972
Most assists
1,995 in 1966
Fewest assists
1,462 in 1989
Most chances accepted
6,309 in 1965
Fewest chances accepted
5,783 in 1972
Most errors
210 in 1962, 1963
Fewest errors
114 in 1971
Most errorless games
88 in 1985
Most consecutive errorless games
9 in 1977
Most double plays
171 in 1966, 1983
Fewest double plays
107 in 1990
Most passed balls
32 in 1964
Fewest passed balls
2 in 1980
Highest fielding average
.982 in 1985
Lowest fielding average
.967 in 1962, 1963
Highest home attendance
3,055,445 in 1988
Highest road attendance
2,660,426 in 1993
Most games won
108 in 1986
Most games lost
120 in 1962
Most games won, month
23 in September 1969
Most games lost, month
26 in August 1962

Games won, league
2,427 in 33 years
Games lost, league
2,798 in 33 years
Highest percentage games won
.667 in 1986 (won 108, lost 54)
Lowest percentage games won
.250 in 1962 (won 40, lost 120)
Most shutouts won
28 in 1969
Most shutouts lost
30 in 1963
Most 1-0 games won
9 in 1969
Most 1-0 games lost
8 in 1963
Most consecutive games won
11 in 1969, 1972, 1986, 1990
Most consecutive games lost
17 in 1962
Number of times league champions
3
Number of last-place finishes
9
Most runs, game
23 vs. Chicago, August 16, 1987
Most runs by opponent, game
26 by Philadelphia, June 11, 1985
Most runs, shutout game
14 vs. Chicago, July 29, 1965, first game
Most runs by opponent, shutout game
12 by Chicago, May 30, 1963, first game
by Pittsburgh, May 30, 1965, second game
by Pittsburgh, July 1, 1966
by Chicago, September 14, 1974
Most runs, doubleheader shutout
2 vs. Pittsburgh, September 12, 1969
Most runs, inning
10 vs. Cincinnati, June 12, 1979, sixth inning
Longest 1-0 game won
15 innings vs. Los Angeles, July 4, 1969
Longest 1-0 game lost
24 innings vs. Houston, April 15, 1968
Most hits, extra-inning game
28 vs. Atlanta, July 4, 1985, 19 innings
Most hits, nine-inning game
23 vs. Chicago, May 26, 1964
Most home runs, game
6 vs. Montreal, April 4, 1988
Most consecutive games with one or more homers
10 (14 homers), 1970
(15 homers), 1975
Most total bases, extra-inning game
38 vs. Atlanta, July 4, 1985, 19 innings
Most total bases, nine-inning game
37 vs. Atlanta, July 20, 1985
Largest crowd, day game
56,738 vs. Los Angeles, June 23, 1968
Largest crowd, doubleheader
57,175 vs. Los Angeles, June 13, 1965
Largest crowd, night game
56,658 vs. San Francisco, May 13, 1966
Largest crowd, home opener
53,134 vs. Colorado, April 5, 1993

PHILADELPHIA PHILLIES

YEARLY FINISHES

Year	Position	W	L	Pct.	*GB	Manager	Attendance
1901 —2nd		83	57	.593	7 ½	Bill Shettsline	234,937
1902 —7th		56	81	.409	46	Bill Shettsline	112,066
1903 —7th		49	86	.363	39 ½	Chief Zimmer	151,729
1904 —8th		52	100	.342	53 ½	Hugh Duffy	140,771

Year	Position	W	L	Pct.	*GB	Manager	Attendance
1905	4th	83	69	.546	21½	Hugh Duffy	317,932
1906	4th	71	82	.464	45½	Hugh Duffy	294,680
1907	3rd	83	64	.565	21½	Bill Murray	341,216
1908	4th	83	71	.539	16	Bill Murray	420,660
1909	5th	74	79	.484	36½	Bill Murray	303,177
1910	4th	78	75	.510	25½	Red Dooin	296,597
1911	4th	79	73	.520	19½	Red Dooin	416,000
1912	5th	73	79	.480	30½	Red Dooin	250,000
1913	2nd	88	63	.583	12½	Red Dooin	470,000
1914	6th	74	80	.481	20½	Red Dooin	138,474
1915	1st	90	62	.592	+ 7	Pat Moran	449,898
1916	2nd	91	62	.595	2½	Pat Moran	515,365
1917	2nd	87	65	.572	10	Pat Moran	354,428
1918	6th	55	68	.447	26	Pat Moran	122,266
1919	8th	47	90	.343	47½	Jack Coombs, Gavvy Cravath	240,424
1920	8th	62	91	.405	30½	Gavvy Cravath	330,998
1921	8th	51	103	.331	43½	Bill Donovan, Kaiser Wilhelm	273,961
1922	7th	57	96	.373	35½	Kaiser Wilhelm	232,471
1923	8th	50	104	.325	45½	Art Fletcher	228,168
1924	7th	55	96	.364	37	Art Fletcher	299,818
1925	6th (tied)	68	85	.444	27	Art Fletcher	304,905
1926	8th	58	93	.384	29½	Art Fletcher	240,600
1927	8th	51	103	.331	43	Stuffy McInnis	305,420
1928	8th	43	109	.283	51	Burt Shotton	182,168
1929	5th	71	82	.464	27½	Burt Shotton	281,200
1930	8th	52	102	.338	40	Burt Shotton	299,007
1931	6th	66	88	.429	35	Burt Shotton	284,849
1932	4th	78	76	.506	12	Burt Shotton	268,914
1933	7th	60	92	.395	31	Burt Shotton	156,421
1934	7th	56	93	.376	37	Jimmy Wilson	169,885
1935	7th	64	89	.418	35½	Jimmy Wilson	205,470
1936	8th	54	100	.351	38	Jimmy Wilson	249,219
1937	7th	61	92	.399	34½	Jimmy Wilson	212,790
1938	8th	45	105	.300	43	Jimmy Wilson, Hans Lobert	166,111
1939	8th	45	106	.298	50½	Doc Prothro	277,973
1940	8th	50	103	.327	50	Doc Prothro	207,177
1941	8th	43	111	.279	57	Doc Prothro	231,401
1942	8th	42	109	.278	62½	Hans Lobert	230,183
1943	7th	64	90	.416	41	Bucky Harris, Fred Fitzsimmons	466,975
1944	8th	61	92	.399	43½	Fred Fitzsimmons	369,586
1945	8th	46	108	.299	52	Fred Fitzsimmons, Ben Chapman	285,057
1946	5th	69	85	.448	28	Ben Chapman	1,045,247
1947	7th (tied)	62	92	.403	32	Ben Chapman	907,332
1948	6th	66	88	.429	25½	Ben Chapman, Dusty Cooke, Eddie Sawyer	767,429
1949	3rd	81	73	.526	16	Eddie Sawyer	819,698
1950	1st	91	63	.591	+ 2	Eddie Sawyer	1,217,035
1951	5th	73	81	.474	23½	Eddie Sawyer	937,658
1952	4th	87	67	.565	9½	Eddie Sawyer, Steve O'Neill	775,417
1953	3rd (tied)	83	71	.539	22	Steve O'Neill	853,644
1954	4th	75	79	.487	22	Steve O'Neill, Terry Moore	738,991
1955	4th	77	77	.500	21½	Mayo Smith	922,886
1956	5th	71	83	.461	22	Mayo Smith	934,798
1957	5th	77	77	.500	19	Mayo Smith	1,146,230
1958	8th	69	85	.448	23	Mayo Smith, Eddie Sawyer	931,110
1959	8th	64	90	.416	23	Eddie Sawyer	802,815
1960	8th	59	95	.383	36	Eddie Sawyer, Andy Cohen, Gene Mauch	862,205
1961	8th	47	107	.305	46	Gene Mauch	590,039
1962	7th	81	80	.503	20	Gene Mauch	762,034
1963	4th	87	75	.537	12	Gene Mauch	907,141
1964	2nd (tied)	92	70	.568	1	Gene Mauch	1,425,891
1965	6th	85	76	.528	11½	Gene Mauch	1,166,376
1966	4th	87	75	.537	8	Gene Mauch	1,108,201
1967	5th	82	80	.506	19½	Gene Mauch	828,888
1968	7th (tied)	76	86	.469	21	Gene Mauch, George Myatt, Bob Skinner	664,546

EAST DIVISION

Year	Position	W	L	Pct.	*GB	Manager	Attendance
1969	5th	63	99	.389	37	Bob Skinner, George Myatt	519,414
1970	5th	73	88	.453	15½	Frank Lucchesi	708,247
1971	6th	67	95	.414	30	Frank Lucchesi	1,511,223
1972	6th	59	97	.378	37½	Frank Lucchesi, Paul Owens	1,343,329
1973	6th	71	91	.438	11½	Danny Ozark	1,475,934
1974	3rd	80	82	.494	8	Danny Ozark	1,808,648
1975	2nd	86	76	.531	6½	Danny Ozark	1,909,233
1976	1st†	101	61	.623	+ 9	Danny Ozark	2,480,150

Year — Position	W	L	Pct.	*GB	Manager	Attendance
1977 — 1st†	101	61	.623	+ 5	Danny Ozark	2,700,070
1978 — 1st†	90	72	.556	+1½	Danny Ozark	2,583,389
1979 — 4th	84	78	.519	14	Danny Ozark, Dallas Green	2,775,011
1980 — 1st‡	91	71	.562	+ 1	Dallas Green	2,651,650
1981 — 1st/3rd	59	48	.551	§	Dallas Green	1,638,752
1982 — 2nd	89	73	.549	3	Pat Corrales	2,376,394
1983 — 1st‡	90	72	.556	+ 6	Pat Corrales, Paul Owens	2,128,339
1984 — 4th	81	81	.500	15½	Paul Owens	2,062,693
1985 — 5th	75	87	.463	26	John Felske	1,830,350
1986 — 2nd	86	75	.534	21½	John Felske	1,933,335
1987 — 4th (tied)	80	82	.494	15	John Felske, Lee Elia	2,100,110
1988 — 6th	65	96	.404	35½	Lee Elia, John Vukovich	1,990,041
1989 — 6th	67	95	.414	26	Nick Leyva	1,861,985
1990 — 4th (tied)	77	85	.475	18	Nick Leyva	1,992,484
1991 — 3rd	78	84	.481	20	Nick Leyva, Jim Fregosi	2,050,012
1992 — 6th	70	92	.432	26	Jim Fregosi	1,927,448
1993 — 1st‡	97	65	.599	3	Jim Fregosi	3,137,674
1994 — 4th	54	61	.470	20½	Jim Fregosi	2,290,971

*Games behind winner.   †Lost Championship Series.   ‡Won Championship Series.   §First half 34-21; second 25-27.

INDIVIDUAL RECORDS (1883 TO DATE)

SERVICE

Most years by non-pitcher
18—Mike Schmidt
Most years by pitcher
15—Steve Carlton

BATTING

Most games
163—Pete Rose, 1979
Most games, career
2,404—Mike Schmidt
Most at-bats
701—Juan Samuel, 160 games, 1984
Most at-bats, career
8,352—Mike Schmidt
Most runs
196—Billy Hamilton, 131 games, 1894
Most runs (since 1900)
158—Chuck Klein, 156 games, 1930
Most runs, career
1,506—Mike Schmidt
Most hits
254—Lefty O'Doul, 154 games, 1929
Most hits, career
2,234—Mike Schmidt
Most singles
181—Lefty O'Doul, 154 games, 1929
      Richie Ashburn, 154 games, 1951
Most singles, career
1,811—Richie Ashburn
Most doubles
59—Chuck Klein, 156 games, 1930
Most doubles, career
432—Ed Delahanty
Most doubles, career (since 1900)
408—Mike Schmidt
Most triples
26—Sam Thompson, 102 games, 1894
Most triples (since 1900)
19—Juan Samuel, 160 games, 1984
Most triples, career
151—Ed Delahanty
Most triples, career (since 1900)
127—Sherry Magee
Most homers by lefthander
43—Chuck Klein, 149 games, 1929
Most homers by righthander
48—Mike Schmidt, 150 games, 1980
Most homers by rookie
30—Willie Montanez, 158 games, 1971
Most homers, month
15—Cy Williams, May, 1923

Most homers at home
29—Chuck Klein, 1932
Most homers on road
29—Mike Schmidt, 1979
Most homers by righthander, career
548—Mike Schmidt
Most homers by lefthander, career
243—Chuck Klein
Most grand slams
4—Vince DiMaggio, 127 games, 1945
Most grand slams, career
7—Mike Schmidt
Most total bases
445—Chuck Klein, 156 games, 1930
Most total bases, career
4,404—Mike Schmidt
Most long hits
107—Chuck Klein, 156 games, 1930
Most long hits, career
1,015—Mike Schmidt
Most extra bases on long hits
195—Chuck Klein, 156 games, 1930
Most extra bases on long hits, career
2,170—Mike Schmidt
Most sacrifice hits
43—Kid Gleason, 155 games, 1905
Most sacrifice flies
13—Willie Montanez, 158 games, 1971
      Mike Schmidt, 150 games, 1980
Most bases on balls
129—Lenny Dykstra, 161 games, 1993
Most bases on balls, career
1,507—Mike Schmidt
Most strikeouts
180—Mike Schmidt, 158 games, 1975
Fewest strikeouts
8—Emil Verban, 155 games, 1947
Most strikeouts, career
1,883—Mike Schmidt
Most hit by pitch
19—Dave Hollins, 156 games, 1992
Most runs batted in
170—Chuck Klein, 154 games, 1930
Most runs batted in, career
1,595—Mike Schmidt
Most game-winning RBIs
17—Mike Schmidt, 150 games, 1980
      Gary Matthews, 162 games, 1982
Highest batting average
.408—Ed Delahanty, 145 games, 1899
Highest batting average (since 1900)
.398—Lefty O'Doul, 154 games, 1929
Highest batting average, career
.362—Billy Hamilton

Highest batting average, career (since 1900)
.326—Chuck Klein
Highest slugging average
.687—Chuck Klein, 156 games, 1930
Longest batting streak
36 games—Billy Hamilton, 1894
Longest batting streak (since 1900)
26 games—Chuck Klein, 1930 (twice)
Most grounded into double play
25—Del Ennis, 153 games, 1950
Ted Sizemore, 152 games, 1977
Fewest grounded into double play
3—Chuck Klein, 152 games, 1933
Richie Ashburn, 156 games, 1953
Richie Ashburn, 153 games, 1954

BASERUNNING

Most stolen bases
115—Billy Hamilton, 133 games, 1891
Most stolen bases (since 1900)
72—Juan Samuel, 160 games, 1984
Most stolen bases, career
437—Ed Delahanty
Most stolen bases, career (since 1900)
387—Sherry Magee
Most caught stealing
19—Juan Samuel, 161 games, 1985

PITCHING (SINCE 1900)

Most games
90—Kent Tekulve, 1987
Most games, career
529—Robin Roberts
Most games started
45—Grover Alexander, 1916
Most games started, career
499—Steve Carlton
Most complete games
38—Grover Alexander, 1916
Most complete games, career
272—Robin Roberts
Most games finished
62—Jim Konstanty, 1950
Most innings
389—Grover Alexander, 1916
Most innings, career
3,740—Robin Roberts
Most games won
33—Grover Alexander, 1916
Most games won, career
241—Steve Carlton
Most 20-victory seasons
6—Grover Alexander, Robin Roberts
Most games lost
24—Chick Fraser, 1904

Most games lost, career
199—Robin Roberts
Highest winning percentage
.800—Robin Roberts (28-7), 1952
Tommy Greene (16-4), 1993
Longest winning streak
15 games—Steve Carlton, 1972
Longest losing streak
12 games—Russ Miller, 1928
Hugh Mulcahy, 1940
Ken Reynolds, 1972
Most saves, season
43—Mitch Williams, 1993
Most bases on balls
164—Earl Moore, 1911
Most bases on balls, career
1,252—Steve Carlton
Most strikeouts
310—Steve Carlton, 1972
Most strikeouts, game
18—Chris Short, October 2, 1965, second game, first 15
innings of 18-inning game
17—Art Mahaffey, April 23, 1961, second game
Most strikeouts, career
3,031—Steve Carlton
Most shutouts
16—Grover Alexander, 1916
Most shutouts, career
61—Grover Alexander
Most 1-0 shutouts won
4—Grover Alexander, 1916
Most runs
178—Ray Benge, 1930
Most earned runs
147—Robin Roberts, 1956
Most hits
348—Claude Passeau, 1937
Most hit batsmen
19—Fred Mitchell, 1903
Jim Bunning, 1966
Most wild pitches
22—Jack Hamilton, 1962
Most home runs
46—Robin Roberts, 1956
Most sacrifice hits
21—Curt Simmons, 1954
Dennis Bennett, 1964
Jim Bunning, 1965
Wayne Twitchell, 1973
Most sacrifice flies
15—Randy Lerch, 1979
Lowest ERA
1.22—Grover Alexander, 376 innings, 1915

CLUB RECORDS

Most players
49 in 1946
Fewest players
23 in 1915
Most games
163 in 1979, 1983, 1989
Most at-bats
5,685 in 1993
Most runs
944 in 1930
Fewest runs
394 in 1942
Most opponents' runs
1,199 in 1930
Most hits
1,783 in 1930
Fewest hits
1,113 in 1907

Most singles
1,338 in 1894
Most singles (since 1900)
1,268 in 1930
Most doubles
345 in 1930
Most triples
148 in 1894
Most triples (since 1900)
82 in 1905
Most homers
186 in 1977
Fewest homers (154 or 162-game schedule)
11 in 1908
Most homers at Baker Bowl, home and opponents
160 in 1929
Most homers at Shibe Park, home and opponents
154 in 1955

Most homers at Veterans Stadium, home and opponents
164 in 1977
Most pinch home runs
11 in 1958
Most grand slams
8 in 1993
Most total bases
2,594 in 1930
Most long hits
519 in 1932
Most extra bases on long hits
936 in 1977
Most sacrifices (sacrifice hits and sacrifice flies)
239 in 1909
Most sacrifice hits
174 in 1905
Most sacrifice flies
74 in 1977
Most stolen bases
200 in 1908
Most caught stealing
80 in 1921
Most bases on balls
665 in 1993
Most strikeouts
1,154 in 1986
Fewest strikeouts
452 in 1924
Most hit by pitch
53 in 1962
Fewest hit by pitch
9 in 1939
Most runs batted in
884 in 1930
Most game-winning RBIs
86 in 1980
Highest batting average
.343 in 1894
Highest batting average (since 1900)
.315 in 1930
Lowest batting average
.232 in 1942
Highest slugging average
.467 in 1929
Lowest slugging average
.305 in 1907
Most grounded into double play
144 in 1950
Fewest grounded into double play
91 in 1935, 1973
Most left on bases
1,281 in 1993
Fewest left on bases
991 in 1920
Most .300 hitters
10 in 1925
Most putouts
4,440 in 1980
Fewest putouts
3,887 in 1907
Most assists
2,176 in 1921
Fewest assists
1,437 in 1957
Most chances accepted
6,440 in 1913
Fewest chances accepted
5,545 in 1955
Most errors
403 in 1904
Fewest errors
104 in 1978
Most errorless games
89 in 1966
Most consecutive errorless games
11 in 1967

Most double plays
179 in 1961, 1973
Fewest double plays
111 in 1991
Most passed balls
27 in 1947, 1971
Fewest passed balls
3 in 1952, 1956
Highest fielding average
.983 in 1978, 1979
Lowest fielding average
.936 in 1904
Highest home attendance
3,137,674 in 1993
Highest road attendance
2,666,219 in 1993
Most games won
101 in 1976, 1977
Most games lost
111 in 1941
Most games won, month
22 in September 1916, July 1950, July 1952, May 1976, August 1977, September 1983
Most games lost, month
27 in September 1939
Highest percentage games won
.623 in 1886 (won 71, lost 43)
in 1976 and 1977 (won 101, lost 61)
Lowest percentage games won
.173 in 1883 (won 17, lost 81)
Lowest percentage games won (since 1900)
.279 in 1941 (won 43, lost 111)
Games won, league
7,832 in 112 years
Games lost, league
8,963 in 112 years
Most shutouts won
24 in 1916
Most shutouts lost
23 in 1908, 1909
Most 1-0 games won
7 in 1913
Most 1-0 games lost
10 in 1967
Most consecutive games won
16 in 1887, 1890, 1892
Most consecutive games won (since 1900)
13 in 1977, 1991
Most consecutive games lost
23 in 1961
Number of times league champions
5
Number of last-place finishes
24 (tied in 1947)
Most runs, game
29 vs. Louisville, August 17, 1894
Most runs, game (since 1900)
26 vs. New York, June 11, 1985
Most runs by opponent, game
29 by Boston, June 20, 1883
by New York, June 15, 1887
Most runs by opponent, game (since 1900)
28 by St. Louis, July 6, 1929, second game
Most runs, shutout game
24 vs. Indianapolis, June 28, 1887
Most runs, shutout game (since 1900)
18 vs. Pittsburgh, July 11, 1910
vs. Cincinnati, August 10, 1930, first game
vs. Cincinnati, July 14, 1934, first game
Most runs by opponent, shutout game
28 by Providence, August 21, 1883
Most runs by opponent, shutout game (since 1900)
16 by Chicago, May 4, 1929, first game
Most runs doubleheader shutout
18 vs. Brooklyn, September 26, 1912

Most runs, inning
  12 vs. New York, October 2, 1897, second inning
    vs. Chicago, July 21, 1923, first game, sixth inning
Longest 1-0 game won
  16 innings vs. Chicago, May 17, 1991
Longest 1-0 game lost
  17 innings vs. Montreal, September 21, 1981
Most hits, game
  36 vs. Louisville, August 17, 1894
Most hits, game (since 1900)
  27 vs. New York, June 11, 1985
Most home runs, game
  6 vs. St. Louis, May 11, 1923
    vs. Pittsburgh, August 28, 1948, second game
    vs. Cincinnati, June 2, 1949
    vs. San Francisco, April 27, 1965
    vs. Chicago, October 3, 1972
    vs. Chicago, April 17, 1976, 10 innings

    vs. Chicago, August 12, 1977
    vs. Chicago, August 17, 1985
    vs. Colorado, May 30, 1993
Most consecutive games with one or more homers
  13 (16 homers), 1964
Most total bases, game
  49 vs. Louisville, August 17, 1894
  48 vs. Pittsburgh, July 23, 1930, second game, 13 innings
    vs. Chicago, May 17, 1979, 10 innings
  47 vs. New York, June 11, 1985
Largest crowd, day game
  60,985 vs. Chicago, April 9, 1993
Largest crowd, doubleheader
  63,346 vs. Pittsburgh, August 10, 1979
Largest crowd, night game
  63,816 vs. Cincinnati, July 3, 1984
Largest crowd, home opener
  60,985 vs. Chicago, April 9, 1993

PITTSBURGH PIRATES

YEARLY FINISHES

Year	Position	W	L	Pct.	*GB	Manager	Attendance
1901	1st	90	49	.647	+ 7½	Fred Clarke	251,955
1902	1st	103	36	.741	+27½	Fred Clarke	243,826
1903	1st	91	49	.650	+ 6½	Fred Clarke	326,855
1904	4th	87	66	.569	19	Fred Clarke	340,615
1905	2nd	96	57	.627	9	Fred Clarke	369,124
1906	3rd	93	60	.608	23½	Fred Clarke	394,877
1907	2nd	91	63	.591	17	Fred Clarke	319,506
1908	2nd	98	56	.636	1	Fred Clarke	382,444
1909	1st	110	42	.724	+ 6½	Fred Clarke	534,950
1910	3rd	86	67	.562	17½	Fred Clarke	436,586
1911	3rd	85	69	.552	14½	Fred Clarke	432,000
1912	2nd	93	58	.616	10	Fred Clarke	384,000
1913	4th	78	71	.523	21½	Fred Clarke	296,000
1914	7th	69	85	.448	25½	Fred Clarke	139,620
1915	5th	73	81	.474	18	Fred Clarke	225,743
1916	6th	65	89	.422	29	Jimmy Callahan	289,132
1917	8th	51	103	.331	47	Jimmy Callahan, Honus Wagner, Hugo Bezdek	192,807
1918	4th	65	60	.520	17	Hugo Bezdek	213,610
1919	4th	71	68	.511	24½	Hugo Bezdek	276,810
1920	4th	79	75	.513	14	George Gibson	429,037
1921	2nd	90	63	.588	4	George Gibson	701,567
1922	3rd (tied)	85	69	.552	8	George Gibson, Bill McKechnie	523,675
1923	3rd	87	67	.565	8½	Bill McKechnie	611,082
1924	3rd	90	63	.588	3	Bill McKechnie	736,883
1925	1st	95	58	.621	+ 8½	Bill McKechnie	804,354
1926	3rd	84	69	.549	4½	Bill McKechnie	798,542
1927	1st	94	60	.610	+ 1½	Donie Bush	869,720
1928	4th	85	67	.559	9	Donie Bush	495,070
1929	2nd	88	65	.575	10½	Donie Bush, Jewel Ens	491,377
1930	5th	80	74	.519	12	Jewel Ens	357,795
1931	5th	75	79	.487	26	Jewel Ens	260,392
1932	2nd	86	68	.558	4	George Gibson	287,262
1933	2nd	87	67	.565	5	George Gibson	288,747
1934	5th	74	76	.493	19½	George Gibson, Pie Traynor	322,622
1935	4th	86	67	.562	13½	Pie Traynor	352,885
1936	4th	84	70	.545	8	Pie Traynor	372,524
1937	3rd	86	68	.558	10	Pie Traynor	459,679
1938	2nd	86	64	.573	2	Pie Traynor	641,033
1939	6th	68	85	.444	28½	Pie Traynor	376,734
1940	4th	78	76	.506	22½	Frankie Frisch	507,934
1941	4th	81	73	.526	19	Frankie Frisch	482,241
1942	5th	66	81	.449	36½	Frankie Frisch	448,897
1943	4th	80	74	.519	25	Frankie Frisch	604,278
1944	2nd	90	63	.588	14½	Frankie Frisch	498,740
1945	4th	82	72	.532	16	Frankie Frisch	604,694
1946	7th	63	91	.409	34	Frankie Frisch, Spud Davis	749,962
1947	7th (tied)	62	92	.403	32	Billy Herman, Bill Burwell	1,283,531
1948	4th	83	71	.539	8½	Billy Meyer	1,517,021
1949	6th	71	83	.461	26	Billy Meyer	1,499,435
1950	8th	57	96	.373	33½	Billy Meyer	1,166,267
1951	7th	64	90	.416	32½	Billy Meyer	980,590
1952	8th	42	112	.273	54½	Billy Meyer	686,673

Year Position	W	L	Pct.	*GB	Manager	Attendance
1953 — 8th	50	104	.325	55	Fred Haney	572,757
1954 — 8th	53	101	.344	44	Fred Haney	475,494
1955 — 8th	60	94	.390	38½	Fred Haney	469,397
1956 — 7th	66	88	.429	27	Bobby Bragan	949,878
1957 — 7th (tied)	62	92	.403	33	Bobby Bragan, Danny Murtaugh	850,732
1958 — 2nd	84	70	.545	8	Danny Murtaugh	1,311,988
1959 — 4th	78	76	.506	9	Danny Murtaugh	1,359,917
1960 — 1st	95	59	.617	+ 7	Danny Murtaugh	1,705,828
1961 — 6th	75	79	.487	18	Danny Murtaugh	1,199,128
1962 — 4th	93	68	.578	8	Danny Murtaugh	1,090,648
1963 — 8th	74	88	.457	25	Danny Murtaugh	783,648
1964 — 6th (tied)	80	82	.494	13	Danny Murtaugh	759,496
1965 — 3rd	90	72	.556	7	Harry Walker	909,279
1966 — 3rd	92	70	.568	3	Harry Walker	1,196,618
1967 — 6th	81	81	.500	20½	Harry Walker, Danny Murtaugh	907,012
1968 — 6th	80	82	.494	17	Larry Shepard	693,485

EAST DIVISION

Year Position	W	L	Pct.	*GB	Manager	Attendance
1969 — 3rd	88	74	.543	12	Larry Shepard, Alex Grammas	769,369
1970 — 1st†	89	73	.549	+ 5	Danny Murtaugh	1,341,947
1971 — 1st‡	97	65	.599	+ 7	Danny Murtaugh	1,501,132
1972 — 1st†	96	59	.619	+11	Bill Virdon	1,427,460
1973 — 3rd	80	82	.494	2½	Bill Virdon, Danny Murtaugh	1,319,913
1974 — 1st†	88	74	.543	+ 1½	Danny Murtaugh	1,110,552
1975 — 1st†	92	69	.571	+ 6½	Danny Murtaugh	1,270,018
1976 — 2nd	92	70	.568	9	Danny Murtaugh	1,025,945
1977 — 2nd	96	66	.593	5	Chuck Tanner	1,237,349
1978 — 2nd	88	73	.547	1½	Chuck Tanner	964,106
1979 — 1st‡	98	64	.605	+ 2	Chuck Tanner	1,435,454
1980 — 3rd	83	79	.512	8	Chuck Tanner	1,646,757
1981 — 4th/6th	46	56	.451	§	Chuck Tanner	541,789
1982 — 4th	84	78	.519	8	Chuck Tanner	1,024,106
1983 — 2nd	84	78	.519	6	Chuck Tanner	1,225,916
1984 — 6th	75	87	.463	21½	Chuck Tanner	773,500
1985 — 6th	57	104	.354	43½	Chuck Tanner	735,900
1986 — 6th	64	98	.395	44	Jim Leyland	1,000,917
1987 — 4th (tied)	80	82	.494	15	Jim Leyland	1,161,193
1988 — 2nd	85	75	.531	15	Jim Leyland	1,866,713
1989 — 5th	74	88	.457	19	Jim Leyland	1,374,141
1990 — 1st†	95	67	.586	+ 4	Jim Leyland	2,049,908
1991 — 1st†	98	64	.605	+14	Jim Leyland	2,065,302
1992 — 1st†	96	66	.593	+ 9	Jim Leyland	1,829,395
1993 — 5th	75	87	.463	22	Jim Leyland	1,650,593

CENTRAL DIVISION

Year Position	W	L	Pct.	*GB	Manager	Attendance
1994 — 3rd (tied)	53	61	.465	13	Jim Leyland	1,222,520

*Games behind winner.   †Lost Championship Series.   ‡Won Championship Series.   §First half 25-23; second half 21-33.

INDIVIDUAL RECORDS (1887 TO DATE)

SERVICE

Most years by non-pitcher
21—Willie Stargell
Most years by pitcher
18—Babe Adams

BATTING

Most games
163—Bill Mazeroski, 1967
Bobby Bonilla, 1989
Most games, career
2,433—Roberto Clemente
Most at-bats
698—Matty Alou, 162 games, 1969
Most at-bats, career
9,454—Roberto Clemente
Most runs
148—Jake Stenzel, 131 games, 1894
Most runs (since 1900)
144—Kiki Cuyler, 153 games, 1925

Most runs, career
1,520—Honus Wagner
Most hits
237—Paul Waner, 155 games, 1927
Most hits, career
3,000—Roberto Clemente
Most singles
198—Lloyd Waner, 150 games, 1927
Most singles, career
2,154—Roberto Clemente
Most doubles
62—Paul Waner, 154 games, 1932
Most doubles, career
556—Honus Wagner, Paul Waner
Most triples
36—Owen Wilson, 152 games, 1912
Most triples, career
231—Honus Wagner
Most homers by righthander
54—Ralph Kiner, 152 games, 1949
Most homers by lefthander
48—Willie Stargell, 141 games, 1971

Most homers by rookie
23—Johnny Rizzo, 143 games, 1938
    Ralph Kiner, 144 games, 1946
Most homers, month
16—Ralph Kiner, September, 1949
Most homers at home
31—Ralph Kiner, 1948
Most homers on road
27—Willie Stargell, 1971
Most homers by righthander, career
301—Ralph Kiner
Most homers by lefthander, career
475—Willie Stargell
Most grand slams
4—Ralph Kiner, 152 games, 1949
Most grand slams, career
11—Ralph Kiner, Willie Stargell
Most total bases
366—Kiki Cuyler, 153 games, 1925
Most total bases, career
4,492—Roberto Clemente
Most long hits, career
953—Willie Stargell
Most long hits
90—Willie Stargell, 148 games, 1973
Most extra bases on long hits
191—Ralph Kiner, 152 games, 1949
Most extra bases on long hits, career
1,958—Willie Stargell
Most sacrifice hits
39—Jay Bell, 159 games, 1990
Most sacrifice flies
15—Bobby Bonilla, 160 games, 1990
Most bases on balls
137—Ralph Kiner, 151 games, 1951
Most bases on balls, career
937—Willie Stargell
Most strikeouts
163—Donn Clendenon, 158 games, 1968
Most strikeouts, career
1,936—Willie Stargell
Fewest strikeouts
13—Carson Bigbee, 150 games, 1922
    Lloyd Waner, 152 games, 1928
Most hit by pitch
14—Al Oliver, 151 games, 1970
Most runs batted in
131—Paul Waner, 155 games, 1927
Most runs batted in, career
1,540—Willie Stargell
Most game-winning RBIs
16—Andy Van Slyke, 154 games, 1988
Most consecutive games with RBI
12—Paul Waner (23 RBIs), 1927
Highest batting average
.385—Arky Vaughan, 137 games, 1935
Highest batting average, career
.340—Paul Waner
Highest slugging average
.658—Ralph Kiner, 152 games, 1949
Longest batting streak
27 games—Jimmy Williams, 1899
Longest batting streak (since 1900)
26 games—Danny O'Connell, 1953
Longest batting streak, two seasons
30 games—Charlie Grimm, 1922 (5), 1923 (25)
Most grounded into double play
25—Al Todd, 133 games, 1938
Fewest grounded into double play
4—Omar Moreno, 150 games, 1977
    Frank Taveras, 157 games, 1978
    Barry Bonds, 150 games, 1987
    Bobby Bonilla, 159 games, 1988

BASERUNNING

Most stolen bases
96—Omar Moreno, 162 games, 1980
Most stolen bases, career
688—Max Carey
Most caught stealing
33—Omar Moreno, 162 games, 1980

PITCHING (SINCE 1900)

Most games
94—Kent Tekulve, 1979
Most games, career
802—Roy Face
Most games, started
42—Bob Friend, 1956
Most games, started, career
477—Bob Friend
Most complete games
32—Vic Willis, 1906
Most complete games, career
263—Wilbur Cooper
Most games finished
67—Kent Tekulve, 1979
Most innings
331—Burleigh Grimes, 1928
Most innings, career
3,481—Bob Friend
Most games won
28—Jack Chesbro, 1902
Most games won, career
202—Wilbur Cooper
Most 20-victory seasons
4—Deacon Phillippe, Vic Willis, Wilbur Cooper, Jesse Tannehill
Most games lost
21—Murry Dickson, 1952
Most games lost, career
218—Bob Friend
Highest winning percentage
.947—Roy Face (18-1), 1959
Longest winning streak
17 games, Roy Face, 1959
Longest losing streak
13 games—Burleigh Grimes, 1917
Most saves, season
34—Jim Gott, 1988
Most bases on balls
159—Marty O'Toole, 1912
Most bases on balls, career
869—Bob Friend
Most strikeouts
276—Bob Veale, 1965
Most strikeouts, game
16—Bob Veale, June 1, 1965
Most strikeouts, career
1,682—Bob Friend
Most shutouts
8—Jack Chesbro, 1902
    Lefty Leifield, 1906
    Al Mamaux, 1915
    Babe Adams, 1920
Most shutouts, career
45—Babe Adams
Most 1-0 shutouts won
3—Vic Willis, 1908
    Claude Hendrix, 1912
    Wilbur Cooper, 1917
    Ed Brandt, 1937
Most runs
181—Ray Kremer, 1930
Most earned runs
154—Ray Kremer, 1930
Most hits
366—Ray Kremer, 1930
Most hit batsmen
21—Jack Chesbro, 1902

Most wild pitches
18—Bob Veale, 1964
Most home runs
32—Murry Dickson, 1951
Most sacrifice hits
20—Max Surkont, 1954
Jerry Reuss, 1974

Most sacrifice flies
12—Vern Law, 1954
John Candelaria, 1974
Lowest ERA
1.87—Wilbur Cooper, 246 innings, 1916

CLUB RECORDS

Most players
49 in 1987
Fewest players
25 in 1938
Most games
164 in 1989
Most at-bats
5,724 in 1967
Most runs
912 in 1925
Fewest runs
464 in 1917
Most opponents' runs
928 in 1930
Most hits
1,698 in 1922
Fewest hits
1,197 in 1914
Most singles
1,297 in 1922
Most doubles
316 in 1925
Most triples
129 in 1912
Most homers
158 in 1966
Fewest homers (154 or 162-game schedule)
9 in 1917
Most homers at Forbes Field, home and opponents
182 in 1947
Most homers at Three Rivers Stadium, home and opponents
155 in 1987
Most grand slams
7 in 1978
Most pinch home runs
8 in 1944
Most total bases
2,430 in 1966
Most long hits
498 in 1925
Most extra bases on long hits
844 in 1966
Most sacrifices (sacrifice hits and sacrifice flies)
214 in 1927
Most sacrifice hits
190 in 1906
Most sacrifice flies
67 in 1982
Most stolen bases
264 in 1907
Most caught stealing
120 in 1977
Most bases on balls
620 in 1991
Most strikeouts
1,011 in 1966
Fewest strikeouts
326 in 1922
Most hit by pitch
55 in 1993
Fewest hit by pitch
11 in 1937
Most runs batted in
844 in 1930
Most game-winning RBIs
80 in 1980, 1982

Highest batting average
.309 in 1928
Lowest batting average
.231 in 1952
Highest slugging average
.449 in 1930
Lowest slugging average
.298 in 1917
Most grounded into double play
142 in 1950
Fewest grounded into double play
95 in 1978
Most left on bases
1,241 in 1936
Fewest left on bases
992 in 1924
Most .300 hitters
9 in 1928
Most putouts
4,480 in 1979
Fewest putouts
3,983 in 1934
Most assists
2,089 in 1905
Fewest assists
1,584 in 1934
Most chances accepted
6,462 in 1968
Fewest chances accepted
5,567 in 1934
Most errors
291 in 1904
Fewest errors
101 in 1992
Most errorless games
87 in 1992
Most consecutive errorless games
9 in 1983, 1992, 1993
Most double plays
215 in 1966
Fewest double plays
94 in 1935
Most passed balls
32 in 1953
Fewest passed balls
3 in 1941, 1943
Highest fielding average
.984 in 1992
Lowest fielding average
.955 in 1904
Highest home attendance
2,065,302 in 1991
Highest road attendance
2,507,346 in 1993
Most games won
110 in 1909
Most games lost
113 in 1890
Most games lost (since 1900)
112 in 1952
Most games won, month
25 in September 1901, September 1908, July 1932
Most games lost, month
24 in September 1916
Highest percentage games won
.741 in 1902 (won 103, lost 36)

— 332 —

Lowest percentage games won
.169 in 1890 (won 23, lost 113)
Lowest percentage games won (since 1900)
.273 in 1952 (won 42, lost 112)
Games won, league
8,479 in 108 years
Games lost, league
7,913 in 108 years
Most shutouts won
26 in 1906
Most shutouts lost
27 in 1916
Most 1-0 games won
10 in 1908
Most 1-0 games lost
10 in 1914
Most consecutive games won
16 in 1909
Most consecutive games lost
23 in 1890
Most consecutive games lost (since 1900)
12 in 1939
Number of times league champions
9
Number of last-place finishes
12 (tied in 1947, 1957)
Most runs, game
27 vs. Boston, June 6, 1894
Most runs, game (since 1900)
24 vs. St. Louis, June 22, 1925
Most runs by opponent, game
28 by Boston, August 27, 1887
Most runs by opponent, game (since 1900)
23 by Philadelphia, July 13, 1900, eight innings
by Brooklyn, July 10, 1943

Most runs, shutout game
22 vs. Chicago, September 16, 1975
Most runs by opponent, shutout game
18 by Philadelphia, July 11, 1910
Most runs, doubleheader shutout
15 vs. Philadelphia, August 7, 1915
Most runs, inning
12 vs. St. Louis, April 22, 1892, first inning
vs. Boston, June 6, 1894, third inning
Most runs, inning (since 1900)
11 vs. St. Louis, September 7, 1942, first game, sixth inning
vs. Cincinnati, May 4, 1992, sixth inning
Longest 1-0 game won
18 innings vs. San Diego, June 7, 1972, second game
Longest 1-0 game lost
14 innings vs. Cincinnati, June 18, 1943
Most hits, game
27 vs. Philadelphia, August 8, 1922, first game
Most home runs, game
7 vs. Boston, June 8, 1894
vs. St. Louis, August 16, 1947
Most consecutive games with one or more homers
13 (21 homers), 1994
Most total bases, game
47 vs. Atlanta, August 1, 1970
Largest crowd, day game
51,726 vs. San Diego, June 6, 1976
Largest crowd, doubleheader
49,886 vs. New York, July 27, 1972
Largest crowd, night game
54,274 vs. Montreal, April 8, 1991
Largest crowd, home opener
54,274 vs. Montreal, April 8, 1991

ST. LOUIS CARDINALS

YEARLY FINISHES

Year	Position	W	L	Pct.	*GB	Manager	Attendance
1901	4th	76	64	.543	14½	Patsy Donovan	379,988
1902	6th	56	78	.418	44½	Patsy Donovan	226,417
1903	8th	43	94	.314	46½	Patsy Donovan	226,538
1904	5th	75	79	.487	31½	Kid Nichols	386,750
1905	6th	58	96	.377	47½	Kid Nichols, Jimmy Burke, Matt Robison	292,800
1906	7th	52	98	.347	63	John McCloskey	283,770
1907	8th	52	101	.340	55½	John McCloskey	185,377
1908	8th	49	105	.318	50	John McCloskey	205,129
1909	7th	54	98	.355	56	Roger Bresnahan	299,982
1910	7th	63	90	.412	40½	Roger Bresnahan	355,668
1911	5th	75	74	.503	22	Roger Bresnahan	447,768
1912	6th	63	90	.412	41	Roger Bresnahan	241,759
1913	8th	51	99	.340	49	Miller Huggins	203,531
1914	3rd	81	72	.529	13	Miller Huggins	256,099
1915	6th	72	81	.471	18½	Miller Huggins	252,666
1916	7th (tied)	60	93	.392	33½	Miller Huggins	224,308
1917	3rd	82	70	.539	15	Miller Huggins	288,491
1918	8th	51	78	.395	33	Jack Hendricks	110,599
1919	7th	54	83	.394	40½	Branch Rickey	167,059
1920	5th (tied)	75	79	.487	18	Branch Rickey	326,836
1921	3rd	87	66	.569	7	Branch Rickey	384,773
1922	3rd (tied)	85	69	.552	8	Branch Rickey	536,998
1923	5th	79	74	.516	16	Branch Rickey	338,551
1924	6th	65	89	.422	28½	Branch Rickey	272,885
1925	4th	77	76	.503	18	Branch Rickey, Rogers Hornsby	404,959
1926	1st	89	65	.578	+ 2	Rogers Hornsby	668,428
1927	2nd	92	61	.601	1½	Bob O'Farrell	749,340
1928	1st	95	59	.617	+ 2	Bill McKechnie	761,574
1929	4th	78	74	.513	20	Bill McKechnie, Billy Southworth	399,887
1930	1st	92	62	.597	+ 2	Gabby Street	508,501
1931	1st	101	53	.656	+13	Gabby Street	608,535
1932	6th (tied)	72	82	.468	18	Gabby Street	279,219
1933	5th	82	71	.536	9½	Gabby Street, Frankie Frisch	256,171
1934	1st	95	58	.621	+ 2	Frankie Frisch	325,056
1935	2nd	96	58	.623	4	Frankie Frisch	506,084

Year	Position	W	L	Pct.	*GB	Manager	Attendance
1936	2nd (tied) ...	87	67	.565	5	Frankie Frisch	448,078
1937	4th	81	73	.526	15	Frankie Frisch	430,811
1938	6th	71	80	.470	17½	Frankie Frisch, Mike Gonzalez	291,418
1939	2nd	92	61	.601	4½	Ray Blades	400,245
1940	3rd	84	69	.549	16	Ray Blades, Mike Gonzalez, Billy Southworth	324,078
1941	2nd	97	56	.634	2½	Billy Southworth	633,645
1942	1st	106	48	.688	+ 2	Billy Southworth	553,552
1943	1st	105	49	.682	+18	Billy Southworth	517,135
1944	1st	105	49	.682	+14½	Billy Southworth	461,968
1945	2nd	95	59	.617	3	Billy Southworth	594,630
1946	1st†	98	58	.628	+ 2	Eddie Dyer	1,061,807
1947	2nd	89	65	.578	5	Eddie Dyer	1,247,913
1948	2nd	85	69	.552	6½	Eddie Dyer	1,111,440
1949	2nd	96	58	.623	1	Eddie Dyer	1,430,676
1950	5th	78	75	.510	12½	Eddie Dyer	1,093,411
1951	3rd	81	73	.526	15½	Marty Marion	1,013,429
1952	3rd	88	66	.571	8½	Eddie Stanky	913,113
1953	3rd (tied)	83	71	.539	22	Eddie Stanky	880,242
1954	6th	72	82	.468	25	Eddie Stanky	1,039,698
1955	7th	68	86	.442	30½	Eddie Stanky, Harry Walker	849,130
1956	4th	76	78	.494	17	Fred Hutchinson	1,029,773
1957	2nd	87	67	.565	8	Fred Hutchinson	1,183,575
1958	5th (tied)	72	82	.468	20	Fred Hutchinson, Stan Hack	1,063,730
1959	7th	71	83	.461	16	Solly Hemus	929,953
1960	3rd	86	68	.558	9	Solly Hemus	1,096,632
1961	5th	80	74	.519	13	Solly Hemus, Johnny Keane	855,305
1962	6th	84	78	.519	17½	Johnny Keane	953,895
1963	2nd	93	69	.574	6	Johnny Keane	1,170,546
1964	1st	93	69	.574	+ 1	Johnny Keane	1,143,294
1965	7th	80	81	.497	16½	Red Schoendienst	1,241,201
1966	6th	83	79	.512	12	Red Schoendienst	1,712,980
1967	1st	101	60	.627	+10½	Red Schoendienst	2,090,145
1968	1st	97	65	.599	+ 9	Red Schoendienst	2,011,167

EAST DIVISION

Year	Position	W	L	Pct.	*GB	Manager	Attendance
1969	4th	87	75	.537	13	Red Schoendienst	1,682,783
1970	4th	76	86	.469	13	Red Schoendienst	1,629,736
1971	2nd	90	72	.556	7	Red Schoendienst	1,604,671
1972	4th	75	81	.481	21½	Red Schoendienst	1,196,894
1973	2nd	81	81	.500	1½	Red Schoendienst	1,574,046
1974	2nd	86	75	.534	1½	Red Schoendienst	1,838,413
1975	3rd (tied)	82	80	.506	10½	Red Schoendienst	1,695,270
1976	5th	72	90	.444	29	Red Schoendienst	1,207,079
1977	3rd	83	79	.512	18	Vern Rapp	1,659,287
1978	5th	69	93	.426	21	Vern Rapp, Jack Krol, Ken Boyer	1,278,215
1979	3rd	86	76	.531	12	Ken Boyer	1,627,256
1980	4th	74	88	.457	17	Ken Boyer, Jack Krol, Whitey Herzog, Red Schoendienst	1,385,147
1981	2nd/2nd	59	43	.578	‡	Whitey Herzog	1,010,247
1982	1st§	92	70	.568	+ 3	Whitey Herzog	2,111,906
1983	4th	79	83	.488	11	Whitey Herzog	2,317,914
1984	3rd	84	78	.519	12½	Whitey Herzog	2,037,448
1985	1st§	101	61	.623	+ 3	Whitey Herzog	2,637,563
1986	3rd	79	82	.491	28½	Whitey Herzog	2,471,974
1987	1st§	95	67	.586	+ 3	Whitey Herzog	3,072,122
1988	5th	76	86	.469	25	Whitey Herzog	2,892,799
1989	3rd	86	76	.531	7	Whitey Herzog	3,080,980
1990	6th	70	92	.432	25	Whitey Herzog, Red Schoendienst, Joe Torre	2,573,225
1991	2nd	84	78	.519	14	Joe Torre	2,448,699
1992	3rd	83	79	.512	13	Joe Torre	2,418,483
1993	3rd	87	75	.537	10	Joe Torre	2,844,328

CENTRAL DIVISION

Year	Position	W	L	Pct.	*GB	Manager	Attendance
1994	3rd (tied)	53	61	.465	13	Joe Torre	1,866,544

*Games behind winner.   †Won pennant playoff.   ‡First half 30-20; second 29-23.   §Won Championship Series.

INDIVIDUAL RECORDS (1876 TO 1877, 1885 TO 1886, 1892 TO DATE)

SERVICE

Most years by non-pitcher
22—Stan Musial
Most years by pitcher
18—Jesse Haines

BATTING

Most games, season
163—Jose Oquendo, 1989
Most games, career
3,026—Stan Musial

Most at-bats
689—Lou Brock, 159 games, 1967
Most at-bats, career
10,972—Stan Musial
Most runs
141—Rogers Hornsby, 154 games, 1922
Most runs, career
1,949—Stan Musial
Most hits
250—Rogers Hornsby, 154 games, 1922
Most hits, career
3,630—Stan Musial
Most singles
180—Jesse Burkett, 142 games, 1901
Most singles, career
2,253—Stan Musial
Most doubles
64—Joe Medwick, 155 games, 1936
Most doubles, career
725—Stan Musial
Most triples
33—Perry Werden, 124 games, 1893
Most triples (since 1900)
25—Tommy Long, 140 games, 1915
Most triples, career
177—Stan Musial
Most homers by lefthander
43—Johnny Mize, 155 games, 1940
Most homers by righthander
42—Rogers Hornsby, 154 games, 1922
Most homers by rookie
21—Ray Jablonski, 157 games, 1953
Most homers, month
12—Whitey Kurowski, August 1947
Most homers at home
25—Johnny Mize, 1940
Most homers on road
23—Stan Musial, 1948
Most homers by lefthander, career
475—Stan Musial
Most homers by righthander, career
255—Ken Boyer
Most grand slams
3—Jim Bottomley, 153 games, 1925
Keith Hernandez, 161 games, 1977
Most grand slams, career
9—Stan Musial
Most total bases
450—Rogers Hornsby, 154 games, 1922
Most total bases, career
6,134—Stan Musial
Most long hits
103—Stan Musial, 155 games, 1948
Most long hits, career
1,377—Stan Musial
Most extra bases on long hits
200—Rogers Hornsby, 154 games, 1922
Most extra bases on long hits, career
2,504—Stan Musial
Most sacrifices (sacrifice hits and sacrifice flies)
37—Taylor Douthit, 139 games, 1926
Most sacrifice hits
36—Harry Walker, 148 games, 1943
Most sacrifice flies
14—George Hendrick, 136 games, 1982
Most bases on balls
136—Jack Clark, 131 games, 1987
Most bases on balls, career
1,599—Stan Musial
Most intentional bases on balls
26—Stan Musial, 135 games, 1958
Most strikeouts
147—Ray Lankford, 153 games, 1992
Most strikeouts, career
1,469—Lou Brock
Fewest strikeouts
10—Frankie Frisch, 153 games, 1927

Most hit by pitch
31—Steve Evans, 151 games, 1910
Most runs batted in
154—Joe Medwick, 156 games, 1937
Most runs batted in, career
1,951—Stan Musial
Most game-winning RBIs
21—Keith Hernandez, 160 games, 1982
Most consecutive games with RBI
10—Bill White (15 RBIs), 1961
Highest batting average
.424—Rogers Hornsby, 143 games, 1924
Highest batting average, career
.359—Rogers Hornsby
Highest slugging average
.756—Rogers Hornsby, 138 games, 1925
Longest batting streak
33 games—Rogers Hornsby, 1922
Most grounded into double play
29—Ted Simmons, 161 games, 1973
Fewest grounded into double play
2—Lou Brock, 155 games, 1965

BASERUNNING

Most stolen bases
118—Lou Brock, 153 games, 1974
Most stolen bases, career
888—Lou Brock
Most caught stealing
36—Miller Huggins, 148 games, 1914

PITCHING (SINCE 1900)

Most games
77—Mike Perez, 1992
Most games, career
554—Jesse Haines
Most games started
41—Bob Harmon, 1911
Most games started, career
482—Bob Gibson
Most complete games
39—Jack W. Taylor, 1904
Most complete games, career
255—Bob Gibson
Most games finished
63—Bruce Sutter, 1984
Most innings
352—Stoney McGlynn, 1907
Most innings, career
3,885—Bob Gibson
Most games won
30—Dizzy Dean, 1934
Most games won, career
251—Bob Gibson
Most 20-victory seasons
5—Bob Gibson
Most games lost
25—Stoney McGlynn, 1907
Bugs Raymond, 1908
Most games lost, career
174—Bob Gibson
Highest winning percentage
.811—Dizzy Dean (30-7), 1934
Longest winning streak
15 games—Bob Gibson, 1968
Longest losing streak
9 games—Bill McGee, 1938
Tom Poholsky, 1951
Bob Forsch, 1978
Most saves
47—Lee Smith, 1991
Most bases on balls
181—Bob Harmon, 1911
Most bases on balls, career
1,336—Bob Gibson

Most strikeouts
274—Bob Gibson, 1970
Most strikeouts, game
19—Steve Carlton, September 15, 1969
Most strikeouts, career
3,117—Bob Gibson
Most shutouts
13—Bob Gibson, 1968
Most shutouts, career
56—Bob Gibson
Most 1-0 shutouts won
4—Bob Gibson, 1968
Most runs
162—Stoney McGlynn, 1907
Most earned runs
129—Bill Sherdel, 1929

Most hits
337—Cy Young, 1900
Most hits batsmen
17—Gerry Staley, 1953
Most wild pitches
15—Fred Beebe, 1907, 1909
        Dave LaPoint, 1984
Most home runs
39—Murry Dickson, 1948
Most sacrifice hits
17—Dave LaPoint, 1983
        Larry McWilliams, 1988
Most sacrifice flies
13—Bob Forsch, 1979
Lowest ERA
1.12—Bob Gibson, 305 innings, 1968

CLUB RECORDS

Most players
49 in 1959
Fewest players
25 in 1904
Most games
164 in 1989
Most at-bats
5,734 in 1979
Most runs
1,004 in 1930
Fewest runs
372 in 1908
Most opponents' runs
806 in 1929
Most hits
1,732 in 1930
Fewest hits
1,105 in 1908
Most singles
1,223 in 1920
Most doubles
373 in 1939
Most triples
96 in 1920
Most homers
143 in 1955
Fewest homers (154 or 162-game schedule)
10 in 1906
Most homers at Sportsman's Park, home and opponents
176 in 1955
Most homers at Busch Memorial Stadium, home and opponents
118 in 1993
Most grand slams
7 in 1961
Most pinch home runs
7 in 1946, 1960, 1994
Most total bases
2,595 in 1930
Most long hits
566 in 1930
Most extra bases on long hits
863 in 1930
Most sacrifices (sacrifice hits and sacrifice flies)
212 in 1926
Most sacrifice hits
172 in 1943
Most sacrifice flies
66 in 1954
Most stolen bases
314 in 1985
Most caught stealing
118 in 1992
Most bases on balls
655 in 1910
Most strikeouts
996 in 1992

Fewest strikeouts
414 in 1925
Most hit by pitch
78 in 1910
Fewest hit by pitch
15 in 1925
Most runs batted in
942 in 1930
Most game-winning RBIs
94 in 1985
Highest batting average
.314 in 1930
Lowest batting average
.223 in 1908
Highest slugging average
.471 in 1930
Lowest slugging average
.288 in 1908
Most grounded into double play
166 in 1958
Fewest grounded into double play
75 in 1945
Most left on bases
1,251 in 1939
Fewest left on bases
968 in 1924
Most .300 hitters
11 in 1930
Most putouts
4,460 in 1979
Fewest putouts
3,952 in 1906
Most assists
2,293 in 1917
Fewest assists
1,595 in 1935
Most chances accepted
6,459 in 1917
Fewest chances accepted
5,752 in 1935
Most errors
348 in 1908
Fewest errors
94 in 1992
Most errorless games
100 in 1992
Most consecutive errorless games
16 in 1992
Most double plays
192 in 1974
Fewest double plays
114 in 1990
Most passed balls
38 in 1906
Fewest passed balls
4 in 1925

Highest fielding average
.985 in 1992
Lowest fielding average
.946 in 1908
Highest home attendance
3,080,980 in 1989
Highest road attendance
2,612,017 in 1993
Most games won
106 in 1942
Most games lost
111 in 1898
Most games lost (since 1900)
105 in 1908
Most games won, month
26 in July 1944
Most games lost, month
27 in September 1908
Highest percentage games won
.703 in 1876 (won 45, lost 19)
Highest percentage games won (since 1900)
.688 in 1942 (won 106, lost 48)
Lowest percentage games won
.221 in 1897 (won 29, lost 102)
Lowest percentage games won (since 1900)
.314 in 1903 (won 43, lost 94)
Games won, league
7,945 in 103 years
Games lost, league
7,795 in 103 years
Most shutouts won
30 in 1968
Most shutouts lost
33 in 1908
Most 1-0 games won
8 in 1907, 1968
Most 1-0 games lost
8 in 1918
Most consecutive games won
14 in 1935
Most consecutive games lost
15 in 1909

Number of times league champions
15
Number of last-place finishes
10 (tied in 1916)
Most runs, game
28 vs. Philadelphia, July 6, 1929, second game
Most runs by opponent, game
28 by Boston, September 3, 1896, first game
Most runs by opponent, game (since 1900)
24 by Pittsburgh, June 22, 1925
Most runs, inning
12 vs. Philadelphia, September 16, 1926, first game, third inning
Most runs, shutout game
18 vs. Cincinnati, June 10, 1944
Most runs by opponent, shutout game
19 by Pittsburgh, August 3, 1961
Most runs, doubleheader shutout
16 vs. Brooklyn, September 21, 1934
Most hits, game
30 vs. New York, June 1, 1895
Longest 1-0 game won
14 innings vs. Boston, June 15, 1939
Longest 1-0 game lost
18 innings vs. New York, July 2, 1933, first game
Most hits, game (since 1900)
28 vs. Philadelphia, July 6, 1929, second game
Most home runs, game
7 vs. Brooklyn, May 7, 1940
Most consecutive games with one or more homers
12 (18 homers), 1955
(15 homers), 1994
Most total bases, game
49 vs. Brooklyn, May 7, 1940
Largest crowd, day game
52,298 vs. Chicago, August 8, 1993
Largest crowd, night game
53,415 vs. Chicago, July 30, 1994
Largest crowd, doubleheader
52,657 vs. Atlanta, July 22, 1994
Largest crowd, home opener
51,647 vs. Pittsburgh, April 8, 1988

SAN DIEGO PADRES

YEARLY FINISHES
WEST DIVISION

Year	Position	W	L	Pct.	*GB	Manager	Attendance
1969	6th	52	110	.321	41	Preston Gomez	512,970
1970	6th	63	99	.389	39	Preston Gomez	643,679
1971	6th	61	100	.379	28½	Preston Gomez	557,513
1972	6th	58	95	.379	36½	Preston Gomez, Don Zimmer	644,273
1973	6th	60	102	.370	39	Don Zimmer	611,826
1974	6th	60	102	.370	42	John McNamara	1,075,399
1975	4th	71	91	.438	37	John McNamara	1,281,747
1976	5th	73	89	.451	29	John McNamara	1,458,478
1977	5th	69	93	.426	29	John McNamara, Bob Skinner, Alvin Dark	1,376,269
1978	4th	84	78	.519	11	Roger Craig	1,670,107
1979	5th	68	93	.422	22	Roger Craig	1,456,967
1980	6th	73	89	.451	19½	Jerry Coleman	1,139,026
1981	6th/6th	41	69	.373	†	Frank Howard	519,161
1982	4th	81	81	.500	8	Dick Williams	1,607,516
1983	4th	81	81	.500	10	Dick Williams	1,539,815
1984	1st‡	92	70	.568	+12	Dick Williams	1,983,904
1985	3rd (tied)	83	79	.512	12	Dick Williams	2,210,352
1986	4th	74	88	.457	22	Steve Boros	1,805,716
1987	6th	65	97	.401	25	Larry Bowa	1,454,061
1988	3rd	83	78	.516	11	Larry Bowa, Jack McKeon	1,506,896
1989	2nd	89	73	.549	3	Jack McKeon	2,009,031
1990	4th (tied)	75	87	.463	16	Jack McKeon, Greg Riddoch	1,856,396
1991	3rd	84	78	.519	10	Greg Riddoch	1,804,289
1992	3rd	82	80	.506	16	Greg Riddoch, Jim Riggleman	1,722,102
1993	7th	61	101	.377	43	Jim Riggleman	1,375,432
1994	4th	47	70	.402	12½	Jim Riggleman	953,857

*Games behind winner.   †First half 23-33; second 18-36.   ‡Won Championship Series.

SERVICE

Most years by non-pitcher
13—Tony Gwynn
Most years by pitcher
10—Eric Show

BATTING

Most games
162—Dave Winfield, 1980
Steve Garvey, 1985
Joe Carter, 1990
Most games, career
1,695—Tony Gwynn
Most at-bats
654—Steve Garvey, 162 games, 1985
Most at-bats, career
6,609—Tony Gwynn
Most runs
119—Tony Gwynn, 157 games, 1987
Most runs, career
991—Tony Gwynn
Most hits
218—Tony Gwynn, 157 games, 1987
Most hits, career
2,204—Tony Gwynn
Most singles
177—Tony Gwynn, 158 games, 1984
Most singles, career
1,696—Tony Gwynn
Most doubles
42—Terry Kennedy, 153 games, 1982
Most doubles, career
351—Tony Gwynn
Most triples
13—Tony Gwynn, 157 games, 1987
Most triples, career
79—Tony Gwynn
Most homers by righthander
38—Nate Colbert, 156 games, 1970
Nate Colbert, 151 games, 1972
Most homers by lefthander
35—Fred McGriff, 152 games, 1992
Most homers by rookie
18—Benito Santiago, 146 games, 1987
Most homers, month
11—Nate Colbert, May 1970
Nate Colbert, July 1972
Nate Colbert, August 1972
Most homers at home
18—Fred McGriff, 1991
Most homers on road
22—Nate Colbert, 1970, 1972
Most homers by righthander, career
163—Nate Colbert
Most homers by lefthander, career
84—Fred McGriff
Most grand slams
2—Held by many players
Most grand slams, career
5—Nate Colbert
Most total bases
333—Dave Winfield, 159 games, 1979
Most total bases, career
2,947—Tony Gwynn
Most long hits
71—Dave Winfield 159 games, 1979
Most long hits, career
508—Tony Gwynn
Most extra bases on long hits
149—Dave Winfield, 159 games, 1979
Most extra bases on long hits, career
787—Dave Winfield

Most sacrifice hits
28—Ozzie Smith, 159 games, 1978
Most sacrifice flies
10—Steve Garvey, 161 games, 1984
Carmelo Martinez, 149 games, 1984
Most bases on balls
132—Jack Clark, 142 games, 1989
Most bases on balls, career
590—Tony Gwynn
Most strikeouts
150—Nate Colbert, 156 games, 1970
Most strikeouts, career
856—Nate Colbert
Fewest strikeouts
23—Tony Gwynn, 158 games, 1984
Most hit by pitch
13—Gene Tenace, 147 games, 1977
Most runs batted in
118—Dave Winfield, 159 games, 1979
Most runs batted in, career
714—Tony Gwynn
Most game-winning RBIs
15—Terry Kennedy, 153 games, 1982
Steve Garvey, 161 games, 1984
Highest batting average
.370—Tony Gwynn, 157 games, 1987
Highest batting average, career
.333—Tony Gwynn
Highest slugging average
.580—Gary Sheffield, 146 games, 1992
Longest batting streak
34 games—Benito Santiago, 1987
Most grounded into double play
25—Steve Garvey, 161 games, 1984
Steve Garvey, 162 games, 1985
Fewest grounded into double play
2—Alan Wiggins, 158 games, 1984

BASERUNNING

Most stolen bases
70—Alan Wiggins, 158 games, 1984
Most stolen bases, career
268—Tony Gwynn
Most caught stealing
21—Alan Wiggins, 158 games, 1984

PITCHING

Most games
83—Craig Lefferts, 1986
Most games, career
375—Craig Lefferts
Most games started
40—Randy Jones, 1976
Most games started, career
253—Randy Jones
Most complete games
25—Randy Jones, 1976
Most complete games, career
71—Randy Jones
Most games finished
69—Rollie Fingers, 1977
Most innings
315—Randy Jones, 1976
Most innings, career
1,765—Randy Jones
Most games won
22—Randy Jones, 1976
Most games won, career
100—Eric Show
Most 20-victory seasons
2—Randy Jones
Most games lost
22—Randy Jones, 1974

Most games lost, career
105—Randy Jones
Highest winning percentage
.778—Gaylord Perry (21-6), 1978
Most saves
44—Mark Davis, 1989
Longest winning streak
11 games—Andy Hawkins, 1985
        LaMarr Hoyt, 1985
Longest losing streak
11 games—Gary Ross, 1969
Most bases on balls
122—Steve Arlin, 1972
Most bases on balls, career
593—Eric Show
Most strikeouts
231—Clay Kirby, 1971
Most strikeouts, career
951—Eric Show
Most strikeouts, game
15—Fred Norman, September 15, 1972
Most shutouts won
6—Fred Norman, 1972
    Randy Jones, 1975
Most shutouts won, career
18—Randy Jones

Most 1-0 shutouts won
2—Joe Niekro, 1969
    Randy Jones, 1978
    Greg W. Harris, 1991
Most runs, allowed
126—Pat Dobson, 1970
      Bill Greif, 1974
Most earned runs
117—Bill Greif, 1974
Most hits
274—Randy Jones, 1976
Most wild pitches
15—Steve Arlin, 1972
Most hit batsmen
14—Bill Greif, 1974
Most homers
36—Ed Whitson, 1987
Most sacrifice hits
23—Randy Jones, 1979
Most sacrifice flies
12—David Roberts, 1971
      Andy Hawkins, 1985
Lowest ERA
2.10—David Roberts, 270 innings, 1971

CLUB RECORDS

Most players
48 in 1991
Fewest players
31 in 1984
Most games
163 in 1980, 1983
Most at-bats
5,602 in 1977
Most runs
692 in 1977
Fewest runs
468 in 1969
Most opponents' runs
834 in 1977
Most hits
1,442 in 1986
Fewest hits
1,181 in 1972
Most singles
1,105 in 1980
Most doubles
255 in 1992
Most triples
53 in 1979
Most homers
172 in 1970
Fewest homers
64 in 1976
Most homers at San Diego Stadium, home and opponents
166 in 1993
Most grand slams
5 in 1989
Most pinch home runs
8 in 1986
Most total bases
2,149 in 1970
Most long hits
420 in 1993
Most extra bases on long hits
796 in 1970
Most sacrifice hits
133 in 1975
Most sacrifice flies
55 in 1984
Most stolen bases
239 in 1980

Most caught stealing
91 in 1987
Most bases on balls
602 in 1977
Most strikeouts
1,164 in 1970
Fewest strikeouts
716 in 1976
Most hit by pitch
59 in 1993
Fewest hit by pitch
9 in 1989
Most runs batted in
652 in 1977
Most game-winning RBIs
83 in 1984
Most .300 hitters
3 in 1987
Highest batting average
.261 in 1986
Lowest batting average
.225 in 1969
Highest slugging average
.391 in 1970
Lowest slugging average
.329 in 1969
Most grounded into double play
134 in 1971
Fewest grounded into double play
81 in 1978
Most left on bases
1,239 in 1980
Fewest left on bases
1,006 in 1972
Most putouts
4,428 in 1982
Fewest putouts
4,211 in 1972
Most assists
2,012 in 1980
Fewest assists
1,616 in 1993
Most chances accepted
6,411 in 1980
Fewest chances accepted
5,832 in 1972

Most errors
189 in 1977
Fewest errors
113 in 1991
Most errorless games
83 in 1991
Most consecutive errorless games
9 in 1979
Most double plays
171 in 1978
Fewest double plays
126 in 1974
Most passed balls
22 in 1987
Fewest passed balls
2 in 1992
Highest fielding average
.982 in 1991, 1992
Lowest fielding average
.971 in 1975, 1977
Highest home attendance
2,210,352 in 1985
Highest road attendance
2,534,072 in 1993
Most games won
92 in 1984
Most games lost
110 in 1969
Most games won, month
19 in June 1984, July 1984, September 1989
Most games lost, month
22 in June 1969, August 1969, May 1974
Games won, league
1,830 in 26 years
Games lost, league
2,273 in 26 years
Highest percentage games won
.568 in 1984 (won 92, lost 70)
Lowest percentage games won
.321 in 1969 (won 52, lost 110)
Most shutouts won
19 in 1985
Most shutouts lost
23 in 1969, 1976
Most 1-0 shutouts won
6 in 1985
Most 1-0 shutouts lost
5 in 1976

Most consecutive games won
11 in 1982
Most consecutive games lost
13 in 1994
Number of times league champions
1
Number of last-place finishes
7 (tied in 1969)
Most runs, inning
13 vs. St. Louis, August 24, 1993, first inning
vs. Pittsburgh, May 31, 1994, second inning
Most runs, game
17 vs. San Francisco, May 23, 1970, 15 innings
vs. Pittsburgh, July 18, 1989
vs. St. Louis, August 24, 1993
Most runs by opponent, game
23 by Chicago, May 17, 1977
Most runs, shutout game
13 vs. Cincinnati, August 11, 1991
Most runs by opponent, shutout game
19 by Chicago, May 13, 1969
by Los Angeles, June 28, 1969
Most runs, doubleheader shutout
No performance
Longest 1-0 game won
14 innings vs. Cincinnati, August 4, 1974, second game
Longest 1-0 game lost
18 innings vs. Pittsburgh, June 7, 1972, second game
Most hits, game
24 vs. San Francisco, April 19, 1982
Most home runs, game
5 vs. San Francisco, May 23, 1970, 15 innings
vs. Cincinnati, August 11, 1991
vs. St. Louis, August 24, 1993
Most consecutive games with one or more homers
10 (15 homers), 1970
Most total bases, game
39 vs. San Francisco, May 23, 1970, 15 innings
33 vs. Pittsburgh, June 2, 1970
vs. Colorado, June 28, 1994, first game
Largest crowd, day game
53,375 vs. San Francisco, June 22, 1985
Largest crowd, doubleheader
43,473 vs. Philadelphia, June 13, 1976
Largest crowd, night game
54,841 vs. Montreal, May 10, 1991
Largest crowd, home opener
54,490 vs. San Francisco, April 15, 1985

SAN FRANCISCO GIANTS

YEARLY FINISHES

Year	Position	W	L	Pct.	*GB	Manager	Attendance
1958	—3rd	80	74	.519	12	Bill Rigney	1,272,625
1959	—3rd	83	71	.539	4	Bill Rigney	1,422,130
1960	—5th	79	75	.513	16	Bill Rigney, Tom Sheehan	1,795,356
1961	—3rd	85	69	.552	8	Alvin Dark	1,390,679
1962	—1st†	103	62	.624	+ 1	Alvin Dark	1,592,594
1963	—3rd	88	74	.543	11	Alvin Dark	1,571,306
1964	—4th	90	72	.556	3	Alvin Dark	1,504,364
1965	—2nd	95	67	.586	2	Herman Franks	1,546,075
1966	—2nd	93	68	.578	1½	Herman Franks	1,657,192
1967	—2nd	91	71	.562	10½	Herman Franks	1,242,480
1968	—2nd	88	74	.543	9	Herman Franks	837,220

WEST DIVISION

Year	Position	W	L	Pct.	*GB	Manager	Attendance
1969	—2nd	90	72	.556	3	Clyde King	873,603
1970	—3rd	86	76	.531	16	Clyde King, Charlie Fox	740,720
1971	—1st‡	90	72	.556	+ 1	Charlie Fox	1,106,043
1972	—5th	69	86	.445	26½	Charlie Fox	647,744
1973	—3rd	88	74	.543	11	Charlie Fox	834,193
1974	—5th	72	90	.444	30	Charlie Fox, Wes Westrum	519,987
1975	—3rd	80	81	.497	27½	Wes Westrum	522,919

Year	Position	W	L	Pct.	*GB	Manager	Attendance
1976	—4th	74	88	.457	28	Bill Rigney	626,868
1977	—4th	75	87	.463	23	Joe Altobelli	700,056
1978	—3rd	89	73	.549	6	Joe Altobelli	1,740,477
1979	—4th	71	91	.438	19½	Joe Altobelli, Dave Bristol	1,456,402
1980	—5th	75	86	.466	17	Dave Bristol	1,096,115
1981	—5th/3rd	56	55	.505	§	Frank Robinson	632,274
1982	—3rd	87	75	.537	2	Frank Robinson	1,200,948
1983	—5th	79	83	.488	12	Frank Robinson	1,251,530
1984	—6th	66	96	.407	26	Frank Robinson, Danny Ozark	1,001,545
1985	—6th	62	100	.383	33	Jim Davenport, Roger Craig	818,697
1986	—3rd	83	79	.512	13	Roger Craig	1,528,748
1987	—1st‡	90	72	.556	+ 6	Roger Craig	1,917,168
1988	—4th	83	79	.512	11½	Roger Craig	1,785,297
1989	—1st★	92	70	.568	+ 3	Roger Craig	2,059,701
1990	—3rd	85	77	.525	6	Roger Craig	1,975,528
1991	—4th	75	87	.463	19	Roger Craig	1,737,478
1992	—5th	72	90	.444	26	Roger Craig	1,561,987
1993	—2nd	103	59	.636	1	Dusty Baker	2,606,354
1994	—2nd	55	60	.478	3½	Dusty Baker	1,704,608

*Games behind winner. †Won pennant playoff. ‡Lost Championship Series. §First half 27-32; second half 29-23.
★Won Championship Series.

INDIVIDUAL RECORDS (1958 TO DATE)

SERVICE

Most years by non-pitcher
19—Willie McCovey
Most years by pitcher
14—Juan Marichal

BATTING

Most games
164—Jose Pagan, 1962
Most games, career
2,256—Willie McCovey
Most at-bats
663—Bobby Bonds, 157 games, 1970
Most at-bats, career
7,578—Willie Mays
Most runs
134—Bobby Bonds, 157 games, 1970
Most runs, career
1,480—Willie Mays
Most hits
208—Willie Mays, 152 games, 1958
Most hits, career
2,284—Willie Mays
Most singles
146—Tito Fuentes, 160 games, 1973
Most singles, career
1,373—Willie Mays
Most doubles
46—Jack Clark, 156 games, 1978
Most doubles, career
376—Willie Mays
Most triples
12—Willie Mays, 153 games, 1960
Most triples, career
76—Willie Mays
Most homers by righthander
52—Willie Mays, 157 games, 1965
Most homers by lefthander
46—Barry Bonds, 159 games, 1993
Most homers by rookie
31—Jim Hart, 153 games, 1964
Most homers, month
17—Willie Mays, August, 1965
Most homers at home
28—Willie Mays, 1962
Most homers on road
28—Willie Mays, 1965
Most homers by righthander, career
459—Willie Mays

Most homers by lefthander, career
469—Willie McCovey
Most grand slams
3—Willie McCovey, 135 games, 1967
Most grand slams, career
16—Willie McCovey
Most total bases
382—Willie Mays, 162 games, 1962
Most total bases, career
4,189—Willie Mays
Most long hits
90—Willie Mays, 162 games, 1962
Most long hits, career
911—Willie Mays
Most extra bases on long hits
193—Willie Mays, 162 games, 1962
Most extra bases on long hits, career
1,905—Willie Mays
Most sacrifice hits
19—Rick Reuschel, 36 games, 1988
Most sacrifice flies
13—Will Clark, 154 games, 1990
Most bases on balls
137—Willie McCovey, 152 games, 1970
Most intentional bases on balls
45—Willie McCovey, 149 games, 1969
Most bases on balls, career
1,168—Willie McCovey
Most strikeouts
189—Bobby Bonds, 157 games, 1970
Most strikeouts, career
1,351—Willie McCovey
Fewest strikeouts
48—Ken Reitz, 155 games, 1976
Most hit by pitch
26—Ron Hunt, 117 games, 1970
Most runs batted in
142—Orlando Cepeda, 152 games, 1961
Most runs batted in, career
1,388—Willie McCovey
Most game-winning RBIs
21—Jack Clark, 157 games, 1982
Highest batting average
.347—Willie Mays, 152 games, 1958
Highest slugging average
.677—Barry Bonds, 159 games, 1993
Longest batting streak
26 games—Jack Clark, 1978
Most grounded into double play, season
25—Bill Madlock, 140 games, 1977

Fewest grounded into double play
2—Jose Uribe, 157 games, 1986
Will Clark, 150 games, 1987
Brett Butler, 157 games, 1988

BASERUNNING

Most stolen bases
58—Bill North, 142 games, 1979
Most stolen bases, career
263—Bobby Bonds
Most caught stealing
24—Bill North, 142 games, 1979

PITCHING

Most games
81—Mike Jackson, 1993
Most games, career
647—Gary Lavelle
Most games started
42—Jack Sanford, 1963
Most games started—career
446, Juan Marichal
Most complete games
30—Juan Marichal, 1968
Most complete games, career
244—Juan Marichal
Most games finished
71—Rod Beck, 1993
Most innings
329—Gaylord Perry, 1970
Most innings, career
3,443—Juan Marichal
Most games won, season
26—Juan Marichal, 1968
Most games won, career
238—Juan Marichal
Most games lost, career
140—Juan Marichal
Most 20-victory season
6—Juan Marichal
Most games lost, season
18—Ray Sadecki, 1968

Highest winning percentage
.806—Juan Marichal (25-6), 1966
Longest winning streak
16—Jack Sanford, 1962
Longest losing streak
9—Mark Davis, 1984
Most saves
48—Rod Beck, 1993
Most bases on balls
124—John D'Acquisto, 1974
Most bases on balls, career
690—Juan Marichal
Most strikeouts
248—Juan Marichal, 1963
Most strikeouts, career
2,281—Juan Marichal
Most strikeouts, game
15—Gaylord Perry, July 22, 1966
Most shutouts, season
10—Juan Marichal, 1965
Most 1-0 shutouts won
2—Held by many pitchers
Most shutouts, career
52—Juan Marichal
Most runs
143—Vida Blue, 1979
Most earned runs
132—Vida Blue, 1979
Most hits
295—Juan Marichal, 1968
Most hits batsmen
11—Gaylord Perry, 1969
John Burkett, 1993
Most wild pitches
18—Rich Robertson, 1970
Most home runs
34—Juan Marichal, 1962
Most sacrifice hits
18—Mike F. McCormick, 1959
Ron Bryant, 1974
Most sacrifice flies
14—Rick Reuschel, 1988
Lowest ERA
1.98—Bobby Bolin, 177 innings, 1968

CLUB RECORDS

Most players
51 in 1990
Fewest players
31 in 1968
Most games
165 in 1962
Most at-bats
5,650 in 1984
Most runs
878 in 1962
Fewest runs
556 in 1985
Most opponents' runs
826 in 1970
Most hits
1,552 in 1962
Fewest hits
1,263 in 1985
Most singles
1,132 in 1984
Most doubles
274 in 1987
Most triples
62 in 1960
Most homers
205 in 1987
Fewest homers
80 in 1980

Most homers at Seals Stadium, home and opponents
173 in 1958
Most homers at Candlestick Park, home and opponents
190 in 1987
Most grand slams
7 in 1970
Most pinch home runs
11 in 1977, 1987
Most long hits
511 in 1987
Most extra bases on long hits
953 in 1987
Most total bases
2,463 in 1962
Most sacrifice hits
127 in 1978
Most sacrifice flies
54 in 1980
Most stolen bases
148 in 1986
Most caught stealing
97 in 1987
Most bases on balls
729 in 1970
Most strikeouts
1,094 in 1987
Fewest strikeouts
764 in 1961

Most hit by pitch
66 in 1969
Fewest hit by pitch
14 in 1980
Most runs batted in
807 in 1962
Most game-winning RBIs
83 in 1987
Highest batting average
.278 in 1962
Lowest batting average
.233 in 1985
Highest slugging average
.441 in 1962
Lowest slugging average
.341 in 1968
Most left on bases
1,280 in 1969
Fewest left on bases
983 in 1961
Most grounded into double play
149 in 1965
Fewest grounded into double play
83 in 1986, 1990
Most .300 hitters
4 in 1962
Most putouts
4,429 in 1966
Fewest putouts
4,129 in 1959
Most assists
1,940 in 1976
Fewest assists
1,513 in 1961
Most chances accepted
6,349 in 1969
Fewest chances accepted
5,677 in 1961
Most errors
186 in 1976
Fewest errors
107 in 1990
Most errorless games
89 in 1991, 1993
Most consecutive errorless games
10 in 1994
Most double plays
183 in 1987
Fewest double plays
109 in 1983
Most passed balls
30 in 1970
Fewest passed balls
6 in 1978
Highest fielding average
.984 in 1993
Lowest fielding average
.971 in 1976
Highest home attendance
2,606,354 in 1993
Highest road attendance
2,772,975 in 1993
Most games won
103 in 1962, 1993

Most games lost
100 in 1985
Most games won, month
21 in September 1965, August 1968
Most games lost, month
21 in May 1972
Highest percentage games won
.636 in 1993 (won 103, lost 59)
Lowest percentage games won
.383 in 1985 (won 62, lost 100)
Games won, league
3,022 in 37 years
Games lost, league
2,835 in 37 years
Most shutouts won
20 in 1968
Most shutouts lost
18 in 1992
Most 1-0 games won
6 in 1968
Most 1-0 games lost
4 in 1972, 1978, 1985, 1989
Most consecutive games won
14 in 1965
Most consecutive games lost
10 in 1985
Number of times league champions
2
Number of last-place finishes
1
Most runs, inning
13 vs. St. Louis, May 7, 1966, third inning
Most runs, game
23 vs. Atlanta, June 8, 1990
Most runs by opponent, game
20 by Chicago, August 13, 1959
Most runs, shutout game
14 vs. Cincinnati, August 23, 1961
Most runs by opponent, shutout game
15 by Chicago, August 22, 1970
Most runs, doubleheader shutout
13 vs. Chicago, April 29, 1962
Longest 1-0 game won
21 innings vs. Cincinnati, September 1, 1967
Longest 1-0 game lost
14 innings vs. New York, August 19, 1969
Most hits, game
27 vs. Atlanta, June 8, 1990
Most home runs, game
8 vs. Milwaukee, April 30, 1961
Most consecutive games with one or more homers
16 (22 homers), 1962
(30 homers), 1963
Most total bases, game
50 vs. Los Angeles, May 13, 1958
Largest crowd, day game
58,077 vs. Pittsburgh, April 4, 1994
Largest crowd, doubleheader
53,178 vs. Los Angeles, July 31, 1983
Largest crowd, night game
55,920 vs. Cincinnati, June 20, 1978
Largest crowd, home opener
58,077 vs. Pittsburgh, April 4, 1994

CHAMPIONSHIP SERIES

Service (Individual, Club)

Batting (Individual, Club)

Baserunning (Individual, Club)

Pitching (Individual, Club)

Fielding (Individual, Club)

Miscellaneous

Non-Playing Personnel

General Reference

INDIVIDUAL SERVICE

ALL PLAYERS

SERIES AND CLUBS

Most series played

A.L.—11—Reggie Jackson, Oakland, 1971, 1972, 1973, 1974, 1975; New York, 1977, 1978, 1980, 1981; California, 1982, 1986.

N.L.—8—Richie Hebner, Pittsburgh, 1970, 1971, 1972, 1974, 1975; Philadelphia, 1977, 1978; Chicago, 1984.

Most consecutive years played in series

A.L.—5—Sal Bando, Vida Blue, Bert Campaneris, Rollie Fingers, Reggie Jackson, Joe Rudi, Gene Tenace, Oakland, 1971 through 1975.

N.L.—4—Sid Bream, Pittsburgh, 1990; Atlanta, 1991, 1992, 1993.

Most series playing in all games

A.L.—9—Reggie Jackson, Oakland, 1971, 1972, 1973, 1974, 1975; New York, 1977, 1978, 1980; California, 1982 (37 games).

N.L.—7—Pete Rose, Cincinnati, 1970, 1972, 1973, 1975, 1976; Philadelphia, 1980, 1983 (28 games).

Most series played with one club

A.L.—7—Jim Palmer, Baltimore, 1969, 1970, 1971, 1973, 1974, 1979, 1983.

N.L.—6

Johnny Bench, Cincinnati, 1970, 1972, 1973, 1975, 1976, 1979.

Willie Stargell, Pittsburgh, 1970, 1971, 1972, 1974, 1975, 1979.

Steve Yeager, Los Angeles, 1974, 1977, 1978, 1981, 1983, 1985.

Most series appeared in as pinch-hitter

M.L.—4

Vic Davalillo, Pittsburgh N.L., 1971, 1972; Oakland A.L., 1973; Los Angeles N.L., 1977 (five games).

Rick Monday, Los Angeles N.L., 1977, 1978, 1981, 1983 (four games).

Richie Hebner, Pittsburgh N.L., 1971; Philadelphia N.L., 1977, 1978; Chicago N.L., 1984 (five games).

Danny Heep, Houston N.L., 1980; New York N.L., 1988; Los Angeles N.L., 1988; Boston A.L., 1990 (10 games).

N.L.—4

Rick Monday, Los Angeles, 1977, 1978, 1981, 1983 (four games).

Richie Hebner, Pittsburgh, 1971; Philadelphia, 1977, 1978; Chicago, 1984 (five games).

A.L.—3

Curt Motton, Baltimore, 1969, 1971, 1974 (four games).

Jim Holt, Minnesota, 1970; Oakland, 1974, 1975 (four games).

Cliff Johnson, New York, 1977, 1978; Toronto, 1985 (five games).

Jamie Quirk, Kansas City, 1976, 1985; Oakland, 1990 (four games).

Most times on series-winning club (playing one or more game each series)

A.L.—6—Reggie Jackson, Oakland, 1972, 1973, 1974; New York, 1977, 1978, 1981.

N.L.—6—Pete Rose, Cincinnati, 1970, 1972, 1975, 1976; Philadelphia, 1980, 1983.

Most times on series-losing club (playing one or more game each series)

N.L.—7—Richie Hebner, Pittsburgh, 1970, 1972, 1974, 1975; Philadelphia, 1977, 1978; Chicago, 1984.

A.L.—5

Bobby Grich, Baltimore, 1973, 1974; California, 1979, 1982, 1986.

Reggie Jackson, Oakland, 1971, 1975; New York, 1980; California, 1982, 1986.

Most clubs, career

A.L.—5—Don Baylor, Baltimore, 1973, 1974; California 1979, 1982; Boston, 1986; Minnesota, 1987; Oakland, 1988.

N.L.—3—Held by many players.

BY POSITION (EXCEPT PITCHERS)

Most series by first baseman

A.L.—5—Boog Powell, Baltimore, 1969, 1970, 1971, 1973, 1974 (12 games).

N.L.—5

Tony Perez, Cincinnati, 1970, 1972, 1973, 1975, 1976 (17 games).

Bob Robertson, Pittsburgh, 1970, 1971, 1972, 1974, 1975 (11 games).

Steve Garvey, Los Angeles, 1974, 1977, 1978, 1981; San Diego, 1984 (22 games).

Most series by second baseman

N.L.—7—Joe Morgan, Cincinnati, 1972, 1973, 1975, 1976, 1979; Houston, 1980; Philadelphia, 1983 (27 games).

A.L.—6—Frank White, Kansas City, 1976, 1977, 1978, 1980, 1984, 1985 (26 games).

Most series by third baseman

M.L.—6

Graig Nettles, New York A.L., 1976, 1977, 1978, 1980, 1981; San Diego N.L., 1984 (23 games).

George Brett, Kansas City A.L., 1976, 1977, 1978, 1980, 1984, 1985 (27 games).

A.L.—6—George Brett, Kansas City, 1976, 1977, 1978, 1980, 1984, 1985 (27 games).

N.L.—5

Richie Hebner, Pittsburgh, 1970, 1971, 1972, 1974, 1975 (18 games).

Mike Schmidt, Philadelphia, 1976, 1977, 1978, 1980, 1983 (20 games).

Terry Pendleton, St. Louis, 1985, 1987; Atlanta, 1991, 1992, 1993 (32 games).

Most series by shortstop

A.L.—6

Mark Belanger, Baltimore, 1969, 1970, 1971, 1973, 1974, 1979 (21 games).

Bert Campaneris, Oakland, 1971, 1972, 1973, 1974, 1975; California, 1979 (18 games).

N.L.—5

Dave Concepcion, Cincinnati, 1970, 1972, 1975, 1976, 1979 (13 games).

Bill Russell, Los Angeles, 1974, 1977, 1978, 1981, 1983 (21 games).

Larry Bowa, Philadelphia, 1976, 1977, 1978, 1980; Chicago, 1984 (21 games).

Most series by outfielder

A.L.—10—Reggie Jackson, Oakland, 1971, 1972, 1973, 1974, 1975; New York, 1977, 1978, 1980, 1981; California, 1982 (32 games).

N.L.—5

Cesar Geronimo, Cincinnati, 1972, 1973, 1975, 1976, 1979 (17 games).

Garry Maddox, Philadelphia, 1976, 1977, 1978, 1980, 1983 (17 games).

Most series by catcher

M.L.—6

Bob Boone, Philadelphia N.L., 1976, 1977, 1978, 1980; California A.L., 1982, 1986 (27 games).

Johnny Bench, Cincinnati N.L., 1970, 1972, 1973, 1975, 1976, 1979 (22 games).

Steve Yeager, Los Angeles N.L., 1974, 1977, 1978, 1981, 1983, 1985 (15 games).

N.L.—6

Johnny Bench, Cincinnati, 1970, 1972, 1973, 1975, 1976,

1979 (22 games).
Steve Yeager, Los Angeles, 1974, 1977, 1978, 1981, 1983, 1985 (15 games).
A.L.—5—Andy Etchebarren, Baltimore, 1969, 1970, 1971, 1973, 1974 (12 games).

YOUNGEST AND OLDEST NON-PITCHERS

Youngest championship series non-pitcher

A.L.—20 years, 1 month, 5 days—Claudell Washington, Oakland, October 5, 1974.
N.L.—21 years, 2 months, 3 days—Gregg Jefferies, New York, October 4, 1988.

Oldest championship series non-pitcher

N.L.—42 years, 5 months, 24 days—Pete Rose, Philadelphiam, October 8, 1983.
A.L.—41 years, 11 days—Dave Winfield, Toronto, October 14, 1992.

YEARS BETWEEN SERIES (INCLUDES PITCHERS)

Most years between first and second series

N.L.—13—Phil Niekro, Atlanta, 1969, 1982.
A.L.—12—Doyle Alexander, Baltimore, 1973; Toronto, 1985. (Bert Blyleven went 17 years between ALCS appearances in 1970 and 1987, but that span was interrupted by a 1979 NLCS appearance with Pittsburgh.)

Most years between first and last series

N.L.—17—Nolan Ryan, New York, 1969; Houston, 1986.
A.L.—17—Bert Blyleven, Minnesota, 1970, 1987.

POSITIONS

Most positions played, career

N.L.—4
Pete Rose, Cincinnati, 1970, 1972, 1973, 1975, 1976; Philadelphia, 1980 (right field, left field, third base, first base; 24 games).
Pedro Guerrero, Los Angeles, 1981, 1983, 1985 (right field, center field, third base, left field; 15 games).
Lloyd McClendon, Chicago, 1989; Pittsburgh, 1991, 1992 (catcher, left field, first base, right field; 11 games).
A.L.—3—Held by many players.

Most positions played, series

A.L.—3—Cesar Tovar, Minnesota, 1970 (center field, second base, left field; 3-game series, three games).
N.L.—2—Held by many players.

PITCHERS

SERIES

Most series pitched

M.L.—8—Bob Welch, Los Angeles N.L., 1978, 1981, 1983, 1985; Oakland A.L., 1988, 1989, 1990, 1992 (10 games).
A.L.—6
Catfish Hunter, Oakland, 1971, 1972, 1973, 1974; New York, 1976, 1978 (10 games).
Jim Palmer, Baltimore, 1969, 1970, 1971, 1973, 1974, 1979 (eight games).
N.L.—6
Tug McGraw, New York, 1969, 1973; Philadelphia, 1976, 1977, 1978, 1980 (15 games).
Ron Reed, Atlanta, 1969; Philadelphia, 1976, 1977, 1978, 1980, 1983 (13 games).

Most series pitched by relief pitcher

M.L.—6
Rick Honeycutt, Los Angeles N.L., 1983, 1985; Oakland A.L., 1988, 1989, 1990, 1992 (15 games as a relief pitcher).
Tug McGraw, New York, 1969, 1973; Philadelphia, 1976, 1977, 1978, 1980 (15 games as a relief pitcher).
N.L.—6—Tug McGraw, New York, 1969, 1973; Philadelphia, 1976, 1977, 1978, 1980 (15 games as a relief pitcher).
A.L.—5—Rollie Fingers, Oakland, 1971, 1972, 1973, 1974, 1975 (11 games as a relief pitcher).

YOUNGEST AND OLDEST PITCHERS

Youngest championship series pitcher

A.L.—19 years, 5 months, 29 days—Bert Blyleven, Minnesota, October 5, 1970.
N.L.—19 years, 8 months, 28 days—Don Gullett, Cincinnati, October 4, 1970.

Oldest championship series pitcher

N.L.—43 years, 6 months, 8 days—Phil Niekro, Atlanta, October 9, 1982.
A.L.—41 years, 6 months, 13 days—Don Sutton, California, October 15, 1986.

CLUB SERVICE

PLAYERS USED

Most players, series

3-game series
A.L.—24—Minnesota vs. Baltimore, 1970.
   Oakland vs. New York, 1981.
N.L.—24—Pittsburgh vs. Cincinnati, 1975.

4-game series
N.L.—23—Los Angeles vs. Philadelphia, 1977.
A.L.—23—California vs. Baltimore, 1979.
   Chicago vs. Baltimore, 1983.
   Boston vs. Oakland, 1990.

5-game series
A.L.—25—Oakland vs. Detroit, 1972.
N.L.—24—Cincinnati vs. New York, 1973.
   Houston vs. Philadelphia, 1980.
   San Diego vs. Chicago, 1984.
   Chicago vs. San Francisco, 1989.
   San Francisco vs. Chicago, 1989.

6-game series
N.L.—25—Los Angeles vs. St. Louis, 1985.
   Philadelphia vs. Atlanta, 1993.
A.L.—25—Oakland vs. Toronto, 1992.

7-game series
N.L.—25—Pittsburgh vs. Atlanta, 1991, 1992.
A.L.—24—Toronto vs. Kansas City, 1985.
   California vs. Boston, 1986.

Most players used by both clubs, series

3-game series
A.L.—46—Oakland 24, New York 22, 1981.
N.L.—42—Pittsburgh 24, Cincinnati 18, 1975.

4-game series
A.L.—45—Chicago 23, Baltimore 22, 1983.
N.L.—44—Los Angeles 22, Pittsburgh 22, 1974.
   Los Angeles 23, Philadelphia 21, 1977.
   Los Angeles 22, Philadelphia 22, 1978.

5-game series
A.L.—49—Oakland 25, Detroit 24, 1972.
N.L.—48—Chicago 24, San Francisco 24, 1989.

6-game series
N.L.—48—Los Angeles 25, St. Louis 23, 1985.
   Philadelphia 25, Atlanta 23, 1993.
A.L.—46—Oakland 25, Toronto 21, 1992.

7-game series
N.L.—50—Pittsburgh 25, Atlanta 25, 1992.
A.L.—46—Toronto 24, Kansas City 22, 1985.

Fewest players, series

3-game series
A.L.—14—Baltimore vs. Minnesota, 1970.
   Boston vs. Oakland, 1975.
N.L.—15—St. Louis vs. Atlanta, 1982.

4-game series
A.L.—20—Oakland vs. Baltimore, 1974.
   Kansas City vs. New York, 1978.
   Baltimore vs. California, 1979.
   Boston vs. Oakland, 1988.
N.L.—20—Philadelphia vs. Los Angeles, 1983.

5-game series
N.L.—17—New York vs. Cincinnati, 1973.
A.L.—18—New York vs. Kansas City, 1977.

6-game series
A.L.—19—Toronto vs. Chicago, 1993.
N.L.—21—Houston vs. New York, 1986.
   Pittsburgh vs. Cincinnati, 1990.

7-game series
A.L.—20—Boston vs. California, 1986.
N.L.—22—New York vs. Los Angeles, 1988.

Fewest players used by both clubs, series

3-game series
A.L.—35—Oakland 20, Baltimore 15, 1971.

   New York 20, Kansas City 15, 1980.
N.L.—35—Atlanta 20, St. Louis 15, 1982.

4-game series
A.L.—41—New York 21, Kansas City 20, 1978.
N.L.—42—Los Angeles 22, Philadelphia 20, 1983.

5-game series
A.L.—40—Kansas City 22, New York 18, 1977.
   Milwaukee 20, California 20, 1982.
N.L.—41—Cincinnati 24, New York 17, 1973.

6-game series
A.L.—41—Chicago 22, Toronto 19, 1993.
N.L.—43—New York 22, Houston 21, 1986.

7-game series
A.L.—44—California 24, Boston 20, 1986.
N.L.—46—St. Louis 23, San Francisco 23, 1987.
   Los Angeles 24, New York 22, 1988.

Most times one club using only nine players in game, series

N.L.—3—New York vs. Cincinnati, 1973 (5-game series).
A.L.—2—Baltimore vs. Minnesota, 1970 (3-game series).

Most players, nine-inning game

N.L.—20—Pittsburgh vs. Atlanta, October 7, 1992.
A.L.—20—Oakland vs. Detroit, October 10, 1972.

Most players, extra-inning game

N.L.—21—Los Angeles vs. New York, October 9, 1988, 12 innings.
A.L.—20—Oakland vs. Detroit, October 11, 1972, 10 innings.

Most players used by both clubs, nine-inning game

N.L.—37—Pittsburgh 20, Atlanta 17, October 7, 1992.
A.L.—35—Oakland 18, New York 17, October 14, 1981.

Most players used by both clubs, extra-inning game

N.L.—38—Los Angeles 21, New York 17, October 9, 1988, 12 innings.
A.L.—Less than nine-inning record.

PINCH-HITTERS

Most pinch-hitters, series

N.L.—15
   Cincinnati vs. New York, 1973 (5-game series).
   Los Angeles vs. New York, 1988 (7-game series).
   Atlanta vs. Pittsburgh, 1992 (7-game series).
A.L.—14—Oakland vs. Detroit, 1972 (5-game series).

Most pinch-hitters used by both clubs, series

N.L.—28—Los Angeles 15, New York 13, 1988.
A.L.—22—Oakland 14, Detroit 8, 1972.

Fewest pinch-hitters, series

A.L.-N.L.—0—Held by many clubs.

Fewest pinch-hitters used by both clubs, series

A.L.—2
   California 2, Milwaukee 0, 1982 (5-game series).
   Chicago 2, Toronto 0, 1993 (6-game series).

Most pinch-hitters, nine-inning game

A.L.—6—Oakland vs. Detroit, October 10, 1972.
N.L.—5
   Los Angeles vs. Pittsburgh, October 8, 1974.
   Philadelphia vs. Los Angeles, October 5, 1983.
   Los Angeles vs. St. Louis, October 12, 1985.
   Pittsburgh vs. Atlanta, October 12, 1991.
   Atlanta vs. Pittsburgh, October 14, 1992.

Most pinch-hitters, extra-inning game

N.L.—6—Los Angeles vs. New York, October 9, 1988, 12 innings.
A.L.—Less than nine-inning record.

Most pinch-hitters used by both clubs, nine-inning game

A.L.—7—Oakland 6, Detroit 1, October 10, 1972.
N.L.—6
   Pittsburgh 3, Cincinnati 3, October 5, 1975.

San Diego 4, Chicago 2, October 6, 1984.
Los Angeles 5, St. Louis 1, October 12, 1985.
Cincinnati 3, Pittsburgh 3, October 4, 1990.
Pittsburgh 4, Atlanta 2, October 7, 1992.
Atlanta 5, Pittsburgh 1, October 14, 1992.

Most pinch-hitters used by both clubs, extra-inning game
N.L.—10—New York 5, Houston 5, October 15, 1986, 16 innings.
A.L.—Less than nine-inning record.

Most pinch-hitters, inning
A.L.—4—Baltimore vs. Chicago, October 7, 1983, ninth inning.
N.L.—4—Philadelphia vs. Los Angeles, October 5, 1983; ninth inning.

PINCH-RUNNERS

Most pinch-runners, series
A.L.—5
Oakland vs. Baltimore, 1974 (4-game series).
Oakland vs. Boston, 1990 (4-game series).
N.L.—3
New York vs. Atlanta, 1969 (3-game series).
Cincinnati vs. Pittsburgh, 1972 (5-game series).
Houston vs. Philadelphia, 1980 (5-game series).
Philadelphia vs. Houston, 1980 (5-game series).
Atlanta vs. Philadelphia, 1993 (6-game series).

Most pinch-runners used by both clubs, series
A.L.—8—Oakland 5, Baltimore 3, 1974 (4-game series).
N.L.—6—Houston 3, Philadelphia 3, 1980 (5-game series).

Fewest pinch-runners used, series
A.L.-N.L.—0—Held by many clubs.

Fewest pinch-runners used by both clubs, series
A.L.—0
Baltimore 0, Minnesota 0, 1969 (3-game series).
Kansas City 0, New York 0, 1980 (3-game series).
N.L.—0—Philadelphia 0, Los Angeles 0, 1978 (4-game series).

Most pinch-runners, nine-inning game
A.L.-N.L.—2—Held by many clubs.

Most pinch-runners, extra-inning game
A.L.—3—Kansas City vs. Detroit, October 3, 1984, 11 innings.
N.L.—2—Held by many clubs.

Most pinch-runners used by both clubs, nine-inning game
A.L.—3—Made in many games.
N.L.—2—Made in many games.

Most pinch-runners used by both clubs, extra-inning game
A.L.—4—Boston 2, California 2, October 12, 1986, 11 innings.
N.L.—3—Philadelphia 2, Houston 1, October 12, 1980, 10 innings.

Most pinch-runners, inning
A.L.—2
Oakland vs. Detroit, October 7, 1972, 11th inning.
Baltimore vs. Oakland, October 9, 1974, ninth inning.
N.L.—1—Held by many clubs.

NUMBER OF PLAYERS USED BY POSITION

FIRST BASEMEN

Most first basemen, series
A.L.-N.L.—3—Held by many clubs.

Most first basemen used by both clubs, series
A.L.—5
Oakland 3, Baltimore 2, 1973 (5-game series).
California 3, Boston 2, 1986 (7-game series).
N.L.—5
Pittsburgh 3, Cincinnati 2, 1990 (6-game series).
Pittsburgh 3, Atlanta 2, 1991 (7-game series).

Most first basemen, game
N.L.—3—Los Angeles vs. St. Louis, October 14, 1985.
A.L.—2—Made in many games.

Most first basemen used by both clubs, game
N.L.—4
Los Angeles 3, St. Louis 1, October 14, 1985.
Atlanta 2, Pittsburgh 2, October 7, 1992.
Atlanta 2, Pittsburgh 2, October 10, 1992.
A.L.—3—Made in many games.

SECOND BASEMEN

Most second basemen, series
A.L.—4—Oakland vs. Detroit, 1972 (5-game series).
N.L.—3—Atlanta vs. Pittsburgh, 1992 (7-game series).

Most second basemen used by both clubs, series
A.L.—6—Oakland 4, Detroit 2, 1972 (5-game series).
N.L.—5—Atlanta 3, Pittsburgh 2, 1992 (7-game series).

Most second basemen, game
A.L.—3
Minnesota vs. Baltimore, October 3, 1970.
Oakland vs. Detroit, October 7, 1972, 11 innings.
Oakland vs. Detroit, October 10, 1972.
Oakland vs. Boston, October 7, 1975.
New York vs. Kansas City, October 4, 1978.
N.L.—2—Made in many games.

Most second basemen used by both clubs, game
A.L.—4
Minnesota 3, Baltimore 1, October 3, 1970.
Oakland 3, Detroit 1, October 7, 1972, 11 innings.
Oakland 3, Detroit 1, October 10, 1972.
Oakland 3, Boston 1, October 7, 1975.
New York 3, Kansas City 1, October 4, 1978.
N.L.—3—Made in many games.

THIRD BASEMEN

Most third basemen, series
A.L.-N.L.—3—Held by many clubs.

Most third basemen used by both clubs, series
N.L.—6—San Francisco 3, Chicago 3, 1989 (5-game series).
A.L.—5—Detroit 3, Kansas City 2, 1984 (3-game series).

Most third basemen, game
A.L.—3
Detroit vs. Kansas City, October 3, 1984, 11 innings.
Minnesota vs. Toronto, October 8, 1991.
N.L.—2—Held by many clubs.

Most third basemen used by both clubs, game
A.L.—5—Detroit 3, Kansas City 2, October 3, 1984, 11 innings.
N.L.—3—Made in many games.

SHORTSTOPS

Most shortstops, series
A.L.—4—Oakland vs. Detroit, 1972 (5-game series).
N.L.—3
Cincinnati vs. New York, 1973 (5-game series).
Pittsburgh vs. Los Angeles, 1974 (4-game series).
Pittsburgh vs. Cincinnati, 1975 (3-game series).

Most shortstops used by both clubs, series
A.L.—6—Oakland 4, Detroit 2, 1972 (5-game series).
N.L.—4—Made in many series.

Most shortstops, nine-inning game
N.L.—3—Pittsburgh vs. Los Angeles, October 6, 1974.
A.L.—2—Held by many clubs.

Most shortstops, extra-inning game
N.L.—3
Cincinnati vs. New York, October 9, 1973, 12 innings.
Pittsburgh vs. Cincinnati, October 7, 1975, 10 innings.
A.L.—3—Oakland vs. Detroit, October 11, 1972, 10 innings.

Most shortstops used by both clubs, game
A.L.-N.L.—4—Occurred in many games.

LEFT FIELDERS

Most left fielders, series
N.L.—5—Philadelphia vs. Houston, 1980 (5-game series).
A.L.—4—Oakland vs. Boston, 1988 (4-game series).

Most left fielders used by both clubs, series
N.L.—6—
Cincinnati 4, Pittsburgh 2, 1970 (3-game series).
Philadelphia 5, Houston 1, 1980 (5-game series).
A.L.—6—
Kansas City 3, New York 3, 1978 (4-game series).
Baltimore 3, California 3, 1979 (4-game series).

Most left fielders, game
N.L.—3
Philadelphia vs. Cincinnati, October 12, 1976.
Philadelphia vs. Houston, October 11, 1980, 10 innings.
Philadelphia vs. Los Angeles, October 8, 1983.
Los Angeles vs. New York, October 12, 1988.
Chicago vs. San Francisco, October 8, 1989.
A.L.—3—Detroit vs. Kansas City, October 2, 1984.

Most left fielders used by both clubs, game
A.L.—4
Kansas City 2, New York 2, October 6, 1978.
Detroit 3, Kansas City 1, October 2, 1984.
N.L.—4
Cincinnati 2, Pittsburgh 2, October 3, 1970, 10 innings.
Philadelphia 3, Cincinnati 1, October 12, 1976.
Philadelphia 3, Houston 1, October 11, 1980, 10 innings.
St. Louis 2, Atlanta 2, October 9, 1982.
Philadelphia 3, Los Angeles 1, October 8, 1983.
Los Angeles 3, New York 1, October 12, 1988.
Chicago 3, San Francisco 1, October 8, 1989.
Atlanta 2, Philadelphia 2, October 6, 1993.

CENTER FIELDERS

Most center fielders, series
A.L.—3
Oakland vs. Baltimore, 1973 (5-game series).
New York vs. Kansas City, 1978 (4-game series).
N.L.—3
Philadelphia vs. Los Angeles, 1983 (4-game series).
San Diego vs. Chicago, 1984 (5-game series).

Most center fielders used by both clubs, series
A.L.—5—Oakland 3, Baltimore 2, 1973 (5-game series).
N.L.—4—Made in many series.

Most center fielders, game
A.L.-N.L.—2—Held by many clubs.

Most center fielders used by both clubs, game
A.L.-N.L.—3—Made in many games.

RIGHT FIELDERS

Most right fielders, series
N.L.—5—St. Louis vs. San Francisco, 1987 (7-game series).
A.L.—4—New York vs. Oakland, 1981 (3-game series)

Most right fielders used by both clubs, series
N.L.—7—St. Louis 5, San Francisco 2, 1987 (7-game series).
A.L.—5
Kansas City 3, New York 2, 1976 (5-game series).
New York 4, Oakland 1, 1981 (3-game series).
Baltimore 3, Chicago 2, 1983 (4-game series).

Most right fielders, game
N.L.—4—St. Louis vs. San Francisco, October 11, 1987.
A.L.—3—New York vs. Oakland, October 14, 1981.

Most right fielders used by both clubs, game
N.L.—5
St. Louis 4, San Francisco 1, October 11, 1987.

St. Louis 3, San Francisco 2, October 13, 1987.
A.L.—4
Kansas City 2, New York 2, October 13, 1976.
New York 3, Oakland 1, October 14, 1981.

CATCHERS

Most catchers, series
A.L.—3—Kansas City vs. New York, 1976 (5-game series).
N.L.—3
Philadelphia vs. Cincinnati, 1976 (3-game series).
Houston vs. Philadelphia, 1980 (5-game series).
Chicago vs. San Francisco, 1989 (5-game series).
Atlanta vs. Philadelphia, 1993 (6-game series).

Most catchers used by both clubs, series
N.L.—5
Houston 3, Philadelphia 2, 1980 (5-game series).
Chicago 3, San Francisco 2, 1989 (5-game series).
Atlanta 3, Philadelphia 2, 1993 (6-game series).
A.L.—4—Made in many series.

Most catchers, game
A.L.-N.L.—2—Held by many clubs.

Most catchers used by both clubs, nine-inning game
N.L.—4—Chicago 2, San Francisco 2, October 8, 1989.
A.L.—3—Made in many games.

Most catchers used by both clubs, extra-inning game
A.L.—4—Baltimore 2, Minnesota 2, October 4, 1969, 12 innings.
N.L.—4—New York 2, Los Angeles 2, October 9, 1988, 12 innings.

PITCHERS

Most pitchers, series
3-game series
N.L.—10—Pittsburgh vs. Cincinnati, 1975.
A.L.—9—Minnesota vs. Baltimore, 1969, 1970.
4-game series
A.L.—10—Boston vs. Oakland, 1990.
N.L.—9—San Francisco vs. Pittsburgh, 1971.
Los Angeles vs. Philadelphia, 1977, 1978.
5-game series
N.L.—10—Pittsburgh vs. Cincinnati, 1972.
San Diego vs. Chicago, 1984.
A.L.—10—Detroit vs. Minnesota, 1987.
Toronto vs. Minnesota, 1991.
6-game series
A.L.—11—Oakland vs. Toronto, 1992.
N.L.—10—Philadelphia vs. Atlanta, 1993.
7-game series
N.L.—11—Pittsburgh vs. Atlanta, 1991.
A.L.—9—California vs. Boston, 1986.

Most pitchers used by both clubs, series
3-game series
N.L.—17—Pittsburgh 10, Cincinnati 7, 1975.
Cincinnati 9, Pittsburgh 8, 1979.
A.L.—16—Minnesota 9, Baltimore 7, 1969.
4-game series
N.L.—17—Los Angeles 9, Philadelphia 8, 1978.
A.L.—16—Oakland 9, Boston 7, 1988.
Boston 10, Oakland 6, 1990.
5-game series
N.L.—18—Pittsburgh 10, Cincinnati 8, 1972.
San Diego 10, Chicago 8, 1984.
San Francisco 9, Chicago 9, 1989.
A.L.—18—Toronto 10, Minnesota 8, 1991.
6-game series
A.L.—20—Oakland 11, Toronto 9, 1992.
N.L.—18—St. Louis 9, Los Angeles 9, 1985.
Philadelphia 10, Atlanta 8, 1993.
7-game series
N.L.—20—Pittsburgh 11, Atlanta 9, 1991.
Pittsburgh 10, Atlanta 10, 1992.
A.L.—16—California 9, Boston 7, 1986.

Fewest pitchers, series

A.L.—4
  Baltimore vs. Minnesota, 1970 (3-game series).
  Baltimore vs. Oakland, 1971 (3-game series).
  Kansas City vs. New York, 1980 (3-game series).
N.L.—5
  Pittsburgh vs. Cincinnati, 1970 (3-game series).
  St. Louis vs. Atlanta, 1982 (3-game series).
  Philadelphia vs. Los Angeles, 1983 (4-game series).

Fewest pitchers used by both clubs, series

A.L.—10—New York 6, Kansas City 4, 1980 (3-game series).
N.L.—12—Cincinnati 7, Pittsburgh 5, 1970 (3-game series).

Most pitchers, game

A.L.—7—Minnesota vs. Baltimore, October 6, 1969.
N.L.—7
  San Francisco vs. St. Louis, October 14, 1987.
  Los Angeles vs. New York, October 9, 1988, 12 innings.
  Pittsburgh vs. Atlanta, October 7, 1992.

Most pitchers used by winning club, nine-inning game

N.L.—6—Los Angeles vs. Philadelphia, October 7, 1977.
A.L.—6—Oakland vs. Boston, October 8, 1988.

Most pitchers used by winning club, extra-inning game

N.L.—7—Los Angeles vs. New York, October 9, 1988, 12 innings.

A.L.—Less than nine-inning record.

Most pitchers used by losing club, game

A.L.—7—Minnesota vs. Baltimore, October 6, 1969.
N.L.—7
  San Francisco vs. St. Louis, October 14, 1987.
  Pittsburgh vs. Atlanta, October 7, 1992.

Most pitchers used by both clubs, game

N.L.—12—Pittsburgh 7, Atlanta 5, October 7, 1992.
A.L.—10
  Oakland 6, Toronto 4, October 10, 1992.
  Oakland 5, Toronto 5, October 11, 1992, 11 innings.

Most pitchers, inning

A.L.—5—Kansas City vs. New York, October 12, 1976, sixth inning.
N.L.—4—Los Angeles vs. New York, October 8, 1988, eighth inning.

SERIES

Most series played

A.L.—10—Oakland, 1971, 1972, 1973, 1974, 1975, 1981, 1988, 1989, 1990, 1992 (won six, lost four).
N.L.—9—Pittsburgh, 1970, 1971, 1972, 1974, 1975, 1979, 1990, 1991, 1992 (won two, lost seven).

INDIVIDUAL BATTING

GAMES

Most games, career

A.L.—45—Reggie Jackson, Oakland, 1971, 1972, 1973, 1974, 1975; New York, 1977, 1978, 1980, 1981; California, 1982, 1986 (11 series).

N.L.—32—Terry Pendleton, St. Louis, 1985, 1987; Atlanta, 1991, 1992, 1993 (five series).

Most games with one club, career

A.L.—27—George Brett, Kansas City, 1976, 1977, 1978, 1980, 1984, 1985 (six series).

N.L.—22
Johnny Bench, Cincinnati, 1970, 1972, 1973, 1975, 1976, 1979 (six series).
Willie Stargell, Pittsburgh, 1970, 1971, 1972, 1974, 1975, 1979 (six series).

Most games by pinch-hitter, career

M.L.—10—Danny Heep, Houston N.L., 1980 (1); New York N.L., 1986 (4); Los Angeles N.L., 1988 (3); Boston A.L., 1990 (2) (10 plate appearances, seven at-bats).

N.L.—8—Lee Mazzilli, New York, 1986 (5), 1988 (3) (eight plate appearances, seven at-bats).

A.L.—6—Dane Iorg, Kansas City, 1984 (2), 1985 (4); (six plate appearances, four at-bats).

Most games by pinch-hitter, series

N.L.—6—Lonnie Smith, Atlanta, 1992 (7-game series).

A.L.—4
George Hendrick, Oakland, 1972 (5-game series).
Dane Iorg, Kansas City, 1985 (7-game series).

Most games by pinch-runner, career

A.L.—4—Lance Blankenship, Oakland, 1990, 1992; (two series).

N.L.—3—Dave Concepcion, Cincinnati, 1970, 1972 (two series).

Most games by pinch-runner, series

A.L.—3
Dave Stapleton, Boston, 1986.
Lance Blankenship, Oakland, 1990.
Eric Fox, Oakland, 1992.

N.L.—2—Held by many players.

BATTING AVERAGE

Highest batting average, career (50 or more at-bats)

A.L.—.392—Devon White, California, 1986; Toronto, 1991, 1992, 1993 (four series, 21 games, 74 at-bats, 29 hits).

N.L.—.381—Pete Rose, Cincinnati, 1970, 1972, 1973, 1975, 1976; Philadelphia, 1980, 1983 (seven series, 28 games, 118 at-bats, 45 hits).

Highest batting average, series (playing all games and having eight or more at-bats)

3-game series
N.L.—.778—Jay Johnstone, Philadelphia, 1976.
A.L.—.583—Brooks Robinson, Baltimore, 1970.

4-game series
A.L.—.500—Ron Hassey, Oakland, 1988.
N.L.—.467—Dusty Baker, Los Angeles, 1978.
Mike Schmidt, Philadelphia, 1983.

5-game series
N.L.—.650—Will Clark, San Francisco, 1989.
A.L.—.611—Fred Lynn, California, 1982.

6-game series
A.L.—.444—Tim Raines, Chicago, 1993.
Devon White, Toronto, 1993.
N.L.—.435—Ozzie Smith, St. Louis, 1985.
Fred McGriff, Atlanta, 1993.

7-game series
A.L.—.455—Bob Boone, California, 1986.
N.L.—.429—Lenny Dykstra, New York, 1988.

SLUGGING AVERAGE

Highest slugging average, career (50 or more at-bats)

A.L.—.728—George Brett, Kansas City, 1976, 1977, 1978, 1980, 1984, 1985 (six series, 27 games, 103 at-bats, 35 hits, five doubles, four triples, nine home runs, 75 total bases).

N.L.—.678—Steve Garvey, Los Angeles, 1974, 1977, 1978, 1981; San Diego, 1984 (five series, 22 games, 90 at-bats, 32 hits, three doubles, one triple, eight home runs, 61 total bases).

Highest slugging average, series (10 or more at-bats)

3-game series
N.L.—1.182—Willie Stargell, Pittsburgh, 1979.
A.L.—.917—Tony Oliva, Minnesota, 1970.
Reggie Jackson, Oakland, 1971.
Bob Watson, New York, 1980.
Graig Nettles, New York, 1981.

4-game series
N.L.—1.250—Bob Robertson, Pittsburgh, 1971.
A.L.—1.056—George Brett, Kansas City, 1978.

5-game series
N.L.—1.200—Will Clark, San Francisco, 1989.
A.L.—1.000—Tom Brunansky, Minnesota, 1987.
Rickey Henderson, Oakland, 1989.

6-game series
N.L.—.824—Paul O'Neill, Cincinnati, 1990.
A.L.—.692—Roberto Alomar, Toronto, 1992.

7-game series
N.L.—1.182—Lloyd McClendon, Pittsburgh, 1992.
A.L.—.826—George Brett, Kansas City, 1985.

AT-BATS AND PLATE APPEARANCES

Most at-bats, career

A.L.—163—Reggie Jackson, Oakland, 1971, 1972, 1973, 1974, 1975; New York, 1977, 1978, 1980, 1981; California, 1982, 1986 (11 series, 45 games).

N.L.—129—Terry Pendleton, St. Louis, 1985, 1987; Atlanta, 1991, 1992, 1993 (five series, 32 games).

Most at-bats by pinch-hitter, career

M.L.—7
Lee Mazzilli, New York N.L., 1986 (5), 1988 (2).
Danny Heep, Houston N.L., 1980 (1), New York N.L., 1986 (3), Los Angeles N.L., 1988 (1), Boston A.L., 1990 (2).

N.L.—7—Lee Mazzilli, New York, 1986 (5), 1988 (2).

A.L.—5—Cliff Johnson, New York, 1977 (1), 1978 (1), Toronto, 1985 (3).

Most plate appearances by pinch-hitter, career

M.L.—10—Danny Heep, Houston N.L., 1980 (1), New York N.L., 1986 (4); Los Angeles N.L., 1988 (3); Boston A.L., 1990 (2).

N.L.—8—Lee Mazzilli, New York, 1986 (5), 1988 (3).

A.L.—6—Dane Iorg, Kansas City, 1984 (2), 1985 (4).

Most consecutive hitless times at bat, career

M.L.—31—Billy North, Oakland A.L., 1974 (last 13 times at bat), 1975 (all 10 times at bat); Los Angeles N.L., 1978 (all eight times at bat).

N.L.—30—Cesar Geronimo, Cincinnati, 1973 (last 13 times at bat), 1975 (all 10 times at bat), 1976 (first seven times at bat).

A.L.—24—Bert Campaneris, Oakland, 1974 (last 13 times at bat), 1975 (all 11 times at bat); California, 1979 (no times at bat).

Most at-bats, series

3-game series
A.L.—15—Mark Belanger, Baltimore, 1969.
Paul Blair, Baltimore, 1969.

N.L.—15—Ken Oberkfell, St. Louis, 1982.
4-game series
 N.L.—19—Dave Cash, Pittsburgh, 1971.
    Garry Maddox, Philadelphia, 1978.
 A.L.—18—George Brett, Kansas City, 1978.
    Thurman Munson, New York, 1978.
    Rudy Law, Chicago, 1983.
5-game series
 N.L.—24—Mike Schmidt, Philadelphia, 1980.
 A.L.—24—Kirby Puckett, Minnesota, 1987.
6-game series
 N.L.—27—Gary Carter, New York, 1986.
    Bill Doran, Houston, 1986.
    Ron Gant, Atlanta, 1993.
 A.L.—27—Joe Carter, Toronto, 1993.
    Tim Raines, Chicago, 1993.
    Devon White, Toronto, 1993.
7-game series
 A.L.—32—Doug DeCinces, California, 1986.
 N.L.—30—Kevin Mitchell, San Francisco, 1987.
    Mike A. Marshall, Los Angeles, 1988.
    Darryl Strawberry, New York, 1988.
    Steve Sax, Los Angeles, 1988.
    Terry Pendleton, Atlanta, 1991, 1992.

Most at-bats by pinch-hitter, series

N.L.—6—Lonnie Smith, Atlanta, 1992.
A.L.—4—George Hendrick, Oakland, 1972.

Most at-bats by player with no hits, career

A.L.—15
 Tom Brookens, Detroit, 1984 (2), 1987 (13).
 Ron Karkovice, Chicago, 1993.
N.L.—11
 Bob Didier, Atlanta, 1969.
 Ed Kirkpatrick, Pittsburgh, 1974 (9), 1975 (2).

Most at-bats, nine-inning game

A.L.—6
 Paul Blair, Baltimore, October 6, 1969.
 Kirby Puckett, Minnesota, October 12, 1987.
 Rickey Henderson, Toronto, October 5, 1993.
N.L.—5—Held by many players.

Most at-bats, extra-inning game

N.L.—7
 Glenn Davis, Houston, October 15, 1986, 16 innings.
 Bill Doran, Houston, October 15, 1986, 16 innings.
 Billy Hatcher, Houston, October 15, 1986, 16 innings.
 Keith Hernandez, New York, October 15, 1986, 16 innings.
 Mookie Wilson, New York, October 15, 1986, 16 innings.
A.L.—6
 Don Buford, Baltimore, October 4, 1969, 12 innings.
 Bobby Grich, California, October 11, 1986, 11 innings.
 Joe Carter, Toronto, October 11, 1992, 11 innings.
 Devon White, Toronto, October 11, 1992, 11 innings.
 Dave Winfield, Toronto, October 11, 1992, 11 innings.

Most at-bats by player with no hits, nine-inning game

A.L.—6—Rickey Henderson, Toronto, October 5, 1993.
N.L.—5—Held by many players.

Most at-bats by player with no hits, extra-inning game

A.L.—6—Don Buford, Baltimore, October 4, 1969, 12 innings.
N.L.—6—Alan Ashby, Houston, October 15, 1986, 16 innings.

Most at-bats, inning

A.L.-N.L.—2—Held by many players.

Most times faced pitcher, inning

A.L.-N.L.—2—Held by many players.

RUNS

Most runs, career

A.L.—22—George Brett, Kansas City, 1976, 1977, 1978, 1980, 1984, 1985 (six series, 27 games).
N.L.—17—Pete Rose, Cincinnati, 1970, 1972, 1973, 1975, 1976; Philadelphia, 1980, 1983 (seven series, 28 games).

Most runs by pinch-hitter, career

N.L.—2—Ty Cline, Cincinnati, 1970 (one series, two games).
A.L.—1—Held by many players.

Most runs by pinch-runner, career

N.L.—2
 Gene Clines, Pittsburgh, 1972, 1974 (two series, two games).
 Rafael Landestoy, Houston, 1980 (one series, two games).
 Jose Gonzalez, Los Angeles, 1988 (one series, two games).
A.L.—2
 Marshall Edwards, Milwaukee, 1982 (one series, two games).
 Devon White, California, 1986 (one series, two games).

Most runs, series

3-game series
 A.L.—5—Mark Belanger, Baltimore, 1970.
 N.L.—4—Held by many players.
4-game series
 A.L.—7—George Brett, Kansas City, 1978.
 N.L.—6—Steve Garvey, Los Angeles, 1978.
5-game series
 A.L.—8—Rickey Henderson, Oakland, 1989.
 N.L.—8—Will Clark, San Francisco, 1989.
6-game series
 A.L.—7—Dave Winfield, Toronto, 1992.
    Paul Molitor, Toronto, 1993.
 N.L.—6—Willie McGee, St. Louis, 1985.
    Fred McGriff, Atlanta, 1993.
7-game series
 A.L.—8—Jim Rice, Boston, 1986.
 N.L.—7—Steve Sax, Los Angeles, 1988.

Most runs by pinch-hitter, series

N.L.—2—Ty Cline, Cincinnati, 1970 (two games).
A.L.—1—Held by many players.

Most runs by pinch-runner, series

N.L.—2
 Rafael Landestoy, Houston, 1980 (two games).
 Jose Gonzalez, Los Angeles, 1988 (two games).
A.L.—2
 Marshall Edwards, Milwaukee, 1982 (two games).
 Devon White, California, 1986 (two games).

Most runs, game

N.L.—4
 Bob Robertson, Pittsburgh, October 3, 1971.
 Steve Garvey, Los Angeles, October 9, 1974.
 Will Clark, San Francisco, October 4, 1989.
A.L.—4
 Mark Brouhard, Milwaukee, October 9, 1982.
 Eddie Murray, Baltimore, October 7, 1983.
 George Brett, Kansas City, October 11, 1985.

Most runs, inning

A.L.-N.L.—1—Held by many players.

HITS

CAREER AND SERIES

Most hits, career

N.L.—45—Pete Rose, Cincinnati, 1970, 1972, 1973, 1975, 1976; Philadelphia, 1980, 1983 (seven series, 28 games).
A.L.—37—Reggie Jackson, Oakland, 1971, 1972, 1973, 1974, 1975; New York, 1977, 1978, 1980, 1981; California, 1982, 1986 (11 series, 45 games).

Most hits by pinch-hitter, career

N.L.—3
 Paul Popovich, Pittsburgh, 1974 (one series, three games).
 Manny Mota, Los Angeles, 1974, 1977, 1978 (three series, six games).

Francisco Cabrera, Atlanta, 1992, 1993 (two series, five games).
A.L.—2—Held by many players.

Most hits, series

3-game series
A.L.—7—Brooks Robinson, Baltimore, 1969, 1970.
N.L.—7—Art Shamsky, New York, 1969.
Jay Johnstone, Philadelphia, 1976.

4-game series
N.L.—8—Dave Cash, Pittsburgh, 1971.
A.L.—7—George Brett, Kansas City, 1978.
Rod Carew, California, 1979.
Rudy Law, Chicago, 1983.
Wade Boggs, Boston, 1990.
Carney Lansford, Oakland, 1990.

5-game series
N.L.—13—Will Clark, San Francisco, 1989.
A.L.—11—Chris Chambliss, New York, 1976.
Fred Lynn, California, 1982.

6-game series
A.L.—12—Tim Raines, Chicago, 1993.
Devon White, Toronto, 1993.
N.L.—10—Ozzie Smith, St. Louis, 1985.
Fred McGriff, Atlanta, 1993.

7-game series
N.L.—12—Jay Bell, Pittsburgh, 1991.
A.L.—11—Marty Barrett, Boston, 1986.

Most hits by pinch-hitter, series

N.L.—3—Paul Popovich, Pittsburgh, 1974 (three games).
A.L.—2—Held by many players.

Most hits, two consecutive series

N.L.—22—Will Clark, San Francisco, 1987 (9), 1989 (13).
A.L.—20
Roberto Alomar, Toronto, 1991 (9), 1992 (11).
Devon White, Toronto, 1992 (8), 1993 (12).

Most series with one or more hits

A.L.—10—Reggie Jackson, Oakland, 1971, 1972, 1973, 1974, 1975; New York, 1977, 1978, 1980; California, 1982, 1986.
N.L.—7
Richie Hebner, Pittsburgh, 1970, 1971, 1972, 1974, 1975; Philadelphia, 1977, 1978.
Pete Rose, Cincinnati, 1970, 1972, 1973, 1975, 1976; Philadelphia, 1980, 1983.

Most consecutive hits, career

N.L.—6—Steve Garvey, Los Angeles, October 9, 1974 (4), October 4, 1977 (2).
A.L.—6—Paul Molitor, Toronto, October 5 (4), 6 (2), 1993.

Most consecutive hits by pinch-hitter, career

N.L.—3—Paul Popovich, Pittsburgh, October 5, 6, 9, 1974.
A.L.—2—Held by many players.

Most consecutive hits, series

A.L.—6—Paul Molitor, Toronto, October 5 (4), 6 (2), 1993.
N.L.—5
Gary Matthews, Philadelphia, October 5 (1), 7 (3), 8 (1), 1983 (one base on balls during streak).
Will Clark, San Francisco, October 4 (4), 5 (1), 1989 (two bases on balls during streak).
Steve Buechele, Pittsburgh, October 12 (2), 13 (3), 1991.

GAME AND INNING

Most hits, game

A.L.—5—Paul Blair, Baltimore, October 6, 1969.
N.L.—4
Bob Robertson, Pittsburgh, October 3, 1971.
Ron Cey, Los Angeles, October 6, 1974.
Steve Garvey, Los Angeles, October 9, 1974.
Dusty Baker, Los Angeles, October 7, 1978, 10 innings.
Terry Puhl, Houston, October 12, 1980, 10 innings.
Steve Garvey, San Diego, October 6, 1984.
Tito Landrum, St. Louis, October 13, 1985.
Kevin McReynolds, New York, October 11, 1988.
Will Clark, San Francisco, October 4, 1989.

Otis Nixon, Atlanta, October 10, 1992.

Most times reached base safely, game (batting 1.000)

A.L.—5
Reggie Jackson, New York, October 3, 1978 (two bases on balls, one single, one double, one home run).
Graig Nettles, New York, October 14, 1981 (one hit by pitch, three singles, one home run).
Don Baylor, Boston, October 8, 1986 (two singles, three bases on balls).
Rich Gedman, Boston, October 12, 1986 (two singles, one double, one home run, one hit by pitch).
Frank Thomas, Chicago, October 5, 1993 (one single, four bases on balls).
Roberto Alomar, Toronto, October 10, 1993 (three singles, two bases on balls).
N.L.—5
Felix Millan, Atlanta, October 5, 1969 (three bases on balls, two singles).
Will Clark, San Francisco, October 4, 1989 (one base on balls, one single, one double, two home runs).

Most hits accounting for all club's hits, game

N.L.—2
Roberto Clemente, Pittsburgh, October 10, 1972.
Andy Kosco, Cincinnati, October 7, 1973.
A.L.—2—Willie Wilson, Kansas City, October 12, 1985.

Most consecutive games with one or more hits, career

N.L.—15—Pete Rose, Cincinnati, 1973 (last 3), 1975 (3), 1976 (3); Philadelphia, 1980 (5), 1983 (first 1).
A.L.—12—Don Baylor, California, 1982 (last 3); Boston, 1986 (7); Minnesota, 1987 (2).

Most hits in two consecutive games, series

A.L.—7—Tim Raines, Chicago, October 8 (4), October 9 (3), 1993.
N.L.—6
Art Shamsky, New York, October 4 (3), October 5 (3), 1969.
Bob Robertson, Pittsburgh, October 2 (2), October 3 (4), 1971.
Jay Johnstone, Philadelphia, October 10 (3), October 12 (3), 1976.
Dave Lopes, Los Angeles, October 4 (3), October 5 (3), 1978.
Mark Grace, Chicago, October 4 (3), October 5 (3), 1989.
Will Clark, San Francisco, October 8 (3), October 9 (3), 1989.
Jay Bell, Pittsburgh, October 12 (3), October 13 (3), 1991.
Lloyd McClendon, Pittsburgh, October 11 (3), October 13 (3), 1992.

Most hits, inning

A.L.—2
Graig Nettles, New York, October 14, 1981, fourth inning.
Rickey Henderson, Oakland, October 6, 1990, ninth inning.
N.L.—2
Jack Clark, St. Louis, October 13, 1985, second inning.
Tito Landrum, St. Louis, October 13, 1985, second inning.
Jerome Walton, Chicago, October 5, 1989, first inning.
Barry Bonds, Pittsburgh, October 13, 1992, second inning.
Lloyd McClendon, Pittsburgh, October 13, 1992, second inning.

SINGLES

Most singles, career

N.L.—34—Pete Rose, Cincinnati, 1970, 1972, 1973, 1975, 1976; Philadelphia, 1980, 1983 (seven series, 28 games).
A.L.—24—Reggie Jackson, Oakland, 1971, 1972, 1973, 1974, 1975; New York, 1977, 1978, 1980, 1981; California 1982, 1986 (11 series, 45 games).

Most singles by pinch-hitter, career

N.L.—3—Paul Popovich, Pittsburgh, 1974 (one series, three games).

A.L.—2—Held by many players.

Most singles, series
3-game series
N.L.—7—Art Shamsky, New York, 1969.
A.L.—6—Brooks Robinson, Baltimore, 1969.
4-game series
N.L.—7—Bill Russell, Los Angeles, 1974.
A.L.—6—Chris Chambliss, New York, 1978.
Rudy Law, Chicago, 1983.
Carney Lansford, Oakland, 1990.
5-game series
A.L.—9—Roberto Alomar, Toronto, 1991.
N.L.—8—Pete Rose, Philadelphia, 1980.
Terry Puhl, Houston, 1980.
Jerome Walton, Chicago, 1989.
6-game series
A.L.—10—Tim Raines, Chicago, 1993.
N.L.—7—Jack Clark, St. Louis, 1985.
Ozzie Smith, St. Louis, 1985.
Terry Pendleton, Atlanta, 1993.
Fred McGriff, Atlanta, 1993.
7-game series
A.L.—9—Marty Barrett, Boston, 1986.
Bob Boone, California, 1986.
N.L.—9—Jay Bell, Pittsburgh, 1991.

Most singles by pinch-hitter, series
N.L.—3—Paul Popovich, Pittsburgh, 1974 (three games).
A.L.—2—Held by many players.

Most singles, game
A.L.—4
Brooks Robinson, Baltimore, October 4, 1969, 12 innings.
Chris Chambliss, New York, October 4, 1978.
Kelly Gruber, Toronto, October 7, 1989.
Jerry Browne, Oakland, October 12, 1992.
N.L.—4
Terry Puhl, Houston, October 12, 1980, 10 innings.
Tito Landrum, St. Louis, October 13, 1985.

Most singles, inning
A.L.—2
Graig Nettles, New York, October 14, 1981, fourth inning.
Rickey Henderson, Oakland, October 6, 1990, ninth inning.
N.L.—2
Jack Clark, St. Louis, October 13, 1985, second inning.
Tito Landrum, St. Louis, October 13, 1985, second inning.
Jerome Walton, Chicago, October 5, 1989, first inning.
Lloyd McClendon, Pittsburgh, October 13, 1992, second inning.

DOUBLES

Most doubles, career
N.L.—7
Pete Rose, Cincinnati, 1970, 1972, 1973, 1975, 1976; Philadelphia, 1980, 1983 (seven series, 28 games).
Richie Hebner, Pittsburgh, 1970, 1971, 1972, 1974, 1975; Philadelphia, 1977, 1978; Chicago, 1984 (eight series, 27 games).
Mike Schmidt, Philadelphia, 1976, 1977, 1978, 1980, 1983 (five series, 20 games).
Ron Cey, Los Angeles, 1974, 1977, 1978, 1981; Chicago, 1984 (five series, 22 games).
A.L.—7
Hal McRae, Kansas City, 1976, 1977, 1978, 1980, 1984, 1985 (six series, 25 games).
Reggie Jackson, Oakland, 1971, 1972, 1973, 1974, 1975; New York, 1977, 1978, 1980, 1981; California, 1982, 1986 (11 series, 45 games).

Most doubles by pinch-hitter, career
N.L.—2—Manny Mota, Los Angeles, 1974, 1977, 1978 (three series, six games).
A.L.—1—Held by many players.

Most doubles, series
3-game series
N.L.—3—Joe Morgan, Cincinnati, 1975.
Darrell Porter, St. Louis, 1982.
A.L.—3—Bob Watson, New York, 1980.
4-game series
N.L.—3—Ron Cey, Los Angeles, 1974.
A.L.—3—Rod Carew, California, 1979.
5-game series
A.L.—4—Matty Alou, Oakland, 1972.
Tom Brunansky, Minnesota, 1987.
N.L.—4—Pete Rose, Cincinnati, 1972.
6-game series
N.L.—4—Tom Herr, St. Louis, 1985.
A.L.—2—Held by many players.
7-game series
A.L.—4—Damaso Garcia, Toronto, 1985.
N.L.—4—Jeff King, Pittsburgh, 1992.
Gary Redus, Pittsburgh, 1992.

Most doubles, game
A.L.-N.L.—2—Held by many players.

Most doubles, inning
A.L.-N.L.—1—Held by many players.

TRIPLES

Most triples, career
A.L.—4—George Brett, Kansas City, 1976, 1977, 1978, 1980, 1984, 1985 (six series, 27 games).
N.L.—3
Willie McGee, St. Louis, 1982, 1985, 1987 (three series, 16 games).
Mariano Duncan, Los Angeles, Cincinnati, Philadelphia, 1985, 1990, 1993 (three series, 14 games).

Most triples by pinch-hitter, career
N.L.—1
Ty Cline, Cincinnati, 1970 (one series, two games).
Lenny Dykstra, New York, 1986 (one series, two games).
Lonnie Smith, Atlanta, 1992 (one series, six games).
A.L.—Never accomplished.

Most triples, series
A.L.—2—George Brett, Kansas City, 1977 (5-game series).
N.L.—2
Willie McGee, St. Louis, 1982 (3-game series).
Mariano Duncan, Philadelphia, 1993 (6-game series).

Most triples, game
N.L.—2—Mariano Duncan, October 9, 1993.
A.L.—1—Held by many players.

Most bases-loaded triples, game
A.L.—1—Jim Sundberg, Kansas City, October 16, 1985.
N.L.—Never accomplished.

HOME RUNS

CAREER AND SERIES

Most home runs, career
A.L.—9—George Brett, Kansas City, 1976, 1977, 1978, 1980, 1984, 1985 (six series, 27 games).
N.L.—8—Steve Garvey, Los Angeles, 1974, 1977, 1978, 1981; San Diego, 1984 (five series, 22 games).

Most home runs, series
3-game series
N.L.—3—Hank Aaron, Atlanta, 1969.
A.L.—2—Held by many players.
4-game series
N.L.—4—Bob Robertson, Pittsburgh, 1971.
Steve Garvey, Los Angeles, 1978.
A.L.—3—George Brett, Kansas City, 1978.
Jose Canseco, Oakland, 1988.

5-game series
N.L.—3—Rusty Staub, New York, 1973.
A.L.—2—Held by many players.
6-game series
N.L.—3—Bill Madlock, Los Angeles, 1985.
A.L.—2—Held by many players.
7-game series
N.L.—4—Jeffrey Leonard, San Francisco, 1987.
A.L.—3—George Brett, Kansas City, 1985.

Most series with one or more home runs

N.L.—5—Johnny Bench, Cincinnati, 1970 (1), 1972 (1), 1973 (1), 1976 (1), 1979 (1).
A.L.—4
Graig Nettles, New York, 1976 (2), 1978 (1), 1980 (1), 1981 (1).
Reggie Jackson, Oakland, 1971 (2), 1975 (1); New York, 1978 (2); California, 1982 (1).
George Brett, Kansas City, 1976 (1), 1978 (3), 1980 (2), 1985 (3).

Most series with two or more home runs

A.L.—3—George Brett, Kansas City, 1978 (3), 1980 (2), 1985 (3).
N.L.—2
Steve Garvey, Los Angeles, 1974 (2), 1978 (4).
Willie Stargell, Pittsburgh, 1974 (2), 1979 (2).
Gary Matthews, Philadelphia, 1983 (3); Chicago, 1984 (2).

GAME AND INNING

Most home runs, game

N.L.—3—Bob Robertson, Pittsburgh, October 3, 1971.
A.L.—3—George Brett, Kansas City, October 6, 1978.

Most grand slams, game

A.L.—1
Mike Cuellar, Baltimore, October 3, 1970, fourth inning.
Don Baylor, California, October 9, 1982, eighth inning.
N.L.—1
Ron Cey, Los Angeles, October 4, 1977, seventh inning.
Dusty Baker, Los Angeles, October 5, 1977, fourth inning.
Will Clark, San Francisco, October 4, 1989, fourth inning.
Ron Gant, Atlanta, October 7, 1992, fifth inning.

Inside-the-park home runs

A.L.—Graig Nettles, New York, October 9, 1980, fifth inning (none on base).
Paul Molitor, Milwaukee, October 6, 1982, fifth inning (one on base).
N.L.—Never accomplished.

Most home runs by pinch-hitter, game

N.L.—1
Jerry Martin, Philadelphia, October 4, 1978, ninth inning.
Bake McBride, Philadelphia, October 7, 1978, seventh inning.
Harry Spilman, San Francisco, October 9, 1987, ninth inning.
A.L.—1
John Lowenstein, Baltimore, October 3, 1979, 10th inning.
Pat Sheridan, Kansas City, October 9, 1985, ninth inning.
Mike Pagliarulo, Minnesota, October 11, 1991, 10th inning.

Home runs by leadoff batter, start of game

A.L.—Bert Campaneris, Oakland, October 7, 1973 (at Baltimore).
George Brett, Kansas City, October 6, 1978 (at New York).
N.L.—Bob Dernier, Chicago, October 2, 1984 (at Chicago).
Orlando Merced, Pittsburgh, October 12, 1991 (at Atlanta).

Home runs winning 1-0 games

A.L.—Sal Bando, Oakland, October 8, 1974, fourth inning.
N.L.—Mike Schmidt, Philadelphia, October 4, 1983, first inning.
Glenn Davis, Houston, October 8, 1986, second inning.

Most home runs by pitcher, game

A.L.—1—Mike Cuellar, Baltimore, October 3, 1970 (three on base).

N.L.—1
Don Gullett, Cincinnati, October 4, 1975 (one on base).
Steve Carlton, Philadelphia, October 6, 1978 (two on base).
Rick Sutcliffe, Chicago, October 2, 1984 (none on base).

Most home runs by rookie, game

A.L.-N.L.—1—Held by many players.

Most consecutive games hitting one or more home runs, series

N.L.—4—Jeffrey Leonard, San Francisco, October 6, 7, 9, 10, 1987.
A.L.—2
Harmon Killebrew, Minnesota, October 3, 4, 1970.
Dave Johnson, Baltimore, October 4, 5, 1970.
Bert Campaneris, Oakland, October 7, 9, 1973, second game 11 innings.
Sal Bando, Oakland, October 6, 8, 1974.
Dan Ford, California, October 3, 4, 1979.
Paul Molitor, Milwaukee, October 6, 8, 1982.
Greg Gagne, Minnesota, October 10, 11, 1987.
Jose Canseco, Oakland, October 5, 6, 1988.
Dave Parker, Oakland, October 4, 6, 1989.
Kirby Puckett, Minnesota, October 12, 13, 1991.
Roberto Alomar, Toronto, October 10, 11, 1992.

Most home runs in two consecutive games, series (homering each game)

N.L.—4—Bob Robertson, Pittsburgh, October 3 (3), October 5 (1), 1971.
A.L.—2
Harmon Killebrew, Minnesota, October 3, 4, 1970.
Dave Johnson, Baltimore, October 4, 5, 1970.
Bert Campaneris, Oakland, October 7, 9, 1973, second game 11 innings.
Sal Bando, Oakland, October 6, 8, 1974.
Dan Ford, California, October 3, 4, 1979.
Paul Molitor, Milwaukee, October 6, 8, 1982.
Greg Gagne, Minnesota, October 10, 11, 1987.
Jose Canseco, Oakland, October 5, 6, 1988.
Dave Parker, Oakland, October 4, 6, 1989.
Kirby Puckett, Minnesota, October 12, 13, 1991.
Roberto Alomar, Toronto, October 10, 11, 1992.

Hitting home run in first championship series at-bat

A.L.—Frank Robinson, Baltimore, October 4, 1969, fourth inning (received base on balls in first inning).
Norm Cash, Detroit, October 7, 1972, second inning.
Dan Ford, California, October 3, 1979, first inning.
John Lowenstein, Baltimore, October 3, 1979, 10th inning (pinch-hit).
Rich Cerone, New York, October 8, 1980, first inning.
Gorman Thomas, Milwaukee, October 5, 1982, second inning.
Gary Gaetti, Minnesota, October 7, 1987, second inning.
N.L.—Joe Morgan, Cincinnati, October 7, 1972, first inning.
Bob Dernier, Chicago, October 2, 1984, first inning.
Rick Sutcliffe, Chicago, October 2, 1984, third inning.
Glenn Davis, Houston, October 8, 1986, second inning.
Mark Grace, Chicago, October 4, 1989, first inning.
Orlando Merced, Pittsburgh, October 12, 1991, first inning.

Hitting home runs in first two championship series at-bats

AL.—Gary Gaetti, Minnesota, October 7, 1987, second and fifth innings.
N.L.—Never accomplished.

Most home runs, inning

A.L.-N.L.—1—Held by many players.

Most home runs, two consecutive innings

N.L.—2
Rusty Staub, New York, October 8, 1973, first and second innings.
Will Clark, San Francisco, October 4, 1989, third and fourth innings.
A.L.—Never accomplished.

TOTAL BASES

Most total bases, career

A.L.—75—George Brett, Kansas City, 1976, 1977, 1978, 1980, 1984, 1985 (six series, 27 games).
N.L.—63—Pete Rose, Cincinnati, 1970, 1972, 1973, 1975, 1976; Philadelphia, 1980, 1983 (seven series, 28 games).

Most total bases by pinch-hitter, career

N.L.—6—Jerry Martin, Philadelphia, 1977, 1978 (two series, three games).
A.L.—4
John Lowenstein, Baltimore, 1979 (one series, two games).
Pat Sheridan, Kansas City, 1985 (one series, two games).
Mike Pagliarulo, Minnesota, 1991 (one series, one game).

Most total bases, series

3-game series
  N.L.—16—Hank Aaron, Atlanta, 1969.
  A.L.—11—Held by many players.
4-game series
  N.L.—22—Steve Garvey, Los Angeles, 1978.
  A.L.—19—George Brett, Kansas City, 1978.
5-game series
  N.L.—24—Will Clark, San Francisco, 1989.
  A.L.—20—Chris Chambliss, New York, 1976.
6-game series
  N.L.—18—Bill Madlock, Los Angeles, 1985.
  A.L.—18—Roberto Alomar, Toronto, 1992.
           Devon White, Toronto, 1993.
7-game series
  N.L.—22—Jeffrey Leonard, San Francisco, 1987.
  A.L.—19—George Brett, Kansas City, 1985.

Most total bases by pinch-hitter, series

N.L.—6—Jerry Martin, Philadelphia, 1978 (two games).
A.L.—4
John Lowenstein, Baltimore, 1979 (two games).
Pat Sheridan, Kansas City, 1985 (two games).
Mike Pagliarulo, Minnesota, 1991 (two game).

Most total bases, game

N.L.—14—Bob Robertson, Pittsburgh, October 3, 1971 (one double, three home runs).
A.L.—12—George Brett, Kansas City, October 6, 1978 (three home runs).

Most total bases, inning

A.L.-N.L.—4—Held by many players.

LONG HITS

Most long hits, career

A.L.—18—George Brett, Kansas City, 1976, 1977, 1978, 1980, 1984, 1985 (six series, 27 games).
N.L.—12—Steve Garvey, Los Angeles, 1974, 1977, 1978, 1981; San Diego, 1984 (five series, 22 games).

Most long hits, series

3-game series
  N.L.—5—Hank Aaron, Atlanta, 1969.
  A.L.—4—Bob Watson, New York, 1980.
4-game series
  N.L.—6—Steve Garvey, Los Angeles, 1978.
  A.L.—5—George Brett, Kansas City, 1978.
5-game series
  A.L.—6—Tom Brunansky, Minnesota, 1987.
  N.L.—6—Will Clark, San Francisco, 1989.
6-game series
  N.L.—5—Tom Herr, St. Louis, 1985.
  A.L.—4—Ruben Sierra, Oakland, 1992.
          Paul Molitor, Toronto, 1993.
7-game series
  A.L.—5—George Brett, Kansas City, 1985.
  N.L.—5—Gary Redus, Pittsburgh, 1992.

Most long hits, game

N.L.—4—Bob Robertson, Pittsburgh, October 3, 1971 (one double, three home runs).
A.L.—3
Paul Blair, Baltimore, October 6, 1969 (two doubles, one home run).
George Brett, Kansas City, October 6, 1978 (three home runs).
George Brett, Kansas City, October 11, 1985 (one double, two home runs).

Most long hits in two consecutive games, series

N.L.—5—Bob Robertson, Pittsburgh, October 3 (4; one double, three home runs); October 5 (1; one home run), 1971.
A.L.—4—George Brett, Kansas City, October 6 (3; three home runs); October 7 (1; one triple), 1978.

Most long hits, inning

A.L.-N.L.—1—Held by many players.

RUNS BATTED IN

Most runs batted in, career

N.L.—21—Steve Garvey, Los Angeles, 1974, 1977, 1978, 1981; San Diego, 1984 (five series, 22 games).
A.L.—20—Reggie Jackson, Oakland, 1971, 1972, 1973, 1974, 1975; New York, 1977, 1978, 1980, 1981; California, 1982, 1986 (11 series, 45 games).

Most runs batted in by pinch-hitter, career

A.L.—3—John Lowenstein, Baltimore, 1979 (one series, two games).
N.L.—2
J.C. Martin, New York, 1969 (one series, two games).
Jerry Martin, Philadelphia, 1977, 1978 (two series, three games).
Luis Quinones, Cincinnati, 1990 (one series, three games).

Most runs batted in, series

3-game series
  A.L.—9—Graig Nettles, New York, 1981.
  N.L.—7—Hank Aaron, Atlanta, 1969.
4-game series
  N.L.—8—Dusty Baker, Los Angeles, 1977.
          Gary Matthews, Philadelphia, 1983.
  A.L.—6—Reggie Jackson, New York, 1978.
5-game series
  A.L.—10—Don Baylor, California, 1982.
  N.L.—9—Matt Williams, San Francisco, 1989.
6-game series
  N.L.—7—Bill Madlock, Los Angeles, 1985.
  A.L.—7—Ruben Sierra, Oakland, 1992.
7-game series
  A.L.—7—Brian Downing, California, 1986.
  N.L.—7—Jeffrey Leonard, San Francisco, 1987.

Most runs batted in by pinch-hitter, series

A.L.—3—John Lowenstein, Baltimore, 1979 (two games).
N.L.—2
J.C. Martin, New York, 1969 (two games).
Jerry Martin, Philadelphia, 1978 (two games).
Luis Quinones, Cincinnati, 1990 (three games).

Most runs batted in, game

N.L.—6—Will Clark, San Francisco, October 4, 1989.
A.L.—5
Paul Blair, Baltimore, October 6, 1969.
Don Baylor, California, October 5, 1982.

Most runs batted in by pinch-hitter, game

A.L.—3—John Lowenstein, Baltimore, 1979, 10th inning.
N.L.—2—J.C. Martin, New York, October 4, 1969, eighth inning.

Most consecutive games with one or more runs batted in, career

N.L.-A.L.—4—Held by many players.

Most runs batted in accounting for all club's runs, game

A.L.—3
Bert Campaneris, Oakland, October 5, 1974.

Graig Nettles, New York, October 13, 1981.
N.L.—3
Keith Hernandez, New York, October 5, 1988.
Jeff Blauser, Atlanta, October 13, 1993.

Most runs batted in, inning

A.L.—4
Mike Cuellar, Baltimore, October 3, 1970, fourth inning.
Don Baylor, California, October 9, 1982, eighth inning.
N.L.—4
Ron Cey, Los Angeles, October 4, 1977, seventh inning.
Dusty Baker, Los Angeles, October 5, 1977, fourth inning.
Will Clark, San Francisco, October 4, 1989, fourth inning.
Ron Gant, Atlanta, October 7, 1992, fifth inning.

Most game-winning RBIs, career (1980-88)

A.L.—3—George Brett, Kansas City, 1980, 1985 (2).
N.L.—3—Gary Carter, Montreal, 1981; New York, 1986, 1988.

Most game-winning RBIs, series (1980-88)

N.L.—2
Greg Luzinski, Philadelphia, 1980.
Gary Carter, New York, 1986.
Kirk Gibson, Los Angeles, 1988.
A.L.—2
Cecil Cooper, Milwaukee, 1982.
Al Oliver, Toronto, 1985.
George Brett, Kansas City, 1985.

BASES ON BALLS

Most bases on balls, career

N.L.—23—Joe Morgan, Cincinnati, 1972, 1973, 1975, 1976, 1979; Houston, 1980; Philadelphia, 1983 (seven series, 27 games).
A.L.—17
Reggie Jackson, Oakland, 1971, 1972, 1973, 1974, 1975; New York, 1977, 1978, 1980, 1981; California, 1982, 1986 (11 series, 45 games).
Rickey Henderson, Oakland, 1981, 1989, 1990, 1992; Toronto, 1993 (five series, 24 games).

Most bases on balls, series

3-game series
A.L.—6—Harmon Killebrew, Minnesota, 1969.
N.L.—6—Joe Morgan, Cincinnati, 1976.
4-game series
N.L.—9—Jim Wynn, Los Angeles, 1974.
A.L.—5—Reggie Jackson, Oakland, 1974.
Eddie Murray, Baltimore, 1979.
Gary Roenicke, Baltimore 1983.
Jose Canseco, Oakland, 1990.
5-game series
N.L.—8—Jose Cruz, Houston, 1980.
A.L.—7—Lou Whitaker, Detroit, 1987.
Rickey Henderson, Oakland, 1989.
6-game series
A.L.—10—Frank Thomas, Chicago, 1993.
N.L.—5—Barry Bonds, Pittsburgh, 1990.
Darren Daulton, Philadelphia, 1993.
7-game series
A.L.—7—George Brett, Kansas City, 1985.
N.L.—6—Held by many players.

Most consecutive bases on balls, series

A.L.—4
Harmon Killebrew, Minnesota, October 4 (3), October 5 (1), 1969.
Gary Roenicke, Baltimore, October 6 (1), October 7 (1), October 8 (2), 1983.
N.L.—4—Darren Daulton, Philadelphia, October 10 (3), October 11 (1), 1993.

Most bases on balls, game

N.L.—4—Darren Daulton, Philadelphia, October 10, 1993.
A.L.—4
Ruppert Jones, California, October 11, 1986, 11 innings.
Frank Thomas, Chicago, October 5, 1993.

Most bases on balls with bases filled, game

A.L.-N.L.—1—Held by many players.

Bases on balls with bases filled by pinch-hitters, game

N.L.—Duffy Dyer, Pittsburgh, October 7, 1975, ninth inning.
Mike Sharperson, Los Angeles, October 8, 1988, eighth inning.
A.L.—Never accomplished.

Most bases on balls, two consecutive games

A.L.—5
Harmon Killebrew, Minnesota, October 4 (3), October 5 (2), 1969, first game 12 innings, second game 11 innings.
Frank Thomas, Chicago, October 5 (4), October 6 (1), 1993.
N.L.—5
Jim Wynn, Los Angeles, October 5 (2), October 6 (3), 1974.
Darren Daulton, Philadelphia, October 10 (4), October 11 (1), 1993, second game 10 innings.

Most bases on balls, inning

A.L.-N.L.—1—Held by many players.

STRIKEOUTS

Most strikeouts, career

A.L.—41—Reggie Jackson, Oakland, 1971, 1972, 1973, 1974, 1975; New York, 1977, 1978, 1980, 1981; California, 1982, 1986 (11 series, 45 games).
N.L.—24—Cesar Geronimo, Cincinnati, 1972, 1973, 1975, 1976, 1979 (five series, 17 games).

Most strikeouts, series

3-game series
A.L.—7—Leo Cardenas, Minnesota, 1969.
N.L.—7—Cesar Geronimo, Cincinnati, 1975.
4-game series
A.L.—7—Dave Henderson, Oakland, 1988.
N.L.—6—Roberto Clemente, Pittsburgh, 1971.
Willie Stargell, Pittsburgh, 1971.
Mike A. Marshall, Los Angeles, 1983.
5-game series
A.L.—8—Kirk Gibson, Detroit, 1987.
Chili Davis, Minnesota, 1991.
N.L.—7—Tony Perez, Cincinnati, 1972.
Cesar Geronimo, Cincinnati, 1973.
6-game series
N.L.—12—Darryl Strawberry, New York, 1986.
A.L.—7—Terry Steinbach, Oakland, 1992.
Ron Karkovice, Chicago, 1993.
7-game series
N.L.—12—John Shelby, Los Angeles, 1988.
A.L.—8—Steve Balboni, Kansas City, 1985.
Bobby Grich, California, 1986.
Jim Rice, Boston, 1986.

Most strikeouts by pinch-hitter, series

N.L.—3
Lee Mazzilli, New York, 1986 (five games).
Curtis Wilkerson, Pittsburgh, 1991 (four games).
A.L.—2
Matt Nokes, Detroit, 1987 (two games).
Larry Parrish, Boston, 1988 (three games).

Most consecutive strikeouts, series (consecutive at-bats)

N.L.—7—Cesar Geronimo, Cincinnati, October 4 (1), October 5 (3), October 7 (3), 1975, first game 10 innings (one base on balls during streak).
A.L.—5—Ron Karkovice, Chicago, October 5 (1), October 6 (1), October 8 (3), 1993 (one sacrifice hit during streak).

Most consecutive strikeouts, series (consecutive plate appearances)

N.L.—5—Cesar Geronimo, Cincinnati, October 6 (1), October 7 (3), October 9 (1), 1973, third game 12 innings.
A.L.—4
Leo Cardenas, Minnesota, October 4 (2), 5 (2), 1969, first

game 12 innings, second game 11 innings.
Dave Boswell, Minnesota, October 5, 1969, 11 innings.
Bobby Grich, California, October 6 (1), October 8 (3), 1982.
Jose Canseco, Oakland, October 3 (3), October 4 (1), 1989.
Ron Karkovice, Chicago, October 6 (1), October 8 (3), 1993.

Most strikeouts, nine-inning game
A.L.-N.L.—3—Held by many players.

Most strikeouts, extra-inning game
A.L.—4—Dave Boswell, Minnesota, October 5, 1969, 11 innings (consecutive).
N.L.—3—Held by many players.

Most strikeouts, inning
A.L.-N.L.—1—Held by many players.

SACRIFICE HITS

Most sacrifice hits, career
M.L.—5—Bob Boone, Philadelphia N.L., 1976, 1977, 1978, 1980; California A.L., 1982, 1986; six series, 27 games.
A.L.—3
Dick Green, Oakland, 1971, 1972, 1973, 1974; four series, 17 games.
Bob Boone, California, 1982, 1986; two series, 12 games.
N.L.—3
Enos Cabell, Houston, 1980; Los Angeles, 1985; two series, 10 games.
Bill Russell, Los Angeles, 1974, 1977, 1978, 1981, 1983; five series, 21 games.
Billy Hatcher, Houston, 1986; Cincinnati, 1990; two series, 10 games.
Rafael Belliard, Atlanta, 1991, 1992, 1993; three series, 13 games.

Most sacrifice hits, series
A.L.—3—Enos Cabell, Houston, 1980 (5-game series).
N.L.—2—Held by many players.

Most sacrifice hits, game
A.L.-N.L.—2—Held by many players.

SACRIFICE FLIES

Most sacrifice flies, career
A.L.-N.L.—2—Held by many players.

Most sacrifice flies, series
A.L.-N.L.—2—Held by many players.

Most sacrifice flies, game
A.L.-N.L.—1—Held by many players.

HIT BY PITCH

Most hit by pitch, career
N.L.—4—Richie Hebner, Pittsburgh, 1971 (1), 1972 (1), 1974 (1); Chicago, 1984 (1).
A.L.—3
Hal McRae, Kansas City, 1976 (1), 1980 (1), 1985 (1).
Bobby Grich, California, 1982 (1), 1986 (2).
Don Baylor, Boston, 1986 (2); Minnesota, 1987 (1).

Most hit by pitch, series
A.L.—2
Don Baylor, Boston, 1986.
Bobby Grich, California, 1986.
Dan Gladden, Minnesota, 1987.
Pat Sheridan, Detroit, 1987.
N.L.—2—Lenny Dykstra, New York, 1988.

Most hit by pitch, game
A.L.—2
Dan Gladden, Minnesota, October 11, 1987.
Pat Sheridan, Detroit, October 12, 1987.
N.L.—1—Held by many players.

GROUNDING INTO DOUBLE PLAYS

Most grounding into double plays, career
N.L.—5—Pedro Guerrero, Los Angeles, 1981, 1983, 1985; three series, 15 games.
A.L.—5—Willie Randolph, New York, 1976, 1977, 1980, 1981, 1990; five series, 22 games.

Most grounding into double plays, series
N.L.—4—Pedro Guerrero, Los Angeles, 1981 (5-game series).
A.L.—3
Tony Taylor, Detroit, 1972 (5-game series).
Doug DeCinces, California, 1986 (7-game series).

Most grounding into double plays, game
A.L.—3—Tony Taylor, Detroit, October 10, 1972.
N.L.—2
Cleon Jones, New York, October 4, 1969.
Pedro Guerrero, Los Angeles, October 16, 1981.
Jerry Royster, Atlanta, October 10, 1982.

REACHING BASE ON INTERFERENCE

Most times awarded first base on catcher's interference, game
N.L.—1
Richie Hebner, Pittsburgh, October 8, 1974, fifth inning.
Mike Scioscia, Los Angeles, October 14, 1985, fourth inning.
A.L.—Never accomplished.

CLUB BATTING

GAMES

Most games played, total series
A.L.—42—Oakland (10 series; won 23, lost 19).
N.L.—42—Pittsburgh (nine series; won 17, lost 25).

BATTING AVERAGE

Highest batting average, series
3-game series
  A.L.—.336—New York vs. Oakland, 1981.
  N.L.—.330—St. Louis vs. Atlanta, 1982.
4-game series
  A.L.—.300—New York vs. Kansas City, 1978.
  N.L.—.286—Los Angeles vs. Philadelphia, 1978.
5-game series
  A.L.—.316—New York vs. Kansas City, 1976.
  N.L.—.303—Chicago vs. San Francisco, 1989.
6-game series
  A.L.—.301—Toronto vs. Chicago, 1993.
  N.L.—.279—St. Louis vs. Los Angeles, 1985.
7-game series
  A.L.—.277—California vs. Boston, 1986.
  N.L.—.260—St. Louis vs. San Francisco, 1987.

Highest batting average by both clubs, series
3-game series
  N.L.—.292—New York .327, Atlanta .255, 1969.
  A.L.—.286—Baltimore .330, Minnesota .238, 1970.
4-game series
  A.L.—.282—New York .300, Kansas City .263, 1978.
  N.L.—.268—Los Angeles .286, Philadelphia .250, 1978.
5-game series
  N.L.—.285—Chicago .303, San Francisco .267, 1989.
  A.L.—.283—New York .316, Kansas City .247, 1976.
6-game series
  A.L.—.271—Toronto .301, Chicago .237, 1993.
  N.L.—.256—St. Louis .279, Los Angeles .234, 1985.
7-game series
  A.L.—.275—California .277, Boston .272, 1986.
  N.L.—.2495—Pittsburgh .255, Atlanta .244, 1992.

Highest batting average by losing club, series
N.L.—.303—Chicago vs. San Francisco, 1989 (5-game series).
A.L.—.277—California vs. Boston, 1986 (7-game series).

Lowest batting average, series
3-game series
  A.L.—.155—Minnesota vs. Baltimore, 1969.
  N.L.—.169—Atlanta vs. St. Louis, 1982.
4-game series
  A.L.—.177—Baltimore vs. Oakland, 1974.
  N.L.—.194—Pittsburgh vs. Los Angeles, 1974.
5-game series
  N.L.—.186—Cincinnati vs. New York, 1973.
  A.L.—.198—Detroit vs. Oakland, 1972.
6-game series
  N.L.—.189—New York vs. Houston, 1986.
  A.L.—.237—Chicago vs. Toronto, 1993.
7-game series
  N.L.—.214—Los Angeles vs. New York, 1988.
  A.L.—.225—Kansas City vs. Toronto, 1985.

Lowest batting average by both clubs, series
3-game series
  A.L.—.202—Detroit .234, Kansas City .170, 1984.
  N.L.—.223—Pittsburgh .225, Cincinnati .220, 1970.
4-game series
  A.L.—.180—Oakland .183, Baltimore .177, 1974.
  N.L.—.232—Los Angeles .268, Pittsburgh .194, 1974.
5-game series
  N.L.—.203—New York .220, Cincinnati .186, 1973.
  A.L.—.205—Baltimore .211, Oakland .200, 1973.

6-game series
  N.L.—.204—Houston .218, New York .189, 1986.
  A.L.—.266—Toronto .281, Oakland .251, 1992.
7-game series
  N.L.—.228—New York .242, Los Angeles .214, 1988.
             Atlanta .231, Pittsburgh .224, 1991.
  A.L.—.247—Toronto .269, Kansas City .225, 1985.

Lowest batting average by winning club, series
A.L.—.183—Oakland vs. Baltimore, 1974 (4-game series).
N.L.—.189—New York vs. Houston, 1986 (6-game series).

SLUGGING AVERAGE

Highest slugging average, series
3-game series
  N.L.—.575—New York vs. Atlanta, 1969.
  A.L.—.560—Baltimore vs. Minnesota, 1970.
4-game series
  N.L.—.544—Los Angeles vs. Philadelphia, 1978.
  A.L.—.511—Oakland vs. Boston, 1988.
5-game series
  A.L.—.497—Minnesota vs. Detroit, 1987.
  N.L.—.494—Chicago vs. San Diego, 1984.
6-game series
  A.L.—.471—Toronto vs. Oakland, 1992.
  N.L.—.420—Philadelphia vs. Atlanta, 1993.
7-game series
  N.L.—.433—Pittsburgh vs. Atlanta, 1992.
  A.L.—.4023—California vs. Boston, 1986.

Highest slugging average by both clubs, series
3-game series
  N.L.—.530—New York .575, Atlanta .481, 1969.
  A.L.—.476—Baltimore .560, Minnesota .386, 1970.
4-game series
  N.L.—.477—Los Angeles .544, Philadelphia .407, 1978.
  A.L.—.443—Kansas City .4436, New York .4428, 1978.
5-game series
  N.L.—.456—San Francisco .473, Chicago .440, 1989.
  A.L.—.444—Minnesota .497, Detroit .389, 1987.
6-game series
  N.L.—.415—Philadelphia .420, Atlanta .409, 1993.
  A.L.—.408—Toronto .471, Oakland .343, 1992.
7-game series
  N.L.—.409—Pittsburgh .433, Atlanta .385, 1992.
  A.L.—.402—California .402, Boston .402, 1986.

Lowest slugging average, series
3-game series
  N.L.—.180—Atlanta vs. St. Louis, 1982.
  A.L.—.198—Kansas City vs. Detroit, 1984.
4-game series
  A.L.—.241—Chicago vs. Baltimore, 1983.
  N.L.—.271—Pittsburgh vs. Los Angeles, 1974.
5-game series
  A.L.—.288—Oakland vs. Detroit, 1972.
  N.L.—.278—Montreal vs. Los Angeles, 1981.
6-game series
  N.L.—.264—New York vs. Houston, 1986.
  A.L.—.343—Oakland vs. Toronto, 1992.
7-game series
  N.L.—.288—Los Angeles vs. New York, 1988.
  A.L.—.366—Kansas City vs. Toronto, 1985.

Lowest slugging average by both clubs, series
3-game series
  A.L.—.300—Detroit .402, Kansas City .198, 1984.
  N.L.—.318—St. Louis .437, Atlanta .180, 1982.
4-game series
  A.L.—.283—Oakland .308, Baltimore .258, 1974.
  N.L.—.339—Los Angeles .391, Philadelphia .290, 1977.
5-game series
  A.L.—.304—Detroit .321, Oakland .288, 1972.

N.L.—.307—Cincinnati .311, New York .304, 1973.
6-game series
N.L.—.288—Houston .311, New York .264, 1986.
A.L.—.373—Toronto .394, Chicago .351, 1993.
7-game series
N.L.—.325—New York .363, Los Angeles .288, 1988.
A.L.—.369—Toronto .372, Kansas City .366, 1985.

AT-BATS AND PLATE APPEARANCES

Most at-bats, total series
N.L.—1,384—Pittsburgh, 9 series, 42 games.
A.L.—1,372—Oakland, 10 series, 42 games.

Most at-bats, series
3-game series
A.L.—123—Baltimore vs. Minnesota, 1969.
N.L.—113—New York vs. Atlanta, 1969.
4-game series
N.L.—147—Los Angeles vs. Philadelphia, 1978.
A.L.—140—New York vs. Kansas City, 1978.
5-game series
N.L.—190—Philadelphia vs. Houston, 1980.
A.L.—181—Minnesota vs. Toronto, 1991.
6-game series
N.L.—227—New York vs. Houston, 1986.
A.L.—216—Toronto vs. Chicago, 1993.
7-game series
A.L.—256—California vs. Boston, 1986.
N.L.—243—Los Angeles vs. New York, 1988.

Most at-bats by both clubs, series
3-game series
A.L.—233—Baltimore 123, Minnesota 110, 1969.
N.L.—219—New York 113, Atlanta 106, 1969.
4-game series
N.L.—287—Los Angeles 147, Philadelphia 140, 1978.
A.L.—273—New York 140, Kansas City 133, 1978.
5-game series
N.L.—362—Philadelphia 190, Houston 172, 1980.
A.L.—354—Minnesota 181, Toronto 173, 1991.
6-game series
N.L.—452—New York 227, Houston 225, 1986.
A.L.—417—Toronto 210, Oakland 207, 1992.
7-game series
A.L.—510—California 256, Boston 254, 1986.
N.L.—483—Los Angeles 243, New York 240, 1988.

Most at-bats by pinch-hitters, series
N.L.—15—Atlanta vs. Pittsburgh, 1992 (7-game series).
A.L.—13
Oakland vs. Detroit, 1972 (5-game series).
Toronto vs. Kansas City, 1985 (7-game series).

Most at-bats by pinch-hitters on both clubs, series
N.L.—25—Atlanta 15, Pittsburgh 10, 1992 (7-game series).
A.L.—20—Oakland 13, Detroit 7, 1972 (5-game series).

Most plate appearances by pinch-hitters, series
N.L.—15
Cincinnati vs. New York, 1973 (5-game series).
Atlanta vs. Pittsburgh, 1992 (7-game series).
A.L.—14—Oakland vs. Detroit, 1972.

Most plate appearances by pinch-hitters on both clubs, series
N.L.—27—Atlanta 15, Pittsburgh 12, 1992 (7-game series).
A.L.—22—Oakland 14, Detroit 8, 1972 (5-game series).

Fewest at-bats, series
3-game series
N.L.—89—Atlanta vs. St. Louis, 1982.
A.L.—95—Baltimore vs. Oakland, 1971.
4-game series
A.L.—120—Oakland vs. Baltimore, 1974.
N.L.—129—Pittsburgh vs. Los Angeles, 1974.
Los Angeles vs. Philadelphia, 1983.
5-game series
A.L.—151—Milwaukee vs. California, 1982.
N.L.—155—San Diego vs. Chicago, 1984.

6-game series
A.L.—194—Chicago vs. Toronto, 1993.
N.L.—197—Los Angeles vs. St. Louis, 1985.
7-game series
N.L.—215—St. Louis vs. San Francisco, 1987.
A.L.—227—Kansas City vs. Toronto, 1985.

Fewest at-bats by both clubs, series
3-game series
A.L.—191—Oakland 96, Baltimore 95, 1971.
N.L.—192—St. Louis 103, Atlanta 89, 1982.
4-game series
A.L.—244—Baltimore 124, Oakland 120, 1974.
N.L.—259—Philadelphia 130, Los Angeles 129, 1983.
5-game series
A.L.—308—California 157, Milwaukee 151, 1982.
N.L.—317—Chicago 162, San Diego 155, 1984.
6-game series
N.L.—398—St. Louis 201, Los Angeles 197, 1985.
A.L.—410—Toronto 216, Chicago 194, 1993.
7-game series
N.L.—441—San Francisco 226, St. Louis 215, 1987.
A.L.—469—Toronto 242, Kansas City 227, 1985.

Most at-bats by club, nine-inning game
A.L.—44
Baltimore vs. Minnesota, October 6, 1969.
Toronto vs. Chicago, October 5, 1993.
N.L.—43—Atlanta vs. Philadelphia, October 7, 1993.

Most at-bats by club, extra-inning game
N.L.—56—Houston vs. New York, October 15, 1986, 16 innings.
A.L.—49—Toronto vs. Oakland, October 11, 1992, 11 innings.

Most at-bats by both clubs, nine-inning game
A.L.—80—Baltimore 44, Minnesota 36, October 6, 1969.
N.L.—77
New York 42, Atlanta 35, October 5, 1969.
Los Angeles 39, Philadelphia 38, October 4, 1978.
Atlanta 43, Philadelphia 34, October 7, 1993.

Most at-bats by both clubs, extra-inning game
N.L.—110—Houston 56, New York 54, October 15, 1986, 16 innings.
A.L.—91—Toronto 49, Oakland 42, October 11, 1992, 11 innings.

Most at-bats by pinch-hitters, game
A.L.—6—Oakland vs. Detroit, October 10, 1972.
N.L.—5—Atlanta vs. Pittsburgh, October 14, 1992.

Most at-bats by pinch-hitters on both clubs, nine-inning game
A.L.—7—Oakland 6, Detroit 1, October 10, 1972.
N.L.—6—Pittsburgh 3, Cincinnati 3, October 4, 1990.

Most at-bats by pinch-hitters on both clubs, extra-inning game
N.L.—8—New York 4, Houston 4, October 15, 1986, 16 innings.
A.L.—Less than nine-inning record.

Most plate appearances by pinch-hitters, game
A.L.—6—Oakland vs. Detroit, October 10, 1972.
N.L.—6—Pittsburgh vs. Cincinnati, October 4, 1990.

Most plate appearances by pinch-hitters on both clubs, nine-inning game
A.L.—7—Oakland 6, Detroit 1, October 10, 1972.
N.L.—6
San Diego 4, Chicago 2, October 6, 1984.
Pittsburgh 3, Cincinnati 3, October 4, 1990.
Atlanta 5, Pittsburgh 1, October 14, 1992.

Most plate appearances by pinch-hitters on both clubs extra-inning game
N.L.—10—New York 5, Houston 5, October 15, 1986, 16 innings.
A.L.—Less than nine-inning record.

Fewest at-bats, game
N.L.—26—St. Louis vs. San Francisco, October 7, 1987.
A.L.—25
California vs. Milwaukee, October 6, 1982 (batted eight innings).
Toronto vs. Oakland, October 8, 1992 (batted eight innings).

Fewest at-bats by both clubs, game
A.L.—56
Kansas City 30, Detroit 26, October 5, 1984.
Oakland 31, Toronto 25, October 8, 1992.
N.L.—58
Cincinnati 30, New York 28, October 6, 1973.
New York 31, Cincinnati 27, October 7, 1973.
Chicago 29, San Diego 29, October 3, 1984.
St. Louis 30, San Francisco 28, October 11, 1987.

Most at-bats, inning
N.L.—12—St. Louis vs. Los Angeles, October 13, 1985, second inning.
A.L.—10
New York vs. Oakland, October 14, 1981, fourth inning.
Toronto vs. Kansas City, October 11, 1985, fifth inning.

Most at-bats by both clubs, inning
A.L.—16—New York 10, Oakland 6, October 14, 1981, fourth inning.
N.L.—15
Philadelphia 8, Houston 7, October 12, 1980, eighth inning.
St. Louis 12, Los Angeles 3, October 13, 1985, second inning.
Pittsburgh 8, Atlanta 7, October 7, 1992, seventh inning.

Most batters facing pitcher, inning
N.L.—14—St. Louis vs. Los Angeles, October 13, 1985, second inning.
A.L.—12—New York vs. Oakland, October 14, 1981, fourth inning.

Most batters facing pitcher by both clubs, inning
A.L.—19—New York 12, Oakland 7, October 14, 1981, fourth inning.
N.L.—19—Atlanta 10, Pittsburgh 9, October 7, 1992, seventh inning.

RUNS

SERIES AND GAMES

Most runs, total series
A.L.—147—Oakland (10 series, 42 games).
N.L.—140—Los Angeles (7 series, 34 games).

Most runs, series
3-game series
A.L.—27—Baltimore vs. Minnesota, 1970.
N.L.—27—New York vs. Atlanta, 1969.
4-game series
A.L.—26—Baltimore vs. California, 1979.
N.L.—24—Pittsburgh vs. San Francisco, 1971.
5-game series
A.L.—34—Minnesota vs. Detroit, 1987.
N.L.—30—San Francisco vs. Chicago, 1989.
6-game series
N.L.—33—Atlanta vs. Philadelphia, 1993.
A.L.—31—Toronto vs. Oakland, 1992.
7-game series
A.L.—41—Boston vs. California, 1986.
N.L.—35—Pittsburgh vs. Atlanta, 1992.

Most runs by both clubs, series
3-game series
N.L.—42—New York 27, Atlanta 15, 1969.
A.L.—37—Baltimore 27, Minnesota 10, 1970.
4-game series
A.L.—41—Baltimore 26, California 15, 1979.
N.L.—39—Pittsburgh 24, San Francisco 15, 1971.
5-game series
A.L.—57—Minnesota 34, Detroit 23, 1987.
N.L.—52—San Francisco 30, Chicago 22, 1989.
6-game series
N.L.—56—Atlanta 33, Philadelphia 23, 1993.
A.L.—55—Toronto 31, Oakland 24, 1992.
7-game series
A.L.—71—Boston 41, California 30, 1986.
N.L.—69—Pittsburgh 35, Atlanta 34, 1992.

Most runs by losing club, series
N.L.—35—Pittsburgh vs. Atlanta, 1992 (7-game series).
A.L.—30—California vs. Boston, 1986 (7-game series).

Fewest runs, series
3-game series
N.L.—3—Pittsburgh vs. Cincinnati, 1970.
A.L.—4—Oakland vs. New York, 1981.
Kansas City vs. Detroit, 1984.
4-game series
A.L.—3—Chicago vs. Baltimore, 1983.
N.L.—10—Pittsburgh vs. Los Angeles, 1974.
5-game series
N.L.—8—Cincinnati vs. New York, 1973.
A.L.—10—Detroit vs. Oakland, 1972.
6-game series
N.L.—15—Pittsburgh vs. Cincinnati, 1990.
A.L.—23—Chicago vs. Toronto, 1993.
7-game series
N.L.—12—Pittsburgh vs. Atlanta, 1991.
A.L.—25—Toronto vs. Kansas City, 1985.

Fewest runs by both clubs, series
3-game series
N.L.—12—Cincinnati 9, Pittsburgh 3, 1970.
A.L.—18—Detroit 14, Kansas City 4, 1984.
4-game series
A.L.—18—Oakland 11, Baltimore 7, 1974.
N.L.—30—Los Angeles 20, Pittsburgh 10, 1974.
5-game series
A.L.—23—Oakland 13, Detroit 10, 1972.
N.L.—25—Los Angeles 15, Montreal 10, 1981.
6-game series
N.L.—35—Cincinnati 20, Pittsburgh 15, 1990.
A.L.—49—Toronto 26, Chicago 23, 1993.
7-game series
N.L.—31—Atlanta 19, Pittsburgh 12, 1991.
A.L.—51—Kansas City 26, Toronto 25, 1985.

Most runs, game
N.L.—14—Atlanta vs. Philadelphia, October 7, 1993.
A.L.—13—New York vs. Oakland, October 14, 1981.

Most earned runs, game
A.L.—13—New York vs. Oakland, October 14, 1981.
N.L.—13
Atlanta vs. Pittsburgh, October 7, 1992.
Atlanta vs. Philadelphia, October 7, 1993.

Most runs by both clubs, game
N.L.—18—Atlanta 13, Pittsburgh 5, October 7, 1992.
A.L.—17—Baltimore 9, California 8, October 4, 1979.

Largest score, shutout game
N.L.—Chicago 13, San Diego 0, October 2, 1984.
A.L.—Baltimore 8, California 0, October 6, 1979.

Most players scoring one or more runs, game
N.L.—11—Atlanta vs. Philadelphia, October 7, 1993.
A.L.—9
Baltimore vs. Minnesota, October 3, 1970.
New York vs. Oakland, October 14, 1981.

Most players from both clubs scoring one or more runs, game
A.L.—14—Baltimore 9, Minnesota 5, October 3, 1970.
California 7, Baltimore 7, October 4, 1979.
N.L.—14—Atlanta 10, Pittsburgh 4, October 7, 1992.
Atlanta 11, Philadelphia 3, October 7, 1993.

INNING

Most runs, inning
N.L.—9—St. Louis vs. Los Angeles, October 13, 1985, second inning.
A.L.—7
Baltimore vs. Minnesota, October 3, 1970, fourth inning.
Baltimore vs. Minnesota, October 4, 1970, ninth inning.
New York vs. Oakland, October 14, 1981, fourth inning.
Oakland vs. Boston, October 6, 1990, ninth inning.

Most runs by both clubs, inning
A.L.—9—New York 7, Oakland 2, October 14, 1981, fourth inning.
N.L.—9
St. Louis 9, Los Angeles 0, October 13, 1985, second inning.
Atlanta 5, Pittsburgh 4, October 7, 1992, seventh inning.

Most runs, extra inning
N.L.—4—Houston vs. Philadelphia, October 8, 1980, 10th inning.
A.L.—3
Detroit vs. Oakland, October 11, 1972, 10th inning.
Baltimore vs. California, October 3, 1979, 10th inning.
Baltimore vs. Chicago, October 8, 1983, 10th inning.

Most runs by both clubs, extra inning
A.L.—5—Detroit 3, Oakland 2, October 11, 1972, 10th inning.
N.L.—5
Houston 4, Philadelphia 1, October 8, 1980, 10th inning.
New York 3, Houston 2, October 15, 1986, 16th inning.

Most innings scored, game
N.L.—6
New York vs. Atlanta, October 5, 1969.
Los Angeles vs. Pittsburgh, October 9, 1974.
A.L.—6—Detroit vs. Kansas City, October 2, 1984.

Most innings scored by both clubs, game
A.L.—8
New York 4, Kansas City 4, October 6, 1978.
California 5, Baltimore 3, October 4, 1979.
Kansas City 4, Toronto 4, October 9, 1985.
Minnesota 5, Detroit 3, October 11, 1987.
Oakland 5, Boston 3, October 8, 1988.
Minnesota 5, Toronto 3, October 12, 1991.
N.L.—8
New York 6, Atlanta 2, October 5, 1969.
Pittsburgh 5, San Francisco 3, October 3, 1971.
Los Angeles 5, Philadelphia 3, October 4, 1978.
Atlanta 5, Pittsburgh 3, October 12, 1991.

Most runs, first inning
N.L.—6—Chicago vs. San Francisco, October 5, 1989.
A.L.—4
Baltimore vs. Oakland, October 6, 1973.
Baltimore vs. California, October 4, 1979.

Most runs, second inning
N.L.—9—St. Louis vs. Los Angeles, October 13, 1985.
A.L.—4
Kansas City vs. New York, October 4, 1978.
Baltimore vs. California, October 4, 1979.
California vs. Boston, October 7, 1986.
Minnesota vs. Detroit, October 12, 1987.
Oakland vs. Boston, October 8, 1988.

Most runs, third inning
A.L.—5
Boston vs. California, October 14, 1986.
Minnesota vs. Detroit, October 10, 1987.
Oakland vs. Toronto, October 11, 1992.
Chicago vs. Toronto, October 8, 1993.
N.L.—6—Atlanta vs. Philadelphia, October 7, 1993.

Most runs, fourth inning
A.L.—7
Baltimore vs. Minnesota, October 3, 1970.
New York vs. Oakland, October 14, 1981.
N.L.—4
Los Angeles vs. Philadelphia, October 5, 1977.
San Francisco vs. St. Louis, October 11, 1987.
San Francisco vs. Chicago, October 4, 1989.

Most runs, fifth inning
N.L.—6—Chicago vs. San Diego, October 2, 1984.
A.L.—5—Toronto vs. Kansas City, October 11, 1985.

Most runs, sixth inning
N.L.—5
St. Louis vs. Atlanta, October 7, 1982.
Atlanta vs. Philadelphia, October 9, 1993.

A.L.—4—Kansas City vs. Toronto, October 16, 1985.

Most runs, seventh inning
A.L.—5
Boston vs. Oakland, October 4, 1975.
Baltimore vs. California, October 6, 1979.
N.L.—5—Atlanta vs. Pittsburgh, October 7, 1992.

Most runs, eighth inning
N.L.—5
New York vs. Atlanta, October 4, 1969.
Philadelphia vs. Houston, October 12, 1980.
New York vs. Los Angeles, October 8, 1988.
A.L.—4
California vs. Milwaukee, October 9, 1982.
Minnesota vs. Detroit, October 7, 1987.

Most runs, ninth inning
A.L.—7
Baltimore vs. Minnesota, October 4, 1970.
Oakland vs. Boston, October 6, 1990.
N.L.—4
New York vs. Cincinnati, October 7, 1973.
Los Angeles vs. Montreal, October 17, 1981.

Most runs, 10th inning
N.L.—4—Houston vs. Philadelphia, October 8, 1980.
A.L.—3
Detroit vs. Oakland, October 11, 1972.
Baltimore vs. California, October 3, 1979.
Baltimore vs. Chicago, October 8, 1983.

Most runs, 11th inning
N.L.—3—Pittsburgh vs. Cincinnati, October 2, 1979.
A.L.—2
Oakland vs. Detroit, October 7, 1972.
Detroit vs. Kansas City, October 3, 1984.

Most runs, 12th inning
A.L.—1—Baltimore vs. Minnesota, October 4, 1969.
N.L.—1
Cincinnati vs. New York, October 9, 1973.
New York vs. Houston, October 14, 1986.
Los Angeles vs. New York, October 9, 1988.

Most runs, 14th inning
N.L.—1
Houston vs. New York, October 15, 1986.
New York vs. Houston, October 15, 1986.
A.L.—Never accomplished.

Most runs, 16th inning
N.L.—3—New York vs. Houston, October 15, 1986.
A.L.—Never accomplished.

GAMES BEING SHUT OUT

Most times being shut out, total series
N.L.—5—Pittsburgh, 1970, 1974, 1991 (3).
A.L.—3
Baltimore, 1973, 1974 (2).
Oakland, 1972, 1973, 1981.

Most consecutive games without being shut out, total series
A.L.—24—Toronto, October 15, 1985 through October 12, 1993.
N.L.—16
Los Angeles, October 5, 1983 through October 12, 1988.
Pittsburgh, October 6, 1974 through October 9, 1991.

HITS

SERIES

Most hits, total series
A.L.—329—Oakland (10 series, 42 games).
N.L.—311—Pittsburgh (nine series, 42 games).

Most hits, series

3-game series
N.L.—37—New York vs. Atlanta, 1969.
A.L.—36—Baltimore vs. Minnesota, 1969, 1970.
New York vs. Oakland, 1981.

4-game series
N.L.—42—Los Angeles vs. Philadelphia, 1978.
A.L.—42—New York vs. Kansas City, 1978.

5-game series
A.L.—55—New York vs. Kansas City, 1976.
N.L.—55—Philadelphia vs. Houston, 1980.

6-game series
A.L.—65—Toronto vs. Chicago, 1993.
N.L.—59—Atlanta vs. Philadelphia, 1993.

7-game series
A.L.—71—California vs. Boston, 1986.
N.L.—59—Pittsburgh vs. Atlanta, 1992.

Most hits by both clubs, series

3-game series
N.L.—64—New York 37, Atlanta 27, 1969.
A.L.—60—Baltimore 36, Minnesota 24, 1970.

4-game series
N.L.—77—Los Angeles 42, Philadelphia 35, 1978.
A.L.—77—New York 42, Kansas City 35, 1978.

5-game series
N.L.—97—Chicago 53, San Francisco 44, 1989.
A.L.—95—New York 55, Kansas City 40, 1976.

6-game series
A.L.—111—Toronto 59, Oakland 52, 1992.
Toronto 65, Chicago 46, 1993.
N.L.—106—Atlanta 59, Philadelphia 47, 1993.

7-game series
A.L.—140—California 71, Boston 69, 1986.
N.L.—116—Pittsburgh 59, Atlanta 57, 1992.

Fewest hits, series

3-game series
N.L.—15—Atlanta vs. St. Louis, 1982.
A.L.—17—Minnesota vs. Baltimore, 1969.

4-game series
A.L.—22—Baltimore vs. Oakland, 1974.
Oakland vs. Baltimore, 1974.
N.L.—25—Pittsburgh vs. Los Angeles, 1974.

5-game series
N.L.—30—Pittsburgh vs. Cincinnati, 1972.
A.L.—32—Detroit vs. Oakland, 1972.
Oakland vs. Baltimore, 1973.

6-game series
N.L.—43—New York vs. Houston, 1986.
A.L.—46—Chicago vs. Toronto, 1993.

7-game series
A.L.—51—Kansas City vs. Toronto, 1985.
N.L.—51—Pittsburgh vs. Atlanta, 1991.

Fewest hits by both clubs, series

3-game series
A.L.—43—Detroit 25, Kansas City 18, 1984.
N.L.—45—Pittsburgh 23, Cincinnati 22, 1970.

4-game series
A.L.—44—Baltimore 22, Oakland 22, 1974.
N.L.—62—Los Angeles 37, Pittsburgh 25, 1974.

5-game series
A.L.—68—Baltimore 36, Oakland 32, 1973.
N.L.—68—New York 37, Cincinnati 31, 1973.

6-game series
N.L.—92—Houston 49, New York 43, 1986.
A.L.—111—Toronto 59, Oakland 52, 1992.
Toronto 65, Chicago 46, 1993.

7-game series
N.L.—104—Atlanta 53, Pittsburgh 51, 1991.
A.L.—116—Toronto 65, Kansas City 51, 1985.

Most hits by pinch-hitters, series

A.L.—6—Toronto vs. Kansas City, 1985 (7-game series).
N.L.—4
Pittsburgh vs. Los Angeles, 1974 (4-game series).
Los Angeles vs. Pittsburgh, 1974 (4-game series).

Philadelphia vs. Houston, 1980 (5-game series).
Cincinnati vs. Pittsburgh, 1990 (6-game series).
Atlanta vs. Pittsburgh, 1992 (7-game series).

Most hits by pinch-hitters on both clubs, series

N.L.—8—Pittsburgh 4, Los Angeles 4, 1974 (4-game series).
A.L.—8—Toronto 6, Kansas City 2, 1985 (7-game series).

GAME AND INNING

Most hits, game

A.L.—19—New York vs. Oakland, October 14, 1981.
N.L.—16—Chicago vs. San Diego, October 2, 1984.

Most hits by both clubs, nine-inning game

A.L.—30—New York 19, Oakland 11, October 14, 1981.
N.L.—25—Los Angeles 13, Philadelphia 12, October 4, 1978.

Most hits by both clubs, extra-inning game

N.L.—27—Houston 14, Philadelphia 13, October 12, 1980 (10 innings).
A.L.—Less than nine-inning record.

Most hits by pinch-hitters, game

A.L.—3—Kansas City vs. Detroit, October 3, 1984, 11 innings.
N.L.—2—Held by many clubs.

Most hits by pinch-hitters on both clubs, game

N.L.—4—Los Angeles 2, Pittsburgh 2, October 6, 1974.
A.L.—3
Kansas City 3, Detroit 0, October 3, 1984, 11 innings.
Detroit 2, Minnesota 1, October 11, 1987.

Fewest hits, game

A.L.—1—Oakland vs. Baltimore, October 9, 1974.
N.L.—1—Pittsburgh vs. Cincinnati, October 12, 1990.

Fewest hits by both clubs, game

A.L.—6
Oakland 4, Baltimore 2, October 8, 1974.
Baltimore 5, Oakland 1, October 9, 1974.
Detroit 3, Kansas City 3, October 5, 1984.
N.L.—7—Houston 4, New York 3, October 12, 1986.

Most players with one or more hits, game

N.L.—11—Chicago vs. San Diego, October 2, 1984.
A.L.—10
New York vs. Oakland, October 14, 1981.
Toronto vs. Kansas City, October 11, 1985.

Most players with one or more hits by both clubs, game

A.L.—18
New York 10, Oakland 8, October 14, 1981.
Boston 9, California 9, October 12, 1986, 11 innings.
N.L.—16
Los Angeles 8, Philadelphia 8, October 4, 1978.
Houston 8, Philadelphia 8, October 12, 1980, 10 innings.

Most hits, inning

N.L.—8
St. Louis vs. Los Angeles, October 13, 1985, second inning.
Pittsburgh vs. Atlanta, October 13, 1992, second inning.
A.L.—7
Baltimore vs. Minnesota, October 3, 1970, fourth inning.
New York vs. Oakland, October 14, 1981, fourth inning.
Toronto vs. Kansas City, October 11, 1985, fifth inning.

Most hits by pinch-hitters, inning

A.L.-N.L.—2—Occurred many times.

Most hits by both clubs, inning

A.L.—11—New York 7, Oakland 4, October 14, 1981, fourth inning.
N.L.—9—Philadelphia 5, Houston 4, October 12, 1980, eighth inning.

Most consecutive hits, inning (consecutive at-bats)

A.L.—7—Baltimore vs. Minnesota, October 3, 1970, fourth inning (one sacrifice fly during streak).
N.L.—6—St. Louis vs. Atlanta, October 7, 1982, sixth inning (one base on balls during streak).

Most consecutive hits, inning (consecutive plate appearances)
N.L.—5
  Cincinnati vs. Pittsburgh, October 8, 1972, first inning.
  Los Angeles vs. Pittsburgh, October 6, 1974, eighth inning.
  St. Louis vs. San Francisco, October 9, 1987, seventh inning.
A.L.—5
  New York vs. Oakland, October 14, 1981, fourth inning.
  Toronto vs. Minnesota, October 8, 1991, sixth inning.

SINGLES

Most singles, total series
A.L.—231—Oakland (10 series, 42 games).
N.L.—211—Pittsburgh (nine series, 42 games).

Most singles, series
3-game series
  A.L.—29—New York vs. Oakland, 1981.
  N.L.—27—St. Louis vs. Atlanta, 1982.
4-game series
  A.L.—34—Oakland vs. Boston, 1990.
  N.L.—27—Pittsburgh vs. San Francisco, 1971.
5-game series
  N.L.—45—Philadelphia vs. Houston, 1980.
  A.L.—37—Minnesota vs. Toronto, 1991.
6-game series
  A.L.—52—Toronto vs. Chicago, 1993.
  N.L.—42—St. Louis vs. Los Angeles, 1985.
7-game series
  A.L.—53—California vs. Boston, 1986.
  N.L.—46—St. Louis vs. San Francisco, 1987.

Most singles by both clubs, series
3-game series
  A.L.—46—New York 29, Oakland 17, 1981.
  N.L.—41—St. Louis 27, Atlanta 14, 1982.
4-game series
  A.L.—55—New York 33, Kansas City 22, 1978.
  N.L.—51—Philadelphia 26, Los Angeles 25, 1977.
5-game series
  N.L.—73—Philadelphia 45, Houston 28, 1980.
  A.L.—73—Minnesota 37, Toronto 36, 1991.
6-game series
  A.L.—87—Toronto 52, Chicago 35, 1993.
  N.L.—72—Houston 38, New York 34, 1986.
7-game series
  A.L.— 103—California 53, Boston 50, 1986.
  N.L.—83—St. Louis 46, San Francisco 37, 1987.

Fewest singles, series
3-game series
  A.L.— 10—Oakland vs. Baltimore, 1971.
  N.L.— 13—Atlanta vs. New York, 1969.
4-game series
  A.L.— 14—Oakland vs. Baltimore, 1974.
  N.L.— 19—Los Angeles vs. Philadelphia, 1983.
5-game series
  N.L.—20—Pittsburgh vs. Cincinnati, 1972.
           Cincinnati vs. New York, 1973.
  A.L.—21—Detroit vs. Oakland, 1972.
           Oakland vs. Baltimore, 1973.
6-game series
  N.L.—25—Philadelphia vs. Atlanta, 1993.
  A.L.—35—Chicago vs. Toronto, 1993.
7-game series
  A.L.—34—Kansas City vs. Toronto, 1985.
  N.L.—31—Pittsburgh vs. Atlanta, 1992.

Fewest singles by both clubs, series
3-game series
  A.L.—24—Baltimore 14, Oakland 10, 1971.
  N.L.—31—Philadelphia 17, Cincinnati 14, 1976.
4-game series
  A.L.—32—Baltimore 18, Oakland 14, 1974.
  N.L.—44—Philadelphia 25, Los Angeles 19, 1983.
5-game series
  A.L.—47—Baltimore 26, Oakland 21, 1973.
  N.L.—47—Cincinnati 27, Pittsburgh 20, 1972.

6-game series
  N.L.—65—Atlanta 40, Philadelphia 25, 1993.
  A.L.—82—Oakland 42, Toronto 40, 1992.
7-game series
  N.L.—69—Atlanta 38, Pittsburgh 31, 1992.
  A.L.—78—Toronto 44, Kansas City 34, 1985.

Most singles by pinch-hitters, series
N.L.—4
  Pittsburgh vs. Los Angeles, 1974 (4-game series).
  Cincinnati vs. Pittsburgh, 1990 (6-game series).
  Atlanta vs. Philadelphia, 1993 (6-game series).
A.L.—4—Toronto vs. Kansas City, 1985 (7-game series).

Most singles by pinch-hitters on both clubs, series
N.L.—7—Pittsburgh 4, Los Angeles 3, 1974 (4-game series).
A.L.—4
  Oakland 3, Detroit 1, 1972 (5-game series).
  Toronto 4, Kansas City 0, 1985 (7-game series).
  Detroit 3, Minnesota 1, 1987 (5-game series).

Most singles, game
A.L.— 15—New York vs. Oakland, October 14, 1981.
N.L.— 13—St. Louis vs. Los Angeles, October 13, 1985.

Most singles by both clubs, game
A.L.—25—Kansas City 13, New York 12, October 4, 1978.
N.L.— 18—St. Louis 10, San Francisco 8, October 14, 1987.

Fewest singles, game
A.L.—0—Oakland vs. Baltimore, October 9, 1974.
N.L.—0—Pittsburgh vs. Cincinnati, October 12, 1990.

Fewest singles by both clubs, game
N.L.—4
  New York 2, Cincinnati 2, October 6, 1973.
  New York 3, Houston 1, October 12, 1986.
A.L.—4—Toronto 2, Kansas City 2, October 12, 1985.

Most singles, inning
N.L.—8—St. Louis vs. Los Angeles, October 13, 1985, second inning.
A.L.—5
  Kansas City vs. New York, October 4, 1978, second inning.
  New York vs. Oakland, October 14, 1981, fourth inning.
  Boston vs. California, October 14, 1986, third inning.
  Toronto vs. Minnesota, October 8, 1991, sixth inning (consecutive).
  Toronto vs. Chicago, October 8, 1993, third inning.

Most singles by both clubs, inning
A.L.—9—New York 5, Oakland 4, October 14, 1981, fourth inning.
N.L.—8
  Philadelphia 4, Houston 4, October 12, 1980, eighth inning.
  St. Louis 8, Los Angeles 0, October 13, 1985, second inning.

DOUBLES

Most doubles, total series
A.L.—61—Oakland (10 series, 42 games).
N.L.—62—Pittsburgh (nine series, 42 games).

Most doubles, series
3-game series
  N.L.—9—Atlanta vs. New York, 1969.
  A.L.—8—Baltimore vs. Minnesota, 1969.
          Oakland vs. Baltimore, 1971.
          Boston vs. Oakland, 1975.
4-game series
  A.L.—9—Baltimore vs. Chicago, 1983.
  N.L.—8—Los Angeles vs. Pittsburgh, 1974.
          Los Angeles vs. Philadelphia, 1978.
5-game series
  A.L.— 13—New York vs. Kansas City, 1976.
          Minnesota vs. Detroit, 1987.
  N.L.— 11—Chicago vs. San Diego, 1984.
6-game series
  N.L.— 14—Atlanta vs. Philadelphia, 1993.

A.L.—8—Toronto vs. Oakland, 1992.
Toronto vs. Chicago, 1993.
7-game series
N.L.—20—Pittsburgh vs. Atlanta, 1992.
A.L.—19—Toronto vs. Kansas City, 1985.

Most doubles by both clubs, series
3-game series
N.L.—17—Atlanta 9, New York 8, 1969.
A.L.—15—Oakland 8, Baltimore 7, 1971.
4-game series
A.L.—13—Baltimore 9, Chicago 4, 1983.
N.L.—11—Los Angeles 8, Philadelphia 3, 1978.
5-game series
A.L.—21—New York 12, Kansas City 9, 1977.
N.L.—16—Chicago 11, San Diego 5, 1984.
6-game series
N.L.—25—Atlanta 14, Philadelphia 11, 1993.
A.L.—13—Toronto 8, Oakland 5, 1992.
Toronto 8, Chicago 5, 1993.
7-game series
N.L.—31—Pittsburgh 20, Atlanta 11, 1992.
A.L.—28—Toronto 19, Kansas City 9, 1985.

Fewest doubles, series
3-game series
N.L.—1—Atlanta vs. St. Louis, 1982.
A.L.—1—Kansas City vs. Detroit, 1984.
4-game series
A.L.—1—Baltimore vs. Oakland, 1974.
N.L.—1—Pittsburgh vs. Los Angeles, 1974.
5-game series
N.L.—3—Los Angeles vs. Montreal, 1981.
A.L.—4—Milwaukee vs. California, 1982.
Detroit vs. Minnesota, 1987.
6-game series
N.L.—4—New York vs. Houston, 1986.
A.L.—5—Oakland vs. Toronto, 1992.
7-game series
N.L.—4—St. Louis vs. San Francisco, 1987.
A.L.—9—Kansas City vs. Toronto, 1985.

Fewest doubles by both clubs, series
3-game series
N.L.—5—St. Louis 4, Atlanta 1, 1982.
A.L.—5—Detroit 4, Kansas City 1, 1984.
4-game series
A.L.—5—Oakland 4, Baltimore 1, 1974.
N.L.—9—San Francisco 5, Pittsburgh 4, 1971.
Los Angeles 8, Pittsburgh 1, 1974.
Los Angeles 6, Philadelphia 3, 1977.
Los Angeles 5, Philadelphia 3, 1983.
5-game series
N.L.—10—Montreal 7, Los Angeles 3, 1981.
A.L.—12—Baltimore 7, Oakland 5, 1973.
California 8, Milwaukee 4, 1982.
6-game series
N.L.—10—Houston 6, New York 4, 1986.
A.L.—13
Toronto 8, Oakland 5, 1992.
Toronto 8, Chicago 5, 1993.
7-game series
N.L.—11—San Francisco 7, St. Louis 4, 1987.
A.L.—22—Boston 11, California 11, 1986.

Most doubles by pinch-hitters, series
A.L.—2—Toronto vs. Kansas City, 1985 (7-game series).
N.L.—1—Held by many clubs.

Most doubles by pinch-hitters on both clubs, series
A.L.—3—Toronto 2, Kansas City 1, 1985 (7-game series).
N.L.—2—Los Angeles 1, Philadelphia 1, 1978 (4-game series).

Most doubles, game
A.L.—6—Baltimore vs. Minnesota, October 6, 1969.
N.L.—6—Philadelphia vs. Cincinnati, October 12, 1976.

Most doubles by both clubs, game
A.L.—9—Oakland 5, Baltimore 4, October 3, 1971.

N.L.—8
Los Angeles 5, St. Louis 3, October 12, 1985.
Philadelphia 5, Atlanta 3, October 6, 1993, 10 innings.
Atlanta 5, Philadelphia 3, October 9, 1993.

Most doubles, inning
N.L.—4—Pittsburgh vs. Atlanta, October 11, 1992, first inning.
A.L.—3
Oakland vs. Baltimore, October 10, 1973, second inning.
Boston vs. Oakland, October 4, 1975, seventh inning.
Minnesota vs. Detroit, October 8, 1987, second inning.

TRIPLES

Most triples, total series
A.L.—13—Kansas City (six series, 27 games).
N.L.—9—Los Angeles (seven series, 34 games).

Most triples, series
3-game series
N.L.—3—Cincinnati vs. Philadelphia, 1976.
A.L.—1—Held by many clubs.
4-game series
A.L.—3—Kansas City vs. New York, 1978.
N.L.—3—Los Angeles vs. Philadelphia, 1978.
5-game series
N.L.—5—Houston vs. Philadelphia, 1980.
A.L.—4—Kansas City vs. New York, 1976.
6-game series
N.L.—4—Philadelphia vs. Atlanta, 1993.
A.L.—3—Toronto vs. Chicago, 1993.
7-game series
N.L.—4—St. Louis vs. San Francisco, 1987.
A.L.—2—Boston vs. California, 1986.

Most triples by both clubs, series
3-game series
N.L.—4—Cincinnati 3, Philadelphia 1, 1976.
A.L.—2—Baltimore 1, Minnesota 1, 1969.
Baltimore 1, Oakland 1, 1971.
Kansas City 1, New York 1, 1980.
4-game series
N.L.—5—Los Angeles 3, Philadelphia 2, 1978.
A.L.—4—Kansas City 3, New York 1, 1978.
5-game series
A.L.—6—Kansas City 4, New York 2, 1976.
N.L.—6—Houston 5, Philadelphia 1, 1980.
6-game series
N.L.—4—Philadelphia 4, Atlanta 0, 1993.
A.L.—4—Toronto 3, Chicago 1, 1993.
7-game series
N.L.—5—St. Louis 4, San Francisco 1, 1987.
Pittsburgh 3, Atlanta 2, 1992.
A.L.—2—Boston 2, California 0, 1986.

Fewest triples, series
A.L.-N.L.—0—Held by many clubs.

Fewest triples by both clubs, series
3-game series
N.L.—0—Cincinnati 0, Pittsburgh 0, 1975.
A.L.—0—Boston 0, Oakland 0, 1975.
4-game series
N.L.—0—Pittsburgh 0, San Francisco 0, 1971.
A.L.—0—Baltimore 0, Chicago 0, 1983.
Oakland 0, Boston 0, 1990.
5-game series
N.L.—0—Cincinnati 0, New York 0, 1973.
A.L.—1—Made in many series.
6-game series
N.L.—2—Los Angeles 1, St. Louis 1, 1985.
A.L.—2—Toronto 1, Oakland 1, 1992.
7-game series
A.L.—1—Kansas City 1, Toronto 0, 1985.
N.L.—1—Atlanta 1, Pittsburgh 0, 1991.

Most triples by pinch-hitters, series
N.L.—1
Cincinnati vs. Pittsburgh, 1970 (3-game series).

— 366 —

New York vs. Houston, 1986 (6-game series).
Atlanta vs. Pittsburgh, 1992 (7-game series).
A.L.—Never accomplished.

Most triples, game
N.L.—3—Philadelphia vs. Atlanta, October 9, 1993.
A.L.—2
Kansas City vs. New York, October 13, 1976.
Kansas City vs. New York, October 8, 1977.

Most triples by both clubs, game
N.L.—3
Los Angeles 2, Philadelphia 1, October 4, 1978.
Philadelphia 3, Atlanta 0, October 9, 1993.
A.L.—2
Baltimore 1, Minnesota 1, October 6, 1969.
Kansas City 1, New York 1, October 9, 1976.
Kansas City 2, New York 0, October 13, 1976.
Kansas City 2, New York 0, October 8, 1977.
Detroit 1, Kansas City 1, October 2, 1984.
Toronto 1, Chicago 1, October 9, 1993.

Most triples, inning
A.L.—2—Kansas City vs. New York, October 8, 1977, third inning.
N.L.—2—Philadelphia vs. Atlanta, October 9, 1993, fourth inning.

HOME RUNS

SERIES

Most home runs, total series
A.L.—31—Oakland (10 series, 42 games).
N.L.—30—Pittsburgh (nine series, 42 games).

Most grand slams, total series
N.L.—2—Los Angeles, 1977 (2).
A.L.—1
Baltimore, 1970.
California, 1982.

Most home runs, series
3-game series
N.L.—6—New York vs. Atlanta, 1969.
A.L.—6—Baltimore vs. Minnesota, 1970.
4-game series
N.L.—8—Pittsburgh vs. San Francisco, 1971.
Los Angeles vs. Philadelphia, 1978.
A.L.—7—Oakland vs. Boston, 1988.
5-game series
N.L.—9—Chicago vs. San Diego, 1984.
A.L.—8—Minnesota vs. Detroit, 1987.
6-game series
A.L.—10—Toronto vs. Oakland, 1992.
N.L.—7—Philadelphia vs. Atlanta, 1993.
7-game series
N.L.—9—San Francisco vs. St. Louis, 1987.
A.L.—7—California vs. Boston, 1986.

Most home runs by both clubs, series
3-game series
N.L.—11—New York 6, Atlanta 5, 1969.
A.L.—9—Baltimore 6, Minnesota 3, 1970.
4-game series
N.L.—13—Pittsburgh 8, San Francisco 5, 1971.
Los Angeles 8, Philadelphia 5, 1978.
A.L.—9—New York 5, Kansas City 4, 1978.
Oakland 7, Boston 2, 1988.
5-game series
A.L.—15—Minnesota 8, Detroit 7, 1987.
N.L.—11—Chicago 9, San Diego 2, 1984.
San Francisco 8, Chicago 3, 1989.
6-game series
A.L.—14—Toronto 10, Oakland 4, 1992.
N.L.—12—Philadelphia 7, Atlanta 5, 1993.
7-game series
A.L.—13—California 7, Boston 6, 1986.
N.L.—11—San Francisco 9, St. Louis 2, 1987.

Atlanta 6, Pittsburgh 5, 1992.

Fewest home runs, series
3-game series
N.L.—0—Pittsburgh vs. Cincinnati, 1970.
Atlanta vs. St. Louis, 1982.
A.L.—0—Oakland vs. New York, 1981.
Kansas City vs. Detroit, 1984.
4-game series
N.L.—0—Philadelphia vs. Los Angeles, 1977.
A.L.—0—Chicago vs. Baltimore, 1983.
Oakland vs. Boston, 1990.
5-game series
N.L.—0—Houston vs. Philadelphia, 1980.
A.L.—1—Oakland vs. Detroit, 1972.
Toronto vs. Minnesota, 1991.
6-game series
A.L.—2—Toronto vs. Chicago, 1993.
N.L.—3—St. Louis vs. Los Angeles, 1985.
New York vs. Houston, 1986.
7-game series
A.L.—2—Toronto vs. Kansas City, 1985.
N.L.—2—St. Louis vs. San Francisco, 1987.

Fewest home runs by both clubs, series
3-game series
N.L.—1—St. Louis 1, Atlanta 0, 1982.
A.L.—2—New York 2, Oakland 0, 1981.
4-game series
A.L.—1—Boston 1, Oakland 0, 1990.
N.L.—5—Los Angeles 3, Philadelphia 2, 1977.
5-game series
N.L.—1—Philadelphia 1, Houston 0, 1980.
A.L.—4—Minnesota 3, Toronto 1, 1991.
6-game series
A.L.—7—Chicago 5, Toronto 2, 1993.
N.L.—8—Los Angeles 5, St. Louis 3, 1985.
Houston 5, New York 3, 1986.
7-game series
N.L.—8—New York 5, Los Angeles 3, 1988.
Atlanta 5, Pittsburgh 3, 1991.
A.L.—9—Kansas City 7, Toronto 2, 1985.

Most grand slams, series
N.L.—2—Los Angeles vs. Philadelphia, 1977.
A.L.—1
Baltimore vs. Minnesota, 1970.
California vs. Milwaukee, 1982.

Most home runs by pinch-hitters, series
N.L.—2—Philadelphia vs. Los Angeles, 1978 (4-game series).
A.L.—1
Baltimore vs. California, 1979 (4-game series).
Kansas City vs. Toronto, 1985 (7-game series).
Minnesota vs. Toronto, 1991 (5-game series).

GAME AND INNING

Most home runs, game
N.L.—5—Chicago vs. San Diego, October 2, 1984.
A.L.—4
Baltimore vs. Oakland, October 4, 1971.
Oakland vs. Baltimore, October 7, 1973.
Oakland vs. Boston, October 8, 1988.

Most home runs by both clubs, game
A.L.—5
Kansas City 3, New York 2, October 6, 1978.
Kansas City 3, Toronto 2, October 11, 1985.
Oakland 4, Boston 1, October 8, 1988.
Oakland 3, Toronto 2, October 7, 1992.
N.L.—6—Atlanta 4, Philadelphia 2, 1993.

Most consecutive games with one or more home runs, total series
A.L.—8—Oakland, all four games vs. Boston, 1988 (seven home runs), first four games vs. Toronto, 1989 (seven home runs).
N.L.—7
Philadelphia, all four games vs. Los Angeles, 1983 (five

home runs), first three games vs. Atlanta, 1993 (four home runs).

Most consecutive games with one or more home runs, series

A.L.—6—Toronto vs. Oakland, October 7, 8, 10, 11, 12, 14, 1992 (10 home runs).

N.L.—5—San Francisco vs. St. Louis, October 6, 7, 9, 10, 11, 1987 (nine home runs).

Most home runs, inning

A.L.—3—Baltimore vs. Minnesota, October 3, 1970, fourth inning (first two consecutive).

N.L.—2

Cincinnati vs. Pittsburgh, October 5, 1970, first inning (consecutive).

San Francisco vs. Pittsburgh, October 2, 1971, fifth inning.

San Francisco vs. Pittsburgh, October 6, 1971, second inning.

Pittsburgh vs. Los Angeles, October 8, 1974, first inning.

Cincinnati vs. Philadelphia, October 12, 1976, ninth inning (consecutive).

Pittsburgh vs. Cincinnati, October 5, 1979, third inning.

Los Angeles vs. Montreal, October 13, 1981, eighth inning (consecutive).

Chicago vs. San Diego, October 2, 1984, first inning.

Chicago vs. San Diego, October 6, 1984, fourth inning (consecutive).

New York vs. Los Angeles, October 9, 1988, fourth inning (consecutive).

Pittsburgh vs. Atlanta, October 13, 1992, second inning.

Atlanta vs. Philadelphia, October 7, 1993, third inning.

Most home runs by both clubs, inning

A.L.—3

Baltimore 3, Minnesota 0, October 3, 1970, fourth inning.

Toronto 2, Kansas City 1, October 11, 1985, fifth inning.

Oakland 2, Boston 1, October 8, 1988, second inning.

N.L.—3—San Francisco 2, Pittsburgh 1, October 6, 1971, second inning.

Most consecutive home runs, inning

A.L.—2

Baltimore (Cuellar and Buford) vs. Minnesota, October 3, 1970, fourth inning.

Minnesota (Killebrew and Oliva) vs. Baltimore, October 4, 1970, fourth inning.

Oakland (Rudi and Bando) vs. Baltimore, October 7, 1973, sixth inning.

New York (Cerone and Piniella) vs. Kansas City, October 8, 1980, second inning.

Oakland (McGwire and Steinbach) vs. Toronto, October 7, 1992, second inning.

N.L.—2

Cincinnati (Perez and Bench) vs. Pittsburgh, October 5, 1970, first inning.

Cincinnati (Foster and Bench) vs. Philadelphia, October 12, 1976, ninth inning.

Los Angeles (Guerrero and Scioscia) vs. Montreal, October 13, 1981, eighth inning.

Chicago (Davis and Durham) vs. San Diego, October 6, 1984, fourth inning.

New York (Strawberry and McReynolds) vs. Los Angeles, October 9, 1988, fourth inning.

TOTAL BASES

Most total bases, total series

A.L.—495—Oakland (10 series, 42 games).

N.L.—479—Pittsburgh (nine series, 42 games).

Most total bases, series

3-game series

N.L.—65—New York vs. Atlanta, 1969.

A.L.—61—Baltimore vs. Minnesota, 1970.

4-game series

N.L.—80—Los Angeles vs. Philadelphia, 1978.

A.L.—70—Oakland vs. Boston, 1988.

5-game series

A.L.—85—Minnesota vs. Detroit, 1987.

N.L.—80—Chicago vs. San Diego, 1984.

6-game series

A.L.—99—Toronto vs. Oakland, 1992.

N.L.—88—Atlanta vs. Philadelphia, 1993.

7-game series

A.L.—103—California vs. Boston, 1986.

N.L.—100—Pittsburgh vs. Atlanta, 1992.

Most total bases by both clubs, series

3-game series

N.L.—116—New York 65, Atlanta 51, 1969.

A.L.—100—Baltimore 61, Minnesota 39, 1970.

4-game series

N.L.—137—Los Angeles 80, Philadelphia 57, 1978.

A.L.—121—New York 62, Kansas City 59, 1978.

5-game series

N.L.—155—San Francisco 78, Chicago 77, 1989.

A.L.—150—Minnesota 85, Detroit 65, 1987.

6-game series

N.L.—175—Atlanta 88, Philadelphia 87, 1993.

A.L.—170—Toronto 99, Oakland 71, 1992.

7-game series

A.L.—205—California 103, Boston 102, 1986.

N.L.—190—Pittsburgh 100, Atlanta 90, 1992.

Fewest total bases, series

3-game series

N.L.—16—Atlanta vs. St. Louis, 1982.

A.L.—21—Kansas City vs. Detroit, 1984.

4-game series

A.L.—31—Boston vs. Oakland, 1990.

N.L.—35—Pittsburgh vs. Los Angeles, 1974.

5-game series

N.L.—44—Montreal vs. Los Angeles, 1981.

A.L.—49—Oakland vs. Detroit, 1972.

6-game series

N.L.—58—Pittsburgh vs. Cincinnati, 1990.

A.L.—68—Chicago vs. Toronto, 1993.

7-game series

N.L.—70—Los Angeles vs. New York, 1988.

Pittsburgh vs. Atlanta, 1991.

A.L.—83—Kansas City vs. Toronto, 1985.

Fewest total bases by both clubs, series

3-game series

N.L.—61—St. Louis 45, Atlanta 16, 1982.

A.L.—64—Detroit 43, Kansas City 21, 1984.

4-game series

A.L.—69—Oakland 37, Baltimore 32, 1974.

N.L.—91—Los Angeles 56, Pittsburgh 35, 1974.

5-game series

N.L.—99—Los Angeles 55, Montreal 44, 1981.

A.L.—101—Detroit 52, Oakland 49, 1972.

6-game series

N.L.—128—Cincinnati 70, Pittsburgh 58, 1990.

A.L.—153—Toronto 85, Chicago 68, 1993.

7-game series

N.L.—150—Atlanta 80, Pittsburgh 70, 1991.

A.L.—173—Toronto 90, Kansas City 83, 1985.

Most total bases, game

N.L.—34—Chicago vs. San Diego, October 2, 1984.

A.L.—30—Oakland vs. Boston, October 8, 1988.

Most total bases by both clubs, game

N.L.—47—Los Angeles 30, Philadelphia 17, October 4, 1978.

A.L.—47—Oakland 30, Boston 17, October 8, 1988.

Fewest total bases, game

N.L.—2

Cincinnati vs. New York, October 7, 1973.

St. Louis vs. San Francisco, October 7, 1987.

Pittsburgh vs. Cincinnati, October 12, 1990.

A.L.—2

Baltimore vs. Oakland, October 8, 1974.

Oakland vs. Baltimore, October 9, 1974.

Kansas City vs. Toronto, October 12, 1985.

Fewest total bases by both clubs, game

A.L.—6—Detroit 3, Kansas City 3, October 5, 1984.
N.L.—11—Cincinnati 9, Pittsburgh 2, October 12, 1990.

Most total bases, inning

A.L.—16—Baltimore vs. Minnesota, October 3, 1970, fourth inning.
N.L.—16—Pittsburgh vs. Atlanta, October 13, 1992, second inning.

Most total bases by both clubs, inning

A.L.—18—Baltimore 16, Minnesota 2, October 3, 1970, fourth inning.
N.L.—17—San Francisco 11, Pittsburgh 6, October 6, 1971, second inning.

LONG HITS

Most long hits, total series

N.L.—100—Pittsburgh (nine series, 42 games).
A.L.—98—Oakland (10 series, 42 games).

Most long hits, series

3-game series
  N.L.—15—New York vs. Atlanta, 1969.
  A.L.—13—Baltimore vs. Minnesota, 1969, 1970.
4-game series
  N.L.—19—Los Angeles vs. Philadelphia, 1978.
  A.L.—15—Oakland vs. Boston, 1988.
5-game series
  A.L.—22—Minnesota vs. Detroit, 1987.
  N.L.—20—Chicago vs. San Diego, 1984.
6-game series
  N.L.—22—Philadelphia vs. Atlanta, 1993.
  A.L.—19—Toronto vs. Oakland, 1992.
7-game series
  N.L.—28—Pittsburgh vs. Atlanta, 1992.
  A.L.—21—Toronto vs. Kansas City, 1985.

Most long hits by both clubs, series

3-game series
  N.L.—29—New York 15, Atlanta 14, 1969.
  A.L.—24—Baltimore 12, Oakland 12, 1971.
4-game series
  N.L.—29—Los Angeles 19, Philadelphia 10, 1978.
  A.L.—22—Kansas City 13, New York 9, 1978.
5-game series
  A.L.—33—Minnesota 22, Detroit 11, 1987.
  N.L.—28—Chicago 20, San Diego 8, 1984.
6-game series
  N.L.—41—Philadelphia 22, Atlanta 19, 1993.
  A.L.—29—Toronto 19, Oakland 10, 1992.
7-game series
  N.L.—47—Pittsburgh 28, Atlanta 19, 1992.
  A.L.—38—Toronto 21, Kansas City 17, 1985.

Fewest long hits, series

3-game series
  N.L.—1—Atlanta vs. St. Louis, 1982.
  A.L.—2—Kansas City vs. Detroit, 1984.
4-game series
  N.L.—4—Pittsburgh vs. Los Angeles, 1974.
  A.L.—4—Baltimore vs. Oakland, 1974.
      Chicago vs. Baltimore, 1983.
      Oakland vs. Boston, 1990.
5-game series
  N.L.—8—New York vs. Cincinnati, 1973.
      Los Angeles vs. Montreal, 1981.
      Montreal vs. Los Angeles, 1981.
      San Diego vs. Chicago, 1984.
  A.L.—7—Toronto vs. Minnesota, 1991.
6-game series
  N.L.—9—New York vs. Houston, 1986.
  A.L.—10—Oakland vs. Toronto, 1992.
7-game series
  N.L.—10—St. Louis vs. San Francisco, 1987.
  A.L.—17—Kansas City vs. Toronto, 1985.

Fewest long hits by both clubs, series

3-game series
  N.L.—8—St. Louis 7, Atlanta 1, 1982.
  A.L.—11—Detroit 9, Kansas City 2, 1984.
4-game series
  A.L.—10—Boston 6, Oakland 4, 1990.
  N.L.—15—Los Angeles 10, Philadelphia 5, 1977.
5-game series
  N.L.—16—Los Angeles 8, Montreal 8, 1981.
  A.L.—20—Detroit 11, Oakland 9, 1972.
      Minnesota 13, Toronto 7, 1991.
6-game series
  N.L.—20—Houston 11, New York 9, 1986.
  A.L.—24—Toronto 13, Chicago 11, 1993.
7-game series
  N.L.—27—San Francisco 17, St. Louis 10, 1987.
  A.L.—37—Boston 19, California 18, 1986.

Most long hits, game

A.L.—8—Baltimore vs. Minnesota, October 6, 1969 (six doubles, one triple, one home run).
N.L.—8
  Cincinnati vs. Philadelphia, October 9, 1976 (five doubles, two triples, one home run).
  Chicago vs. San Diego, October 2, 1984 (three doubles, five home runs).

Most long hits by both clubs, game

A.L.—12—Oakland 6 (five doubles, one home run), Boston 6 (four doubles, two home runs), October 5, 1975.
N.L.—12—Philadelphia 7 (three doubles, three triples, one home run), Atlanta 5 (five doubles), October 9, 1993.

EXTRA BASES ON LONG HITS

Most extra bases on long hits, total series

N.L.—168—Pittsburgh (nine series, 42 games; 62 on doubles, 16 on triples, 90 on home runs).
A.L.—166—Oakland (10 series, 42 games; 61 on doubles, 12 on triples, 93 on home runs).

Most extra bases on long hits, series

3-game series
  N.L.—28—New York vs. Atlanta, 1969.
  A.L.—25—Baltimore vs. Minnesota, 1970.
4-game series
  N.L.—38—Los Angeles vs. Philadelphia, 1978.
  A.L.—29—Oakland vs. Boston, 1988.
5-game series
  A.L.—39—Minnesota vs. Detroit, 1987.
  N.L.—38—Chicago vs. San Diego, 1984.
6-game series
  A.L.—40—Toronto vs. Oakland, 1992.
  N.L.—40—Philadelphia vs. Atlanta, 1993.
7-game series
  N.L.—41—Pittsburgh vs. Atlanta, 1992.
  A.L.—33—Boston vs. California, 1986.

Most extra bases on long hits by both clubs, series

3-game series
  N.L.—52—New York 28, Atlanta 24, 1969.
  A.L.—40—Baltimore 25, Minnesota 15, 1970.
      Baltimore 21, Oakland 19, 1971.
4-game series
  N.L.—60—Los Angeles 38, Philadelphia 22, 1978.
  A.L.—44—Kansas City 24, New York 20, 1978.
5-game series
  A.L.—64—Minnesota 39, Detroit 25, 1987.
  N.L.—58—San Francisco 34, Chicago 24, 1989.
6-game series
  N.L.—69—Philadelphia 40, Atlanta 29, 1993.
  A.L.—59—Toronto 40, Oakland 19, 1992.
7-game series
  N.L.—74—Pittsburgh 41, Atlanta 33, 1992.
  A.L.—65—Boston 33, California 32, 1986.

Fewest extra bases on long hits, series

3-game series
N.L.—1—Atlanta vs. St. Louis, 1982.
A.L.—3—Kansas City vs. Detroit, 1984.
4-game series
A.L.—4—Chicago vs. Baltimore, 1983.
Oakland vs. Boston, 1990.
N.L.—9—Philadelphia vs. Los Angeles, 1977.
5-game series
A.L.—9—Toronto vs. Minnesota, 1991.
N.L.—10—Montreal vs. Los Angeles, 1981.
6-game series
N.L.—17—New York vs. Houston, 1986.
A.L.—19—Oakland vs. Toronto, 1992.
7-game series
N.L.—18—St. Louis vs. San Francisco, 1987.
Los Angeles vs. New York, 1988.
A.L.—25—Toronto vs. Kansas City, 1985.

Fewest extra bases on long hits by both clubs, series

3-game series
N.L.—12—St. Louis 11, Atlanta 1, 1982.
A.L.—17—New York 11, Oakland 6, 1981.
4-game series
A.L.—12—Boston 8, Oakland 4, 1990.
N.L.—26—Los Angeles 17, Philadelphia 9, 1977.
5-game series
N.L.—27—Los Angeles 17, Montreal 10, 1981.
A.L.—29—Minnesota 20, Toronto 9, 1991.
6-game series
N.L.—38—Houston 21, New York 17, 1986.
A.L.—42—Chicago 22, Toronto 20, 1993.
7-game series
N.L.—46—Atlanta 27, Pittsburgh 19, 1991.
A.L.—57—Kansas City 32, Toronto 25, 1985.

RUNS BATTED IN

Most runs batted in, total series

A.L.—138—Oakland (10 series, 42 games).
N.L.—137—Pittsburgh (nine series, 42 games).

Most runs batted in, series

3-game series
A.L.—24—Baltimore vs. Minnesota, 1970.
N.L.—24—New York vs. Atlanta, 1969.
4-game series
A.L.—25—Baltimore vs. California, 1979.
N.L.—23—Pittsburgh vs. San Francisco, 1971.
5-game series
A.L.—33—Minnesota vs. Detroit, 1987.
N.L.—29—San Francisco vs. Chicago, 1989.
6-game series
N.L.—32—Atlanta vs. Philadelphia, 1993.
A.L.—30—Toronto vs. Oakland, 1992.
7-game series
A.L.—35—Boston vs. California, 1986.
N.L.—32—Atlanta vs. Pittsburgh, 1992.
Pittsburgh vs. Atlanta, 1992.

Most runs batted in by both clubs, series

3-game series
N.L.—39—New York 24, Atlanta 15, 1969.
A.L.—34—Baltimore 24, Minnesota 10, 1970.
4-game series
A.L.—39—Baltimore 25, California 14, 1979.
N.L.—37—Pittsburgh 23, San Francisco 14, 1971.
Los Angeles 21, Philadelphia 16, 1978.
5-game series
A.L.—54—Minnesota 33, Detroit 21, 1987.
N.L.—50—San Francisco 29, Chicago 21, 1989.
6-game series
N.L.—54—Atlanta 32, Philadelphia 22, 1993.
A.L.—53—Toronto 30, Oakland 23, 1992.
7-game series
A.L.—64—Boston 35, California 29, 1986.
N.L.—64—Atlanta 32, Pittsburgh 32, 1992.

Fewest runs batted in, series

3-game series
N.L.—3—Pittsburgh vs. Cincinnati, 1970.
Atlanta vs. St. Louis, 1982.
A.L.—4—Oakland vs. New York, 1981.
Kansas City vs. Detroit, 1984.
4-game series
A.L.—2—Chicago vs. Baltimore, 1983.
N.L.—7—Los Angeles vs. Philadelphia, 1983.
5-game series
N.L.—8—Cincinnati vs. New York, 1973.
Montreal vs. Los Angeles, 1981.
A.L.—10—Oakland vs. Detroit, 1972.
Detroit vs. Oakland, 1972.
6-game series
N.L.—17—Houston vs. New York, 1986.
A.L.—22—Chicago vs. Toronto, 1993.
7-game series
N.L.—11—Pittsburgh vs. Atlanta, 1991.
A.L.—23—Toronto vs. Kansas City, 1985.

Fewest runs batted in by both clubs, series

3-game series
N.L.—11—Cincinnati 8, Pittsburgh 3, 1970.
A.L.—18—Detroit 14, Kansas City 4, 1984.
4-game series
A.L.—18—Oakland 11, Baltimore 7, 1974.
N.L.—22—Philadelphia 15, Los Angeles 7, 1983.
5-game series
A.L.—20—Oakland 10, Detroit 10, 1972.
N.L.—23—Los Angeles 15, Montreal 8, 1981.
6-game series
N.L.—36—New York 19, Houston 17, 1986.
A.L.—46—Toronto 24, Chicago 22, 1993.
7-game series
N.L.—30—Atlanta 19, Pittsburgh 11, 1991.
A.L.—49—Kansas City 26, Toronto 23, 1985.

Most runs batted in by pinch-hitters, series

A.L.—4
Baltimore vs. California, 1979 (4-game series).
Toronto vs. Kansas City, 1985 (7-game series).
Detroit vs. Minnesota, 1987 (5-game series).
N.L.—4—Philadelphia vs. Houston, 1980 (5-game series).

Most runs batted in by pinch-hitters on both clubs, series

A.L.—6—Detroit 4, Minnesota 2, 1987 (5-game series).
N.L.—5—Philadelphia 4, Houston 1, 1980 (5-game series).

Most runs batted in, game

N.L.—14—Atlanta vs. Philadelphia, October 7, 1993.
A.L.—13—New York vs. Oakland, October 14, 1981.

Most runs batted in by both clubs, game

N.L.—17
New York 11, Atlanta 6, October 5, 1969.
Atlanta 13, Pittsburgh 4, October 7, 1992.
Atlanta 14, Philadelphia 3, October 7, 1993.
A.L.—16
Baltimore 8, California 8, October 4, 1979.
New York 13, Oakland 3, October 14, 1981.
Oakland 10, Boston 6, October 8, 1988.

Fewest runs batted in by both clubs, game

A.L.-N.L.—1—Held by many clubs.

Most runs batted in, inning

N.L.—8—St. Louis vs. Los Angeles, October 13, 1985, second inning.
A.L.—7
Baltimore vs. Minnesota, October 3, 1970, fourth inning.
New York vs. Oakland, October 14, 1981, fourth inning.

Most runs batted in by both clubs, inning

A.L.—9—New York 7, Oakland 2, October 14, 1981, fourth inning.
N.L.—8—St. Louis 8, Los Angeles 0, October 13, 1985, second inning.

Most runs batted in by pinch-hitters, inning

A.L.—3—Baltimore vs. California, October 3, 1979, 10th inning.

N.L.—2
  New York vs. Atlanta, October 4, 1969, eighth inning.
  Los Angeles vs. Pittsburgh, October 6, 1974, eighth inning.

BASES ON BALLS

Most bases on balls, total series
A.L.— 144—Oakland (10 series, 42 games).
N.L.— 120—Los Angeles (seven series, 34 games).

Most bases on balls, series
3-game series
  N.L.— 15—Cincinnati vs. Philadelphia, 1976.
  A.L.— 13—Baltimore vs. Minnesota, 1969.
      Baltimore vs. Oakland, 1971.
4-game series
  N.L.—30—Los Angeles vs. Pittsburgh, 1974.
  A.L.—22—Oakland vs. Baltimore, 1974.
5-game series
  N.L.—31—Houston vs. Philadelphia, 1980.
  A.L.—20—Minnesota vs. Detroit, 1987.
      Oakland vs. Toronto, 1989.
6-game series
  A.L.—32—Chicago vs. Toronto, 1993.
  N.L.—30—St. Louis vs. Los Angeles, 1985.
7-game series
  N.L.—29—Atlanta vs. Pittsburgh, 1992.
      Pittsburgh vs. Atlanta, 1992.
  A.L.—22—Kansas City vs. Toronto, 1985.

Most bases on balls by both clubs, series
3-game series
  N.L.—27—Cincinnati 15, Philadelphia 12, 1976.
  A.L.—25—Baltimore 13, Minnesota 12, 1969.
4-game series
  N.L.—38—Los Angeles 30, Pittsburgh 8, 1974.
  A.L.—28—Baltimore 16, Chicago 12, 1983.
      Boston 18, Oakland 10, 1988.
5-game series
  N.L.—44—Houston 31, Philadelphia 13, 1980.
  A.L.—38—Minnesota 20, Detroit 18, 1987.
6-game series
  A.L.—53—Chicago 32, Toronto 21, 1993.
  N.L.—49—St. Louis 30, Los Angeles 19, 1985.
7-game series
  N.L.—58—Atlanta 29, Pittsburgh 29, 1992.
  A.L.—39—California 20, Boston 19, 1986.

Fewest bases on balls, series
3-game series
  A.L.—3—Boston vs. Oakland, 1975.
  N.L.—6—Atlanta vs. St. Louis, 1982.
4-game series
  A.L.—5—Baltimore vs. Oakland, 1974.
  N.L.—5—Pittsburgh vs. San Francisco, 1971.
5-game series
  A.L.—9—New York vs. Kansas City, 1977.
  N.L.—9—Pittsburgh vs. Cincinnati, 1972.
6-game series
  N.L.— 10—Cincinnati vs. Pittsburgh, 1990.
  A.L.—21—Toronto vs. Chicago, 1993.
7-game series
  A.L.— 16—Toronto vs. Kansas City, 1985.
  N.L.— 16—St. Louis vs. San Francisco, 1987.

Fewest bases on balls by both clubs, series
3-game series
  A.L.— 12—Oakland 9, Boston 3, 1975.
  N.L.— 18—St. Louis 12, Atlanta 6, 1982.
4-game series
  N.L.— 18—Los Angeles 9, Philadelphia 9, 1978.
  A.L.—21—Kansas City 14, New York 7, 1978.
5-game series
  N.L.— 19—Cincinnati 10, Pittsburgh 9, 1972.
  A.L.—24—Kansas City 15, New York 9, 1977.

6-game series
  N.L.—31—Houston 17, New York 14, 1986.
  A.L.—47—Oakland 24, Toronto 23, 1992.
7-game series
  N.L.—33—San Francisco 17, St. Louis 16, 1987.
  A.L.—38—Kansas City 22, Toronto 16, 1985.

Most bases on balls by pinch-hitters, series
N.L.—4—Los Angeles vs. New York, 1988 (7-game series).
A.L.—2
  Oakland vs. Boston, 1975 (3-game series).
  California vs. Baltimore, 1979 (4-game series).
  Baltimore vs. Chicago, 1983 (4-game series).
  Kansas City vs. Toronto, 1985 (7-game series).
  Toronto vs. Minnesota, 1991 (5-game series).
  Oakland vs. Toronto, 1992 (6-game series).

Most bases on balls by pinch-hitters on both clubs, series
N.L.—6—Los Angeles 4, New York 2, 1988 (7-game series).
A.L.—3
  California 2, Baltimore 1, 1979 (4-game series).
  Toronto 2, Minnesota 1, 1991 (5-game series).

Most bases on balls, game
A.L.— 11—Oakland vs. Baltimore, October 9, 1974.
N.L.— 11—Los Angeles vs. Pittsburgh, October 9, 1974.

Most bases on balls by both clubs, game
A.L.— 14—Oakland 11, Baltimore 3, October 9, 1974.
N.L.— 13—Atlanta 8, Pittsburgh 5, October 7, 1992.

Fewest bases on balls, game
A.L.-N.L.—0—Held by many clubs.

Fewest bases on balls by both clubs, game
A.L.— 1
  Oakland 1, Baltimore 0, October 8, 1974.
  New York 1, Kansas City 0, October 9, 1976.
N.L.—2
  Cincinnati 2, Pittsburgh 0. October 10, 1072.
  Los Angeles 1, Montreal 1, October 16, 1981.
  Chicago 2, San Diego 0, October 4, 1984.
  Houston 2, New York 0, October 12, 1986.

Most bases on balls by pinch-hitters, game
N.L.—2
  Pittsburgh vs. Cincinnati, October 7, 1975, 10 innings.
  Los Angeles vs. New York, October 8, 1988.
  Los Angeles vs. New York, October 9, 1988, 12 innings.
A.L.—2
  California vs. Baltimore, October 4, 1979.
  Baltimore vs. Chicago, October 7, 1983.

Most bases on balls by pinch-hitters on both clubs, game
N.L.—3
  Pittsburgh 2, Cincinnati 1, October 7, 1975, 10 innings.
  Los Angeles 2, New York 1, October 8, 1988.
A.L.—2
  Detroit 1, Oakland 1, October 11, 1972, 10 innings.
  California 2, Baltimore 0, October 4, 1979.
  Baltimore 2, Chicago 0, October 7, 1983.

Most bases on balls, inning
A.L.—4—Oakland vs. Baltimore, October 9, 1974, fifth inning
      (consecutive).
N.L.—4
  Philadelphia vs. Los Angeles, October 7, 1977, second in-
      ning (consecutive).
  St. Louis vs. Los Angeles, October 12, 1985, first inning.
  San Francisco vs. Chicago, October 9, 1989, eighth inning.

Most bases on balls by both clubs, inning
N.L.—6—St. Louis 4, Los Angeles 2, October 12, 1985, first
      inning.
A.L.—4—Made in many innings.

Most bases on balls by pinch-hitters, inning
N.L.—2
  Pittsburgh vs. Cincinnati, October 7, 1975, ninth inning.
  Los Angeles vs. New York, October 8, 1988, eighth inning.
A.L.—2—Baltimore vs. Chicago, October 7, 1983, ninth inning.

Most strikeouts, total series
N.L.—275—Pittsburgh (nine series, 42 games).
A.L.—264—Oakland (10 series, 42 games).

Most strikeouts, series
3-game series
  N.L.—28—Cincinnati vs. Pittsburgh, 1975.
  A.L.—27—Minnesota vs. Baltimore, 1969.
4-game series
  A.L.—35—Oakland vs. Boston, 1988.
  N.L.—33—Pittsburgh vs. San Francisco, 1971.
5-game series
  N.L.—42—Cincinnati vs. New York, 1973.
  A.L.—39—Oakland vs. Baltimore, 1973.
6-game series
  N.L.—57—New York vs. Houston, 1986.
  A.L.—43—Chicago vs. Toronto, 1993.
7-game series
  N.L.—57—Pittsburgh vs. Atlanta, 1991.
  A.L.—51—Kansas City vs. Toronto, 1985.

Most strikeouts by both clubs, series
3-game series
  N.L.—46—Cincinnati 28, Pittsburgh 18, 1975.
  A.L.—41—Minnesota 27, Baltimore 14, 1969.
       Minnesota 22, Baltimore 19, 1970.
4-game series
  N.L.—61—Pittsburgh 33, San Francisco 28, 1971.
  A.L.—58—Oakland 35, Boston 23, 1988.
5-game series
  N.L.—70—Cincinnati 42, New York 28, 1973.
  A.L.—67—Minnesota 37, Toronto 30, 1991.
6-game series
  N.L.— 105—Atlanta 54, Philadelphia 51, 1993.
  A.L.—79—Chicago 43, Toronto 36, 1993.
7-game series
  N.L.—99—Pittsburgh 57, Atlanta 42, 1991.
  A.L.—88—Kansas City 51, Toronto 37, 1985.

Fewest strikeouts, series
3-game series
  N.L.—9—Philadelphia vs. Cincinnati, 1976.
  A.L.— 10—New York vs. Oakland, 1981.
4-game series
  A.L.—13—California vs. Baltimore, 1979.
  N.L.— 16—Los Angeles vs. Pittsburgh, 1974.
5-game series
  A.L.— 15—New York vs. Kansas City, 1976.
  N.L.— 19—Houston vs. Philadelphia, 1980.
6-game series
  A.L.—29—Toronto vs. Oakland, 1992.
  N.L.—31—Los Angeles vs. St. Louis, 1985.
7-game series
  N.L.—28—Atlanta vs. Pittsburgh, 1992.
  A.L.—31—Boston vs. California, 1986.

Fewest strikeouts by both clubs, series
3-game series
  N.L.—25—Cincinnati 16, Philadelphia 9, 1976.
  A.L.—26—Oakland 14, Boston 12, 1975.
4-game series
  N.L.—33—Pittsburgh 17, Los Angeles 16, 1974.
  A.L.—36—Baltimore 20, Oakland 16, 1974.
5-game series
  A.L.—33—Kansas City 18, New York 15, 1976.
  N.L.—48—Montreal 25, Los Angeles 23, 1981.
6-game series
  A.L.—62—Oakland 33, Toronto 29, 1992.
  N.L.—65—St. Louis 34, Los Angeles 31, 1985.
7-game series
  N.L.—70—Pittsburgh 42, Atlanta 28, 1992.
  A.L.—75—California 44, Boston 31, 1986.

Most strikeouts by pinch-hitters, series
N.L.—7—Cincinnati vs. New York, 1973 (5-game series).

A.L.—4
  Minnesota vs. Baltimore, 1970 (3-game series).
  Oakland vs. Detroit, 1972 (5-game series).

Most strikeouts by pinch-hitters on both clubs, series
N.L.—9—Pittsburgh 6, Atlanta 3, 1992 (7-game series).
A.L.—4
  Minnesota 4, Baltimore 0, 1970 (3-game series).
  Oakland 4, Detroit 0, 1972 (5-game series).

Most strikeouts, nine-inning game
N.L.— 15—Philadelphia vs. Atlanta, October 10, 1993.
A.L.— 14
  Oakland vs. Detroit, October 10, 1972.
  Chicago vs. Baltimore, October 6, 1983.

Most strikeouts, extra-inning game
N.L.— 15
  Cincinnati vs. Pittsburgh, October 7, 1975, 10 innings.
  New York vs. Houston, October 14, 1986, 12 innings.
A.L.—Less than nine-inning record.

Most strikeouts by pinch-hitters, game
A.L.—4—Oakland vs. Detroit, October 10, 1972.
N.L.—4—Pittsburgh vs. Atlanta, October 10, 1992.

Most strikeouts by both clubs, nine-inning game
N.L.— 21
  Pittsburgh 12, Cincinnati 9, October 4, 1990.
  Philadelphia 15, Atlanta 6, October 10, 1993.
A.L.— 19
  Minnesota 12, Baltimore 7, October 5, 1970.
  Oakland 12, Baltimore 7, October 6, 1973.

Most strikeouts by both clubs, extra-inning game
N.L.—23—Cincinnati 15, Pittsburgh 8, October 7, 1975, 10
       innings.
A.L.—Less than nine-inning record.

Fewest strikeouts, game
N.L.—0—Pittsburgh vs. Los Angeles, October 6, 1974.
A.L.— 1
  Baltimore vs. Oakland, October 11, 1973.
  New York vs. Kansas City, October 13, 1976.
  Kansas City vs. New York, October 4, 1978.
  Toronto vs. Kansas City, October 12, 1985.
  Boston vs. Oakland, October 10, 1990.

Fewest strikeouts by both clubs, game
A.L.—3
  Oakland 2, Baltimore 1, October 11, 1973.
  Kansas City 2, New York 1, October 13, 1976.
N.L.—4—Philadelphia 2, Cincinnati 2, October 12, 1976.

Most consecutive strikeouts, game
A.L.—4
  Oakland vs. Detroit, October 10, 1972 (one in fourth inning,
       three in fifth inning).
  Baltimore vs. California, October 3, 1979 (three in first in-
       ning, one in second inning).
  Kansas City vs. Detroit, October 5, 1984 (two in fourth in-
       ning, two in fifth inning).
  Oakland vs. Boston, October 6, 1988 (two in second inning,
       two in third inning).
N.L.—5—Atlanta vs. Philadelphia, October 6, 1993 (three in
       first inning, two in second inning).

Most strikeouts, inning
A.L.-N.L.—3—Held by many clubs.

Most strikeouts by both clubs, inning
A.L.—5
  Oakland 3, Baltimore 2, October 6, 1973, first inning.
  Boston 3, Oakland 2, October 4, 1975, second inning.
  Baltimore 3, Chicago 2, October 6, 1983, first inning.
  Kansas City 3, Toronto 2, October 15, 1985, eighth inning.
N.L.—5
  New York 3, Atlanta 2, October 5, 1969, third inning.
  New York 3, Atlanta 2, October 6, 1969, third inning.
  Philadelphia 3, Los Angeles 2, October 4, 1977, seventh in-
       ning.

Most strikeouts by pinch-hitters, inning

A.L.—2—Oakland vs. Baltimore, October 5, 1971, ninth inning (consecutive).

N.L.—2

Cincinnati vs. New York, October 7, 1973, eighth inning (consecutive).

Pittsburgh vs. Atlanta, October 10, 1992, eighth inning.

SACRIFICE HITS

Most sacrifice hits, total series

A.L.—22—Oakland (10 series, 42 games).

N.L.—19—Pittsburgh (nine series, 42 games).

Most sacrifice hits, series

N.L.—7—Houston vs. Philadelphia, 1980 (5-game series).

A.L.—5

Boston vs. Oakland, 1975 (3-game series).

California vs. Milwaukee, 1982 (5-game series).

Chicago vs. Toronto, 1993 (6-game series).

Most sacrifice hits by both clubs, series

N.L.—12—Houston 7, Philadelphia 5, 1980 (5-game series).

A.L.—7

Oakland 4, Detroit 3, 1972 (5-game series).

California 5, Milwaukee 2, 1982 (5-game series).

California 4, Boston 3, 1986 (7-game series).

Fewest sacrifice hits, series

A.L.-N.L.—0—Held by many clubs.

Fewest sacrifice hits by both clubs, series

N.L.—0—Cincinnati 0, Pittsburgh 0, 1975 (3-game series).

A.L.—1

New York 1, Kansas City 0, 1980 (3-game series).

Kansas City 1, New York 0, 1978 (4-game series).

Baltimore 1, California 0, 1979 (4-game series).

Most sacrifice hits, game

N.L.—3

Pittsburgh vs. Cincinnati, October 3, 1979, 10 innings.

Philadelphia vs. Houston, October 8, 1980, 10 innings.

Los Angeles vs. Montreal, October 17, 1981.

St. Louis vs. Atlanta, October 9, 1982.

A.L.—3

California vs. Milwaukee, October 10, 1982.

California vs. Boston, October 12, 1986, 11 innings.

Most sacrifice hits by both clubs, game

N.L.—4

Pittsburgh 3, Cincinnati 1, October 3, 1979, 10 innings.

Los Angeles 3, Montreal 1, October 17, 1981.

St. Louis 2, Atlanta 2, October 9, 1982.

Atlanta 2, Philadelphia 2, October 13, 1993.

A.L.—3

California 3, Milwaukee 0, October 10, 1982.

Boston 2, California 1, October 11, 1986, 11 innings.

California 3, Boston 0, October 12, 1986, 11 innings.

Oakland 2, Boston 1, October 6, 1990.

Most sacrifice hits, inning

N.L.—2—Philadelphia vs. Cincinnati, October 10, 1976,

fourth inning.

A.L.—1—Held by many clubs.

SACRIFICE FLIES

Most sacrifice flies, total series

N.L.—12—Cincinnati (seven series, 28 games).

A.L.—11

Oakland (10 series, 42 games).

Toronto (five series, 29 games).

Most sacrifice flies, series

A.L.—4

Kansas City vs. New York, 1976 (5-game series).

Toronto vs. Oakland, 1992 (6-game series).

N.L.—4

San Diego vs. Chicago, 1984 (5-game series).

St. Louis vs. San Francisco, 1987 (7-game series).

Most sacrifice flies by both clubs, series

N.L.—6—San Diego 4, Chicago 2, 1984 (5-game series).

A.L.—6—Toronto 4, Oakland 2, 1992 (6-game series).

Most sacrifice flies, game

N.L.—3—St. Louis vs. Atlanta, October 7, 1982.

A.L.—2—Held by many clubs.

Most sacrifice flies by both clubs, game

N.L.—3

St. Louis 3, Atlanta 0, October 7, 1982.

St. Louis 2, San Francisco 1, October 11, 1987.

A.L.—2—Occurred many times.

Most sacrifice flies, inning

A.L.—2

Baltimore vs. Chicago, October 7, 1983, ninth inning.

Detroit vs. Minnesota, October 7, 1987, eighth inning.

N.L.—2—

San Diego vs. Chicago, October 7, 1984, sixth inning.

HIT BY PITCH

Most hit by pitch, total series

A.L.—12—Oakland (10 series, 42 games).

N.L.—10—Pittsburgh (nine series, 42 games).

Most hit by pitch, series

A.L.—5—Minnesota vs. Detroit, 1987 (5-game series).

N.L.—4—New York vs. Los Angeles, 1988 (7-game series).

Most hit by pitch by both clubs, series

A.L.—8—Minnesota 5, Detroit 3, 1987 (5-game series).

N.L.—6—New York 4, Los Angeles 2, 1988 (7-game series).

Most hit by pitch, game

A.L.—3—Minnesota vs. Detroit, October 11, 1987.

N.L.—2—New York vs. Los Angeles, October 12, 1988.

Most hit by pitch by both clubs, game

A.L.—4—Detroit 2, Minnesota 2, October 12, 1987.

N.L.—2—Occurred in many games.

Most hit by pitch, inning

A.L.-N.L.—1—Held by many clubs.

INDIVIDUAL BASERUNNING

STOLEN BASES

Most stolen bases, career
A.L.—16—Rickey Henderson, Oakland, 1981, 1989, 1990, 1992, 1993; five series, 24 games.
N.L.—9—Dave Lopes, Los Angeles, 1974, 1977, 1978, 1981; Chicago, 1984; Houston, 1986; six series, 22 games.

Most stolen bases, series
3-game series
N.L.—4—Joe Morgan, Cincinnati, 1975.
A.L.—2—Juan Beniquez, Boston, 1975.
Amos Otis, Kansas City, 1980.
Rickey Henderson, Oakland, 1981.
4-game series
A.L.—4—Amos Otis, Kansas City, 1978.
N.L.—3—Dave Lopes, Los Angeles, 1974.
5-game series
A.L.—8—Rickey Henderson, Oakland, 1989.
N.L.—5—Dave Lopes, Los Angeles, 1981.
6-game series
A.L.—7—Willie Wilson, Oakland, 1992.
N.L.—3—Billy Hatcher, Houston, 1986.
Barry Larkin, Cincinnati, 1990.
7-game series
N.L.—7—Ron Gant, Atlanta, 1991.
A.L.—1—Held by many players.

Most stolen bases, game
A.L.—4—Rickey Henderson, Oakland, October 4, 1989.
N.L.—3
Joe Morgan, Cincinnati, October 4, 1975.
Ken Griffey Sr., Cincinnati, October 5, 1975.
Steve Sax, Los Angeles, October 9, 1988, 12 innings.
Ron Gant, Atlanta, October 10, 1991.

Most stolen bases by pinch-runner, game
A.L.-N.L.—1—Held by many players.

Most times stealing home, game
A.L.—1—Reggie Jackson, Oakland, October 12, 1972, second inning (front end of double steal).
N.L.—Never accomplished.

Most stolen bases, inning
A.L.-N.L.—2—Held by many players.

CAUGHT STEALING

Most caught stealing, career
A.L.—6—Hal McRae, Kansas City, 1976, 1977, 1978, 1980, 1984, 1985; six series, 28 games.
N.L.—4
Willie McGee, St. Louis, 1982, 1985, 1987; three series, 16 games.
Vince Coleman, St. Louis, 1985, 1987; two series, 10 games.

Most caught stealing by pinch-runner, career
A.L.—2—Herb Washington, Oakland, 1974; one series, two games.
N.L.—Never accomplished.

Most caught stealing, series
A.L.—4—Devon White, Toronto, 1992 (no stolen bases; 6-game series).
N.L.—3
Willie McGee, St. Louis, 1985 (two stolen bases; 6-game series).
Kevin Bass, Houston, 1986 (two stolen bases; 6-game series).

Most caught stealing by pinch-runner, series
A.L.—2—Herb Washington, Oakland, 1974; two games.
N.L.—Never accomplished.

Most caught stealing, nine-inning game
A.L.-N.L.—1—Held by many players.

Most caught stealing, extra-inning game
A.L.—2—Brooks Robinson, Baltimore, October 4, 1969, 12 innings.
N.L.—2—Kevin Bass, Houston, October 15, 1986, 16 innings.

Most caught stealing by pinch-runner, game
A.L.—1
Herb Washington, Oakland, October 6, 8, 1974.
Sandy Alomar Sr., New York, October 14, 1976.
Onix Concepcion, Kansas City, October 9, 1985.
N.L.—Never accomplished.

Most caught stealing, inning
A.L.-N.L.—1—Held by many players.

CLUB BASERUNNING

STOLEN BASES

Most stolen bases, total series
A.L.—54—Oakland (10 series, 42 games).
N.L.—31
  Los Angeles (seven series, 34 games).
  Cincinnati (seven series, 28 games).

Most stolen bases, series
3-game series
  N.L.—11—Cincinnati vs. Pittsburgh, 1975.
  A.L.—4—Detroit vs. Kansas City, 1984.
4-game series
  A.L.—9—Oakland vs. Boston, 1990.
  N.L.—5—Los Angeles vs. Pittsburgh, 1974.
5-game series
  A.L.—13—Oakland vs. Toronto, 1989.
  N.L.—7—Philadelphia vs. Houston, 1980.
6-game series
  A.L.—16—Oakland vs. Toronto, 1992.
  N.L.—8—Houston vs. New York, 1986.
7-game series
  N.L.—10—Atlanta vs. Pittsburgh, 1991.
  A.L.—2—Kansas City vs. Toronto, 1985.
    Toronto vs. Kansas City, 1985.

Most stolen bases by both clubs, series
3-game series
  N.L.—11—Cincinnati 11, Pittsburgh 0, 1975.
  A.L.—4—New York 2, Oakland 2, 1981.
    Detroit 4, Kansas City 0, 1984.
4-game series
  A.L.—10—Oakland 9, Boston 1, 1990.
  N.L.—6—Los Angeles 5, Pittsburgh 1, 1974.
5-game series
  A.L.—24—Oakland 13, Toronto 11, 1989.
  N.L.—11—Philadelphia 7, Houston 4, 1980.
6-game series
  A.L.—23—Oakland 16, Toronto 7, 1992.
  N.L.—12—Houston 8, New York 4, 1986.
    Cincinnati 6, Pittsburgh 6, 1990.
7-game series
  N.L.—16—Atlanta 10, Pittsburgh 6, 1991.
  A.L.—4—Toronto 2, Kansas City 2, 1985.

Fewest stolen bases, series
A.L.-N.L.—0—Held by many clubs.

Fewest stolen bases by both clubs, series
3-game series
  A.L.—0—Baltimore 0, Oakland 0, 1971.
  N.L.—1—Cincinnati 1, Pittsburgh 0, 1970.
4-game series
  N.L.—2—Los Angeles 2, Philadelphia 0, 1978.
  A.L.—1—Oakland 1, Boston 0, 1988.
5-game series
  N.L.—0—Cincinnati 0, New York 0, 1973.
  A.L.—3—Milwaukee 2, California 1, 1982.
6-game series
  N.L.—2—Philadelphia 2, Atlanta 0, 1993.
  A.L.—10—Toronto 7, Chicago 3, 1993.
7-game series
  A.L.—2—Boston 1, California 1, 1986.
  N.L.—9—San Francisco 5, St. Louis 4, 1987.

Most stolen bases, game
N.L.—7—Cincinnati vs. Pittsburgh, October 5, 1975.
A.L.—6
  Oakland vs. Toronto, October 4, 1989.
  Oakland vs. Toronto, October 8, 1992.

Most stolen bases by both clubs, game
A.L.—8
  Oakland 6, Toronto 2, October 4, 1989.
  Oakland 6, Toronto 2, October 8, 1992.
N.L.—7—Cincinnati 7, Pittsburgh 0, October 5, 1975.

Longest game with no stolen bases
N.L.—16 innings—New York vs. Houston, October 15, 1986.
A.L.—12 innings—Baltimore vs. Minnesota, October 4, 1969.

Longest game with no stolen bases by either club
N.L.—12 innings—New York 0, Cincinnati 0, October 9, 1973.
A.L.—11 innings
  Detroit 0, Oakland 0, October 7, 1972.
  Baltimore 0, Oakland 0, October 9, 1973.
  Boston 0, California 0, October 11, 1986.
  Boston 0, California 0, October 12, 1986.

Most stolen bases, inning
A.L.—3
  Oakland vs. Detroit, October 12, 1972, second inning.
  Oakland vs. Toronto, October 8, 1992, fifth inning.
N.L.—2—Held by many clubs.

CAUGHT STEALING

Most caught stealing, series
3-game series
  A.L.—5—Kansas City vs. New York, 1980.
  N.L.—2—Pittsburgh vs. Cincinnati, 1970.
    Cincinnati vs. Pittsburgh, 1979.
    Atlanta vs. St. Louis, 1982.
4-game series
  A.L.—3—Oakland vs. Baltimore, 1974.
    Baltimore vs. Oakland, 1974.
    Kansas City vs. New York, 1978.
    Oakland vs. Boston, 1988, 1990.
  N.L.—2—Los Angeles vs. Philadelphia, 1983.
5-game series
  A.L.—5—Kansas City vs. New York, 1976.
  N.L.—3—Philadelphia vs. Houston, 1980.
    Chicago vs. San Diego, 1984.
6-game series
  N.L.—6—St. Louis vs. Los Angeles, 1985.
  A.L.—5—Toronto vs. Oakland, 1992.
7-game series
  A.L.—4—Kansas City vs. Toronto, 1985.
    California vs. Boston, 1986.
  N.L.—4—San Francisco vs. St. Louis, 1987.
    St. Louis vs. San Francisco, 1987.
    Atlanta vs. Pittsburgh, 1991.

Most caught stealing by both clubs, series
3-game series
  A.L.—5—Kansas City 5, New York 0, 1980.
  N.L.—3—Pittsburgh 2, Cincinnati 1, 1970.
4-game series
  A.L.—6—Oakland 3, Baltimore 3, 1974.
  N.L.—3—Los Angeles 2, Philadelphia 1, 1983.
5-game series
  A.L.—8—Kansas City 5, New York 3, 1976.
  N.L.—5—Chicago 3, San Diego 2, 1984.
6-game series
  N.L.—7—St. Louis 6, Los Angeles 1, 1985.
  A.L.—7—Toronto 5, Oakland 2, 1992.
7-game series
  N.L.—8—San Francisco 4, St. Louis 4, 1987.
  A.L.—6—Kansas City 4, Toronto 2, 1985.

Fewest caught stealing, series
A.L.-N.L.—0—By many clubs.

Fewest caught stealing by both clubs, series
3-game series
  N.L.—0—Cincinnati 0, Pittsburgh 0, 1975.
  A.L.—0—Baltimore 0, Minnesota 0, 1970.
    Boston 0, Oakland 0, 1975.
4-game series
  N.L.—0—Los Angeles 0, Pittsburgh 0, 1974.
  A.L.—1—Chicago 1, Baltimore 0, 1983.

5-game series
N.L.—0—Chicago 0, San Francisco 0, 1989.
A.L.—1—Minnesota 1, Detroit 0, 1987.
6-game series
N.L.—3—Houston 3, New York 0, 1986.
    Atlanta 3, Philadelphia 0, 1993.
A.L.—4—Toronto 2, Chicago 2, 1993.
7-game series
A.L.—4—California 4, Boston 0, 1986.
N.L.—3—New York 2, Los Angeles 1, 1988.

Most caught stealing, game

A.L.-N.L.—2—Held by many clubs.

Most caught stealing by both clubs, game

A.L.—3
    Baltimore 2, Oakland 1, October 10, 1973.
    Kansas City 2, New York 1, October 12, 1976.
    Milwaukee 2, California 1, October 9, 1982.
N.L.—3
    Chicago 2, San Diego 1, October 7, 1984.
    St. Louis 2, Los Angeles 1, October 12, 1985.

Most caught stealing, inning

N.L.—2
    St. Louis vs. Los Angeles, October 10, 1985, first inning.
    St. Louis vs. Los Angeles, October 12, 1985, second inning.
A.L.—1—Held by many clubs.

LEFT ON BASE

Most left on base, total series

A.L.—294—Oakland (10 series, 42 games).
N.L.—293—Pittsburgh (nine series, 42 games).

Most left on base, series

3-game series
N.L.—31—St. Louis vs. Atlanta, 1982.
A.L.—30—New York vs. Oakland, 1981.
4-game series
N.L.—44—Los Angeles vs. Pittsburgh, 1974.
A.L.—35—Chicago vs. Baltimore, 1983.
    Oakland vs. Boston, 1990.
5-game series
N.L.—45—Houston vs. Philadelphia, 1980.
A.L.—41—New York vs. Kansas City, 1976.
6-game series
A.L.—56—Toronto vs. Chicago, 1993.
N.L.—52—Philadelphia vs. Atlanta, 1993.
7-game series
A.L.—60—California vs. Boston, 1986.
N.L.—54—New York vs. Los Angeles, 1988.
    Pittsburgh vs. Atlanta, 1991.

Most left on base by both clubs, series

3-game series
A.L.—50—Baltimore 28, Minnesota 22, 1969.
    New York 30, Oakland 20, 1981.
N.L.—49—Cincinnati 25, Pittsburgh 24, 1979.
4-game series
N.L.—68—Los Angeles 44, Pittsburgh 24, 1974.
A.L.—59—Chicago 35, Baltimore 24, 1983.
5-game series
N.L.—88—Houston 45, Philadelphia 43, 1980.
A.L.—74—Detroit 37, Minnesota 37, 1987.
6-game series
A.L.—106—Toronto 56, Chicago 50, 1993.
N.L.—99—Philadelphia 52, Atlanta 47, 1993.
7-game series
A.L.—108—California 60, Boston 48, 1986.
N.L.—105—Pittsburgh 54, Atlanta 51, 1991.

Fewest left on base, series

3-game series
N.L.—12—Atlanta vs. St. Louis, 1982.
A.L.—14—Boston vs. Oakland, 1975.
4-game series
A.L.—16—Baltimore vs. Oakland, 1974.
N.L.—22—Los Angeles vs. Philadelphia, 1977.
5-game series
A.L.—22—Kansas City vs. New York, 1976.

N.L.—24—Pittsburgh vs. Cincinnati, 1972.
6-game series
N.L.—33—Cincinnati vs. Pittsburgh, 1990.
A.L.—45—Toronto vs. Oakland, 1992.
7-game series
N.L.—37—St. Louis vs. San Francisco, 1987.
A.L.—44—Kansas City vs. Toronto, 1985.

Fewest left on base by both clubs, series

3-game series
A.L.—33—Oakland 19, Boston 14, 1975.
N.L.—38—Pittsburgh 21, Cincinnati 17, 1975.
4-game series
A.L.—45—Baltimore 23, California 22, 1979.
N.L.—52—Los Angeles 28, Philadelphia 24, 1978.
5-game series
N.L.—54—Cincinnati 30, Pittsburgh 24, 1972.
A.L.—62—New York 34, Kansas City 28, 1977.
6-game series
N.L.—74—Pittsburgh 41, Cincinnati 33, 1990.
A.L.—93—Oakland 48, Toronto 45, 1992.
7-game series
N.L.—80—San Francisco 43, St. Louis 37, 1987.
A.L.—94—Toronto 50, Kansas City 44, 1985.

Most left on bases, nine-inning game

N.L.—15—Philadelphia vs. Atlanta, October 10, 1993.
A.L.—13
    Baltimore vs. Oakland, October 5, 1971.
    Chicago vs. Toronto, October 5, 1993.

Most left on base, extra-inning game

A.L.—14—Toronto vs. Oakland, October 11, 1992, 11 innings.
N.L.—14—Philadelphia vs. Houston, October 8, 1980, 10 innings.

Most left on base by both clubs, nine-inning game

N.L.—26—Philadelphia 15, Atlanta 11, October 10, 1993.
A.L.—25—Chicago 13, Toronto 12, October 5, 1993.

Most left on base by both clubs, extra-inning game

A.L.—25—Toronto 14, Oakland 11, October 11, 1992, 11 innings.
N.L.—22—Philadelphia 14, Houston 8, October 8, 1980, 10 innings.

Fewest left on base, game

N.L.—1
    Pittsburgh vs. Cincinnati, October 7, 1972.
    Pittsburgh vs. Los Angeles, October 9, 1974.
    San Diego vs. Chicago, October 4, 1984.
A.L.—2
    Detroit vs. Oakland, October 8, 1972.
    Kansas City vs. New York, October 9, 1976.
    New York vs. Kansas City, October 6, 1978.

Fewest left on base by both clubs, game

A.L.—6—Oakland 4, Detroit 2, October 8, 1972.
N.L.—6
    Chicago 5, San Diego 1, October 4, 1984.
    Houston 3, New York 3, October 12, 1986.

Most left on base, nine-inning shutout defeat

A.L.—10—Oakland vs. Detroit, October 10, 1972 (lost 3-0).
N.L.—10
    Los Angeles vs. Pittsburgh, October 8, 1974 (lost 7-0).
    San Diego vs. Chicago, October 2, 1984 (lost 13-0).

Most left on base, extra-inning shutout defeat

A.L.—11—Chicago vs. Baltimore, October 8, 1983, 10 innings (lost 3-0).
N.L.—11—Philadelphia vs. Houston, October 10, 1980, 11 innings (lost 1-0).

Most left on base, two consecutive games

N.L.—25—Los Angeles vs. Pittsburgh, October 5 (13), October 6 (12), 1974.
A.L.—23
    Minnesota vs. Detroit, October 11 (11), October 12 (12), 1987.
    Chicago vs. Toronto, October 5 (13), October 6 (10), 1993.

INDIVIDUAL PITCHING

GAMES

Most games pitched, career

M.L. — 15
  Tug McGraw, New York, 1969, 1973; Philadelphia, 1976, 1977, 1978, 1980; six series.
  Dennis Eckersley, Chicago N.L., 1984; Oakland A.L., 1988, 1989, 1990, 1992; five series.
  Rick Honeycutt, Los Angeles N.L., 1983, 1985; Oakland A.L., 1988, 1989, 1990, 1992; six series.
N.L. — 15—Tug McGraw, New York, 1969, 1973; Philadelphia, 1976, 1977, 1978, 1980; six series.
A.L. — 14—Dennis Eckersley, Oakland, 1988, 1989, 1990, 1992; four series.

Most games pitched, series

3-game series
  A.L.-N.L. — 3—Held by many pitchers.
4-game series
  N.L. — 4—Dave Giusti, Pittsburgh, 1971.
  A.L. — 4—Dennis Eckersley, Oakland, 1988.
5-game series
  N.L. — 5—Tug McGraw, Philadelphia, 1980.
  A.L. — 5—Jim Acker, Toronto, 1989.
6-game series
  N.L. — 5—Ken Dayley, St. Louis, 1985.
            Kent Mercker, Atlanta, 1993.
  A.L. — 4—Held by many pitchers.
7-game series
  N.L. — 5—Mike Stanton, Atlanta, 1992.
  A.L. — 4—Held by many pitchers.

Most consecutive games pitched, series

N.L. — 5—Tug McGraw, Philadelphia, October 7, 8, 10, 11, 12, 1980.
A.L. — 5—Jim Acker, Toronto, October 3, 4, 6, 7, 8, 1989.

GAMES STARTED

Most games started, career

A.L. — 10
  Catfish Hunter, Oakland, 1971, 1972, 1973, 1974; New York, 1976, 1978; six series.
  Dave Stewart, Oakland, 1988, 1989, 1990, 1992; Toronto, 1993; five series.
N.L. — 8—Steve Carlton, Philadelphia, 1976, 1977, 1978, 1980, 1983; five series.

Most opening games started, career

M.L. — 4
  Don Gullett, Cincinnati N.L., 1972, 1975, 1976; New York A.L., 1977 (won 2, lost 2).
  Steve Carlton, Philadelphia N.L., 1976, 1977, 1980, 1983 (won 2, lost 1).
  Dave Stewart, Oakland A.L., 1988, 1989, 1990, 1992 (won 2).
N.L. — 4—Steve Carlton, Philadelphia, 1976, 1977, 1980, 1983 (won 2, lost 1).
A.L. — 4—Dave Stewart, Oakland, 1988, 1989, 1990, 1992 (won 2).

Most games started, series

A.L.-N.L. — 3—Held by many pitchers.

GAMES RELIEVED AND FINISHED

Most games by relief pitcher, career

M.L. — 15
  Rick Honeycutt, Los Angeles N.L., 1983, 1985; Oakland A.L., 1988, 1989, 1990, 1992; 10⅓ innings.
  Tug McGraw, New York, 1969, 1973; Philadelphia, 1976, 1977, 1978, 1980; 27 innings.

N.L. — 15—Tug McGraw, New York, 1969, 1973; Philadelphia, 1976, 1977, 1978, 1980; 27 innings.
A.L. — 14—Dennis Eckersley, Oakland, 1988, 1989, 1990, 1992; 18 innings.

Most games by relief pitcher, series

A.L. — 5—Jim Acker, Toronto, 1989 (5-game series).
N.L. — 5
  Tug McGraw, Philadelphia, 1980 (5-game series).
  Ken Dayley, St. Louis, 1985 (6-game series).
  Mike Stanton, Atlanta, 1992 (7-game series).
  Kent Mercker, Atlanta, 1993 (6-game series).

Most games finished, career

A.L. — 13—Dennis Eckersley, Oakland, 1988, 1989, 1990, 1992; four series, 14 games.
N.L. — 9
  Dave Giusti, Pittsburgh, 1970, 1971, 1972, 1974, 1975; five series, 13 games.
  Tug McGraw, New York, Philadelphia, 1969, 1973, 1976, 1977, 1978, 1980; six series, 15 games.

Most games finished, series

A.L.-N.L. — 4—Held by many pitchers.

COMPLETE GAMES

Most complete games pitched, career

A.L. — 5—Jim Palmer, Baltimore, 1969, 1970, 1971, 1973, 1974.
N.L. — 2
  Don Sutton, Los Angeles, 1974, 1977.
  Tommy John, Los Angeles, 1977, 1978.
  Mike Scott, Houston, 1987 (2).
  Danny Cox, St. Louis, 1987 (2).
  Orel Hershiser, Los Angeles, 1985, 1988.
  Doug Drabek, Pittsburgh, 1990, 1991.
  Tim Wakefield, Pittsburgh, 1992 (2).

Most consecutive complete games pitched, career

A.L. — 4—Jim Palmer, Baltimore, 1969 (1), 1970 (1), 1971 (1), 1973 (1; won four).
N.L. — 2
  Tommy John, Los Angeles, 1977 (1), 1978 (1; won two).
  Mike Scott, Houston, 1986 (2; won two).
  Danny Cox, St. Louis, 1987 (2; won one, lost one).
  Tim Wakefield, Pittsburgh, 1992 (2; won two).

Most complete games, series

N.L. — 2
  Mike Scott, Houston, 1986 (6-game series).
  Danny Cox, St. Louis, 1987 (7-game series).
  Tim Wakefield, Pittsburgh, 1992 (7-game series).
A.L. — 1—Held by many pitchers.

INNINGS

Most innings pitched, career

A.L. — 75⅓—Dave Stewart, Oakland, 1988, 1989, 1990, 1992; Toronto, 1993; five series, 10 games.
N.L. — 53⅔—Steve Carlton, Philadelphia, 1976, 1977, 1978, 1980, 1983; five series, eight games.

Most innings pitched, series

3-game series
  A.L. — 11—Dave McNally, Baltimore, 1969.
           Ken Holtzman, Oakland, 1975.
  N.L. — 9⅔—Dock Ellis, Pittsburgh, 1970.
4-game series
  N.L. — 17—Don Sutton, Los Angeles, 1974.
  A.L. — 16—Dave Stewart, Oakland, 1990.
5-game series
  A.L. — 19—Mickey Lolich, Detroit, 1972.
  N.L. — 17—Ray Burris, Montreal, 1981.

6-game series
N.L.— 18—Mike Scott, Houston, 1986.
A.L.— 16⅔—Dave Stewart, Oakland, 1992.
7-game series
N.L.—24⅔—Orel Hershiser, Los Angeles, 1988.
A.L.—22⅔—Roger Clemens, Boston, 1986.

Most innings pitched, game

A.L.—11
Dave McNally, Baltimore, October 5, 1969 (complete game, won 1-0).
Ken Holtzman, Oakland, October 9, 1973 (complete game, won 2-1).
N.L.— 10
Joe Niekro, Houston, October 10, 1980 (incomplete game, no decision).
Dwight Gooden, New York, October 14, 1986 (incomplete game, no decision).

GAMES WON

Most games won, career

A.L.—8—Dave Stewart, Oakland, 1988, 1989, 1990, 1992; Toronto, 1993; five series, ten games (lost none).
N.L.—4
Steve Carlton, Philadelphia, 1976, 1977, 1978, 1980, 1983; five series, eight games (lost two).
John Smoltz, Atlanta, 1991, 1992, 1993; three series, six games (lost one).

Most games won by undefeated pitcher, career

A.L.—8—Dave Stewart, Oakland, 1988, 1989, 1990, 1992; Toronto, 1993.
N.L.—3—Jesse Orosco, New York, 1986; Los Angeles, 1988.

Most opening games won, career

N.L.—2
Don Gullett, Cincinnati, 1975, 1976.
Steve Carlton, Philadelphia, 1980, 1983.
A.L.—2
Dick Hall, Baltimore, 1969, 1970.
Tommy John, New York, 1981; California, 1982.
Dave Stewart, Oakland, 1989, 1990.
Jack Morris, Detroit, 1984; Minnesota, 1991.

Most consecutive games won, career

A.L.—8—Dave Stewart, Oakland, October 9, 1988; October 3, 8, 1989; October 6, 10, 1990; October 12, 1992; Toronto, October 6, 12, 1993 (one complete).
N.L.—4
Steve Carlton, Philadlephia, October 6, 1978; October 7, 1980; October 4, 8, 1983 (one complete).
John Smoltz, Atlanta, October 6, 10, 1991; October 6, 10, 1992 (none complete).

Most consecutive complete games won, career

A.L.—4—Jim Palmer, Baltimore, October 6, 1969; October 5, 1970; October 5, 1971; October 6, 1973.
N.L.—2
Tommy John, Los Angeles, October 8, 1977; October 5, 1978.
Mike Scott, Houston, October 8, 12, 1986.
Tim Wakefield, Pittsburgh, October 9, 13, 1992.

Most games won, series

N.L.—3—Jesse Orosco, New York, 1986 (6-game series).
A.L.—2—Held by many pitchers.

Most games won by relief pitcher, series

N.L.—3—Jesse Orosco, New York, 1986 (6-game series).
A.L.—2
Sparky Lyle, New York, 1977 (5-game series).
Tom Henke, Toronto, 1985 (7-game series).
Jeff Reardon, Minnesota, 1987 (5-game series).

SAVES

Most saves, career

A.L.— 10—Dennis Eckersley, Oakland, 1988, 1989, 1990, 1992.

N.L.—5—Tug McGraw, New York, 1969, 1973; Philadelphia, 1977, 1980 (2).

Most saves, series

3-game series
A.L.—2—Dick Drago, Boston, 1975.
N.L.—2—Don Gullett, Cincinnati, 1970.
4-game series
A.L.—4—Dennis Eckersley, Oakland, 1988.
N.L.—3—Dave Giusti, Pittsburgh, 1971.
5-game series
N.L.—3—Steve Bedrosian, San Francisco, 1989.
A.L.—3—Dennis Eckersley, Oakland, 1989.
Rick Aguilera, Minnesota, 1991.
6-game series
N.L.—3—Randy Myers, Cincinnati, 1990.
A.L.—3—Tom Henke, Toronto, 1992.
7-game series
N.L.—3—Alejandro Pena, Atlanta, 1991.
A.L.—1—Held by many pitchers.

GAMES LOST

Most games lost, career

N.L.—7—Jerry Reuss, Pittsburgh, 1974, 1975; Los Angeles, 1981, 1983, 1985; five series, seven games (won none).
A.L.—4—Doyle Alexander, Baltimore, 1973; Toronto, 1985; Detroit, 1987; three series, five games (won none).

Most games lost by winless pitcher, career

N.L.—7—Jerry Reuss, Pittsburgh, 1974 (2), 1975; Los Angeles, 1981, 1983 (2), 1985.
A.L.—4—Doyle Alexander, Baltimore, 1973; Toronto, 1985; Detroit, 1987 (2).

Most consecutive games lost, career

N.L.—7—Jerry Reuss, Pittsburgh, 1974 (2), 1975; Los Angeles, 1981, 1983 (2), 1985.
A.L.—4—Doyle Alexander, Baltimore, 1973; Toronto, 1985; Detroit, 1987 (2).

Most games lost, series

N.L.—3—Doug Drabek, Pittsburgh, 1992.
A.L.—2—Held by many pitchers.

RUNS

Most runs allowed, career

A.L.—25—Catfish Hunter, Oakland, 1971, 1972, 1973, 1974; New York, 1976, 1978; six series, 10 games.
N.L.—25—Jerry Reuss, Pittsburgh, 1974, 1975; Los Angeles, 1981, 1983; five series, seven games.

Most runs allowed, series

3-game series
A.L.—9—Jim Perry, Minnesota, 1970.
N.L.—9—Phil Niekro, Atlanta, 1969.
4-game series
N.L.— 11—Gaylord Perry, San Francisco, 1971.
A.L.— 10—Dave Frost, California, 1979.
5-game series
N.L.— 12—Greg Maddux, Chicago, 1989.
A.L.— 10—Doyle Alexander, Detroit, 1987.
6-game series
N.L.— 10—Joaquin Andujar, St. Louis, 1985.
Tommy Greene, Philadelphia, 1993.
A.L.— 10—Jack McDowell, Chicago, 1993.
7-game series
A.L.— 13—Kirk McCaskill, California, 1986.
N.L.— 11—Doug Drabek, Pittsburgh, 1992.
Tom Glavine, Atlanta, 1992.

Most runs allowed, game

N.L.—9—Phil Niekro, Atlanta, October 4, 1969.
A.L.—8
Jim Perry, Minnesota, October 3, 1970.
Roger Clemens, Boston, October 7, 1986.

Most runs allowed, inning
N.L.—8—Tom Glavine, Atlanta, October 13, 1992, second inning.
A.L.—6—Jim Perry, Minnesota, October 3, 1970, fourth inning.

EARNED RUNS

Most earned runs allowed, career
A.L.—25—Catfish Hunter, Oakland, 1971, 1972, 1973, 1974; New York, 1976, 1978; six series, 10 games.
N.L.—21—Steve Carlton, Philadelphia, 1976, 1977, 1978, 1980, 1983; five series, eight games.

Most earned runs allowed, series
3-game series
　A.L.—8—Jim Perry, Minnesota, 1970.
　N.L.—6—Jerry Koosman, New York, 1969.
　　　Pat Jarvis, Atlanta, 1969.
4-game series
　N.L.—10—Gaylord Perry, San Francisco, 1971.
　A.L.—9—Dave Frost, California, 1979.
5-game series
　N.L.—11—Greg Maddux, Chicago, 1989.
　A.L.—10—Doyle Alexander, Detroit, 1987.
6-game series
　N.L.—10—Tommy Greene, Philadelphia, 1993.
　A.L.—10—Jack McDowell, Chicago, 1993.
7-game series
　A.L.—11—Roger Clemens, Boston, 1986.
　N.L.—10—Tom Glavine, Atlanta, 1992.

Most earned runs allowed, game
A.L.—7—
　Jim Perry, Minnesota, October 3, 1970.
　Roger Clemens, Boston, October 7, 1986.
　Jack McDowell, Chicago, October 5, 1993.
N.L.—7—
　Gaylord Perry, San Francisco, October 6, 1971.
　Greg A. Harris, San Diego, October 2, 1984.
　Tom Glavine, Atlanta, October 13, 1992.
　Tommy Greene, Philadelphia, October 7, 1993.

Most earned runs allowed, inning
N.L.—7—Tom Glavine, Atlanta, October 13, 1992, second inning.
A.L.—6—Jim Perry, Minnesota, October 3, 1970, fourth inning.

SHUTOUTS AND SCORELESS INNINGS

Most shutouts, series
A.L.-N.L.—1—Held by many pitchers.

Most consecutive scoreless innings, career
N.L.—22⅓—Steve Avery, Atlanta, October 10 (8⅓ innings), October 16 (eight innings), 1991; October 7 (six innings), 1992.
A.L.—18—Ken Holtzman, Oakland, 1973 (nine innings); October 6 (nine innings), 1974.

Most consecutive scoreless innings, series
N.L.—16⅓—Steve Avery, Atlanta, October 10, 16, 1991.
A.L.—11—Dave McNally, Baltimore, October 5, 1969.

HITS

Most hits allowed, career
A.L.—57—Catfish Hunter, Oakland, 1971, 1972, 1973, 1974; New York, 1976, 1978; six series, 10 games.
N.L.—53—Steve Carlton, Philadelphia, 1976, 1977, 1978, 1980, 1983; five series, eight games.

Most consecutive hitless innings, career
A.L.—10—Dave McNally, Baltimore, October 5 (7 innings), 1969; October 4 (3 innings), 1970.
N.L.—6—Jack Billingham, Cincinnati, October 6 (6 innings), 1973.

Most hits allowed, series
3-game series
　A.L.—12—Ken Holtzman, Oakland, 1975.
　N.L.—10—Pat Jarvis, Atlanta, 1969.
4-game series
　N.L.—19—Gaylord Perry, San Francisco, 1971.
　A.L.—13—Dennis Leonard, Kansas City, 1978.
5-game series
　A.L.—18—Larry Gura, Kansas City, 1976.
　N.L.—16—Nolan Ryan, Houston, 1980.
　　　Scott Garrelts, San Francisco, 1989.
6-game series
　A.L.—18—Jack McDowell, Chicago, 1993.
　N.L.—17—Orel Hershiser, Los Angeles, 1985.
7-game series
　A.L.—22—Roger Clemens, Boston, 1986.
　N.L.—18—Orel Hershiser, Los Angeles, 1988.
　　　Doug Drabek, Pittsburgh, 1992.

Most hits allowed, game
A.L.—13—Jack McDowell, Chicago, October 5, 1993.
N.L.—10—
　Pat Jarvis, Atlanta, October 6, 1969.
　Gaylord Perry, San Francisco, October 6, 1971.
　Burt Hooton, Los Angeles, October 4, 1978.
　Bob Ojeda, New York, October 9, 1986.
　John Tudor, St. Louis, October 7, 1987.

Most consecutive hitless innings, game
A.L.—7—Dave McNally, Baltimore, October 5, 1969, 11-inning game.
N.L.—6—Jack Billingham, Cincinnati, October 6, 1973.

Fewest hits allowed, nine-inning game
A.L.—2—Vida Blue, Oakland, October 8, 1974.
N.L.—2
　Ross Grimsley, Cincinnati, October 10, 1972.
　Jon Matlack, New York, October 7, 1973.
　Dave Dravecky, San Francisco, October 7, 1987.

Most hits allowed, inning
A.L.—6—
　Jim Perry, Minnesota, October 3, 1970; fourth inning.
　Kirk McCaskill, California, October 14, 1966, third inning.
N.L.—6—
　Greg A. Harris, San Diego, October 2, 1984, fifth inning.
　Tom Glavine, Atlanta, October 13, 1992, second inning.

Most consecutive hits allowed, inning (consecutive at-bats)
A.L.—6—Jim Perry, Minnesota, October 3, 1970, fourth inning (sacrifice fly during streak).
N.L.—5—Bob Moose, Pittsburgh, October 8, 1972, first inning.

Most consecutive hits allowed, inning (consecutive plate appearances)
N.L.—5—Bob Moose, Pittsburgh, October 8, 1972, first inning.
A.L.—5—
　Dave Beard, Oakland, October 14, 1981, fourth inning.
　Jack Morris, Minnesota, October 8, 1991, sixth inning.

DOUBLES, TRIPLES AND HOME RUNS

Most doubles allowed, game
N.L.—4—
　Tom Seaver, New York, October 4, 1969.
　Tom Glavine, Atlanta, October 9, 1992.
　Steve Avery, Atlanta, October 11, 1992.
A.L.—4—
　Dave McNally, Baltimore, October 3, 1971.
　Vida Blue, Oakland, October 3, 1971.

Most triples allowed, game
A.L.—2—Ed Figueroa, New York, October 8, 1977.
N.L.—2
　Steve Carlton, Philadelphia, October 9, 1976.
　Larry Christenson, Philadelphia, October 4, 1978.
　Tom Glavine, Atlanta, October 9, 1993.

Most home runs allowed, career

A.L.—12—Catfish Hunter, Oakland, 1971 (4), 1972 (2), 1974 (3); New York, 1978 (3).
N.L.—6—Steve Blass, Pittsburgh, 1971 (4), 1972 (2).

Most home runs allowed, series

3-game series
A.L.—4—Catfish Hunter, Oakland, 1971.
N.L.—3—Pat Jarvis, Atlanta, 1969.
4-game series
N.L.—4—Steve Blass, Pittsburgh, 1971.
A.L.—3—Catfish Hunter, Oakland, 1974; New York, 1978.
Mike Boddicker, Boston, 1988.
5-game series
N.L.—5—Eric Show, San Diego, 1984.
A.L.—4—Dave McNally, Baltimore, 1973.
6-game series
A.L.—3—Mike Moore, Oakland, 1992.
Jack Morris, Toronto, 1992.
Dave Stewart, Oakland, 1992.
N.L.—3—Tommy Greene, Philadelphia, 1993.
7-game series
A.L.—4—Doyle Alexander, Toronto, 1985.
N.L.—4—Tim Wakefield, Pittsburgh, 1992.

Most home runs allowed, game

A.L.—4
Catfish Hunter, Oakland, October 4, 1971.
Dave McNally, Baltimore, October 7, 1973.
N.L.—3
Pat Jarvis, Atlanta, October 6, 1969.
Eric Show, San Diego, October 2, 1984.
Danny Cox, St. Louis, October 10, 1987.

Most grand slams allowed, game

A.L.—1
Jim Perry, Minnesota, October 3, 1970, fourth inning.
Bryan Haas, Milwaukee, October 9, 1982, eighth inning.
N.L.—1
Steve Carlton, Philadelphia, October 4, 1977, seventh inning.
Jim Lonborg, Philadelphia, October 5, 1977, fourth inning.
Greg Maddux, Chicago, October 4, 1989, fourth inning.
Bob Walk, Pittsburgh, October 7, 1992, fifth inning.

Most home runs allowed, inning

A.L.-N.L.—2—Held by many pitchers.

Most consecutive home runs allowed, inning

A.L.-N.L.—2—Held by many pitchers.

TOTAL BASES

Most total bases allowed, game

N.L.—22—Pat Jarvis, Atlanta, October 6, 1969.
A.L.—20—Catfish Hunter, New York, October 6, 1978.

BASES ON BALLS

Most bases on balls, career

N.L.—28—Steve Carlton, Philadelphia, 1976, 1977, 1978, 1980, 1983; five series, eight games.
A.L.—25—Dave Stewart, Oakland, 1988, 1989, 1990, 1992; Toronto, 1993; five series, 10 games.

Most bases on balls, series

3-game series
A.L.—7—Dave Boswell, Minnesota, 1969.
N.L.—5—Fred Norman, Cincinnati, 1975.
Steve Carlton, Philadelphia, 1976.
4-game series
A.L.—13—Mike Cuellar, Baltimore, 1974.
N.L.—8—Jerry Reuss, Pittsburgh, 1974.
Steve Carlton, Philadelphia, 1977.
5-game series
A.L.—8—Jim Palmer, Baltimore, 1973.
N.L.—8—Steve Carlton, Philadelphia, 1980.
Rick Sutcliffe, Chicago, 1984.

6-game series
N.L.—10—Fernando Valenzuela, Los Angeles, 1985.
A.L.—9—Jack Morris, Toronto, 1992.
Juan Guzman, Toronto, 1993.
7-game series
A.L.—10—Dave Stieb, Toronto, 1985.
N.L.—10—John Smoltz, Atlanta, 1992.

Most bases on balls, game

A.L.—9—Mike Cuellar, Baltimore, October 9, 1974.
N.L.—8—Fernando Valenzuela, Los Angeles, October 14, 1985.

Most bases on balls, inning

A.L.—4—Mike Cuellar, Baltimore, October 9, 1974, fifth inning (consecutive).
N.L.—4
Burt Hooton, Los Angeles, October 7, 1977, second inning (consecutive).
Bob Welch, Los Angeles, October 12, 1985, first inning.

Most consecutive bases on balls, inning

A.L.—4—Mike Cuellar, Baltimore, October 9, 1974, fifth inning.
N.L.—4—Burt Hooton, Los Angeles, October 7, 1977, second inning.

STRIKEOUTS

Most strikeouts, career

M.L.—46
Nolan Ryan, New York N.L., 1969; California A.L., 1979; Houston N.L., 1980, 1986; four series, six games.
Jim Palmer, Baltimore A.L., 1969, 1970, 1971, 1973, 1974, 1979; eight series, six games.
A.L.—46—Jim Palmer, Baltimore, 1969, 1970, 1971, 1973, 1974, 1979; eight series, six games.
N.L.—44—John Smoltz, Atlanta, 1991, 1992, 1993; three series, six games.

Most strikeouts, series

3-game series
N.L.—14—John Candelaria, Pittsburgh, 1975.
A.L.—12—Jim Palmer, Baltimore, 1970.
4-game series
A.L.—14—Mike Boddicker, Baltimore, 1983.
N.L.—13—Don Sutton, Los Angeles, 1974.
Steve Carlton, Philadelphia, 1983.
5-game series
N.L.—17—Tom Seaver, New York, 1973.
A.L.—15—Jim Palmer, Baltimore, 1973.
6-game series
N.L.—19—Mike Scott, Houston, 1986.
Curt Schilling, Philadelphia, 1993.
A.L.—11—Juan Guzman, Toronto, 1992.
7-game series
N.L.—20—Dwight Gooden, New York, 1988.
A.L.—18—Dave Stieb, Toronto, 1985.

Most strikeouts, game

A.L.—14
Joe Coleman, Detroit, October 10, 1972.
Mike Boddicker, Baltimore, October 6, 1983.
N.L.—14
John Candelaria, Pittsburgh, October 7, 1975, pitched first 7⅔ innings of 10-inning game.
Mike Scott, Houston, October 8, 1986.

Most strikeouts, game, relief pitcher

A.L.—8—Wes Gardner, Boston, October 8, 1988, pitched 4⅔ innings.
N.L.—7—Nolan Ryan, New York, October 6, 1969, pitched seven innings.

Most consecutive strikeouts, game

N.L.—5—Curt Schilling, Philadelphia, October 6, 1993 (three in first inning, two in second inning).
A.L.—4
Joe Coleman, Detroit, October 10, 1972 (one in fourth in-

ning, three in fifth inning).
Nolan Ryan, California, October 3, 1979 (three in first inning, one in second inning).
Milt Wilcox, Detroit, October 5, 1984 (two in fourth inning, two in fifth inning).
Roger Clemens, Boston, October 6, 1988 (two in second inning, two in third inning).

Most consecutive strikeouts from start of game

N.L.—5—Curt Schilling, Philadelphia, October 6, 1993 (three in first inning, two in second inning).
A.L.—4—Nolan Ryan, California, October 3, 1979.

Most strikeouts, inning

A.L.-N.L.—3—Held by many pitchers.

HIT BATSMEN, WILD PITCHES AND BALKS

Most hit batsmen, career

A.L.—4
Frank Tanana, California, 1979; Detroit, 1987 (3).
Mike Boddicker, Baltimore, 1983 (2); Boston, 1990 (2).
N.L.—2
Tom Seaver, New York, 1969, 1973.
Tommy John, Los Angeles, 1977 (2).
Orel Hershiser, Los Angeles, 1988 (2).
Tom Glavine, Atlanta, 1992 (2).

Most hit batsmen, series

A.L.—3—Frank Tanana, Detroit, 1987 (5-game series).
N.L.—2
Tommy John, Los Angeles, 1977 (4-game series).
Orel Hershiser, Los Angeles, 1988 (7-game series).
Tom Glavine, Atlanta, 1992 (7-game series).

Most hit batsmen, game

A.L.—3—Frank Tanana, Detroit, October 11, 1987.
N.L.—2—Orel Hershiser, Los Angeles, October 12, 1988.

Most hit batsmen, inning

A.L.-N.L.—1—Held by many pitchers.

Most wild pitches, career

A.L.—4
Tommy John, New York, 1980; California, 1982.
Juan Guzman, Toronto, 1991, 1992, 1993.
N.L.—4—Alejandro Pena, Los Angeles, 1983 (2); Atlanta 1991 (2).

Most wild pitches, series

A.L.—3
Tommy John, California, 1982 (5-game series).
Juan Guzman, Toronto, 1993 (6-game series).
N.L.—2—Held by many pitchers.

Most wild pitches, game

A.L.—3
Tommy John, California, October 9, 1982.
Juan Guzman, Toronto, October 5, 1993.
N.L.—2—Held by many pitchers.

Most wild pitches, inning

A.L.—2
Chris Zachary, Detroit, October 8, 1972, fifth inning.
Tommy John, California, October 9, 1982, fourth inning.
Juan Guzman, Toronto, October 5, 1993, first inning.
N.L.—2—Jeff Calhoun, Houston, October 15, 1986, 16th inning.

Most balks, game

A.L.-N.L.—1—Held by many pitchers.

CLUB PITCHING

APPEARANCES

Most appearances by pitchers, series

3-game series
A.L.—14—Minnesota vs. Baltimore, 1970.
N.L.—13—Cincinnati vs. Pittsburgh, 1979.
4-game series
A.L.—16—Oakland vs. Boston, 1988.
N.L.—14—Philadelphia vs. Los Angeles, 1977.
5-game series
N.L.—21—Philadelphia vs. Houston, 1980.
A.L.—19—Toronto vs. Minnesota, 1991.
6-game series
N.L.—23—St. Louis vs. Los Angeles, 1985.
A.L.—23—Oakland vs. Toronto, 1992.
7-game series
N.L.—28—Atlanta vs. Pittsburgh, 1992.
A.L.—22—California vs. Boston, 1986.

Most appearances by pitchers of both clubs, series

3-game series
N.L.—25—Cincinnati 13, Pittsburgh 12, 1979.
A.L.—18—Minnesota 11, Baltimore 7, 1969.
      Minnesota 14, Baltimore 4, 1970.
4-game series
N.L.—26—Philadelphia 14, Los Angeles 12, 1977.
A.L.—26—Oakland 16, Boston 10, 1988.
      Boston 15, Oakland 11, 1990.
5-game series
N.L.—36—Philadelphia 21, Houston 15, 1980.
A.L.—36—Toronto 19, Minnesota 17, 1991.
6-game series
A.L.—41—Oakland 23, Toronto 18, 1992.
N.L.—41—Philadelphia 21, Atlanta 20, 1993.
7-game series
N.L.—48—Atlanta 28, Pittsburgh 20, 1992.
A.L.—40—California 22, Boston 18, 1986.

COMPLETE GAMES

Most complete games, series
A.L.-N.L.—2—Held by many clubs.

Most complete games by both clubs, series
A.L.—4—Baltimore 2, Oakland 2, 1973 (5-game series).
N.L.—4—San Francisco 2, St. Louis 2, 1987 (7-game series).

SAVES

Most saves, series

3-game series
N.L.—3—Cincinnati vs. Pittsburgh, 1970.
A.L.—2—Boston vs. Oakland, 1975.
4-game series
A.L.—4—Oakland vs. Boston, 1988.
N.L.—3—Pittsburgh vs. San Francisco, 1971.
5-game series
A.L.—3—Milwaukee vs. California, 1982.
         Minnesota vs. Detroit, 1987.
         Oakland vs. Toronto, 1989.
         Minnesota vs. Toronto, 1991.
N.L.—3—San Francisco vs. Chicago, 1989.
6-game series
N.L.—4—Cincinnati vs. Pittsburgh, 1990.
A.L.—3—Toronto vs. Oakland, 1992.
7-game series
N.L.—3—St. Louis vs. San Francisco, 1987.
         Los Angeles vs. New York, 1988.

Atlanta vs. Pittsburgh, 1991.
A.L.—1—Held by many clubs.

Most saves by both clubs, series

3-game series
N.L.—3—Cincinnati 3, Pittsburgh 0, 1970.
A.L.—2—Boston 2, Oakland 0, 1975.
4-game series
A.L.—4—Oakland 4, Boston 0, 1988.
N.L.—3—Pittsburgh 3, San Francisco 0, 1971.
5-game series
N.L.—5—Houston 3, Philadelphia 2, 1980.
A.L.—4—Minnesota 3, Toronto 1, 1991.
6-game series
N.L.—6—Cincinnati 4, Pittsburgh 2, 1990.
A.L.—4—Toronto 3, Oakland 1, 1992.
7-game series
N.L.—5—Atlanta 3, Pittsburgh 2, 1991.
A.L.—2—California 1, Boston 1, 1986.

Fewest saves by one and both clubs, series
A.L.-N.L.—0—Held by many clubs.

RUNS AND SHUTOUTS

Most runs allowed, total series
N.L.—170—Pittsburgh (nine series, 42 games).
A.L.—152—Oakland (10 series, 42 games).

Most shutouts won, total series
A.L.—5—Baltimore, 1969, 1973, 1979, 1983 (2).
N.L.—3
St. Louis, 1982, 1987 (2).
Los Angeles, 1974, 1978, 1988.
Atlanta, 1991 (3).

Most shutouts won, series
N.L.—3—Atlanta vs. Pittsburgh, 1991 (7-game series).
A.L.—2
Oakland vs. Baltimore, 1974 (4-game series).
Baltimore vs. Chicago, 1983 (4-game series).

Most consecutive shutouts won, series
A.L.—2—Oakland vs. Baltimore, October 6, 8, 1974.
N.L.—2
St. Louis vs. San Francisco, October 13, 14, 1987.
Atlanta vs. Pittsburgh, October 16, 17, 1991.

Most shutouts by both clubs, series
N.L.—4—Atlanta 3, Pittsburgh 1, 1991 (7-game series).
A.L.—2
Oakland 1, Detroit 1, 1972 (5-game series).
Oakland 1, Baltimore 1, 1973 (5-game series).
Oakland 2, Baltimore 0, 1974 (4-game series).
Baltimore 2, Chicago 0, 1983 (4-game series).

Largest score, shutout game
N.L.—13-0—Chicago 13, San Diego 0, October 2, 1984.
A.L.—8-0—Baltimore 8, California 0, October 6, 1979.

Longest shutout game
A.L.—11 innings—Baltimore 1, Minnesota 0, October 5, 1969.
N.L.—11 innings—Houston 1, Philadelphia 0, October 10, 1980.

Most consecutive innings shutting out opponent, total series
A.L.—30—Oakland vs. Baltimore, October 5 (sixth inning) through October 9 (eighth inning), 1974.
N.L.—26—Pittsburgh vs. Atlanta, October 13 (second inning) through October 16 (eighth inning), 1991.

Most consecutive innings shutting out opponent, series
A.L.—30—Oakland vs. Baltimore, October 5 (sixth inning) through October 9 (eighth inning), 1974.
N.L.—26—Pittsburgh vs. Atlanta, October 13 (second inning) through October 16 (eighth inning), 1991.

WILD PITCHES AND BALKS

Most wild pitches, series
A.L.—5—Toronto vs. Chicago, 1993 (6-game series).
N.L.—4—Los Angeles vs. Philadelphia, 1983 (4-game series).

Most wild pitches by both clubs, series
A.L.—7—Toronto 5, Chicago 2, 1993 (6-game series).
N.L.—6—Los Angeles 4, Philadelphia 2, 1983 (4-game series).

Most balks, series
N.L.—2
   Pittsburgh vs. Cincinnati, 1975 (3-game series).

New York vs. Los Angeles, 1988 (7-game series).
A.L.—2—Baltimore vs. Chicago, 1983 (4-game series).

Most balks by both clubs, series
N.L.—2
   Pittsburgh 2, Cincinnati 0, 1975 (3-game series).
   Philadelphia 1, Los Angeles 1, 1977 (4-game series).
   New York 2, Los Angeles 0, 1988 (7-game series).
A.L.—2
   Baltimore 2, Chicago 0, 1983 (4-game series).
   Boston 1, Oakland 1, 1988 (4-game series).

INDIVIDUAL FIELDING

FIRST BASEMEN

GAMES

Most games played, career

N.L.—22—Steve Garvey, Los Angeles, 1974, 1977, 1978, 1981; San Diego, 1984; five series.
A.L.—19—Mark McGwire, Oakland, 1988, 1989, 1990, 1992; four series.

PUTOUTS, ASSISTS AND CHANCES ACCEPTED

Most putouts, career

N.L.—208—Steve Garvey, Los Angeles, 1974, 1977, 1978, 1981; San Diego, 1984; five series, 22 games.
A.L.—156—Mark McGwire, Oakland, 1988, 1989, 1990, 1992; four series, 19 games.

Most putouts, series

3-game series
N.L.—35—Keith Hernandez, St. Louis, 1982.
A.L.—34—Boog Powell, Baltimore, 1969.
4-game series
N.L.—44—Steve Garvey, Los Angeles, 1978.
A.L.—44—Eddie Murray, Baltimore, 1979.
5-game series
A.L.—55—Mike Epstein, Oakland, 1972.
N.L.—53—Pete Rose, Philadelphia, 1980.
6-game series
N.L.—67—Keith Hernandez, New York, 1986.
A.L.—51—John Olerud, Toronto, 1992.
7-game series
A.L.—72—Steve Balboni, Kansas City, 1985.
N.L.—63—Will Clark, San Francisco, 1987.

Most putouts, nine-inning game

N.L.—16
Steve Garvey, Los Angeles, October 5, 1978.
Steve Garvey, Los Angeles, October 6, 1978.
A.L.—15
Chris Chambliss, New York, October 14, 1976.
Mark McGwire, Oakland, October 4, 1989.

Most putouts, extra-inning game

N.L.—21—Glenn Davis, Houston, October 15, 1986, 16 innings.
A.L.—16—John Olerud, Toronto, October 11, 1991, 10 innings.

Fewest putouts, nine-inning game

N.L.—1—Bob Robertson, Pittsburgh, October 2, 1971.
A.L.—2
Norm Cash, Detroit, October 8, 1972.
Cecil Cooper, Boston, October 4, 1975.
Carlos Quintana, Boston, October 6, 1990.

Most putouts, inning

A.L.-N.L.—3—Held by many first basemen.

Most assists, career

N.L.—17—Keith Hernandez, St. Louis, 1982; New York, 1986, 1988; three series, 16 games.
A.L.—11—Chris Chambliss, New York, 1976, 1977, 1978; three series, 14 games.

Most assists, series

3-game series
A.L.—5—Rich Reese, Minnesota, 1969.
Bob Watson, New York, 1980.
N.L.—5—Tony Perez, Cincinnati, 1975.
Chris Chambliss, Atlanta, 1982.
4-game series
N.L.—5—Steve Garvey, Los Angeles, 1978.
A.L.—3—Eddie Murray, Baltimore, 1979, 1983.
Tom Paciorek, Chicago, 1983.
5-game series
A.L.—8—Kent Hrbek, Minnesota, 1991.
N.L.—7—Pete Rose, Philadelphia, 1980.

6-game series
N.L.—12—Keith Hernandez, New York, 1986.
A.L.—9—John Olerud, Toronto, 1993.
7-game series
A.L.—7—Steve Balboni, Kansas City, 1985.
Willie Upshaw, Toronto, 1985.
N.L.—7—Will Clark, San Francisco, 1987.

Most assists, nine-inning game

A.L.—4—Steve Balboni, Kansas City, October 12, 1985.
N.L.—3
Tony Perez, Cincinnati, October 4, 1975.
Chris Chambliss, Atlanta, October 10, 1982.
Greg Brock, Los Angeles, October 16, 1985.
Will Clark, San Francisco, October 10, 1987.
Will Clark, San Francisco, October 7, 1989.

Most assists, extra-inning game

N.L.—7—Keith Hernandez, New York, October 15, 1986, 16 innings.
A.L.—Less than nine-inning record.

Most assists, inning

A.L.-N.L.—2—Held by many first basemen.

Most chances accepted, career

N.L.—221—Steve Garvey, Los Angeles, 1974, 1977, 1978, 1981; San Diego, 1984; five series, 22 games.
A.L.—124—Chris Chambliss, New York, 1976, 1977, 1978; three series, 14 games.

Most chances accepted, series

3-game series
N.L.—36—Keith Hernandez, St. Louis, 1982.
A.L.—34—Boog Powell, Baltimore, 1969.
4-game series
N.L.—49—Steve Garvey, Los Angeles, 1978.
A.L.—47—Eddie Murray, Baltimore, 1979.
5-game series
N.L.—60—Pete Rose, Philadelphia, 1980.
A.L.—57—Mike Epstein, Oakland, 1972.
6-game series
N.L.—79—Keith Hernandez, New York, 1986.
A.L.—57—John Olerud, Toronto, 1993.
7-game series
A.L.—79—Steve Balboni, Kansas City, 1985.
N.L.—70—Will Clark, San Francisco, 1987.

Most chances accepted, nine-inning game

N.L.—18—Steve Garvey, Los Angeles, October 6, 1978 (16 putouts, two assists).
A.L.—16
Steve Balboni, Kansas City, October 12, 1985 (12 putouts, four assists).
George Hendrick, California, October 11, 1986, 11 innings (14 putouts, two assists).

Most chances accepted, extra-inning game

N.L.—27—Keith Hernandez, New York, October 15, 1986, 16 innings (20 putouts, seven assists).
A.L.—16—John Olerud, Toronto, October 11, 1991, 10 innings (16 putouts).

Fewest chances offered, nine-inning game

N.L.—2—Bob Robertson, Pittsburgh, October 2, 1971 (one putout, one assist).
A.L.—2—Carlos Quintana, Boston, October 6, 1990 (two putouts).

Most chances accepted, inning

A.L.-N.L.—3—Held by many first basemen.

ERRORS AND DOUBLE PLAYS

Most errors, career

A.L.—3
Cecil Cooper, Boston, 1975; Milwaukee, 1982; two series, eight games.

Steve Balboni, Kansas City, 1984, 1985; two series, 10 games.
N.L.—2
Orlando Cepeda, Atlanta, 1969; one series, three games.
Mickey Hatcher, Los Angeles, 1988; one series, six games.
Orlando Merced, Pittsburgh, 1991, 1992; two series, six games.

Most consecutive errorless games, career
N.L.— 19—Steve Garvey, Los Angeles, San Diego, October 9, 1974 through October 7, 1984.
A.L.— 12
Boog Powell, Baltimore, October 4, 1969 through October 9, 1974.
Chris Chambliss, New York, October 12, 1976 through October 7, 1978.

Most errors, series
A.L.-N.L.—2—Held by many first basemen.

Most chances accepted, errorless series
N.L.—79—Keith Hernandez, New York, 1986 (6-game series).
A.L.—57—Mike Epstein, Oakland, 1972 (5-game series).

Most errors, game
A.L.-N.L.—1—Held by many first basemen.

Most double plays, career
N.L.—21—Steve Garvey, Los Angeles, 1974, 1977, 1978, 1981; San Diego, 1984; five series, 22 games.
A.L.— 15
Mark McGwire, Oakland, 1988, 1989, 1990, 1992; four series, 19 games.
John Olerud, Toronto, 1991, 1992, 1993; three series, 17 games.

Most double plays, series
N.L.— 10—Will Clark, San Francisco, 1987 (7-game series).
A.L.—6
Rod Carew, California, 1979 (4-game series).
Bob Watson, New York, 1981 (3-game series).

Most double plays started, series
N.L.-A.L.—1—Held by many first basemen.

Most double plays, game
N.L.—4—Will Clark, San Francisco, October 10, 1987.
A.L.—3
Rich Reese, Minnesota, October 3, 1970.
Mike Epstein, Oakland, October 10, 1972.
Gene Tenace, Oakland, October 5, 1975.
Eddie Murray, Baltimore, October 6, 1979.
Bobby Grich, California, October 14, 1986.

Most double plays started, game
A.L.-N.L.—1—Held by many first basemen.

Most unassisted double plays, game
A.L.-N.L.—Never accomplished.

SECOND BASEMEN

GAMES

Most games played, career
N.L.—27—Joe Morgan, Cincinnati, 1972, 1973, 1975, 1976, 1979; Houston, 1980; Philadelphia, 1983; seven series.
A.L.—26—Frank White, Kansas City, 1976, 1977, 1978, 1980, 1984, 1985; six series.

PUTOUTS, ASSISTS AND CHANCES ACCEPTED

Most putouts, career
N.L.—63—Joe Morgan, Cincinnati, 1972, 1973, 1975, 1976, 1979; Houston, 1980; Philadelphia, 1983; seven series, 27 games.
A.L.—53—Frank White, Kansas City, 1976, 1977, 1978, 1980, 1984, 1985; six series, 26 games.

Most putouts, series
3-game series
N.L.— 12—Joe Morgan, Cincinnati, 1979.

A.L.— 12—Willie Randolph, New York, 1981.
4-game series
A.L.— 13—Bobby Grich, Baltimore, 1974.
N.L.— 11—Dave Cash, Pittsburgh, 1971.
Steve Sax, Los Angeles, 1983.
5-game series
A.L.— 16—Bobby Grich, Baltimore, 1973.
N.L.— 18—Manny Trillo, Philadelphia, 1980.
6-game series
N.L.— 19—Jose Lind, Pittsburgh, 1990.
A.L.— 18—Joey Cora, Chicago, 1993.
7-game series
A.L.— 19—Marty Barrett, Boston, 1986.
N.L.— 16—Jose Lind, Pittsburgh, 1992.

Most putouts, nine-inning game
A.L.—7—Bobby Grich, Baltimore, October 6, 1974.
N.L.—6
Dave Cash, Philadelphia, October 12, 1976.
Dave Lopes, Los Angeles, October 13, 1981.

Most putouts, extra-inning game
A.L.—8—Roberto Alomar, Toronto, October 11, 1992, 11 innings.
N.L.—7—Steve Sax, Los Angeles, October 9, 1988, 12 innings.

Most putouts, inning
N.L.—3
Joe Morgan, Cincinnati, October 10, 1976, eighth inning.
Ryne Sandberg, Chicago, October 4, 1984, fifth inning.
A.L.—3
Bobby Grich, Baltimore, October 11, 1973, third inning.
Dick Green, Oakland, October 8, 1974, seventh inning.

Most assists, career
N.L.—85—Joe Morgan, Cincinnati, 1972, 1973, 1975, 1976, 1979; Houston, 1980; Philadelphia, 1983; seven series, 27 games.
A.L.—80—Frank White, Kansas City, 1976, 1977, 1978, 1980, 1984, 1985; six series, 26 games.

Most assists, series
3-games series
N.L.— 12—Tommy Helms, Cincinnati, 1970.
A.L.— 12—Willie Randolph, New York, 1981.
4-game series
N.L.— 18—Dave Lopes, Los Angeles, 1974.
A.L.— 14—Julio Cruz, Chicago, 1983.
5-game series
N.L.—27—Joe Morgan, Cincinnati, 1973.
A.L.— 17—Bobby Grich, California, 1982.
6-game series
N.L.—21—Steve Sax, Los Angeles, 1985.
A.L.—20—Joey Cora, Chicago, 1993.
7-game series
A.L.—28—Frank White, Kansas City, 1985.
N.L.—24—Jose Lind, Pittsburgh, 1991.

Most assists, nine-inning game
A.L.—9—Joey Cora, Chicago, October 6, 1993.
N.L.—8—Manny Trillo, Philadelphia, October 7, 1980.

Most assists, extra-inning game
N.L.—9—Wally Backman, October 14, 1986, 12 innings.
A.L.—Less than nine-inning record.

Most assists, inning
A.L.-N.L.—2—Held by many second basemen.

Most chances accepted, career
N.L.— 148—Joe Morgan, Cincinnati, 1972, 1973, 1975, 1976, 1979; Houston, 1980; Philadelphia, 1983; seven series, 27 games.
A.L.— 133—Frank White, Kansas City, 1976, 1977, 1978, 1980, 1984, 1985; six series, 26 games.

Most chances accepted, series
3-game series
A.L.—24—Willie Randolph, New York, 1981.
N.L.—23—Tommy Helms, Cincinnati, 1970.
Joe Morgan, Cincinnati, 1979.

4-game series
N.L.—27—Dave Lopes, Los Angeles, 1974.
A.L.—25—Bobby Grich, Baltimore, 1974.
5-game series
N.L.—43—Manny Trillo, Philadelphia, 1980.
A.L.—29—Frank White, Kansas City, 1977.
6-game series
N.L.—38—Jose Lind, Pittsburgh, 1990.
A.L.—38—Joey Cora, Chicago, 1993.
7-game series
N.L.—39—Jose Lind, Pittsburgh, 1992.
A.L.—37—Frank White, Kansas City, 1985.

Most chances accepted, nine-inning game

N.L.—13—Manny Trillo, Philadelphia, October 7, 1980 (five putouts, eight assists).
A.L.—12—Bobby Grich, Baltimore, October 6, 1974 (seven putouts, five assists, one error).

Most chances accepted, extra-inning game

A.L.—13—Roberto Alomar, Toronto, October 11, 1992 (eight putouts, five assists).
N.L.—Less than nine-inning record.

Fewest chances offered, game

A.L.—0
Danny Thompson, Minnesota, October 4, 1970.
Bobby Grich, California, October 10, 1986.
N.L.—0—Ryne Sandberg, Chicago, October 9, 1989.

Most chances accepted, inning

A.L.-N.L.—3—Held by many second basemen.

ERRORS AND DOUBLE PLAYS

Most errors, career

A.L.—4
Dick Green, Oakland, 1971, 1972, 1973, 1974; four series, 17 games.
Bobby Grich, Baltimore, 1973, 1974; California, 1979, 1982, 1986; five series, 21 games.
N.L.—4—Dave Lopes, Los Angeles, 1974, 1977, 1978, 1981; four series, 17 games.

Most consecutive errorless games, career

N.L.—27—Joe Morgan, Cincinnati, Houston, Philadelphia, October 7, 1972 through October 8, 1983.
A.L.—20—Willie Randolph, New York, Oakland, October 9, 1976 through October 10, 1990.

Most errors, series

A.L.-N.L.—2—Held by many second basemen.

Most chances accepted, errorless series

A.L.—40—Marty Barrett, Boston, 1986 (7-game series).
N.L.—39—Joe Morgan, Cincinnati, 1973 (5-game series).

Most errors, game

A.L.—2
Dick Green, Oakland, October 9, 1973, 11 innings.
Dick Green, Oakland, October 8, 1974.
Lance Blankenship, Oakland, October 10, 1992.
N.L.—1—Held by many second basemen.

Most errors, inning

A.L.-N.L.—1—Held by many second basemen.

Most double plays, career

N.L.—14—Joe Morgan, Cincinnati, 1972, 1973, 1975, 1976, 1979; Houston, 1980; Philadelphia, 1983; seven series, 27 games.
A.L.—14—Frank White, Kansas City, 1976, 1977, 1978, 1980, 1984, 1985; six series, 26 games.

Most double plays, series

N.L.—7—Rodney Scott, Montreal, 1981 (5-game series).
A.L.—5—Roberto Alomar, Toronto, 1993 (6-game series).

Most double plays started, series

N.L.—5—Steve Sax, Los Angeles, 1988 (7-game series).
A.L.—2—Held by many second basemen.

Most double plays, game

N.L.—4—Dave Lopes, Los Angeles, October 13, 1981.
A.L.—3—Rob Wilfong, California, October 14, 1986.

Most double plays started, game

N.L.—2
Rennie Stennett, Pittsburgh, October 6, 1975.
Ted Sizemore, Philadelphia, October 6, 1978.
Rodney Scott, Montreal, October 17, 1981.
Tom Herr, St. Louis, October 10, 1982.
Ryne Sandberg, Chicago, October 2, 1984.
Robby Thompson, San Francisco, October 10, 1987.
A.L.—1—Held by many second basemen.

Most unassisted double plays, game

N.L.—1—Joe Morgan, Cincinnati, October 10, 1976.
A.L.—Never accomplished.

THIRD BASEMEN

GAMES

Most games played, career

N.L.—32—Terry Pendleton, St. Louis, 1985, 1987; Atlanta, 1991, 1992, 1993; five series.
A.L.—27—George Brett, Kansas City, 1976, 1977, 1978, 1980, 1984, 1985; six series.

PUTOUTS, ASSISTS AND CHANCES ACCEPTED

Most putouts, career

A.L.—25—Sal Bando, Oakland, 1971, 1972, 1973, 1974, 1975; five series, 20 games.
N.L.—25—Terry Pendleton, St. Louis, 1985, 1987; Atlanta, 1991, 1992, 1993; five series, 32 games.

Most putouts, series

3-game series
A.L.—6—Brooks Robinson, Baltimore, 1969.
Harmon Killebrew, Minnesota, 1969.
Sal Bando, Oakland, 1971.
N.L.—5—Tony Perez, Cincinnati, 1970.
4-game series
N.L.—7—Ron Cey, Los Angeles, 1977.
A.L.—7—Carney Lansford, Oakland, 1988.
5-game series
A.L.—9—Doug DeCinces, California, 1982.
N.L.—5—Richie Hebner, Pittsburgh, 1972.
Ron Cey, Los Angeles, 1981.
Graig Nettles, San Diego, 1984.
Matt Williams, San Francisco, 1989.
6-game series
N.L.—7—Terry Pendleton, Atlanta, 1993.
A.L.—5—Kelly Gruber, Toronto, 1992.
Ed Sprague Jr., Toronto, 1993.
7-game series
N.L.—11—Jeff King, Pittsburgh, 1992.
A.L.—7—George Brett, Kansas City, 1985.
Wade Boggs, Boston, 1986.

Most putouts, game

A.L.—4
Carney Lansford, California, October 6, 1979.
Wade Boggs, Boston, October 10, 1990.
N.L.—3—Held by many players.

Most putouts, inning

A.L.-N.L.—2—Held by many third basemen.

Most assists, career

N.L.—66—Mike Schmidt, Philadelphia, 1976, 1977, 1978, 1980, 1983; five series, 20 games.
A.L.—49
Brooks Robinson, Baltimore, 1969, 1970, 1971, 1973, 1974; five series, 18 games.
George Brett, Kansas City, 1976, 1977, 1978, 1980, 1984, 1985; six series, 27 games.

Most assists, series

3-game series
A.L.—11—Sal Bando, Oakland, 1975.
N.L.—9—Mike Schmidt, Philadelphia, 1976.
4-game series
N.L.—18—Mike Schmidt, Philadelphia, 1978.
A.L.—13—Brooks Robinson, Baltimore, 1974.
   Todd Cruz, Baltimore, 1983.
5-game series
N.L.—17—Mike Schmidt, Philadelphia, 1980.
A.L.—16—Sal Bando, Oakland, 1972.
6-game series
N.L.—19—Ray Knight, New York, 1986.
A.L.—16—Kelly Gruber, Toronto, 1992.
7-game series
N.L.—19—Jeff King, Pittsburgh, 1992.
A.L.—18—Doug DeCinces, California, 1986.

Most assists, nine-inning game

N.L.—8—Ron Cey, Los Angeles, October 16, 1981.
A.L.—6
Sal Bando, Oakland, October 8, 1972.
Todd Cruz, Baltimore, October 5, 1983.
Tom Brookens, Detroit, October 11, 1987.

Most assists, extra-inning game

A.L.—7—Aurelio Rodriguez, Detroit, October 11, 1972, 10 innings.
N.L.—Less than nine-inning record.

Most assists, inning

N.L.—3
Ron Cey, Los Angeles, October 4, 1977, fourth inning.
Ron Cey, Los Angeles, October 16, 1981, eighth inning.
A.L.—3—Todd Cruz, Baltimore, October 5, 1983, fifth inning.

Most chances accepted, career

N.L.—88—Terry Pendleton, St. Louis, 1985, 1987; Atlanta, 1991, 1992, 1993; five series, 32 games.
A.L.—72—Sal Bando, Oakland, 1971, 1972, 1973, 1974, 1975; five series, 20 games.

Most chances accepted, series

3-game series
A.L.—16—Brooks Robinson, Baltimore, 1969.
N.L.—13—Mike Schmidt, Philadelphia, 1976.
4-game series
N.L.—21—Ron Cey, Los Angeles, 1977.
   Mike Schmidt, Philadelphia, 1978.
A.L.—19—Todd Cruz, Baltimore, 1983.
5-game series
A.L.—22—Sal Bando, Oakland, 1972.
N.L.—21—Ron Cey, Los Angeles, 1981.
6-game series
N.L.—24—Terry Pendleton, St. Louis, 1985.
   Ray Knight, New York, 1986.
A.L.—21—Kelly Gruber, Toronto, 1992.
7-game series
A.L.—24—Doug DeCinces, California, 1986.
N.L.—22—Steve Buechele, Pittsburgh, 1991.

Most chances accepted, game

N.L.—10—Ron Cey, Los Angeles, October 16, 1981 (two putouts, eight assists).
A.L.—9
Todd Cruz, Baltimore, October 5, 1983 (three putouts, six assists).
Wade Boggs, Boston, October 10, 1990 (four putouts, five assists).

Fewest chances offered, game

A.L.-N.L.—0—Held by many players.

Most chances accepted, inning

A.L.-N.L.—3—Held by many third basemen.

[ ] ERRORS AND DOUBLE PLAYS [ ]

Most errors, career

A.L.—8—George Brett, Kansas City, 1976, 1977, 1978, 1980,

1984, 1985; six series, 27 games.
N.L.—5—Mike Schmidt, Philadelphia, 1976, 1977, 1978, 1980, 1983; five series, 20 games.

Most consecutive errorless games, career

N.L.—31—Terry Pendleton, St. Louis, Atlanta, October 10, 1985 through October 13, 1993.
A.L.—17
Sal Bando, Oakland, October 3, 1971 through October 9, 1974.
Carney Lansford, California, Oakland, October 3, 1979 through October 8, 1992.

Most errors, series

A.L.—3
George Brett, Kansas City, 1976 (5-game series).
Doug DeCinces, California, 1982 (5-game series).
Kelly Gruber, Toronto, 1991 (5-game series).
N.L.—2—Held by many third basemen.

Most chances accepted, errorless series

A.L.—22—Sal Bando, Oakland, 1972 (5-game series).
N.L.—22
Steve Buechele, Pittsburgh, 1991 (7-game series).
Terry Pendleton, Atlanta, 1992 (7-game series).

Most errors, game

A.L.—2
George Brett, Kansas City, October 9, 1976.
Doug DeCinces, California, October 9, 1982.
Darrell Evans, Detroit, October 11, 1987.
Kelly Gruber, Toronto, October 8, 1991.
N.L.—2—Ron Cey, Los Angeles, October 5, 1974.

Most errors, inning

A.L.—2—George Brett, Kansas City, October 9, 1976, first inning.
N.L.—1—Held by many third basemen.

Most double plays, career

A.L.—7—Doug DeCinces, Baltimore, 1979; California, 1982, 1986; three series, 16 games.
N.L.—7—Terry Pendleton, St. Louis, 1985, 1987; Atlanta, 1991, 1992, 1993; five series, 32 games.

Most double plays, series

N.L.—5—Jeff King, Pittsburgh, 1992 (7-game series).
A.L.—3
Carney Lansford, California, 1979 (4-game series).
Doug DeCinces, California, 1982 (5-game series).

Most double plays started, series

N.L.—5—Jeff King, Pittsburgh, 1992 (7-game series).
A.L.—3—Carney Lansford, California, 1979 (4-game series).

Most double plays, game

A.L.-N.L.—2—Held by many third basemen.

Most double plays started, game

A.L.-N.L.—2—Held by many third basemen.

Most unassisted double plays, game

N.L.—1
Mike Schmidt, Philadelphia, October 9, 1976.
Jeff King, Pittsburgh, October 14, 1992.
A.L.—Never accomplished.

[SHORTSTOPS]
[ ] GAMES [ ]

Most games played, career

A.L.—21—Mark Belanger, Baltimore, 1969, 1970, 1971, 1973, 1974, 1979; six series.
N.L.—21
Bill Russell, Los Angeles, 1974, 1977, 1978, 1981, 1983; five series.
Larry Bowa, Philadelphia, 1976, 1977, 1978, 1980; Chicago, 1984; five series.

☐ PUTOUTS, ASSISTS AND CHANCES ACCEPTED ☐

Most putouts, career

N.L.—42—Bill Russell, Los Angeles, 1974, 1977, 1978, 1981, 1983; five series, 21 games.

A.L.—31—Mark Belanger, Baltimore, 1969, 1970, 1971, 1973, 1974, 1979; six series, 21 games.

Most putouts, series

3-game series
A.L.—13—Leo Cardenas, Minnesota, 1969.
N.L.—6—Held by many shortstops.

4-game series
N.L.—13—Bill Russell, Los Angeles, 1974.
A.L.—9—Fred Patek, Kansas City, 1978.

5-game series
N.L.—19—Garry Templeton, San Diego, 1984.
A.L.—13—Fred Patek, Kansas City, 1976.

6-game series
N.L.—21—Barry Larkin, Cincinnati, 1990.
A.L.—12—Manny Lee, Toronto, 1992.
        Tony Fernandez, Toronto, 1993.
        Ozzie Guillen, Chicago, 1993.

7-game series
N.L.—17—Alfredo Griffin, Los Angeles, 1988.
A.L.—13—Dick Schofield, California, 1986.

Most putouts, game

N.L.—7—Garry Templeton, San Diego, October 4, 1984.
A.L.—6
Mark Belanger, Baltimore, October 5, 1974.
Bucky Dent, New York, October 5, 1977.
Fred Patek, Kansas City, October 5, 1977.
Manny Lee, Toronto, October 8, 1992.

Most putouts, inning

A.L.—3
Mark Belanger, Baltimore, October 5, 1974, third inning.
Fred Patek, Kansas City, October 5, 1977, second inning.
N.L.—3—Chris Speier, Montreal, October 14, 1981, fifth inning.

Most assists, career

N.L.—70—Larry Bowa, Philadelphia, 1976, 1977, 1978, 1980; Chicago, 1984; five series, 21 games.

A.L.—69—Mark Belanger, Baltimore, 1969, 1970, 1971, 1973, 1974, 1979; six series, 21 games.

Most assists, series

3-game series
A.L.—14—Mark Belanger, Baltimore, 1970.
N.L.—14—Dave Concepcion, Cincinnati, 1979.

4-game series
A.L.—17—Bert Campaneris, Oakland, 1974.
N.L.—17—Larry Bowa, Philadelphia, 1977.

5-game series
A.L.—18—Fred Patek, Kansas City, 1976, 1977.
N.L.—16—Darrel Chaney, Cincinnati, 1972.
        Chris Speier, Montreal, 1981.

6-game series
N.L.—22—Jay Bell, Pittsburgh, 1990.
A.L.—15—Manny Lee, Toronto, 1992.

7-game series
A.L.—23—Dick Schofield, California, 1986.
N.L.—20—Jose Uribe, San Francisco, 1987.

Most assists, game

N.L.—9—Bill Russell, Los Angeles, October 5, 1978.
A.L.—9—Kiko Garcia, Baltimore, October 4, 1979.

Most assists, inning

A.L.-N.L.—3—Held by many shortstops.

Most chances accepted, career

N.L.—107—Bill Russell, Los Angeles, 1974, 1977, 1978, 1981, 1983; five series, 21 games.

A.L.—100—Mark Belanger, Baltimore, 1969, 1970, 1971, 1973, 1974, 1979; six series, 21 games.

Most chances accepted, series

3-game series
A.L.—25—Leo Cardenas, Minnesota, 1969.
N.L.—17—Dave Concepcion, Cincinnati, 1979.

4-game series
N.L.—29—Bill Russell, Los Angeles, 1974.
A.L.—22—Kiko Garcia, Baltimore, 1979.

5-game series
A.L.—31—Fred Patek, Kansas City, 1976.
N.L.—31—Chris Speier, Montreal, 1981.

6-game series
N.L.—36—Barry Larkin, Cincinnati, 1990.
A.L.—27—Manny Lee, Toronto, 1992.

7-game series
A.L.—36—Dick Schofield, California, 1986.
N.L.—32—Jay Bell, Pittsburgh, 1991.

Most chances accepted, game

N.L.—13—Bill Russell, Los Angeles, October 8, 1974 (six putouts, seven assists).

A.L.—11
Leo Cardenas, Minnesota, October 5, 1969, 11 innings (six putouts, five assists, one error).
Kiko Garcia, Baltimore, October 4, 1979 (two putouts, nine assists).

Fewest chances offered, game

A.L.-N.L.-0—Held by many shortstops.

Most chances accepted, inning

A.L.-N.L.—3—Held by many shortstops.

☐ ERRORS AND DOUBLE PLAYS ☐

Most errors, career

A.L.—5—Spike Owen, Boston. 1986; one series, seven games.

N.L.—4—Craig Reynolds, Pittsburgh, 1975; Houston, 1980, 1986; three series, nine games.

Most consecutive errorless games, career

A.L.—17—Mark Belanger, Baltimore, October 4, 1969 through October 8, 1974.

N.L.—13—Bill Russell, Los Angeles, October 5, 1977 through October 4, 1983.

Most errors, series

A.L.—5—Spike Owen, Boston, 1986 (7-game series).
N.L.—3—Darrel Chaney, Cincinnati, 1972 (5-game series).

Most chances accepted, errorless series

A.L.—31—Fred Patek, Kansas City, 1976 (5-game series).
N.L.—31—Rafael Santana, New York, 1986. (6-game series).

Most errors, game

A.L.—2
Leo Cardenas, Minnesota, October 4, 1970.
Manny Lee, Toronto, October 11, 1992; 11 innings.
N.L.—2
Gene Alley, Pittsburgh, October 10, 1972.
Bill Russell, Los Angeles, October 4, 1977.
Kevin Elster, New York, October 9, 1988; 12 innings.

Most errors, inning

N.L.—2
Gene Alley, Pittsburgh, October 10, 1972, fourth inning.
Kevin Elster, New York, October 9, 1988, fifth inning.
A.L.—1—Held by many shortstops.

Most double plays, career

N.L.—18—Bill Russell, Los Angeles, 1974, 1977, 1978, 1981, 1983; five series, 21 games.

A.L.—10—Tony Fernandez, Toronto, 1985, 1989, 1993; three series, 18 games.

Most double plays, series

N.L.—7
Jose Uribe, San Francisco, 1987 (7-game series).
Alfredo Griffin, Los Angeles, 1988 (7-game series).
A.L.—5
Manny Lee, Toronto, 1992 (6-game series).
Tony Fernandez, Toronto, 1993 (6-game series).

Most double plays started, series

A.L.-N.L.—3—Held by many shortstops.

Most double plays, game
A.L.—3—Bert Campaneris, Oakland, October 5, 1975.
N.L.—3
  Bill Russell, Los Angeles, October 8, 1974.
  Bill Russell, Los Angeles, October 5, 1983.
  Jose Uribe, San Francisco, October 10, 1987.
  Ozzie Smith, St. Louis, October 14, 1987.

Most double plays started, game
N.L.—3—Bill Russell, Los Angeles, October 5, 1983.
A.L.—2—Held by many shortstops.

Most unassisted double plays, game
N.L.—1
  Bill Russell, Los Angeles, October 8, 1974.
  Alfredo Griffin, Los Angeles, October 5, 1988.
A.L.—1
  Robin Yount, Milwaukee, October 5, 1982.
  Buddy Biancalana, Kansas City, October 12, 1985.
  Tony Fernandez, Toronto, October 4, 1989.

OUTFIELDERS

GAMES

Most games played, career
A.L.—32—Reggie Jackson, Oakland, 1971, 1972, 1973, 1974, 1975; New York, 1977, 1978, 1980, 1981; California, 1982; 10 series.
N.L.—25—Andy Van Slyke, St. Louis, 1985; Pittsburgh, 1990, 1991, 1992; four series.

☐ PUTOUTS, ASSISTS AND CHANCES ACCEPTED ☐

Most putouts, career
A.L.—69—Reggie Jackson, Oakland, 1971, 1972, 1973, 1974, 1975; New York, 1977, 1978, 1980, 1981; California, 1982; 10 series, 32 games.
N.L.—62—Garry Maddox, Philadelphia, 1976, 1977, 1978, 1980, 1983; five series, 17 games.

Most putouts, series
3-game series
  N.L.—13—Cesar Geronimo, Cincinnati, 1975.
             Dave Parker, Pittsburgh, 1975.
  A.L.—12—Fred Lynn, Boston, 1975
4-game series
  N.L.—16—Garry Maddox, Philadelphia, 1978.
  A.L.—14—Bill North, Oakland, 1974.
5-game series
  N.L.—23—Garry Maddox, Philadelphia, 1980.
  A.L.—22—Dave Henderson, Oakland, 1989.
6-game series
  N.L.—18—Willie McGee, St. Louis, 1985.
  A.L.—16—Devon White, Toronto, 1992.
7-game series
  A.L.—28—Gary Pettis, California, 1986.
  N.L.—20—Andy Van Slyke, Pittsburgh, 1992.

Most putouts by left fielder, game
A.L.—7—Roy White, New York, October 13, 1976.
N.L.—7
  Rennie Stennett, Pittsburgh, October 7, 1972.
  Jose Cruz, Houston, October 10, 1980, 11 innings.

Most putouts by center fielder, game
A.L.—9—Gary Pettis, California, October 10. 1986.
N.L.—8
  Al Oliver, Pittsburgh, October 7, 1972.
  Don Hahn, New York, October 8, 1973.

Most putouts by right fielder, game
A.L.—9—Jesse Barfield, Toronto, October 11, 1985.
N.L.—6
  Kevin Bass, Houston, October 14, 1986, 12 innings.
  David Justice, Atlanta, October 14, 1992.
  David Justice, Atlanta, October 11, 1993, 10 innings.

Most consecutive putouts, game
A.L.—4
  Oscar Gamble, New York, October 15, 1981, 3 in sixth inning, 1 in seventh inning (right fielder).
  Dan Gladden, Minnesota, October 9, 1991, 3 in eighth inning, 1 in ninth inning (left fielder).
N.L.—4—Andre Dawson, Montreal, October 19, 1981, 1 in sixth inning, 3 in seventh inning (center fielder).

Most putouts, inning
A.L.-N.L.—3—Held by many outfielders.

Most assists, career
M.L.—6—Lonnie Smith, Philadelphia N.L., 1980; St. Louis N.L., 1982; Kansas City A.L., 1985; Atlanta N.L., 1991; four series, 19 games.
N.L.—5—Bake McBride, Philadelphia, 1977, 1978, 1980; three series, 11 games.
A.L.—3
  Tony Oliva, Minnesota, 1969, 1970; two series, six games.
  Reggie Jackson, Oakland, 1971, 1972, 1973, 1974, 1975; New York, 1977, 1978, 1980, 1981; nine series, 27 games.
  Lonnie Smith, Kansas City, 1985; one series, seven games.

Most games played with no assists, career
A.L.—24—Paul Blair, Baltimore, 1969, 1970, 1971, 1973, 1974,; New York, 1977, 1978; seven series.
N.L.—17—Garry Maddox, Philadelphia, 1976, 1977, 1978, 1980, 1983; five series.

Most assists, series
3-game series
  A.L.—2—Tony Oliva, Minnesota, 1970.
           Carl Yastrzemski, Boston, 1975.
           Tony Armas, Oakland, 1981.
  N.L.—2—George Foster, Cincinnati, 1979.
4-game series
  N.L.—2—Bake McBride, Philadelphia, 1977.
  A.L.—2—Rick Miller, California, 1979.
5-game series
  N.L.—3—Bake McBride, Philadelphia, 1980.
  A.L.—1—Held by many outfielders.
6-game series
  N.L.—2—Paul O'Neill, Cincinnati, 1990.
           Wes Chamberlain, Philadelphia, 1993.
  A.L.—1—Held by many outfielders.
7-game series
  A.L.—3—Lonnie Smith, Kansas City, 1985.
  N.L.—3—David Justice, Atlanta, 1992.

Most assists, game
A.L.—2—Tony Oliva, Minnesota, October 4, 1970.
N.L.—2
  George Foster, Cincinnati, October 3, 1979, 10 innings.
  Bake McBride, Philadelphia, October 11, 1980, 10 innings.

Most chances accepted, career
A.L.—72—Reggie Jackson, Oakland, 1971, 1972, 1973, 1974, 1975; New York, 1977, 1978, 1980, 1981; California, 1982; 10 series, 32 games.
N.L.—62—Garry Maddox, Philadelphia, 1976, 1977, 1978, 1980, 1983; five series, 17 games.

Most chances accepted, series
3-game series
  N.L.—14—Dave Parker, Pittsburgh, 1975.
  A.L.—13—Fred Lynn, Boston, 1975.
4-game series
  N.L.—16—Garry Maddox, Philadelphia, 1978.
  A.L.—16—Rick Miller, California, 1979.
5-game series
  N.L.—23—Garry Maddox, Philadelphia, 1980.
  A.L.—22—Dave Henderson, Oakland, 1989.
6-game series
  N.L.—18—Willie McGee, St. Louis, 1985.
  A.L.—16—Devon White, Toronto, 1992.
           Willie Wilson, Oakland, 1992.
7-game series
  A.L.—28—Gary Pettis, California, 1986.

N.L.—22—David Justice, Atlanta, 1992.

Most chances accepted by left fielder, game

A.L.—7
  Roy White, New York, October 13, 1976 (seven putouts).
  Clint Hurdle, Kansas City, October 6, 1978 (six putouts, one assist).
N.L.—7
  Rennie Stennett, Pittsburgh, October 7, 1972 (seven putouts).
  Jose Cruz, Houston, October 10, 1980 (seven putouts).
  Kevin Mitchell, San Francisco, October 7, 1989 (six putouts, one assist).

Most chances accepted by center fielder, game

A.L.—9—Gary Pettis, California, October 10, 1986 (nine putouts).
N.L.—8
  Al Oliver, Pittsburgh, October 7, 1972 (eight putouts).
  Don Hahn, New York, October 8, 1973 (eight putouts).

Most chances accepted by right fielder, game

A.L.—9—Jesse Barfield, Toronto, October 11, 1985 (nine putouts).
N.L.—7—David Justice, Atlanta, October 14, 1992 (six putouts, one assist).

Longest game with no chances offered to outfielder

N.L.—12 innings
  Don Hahn, New York, October 9, 1973.
  Billy Hatcher, Houston, October 14, 1986.
A.L.—11 innings
  Matty Alou, Oakland, October 7, 1972.
  Jim Rice, Boston, October 11, 1986.
  Ruben Sierra, Oakland, October 11, 1992.

Most chances accepted, inning

A.L.-N.L.—3—Held by many players.

ERRORS AND DOUBLE PLAYS

Most errors, career

A.L.—6—Rickey Henderson, Oakland, 1981, 1989, 1990, 1992; Toronto, 1993; five series, 24 games.
N.L.—2—Reggie Smith, Los Angeles, 1977, 1978; two series, eight games.

Most consecutive errorless games, career

A.L.—25—Reggie Jackson, Oakland, New York, California, October 12, 1972 through October 10, 1982 (48 chances accepted).
N.L.—25—Andy Van Slyke, Pittsburgh, October 10, 1985 through October 14, 1992 (59 chances accepted).

Most errors, series

A.L.—3—Rickey Henderson, Oakland, 1992 (6-game series).
N.L.—1—Held by many outfielders.

Most chances accepted, errorless series

N.L.—23—Garry Maddox, Philadelphia, 1980 (5-game series).
A.L.—22—Dave Henderson, Oakland, 1989 (5-game series).

Most errors, game

A.L.—2
  Tony Oliva, Minnesota, October 6, 1969.
  Ben Oglivie, Milwaukee, October 10, 1982.
N.L.—1—Held by many outfielders.

Most errors, inning

A.L.-N.L.—1—Held by many outfielders.

Most double plays, career

N.L.—3—Bake McBride, Philadelphia, 1977, 1978, 1980; three series, 11 games.
A.L.—2—Rick Miller, California, 1979; one series, four games.

Most double plays, nine-inning game

A.L.-N.L.—1—Held by many outfielders.

Most double plays, extra-inning game

N.L.—2—Bake McBride, Philadelphia, October 11, 1980, 10 innings.

A.L.—1—Held by many outfielders.

Most double plays started, nine-inning game

A.L.-N.L.—1—Held by many outfielders.

Most double plays started, extra-inning game

N.L.—2—Bake McBride, Philadelphia, October 11, 1980, 10 innings.
A.L.—1—Held by may outfielders.

Most unassisted double plays, game

A.L.-N.L.—Never accomplished.

CATCHERS

GAMES

Most games caught, career

M.L.—27—Bob Boone, Philadelphia N.L., 1976, 1977, 1978, 1980; California A.L., 1982, 1986; six series.
N.L.—22—Johnny Bench, Cincinnati, 1970, 1972, 1973, 1975, 1976, 1979; six series.
A.L.—18—Pat Borders, Toronto, 1989, 1991, 1992, 1993; four series.

PUTOUTS, ASSISTS AND CHANCES ACCEPTED

Most putouts, career

M.L.—127
  Bob Boone, Philadelphia N.L., 1976, 1977, 1978, 1980; California A.L., 1982, 1986; six series, 27 games.
  Gary Carter, Montreal N.L., 1981; New York N.L., 1986, 1988; three series, 18 games.
N.L.—127—Gary Carter, Montreal, 1981; New York, 1986, 1988; three series, 18 games.
A.L.—118—Pat Borders, Toronto, 1989, 1991, 1992, 1993; four series, 18 games.

Most putouts, series

3-game series
  N.L.—29—Manny Sanguillen, Pittsburgh, 1975.
  A.L.—23—Rick Cerone, New York, 1981.
4-game series
  N.L.—34—Dick Dietz, San Francisco, 1971.
  A.L.—34—Rich Gedman, Boston, 1988.
5-game series
  N.L.—42—Jerry Grote, New York, 1973.
  A.L.—36—Ted Simmons, Milwaukee, 1982.
6-game series
  N.L.—59—Alan Ashby, Houston, 1986.
  A.L.—41—Pat Borders, Toronto, 1993.
7-game series
  N.L.—62—Greg Olson, Atlanta, 1991.
  A.L.—50—Ernie Whitt, Toronto, 1985.

Most putouts, nine-inning game

A.L.—15—Rick Dempsey, Baltimore, October 6, 1983.
N.L.—14
  Dick Dietz, San Francisco, October 3, 1971.
  Alan Ashby, Houston, October 8, 1986.

Most putouts, extra-inning game

N.L.—15
  Manny Sanguillen, Pittsburgh, October 7, 1975, 10 innings.
  Alan Ashby, Houston, October 14, 1986, 12 innings.
A.L.—Less than nine-inning record.

Fewest putouts, game

A.L.—1
  Ray Fosse, Oakland, October 11, 1973.
  Buck Martinez, Kansas City, October 13, 1976.
  Jim Sundberg, Kansas City, October 12, 1985.
  Terry Steinbach, Oakland, October 10, 1990.
N.L.—1—Terry Kennedy, San Diego, October 3, 1984.

Most putouts, inning

A.L.-N.L.—3—Held by many catchers.

Most assists, career

N.L.—18—Johnny Bench, Cincinnati, 1970, 1972, 1973,

1975, 1976, 1979; six series, 22 games.
A.L.—14—Thurman Munson, New York, 1976, 1977, 1978;
three series, 14 games.

Most assists, series
3-game series
A.L.—4—George Mitterwald, Minnesota, 1969.
Rick Cerone, New York, 1980.
N.L.—4—Johnny Bench, Cincinnati, 1975, 1976.
4-game series
A.L.—5—Rick Dempsey, Baltimore, 1983.
Rich Gedman, Boston, 1988.
N.L.—2—Held by many catchers.
5-game series
A.L.—6—Thurman Munson, New York, 1976.
N.L.—4—Terry Kennedy, San Diego, 1984.
6-game series
A.L.—7—Terry Steinbach, Oakland, 1992.
N.L.—5—Gary Carter, New York, 1986.
7-game series
N.L.—5—Tony Pena, St. Louis, 1987.
Don Slaught, Pittsburgh, 1991.
A.L.—4—Rich Gedman, Boston, 1986.

Most assists, game
N.L.—3
Johnny Bench, Cincinnati, October 3, 1970, 10 innings.
Johnny Bench, Cincinnati, October 5, 1975.
Gary Carter, New York, October 15, 1986, 16 innings.
A.L.—3
Rich Gedman, Boston, October 8, 1988.
Terry Steinbach, Oakland, October 10, 1992.
Pat Borders, Toronto, October 8, 1993.

Most assists, inning
N.L.—2
Johnny Bench, Cincinnati, October 7, 1973, eighth inning.
Mike Scioscia, Los Angeles, October 10, 1985, first inning.
Gary Carter, New York, October 15, 1986, 12th inning.
A.L.—2—Rich Gedman, Boston, October 8, 1988, first inning.

Most chances accepted, career
N.L.—143—Johnny Bench, Cincinnati, 1970, 1972, 1973,
1975, 1976, 1979; six series, 22 games.
A.L.—129—Pat Borders, Toronto, 1989, 1991, 1992, 1993;
four series, 18 games.

Most chances accepted, series
3-game series
N.L.—30—Manny Sanguillen, Pittsburgh, 1975.
A.L.—25—Rick Cerone, New York, 1981.
4-game series
A.L.—39—Rich Gedman, Boston, 1988.
N.L.—36—Dick Dietz, San Francisco, 1971.
5-game series
N.L.—43—Jerry Grote, New York, 1973.
A.L.—42—Pat Borders, Toronto, 1991.
6-game series
N.L.—60—Alan Ashby, Houston, 1986.
A.L.—45—Pat Borders, Toronto, 1993.
7-game series
N.L.—62—Greg Olson, Atlanta, 1991.
A.L.—53—Ernie Whitt, Toronto, 1985.

Most chances accepted, game
A.L.—16—Rick Dempsey, Baltimore, October 6, 1983 (15
putouts, 1 assist).
N.L.—15
Dick Dietz, San Francisco, October 3, 1971 (14 putouts, 1
assist).
Manny Sanguillen, Pittsburgh, October 7, 1975, 10 innings
(15 putouts, 1 error).
Alan Ashby, Houston, October 14, 1986, 12 innings (15
putouts).

Fewest chances offered, game
A.L.-N.L.—2—Held by many catchers.

Most chances accepted, inning
A.L.-N.L.—3—Held by many catchers.

ERRORS AND PASSED BALLS

Most errors, career
N.L.—5—Manny Sanguillen, Pittsburgh, 1970, 1971, 1972,
1974, 1975; five series, 19 games.
A.L.—3
Don Slaught, Kansas City, 1984; one series, three games.
Pat Borders, Toronto, 1989, 1991, 1992, 1993; four series,
18 games.

Most consecutive errorless games, career
M.L.—18
Darrell Porter, Kansas City A.L., October 5, 1977 through
October 10, 1980, 12 games; St. Louis N.L., October 7,
1982 through October 12, 1985, six games.
Gary Carter, Montreal, New York, October 13, 1981 through
October 12, 1988.
N.L.—18—Gary Carter, Montreal, New York, October 13,
1981 through October 12, 1988.
A.L.—15—Terry Steinbach, Oakland, October 5, 1988
through October 14, 1992.

Most errors, series
A.L.—3—Don Slaught, Kansas City, 1984 (3-game series).
N.L.—2—Manny Sanguillen, Pittsburgh, 1974 (4-game series).

Most chances accepted, errorless series
N.L.—63—Greg Olson, Atlanta, 1991 (7-game series).
A.L.—53—Ernie Whitt, Toronto, 1985 (7-game series).

Most errors, game
A.L.—2
Thurman Munson, New York, October 10, 1976.
Don Slaught, Kansas City, October 5, 1984.
N.L.—2—Manny Sanguillen, Pittsburgh, October 6, 1974.

Most errors, inning
A.L.-N.L.—1—Held by many catchers.

Most passed balls, career
M.L.—4
Manny Sanguillen, Pittsburgh N.L., 1970, 1971, 1972, 1974,
1975; five series, 19 games.
Bob Boone, Philadelphia N.L., 1976, 1977, 1978, 1980; Cali-
fornia A.L., 1982, 1986; six series, 27 games.
N.L.—4—Manny Sanguillen, Pittsburgh, 1970, 1971, 1972,
1974, 1975; five series, 19 games.
A.L.—3
Bob Boone, California, 1982, 1986; two series, 12 games.
Pat Borders, Toronto, 1989, 1991, 1992, 1993; four series,
18 games.

Most passed balls, series
A.L.—3—Pat Borders, Toronto, 1992 (6-game series).
N.L.—2
Manny Sanguillen, Pittsburgh, 1975 (3-game series).
Alan Ashby, Houston, 1986 (6-game series).
Don Slaught, Pittsburgh, 1992 (7-game series).
Darren Daulton, Philadelphia, 1993 (6-game series).

Most passed balls, game
N.L.—2
Manny Sanguillen, Pittsburgh, October 4, 1975.
Alan Ashby, Houston, October 11, 1986.
Don Slaught, Pittsburgh, October 13, 1992.
A.L.—2—Pat Borders, Toronto, October 14, 1992.

Most passed balls, inning
A.L.-N.L.—1—Held by many catchers.

DOUBLE PLAYS AND RUNNERS CAUGHT STEALING

Most double plays, career
A.L.—4—Ray Fosse, Oakland, 1973, 1974, 1975; three series, 10 games.
N.L.—3—Manny Sanguillen, Pittsburgh, 1970, 1971, 1972,
1974, 1975; five series, 19 games.

Most double plays, series
A.L.—2
George Mitterwald, Minnesota, 1970 (3-game series).

Ray Fosse, Oakland, 1973 (5-game series).
N.L.—1—Held by many catchers.

Most double plays started, series
A.L.—2—Ray Fosse, Oakland, 1973 (5-game series).
N.L.—1—Held by many catchers.

Most double plays, game
A.L.-N.L.—1—Held by many catchers.

Most double plays started, game
A.L.-N.L.—1—Held by many catchers.

Most unassisted double plays, game
A.L.-N.L.—Never accomplished.

Most runners caught stealing, career
A.L.—12—Thurman Munson, New York, 1976, 1977, 1978;
three series, 14 games.
N.L.—6—Mike Scioscia, Los Angeles, 1981, 1985, 1988;
three series, 18 games.

Most runners caught stealing, series
A.L.—5
Thurman Munson, New York, 1976 (5-game series).
Terry Steinbach, Oakland, 1992 (6-game series).
N.L.—4—Mike Scioscia, Los Angeles, 1985 (6-game series).

Most runners caught stealing, game
A.L.-N.L.—2—Held by many catchers.

Most runners caught stealing, inning
N.L.—2—Mike Scioscia, Los Angeles, October 10, 1985, first
inning.
A.L.—1—Held by many catchers.

PITCHERS

GAMES

Most games pitched, career
M.L.—15
Tug McGraw, New York N.L., 1969, 1973; Philadelphia N.L.,
1976, 1977, 1978, 1980; six series.
Dennis Eckersley, Chicago N.L., 1984; Oakland A.L., 1988,
1989, 1990, 1992; five series.
Rick Honeycutt, Los Angeles N.L., 1983, 1985; Oakland
A.L., 1988, 1989, 1990, 1992; six series.
N.L.—15—Tug McGraw, New York, 1969, 1973; Philadelphia,
1976, 1977, 1978, 1980; six series.
A.L.—14—Dennis Eckersley, Oakland, 1988, 1989, 1990,
1992; four series.

Most games pitched, series
3-game series
N.L.—3—Cecil Upshaw, Atlanta, 1969.
Dave Tomlin, Cincinnati, 1979.
Tom Hume, Cincinnati, 1979.
A.L.—3—Ron Perranoski, Minnesota, 1969.
Jim Todd, Oakland, 1975.
Willie Hernandez, Detroit, 1984.
4-game series
N.L.—4—Dave Giusti, Pittsburgh, 1971.
A.L.—4—Dennis Eckersley, Oakland, 1988.
5-game series
N.L.—5—Tug McGraw, Philadelphia, 1980.
A.L.—5—Jim Acker, Toronto, 1989.
6-game series
N.L.—5—Ken Dayley, St. Louis, 1985.
Kent Mercker, Atlanta, 1993.
A.L.—4—Held by many pitchers.
7-game series
N.L.—5—Mike Stanton, Atlanta, 1992.
A.L.—4—Held by many pitchers.

☐ PUTOUTS, ASSISTS AND CHANCES ACCEPTED ☐

Most putouts, career
N.L.—5
Don Gullett, Cincinnati, 1970, 1972, 1973, 1975, 1976; five

series, nine games.
Orel Hershiser, Los Angeles, 1985, 1988; two series, s ‹
games.
A.L.—4
Catfish Hunter, Oakland, 1971, 1972, 1973, 1974; New
York, 1976, 1978; six series, 10 games.
Jim Palmer, Baltimore, 1969, 1970, 1971, 1973, 1974, 1979;
six series, eight games.
Charlie Leibrandt, Kansas City, 1984, 1985; two series, four
games.
Jack Morris, Detroit, 1984, 1987; Minnesota, 1991; Toron-
to, 1992; four series, six games.

Most putouts, series
3-game series
N.L.—4—Don Gullett, Cincinnati, 1975.
A.L.—2—Rick Wise, Boston, 1975.
Milt Wilcox, Detroit, 1984.
4-game series
A.L.—3—Jim Hunter, Oakland, 1974.
N.L.—2—Juan Marichal, San Francisco, 1971.
Don Sutton, Los Angeles, 1974.
5-game series
A.L.—3—Tommy John, California, 1982.
N.L.—2—Tug McGraw, New York, 1973.
Dick Ruthven, Philadelphia, 1980.
6-game series
N.L.—3—Dwight Gooden, New York, 1986.
Roger McDowell, New York, 1986.
A.L.—2—Held by many pitchers.
7-game series
N.L.—4—Danny Cox, St. Louis, 1987.
A.L.—3—Charlie Leibrandt, Kansas City, 1985.

Most putouts, game
N.L.—4—Don Gullett, Cincinnati, October 4, 1975.
A.L.—3
Tommy John, California, October 5, 1982.
Charlie Leibrandt, Kansas City, October 12, 1985.

Most putouts, inning
A.L.—2
Mike Torrez, New York, October 7, 1977, second inning.
Charlie Leibrandt, Kansas City, October 12, 1985, fifth inning.
Mike Witt, California, October 12, 1986, first inning.
N.L.—2
Don Gullett, Cincinnati, October 4, 1975, third inning.
Roger McDowell, New York, October 15, 1986, 10th inning.

Most assists, career
A.L.—12—Mike Cuellar, Baltimore, 1969, 1970, 1971, 1973,
1974; five series, six games.
N.L.—6
Don Sutton, Los Angeles, 1974, 1977, 1978; three series,
four games.
Steve Carlton, Philadelphia, 1976, 1977, 1978, 1980, 1983;
five series, eight games.

Most assists, series
3-game series
A.L.—4—Dave Boswell, Minnesota, 1969.
Paul Lindblad, Oakland, 1975.
N.L.—3—Phil Niekro, Atlanta, 1969.
Dock Ellis, Pittsburgh, 1970.
Pat Zachry, Cincinnati, 1976.
4-game series
A.L.—5—Mike Cuellar, Baltimore, 1974.
N.L.—5—Steve Carlton, Philadelphia, 1983.
5-game series
N.L.—3—Steve Blass, Pittsburgh, 1972.
Tom Seaver, New York, 1973.
Nolan Ryan, Houston, 1980.
A.L.—3—Held by many pitchers.
6-game series
N.L.—6—Doug Drabek, Pittsburgh, 1990.
A.L.—4—Jack Morris, Toronto, 1992.
Juan Guzman, Toronto, 1993.
7-game series
A.L.—7—Charlie Leibrandt, Kansas City, 1985.
N.L.—5—Danny Cox, St. Louis, 1987.

Most assists, game

A.L.—5—Charlie Leibrandt, Kansas City, October 12, 1985.
N.L.—4—Juan Marichal, San Francisco, October 5, 1971.

Most assists, inning

N.L.—3—Pat Zachry, Cincinnati, October 10, 1976, fourth inning.
A.L.—2—Held by many pitchers.

Most chances accepted, career

A.L.—13
   Mike Cuellar, Baltimore, 1969, 1970, 1971, 1973, 1974; five series, six games.
   Charlie Leibrandt, Kansas City, 1984, 1985; two series, four games.
N.L.—10
   Orel Hershiser, Los Angeles, 1985, 1988; two series, six games.
   Doug Drabek, Pittsburgh, 1990, 1991; two series, four games.

Most chances accepted, series

3-game series
   N.L.—5—Don Gullett, Cincinnati, 1975.
   A.L.—5—Dave Boswell, Minnesota, 1969.
          Rick Wise, Boston, 1975.
          Paul Lindblad, Oakland, 1975.
4-game series
   N.L.—6—Juan Marichal, San Francisco, 1971.
          Steve Carlton, Philadelphia, 1983.
   A.L.—5—Catfish Hunter, Oakland, 1974.
          Mike Cuellar, Baltimore, 1974.
          Larry Gura, Kansas City, 1978.
5-game series
   N.L.—4—Steve Blass, Pittsburgh, 1972.
          Nolan Ryan, Houston, 1980.
   A.L.—5—Mike Flanagan, Toronto, 1989.
6-game series
   N.L.—7—Doug Drabek, Pittsburgh, 1990.
   A.L.—4—Jack Morris, Toronto, 1992.
          Juan Guzman, Toronto, 1993.
7-game series
   A.L.—10—Charlie Leibrandt, Kansas City, 1985.
   N.L.—9—Danny Cox, St. Louis, 1987.

Most chances accepted, game

A.L.—8—Charlie Leibrandt, Kansas City, October 12, 1985.
N.L.—6—Juan Marichal, San Francisco, October 5, 1971.

Most chances accepted, inning

N.L.—3—Pat Zachry, Cincinnati, October 10, 1976, fourth inning.
A.L.—2—Held by many pitchers.

ERRORS AND DOUBLE PLAYS

Most errors, career

N.L.—2—Joaquin Andujar, St. Louis, 1982, 1985; two series, four games.
A.L.—1—Held by many pitchers.

Most consecutive errorless games, career

M.L.—15—Dennis Eckersley, Chicago N.L., Oakland A.L., October 4, 1984 through October 11, 1992.
A.L.—14—Dennis Eckersley, Oakland, October 5, 1988 through October 11, 1992.
N.L.—13
   Dave Giusti, Pittsburgh, October 4, 1970 through October 7, 1975.
   Tug McGraw, New York, Philadelphia, October 10, 1973 through October 12, 1980.
   Ron Reed, Atlanta, Philadelphia, October 5, 1969 through October 8, 1983.

Most errors, series

N.L.—2—Joaquin Andujar, St. Louis, 1985.
A.L.—1—Held by many pitchers.

Most chances accepted, errorless series

A.L.—10—Charlie Leibrandt, Kansas City, 1985 (7-game series).
N.L.—9—Danny Cox, St. Louis, 1987 (7-game series).

Most errors, game

A.L.-N.L.—1—Held by many pitchers.

Most double plays, career

N.L.—2—Ricky Horton, St. Louis, 1985, 1987; Los Angeles, 1988; three series, eight games.
A.L.—2—Mike Flanagan, Baltimore, 1979, 1983; Toronto, 1989; three series, three games.

Most double plays started, career

N.L.—2—Ricky Horton, St. Louis, 1985, 1987; Los Angeles, 1988; three series, eight games.
A.L.—2—Mike Flanagan, Baltimore, 1979, 1983; Toronto, 1989; three series, three games.

Most unassisted double plays, game

A.L.-N.L.—Never accomplished.

CLUB FIELDING

AVERAGE

Highest fielding average, series
3-game series
A.L.—1.000—Baltimore vs. Minnesota, 1970.
Oakland vs. Baltimore, 1971.
N.L.—1.000—Pittsburgh vs. Cincinnati, 1979.
4-game series
A.L.—.993—New York vs. Kansas City, 1978.
Boston vs. Oakland, 1988.
Oakland vs. Boston, 1990.
N.L.—.993—Los Angeles vs. Philadelphia, 1983.
5-game series
N.L.—.994—San Diego vs. Chicago, 1984.
A.L.—.989—Baltimore vs. Oakland, 1973.
New York vs. Kansas City, 1977.
6-game series
N.L.—.996—New York vs. Houston, 1986.
A.L.—.991—Toronto vs. Chicago, 1993.
7-game series
N.L.—.992—Atlanta vs. Pittsburgh, 1992.
A.L.—.984—Toronto vs. Kansas City, 1985.

Highest fielding average by both clubs, series
3-game series
N.L.—.996—Pittsburgh 1.000, Cincinnati .992, 1979.
A.L.—.995—Oakland 1.000, Baltimore .991, 1971.
4-game series
A.L.—.986—Boston .993, Oakland .979, 1988.
N.L.—.979—Los Angeles .993, Philadelphia .966, 1983.
5-game series
N.L.—.989—San Diego .994, Chicago .983, 1984.
A.L.—.986—Toronto .988, Oakland .983, 1989.
6-game series
N.L.—.985—New York .996, Houston .973, 1986.
A.L.—.984—Toronto .991, Chicago .968, 1993.
7-game series
N.L.—.986—Atlanta .992, Pittsburgh .980, 1992.
A.L.—.981—Toronto .984, Kansas City .979, 1985.

Lowest fielding average, series
3-game series
A.L.—.940—Kansas City vs. Detroit, 1984.
N.L.—.950—Atlanta vs. New York, 1969.
4-game series
N.L.—.957—Los Angeles vs. Pittsburgh, 1974.
A.L.—.968—Boston vs. Oakland, 1990.
5-game series
A.L.—.956—Milwaukee vs. California, 1982.
N.L.—.973—Philadelphia vs. Houston, 1980.
San Francisco vs. Chicago, 1989.
6-game series
A.L.—.966—Toronto vs. Oakland, 1992.
N.L.—.968—Philadelphia vs. Atlanta, 1993.
7-game series
N.L.—.969—New York vs. Los Angeles, 1988.
A.L.—.971—California vs. Boston, 1986.

Lowest fielding average by both clubs, series
3-game series
A.L.—.958—Boston .966, Oakland .950, 1975.
N.L.—.965—New York .981, Atlanta .950, 1969.
4-game series
N.L.—.964—Pittsburgh .973, Los Angeles .957, 1974.
A.L.—.978—California .986, Baltimore .970, 1979.
5-game series
A.L.—.966—California .977, Milwaukee .956, 1982.
N.L.—.977—San Francisco .973, Chicago .982, 1989.
6-game series
A.L.—.967—Oakland .969, Toronto .966, 1992.
N.L.—.973—Atlanta .977, Philadelphia .968, 1993.
7-game series
A.L.—.973—Boston .975, California .971, 1986.
N.L.—.975—New York .969, Los Angeles .981, 1988.

PUTOUTS

Most putouts, total series
A.L.—1,119—Oakland (10 series, 42 games).
N.L.—1,117—Pittsburgh (nine series, 42 games).

Most putouts, series
3-game series
A.L.—96—Baltimore vs. Minnesota, 1969.
N.L.—90—Pittsburgh vs. Cincinnati, 1979.
4-game series
N.L.—111—Los Angeles vs. Philadelphia, 1978.
A.L.—111—Baltimore vs. Chicago, 1983.
5-game series
N.L.—148—Philadelphia vs. Houston, 1980.
A.L.—139—Detroit vs. Oakland, 1972.
6-game series
N.L.—189—New York vs. Houston, 1986.
A.L.—165—Toronto vs. Oakland, 1992.
7-game series
A.L.—196—Boston vs. California, 1986.
N.L.—195—Los Angeles vs. New York, 1988.

Most putouts by both clubs, series
3-game series
A.L.—190—Baltimore 96, Minnesota 94, 1969.
N.L.—177—Pittsburgh 90, Cincinnati 87, 1979.
4-game series
N.L.—221—Los Angeles 111, Philadelphia 110, 1978.
A.L.—219—Baltimore 111, Chicago 108, 1983.
5-game series
N.L.—295—Philadelphia 148, Houston 147, 1980.
A.L.—277—Detroit 139, Oakland 138, 1972.
6-game series
N.L.—377—New York 189, Houston 188, 1986.
A.L.—327—Toronto 165, Oakland 162, 1992.
7-game series
A.L.—388—Boston 196, California 192, 1986.
N.L.—387—Los Angeles 195, New York 192, 1988.

Fewest putouts, series
3-game series
A.L.—75—Oakland vs. Baltimore, 1971.
Oakland vs. Boston, 1975.
New York vs. Kansas City, 1980.
Oakland vs. New York, 1981.
N.L.—76—Atlanta vs. St. Louis, 1982.
4-game series
A.L.—102—Kansas City vs. New York, 1978.
Boston vs. Oakland, 1988, 1990.
N.L.—102—San Francisco vs. Pittsburgh, 1971.
Los Angeles vs. Philadelphia, 1983.
5-game series
A.L.—126—California vs. Milwaukee, 1982.
N.L.—126—Chicago vs. San Francisco, 1989.
6-game series
N.L.—154—Los Angeles vs. St. Louis, 1985.
A.L.—159—Chicago vs. Toronto, 1993.
7-game series
N.L.—180—San Francisco vs. St. Louis, 1987.
A.L.—186—Toronto vs. Kansas City, 1985.

Fewest putouts by both clubs, series
3-game series
A.L.—156—Baltimore 81, Oakland 75, 1971.
Boston 81, Oakland 75, 1975.
Kansas City 81, New York 75, 1980.
New York 81, Oakland 75, 1981.
N.L.—157—St. Louis 81, Atlanta 76, 1982.
4-game series
A.L.—207—New York 105, Kansas City 102, 1978.
N.L.—207—Pittsburgh 105, San Francisco 102, 1971.
Philadelphia 105, Los Angeles 102, 1983.

5-game series
A.L.—255—Milwaukee 129, California 126, 1982.
N.L.—256—Chicago 129, San Diego 127, 1984.
6-game series
N.L.—310—St. Louis 156, Los Angeles 154, 1985.
A.L.—321—Toronto 162, Chicago 159, 1993.
7-game series
N.L.—363—St. Louis 183, San Francisco 180, 1987.
A.L.—374—Kansas City 188, Toronto 186, 1985.

Most players with one or more putouts, nine-inning game
A.L.—11
 Oakland vs. New York, October 14, 1981.
 Toronto vs. Oakland, October 7, 1989.
N.L.— 10—Held by many clubs.

Most players with one or more putouts, extra-inning game
N.L.— 14—New York vs. Houston, October 15, 1986, 16 innings.
A.L.—11
 Kansas City vs. Detroit, October 3, 1984, 11 innings.
 California vs. Boston, October 12, 1986, 11 innings.
 Boston vs. California, October 12, 1986, 11 innings.

Most players with one or more putouts by both clubs, nine-inning game
N.L.—20—Cincinnati 10, Pittsburgh 10, October 8, 1972.
A.L.—20—Toronto 11, Oakland 9, October 7, 1989.

Most players with one or more putouts by both clubs, extra-inning game
N.L.—23—New York 14, Houston 9, October 15, 1986, 16 innings.
A.L.—22—Boston 11, California 11, October 12, 1986, 11 innings.

Most putouts by outfield, game
N.L.— 18—Pittsburgh vs. Cincinnati, October 7, 1972.
A.L.— 14
 Boston vs. Oakland, October 4, 1975.
 New York vs. Kansas City, October 13, 1976.

Most putouts by outfield of both clubs, game
A.L.—26—New York 14, Kansas City 12, October 13, 1976.
N.L.—25—Pittsburgh 18, Cincinnati 7, October 7, 1972.

Fewest putouts by outfield, nine-inning game
N.L.—1
 Atlanta vs. New York, October 4, 1969.
 Cincinnati vs. Pittsburgh, October 5, 1970.
 Montreal vs. Los Angeles, October 16, 1981.
A.L.—2
 Oakland vs. Boston, October 5, 1975 (fielded eight innings).
 Milwaukee vs. California, October 8, 1982.
 Baltimore vs. Chicago, October 5, 1983.
 Boston vs. Oakland, October 10, 1990 (fielded eight innings).

Fewest putouts by outfield, extra-inning game
N.L.—3—Cincinnati vs. Pittsburgh, October 3, 1970, 10 innings.
A.L.—4—Baltimore vs. Oakland, October 9, 1973, fielded 10 innings of 11-inning game.

Fewest putouts by outfield of both clubs, nine-inning game
N.L.—5—Pittsburgh 4, Cincinnati 1, October 5, 1970.
A.L.—7—Minnesota 4, Baltimore 3, October 3, 1970.

Fewest putouts by outfield of both clubs, extra-inning game
A.L.— 10—Baltimore 7, Chicago 3, October 8, 1983, 10 innings.
N.L.— 12
 Cincinnati 7, Pittsburgh 5, October 2, 1979, 11 innings.
 New York 6, Houston 6, October 15, 1986, 16 innings.

Most putouts by outfield, inning
A.L.-N.L.—3—Held by many clubs.

Most putouts by outfield of both clubs, inning
A.L.—6—Baltimore 3, Oakland 3, October 11, 1973, seventh inning.
N.L.—5
 New York 3, Atlanta 2, October 5, 1969, seventh inning.
 Pittsburgh 3, Cincinnati 2, October 7, 1972, third inning.
 Los Angeles 3, Philadelphia 2, October 7, 1978, third inning.

Most putouts by catchers of both clubs, inning
A.L.—5
 Baltimore 3, Oakland 2, October 6, 1973, first inning.

Oakland 3, Boston 2, October 4, 1975, second inning.
Chicago 3, Baltimore 2, October 6, 1983, first inning.
N.L.—5
 Atlanta 3, New York 2, October 5, 1969, third inning.
 Atlanta 3, New York 2, October 6, 1969, third inning.
 Los Angeles 3, Philadelphia 2, October 4, 1977, seventh inning.

ASSISTS

Most assists, total series
A.L.—410—Oakland (10 series, 42 games).
N.L.—407—Pittsburgh (nine series, 42 games).

Most assists, series
3-game series
A.L.—41—New York vs. Kansas City, 1980.
 N.L.—39—Cincinnati vs. Pittsburgh, 1970, 1979.
  Atlanta vs. St. Louis, 1982.
4-game series
A.L.—52—Baltimore vs. California, 1979.
N.L.—50—Los Angeles vs. Philadelphia, 1978.
5-game series
N.L.—71—Philadelphia vs. Houston, 1980.
A.L.—60—New York vs. Kansas City, 1976.
6-game series
N.L.—94—New York vs. Houston, 1986.
A.L.—60—Toronto vs. Oakland, 1992.
7-game series
A.L.—87—Kansas City vs. Toronto, 1985.
N.L.—77—San Francisco vs. St. Louis, 1987.

Most assists by both clubs, series
3-game series
N.L.—76—Cincinnati 39, Pittsburgh 37, 1970.
A.L.—73—Oakland 40, Boston 33, 1975.
4-game series
A.L.— 100—Chicago 51, Baltimore 49, 1983.
N.L.—96—Los Angeles 50, Philadelphia 46, 1978.
5-game series
A.L.— 111—New York 60, Kansas City 51, 1976.
N.L.— 123—Philadelphia 71, Houston 52, 1980.
6-game series
N.L.— 160—New York 94, Houston 66, 1986.
A.L.— 115—Toronto 60, Oakland 55, 1992.
7-game series
A.L.— 151—California 78, Boston 73, 1986.
N.L.— 144—San Francisco 77, St. Louis 67, 1987.

Fewest assists, series
3-game series
A.L.— 15—Oakland vs. Baltimore, 1971.
N.L.—20—Pittsburgh vs. Cincinnati, 1975.
4-game series
A.L.—30—Oakland vs. Boston, 1988.
N.L.—32-Pittsburgh vs. San Francisco, 1971.
5-game series
N.L.—38—Pittsburgh vs. Cincinnati, 1972.
A.L.—40—Toronto vs. Oakland, 1989.
6-game series
N.L.—45—Cincinnati vs. Pittsburgh, 1980.
A.L.—55—Oakland vs. Toronto, 1992.
7-game series
A.L.—61—Toronto vs. Kansas City, 1985.
N.L.—61—Los Angeles vs. New York, 1988.

Fewest assists by both clubs, series
3-game series
A.L.—46—Baltimore 31, Oakland 15, 1971.
N.L.—51—Cincinnati 31, Pittsburgh 20, 1975.
4-game series
A.L.—64—Boston 34, Oakland 30, 1988.
N.L.—69—San Francisco 37, Pittsburgh 32, 1971.
5-game series
A.L.—85—Oakland 45, Toronto 40, 1989.
N.L.—89—San Francisco 49, Chicago 40, 1989.
6-game series
N.L.— 101—Atlanta 54, Philadelphia 47, 1993.
A.L.— 113—Toronto 57, Chicago 56, 1993.

7-game series
N.L.— 123—New York 62, Los Angeles 61, 1988.
A.L.— 148—Kansas City 87, Toronto 61, 1985.

Most assists, nine-inning game
N.L.—21—Los Angeles vs. Philadelphia, October 5, 1978.
A.L.— 18—Boston vs. Oakland, October 7, 1975.

Most assists, extra-inning game
N.L.—31—New York vs. Houston, October 15, 1986, 16 innings.
A.L.— 18—Toronto vs. Oakland, October 11, 1992, 11 innings.

Most assists by both clubs, nine-inning game
A.L.—33—Boston 18, Oakland 15, October 7, 1975.
N.L.—30—Los Angeles 21, Philadelphia 9, October 5, 1978.

Most assists by both clubs, extra-inning game
N.L.—56—New York 31, Houston 25, October 15, 1986, 16 innings.
A.L.—Less than nine-inning record.

Most players with one or more assists, nine-inning game
N.L.—9
Los Angeles vs. Montreal, October 14, 1981.
Atlanta vs. Pittsburgh, October 13, 1992.
A.L.—9—Oakland vs. New York, October 14, 1981.

Most players with one or more assists, extra-inning game
N.L.— 10—New York vs. Houston, October 15, 1986, 16 innings.
A.L.—Less than nine-inning record.

Most players with one or more assists by both clubs, nine-inning game
N.L.— 13
New York 7, Atlanta 6, October 4, 1969.
Pittsburgh 7, Cincinnati 6, October 9, 1972.
Cincinnati 8, New York 5, October 10, 1973.
Los Angeles 9, Montreal 4, October 14, 1981.
Atlanta 7, St. Louis 6, October 9, 1982.
San Francisco 7, St. Louis 6, October 14, 1987.
A.L.— 15—Oakland 9, New York 6, October 14, 1981.

Most players with one or more assists by both clubs, extra-inning game
N.L.— 19—New York 10, Houston 9, October 15, 1986, 16 innings.
A.L.—Less than nine-inning record.

Fewest assists, game
A.L.—2—Boston vs. Oakland, October 4, 1975.
N.L.—2
Pittsburgh vs. Cincinnati, October 7, 1972.
Pittsburgh vs. Cincinnati, October 7, 1975, 10 innings.

Fewest assists by both clubs, game
N.L.— 10
Cincinnati 8, Pittsburgh 2, October 7, 1975, 10 innings.
Los Angeles 5, Philadelphia 5, October 7, 1983.
San Diego 5, Chicago 5, October 2, 1984.
New York 6, Los Angeles 4, October 10, 1988.
San Francisco 5, Chicago 5, October 5, 1989.
Pittsburgh 7, Atlanta 3, October 12, 1991.
A.L.— 10—Toronto 6, Oakland 4, October 3, 1989.

Most assists by outfield, nine-inning game
N.L.—2
Pittsburgh vs. Cincinnati, October 9, 1972.
Cincinnati vs. New York, October 10, 1973.
Philadelphia vs. Los Angeles, October 7, 1977.
Cincinnati vs. Pittsburgh, October 9, 1990.
A.L.—2
Minnesota vs. Baltimore, October 4, 1970.
Boston vs. Oakland, October 5, 1975.
Baltimore vs. California, October 5, 1979.

Most assists by outfield, extra-inning game
N.L.—3—Philadelphia vs. Houston, October 11, 1980, 10 innings.
A.L.—Less than nine-inning record.

Most assists by outfield of both clubs, nine-inning game
N.L.—3—Pittsburgh 2, Cincinnati 1, October 9, 1972.
A.L.—3
Minnesota 2, Baltimore 1, October 4, 1970.
Boston 2, Oakland 1, October 5, 1975.

Baltimore 2, California 1, October 5, 1979.

Most assists by outfield of both clubs, extra-inning game
N.L.—4—Philadelphia 3, Houston 1, October 11, 1980, 10 innings.
A.L.—Less than nine-inning record.

Most assists by outfield, inning
N.L.—2—Cincinnati vs. New York, October 10, 1973, fifth inning.
A.L.— 1—Held by many clubs.

CHANCES OFFERED

Fewest chances offered to outfield, nine-inning game
N.L.— 1
Cincinnati vs. Pittsburgh, October 5, 1970.
Montreal vs. Los Angeles, October 16, 1981.
A.L.—2
Kansas City vs. New York, October 7, 1978.
Milwaukee vs. California, October 8, 1982.

Fewest chances offered to outfield, extra-inning game
N.L.—3—Cincinnati vs. Pittsburgh, October 3, 1970, 10 innings.
A.L.—4—Baltimore vs. Oakland, October 9, 1973, fielded 10 innings of 11-inning game.

Fewest chances offered to outfields of both clubs, nine-inning game
N.L.—5—Pittsburgh 4, Cincinnati 1, October 5, 1970.
A.L.—7—Minnesota 4, Baltimore 3, October 3, 1970.

Fewest chances offered to outfields of both clubs, extra-inning game
A.L.— 10—Baltimore 7, Chicago 3, October 8, 1983, 10 innings.
N.L.— 12—Cincinnati 7, Pittsburgh 5, October 2, 1979, 11 innings.

ERRORS

Most errors, total series
A.L.—33—Oakland (10 series, 42 games).
N.L.—31—Pittsburgh (nine series, 42 games).

Most errors, series
3-game series
A.L.—7—Kansas City vs. Detroit, 1984.
N.L.—6—Atlanta vs. New York, 1969.
4-game series
N.L.—7—Los Angeles vs. Pittsburgh, 1974.
A.L.—5—Baltimore vs. California, 1979.
Boston vs. Oakland, 1990.
5-game series
A.L.—8—Milwaukee vs. California, 1982.
N.L.—6—Philadelphia vs. Houston, 1980.
6-game series
A.L.—8—Toronto vs. Oakland, 1992.
N.L.—7—Houston vs. New York, 1986.
Philadelphia vs. Atlanta, 1993.
7-game series
A.L.—8—California vs. Boston, 1986.
N.L.—8—New York vs. Los Angeles, 1988.

Most errors by both clubs, series
3-game series
A.L.— 10—Oakland 6, Boston 4, 1975.
N.L.—8—Atlanta 6, New York 2, 1969.
4-game series
N.L.— 11—Los Angeles 7, Pittsburgh 4, 1974.
A.L.—7—Baltimore 5, California 2, 1979.
5-game series
A.L.— 12—Milwaukee 8, California 4, 1982.
N.L.—9—Philadelphia 6, Houston 3, 1980.
6-game series
A.L.— 15—Toronto 8, Oakland 7, 1992.
N.L.— 12—Philadelphia 7, Atlanta 5, 1993.
7-game series
A.L.— 15—California 8, Boston 7, 1986.
N.L.— 13—New York 8, Los Angeles 5, 1988.

Fewest errors, series

3-game series
 A.L.—0—Baltimore vs. Minnesota, 1970.
  Oakland vs. Baltimore, 1971.
 N.L.—0—Pittsburgh vs. Cincinnati, 1970.
4-game series
 A.L.—1—New York vs. Kansas City, 1978.
  Boston vs. Oakland, 1988.
  Oakland vs. Boston, 1990.
 N.L.—1—Los Angeles vs. Philadelphia, 1983.
5-game series
 N.L.—1—San Diego vs. Chicago, 1984.
 A.L.—2—Baltimore vs. Oakland, 1973.
  New York vs. Kansas City, 1977.
  Toronto vs. Oakland, 1989.
6-game series
 N.L.—1—New York vs. Houston, 1986.
 A.L.—2—Toronto vs. Chicago, 1993.
7-game series
 N.L.—3—St. Louis vs. San Francisco, 1987.
 A.L.—4—Toronto vs. Kansas City, 1985.

Fewest errors by both clubs, series

3-game series
 A.L.—1—Baltimore 1, Oakland 0, 1971.
 N.L.—1—Cincinnati 1, Pittsburgh 0, 1979.
4-game series
 A.L.—4—Oakland 3, Boston 1, 1988.
 N.L.—6—Philadelphia 5, Los Angeles 1, 1983.
5-game series
 N.L.—4—Chicago 3, San Diego 1, 1984.
 A.L.—5—Oakland 3, Toronto 2, 1989.
6-game series
 N.L.—7—Pittsburgh 5, Cincinnati 2, 1990.
 A.L.—9—Chicago 7, Toronto 2, 1993.
7-game series
 N.L.—9—San Francisco 6, St. Louis 3, 1987.
 A.L.—10—Kansas City 6, Toronto 4, 1985.

Most errors, game

A.L.—5—New York vs. Kansas City, October 10, 1976.
N.L.—5—Los Angeles vs. Pittsburgh, October 8, 1974.

Most errors by both clubs, game

A.L.—7—Oakland 4, Boston 3, October 4, 1975.
N.L.—5—Los Angeles 5, Pittsburgh 0, October 8, 1974.

Most errors by infield, game

A.L.—3
 Oakland vs. Baltimore, October 9, 1973, 11 innings.
 California vs. Boston, October 8, 1986.
N.L.—2—Held by many clubs.

Most errors by infields of both clubs, game

A.L.—5—California 3, Boston 2, October 8, 1986.
N.L.—3
 Atlanta 2, New York 1, October 5, 1969.
 Pittsburgh 2, Cincinnati 1, October 10, 1972.
 New York 2, Los Angeles 1, October 9, 1988, 12 innings.

Most errors by outfield, game

A.L.—2
 Minnesota vs. Baltimore, October 6, 1969.
 Oakland vs. Boston, October 4, 1975.
 Milwaukee vs. California, October 10, 1982.
N.L.—1—Held by many clubs.

Most errors by outfields of both clubs, game

A.L.—3—Oakland 2, Boston 1, October 4, 1975.
N.L.—1—Made in many games.

Longest errorless game

N.L.—16 innings—New York vs. Houston, October 15, 1986.
A.L.—11 innings
 Baltimore vs. Minnesota, October 5, 1969.
 Baltimore vs. Oakland, October 9, 1973, fielded 10 innings
  of 11-inning game.
 California vs. Boston, October 12, 1986.
 Boston vs. California, October 12, 1986.

Longest errorless game by both clubs

N.L.—11 innings—Pittsburgh vs. Cincinnati, October 2, 1979.
A.L.—11 innings—California vs. Boston, October 12, 1986.

Most errors, inning

A.L.—3
 Oakland vs. Boston, October 4, 1975, first inning.
 California vs. Boston, October 8, 1986, seventh inning.
N.L.—2—Held by many clubs.

PASSED BALLS

Most passed balls, total series

N.L.—6—Pittsburgh (nine series, 42 games).
A.L.—4
 Oakland (10 series, 42 games).
 Toronto (four series, 23 games).

Most passed balls, series

A.L.—3—Toronto vs. Oakland, 1992 (6-game series).
N.L.—2
 Pittsburgh vs. Cincinnati, 1975 (3-game series).
 Houston vs. New York, 1986 (6-game series).
 Chicago vs. San Francisco, 1989 (5-game series).
 Pittsburgh vs. Atlanta, 1992 (7-game series).
 Philadelphia vs. Atlanta, 1993 (6-game series).

Most passed balls by both clubs, series

N.L.—3
 Chicago 2, San Francisco 1, 1989 (5-game series).
 Pittsburgh 2, Atlanta 1, 1992 (7-game series).
A.L.—3—Toronto 3, Oakland 0, 1992 (6-game series).

Most passed balls, game

N.L.—2
 Pittsburgh vs. Cincinnati, October 4, 1975.
 Houston vs. New York, October 11, 1986.
 Pittsburgh vs. Atlanta, October 13, 1992.
A.L.—2—Toronto vs. Oakland, October 14, 1992.

Most passed balls, inning

A.L.-N.L.—1—Held by many clubs.

DOUBLE AND TRIPLE PLAYS

Most double plays, total series

A.L.—39—Oakland (10 series, 42 games).
N.L.—35—Los Angeles (seven series, 34 games).

Most double plays, series

3-game series
 A.L.—6—New York vs. Oakland, 1981.
 N.L.—4—Atlanta vs. New York, 1969.
4-game series
 N.L.—8—Los Angeles vs. Pittsburgh, 1974.
 A.L.—7—California vs. Baltimore, 1979.
5-game series
 N.L.—8—Montreal vs. Los Angeles, 1981.
 A.L.—5—Held by many clubs.
6-game series
 A.L.—7—Toronto vs. Oakland, 1992.
  Toronto vs. Chicago, 1993.
 N.L.—6—New York vs. Houston, 1986.
7-game series
 N.L.—10—San Francisco vs. St. Louis, 1987.
 A.L.—7—Kansas City vs. Toronto, 1985.
  California vs. Boston, 1986.

Most double plays by both clubs, series

3-game series
 A.L.—8—Minnesota 5, Baltimore 3, 1970.
 N.L.—6—Atlanta 4, New York 2, 1969.
  Cincinnati 3, Philadelphia 3, 1976.
4-game series
 A.L.—12—California 7, Baltimore 5, 1979.
 N.L.—10—Los Angeles 8, Pittsburgh 2, 1974.

5-game series
N.L.—13—Montreal 8, Los Angeles 5, 1981.
A.L.—9—Oakland 5, Detroit 4, 1972.
Toronto 5, Oakland 4, 1989.
6-game series
A.L.—12—Toronto 7, Oakland 5, 1992.
Toronto 7, Chicago 5, 1993.
N.L.—9—New York 6, Houston 3, 1986.
7-game series
N.L.—15—San Francisco 10, St. Louis 5, 1987.
A.L.—12—California 7, Boston 5, 1986.

Fewest double plays, series

3-game series
N.L.—0—Atlanta vs. St. Louis, 1982.
A.L.—0—Detroit vs. Kansas City, 1984.
4-game series
N.L.—0—Philadelphia vs. Los Angeles, 1983.
A.L.—2—New York vs. Kansas City, 1978.
Boston vs. Oakland, 1988.
5-game series
A.L.—1—Detroit vs. Minnesota, 1987.
N.L.—1—Chicago vs. San Francisco, 1989.
6-game series
N.L.—1—Atlanta vs. Philadelphia, 1993.
A.L.—5—Oakland vs. Toronto, 1992.
Chicago vs. Toronto, 1993.
7-game series
N.L.—2—New York vs. Los Angeles, 1988.
A.L.—4—Toronto vs. Kansas City, 1985.

Fewest double plays by both clubs, series

3-game series
A.L.—2—Kansas City 2, Detroit 0, 1984.

N.L.—3—St. Louis 3, Atlanta 0, 1982.
4-game series
N.L.—3—Los Angeles 3, Philadelphia 0, 1983.
A.L.—6—Kansas City 4, New York 2, 1978.
5-game series
A.L.—4—Kansas City 2, New York 2, 1977.
Minnesota 3, Detroit 1, 1987.
N.L.—6—Cincinnati 3, Pittsburgh 3, 1972.
Cincinnati 3, New York 3, 1973.
6-game series
N.L.—3—Philadelphia 2, Atlanta 1, 1993.
A.L.—12—Toronto 7, Oakland 5, 1992.
Toronto 7, Chicago 5, 1993.
7-game series
N.L.—9—Atlanta 6, Pittsburgh 3, 1991.
Pittsburgh 6, Atlanta 3, 1992.
A.L.—10—Boston 5, California 5, 1986.

Most double plays, game

A.L.—4—Oakland vs. Boston, October 5, 1975.
N.L.—4
Los Angeles vs. Montreal, October 13, 1981.
San Francisco vs. St. Louis, October 10, 1987.

Most double plays by both clubs, game

A.L.—6—Oakland 4, Boston 2, October 5, 1975.
N.L.—5
Pittsburgh 3, Cincinnati 2, October 5, 1975.
Philadelphia 3, Houston 2, October 11, 1980, 10 innings.

Most triple plays, series

A.L.-N.L.—Never accomplished.

MISCELLANEOUS

CLUB AND DIVISION

ONE-RUN DECISIONS

Most one-run games won, series
N.L.—3—New York vs. Houston, 1986 (6-game series).
A.L.—2—Held by many clubs.

Most one-run games by both clubs, series
3-game series
  A.L.—2—Baltimore (won two) vs. Minnesota, 1969.
  N.L.—1—Occurred often.
4-game series
  A.L.-N.L.—2—Occurred often.
5-game series
  A.L.—3—Oakland (won two) vs. Detroit (won one), 1972.
  N.L.—2—Occurred often.
6-game series
  N.L.—4—New York (won three) vs. Houston (won one), 1986.
      Pittsburgh (won two) vs. Cincinnati (won two), 1990.
  A.L.—2—Oakland (won one) vs. Toronto (won one), 1992.
7-game series
  N.L.—4—Pittsburgh (won two) vs. Atlanta (won two), 1991.
  A.L.—2—Toronto (won one) vs. Kansas City (won one), 1985.
      California (won one) vs. Boston (won one), 1986.

LENGTH OF GAMES
BY INNINGS

Longest game
N.L.—16 innings—New York 7, Houston 6, October 15, 1986 (at Houston).
A.L.—12 innings—Baltimore 4, Minnesota 3, October 4, 1969 (at Baltimore).

Most extra-inning games, total series
N.L.—6—Houston (two series, 11 games; won two, lost four).
A.L.—5—Baltimore (seven series, 26 games; won four, lost one).

Most extra-inning games won, total series
A.L.—4—Baltimore (seven series, 26 games; lost one).
N.L.—4—Philadelphia (six series, 26 games; lost none).

Most extra-inning games lost, total series
N.L.—4—Houston (four series, 11 games; won two).
A.L.—2
  Minnesota (two series, six games; won none).
  Kansas City (six series, 27 games; won none).
  California (three series, 16 games; won one).
  Oakland (10 series, 42 games; won two).

Most extra-inning games by both clubs, series
3-game series
  A.L.—2—Baltimore vs. Minnesota, 1969.
  N.L.—2—Cincinnati vs. Pittsburgh, 1979.
4-game series
  N.L.-A.L.—1—Occurred often.
5-game series
  N.L.—4—Philadelphia vs. Houston, 1980.
  A.L.—2—Detroit vs. Oakland, 1972.
6-game series
  N.L.—2—New York vs. Houston, 1986.
      Philadelphia vs. Atlanta, 1993.
  A.L.—1—Toronto vs. Oakland, 1992.
7-game series
  A.L.—2—Boston vs. California, 1986.
  N.L.—1—Occurred often.

BY TIME

Longest nine-inning game
N.L.—3 hours, 44 minutes—New York 8, Los Angeles 4, October 8, 1988 (at New York).

A.L.—3 hours, 40 minutes—Toronto 7, Oakland 5, October 10, 1992 (at Oakland).

Longest extra-inning game
N.L.—4 hours, 42 minutes—New York 7, Houston 6, October 15, 1986, 16 innings (at Houston).
A.L.—4 hours, 25 minutes—Toronto 7, Oakland 6, October 11, 1992, 11 innings (at Oakland).

Shortest game
A.L.—1 hour, 57 minutes—Oakland 1, Baltimore 0, October 8, 1974 (at Baltimore).
N.L.—1 hour, 57 minutes—Pittsburgh 5, Cincinnati 1, October 7, 1972 (at Pittsburgh).

SERIES STARTING AND FINISHING DATES

Earliest date for series game
N.L.—October 2, 1971—Pittsburgh at San Francisco.
    October 2, 1979—Pittsburgh at Cincinnati, 11 innings.
    October 2, 1984—San Diego at Chicago.
A.L.—October 2, 1984—Detroit at Kansas City.

Earliest date for series final game
N.L.—October 5, 1970—Pittsburgh at Cincinnati (3-game series).
    October 5, 1979—Cincinnati at Pittsburgh (3-game series).
A.L.—October 5, 1970—Minnesota at Baltimore (3-game series).
    October 5, 1971—Baltimore at Oakland (3-game series).
    October 5, 1984—Kansas City at Detroit (3-game series).

Latest date for series start
N.L.—October 13, 1981—Los Angeles at Montreal.
A.L.—October 13, 1981—Oakland at New York.

Latest date for series finish
N.L.—October 19, 1981—Los Angeles at Montreal (5-game series).
A.L.—October 16, 1985—Kansas City at Toronto (7-game series).

SERIES AND GAMES WON

Most series won
A.L.—6—Oakland, 1972, 1973, 1974, 1988, 1989, 1990 (lost four).
N.L.—5
  Los Angeles, 1974, 1977, 1978, 1981, 1988 (lost two).
  Cincinnati, 1970, 1972, 1975, 1976, 1990 (lost two).

Most consecutive years winning series
A.L.—3
  Baltimore, 1969, 1970, 1971.
  Oakland, 1972, 1973, 1974.
  New York, 1976, 1977, 1978.
  Oakland, 1988, 1989, 1990.
N.L.—2
  Cincinnati, 1975, 1976.
  Los Angeles, 1977, 1978.
  Atlanta, 1991, 1992.

Most consecutive series won, division
N.L.—5
  West Division, 1974, 1975, 1976, 1977, 1978.
  West Division, 1988, 1989, 1990, 1991, 1992.
A.L.—5
  East Division, 1975, 1976, 1977, 1978, 1979.
  West Division, 1987, 1988, 1989, 1990, 1991.

Most times winning series in four consecutive games
A.L.—2—Oakland, 1988, 1990.
N.L.—Never occurred.

Most times winning series in three consecutive games
A.L.—3—Baltimore, 1969, 1970, 1971.
N.L.—3—Cincinnati, 1970, 1975, 1976.

Winning series after winning first game
A.L.—Accomplished 17 times.
N.L.—Accomplished 15 times.

Winning series after losing first game
N.L.—Accomplished 10 times.
A.L.—Accomplished eight times.

Winning series after winning one game and losing two
N.L.—Cincinnati vs. Pittsburgh, 1972 (5-game series).
   Philadelphia vs. Houston, 1980 (5-game series).
   Los Angeles vs. Montreal, 1981 (5-game series).
   San Diego vs. Chicago, 1984 (5-game series).
   St. Louis vs. Los Angeles, 1985 (6-game series).
   Los Angeles vs. New York, 1988 (7-game series).
   Philadelphia vs. Atlanta, 1993 (6-game series).
A.L.—New York vs. Kansas City, 1977 (5-game series).
   Milwaukee vs. California, 1982 (5-game series).
   Kansas City vs. Toronto, 1985 (7-game series).
   Boston vs. California, 1986 (7-game series).

Winning series after winning one game and losing three
A.L.—Kansas City vs. Toronto, 1985.
   Boston vs. California, 1986.
N.L.—Never accomplished.

Winning series after losing first two games
A.L.—Milwaukee vs. California, 1982 (5-game series).
   Kansas City vs. Toronto, 1985 (7-game series).
N.L.—San Diego vs. Chicago, 1984 (5-game series).
   St. Louis vs. Los Angeles, 1985 (6-game series).

Most games won, total series
A.L.—23—Oakland (10 series; won 23, lost 19).
N.L.—19—Los Angeles (seven series; won 19, lost 15).

Most consecutive games won, total series
A.L.—10—Baltimore, 1969 (3), 1970 (3), 1971 (3), 1973 (first 1).
N.L.—6—Cincinnati, 1975 (3), 1976 (3).

Most consecutive games won, division
A.L.—9—East Division, 1969 (3), 1970 (3), 1971 (3).
N.L.—7—West Division, 1974 (last 1), 1975 (3), 1976 (3).

SERIES AND GAMES LOST

Most series lost
N.L.—7—Pittsburgh, 1970, 1972, 1974, 1975, 1990, 1991, 1992 (won two).
A.L.—4
   Kansas City, 1976, 1977, 1978, 1984 (won two).
   Oakland, 1971, 1975, 1981, 1992 (won six).

Most consecutive years losing series
A.L.—3—Kansas City, 1976, 1977, 1978.
N.L.—3
   Philadelphia, 1976, 1977, 1978.
   Pittsburgh, 1990, 1991, 1992.

Most games lost, total series
N.L.—25—Pittsburgh (nine series; won 17, lost 25).
A.L.—19—Oakland (10 series; won 23, lost 19).

Most consecutive games lost, total series
A.L.—8—Boston, 1988 (4), 1990 (4).
N.L.—7—Atlanta, 1969 (3), 1982 (3), 1991 (1).

ATTENDANCE

Largest attendance, series
3-game series
   N.L.—180,338—Cincinnati vs. Philadelphia, 1976.
   A.L.—151,539—Oakland vs. New York, 1981.
4-game series
   N.L.—240,584—Philadelphia vs. Los Angeles, 1977.
   A.L.—195,748—Baltimore vs. Chicago, 1983.
5-game series
   A.L.—284,691—California vs. Milwaukee, 1982.
   N.L.—264,950—Philadelphia vs. Houston, 1980.

6-game series
   N.L.—343,046—Philadelphia vs. Atlanta, 1993.
   A.L.—293,086—Toronto vs. Oakland, 1992.
7-game series
   N.L.—396,597—St. Louis vs. San Francisco, 1987.
   A.L.—324,430—Boston vs. California, 1986.

Smallest attendance, series
3-game series
   A.L.—81,945—Baltimore vs. Minnesota, 1970.
   N.L.—112,943—Pittsburgh vs. Cincinnati, 1970.
4-game series
   A.L.—144,615—Baltimore vs. Oakland, 1974.
   N.L.—157,348—San Francisco vs. Pittsburgh, 1971.
5-game series
   A.L.—175,833—Baltimore vs. Oakland, 1973.
   N.L.—234,814—Pittsburgh vs. Cincinnati, 1972.
6-game series
   A.L.—292,921—Toronto vs. Chicago, 1993.
   N.L.—299,316—New York vs. Houston, 1986.
7-game series
   A.L.—264,167—Kansas City vs. Toronto, 1985.
   N.L.—369,443—Atlanta vs. Pittsburgh, 1991.

Largest attendance, game
N.L.—64,924—At Philadelphia, October 8, 1977 (Los Angeles 4, Philadelphia 1).
A.L.—64,406—At California, October 5, 1982 (California 8, Milwaukee 3).

Smallest attendance, game
A.L.—24,265—At Oakland, October 11, 1973 (Oakland 3, Baltimore 0).
N.L.—33,088—At Pittsburgh, October 3, 1970 (Cincinnati 3, Pittsburgh 0).

Largest attendance by each club, game

AMERICAN LEAGUE

Club	Attendance		
Baltimore	52,787	(Oct.	3, 1979)
Boston	35,578	(Oct.	4, 1975)
		(Oct.	5, 1975)
California	64,406	(Oct.	5, 1982)
Chicago	46,635	(Oct.	7, 1983)
Detroit	52,168	(Oct.	5, 1984)
Kansas City	42,633	(Oct.	9, 1980)
Milwaukee	54,968	(Oct.	10, 1982)
Minnesota	55,245	(Oct.	8, 1987)
New York	56,821	(Oct.	14, 1976)
Oakland	49,444	(Oct.	4, 1989)
Toronto	51,889	(Oct.	9, 1993)

NATIONAL LEAGUE

Club	Attendance		
Atlanta	52,173	(Oct.	10, 1982)
Chicago	39,195	(Oct.	4, 1989)
		(Oct.	5, 1989)
Cincinnati	56,079	(Oct.	12, 1990)
Houston	45,718	(Oct.	15, 1986)
Los Angeles	55,973	(Oct.	5, 1977)
Montreal	54,499	(Oct.	17, 1981)
New York	55,052	(Oct.	11, 1986)
Philadelphia	65,476	(Oct.	8, 1980)
Pittsburgh	57,533	(Oct.	10, 1991)
St. Louis	55,331	(Oct.	6, 1987)
		(Oct.	7, 1987)
		(Oct.	13, 1987)
		(Oct.	14, 1987)
San Diego	58,359	(Oct.	7, 1984)
San Francisco	62,084	(Oct.	9, 1989)

Smallest attendance by each club, game

AMERICAN LEAGUE

Club	Attendance		
Baltimore	27,608	(Oct.	5, 1970)
Boston	32,786	(Oct.	8, 1986)
California	43,199	(Oct.	5, 1979)

Club	Attendance	
		(Oct. 6, 1979)
Chicago	45,477	(Oct. 8, 1983)
Detroit	37,615	(Oct. 11, 1972)
Kansas City	40,046	(Oct. 13, 1985)
Milwaukee	50,135	(Oct. 8, 1982)
Minnesota	26,847	(Oct. 3, 1970)
New York	48,497	(Oct. 14, 1981)
Oakland	24,265	(Oct. 11, 1973)
Toronto	32,084	(Oct. 16, 1985)

NATIONAL LEAGUE

Club	Attendance	
Atlanta	50,122	(Oct. 4, 1969)
Chicago	36,282	(Oct. 2, 1984)
		(Oct. 3, 1984)
Cincinnati	39,447	(Oct. 10, 1972)
Houston	44,131	(Oct. 8, 1986)
Los Angeles	49,963	(Oct. 4, 1983)
Montreal	36,491	(Oct. 19, 1981)
New York	44,672	(Oct. 8, 1988)
Philadelphia	53,490	(Oct. 7, 1983)
Pittsburgh	33,088	(Oct. 3, 1970)
St. Louis	53,008	(Oct. 7, 1982)
San Diego	58,346	(Oct. 4, 1984)
San Francisco	40,977	(Oct. 2, 1971)

NON-PLAYING PERSONNEL

MANAGERS

Most series by manager

M.L.—7—Sparky Anderson, Cincinnati N.L.; Detroit A.L. (won five, lost two).

A.L.—6—Earl Weaver, Baltimore, 1969, 1970, 1971, 1973, 1974, 1979 (won four, lost two).

N.L.—6—Tom Lasorda, Los Angeles, 1977, 1978, 1981, 1983, 1985, 1988 (won four, lost two).

Most championship series winners managed

M.L.—5—Sparky Anderson, Cincinnati N.L., 1970, 1972, 1975, 1976; Detroit A.L., 1984.

N.L.—4

Sparky Anderson, Cincinnati, 1970, 1972, 1975, 1976.

Tom Lasorda, Los Angeles, 1977, 1978, 1981, 1988.

A.L.—4—Earl Weaver, Baltimore, 1969, 1970, 1971, 1979.

Most championship series losers managed

A.L.—3

Whitey Herzog, Kansas City, 1976, 1977, 1978.

Billy Martin, Minnesota, 1969; Detroit, 1972; Oakland, 1981.

N.L.—3

Danny Murtaugh, Pittsburgh, 1970, 1974, 1975.

Danny Ozark, Philadelphia, 1976, 1977, 1978.

Jim Leyland, Pittsburgh, 1990, 1991, 1992.

Most different clubs managed, league

A.L.—4—Billy Martin, Minnesota 1970, Detroit 1972, New York 1976, 1977, Oakland 1981.

N.L.—2—Bill Virdon, Pittsburgh 1972, Houston 1980.

UMPIRES

Most series umpired

N.L.—9—Doug Harvey (38 games).

A.L.—6

Larry Barnett (31 games).

Don Denkinger (27 games).

Jim Evans (28 games).

Most games umpired

N.L.—41—Bruce Froemming (eight series).

A.L.—31—Larry Barnett (six series).

GENERAL REFERENCE

YEAR BY YEAR

AMERICAN LEAGUE

Year	Winner	Loser	Games
1969	Baltimore (East)	Minnesota (West)	3-0
1970	Baltimore (East)	Minnesota (West)	3-0
1971	Baltimore (East)	Oakland (West)	3-0
1972	Oakland (West)	Detroit (East)	3-2
1973	Oakland (West)	Baltimore (East)	3-2
1974	Oakland (West)	Baltimore (East)	3-1
1975	Boston (East)	Oakland (West)	3-0
1976	New York (East)	Kansas City (West)	3-2
1977	New York (East)	Kansas City (West)	3-2
1978	New York (East)	Kansas City (West)	3-1
1979	Baltimore (East)	California (West)	3-1
1980	Kansas City (West)	New York (East)	3-0
1981	New York (East)	Oakland (West)	3-0
1982	Milwaukee (East)	California (West)	3-2
1983	Baltimore (East)	Chicago (West)	3-1
1984	Detroit (East)	Kansas City (West)	3-0
1985	Kansas City (West)	Toronto (East)	4-3
1986	Boston (East)	California (West)	4-3
1987	Minnesota (West)	Detroit (East)	4-1
1988	Oakland (West)	Boston (East)	4-0
1989	Oakland (West)	Toronto (East)	4-1
1990	Oakland (West)	Boston (East)	4-0
1991	Minnesota (West)	Toronto (East)	4-1
1992	Toronto (East)	Oakland (West)	4-2
1993	Toronto (East)	Chicago (West)	4-2
1994	No series played.		

NATIONAL LEAGUE

Year	Winner	Loser	Games
1969	New York (East)	Atlanta (West)	3-0
1970	Cincinnati (West)	Pittsburgh (East)	3-0
1971	Pittsburgh (East)	San Francisco (West)	3-1
1972	Cincinnati (West)	Pittsburgh (East)	3-2
1973	New York (East)	Cincinnati (West)	3-2
1974	Los Angeles (West)	Pittsburgh (East)	3-1
1975	Cincinnati (West)	Pittsburgh (East)	3-0
1976	Cincinnati (West)	Philadelphia (East)	3-0
1977	Los Angeles (West)	Philadelphia (East)	3-1
1978	Los Angeles (West)	Philadelphia (East)	3-1
1979	Pittsburgh (East)	Cincinnati (West)	3-0
1980	Philadelphia (East)	Houston (West)	3-2
1981	Los Angeles (West)	Montreal (East)	3-2
1982	St. Louis (East)	Atlanta (West)	3-0
1983	Philadelphia (East)	Los Angeles (West)	3-1
1984	San Diego (West)	Chicago (East)	3-2
1985	St. Louis (East)	Los Angeles (West)	4-2
1986	New York (East)	Houston (West)	4-2
1987	St. Louis (East)	San Francisco (West)	4-3
1988	Los Angeles (West)	New York (East)	4-3
1989	San Francisco (West)	Chicago (East)	4-1
1990	Cincinnati (West)	Pittsburgh (East)	4-2
1991	Atlanta (West)	Pittsburgh (East)	4-3
1992	Atlanta (West)	Pittsburgh (East)	4-3
1993	Philadelphia (East)	Atlanta (West)	4-2
1994	No series played.		

SERIES WON AND LOST BY TEAMS

AMERICAN LEAGUE—EAST DIVISION

	W	L	Pct.
Milwaukee	1	0	1.000
New York	4	1	.800
Baltimore	5	2	.714
Boston	2	2	.500

	W	L	Pct.
Toronto	2	3	.400
Detroit	1	2	.333
Totals	15	10	.600

AMERICAN LEAGUE—WEST DIVISION

	W	L	Pct.
Oakland	6	4	.600
Minnesota	2	2	.500
Kansas City	2	4	.333
Chicago	0	2	.000
California	0	3	.000
Totals	10	15	.400

NATIONAL LEAGUE—EAST DIVISION

	W	L	Pct.
St. Louis	3	0	1.000
New York	3	1	.750
Philadelphia	3	3	.500
Pittsburgh	2	7	.222
Montreal	0	1	.000
Chicago	0	2	.000
Totals	11	14	.440

NATIONAL LEAGUE—WEST DIVISION

	W	L	Pct.
San Diego	1	0	1.000
Los Angeles	5	2	.714
Cincinnati	5	2	.714
Atlanta	2	3	.400
San Francisco	1	2	.333
Houston	0	2	.000
Totals	14	11	.550

GAMES WON AND LOST BY TEAMS

AMERICAN LEAGUE—EAST DIVISION

	W	L	Pct.
Baltimore	18	8	.692
New York	12	8	.600
Milwaukee	3	2	.600
Detroit	6	7	.462
Toronto	13	16	.448
Boston	7	11	.389
Totals	59	52	.532

AMERICAN LEAGUE—WEST DIVISION

	W	L	Pct.
Oakland	23	19	.548
Minnesota	8	8	.500
Kansas City	12	15	.444
California	6	10	.375
Chicago	3	7	.300
Totals	52	59	.468

NATIONAL LEAGUE—EAST DIVISION

	W	L	Pct.
St. Louis	11	5	.688
New York	13	8	.619
Philadelphia	12	14	.462
Pittsburgh	17	25	.405
Montreal	2	3	.400
Chicago	3	7	.300
Totals	58	62	.483

NATIONAL LEAGUE—WEST DIVISION

	W	L	Pct.
Cincinnati	18	10	.643
San Diego	3	2	.600
Los Angeles	19	15	.559
San Francisco	8	8	.500
Atlanta	10	16	.385
Houston	4	7	.364
Totals	62	58	.517

HOME AND ROAD GAMES BY TEAMS

AMERICAN LEAGUE—EAST DIVISION

	Years	Game	Home	Away
Toronto	5	29	16	13
Baltimore	7	26	13	13
New York	5	20	10	10
Boston	4	18	10	8
Detroit	3	13	7	6
Milwaukee	1	5	3	2
Totals	25	111	59	52

AMERICAN LEAGUE—WEST DIVISION

	Years	Game	Home	Away
Oakland	10	42	19	23
Kansas City	6	27	14	13
Minnesota	4	16	7	9
California	3	16	7	9
Chicago	2	10	5	5
Totals	25	111	52	59

NATIONAL LEAGUE—EAST DIVISION

	Years	Game	Home	Away
Pittsburgh	9	42	20	22
Philadelphia	6	26	13	13
New York	4	21	10	11
St. Louis	3	16	9	7
Chicago	2	10	4	6
Montreal	1	5	3	2
Totals	25	120	59	61

NATIONAL LEAGUE—WEST DIVISION

	Years	Game	Home	Away
Los Angeles	7	34	17	17
Cincinnati	7	28	14	14
Atlanta	5	26	13	13
San Francisco	3	16	8	8
Houston	2	11	6	5
San Diego	1	5	3	2
Totals	25	120	61	59

SHUTOUTS

AMERICAN LEAGUE

Oct. 5, 1969—Dave McNally, Baltimore 1, Minnesota 0, 11 innings (three hits).

Oct. 8, 1972—Blue Moon Odom, Oakland 5, Detroit 0 (three hits).

Oct. 10, 1972—Joe Coleman, Detroit 3, Oakland 0 (seven hits).

Oct. 6, 1973—Jim Palmer, Baltimore 6, Oakland 0 (five hits).

Oct. 11, 1973—Catfish Hunter, Oakland 3, Baltimore 0 (five hits).

Oct. 6, 1974—Ken Holtzman, Oakland 5, Baltimore 0 (five hits).

Oct. 8, 1974—Vida Blue, Oakland 1, Baltimore 0 (two hits).

Oct. 6, 1979—Scott McGregor, Baltimore 8, California 0 (six hits).

Oct. 15, 1981—Dave Righetti, Ron Davis and Rich Gossage, New York 4, Oakland 0 (five hits).

Oct. 6, 1983—Mike Boddicker, Baltimore 4, Chicago 0 (five hits).

Oct. 8, 1983—Storm Davis and Tippy Martinez, Baltimore 3, Chicago 0, 10 innings (10 hits).

Oct. 5, 1984—Milt Wilcox and Willie Hernandez, Detroit 1, Kansas City 0 (three hits).

Oct. 13, 1985—Danny Jackson, Kansas City 2, Toronto 0 (eight hits).

Total number of shutouts: (13)

NATIONAL LEAGUE

Oct. 3, 1970—Gary Nolan and Clay Carroll, Cincinnati 3, Pittsburgh 0, 10 innings (eight hits).

Oct. 7, 1973—Jon Matlack, New York 5, Cincinnati 0 (two hits).

Oct. 5, 1974—Don Sutton, Los Angeles 3, Pittsburgh 0 (four hits).

Oct. 8, 1974—Bruce Kison and Ramon Hernandez, Pittsburgh 7, Los Angeles 0 (four hits).

Oct. 4, 1978—Tommy John, Los Angeles 4, Philadelphia 0 (four hits).

Oct. 10, 1980—Joe Niekro and Dave Smith, Houston 1, Philadelphia 0, 11 innings (seven hits).

Oct. 14, 1981—Ray Burris, Montreal 3, Los Angeles 0 (five hits).

Oct. 7, 1982—Bob Forsch, St. Louis 7, Atlanta 0 (three hits).

Oct. 4, 1983—Steve Carlton and Al Holland, Philadelphia 1, Los Angeles 0 (seven hits).

Oct. 2, 1984—Rick Sutcliffe and Warren Brusstar, Chicago 13, San Diego 0 (six hits).

Oct. 8, 1986—Mike Scott, Houston 1, New York 0 (five hits).

Oct. 7, 1987—Dave Dravecky, San Francisco 5, St. Louis 0 (two hits).

Oct. 13, 1987—John Tudor, Todd Worrell and Ken Dayley, St. Louis 1, San Francisco 0 (six hits).

Oct. 14, 1987—Danny Cox, St. Louis 6, San Francisco 0 (eight hits).

Oct. 12, 1988—Orel Hershiser, Los Angeles 6, New York 0 (five hits).

Oct. 10, 1991—Steve Avery and Alejandro Pena, Atlanta 1, Pittsburgh 0 (six hits).

Oct. 14, 1991—Zane Smith and Roger Mason, Pittsburgh 1, Atlanta 0 (nine hits).

Oct. 16, 1991—Steve Avery and Alejandro Pena, Atlanta 1, Pittsburgh 0 (four hits).

Oct. 17, 1991—John Smoltz, Atlanta 4, Pittsburgh 0 (six hits).

Total number of shutouts: (19)

EXTRA-INNING GAMES

AMERICAN LEAGUE

Oct. 4, 1969— 12 innings, Baltimore 4, Minnesota 3.

Oct. 5, 1969— 11 innings, Baltimore 1, Minnesota 0.

Oct. 7, 1972— 11 innings, Oakland 3, Detroit 2.

Oct. 11, 1972— 10 innings, Detroit 4, Oakland 3.

Oct. 9, 1973— 11 innings, Oakland 2, Baltimore 1.

Oct. 3, 1979— 10 innings, Baltimore 6, California 2.

Oct. 8, 1983— 10 innings, Baltimore 3, Chicago 0.

Oct. 3, 1984— 11 innings, Detroit 5, Kansas City 3.

Oct. 9, 1985— 10 innings, Toronto 6, Kansas City 5.

Oct. 11, 1986— 11 innings, California 4, Boston 3.

Oct. 12, 1986— 11 innings, Boston 7, California 6.

Oct. 11, 1991— 10 innings, Minnesota 3, Toronto 2.

Oct. 11, 1992— 11 innings, Toronto 7, Oakland 6.

Total number of extra-inning games: (13)

NATIONAL LEAGUE

Oct. 3, 1970— 10 innings, Cincinnati 3, Pittsburgh 0.

Oct. 9, 1973— 12 innings, Cincinnati 2, New York 1.

Oct. 7, 1975— 10 innings, Cincinnati 5, Pittsburgh 3.

Oct. 7, 1978— 10 innings, Los Angeles 4, Philadelphia 3.

Oct. 2, 1979— 11 innings, Pittsburgh 5, Cincinnati 2.

Oct. 3, 1979— 10 innings, Pittsburgh 3, Cincinnati 2.

Oct. 8, 1980—10 innings, Houston 7, Philadelphia 4.
Oct. 10, 1980—11 innings, Houston 1, Philadelphia 0.
Oct. 11, 1980—10 innings, Philadelphia 5, Houston 3.
Oct. 12, 1980—10 innings, Philadelphia 8, Houston 7.
Oct. 14, 1986—12 innings, New York 2, Houston 1.
Oct. 15, 1986—16 innings, New York 7, Houston 6.
Oct. 9, 1988—12 innings, Los Angeles 5, New York 4.
Oct. 13, 1991—10 innings, Pittsburgh 3, Atlanta 2.
Oct. 6, 1993—10 innings, Philadelphia 4, Atlanta 3.
Oct. 11, 1993—10 innings, Philadelphia 4, Atlanta 3.

Total number of extra-inning games: (16)

ATTENDANCE

AMERICAN LEAGUE

Year	Games	Total	Year	Games	Total
1969	3	113,763	1982	5	284,691
1970	3	81,945	1983	4	195,748
1971	3	110,800	1984	3	136,160
1972	5	189,671	1985	7	264,167
1973	5	175,833	1986	7	324,430
1974	4	144,615	1987	5	257,631
1975	3	120,514	1988	4	167,376
1976	5	252,152	1989	5	249,247
1977	5	234,713	1990	4	168,340
1978	4	194,192	1991	5	263,987
1979	4	191,293	1992	6	293,086
1980	3	141,819	1993	6	292,921
1981	3	151,539			

NATIONAL LEAGUE

Year	Games	Total	Year	Games	Total
1969	3	153,587	1982	3	158,589
1970	3	112,943	1983	4	223,914
1971	4	157,348	1984	5	247,623
1972	5	234,814	1985	6	326,824
1973	5	262,548	1986	6	299,316
1974	4	200,262	1987	7	396,597
1975	3	155,740	1988	7	373,695
1976	3	180,338	1989	5	264,617
1977	4	240,584	1990	6	310,528
1978	4	234,269	1991	7	369,443
1979	3	152,246	1992	7	374,599
1980	5	264,950	1993	6	343,046
1981	5	250,098			

INDIVIDUAL BATTING

LEADING BATTERS

**(Playing in all games, each series,
with four or more hits)**

AMERICAN LEAGUE

Year	Player, Club	AB	H	TB	Avg.
1969—Brooks Robinson, Baltimore		14	7	8	.500
1970—Brooks Robinson, Baltimore		12	7	9	.583
1971—Brooks Robinson, Baltimore		11	4	8	.364
—Sal Bando, Oakland		11	4	9	.364
1972—Matty Alou, Oakland		21	8	12	.381
1973—Bert Campaneris, Oakland		21	7	14	.333
1974—Ray Fosse, Oakland		12	4	8	.333
1975—Sal Bando, Oakland		12	6	8	.500
1976—Chris Chambliss, New York		21	11	20	.524
1977—Hal McRae, Kansas City		18	8	14	.444
1978—Reggie Jackson, New York		13	6	13	.462
1979—Eddie Murray, Baltimore		12	5	8	.417
1980—Frank White, Kansas City		11	6	10	.545
1981—Graig Nettles, New York		12	6	11	.500
—Jerry Mumphrey, New York		12	6	7	.611
1982—Fred Lynn, California		18	11	16	.611
1983—Cal Ripken Jr., Baltimore		15	6	8	.400
1984—Kirk Gibson, Detroit		12	5	9	.417
1985—Cliff Johnson, Toronto		19	7	9	.368
1986—Bob Boone, California		22	10	13	.455

Year	Player, Club	AB	H	TB	Avg.
1987—Tom Brunansky, Minnesota		17	7	17	.412
1988—Ron Hassey, Oakland		8	4	8	.500
1989—Rickey Henderson, Oakland		15	6	15	.400
1990—Wade Boggs, Boston		16	7	11	.438
—Carney Lansford, Oakland		16	7	8	.438
1991—Roberto Alomar, Toronto		19	9	9	.474
1992—Harold Baines, Oakland		25	11	16	.440
1993—Tim Raines, Chicago		27	12	14	.444
—Devon White, Toronto		27	12	18	.444
1994—No series played.					

NATIONAL LEAGUE

Year	Player, Club	AB	H	TB	Avg.
1969—Art Shamsky, New York		13	7	7	.538
1970—Willie Stargell, Pittsburgh		12	6	7	.500
1971—Bob Robertson, Pittsburgh		16	7	20	.438
1972—Pete Rose, Cincinnati		20	9	13	.450
1973—Pete Rose, Cincinnati		21	8	15	.381
1974—Willie Stargell, Pittsburgh		15	6	12	.400
1975—Richie Zisk, Pittsburgh		10	5	6	.500
1976—Jay Johnstone, Philadelphia		9	7	10	.778
1977—Bob Boone, Philadelphia		10	4	4	.400
1978—Dusty Baker, Los Angeles		15	7	9	.467
1979—Willie Stargell, Pittsburgh		11	5	13	.455
1980—Terry Puhl, Houston		19	10	12	.526
1981—Gary Carter, Montreal		16	7	87	.438
1982—Darrell Porter, St. Louis		9	5	8	.556
—Ozzie Smith, St. Louis		9	5	5	.556
1983—Mike Schmidt, Philadelphia		15	7	12	.467
1984—Steve Garvey, San Diego		20	8	12	.400
1985—Ozzie Smith, St. Louis		23	10	16	.435
1986—Lenny Dykstra, New York		23	7	13	.304
1987—Jeffrey Leonard, San Francisco		24	10	22	.417
1988—Lenny Dykstra, New York		14	6	12	.439
1989—Will Clark, San Francisco		20	13	24	.650
1990—Mariano Duncan, Cincinnati		20	6	9	.300
1991—Jay Bell, Pittsburgh		29	12	17	.414
1992—Mark Lemke, Atlanta		21	7	8	.333
1993—Fred McGriff, Atlanta		23	10	15	.435
1994—No series played.					

HOME RUNS

AMERICAN LEAGUE

1969—4—Baltimore (East), Frank Robinson (1), Mark Belanger (1), Boog Powell (1), Paul Blair (1).
1—Minnesota (West), Tony Oliva (1).
1970—6—Baltimore (East), Dave Johnson (2), Mike Cuellar (1), Don Buford (1), Boog Powell (1), Frank Robinson (1).
3—Minnesota (West), Harmon Killebrew (2), Tony Oliva (1).
1971—4—Baltimore (East), Boog Powell (2), Brooks Robinson (1), Elrod Hendricks (1).
3—Oakland (West), Reggie Jackson (2), Sal Bando (1).
1972—4—Detroit (East), Norm Cash (1), Al Kaline (1), Bill Freehan (1), Dick McAuliffe (1).
1—Oakland (West), Mike Epstein (1).
1973—5—Oakland (West), Sal Bando (2), Bert Campaneris (2), Joe Rudi (1).
3—Baltimore (East), Earl Williams (1), Andy Etchebarren (1), Bobby Grich (1).
1974—3—Baltimore (East), Paul Blair (1), Brooks Robinson (1), Bobby Grich (1).
3—Oakland (West), Sal Bando (2), Ray Fosse (1).
1975—2—Boston (East), Carl Yastrzemski (1), Rico Petrocelli (1).
1—Oakland (West), Reggie Jackson (1).
1976—4—New York (East), Graig Nettles (2), Chris Chambliss (2).
2—Kansas City (West), John Mayberry (1), George Brett (1).
1977—3—Kansas City (West), Hal McRae (1), John Mayberry (1), Al Cowens (1).

2—New York (East), Thurman Munson (1), Cliff Johnson (1).
1978—5—New York (East), Reggie Jackson (2), Thurman Munson (1), Graig Nettles (1), Roy White (1).
4—Kansas City (West), George Brett (3), Fred Patek (1).
1979—3—Baltimore (East), John Lowenstein (1), Eddie Murray (1), Pat Kelly (1).
3—California (West), Dan Ford (2), Don Baylor (1).
1980—3—New York (East), Rick Cerone (1), Lou Piniella (1), Graig Nettles (1).
3—Kansas City (West), George Brett (2), Frank White (1).
1981—3—New York (East), Lou Piniella (1), Graig Nettles (1), Willie Randolph (1).
0—Oakland (West).
1982—5—Milwaukee (East), Paul Molitor (2), Gorman Thomas (1), Mark Brouhard (1), Ben Oglivie (1).
4—California (West), Fred Lynn (1), Reggie Jackson (1), Bob Boone (1), Don Baylor (1).
1983—3—Baltimore (East), Gary Roenicke (1), Eddie Murray (1), Tito Landrum (1).
0—Chicago (West).
1984—4—Detroit (East), Kirk Gibson (1), Larry Herndon (1), Lance Parrish (1), Alan Trammell (1).
0—Kansas City (West).
1985—7—Kansas City (West), George Brett (3), Pat Sheridan (2), Willie Wilson (1), Jim Sundberg (1).
2—Toronto (East), Jesse Barfield (1), Rance Mulliniks (1).
1986—7—California (West), Bob Boone (1), Doug DeCinces (1), Brian Downing (1), Bobby Grich (1), Wally Joyner (1), Gary Pettis (1), Dick Schofield (1).
6—Boston (East), Jim Rice (2), Don Baylor (1), Dwight Evans (1), Rich Gedman (1), Dave Henderson (1).
1987—8—Minnesota (West), Tom Brunansky (2), Gary Gaetti (2), Greg Gagne (2), Kent Hrbek (1), Kirby Puckett (1).
7—Detroit (East), Chet Lemon (2), Kirk Gibson (1), Mike Heath (1), Matt Nokes (1), Pat Sheridan (1), Lou Whitaker (1).
1988—7—Oakland (West), Jose Canseco (3), Ron Hassey (1), Dave Henderson (1), Carney Lansford (1), Mark McGwire (1).
2—Boston (East), Rich Gedman (1), Mike Greenwell (1).
1989—7—Oakland (West), Rickey Henderson (2), Dave Parker (2), Jose Canseco (1), Dave Henderson (1), Mark McGwire (1).
3—Toronto (East), George Bell (1), Lloyd Moseby (1), Ernie Whitt (1).
1990—1—Boston (East), Wade Boggs (1).
0—Oakland (West).
1991—3—Minnesota (West), Kirby Puckett (2), Mike Pagliarulo (1).
1—Toronto (East), Joe Carter (1).
1992—10—Toronto (East), Roberto Alomar (2), Candy Maldonado (2), Dave Winfield (2), Pat Borders (1), Joe Carter (1), Kelly Gruber (1), John Olerud (1).
4—Oakland (West), Harold Baines (1), Mark McGwire (1), Ruben Sierra (1), Terry Steinbach (1).
1993—5—Chicago (West), Ellis Burks (1), Lance Johnson (1), Warren Newson (1), Frank Thomas (1), Robin Ventura (1).
2—Toronto (East), Paul Molitor (1), Devon White (1).
1994—No series played.
Total number of home runs: (176)

NATIONAL LEAGUE

1969—6—New York (East), Tommie Agee (2), Ken Boswell (2), Cleon Jones (1), Wayne Garrett (1).

5—Atlanta (West), Hank Aaron (3), Tony Gonzalez (1), Orlando Cepeda (1).
1970—3—Cincinnati (West), Bobby Tolan (1), Tony Perez (1), Johnny Bench (1).
0—Pittsburgh (East).
1971—8—Pittsburgh (East), Bob Robertson (4), Richie Hebner (2), Gene Clines (1), Al Oliver (1).
5—San Francisco (West), Willie McCovey (2), Tito Fuentes (1), Willie Mays (1), Chris Speier (1).
1972—4—Cincinnati (West), Joe Morgan (2), Cesar Geronimo (1), Johnny Bench (1).
3—Pittsburgh (East), Al Oliver (1), Manny Sanguillen (1), Roberto Clemente (1).
1973—5—Cincinnati (West), Pete Rose (2), Johnny Bench (1), Denis Menke (1), Tony Perez (1).
3—New York (East), Rusty Staub (3).
1974—3—Los Angeles (West), Steve Garvey (2), Ron Cey (1).
3—Pittsburgh (East), Willie Stargell (2), Richie Hebner (1).
1975—4—Cincinnati (West), Don Gullett (1), Tony Perez (1), Dave Concepcion (1), Pete Rose (1).
1—Pittsburgh (East), Al Oliver (1).
1976—3—Cincinnati (West), George Foster (2), Johnny Bench (1).
1—Philadelphia (East), Greg Luzinski (1).
1977—3—Los Angeles (West), Dusty Baker (2), Ron Cey (1).
2—Philadelphia (East), Greg Luzinski (1), Bake McBride (1).
1978—8—Los Angeles (West), Steve Garvey (4), Dave Lopes (2), Steve Yeager (1), Ron Cey (1).
5—Philadelphia (East), Greg Luzinski (1), Jerry Martin (1), Steve Carlton (1), Bake McBride (1).
1979—4—Pittsburgh (East), Willie Stargell (2), Phil Garner (1), Bill Madlock (1).
2—Cincinnati (West), George Foster (1), Johnny Bench (1).
1980—1—Philadelphia (East), Greg Luzinski (1).
0—Houston (West).
1981—4—Los Angeles (West), Pedro Guerrero (1), Mike Scioscia (1), Steve Garvey (1), Rick Monday (1).
1—Montreal (East), Jerry White (1).
1982—1—St. Louis (East), Willie McGee (1).
0—Atlanta (West).
1983—5—Philadelphia (East), Gary Matthews (3), Mike Schmidt (1), Sixto Lezcano (1).
2—Los Angeles (West), Mike A. Marshall (1), Dusty Baker (1).
1984—9—Chicago (East), Jody Davis (2), Leon Durham (2), Gary Matthews (2), Ron Cey (1), Bob Dernier (1), Rick Sutcliffe (1).
2—San Diego (West), Steve Garvey (1), Kevin McReynolds (1).
1985—5—Los Angeles (West), Bill Madlock (3), Greg Brock (1), Mike A. Marshall (1).
3—St. Louis (East), Tom Herr (1), Ozzie Smith (1), Jack Clark (1).
1986—5—Houston (West), Alan Ashby (1), Glenn Davis (1), Bill Doran (1), Billy Hatcher (1), Dickie Thon (1).
3—New York (East), Darryl Strawberry (2), Lenny Dykstra (1).
1987—9—San Francisco (West), Jeffrey Leonard (4), Bob Brenly (1), Will Clark (1), Kevin Mitchell (1), Harry Spilman (1), Robby Thompson (1).
2—St. Louis (East), Jim Lindeman (1), Jose Oquendo (1).
1988—5—New York (East), Kevin McReynolds (2), Lenny Dykstra (1), Keith Hernandez (1), Darryl Strawberry (1).
3—Los Angeles (West), Kirk Gibson (2), Mike Scioscia (1).
1989—8—San Francisco (West), Will Clark (2), Kevin Mitchell (2), Robby Thompson (2), Matt Williams (2).
3—Chicago (East), Mark Grace (1), Luis Salazar

(1), Ryne Sandberg (1).

1990—4—Cincinnati (West), Mariano Duncan (1), Billy Hatcher (1), Paul O'Neill (1), Chris Sabo (1).
    3—Pittsburgh (East), Jay Bell (1), Sid Bream (1), Jose Lind (1).

1991—5—Atlanta (West), Sid Bream (1), Ron Gant (1), Brian Hunter (1), David Justice (1), Greg Olson (1).
    3—Pittsburgh (East), Jay Bell (1), Orlando Merced (1), Andy Van Slyke (1).

1992—6—Atlanta (West), Ron Gant (2), David Justice (2), Jeff Blauser (1), Sid Bream (1).
    5—Pittsburgh (East), Jay Bell (1), Barry Bonds (1), Jose Lind (1), Lloyd McClendon (1), Don Slaught (1).

1993—7—Philadelphia (East), Lenny Dykstra (2), Dave Hollins (2), Darren Daulton (1), Pete Incaviglia (1), John Kruk (1).
    5—Atlanta (West), Jeff Blauser (2), Damon Berryhill (1), Fred McGriff (1), Terry Pendleton (1).

1994—No series played.

Total number of home runs: (190)

PLAYERS WITH FOUR HOME RUNS
BOTH LEAGUES

Player	Series	No.
Kirk Gibson	3	4

Total number of players: (1)

AMERICAN LEAGUE

Player	Series	No.
George Brett	6	9
Reggie Jackson	11	6
Sal Bando	5	5
Graig Nettles	6	5
Jose Canseco	3	4
Boog Powell	5	4

Total number of players: (6)

NATIONAL LEAGUE

Player	Series	No.
Steve Garvey	5	8
Gary Matthews	2	5
Greg Luzinski	5	5
Johnny Bench	6	5
Jeffrey Leonard	2	4
Bill Madlock	2	4
Lenny Dykstra	3	4
Bob Robertson	5	4
Ron Cey	5	4
Willie Stargell	6	4

Total number of players: (10)

.450 HITTERS
(Playing in all games and having nine or more at-bats)

AMERICAN LEAGUE

Player, Club	Year	AB	H	TB	Avg.
Fred Lynn, California	1982	18	11	16	.611
Brooks Robinson, Baltimore	1970	12	7	9	.583
Frank White, Kansas City	1980	11	6	10	.545
Chris Chambliss, New York	1976	21	11	20	.524
Brooks Robinson, Baltimore	1969	14	7	8	.500
Tony Oliva, Minnesota	1970	12	6	11	.500
Sal Bando, Oakland	1975	12	6	8	.500
Bob Watson, New York	1980	12	6	11	.500
Graig Nettles, New York	1981	12	6	11	.500
Jerry Mumphrey, New York	1981	12	6	7	.500
Roberto Alomar, Toronto	1991	19	9	9	.474
Reggie Jackson, New York	1978	13	6	13	.462
Larry Milbourne, New York	1981	13	6	6	.462
Charlie Moore, Milwaukee	1982	13	6	6	.462

Player, Club	Year	AB	H	TB	Avg.
Carl Yastrzemski, Boston	1975	11	5	9	.455
Mickey Rivers, New York	1978	11	5	5	.455
Bob Boone, California	1986	22	10	13	.455

Total number of occurrences: (17)

NATIONAL LEAGUE

Player, Club	Year	AB	H	TB	Avg.
Jay Johnstone, Philadelphia	1976	9	7	7	.778
Will Clark, San Francisco	1989	20	13	24	.650
Mark Grace, Chicago	1989	17	11	19	.647
Darrell Porter, St. Louis	1982	9	5	8	.556
Ozzie Smith, St. Louis	1982	9	5	5	.556
Art Shamsky, New York	1969	13	7	7	.538
Terry Puhl, Houston	1980	19	10	12	.526
Willie Stargell, Pittsburgh	1970	12	6	7	.500
Richie Zisk, Pittsburgh	1975	10	5	6	.500
Dusty Baker, Los Angeles	1978	15	7	9	.467
Mike Schmidt, Philadelphia	1983	15	7	12	.467
Orlando Cepeda, Atlanta	1969	11	5	10	.455
Dave Concepcion, Cincinnati	1975	11	5	8	.455
Willie Stargell, Pittsburgh	1979	11	5	13	.455
Pete Rose, Cincinnati	1972	20	9	13	.450

Total number of occurrences: (15)

INDIVIDUAL PITCHING

PITCHERS WITH FOUR VICTORIES
BOTH LEAGUES

Pitcher, Club	Yrs.	W	L
Bruce Kison, Pit. N.L., Cal. A.L.	5	4	0
Tommy John, L.A. N.L., N.Y. A.L., Cal. A.L.	5	4	1
Don Sutton, L.A. N.L., Mil. A.L., Cal. A.L.	5	4	1

Total number of pitchers: (3)

AMERICAN LEAGUE

Pitcher, Club	Yrs.	W	L
Dave Stewart, Oakland, Toronto	5	8	0
Juan Guzman, Toronto	3	5	0
Jim Palmer, Baltimore	6	4	1
Catfish Hunter, Oakland, New York	6	4	3

Total number of pitchers: (4)

NATIONAL LEAGUE

Pitcher, Club	Yrs.	W	L
Steve Carlton, Philadelphia	5	4	2
John Smoltz, Atlanta	2	4	0

Total number of pitchers: (2)

10-STRIKEOUT GAMES BY PITCHERS
AMERICAN LEAGUE

Date	Pitcher, Club	No.
Oct. 5, 1969	Dave McNally, Bal. vs. Min. (11 inn.)	11
Oct. 5, 1970	Jim Palmer, Bal. vs. Min.	12
Oct. 10, 1972	Joe Coleman, Det. vs. Oak.	14
Oct. 6, 1973	Jim Palmer, Bal. vs. Oak.	12
Oct. 9, 1973	Mike Cuellar, Bal. vs. Oak. (10 inn.)	11
Oct. 6, 1983	Mike Boddicker, Bal. vs. Chi.	14

Total number of occurrences: (6)

NATIONAL LEAGUE

Date	Pitcher, Club	No.
Oct. 6, 1973	Tom Seaver, N.Y. vs. Cin. (8⅓ inn.)	13
Oct. 7, 1975	John Candelaria, Pit. vs. Cin. (7⅔ inn.)	14
Oct. 8, 1986	Mike Scott, Hou. vs. New York	14

Date	Pitcher, Club	No.
Oct. 14, 1986—Nolan Ryan, Hou. vs. N.Y.		12
Oct. 4, 1988—Dwight Gooden, N.Y. vs. L.A.		10
Oct. 5, 1988—Tim Belcher, L.A. vs. N.Y.		10

Date	Pitcher, Club	No.
Oct. 6, 1993—Curt Schilling, Phi. vs. Atl. (8 inn.)		10
Oct. 10, 1993—John Smoltz, Atl. vs. Phi. (6⅓ inn.)		10

Total number of occurrences: (8)

CLUB BATTING

AMERICAN LEAGUE

Year	Club, Division	G	AB	R	H	TB	2B	3B	HR	SH	SF	SB	BB	SO	RBI	Avg.	LOB
1969	Baltimore, East	3	123	16	36	58	8	1	4	2	0	0	13	14	15	.293	28
	Minnesota, West	3	110	5	17	25	3	1	1	0	1	2	12	27	5	.155	22
1970	Baltimore, East	3	109	27	36	61	7	0	6	1	2	1	12	19	24	.330	20
	Minnesota, West	3	101	10	24	39	4	1	3	1	0	0	9	22	10	.238	20
1971	Baltimore, East	3	95	15	26	47	7	1	4	0	1	0	13	22	14	.274	19
	Oakland, West	3	96	7	22	41	8	1	3	2	0	0	5	16	7	.229	15
1972	Detroit, East	5	162	10	32	52	6	1	4	3	0	0	13	25	10	.198	30
	Oakland, West	5	170	13	38	49	8	0	1	4	1	7	12	35	10	.224	38
1973	Baltimore, East	5	171	15	36	52	7	0	3	0	0	1	16	25	15	.211	36
	Oakland, West	5	160	15	32	54	5	1	5	4	1	3	17	39	15	.200	34
1974	Baltimore, East	4	124	7	22	32	1	0	3	2	0	0	5	20	7	.177	16
	Oakland, West	4	120	11	22	37	4	1	3	2	1	3	22	16	11	.183	30
1975	Boston, East	3	98	18	31	45	8	0	2	5	1	3	3	12	14	.316	14
	Oakland, West	3	98	7	19	28	6	0	1	0	0	0	9	14	7	.194	19
1976	New York, East	5	174	23	55	84	13	2	4	2	1	4	16	15	21	.316	41
	Kansas City, West	5	162	24	40	60	6	4	2	0	4	5	11	18	24	.247	22
1977	New York, East	5	175	21	46	64	12	0	2	1	2	2	9	16	17	.263	34
	Kansas City, West	5	163	22	42	66	9	3	3	2	2	5	15	22	21	.258	28
1978	New York, East	4	140	19	42	62	3	1	5	0	1	0	7	18	18	.300	27
	Kansas City, West	4	133	17	35	59	6	3	4	1	2	6	14	21	16	.263	28
1979	Baltimore, East	4	133	26	37	53	5	1	3	1	3	5	18	24	25	.278	22
	California, West	4	137	15	32	48	7	0	3	0	2	2	7	13	14	.234	22
1980	New York, East	3	102	6	26	44	7	1	3	1	0	0	6	16	5	.255	22
	Kansas City, West	3	97	14	28	45	6	1	3	0	0	3	9	15	14	.289	18
1981	New York, East	3	107	20	36	49	4	0	3	2	1	2	13	10	20	.336	30
	Oakland, West	3	99	4	22	28	4	1	0	0	0	2	6	23	4	.222	20
1982	Milwaukee, East	5	151	23	33	52	4	0	5	2	3	2	15	28	20	.219	24
	California, West	5	157	23	40	62	8	1	4	5	2	1	16	34	23	.255	29
1983	Baltimore, East	4	129	19	28	46	9	0	3	1	3	2	16	24	17	.217	24
	Chicago, West	4	133	4	28	32	4	0	0	1	0	4	12	26	2	.211	35
1984	Detroit, East	3	107	14	25	43	4	1	4	2	1	4	8	17	14	.234	20
	Kansas City, West	3	106	4	18	21	1	1	0	0	0	0	6	21	4	.170	21
1985	Toronto, East	7	242	25	65	90	19	0	2	0	2	2	16	37	23	.269	50
	Kansas City, West	7	227	26	51	83	9	1	7	4	2	2	22	51	26	.225	44
1986	Boston, East	7	254	41	69	102	11	2	6	3	2	1	19	31	35	.272	48
	California, West	7	256	30	71	103	11	0	7	4	2	1	20	44	29	.277	60
1987	Detroit, East	5	167	23	40	65	4	0	7	2	2	5	18	35	21	.240	37
	Minnesota, West	5	171	34	46	85	13	1	8	2	2	4	20	25	33	.269	47
1988	Boston, East	4	126	11	26	36	4	0	2	2	2	0	18	23	10	.206	30
	Oakland, West	4	137	20	41	70	8	0	7	0	1	1	10	35	20	.299	26
1989	Toronto, East	5	165	21	40	54	5	0	3	0	3	11	15	24	19	.242	30
	Oakland, West	5	158	26	43	75	9	1	7	3	2	13	20	32	23	.272	24
1990	Boston, East	4	126	4	23	31	5	0	1	1	2	1	6	16	4	.183	23
	Oakland, West	4	127	20	38	42	4	0	4	0	3	9	19	21	18	.299	35
1991	Toronto, East	5	173	19	43	52	6	0	1	3	1	7	15	30	18	.249	35
	Minnesota, West	5	181	27	50	70	9	1	3	1	2	8	15	37	25	.276	38
1992	Toronto, East	6	210	31	59	99	8	1	10	1	4	7	23	29	30	.281	45
	Oakland, West	6	207	24	52	71	5	1	4	3	2	16	24	33	23	.251	48
1993	Toronto, East	6	216	26	65	85	8	3	2	1	1	7	21	36	24	.301	56
	Chicago, West	6	194	23	46	68	5	1	5	5	1	3	32	43	22	.237	50
1994	No series played.																

NATIONAL LEAGUE

Year	Club	G	AB	R	H	TB	2B	3B	HR	SH	SF	SB	BB	SO	RBI	Avg.	LOB
1969	New York, East	3	113	27	37	65	8	1	6	1	0	5	10	25	24	.327	19
	Atlanta, West	3	106	15	27	51	9	0	5	0	1	1	11	20	15	.255	23
1970	Pittsburgh, East	3	102	3	23	29	6	0	0	2	0	0	12	19	3	.225	29
	Cincinnati, West	3	100	9	22	36	3	1	3	0	0	1	8	12	8	.220	18
1971	Pittsburgh, East	4	144	24	39	67	4	0	8	1	0	2	5	33	23	.271	26
	San Francisco, West	4	132	15	31	51	5	0	5	4	0	2	16	28	14	.235	33
1972	Pittsburgh, East	5	158	15	30	47	6	1	3	2	0	0	9	27	14	.190	24
	Cincinnati, West	5	166	19	42	67	9	2	4	3	1	4	10	28	16	.253	30
1973	New York, East	5	168	23	37	51	5	0	3	3	1	0	19	28	22	.220	30
	Cincinnati, West	5	167	8	31	52	6	0	5	3	1	0	13	42	8	.186	35

Year	Club, Division	G	AB	R	H	TB	2B	3B	HR	SH	SF	SB	BB	SO	RBI	Avg.	LOB
1974—	Pittsburgh, East	4	129	10	25	35	1	0	3	2	0	1	8	17	10	.194	24
	Los Angeles, West	4	138	20	37	56	8	1	3	1	0	5	30	16	19	.268	44
1975—	Pittsburgh, East	3	101	7	20	26	3	0	1	0	0	0	10	18	7	.198	21
	Cincinnati, West	3	102	19	29	45	4	0	4	0	3	11	9	28	18	.284	17
1976—	Philadelphia, East	3	100	11	27	40	8	1	1	3	2	0	12	9	11	.270	25
	Cincinnati, West	3	99	19	25	45	5	3	3	1	3	5	15	16	17	.253	20
1977—	Philadelphia, East	4	138	14	31	40	3	0	2	2	0	1	11	21	12	.225	32
	Los Angeles, West	4	133	22	35	52	6	1	3	2	0	3	14	22	20	.263	22
1978—	Philadelphia, East	4	140	17	35	37	3	2	5	2	1	0	9	21	16	.250	24
	Los Angeles, West	4	147	21	42	80	8	3	8	2	0	2	9	22	21	.286	28
1979—	Pittsburgh, East	3	105	15	28	47	3	2	4	5	3	4	13	13	14	.267	24
	Cincinnati, West	3	107	5	23	35	4	1	2	1	1	4	11	26	5	.215	25
1980—	Philadelphia, East	5	190	20	55	68	8	1	1	5	1	7	13	37	19	.291	43
	Houston, West	5	172	19	40	57	7	5	0	7	2	4	31	19	18	.233	45
1981—	Montreal, East	5	158	10	34	44	7	0	1	3	0	2	12	25	8	.215	31
	Los Angeles, West	5	163	15	38	55	3	1	4	4	0	5	12	23	15	.233	33
1982—	St. Louis, East	3	103	17	34	45	4	2	1	5	3	1	12	16	16	.330	31
	Atlanta, West	3	89	5	15	16	1	0	0	2	1	1	6	15	3	.169	12
1983—	Philadelphia, East	4	130	16	34	53	4	0	5	3	1	2	15	22	15	.262	31
	Los Angeles, West	4	129	8	27	40	5	1	2	2	0	3	11	31	7	.209	31
1984—	Chicago, East	5	162	26	42	80	11	0	9	1	2	6	20	28	25	.259	32
	San Diego, West	5	155	22	41	54	5	1	2	2	4	2	14	22	20	.265	27
1985—	St. Louis, East	6	201	29	56	77	10	1	3	2	1	6	30	34	26	.279	51
	Los Angeles, West	6	197	23	46	75	12	1	5	1	1	4	19	31	23	.234	40
1986—	New York, East	6	227	21	43	60	4	2	3	1	3	4	14	57	19	.189	36
	Houston, West	6	225	17	49	70	6	0	5	2	0	8	17	40	17	.218	39
1987—	St. Louis, East	7	215	23	56	74	4	4	2	5	4	4	16	42	22	.260	37
	San Francisco, West	7	226	23	54	90	7	1	9	3	1	5	17	51	20	.239	43
1988—	New York, East	7	240	27	58	87	12	1	5	3	1	6	28	42	27	.242	54
	Los Angeles, West	7	243	31	52	70	7	1	3	1	2	9	25	54	30	.214	50
1989—	Chicago, East	5	175	22	53	77	9	3	3	3	2	3	16	27	21	.303	43
	San Francisco, West	5	165	30	44	78	6	2	8	2	1	2	17	29	29	.267	30
1990—	Pittsburgh, East	6	186	15	36	58	9	2	3	0	1	6	27	49	14	.194	41
	Cincinnati, West	6	192	20	49	70	9	0	4	3	3	6	10	37	20	.255	33
1991—	Pittsburgh, East	7	228	12	51	70	10	0	3	4	1	6	22	57	11	.224	54
	Atlanta, West	7	229	19	53	80	10	1	5	5	1	10	22	42	19	.231	51
1992—	Pittsburgh, East	7	231	35	59	100	20	3	5	3	3	1	29	42	32	.255	50
	Atlanta, West	7	234	34	57	90	11	2	6	2	2	5	29	28	32	.244	51
1993—	Philadelphia, East	6	207	23	47	87	11	4	7	3	2	2	26	51	22	.227	52
	Atlanta, West	6	215	33	59	88	14	0	5	5	2	0	22	54	32	.274	47
1994—	No series played.																

CLUB FIELDING AND PLAYERS USED

AMERICAN LEAGUE

Year	Team, Division	G	PO	A	E	DP	PB	Fielding Avg.	Players Used	Pitchers Used
1969—	Baltimore, East	3	96	31	1	2	0	.992	20	7
	Minnesota, West	3	94	34	5	3	0	.962	22	9
1970—	Baltimore, East	3	81	29	0	3	0	1.000	14	4
	Minnesota, West	3	78	28	6	5	0	.946	24	9
1971—	Baltimore, East	3	81	31	1	3	0	.991	15	4
	Oakland, West	3	75	15	0	4	0	1.000	20	7
1972—	Detroit, East	5	139	48	7	4	0	.964	24	8
	Oakland, West	5	138	59	3	5	1	.985	25	8
1973—	Baltimore, East	5	135	51	2	2	1	.989	23	7
	Oakland, West	5	138	47	4	4	0	.979	22	6
1974—	Baltimore, East	4	105	50	4	4	0	.975	22	7
	Oakland, West	4	108	43	2	4	1	.987	20	5
1975—	Boston, East	3	81	33	4	3	0	.966	14	5
	Oakland, West	3	75	40	6	4	0	.950	22	7
1976—	New York, East	5	132	60	6	3	1	.970	22	6
	Kansas City, West	5	129	51	4	5	0	.978	24	9
1977—	New York, East	5	132	51	2	2	0	.989	18	6
	Kansas City, West	5	132	54	5	2	0	.974	22	8
1978—	New York, East	4	105	35	1	2	1	.993	21	8
	Kansas City, West	4	102	36	4	4	1	.972	20	7
1979—	Baltimore, East	4	109	52	5	5	1	.970	20	5
	California, West	4	107	37	2	7	0	.986	23	9
1980—	New York, East	3	75	42	1	2	0	.991	20	6
	Kansas City, West	3	81	29	1	3	0	.991	15	4
1981—	New York, East	3	81	30	1	6	1	.991	22	6
	Oakland, West	3	75	33	4	1	0	.964	24	8

Year	Team, Division	G	PO	A	E	DP	PB	Fielding Avg.	Players Used	Pitchers Used
1982—	Milwaukee, East	5	129	45	8	5	0	.956	20	8
	California, West	5	126	46	4	3	1	.977	20	7
1983—	Baltimore, East	4	111	49	2	4	0	.988	22	6
	Chicago, West	4	108	51	3	5	0	.981	23	9
1984—	Detroit, East	3	87	27	1	0	0	.991	20	5
	Kansas City, West	3	84	26	7	2	0	.940	22	6
1985—	Toronto, East	7	186	61	4	4	0	.984	24	8
	Kansas City, West	7	188	87	6	7	0	.979	22	7
1986—	Boston, East	7	196	73	7	5	0	.975	20	7
	California, West	7	192	78	8	5	2	.971	24	9
1987—	Detroit, East	5	129	56	5	1	1	.974	24	10
	Minnesota, West	5	132	41	3	3	0	.983	21	7
1988—	Boston, East	4	102	34	1	2	1	.993	20	7
	Oakland, West	4	108	30	3	5	1	.979	22	9
1989—	Toronto, East	5	129	40	2	5	1	.988	22	9
	Oakland, West	5	132	45	3	4	1	.983	22	8
1990—	Boston, East	4	102	47	5	6	1	.968	23	10
	Oakland, West	4	108	43	1	3	0	.993	21	6
1991—	Toronto, East	5	135	49	7	4	0	.963	23	10
	Minnesota, West	5	138	51	4	3	0	.979	23	8
1992—	Toronto, East	6	165	60	8	7	3	.966	21	9
	Oakland, West	6	162	55	7	5	0	.969	25	11
1993—	Toronto, East	6	162	57	2	7	0	.991	19	10
	Chicago, West	6	159	56	7	5	0	.968	22	9
1994—	No series played.									

```
                        NATIONAL LEAGUE
```

Year	Team, Division	G	PO	A	E	DP	PB	Fielding Avg.	Players Used	Pitchers Used
1969—	New York, East	3	81	23	2	2	1	.981	17	6
	Atlanta, West	3	78	37	6	4	1	.950	23	9
1970—	Pittsburgh, East	3	81	37	2	3	0	.983	18	5
	Cincinnati, West	3	84	39	1	1	0	.992	20	7
1971—	Pittsburgh, East	4	105	32	3	3	1	.979	21	7
	San Francisco, West	4	102	37	4	1	1	.972	22	9
1972—	Pittsburgh, East	5	131	38	4	3	0	.977	23	10
	Cincinnati, West	5	132	53	4	3	1	.979	21	8
1973—	New York, East	5	142	44	4	3	0	.979	17	6
	Cincinnati, West	5	138	59	2	3	0	.990	24	9
1974—	Pittsburgh, East	4	105	37	4	2	1	.973	22	8
	Los Angeles, West	4	108	46	7	8	1	.957	22	7
1975—	Pittsburgh, East	3	78	20	2	3	2	.980	24	10
	Cincinnati, West	3	84	31	1	2	0	.991	18	7
1976—	Philadelphia, East	3	79	34	2	3	0	.983	22	7
	Cincinnati, West	3	81	32	2	3	0	.983	18	6
1977—	Philadelphia, East	4	105	49	3	3	1	.981	21	7
	Los Angeles, West	4	108	44	5	3	0	.968	23	9
1978—	Philadelphia, East	4	110	46	4	4	0	.975	22	8
	Los Angeles, West	4	111	50	3	4	0	.982	22	9
1979—	Pittsburgh, East	3	90	34	0	2	0	1.000	20	8
	Cincinnati, West	3	87	39	1	2	0	.992	20	9
1980—	Philadelphia, East	5	148	71	6	7	0	.973	23	9
	Houston, West	5	147	52	3	4	1	.985	24	7
1981—	Montreal, East	5	132	52	4	8	0	.979	19	7
	Los Angeles, West	5	132	53	2	5	1	.989	23	9
1982—	St. Louis, East	3	81	35	2	3	0	.983	15	5
	Atlanta, West	3	76	39	1	0	1	.991	20	8
1983—	Philadelphia, East	4	105	36	5	0	0	.966	20	5
	Los Angeles, West	4	102	38	1	3	1	.993	22	8
1984—	Chicago, East	5	127	49	3	6	1	.983	23	8
	San Diego, West	5	129	43	1	4	0	.994	24	10
1985—	St. Louis, East	6	156	54	4	4	1	.981	23	9
	Los Angeles, West	6	154	72	6	3	0	.974	25	9
1986—	New York, East	6	189	94	1	6	0	.996	22	8
	Houston, West	6	188	66	7	3	2	.973	21	8
1987—	St. Louis, East	7	183	67	3	5	0	.988	23	8
	San Francisco, West	7	180	77	6	10	1	.977	23	10
1988—	New York, East	7	192	62	8	2	0	.969	22	8
	Los Angeles, West	7	195	61	5	9	1	.981	24	9
1989—	Chicago, East	5	126	40	3	1	2	.982	24	9
	San Francisco, West	5	132	49	5	7	1	.973	24	9
1990—	Pittsburgh, East	6	156	71	5	4	0	.978	21	8
	Cincinnati, West	6	159	45	2	3	0	.990	23	8

Year	Team, Division	G	PO	A	E	DP	PB	Fielding Avg.	Players Used	Pitchers Used
1991—Pittsburgh, East		7	189	75	6	3	0	.978	25	11
Atlanta, West		7	189	62	4	6	0	.984	23	9
1992—Pittsburgh, East		7	182	63	5	6	2	.980	25	10
Atlanta, West		7	183	74	2	3	1	.992	25	10
1993—Philadelphia, East		6	165	47	7	2	2	.968	25	10
Atlanta, West		6	163	54	5	1	0	.977	23	8
1994—No series played.										

MANAGERIAL RECORDS

AMERICAN LEAGUE

	Series W	L	Games W	L
Joe Altobelli, Baltimore (East)	1	0	3	1
Sparky Anderson, Detroit (East)	1	1	4	4
Bobby Cox, Toronto (East)	0	1	3	4
Alvin Dark, Oakland (West)	1	1	3	4
Jim Fregosi, California (West)	0	1	1	3
Jim Frey, Kansas City (West)	1	0	3	0
Cito Gaston, Toronto (East)	2	2	10	12
Whitey Herzog, Kansas City, (West)	0	3	5	9
Dick Howser, New York (East), Kansas City (West)	1	2	4	9
Darrell Johnson, Boston (East)	1	0	3	0
Tom Kelly, Minnesota (West)	2	0	8	2
Harvey Kuenn, Milwaukee (East)	1	0	3	2
Gene Lamont, Chicago (West)	0	1	2	4
Tony La Russa, Chicago (West), Oakland (West)	3	2	15	8
Bob Lemon, New York (East)	2	0	6	1
Billy Martin, Minnesota (West), Detroit (East), New York (East), Oakland (West)	2	3	8	13
Gene Mauch, California (West)	0	2	5	7
John McNamara, Boston (East)	1	0	4	3
Joe Morgan, Boston (East)	0	2	0	8
Bill Rigney, Minnesota (West)	0	1	0	3
Earl Weaver, Baltimore (East)	4	2	15	7
Dick Williams, Oakland (West)	2	1	6	7

Total number of managers: (22)

NATIONAL LEAGUE

	Series W	L	Games W	L
Walter Alston, Los Angeles (West)	1	0	3	1
Sparky Anderson, Cincinnati (West)	4	1	14	5
Yogi Berra, New York (East)	1	0	3	2
Bobby Cox, Atlanta (West)	2	1	10	10
Roger Craig, San Francisco (West)	1	1	7	5
Jim Fanning, Montreal (East)	0	1	2	3
Jim Fregosi, Philadelphia (East)	1	0	4	2
Jim Frey, Chicago (East)	0	1	2	3
Charlie Fox, San Francisco (West)	0	1	1	3
Dallas Green, Philadelphia (East)	1	0	3	2
Lum Harris, Atlanta (West)	0	1	0	3
Whitey Herzog, St. Louis (East)	3	0	11	5
Gil Hodges, New York (East)	1	0	3	0
Dave Johnson, New York (East)	1	1	7	6
Hal Lanier, Houston (West)	0	1	2	4
Tom Lasorda, Los Angeles, (West)	4	2	16	14
Jim Leyland, Pittsburgh (East)	0	3	8	12
John McNamara, Cincinnati (West)	0	1	0	3
Danny Murtaugh, Pittsburgh (East)	1	3	4	10
Paul Owens, Philadelphia (East)	1	0	3	1
Danny Ozark, Philadelphia (East)	0	3	2	9
Lou Piniella, Cincinnati (West)	1	0	4	2
Chuck Tanner, Pittsburgh (East)	1	0	3	0
Joe Torre, Atlanta (West)	0	1	0	3
Bill Virdon, Pittsburgh (East), Houston (West)	0	2	4	6
Dick Williams, San Diego (West)	1	0	3	2
Don Zimmer, Chicago (East)	0	1	1	4

Total number of managers: (27)

COMBINED RECORDS FOR BOTH LEAGUES

	Series W	L	Games W	L
Sparky Anderson, Cincinnati N.L., Detroit A.L.	5	2	18	9
Bobby Cox, Toronto A.L., Atlanta N.L.	2	2	13	14
Jim Fregosi, California A.L., Philadelphia N.L.	1	1	5	5
Jim Frey, Kansas City A.L., Chicago N.L.	1	1	5	3
Whitey Herzog, Kansas City A.L., St. Louis N.L.	3	3	16	14
John McNamara, Cincinnati N.L., Boston A.L.	1	1	4	6
Dick Williams, Oakland A.L., San Diego N.L.	3	1	9	9

Total number of managers: (7)

WORLD SERIES

Service (Individual, Club)

Batting (Individual, Club)

Baserunning (Individual, Club)

Pitching (Individual, Club)

Fielding (Individual, Club)

Miscellaneous

Non-Playing Personnel

General Reference

INDIVIDUAL SERVICE

SERIES AND CLUBS

Most series played

14—Yogi Berra, New York A.L., 1947, 1949, 1950, 1951, 1952, 1953, 1955, 1956, 1957, 1958, 1960, 1961, 1962, 1963, 75 games (65 consecutive).

Most series eligible, but did not play

6—Charlie Silvera, New York A.L., 1950, 1951, 1952, 1953, 1955, 1956, 37 games (played one game in 1949).

Most consecutive series played (17 times)

5—Hank Bauer, New York A.L., 1949 through 1953.
Yogi Berra, New York A.L., 1949 through 1953.
Ed Lopat, New York A.L., 1949 through 1953.
Johnny Mize, New York A.L., 1949 through 1953.
Vic Raschi, New York A.L., 1949 through 1953.
Allie Reynolds, New York A.L., 1949 through 1953.
Phil Rizzuto, New York A.L., 1949 through 1953.
Gene Woodling, New York A.L., 1949 through 1953.
Johnny Blanchard, New York A.L., 1960 through 1964.
Clete Boyer, New York A.L., 1960 through 1964.
Ralph Terry, New York A.L., 1960 through 1964.
Whitey Ford, New York A.L., 1960 through 1964.
Elston Howard, New York A.L., 1960 through 1964.
Hector Lopez, New York A.L., 1960 through 1964.
Mickey Mantle, New York A.L., 1960 through 1964.
Roger Maris, New York A.L., 1960 through 1964.
Bobby Richardson, New York A.L., 1960 through 1964.

Most series played with one club

14—Yogi Berra, New York A.L., 1947, 1949, 1950, 1951, 1952, 1953, 1955, 1956, 1957, 1958, 1960, 1961, 1962, 1963, 75 games (65 consecutive).

Most series playing in all games

10—Joe DiMaggio, New York A.L., 1936, 1937, 1938, 1939, 1941, 1942, 1947, 1949, 1950, 1951, 51 games.

Most times on series-winning club (playing one or more games each series)

10—Yogi Berra, New York A.L., 1947, 1949, 1950, 1951, 1952, 1953, 1956, 1958, 1961, 1962.

Most times on series-losing club (playing one or more games each series)

6—Pee Wee Reese, Brooklyn N.L., 1941, 1947, 1949, 1952, 1953, 1956.
Elston Howard, New York A.L., 1955, 1957; 1960, 1963, 1964; Boston A.L., 1967.

Most series played in first four major league seasons

4—Joe DiMaggio, New York A.L., 1936 through 1939.
Elston Howard, New York A.L., 1955 through 1958.
Johnny Kucks, New York A.L., 1955 through 1958.

Most clubs, career

4—Lonnie Smith, Philadelphia N.L., 1980; St. Louis N.L., 1982; Kansas City A.L., 1985; Atlanta N.L., 1991, 1992.

BY POSITION (EXCEPT PITCHERS)

Most series by first baseman

8—Bill Skowron, New York A.L., 1955, 1956, 1957, 1958, 1960, 1961, 1962; Los Angeles N.L., 1963, 37 games.

Most series by second baseman

7—Frankie Frisch, New York N.L., 1922, 1923, 1924; St. Louis N.L., 1928, 1930, 1931, 1934, 42 games.

Most series by third baseman

6—Red Rolfe, New York A.L., 1936, 1937, 1938, 1939, 1941, 1942, 28 games.

Most series by shortstop

9—Phil Rizzuto, New York A.L., 1941, 1942, 1947, 1949, 1950, 1951, 1952, 1953, 1955, 52 games.

Most series by outfielder

12—Mickey Mantle, New York A.L., 1951, 1952, 1953, 1955, 1956, 1957, 1958, 1960, 1961, 1962, 1963, 1964, 63 games.

Most series by catcher

12—Yogi Berra, New York A.L., 1947, 1949, 1950, 1951, 1952, 1953, 1955, 1956, 1957, 1958, 1960, 1962, 63 games.

YOUNGEST AND OLDEST NON-PITCHERS

Youngest World Series non-pitcher

18 years, 10 months, 13 days—Fred Lindstrom, New York N.L., October 4, 1924.

Oldest World Series non-pitcher

42 years, 6 months, 2 days—Pete Rose, Philadelphia N.L., October 16, 1983.

YEARS BETWEEN SERIES (INCLUDES PITCHERS)

Most years between first and second series

17—Jim Kaat, Minnesota A.L., 1965; St. Louis N.L., 1982.

Most years between first and last series

22—Willie Mays, New York (Giants) N.L., 1951; New York (Mets) N.L., 1973.

Most years played in majors before playing in series

21—Joe Niekro, Minnesota, October 21, 1987.

POSITIONS

Most positions played, career

4—Babe Ruth, Boston A.L., 1915, 1916, 1918; New York A.L., 1921, 1922, 1923, 1926, 1927, 1928, 1932, 41 games (pitcher, left field, right field, first base).
Jackie Robinson, Brooklyn N.L., 1947, 1949, 1952, 1953, 1955, 1956, 38 games (first base, second base, left field, third base).
Elston Howard, New York A.L., 1955, 1956, 1957, 1958, 1960, 1961, 1962, 1964; Boston A.L., 1967, 54 games (left field, right field, first base, catcher).
Tony Kubek, New York A.L., 1957, 1958, 1960, 1961, 1962, 1963, 37 games (left field, third base, center field, shortstop).
Pete Rose, Cincinnati N.L., 1970, 1972, 1975, 1976, Philadelphia N.L., 1980, 1983, 34 games (right field, left field, third base, first base).

Most positions played, series

3—Held by many players.

SERIES

Most series pitched

11—Whitey Ford, New York A.L., 1950, 1953, 1955, 1956, 1957, 1958, 1960, 1961, 1962, 1963, 1964, 22 games.

Most series pitched by relief pitcher

6—Johnny Murphy, New York A.L., 1936, 1937, 1938, 1939, 1941, 1943, eight games as a relief pitcher.

YOUNGEST AND OLDEST PITCHERS

Youngest World Series pitcher

19 years, 20 days—Ken Brett, Boston A.L., October 8, 1967.

Oldest World Series pitcher

46 years, 2 months, 29 days—Jack Quinn, Philadelphia A.L., October 4, 1930.

CLUB SERVICE

PLAYERS USED

Most players, series
4-game series—25—Oakland A.L. vs. Cincinnati N.L., 1990.
5-game series—25—Brooklyn N.L. vs. New York A.L., 1949.
6-game series—25—Los Angeles N.L. vs. New York A.L., 1977.
7-game series—26
Detroit A.L. vs. Chicago N.L., 1945.
Boston A.L. vs. St. Louis N.L., 1946.
8-game series— 19
Chicago A.L. vs. Cincinnati N.L., 1919.
New York A.L. vs. New York N.L., 1921.

Most players used by both clubs, series
4-game series—46—Oakland A.L. 25, Cincinnati N.L. 21, 1990.
5-game series—46
Baltimore A.L. 23, Philadelphia N.L. 23, 1983.
San Diego N.L. 24, Detroit A.L. 22, 1984.
Oakland A.L. 24, Los Angeles N.L. 22, 1988.
6-game series—48—New York A.L. 24, Los Angeles N.L. 24, 1981.
7-game series—51—Detroit A.L. 26, Chicago N.L. 25, 1945.
8-game series—36—Chicago A.L. 19 Cincinnati N.L. 17, 1919.

Fewest players, series
4-game series— 13
Los Angeles N.L. vs. New York A.L., 1963.
Baltimore A.L. vs. Los Angeles N.L., 1966.
5-game series— 12
New York N.L. vs. Philadelphia A.L., 1905.
Philadelphia A.L. vs. Chicago N.L., 1910.
Philadelphia A.L. vs. New York N.L., 1913.
6-game series— 14
Chicago N.L. vs. Chicago A.L., 1906.
Philadelphia A.L. vs. New York N.L., 1911.
7-game series— 16—Detroit A.L. vs. Pittsburgh N.L., 1909.
8-game series— 13
Boston A.L. vs. Pittsburgh N.L., 1903.
New York N.L. vs. New York A.L., 1921.

Fewest players used by both clubs, series
4-game series—31—Philadelphia A.L. 16, Boston N.L. 15, 1914.
5-game series—25—Philadelphia A.L. 13, New York N.L. 12, 1905.
6-game series—29—New York N.L. 15, Philadelphia A.L. 14, 1911.
7-game series—33—Pittsburgh N.L. 17, Detroit A.L. 16, 1909.
8-game series—27—Pittsburgh N.L. 14, Boston A.L. 13, 1903.

Most times one club using only nine players in game, series
5-game series—5
Philadelphia A.L. vs. Chicago N.L., 1910.
Philadelphia A.L. vs. New York N.L., 1913.
7-game series—5—New York A.L. vs. Brooklyn N.L., 1956.
8-game series—6—Pittsburgh N.L. vs. Boston A.L., 1903.

Most times both clubs using only nine players in game, series
7-game series—7—New York A.L. 5, Brooklyn N.L. 2, 1956.
8-game series—11—Pittsburgh N.L. 6, Boston A.L. 5, 1903.

Most players, nine-inning game
21—New York A.L. vs. Brooklyn N.L. October 5, 1947.
Cincinnati N.L. vs. New York A.L. October 9, 1961.

Most players, extra-inning game
23—Minnesota A.L. vs. Atlanta N.L. October 22, 1991, 12 innings.

Most players used by both clubs, nine-inning game
38—New York A.L. 21, Brooklyn N.L. 17, October 5, 1947.

Most players used by both clubs, extra-inning game
42—Minnesota A.L. 23, Atlanta N.L. 19, October 22, 1991, 12 innings.

PINCH-HITTERS

Most times pinch-hitters used, series
23—Baltimore A.L. vs. Pittsburgh N.L., 1979 (7-game series).

Most pinch-hitters used by both clubs, series
37—Minnesota A.L. 21, Atlanta N.L. 16, 1991 (7-game series).

Fewest times pinch-hitters used, series
0—Held by many clubs. Last club—Cincinnati N.L. vs. New York A.L., 1976 (4-game series).

Fewest pinch-hitters used by both clubs, series
2—New York N.L. 1, Philadelphia A.L. 1, 1905 (5-game series).

Most pinch-hitters, nine-inning game
6—Los Angeles N.L. vs. Chicago A.L. October 6, 1959.

Most pinch-hitters, extra-inning game
8—Minnesota A.L. vs. Atlanta N.L. October 22, 1991, 12 innings.

Most pinch-hitters used by both clubs, nine-inning game
8—Oakland A.L. 5, New York N.L. 3, October 14, 1973.
Baltimore A.L. 4, Philadelphia N.L. 4, October 15, 1983.

Most pinch-hitters used by both clubs, extra-inning game
12—Minnesota A.L. 8, Atlanta N.L. 4, October 22, 1991, 12 innings.

Most pinch-hitters, inning
4—New York N.L. vs. Oakland A.L. October 13, 1973, ninth inning.
Baltimore A.L. vs. Philadelphia N.L. October 15, 1983, sixth inning.
Minnesota A.L. vs. St. Louis N.L. October 22, 1987, ninth inning.

PINCH-RUNNERS

Most times pinch-runners used, series
8—Oakland A.L. vs. Cincinnati N.L., 1972 (7-game series).

Most pinch-runners used by both clubs, series
10—Oakland A.L. 8, Cincinnati N.L. 2, 1972 (7-game series).

Fewest times pinch-runners used, series
0—Held by many clubs.

Most pinch-runners, game
2—Made in many games.

Most pinch-runners used by both clubs, game
4—St. Louis N.L. 2, Kansas City A.L. 2, October 26, 1985.

Most pinch-runners, inning
2—New York N.L. vs. New York A.L. October 10, 1923, third inning.
New York A.L. vs. New York N.L. October 15, 1923, eighth inning.
Brooklyn N.L. vs. New York A.L. October 3, 1947, ninth inning.
Boston N.L. vs. Cleveland A.L. October 6, 1948, eighth inning.
Philadelphia N.L. vs. New York A.L. October 7, 1950, ninth inning.
Los Angeles N.L. vs. Chicago A.L. October 6, 1959, seventh inning.
Oakland A.L. vs. Cincinnati N.L. October 19, 1972, ninth inning.
St. Louis N.L. vs. Kansas City A.L. October 26, 1985, eighth inning.
Kansas City A.L. vs. St. Louis N.L. October 26, 1985, ninth inning.

Most pinch-runners used by both clubs, inning
2—Made in many games.

NUMBER OF PLAYERS USED BY POSITION

FIRST BASEMEN

Most first basemen, series

4—New York A.L. vs. Milwaukee N.L., 1957 (7-game series).
Oakland A.L. vs. New York N.L., 1973 (7-game series).

Most first basemen used by both clubs, series

6—New York A.L. 4, Milwaukee N.L. 2, 1957 (7-game series).

Most first basemen, game

3—New York A.L. vs. Milwaukee N.L. October 2, 1957.
New York A.L. vs. Milwaukee N.L. October 5, 1957.

Most first basemen used by both clubs, game

5—New York A.L. 3, Milwaukee N.L. 2, October 2, 1957.
New York A.L. 3, Milwaukee N.L. 2, October 5, 1957.

SECOND BASEMEN

Most second basemen, series

3—St. Louis N.L. vs. New York A.L., 1964 (7-game series).
Oakland A.L. vs. New York N.L., 1973 (7-game series).
Oakland A.L. vs. Los Angeles N.L., 1988 (5-game series).
Oakland A.L. vs. San Francisco N.L., 1989 (4-game series).

Most second basemen used by both clubs, series

5—Oakland A.L. 3, San Francisco N.L. 2, 1989 (4-game series).

Most second basemen, game

3—St. Louis N.L. vs. New York A.L., October 7, 1964.
Oakland A.L. vs. New York N.L., October 14, 1973, 12 innings.

Most second basemen used by both clubs, game

4—New York A.L. 2, Milwaukee N.L. 2, October 7, 1957.
St. Louis N.L. 3, New York A.L. 1, October 7, 1964.
Oakland A.L. 3, New York N.L. 1, October 14, 1973, 12 innings.
Oakland A.L. 2, San Francisco N.L. 2, October 27, 1989.

THIRD BASEMEN

Most third basemen, series

3—Held by many clubs. Last club—Toronto vs. Philadelphia, 1993 (6-game series).

Most third basemen used by both clubs, series

6—Oakland A.L. 3, San Francisco N.L. 3, 1989 (4-game series).

Most third basemen, game

3—Oakland A.L. vs. San Francisco N.L., October 27, 1989.
San Francisco N.L. vs. Oakland A.L., October 28, 1989.
Minnesota A.L. vs. Atlanta N.L., October 22, 1991, 12 innings.
Minnesota A.L. vs. Atlanta N.L., October 23, 1991.

Most third basemen used by both clubs, game

4—Made in many games.

SHORTSTOPS

Most shortstops, series

3—Chicago N.L. vs. Detroit A.L., 1945 (7-game series).
New York A.L. vs. Pittsburgh N.L., 1960 (7-game series).
Cincinnati N.L. vs. Baltimore A.L., 1970 (5-game series).
Minnesota A.L. vs. Atlanta N.L., 1991 (7-game series).

Most shortstops used by both clubs, series

5—Chicago N.L. 3, Detroit A.L. 2, 1945 (7-game series).
New York A.L. 3, Pittsburgh N.L. 2, 1960 (7-game series).
Minnesota A.L. 3, Atlanta N.L. 2, 1991 (7-game series).

Most shortstops, game

3—New York A.L. vs. Pittsburgh N.L., October 13, 1960.
Cincinnati N.L. vs. Baltimore A.L., October 14, 1970.
Minnesota A.L. vs. Atlanta N.L. October 27, 1991, 10 innings.

Most shortstops used by both clubs, nine-inning game

4—Made in many games.

Most shortstops used by both clubs, extra-inning game

5—Minnesota A.L. 3, Atlanta N.L. 2, October 27, 1991, 10 innings.

LEFT FIELDERS

Most left fielders, series

4—Held by many clubs. Last club—Oakland A.L. vs. Los Angeles N.L., 1988 (5-game series).

Most left fielders used by both clubs, series

7—Oakland A.L. 4, Los Angeles N.L. 3, 1988 (5-game series).

Most left fielders, game

3—New York N.L. vs. Washington A.L., October 10, 1924, 12 innings.
Brooklyn N.L. vs. New York A.L., October 5, 1947.
Brooklyn N.L. vs. New York A.L., October 5, 1952, 11 innings.
Philadelphia N.L. vs. Kansas City A.L., October 19, 1980.
New York A.L. vs. Los Angeles N.L., October 24, 1981.

Most left fielders used by both clubs, game

5—Brooklyn N.L. 3, New York A.L. 2, October 5, 1947.

CENTER FIELDERS

Most center fielders, series

4—Los Angeles N.L. vs. Chicago A.L., 1959 (6-game series).

Most center fielders used by both clubs, series

6—New York A.L. 3, Los Angeles N.L. 3, 1981 (6-game series).

Most center fielders, game

3—New York N.L. vs. New York A.L., October 5, 1922, 10 innings.

Most center fielders used by both clubs, game

4—New York N.L. 3, New York A.L. 1, October 5, 1922, 10 innings.
New York A.L. 2, New York N.L. 2, October 15, 1923.
New York A.L. 2, Los Angeles N.L. 2, October 11, 1978.
New York A.L. 2, Los Angeles N.L. 2, October 24, 25, 1981.

RIGHT FIELDERS

Most right fielders, series

5—Los Angeles N.L. vs. Chicago A.L., 1959 (6-game series).

Most right fielders used by both clubs, series

9—Los Angeles N.L. 5, Chicago A.L. 4, 1959 (6-game series).

Most right fielders, game

3—Held by many clubs.

Most right fielders used by both clubs, game

5—Los Angeles N.L. 3, Chicago A.L. 2, October 8, 1959.

CATCHERS

Most catchers, series

4—Los Angeles N.L. vs. New York A.L., 1978 (6-game series).

Most catchers used by both clubs, series

6—New York A.L. 3, Pittsburgh N.L. 3, 1927 (4-game series).
Los Angeles N.L. 4, New York A.L. 2, 1978 (6-game series).
New York A.L. 3, Pittsburgh N.L. 3, 1960 (7-game series).

Most catchers, game

3—Philadelphia N.L. vs. New York A.L., October 5, 1950, 10 innings.
Los Angeles N.L. vs. New York A.L., October 13, 1978.

Most catchers used by both clubs, game

4—Detroit A.L. 2, Chicago N.L. 2, October 8, 1945, 12 innings.
Boston A.L. 2, St. Louis N.L. 2, October 15, 1946.
Philadelphia N.L. 3, New York A.L. 1, October 5, 1950, 10 innings.

Los Angeles N.L. 3, New York A.L. 1, October 13, 1978.
Los Angeles N.L. 2, New York A.L. 2, October 15, 1978.

PITCHERS

Most pitchers, series

4-game series—10—Oakland A.L. vs. Cincinnati N.L., 1990.
5-game series—10
San Diego N.L. vs. Detroit A.L., 1984.
Oakland A.L. vs. Los Angeles N.L., 1988.
6-game series—10
Brooklyn N.L. vs. New York A.L., 1953.
Philadelphia N.L. vs. Kansas City A.L., 1980.
Los Angeles N.L. vs. New York A.L., 1981.
Toronto A.L. vs. Atlanta N.L., 1992.
Toronto A.L. vs. Philadelphia N.L., 1993.
Philadelphia N.L. vs. Toronto A.L., 1993.
7-game series—11—Boston A.L. vs. St. Louis N.L., 1946.
8-game series—8—New York A.L. vs. New York N.L., 1921.

Most pitchers used by both clubs, series

4-game series—18—Oakland A.L. 10, Cincinnati N.L. 8, 1990.
5-game series—18—Baltimore A.L. 9, Cincinnati N.L. 9, 1970.
6-game series—20—Toronto A.L. 10, Philadelphia N.L. 10, 1993.
7-game series—20
Pittsburgh N.L. 10, New York A.L. 10, 1960.
St. Louis N.L. 10, Boston A.L. 10, 1967.
Pittsburgh N.L. 10, Baltimore A.L. 10, 1971.
8-game series—12—New York A.L. 8, New York N.L. 4, 1921.

Fewest pitchers, series

2—Philadelphia A.L. vs. Chicago N.L. 1910 (5-game series).

Fewest pitchers used by both clubs, series

6—Philadelphia A.L. 3, New York N.L. 3, 1905 (5-game series).

Most different starting pitchers, series

6—Brooklyn N.L. vs. New York A.L., 1947.
Brooklyn N.L. vs. New York A.L., 1955.
Pittsburgh N.L. vs. Baltimore A.L., 1971.

Most different starting pitchers used by both clubs, series

11—Brooklyn N.L. 6, New York A.L. 5, 1955.

Most pitchers, game

8—Cincinnati N.L. vs. New York A.L., October 9, 1961.

St. Louis N.L. vs. Boston A.L., October 11, 1967.
Cincinnati N.L. vs. Boston A.L., October 21, 1975, 12 innings.

Most pitchers used by winning club, nine-inning game

6—Cincinnati N.L. vs. Oakland A.L., October 20, 1972 (won 5-4).

Most pitchers used by winning club, extra-inning game

7—Toronto A.L. vs. Atlanta N.L., October 24, 1992, 11 innings (won 4-3).

Most pitchers used by losing club, game

8—Cincinnati N.L. vs. New York A.L., October 9, 1961 (lost 13-5).
St. Louis N.L. vs. Boston A.L., October 11, 1967 (lost 8-4).
Cincinnati N.L. vs. Boston A.L., October 21, 1975, 12 innings (lost 7-6).

Most pitchers used by both clubs, nine-inning game

11—St. Louis N.L. 8, Boston A.L. 3, October 11, 1967.
San Francisco N.L. 6, Oakland A.L. 5, October 28, 1989.

Most pitchers used by both clubs, extra-inning game

13—Minnesota A.L. 7, Atlanta N.L. 6, October 22, 1991, 12 innings.

Most pitchers, inning

5—Baltimore A.L. vs. Pittsburgh N.L., October 17, 1979, ninth inning.
St. Louis N.L. vs. Kansas City A.L., October 27, 1985, fifth inning.

SERIES

Most series played

33—New York A.L., 1921, 1922, 1923, 1926, 1927, 1928, 1932, 1936, 1937, 1938, 1939, 1941, 1942, 1943, 1947, 1949, 1950, 1951, 1952, 1953, 1955, 1956, 1957, 1958, 1960, 1961, 1962, 1963, 1964, 1976, 1977, 1978, 1981 (won 22, lost 11).
18—Brooklyn/Los Angeles N.L., 1916, 1920, 1941, 1947, 1949, 1952, 1953, 1955, 1956, 1959, 1963, 1965, 1966, 1974, 1977, 1978, 1981, 1988 (won 6, lost 12).

Most consecutive series played between same clubs

3—New York N.L. vs. New York A.L., 1921, 1922, 1923.

INDIVIDUAL BATTING

GAMES

Most games, career

75—Yogi Berra, New York A.L., 1947, 1949, 1950, 1951, 1952, 1953, 1955, 1956, 1957, 1958, 1960, 1961, 1962, 1963 (14 series, 65 consecutive games).

Most games with one club, career

75—Yogi Berra, New York A.L., 1947, 1949, 1950, 1951, 1952, 1953, 1955, 1956, 1957, 1958, 1960, 1961, 1962, 1963 (14 series, 65 consecutive games).

Most consecutive games played (in consecutive years)

30—Bobby Richardson, New York A.L., October 5, 1960 through October 15, 1964.

Most games by pinch-hitter, career

10—John Blanchard, New York A.L., 1960 (3), 1961 (2), 1962 (1), 1964 (4).

Most games by pinch-runner, career

9—Allan Lewis, Oakland A.L., 1972, 1973; two series (three runs).

Most games by pinch-hitter, series

5—Harry McCormick, New York N.L., 1912.
Ben Paschal, New York A.L., 1926.
Frank Secory, Chicago N.L., 1945.
Cookie Lavagetto, Brooklyn N.L., 1947.
Carl Warwick, St. Louis N.L., 1964.
Tom Shopay, Baltimore A.L., 1971.
Gonzalo Marquez, Oakland A.L., 1972.
Angel Mangual, Oakland A.L., 1973.
Terry Crowley, Baltimore A.L., 1979.
Pat Kelly, Baltimore A.L., 1979.

Most games by pinch-runner, series

6—Allan Lewis, Oakland A.L., 1972 (scored two runs).

BATTING AVERAGE

Highest batting average, career (20 or more games)

.391—Lou Brock, St. Louis N.L., 1964, 1967, 1968; three series, 21 games (87 at-bats, 34 hits).

Highest batting average, series

4-game series—.750—Billy Hatcher, Cincinnati N.L., 1990.
5-game series—.500
Larry McLean, New York N.L., 1913.
Joe Gordon, New York A.L., 1941.
6-game series—.500
Dave Robertson, New York N.L., 1917.
Billy Martin, New York A.L., 1953.
Paul Molitor, Toronto A.L., 1993.
7-game series—.500
Pepper Martin, St. Louis N.L., 1931.
Johnny Lindell, New York A.L., 1947 (played only six games due to broken rib).
Phil Garner, Pittsburgh N.L., 1979.
8-game series—.400—Buck Herzog, New York N.L., 1912.

Most series leading club in batting average

3—Home Run Baker, Philadelphia A.L., 1911, 1913, 1914.
Pee Wee Reese, Brooklyn N.L., 1947, 1949, 1952 (tied).
Duke Snider, Brooklyn N.L., 1952 (tied), 1955, 1956 (tied).
Gil Hodges, Brooklyn N.L., Los Angeles N.L., 1953, 1956 (tied), 1959.
Steve Garvey, Los Angeles N.L., 1974, 1977, 1981.

Most series batting .300 or over

6—Babe Ruth, New York A.L., 1921, 1923, 1926, 1927, 1928, 1932.

SLUGGING AVERAGE

Highest slugging average, career (20 or more games)

.755—Reggie Jackson, Oakland A.L., 1973, 1974; New York A.L., 1977, 1978, 1981; five series, 30 games (98 at-bats, 35 hits, seven doubles, one triple, 10 home runs, 74 total bases).

Highest slugging average, series

4-game series—1.727—Lou Gehrig, New York A.L., 1928.
5-game series—.929—Joe Gordon, New York A.L., 1941. (Donn Clendenon, New York N.L., 1969, had slugging average of 1.071 but played only four games.)
6-game series—1.250—Reggie Jackson, New York A.L., 1977.
7-game series—.913—Gene Tenace, Oakland A.L., 1972.
8-game series—.600—Buck Herzog, New York N.L., 1912.

AT-BATS AND PLATE APPEARANCES

Most at-bats, career

259—Yogi Berra, New York A.L., 1947, 1949, 1950, 1951, 1952, 1953, 1955, 1956, 1957, 1958, 1960, 1961, 1962, 1963; 14 series, 75 games.

Most at-bats, series

4-game series—19
Mark Koenig, New York A.L., 1928.
Rickey Henderson, Oakland A.L., 1989.
5-game series—23
Hal Janvrin, Boston A.L., 1916.
Joe Moore, New York N.L., 1937.
Bobby Richardson, New York A.L., 1961.
6-game series—29—Mariano Duncan, Philadelphia N.L., 1993.
7-game series—33
Bucky Harris, Washington A.L., 1924.
Sam Rice, Washington A.L., 1925.
Omar Moreno, Pittsburgh N.L., 1979.
8-game series—36—Jimmy Collins, Boston A.L., 1903.

Most at-bats, nine-inning game

6—Held by many players. Last player—Rickey Henderson, Oakland A.L., October 28, 1989.

Most at-bats, extra-inning game

7—Don Hahn, New York N.L., October 14, 1973, 12 innings.

Most times faced pitcher with no at-bats, game

5—Fred Clarke, Pittsburgh N.L., October 16, 1909 (four bases on balls, one sacrifice hit).

Most at-bats, inning

2—Held by many players. Last player—Roberto Alomar, Toronto A.L., October 20, 1993, eighth inning.

Most times faced pitcher, inning

2—Held by many players. Last player—Roberto Alomar, Toronto A.L., October 20, 1993, eighth inning.

Most at-bats by pinch-hitter, inning

2—George H. Burns, Philadelphia A.L., October 12, 1929, seventh inning.

Most times faced pitcher twice in an inning, career

3—Joe DiMaggio, New York A.L., October 6, 1936, ninth inning; October 6, 1937, sixth inning; September 30, 1947, fifth inning.

Most times faced pitcher twice in an inning, series

2—Stan Musial, St. Louis N.L., September 30, ninth inning; October 4, 1942, fourth inning.

RUNS

Most runs, career

42—Mickey Mantle, New York A.L., 1951, 1952, 1953, 1955,

1956, 1957, 1958, 1960, 1961, 1962, 1963, 1964; 12 series, 65 games.

Most runs, series

4-game series—9
Babe Ruth, New York A.L., 1928.
Lou Gehrig, New York A.L., 1932.
5-game series—6
Home Run Baker, Philadelphia A.L., 1910.
Dan Murphy, Philadelphia A.L., 1910.
Harry Hooper, Boston A.L., 1916.
Al Simmons, Philadelphia A.L., 1929.
Lee May, Cincinnati N.L., 1970.
Boog Powell, Baltimore A.L., 1970.
Lou Whitaker, Detroit A.L., 1984.
6-game series— 10
Reggie Jackson, New York A.L., 1977.
Paul Molitor, Toronto A.L., 1993.
7-game series—8
Tommy Leach, Pittsburgh N.L., 1909.
Pepper Martin, St. Louis N.L., 1934.
Billy Johnson, New York A.L., 1947.
Mickey Mantle, New York A.L., 1960.
Bobby Richardson, New York A.L., 1960.
Mickey Mantle, New York A.L., 1964.
Lou Brock, St. Louis N.L., 1967.
8-game series—8—Fred Parent, Boston A.L., 1903.

Most series with one or more runs

12—Yogi Berra, New York A.L., 1947, 1949, 1950, 1951, 1952, 1953, 1955, 1956, 1957, 1958, 1960, 1961.

Most at-bats without scoring a run, series

29—Marv Owen, Detroit A.L., 1934 (7-game series).

Most consecutive games with one or more runs, career

9—Babe Ruth, New York A.L., 1927 (last 2), 1928 (4), 1932 (first 3).

Most runs, game

4—Babe Ruth, New York A.L., October 6, 1926.
Earle Combs, New York A.L., October 2, 1932.
Frank Crosetti, New York A.L., October 2, 1936.
Enos Slaughter, St. Louis N.L., October 10, 1946.
Reggie Jackson, New York A.L., October 18, 1977.
Kirby Puckett, Minnesota A.L., October 24, 1987.
Carney Lansford, Oakland A.L., October 27, 1989.
Lenny Dykstra, Philadelphia N.L., October 20, 1993.

Most runs, inning

2—Frankie Frisch, New York N.L., October 7, 1921, seventh inning.
Al Simmons, Philadelphia A.L., October 12, 1929, seventh inning.
Jimmie Foxx, Philadelphia A.L., October 12, 1929, seventh inning.
Dick McAuliffe, Detroit A.L., October 9, 1968, third inning.
Mickey Stanley, Detroit A.L., October 9, 1968, third inning.
Al Kaline, Detroit A.L., October 9, 1968, third inning.

HITS

CAREER AND SERIES

Most hits, career

71—Yogi Berra, New York A.L., 1947, 1949, 1950, 1951, 1952, 1953, 1955, 1956, 1957, 1958, 1960, 1961, 1962, 1963; 14 series, 75 games.

Most hits by pinch-hitter, career

3—Ken O'Dea, Chicago N.L., 1935 (1), 1938 (0); St. Louis N.L., 1942 (1), 1943 (0), 1944 (1; 5 series, 8 games).
Bobby Brown, New York A.L., 1947 (3), 1949 (0), 1950 (0), 1951 (0; four series, seven games).
Johnny Mize, New York A.L., 1949 (2), 1950 (0), 1951 (0), 1952 (1), 1953 (0; five series, eight games).
Dusty Rhodes, New York N.L., 1954 (3; one series, three games).

Carl Furillo, Brooklyn N.L., 1947 (2), 1949 (0); Los Angeles N.L., 1959 (1; three series, seven games).
Bob Cerv, New York A.L., 1955 (1), 1956 (1), 1960 (1; three series, three games).
John Blanchard, New York A.L., 1960 (1), 1961 (1), 1962 (0), 1964 (1; four series, 10 games).
Carl Warwick, St. Louis N.L., 1964 (3; one series, five games).
Gonzalo Marquez, Oakland A.L., 1972 (3; one series, five games).
Ken Boswell, New York N.L., 1973 (3; one series, three games).

Most series with one or more hits

12—Yogi Berra, New York A.L., 1947, 1949, 1950, 1951, 1952, 1953, 1955, 1956, 1957, 1958, 1960, 1961.
Mickey Mantle, New York A.L., 1951, 1952, 1953, 1955, 1956, 1957, 1958, 1960, 1961, 1962, 1963, 1964.

Most consecutive games with one or more hits, career

17—Hank Bauer, New York A.L., 1956 (7), 1957 (7), 1958 (first 3).

Most hits, series

4-game series— 10—Babe Ruth, New York A.L., 1928.
5-game series—9
Home Run Baker, Philadelphia A.L., 1910.
Eddie Collins, Philadelphia A.L., 1910.
Home Run Baker, Philadelphia A.L., 1913.
Heinie Groh, New York N.L., 1922.
Joe Moore, New York N.L., 1937.
Bobby Richardson, New York A.L., 1961.
Paul Blair, Baltimore A.L., 1970.
Brooks Robinson, Baltimore A.L., 1970.
Alan Trammell, Detroit A.L., 1984.
6-game series— 12
Billy Martin, New York A.L., 1953.
Paul Molitor, Toronto A.L., 1993.
Roberto Alomar, Toronto A.L., 1993.
7-game series— 13
Bobby Richardson, New York A.L., 1964.
Lou Brock, St. Louis N.L., 1968.
Marty Barrett, Boston A.L., 1986.
8-game series— 12
Buck Herzog, New York N.L., 1912.
Joe Jackson, Chicago A.L., 1919.

Most hits by pinch-hitter, series

3—Bobby Brown, New York A.L., 1947 (consecutive; four games; one base on balls, one single, two doubles, three runs batted in).
Dusty Rhodes, New York N.L., 1954 (consecutive; three games; one home run, two singles, six runs batted in).
Carl Warwick, St. Louis N.L., 1964 (consecutive; five games; two singles, walk, single, one run batted in).
Gonzalo Marquez, Oakland A.L., 1972 (consecutive' three games; three singles, one run batted in).
Ken Boswell, New York N.L., 1973 (consecutive; three games; three singles).

Most consecutive hits, career

7—Thurman Munson, New York A.L., October 19 (2), October 21 (4), 1976, October 11 (1), 1977.
Billy Hatcher, Cincinnati N.L., October 16 (3), 17 (4), 1990.

Most hits, two consecutive series

25—Lou Brock, St. Louis N.L., 1967 (12), 1968 (13).

Most consecutive hits, series

7—Billy Hatcher, Cincinnati N.L., October 16 (3), 17 (4), 1990.

Most games with four or more hits, series

2—Robin Yount, Milwaukee A.L., October 12 (4), 16 (4), 1982.

Collecting one or more hits in each game, series

Held by many players.

Most at-bats without a hit, career

22—George Earnshaw, Philadelphia A.L., 1929 (5), 1930
(9), 1931 (8).

Most at-bats without a hit, series

22—Dal Maxvill, St. Louis N.L., 1968 (7-game series).

Most consecutive hitless times at bat, career

31—Marv Owen, Detroit A.L., 1934 (last 12), 1935 (first 19).

GAME AND INNING

Most hits, game

5—Paul Molitor, Milwaukee A.L., October 12, 1982.

Most times reached first base safely, nine-inning game (batting 1.000)

5—Babe Ruth, New York A.L., October 6, 1926 (three home
runs, two bases on balls).
Babe Ruth, New York A.L., October 10, 1926 (one home
run, four bases on balls).
Lou Brock, St. Louis N.L., October 4, 1967 (four singles,
one base on balls).
Brooks Robinson, Baltimore A.L., October 11, 1971 (three
singles, two bases on balls).
Rusty Staub, New York N.L., October 17, 1973 (three singles one home run, one base on balls).
Kiko Garcia, Baltimore A.L., October 12, 1979 (two singles, one double, one triple, one base on balls).
Reggie Jackson, New York A.L., October 24, 1981 (two
singles, one home run, two bases on balls).
George Brett, Kansas City A.L., October 22, 1985 (two
singles, three bases on balls).
Kirby Puckett, Minnesota A.L., October 24, 1987 (four
singles, one base on balls).
Billy Hatcher, Cincinnati N.L., October 17, 1990 (one single, two doubles, one triple, one base on balls).

Most hits accounting for all club's hits, game

3—Irish Meusel, New York N.L., October 14, 1923 (one single, one double, one triple).
Dave Parker, Oakland A.L., October 16, 1988 (three singles).

Most at-bats with no hits, nine-inning game

5—Held by many players.

Most at-bats with no hits, extra-inning game

6—Travis Jackson, New York N.L., October 10, 1924, 12 in-
nings.
Hughie Critz, New York N.L., October 6, 1933, 11 innings.
Felix Millan, New York N.L., October 14, 1973, 12 innings.
Mickey Rivers, New York A.L., October 11, 1977, 12 innings.
Ron Gant, Atlanta, October 22, 1991, 12 innings.

Most hits in two consecutive games, series

7—Frank Isbell, Chicago A.L., October 13 (4), 14 (3), 1906.
Fred Lindstrom, New York N.L., October 7 (3), 8 (4), 1924.
Monte Irvin, New York N.L., October 4 (4), 5 (3), 1951.
Thurman Munson, New York A.L., October 19 (3), 21 (4),
1976.
Paul Molitor, Milwaukee A.L., October 12 (5), 13 (2), 1982.
Billy Hatcher, Cincinnati N.L., October 16 (3), 17 (4),
1990.

Most hits, inning (17 times)

2—Ross Youngs, New York N.L., October 7, 1921, seventh in-
ning.
Al Simmons, Philadelphia A.L., October 12, 1929, seventh
inning.
Jimmie Foxx, Philadelphia A.L., October 12, 1929, seventh
inning.
Jimmie Dykes, Philadelphia A.L., October 12, 1929, sev-
enth inning.
Joe Moore, New York N.L., October 4, 1933, sixth inning.
Dizzy Dean, St. Louis N.L., October 9, 1934, third inning.
Joe DiMaggio, New York A.L., October 6, 1936, ninth in-
ning.
Hank Leiber, New York N.L., October 9, 1937, second inning.

Stan Musial, St. Louis N.L., October 4, 1942, fourth in-
ning.
Elston Howard, New York A.L., October 6, 1960, sixth in-
ning.
Bobby Richardson, New York A.L., October 6, 1960, sixth
inning.
Bob Cerv, New York A.L., October 8, 1960, first inning.
Frank Quilici, Minnesota A.L., October 6, 1965, third in-
ning.
Al Kaline, Detroit A.L., October 9, 1968, third inning.
Norm Cash, Detroit A.L., October 9, 1968, third inning.
Merv Rettenmund, Baltimore A.L., October 11, 1971, fifth
inning.
Gary Gaetti, Minnesota A.L., October 17, 1987, fourth in-
ning.

SINGLES

Most singles, career

49—Yogi Berra, New York A.L., 1947, 1949, 1950, 1951,
1952, 1953, 1955, 1956, 1957, 1958, 1960, 1961, 1962,
1963; 14 series, 75 games.

Most singles, series

4-game series—9—Thurman Munson, New York A.L., 1976.
5-game series—8
Frank Chance, Chicago N.L., 1908.
Home Run Baker, Philadelphia A.L., 1913.
Heinie Groh, New York N.L., 1922.
Joe Moore, New York N.L., 1937.
Bobby Richardson, New York A.L., 1961.
Paul Blair, Baltimore A.L., 1970.
Steve Garvey, Los Angeles N.L., 1974.
6-game series—10
Red Rolfe, New York A.L., 1936.
Monte Irvin, New York N.L., 1951.
7-game series—12—Sam Rice, Washington A.L., 1925.
8-game series—9
Jimmy Sebring, Pittsburgh N.L., 1903.
Chief Meyers, New York N.L., 1912.

Most singles, game

5—Paul Molitor, Milwaukee A.L., October 12, 1982.

Most singles, inning

2—Jimmie Foxx, Philadelphia A.L., October 12, 1929, seventh
inning.
Joe Moore, New York N.L., October 4, 1933, sixth inning.
Joe DiMaggio, New York A.L., October 6, 1936, ninth in-
ning.
Hank Leiber, New York N.L., October 9, 1937, second inning.
Bob Cerv, New York A.L., October 8, 1960, first inning.
Al Kaline, Detroit A.L., October 9, 1968, third inning.
Norm Cash, Detroit A.L., October 9, 1968, third inning.
Merv Rettenmund, Baltimore A.L., October 11, 1971, fifth
inning.

DOUBLES

Most doubles, career

10—Frankie Frisch, New York N.L. (5), 1921, 1922, 1923,
1924; St. Louis N.L. (5), 1928, 1930, 1931, 1934; eight
series, 50 games.
Yogi Berra, New York A.L., 1947, 1949, 1950, 1951,
1952, 1953, 1955, 1956, 1957, 1958, 1960, 1961, 1962,
1963; 14 series, 75 games.

Most doubles, series

4-game series—4—Billy Hatcher, Cincinnati, N.L., 1990.
5-game series—4
Eddie Collins, Philadelphia A.L., 1910.
Rick Dempsey, Baltimore A.L., 1983.
6-game series—5—Chick Hafey, St. Louis N.L., 1930.
7-game series—6—Pete Fox, Detroit A.L., 1934.
8-game series—4
Red Murray, New York N.L., 1912.

Buck Herzog, New York N.L., 1912.
Buck Weaver, Chicago A.L., 1919.
George J. Burns, New York N.L., 1921.

Most doubles, game

4—Frank Isbell, Chicago A.L., October 13, 1906.

Most doubles batting in three runs, game

1—Frankie Frisch, St. Louis N.L., October 9, 1934, third inning.
Paul Richards, Detroit A.L., October 10, 1945, first inning.
Lou Brock, St. Louis N.L., October 6, 1968, eighth inning.
Terry Pendleton, St. Louis N.L., October 20, 1985, ninth inning.

Most doubles, inning

1—Held by many players.

TRIPLES

Most triples, career

4—Tommy Leach, Pittsburgh N.L. (4), 1903, 1909; two series, 15 games.
Tris Speaker, Boston A.L. (3), 1912, 1915; Cleveland A.L. (1), 1920; three series, 20 games.
Billy Johnson, New York A.L., 1943, 1947, 1949, 1950; four series, 18 games.

Most games without a triple, career

75—Yogi Berra, New York A.L.; 14 series, 259 at-bats.

Most triples, series

4-game series—2
Lou Gehrig, New York A.L., 1927.
Tommy Davis, Los Angeles N.L., 1963.
Rickey Henderson, Oakland A.L., 1989.
5-game series—2
Eddie Collins, Philadelphia A.L., 1913.
Bobby Brown, New York A.L., 1949.
6-game series—2
George Rohe, Chicago A.L., 1906.
Bob Meusel, New York A.L., 1923.
Billy Martin, New York A.L., 1953.
Paul Molitor, Toronto A.L., 1993.
Devon White, Toronto A.L., 1993.
7-game series—3
Billy Johnson, New York A.L., 1947.
Mark Lemke, Atlanta N.L., 1991.
8-game series—4—Tommy Leach, Pittsburgh N.L., 1903.

Most triples, game

2—Tommy Leach, Pittsburgh N.L., October 1, 1903.
Patsy Dougherty, Boston A.L., October 7, 1903.
Dutch Ruether, Cincinnati N.L., October 1, 1919.
Bobby Richardson, New York A.L., October 12, 1960.
Tommy Davis, Los Angeles N.L., October 3, 1963.
Mark Lemke, Atlanta N.L., October 24, 1991.

Most bases-loaded triples, game

1—George Rohe, Chicago A.L., October 11, 1906, sixth inning.
Ross Youngs, New York N.L., October 7, 1921, seventh inning.
Billy Johnson, New York A.L., October 7, 1943, eighth inning.
Bobby Brown, New York A.L., October 8, 1949, fifth inning.
Hank Bauer, New York A.L., October 10, 1951, sixth inning.
Billy Martin, New York A.L., September 30, 1953, first inning.
Kiko Garcia, Baltimore A.L., October 12, 1979, fourth inning.
Milt Thompson, Philadelphia N.L., October 20, 1993, first inning.

Most triples, inning

1—Held by many players.

HOME RUNS

CAREER AND SERIES

Most home runs, career

18—Mickey Mantle, New York A.L., 1951, 1952, 1953, 1955,

1956, 1957, 1958, 1960, 1961, 1962, 1963, 1964; 12 series, 65 games.

Most home runs by pitcher, career

2—Bob Gibson, St. Louis N.L., 1964 (0), 1967 (1), 1968 (1); three series, nine games.
Dave McNally, Baltimore A.L., 1966 (0), 1969 (1), 1970 (1), 1971 (0); four series, nine games.

Most games without a home run, career

50—Frankie Frisch, New York N.L., St. Louis N.L.; eight series, 197 at-bats.

Most series with one or more home runs

9—Yogi Berra, New York A.L., 1947 (1), 1950 (1), 1952 (2), 1953 (1), 1955 (1), 1956 (3), 1957 (1), 1960 (1), 1961 (1).
Mickey Mantle, New York A.L., 1952 (2), 1953 (2), 1955 (1), 1956 (3), 1957 (1), 1958 (2), 1960 (3), 1963 (1), 1964 (3).

Most home runs, four consecutive games (homering in each game)

6—Reggie Jackson, New York A.L., 1977 (5), last three games; 1978 (1), first game.

Hitting home runs for both leagues

Bill Skowron, A.L. (7), N.L. (1).
Frank Robinson, N.L. (1), A.L. (7).
Roger Maris, A.L. (5), N.L. (1).
Reggie Smith, A.L. (2), N.L. (4).
Enos Slaughter, N.L. (2), A.L. (1).
Kirk Gibson, A.L. (2), N.L. (1).

Most home runs, series

4-game series—4—Lou Gehrig, New York A.L., 1928.
5-game series—3—Donn Clendenon, New York N.L., 1969.
6-game series—5—Reggie Jackson, New York, 1977.
7-game series—4
Babe Ruth, New York A.L., 1926.
Duke Snider, Brooklyn N.L., 1952.
Duke Snider, Brooklyn N.L., 1955.
Hank Bauer, New York A.L., 1958.
Gene Tenace, Oakland A.L., 1972.
8-game series—2—Patsy Dougherty, Boston A.L., 1903.

Most home runs by pinch-hitter, series

2—Chuck Essegian, Los Angeles N.L., 4 games, 1959.
Bernie Carbo, Boston A.L., 3 games, 1975.

Most home runs by rookie, series

3—Charlie Keller, New York A.L., 1939.

Most series with two or more home runs

6—Mickey Mantle, New York A.L., 1952 (2), 1953 (2), 1956 (3), 1958 (2), 1960 (3), 1964 (3).

Most series with three or more home runs

3—Babe Ruth, New York A.L., 1923 (3), 1926 (4), 1928 (3).
Mickey Mantle, New York A.L., 1956 (3), 1960 (3), 1964 (3).

Most series with four or more home runs

2—Duke Snider, Brooklyn N.L., 1952, 1955.

Most home runs, two consecutive series (two consecutive years)

7—Reggie Jackson, New York A.L., 1977 (5), 1978 (2).

Most home runs, three consecutive series (three consecutive years)

9—Babe Ruth, New York A.L., 1926 (4), 1927 (2), 1928 (3).

Most home runs in three consecutive games, series (homering each game)

5—Reggie Jackson, New York A.L., October 15 (1), 16 (1), 18 (3), 1977.

Most home runs in two consecutive games, series (homering each game)

4—Reggie Jackson, New York A.L., October 16 (1), 18 (3), 1977.

Most consecutive home runs in two consecutive games, series

4—Reggie Jackson, New York A.L., October 16 (1), 18 (3), 1977 (one base on balls included).

Most series with two or more home runs in a game

4—Babe Ruth, New York A.L., 1923, 1926, 1928, 1932 (two home runs in one game twice, three home runs in one game twice).

GAME AND INNING

Most home runs, game (3 homers, 3 times; 2 homers, 34 times; *consecutive)

3—Babe Ruth, New York A.L., October 6, 1926 (two consecutive).

Babe Ruth, New York A.L., October 9, 1928, (two consecutive).

Reggie Jackson, New York A.L., October 18, 1977* (each on first pitch).

2—Patsy Dougherty, Boston A.L., October 2, 1903.
Harry Hooper, Boston A.L., October 13, 1915.
Benny Kauff, New York N.L., October 11, 1917.
Babe Ruth, New York A.L., October 11, 1923*.
Lou Gehrig, New York A.L., October 7, 1928*.
Lou Gehrig, New York A.L., October 1, 1932*.
Babe Ruth, New York A.L., October 1, 1932.
Tony Lazzeri, New York A.L., October 2, 1932.
Charlie Keller, New York A.L., October 7, 1939.
Bob Elliott, Boston N.L., October 10, 1948*.
Duke Snider, Brooklyn N.L., October 6, 1952*.
Joe Collins, New York A.L., September 28, 1955*.
Duke Snider, Brooklyn N.L., October 2, 1955*.
Yogi Berra, New York A.L., October 10, 1956*.
Tony Kubek, New York A.L., October 5, 1957.
Mickey Mantle, New York A.L., October 2, 1958.
Ted Kluszewski, Chicago A.L., October 1, 1959*.
Charlie Neal, Los Angeles N.L., October 2, 1959*.
Mickey Mantle, New York A.L., October 6, 1960.
Carl Yastrzemski, Boston A.L., October 5, 1967.
Rico Petrocelli, Boston A.L., October 11, 1967*.
Gene Tenace, Oakland A.L., October 14, 1972*.
Tony Perez, Cincinnati N.L., October 16, 1975*.
Johnny Bench, Cincinnati N.L., October 21, 1976.
Dave Lopes, Los Angeles N.L., October 10, 1978*.
Willie Aikens, Kansas City A.L., October 14, 1980.
Willie Aikens, Kansas City A.L., October 18, 1980.
Willie McGee, St. Louis N.L., October 15, 1982*.
Eddie Murray, Baltimore A.L., October 16, 1983*.
Alan Trammell, Detroit A.L., October 13, 1984*.
Kirk Gibson, Detroit A.L., October 14, 1984.
Gary Carter, New York N.L., October 22, 1986.
Dave Henderson, Oakland A.L., October 27, 1989*.
Chris Sabo, Cincinnati N.L., October 19, 1990*.

Most home runs by rookie, game

2—Charlie Keller, New York A.L., October 7, 1939.
Tony Kubek, New York A.L., October 5, 1957.
Willie McGee, St. Louis N.L., October 15, 1982.

Hitting home runs in first two World Series at-bats

Gene Tenace, Oakland A.L., October 14, 1972, second and fifth innings.

Hitting home runs in first World Series at-bat (23 times; *not first plate appearance)

Joe Harris, Washington A.L., vs. Pittsburgh N.L., October 7, 1925, second inning.
George Watkins, St. Louis N.L., vs. Philadelphia A.L., October 2, 1930, second inning.
Mel Ott, New York N.L., vs. Washington A.L., October 3, 1933, first inning.
George Selkirk, New York A.L., vs. New York N.L., September 30, 1936, third inning.
Dusty Rhodes, New York N.L., vs. Cleveland A.L., September 29, 1954, 10th inning.
Elston Howard, New York A.L., vs. Brooklyn N.L. September 28, 1955, second inning.
Roger Maris, New York A.L., vs. Pittsburgh N.L., October 5, 1960, first inning.
Don Mincher, Minnesota A.L., vs. Los Angeles N.L., October 6, 1965, second inning.

Brooks Robinson, Baltimore A.L., vs. Los Angeles N.L., October 5, 1966, first inning.
Jose R. Santiago, Boston A.L., vs. St. Louis N.L., October 4, 1967, third inning.
Mickey Lolich, Detroit A.L., vs. St. Louis N.L., October 3, 1968, third inning.
Don Buford, Baltimore A.L., vs. New York N.L., October 11, 1969, first inning.
Gene Tenace, Oakland A.L., vs. Cincinnati N.L., October 14, 1972, second inning.
Jim Mason, New York A.L., vs. Cincinnati N.L., October 19, 1976, seventh inning.
Doug DeCinces, Baltimore A.L. vs. Pittsburgh N.L., October 10, 1979, first inning.
Amos Otis, Kansas City A.L. vs. Philadelphia N.L., October 14, 1980, second inning.
Bob Watson, New York A.L. vs. Los Angeles N.L., October 20, 1981, first inning.
Jim Dwyer, Baltimore A.L. vs. Philadelphia N.L., October 11, 1983, first inning.
Mickey Hatcher, Los Angeles N.L. vs. Oakland A.L., October 15, 1988, first inning.
Jose Canseco, Oakland A.L. vs. Los Angeles N.L., October 15, 1988, second inning*.
Bill Bathe, San Francisco N.L. vs. Oakland A.L., October 27, 1989, ninth inning.
Eric Davis, Cincinnati N.L. vs. Oakland A.L., October 16, 1990, first inning.
Ed Sprague Jr., Toronto A.L. vs. Atlanta N.L., October 18, 1992, ninth inning.

Most times hitting home run winning a 1-0 game

1—Casey Stengel, New York N.L., October 12, 1923, seventh inning.
Tommy Henrich, New York A.L., October 5, 1949, ninth inning.
Paul Blair, Baltimore A.L., October 8, 1966, fifth inning.
Frank Robinson, Baltimore A.L., October 9, 1966, fourth inning.

Most times homering as leadoff batter at start of game (15 times)

1—Patsy Dougherty, Boston A.L., October 2, 1903.
Davy Jones, Detroit A.L., October 13, 1909.
Phil Rizzuto, New York A.L., October 5, 1942.
Dale Mitchell, Cleveland A.L., October 10, 1948.
Gene Woodling, New York A.L., October 4, 1953.
Al Smith, Cleveland A.L., September 30, 1954.
Billy Bruton, Milwaukee N.L., October 2, 1958.
Lou Brock, St. Louis N.L., October 6, 1968.
Don Buford, Baltimore A.L., October 11, 1969.
Tommie Agee, New York N.L., October 14, 1969.
Pete Rose, Cincinnati N.L., October 20, 1972.
Wayne Garrett, New York N.L., October 16, 1973.
Dave Lopes, Los Angeles N.L., October 17, 1978.
Lenny Dykstra, New York N.L., October 21, 1986.
Rickey Henderson, Oakland A.L., October 28, 1989.

Most home runs by pitcher, game (14 times)

1—Jim Bagby Sr., Cleveland A.L., October 10, 1920 (two on base).
Rosy Ryan, New York N.L., October 6, 1924 (none on base).
Jack Bentley, New York N.L., October 8, 1924 (one on base).
Jesse Haines, St. Louis N.L., October 5, 1926 (one on base).
Bucky Walters, Cincinnati N.L., October 7, 1940 (none on base).
Lew Burdette, Milwaukee N.L., October 2, 1958 (two on base).
Mudcat Grant, Minnesota A.L., October 13, 1965 (two on base).
Jose R. Santiago, Boston A.L., October 4, 1967 (none on base).
Bob Gibson, St. Louis N.L., October 12, 1967 (none on base).
Mickey Lolich, Detroit A.L., October 3, 1968 (none on base).
Bob Gibson, St. Louis N.L., October 6, 1968 (none on base).
Dave McNally, Baltimore A.L., October 16, 1969 (one on base).
Dave McNally, Baltimore A.L., October 13, 1970 (three on base).

Ken Holtzman, Oakland A.L., October 16, 1974 (none on base).

Most home runs by pinch-hitter, inning or game (17 times)

1—Yogi Berra, New York A.L., October 2, 1947, seventh inning (none on base).
  Johnny Mize, New York A.L., October 3, 1952, ninth inning (none on base).
  George Shuba, Brooklyn N.L., September 30, 1953, sixth inning (one on base).
  Dusty Rhodes, New York N.L., September 29, 1954, 10th inning (two on base).
  Hank Majeski, Cleveland A.L., October 2, 1954, fifth inning (two on base).
  Bob Cerv, New York A.L., October 2, 1955, seventh inning (none on base).
  Chuck Essegian, Los Angeles N.L., October 2, 1959, seventh inning (none on base).
  Chuck Essegian, Los Angeles N.L., October 8, 1959, ninth inning (none on base).
  Elston Howard, New York A.L., October 5, 1960, ninth inning (none on base).
  John Blanchard, New York A.L., October 7, 1961, eighth inning (none on base).
  Bernie Carbo, Boston A.L., October 14, 1975, seventh inning (none on base).
  Bernie Carbo, Boston A.L., October 21, 1975, eighth inning (two on base).
  Jay Johnstone, Los Angeles N.L., October 24, 1981, sixth inning (one on base).
  Kirk Gibson, Los Angeles N.L., October 15, 1988, ninth inning (one on base).
  Bill Bathe, San Francisco N.L., October 27, 1989, ninth inning (two on base).
  Chili Davis, Minnesota A.L., October 22, 1991, eighth inning (one on base).
  Ed Sprague Jr., Toronto A.L., October 18, 1992, ninth inning (one on base).

Most grand slams, game (16 times)

1—Elmer Smith, Cleveland A.L., October 10, 1920, first inning.
  Tony Lazzeri, New York A.L., October 2, 1936, third inning.
  Gil McDougald, New York A.L., October 9, 1951, third inning.
  Mickey Mantle, New York A.L., October 4, 1953, third inning.
  Yogi Berra, New York A.L., October 5, 1956, second inning.
  Bill Skowron, New York A.L., October 10, 1956, seventh inning.
  Bobby Richardson, New York A.L., October 8, 1960, first inning.
  Chuck Hiller, San Francisco N.L., October 8, 1962, seventh inning.
  Ken Boyer, St. Louis N.L., October 11, 1964, sixth inning.
  Joe Pepitone, New York A.L., October 14, 1964, eighth inning.
  Jim Northrup, Detroit A.L., October 9, 1968, third inning.
  Dave McNally, Baltimore A.L., October 13, 1970, sixth inning.
  Dan Gladden, Minnesota A.L., October 17, 1987, fourth inning.
  Kent Hrbek, Minnesota A.L., October 24, 1987, sixth inning.
  Jose Canseco, Oakland A.L., October 15, 1988, second inning.
  Lonnie Smith, Atlanta N.L., October 22, 1992, fifth inning.

Most home runs, inning

1—Held by many players.

Most home runs, two consecutive innings

2—Babe Ruth, New York A.L., October 11, 1923, fourth and fifth innings.
  Babe Ruth, New York A.L., October 9, 1928, seventh and eighth innings.
  Ted Kluszewski, Chicago A.L., October 1, 1959, third and fourth innings.
  Reggie Jackson, New York A.L., October 18, 1977, fourth and fifth innings.
  Willie Aikens, Kansas City A.L., October 18, 1980, first and second innings.

Dave Henderson, Oakland A.L., October 27, 1989, fourth and fifth innings.
Chris Sabo, Cincinnati N.L., October 19, 1990, second and third innings.

TOTAL BASES

Most total bases, career

123—Mickey Mantle, New York A.L., 1951, 1952, 1953, 1955, 1956, 1957, 1958, 1960, 1961, 1962, 1963, 1964; 12 series, 65 games.

Most total bases, series

4-game series—22—Babe Ruth, New York A.L., 1928.
5-game series—17—Brooks Robinson, Baltimore A.L., 1970.
6-game series—25—Reggie Jackson, New York A.L., 1977.
7-game series—25—Willie Stargell, Pittsburgh N.L., 1979.
8-game series—18
  Buck Herzog, New York N.L., 1912.
  Joe Jackson, Chicago A.L., 1919.

Most total bases by pinch-hitter, series

8—Chuck Essegian, Los Angeles N.L., 1959; four games (two home runs).
  Bernie Carbo, Boston A.L., 1975; three games (two home runs).

Most total bases, game

12—Babe Ruth, New York A.L., October 6, 1926 (three home runs).
  Babe Ruth, New York A.L., October 9, 1928 (three home runs).
  Reggie Jackson, New York A.L., October 18, 1977 (three home runs).

Most total bases, inning

5—Ross Youngs, New York N.L., October 7, 1921, seventh inning (double and triple).
  Al Simmons, Philadelphia A.L., October 12, 1929, seventh inning (home run and single).

LONG HITS

Most long hits, career

26—Mickey Mantle, New York A.L., 1951, 1952, 1953, 1955, 1956, 1957, 1958, 1960, 1961, 1962, 1963, 1964; 12 series, 65 games.

Most long hits, series

4-game series—6—Babe Ruth, New York A.L., 1928.
5-game series—5—Rick Dempsey, Baltimore A.L., 1983.
6-game series—6
  Reggie Jackson, New York A.L., 1977.
  Paul Molitor, Toronto A.L., 1993.
  Devon White, Toronto A.L., 1993.
7-game series—7—Willie Stargell, Pittsburgh N.L., 1979.
8-game series—5
  Red Murray, New York N.L., 1912.
  Buck Herzog, New York N.L., 1912.
  Buck Weaver, Chicago A.L., 1919.
  George J. Burns, New York N.L., 1921.

Most long hits, game

4—Frank Isbell, Chicago A.L., October 13, 1906 (four doubles).

Most long hits in two consecutive games, series

5—Lou Brock, St. Louis N.L., October 6 (3—double, triple, home run); October 7 (2—two doubles), 1968.

Most long hits, inning

2—Ross Youngs, New York N.L., October 7, 1921, seventh inning (double and triple).

EXTRA BASES ON LONG HITS

Most extra bases on long hits, career

64—Mickey Mantle, New York A.L., 1951, 1952, 1953, 1955,

1956, 1957, 1958, 1960, 1961, 1962, 1963, 1964; 12 series, 65 games.

Most extra bases on long hits, series

4-game series—13—Lou Gehrig, New York A.L., 1928 (one double, four home runs).
5-game series—10—Donn Clendenon, New York N.L., 1969 (one double, three home runs).
6-game series—16—Reggie Jackson, New York A.L. 1977 (one double, five home runs).
7-game series—14—Duke Snider, Brooklyn N.L., 1952 (two doubles, four home runs).
8-game series—10—Patsy Dougherty, Boston A.L., 1903 (two triples, two home runs).

RUNS BATTED IN

Most runs batted in, career

40—Mickey Mantle, New York A.L., 1951, 1952, 1953, 1955, 1956, 1957, 1958, 1960, 1961, 1962, 1963, 1964; 12 series, 65 games.

Most series with one or more runs batted in

11—Yogi Berra, New York A.L., 1947, 1949, 1950, 1952, 1953, 1955, 1956, 1957, 1958, 1960, 1961.

Most consecutive games with one or more RBIs, career

8—Lou Gehrig, New York A.L., 1928 (4), 1932 (4) (total of 17 runs batted in).
Reggie Jackson, New York A.L., 1977 (4), 1978 (4) (total of 14 runs batted in).

Most runs batted in, series

4-game series—9—Lou Gehrig, New York A.L., 1928.
5-game series—8
Dan Murphy, Philadelphia A.L., 1910.
Lee May, Cincinnati N.L., 1970.
6-game series—10—Ted Kluszewski, Chicago A.L., 1959.
7-game series—12—Bobby Richardson, New York A.L., 1960.
8-game series—8
Tommy Leach, Pittsburgh N.L., 1903.
Pat Duncan, Cincinnati N.L., 1919.

Most runs batted in by pinch-hitter, series

6—Dusty Rhodes, New York N.L., 1954; three games.

Most at-bats without a run batted in, series

34—Fred Clarke, Pittsburgh N.L., 1903; eight games.
Buck Weaver, Chicago A.L., 1919; eight games.

Most runs batted in, game

6—Bobby Richardson, New York A.L., October 8, 1960.

Most runs batted in accounting for all club's runs, game

4—Hank Bauer, New York A.L., October 4, 1958 (won 4-0.
Ken Boyer, St. Louis N.L., October 11, 1964 (won 4-3).
Ron Cey, Los Angeles N.L., October 11, 1978 (won 4-3).
Alan Trammell, Detroit A.L., October 13, 1984 (won 4-2).
Jose Canseco, Oakland A.L., October 15, 1988 (lost 5-4).

Most runs batted in, inning (16 times)

4—Elmer Smith, Cleveland A.L., October 10, 1920, first inning.
Tony Lazzeri, New York A.L., October 2, 1936, third inning.
Gil McDougald, New York A.L., October 9, 1951, third inning.
Mickey Mantle, New York A.L., October 4, 1953, third inning.
Yogi Berra, New York A.L., October 5, 1956, second inning.
Bill Skowron, New York A.L., October 10, 1956, seventh inning.
Bobby Richardson, New York A.L., October 8, 1960, first inning.
Chuck Hiller, San Francisco N.L., October 8, 1962, seventh inning.
Ken Boyer, St. Louis N.L., October 11, 1964, sixth inning.
Joe Pepitone, New York A.L., October 14, 1964, eighth inning.
Jim Northrup, Detroit A.L., October 9, 1968, third inning.
Dave McNally, Baltimore A.L., October 13, 1970, sixth inning.
Dan Gladden, Minnesota A.L., October 17, 1987, fourth inning.

Kent Hrbek, Minnesota A.L., October 24, 1987, sixth inning.
Jose Canseco, Oakland A.L., October 15, 1988, second inning.
Lonnie Smith, Atlanta N.L., October 22, 1992, fifth inning.

BASES ON BALLS

Most bases on balls, career

43—Mickey Mantle, New York A.L., 1951, 1952, 1953, 1955, 1956, 1957, 1958, 1960, 1961, 1962, 1963, 1964; 12 series, 65 games.

Most bases on balls, series

4-game series—7—Hank Thompson, New York N.L., 1954.
5-game series—7
Jimmy Sheckard, Chicago N.L., 1910.
Mickey Cochrane, Philadelphia A.L., 1929.
Joe Gordon, New York A.L., 1941.
6-game series—9—Willie Randolph, New York A.L., 1981.
7-game series—11
Babe Ruth, New York A.L., 1926.
Gene Tenace, Oakland A.L., 1973.
8-game series—7
Josh Devore, New York N.L., 1912.
Ross Youngs, New York N.L., 1921.

Most series with one or more bases on balls, career

13—Yogi Berra, New York A.L., 1947, 1949, 1950, 1951, 1952, 1953, 1955, 1956, 1957, 1958, 1960, 1961, 1962.

Most bases on balls by pinch-hitter, series

3—Bennie Tate, Washington A.L., 1924; three games.

Most at-bats without a base on balls, series

34—Buck Weaver, Chicago A.L., 1919 (8-game series).

Most at-bats without a base on balls or strikeout, series

29—Billy Southworth, St. Louis N.L., 1926 (7-game series).

Most consecutive bases on balls, one series

5—Lou Gehrig, New York A.L., October 7 (2), October 9 (3), 1928.

Most bases on balls, game

4—Fred Clarke, Pittsburgh N.L., October 16, 1909.
Dick Hoblitzell, Boston A.L., October 9, 1916, 14 innings.
Ross Youngs, New York N.L., October 10, 1924, 12 innings.
Babe Ruth, New York A.L., October 10, 1926.
Jackie Robinson, Brooklyn N.L., October 5, 1952, 11 innings.
Doug DeCinces, Baltimore A.L., October 13, 1979.

Most bases on balls with bases filled, game

2—Jim Palmer, Baltimore A.L., October 11, 1971, fourth and fifth innings.

Most bases on balls, two consecutive games

6—Jimmy Sheckard, Chicago N.L., October 18 (3), October 20 (3), 1910.

Most bases on balls, inning

2—Lefty Gomez, New York A.L., October 6, 1937, sixth inning.
Dick McAuliffe, Detroit A.L., October 9, 1968, third inning.

STRIKEOUTS

Most strikeouts, career

54—Mickey Mantle, New York A.L., 1951, 1952, 1953, 1955, 1956, 1957, 1958, 1960, 1961, 1962, 1963, 1964; 12 series, 65 games.

Most strikeouts, series

4-game series—7—Bob Meusel, New York A.L., 1927.
5-game series—9—Carmelo Martinez, San Diego N.L., 1984.
6-game series—12—Willie Wilson, Kansas City A.L., 1980.
7-game series—11
Eddie Mathews, Milwaukee N.L., 1958.
Wayne Garrett, New York N.L., 1973.
8-game series—10—George Kelly, New York N.L., 1921.

Most series with one or more strikeouts

12—Mickey Mantle, New York A.L., 1951, 1952, 1953, 1955, 1956, 1957, 1958, 1960, 1961, 1963, 1964.

Most consecutive strikeouts, one series

5—Josh Devore, New York N.L., October 16 (4), October 17 (1), 1911.
George Mogridge, Washington A.L., October 7 (4), October 10, (1), 1924.
George Pipgras, New York A.L., October 1 (5), 1932.
Mickey Mantle, New York A.L., October 2 (4), October 3 (1), 1953.
Mike Shannon, St. Louis N.L., October 12 (2), October 14 (3), 1964.
Danny Jackson, Kansas City A.L., October 19 (2), October 24 (3), 1985.

Most strikeouts by pinch-hitter, series

3—Gabby Hartnett, Chicago N.L., 1929; three games.
Rollie Hemsley, Chicago N.L., 1932; three games.
Otto Velez, New York A.L., 1976; three games.

Most at-bats without a strikeout, series

30—Tim Foli, Pittsburgh N.L., 1979 (7-game series).

Most strikeouts, game

5—George Pipgras, New York A.L., October 1, 1932 (consecutive).

Most strikeouts, inning

1—Held by many players.

SACRIFICE HITS AND FLIES

Most sacrifices, career

8—Eddie Collins, Philadelphia A.L. (6), 1910, 1911, 1913, 1914; Chicago A.L. (2), 1917, 1919; six series, 34 games.

Most sacrifices, series

4-game series—3—Wes Westrum, New York N.L., 1954 (one sacrifice hit and two sacrifice flies).
5-game series—4—Duffy Lewis, Boston A.L., 1916.
6-game series—3
Jimmy Sheckard, Chicago N.L., 1906.
Harry Steinfeldt, Chicago N.L., 1906.
Joe Tinker, Chicago N.L., 1906.
Jack Barry, Philadelphia A.L., 1911.
Bill Lee, Chicago N.L., 1935.
7-game series—5—Fred Clarke, Pittsburgh N.L., 1909.
8-game series—5—Jake Daubert, Cincinnati N.L., 1919.

Most sacrifices, game

3—Joe Tinker, Chicago N.L., October 12, 1906 (all sacrifice hits).
Wes Westrum, New York N.L., October 2, 1954 (one sacrifice hit and two sacrifice flies).

Most sacrifice hits, inning

1—Held by many players.

Most sacrifice flies, career

4—Joe Carter, Toronto A.L., 1992 (1), 1993 (3); two series, 12 games.

Most sacrifice flies, series

3—Joe Carter, Toronto A.L., 1993 (6-game series).

Most sacrifice flies, game

2—Wes Westrum, New York N.L., October 2, 1954.

Most sacrifice flies, inning

1—Held by many players.

Most runs batted in on sacrifice fly

2—Tommy Herr, St. Louis N.L., October 16, 1982, second inning.

HIT BY PITCH

Most hit by pitch, career

3—Frank Chance, Chicago N.L., 1906 (2), 1907 (1).
Honus Wagner, Pittsburgh N.L., 1903 (1), 1909 (2).
Fred Snodgrass, New York N.L., 1911 (2), 1912 (1).
Max Carey, Pittsburgh N.L., 1925 (3).
Yogi Berra, New York A.L., 1953 (2), 1955 (1).
Elston Howard, New York A.L., 1960 (1), 1962 (1), 1964 (1).
Frank Robinson, Cincinnati N.L., 1961 (2); Baltimore A.L., 1971 (1).
Bert Campaneris, Oakland A.L., 1973 (2), 1974 (1).
Reggie Jackson, New York A.L., 1977 (1), 1978 (2).

Most hit by pitch, series

3—Max Carey, Pittsburgh N.L., 1925 (7-game series).

Most hit by pitch, game

2—Max Carey, Pittsburgh N.L., October 7, 1925.
Yogi Berra, New York A.L., October 2, 1953.
Frank Robinson, Cincinnati N.L., October 8, 1961.

Most hit by pitch, inning

1—Held by many players.

GROUNDING INTO DOUBLE PLAYS

Most grounding into double play, career

7—Joe DiMaggio, New York A.L., 1936, 1937, 1938, 1939, 1941, 1942, 1947, 1949, 1950, 1951; 10 series, 51 games.

Most grounding into double play, series

5—Irv Noren, New York A.L., 1955 (7-game series).

Most grounding into double play, game

3—Willie Mays, New York N.L., October 8, 1951.

REACHING ON ERRORS OR INTERFERENCE

Most times reaching first base on error, game

3—Fred Clarke, Pittsburgh N.L., October 10, 1903.

Most times awarded first base on catcher's interference, game

1—Roger Peckinpaugh, Washington A.L., October 15, 1925, first inning.
Bud Metheny, New York A.L., October 6, 1943, sixth inning.
Ken Boyer, St. Louis N.L., October 12, 1964, first inning.
Pete Rose, Cincinnati N.L., October 10, 1970, fifth inning.
George Hendrick, St. Louis N.L., October 15, 1982, ninth inning.

CLUB BATTING

GAMES

Most games played, total series
187—New York A.L. (33 series, won 109, lost 77, tied 1).

BATTING AVERAGE

Highest batting average, series
4-game series—.317—Cincinnati N.L. vs. Oakland A.L., 1990.
5-game series—.316—Philadelphia A.L. vs. Chicago N.L., 1910.
6-game series—.311—Toronto A.L. vs. Philadelphia N.L., 1993.
7-game series—.338—New York A.L. vs. Pittsburgh N.L., 1960.
8-game series—.270—New York N.L. vs. Boston A.L., 1912.

Highest batting average by both clubs, series
4-game series—.283—New York A.L. .313, Chicago N.L. .253, 1932.
5-game series—.272—Philadelphia A.L. .316, Chicago N.L. .222, 1910.
6-game series—.292
Philadelphia N.L. .294, Kansas City A.L. .290, 1980.
Toronto A.L. .311, Philadelphia N.L. .274, 1993.
7-game series—.300—New York A.L. .338, Pittsburgh N.L. .256, 1960.
8-game series—.245—New York N.L. .270, Boston A.L. .220, 1912.

Highest batting average by series loser
.338—New York A.L. vs. Pittsburgh N.L., 1960 (7-game series).

Lowest batting average, series
4-game series—.142—Los Angeles N.L. vs. Baltimore A.L., 1966.
5-game series—.146—Baltimore A.L. vs. New York N.L., 1969.
6-game series—.175—New York N.L. vs. Philadelphia A.L., 1911.
7-game series—.185—St. Louis N.L. vs. Kansas City A.L., 1985.
8-game series—.207—New York A.L. vs. New York N.L., 1921.

Lowest batting average by both clubs, series
4-game series—.171—Los Angeles N.L. .142, Baltimore A.L. .200, 1966.
5-game series—.184—Baltimore A.L. .146, New York N.L. .220, 1969.
6-game series—.197—Chicago A.L. .198, Chicago N.L. .196, 1906.
7-game series—.209—Oakland A.L. .209, Cincinnati N.L. .209, 1972.
8-game series—.239—Cincinnati N.L. .255, Chicago A.L. .224, 1919.

Lowest batting average by series winner
.186—Boston A.L. vs. Chicago N.L., 1918 (6-game series).

SLUGGING AVERAGE

Highest slugging average, series
4-game series—.582—Oakland A.L. vs. San Francisco N.L., 1989.
5-game series—.509—Baltimore A.L. vs. Cincinnati N.L., 1970.
6-game series—.510—Toronto A.L. vs. Philadelphia N.L., 1993.
7-game series—.528—New York A.L. vs. Pittsburgh N.L., 1960.
8-game series—.401—Boston A.L. vs. Pittsburgh N.L., 1903.

Highest slugging average by both clubs, series
4-game series—.468—Oakland A.L. .582, San Francisco N.L. .343, 1989.
5-game series—.433—Baltimore A.L. .509, Cincinnati N.L. .354, 1970.
6-game series—.467—Toronto A.L. .510, Philadelphia N.L. .425, 1993.
7-game series—.447—New York A.L. .528, Pittsburgh N.L. .355, 1960.
8-game series—.344—New York N.L. .361, Boston A.L. .326, 1912.

Lowest slugging average, series
4-game series—.192—Los Angeles N.L. vs. Baltimore A.L., 1966.
5-game series—.194—Philadelphia A.L. vs. New York N.L., 1905.
6-game series—.233—Boston A.L. vs. Chicago N.L., 1918.
7-game series—.237—Brooklyn N.L. vs. Cleveland A.L., 1920.
8-game series—.270—New York A.L. vs. New York N.L., 1921.

Lowest slugging average by both clubs, series
4-game series—.267—Baltimore A.L. .342, Los Angeles N.L. .192, 1966.
5-game series—.224—New York N.L. .255, Philadelphia A.L. .194, 1905.
6-game series—.241—Chicago N.L. .250, Boston A.L. .233, 1918.
7-game series—.285—Cleveland A.L. .332, Brooklyn N.L. .237, 1920.
8-game series—.323—New York N.L. .371, New York A.L. .270, 1921.

AT-BATS AND PLATE APPEARANCES

Most at-bats, total series
6,255—New York A.L. (33 series, 187 games).

Most at-bats, series
4-game series—146
Chicago N.L. vs. New York A.L., 1932.
Oakland A.L. vs. San Francisco N.L., 1989.
5-game series—178—New York A.L. vs. St. Louis N.L., 1942.
6-game series—222—New York A.L. vs. Los Angeles N.L., 1978.
7-game series—269—New York A.L. vs. Pittsburgh N.L., 1960.
8-game series—282—Boston A.L. vs. Pittsburgh N.L., 1903.

Most at-bats by both clubs, series
4-game series—290—Chicago N.L. 146, New York A.L. 144, 1932.
5-game series—349—New York N.L. 176, Washington A.L. 173, 1933.
6-game series—421—New York A.L. 222, Los Angeles N.L. 199, 1978.
7-game series—512—St. Louis N.L. 262, Detroit A.L. 250, 1934.
8-game series—552—Boston A.L. 282, Pittsburgh N.L. 270, 1903.

Fewest at-bats, series
4-game series—117—Los Angeles N.L. vs. New York A.L., 1963.
5-game series—142—Oakland A.L. vs. Los Angeles N.L., 1974.
6-game series—172—Boston A.L. vs. Chicago N.L., 1918.
7-game series—215
Brooklyn N.L. vs. Cleveland A.L., 1920.
Brooklyn N.L. vs. New York A.L., 1956.
Minnesota A.L. vs. Los Angeles N.L., 1965.
8-game series—241—New York A.L. vs. New York N.L., 1921.

Fewest at-bats by both clubs, series
4-game series—240—Baltimore A.L. 120, Los Angeles N.L. 120, 1966.
5-game series—300—Los Angeles N.L. 158, Oakland A.L. 142, 1974.
6-game series—348—Chicago N.L. 176, Boston A.L. 172, 1918.
7-game series—432—Cleveland A.L. 217, Brooklyn N.L. 215, 1920.
8-game series—505—New York N.L. 264, New York A.L. 241, 1921.

Most at-bats, nine-inning game

45—New York A.L. vs. Chicago N.L., October 2, 1932.
New York A.L. vs. New York N.L., October 6, 1936.
New York A.L. vs. Pittsburgh N.L., October 6, 1960.

Most at-bats, extra-inning game

54—New York N.L. vs. Oakland A.L., October 14, 1973, 12 innings.

Most at-bats by both clubs, nine-inning game

85—Toronto A.L. 44, Philadelphia 41, October 20, 1993.

Most at-bats by both clubs, extra-inning game

101—New York N.L. 54, Oakland A.L. 47, October 14, 1973, 12 innings.

Fewest official at-bats, nine-inning game

25—Philadelphia A.L. vs. Boston N.L., October 10, 1914.

Fewest official at-bats by both clubs, nine-inning game

54—Chicago N.L. 27, Chicago A.L. 27, October 12, 1906.

Most at-bats, inning

13—Philadelphia A.L. vs. Chicago N.L., October 12, 1929, seventh inning.

Most at-bats by both clubs, inning

17—Philadelphia A.L. 13, Chicago N.L. 4, October 12, 1929, seventh inning.

Most men facing pitcher, inning

15—Philadelphia A.L. vs. Chicago N.L., October 12, 1929, seventh inning.
Detroit A.L. vs. St. Louis N.L., October 9, 1968, third inning.

Most men facing pitcher by both clubs, inning

20—Philadelphia A.L. 15, Chicago N.L. 5, October 12, 1929, seventh inning.

RUNS

SERIES AND GAME

Most runs, total series

838—New York A.L. (33 series, 187 games).

Most runs, series

4-game series—37—New York A.L. vs. Chicago N.L., 1932.
5-game series—35—Philadelphia A.L. vs. Chicago N.L., 1910.
6-game series—45—Toronto A.L. vs. Philadelphia N.L., 1993.
7-game series—55—New York A.L. vs. Pittsburgh N.L., 1960.
8-game series—39—Boston A.L. vs. Pittsburgh N.L., 1903.

Most runs by both clubs, series

4-game series—56—New York A.L. 37, Chicago N.L. 19, 1932.
5-game series—53—Baltimore A.L. 33, Cincinnati N.L. 20, 1970.
6-game series—81—Toronto A.L. 45, Philadelphia N.L. 36, 1993.
7-game series—82—New York A.L. 55, Pittsburgh N.L. 27, 1960.
8-game series—63—Boston A.L. 39, Pittsburgh N.L. 24, 1903.

Most runs by series loser

55—New York A.L. vs. Pittsburgh N.L., 1960 (7-game series).

Fewest runs, series

4-game series—2—Los Angeles N.L. vs. Baltimore A.L. 1966.
5-game series—3—Philadelphia A.L. vs. New York N.L. 1905.
6-game series—9—Boston A.L. vs. Chicago N.L., 1918.
7-game series—8—Brooklyn N.L. vs. Cleveland A.L., 1920.
8-game series—20—Chicago A.L. vs. Cincinnati N.L., 1919.

Fewest runs by both clubs, series

4-game series—15—Baltimore A.L. 13, Los Angeles N.L. 2, 1966.
5-game series—18—New York N.L. 15, Philadelphia A.L. 3, 1905.
6-game series—19—Chicago N.L. 10, Boston A.L. 9, 1918.
7-game series—29—Cleveland A.L. 21, Brooklyn N.L. 8, 1920.
8-game series—51—New York N.L. 29, New York A.L. 22, 1921.

Most runs, game

18—New York A.L. vs. New York N.L., October 2, 1936 (won 18-4).

Most runs by pinch-hitters, game

3—New York A.L. vs. Brooklyn N.L., October 2, 1947.

Most earned runs, game

17—New York A.L. vs. New York N.L., October 2, 1936 (won 18-4).

Most runs by both clubs, game

29—Toronto A.L. 15, Philadelphia N.L. 14, October 20, 1993.

Largest score, shutout game

12-0—New York A.L. 12, Pittsburgh N.L. 0, October 12, 1960.

Most players scoring one or more runs, game

9—St. Louis N.L. vs. Detroit A.L., October 9, 1934.
New York A.L. vs. New York N.L., October 2, 1936.
Milwaukee N.L. vs. New York A.L., October 2, 1958.
New York A.L. vs. Pittsburgh N.L., October 6, 1960.
Pittsburgh N.L. vs. New York A.L., October 13, 1960.
Toronto A.L. vs. Philadelphia N.L., October 20, 1993.

Most players from both clubs scoring one or more runs, game

16—Toronto A.L. 9, Philadelphia N.L. 7, October 20, 1993.

INNING

Most runs, inning

10—Philadelphia A.L. vs. Chicago N.L., October 12, 1929, seventh inning.
Detroit A.L. vs. St. Louis N.L., October 9, 1968, third inning.

Most runs by both clubs, inning

11—Philadelphia A.L. 10, Chicago N.L. 1, October 12, 1929, seventh inning.
Brooklyn N.L. 6, New York A.L. 5, October 5, 1956, second inning.

Most runs, extra inning

4—New York N.L. vs. Oakland A.L., October 14, 1973, 12th inning.

Most runs, two consecutive innings

12—Detroit A.L. vs. St. Louis N.L., October 9, 1968 (2 in second inning, 10 in third inning).

Most innings scored, game

6—New York A.L. vs. St. Louis N.L., October 6, 1926.
New York A.L. vs. Brooklyn N.L., October 1, 1947.
New York A.L. vs. Pittsburgh N.L., October 6, 1960.
Philadelphia N.L. vs. Toronto A.L., October 20, 1993.

Most innings scored by both clubs, game

10—Philadelphia N.L. 6, Toronto A.L. 4, October 20, 1993.

Most runs, first inning

7—Milwaukee N.L. vs. New York A.L., October 2, 1958.

Most runs, second inning

6—New York A.L. vs. New York N.L., October 13, 1923.
New York N.L. vs. New York A.L., October 9, 1937.
Brooklyn N.L. vs. New York A.L., October 2, 1947.
Brooklyn N.L. vs. New York A.L., October 5, 1956.

Most runs, third inning

10—Detroit A.L. vs. St. Louis N.L., October 9, 1968.

Most runs, fourth inning

7—Minnesota A.L. vs. St. Louis N.L., October 17, 1987.

Most runs, fifth inning

6—Baltimore A.L. vs. Pittsburgh N.L., October 11, 1971.
Kansas City A.L. vs. St. Louis N.L., October 27, 1985.

Most runs, sixth inning

7—New York A.L. vs. New York N.L., October 6, 1937.
New York A.L. vs. Pittsburgh N.L., October 6, 1960.

Most runs, seventh inning

10—Philadelphia A.L. vs. Chicago N.L., October 12, 1929.

Most runs, eighth inning

6—Chicago A.L. vs. Detroit A.L., October 11, 1908.
Baltimore A.L. vs. Pittsburgh N.L., October 13, 1979.
Toronto A.L. vs. Philadelphia N.L., October 20, 1993.

Most runs, ninth inning

7—New York A.L. vs. New York N.L., October 6, 1936.

Most runs with none on base and two out in ninth inning

4—New York A.L. vs. Brooklyn N.L., October 5, 1941.

Most runs, 10th inning

3—New York N.L. vs. Philadelphia A.L., October 8, 1913.
New York A.L. vs. Cincinnati N.L., October 8, 1939.
New York N.L. vs. Cleveland A.L., September 29, 1954.
Milwaukee N.L. vs. New York A.L., October 6, 1957.
St. Louis N.L. vs. New York A.L., October 12, 1964.
New York N.L. vs. Boston A.L., October 25, 1986.

Most runs, 11th inning

2—Philadelphia A.L. vs. New York N.L., October 17, 1911.
Toronto A.L. vs. Atlanta N.L., October 24, 1992.

Most runs, 12th inning

4—New York N.L. vs. Oakland A.L., October 14, 1973.

GAMES BEING SHUT OUT

Most times shut out, total series

13—New York A.L.

Most times shut out, series

4—Philadelphia A.L. vs. New York N.L., 1905.

Most consecutive times shut out, series

3—Philadelphia A.L. vs. New York N.L., October 12, 13, 14, 1905.
Los Angeles N.L. vs. Baltimore A.L., October 6, 8, 9, 1966.

Most consecutive games without being shut out, total series

42—New York A.L., October 6, 1926 through October 1, 1942.

HITS

SERIES

Most hits, total series

1,568—New York A.L. (33 series, 187 games).

Most hits, series

4-game series—45
New York A.L. vs. Chicago N.L., 1932.
Cincinnati N.L. vs. Oakland A.L., 1990.

5-game series—56—Philadelphia A.L. vs. Chicago N.L., 1910.

6-game series—68—New York A.L. vs. Los Angeles N.L., 1978.

7-game series—91—New York A.L. vs. Pittsburgh N.L., 1960.

8-game series—74—New York N.L. vs. Boston A.L., 1912.

Most hits by both clubs, series

4-game series—82—New York A.L. 45, Chicago N.L. 37, 1932.

5-game series—91—Philadelphia A.L. 56, Chicago N.L. 35, 1910.

6-game series—122—Toronto A.L. 64, Philadelphia N.L. 58, 1993.

7-game series—151—New York A.L. 91, Pittsburgh N.L. 60, 1960.

8-game series—135—Boston A.L. 71, Pittsburgh N.L. 64, 1903.

Fewest hits, series

4-game series—17—Los Angeles N.L. vs. Baltimore A.L., 1966.

5-game series—23—Baltimore A.L. vs. New York N.L., 1969.

6-game series—32—Boston A.L. vs. Chicago N.L., 1918.

7-game series—40—St. Louis N.L. vs. Kansas City A.L., 1985.

8-game series—50—New York A.L. vs. New York N.L., 1921.

Fewest hits by both clubs, series

4-game series—41—Baltimore A.L. 24, Los Angeles N.L. 17, 1966.

5-game series—57—New York N.L. 32, Philadelphia A.L. 25, 1905.

6-game series—69—Chicago N.L. 37, Boston A.L. 32, 1918.

7-game series—92—Oakland A.L. 46, Cincinnati N.L. 46, 1972.

8-game series—121—New York N.L. 71, New York A.L. 50, 1921.

Most hits by pinch-hitters, series

6—New York A.L. vs. Brooklyn N.L., 1947 (7-game series).
New York A.L. vs. Pittsburgh N.L., 1960 (7-game series).
Oakland A.L. vs. Cincinnati N.L., 1972 (7-game series).
Baltimore A.L. vs. Pittsburgh N.L., 1979 (7-game series).

Most hits by pinch-hitters for both clubs, series

11—New York A.L. 6, Brooklyn N.L. 5, 1947 (7-game series).

Most players with one or more hits in each game, series

4—New York A.L. vs. Los Angeles N.L., 1978 (6-game series).

Most consecutive hitless innings, series

9—Brooklyn N.L. vs. New York A.L., October 8, 1956 (all 27 batters).

GAME AND INNING

Most hits, game

20—New York N.L. vs. New York A.L., October 7, 1921.
St. Louis N.L. vs. Boston A.L., October 10, 1946.

Most hits by losing club, game

17—Pittsburgh N.L. vs. Baltimore A.L., October 13, 1979.

Most hits by pinch-hitters, game

3—Oakland A.L. vs. Cincinnati N.L., October 19, 1972.
Baltimore A.L. vs. Pittsburgh N.L., October 13, 1979.

Most hits by both clubs, game

32—New York A.L. 19, Pittsburgh N.L. 13, October 6, 1960.
Toronto A.L. 18, Philadelphia 14, October 20, 1993.

Fewest hits, game

0—Brooklyn N.L. vs. New York A.L., October 8, 1956.

Fewest hits by both clubs, game

5—New York A.L. 3, New York N.L. 2, October 6, 1921.
New York A.L. 5, Brooklyn N.L. 0, October 8, 1956.

Most players with one or more hits, game

11—New York A.L. vs. St. Louis N.L., October 9, 1928.
New York A.L. vs. Pittsburgh N.L., October 6, 1960.

Most players with one or more hits for either club, game

19—New York A.L. 11, Pittsburgh N.L. 8, October 6, 1960.

Most players with one or more hits and runs, game

9—New York A.L. vs. New York N.L., October 2, 1936.
New York A.L. vs. Pittsburgh N.L., October 6, 1960.

Most hits, inning

10—Philadelphia A.L. vs. Chicago N.L., October 12, 1929, seventh inning.

Most hits by pinch-hitters, inning

3—Oakland A.L. vs. Cincinnati N.L., October 19, 1972, ninth inning.

Most hits by both clubs, inning

12—Philadelphia A.L. 10, Chicago N.L. 2, October 12, 1929, seventh inning.

Most consecutive hits, inning

8—New York N.L. vs. New York A.L., October 7, 1921, seventh inning. (base on balls and sacrifice during streak.)

Most consecutive hits, inning (consecutive plate appearances)

6—Chicago N.L. vs. Detroit A.L., October 10, 1908, ninth inning (6 singles).

SINGLES

Most singles, total series

1,116—New York A.L. (33 series, 187 games).

Most singles, series

4-game series—31
New York A.L. vs. Chicago N.L., 1932.
Cincinnati N.L. vs. Oakland A.L., 1990.

5-game series—46—New York N.L. vs. New York A.L., 1922.

6-game series—57—New York A.L. vs. Los Angeles N.L., 1978.

7-game series—64—New York A.L. vs. Pittsburgh N.L., 1960.
8-game series—55—New York N.L. vs. Boston A.L., 1912.

Most singles by both clubs, series
4-game series—55—New York A.L. 31, Chicago N.L. 24, 1932.
5-game series—70—New York N.L. 39, Washington A.L. 31, 1933.
6-game series—95—New York A.L. 57, Los Angeles N.L. 38, 1978.
7-game series—109—New York A.L. 64, Pittsburgh N.L. 45, 1960.
8-game series—96—Boston A.L. 49, Pittsburgh N.L. 47, 1903.

Fewest singles, series
4-game series—13
  Philadelphia A.L. vs. Boston N.L., 1914.
  Los Angeles N.L. vs. Baltimore A.L., 1966.
5-game series—19
  Brooklyn N.L. vs. New York A.L., 1941.
  Baltimore A.L. vs. New York N.L., 1969.
6-game series—17—Philadelphia A.L. vs. St. Louis N.L., 1930.
7-game series—27
  Minnesota A.L. vs. Los Angeles N.L., 1965.
  St. Louis N.L. vs. Kansas City A.L., 1985.
8-game series—39—Boston A.L. vs. New York N.L., 1912.

Fewest singles by both clubs, series
4-game series—29—Baltimore A.L. 16, Los Angeles N.L. 13, 1966.
5-game series—40—New York N.L. 21, Baltimore A.L. 19, 1969.
6-game series—42—St. Louis N.L. 25, Philadelphia A.L. 17, 1930.
7-game series—66—St. Louis N.L. 33, Boston A.L. 33, 1967.
8-game series—92
  Cincinnati N.L. 47, Chicago A.L. 45, 1919.
  New York N.L. 52, New York A.L. 40, 1921.

Most singles, game
16—New York A.L. vs. Los Angeles N.L., October 15, 1978.

Most singles by both clubs, game
24—New York A.L. 16, Los Angeles N.L. 8, October 15, 1978.

Fewest singles, game
0—Philadelphia A.L. vs. St. Louis N.L., October 1, 1930 (batted eight innings).
  Philadelphia A.L. vs. St. Louis N.L., October 8, 1930 (batted eight innings).
  Brooklyn N.L. vs. New York A.L., October 3, 1947 (batted 8⅔ innings).
  New York A.L. vs. Brooklyn N.L., October 4, 1952 (batted eight innings).
  Brooklyn N.L. vs. New York A.L., October 8, 1956.
  St. Louis N.L. vs. Boston A.L., October 5, 1967.

Fewest singles by both clubs, game
2—St. Louis N.L. 2, Philadelphia A.L. 0, October 8, 1930.

Most singles, inning
7—Philadelphia A.L. vs. Chicago N.L., October 12, 1929, seventh inning.
  New York N.L. vs. Washington A.L., October 4, 1933, sixth inning.
  Brooklyn N.L. vs. New York A.L., October 8, 1949, sixth inning.

Most singles by both clubs, inning
8—Philadelphia A.L. 7, Chicago N.L. 1, October 12, 1929, seventh inning.
  New York N.L. 7, Washington A.L. 1, October 4, 1933, sixth inning.
  Brooklyn N.L. 7, New York A.L. 1, October 8, 1949, sixth inning.

DOUBLES

Most doubles, total series
224—New York A.L. (33 series, 187 games).

Most doubles, series
4-game series—9
  Philadelphia A.L. vs. Boston N.L., 1914.
  Cincinnati N.L. vs. Oakland A.L., 1990.
5-game series—19—Philadelphia A.L. vs. Chicago N.L., 1910.
6-game series—15—Philadelphia A.L. vs. New York N.L., 1911.
7-game series—19—St. Louis N.L. vs. Boston A.L., 1946.
8-game series—14
  Boston A.L. vs. New York N.L., 1912.
  New York N.L. vs. Boston A.L., 1912.

Most doubles by both clubs, series
4-game series—15—Philadelphia A.L. 9, Boston N.L. 6, 1914.
5-game series—30—Philadelphia A.L. 19, Chicago N.L. 11, 1910.
6-game series—26—Philadelphia A.L. 15, New York N.L. 11, 1911.
7-game series—29—Detroit A.L. 16, Pittsburgh N.L. 13, 1909.
8-game series—28—Boston A.L. 14, New York N.L. 14, 1912.

Fewest doubles, series
4-game series—3
  Cincinnati N.L. vs. New York A.L., 1939.
  New York A.L. vs. Philadelphia N.L., 1950.
  New York N.L. vs. Cleveland A.L., 1954.
  Los Angeles N.L. vs. New York A.L., 1963.
  New York A.L. vs. Los Angeles N.L., 1963.
  Baltimore A.L. vs. Los Angeles N.L., 1966.
  Los Angeles N.L. vs. Baltimore A.L., 1966.
  New York A.L. vs. Cincinnati N.L., 1976.
5-game series—1
  Detroit A.L. vs. Chicago N.L., 1907.
  Baltimore A.L. vs. New York N.L., 1969.
6-game series—2
  Boston A.L. vs. Chicago N.L., 1918.
  New York N.L. vs. New York A.L., 1923.
7-game series—3—Baltimore A.L. vs. Pittsburgh N.L., 1971.
8-game series—4—Boston A.L. vs. Pittsburgh N.L., 1903.

Fewest doubles by both clubs, series
4-game series—6
  Los Angeles N.L. 3, New York A.L. 3, 1963.
  Baltimore A.L. 3, Los Angeles N.L. 3, 1966.
5-game series—6—Philadelphia N.L. 4, Boston A.L. 2, 1915.
6-game series—7—Chicago N.L. 5, Boston A.L. 2, 1918.
7-game series—11—St. Louis N.L. 7, Detroit A.L. 4, 1968.
8-game series—11—Pittsburgh N.L. 7, Boston A.L. 4, 1903.

Most doubles, game
8—Chicago A.L. vs. Chicago N.L., October 13, 1906.
  Pittsburgh N.L. vs. Washington A.L., October 15, 1925.

Most doubles by both clubs, game
11—Chicago A.L. 8, Chicago N.L. 3, October 13, 1906.

Most doubles, inning
3—Chicago A.L. vs. Chicago N.L., October 13, 1906, fourth inning.
  Philadelphia A.L. vs. Chicago N.L., October 18, 1910, seventh inning.
  Philadelphia A.L. vs. New York N.L., October 24, 1911, fourth inning (consecutive).
  Pittsburgh N.L. vs. Washington A.L., October 15, 1925, eighth inning.
  St. Louis N.L. vs. Detroit A.L., October 9, 1934, third inning.
  Brooklyn N.L. vs. New York A.L., October 2, 1947, second inning.
  Brooklyn N.L. vs. New York A.L., October 5, 1947, third inning (consecutive).
  New York A.L. vs. Brooklyn N.L., October 8, 1949, fourth inning.
  Chicago A.L. vs. Los Angeles N.L., October 1, 1959, third inning.

TRIPLES

Most triples, total series
47—New York A.L. (33 series, 187 games).

Most triples, series
4-game series—3
  Cincinnati N.L. vs. New York A.L., 1976.
  Oakland A.L. vs. San Francisco N.L., 1989.
5-game series—6—Boston A.L. vs. Brooklyn N.L., 1916.
6-game series—5—Toronto A.L. vs. Philadelphia N.L., 1993.
7-game series—5
  St. Louis N.L. vs. Detroit A.L., 1934.
  New York A.L. vs. Brooklyn N.L., 1947.
8-game series—16—Boston A.L. vs. Pittsburgh N.L., 1903.

Most triples by both clubs, series
4-game series—4
  Cincinnati N.L. 3, New York A.L. 1, 1976.
  Oakland A.L. 3, San Francisco N.L. 1, 1989.
5-game series—11—Boston A.L. 6, Brooklyn N.L. 5, 1916.
6-game series—7
  New York A.L. 4, New York N.L. 3, 1923.
  Toronto A.L. 5, Philadelphia N.L. 2, 1993.
7-game series—8—Atlanta N.L. 4, Minnesota A.L. 4, 1991.
8-game series—25—Boston A.L. 16, Pittsburgh N.L. 9, 1903.

Fewest triples, series
4-game series—0—Held by many clubs.
5-game series—0—Held by many clubs. Last club—Oakland A.L., 1988.
6-game series—0—Held by many clubs. Last clubs—Atlanta N.L., Toronto A.L., 1992.
7-game series—0—Held by many clubs. Last club—St. Louis N.L., 1987.
8-game series—1—New York A.L. vs. New York N.L., 1921.

Fewest triples by both clubs, series
4-game series—1
  St. Louis N.L. 1, New York A.L. 0, 1928.
  Cleveland A.L. 1, New York N.L. 0, 1954.
  Baltimore A.L. 1, Los Angeles N.L. 0, 1966.
5-game series—0
  New York N.L. 0, Philadelphia A.L. 0, 1905.
  New York N.L. 0, Washington A.L. 0, 1933.
  New York N.L. 0, Baltimore A.L. 0, 1969.
  Detroit A.L. 0, San Diego N.L. 0, 1984.
6-game series—0
  Cleveland A.L. 0, Boston N.L. 0, 1948.
  New York A.L. 0, Los Angeles N.L. 0, 1978.
  Toronto A.L. 0, Atlanta N.L. 0, 1992.
7-game series—0—St. Louis N.L. 0, Philadelphia A.L. 0, 1931.
8-game series—5—New York N.L. 4, New York A.L. 1, 1921.

Most triples, nine-inning game
5—Boston A.L. vs. Pittsburgh N.L., October 7, 1903.
  Boston A.L. vs. Pittsburgh N.L., October 10, 1903.

Most triples by both clubs, nine-inning game
7—Boston A.L. 5, Pittsburgh N.L. 2, October 10, 1903.

Most triples, inning
2—Boston A.L. vs. Pittsburgh N.L., October 7, 1903, eighth inning.
  Boston A.L. vs. Pittsburgh N.L., October 10, 1903, first inning, also fourth inning.
  Boston A.L. vs. New York N.L., October 12, 1912, third inning.
  Philadelphia A.L. vs. New York N.L., October 7, 1913, fourth inning.
  Boston A.L. vs. Chicago N.L., September 6, 1918, ninth inning.
  New York A.L. vs. Brooklyn N.L., October 1, 1947, third inning.
  New York A.L. vs. Brooklyn N.L., September 30, 1953, first inning.
  Detroit A.L. vs. St. Louis N.L., October 7, 1968, fourth inning.

HOME RUNS
SERIES

Most home runs, total series
181—New York A.L. (33 series, 187 games).

Most grand slams, total series
7—New York A.L. (33 series, 187 games).

Most home runs by pinch-hitters, total series
5—New York A.L. (33 series, 187 games).

Most home runs, series
4-game series—9
  New York A.L. vs. St. Louis N.L., 1928.
  Oakland A.L. vs. San Francisco N.L., 1989.
5-game series—10—Baltimore A.L. vs. Cincinnati N.L., 1970.
6-game series—9
  New York A.L. vs. Brooklyn N.L., 1953.
  Los Angeles N.L. vs. New York A.L., 1977.
7-game series—12—New York A.L. vs. Brooklyn N.L., 1956.
8-game series—2
  Boston A.L. vs. Pittsburgh N.L., 1903.
  New York A.L. vs. New York N.L., 1921.
  New York N.L. vs. New York A.L., 1921.

Most home runs by both clubs, series
4-game series—13—Oakland A.L. 9, San Francisco N.L. 4, 1989.
5-game series—15—Baltimore A.L. 10, Cincinnati N.L. 5, 1970.
6-game series—17
  New York A.L. 9, Brooklyn N.L. 8, 1953.
  Los Angeles N.L. 9, New York A.L. 8, 1977.
7-game series—17—Brooklyn N.L. 9, New York A.L. 8, 1955.
8-game series—4—New York N.L. 2, New York A.L. 2, 1921.

Most grand slams, series
2—New York A.L. vs. Brooklyn N.L., 1956.
  Minnesota A.L. vs. St. Louis N.L., 1987.

Most grand slams by both clubs, series
2—New York A.L. 2, Brooklyn N.L. 0, 1956.
  St. Louis N.L. 1, New York A.L. 1, 1964.
  Minnesota A.L. 2, St. Louis N.L. 0, 1987.

Most home runs by pinch-hitters, series
2—Los Angeles N.L. vs. Chicago A.L., 1959.
  Boston A.L. vs. Cincinnati N.L., 1975.

Most home runs by pinch-hitters for both clubs, series
2—New York N.L. 1, Cleveland A.L. 1, 1954.
  Los Angeles N.L. 2, Chicago A.L. 0, 1959.
  Boston A.L. 2, Cincinnati N.L. 0, 1975.

Most home runs by pitchers as batters, series
2—New York N.L. vs. Washington A.L., 1924.

Most home runs by pitchers as batters for both clubs, series
2—New York N.L. 2, Washington A.L. 0, 1924.
  Boston A.L. 1, St. Louis N.L. 1, 1967.
  Detroit A.L. 1, St. Louis N.L. 1, 1968.

Fewest home runs, series
4-game series—0—Held by many clubs.
5-game series—0—Held by many clubs.
6-game series—0
  Chicago N.L. vs. Chicago A.L., 1906.
  Chicago A.L. vs. Chicago N.L., 1906.
  New York N.L. vs. Philadelphia A.L., 1911.
  Boston A.L. vs. Chicago N.L., 1918.
  Chicago N.L. vs. Boston A.L., 1918.
7-game series—0—Brooklyn N.L. vs. Cleveland A.L., 1920.
8-game series—0—Cincinnati N.L. vs. Chicago A.L., 1919.

Fewest home runs by both clubs, series
4-game series—1—Boston N.L. 1, Philadelphia A.L. 0, 1914.
5-game series—0
  New York N.L. 0, Philadelphia A.L. 0, 1905.
  Chicago N.L. 0, Detroit A.L. 0, 1907.
6-game series—0
  Chicago A.L. 0, Chicago N.L. 0, 1906.
  Boston A.L. 0, Chicago N.L. 0, 1918.
7-game series—2—Cleveland A.L. 2, Brooklyn N.L. 0, 1920.
8-game series—1—Chicago A.L. 1, Cincinnati N.L. 0, 1919.

GAME

Most home runs, game

5—New York A.L. vs. St. Louis N.L., October 9, 1928.
Oakland A.L. vs. San Francisco N.L., October 27, 1989.

Most home runs by both clubs, game

7—Oakland A.L. 5, San Francisco N.L. 2, October 27, 1989.

Most consecutive games with one or more home runs, total series

9—New York A.L., last 2 games vs. Chicago N.L. in 1932 (seven home runs), all 6 games vs. New York N.L. in 1936 (seven home runs) and first game vs. New York N.L. in 1937 (one home run; total 15 home runs).
New York A.L., all 7 games vs. Brooklyn N.L. in 1952 (10 home runs) and first 2 games vs. Brooklyn N.L. in 1953 (four home runs; total 14 home runs).

Most consecutive games with one or more home runs, series

7—Washington A.L. vs. Pittsburgh N.L., October 7 through 15, 1925 (eight home runs).
New York A.L. vs. Brooklyn N.L., October 1 through 7, 1952 (10 home runs).

INNING

Most home runs, inning (two home runs, 30 times)

3—Boston A.L. vs. St. Louis N.L., October 11, 1967, fourth inning, Yastrzemski, Smith, Petrocelli (two consecutive).
2—New York N.L. vs. New York A.L., October 11, 1921, second inning.
Washington A.L. vs. Pittsburgh N.L., October 11, 1925, third inning.
New York A.L. vs. St. Louis N.L., October 9, 1928, seventh inning.
New York A.L. vs. St. Louis N.L., October 9, 1928, eighth inning.
Philadelphia A.L. vs. Chicago N.L., October 12, 1929, seventh inning.
New York A.L. vs. Chicago N.L., October 1, 1932, fifth inning.
New York A.L. vs. Chicago N.L., October 2, 1932, ninth inning.
New York A.L. vs. Cincinnati N.L., October 7, 1939, fifth inning.
New York A.L. vs. Cincinnati N.L., October 8, 1939, seventh inning.
Detroit A.L. vs. Cincinnati N.L., October 4, 1940, seventh inning.
Brooklyn N.L. vs. New York A.L., October 7, 1949, ninth inning.
Brooklyn N.L. vs. New York A.L., September 30, 1953, sixth inning.
Brooklyn N.L. vs. New York A.L., October 1, 1955, fourth inning.
Milwaukee N.L. vs. New York A.L., October 6, 1957, fourth inning.
Milwaukee N.L. vs. New York A.L., October 2, 1958, first inning.
New York A.L. vs. Milwaukee N.L., October 2, 1958, ninth inning.
Los Angeles N.L. vs. Chicago A.L., October 2, 1959, seventh inning.
New York A.L. vs. St. Louis N.L., October 14, 1964, sixth inning.
New York A.L. vs. St. Louis N.L., October 15, 1964, ninth inning.
Baltimore A.L. vs. Los Angeles N.L., October 5, 1966, first inning.
Baltimore A.L. vs. New York N.L., October 16, 1969, third inning.
Oakland A.L. vs. New York N.L., October 21, 1973, third inning.
Cincinnati N.L. vs. Boston A.L., October 14, 1975, fifth inning.
New York A.L. vs. Los Angeles N.L., October 16, 1977, eighth inning.
Los Angeles N.L. vs. New York A.L., October 10, 1978, second inning.
Los Angeles N.L. vs. New York A.L., October 25, 1981, seventh inning.
Boston A.L. vs. New York N.L., October 27, 1986, second inning.
Oakland A.L. vs. San Francisco N.L., October 27, 1989, fourth and fifth innings.
Philadelphia N.L. vs. Toronto A.L., October 20, 1993, fifth inning.

Most home runs by both clubs, inning

3—New York N.L., 2, New York A.L., 1, October 11, 1921, second inning.
Boston A.L., 3, St. Louis N.L. 0, October 11, 1967, fourth inning.

Most consecutive home runs, inning (10 times)

2—Washington A.L. vs. Pittsburgh N.L., October 11, 1925, third inning.
New York A.L. vs. St. Louis N.L., October 9, 1928, seventh inning.
New York A.L. vs. Chicago N.L., October 1, 1932, fifth inning.
New York A.L. vs. St. Louis N.L., October 14, 1964, sixth inning.
Baltimore A.L. vs. Los Angeles N.L., October 5, 1966, first inning.
Boston A.L. vs. St. Louis N.L., October 11, 1967, fourth inning.
Cincinnati N.L. vs. Boston A.L., October 14, 1975, fifth inning.
New York A.L. vs. Los Angeles N.L., October 16, 1977, eighth inning.
Los Angeles N.L. vs. New York A.L., October 25, 1981, seventh inning.
Boston A.L. vs. New York N.L., October 27, 1986, second inning.

Most times hitting two home runs in an inning, total series

10—New York A.L., 1928 (2), 1932 (2), 1939 (2), 1958 (1), 1964 (2), 1977 (1).

Most times hitting two home runs in an inning, series

2—New York A.L., 1928, 1932, 1939, 1964; Oakland A.L., 1989.

Most times hitting two home runs in an inning, game

2—New York A.L. vs. St. Louis N.L., October 9, 1928, seventh and eighth innings.
Oakland A.L. vs. San Francisco N.L., October 27, 1989, fourth and fifth innings.

TOTAL BASES

Most total bases, total series

2,429—New York A.L. (3 series, 187 games)

Most total bases, series

4-game series—85—Oakland A.L. vs. San Francisco N.L., 1989.
5-game series—87—Baltimore A.L. vs. Cincinnati N.L., 1970.
6-game series—105—Toronto A.L. vs. Philadelphia N.L., 1993.
7-game series—142—New York A.L. vs. Pittsburgh N.L., 1960.
8-game series—113—Boston A.L. vs. Pittsburgh N.L., 1903.

Most total bases by both clubs, series

4-game series—133—New York A.L. 75, Chicago N.L. 58, 1932.
5-game series—145—Baltimore A.L. 87, Cincinnati N.L. 58, 1970.
6-game series—200—Brooklyn N.L. 103, New York A.L. 97, 1953.
7-game series—225—New York A.L. 142, Pittsburgh N.L. 83, 1960.
8-game series—205—Boston A.L. 113, Pittsburgh N.L. 92, 1903.

Fewest total bases, series

4-game series—23—Los Angeles N.L. vs. Baltimore A.L., 1966.
5-game series—30—Philadelphia A.L. vs. New York N.L., 1905.
6-game series—40—Boston A.L. vs. Chicago N.L., 1918.
7-game series—51—Brooklyn N.L. vs. Cleveland A.L., 1920.
8-game series—65—New York A.L. vs. New York N.L., 1921.

Fewest total bases by both clubs, series

4-game series—64—Baltimore A.L. 41, Los Angeles N.L. 23, 1966.
5-game series—69—New York N.L. 39, Philadelphia A.L. 30, 1905.
6-game series—84—Chicago N.L. 44, Boston A.L. 40, 1918.
7-game series—123—Cleveland A.L. 72, Brooklyn N.L. 51, 1920.
8-game series—163—New York N.L. 98, New York A.L. 65, 1921.

Most total bases, game

34—Atlanta N.L. vs. Minnesota A.L., October 24, 1991.

Most total bases by both clubs, game

47—New York A.L. 27, Brooklyn N.L. 20, October 4, 1953.

Fewest total bases, game

0—Brooklyn N.L. vs. New York A.L., October 8, 1956.

Fewest total bases by both clubs, game

5—New York A.L. 3, New York N.L. 2, October 6, 1921.

Most total bases, inning

17—Philadelphia A.L. vs. Chicago N.L., October 12, 1929, seventh inning.

Most total bases by both clubs, inning

21—Philadelphia A.L. 17, Chicago N.L. 4, October 12, 1929, seventh inning.

LONG HITS

Most long hits, total series

452—New York A.L. (33 series, 187 games).

Most long hits, series

4-game series—20—Oakland A.L. vs. San Francisco N.L., 1989.

5-game series—21—Philadelphia A.L. vs. Chicago N.L., 1910.

6-game series—24—Toronto A.L. vs. Philadelphia N.L., 1993.

7-game series—27—New York A.L. vs. Pittsburgh N.L., 1960.

8-game series—22—Boston A.L. vs. Pittsburgh N.L., 1903.

Most long hits by both clubs, series

4-game series—29—Oakland A.L. 20, San Francisco N.L. 9, 1989.

5-game series—33—Philadelphia A.L. 21, Chicago N.L. 12, 1910.

6-game series—41—Brooklyn N.L. 22, New York A.L. 19, 1953.

7-game series—42
New York A.L. 27, Pittsburgh N.L. 15, 1960.
St. Louis N.L. 23, Milwaukee A.L. 19, 1982.
Atlanta N.L. 22, Minnesota A.L. 20, 1991.

8-game series—40—Boston A.L. 21, New York N.L. 19, 1912.

Fewest long hits, series

4-game series—4
Cincinnati N.L. vs. New York A.L., 1939.
Los Angeles N.L. vs. Baltimore A.L., 1966.

5-game series—3—Detroit A.L. vs. Chicago N.L., 1907.

6-game series—5—Boston A.L. vs. Chicago N.L., 1918.

7-game series—6—Brooklyn N.L. vs. Cleveland A.L., 1920.

8-game series—10—New York A.L. vs. New York N.L., 1921.

Fewest long hits by both clubs, series

4-game series— 12—Baltimore A.L. 8, Los Angeles N.L. 4, 1966.

5-game series— 10—Chicago N.L. 7, Detroit A.L. 3, 1907.

6-game series—11—Chicago N.L. 6, Boston A.L. 5, 1918.

7-game series— 19—Cleveland A.L. 13, Brooklyn N.L. 6, 1920.

8-game series—29—New York N.L. 19, New York A.L. 10, 1921.

Most long hits, game

9—Pittsburgh N.L. vs. Washington A.L., October 15, 1925 (8 doubles, 1 triple).

Most long hits by both clubs, game

11—Chicago A.L. 8 (eight doubles), Chicago N.L. 3 (3 doubles), October 13, 1906.
Pittsburgh N.L. 9 (8 doubles, 1 triple), Washington A.L. 2 (1 double, 1 home run), October 15, 1925.
New York A.L. 7 (4 doubles, 1 triple, 2 home runs), Cincinnati N.L. 4 (2 doubles, 2 home runs), October 9, 1961.
Oakland A.L. 7 (2 doubles, 5 home runs), San Francisco N.L. 4 (2 doubles, 2 home runs), October 27, 1989.
Atlanta N.L. 8 (2 doubles, 3 triples, 3 home runs), Minnesota A.L. 3 (1 double, 2 triples), October 24, 1991, 12 innings.

Longest extra-inning game without a long hit

12 innings—
Chicago N.L. vs. Detroit A.L., October 8, 1907.
Detroit A.L. vs. Chicago N.L., October 8, 1907.

Longest extra-inning game without a long hit by either club

12 innings—Chicago N.L. 0, Detroit A.L. 0, October 8, 1907.

EXTRA BASES ON LONG HITS

Most extra bases on long hits, total Series

861—New York A.L. (33 series, 187 games; 224 on doubles, 94 on triples, 543 on home runs).

Most extra bases on long hits, series

4-game series—41—Oakland A.L. vs. San Francisco N.L., 1989.

5-game series—37—Baltimore A.L. vs. Cincinnati N.L., 1970.

6-game series—41
New York A.L. vs. Brooklyn N.L., 1953.
Toronto A.L. vs. Philadelphia N.L., 1993.

7-game series—51—New York A.L. vs. Pittsburgh N.L., 1960.

8-game series—42—Boston A.L. vs. Pittsburgh N.L., 1903.

Most extra bases on long hits by both clubs, series

4-game series—59—Oakland A.L. 41, San Francisco N.L. 18, 1989.

5-game series—60—Baltimore A.L. 37, Cincinnati N.L. 23, 1970.

6-game series—80—New York A.L. 41, Brooklyn N.L. 39, 1953.

7-game series—82—Atlanta N.L. 42, Minnesota A.L. 40, 1991.

8-game series—70—Boston A.L. 42, Pittsburgh N.L. 28, 1903.

Fewest extra bases on long hits, series

4-game series—5—Cincinnati N.L. vs. New York A.L., 1939.

5-game series—5
Philadelphia A.L. vs. New York N.L., 1905.
Detroit A.L. vs. Chicago N.L., 1907.
Detroit A.L. vs. Chicago N.L., 1908.

6-game series—7—Chicago N.L. vs. Boston A.L., 1918.

7-game series—7—Brooklyn N.L. vs. Cleveland A.L., 1920.

8-game series— 15—New York A.L. vs. New York N.L., 1921.

Fewest extra bases on long hits by both clubs, series

4-game series— 19—New York A.L. 11, Philadelphia N.L. 8, 1950.

5-game series— 12—New York N.L. 7, Philadelphia A.L. 5, 1905.

6-game series— 15—Boston A.L. 8, Chicago N.L. 7, 1918.

7-game series—26—Cleveland A.L. 19, Brooklyn N.L. 7, 1920.

8-game series—42—New York N.L. 27, New York A.L. 15, 1921.

RUNS BATTED IN

Most runs batted in, total series

791—New York A.L. (33 series, 187 games).

Most runs batted in, series

4-game series—36—New York A.L. vs. Chicago N.L., 1932.

5-game series—32—Baltimore A.L. vs. Cincinnati N.L., 1970.

6-game series—45—Toronto A.L. vs. Philadelphia N.L., 1993.

7-game series—54—New York A.L. vs. Pittsburgh N.L., 1960.

8-game series—35—Boston A.L. vs. Pittsburgh N.L., 1903.

Most runs batted in by both clubs, series

4-game series—52—New York A.L. 36, Chicago N.L. 16, 1932.

5-game series—52—Baltimore A.L. 32, Cincinnati N.L. 20, 1970.

6-game series—80—Toronto A.L. 45, Philadelphia N.L. 35, 1993.

7-game series—80—New York A.L. 54, Pittsburgh N.L. 26, 1960.

8-game series—58—Boston A.L. 35, Pittsburgh N.L. 23, 1903.

Fewest runs batted in, series

4-game series—2—Los Angeles N.L. vs. Baltimore A.L., 1966.

5-game series—2—Philadelphia A.L. vs. New York N.L., 1905.

6-game series—6—Boston A.L. vs. Chicago N.L., 1918.

7-game series—8—Brooklyn N.L. vs. Cleveland A.L., 1920.

8-game series— 17—Chicago A.L. vs. Cincinnati N.L., 1919.

Fewest runs batted in by both clubs, series

4-game series— 12—Los Angeles N.L. 2, Baltimore A.L. 10, 1966.

5-game series— 15—Philadelphia A.L. 2, New York N.L. 13, 1905.

6-game series— 16—Boston A.L. 6, Chicago N.L. 10, 1918.

7-game series—26—Brooklyn N.L. 8, Cleveland A.L. 18, 1920.

8-game series—46—Boston A.L. 21, New York N.L. 25, 1912.

Most runs batted in, game

18—New York A.L. vs. New York N.L., October 2, 1936.

Most runs batted in by both clubs, game

29—Toronto A.L. 15, Philadelphia N.L. 14, October 20, 1993.

Fewest runs batted in, game

0—Held by many clubs.

Most runs batted in, inning

10—Philadelphia A.L. vs. Chicago N.L., October 12, 1929, seventh inning.

Detroit A.L. vs. St. Louis N.L., October 9, 1968, third inning.

Most runs batted in by both clubs, inning

11—Philadelphia A.L. 10, Chicago N.L. 1, October 12, 1929, seventh inning.

Brooklyn N.L. 6, New York A.L. 5, October 5, 1956, second inning.

Fewest runs batted in by both clubs, game

0—New York N.L. 0, Philadelphia A.L. 0, October 13, 1905.
New York N.L. 0, New York A.L. 0, October 13, 1921.
Chicago A.L. 0, Los Angeles N.L. 0, October 6, 1959.
New York A.L. 0, San Francisco N.L. 0, October 16, 1962.

BASES ON BALLS

Most bases on balls, total series

645—New York A.L. (33 series, 187 games).

Most bases on balls, series

4-game series—23—New York A.L. vs. Chicago N.L., 1932.
5-game series—24—New York A.L. vs. Cincinnati N.L., 1961.
6-game series—34—Philadelphia N.L. vs. Toronto A.L., 1993.
7-game series—38—New York A.L. vs. Brooklyn N.L., 1947.
8-game series—27—New York A.L. vs. New York N.L., 1921.

Most bases on balls by both clubs, series

4-game series—34—New York A.L. 23, Chicago N.L. 11, 1932.
5-game series—37—New York A.L. 23, Brooklyn N.L. 14, 1941.
6-game series—59—Philadelphia N.L. 34, Toronto A.L. 25, 1993.
7-game series—68—New York A.L. 38, Brooklyn N.L. 30, 1947.
8-game series—49—New York A.L. 27, New York N.L. 22, 1921.

Fewest bases on balls, series

4-game series—4—Pittsburgh N.L. vs. New York A.L., 1927.
5-game series—5—Philadelphia A.L. vs. New York N.L., 1905.
6-game series—4—Philadelphia A.L. vs. New York A.L., 1911.
7-game series—9—St. Louis N.L. vs. Philadelphia A.L., 1931.
8-game series—13—Boston A.L. vs. Pittsburgh N.L., 1903.

Fewest bases on balls by both clubs, series

4-game series—15—New York A.L. 9, Cincinnati N.L. 6, 1939.
5-game series—15—New York N.L. 8, Philadelphia A.L. 7, 1913.
6-game series—17—Chicago A.L. 11, New York N.L. 6, 1917.
7-game series—30—New York A.L. 18, Pittsburgh N.L. 12, 1960.
8-game series—27—Pittsburgh N.L. 14, Boston A.L. 13, 1903.

Most bases on balls, game

11—Brooklyn N.L. vs. New York A.L., October 5, 1956.
New York A.L. vs. Milwaukee N.L., October 5, 1957.
Detroit A.L. vs. San Diego N.L., October 12, 1984.

Most bases on balls by both clubs, game

19—New York A.L. 11, Milwaukee N.L. 8, October 5, 1957.

Longest game with no bases on balls

12 innings—St. Louis N.L. vs. Detroit A.L., October 4, 1934.

Fewest bases on balls by both clubs, game

0—Philadelphia A.L. 0, New York N.L. 0, October 16, 1911.
New York N.L. 0, Chicago A.L. 0, October 10, 1917.
New York N.L. 0, New York A.L. 0, October 9, 1921.
Boston A.L. 0, St. Louis N.L. 0, October 7, 1967.
Philadelphia N.L. 0, Baltimore A.L. 0, October 11, 1983.

Most bases on balls, inning

5—New York A.L. vs. St. Louis N.L., October 6, 1926, fifth inning.

Most bases on balls by both clubs, inning

6—New York A.L. 3, New York N.L. 3, October 7, 1921, third inning.
New York A.L. 5, St. Louis N.L. 1, October 6, 1926, fifth inning.

Most bases on balls by pinch-hitters, inning

2—New York A.L. vs. New York N.L., October 15, 1923, eighth inning.
Baltimore A.L. vs. Philadelphia N.L., October 15, 1983, sixth inning.

STRIKEOUTS

Most strikeouts, total series

986—New York A.L. (33 series, 187 games).

Most strikeouts, series

4-game series—37—New York A.L. vs. Los Angeles N.L., 1963.
5-game series—50—Chicago N.L. vs. Philadelphia A.L., 1929.
6-game series—50—Philadelphia N.L. vs. Toronto A.L., 1993.
7-game series—62—Oakland A.L. vs. New York N.L., 1973.
8-game series—45—Pittsburgh N.L. vs. Boston A.L., 1903.

Most strikeouts by both clubs, series

4-game series—62—New York A.L. 37, Los Angeles N.L. 25, 1963.
5-game series—77
Chicago N.L. 50, Philadelphia A.L. 27, 1929.
Oakland A.L. 41, Los Angeles N.L. 36, 1988.
6-game series—92—St. Louis A.L. 49, St. Louis N.L. 43, 1944.
7-game series—99—Detroit A.L. 59, St. Louis N.L. 40, 1968.
8-game series—82—New York A.L. 44, New York N.L. 38, 1921.

Fewest strikeouts, series

4-game series—7—Pittsburgh N.L. vs. New York A.L., 1927.
5-game series—15—New York N.L. vs. New York A.L., 1922.
6-game series—14—Chicago N.L. vs. Boston A.L., 1918.
7-game series—20—Brooklyn N.L. vs. Cleveland A.L., 1920.
8-game series—22—Cincinnati N.L. vs. Chicago A.L., 1919.

Fewest strikeouts by both clubs, series

4-game series—32
New York A.L. 25, Pittsburgh N.L. 7, 1927.
Cincinnati N.L. 16, New York A.L. 16, 1976.
5-game series—35
New York N.L. 19, Philadelphia A.L. 16, 1913.
New York A.L. 20, New York N.L. 15, 1922.
6-game series—35—Boston A.L. 21, Chicago N.L. 14, 1918.
7-game series—41—Cleveland A.L. 21, Brooklyn N.L. 20, 1920.
8-game series—52—Chicago A.L. 30, Cincinnati N.L. 22, 1919.

Most strikeouts, game

17—Detroit A.L. vs. St. Louis N.L., October 2, 1968.

Most strikeouts by pinch-hitters, game

4—St. Louis A.L. vs. St. Louis N.L., October 8, 1944 (consecutive) and October 9, 1944 (consecutive).

Most consecutive strikeouts, game

6—Chicago A.L. vs. Cincinnati N.L., October 6, 1919 (3 in second inning, 3 in third inning).
Los Angeles N.L. vs. Baltimore A.L., October 5, 1966 (3 in fourth inning, 3 in fifth inning).
Kansas City A.L. vs. St. Louis N.L., October 24, 1985 (3 in sixth inning, 3 in seventh inning).

Most strikeouts by both clubs, nine-inning game

25—New York A.L. 15, Los Angeles N.L. 10, October 2, 1963.

Most strikeouts by both clubs, extra-inning game

25—Oakland A.L. 15, New York N.L. 10, October 14, 1973, 12 innings.

Fewest strikeouts, game

0—Chicago N.L. vs. Boston A.L., September 6, 1918 (batted eight innings).
  Chicago N.L. vs. Boston A.L., September 9, 1918.
  New York A.L. vs. New York N.L., October 6, 1921 (batted eight innings).
  New York A.L. vs. Philadelphia N.L., October 4, 1950.
  Brooklyn N.L. vs. New York A.L., October 3, 1952.
  Pittsburgh N.L. vs. New York A.L., October 6, 1960.
  Pittsburgh N.L. vs. New York A.L., October 13, 1960.
  New York A.L. vs. Pittsburgh N.L., October 13, 1960.

Fewest strikeouts by both clubs, game

0—Pittsburgh N.L. 0, New York A.L. 0, October 13, 1960.

Most consecutive strikeouts by pinch-hitters, two consecutive games

8—St. Louis A.L. vs. St. Louis N.L., October 8 (4), October 9 (4), 1944.

Most strikeouts, inning

4—Detroit A.L. vs. Chicago N.L., October 14, 1908, first inning.

Most strikeouts by pinch-hitters, inning

3—St. Louis A.L. vs. St. Louis N.L., October 8, 1944, ninth inning.

Most strikeouts by both clubs, inning

6—Cincinnati N.L. 3, Oakland A.L. 3, October 18, 1972, fifth inning.
  Kansas City A.L. 3, St. Louis N.L. 3, October 24, 1985, seventh inning.

SACRIFICE HITS

Most sacrifices, total series

108—New York A.L. (33 series, 187 games).

Most sacrifices, series

14—Chicago N.L. vs. Chicago A.L., 1906 (6-game series).

Most sacrifices by both clubs, series

22—St. Louis N.L. 12, New York A.L. 10, 1926 (7-game series).

Fewest sacrifices, series

0—Held by many clubs. Last club—Toronto A.L. vs. Philadelphia N.L., 1993.

Fewest sacrifices by both clubs, series

0—New York A.L. 0, Brooklyn N.L. 0, 1941 (5-game series).
  Cincinnati N.L. 0, New York A.L. 0, 1976 (4-game series).
  Baltimore A.L. 0, Philadelphia N.L. 0, 1983 (5-game series).
  Oakland A.L. 0, San Francisco N.L. 0, 1989 (4-game series).

Most sacrifices, game

5—Chicago N.L. vs. Chicago A.L., October 12, 1906 (all sacrifice hits).
  Chicago N.L. vs. Detroit A.L., October 10, 1908 (all sacrifice hits).
  Pittsburgh N.L. vs. Detroit A.L., October 16, 1909 (4 sacrifice hits and 1 sacrifice fly).
  New York N.L. vs. Cleveland A.L., October 2, 1954 (3 sacrifice hits and 2 sacrifice flies).

Most sacrifices by both clubs, game

7—Chicago N.L. 5, Detroit A.L. 2, October 10, 1908 (all sacrifice hits).

Most sacrifices, inning

3—Brooklyn N.L. vs. New York A.L., October 4, 1955, sixth inning (2 sacrifice hits, 1 sacrifice fly).

SACRIFICE FLIES (SINCE 1955)

Most sacrifice flies, total series

14—New York A.L., 13 series, 80 games.

Most sacrifice flies, series

7—Toronto A.L. vs. Philadelphia N.L., 1993 (6-game series).

Most sacrifice flies by both clubs, series

8—Toronto A.L. 7, Philadelphia N.L. 1, 1993 (6-game series).

Most sacrifice flies, game

3—Toronto A.L. vs. Philadelphia N.L., October 19, 1993.

Most sacrifice flies by both clubs, game

3—Toronto A.L. 3, Philadelphia N.L. 0, October 19, 1993.
  Toronto A.L. 2, Philadelphia N.L. 1, October 23, 1993.

Most sacrifice flies, inning

2—Baltimore A.L. vs. Pittsburgh N.L., October 13, 1971, first inning.

HIT BY PITCH

Most hit by pitch, total series

39—New York A.L. (33 series, 187 games).

Most hit by pitch, series

6—Pittsburgh N.L. vs. Detroit A.L., 1909 (7-game series).

Most hit by pitch by both clubs, series

10—Pittsburgh N.L. 6, Detroit A.L. 4, 1909 (7-game series).

Fewest hit by pitch, series

0—Held by many clubs.

Most hit by pitch, game

3—Detroit A.L. vs. St. Louis N.L., October 9, 1968.
  Baltimore A.L. vs. Pittsburgh N.L., October 13, 1971.

Most hit by pitch by both clubs, game

3—Philadelphia N.L. 2, Boston A.L. 1, October 13, 1915.
  Cincinnati N.L. 2, Chicago A.L. 1, October 9, 1919.
  Pittsburgh N.L. 2, Washington A.L. 1, October 7, 1925.
  Detroit A.L. 3, St. Louis N.L. 0, October 9, 1968.
  Baltimore A.L. 3, Pittsburgh N.L. 0, October 13, 1971.
  New York N.L. 2, Oakland A.L. 1, October 14, 1973.
  Minnesota A.L. 2, St. Louis N.L. 1, October 21, 1987.

Most hit by pitch, inning

2—Pittsburgh N.L. vs. Detroit A.L., October 11, 1909, second inning (consecutive).
  Detroit A.L. vs. St. Louis N.L., October 9, 1968, eighth inning.
  Pittsburgh N.L. vs. Baltimore A.L., October 17, 1979, ninth inning (consecutive).

REACHING BASE ON ERRORS

Most first on error, game

5—Chicago N.L. vs. Chicago A.L., October 13, 1906.

Most first on error by both clubs, game

6—Pittsburgh N.L. 4, Boston A.L. 2, October 10, 1903.
  Chicago N.L. 4, Philadelphia A.L. 2, October 18, 1910.
  New York N.L. 4, Philadelphia A.L. 2, October 26, 1911.

INDIVIDUAL BASERUNNING

STOLEN BASES

Most stolen bases, career

14—Eddie Collins, Philadelphia A.L. (10), 1910, 1911, 1913, 1914; Chicago A.L. (4), 1917, 1919; six series, 34 games.

Lou Brock, St. Louis N.L., 1964 (0), 1967 (7), 1968 (7); three series, 21 games.

Most stolen bases, series

4-game series—3—Rickey Henderson, Oakland A.L., 1989, 1990.

5-game series—6—Jimmy Slagle, Chicago N.L., 1907.

6-game series—5

Otis Nixon, Atlanta N.L., 1992.

Deion Sanders, Atlanta N.L., 1992.

7-game series—7

Lou Brock, St. Louis N.L., 1967.

Lou Brock, St. Louis N.L., 1968.

8-game series—4—Josh Devore, New York N.L., 1912.

Most stolen bases, game

3—Honus Wagner, Pittsburgh N.L., October 11, 1909.

Willie Davis, Los Angeles N.L., October 11, 1965.

Lou Brock, St. Louis N.L., October 12, 1967.

Lou Brock, St. Louis N.L., October 5, 1968.

Most times stealing home, game (13 times; *part of double steal)

1—Bill Dahlen, New York N.L., October 12, 1905, fifth inning.*

George Davis, Chicago A.L., October 13, 1906, third inning.*

Jimmy Slagle, Chicago N.L., October 11, 1907, seventh inning.

Ty Cobb, Detroit A.L., October 9, 1909, third inning.

Buck Herzog, New York N.L., October 14, 1912, first inning.*

Butch Schmidt, Boston N.L., October 9, 1914, eighth inning.*

Mike McNally, New York A.L., October 5, 1921, fifth inning.

Bob Meusel, New York A.L., October 6, 1921, eighth inning.

Bob Meusel, New York A.L., October 7, 1928, sixth inning.*

Hank Greenberg, Detroit A.L., October 6, 1934, eighth inning.*

Monte Irvin, New York N.L., October 4, 1951, first inning.

Jackie Robinson, Brooklyn N.L., September 28, 1955, eighth inning.

Tim McCarver, St. Louis N.L., October 15, 1964, fourth inning.*

Most stolen bases, inning (seven times)

2—Jimmy Slagle, Chicago N.L., October 8, 1907, 10th inning.

George Browne, New York N.L., October 12, 1905, ninth inning.

Ty Cobb, Detroit A.L., October 12, 1908, ninth inning.

Eddie Collins, Chicago A.L., October 7, 1917, sixth inning.

Babe Ruth, New York A.L., October 6, 1921, fifth inning.

Lou Brock, St. Louis N.L., October 12, 1967, fifth inning.

Dave Lopes, Los Angeles N.L., October 15, 1974, first inning.

CAUGHT STEALING

Most caught stealing, career

9—Frank Schulte, Chicago N.L., 1906, 1907, 1908, 1910; four series, 21 games.

Most caught stealing, series

5—Frank Schulte, Chicago N.L., 1910 (5-game series).

Most times caught stealing, game

2—Frank Schulte, Chicago N.L., October 17, 1910.

Frank Schulte, Chicago N.L., October 23, 1910.

Fred Luderus, Philadelphia N.L., October 8, 1915.

Jimmy Johnston, Brooklyn N.L., October 9, 1916.

Mickey Livingston, Chicago N.L., October 3, 1945.

Billy Martin, New York A.L., September 28, 1955.

Most times caught stealing, inning

1—Held by many players.

Most times caught off base, game

2—Max Flack, Chicago N.L., September 9, 1918 (first base in first inning, second base in third inning).

CLUB BASERUNNING

STOLEN BASES

Most stolen bases, total series
60—New York A.L. (33 series, 187 games).

Most stolen bases, series
4-game series—9—Boston N.L. vs. Philadelphia A.L., 1914.
5-game series—18—Chicago N.L. vs. Detroit A.L., 1907.
6-game series—15—Atlanta N.L. vs. Toronto A.L., 1992.
7-game series—18—Pittsburgh N.L. vs. Detroit A.L., 1909.
8-game series—12—New York N.L. vs. Boston A.L., 1912.

Most stolen bases by both clubs, series
4-game series—11—Boston N.L. 9, Philadelphia A.L. 2, 1914.
5-game series—25—Chicago N.L. 18, Detroit A.L. 7, 1907.
6-game series—20—Atlanta N.L. 15, Toronto A.L. 5, 1992.
7-game series—24—Pittsburgh N.L. 18, Detroit A.L. 6, 1909.
8-game series—18—New York N.L. 12, Boston A.L. 6, 1912.

Fewest stolen bases, series
4-game series—0—Held by many clubs.
5-game series—0—Held by many clubs.
6-game series—0—Held by many clubs.
7-game series—0
Philadelphia A.L. vs. St. Louis N.L., 1931.
Detroit A.L. vs. Cincinnati N.L., 1940.
New York A.L. vs. Pittsburgh N.L., 1960.
Detroit A.L. vs. St. Louis N.L., 1968.
New York N.L. vs. Oakland A.L., 1973.
Boston A.L. vs. Cincinnati N.L., 1975.
Pittsburgh N.L. vs. Baltimore A.L., 1979.
Boston A.L. vs. New York N.L., 1986.
8-game series—5
Boston A.L. vs. Pittsburgh N.L., 1903.
Chicago A.L. vs. Cincinnati N.L., 1919.

Fewest stolen bases by both clubs, series
4-game series—1
Cincinnati N.L. 1, New York A.L. 0, 1939.
New York N.L. 1, Cleveland A.L. 0, 1954.
Los Angeles N.L. 1, Baltimore A.L. 0, 1966.
5-game series—1
Chicago N.L. 1, Philadelphia A.L. 0, 1929.
Washington A.L. 1, New York N.L. 0, 1933.
New York N.L. 1, New York A.L. 0, 1937.
New York A.L. 1, Cincinnati N.L. 0, 1961.
Cincinnati N.L. 1, Baltimore A.L. 0, 1970.
6-game series—0—St. Louis N.L. 0, St. Louis A.L. 0, 1944.
7-game series—1—Cincinnati N.L. 1, Detroit A.L. 0, 1940.
8-game series—12
Pittsburgh N.L. 7, Boston A.L. 5, 1903.
Cincinnati N.L. 7, Chicago A.L. 5, 1919.

Most stolen bases, nine-inning game
5—New York N.L. vs. Philadelphia A.L., October 12, 1905.
Chicago N.L. vs. Chicago A.L., October 10, 1906.
Chicago N.L. vs. Detroit A.L., October 9, 1907.
St. Louis N.L. vs. Minnesota A.L., October 22, 1987.
Atlanta N.L. vs. Toronto A.L., October 18, 1992.

Most stolen bases, extra-inning game
7—Chicago N.L. vs. Detroit A.L., October 8, 1907, 10 innings.

Most stolen bases by both clubs, nine-inning game
6—New York N.L. 5, Philadelphia A.L. 1, October 12, 1905.
Pittsburgh N.L. 4, Detroit A.L. 2, October 13, 1909.
New York N.L. 3, Philadelphia A.L. 3, October 9, 1913.
St. Louis N.L. 5, Minnesota A.L. 1, October 22, 1987.

Most stolen bases by both clubs, extra-inning game
11—Chicago N.L. 7, Detroit A.L. 4, October 8, 1907, 12 innings.

Longest extra-inning game with no stolen bases
14 innings—
Boston A.L. vs. Brooklyn N.L., October 9, 1916.

Brooklyn N.L. vs. Boston A.L., October 9, 1916.

Longest extra-inning game with no stolen bases by either club
14 innings—Boston A.L. vs. Brooklyn N.L., October 9, 1916.

Most stolen bases, inning
3—Pittsburgh N.L. vs. Boston A.L., October 1, 1903, first inning.
New York N.L. vs. Philadelphia A.L., October 12, 1905, ninth inning.
Chicago N.L. vs. Detroit A.L., October 8, 1907, 10th inning.
Chicago N.L. vs. Detroit A.L., October 11, 1908, eighth inning.
New York N.L. vs. Boston A.L., October 14, 1912, first inning.
Chicago A.L. vs. New York N.L., October 7, 1917, sixth inning.

CAUGHT STEALING

Most caught stealing, series
4-game series—5
Boston N.L. vs. Philadelphia A.L., 1914.
Cincinnati N.L. vs. New York, A.L., 1976.
5-game series—8—Chicago N.L. vs. Philadelphia A.L. 1910.
6-game series—13—New York N.L. vs. Philadelphia A.L. 1911.
7-game series—7
Cleveland A.L. vs. Brooklyn N.L., 1920.
Washington A.L. vs. Pittsburgh N.L., 1925.
St. Louis N.L. vs. Detroit A.L., 1968.
8-game series—11—New York N.L. vs. Boston A.L., 1912.

Most caught stealing by both clubs, series
4-game series—7—Cincinnati N.L. 5, New York A.L. 2, 1976.
5-game series—15—Chicago N.L. 8, Philadelphia A.L. 7, 1910.
6-game series—19—New York N.L. 13, Philadelphia A.L. 6, 1911.
7-game series—11—Pittsburgh N.L. 6, Detroit A.L. 5, 1909.
8-game series—16—New York N.L. 11, Boston A.L. 5, 1912.

Fewest caught stealing, series
0—Held by many clubs.

Fewest caught stealing by both clubs, series
4-game series—1
New York A.L. 1, Pittsburgh N.L. 0, 1927.
Cincinnati N.L. 1, New York A.L. 0, 1939.
New York N.L. 1, Philadelphia N.L. 0, 1950.
New York A.L. 1, Cleveland A.L. 0, 1954.
5-game series—0—New York A.L. 0, Brooklyn N.L. 0, 1949.
6-game series—1
St. Louis N.L. 1, St. Louis A.L. 0, 1944.
Cleveland A.L. 1, Boston N.L. 0, 1948.
7-game series—0—St. Louis N.L. 0, New York A.L. 0, 1964.
8-game series—6—Pittsburgh N.L. 4, Boston A.L. 2, 1903.

Most caught stealing, nine-inning game
3—Made in many games. Last time—Los Angeles N.L. vs. Oakland A.L., October 19, 1988.

Most caught stealing, extra-inning game
5—New York N.L. vs. Philadelphia A.L., October 17, 1911, 11 innings (0 stolen bases).

Most caught stealing by both clubs, nine-inning game
5—Philadelphia A.L. 3, Chicago N.L. 2, October 17, 1910.

Most caught stealing, inning
2—Made in many innings.

LEFT ON BASE

Most left on base, total series
1,272—New York A.L. (33 series, 187 games).

Most left on base, series

4-game series—37—Cleveland A.L. vs. New York N.L., 1954.
5-game series—42—New York A.L. vs. Brooklyn N.L., 1941.
6-game series—55—New York A.L. vs. Los Angeles N.L., 1981.
7-game series—72—New York N.L. vs. Oakland A.L., 1973.
8-game series—55
　Boston A.L. vs. Pittsburgh N.L., 1903.
　Boston A.L. vs. New York N.L., 1912.

Most left on base by both clubs, series

4-game series—65—Cleveland A.L. 37, New York N.L. 28, 1954.
5-game series—76—New York N.L. 39, Washington A.L. 37, 1933.
6-game series—101—New York A.L. 55, Los Angeles N.L. 46, 1981.
7-game series—130—New York N.L. 72, Oakland A.L. 58, 1973.
8-game series—108—Boston A.L. 55, New York N.L. 53, 1912.

Fewest left on base, series

4-game series—16—New York A.L. vs. Cincinnati N.L., 1939.
5-game series—23—Philadelphia N.L. vs. Baltimore A.L., 1983.
6-game series—29—Philadelphia A.L. vs. New York N.L., 1911.
7-game series—36—Minnesota A.L. vs. Los Angeles N.L., 1965.
8-game series—43—New York A.L. vs. New York N.L., 1921.

Fewest left on base by both clubs, series

4-game series—39—Cincinnati N.L. 23, New York A.L. 16, 1939.
5-game series—51—Baltimore A.L. 28, Philadelphia N.L. 23, 1983.
6-game series—60—New York N.L. 31, Philadelphia A.L. 29, 1911.
7-game series—82
　Cleveland A.L. 43, Brooklyn N.L. 39, 1920.
　Brooklyn N.L. 42, New York A.L. 40, 1956.
　New York A.L. 43, San Francisco N.L. 39, 1962.
8-game series—97—New York N.L. 54, New York A.L. 43, 1921.

Most left on base, nine-inning game

14—Chicago N.L. vs. Philadelphia A.L., October 18, 1910.
　Detroit A.L. vs. Cincinnati N.L., October 6, 1940 (batted eight innings).
　Milwaukee N.L. vs. New York A.L., October 5, 1957.
　Pittsburgh N.L. vs. Baltimore A.L., October 11, 1971.
　St. Louis N.L. vs. Milwaukee A.L., October 20, 1982 (batted eight innings).
　Detroit A.L. vs. San Diego N.L., October 12, 1984.

Most left on base, extra-inning game

15—New York N.L. vs. Oakland A.L., October 14, 1973, 12 innings.
　Philadelphia N.L. vs. Kansas City A.L., October 17, 1980, 10 innings.

Most left on base, two consecutive nine-inning games

26—Cleveland A.L. vs. New York N.L. September 29 (13), September 30 (13), 1954.

Most left on base, nine-inning shutout defeat

11—Philadelphia A.L. vs. St. Louis N.L., October 4, 1930 (lost 5-0).
　St. Louis N.L. vs. New York A.L., October 11, 1943 (lost 2-0).
　Los Angeles N.L. vs. Chicago A.L., October 6, 1959 (lost 1-0).
　Baltimore A.L. vs. New York N.L., October 14, 1969 (lost 5-0).

Most left on base by both clubs, nine-inning game

24—Detroit A.L. 14, San Diego N.L. 10, October 12, 1984.

Most left on base by both clubs, extra-inning game

27—New York N.L. 15, Oakland A.L. 12, October 14, 1973, 12 innings.

Fewest left on base, game

0—Brooklyn N.L. vs. New York A.L., October 8, 1956.
　Los Angeles N.L. vs. New York A.L., October 6, 1963 (batted eight innings).

Fewest left on base by both clubs, game

3—New York A.L. 3, Brooklyn N.L. 0, October 8, 1956.

INDIVIDUAL PITCHING

GAMES

Most games pitched, career

22—Whitey Ford, New York A.L., 1950, 1953, 1955, 1956, 1957, 1958, 1960, 1961, 1962, 1963, 1964; 11 series.

Most games pitched, series

4-game series—3—Held by many pitchers.

5-game series—5—Mike G. Marshall, Los Angeles N.L., 1974 (nine innings).

6-game series—6—Dan Quisenberry, Kansas City A.L., 1980 (10⅓ innings).

7-game series—7—Darold Knowles, Oakland A.L., 1973 (6⅓ innings).

8-game series—5—Deacon Phillippe, Pittsburgh N.L., 1903 (44 innings).

Most consecutive games pitched, series

7—Darold Knowles, Oakland A.L., October 13, 14, 16, 17, 18, 20, 21, 1973.

GAMES STARTED

Most games started, career

22—Whitey Ford, New York A.L., 1950, 1953, 1955, 1956, 1957, 1958, 1960, 1961, 1962, 1963, 1964; 11 series.

Most opening games started, career

8—Whitey Ford, New York A.L., 1955, 1956, 1957, 1958, 1961, 1962, 1963, 1964 (won 4, lost 3).

Most consecutive games started, series

2—Deacon Phillippe, Pittsburgh N.L., October 3, 6, 1903.
Deacon Phillippe, Pittsburgh N.L., October 10, 13, 1903.
Jack Coombs, Philadelphia A.L., October 18, 20, 1910.
Christy Mathewson, New York N.L., October 17, 24, 1911.
George Earnshaw, Philadelphia A.L., October 9, 11, 1929.
George Earnshaw, Philadelphia A.L., October 6, 8, 1930.

Most series with three games started, career

3—Bob Gibson, St. Louis N.L., 1964, 1967, 1968.

Most games started, series

5—Deacon Phillippe, Pittsburgh N.L., 1903 (8-game series).

Oldest pitcher to start a game

45 years, 3 months, 7 days—Jack Quinn, Philadelphia A.L., October 12, 1929 (pitched five innings).

GAMES RELIEVED AND FINISHED

Most games by relief pitcher, career

16—Rollie Fingers, Oakland A.L., 1972, 1973, 1974 (33⅓ innings).

Most games pitched by relief pitcher, series

7—Darold Knowles, Oakland A.L., 1973 (7-game series).

Most games finished, series

6—Hugh Casey, Brooklyn N.L., 1947 (7-game series).
Dan Quisenberry, Kansas City A.L., 1980 (6-game series).

Oldest pitcher to finish game

46 years, 2 months, 29 days—Jack Quinn, Philadelphia A.L., October 4, 1930 (pitched two innings).

COMPLETE GAMES

Most complete games pitched, career

10—Christy Mathewson, New York N.L. 1905, 1911, 1912, 1913.

Most consecutive complete games pitched, career

8—Bob Gibson, St. Louis N.L., 1964, 1967, 1968 (won 7, lost 1).

Most consecutive complete games won, career

7—Bob Gibson, St. Louis N.L., October 12, 15, 1964; October 4, 8, 12, 1967; October 2, 6, 1968.

Most complete games, series

5—Deacon Phillippe, Pittsburgh N.L., 1903 (8-game series).

Youngest pitcher to pitch a complete game

20 years, 10 months, 12 days—Joe Bush, Philadelphia A.L., October 9, 1913 (Philadelphia A.L. 8, New York N.L. 2).

Youngest pitcher to win a complete game

20 years, 10 months, 12 days—Joe Bush, Philadelphia A.L., October 9, 1913 (Philadelphia A.L. 8, New York N.L. 2).

Oldest pitcher to pitch a complete game

39 years, 7 months, 13 days—Grover Alexander, St. Louis N.L., October 9, 1926 (St. Louis N.L. 10, New York A.L. 2).

INNINGS

Most innings pitched, career

146—Whitey Ford, New York A.L., 1950, 1953, 1955, 1956, 1957, 1958, 1960, 1961, 1962, 1963, 1964; 11 series, 22 games.

Most innings pitched, series

4-game series—18
Dick Rudolph, Boston N.L., 1914.
Waite Hoyt, New York A.L., 1928.
Red Ruffing, New York A.L., 1938.
Sandy Koufax, Los Angeles N.L., 1963.

5-game series—27
Christy Mathewson, New York N.L., 1905.
Jack Coombs, Philadelphia A.L., 1910.

6-game series—27
Christy Mathewson, New York N.L. 1911.
Red Faber, Chicago A.L., 1917.
Hippo Vaughn, Chicago N.L., 1918.

7-game series—32—George Mullin, Detroit A.L., 1909.

8-game series—44—Deacon Phillippe, Pittsburgh N.L., 1903.

Most innings pitched, game

14—Babe Ruth, Boston A.L., October 9, 1916 (complete game, won 2-1).

GAMES WON

Most games won, career

10—Whitey Ford, New York A.L., 1950, 1953, 1955, 1956, 1957, 1958, 1960, 1961, 1962, 1963, 1964; 11 series, 22 games (lost 8).

Most consecutive games won, career

7—Bob Gibson, St. Louis N.L., October 12, 15, 1964; October 4, 8, 12, 1967; October 2, 6, 1968 (seven complete).

Most games won by undefeated pitcher, career

6—Lefty Gomez, New York A.L., 1932, 1936, 1937, 1938.

Most series-opening games won, career

5—Red Ruffing, New York A.L., 1932, 1938, 1939, 1941, 1942, four complete (lost complete-game opener in 1936).

Most games won, series

4-game series—2—Held by many pitchers.

5-game series—3
Christy Mathewson, New York N.L., 1905.
Jack Coombs, Philadelphia A.L., 1910.

6-game series—3—Red Faber, Chicago A.L., 1917.

7-game series—3
Babe Adams, Pittsburgh N.L., 1909.
Stan Coveleski, Cleveland A.L., 1920.
Harry Brecheen, St. Louis N.L., 1946.

Lew Burdette, Milwaukee N.L., 1957.
Bob Gibson, St. Louis N.L., 1967.
Mickey Lolich, Detroit A.L., 1968.
8-game series—3
Bill Dinneen, Boston A.L., 1903.
Deacon Phillippe, Pittsburgh N.L., 1903.
Joe Wood, Boston A.L., 1912.

Most games won by relief pitcher, series

2—Jesse Barnes, New York N.L., 1921 (8-game series).
Hugh Casey, Brooklyn N.L., 1947 (7-game series).
Larry Sherry, Los Angeles N.L., 1959 (6-game series).
Ross Grimsley, Cincinnati N.L., 1972 (6-game series).
Rawly Eastwick, Cincinnati N.L., 1975 (7-game series).
Duane Ward, Toronto A.L., 1992 (6-game series).

Most games won by undefeated pitcher, series

4-game series—2—Held by many pitchers.
5-game series—3
Christy Mathewson, New York N.L., 1905.
Jack Coombs, Philadelphia A.L., 1910.
6-game series—2—Held by many pitchers.
7-game series—3
Babe Adams, Pittsburgh N.L., 1909.
Stan Coveleski, Cleveland A.L., 1920.
Harry Brecheen, St. Louis N.L., 1946.
Lew Burdette, Milwaukee N.L., 1957.
Bob Gibson, St. Louis N.L., 1967.
Mickey Lolich, Detroit A.L., 1968.
8-game series—2
Rube Marquard, New York N.L., 1912.
Hod Eller, Cincinnati N.L., 1919.
Dickie Kerr, Chicago A.L., 1919.
Jesse Barnes, New York N.L., 1921.

SAVES (SINCE 1969)

Most saves, career

6—Rollie Fingers, Oakland A.L., 1972, 1973, 1974.

Most saves, series

4-game series—2—Will McEnaney, Cincinnati N.L., 1976.
5-game series—2
Rollie Fingers, Oakland A.L., 1974.
Tippy Martinez, Baltimore A.L., 1983.
Willie Hernandez, Detroit A.L., 1984.
6-game series—2
Tug McGraw, Philadelphia N.L., 1980.
Rich Gossage, New York A.L., 1981.
Tom Henke, Toronto A.L., 1992.
Duane Ward, Toronto A.L., 1993.
7-game series—3—Kent Tekulve, Pittsburgh N.L., 1979.

GAMES LOST

Most games lost, career

8—Whitey Ford, New York A.L., 1950, 1953, 1955, 1956,
1957, 1958, 1960, 1961, 1962, 1963, 1964; 11 series, 22
games (won 10).

Most consecutive games lost, career

5—Joe Bush, Philadelphia A.L., Boston A.L., New York A.L.,
1914 (1), 1918 (1), 1922 (2), 1923 (1).

Most games lost by winless pitcher, career

4—Ed Summers, Detroit A.L., 1908 (2), 1909 (2).
Willie Sherdel, St. Louis N.L., 1926 (2), 1928 (2).
Don Newcombe, Brooklyn N.L., 1949 (2), 1955 (1), 1956
(1).
Charlie Leibrandt, Kansas City A.L., 1985 (1); Atlanta
N.L., 1991 (2), 1992 (1).

Most games lost, series

4-game series—2—Held by many pitchers.
5-game series—2—Held by many pitchers.
6-game series—3—George Frazier, New York N.L., 1981.
7-game series—2—Held by many pitchers
8-game series—3—Lefty Williams, Chicago A.L., 1919.

RUNS. EARNED RUNS AND ERA

Most runs allowed, series

4-game series—11
Grover Alexander, St. Louis N.L., 1928.
Bob Lemon, Cleveland A.L., 1954.
5-game series—16—Mordecai Brown, Chicago N.L., 1910.
6-game series—10
Slim Sallee, New York N.L., 1917.
Red Ruffing, New York A.L., 1936.
Don Gullett, New York A.L., 1977.
Don Sutton, Los Angeles N.L., 1978.
Jack Morris, Toronto A.L., 1992.
7-game series—17—Lew Burdette, Milwaukee N.L., 1958.
8-game series—19—Deacon Phillippe, Pittsburgh N.L., 1903.

Most runs allowed, nine-inning game

9—Andy Coakley, Philadelphia A.L., October 12, 1905.
Mordecai Brown, Chicago N.L., October 18, 1910.
Walter Johnson, Washington A.L., October 15, 1925.

Most earned runs allowed, nine-inning game

7—Mordecai Brown, Chicago N.L., October 18, 1910.
Danny Cox, St. Louis N.L., October 19, 1987.
Jack Morris, Toronto A.L., October 22, 1992.

Most runs allowed, inning

7—Hooks Wiltse, New York N.L., October 26, 1911, seventh
inning.
Carl Hubbell, New York N.L., October 6, 1937, sixth inning.

Most earned runs allowed, inning

6—Hooks Wiltse, New York N.L., October 26, 1911, seventh
inning.
Danny Cox, St. Louis N.L., October 18, 1987, fourth inning.

Lowest earned-run average, series (14 or more innings)

0.00—Christy Mathewson, New York N.L., 1905 (27 innings).
Waite Hoyt, New York A.L., 1921 (27 innings).
Carl Hubbell, New York N.L., 1933 (20 innings).
Whitey Ford, New York A.L., 1960 (18 innings).
Joe McGinnity, New York N.L., 1905 (17 innings).
Duster Mails, Cleveland A.L., 1920 (15⅔ innings).
Rube Benton, New York N.L., 1917 (14 innings).
Whitey Ford, New York A.L., 1961 (14 innings).

SHUTOUTS AND SCORELESS INNINGS

Most shutouts won, career

4—Christy Mathewson, New York N.L., 1905 (3), 1913 (1).

Most shutouts won, series

3—Christy Mathewson, New York N.L., October 9, 12, 14,
1905 (consecutive).

Most 1-0 shutouts won, career

2—Art Nehf, New York N.L., October 13, 1921, October 12, 1923.

Most shutouts lost, career

3—Eddie Plank, Philadelphia A.L., 1905 (2), 1914 (1).

Most 1-0 shutouts lost, career

2—Eddie Plank, Philadelphia A.L., October 13, 1905, October
10, 1914.

Youngest pitcher to win a complete World Series shutout game

20 years, 11 months, 21 days—Jim Palmer, Baltimore A.L.,
October 6, 1966; Baltimore A.L., 6, Los Angeles N.L., 0.

Oldest pitcher to win a complete World Series shutout game

37 years, 11 months, 5 days—Walter Johnson, Washington A.L.,
October 11, 1925; Washington A.L. 4, Pittsburgh N.L. 0.

Most consecutive scoreless innings, career

33—Whitey Ford, New York A.L., October 8, 1960 (9); October 12, 1960 (9); October 4, 1961 (9) innings; October 8, 1961 (5); October 4, 1962 (1).

Most consecutive scoreless innings, series

27—Christy Mathewson, New York N.L., October 9, 12, 14, 1905.

Retiring side on three pitched balls

Christy Mathewson, New York N.L., October 9, 1912, 11th inning.

Christy Mathewson, New York N.L., October 16, 1912, fifth inning.

Rube Walberg, Philadelphia A.L., October 14, 1929, seventh inning.

Tiny Bonham, New York A.L., October 6, 1941, seventh inning.

HITS

Most hits allowed, series

4-game series— 17—Red Ruffing, New York A.L., 1938.

5-game series—23
Jack Coombs, Philadelphia A.L., 1910.
Mordecai Brown, Chicago N.L., 1910.

6-game series—25—Christy Mathewson, New York N.L., 1911.

7-game series—30—Walter Johnson, Washington A.L., 1924.

8-game series—38—Deacon Phillippe, Pittsburgh N.L., 1903.

Most hits allowed, nine-inning game

15—Walter Johnson, Washington A.L., October 15, 1925.

Fewest hits allowed, nine-inning game

0—Don Larsen, New York A.L., October 8, 1956 (perfect game).

One and two-hit games of nine innings (pitching complete game)

1—Ed Reulbach, Chicago N.L., October 10, 1906 (hit came with none out in seventh).
Claude Passeau, Chicago N.L., October 5, 1945 (hit came with two out in second).
Bill Bevens, New York A.L., October 3, 1947 (hit came with two out in ninth).
Jim Lonborg, Boston A.L., October 5, 1967 (hit came with two out in eighth).

2—Ed Walsh, Chicago A.L., October 11, 1906.
Mordecai Brown, Chicago A.L., October 12, 1906.
Eddie Plank, Philadelphia A.L., October 11, 1913.
Bill James, Boston N.L., October 10, 1914.
Waite Hoyt, New York A.L., October 6, 1921.
Burleigh Grimes, St. Louis N.L., October 5, 1931.
George Earnshaw, Philadelphia A.L., October 6, 1931.
Monte Pearson, New York A.L., October 5, 1939.
Mort Cooper, St. Louis N.L., October 4, 1944.
Bob Feller, Cleveland A.L., October 6, 1948.
Allie Reynolds, New York A.L., October 5, 1949.
Vic Raschi, New York A.L., October 4, 1950.
Warren Spahn, Milwaukee N.L., October 5, 1958.
Whitey Ford, New York A.L., October 4, 1961.
Nelson Briles, Pittsburgh N.L., October 14, 1971.

Fewest hits allowed, two consecutive complete games

4—Jim Lonborg, Boston A.L., October 5 (1), October 9 (3), 1967.

Fewest hits allowed, three consecutive complete games

14—Christy Mathewson, New York N.L., October 5 (4), October 12 (4), October 14 (6), 1905.
Bob Gibson, St. Louis N.L., October 4 (6), October 8 (5), October 12 (3), 1967.

Most consecutive hitless innings, career

11—Don Larsen, New York A.L., October 8, 1956 (9), October 5, 1957 (2).

Most consecutive hitless innings, game

9—Don Larsen, New York A.L., October 8, 1956.

Most consecutive innings allowing no players to reach first base, career

11—Don Larsen, New York A.L., October 8, 1956 (9), October 5, 1957 (2).

Most consecutive innings allowing no players to reach first base, series

9—Don Larsen, New York A.L., October 8, 1956.

Most consecutive innings allowing no player to reach first base, game

9—Don Larsen, New York A.L., October 8, 1956 (perfect game).

Most hits allowed, inning

7—Joe Wood, Boston A.L., October 15, 1912, first inning.

Most consecutive hits allowed, inning (consecutive plate appearances)

6—Ed Summers, Detroit A.L., October 10, 1908, ninth inning (6 singles).

DOUBLES, TRIPLES AND HOME RUNS

Most doubles allowed, game

8—Walter Johnson, Washington A.L., October 15, 1925.

Most triples allowed, game

5—Deacon Phillippe, Pittsburgh N.L., October 10, 1903.

Most home runs allowed, career

9—Catfish Hunter, Oakland A.L., 1972, 1973, 1974; New York A.L., 1976, 1977, 1978; six series, 12 games.

Most home runs allowed, series

4-game series—4
Willie Sherdel, St. Louis N.L., 1928.
Charlie Root, Chicago N.L., 1932.
Junior Thompson, Cincinnati N.L., 1939.
Scott Garrelts, San Francisco N.L., 1989.

5-game series—4
Gary Nolan, Cincinnati N.L., 1970.
Charles Hudson, Philadelphia N.L., 1983.

6-game series—4—Allie Reynolds, New York A.L., 1953.

7-game series—5
Lew Burdette, Milwaukee N.L., 1958.
Dick Hughes, St. Louis N.L., 1967.

8-game series—2
Babe Adams, Pittsburgh N.L., 1909.
Harry Harper, New York A.L., 1921.

Most home runs allowed, game

4—Charlie Root, Chicago N.L., October 1, 1932.
Junior Thompson, Cincinnati N.L., October 7, 1939.
Dick Hughes, St. Louis N.L., October 11, 1967.

Most home runs allowed, inning

3—Dick Hughes, St. Louis N.L., October 11, 1967, fourth inning.

Most consecutive home runs allowed, inning (nine times)

2—Emil Yde, Pittsburgh N.L., October 11, 1925, third inning.
Bill Sherdel, St. Louis N.L., October 9, 1928, seventh inning.
Charlie Root, Chicago N.L., October 1, 1932, fifth inning.
Curt Simmons, St. Louis N.L., October 14, 1964, sixth inning.
Don Drysdale, Los Angeles N.L., October 5, 1966, first inning.
Dick Hughes, St. Louis N.L., October 11, 1967, fourth inning.
Rick Wise, Boston A.L., October 14, 1975, fifth inning.
Don Sutton, Los Angeles N.L., October 16, 1977, eighth inning.
Ron Guidry, New York A.L., October 25, 1981, seventh inning.
Ron Darling, New York N.L., October 27, 1986, second inning.

TOTAL BASES AND LONG HITS

Most total bases allowed, game

25—Walter Johnson, Washington A.L., October 15, 1925.

Most long hits allowed, game

9—Walter Johnson, Washington A.L., October 15, 1925.

BASES ON BALLS

Most bases on balls, career

34—Whitey Ford, New York A.L., 1950, 1953, 1955, 1956, 1957, 1958, 1960, 1961, 1962, 1963, 1964; 11 series, 22 games.

Most innings pitched without allowing a base on balls, series

26—Carl Mays, New York A.L., 1921.

Most bases on balls, series

4-game series—8—Bob Lemon, Cleveland A.L., 1954.
5-game series—14—Jack Coombs, Philadelphia A.L., 1910.
6-game series—11
  Lefty Tyler, Chicago N.L., 1918.
  Lefty Gomez, New York A.L., 1936.
  Allie Reynolds, New York A.L., 1951.
7-game series—11
  Walter Johnson, Washington A.L., 1924.
  Bill Bevens, New York A.L., 1947.
8-game series—13—Art Nehf, New York N.L., 1921.

Most bases on balls, game

10—Bill Bevens, New York A.L., October 3, 1947.

Longest game without allowing base on balls

12 innings—Schoolboy Rowe, Detroit A.L., October 4, 1934.

Most bases on balls, inning

4—Bill Donovan, Detroit A.L., October 16, 1909, second inning.
  Art Reinhart, St. Louis N.L., October 6, 1926, fifth inning.
  (one base on balls with bases full).
  Guy Bush, Chicago N.L., September 28, 1932, sixth inning.
  Don Gullett, Cincinnati N.L., October 22, 1975, third in-
  ning (two bases on balls with bases full).
  Tom Glavine, Atlanta N.L., October 24, 1991, sixth inning
  (two bases on balls with bases full).
  Todd Stottlemyre, Toronto A.L., October 20, 1993, first in-
  ning (one base on balls with bases full).

Most consecutive bases on balls, inning

3—Bob Shawkey, New York A.L., October 7, 1921, fourth inning (two bases on balls with bases full).
  Art Reinhart, St. Louis N.L., October 6, 1926, fifth inning
  (one base on balls with bases full).
  Guy Bush, Chicago N.L., September 28, 1932, sixth inning.
  Joe Hoerner, St. Louis N.L., October 3, 1968, ninth inning
  (two bases on balls with bases full).
  Tom Glavine, Atlanta N.L., October 24, 1991, sixth inning
  (two bases on balls with bases full).
  Todd Stottlemyre, Toronto A.L., October 20, 1993, first inning (one base on balls with bases full).

STRIKEOUTS

Most strikeouts, career

94—Whitey Ford, New York A.L., 1950, 1953, 1955, 1956,
  1957, 1958, 1960, 1961, 1962, 1963, 1964; 11 series,
  22 games.

Most strikeouts, series

4-game series—23—Sandy Koufax, Los Angeles N.L., 1963.
5-game series—18—Christy Mathewson, New York N.L., 1905.
6-game series—20—Chief Bender, Philadelphia A.L., 1911.
7-game series—35—Bob Gibson, St. Louis N.L., 1968.
8-game series—28—Bill Dinneen, Boston A.L., 1903.

Most strikeouts, game

17—Bob Gibson, St. Louis N.L., October 2, 1968.

Most games with 10 or more strikeouts, career

5—Bob Gibson, St. Louis N.L., 1964 (1), 1967 (2), 1968 (2).

Most strikeouts by losing pitcher, nine-inning game

11—Chief Bender, Philadelphia A.L., October 14, 1911.
  Don Newcombe, Brooklyn N.L., October 5, 1949.
  Blue Moon Odom, Oakland A.L., October 18, 1972,
  pitched first seven innings.

Most strikeouts by losing pitcher, extra-inning game

12—Walter Johnson, Washington A.L., October 4, 1924, 12
  innings.

Most strikeouts by relief pitcher, game

11—Moe Drabowsky, Baltimore A.L., October 5, 1966,
  pitched 6⅔ innings.

Most consecutive strikeouts, game

6—Hod Eller, Cincinnati N.L., October 6, 1919 (three in second inning, three in third inning).
  Moe Drabowsky, Baltimore A.L., October 5, 1966 (three in
  fourth inning, three in fifth inning).
  Todd Worrell, St. Louis N.L., October 24, 1985 (three in
  sixth inning, three in seventh inning).

Most consecutive strikeouts at start of game

5—Mort Cooper, St. Louis N.L., October 11, 1943.
  Sandy Koufax, Los Angeles N.L., October 23, 1963.

Most innings with one or more strikeouts, nine-inning game

9—Ed Walsh, Chicago A.L., October 11, 1906 (12 strikeouts).
  Bob Gibson, St. Louis N.L., October 2, 1968 (17 strikeouts).

Most strikeouts, inning

4—Orval Overall, Chicago N.L., October 14, 1908, first inning.

HIT BATSMEN, WILD PITCHES AND BALKS

Most hit batsmen, career

4—Bill Donovan, Detroit A.L., 1907 (3), 1908 (0), 1909 (1).
  Eddie Plank, Philadelphia A.L., 1905 (1), 1911 (1), 1913
  (1), 1914 (1).

Most hit batsmen, series

3—Bill Donovan, Detroit A.L., 1907.
  Bruce Kison, Pittsburgh N.L., 1971.

Most hit batsmen, game

3—Bruce Kison, Pittsburgh N.L., October 13, 1971, 6⅓ innings.

Most hit batsmen, inning

2—Ed Willett, Detroit A.L., October 11, 1909, second inning
  (consecutive).
  Wayne Granger, St. Louis N.L., October 9, 1968, eighth
  inning.

Most wild pitches, career

5—Hal Schumacher, New York N.L., 1933 (2), 1936 (2),
  1937 (1).

Most wild pitches, series

3—Jeff Tesreau, New York N.L., 1912.
  John Stuper, St. Louis N.L., 1982.

Most wild pitches, game

2—Jeff Tesreau, New York N.L., October 15, 1912.
  Jeff Pfeffer, Brooklyn N.L., October 12, 1916.
  Bob Shawkey, New York A.L., October 5, 1922.
  Vic Aldridge, Pittsburgh N.L., October 15, 1925.
  Johnny Miljus, Pittsburgh N.L., October 8, 1927.
  Tex Carleton, Chicago N.L., October 9, 1938.
  Jim Bouton, New York A.L., October 5, 1963.
  John Stuper, St. Louis N.L., October 13, 1982.
  George Medich, Milwaukee A.L., October 19, 1982.
  Jack Morris, Detroit A.L., October 13, 1984.
  Ron Darling, New York N.L., October 18, 1986.
  Mike Moore, Oakland A.L., October 15, 1989.
  John Smoltz, Atlanta N.L., October 18, 1992.

Most wild pitches, inning

2—Bob Shawkey, New York A.L., October 5, 1922, fifth inning.
  Vic Aldridge, Pittsburgh N.L., October 15, 1925, first inning.
  Johnny Miljus, Pittsburgh N.L., October 8, 1927, ninth inning.
  Tex Carleton, Chicago N.L., October 9, 1938, eighth inning.
  Doc Medich, Milwaukee A.L., October 19, 1982, sixth inning.

Most balks, inning, game, series or career

1—Held by many pitchers.

CLUB PITCHING

APPEARANCES

Most appearances by pitchers, series
4-game series—19—San Francisco N.L. vs. Oakland A.L., 1989.
5-game series—20—Oakland A.L. vs. Los Angeles N.L., 1988.
6-game series—25—Toronto A.L. vs. Atlanta N.L., 1992.
7-game series—30—Cincinnati N.L. vs. Boston A.L., 1975.
8-game series—14—Boston A.L. vs. New York N.L., 1912.

Most appearances by pitchers from both clubs, series
4-game series—32—San Francisco N.L. 19, Oakland A.L. 13, 1989.
5-game series—32—Oakland A.L. 20, Los Angeles N.L. 12, 1988.
6-game series—44—Philadelphia N.L. 23, Toronto A.L. 21, 1993.
7-game series—52—Cincinnati N.L. 30, Boston A.L. 22, 1975.
8-game series—25—Chicago A.L. 13, Cincinnati N.L. 12, 1919.

COMPLETE GAMES

Most complete games, series
7—Boston A.L. vs. Pittsburgh N.L., 1903 (8-game series).

Most complete games from both clubs, series
13—Boston A.L. 7, Pittsburgh N.L. 6, 1903 (8-game series).

Fewest complete games, series
0—Held by many clubs.

Fewest complete games by both clubs, series
0—Occurred many times. Last time—St. Louis N.L. 0, Minnesota A.L. 0, 1987 (7-game series).

SAVES (SINCE 1969)

Most saves, series
4-game series—2—Cincinnati N.L. vs. New York A.L., 1976.
5-game series—3—Oakland A.L. vs. Los Angeles N.L., 1974.
6-game series—3
 Philadelphia N.L. vs. Kansas City A.L., 1980.
 Toronto A.L. vs. Atlanta N.L., 1992.
7-game series—4—Oakland A.L. vs. New York N.L., 1973.

Most saves by both clubs, series
4-game series—2—Cincinnati N.L. 2, New York A.L. 0, 1976.
5-game series—4—Oakland A.L. 3, Los Angeles N.L. 1, 1974.
6-game series—4
 Philadelphia N.L. 3, Kansas City A.L. 1, 1980.
 Toronto A.L. 3, Atlanta N.L. 1, 1992.
7-game series—7—Oakland A.L. 4, New York N.L. 3, 1973.

Fewest saves, series
0—Held by many clubs.

Fewest saves by both clubs, series
0—New York A.L. 0, Los Angeles N.L. 0, 1977 (6-game series).

RUNS AND SHUTOUTS

Most runs allowed, total series
651—New York A.L., 33 series, 187 games.

Most shutouts won, total series
17—New York A.L.

Most shutouts won, series
4—New York N.L. vs. Philadelphia A.L., 1905.

Most consecutive shutouts won, series
3—New York N.L. vs. Philadelphia A.L., October 12, 13, 14, 1905.
 Baltimore A.L., vs. Los Angeles N.L., October 6, 8, 9, 1966.

Most shutouts by both clubs, series
5—New York N.L. 4, Philadelphia A.L. 1, 1905.

Fewest shutouts, series
0—Held by many clubs in series of all lengths.

Fewest shutouts by both clubs, series
0—Held by many clubs in series of all lengths.

Longest shutout game
10 innings—New York N.L. 3, Philadelphia A.L. 0, October 8, 1913.
 Brooklyn N.L. 1, New York A.L. 0, October 9, 1956.
 Minnesota A.L. 1, Atlanta N.L. 0, October 27, 1991.

Largest score, shutout game
12-0—New York A.L. 12, Pittsburgh N.L. 0, October 12, 1960.

Most consecutive innings shut out opponents, total series
39—Baltimore A.L., October 5, 1966, fourth inning, through October 11, 1969, first six innings.

Most consecutive innings shut out opponent, series
33—Baltimore A.L. vs. Los Angeles N.L., October 5, fourth inning, through end of game, October 6, 8, 9, 1966.

1-0 GAMES

Most 1-0 games won, total series
3—New York A.L.
 New York (Giants) N.L.

Most 1-0 games won, series
2—Baltimore A.L. vs. Los Angeles N.L., 1966.

Most 1-0 games won by both clubs, series
2—New York A.L. 1, Brooklyn N.L. 1, 1949.
 Baltimore A.L. 2, Los Angeles N.L. 0, 1966.

WILD PITCHES AND BALKS

Most wild pitches, series
5—Pittsburgh N.L. vs. New York A.L., 1960.

Most wild pitches by both clubs, series
8—New York A.L. 4, Brooklyn N.L. 4, 1947.

Fewest wild pitches by both clubs, series
0—Made in series of all lengths.

Most balks, series
2—Cleveland A.L. vs. Boston N.L., 1948.
 Minnesota A.L. vs. St. Louis N.L., 1987.

Most balks by both clubs, series
2—Cleveland A.L. 2, Boston N.L. 0, 1948.
 Minnesota A.L. 2, St. Louis N.L. 0, 1987.
 Los Angeles N.L. 1, Oakland A.L. 1, 1988.

Fewest balks by both clubs, series
0—Made in series of all lengths.

INDIVIDUAL FIELDING

FIRST BASEMEN

	GAMES	

Most games played, career

38—Gil Hodges, Brooklyn N.L., Los Angeles N.L., 1949, 1952, 1953, 1955, 1956, 1959; six series.

☐ PUTOUTS, ASSISTS AND CHANCES ACCEPTED ☐

Most putouts, career

326—Gil Hodges, Brooklyn N.L., Los Angeles N.L., 1949, 1952, 1953, 1955, 1956, 1959; six series, 38 games.

Most putouts, series

4-game series—52—Butch Schmidt, Boston N.L., 1914.
5-game series—69—Dick Hoblitzel, Boston A.L., 1916.
6-game series—79—Jiggs Donahue, Chicago A.L., 1906.
7-game series—79—Jim Bottomley, St. Louis N.L., 1926.
8-game series—92—Wally Pipp, New York A.L., 1921.

Most putouts, nine-inning game

19—George Kelly, New York N.L., October 15, 1923.

Fewest putouts, nine-inning game

1—Orlando Cepeda, St. Louis N.L., October 2, 1968.

Most putouts, inning

3—Held by many first basemen.

Most assists, career

29—Bill Skowron, New York A.L., 1955, 1956, 1957, 1958, 1960, 1961, 1962; Los Angeles N.L., 1963; eight series, 37 games.

Most assists, series

4-game series—6
Vic Wertz, Cleveland A.L., 1954.
Joe Pepitone, New York A.L., 1963.
5-game series—5
Claude Rossman, Detroit A.L., 1908.
Dolph Camilli, Brooklyn N.L., 1941.
Ray Sanders, St. Louis N.L., 1943.
Bill Skowron, New York A.L., 1961.
6-game series—9—Fred Merkle, Chicago N.L., 1918.
7-game series—10—Cecil Cooper, Milwaukee A.L., 1982.
8-game series—7—George Kelly, New York N.L., 1921.

Most assists, nine-inning game

4—Marv Owen, Detroit A.L., October 6, 1935.
Don Mincher, Minnesota A.L., October 7, 1965.

Most assists, inning

2—Held by many first basemen.

Most chances accepted, career

350—Gil Hodges, Brooklyn N.L., Los Angeles N.L., 1949, 1952, 1953, 1955, 1956, 1959; six series, 38 games.

Most chances accepted, series

4-game series—55—Butch Schmidt, Boston N.L., 1914.
5-game series—73—Dick Hoblitzel, Boston A.L., 1916.
6-game series—87—Jiggs Donahue, Chicago A.L., 1906.
7-game series—81—Cecil Cooper, Milwaukee A.L., 1982.
8-game series—93
George Kelly, New York N.L., 1921.
Wally Pipp, New York A.L., 1921.

Most chances accepted, nine-inning game

19—Ed Konetchy, Brooklyn N.L., October 7, 1920 (17 putouts, 2 assists).
George Kelly, New York N.L., October 15, 1923 (19 putouts).

Fewest chances offered, nine-inning game

2—Wally Pipp, New York A.L., October 11, 1921 (2 putouts).
Orlando Cepeda, St. Louis N.L., October 2, 1968 (1 putout, 1 assist).

Most chances accepted, inning

3—Held by many first basemen.

| | ERRORS AND DOUBLE PLAYS | |

Most errors, career

8—Fred Merkle, New York N.L., 1911, 1912, 1913 (7); Brooklyn N.L., 1916 (1), Chicago N.L., 1918 (0); five series, 25 games.

Most consecutive errorless games, career

31—Bill Skowron, New York A.L., Los Angeles N.L., October 10, 1956 through October 6, 1963.

Most errors, series

4-game series—2—Mark McGwire, Oakland A.L., 1990.
5-game series—3
Frank Chance, Chicago N.L., 1908.
Harry Davis, Philadelphia A.L., 1910.
6-game series—3—Hank Greenberg, Detroit A.L., 1935.
7-game series—5—Bill Abstein, Pittsburgh N.L., 1909.
8-game series—3—Fred Merkle, New York N.L., 1912.

Most chances accepted, errorless series

93—George Kelly, New York N.L., 1921 (8-game series).
Wally Pipp, New York A.L., 1921 (8-game series).

Most errors, nine-inning game

2—Held by many first basemen.

Most errors, inning

2—Hank Greenberg, Detroit A.L., October 3, 1935, fifth inning.
Johnny McCarthy, New York N.L., October 8, 1937, fifth inning.
Frank Torre, Milwaukee N.L., October 9, 1958, second inning.

Most double plays, career

31—Gil Hodges, Brooklyn N.L., Los Angeles N.L., 1949, 1952, 1953, 1955, 1956, 1959; six series, 38 games.

Most double plays, series

11—Gil Hodges, Brooklyn N.L., 1955 (7-game series).

Most double plays started, series

3—Gil Hodges, Brooklyn N.L., 1955 (7-game series).

Most double plays, nine-inning game

4—Stuffy McInnis, Philadelphia A.L., October 9, 1914.
Joe Collins, New York A.L., October 8, 1951.
Gene Tenace, Oakland A.L., October 17, 1973.
Pete Rose, Philadelphia N.L., October 15, 1980.

Most double plays started, game

2—Eddie Murray, Baltimore A.L., October 11, 1979.

Most unassisted double plays, game

1—George Grantham, Pittsburgh N.L., October 7, 1925.
Joe Judge, Washington A.L., October 13, 1925.
Jimmie Foxx, Philadelphia A.L., October 8, 1930.
Jim Bottomley, St. Louis N.L., October 1, 1931.
Lou Gehrig, New York A.L., October 10, 1937.
Rip Collins, Chicago N.L., October 5, 1938.
Joe Collins, New York A.L., October 7, 1956.
Gordy Coleman, Cincinnati N.L., October 8, 1961.
Tony Perez, Cincinnati N.L., October 11, 1975.
Steve Garvey, San Diego N.L., October 9, 1984.

SECOND BASEMEN

	GAMES	

Most games played, career

42—Frankie Frisch, New York N.L. (18), 1922, 1923, 1924; St. Louis N.L. (24), 1928, 1930, 1931, 1934; seven series.

☐ PUTOUTS, ASSISTS AND CHANCES ACCEPTED ☐

Most putouts, career

104—Frankie Frisch, New York N.L., St. Louis N.L., 1922, 1923, 1924, 1928, 1930, 1931, 1934; seven series, 42 games.

Most putouts, series

4-game series—14—Willie Randolph, Oakland A.L., 1990.
5-game series—20—Joe Gordon, New York A.L., 1943.
6-game series—26—Dave Lopes, Los Angeles N.L., 1981.
7-game series—26—Bucky Harris, Washington A.L., 1924.
8-game series—22—Morrie Rath, Cincinnati N.L., 1919.

Most putouts, nine-inning game

8—Bucky Harris, Washington A.L., October 8, 1924.
   Dave Lopes, Los Angeles N.L., October 16, 1974.

Most putouts, extra-inning game

9—Hughie Critz, New York N.L., October 6, 1933, 11 innings.

Most putouts, inning

3—Larry Doyle, New York N.L., October 9, 1913, seventh inning.
   Bill Wambsganss, Cleveland A.L., October 10, 1920, fifth inning.
   Johnny Rawlings, New York N.L., October 11, 1921, ninth inning.
   Dave Lopes, Los Angeles N.L., October 16, 1974, sixth inning.
   Dave Lopes, Los Angeles N.L., October 21, 1981, fourth inning.

Most assists, career

135—Frankie Frisch, New York N.L., St. Louis N.L., 1922, 1923, 1924, 1928, 1930, 1931, 1934; seven series, 42 games.

Most assists, series

4-game series—18—Tony Lazzeri, New York A.L., 1927.
5-game series—23—Joe Gordon, New York A.L., 1943.
6-game series—27—Aaron Ward, New York A.L., 1923.
7-game series—33—Jim Gantner, Milwaukee A.L., 1982.
8-game series—34—Aaron Ward, New York A.L., 1921.

Most assists, nine-inning game

8—Claude Ritchey, Pittsburgh, N.L., October 10, 1903.
   Germany Schaefer, Detroit A.L., October 12, 1907.
   Hal Janvrin, Boston A.L., October 7, 1916.
   Eddie Collins, Chicago A.L., October 15, 1917.
   Bucky Harris, Washington A.L., October 7, 1924.
   Joe Gordon, New York A.L., October 5, 1943.
   Bobby Doerr, Boston A.L., October 9, 1946.

Most assists, inning

3—Eddie Collins, Philadelphia A.L., October 12, 1914, fourth inning.
   Pete Kilduff, Brooklyn N.L., October 10, 1920, third inning.
   Aaron Ward, New York A.L., October 12, 1921, sixth inning.
   Joe Gordon, New York A.L., October 11, 1943, eighth inning.
   Jackie Robinson, Brooklyn N.L., October 8, 1949, seventh inning.
   Phil Garner, Pittsburgh N.L., October 13, 1979, ninth inning.
   Marty Barrett, Boston A.L., October 23, 1986; first inning.

Most chances accepted, career

239—Frankie Frisch, New York N.L., St. Louis N.L., 1922, 1923, 1924, 1928, 1930, 1931, 1934; seven series, 42 games.

Most chances accepted, series

4-game series—28—Tony Lazzeri, New York A.L., 1927.
5-game series—43—Joe Gordon, New York A.L., 1943.
6-game series—40—Dave Lopes, Los Angeles N.L., 1981.
7-game series—54—Bucky Harris, Washington A.L., 1924.
8-game series—52
   Eddie Collins, Chicago A.L., 1919.
   Aaron Ward, New York A.L., 1921.

Most chances accepted, nine-inning game

13—Claude Ritchey, Pittsburgh N.L., October 10, 1903 (5 putouts, 8 assists).
   Bucky Harris, Washington A.L., October 11, 1925 (6 putouts, 7 assists).
   Dave Lopes, Los Angeles N.L., October 16, 1974 (8 putouts, 5 assists).

Most chances accepted, extra-inning game

14—Hughie Critz, New York N.L., October 6, 1933, 11 innings (9 putouts, 5 assists).

Fewest chances offered, nine-inning game

0—Charlie Pick, Chicago N.L., September 7, 1918.
   Max Bishop, Philadelphia A.L., October 6, 1931.
   Jerry Coleman, New York A.L., October 8, 1949.
   Willie Randolph, New York A.L., October 25, 1981.
   Frank White, Kansas City A.L., October 20, 1985.
   Mariano Duncan, Cincinnati N.L., October 19, 1990.

Most chances accepted, inning

3—Held by many second basemen.

☐ ERRORS AND DOUBLE PLAYS ☐

Most errors, career

8—Larry Doyle, New York N.L., 1911, 1912, 1913; three series, 19 games.
   Eddie Collins, Philadelphia A.L., 1910, 1911, 1913, 1914, Chicago A.L., 1917, 1919; six series, 34 games.

Most consecutive errorless games, career

23—Billy Martin, New York A.L., October 5, 1952 through October 10, 1956.

Most errors, series

4-game series—2
   Tony Lazzeri, New York A.L., 1928.
   Joe Gordon, New York A.L., 1938.
   Billy Herman, Chicago N.L., 1938.
   Joe Morgan, Cincinnati N.L., 1976.
5-game series—4—Danny Murphy, Philadelphia A.L., 1905.
6-game series—6—Dave Lopes, Los Angeles N.L., 1981.
7-game series—5—Jim Gantner, Milwaukee A.L., 1982.
8-game series—4—Larry Doyle, New York N.L., 1912.

Most chances accepted, errorless series

49—Bobby Doerr, Boston A.L., 1946 (7-game series).

Most errors, nine-inning game

3—Danny Murphy, Philadelphia A.L., October 12, 1905.
   Buddy Myer, Washington A.L., October 3, 1933.
   Dave Lopes, Los Angeles N.L., October 25, 1981.

Most errors, inning

2—Danny Murphy, Philadelphia A.L., October 12, 1905, fifth inning.
   Mike Andrews, Oakland A.L., October 14, 1973, 12th inning.
   Dave Lopes, Los Angeles N.L., October 25, 1981, fourth inning.

Most double plays, career

24—Frankie Frisch, New York N.L., St. Louis N.L., 1922, 1923, 1924, 1928, 1930, 1931, 1934; seven series, 42 games.

Most double plays, series

9—Phil Garner, Pittsburgh N.L., 1979 (7-game series).

Most double plays started, series

5—Billy Herman, Chicago N.L., 1932 (4-game series).
   Tom Herr, St. Louis N.L., 1985 (7-game series).

Most double plays, nine-inning game

3—Held by many second basemen.

Most double plays started, nine-inning game

3—Dick Green, Oakland A.L., October 15, 1974.

Most unassisted double plays, game

1—Hobe Ferris, Boston A.L., October 2, 1903.
   Larry Doyle, New York N.L., October 9, 1913.
   Buck Herzog, New York N.L., October 7, 1917.
   Frank White, Kansas City A.L., October 17, 1980.
   Mark Lemke, Atlanta N.L., October 27, 1991, 10 innings.

Unassisted triple play

1—Bill Wambsganss, Cleveland A.L., October 10, 1920.

THIRD BASEMEN

GAMES

Most games played, career
31—Gil McDougald, New York A.L., 1951, 1952, 1953, 1955, 1960; five series.

PUTOUTS, ASSISTS AND CHANCES ACCEPTED

Most putouts, career
37—Home Run Baker, Philadelphia A.L., New York A.L., 1910, 1911, 1913, 1914, 1921; five series, 22 games.

Most putouts, series
4-game series— 10—Home Run Baker, Philadelphia A.L., 1914.
5-game series— 10—Harry Steinfeldt, Chicago N.L., 1907.
6-game series— 14—Red Rolfe, New York A.L. 1936.
7-game series— 13—Whitey Kurowski, St. Louis N.L., 1946.
8-game series— 13—Frankie Frisch, New York N.L., 1921.

Most putouts, nine-inning game
4—Art Devlin, New York N.L., October 13, 1905.
  Bill Coughlin, Detroit A.L., October 10, 1907.
  Bobby Byrne, Pittsburgh N.L., October 9, 1909.
  Tommy Leach, Pittsburgh N.L., October 16, 1909.
  Home Run Baker, Philadelphia A.L., October 24, 1911.
  Heinie Zimmerman, New York N.L., October 7, 1917.
  Jimmie Dykes, Philadelphia A.L., October 2, 1930.
  Bob Elliott, Boston N.L., October 11, 1948.
  Willie Jones, Philadelphia N.L. October 4, 1950.

Most putouts, inning
2—Held by many third basemen.

Most assists, career
68—Graig Nettles, New York A.L., 1976, 1977, 1978, 1981; San Diego N.L., 1984; five series, 24 games.

Most assists, series
4-game series— 15—Home Run Baker, Philadelphia A.L., 1914.
5-game series— 18—Larry Gardner, Boston A.L., 1916.
6-game series— 20—Graig Nettles, New York A.L., 1977.
7-game series— 30—Pinky Higgins, Detroit A.L., 1940.
8-game series— 24—Frankie Frisch, New York N.L., 1921.

Most assists, nine-inning game
9—Pinky Higgins, Detroit A.L., October 5, 1940.

Most assists, inning
3—Jose Pagan, Pittsburgh N.L., October 14, 1971, ninth inning.
  Sal Bando, Oakland A.L., October 16, 1974, sixth inning.
  Wade Boggs, Boston A.L., October 19, 1986, third inning.
  Terry Pendleton, Atlanta N.L., October 27, 1991, seventh inning.

Most chances accepted, career
96—Graig Nettles, New York A.L., 1976, 1977, 1978, 1981; San Diego N.L., 1984; five series, 24 games.

Most chances accepted, series
4-game series—25—Home Run Baker, Philadelphia A.L., 1914.
5-game series—25—Larry Gardner, Boston A.L., 1916.
6-game series—27—Bobby Thomson, New York N.L., 1951.
7-game series—34—Pinky Higgins, Detroit A.L., 1940.
8-game series—37—Frankie Frisch, New York N.L., 1921.

Most chances accepted, nine-inning game
10—Pinky Higgins, Detroit A.L., October 5, 1940 (1 putout, 9 assists).
  Chris Sabo, Cincinnati N.L., October 19, 1990 (3 putouts, 7 assists).

Fewest chances offered, nine-inning game
0—Held by many third basemen.

Most chances accepted, inning
4—Eddie Mathews, Milwaukee N.L., October 5, 1957, third inning.

ERRORS AND DOUBLE PLAYS

Most errors, career
8—Larry Gardner, Boston A.L., 1912, 1915, 1916 (6); Cleveland A.L., 1920 (2); four series, 25 games.

Most consecutive errorless games, career
22—Ron Cey, Los Angeles N.L., October 13, 1974 through October 28, 1981.

Most errors, series
4-game series—2—Red Rolfe, New York A.L., 1938.
5-game series—4—Harry Steinfeldt, Chicago N.L., 1910.
6-game series—3
  George Rohe, Chicago A.L., 1906.
  Buck Herzog, New York N.L., 1911.
  Travis Jackson, New York N.L., 1936.
  Bob Elliott, Boston N.L., 1948.
7-game series—4
  Pepper Martin, St. Louis N.L., 1934.
  Gil McDougald, New York A.L., 1952.
8-game series—4
  Tommy Leach, Pittsburgh N.L., 1903.
  Larry Gardner, Boston A.L., 1912.

Most chances accepted, errorless series
29—Denis Menke, Cincinnati N.L., 1972 (7-game series).

Most errors, nine-inning game
3—Pepper Martin, St. Louis N.L., October 6, 1934.

Most errors, inning
2—Harry Steinfeldt, Chicago N.L., October 18, 1910, third inning.
  Doug DeCinces, Baltimore A.L., October 10, 1979, sixth inning.

Most double plays, career
7—Graig Nettles, New York A.L., 1976, 1977, 1978, 1981; San Diego N.L., 1984; five series, 24 games.

Most double plays, series
4—Jim Davenport, San Francisco N.L., 1962 (7-game series).
  Bill Madlock, Pittsburgh N.L., 1979 (7-game series).

Most double plays started, series
4—Jim Davenport, San Francisco N.L., 1962 (7-game series).

Most double plays, nine-inning game
2—Held by many third basemen.

Most double plays started, nine-inning game
2—Fred McMullin, Chicago A.L., October 13, 1917.
  Ossie Bluege, Washington A.L., October 5, 1924.
  Whitey Kurowski, St. Louis N.L., October 13, 1946.
  Clete Boyer, New York A.L., October 12, 1960.
  Dalton Jones, Boston A.L., October 4, 1967.
  Graig Nettles, New York A.L., October 19, 1976.

Most unassisted double plays, game
Never accomplished.

SHORTSTOPS

GAMES

Most games played, career
52—Phil Rizzuto, New York A.L., 1941, 1942, 1947, 1949, 1950, 1951, 1952, 1953, 1955; nine series.

PUTOUTS, ASSISTS AND CHANCES ACCEPTED

Most putouts, career
107—Phil Rizzuto, New York A.L., 1941, 1942, 1947, 1949, 1950, 1951, 1952, 1953, 1955; nine series, 52 games.

Most putouts, series
4-game series— 16—Frank Crosetti, New York A.L., 1938.
5-game series— 15
  Joe Tinker, Chicago N.L., 1907.
  Phil Rizzuto, New York A.L., 1942.

6-game series—16—Billy Jurges, Chicago N.L., 1935.
7-game series—22—Ozzie Smith, St. Louis N.L., 1982.
8-game series—24—Heinie Wagner, Boston A.L., 1912.

Most putouts, nine-inning game

7—Buck Weaver, Chicago A.L., October 7, 1917.
  Phil Rizzuto, New York A.L., October 5, 1942.

Most putouts, inning

3—Mickey Stanley, Detroit A.L., October 10, 1968, sixth inning.

Most assists, career

143—Phil Rizzuto, New York A.L., 1941, 1942, 1947, 1949,
  1950, 1951, 1952, 1953, 1955; nine series, 52 games.

Most assists, series

4-game series—21—Jack Barry, Philadelphia A.L., 1914.
5-game series—25—Everett Scott, Boston A.L., 1916.
6-game series—26—Bill Russell, Los Angeles N.L., 1981.
7-game series—32—Tim Foli, Pittsburgh N.L., 1979.
8-game series—30—Freddy Parent, Boston A.L., 1903.

Most assists, nine-inning game

9—Roger Peckinpaugh, New York A.L., October 5, 1921.

Most assists, extra-inning game

10—Johnny Logan, Milwaukee N.L., October 6, 1957, 10 innings.

Most assists, inning

3—Dave Bancroft, New York N.L., October 8, 1922, third inning.
  Ossie Bluege, Washington, A.L., October 7, 1924, sixth inning.
  Glenn Wright, Pittsburgh N.L., October 8, 1927, second inning.
  Blondy Ryan, New York N.L., October 7, 1933, third inning.
  Phil Rizzuto, New York A.L., October 3, 1942, second inning.
  Ernie Bowman, San Francisco N.L., October 8, 1962, ninth in-
  ning.
  Bud Harrelson, New York N.L., October 14, 1969, fifth inning.
  Mark Belanger, Baltimore A.L., October 16, 1971, seventh in-
  ning.
  Bud Harrelson, New York N.L., October 13, 1973, seventh in-
  ning.
  Tim Foli, Pittsburgh N.L., October 12, 1979, second inning.

Most chances accepted, career

250—Phil Rizzuto, New York A.L., 1941, 1942, 1947, 1949,
  1950, 1951, 1952, 1953, 1955; nine series, 52 games.

Most chances accepted, series

4-game series—27—Maury Wills, Los Angeles N.L., 1966.
5-game series—38—Joe Tinker, Chicago N.L., 1907.
6-game series—37—Phil Rizzuto, New York A.L., 1951.
7-game series—42—Charlie Gelbert, St. Louis N.L., 1931.
8-game series—51—Swede Risberg, Chicago A.L., 1919.

Most chances accepted, nine-inning game

13—Buck Weaver, Chicago A.L., October 7, 1917 (7 putouts,
  6 assists).

Fewest chances offered, nine-inning game

0—Joe Boley, Philadelphia A.L., October 8, 1929.
  Phil Rizzuto, New York A.L., October 7, 1949.
  Zoilo Versalles, Minnesota A.L., October 7, 1965.
  Rico Petrocelli, Boston A.L., October 4, 1967.
  Bert Campaneris, Oakland A.L., October 18, 1972.
  Dave Concepcion, Cincinnati N.L., October 16, 1975.
  Ozzie Smith, St. Louis N.L., October 23, 1985.

Fewest chances offered, eight-inning game

0—Dave Bancroft, New York N.L., October 12, 1915.
  Pee Ree Reese, Brooklyn N.L., October 1, 1947.

Most chances accepted, inning

3—Held by many shortstops.

| ERRORS AND DOUBLE PLAYS |

Most errors, career

12—Art Fletcher, New York N.L., 1911, 1912, 1913, 1917;
  four series, 25 games.

Most consecutive errorless games, career

21—Phil Rizzuto, New York A.L., October 3, 1942 through
  October 5, 1951.

Most errors, series

4-game series—4—Frank Crosetti, New York A.L., 1932.
5-game series—4
  Ivy Olson, Brooklyn N.L., 1916.
  Woody English, Chicago N.L., 1929.
6-game series—4
  Art Fletcher, New York N.L., 1911.
  Buck Weaver, Chicago A.L., 1917.
7-game series—6—Roger Peckinpaugh, Washington A.L., 1925.
8-game series—6—Honus Wagner, Pittsburgh N.L., 1903.

Most chances accepted, errorless series

42—Charlie Gelbert, St. Louis N.L., 1931 (7-game series).

Most errors, nine-inning game

3—Jack Barry, Philadelphia A.L., October 26, 1911.
  Art Fletcher, New York N.L., October 9, 1912.
  Buck Weaver, Chicago A.L., October 13, 1917.

Most errors, inning

2—Roger Peckinpaugh, Washington A.L., October 8, 1925,
  eighth inning.
  Woody English, Chicago N.L., October 8, 1929, ninth inning.
  Dick Bartell, New York N.L., October 9, 1937, third inning.
  Pee Ree Reese, Brooklyn N.L., October 2, 1941, eighth in-
  ning.

Most double plays, career

32—Phil Rizzuto, New York A.L., 1941, 1942, 1947, 1949,
  1950, 1951, 1952, 1953, 1955; nine series, 52 games.

Most double plays, series

8—Phil Rizzuto, New York A.L., 1951 (6-game series).

Most double plays started, series

7—Larry Bowa, Philadelphia N.L., 1980 (6-game series).

Most unassisted double plays, series

2—Joe Tinker, Chicago N.L., October 10, 11, 1907.

Most double plays, nine-inning game

4—Phil Rizzuto, New York A.L., October 8, 1951.

Most double plays started, nine-inning game

3—Phil Rizzuto, New York A.L., October 10, 1951.
  Maury Wills, Los Angeles N.L., October 11, 1965.
  Larry Bowa, Philadelphia N.L., October 15, 1980.

Most unassisted double plays, game

1—Joe Tinker, Chicago N.L., October 10, 1907.
  Joe Tinker, Chicago N.L., October 11, 1907.
  Charlie Gelbert, St. Louis N.L., October 2, 1930.
  Eddie Kasko, Cincinnati N.L., October 7, 1961.
  Greg Gagne, Minnesota A.L., October 26, 1991, 11 innings.

OUTFIELDERS

| GAMES |

Most games played, career

63—Mickey Mantle, New York A.L., 1951, 1952, 1953, 1955, 1956,
  1957, 1958, 1960, 1961, 1962, 1963, 1964; 12 series.

| PUTOUTS, ASSISTS AND CHANCES ACCEPTED |

Most putouts, career

150—Joe DiMaggio, New York A.L., 1936, 1937, 1938, 1939, 1941,
  1942, 1947, 1949, 1950, 1951; 10 series, 51 games.

Most putouts, series

4-game series—16—Earle Combs, New York A.L., 1927.
5-game series—20—Joe DiMaggio, New York A.L., 1942.
6-game series—24—Mickey Rivers, New York A.L., 1977.
7-game series—25—Dan Gladden, Minnesota A.L., 1991.
8-game series—30—Edd Roush, Cincinnati N.L., 1919.

Most putouts, game

8—Edd Roush, Cincinnati N.L., October 1, 1919.
  George Foster, Cincinnati N.L., October 21, 1976.

Most putouts by left fielder, game

8—George Foster, Cincinnati N.L., October 21, 1976.

Most putouts by center fielder, game

9—Amos Otis, Kansas City A.L., October 17, 1980, 10 innings.
8—Edd Roush, Cincinnati N.L., October 1, 1919.

Most putouts by right fielder, game

7—Red Murray, New York N.L., October 14, 1912.
   Bing Miller, Philadelphia A.L., October 5, 1930.
   Ray Blades, St. Louis N.L., October 5, 1930.
   Tony Oliva, Minnesota A.L., October 6, 1965.
   Al Kaline, Detroit A.L., October 9, 1968.
   Frank Robinson, Baltimore A.L., October 14, 1969.

Most consecutive putouts, game

4—Mike Donlin, New York N.L., October 13, 1905 (1 in third inning, 3 in fourth inning, center field).
   Dode Paskert, Philadelphia N.L., October 11, 1915 (3 in fourth inning, 1 in fifth inning, center field).
   Charlie Keller, New York A.L., October 1, 1941 (1 in second inning, 3 in third inning, left field).
   Monte Irvin, New York N.L., September 29, 1954 (1 in eighth inning, 3 in ninth inning, left field; Irvin dropped fly for error after second putout in ninth inning).
   Tommie Agee, New York N.L., October 14, 1969 (3 in seventh inning, 1 in eighth inning, center field).
   Ben Oglivie, Milwaukee A.L., October 19, 1982 (1 in sixth inning, 3 in seventh inning, left field).

Most putouts by left fielder, inning

3—Charlie Keller, New York A.L., October 1, 1941, third inning.
   Monte Irvin, New York N.L., September 29, 1954, ninth inning.
   Tommy Davis, Los Angeles N.L., October 3, 1963, seventh inning.
   Ben Oglivie, Milwaukee A.L., October 19, 1982, seventh inning.
   Deion Sanders, Atlanta N.L., October 22, 1992, fifth inning.

Most putouts by center fielder, inning

3—Mike Donlin, New York N.L., October 13, 1905, fourth inning.
   Dode Paskert, Philadelphia N.L., October 11, 1915, fourth inning.
   Ernie Orsatti, St. Louis N.L., October 8, 1934, fifth inning.
   Joe DiMaggio, New York A.L., October 2, 1936, ninth inning, and October 7, 1937, sixth inning.
   Roger Maris, New York A.L., October 11, 1964, third inning.
   Reggie Smith, Boston A.L., October 11, 1967, seventh inning.
   Tommie Agee, New York N.L., October 14, 1969, seventh inning.
   Willie McGee, St. Louis N.L., October 22, 1987, eighth inning.

Most putouts right fielder, inning

3—Mel Ott, New York N.L., October 4, 1933, seventh inning.
   Bob Hazle, Milwaukee N.L., October 10, 1957, fourth inning.
   Ron Swoboda, New York N.L., October 15, 1969, ninth inning.
   Charlie Moore, Milwaukee A.L., October 12, 1982, eighth inning.

Most assists, career

5—Harry Hooper, Boston A.L., 1912, 1915, 1916, 1918; four series, 24 games.
   Ross Youngs, New York N.L., 1921, 1922, 1923, 1924; four series, 26 games.

Most games by outfielder with no assists, career

51—Joe DiMaggio, New York A.L., 1936, 1937, 1938, 1939, 1941, 1942, 1947, 1949, 1950, 1951; 10 series.

Most assists, series

4-game series—2—Joe Connally, Boston, N.L., 1914.
5-game series—2—Held by many outfielders.
6-game series—2—Held by many outfielders.
7-game series—4—Edgar Rice, Washington A.L., 1924.
8-game series—3
   Patsy Dougherty, Boston A.L., 1903.
   Harry Hooper, Boston A.L., 1912.
   Edd Roush, Cincinnati N.L., 1919.

Most assists, game

2—Held by many outfielders.

Most chances accepted, career

150—Joe DiMaggio, New York A.L., 1936, 1937, 1938, 1939, 1941, 1942, 1947, 1949, 1950, 1951; 10 series, 51 games.

Most chances accepted, series

4-game series—16—Earle Combs, New York A.L., 1927.
5-game series—20—Joe DiMaggio, New York A.L., 1942.
6-game series—25—Mickey Rivers, New York A.L., 1977.
7-game series—26
   Andy Pafko, Chicago N.L., 1945.
   Dan Gladden, Minnesota A.L., 1991.
8-game series—33—Edd Roush, Cincinnati N.L., 1919.

Most chances accepted by left fielder, game

8—George Foster, Cincinnati N.L., October 21, 1976 (8 putouts).

Most chances accepted by center fielder, nine-inning game

8—Edd Roush, Cincinnati N.L., October 1, 1919 (8 putouts).
   Hank Leiber, New York N.L., October 2, 1936 (7 putouts, 1 assist).

Most chances accepted by center fielder, extra-inning game

9—Edd Roush, Cincinnati N.L., October 7, 1919, 10 innings (7 putouts, 2 assists).
   Amos Otis, Kansas City A.L., October 17, 1980, 10 innings (9 putouts).

Most chances accepted by right fielder, game

7—Red Murray, New York N.L., October 14, 1912 (7 putouts).
   Bing Miller, Philadelphia A.L., October 5, 1930 (7 putouts).
   Ray Blades, St. Louis N.L., October 5, 1930 (7 putouts).
   Tony Oliva, Minnesota A.L., October 6, 1965 (7 putouts).
   Al Kaline, Detroit A.L., October 9, 1968 (7 putouts).
   Frank Robinson, Baltimore A.L., October 14, 1969 (7 putouts).

Longest game with no chances offered

12 innings—Ty Cobb, Detroit A.L., right field, October 8, 1907 (right field).
   Earl McNeely, Washington A.L., October 10, 1924 (center field).
   Joe Medwick, St. Louis N.L., October 4, 1934 (played 11⅓ innings in left field).
   Don Hahn, New York N.L., October 14, 1973 (center and right field).
   Cleon Jones, New York N.L., October 14, 1973 (left field).
   Ken Griffey Sr., Cincinnati N.L., October 21, 1975 (played 11 innings in right field).

Fewest chances offered, three consecutive games

0—George Browne, New York N.L., October 12, 1905 (nine innings); October 13, 1905 (nine innings); October 14, 1905 (nine innings; right field).
   Max Carey, Pittsburgh N.L., October 11, 1925 (eight innings); October 12, 1925 (nine innings); October 13, 1925 (nine innings; center field).
   Al Simmons, Philadelphia A.L., October 11, 1929 (nine innings); October 12, 1929 (nine innings); October 14, 1929 (nine innings; left field).
   Chief Wilson, Pittsburgh N.L., October 8, 1909 (nine innings); October 9, 1909 (nine innings); October 11, 1909 (nine innings; right field).

Fewest chances offered, four consecutive games

0—Chief Wilson, Pittsburgh N.L., October 8, 1909 (nine innings); October 9, 1909 (nine innings); October 11, 1909 (nine innings); October 12, 1909 (eight innings; right field).

Most chances accepted, inning

3—Held by many outfielders.

ERRORS AND DOUBLE PLAYS

Most errors, career

4—Ross Youngs, New York N.L., 1921, 1922, 1923, 1924; four series, 26 games.

Most consecutive errorless games, career

45—Joe DiMaggio, New York A.L., October 6, 1937 through October 10, 1951.

Most errors, series

4-game series—3—Willie Davis, Los Angeles N.L., 1966.
5-game series—2—Held by many outfielders.
6-game series—3
  Red Murray, New York N.L., 1911.
  Shano Collins, Chicago A.L., 1917.
7-game series—2
  Zack Wheat, Brooklyn N.L., 1920.
  Ernie Orsatti, St. Louis N.L., 1934.
  Goose Goslin, Detroit A.L., 1934.
  Mickey Mantle, New York A.L., 1964.
  Jim Northrup, Detroit A.L., 1968.
8-game series—2—Held by many outfielders.

Most chances accepted, errorless series

25—Mickey Rivers, New York A.L., 1977 (6-game series).

Most errors, game

3—Willie Davis, Los Angeles N.L., October 6, 1966.

Most errors, inning

3—Willie Davis, Los Angeles N.L., October 6, 1966, fifth inning.

Most double plays, career

2—Held by many outfielders.

Most double plays, series

2—Danny Murphy, Philadelphia A.L., 1910 (5-game series).
  Tris Speaker, Boston A.L., 1912 (8-game series).
  Edd Roush, Cincinnati N.L., 1919 (8-game series).
  Elston Howard, New York A.L., 1958 (7-game series).

Most double plays started, series

2—Danny Murphy, Philadelphia A.L., 1910 (5-game series).
  Tris Speaker, Boston A.L., 1912 (8-game series).
  Edd Roush, Cincinnati N.L., 1919 (8-game series).
  Elston Howard, New York A.L., 1958 (7-game series).

Most double plays, game

2—Edd Roush, Cincinnati N.L., October 7, 1919 (fifth and eighth innings of 10-inning game).

Most double plays started, game

2—Edd Roush, Cincinnati N.L., October 7, 1919 (fifth and eighth innings of 10-inning game).

Most unassisted double plays, game

1—Tris Speaker, Boston A.L., October 15, 1912.

CATCHERS

GAMES

Most games caught, career

63—Yogi Berra, New York A.L., 1947, 1949, 1950, 1951, 1952, 1953, 1955, 1956, 1957, 1958, 1960, 1962; 12 series.

PUTOUTS, ASSISTS AND CHANCES ACCEPTED

Most putouts, career

421—Yogi Berra, New York A.L., 1947, 1949, 1950, 1951, 1952, 1953, 1955, 1956, 1957, 1958, 1960, 1962; 12 series, 63 games.

Most putouts, series

4-game series—43—John Roseboro, Los Angeles N.L., 1963.
5-game series—59—Mickey Cochrane, Philadelphia A.L., 1929.
6-game series—55—Walker Cooper, St. Louis N.L., 1944.
7-game series—67—Jerry Grote, New York N.L., 1973.
8-game series—54—Lou Criger, Boston A.L., 1903.

Most putouts, nine-inning game

18—John Roseboro, Los Angeles N.L., October 2, 1963 (15 strikeouts).

Fewest putouts, nine-inning game

1—Held by many catchers.

Most putouts, inning

3—Held by many catchers.

Most assists, career

36—Yogi Berra, New York A.L., 1947, 1949, 1950, 1951,

1952, 1953, 1955, 1956, 1957, 1958, 1960, 1962; 12 series, 63 games.

Most assists, series

4-game series—7—Thurman Munson, New York A.L., 1976.
5-game series—9
  Boss Schmidt, Detroit A.L., 1907.
  Johnny Kling, Chicago N.L., 1907.
  Ed Burns, Philadelphia N.L., 1915.
6-game series—12—Chief Meyers, New York N.L., 1911.
7-game series—11—Boss Schmidt, Detroit A.L., 1909.
8-game series—15—Ray Schalk, Chicago A.L., 1919.

Most assists, nine-inning game

4—Johnny Kling, Chicago N.L., October 9, 1907.
  Boss Schmidt, Detroit A.L., October 11, 1907
  Boss Schmidt, Detroit A.L., October 14, 1908
  George Gibson, Pittsburgh N.L., October 12, 1909.
  Bill Rariden, New York N.L., October 10, 1917.
  Sam Agnew, Boston A.L., September 6, 1918.
  Bill DeLancey, St. Louis N.L., October 8, 1934.

Most assists, extra-inning game

6—Jack Lapp, Philadelphia A.L., October 17, 1911, 11 innings.

Most assists, inning

2—Held by many catchers.

Most chances accepted, career

457—Yogi Berra, New York A.L., 1947, 1949, 1950, 1951, 1952, 1953, 1955, 1956, 1957, 1958, 1960, 1962; 12 series, 63 games.

Most chances accepted, series

4-game series—43—John Roseboro, Los Angeles N.L., 1963.
5-game series—61—Mickey Cochrane, Philadelphia A.L., 1929.
6-game series—56
  Johnny Kling, Chicago N.L., 1906.
  Roy Campanella, Brooklyn N.L., 1953.
7-game series—71—Jerry Grote, New York N.L., 1973.
8-game series—62—Lou Criger, Boston A.L., 1903.

Most chances accepted, nine-inning game

18—John Roseboro, Los Angeles N.L., October 2, 1963, (18 putouts, 15 strikeouts).
  Tim McCarver, St. Louis N.L., October 2, 1968 (17 putouts, 1 assist, 17 strikeouts).

Fewest chances offered, nine-inning game

1—Wally Schang, Philadelphia A.L., October 11, 1913 (strikeout).
  Wally Schang, New York A.L., October 11, 1923 (strikeout).
  Muddy Ruel, Washington A.L., October 5, 1924 (strikeout).
  Mickey Cochrane, Detroit A.L., October 6, 1934 (strikeout).
  Gabby Hartnett, Chicago N.L., October 2, 1935 (strikeout).
  Sherm Lollar, Chicago A.L., October 6, 1959 (strikeout).
  Elston Howard, New York A.L., October 6, 1960.

Fewest chances offered, eight-inning game

1—Bill Killefer, Chicago N.L., September 9, 1918 (strikeout).

Most chances accepted, inning

4—Tim McCarver, St. Louis N.L., October 9, 1967, ninth inning (3 putouts, 1 assist, 2 strikeouts).

ERRORS AND PASSED BALLS

Most errors, career

7—Boss Schmidt, Detroit A.L., 1907, 1908, 1909; three series, 13 games.

Most consecutive errorless games, career

30—Yogi Berra, New York A.L., October 4, 1952 through October 9, 1957.

Most errors, series

4-game series—3—Joe Oliver, Cincinnati N.L., 1990.
5-game series—2
  Boss Schmidt, Detroit A.L., 1907.
  Walker Cooper, St. Louis N.L., 1943.
  Joe Ferguson, Los Angeles N.L., 1974.
6-game series—2—Ray Schalk, Chicago A.L., 1917.

7-game series—5—Boss Schmidt, Detroit A.L., 1909.
8-game series—3—Lou Criger, Boston A.L., 1909.

Most chances accepted, errorless series
71—Jerry Grote, New York N.L., 1973 (7-game series).

Most errors, nine-inning game
2—Lou Criger, Boston A.L., October 1, 1903.
Jimmie Wilson, St. Louis N.L., October 7, 1928.
Joe Ferguson, Los Angeles N.L., October 15, 1974.
Carlton Fisk, Boston A.L., October 14, 1975, 9⅓ innings.

Most errors, inning
2—Lou Criger, Boston A.L., October 1, 1903, first inning.
Jimmie Wilson, St. Louis N.L., October 7, 1928, sixth inning.

Most passed balls, career
5—Johnny Kling, Chicago N.L., 1906 (3), 1907, 1908.

Most passed balls, series
3—Johnny Kling, Chicago N.L., 1906.
Smoky Burgess, Pittsburgh N.L., 1960.
Elston Howard, New York A.L., 1964.

Most passed balls, nine-inning game
2—Johnny Kling, Chicago N.L., October 9, 1906.
Bill Killefer, Chicago N.L., September 9, 1918.
Paul Richards, Detroit A.L., October 3, 1945.
Bruce Edwards, Brooklyn N.L., October 4, 1947.
Smoky Burgess, Pittsburgh N.L., October 6, 1960.
Elston Howard, New York A.L., October 7, 1964.

Most passed balls, inning
1—Held by many catchers.

DOUBLE PLAYS AND RUNNERS CAUGHT STEALING

Most double plays, career
6—Yogi Berra, New York A.L., 1947, 1949, 1950, 1951, 1952, 1953, 1955, 1956, 1957, 1958, 1960, 1962; 12 series, 63 games.
Johnny Bench, Cincinnati N.L., 1970 (1), 1972 (2), 1975 (3), 1976 (0); four series, 23 games.

Most double plays, series
3—Johnny Kling, Chicago N.L., 1906 (6-game series).
Boss Schmidt, Detroit A.L., 1909 (7-game series).
Wally Schang, New York A.L., 1921 (8-game series).
Johnny Bench, Cincinnati N.L., 1975 (7-game series).

Most double plays started, series
3—Wally Schang, New York A.L., 1921 (8-game series).

Most double plays, nine-inning game
2—Boss Schmidt, Detroit A.L., October 14, 1909.
Wally Schang, New York A.L., October 11, 1921.
Gabby Hartnett, Chicago N.L., September 29, 1932.
Del Rice, Milwaukee N.L., October 9, 1957.
Rich Gedman, Boston A.L., October 22, 1986.

Most double plays started, nine-inning game
2—Boss Schmidt, Detroit A.L., October 14, 1909.
Wally Schang, New York A.L., October 11, 1921.

Most unassisted double plays, game
Never accomplished.

Most runners caught stealing, career
20—Wally Schang, Philadelphia A.L., 1913, 1914; Boston A.L., 1918; New York A.L., 1921, 1922, 1923, six series, 32 games.

Most runners caught stealing, series
10—Ray Schalk, Chicago A.L., 1919 (8-game series).

Most runners caught stealing, nine-inning game
3—Performed nine times by eight catchers. Last time—Terry Steinbach, Oakland A.L., October 19, 1988.

Most runners caught stealing, extra-inning game
5—Jack Lapp, Philadelphia A.L., October 17, 1911, 11 innings.

Most runners caught stealing, inning
2—Jack Lapp, Philadelphia A.L., October 17, 1911, 10th inning.
Aaron Robinson, New York A.L., October 6, 1947, first inning.

Bill Carrigan, Boston A.L., October 9, 1912, 11th inning.
Roy Campanella, Brooklyn N.L., October 2, 1952, first inning.

PITCHERS

GAMES

Most games pitched, career
22—Whitey Ford, New York A.L., 1950, 1953, 1955, 1956, 1957, 1958, 1960, 1961, 1962, 1963, 1964; 11 series.

Most games pitched, series
4-game series—3—Held by many pitchers.
5-game series—5—Mike G. Marshall, Los Angeles N.L., 1974, nine innings.
6-game series—6—Dan Quisenberry, Kansas City A.L., 1980, 10⅓ innings.
7-game series—7—Darold Knowles, Oakland A.L., 1973, 6⅓ innings.
8-game series—5—Deacon Phillippe, Pittsburgh N.L., 1903, 44 innings.

PUTOUTS, ASSISTS AND CHANCES ACCEPTED

Most putouts, career
11—Whitey Ford, New York A.L., 1950, 1953, 1955, 1956, 1957, 1958, 1960, 1961, 1962, 1963, 1964; 11 series, 22 games.

Most putouts, series
4-game series—3—Whitey Ford, New York A.L., 1963.
5-game series—5—Jack Morris, Detroit, A.L., 1984.
6-game series—6
Nick Altrock, Chicago A.L., 1906.
Hippo Vaughn, Chicago N.L., 1918.
7-game series—5—Jim Kaat, Minnesota A.L., 1965.
8-game series—2
Deacon Phillippe, Pittsburgh N.L., 1903.
Phil Douglas, New York N.L., 1921.

Most putouts, nine-inning game
5—Jim Kaat, Minnesota A.L., October 7, 1965.

Most putouts, inning
2—Johnny Beazley, St. Louis N.L., October 5, 1942, eighth inning.
Bob Turley, New York A.L., October 9, 1957, seventh inning.
Whitey Ford, New York A.L., October 8, 1960, ninth inning.
Bob Purkey, Cincinnati N.L., October 7, 1961, ninth inning.
John Denny, Philadelphia N.L., October 15, 1983, fifth inning.
Dave Stewart, Oakland A.L., October 16, 1990, third inning.

Most assists, career
34—Christy Mathewson, New York N.L., 1905, 1911, 1912, 1913; four series, 11 games.

Most assists, series
4-game series—5
Joe Bush, Philadelphia A.L., 1914.
Lefty Tyler, Boston N.L., 1914.
Bill James, Boston N.L., 1914.
Wilcy Moore, New York A.L., 1927.
Monte Pearson, New York A.L., 1939.
5-game series—10—Mordecai Brown, Chicago N.L., 1910.
6-game series—12—Mordecai Brown, Chicago N.L., 1906.
7-game series—12—George Mullin, Detroit A.L., 1909.
8-game series—12—Christy Mathewson, New York N.L., 1912.

Most assists, nine-inning game
8—Nick Altrock, Chicago A.L., October 12, 1906.
Lon Warneke, Chicago N.L., October 2, 1935.

Most assists, inning
3—Eddie Plank, Philadelphia A.L., October 13, 1905, eighth inning.
Rube Marquard, New York N.L., October 7, 1913, fourth inning.
Lon Warneke, Chicago N.L., October 2, 1935, third inning.
Johnny Murphy, New York A.L., October 8, 1939, eighth inning.
Bob Rush, Milwaukee N.L., October 4, 1958, third inning.

Most chances accepted, career

40—Christy Mathewson, New York N.L., 1905, 1911, 1912, 1913; four series, 11 games.

Most chances accepted, series

4-game series—6
Lefty Tyler, Boston N.L., 1914.
Red Ruffing, New York A.L., 1938.
5-game series—10
Christy Mathewson, New York N.L., 1905.
Mordecai Brown, Chicago N.L., 1910.
6-game series—17
Nick Altrock, Chicago A.L., 1906.
Hippo Vaughn, Chicago N.L., 1918.
7-game series—12—George Mullin, Detroit A.L., 1909.
8-game series—13—Christy Mathewson, New York N.L., 1912.

Most innings pitched with no chances offered, series

26—Lefty Grove, Philadelphia A.L., 1931; three games.

Most chances accepted, nine-inning game

11—Nick Altrock, Chicago A.L., October 12, 1906 (3 putouts, 8 assists).

Fewest chances offered, extra-inning game

0—Howie Pollet, St. Louis N.L., October 6, 1946, 10 innings.
Robin Roberts, Philadelphia N.L., October 5, 1950, 10 innings.

Most chances accepted, inning

3—Held by many pitchers.

| **ERRORS AND DOUBLE PLAYS** |

Most errors, career

3—Deacon Phillippe, Pittsburgh N.L., 1903, 1909; two series, seven games.
Ed Cicotte, Chicago A.L., 1917, 1919; two series, six games.
Max Lanier, St. Louis N.L., 1942, 1943, 1944; three series, seven games.

Most errors, series

4-game series—1—Held by many pitchers.
5-game series—2
Jack Coombs, Philadelphia A.L., 1910.
Max Lanier, St. Louis N.L., 1942.

6-game series—2—Nels Potter, St. Louis A.L., 1944.
7-game series—2
Deacon Phillippe, Pittsburgh N.L., 1909.
Allie Reynolds, New York A.L., 1952.
8-game series—2—Ed Cicotte, Chicago A.L., 1919.

Most chances accepted, errorless series

17—Nick Altrock, Chicago A.L., 1906 (6-game series).
Hippo Vaughn, Chicago N.L., 1918 (6-game series).

Most errors, nine-inning game

2—Deacon Phillippe, Pittsburgh N.L., October 12, 1909.
Jack Coombs, Philadelphia A.L., October 18, 1910.
Ed Cicotte, Chicago A.L., October 4, 1919.
Max Lanier, St. Louis N.L., September 30, 1942.
Nels Potter, St. Louis A.L., October 5, 1944.

Most errors, inning

2—Jack Coombs, Philadelphia A.L., October 18, 1910, fifth inning.
Ed Cicotte, Chicago A.L., October 4, 1919, fifth inning.
Max Lanier, St. Louis N.L., September 30, 1942, ninth inning.
Nels Potter, St. Louis A.L., October 5, 1944, third inning.

Most consecutive errorless games, career

18—Whitey Ford, New York A.L., October 7, 1950 through October 8, 1962.

Most double plays, career

3—Chief Bender, Philadelphia A.L., 1905, 1910, 1911, 1913, 1914; five series, 10 games.
Joe Bush, Philadelphia A.L., Boston A.L., New York A.L., 1913, 1914, 1918, 1922, 1923; five series, nine games.
Allie Reynolds, New York A.L., 1947, 1949, 1950, 1951, 1952, 1953; six series, 15 games.

Most double plays, series

2—Held by many pitchers.

Most double plays started, series

2—Held by many pitchers.

Most unassisted double plays, game

Never accomplished.

Most double plays started, game

2—Chief Bender, Philadelphia A.L., October 9, 1914.
Joe Bush, New York A.L., October 8, 1922.
Allie Reynolds, New York A.L., October 8, 1951.

CLUB FIELDING

Highest fielding average, series
4-game series—1.000—Baltimore A.L. vs. Los Angeles N.L., 1966.
5-game series—1.000—New York A.L. vs. New York N.L., 1937.
6-game series—.996
Boston A.L. vs. Chicago N.L., 1918.
St. Louis N.L. vs. St. Louis A.L., 1944.
Los Angeles N.L. vs. New York A.L., 1977.
7-game series—.993—Cincinnati N.L. vs. Boston A.L., 1975.
8-game series—.984—New York N.L. vs. New York A.L., 1921.

Highest fielding average by both clubs, series
4-game series—.986—New York A.L. .993, Los Angeles N.L. .979, 1963.
5-game series—.986—Oakland A.L. .989, Los Angeles N.L. .983, 1988.
6-game series—.991—Los Angeles N.L. .996, New York A.L. .987, 1977.
7-game series—.990—St. Louis N.L. .992, Kansas City A.L. .989, 1985.
8-game series—.983—New York N.L. .984, New York A.L. .981, 1921.

Lowest fielding average, series
4-game series—.949—New York A.L. vs. Chicago N.L., 1932.
5-game series—.942—Brooklyn N.L. vs. Boston A.L., 1916.
6-game series—.938—New York N.L. vs. Philadelphia A.L., 1911.
7-game series—.934—Detroit A.L. vs. Pittsburgh N.L., 1909.
8-game series—.944—Pittsburgh N.L. vs. Boston A.L., 1903.

Lowest fielding average by both clubs, series
4-game series—.954—Chicago N.L. .959, New York A.L. .949, 1932.
5-game series—.946—Philadelphia A.L. .947, Chicago N.L. .946, 1910.
6-game series—.947—Philadelphia A.L. .956, New York N.L. .938, 1911.
7-game series—.941—Pittsburgh N.L. .947, Detroit A.L. .934, 1909.
8-game series—.951—Boston A.L. .957, Pittsburgh N.L. .944, 1903.

Most putouts, total series
4,983—New York A.L. (33 series, 187 games).

Most putouts, series
4-game series—117—Boston N.L. vs. Philadelphia A.L., 1914.
5-game series—147—Boston A.L. vs. Brooklyn N.L., 1916.
6-game series—168—New York A.L. vs. Los Angeles N.L., 1977.
7-game series—202—Minnesota A.L. vs. Atlanta N.L., 1991.
8-game series—222—Boston A.L. vs. New York N.L., 1912.

Most putouts by both clubs, series
4-game series—228—Boston N.L. 117, Philadelphia A.L. 111, 1914.
5-game series—289—Boston A.L. 147, Brooklyn N.L. 142, 1916.
6-game series—333—New York A.L. 168, Los Angeles N.L. 165, 1977.
7-game series—401—Washington A.L. 201, New York N.L. 200, 1924.
8-game series—443—Boston A.L. 222, New York N.L. 221, 1912.

Fewest putouts, series
4-game series—102
St. Louis N.L. vs. New York A.L., 1928.
Chicago N.L. vs. New York A.L., 1932.
Chicago N.L. vs. New York A.L., 1938.
New York A.L. vs. Los Angeles N.L., 1963.
Los Angeles N.L. vs. Baltimore A.L., 1966.
San Francisco N.L. vs. Oakland A.L., 1989.
5-game series—126
Los Angeles N.L. vs. Oakland A.L., 1974.
San Diego N.L. vs. Detroit A.L., 1984.
6-game series—153
New York N.L. vs. Chicago A.L., 1917.
St. Louis N.L. vs. Philadelphia A.L., 1930.
New York A.L. vs. Los Angeles N.L., 1981.
7-game series—177
Brooklyn N.L. vs. Cleveland A.L., 1920.
St. Louis N.L. vs. Minnesota A.L., 1987.
8-game series—210
Pittsburgh N.L. vs. Boston A.L., 1903.
New York A.L. vs. New York N.L., 1921.

Fewest putouts by both clubs, series
4-game series—210
New York A.L. 108, St. Louis N.L. 102, 1928.
New York A.L. 108, Chicago N.L. 102, 1932.
New York A.L. 108, Chicago N.L. 102, 1938.
Los Angeles N.L. 108, New York A.L. 102, 1963.
Baltimore A.L. 108, Los Angeles N.L. 102, 1966.
Oakland A.L. 108, San Francisco N.L. 102, 1989.
5-game series—258
Oakland A.L. 132, Los Angeles N.L. 126, 1974.
Detroit A.L. 132, San Diego N.L. 126, 1984.
6-game series—309
Chicago A.L. 156, New York N.L. 153, 1917.
Philadelphia A.L. 156, St. Louis N.L. 153, 1930.
Los Angeles N.L. 156, New York A.L. 153, 1981.
7-game series—357—Minnesota A.L. 180, St. Louis N.L. 177, 1987.
8-game series—422—New York N.L. 212, New York A.L. 210, 1921.

Most players with one or more putouts, nine-inning game
11—New York A.L. vs. Milwaukee N.L., October 2, 1957.
Baltimore A.L. vs. Pittsburgh N.L., October 16, 1979.

Most players with one or more putouts by both clubs, nine-inning game
19—New York A.L. 11, Milwaukee N.L. 8, October 2, 1957.
Baltimore A.L. 10, Pittsburgh N.L. 9, October 11, 1971.

Most players with one or more putouts by both clubs, extra-inning game
20—Chicago N.L. 10, Detroit A.L. 10, October 8, 1945, 12 innings.

Most putouts by outfield, nine-inning game
15—New York N.L. vs. Boston A.L., October 14, 1912.
Boston N.L. vs. Cleveland A.L., October 6, 1948.

Most putouts by outfield, extra-inning game
16—Brooklyn N.L. vs. New York A.L., October 5, 1952, 11 innings.

Most putouts by outfields of both clubs, game
23—Pittsburgh N.L. 13, New York A.L. 10, October 6, 1927.
Brooklyn N.L. 16, New York A.L. 7, October 5, 1952, 11 innings.

Fewest putouts by outfield, nine-inning game
0—New York N.L. vs. New York A.L., October 5, 1921.
New York N.L. vs. New York A.L., September 30, 1936.

Fewest putouts by outfield, extra-inning game
1—New York N.L. vs. Oakland A.L., October 14, 1973, 12 innings.

Fewest putouts by outfields of both clubs, nine-inning game
3—New York A.L. 2, Brooklyn N.L. 1, October 10, 1956.
Most putouts by outfield, inning
3—Made in many games.
Most putouts by outfields of both clubs, inning
6—Kansas City A.L. 3, St. Louis N.L. 3, October 27, 1985, seventh inning.
Most putouts by catchers of both clubs, inning
6—Chicago A.L. 3, Cincinnati N.L. 3, October 6, 1919, second inning.
Cincinnati N.L. 3, Oakland A.L. 3, October 18, 1972, fifth inning.
St. Louis N.L. 3, Kansas City A.L. 3, October 24, 1985, seventh inning.

ASSISTS

Most assists, total series
1,978—New York A.L. (33 series, 187 games).
Most assists, series
4-game series—67—Philadelphia A.L. vs. Boston N.L., 1914.
5-game series—90—Boston A.L. vs. Brooklyn N.L., 1916.
6-game series—99—Chicago A.L. vs. Chicago N.L., 1906.
7-game series—99
Washington A.L. vs. New York N.L., 1924.
St. Louis N.L. vs. New York A.L., 1926.
8-game series—116—Chicago A.L. vs. Cincinnati N.L., 1919.
Most assists by both clubs, series
4-game series—129—Philadelphia A.L. 67, Boston N.L. 62, 1914.
5-game series—160—Boston A.L. 90, Brooklyn N.L. 70, 1916.
6-game series—183—Chicago A.L. 99, Chicago N.L. 84, 1906.
7-game series—193—Washington A.L. 99, New York N.L. 94, 1924.
8-game series—212—Chicago A.L. 116, Cincinnati N.L. 96, 1919.
Fewest assists, series
4-game series—28—New York A.L. vs. St. Louis N.L., 1928.
5-game series—36—Los Angeles N.L. vs. Oakland A.L., 1988.
6-game series—41—Philadelphia A.L. vs. St. Louis N.L., 1930.
7-game series—48—St. Louis N.L. vs. Detroit A.L., 1968.
8-game series—96
Pittsburgh N.L. vs. Boston A.L., 1903.
Cincinnati N.L. vs. Chicago A.L., 1919.
Fewest assists by both clubs, series
4-game series—64—St. Louis N.L. 36, New York A.L. 28, 1928.
5-game series—79—Oakland A.L. 43, Los Angeles N.L. 36, 1988.
6-game series—96—St. Louis N.L. 55, Philadelphia A.L. 41, 1930.
7-game series—120—Detroit A.L. 72, St. Louis N.L. 48, 1968.
8-game series—198—Boston A.L. 102, Pittsburgh N.L. 96, 1903.
Most players with one or more assists, nine-inning game
9—Chicago A.L. vs. New York N.L., October 7, 1917.
New York A.L. vs. New York N.L., October 6, 1922.
Chicago N.L. vs. Detroit A.L., October 8, 1945, 12 innings.
Brooklyn N.L. vs. New York A.L., October 3, 1947.
Most players with one or more assists by both clubs, nine-inning game
15—New York A.L. 9, New York N.L. 6, October 6, 1922.
Chicago N.L. 9, Detroit A.L. 6, October 8, 1945, 12 innings.

Most players with one or more assists by both clubs, extra-inning game
16—Los Angeles N.L. 9, New York A.L. 7, October 11, 1977, 12 innings.
Most assists, nine-inning game
21—Chicago A.L. vs. New York N.L., October 7, 1917.
Boston A.L. vs. Chicago N.L., September 9, 1918.
Most assists by both clubs, nine-inning game
38—Chicago A.L. 20, Chicago N.L. 18, October 12, 1906.
Fewest assists, nine-inning game
2—St. Louis N.L. vs. Detroit A.L., October 2, 1968.
Fewest assists by both clubs, nine-inning game
8—Philadelphia A.L. 5, St. Louis N.L. 3, October 2, 1930.
Boston A.L. 5, Cincinnati N.L. 3, October 16, 1975.
Fewest assists by infield, nine-inning game
1—St. Louis N.L. vs. Detroit A.L., October 2, 1968.
Most assists by outfield, inning
2—Boston A.L. vs. St. Louis N.L., October 10, 1946, fifth inning.

CHANCES OFFERED

Fewest chances offered to outfield, nine-inning game
0—New York N.L. vs. New York A.L., September 30, 1936.
Fewest chances offered to outfield, extra-inning game
1—New York N.L. vs. Oakland A.L., October 14, 1973, 12 innings.
Fewest chances offered to outfield by both clubs, nine-inning game
3—New York A.L., 2, Brooklyn N.L., 1, October 10, 1956.
Fewest chances offered to infield, game (excluding first base)
2—Philadelphia A.L. vs. St. Louis N.L., October 6, 1931.

ERRORS

Most errors, total series
140—New York A.L. (33 series, 187 games).
Most errors, series
4-game series—8—New York A.L. vs. Chicago N.L., 1932.
5-game series—13—Brooklyn N.L. vs. Boston A.L., 1916.
6-game series—16—New York N.L. vs. Philadelphia A.L., 1911.
7-game series—19—Detroit A.L. vs. Pittsburgh N.L., 1909.
8-game series—18—Pittsburgh N.L. vs. Boston A.L., 1903.
Most errors by both clubs, series
4-game series—14—New York A.L. 8, Chicago N.L. 6, 1932.
5-game series—23—Chicago N.L. 12, Philadelphia A.L. 11, 1910.
6-game series—27—New York N.L. 16, Philadelphia A.L. 11, 1911.
7-game series—34—Detroit A.L. 19, Pittsburgh N.L. 15, 1909.
8-game series—32—Pittsburgh N.L. 18, Boston A.L. 14, 1903.
Fewest errors, series
4-game series—0—Baltimore A.L. vs. Los Angeles N.L., 1966.
5-game series—0—New York A.L. vs. New York N.L., 1937.
6-game series—1
Boston A.L. vs. Chicago N.L., 1918.
St. Louis N.L. vs. St. Louis A.L., 1944.
New York A.L. vs. Brooklyn N.L., 1953.
Los Angeles N.L. vs. New York A.L., 1977.
7-game series—2
Philadelphia A.L. vs. St. Louis N.L., 1931.
New York A.L. vs. Brooklyn N.L., 1955.
Brooklyn N.L. vs. New York A.L., 1956.
St. Louis N.L. vs. Detroit A.L., 1968.

Cincinnati N.L. vs. Boston A.L., 1975.
St. Louis N.L. vs. Kansas City A.L., 1985.
8-game series—5—New York N.L. vs. New York A.L., 1921.

Fewest errors by both clubs, series

4-game series—4—Los Angeles N.L. 3, New York A.L. 1, 1963.
5-game series—5—Los Angeles N.L. 3, Oakland A.L. 2, 1988.
6-game series—4—New York A.L. 3, Los Angeles N.L. 1, 1977.
7-game series—5—Kansas City A.L. 3, St. Louis N.L. 2, 1985.
8-game series—11—New York A.L. 6, New York N.L. 5, 1921.

Most errors, nine-inning game

6—Chicago A.L. vs. Chicago N.L., October 13, 1906.
Pittsburgh N.L. vs. Detroit A.L., October 12, 1909.
Chicago A.L. vs. New York N.L., October 13, 1917.
Los Angeles N.L. vs. Baltimore A.L., October 6, 1966.

Most errors by both clubs, nine-inning game

9—Chicago A.L. 6, New York N.L. 3, October 13, 1917.

Most errors by outfield, game

4—Los Angeles N.L. vs. Baltimore A.L., October 6, 1966.

Most errors by outfields of both clubs, game

4—Los Angeles N.L. 4, Baltimore A.L. 0, October 6, 1966.

Most errors by infield, game

5—Chicago A.L. vs. Chicago N.L., October 13, 1906.
New York N.L. vs. Philadelphia A.L., October 17, 1911, 11 innings.
Detroit A.L. vs. St. Louis N.L., October 3, 1934.

Most errors by infields of both clubs, game

7—New York N.L. 5, Philadelphia A.L. 2, October 17, 1911, 11 innings.
Chicago A.L. 4, New York N.L. 3, October 13, 1917.

Most errors, inning

3—Chicago A.L., October 13, 1917, fourth inning.
New York N.L., October 8, 1937, fifth inning.
New York N.L., October 9, 1937, third inning.
Cincinnati N.L., October 8, 1939, 10th inning.
Los Angeles N.L., October 1, 1959, third inning.
Los Angeles N.L., October 6, 1966, fifth inning.

Most errorless games, total series

89—New York A.L. (33 series, 187 games).

Most consecutive errorless games, total series

7—Philadelphia A.L. vs. St. Louis N.L., October 6, 7, 1930; October 1, 2, 5, 6, 7, 1931.

Most errorless games, series

4-game series—4—Baltimore A.L. vs. Los Angeles N.L., 1966.
5-game series—5—New York A.L. vs. New York N.L., 1937.
6-game series—5
Boston A.L. vs. Chicago N.L., 1918.
St. Louis N.L. vs. St. Louis A.L., 1944.
New York A.L. vs. Brooklyn N.L., 1953.
Los Angeles N.L. vs. New York A.L., 1977.
7-game series—5
Philadelphia A.L. vs. St. Louis N.L., 1931.
New York A.L. vs. Brooklyn N.L., 1955.
Brooklyn N.L. vs. New York A.L., 1956.
St. Louis N.L. vs. Detroit A.L., 1968.
Cincinnati N.L. vs. Boston A.L., 1975.
St. Louis N.L. vs. Kansas City A.L., 1985.
Kansas City A.L. vs. St. Louis N.L., 1985.
Boston A.L. vs. New York N.L., 1986.
8-game series—5—New York N.L. vs. New York A.L., 1921.

Most consecutive errorless games, series

5—Philadelphia A.L. vs. St. Louis N.L., October 1, 2, 5, 6, 7, 1931 (first five games).
New York A.L. vs. New York N.L., October 6, 7, 8, 9, 10, 1937 (full series).
New York A.L. vs. Brooklyn N.L., September 29, 30, October 1, 2, 3, 1955.

Most errorless games by both clubs, series

4-game series—7—Baltimore A.L. 4, Los Angeles N.L. 3, 1966.
5-game series—7—New York A.L. 5, New York N.L. 2, 1937.
6-game series—9—Los Angeles N.L. 5, New York A.L. 4, 1977.
7-game series—10—St. Louis N.L. 5, Kansas City A.L. 5, 1985.
8-game series—8—New York N.L. 5, New York A.L. 3, 1921.

Fewest errorless games, series

0—Held by many clubs.

Longest errorless game

12 innings—
Detroit A.L. vs. St. Louis N.L., October 4, 1934.
New York A.L. vs. Los Angeles N.L., October 11, 1977.

Longest errorless game by both clubs

12 innings—New York A.L. vs. Los Angeles N.L., October 11, 1977 (Los Angeles fielded 11 innings).

PASSED BALLS

Most passed balls, total series

13—New York A.L. (33 series, 187 games).

Most passed balls, series

3—Chicago N.L. vs. Chicago A.L., 1906.
Pittsburgh N.L. vs. New York A.L., 1960.
New York A.L. vs. St. Louis N.L., 1964.

Most passed balls by both clubs, series

4—Chicago N.L., 3, Chicago A.L., 1, 1906 (6-game series).
New York A.L. 2, Brooklyn N.L. 2, 1947 (7-game series).

Fewest passed balls, series

0—Held by many clubs.

Fewest passed balls by both clubs, series

0—Held by many clubs.

DOUBLE AND TRIPLE PLAYS

Most double plays, total series

163—New York A.L. (33 series, 187 games).

Most double plays, series

4-game series—7
Chicago N.L. vs. New York A.L., 1932.
New York A.L. vs. Los Angeles N.L., 1963.
5-game series—7
New York A.L. vs. New York N.L., 1922.
New York A.L. vs. Brooklyn N.L., 1941.
Cincinnati N.L. vs. New York A.L., 1961.
6-game series—10—New York A.L. vs. New York N.L., 1951.
7-game series—12—Brooklyn N.L. vs. New York A.L., 1955.
8-game series—9—Chicago A.L. vs. Cincinnati N.L., 1919.

Most double plays by both clubs, series

4-game series—10—New York A.L. 6, Cincinnati N.L. 4, 1976.
5-game series—12—New York A.L. 7, Brooklyn N.L. 5, 1941.
6-game series—16—Philadelphia N.L. 8, Kansas City A.L. 8, 1980.
7-game series—19—Brooklyn N.L. 12, New York A.L. 7, 1955.
8-game series—16—Chicago A.L. 9, Cincinnati N.L. 7, 1919.

Fewest double plays, series

4-game series—1
New York A.L. vs. Chicago N.L., 1932.
Cincinnati N.L. vs. New York A.L., 1939.
Philadelphia N.L. vs. New York A.L., 1950.
Los Angeles N.L. vs. New York A.L., 1963.
Oakland A.L. vs. San Francisco N.L., 1989.
5-game series—0—New York N.L. vs. Baltimore A.L., 1969.
6-game series—2
Chicago A.L. vs. Chicago N.L., 1906.

New York N.L. vs. Philadelphia A.L., 1911.
Philadelphia A.L. vs. New York N.L., 1911.
Philadelphia A.L. vs. St. Louis N.L., 1930.
New York A.L. vs. New York N.L., 1936.
Chicago A.L. vs. Los Angeles N.L., 1959.
New York A.L. vs. Los Angeles N.L., 1977, 1981.
7-game series—2
St. Louis N.L. vs. Detroit A.L., 1934.
Baltimore A.L. vs. Pittsburgh N.L., 1971.
St. Louis N.L. vs. Minnesota A.L., 1987.
8-game series—4—New York N.L. vs. Boston A.L., 1912.

Fewest double plays by both clubs, series

4-game series—4
New York N.L. 2, Cleveland A.L. 2, 1954.
San Francisco N.L. 3, Oakland A.L. 1, 1989.
5-game series—4
New York N.L. 2, Philadelphia A.L. 2, 1905.
Baltimore A.L. 4, New York N.L. 0, 1969.

6-game series—4—Philadelphia A.L. 2, New York N.L. 2, 1911.
7-game series—6—Minnesota A.L. 4, St. Louis N.L. 2, 1987.
8-game series—9—Boston A.L. 5, New York N.L. 4, 1912.

Most double plays, nine-inning game

4—Philadelphia A.L. vs. Boston N.L., October 9, 1914.
Boston A.L. vs. Brooklyn N.L., October 7, 1916.
Chicago N.L. vs. New York A.L., September 29, 1932.
Cleveland A.L. vs. Boston N.L., October 11, 1948.
New York A.L. vs. New York N.L., October 8, 1951.
Oakland A.L. vs. New York N.L., October 17, 1973.
Philadelphia N.L. vs. Kansas City A.L., October 15, 1980.

Most double plays by both clubs, nine-inning game

6—New York A.L. 3, Brooklyn N.L. 3, September 29, 1955.
Philadelphia N.L. 4, Kansas City A.L. 2, October 15, 1980.

Most triple plays, series

1—Cleveland A.L. vs. Brooklyn N.L., 1920.

MISCELLANEOUS

CLUB

ONE-RUN DECISIONS

Most one-run games, total series
56—New York A.L. (33 series; won 27, lost 29).

Most one-run games won, total series
27—New York A.L. (33 series; lost 29).

Most one-run games lost, total series
29—New York A.L. (33 series; won 27).

Most one-run games won, series
4—Boston A.L. vs. Philadelphia N.L., 1915 (lost one).
Boston A.L. vs. Chicago N.L., 1918 (lost none).
Oakland A.L. vs. Cincinnati N.L., 1972 (lost two).

Most one-run games by both clubs, series
4-game series—3—New York A.L. (won three) vs. Philadelphia N.L., 1950.
5-game series—5
Boston A.L. (won four) vs. Philadelphia N.L., 1915.
Oakland A.L. (won three) vs. Los Angeles N.L. (won one), 1974.
6-game series—4
Boston A.L. (won four) vs. Chicago N.L., 1918.
Toronto A.L. (won four) vs. Atlanta N.L., 1992.
7-game series—6—Oakland A.L. (won four) vs. Cincinnati N.L. (won two), 1972.
8-game series—4—Boston A.L. (won three) vs. New York N.L. (won one), 1912.

Most one-run games won, series
4-game series—3—New York A.L. vs. Philadelphia N.L., 1950.
5-game series—4—Boston A.L. vs. Philadelphia N.L., 1915.
6-game series—4
Boston A.L. vs. Chicago N.L., 1918.
Toronto A.L. vs. Atlanta N.L., 1992.
7-game series—4—Oakland A.L. vs. Cincinnati N.L., 1972.
8-game series—3—Boston A.L. vs. New York N.L., 1912.

Most consecutive one-run games won, total series
6—Boston A.L., 1915 (last 4), 1916 (first 2).

Most consecutive one-run games lost, total series
7—Philadelphia N.L., 1915 (last 4), 1950 (first 3).

LENGTH OF GAMES

BY INNINGS

Longest tie game
12 innings—Chicago N.L., 3, Detroit A.L., 3, October 8, 1907 (at Chicago).

Longest day game
14 innings—Boston A.L., 2, Brooklyn N.L., 1, October 9, 1916 (at Boston).

Longest night game
12 innings—
Boston A.L., 7, Cincinnati N.L., 6, October 21, 1975 (at Boston).
New York A.L., 4, Los Angeles N.L., 3, October 11, 1977 (at New York).

Most extra-inning games, total series
13—New York A.L. (33 series, 187 games; won six, lost six, tied one).

Most extra-inning games won, total series
7—New York N.L. (14 series, 82 games; won seven, lost three, tied two).

Most extra-inning games lost, total series
6—New York A.L. (33 series, 187 games; won six, lost six, tied one).

Most extra-inning games, series
4-game series—1
Boston N.L. vs. Philadelphia A.L., 1914.
New York A.L. vs. Cincinnati N.L., 1939.
New York A.L. vs. Philadelphia N.L., 1950.
New York N.L. vs. Cleveland A.L., 1954.
5-game series—2—New York N.L. vs. Washington A.L., 1933.
6-game series—2—Philadelphia A.L. vs. New York N.L., 1911.
7-game series—3—Minnesota A.L. vs. Atlanta N.L., 1991.
8-game series—2—Boston A.L. vs. New York N.L., 1912.

BY TIME

Longest average time per game, series
4-game series—3 hours—Oakland A.L. vs. Cincinnati N.L., 1990.
5-game series—2 hours, 58 minutes—Los Angeles N.L. vs. Oakland A.L., 1988.
6-game series—3 hours, 29 minutes—Toronto A.L. vs. Philadelphia N.L., 1993.
7-game series—3 hours, 20 minutes—New York N.L. vs. Boston A.L., 1986.
8-game series—2 hours, 14 minutes—Boston A.L. vs. New York N.L., 1912.

Shortest average time per game, series
4-game series—1 hour, 46 minutes—New York A.L. vs. Cincinnati N.L., 1939.
5-game series—1 hour, 46 minutes—Detroit A.L. vs. Chicago N.L., 1908.
6-game series—1 hour, 49 minutes—Philadelphia A.L. vs. St. Louis N.L., 1930.
7-game series—1 hour, 47 minutes—Cleveland A.L. vs. Brooklyn N.L., 1920.
8-game series—1 hour, 48 minutes—Boston A.L. vs. Pittsburgh N.L., 1903.

Shortest game
1 hour, 25 minutes—Chicago N.L., 2, Detroit A.L., 0, October 14, 1908 (at Detroit).

Longest nine-inning day game
3 hours, 48 minutes—Baltimore A.L., 9, Pittsburgh N.L., 6, October 13, 1979 (at Pittsburgh).

Longest nine-inning night game
4 hours, 14 minutes—Toronto A.L., 15, Philadelphia N.L., 14, October 20, 1993 (at Philadelphia).

Longest extra-inning day game
4 hours, 13 minutes—New York N.L., 10, Oakland A.L., 7, October 14, 1973, 12 innings (at Oakland).

Longest extra-inning night game
4 hours, 7 minutes—Toronto A.L., 4, Atlanta N.L., 3, October 24, 1992, 11 innings (at Atlanta).

SERIES STARTING AND FINISHING DATES

Earliest date for series game (except 1918)
September 28, 1932—Chicago N.L. at New York A.L.
September 28, 1955—Brooklyn N.L. at New York A.L.

Earliest date for series final game (except 1918)
October 2, 1932—New York A.L. at Chicago N.L. (4-game series).
October 2, 1954—New York N.L. at Cleveland A.L. (4-game series).

Latest date for series start
October 20, 1981—Los Angeles N.L. at New York A.L.

Latest date for series finish

October 28, 1981—Los Angeles N.L. at New York A.L. (6-game series).

October 28, 1989—Oakland A.L. at San Francisco N.L. (4-game series).

NIGHT GAMES

First night game

October 13, 1971—Pittsburgh N.L., 4, Baltimore A.L., 3 (at Pittsburgh).

First year the entire series played at night

1985—St. Louis N.L. vs. Kansas City A.L., October 19 through 27 (7-game series).

SERIES AND GAMES WON

Most series won

22—New York A.L., 1923, 1927, 1928, 1932, 1936, 1937, 1938, 1939, 1941, 1943, 1947, 1949, 1950, 1951, 1952, 1953, 1956, 1958, 1961, 1962, 1977, 1978 (lost 11).

Most consecutive series won

8—New York A.L., 1927, 1928, 1932, 1936, 1937, 1938, 1939, 1941.

Most consecutive years winning series

5—New York A.L., 1949, 1950, 1951, 1952, 1953.

Most times winning series in four consecutive games

6—New York A.L., 1927, 1928, 1932, 1938, 1939, 1950.

Winning series after winning first game

Accomplished 53 times.

Winning series after losing first game

Accomplished 37 times.

Winning series after winning one game and losing three

Boston A.L. vs. Pittsburgh N.L., 1903 (8-game series; needed five wins).

Pittsburgh N.L. vs. Washington A.L., 1925 (7-game series).

New York A.L. vs. Milwaukee N.L., 1958 (7-game series).

Detroit A.L. vs. St. Louis N.L., 1968 (7-game series).

Pittsburgh N.L. vs. Baltimore A.L., 1979 (7-game series).

Kansas City A.L. vs. St. Louis N.L., 1985 (7-game series).

Winning series after losing first two games

New York N.L. vs. New York A.L., 1921 (8-game series; needed five wins).

Brooklyn N.L. vs. New York A.L., 1955 (7-game series).

New York A.L. vs. Brooklyn N.L., 1956 (7-game series).

New York A.L. vs. Milwaukee N.L., 1958 (7-game series).

Los Angeles N.L. vs. Minnesota A.L., 1965 (7-game series).

Pittsburgh N.L. vs. Baltimore A.L., 1971 (7-game series).

New York A.L. vs. Los Angeles N.L., 1978 (6-game series).

Los Angeles N.L. vs. New York A.L., 1981 (6-game series).

Kansas City A.L. vs. St. Louis N.L., 1985 (7-game series).

New York N.L. vs. Boston A.L., 1986 (7-game series).

Winning series after losing first three games

Never accomplished.

Most games won, total series

109—New York A.L. (33 series; lost 77, tied one).

Most consecutive games won, total series

12—New York A.L., 1927 (4), 1928 (4), 1932 (4).

SERIES AND GAMES LOST

Most series lost

12—Brooklyn/Los Angeles N.L., 1916, 1920, 1941, 1947, 1949, 1952, 1953, 1956, 1966, 1974, 1977, 1978 (won six).

11—New York A.L., 1921, 1922, 1926, 1942, 1955, 1957, 1960, 1963, 1964, 1976, 1981 (won 22).

Most consecutive series lost

7—Chicago N.L., 1910, 1918, 1929, 1932, 1935, 1938, 1945.

Brooklyn N.L., 1916, 1920, 1941, 1947, 1949, 1952, 1953.

Most consecutive years losing series

3—Detroit A.L., 1907, 1908, 1909.

New York N.L., 1911, 1912, 1913.

Most games lost, total series

77—New York A.L., 33 series (won 109, tied one).

Most consecutive games lost, total series

8—New York A.L., 1921 (last 3), 1922 (4), 1923 (first 1). (In 1922 there was one tie during the streak.)

Philadelphia N.L., 1915 (last 4), 1950 (4).

ATTENDANCE

Largest attendance, series

4-game series—251,507—New York N.L. vs. Cleveland A.L., 1954.

5-game series—304,139—Baltimore A.L. vs. Philadelphia N.L., 1983.

6-game series—420,784—Los Angeles N.L. vs. Chicago A.L., 1959.

7-game series—394,712—Milwaukee N.L. vs. New York A.L., 1957.

8-game series—269,976—New York N.L. vs. New York A.L., 1921.

Smallest attendance, series

4-game series—111,009—Boston N.L. vs. Philadelphia A.L., 1914.

5-game series—62,232—Chicago N.L. vs. Detroit A.L., 1908.

6-game series—99,845—Chicago A.L. vs. Chicago N.L., 1906.

7-game series—145,295—Pittsburgh N.L. vs. Detroit A.L., 1909.

8-game series—100,429—Pittsburgh N.L. vs. Boston A.L., 1903.

Largest attendance, game

92,706—At Los Angeles, October 6, 1959, Chicago A.L. 1, Los Angeles N.L. 0.

Smallest attendance, game

6,210—At Detroit, October 14, 1908; Chicago N.L. 2, Detroit A.L. 0.

LEAGUE

SERIES AND GAMES WON AND LOST

Most consecutive series won, league

7—American League, 1947, 1948, 1949, 1950, 1951, 1952, 1953.

Most consecutive series lost, league

7—National League, 1947, 1948, 1949, 1950, 1951, 1952, 1953.

Most consecutive games won, league

10—American League, 1927 (4) 1928 (4), 1929 (first 2).

American League, 1937 (last 1), 1938 (4), 1939 (4), 1940 (first 1).

SHUTOUTS

Most consecutive series with shutouts

9—1955 through 1963.

Most consecutive series ending in shutouts

3—1907, 1908, 1909.

1955, 1956, 1957.

Most consecutive series without shutouts

3—1910, 1911, 1912.

1927, 1928, 1929.

1936, 1937, 1938.

1976, 1977, 1978.

NON-PLAYING PERSONNEL

MANAGERS AND COACHES

Most series by manager

10—Casey Stengel, New York A.L., 1949, 1950, 1951, 1952, 1953, 1955, 1956, 1957, 1958, 1960 (won seven, lost three).

Most series by coach

15—Frank Crosetti, New York A.L., 1947, 1949, 1950, 1951, 1952, 1953, 1955, 1956, 1957, 1958, 1960, 1961, 1962, 1963, 1964 (10 World Series winners).

Most series eligible as player and coach

23—Frank Crosetti, New York A.L., 1932, 1936, 1937, 1938, 1939, 1941, 1942, 1943 (eight series as player, seven winners); 1947, 1949, 1950, 1951, 1952, 1953, 1955, 1956, 1957, 1958, 1960, 1961, 1962, 1963, 1964 (15 series as coach, 10 winners).

Most series winners managed

7—Joe McCarthy, New York A.L., 1932, 1936, 1937, 1938, 1939, 1941, 1943.
    Casey Stengel, New York A.L., 1949, 1950, 1951, 1952, 1953, 1956, 1958.

Most consecutive years managing series winners

5—Casey Stengel, New York A.L., 1949, 1950, 1951, 1952, 1953 (his first five years as New York A.L. manager).

Most consecutive series winners managed, career

6—Joe McCarthy, New York A.L., 1932, 1936, 1937, 1938, 1939, 1941.

Most series losers managed

6—John McGraw, New York N.L., 1911, 1912, 1913, 1917, 1923, 1924.

Most consecutive years managing series losers

3—Hughey Jennings, Detroit A.L., 1907, 1908, 1909.
    John McGraw, New York N.L., 1911, 1912, 1913.

Most consecutive series losers managed, career

4—John McGraw, New York N.L., 1911, 1912, 1913, 1917.

Most different series winners managed

2—Bill McKechnie, Pittsburgh N.L., 1925; Cincinnati N.L., 1940.
    Bucky Harris, Washington A.L., 1924; New York A.L., 1947.
    Sparky Anderson, Cincinnati N.L., 1975, 1976; Detroit A.L., 1984.

Most different clubs managed

3—Bill McKechnie, Pittsburgh N.L., 1925; St. Louis N.L., 1928; Cincinnati N.L., 1939, 1940.
    Dick Williams, Boston A.L., 1967; Oakland A.L., 1972, 1973; San Diego N.L., 1984.

Most games by manager

63—Casey Stengel, New York A.L., 10 series.

Most games won by manager

37—Casey Stengel, New York A.L., 10 series.

Most games lost by manager

28—John McGraw, New York N.L., 10 series.

Youngest manager

26 years, 11 months, 21 days—Joe Cronin, Washington A.L. vs. New York N.L., October 3, 1933.

Youngest manager of a series winner

27 years, 11 months, 2 days—Bucky Harris, Washington A.L. vs. New York N.L., October 10, 1924.

UMPIRES

Most series umpired

18—Bill Klem, 1908, 1909, 1911, 1912, 1913, 1914, 1915, 1917, 1918, 1920, 1922, 1924, 1926, 1929, 1931, 1932, 1934, 1940.

Most consecutive series umpired

5—Bill Klem, 1911, 1912, 1913, 1914, 1915.

Most games umpired

104—Bill Klem, 18 series.

GENERAL REFERENCE

YEAR BY YEAR

*Also one tie

Year	Winner	Loser	Games
1903—Boston A.L.	Pittsburgh N.L.	5-3
1904—No series played.		
1905—New York N.L.	Philadelphia A.L.	4-1
1906—Chicago A.L.	Chicago N.L.	4-2
1907—Chicago N.L.	Detroit A.L.	*4-0
1908—Chicago N.L.	Detroit A.L.	4-1
1909—Pittsburgh N.L.	Detroit A.L.	4-3
1910—Philadelphia A.L.	Chicago N.L.	4-1
1911—Philadelphia A.L.	New York N.L.	4-2
1912—Boston A.L.	New York N.L.	*4-3
1913—Philadelphia A.L.	New York N.L.	4-1
1914—Boston N.L.	Philadelphia A.L.	4-0
1915—Boston A.L.	Philadelphia N.L.	4-1
1916—Boston A.L.	Brooklyn N.L.	4-1
1917—Chicago A.L.	New York N.L.	4-2
1918—Boston A.L.	Chicago N.L.	4-2
1919—Cincinnati N.L.	Chicago A.L.	5-3
1920—Cleveland A.L.	Brooklyn N.L.	5-2
1921—New York N.L.	New York A.L.	5-3
1922—New York N.L.	New York A.L.	*4-0
1923—New York A.L.	New York N.L.	4-2
1924—Washington A.L.	New York N.L.	4-3
1925—Pittsburgh N.L.	Washington A.L.	4-3
1926—St. Louis N.L.	New York A.L.	4-3
1927—New York A.L.	Pittsburgh N.L.	4-0
1928—New York A.L.	St. Louis N.L.	4-0
1929—Philadelphia A.L.	Chicago N.L.	4-1
1930—Philadelphia A.L.	St. Louis N.L.	4-2
1931—St. Louis N.L.	Philadelphia A.L.	4-3
1932—New York A.L.	Chicago N.L.	4-0
1933—New York N.L.	Washington A.L.	4-1
1934—St. Louis N.L.	Detroit A.L.	4-3
1935—Detroit A.L.	Chicago N.L.	4-2
1936—New York A.L.	New York N.L.	4-2
1937—New York A.L.	New York N.L.	4-1
1938—New York A.L.	Chicago N.L.	4-0
1939—New York A.L.	Cincinnati N.L.	4-0
1940—Cincinnati N.L.	Detroit A.L.	4-3
1941—New York A.L.	Brooklyn N.L.	4-1
1942—St. Louis N.L.	New York A.L.	4-1
1943—New York A.L.	St. Louis N.L.	4-1
1944—St. Louis N.L.	St. Louis A.L.	4-2
1945—Detroit A.L.	Chicago N.L.	4-3
1946—St. Louis N.L.	Boston A.L.	4-3
1947—New York A.L.	Brooklyn N.L.	4-3
1948—Cleveland A.L.	Boston N.L.	4-2
1949—New York A.L.	Brooklyn N.L.	4-1
1950—New York A.L.	Philadelphia N.L.	4-0
1951—New York A.L.	New York N.L.	4-2
1952—New York A.L.	Brooklyn N.L.	4-3
1953—New York A.L.	Brooklyn N.L.	4-2
1954—New York N.L.	Cleveland A.L.	4-0
1955—Brooklyn N.L.	New York A.L.	4-3
1956—New York A.L.	Brooklyn N.L.	4-3
1957—Milwaukee N.L.	New York A.L.	4-3
1958—New York A.L.	Milwaukee N.L.	4-3
1959—Los Angeles N.L.	Chicago A.L.	4-2
1960—Pittsburgh N.L.	New York A.L.	4-3
1961—New York A.L.	Cincinnati N.L.	4-1
1962—New York A.L.	San Francisco N.L.	4-3
1963—Los Angeles N.L.	New York A.L.	4-0
1964—St. Louis N.L.	New York A.L.	4-3
1965—Los Angeles N.L.	Minnesota A.L.	4-3
1966—Baltimore A.L.	Los Angeles N.L.	4-0
1967—St. Louis N.L.	Boston A.L.	4-3
1968—Detroit A.L.	St. Louis N.L.	4-3
1969—New York N.L.	Baltimore A.L.	4-1

Year	Winner	Loser	Games
1970—Baltimore A.L.	Cincinnati N.L.	4-1
1971—Pittsburgh N.L.	Baltimore A.L.	4-3
1972—Oakland A.L.	Cincinnati N.L.	4-3
1973—Oakland A.L.	New York N.L.	4-3
1974—Oakland A.L.	Los Angeles N.L.	4-1
1975—Cincinnati N.L.	Boston A.L.	4-3
1976—Cincinnati N.L.	New York A.L.	4-0
1977—New York A.L.	Los Angeles N.L.	4-2
1978—New York A.L.	Los Angeles N.L.	4-2
1979—Pittsburgh N.L.	Baltimore A.L.	4-3
1980—Philadelphia N.L.	Kansas City A.L.	4-2
1981—Los Angeles N.L.	New York A.L.	4-2
1982—St. Louis N.L.	Milwaukee A.L.	4-3
1983—Baltimore A.L.	Philadelphia N.L.	4-1
1984—Detroit A.L.	San Diego N.L.	4-1
1985—Kansas City A.L.	St. Louis N.L.	4-3
1986—New York N.L.	Boston A.L.	4-3
1987—Minnesota A.L.	St. Louis N.L.	4-3
1988—Los Angeles N.L.	Oakland A.L.	4-1
1989—Oakland A.L.	San Francisco N.L.	4-0
1990—Cincinnati N.L.	Oakland A.L.	4-0
1991—Minnesota A.L.	Atlanta N.L.	4-3
1992—Toronto A.L.	Atlanta N.L.	4-2
1993—Toronto A.L.	Philadelphia N.L.	4-2
1994—No series played.		

SERIES WON AND LOST BY TEAMS

AMERICAN LEAGUE

	W	L	Pct.
Toronto	2	0	1.000
New York	22	11	.667
Oakland	4	2	.667
Cleveland	2	1	.667
Minnesota	2	1	.667
Philadelphia	5	3	.625
Boston	5	4	.556
Baltimore	3	3	.500
Chicago	2	2	.500
Kansas City	1	1	.500
Detroit	4	5	.444
Washington	1	2	.333
Milwaukee	0	1	.000
St. Louis	0	1	.000
Totals	53	37	.589

NATIONAL LEAGUE

	W	L	Pct.
Pittsburgh	5	2	.714
New York Mets	2	1	.667
St. Louis	9	6	.600
Cincinnati	5	4	.556
Los Angeles	5	4	.555
Boston	1	1	.500
Milwaukee	1	1	.500
New York Giants	5	9	.357
Philadelphia	1	4	.200
Chicago	2	8	.200
Brooklyn	1	8	.111
San Diego	0	1	.000
Atlanta	0	2	.000
San Francisco	0	2	.000
Totals	37	53	.411

GAMES WON AND LOST BY TEAMS

AMERICAN LEAGUE

	W	L	Tie	Pct.
Toronto	8	4		.667
New York	109	77	1	.586

	W	L	Tie	Pct.
Baltimore	19	14		.576
Boston	33	26	1	.559
Philadelphia	24	19		.558
Oakland	17	15		.531
Cleveland	9	8		.529
Minnesota	11	10		.524
Chicago	13	13		.500
Detroit	26	29	1	.473
Kansas City	6	7		.462
Milwaukee	3	4		.429
Washington	8	11		.421
St. Louis	2	4		.333
Totals	288	241	3	.544

NATIONAL LEAGUE

	W	L	Tie	Pct.
Boston	6	4		.600
New York Mets	11	8		.579
Los Angeles	25	24		.510
Cincinnati	26	25		.510
St. Louis	48	48		.500
Milwaukee	7	7		.500
Pittsburgh	23	24		.489
New York Giants	39	41	2	.488
Atlanta	5	8		.385
Chicago	19	33	1	.365
Brooklyn	20	36		.357
Philadelphia	8	18		.308
San Francisco	3	8		.273
San Diego	1	4		.200
Totals	241	288	3	.456

☐ HOME AND ROAD GAMES BY TEAMS ☐

AMERICAN LEAGUE

	Years	Game	Home	Away
New York	33	187	91	96
Boston	9	60	31	29
Detroit	9	56	28	28
Philadelphia	8	43	20	23
Baltimore	6	33	17	16
Oakland	6	32	17	15
Chicago	4	26	13	13
Minnesota	3	21	12	9
Washington	3	19	10	9
Cleveland	3	17	9	8
Kansas City	2	13	7	6
Toronto	2	12	6	6
Milwaukee	1	7	3	4
St. Louis	1	6	3	3
Totals	90	532	267	265

NATIONAL LEAGUE

	Years	Game	Home	Away
St. Louis	15	96	47	49
New York Giants	14	82	41	41
Brooklyn	9	56	28	28
Chicago	10	53	27	26
Cincinnati	9	51	26	25
Los Angeles	9	49	23	26
Pittsburgh	7	47	23	24
Philadelphia	5	26	14	12
New York Mets	3	19	10	9
Milwaukee	2	14	7	7
Atlanta	2	13	6	7
San Francisco	2	11	6	5
Boston	2	10	5	5
San Diego	1	5	2	3
Totals	90	532	265	267

☐ TIE GAMES ☐

Oct. 8, 1907 — 12 innings, Chicago N.L. 3, Detroit A.L. 3.
Oct. 9, 1912 — 11 innings, Boston A.L. 6, New York N.L. 6.
Oct. 5, 1922 — 10 innings, New York A.L. 3, New York N.L. 3.

Total number of ties: (3)

☐ SHUTOUTS ☐

Oct. 2, 1903 — Bill Dinneen, Boston A.L. 3, Pittsburgh N.L. 0 (three hits).
Oct. 13, 1903 — Bill Dinneen, Boston A.L. 3, Pittsburgh N.L. 0 (four hits).
Oct. 9, 1905 — Christy Mathewson, New York N.L. 3, Philadelphia A.L. 0 (four hits).
Oct. 10, 1905 — Chief Bender, Philadelphia A.L. 3, New York N.L. 0 (four hits).
Oct. 12, 1905 — Christy Mathewson, New York N.L. 9, Philadelphia A.L. 0 (four hits).
Oct. 13, 1905 — Joe McGinnity, New York N.L. 1, Philadelphia A.L. 0 (five hits).
Oct. 14, 1905 — Christy Mathewson, New York N.L. 2, Philadelphia A.L. 0 (six hits).
Oct. 11, 1906 — Ed Walsh, Chicago A.L. 3, Chicago N.L. 0 (two hits).
Oct. 12, 1906 — Mordecai Brown, Chicago N.L. 1, Chicago A.L. 0 (two hits).
Oct. 12, 1907 — Mordecai Brown, Chicago N.L. 2, Detroit A.L. 0 (seven hits).
Oct. 13, 1908 — Mordecai Brown, Chicago N.L. 3, Detroit A.L. 0 (four hits).
Oct. 14, 1908 — Orval Overall, Chicago N.L. 2, Detroit A.L. 0 (three hits).
Oct. 12, 1909 — George Mullin, Detroit A.L. 5, Pittsburgh N.L. 0 (five hits).
Oct. 16, 1909 — Babe Adams, Pittsburgh N.L. 8, Detroit A.L. 0 (six hits).
Oct. 8, 1913 — Christy Mathewson, New York N.L. 3, Philadelphia A.L. 0, 10 innings (eight hits).
Oct. 10, 1914 — Bill James, Boston N.L. 1, Philadelphia A.L. 0 (two hits).
Oct. 10, 1917 — Rube Benton, New York N.L. 2, Chicago A.L. 0 (five hits).
Oct. 11, 1917 — Ferdie Schupp, New York N.L. 5, Chicago A.L. 0 (seven hits).
Sept. 5, 1918 — Babe Ruth, Boston A.L. 1, Chicago N.L. 0 (six hits).
Sept. 10, 1918 — Hippo Vaughn, Chicago N.L. 3, Boston A.L. 0 (five hits).
Oct. 3, 1919 — Dickie Kerr, Chicago A.L. 3, Cincinnati N.L. 0 (three hits).
Oct. 4, 1919 — Jimmy Ring, Cincinnati N.L. 2, Chicago A.L. 0 (three hits).
Oct. 6, 1919 — Hod Eller, Cincinnati N.L. 5, Chicago A.L. 0 (three hits).
Oct. 6, 1920 — Burleigh Grimes, Brooklyn N.L. 3, Cleveland A.L. 0 (seven hits).
Oct. 11, 1920 — Duster Mails, Cleveland A.L. 1, Brooklyn N.L. 0 (three hits).
Oct. 12, 1920 — Stan Coveleski, Cleveland A.L. 3, Brooklyn N.L. 0 (five hits).
Oct. 5, 1921 — Carl Mays, New York A.L. 3, New York N.L. 0 (five hits).
Oct. 6, 1921 — Waite Hoyt, New York A.L. 3, New York N.L. 0 (two hits).
Oct. 13, 1921 — Art Nehf, New York N.L. 1, New York A.L. 0 (four hits).
Oct. 6, 1922 — Jack Scott, New York N.L. 3, New York A.L. 0 (four hits).
Oct. 12, 1923 — Art Nehf, New York N.L. 1, New York A.L. 0 (six hits).
Oct. 11, 1925 — Walter Johnson, Washington A.L. 4, Pittsburgh N.L. 0 (six hits).
Oct. 5, 1926 — Jesse Haines, St. Louis N.L. 4, New York A.L. 0 (five hits).
Oct. 4, 1930 — Bill Hallahan, St. Louis N.L. 5, Philadelphia A.L. 0 (seven hits).

Oct. 6, 1930—George Earnshaw and Lefty Grove, Philadelphia A.L. 2, St. Louis N.L. 0 (three hits).

Oct. 2, 1931—Bill Hallahan, St. Louis N.L. 2, Philadelphia A.L. 0 (three hits).

Oct. 6, 1931—George Earnshaw, Philadelphia A.L. 3, St. Louis N.L. 0 (two hits).

Oct. 5, 1933—Earl Whitehill, Washington A.L. 4, New York N.L. 0 (five hits).

Oct. 9, 1934—Dizzy Dean, St. Louis N.L. 11, Detroit A.L. 0 (six hits).

Oct. 2, 1935—Lon Warneke, Chicago N.L. 3, Detroit A.L. 0 (four hits).

Oct. 5, 1939—Monte Pearson, New York A.L. 4, Cincinnati N.L. 0 (two hits).

Oct. 6, 1940—Bobo Newsom, Detroit A.L. 8, Cincinnati N.L. 0 (three hits).

Oct. 7, 1940—Bucky Walters, Cincinnati N.L. 4, Detroit A.L. 0 (five hits).

Oct. 3, 1942—Ernie White, St. Louis N.L. 2, New York A.L. 0 (six hits).

Oct. 11, 1943—Spud Chandler, New York A.L. 2, St. Louis N.L. 0 (10 hits).

Oct. 8, 1944—Mort Cooper, St. Louis N.L. 2, St. Louis A.L. 0 (seven hits).

Oct. 3, 1945—Hank Borowy, Chicago N.L. 9, Detroit A.L. 0 (six hits).

Oct. 5, 1945—Claude Passeau, Chicago N.L. 3, Detroit A.L. 0 (one hit).

Oct. 7, 1946—Harry Brecheen, St. Louis N.L. 3, Boston A.L. 0 (four hits).

Oct. 9, 1946—Boo Ferriss, Boston A.L. 4, St. Louis N.L. 0 (six hits).

Oct. 6, 1948—Johnny Sain, Boston N.L. 1, Cleveland A.L. 0 (four hits).

Oct. 8, 1948—Gene Bearden, Cleveland A.L. 2, Boston N.L. 0 (five hits).

Oct. 5, 1949—Allie Reynolds, New York A.L. 1, Brooklyn N.L. 0 (two hits).

Oct. 6, 1949—Preacher Roe, Brooklyn N.L. 1, New York A.L. 0 (six hits).

Oct. 4, 1950—Vic Raschi, New York A.L. 1, Philadelphia N.L. 0 (two hits).

Oct. 4, 1952—Allie Reynolds, New York A.L. 2, Brooklyn N.L. 0 (four hits).

Oct. 4, 1955—Johnny Podres, Brooklyn N.L. 2, New York A.L. 0 (eight hits).

Oct. 8, 1956—Don Larsen, New York A.L. 2, Brooklyn N.L. 0 (no hits).

Oct. 9, 1956—Clem Labine, Brooklyn N.L. 1, New York A.L. 0, 10 innings (seven hits).

Oct. 10, 1956—Johnny Kucks, New York A.L. 9, Brooklyn N.L. 0 (three hits).

Oct. 7, 1957—Lew Burdette, Milwaukee N.L. 1, New York A.L. 0 (seven hits).

Oct. 10, 1957—Lew Burdette, Milwaukee N.L. 5, New York A.L. 0 (seven hits).

Oct. 4, 1958—Don Larsen and Ryne Duren, New York A.L. 4, Milwaukee N.L. 0 (six hits).

Oct. 5, 1958—Warren Spahn, Milwaukee N.L. 3, New York A.L., 0 (two hits).

Oct. 6, 1958—Bob Turley, New York A.L. 7, Milwaukee N.L. 0 (five hits).

Oct. 1, 1959—Early Wynn and Gerry Staley, Chicago A.L. 11, Los Angeles N.L. 0 (eight hits).

Oct. 6, 1959—Bob Shaw, Billy Pierce and Dick Donovan, Chicago A.L. 1, Los Angeles N.L. 0 (nine hits).

Oct. 8, 1960—Whitey Ford, New York A.L. 10, Pittsburgh N.L. 0 (four hits).

Oct. 12, 1960—Whitey Ford, New York A.L. 12, Pittsburgh N.L. 0 (seven hits).

Oct. 4, 1961—Whitey Ford, New York A.L. 2, Cincinnati N.L. 0 (two hits).

Oct. 8, 1961—Whitey Ford and Jim Coates, New York A.L. 7, Cincinnati N.L. 0 (five hits).

Oct. 5, 1962—Jack Sanford, San Francisco N.L. 2, New York A.L. 0 (three hits).

Oct. 16, 1962—Ralph Terry, New York A.L. 1, San Francisco N.L. 0 (four hits).

Oct. 5, 1963—Don Drysdale, Los Angeles N.L. 1, New York A.L. 0 (three hits).

Oct. 9, 1965—Claude Osteen, Los Angeles N.L. 4, Minnesota A.L. 0 (five hits).

Oct. 11, 1965—Sandy Koufax, Los Angeles N.L. 7, Minnesota A.L. 0 (four hits).

Oct. 14, 1965—Sandy Koufax, Los Angeles N.L. 2, Minnesota A.L. 0 (three hits).

Oct. 6, 1966—Jim Palmer, Baltimore A.L. 6, Los Angeles N.L. 0 (four hits).

Oct. 8, 1966—Wally Bunker, Baltimore A.L. 1, Los Angeles N.L. 0 (six hits).

Oct. 9, 1966—Dave McNally, Baltimore A.L. 1, Los Angeles N.L. 0 (four hits).

Oct. 5, 1967—Jim Lonborg, Boston A.L. 5, St. Louis N.L. 0 (one hit).

Oct. 8, 1967—Bob Gibson, St. Louis N.L. 6, Boston A.L. 0 (five hits).

Oct. 2, 1968—Bob Gibson, St. Louis N.L. 4, Detroit A.L. 0 (five hits).

Oct. 14, 1969—Gary Gentry and Nolan Ryan, New York N.L. 5, Baltimore A.L. 0 (four hits).

Oct. 14, 1971—Nelson Briles, Pittsburgh N.L. 4, Baltimore A.L. 0 (two hits).

Oct. 18, 1972—Jack Billingham and Clay Carroll, Cincinnati N.L. 1, Oakland A.L. 0 (three hits).

Oct. 18, 1973—Jerry Koosman and Tug McGraw, New York N.L. 2, Oakland A.L. 0 (three hits).

Oct. 11, 1975—Luis Tiant, Boston A.L. 6, Cincinnati N.L. 0 (five hits).

Oct. 16, 1979—John Candelaria and Kent Tekulve, Pittsburgh N.L. 4, Baltimore A.L. 0 (seven hits).

Oct. 21, 1981—Tommy John and Rich Gossage, New York A.L., 3 Los Angeles N.L. 0 (four hits).

Oct. 12, 1982—Mike Caldwell, Milwaukee A.L. 10, St. Louis N.L. 0 (three hits).

Oct. 16, 1983—Scott McGregor, Baltimore A.L. 5, Philadelphia N.L. 0 (five hits).

Oct. 23, 1985—John Tudor, St. Louis N.L. 3, Kansas City A.L. 0 (five hits).

Oct. 27, 1985—Bret Saberhagen, Kansas City A.L. 11, St. Louis N.L. 0 (five hits).

Oct. 18, 1986—Bruce Hurst and Calvin Schiraldi, Boston A.L. 1, New York N.L. 0 (five hits).

Oct. 16, 1988—Orel Hershiser, Los Angeles N.L. 6, Oakland A.L. 0 (three hits).

Oct. 14, 1989—Dave Stewart, Oakland A.L. 5, San Francisco N.L. 0 (five hits).

Oct. 16, 1990—Jose Rijo, Rob Dibble and Randy Myers, Cincinnati N.L. 7, Oakland A.L. 0 (nine hits).

Oct. 27, 1991—Jack Morris, Minnesota A.L. 1, Atlanta N.L. 0, 10 innings (seven hits).

Oct. 21, 1993—Curt Schilling, Philadelphia N.L. 2, Toronto A.L. 0 (five hits).

Total number of shutouts: (100)

EXTRA-INNING GAMES

Oct. 8, 1907— 12 innings, Chicago N.L. 3, Detroit A.L. 3 (tie).

Oct. 22, 1910— 10 innings, Chicago N.L. 4, Philadelphia A.L. 3.

Oct. 17, 1911— 11 innings, Philadelphia A.L. 3, New York N.L. 2.

Oct. 25, 1911— 10 innings, New York N.L. 4, Philadelphia A.L. 3.

Oct. 9, 1912— 11 innings, Boston A.L. 6, New York N.L. 6 (tie).

Oct. 16, 1912— 10 innings, Boston A.L. 3, New York N.L. 2.

Oct. 8, 1913— 10 innings, New York N.L. 3, Philadelphia A.L. 0.

Oct. 12, 1914— 12 innings, Boston N.L. 5, Philadelphia A.L. 4.

Oct. 9, 1916— 14 innings, Boston A.L. 2, Brooklyn N.L. 1.

Oct. 7, 1919— 10 innings, Chicago A.L. 5, Cincinnati N.L. 4.

Oct. 5, 1922— 10 innings, New York N.L. 3, New York A.L. 3 (tie).

Oct. 4, 1924— 12 innings, New York N.L. 4, Washington A.L. 3.

Oct. 10, 1924— 12 innings, Washington A.L. 4, New York N.L. 3.

Oct. 7, 1926— 10 innings, New York A.L. 3, St. Louis N.L. 2.

Oct. 6, 1933— 11 innings, New York N.L. 2, Washington A.L. 1.

Oct. 7, 1933— 10 innings, New York N.L. 4, Washington A.L. 3.

Oct. 4, 1934— 12 innings, Detroit A.L. 3, St. Louis N.L. 2.

Oct. 4, 1935— 11 innings, Detroit A.L. 6, Chicago N.L. 5.
Oct. 5, 1936— 10 innings, New York N.L. 5, New York A.L. 4.
Oct. 8, 1939— 10 innings, New York A.L. 7, Cincinnati N.L. 4.
Oct. 5, 1944— 11 innings, St. Louis N.L. 3, St. Louis A.L. 2.
Oct. 8, 1945— 12 innings, Chicago N.L. 8, Detroit A.L. 7.
Oct. 6, 1946— 10 innings, Boston A.L. 3, St. Louis N.L. 2.
Oct. 5, 1950— 10 innings, New York A.L. 2, Philadelphia N.L. 1.
Oct. 5, 1952— 11 innings, Brooklyn N.L. 6, New York A.L. 5.
Sept. 29, 1954— 10 innings, New York N.L. 5, Cleveland A.L. 2.
Oct. 9, 1956— 10 innings, Brooklyn N.L. 1, New York A.L. 0.
Oct. 6, 1957— 10 innings, Milwaukee N.L. 7, New York A.L. 5.
Oct. 1, 1958— 10 innings, Milwaukee N.L. 4, New York A.L. 3.
Oct. 8, 1958— 10 innings, New York A.L. 4, Milwaukee N.L. 3.
Oct. 12, 1964— 10 innings, St. Louis N.L. 5, New York A.L. 2.
Oct. 15, 1969— 10 innings, New York N.L. 2, Baltimore A.L. 1.
Oct. 16, 1971— 10 innings, Baltimore A.L. 3, Pittsburgh N.L. 2.
Oct. 14, 1973— 12 innings, New York N.L. 10, Oakland A.L. 7.
Oct. 16, 1973— 11 innings, Oakland A.L. 3, New York N.L. 2.
Oct. 14, 1975— 10 innings, Cincinnati N.L. 6, Boston A.L. 5.
Oct. 21, 1975— 12 innings, Boston A.L. 7, Cincinnati N.L. 6.
Oct. 11, 1977— 12 innings, New York A.L. 4, Los Angeles N.L. 3.
Oct. 14, 1978— 10 innings, New York A.L. 4, Los Angeles N.L. 3.
Oct. 17, 1980— 10 innings, Kansas City A.L. 4, Philadelphia N.L. 3.
Oct. 25, 1986— 10 innings, New York N.L. 6, Boston A.L. 5.
Oct. 17, 1990— 10 innings, Cincinnati N.L. 2, Oakland A.L. 1.
Oct. 22, 1991— 12 innings, Atlanta N.L. 5, Minnesota A.L. 4.
Oct. 26, 1991— 11 innings, Minnesota A.L. 4, Atlanta N.L. 3.
Oct. 27, 1991— 10 innings, Minnesota A.L. 1, Atlanta N.L. 0.
Oct. 24, 1992— 11 innings, Toronto A.L. 4, Atlanta N.L. 3.

Total number of occurrences: (45)

Year	Games	Total	Year	Games	Total
1986	7	321,774	1990	4	208,544
1987	7	387,138	1991	7	373,160
1988	5	259,984	1992	6	311,460
1989	4	222,843	1993	6	344,394

INDIVIDUAL BATTING

LEADING BATTERS

(Playing in all games, each series; capitalized name
denotes leader or tied for series, both clubs)

AMERICAN LEAGUE

Year	Player, Club	AB	H	TB	Avg.
1903	Chick Stahl, Boston	33	10	17	.303
1904	No series played.				
1905	Topsy Hartsel, Philadelphia	17	5	6	.294
1906	GEORGE ROHE, Chicago	21	7	12	.333
	JIGGS DONAHUE, Chicago	18	6	10	.333
1907	Claude Rossman, Detroit	20	8	10	.400
1908	Ty Cobb, Detroit	19	7	8	.368
1909	JIM DELAHANTY, Detroit	26	9	13	.346
1910	EDDIE COLLINS, Philadelphia	21	9	13	.429
1911	HOME RUN BAKER, Philadelphia	24	9	17	.375
1912	Tris Speaker, Boston	30	9	14	.300
1913	Home Run Baker, Philadelphia	20	9	12	.450
1914	Home Run Baker, Philadelphia	16	4	6	.250
1915	DUFFY LEWIS, Boston	18	8	12	.444
1916	DUFFY LEWIS, Boston	17	6	10	.353
1917	Eddie Collins, Chicago	22	9	10	.409
1918	Stuffy McInnis, Boston	20	5	5	.250
	George Whiteman, Boston	20	5	7	.250
1919	JOE JACKSON, Chicago	32	12	18	.375
1920	STEVE O'NEILL, Cleveland	21	7	10	.333
1921	Wally Schang, New York	21	6	9	.296
1922	Bob Meusel, New York	20	6	7	.300
1923	AARON WARD, New York	24	10	13	.417
1924	JOE JUDGE, Washington	26	10	11	.385
1925	Bucky Harris, Washington	25	11	22	.440
1926	Earle Combs, New York	28	10	12	.357
1927	MARK KOENIG, New York	18	9	11	.500
1928	BABE RUTH, New York	16	10	22	.625
1929	Jimmie Dykes, Philadelphia	19	8	9	.421
1930	AL SIMMONS, Philadelphia	22	8	16	.364
1931	Jimmie Foxx, Philadelphia	23	8	11	.348
1932	LOU GEHRIG, New York	17	9	19	.529
1933	Fred Schulte, Washington	21	7	21	.333
1934	CHARLIE GEHRINGER, Detroit	29	11	15	.379
1935	PETE FOX, Detroit	26	10	15	.385
1936	JAKE POWELL, New York	22	10	14	.455
1937	TONY LAZZERI, New York	15	6	11	.400
1938	Bill Dickey, New York	15	6	9	.400
	Joe Gordon, New York	15	6	11	.400
1939	CHARLIE KELLER, New York	16	7	19	.438
1940	Bruce Campbell, Detroit	25	9	13	.360
1941	JOE GORDON, New York	14	7	13	.500
1942	PHIL RIZZUTO, New York	21	8	11	.381
1943	Billy Johnson, New York	20	6	9	.300
1944	GEORGE McQUINN, St. Louis	16	7	12	.438
1945	Roger Cramer, Detroit	29	11	11	.379
1946	Rudy York, Boston	23	6	15	.261
1947	TOMMY HENRICH, New York	31	10	15	.323
1948	Larry Doby, Cleveland	22	7	11	.318
1949	Tommy Henrich, New York	19	5	8	.263
1950	GENE WOODLING, New York	14	6	6	.429
1951	Phil Rizzuto, New York	25	8	11	.320
1952	GENE WOODLING, New York	23	8	14	.348
1953	BILLY MARTIN, New York	24	12	23	.500
1954	VIC WERTZ, Cleveland	16	8	15	.500
1955	YOGI BERRA, New York	24	10	14	.417
1956	YOGI BERRA, New York	25	9	20	.360
1957	Jerry Coleman, New York	22	8	10	.364
1958	Hank Bauer, New York	31	10	22	.323
1959	TED KLUSZEWSKI, Chicago	23	9	19	.391
1960	MICKEY MANTLE, New York	25	10	20	.400

ATTENDANCE

Year	Games	Total	Year	Games	Total
1903	8	100,429	1945	7	333,457
1905	5	91,723	1946	7	250,071
1906	6	99,845	1947	7	389,763
1907	5	78,068	1948	6	358,362
1908	5	62,232	1949	5	236,716
1909	7	145,295	1950	4	196,009
1910	5	124,222	1951	6	341,977
1911	6	179,851	1952	7	340,706
1912	8	252,037	1953	6	307,350
1913	5	151,000	1954	4	251,507
1914	4	111,009	1955	7	362,310
1915	5	143,351	1956	7	345,903
1916	5	162,859	1957	7	394,712
1917	6	186,654	1958	7	393,909
1918	6	128,483	1959	6	420,784
1919	8	236,928	1960	7	349,813
1920	7	178,737	1961	5	223,247
1921	8	269,976	1962	7	376,864
1922	5	185,947	1963	4	247,279
1923	6	301,430	1964	7	321,807
1924	7	283,665	1965	7	364,326
1925	7	282,848	1966	4	220,791
1926	7	328,051	1967	7	304,085
1927	4	201,705	1968	7	379,670
1928	4	199,072	1969	5	272,378
1929	5	190,490	1970	5	253,183
1930	6	212,619	1971	7	351,091
1931	7	231,567	1972	7	363,149
1932	4	191,998	1973	7	358,289
1933	5	163,076	1974	5	260,004
1934	7	281,510	1975	7	308,272
1935	6	286,672	1976	4	223,009
1936	6	302,924	1977	6	337,708
1937	5	238,142	1978	6	337,304
1938	4	200,833	1979	7	367,597
1939	4	183,849	1980	6	324,516
1940	7	281,927	1981	6	338,081
1941	5	235,773	1982	7	384,570
1942	5	277,101	1983	5	304,139
1943	5	277,312	1984	5	271,820
1944	6	206,708	1985	7	327,494

Year	Player, Club	AB	H	TB	Avg.
1961	BOBBY RICHARDSON, New York	23	9	10	.391
1962	Tom Tresh, New York	28	9	13	.321
1963	Elston Howard, New York	15	5	5	.333
1964	Bobby Richardson, New York	32	13	15	.406
1965	Zoilo Versalles, Minnesota	28	8	14	.286
	—Harmon Killebrew, Minnesota	21	6	9	.286
1966	BOOG POWELL, Baltimore	14	5	6	.357
1967	Carl Yastrzemski, Boston	25	10	21	.400
1968	Norm Cash, Detroit	26	10	13	.385
1969	Boog Powell, Baltimore	19	5	5	.263
1970	PAUL BLAIR, Baltimore	19	9	10	.474
1971	Brooks Robinson, Baltimore	22	7	7	.318
1972	Gene Tenace, Oakland	23	8	21	.348
1973	Joe Rudi, Oakland	27	9	11	.333
1974	Bert Campaneris, Oakland	17	6	8	.353
1975	Carl Yastrzemski, Boston	29	9	10	.310
1976	Thurman Munson, New York	17	9	9	.529
1977	REGGIE JACKSON, New York	20	9	25	.450
1978	BRIAN DOYLE, New York	16	7	8	.438
1979	Ken Singleton, Baltimore	28	10	11	.357
1980	AMOS OTIS, Kansas City	23	11	22	.478
1981	LOU PINIELLA, New York	16	7	8	.438
1982	ROBIN YOUNT, Milwaukee	29	12	18	.414
1983	JOHN SHELBY, Baltimore	9	4	4	.444
1984	ALAN TRAMMELL, Detroit	20	9	16	.450
1985	GEORGE BRETT, Kansas City	27	10	11	.370
1986	MARTY BARRETT, Boston	30	13	15	.433
1987	Kirby Puckett, Minnesota	28	10	13	.357
1988	Dave Henderson, Oakland	20	6	8	.300
1989	RICKEY HENDERSON, Oakland	19	9	17	.474
1990	Rickey Henderson, Oakland	15	5	10	.333
1991	BRIAN HARPER, Minnesota	21	8	10	.381
1992	PAT BORDERS, Toronto	20	9	15	.450
1993	PAUL MOLITOR, Toronto	24	12	24	.500
1994	No series played.				

NATIONAL LEAGUE

Year	Player, Club	AB	H	TB	Avg.
1903	JIMMY SEBRING, Pittsburgh	30	11	16	.367
1904	No series played.				
1905	MIKE DONLIN, New York	19	6	7	.316
1906	Solly Hofman, Chicago	23	7	8	.304
1907	HARRY STEINFELDT, Chicago	17	8	11	.471
1908	FRANK CHANCE, Chicago	19	8	8	.421
1909	Honus Wagner, Pittsburgh	24	8	12	.333
1910	Frank Schulte, Chicago	17	6	9	.353
	—Frank Chance, Chicago	17	6	9	.353
1911	Larry Doyle, New York	23	7	12	.304
1912	BUCK HERZOG, New York	30	12	18	.400
1913	LARRY McLEAN, New York	12	6	6	.500
1914	HANK GOWDY, Boston	11	6	14	.545
1915	Fred Luderus, Philadelphia	16	7	12	.438
1916	Ivy Olson, Brooklyn	16	4	6	.250
1917	DAVE ROBERTSON, New York	22	11	14	.500
1918	CHARLIE PICK, Chicago	18	7	8	.389
1919	Greasy Neale, Cincinnati	28	10	13	.357
1920	ZACH WHEAT, Brooklyn	27	9	11	.333
1921	IRISH MEUSEL, New York	29	10	17	.345
1922	HEINIE GROH, New York	19	9	11	.474
1923	CASEY STENGEL, New York	12	5	11	.417
1924	Frankie Frisch, New York	30	10	16	.333
	—Fred Lindstrom, New York	30	10	12	.333
1925	MAX CAREY, Pittsburgh	24	11	15	.458
1926	TOMMY THEVENOW, St. Louis	24	10	14	.417
1927	Lloyd Waner, Pittsburgh	15	6	9	.400
1928	Rabbit Maranville, St. Louis	13	4	8	.308
1929	Hack Wilson, Chicago	17	8	10	.471
1930	Charlie Gelbert, St. Louis	17	6	8	.353
1931	PEPPER MARTIN, St. Louis	24	12	19	.500
1932	Riggs Stephenson, Chicago	18	8	9	.444
1933	MEL OTT, New York	18	7	13	.389
1934	JOE MEDWICK, St. Louis	29	11	16	.379
1935	Billy Herman, Chicago	24	8	15	.333
1936	Dick Bartell, New York	21	8	14	.381
1937	Joe Moore, New York	23	9	10	.391

Year	Player, Club	AB	H	TB	Avg.
1938	STAN HACK, Chicago	17	8	9	.471
1939	Frank McCormick, Cincinnati	15	6	7	.400
1940	BILL WERBER, Cincinnati	27	10	14	.370
1941	Joe Medwick, Brooklyn	17	4	5	.235
1942	Jimmy Brown, St. Louis	20	6	6	.300
1943	MARTY MARION, St. Louis	14	5	10	.357
1944	Emil Verban, St. Louis	17	7	7	.412
1945	PHIL CAVARRETTA, Chicago	26	11	16	.423
1946	HARRY WALKER, St. Louis	17	7	9	.412
1947	Pee Wee Reese, Brooklyn	23	7	8	.304
1948	BOB ELLIOTT, Boston	21	7	13	.333
1949	PEE WEE REESE, Brooklyn	19	6	10	.316
1950	GRANNY HAMNER, Philadelphia	14	6	10	.429
1951	MONTE IRVIN, New York	24	11	13	.458
1952	Duke Snider, Brooklyn	29	10	24	.345
	—Pee Wee Reese, Brooklyn	29	10	13	.345
1953	Gil Hodges, Brooklyn	22	8	11	.364
1954	Alvin Dark, New York	17	7	7	.412
1955	Duke Snider, Brooklyn	25	8	21	.320
1956	Duke Snider, Brooklyn	23	7	11	.304
	—Gil Hodges, Brooklyn	23	7	12	.304
1957	HANK AARON, Milwaukee	28	11	22	.393
1958	BILL BRUTON, Milwaukee	17	7	10	.412
1959	GIL HODGES, Los Angeles	23	9	14	.391
1960	Bill Mazeroski, Pittsburgh	25	8	16	.320
1961	Wally Post, Cincinnati	18	6	10	.333
1962	JOSE PAGAN, San Francisco	19	7	10	.368
1963	TOMMY DAVIS, Los Angeles	15	6	10	.400
1964	TIM McCARVER, St. Louis	23	11	17	.478
1965	RON FAIRLY, Los Angeles	29	11	20	.379
1966	Lou Johnson, Los Angeles	15	4	5	.267
1967	LOU BROCK, St. Louis	29	12	19	.414
1968	LOU BROCK, St. Louis	28	13	24	.464
1969	AL WEIS, New York	11	5	8	.455
1970	Lee May, Cincinnati	18	7	15	.389
1971	ROBERTO CLEMENTE, Pittsburgh	29	12	22	.414
1972	TONY PEREZ, Cincinnati	23	10	12	.435
1973	RUSTY STAUB, New York	26	11	16	.423
1974	STEVE GARVEY, Los Angeles	21	8	8	.381
1975	PETE ROSE, Cincinnati	27	10	13	.370
1976	JOHNNY BENCH, Cincinnati	15	8	17	.533
1977	Steve Garvey, Los Angeles	24	9	15	.375
1978	Bill Russell, Los Angeles	26	11	13	.423
1979	PHIL GARNER, Pittsburgh	24	12	16	.500
1980	Bob Boone, Philadelphia	17	7	9	.412
1981	Steve Garvey, Los Angeles	24	10	11	.417
1982	George Hendrick, St. Louis	28	9	9	.321
	—Lonnie Smith, St. Louis	28	9	15	.321
1983	Bo Diaz, Philadelphia	15	5	6	.333
1984	Kurt Bevacqua, San Diego	17	7	15	.412
1985	Tito Landrum, St. Louis	25	9	14	.360
1986	Lenny Dykstra, New York	27	8	14	.296
1987	TONY PENA, St. Louis	22	9	10	.409
1988	MICKEY HATCHER, Los Angeles	19	7	14	.368
1989	Ken Oberkfell, San Francisco	6	2	2	.333
1990	BILLY HATCHER, Cincinnati	12	9	15	.750
1991	Rafael Belliard, Atlanta	16	6	7	.375
1992	Otis Nixon, Atlanta	27	8	9	.296
1993	Lenny Dykstra, Philadelphia	23	8	21	.348
	—John Kruk, Philadelphia	23	8	9	.348
1994	No series played.				

HOME RUNS

AMERICAN LEAGUE

1903—2—Boston, Patsy Dougherty (2).
1904—No series played.
1905—0—Philadelphia.
1906—0—Chicago.
1907—0—Detroit.
1908—0—Detroit.
1909—2—Detroit, Davy Jones (1), Sam Crawford (1).
1910—1—Philadelphia, Danny Murphy (1).
1911—3—Philadelphia, Home Run Baker (2), Rube Oldring (1).

1912—1—Boston, Larry Gardner (1).
1913—2—Philadelphia, Home Run Baker (1), Wally Schang (1).
1914—0—Philadelphia.
1915—3—Boston, Harry Hooper (2), Duffy Lewis (1).
1916—2—Boston, Larry Gardner (2).
1917—1—Chicago, Happy Felsch (1).
1918—0—Boston.
1919—1—Chicago, Joe Jackson (1).
1920—2—Cleveland, Elmer Smith (1), Jim Bagby (1).
1921—2—New York, Babe Ruth (1), Chick Fewster (1).
1922—2—New York, Aaron Ward (2).
1923—5—New York, Babe Ruth (3), Aaron Ward (1), Joe Dugan (1).
1924—5—Washington, Goose Goslin (3), Bucky Harris (2).
1925—8—Washington, Bucky Harris (3), Goose Goslin (3), Joe Judge (1), Roger Peckinpaugh (1).
1926—4—New York, Babe Ruth (4).
1927—2—New York, Babe Ruth (2).
1928—9—New York, Lou Gehrig (4), Babe Ruth (3), Bob Meusel (1), Cedric Durst (1).
1929—6—Philadelphia, Jimmie Foxx (2), Al Simmons (2), Mule Haas (2).
1930—6—Philadelphia, Mickey Cochrane (2), Al Simmons (2), Jimmie Foxx (1), Jimmie Dykes (1).
1931—3—Philadelphia, Al Simmons (2), Jimmie Foxx (1).
1932—8—New York, Lou Gehrig (3), Babe Ruth (2), Tony Lazzeri (1), Earle Combs (1).
1933—2—Washington, Goose Goslin (1), Fred Schulte (1).
1934—2—Detroit, Hank Greenberg (1), Charlie Gehringer (1).
1935—1—Detroit, Hank Greenberg (1).
1936—7—New York, Lou Gehrig (2), George Selkirk (2), Tony Lazzeri (1), Bill Dickey (1), Jake Powell (1).
1937—4—New York, Tony Lazzeri (1), Lou Gehrig (1), Myril Hoag (1), Joe DiMaggio (1).
1938—5—New York, Frank Crosetti (1), Joe DiMaggio (1), Joe Gordon (1), Bill Dickey (1), Tommy Henrich (1).
1939—7—New York, Charlie Keller (3), Bill Dickey (2), Babe Dahlgren (1), Joe DiMaggio (1).
1940—4—Detroit, Bruce Campbell (1), Rudy York (1), Pinky Higgins (1), Hank Greenberg (1).
1941—2—New York, Joe Gordon (1), Tommy Henrich (1).
1942—3—New York, Charlie Keller (2), Phil Rizzuto (1).
1943—2—New York, Joe Gordon (1), Bill Dickey (1).
1944—1—St. Louis, Babe McQuinn (1).
1945—2—Detroit, Hank Greenberg (2).
1946—4—Boston, Rudy York (2), Bobby Doerr (1), Leon Culberson (1).
1947—4—New York, Joe DiMaggio (2), Tommy Henrich (1), Yogi Berra (1).
1948—4—Cleveland, Larry Doby (1), Dale Mitchell (1), Jim Hegan (1), Joe Gordon (1).
1949—2—New York, Tommy Henrich (1), Joe DiMaggio (1).
1950—2—New York, Joe DiMaggio (1), Yogi Berra (1).
1951—5—New York, Joe Collins (1), Gene Woodling (1), Joe DiMaggio (1), Gil McDougald (1), Phil Rizzuto (1).
1952—10—New York, Johnny Mize (3), Mickey Mantle (2), Yogi Berra (2), Gil McDougald (1), Billy Martin (1), Gene Woodling (1).
1953—9—New York, Mickey Mantle (2), Gil McDougald (2), Billy Martin (2), Yogi Berra (1), Joe Collins (1), Gene Woodling (1).
1954—3—Cleveland, Al Smith (1), Vic Wertz (1), Hank Majeski (1).
1955—8—New York, Joe Collins (2), Yogi Berra (1), Bob Cerv (1), Elston Howard (1), Mickey Mantle (1), Gil McDougald (1), Bill Skowron (1).
1956—12—New York, Mickey Mantle (3), Yogi Berra (3), Billy Martin (2), Enos Slaughter (1), Hank Bauer (1), Elston Howard (1), Bill Skowron (1).
1957—7—New York, Hank Bauer (2), Tony Kubek (2), Mickey Mantle (1), Yogi Berra (1), Elston Howard (1).

1958—10—New York, Hank Bauer (4), Gil McDougald (2), Mickey Mantle (2), Bill Skowron (2).
1959—4—Chicago, Ted Kluszewski (3), Sherm Lollar (1).
1960—10—New York, Mickey Mantle (3), Roger Maris (2), Bill Skowron (2), Yogi Berra (1), Elston Howard (1), Bobby Richardson (1).
1961—7—New York, Johnny Blanchard (2), Yogi Berra (1), Elston Howard (1), Hector Lopez (1), Roger Maris (1), Bill Skowron (1).
1962—3—New York, Tom Tresh (1), Roger Maris (1), Clete Boyer (1).
1963—2—New York, Tom Tresh (1), Mickey Mantle (1).
1964—10—New York, Mickey Mantle (3), Phil Linz (2), Tom Tresh (2), Roger Maris (1), Joe Pepitone (1), Clete Boyer (1).
1965—6—Minnesota, Zoilo Versalles (1), Tony Oliva (1), Harmon Killebrew (1), Don Mincher (1), Bob Allison (1), Mudcat Grant (1).
1966—4—Baltimore, Frank Robinson (2), Brooks Robinson (1), Paul Blair (1).
1967—8—Boston, Carl Yastrzemski (3), Reggie Smith (2), Rico Petrocelli (2), Jose Santiago (1).
1968—8—Detroit, Al Kaline (2), Jim Northrup (2), Norm Cash (1), Willie Horton (1), Mickey Lolich (1), Dick McAuliffe (1).
1969—3—Baltimore, Don Buford (1), Dave McNally (1), Frank Robinson (1).
1970—10—Baltimore, Boog Powell (2), Frank Robinson (2), Brooks Robinson (2), Don Buford (1), Elrod Hendricks (1), Dave McNally (1), Merv Rettenmund (1).
1971—5—Baltimore, Don Buford (2), Frank Robinson (2), Merv Rettenmund (1).
1972—5—Oakland, Gene Tenace (4), Joe Rudi (1).
1973—2—Oakland, Bert Campaneris (1), Reggie Jackson (1).
1974—4—Oakland, Ray Fosse (1), Ken Holtzman (1), Reggie Jackson (1), Joe Rudi (1).
1975—6—Boston, Bernie Carbo (2), Carlton Fisk (2), Dwight Evans (1), Fred Lynn (1).
1976—1—New York, Jim Mason (1).
1977—8—New York, Reggie Jackson (5), Chris Chambliss (1), Thurman Munson (1), Willie Randolph (1).
1978—3—New York, Reggie Jackson (2), Roy White (1).
1979—4—Baltimore, Doug DeCinces (1), Eddie Murray (1), Benny Ayala (1), Rich Dauer (1).
1980—8—Kansas City, Willie Aikens (4), Amos Otis (3), George Brett (1).
1981—6—New York, Willie Randolph (2), Bob Watson (2), Rich Cerone (1), Reggie Jackson (1).
1982—5—Milwaukee, Ted Simmons (2), Cecil Cooper (1), Ben Oglivie (1), Robin Yount (1).
1983—6—Baltimore, Eddie Murray (2), Jim Dwyer (1), John Lowenstein (1), Dan Ford (1), Rick Dempsey (1).
1984—7—Detroit, Kirk Gibson (2), Alan Trammell (2), Marty Castillo (1), Larry Herndon (1), Lance Parrish (1).
1985—2—Kansas City, Frank White (1), Darryl Motley (1).
1986—5—Boston, Dwight Evans (2), Dave Henderson (2), Rich Gedman (1).
1987—7—Minnesota, Don Baylor (1), Gary Gaetti (1), Greg Gagne (1), Dan Gladden (1), Kent Hrbek (1), Tim Laudner (1), Steve Lombardozzi (1).
1988—2—Oakland, Jose Canseco (1), Mark McGwire (1).
1989—9—Oakland, Dave Henderson (2), Jose Canseco (1), Rickey Henderson (1), Carney Lansford (1), Dave Parker (1), Tony Phillips (1), Terry Steinbach (1), Walt Weiss (1).
1990—3—Oakland, Harold Baines (1), Jose Canseco (1), Rickey Henderson (1).
1991—8—Minnesota, Chili Davis (2), Kirby Puckett (2), Greg Gagne (1), Kent Hrbek (1), Scott Leius (1), Mike Pagliarulo (1).
1992—6—Toronto, Joe Carter (2), Pat Borders (1), Kelly

— 463 —

Gruber (1), Candy Maldonado (1), Ed Sprague (1).
1993—6—Toronto, Joe Carter (2), Paul Molitor (2), John Olerud (1), Devon White (1).
1994—No series played.

Total number of home runs: (395)

NATIONAL LEAGUE

1903—1—Pittsburgh, Jimmy Sebring (1).
1904—No series played.
1905—0—New York.
1906—0—Chicago.
1907—0—Chicago.
1908—1—Chicago, Joe Tinker (1).
1909—2—Pittsburgh, Fred Clarke (2).
1910—0—Chicago.
1911—0—New York.
1912—1—New York, Larry Doyle (1).
1913—1—New York, Fred Merkle (1).
1914—1—Boston, Hank Gowdy (1).
1915—1—Philadelphia, Fred Luderus (1).
1916—1—Brooklyn, Hy Myers (1).
1917—2—New York, Benny Kauff (2).
1918—0—Chicago.
1919—0—Cincinnati.
1920—0—Brooklyn.
1921—2—New York, Frank Snyder (1), Irish Meusel (1).
1922—1—New York, Irish Meusel (1).
1923—5—New York, Casey Stengel (2), Irish Meusel (1), Ross Youngs (1), Frank Snyder (1).
1924—4—New York, George Kelly (1), Bill Terry (1), Rosy Ryan (1), Jack Bentley (1).
1925—4—Pittsburgh, Pie Traynor (1), Glenn Wright (1), Kiki Cuyler (1), Eddie Moore (1).
1926—4—St. Louis, Billy Southworth (1), Tommy Thevenow (1), Jesse Haines (1), Les Bell (1).
1927—0—Pittsburgh.
1928—1—St. Louis, Jim Bottomley (1).
1929—1—Chicago, Charlie Grimm (1).
1930—2—St. Louis, George Watkins (1), Taylor Douthit (1).
1931—2—St. Louis, Pepper Martin (1), George Watkins (1).
1932—3—Chicago, Kiki Cuyler (1), Gabby Hartnett (1), Frank Demaree (1).
1933—3—New York, Mel Ott (2), Bill Terry (1).
1934—2—St. Louis, Joe Medwick (1), Bill DeLancey (1).
1935—5—Chicago, Frank Demaree (2), Gabby Hartnett (1), Chuck Klein (1), Billy Herman (1).
1936—4—New York, Dick Bartell (1), Jimmy Ripple (1), Mel Ott (1), Joe Moore (1).
1937—1—New York, Mel Ott (1).
1938—2—Chicago, Joe Marty (1), Ken O'Dea (1).
1939—0—Cincinnati.
1940—2—Cincinnati, Jimmy Ripple (1), Bucky Walters (1).
1941—1—Brooklyn, Pete Reiser (1).
1942—2—St. Louis, Enos Slaughter (1), Whitey Kurowski (1).
1943—2—St. Louis, Marty Marion (1), Ray Sanders (1).
1944—3—St. Louis, Stan Musial (1), Ray Sanders (1), Danny Litwhiler (1).
1945—1—Chicago, Phil Cavarretta (1).
1946—1—St. Louis, Enos Slaughter (1).
1947—1—Brooklyn, Dixie Walker (1).
1948—4—Boston, Bob Elliott (2), Marv Rickert (1), Bill Salkeld (1).
1949—4—Brooklyn, Pee Wee Reese (1), Luis Olmo (1), Roy Campanella (1), Gil Hodges (1).
1950—0—Philadelphia.
1951—2—New York, Alvin Dark (1), Whitey Lockman (1).
1952—6—Brooklyn, Duke Snider (4), Jackie Robinson (1), Pee Wee Reese (1).
1953—8—Brooklyn, Jim Gilliam (2), Roy Campanella (1), Billy Cox (1), Carl Furillo (1), Gil Hodges (1), George Shuba (1), Duke Snider (1).
1954—2—New York, Dusty Rhodes (2).
1955—9—Brooklyn, Duke Snider (4), Roy Campanella (2),

Sandy Amoros (1), Carl Furillo (1), Gil Hodges (1).
1956—3—Brooklyn, Duke Snider (1), Jackie Robinson (1), Gil Hodges (1).
1957—8—Milwaukee, Hank Aaron (3), Frank Torre (2), Eddie Mathews (1), Johnny Logan (1), Del Crandall (1).
1958—3—Milwaukee, Del Crandall (1), Bill Bruton (1), Lew Burdette (1).
1959—7—Los Angeles, Charlie Neal (2), Chuck Essegian (2), Wally Moon (1), Duke Snider (1), Gil Hodges (1).
1960—4—Pittsburgh, Bill Mazeroski (2), Rocky Nelson (1), Hal Smith (1).
1961—3—Cincinnati, Gordy Coleman (1), Wally Post (1), Frank Robinson (1).
1962—5—San Francisco, Chuck Hiller (1), Willie McCovey (1), Tom Haller (1), Ed Bailey (1), Jose Pagan (1).
1963—3—Los Angeles, John Roseboro (1), Bill Skowron (1), Frank Howard (1).
1964—5—St. Louis, Ken Boyer (2), Lou Brock (1), Mike Shannon (1), Tim McCarver (1).
1965—5—Los Angeles, Ron Fairly (2), Lou Johnson (2), Wes Parker (1).
1966—1—Los Angeles, Jim Lefebvre (1).
1967—5—St. Louis, Lou Brock (1), Bob Gibson (1), Julian Javier (1), Roger Maris (1), Mike Shannon (1).
1968—7—St. Louis, Lou Brock (2), Orlando Cepeda (2), Bob Gibson (1), Tim McCarver (1), Mike Shannon (1).
1969—6—New York, Donn Clendenon (3), Tommie Agee (1), Ed Kranepool (1), Al Weis (1).
1970—5—Cincinnati, Lee May (2), Johnny Bench (1), Pete Rose (1), Bobby Tolan (1).
1971—5—Pittsburgh, Bob Robertson (2), Roberto Clemente (2), Richie Hebner (1).
1972—3—Cincinnati, Johnny Bench (1), Denis Menke (1), Pete Rose (1).
1973—4—New York, Wayne Garrett (2), Cleon Jones (1), Rusty Staub (1).
1974—4—Los Angeles, Bill Buckner (1), Willie Crawford (1), Joe Ferguson (1), Jim Wynn (1).
1975—7—Cincinnati, Tony Perez (3), Cesar Geronimo (2), Johnny Bench (1), David Concepcion (1).
1976—4—Cincinnati, Johnny Bench (2), Dan Driessen (1), Joe Morgan (1).
1977—9—Los Angeles, Reggie Smith (3), Steve Yeager (2), Dusty Baker (1), Ron Cey (1), Steve Garvey (1), Dave Lopes (1).
1978—6—Los Angeles, Dave Lopes (3), Dusty Baker (1), Ron Cey (1), Reggie Smith (1).
1979—3—Pittsburgh, Willie Stargell (3).
1980—3—Philadelphia, Mike Schmidt (2), Bake McBride (1).
1981—6—Los Angeles, Pedro Guerrero (2), Steve Yeager (2), Ron Cey (1), Jay Johnstone (1).
1982—4—St. Louis, Willie McGee (2), Keith Hernandez (1), Darrell Porter (1).
1983—4—Philadelphia, Joe Morgan (2), Garry Maddox (1), Gary Matthews (1).
1984—3—San Diego, Kurt Bevacqua (2), Terry Kennedy (1).
1985—2—St. Louis, Tito Landrum (1), Willie McGee (1).
1986—7—New York, Gary Carter (2), Lenny Dykstra (2), Ray Knight (1), Darryl Strawberry (1), Tim Teufel (1).
1987—2—St. Louis, Tom Herr (1), Tom Lawless (1).
1988—5—Los Angeles, Mickey Hatcher (2), Mike Davis (1), Kirk Gibson (1), Mike A. Marshall (1).
1989—4—San Francisco, Bill Bathe (1), Greg Litton (1), Kevin Mitchell (1), Matt Williams (1).
1990—3—Cincinnati, Chris Sabo (2), Eric Davis (1).
1991—8—Atlanta, Lonnie Smith (3), David Justice (2), Terry Pendleton (2), Brian Hunter (1).
1992—3—Atlanta, Damon Berryhill (1), David Justice (1),

Lonnie Smith (1).
1993—7—Philadelphia, Lenny Dykstra (4), Darren Daulton
  (1), Jim Eisenreich (1), Milt Thompson (1).
1994—No series played.

Total number of home runs: (281)

PLAYERS WITH FIVE HOME RUNS

Player	Series	No.
Mickey Mantle	12	18
Babe Ruth	10	15
Yogi Berra	14	12
Duke Snider	6	11
Reggie Jackson	5	10
Lou Gehrig	7	10
Frank Robinson	5	8
Bill Skowron	8	8
Joe DiMaggio	10	8
Goose Goslin	5	7
Gil McDougald	8	7
Hank Bauer	9	7
Lenny Dykstra	2	6
Al Simmons	4	6
Reggie Smith	4	6
Roger Maris	7	6
Charlie Keller	4	5
Hank Greenberg	4	5
Johnny Bench	4	5
Billy Martin	5	5
Gil Hodges	7	5
Bill Dickey	8	5
Elston Howard	9	5

Total number of players: (23)

.450 HITTERS

(Playing in all games and having 10 or more at-bats)

Player, Club	Year	AB	H	TB	Avg.
Billy Hatcher, Cincinnati N.L.	1990	12	9	15	.750
Babe Ruth, New York A.L.	1928	16	10	22	.625
Chris Sabo, Cincinnati N.L.	1990	16	9	16	.563
Hank Gowdy, Boston N.L.	1914	11	6	14	.545
Lou Gehrig, New York A.L.	1928	11	6	19	.545
Johnny Bench, Cincinnati N.L.	1976	15	8	17	.533
Lou Gehrig, New York A.L.	1932	17	9	19	.529
Thurman Munson, New York A.L.	1976	17	9	9	.529
Larry McLean, New York N.L.	1913	12	6	6	.500
Dave Robertson, New York N.L.	1917	22	11	14	.500
Mark Koenig, New York A.L.	1927	18	9	11	.500
Pepper Martin, St. Louis N.L.	1931	24	12	19	.500
Joe Gordon, New York A.L.	1941	14	7	13	.500
Billy Martin, New York A.L.	1953	24	12	23	.500
Vic Wertz, Cleveland A.L.	1954	16	8	15	.500
Phil Garner, Pittsburgh N.L.	1979	24	12	16	.500
Paul Molitor, Toronto A.L.	1993	24	12	24	.500
Roberto Alomar, Toronto A.L.	1993	25	12	16	.480
Tim McCarver, St. Louis N.L.	1964	23	11	17	.478
Amos Otis, Kansas City A.L.	1980	23	11	22	.478
Heinie Groh, New York N.L.	1922	19	9	11	.474
Paul Blair, Baltimore A.L.	1970	19	9	10	.474
Rickey Henderson, Oakland A.L.	1989	19	9	17	.474
Harry Steinfeldt, Chicago N.L.	1907	17	8	11	.471
Frankie Frisch, New York N.L.	1922	17	8	9	.471
Hack Wilson, Chicago N.L.	1929	17	8	10	.471
Stan Hack, Chicago N.L.	1938	17	8	9	.471
Lou Brock, St. Louis N.L.	1968	28	13	24	.464
Phil Cavarretta, Chicago N.L.	1938	13	6	7	.462
Max Carey, Pittsburgh N.L.	1925	24	11	15	.458
Monte Irvin, New York N.L.	1951	24	11	13	.458
Jake Powell, New York A.L.	1936	22	10	14	.455
Al Weis, New York N.L.	1969	11	5	8	.455
Home Run Baker, Phil. A.L.	1913	20	9	12	.450
Reggie Jackson, New York A.L.	1977	20	9	25	.450
Alan Trammell, Detroit A.L.	1984	20	9	16	.450
Pat Borders, Toronto A.L.	1992	20	9	15	.450

Total number of occurrences: (37)

INDIVIDUAL PITCHING

PITCHERS WITH FIVE VICTORIES

Pitcher, Club	Yrs.	W	L
Whitey Ford, New York A.L.	11	10	8
Red Ruffing, New York A.L.	7	7	2
Allie Reynolds, New York A.L.	6	7	2
Bob Gibson, St. Louis N.L.	3	7	2
Lefty Gomez, New York A.L.	4	6	0
Chief Bender, Philadelphia A.L.	5	6	4
Waite Hoyt, New York A.L., Philadelphia A.L.	6	6	4
Jack Coombs, Philadelphia A.L., Brooklyn N.L.	3	5	0
Herb Pennock, New York A.L.	3	5	0
Vic Raschi, New York A.L.	5	5	3
Catfish Hunter, Oakland A.L., New York A.L.	6	5	3
Mordecai Brown, Chicago N.L.	4	5	4
Christy Mathewson, New York N.L.	4	5	5

Total number of pitchers: (13)

10-STRIKEOUT GAMES BY PITCHERS

Date	Pitcher, Club	No.
Oct. 1,	1903—Deacon Phillippe, Pit. N.L. vs. Bos. A.L.	10
Oct. 2,	1903—Bill Dinneen, Bos. A.L. vs. Pit. N.L.	11
Oct. 11,	1906—Ed Walsh, Chi. A.L. vs. Chi. N.L.	12
Oct. 8,	1907—Bill Donovan, Det. A.L. vs. Chi. N.L. (12 innings)	12
Oct. 14,	1908—Orval Overall, Chi. N.L. vs. Det. A.L.	10
Oct. 12,	1909—George Mullin, Det. A.L. vs. Pit. N.L.	10
Oct. 14,	1911—Chief Bender, Phi. A.L. vs. N.Y. N.L. (eight innings)	11
Oct. 8,	1912—Joe Wood, Bos. A.L. vs. N.Y. N.L.	11
Oct. 11,	1921—Jesse Barnes, N.Y. N.L. vs. N.Y. A.L.	10
Oct. 24,	1924—Walter Johnson, Was. A.L. vs. N.Y. N.L. (12 innings)	12
Oct. 7,	1925—Walter Johnson, Was. A.L. vs. Pit. N.L.	10
Oct. 3,	1926—Grover Alexander, St.L. N.L. vs. N.Y. A.L.	10
Oct. 8,	1929—Howard Ehmke, Phi. A.L. vs. Chi. N.L.	13
Oct. 11,	1929—George Earnshaw, Phi. A.L. vs. Chi. N.L.	10
Sept. 28,	1932—Red Ruffing, N.Y. A.L. vs. Chi. N.L.	10
Oct. 3,	1933—Carl Hubbell, N.Y. N.L. vs. Was. A.L.	10
Oct. 5,	1936—Hal Schumacher, N.Y. N.L. vs. N.Y. A.L. (10 innings)	10
Oct. 6,	1944—Jack Kramer, St.L. A.L. vs. St.L. N.L.	10
Oct. 8,	1944—Denny Galehouse, St.L. A.L. vs. St.L. N.L.	10
Oct. 8,	1944—Mort Cooper, St.L. N.L. vs. St.L. A.L.	12
Oct. 10,	1945—Hal Newhouser, Det. A.L. vs. Chi. N.L.	10
Oct. 5,	1949—Don Newcombe, Bkn. N.L. vs. N.Y. A.L. (eight innings)	11
Oct. 4,	1952—Allie Reynolds, N.Y. A.L. vs. Bkn. N.L.	10
Oct. 2,	1953—Carl Erskine, Bkn. N.L. vs. N.Y. A.L.	14
Oct. 3,	1956—Sal Maglie, Bkn. N.L. vs. N.Y. A.L.	10
Oct. 9,	1956—Bob Turley, N.Y. A.L. vs. Bkn. N.L.	11
Oct. 6,	1958—Bob Turley, N.Y. A.L. vs. Mil. N.L.	10
Oct. 10,	1962—Jack Sanford, S.F. N.L. vs. N.Y. A.L.	10
Oct. 2,	1963—Sandy Koufax, L.A. N.L. vs. N.Y. A.L.	15
Oct. 12,	1964—Bob Gibson, St.L. N.L. vs. N.Y. A.L. (10 innings)	13
Oct. 10,	1965—Don Drysdale, L.A. N.L. vs. Min. A.L.	11
Oct. 11,	1965—Sandy Koufax, L.A. N.L. vs. Min. A.L.	10
Oct. 14,	1965—Sandy Koufax, L.A. N.L. vs. Min. A.L.	10
Oct. 5,	1966—Moe Drabowsky, Bal. A.L. vs. L.A. N.L.	11
Oct. 4,	1967—Bob Gibson, St.L. N.L. vs. Bos. A.L.	10
Oct. 12,	1967—Bob Gibson, St.L. N.L. vs. Bos. A.L.	10
Oct. 2,	1968—Bob Gibson, St.L. N.L. vs. Det. A.L.	17
Oct. 6,	1968—Bob Gibson, St.L. N.L. vs. Det. A.L.	10
Oct. 11,	1971—Jim Palmer, Bal. A.L. vs. Pit. N.L.	10
Oct. 18,	1972—Blue Moon Odom, Oak. A.L. vs. Cin. N.L. (seven innings)	11
Oct. 16,	1973—Tom Seaver, N.Y. N.L. vs. Oak. A.L. (eight innings)	12
Oct. 15,	1980—Steve Carlton, Phi. N.L. vs. K.C. A.L. (eight innings)	10

Total number of performances: (42)

Bill Wambsganss, second baseman, Cleveland A.L. vs. Brooklyn N.L. at Cleveland, October 10, 1920, fifth inning.

Wambsganss caught Clarence Mitchell's line drive, stepped on second to retire Pete Kilduff, then tagged Otto Miller coming from first. (This unassisted triple play was made with runners on first and second bases only.)

Total number of occurrences: (1)

CLUB BATTING

Year	Club, League	G	AB	R	H	TB	2B	3B	HR	SB	BB	SO	RBI	Avg.	LOB
1903—	Pittsburgh N.L.	8	270	24	64	92	7	9	1	7	14	45	23	.237	51
	Boston A.L.	8	282	39	71	113	4	16	2	5	13	27	35	.252	55
1904—	No series played.														
1905—	New York N.L.	5	153	15	32	39	7	0	0	11	15	26	13	.209	31
	Philadelphia A.L.	5	155	3	25	30	5	0	0	2	5	25	2	.161	26
1906—	Chicago N.L.	6	184	18	36	45	9	0	0	8	18	27	11	.196	37
	Chicago A.L.	6	187	22	37	53	10	3	0	6	18	35	19	.198	33
1907—	Chicago N.L.	5	167	19	43	51	6	1	0	18	12	25	16	.257	35
	Detroit A.L.	5	173	6	36	41	1	2	0	7	9	21	6	.208	36
1908—	Chicago N.L.	5	164	24	48	59	4	2	1	13	13	26	21	.293	30
	Detroit A.L.	5	158	15	32	37	5	0	0	5	12	26	14	.203	27
1909—	Pittsburgh N.L.	7	223	34	49	70	12	1	2	18	20	34	26	.220	44
	Detroit A.L.	7	234	28	55	77	16	0	2	6	20	22	25	.235	50
1910—	Chicago N.L.	5	158	15	35	48	11	1	0	3	18	31	13	.222	31
	Philadelphia A.L.	5	177	35	56	80	19	1	1	7	17	24	29	.316	36
1911—	New York N.L.	6	189	13	33	46	11	1	0	4	14	44	10	.175	31
	Philadelphia A.L.	6	205	27	50	74	15	0	3	4	4	31	21	.244	29
1912—	New York N.L.	8	274	31	74	99	14	4	1	12	22	39	25	.270	53
	Boston A.L.	8	273	25	60	89	14	6	1	6	19	36	21	.220	56
1913—	New York N.L.	5	164	15	33	41	3	1	1	5	8	19	15	.201	24
	Philadelphia A.L.	5	174	23	46	64	4	4	2	5	7	16	21	.264	30
1914—	Boston N.L.	4	135	16	33	46	6	2	1	9	15	18	14	.244	27
	Philadelphia A.L.	4	128	6	22	31	9	0	0	2	13	28	5	.172	21
1915—	Philadelphia N.L.	5	148	10	27	36	4	1	1	2	10	25	9	.182	23
	Boston A.L.	5	159	12	42	57	2	2	3	1	11	25	11	.264	35
1916—	Brooklyn N.L.	5	170	13	34	49	2	5	1	1	14	19	11	.200	32
	Boston A.L.	5	164	21	39	64	7	6	2	1	18	25	18	.238	31
1917—	New York N.L.	6	199	17	51	70	5	4	2	4	6	27	16	.256	37
	Chicago A.L.	6	197	21	54	63	6	0	1	6	11	28	18	.274	37
1918—	Chicago N.L.	6	176	10	37	44	5	1	0	3	18	14	10	.210	31
	Boston A.L.	6	172	9	32	40	2	3	0	3	16	21	6	.186	32
1919—	Cincinnati N.L.	8	251	35	64	88	10	7	0	7	25	22	34	.255	46
	Chicago A.L.	8	263	20	59	78	10	3	1	5	15	30	17	.224	52
1920—	Brooklyn N.L.	7	215	8	44	51	5	1	0	1	10	20	8	.205	39
	Cleveland A.L.	7	217	21	53	72	9	2	2	2	21	21	18	.244	43
1921—	New York N.L.	8	264	29	71	98	13	4	2	7	22	38	28	.269	54
	New York A.L.	8	241	22	50	65	7	1	2	6	27	44	20	.207	43
1922—	New York N.L.	5	162	18	50	57	2	1	1	1	12	15	18	.309	32
	New York A.L.	5	158	11	32	46	6	1	2	2	8	20	11	.203	25
1923—	New York N.L.	6	201	17	47	70	2	3	5	1	12	18	17	.234	35
	New York A.L.	6	205	30	60	91	8	4	5	1	20	22	29	.293	43
1924—	New York N.L.	7	253	27	66	91	9	2	4	3	25	40	22	.261	59
	Washington A.L.	7	248	26	61	95	9	0	5	5	29	34	23	.246	57
1925—	Pittsburgh N.L.	7	230	25	61	89	12	2	4	7	17	32	25	.265	54
	Washington A.L.	7	225	26	59	91	8	0	8	2	17	32	25	.262	46
1926—	St. Louis N.L.	7	239	31	65	91	12	1	4	2	11	30	30	.272	43
	New York A.L.	7	223	21	54	78	10	1	4	1	31	31	19	.242	55
1927—	Pittsburgh N.L.	4	130	10	29	37	6	1	0	6	4	7	10	.223	23
	New York A.L.	4	136	23	38	54	6	2	2	2	13	25	19	.279	29
1928—	St. Louis N.L.	4	131	10	27	37	5	1	1	3	11	29	9	.206	27
	New York A.L.	4	134	27	37	71	7	0	9	4	13	12	25	.276	24
1929—	Chicago N.L.	5	173	17	43	56	6	2	1	1	13	50	15	.249	36
	Philadelphia A.L.	5	171	26	48	71	5	0	6	0	13	27	26	.281	35
1930—	St. Louis N.L.	6	190	12	38	56	10	1	2	1	11	33	11	.200	37
	Philadelphia A.L.	6	178	21	35	67	10	2	6	0	24	32	21	.197	36
1931—	St. Louis N.L.	7	229	19	54	71	11	0	2	8	9	41	17	.236	40
	Philadelphia A.L.	7	227	22	50	64	5	0	3	0	28	46	20	.220	52
1932—	Chicago N.L.	4	146	19	37	58	8	2	3	2	11	24	16	.253	31
	New York A.L.	4	144	37	45	75	6	0	8	0	23	26	36	.313	33
1933—	New York N.L.	5	176	16	47	61	5	0	3	0	11	21	16	.267	39
	Washington A.L.	5	173	11	37	47	4	0	2	1	13	25	11	.214	37
1934—	St. Louis N.L.	7	262	34	73	103	14	5	2	2	11	31	32	.279	49
	Detroit A.L.	7	250	23	56	76	12	1	2	4	25	43	20	.224	64
1935—	Chicago N.L.	6	202	18	48	73	6	2	5	1	11	29	17	.238	33
	Detroit A.L.	6	206	21	51	67	11	1	1	1	25	27	18	.248	51

Year	Club, League	G	AB	R	H	TB	2B	3B	HR	SB	BB	SO	RBI	Avg.	LOB
1936—	New York N.L.	6	203	23	50	71	9	0	4	0	21	33	20	.246	46
	New York A.L.	6	215	43	65	96	8	1	7	1	26	35	41	.302	43
1937—	New York N.L.	5	169	12	40	49	6	0	1	1	11	21	12	.237	36
	New York A.L.	5	169	28	42	68	6	4	4	0	21	21	25	.249	36
1938—	Chicago N.L.	4	136	9	33	45	4	1	2	0	6	26	8	.243	26
	New York A.L.	4	135	22	37	60	6	1	5	3	11	16	21	.274	24
1939—	Cincinnati N.L.	4	133	8	27	32	3	1	0	1	6	22	8	.203	23
	New York A.L.	4	131	20	27	54	4	1	7	0	9	20	18	.206	16
1940—	Cincinnati N.L.	7	232	22	58	78	14	0	2	1	15	30	21	.250	49
	Detroit A.L.	7	228	28	56	83	9	3	4	0	30	30	24	.246	50
1941—	Brooklyn N.L.	5	159	11	29	43	7	2	1	0	14	21	11	.182	27
	New York A.L.	5	166	17	41	54	5	1	2	2	23	18	16	.247	42
1942—	St. Louis N.L.	5	163	23	39	53	4	2	2	0	17	19	23	.239	32
	New York A.L.	5	178	18	44	59	6	0	3	3	8	22	14	.247	34
1943—	St. Louis N.L.	5	165	9	37	48	5	0	2	1	11	26	8	.224	37
	St. Louis A.L.	5	159	17	35	50	5	2	2	2	12	30	14	.220	29
1944—	St. Louis N.L.	6	204	16	49	69	9	1	3	0	19	43	15	.240	51
	St. Louis A.L.	6	197	12	36	50	9	1	1	0	23	49	9	.183	44
1945—	Chicago N.L.	7	247	29	65	90	16	3	1	2	19	48	27	.263	50
	Detroit A.L.	7	242	32	54	70	10	0	2	3	33	22	32	.223	53
1946—	St. Louis N.L.	7	232	28	60	86	19	2	1	3	19	30	27	.259	50
	Boston A.L.	7	233	20	56	77	7	1	4	2	22	28	18	.240	53
1947—	Brooklyn N.L.	7	226	29	52	70	13	1	1	7	30	32	26	.230	46
	New York A.L.	7	238	38	67	100	11	5	4	2	38	37	36	.282	63
1948—	Boston N.L.	6	187	17	43	61	6	0	4	1	16	19	16	.230	34
	Cleveland A.L.	6	191	17	38	57	7	0	4	2	12	26	16	.199	34
1949—	Brooklyn N.L.	5	162	14	34	55	7	1	4	2	15	38	14	.210	31
	New York A.L.	5	164	21	37	57	10	2	2	2	18	27	20	.226	32
1950—	Philadelphia N.L.	4	128	5	26	34	6	1	0	1	7	24	3	.203	26
	New York A.L.	4	135	11	30	41	3	1	2	1	13	12	10	.222	33
1951—	New York N.L.	6	194	18	46	61	7	1	2	2	25	22	15	.237	45
	New York A.L.	6	199	29	49	75	7	2	5	0	26	23	25	.246	41
1952—	Brooklyn N.L.	7	233	20	50	75	7	0	6	5	24	49	18	.215	52
	New York A.L.	7	232	26	50	89	5	2	10	1	31	32	24	.216	48
1953—	Brooklyn N.L.	6	213	27	64	103	13	1	8	2	15	30	26	.300	49
	New York A.L.	6	201	33	56	97	6	4	9	2	25	43	32	.279	47
1954—	New York N.L.	4	130	21	33	42	3	0	2	1	17	24	20	.254	28
	Cleveland A.L.	4	137	9	26	42	5	1	3	0	16	23	9	.190	37
1955—	Brooklyn N.L.	7	223	31	58	95	8	1	9	2	33	38	30	.260	55
	New York A.L.	7	222	26	55	87	4	2	8	3	22	39	25	.248	41
1956—	Brooklyn N.L.	7	215	25	42	61	8	1	3	1	32	47	24	.195	42
	New York A.L.	7	229	33	58	100	6	0	12	2	21	43	33	.253	40
1957—	Milwaukee N.L.	7	225	23	47	79	6	1	8	1	22	40	22	.209	46
	New York A.L.	7	230	25	57	87	7	1	7	1	22	34	25	.248	45
1958—	Milwaukee N.L.	7	240	25	60	81	10	1	3	1	27	56	24	.250	58
	New York A.L.	7	233	29	49	86	5	1	10	1	21	42	29	.210	40
1959—	Los Angeles N.L.	6	203	21	53	79	3	1	7	5	12	27	19	.261	42
	Chicago A.L.	6	199	23	52	74	10	0	4	2	20	33	19	.261	43
1960—	Pittsburgh N.L.	7	234	27	60	83	11	0	4	2	12	26	26	.256	42
	New York A.L.	7	269	55	91	142	13	4	10	0	18	40	54	.338	51
1961—	Cincinnati N.L.	5	170	13	35	52	8	0	3	0	8	27	11	.206	33
	New York A.L.	5	165	27	42	73	8	1	7	1	24	25	26	.255	34
1962—	San Francisco N.L.	7	226	21	51	80	10	2	5	1	12	39	19	.226	39
	New York A.L.	7	221	20	44	61	6	1	3	4	21	39	17	.199	43
1963—	Los Angeles N.L.	4	117	12	25	41	3	2	3	2	11	25	12	.214	17
	New York A.L.	4	129	4	22	31	3	0	2	0	5	37	4	.171	24
1964—	St. Louis N.L.	7	240	32	61	90	8	3	5	3	18	39	29	.254	47
	New York A.L.	7	239	33	60	101	11	0	10	2	25	54	33	.251	47
1965—	Los Angeles N.L.	7	234	24	64	91	10	1	5	9	13	31	21	.274	52
	Minnesota A.L.	7	215	20	42	71	7	2	6	2	19	54	19	.195	36
1966—	Los Angeles N.L.	4	120	2	17	23	3	0	1	1	13	28	2	.142	24
	Baltimore A.L.	4	120	13	24	41	3	1	4	0	11	17	10	.200	18
1967—	St. Louis N.L.	7	229	25	51	81	11	2	5	7	17	30	24	.223	40
	Boston A.L.	7	222	21	48	80	6	1	8	1	17	49	19	.216	43
1968—	St. Louis N.L.	7	239	27	61	95	7	3	11	11	21	40	27	.255	49
	Detroit A.L.	7	231	34	56	90	4	3	8	0	27	59	33	.242	44
1969—	New York N.L.	5	159	15	35	61	8	0	6	1	15	35	13	.220	34
	Baltimore A.L.	5	157	9	23	33	1	0	3	1	15	28	9	.146	29
1970—	Cincinnati N.L.	5	164	20	35	58	6	1	5	1	15	23	20	.213	28
	Baltimore A.L.	5	171	33	50	87	7	0	10	0	20	33	32	.292	31
1971—	Pittsburgh N.L.	7	238	23	56	84	9	2	5	5	26	47	21	.235	63
	Baltimore A.L.	7	219	24	45	65	3	1	5	1	20	35	22	.205	39
1972—	Cincinnati N.L.	7	220	21	46	75	8	1	3	12	27	46	21	.209	49
	Oakland A.L.	7	220	16	46	65	4	0	5	1	21	37	16	.209	45
1973—	New York N.L.	7	261	24	66	89	7	2	4	0	26	36	16	.253	72
	Oakland A.L.	7	241	21	51	75	12	3	2	3	28	62	20	.212	58

Year	Club, League	G	AB	R	H	TB	2B	3B	HR	SB	BB	SO	RBI	Avg.	LOB
1974—	Los Angeles N.L.	5	158	11	36	54	4	1	4	3	16	32	10	.228	36
	Oakland A.L.	5	142	16	30	46	4	0	4	3	16	42	14	.211	26
1975—	Cincinnati N.L.	7	244	29	59	95	9	3	7	9	25	30	29	.242	50
	Boston A.L.	7	239	30	60	89	7	2	6	0	30	40	30	.251	52
1976—	Cincinnati N.L.	4	134	22	42	70	10	3	4	7	12	16	21	.313	22
	New York A.L.	4	135	8	30	38	3	1	1	1	12	16	8	.222	33
1977—	Los Angeles N.L.	6	208	28	48	86	5	3	9	2	16	36	28	.231	31
	New York A.L.	6	205	26	50	84	10	0	8	1	11	37	25	.244	32
1978—	Los Angeles N.L.	6	199	23	52	78	8	0	6	5	20	31	22	.261	38
	New York A.L.	6	222	36	68	85	8	0	3	5	16	40	34	.306	47
1979—	Pittsburgh N.L.	7	251	32	81	110	18	1	3	0	16	35	32	.323	60
	Baltimore A.L.	7	233	26	54	78	10	1	4	2	26	41	23	.232	49
1980—	Philadelphia N.L.	6	201	27	59	81	13	0	3	3	15	17	26	.294	41
	Kansas City A.L.	6	207	23	60	97	9	2	8	6	26	49	22	.290	54
1981—	Los Angeles N.L.	6	198	27	51	77	6	1	6	6	20	44	26	.258	46
	New York A.L.	6	193	22	46	74	8	1	6	4	33	24	22	.238	55
1982—	St. Louis N.L.	7	245	39	67	101	16	3	4	7	20	26	34	.273	49
	Milwaukee A.L.	7	238	33	64	95	12	2	5	1	19	28	29	.269	44
1983—	Philadelphia N.L.	5	159	9	31	49	4	1	4	1	7	29	9	.195	23
	Baltimore A.L.	5	164	18	35	61	8	0	6	1	10	37	17	.213	28
1984—	San Diego N.L.	5	166	15	44	60	7	0	3	2	11	26	14	.265	34
	Detroit A.L.	5	158	23	40	65	4	0	7	7	24	27	23	.253	39
1985—	St. Louis N.L.	7	216	13	40	58	10	1	2	2	28	42	13	.185	38
	Kansas City A.L.	7	236	28	68	90	12	2	2	7	18	56	26	.288	56
1986—	New York N.L.	7	240	32	65	92	6	0	7	7	21	43	29	.271	50
	Boston A.L.	7	248	27	69	99	11	2	5	0	28	53	26	.278	69
1987—	St. Louis N.L.	7	232	26	60	74	8	0	2	12	13	44	25	.259	43
	Minnesota A.L.	7	238	38	64	101	10	3	7	6	29	36	38	.269	56
1988—	Los Angeles N.L.	5	167	21	41	66	8	1	5	4	13	36	19	.246	30
	Oakland A.L.	5	158	11	28	37	3	0	2	3	17	41	11	.177	34
1989—	San Francisco N.L.	4	134	14	28	46	4	1	4	2	8	27	14	.209	21
	Oakland A.L.	4	146	32	44	85	8	3	9	4	18	22	30	.301	31
1990—	Cincinnati N.L.	4	142	22	45	67	9	2	3	2	15	9	22	.317	32
	Oakland A.L.	4	135	8	28	41	4	0	3	7	12	28	8	.207	31
1991—	Atlanta N.L.	7	249	29	63	105	10	4	8	5	26	39	29	.253	52
	Minnesota A.L.	7	241	24	56	96	8	4	8	7	21	48	24	.232	47
1992—	Atlanta N.L.	6	200	20	44	59	6	0	3	15	20	48	19	.220	40
	Toronto A.L.	6	196	17	45	71	8	0	6	5	18	33	17	.230	38
1993—	Philadelphia N.L.	6	212	36	58	90	7	2	7	7	34	50	35	.274	54
	Toronto A.L.	6	206	45	64	105	13	5	6	7	25	30	45	.311	39
1994—	No series played.														

CLUB FIELDING AND PLAYERS USED

Year	Team, League	G	PO	A	E	DP	PB	Fielding Avg.	Players Used	Pitchers Used	PH	PR
1903—	Pittsburgh N.L.	8	210	96	18	5	0	.944	14	5	1	0
	Boston A.L.	8	213	102	14	6	2	.957	13	3	4	0
1904—	No series played.											
1905—	New York N.L.	5	135	78	6	2	0	.973	12	3	1	0
	Philadelphia A.L.	5	129	56	9	2	0	.954	13	3	1	0
1906—	Chicago N.L.	6	159	84	7	4	3	.972	14	4	4	0
	Chicago A.L.	6	162	99	14	2	1	.949	16	4	2	1
1907—	Chicago N.L.	5	144	65	10	6	1	.954	15	4	2	0
	Detroit A.L.	5	138	70	9	2	0	.959	14	4	1	1
1908—	Chicago N.L.	5	135	74	5	4	1	.977	13	4	1	0
	Detroit A.L.	5	131	63	10	5	1	.951	16	5	4	1
1909—	Pittsburgh N.L.	7	182	88	15	3	0	.947	17	6	3	0
	Detroit A.L.	7	183	87	19	4	1	.934	16	5	5	0
1910—	Chicago N.L.	5	132	77	12	3	0	.946	18	7	6	1
	Philadelphia A.L.	5	136	59	11	6	0	.947	12	2	0	0
1911—	New York N.L.	6	162	79	16	2	1	.938	15	5	4	0
	Philadelphia A.L.	6	167	72	11	2	0	.956	14	3	0	1
1912—	New York N.L.	8	221	108	17	4	0	.951	17	5	5	3
	Boston A.L.	8	222	101	14	5	0	.958	17	5	5	1
1913—	New York N.L.	5	135	67	7	1	1	.967	20	5	6	5
	Philadelphia A.L.	5	138	54	5	6	0	.975	12	3	0	0
1914—	Boston N.L.	4	117	62	4	4	0	.978	15	3	3	1
	Philadelphia A.L.	4	111	66	3	4	1	.983	16	6	1	0
1915—	Philadelphia N.L.	5	131	54	3	3	0	.984	16	4	2	2
	Boston A.L.	5	132	58	4	2	0	.979	17	3	3	1
1916—	Brooklyn N.L.	5	142	70	13	2	2	.942	20	7	6	1
	Boston A.L.	5	147	90	6	5	1	.975	20	5	3	1
1917—	New York N.L.	6	153	72	11	3	1	.953	17	6	3	0
	Chicago A.L.	6	156	82	12	7	1	.952	16	5	5	0

Year	Team, League	G	PO	A	E	DP	PB	Fielding Avg.	Players Used	Pitchers Used	PH	PR
1918—	Chicago N.L.	6	156	76	5	7	2	.979	17	4	8	2
	Boston A.L.	6	159	88	1	4	1	.996	15	4	5	0
1919—	Cincinnati N.L.	8	216	96	12	7	0	.963	17	6	3	1
	Chicago A.L.	8	213	116	12	9	1	.965	19	7	6	0
1920—	Brooklyn N.L.	7	177	91	6	5	2	.978	21	7	7	3
	Cleveland A.L.	7	182	89	12	8	0	.958	20	5	12	1
1921—	New York N.L.	8	212	102	5	5	2	.984	13	4	2	0
	New York A.L.	8	210	106	6	8	0	.981	19	8	3	2
1922—	New York N.L.	5	138	70	6	4	0	.972	16	5	3	1
	New York A.L.	5	129	62	1	7	1	.995	17	5	4	0
1923—	New York N.L.	6	159	80	6	8	0	.976	22	8	9	3
	New York A.L.	6	162	77	3	6	0	.988	17	5	4	2
1924—	New York N.L.	7	200	94	6	4	0	.980	21	9	7	3
	Washington A.L.	7	201	99	12	10	1	.962	21	8	8	2
1925—	Pittsburgh N.L.	7	182	89	7	4	0	.980	18	7	5	2
	Washington A.L.	7	180	75	9	8	1	.966	21	6	7	4
1926—	St. Louis N.L.	7	189	99	5	6	0	.983	19	8	6	0
	New York A.L.	7	189	82	7	3	1	.975	19	7	7	2
1927—	Pittsburgh N.L.	4	104	46	6	2	0	.962	21	7	5	1
	New York A.L.	4	108	44	3	4	0	.981	15	4	1	0
1928—	St. Louis N.L.	4	102	36	5	3	0	.965	20	6	6	1
	New York A.L.	4	108	28	6	3	0	.958	16	3	4	0
1929—	Chicago N.L.	5	131	44	7	4	0	.962	19	6	8	0
	Philadelphia A.L.	5	135	40	4	2	6	.978	17	6	3	0
1930—	St. Louis N.L.	6	153	55	5	4	1	.977	21	7	7	0
	Philadelphia A.L.	6	156	41	3	2	0	.985	15	5	3	0
1931—	St. Louis N.L.	7	186	73	4	7	0	.985	21	6	6	1
	Philadelphia A.L.	7	183	69	2	4	0	.992	20	6	8	1
1932—	Chicago N.L.	4	102	40	6	7	0	.959	22	8	6	1
	New York A.L.	4	108	41	8	1	0	.949	16	6	6	1
1933—	New York N.L.	5	141	67	4	5	0	.981	15	5	2	0
	Washington A.L.	5	138	65	4	4	0	.981	10	7	5	1
1934—	St. Louis N.L.	7	196	73	15	2	0	.947	20	8	5	2
	Detroit A.L.	7	195	70	12	6	0	.957	17	6	4	0
1935—	Chicago N.L.	6	164	74	6	5	0	.975	18	7	5	0
	Detroit A.L.	6	165	72	9	7	1	.963	15	5	2	0
1936—	New York N.L.	6	159	62	7	7	0	.969	22	8	10	2
	New York A.L.	6	162	57	6	2	0	.973	16	6	2	2
1937—	New York N.L.	5	129	46	9	5	0	.951	20	7	7	0
	New York A.L.	5	132	47	0	2	0	1.000	17	7	1	0
1938—	Chicago N.L.	4	102	35	3	3	0	.979	20	8	8	0
	New York A.L.	4	108	39	6	4	0	.961	14	4	1	0
1939—	Cincinnati N.L.	4	106	34	4	1	0	.972	18	5	3	2
	New York A.L.	4	111	50	2	5	0	.988	15	7	0	0
1940—	Cincinnati N.L.	7	183	67	8	9	1	.969	23	9	9	1
	Detroit A.L.	7	180	80	4	4	0	.985	20	8	6	0
1941—	Brooklyn N.L.	5	132	60	4	5	0	.980	20	7	6	0
	New York A.L.	5	135	55	2	7	0	.990	18	7	2	1
1942—	St. Louis N.L.	5	135	45	10	3	0	.947	18	6	4	1
	New York A.L.	5	132	45	5	2	0	.973	20	7	4	2
1943—	St. Louis N.L.	5	129	53	10	4	0	.948	20	6	6	1
	New York A.L.	5	135	63	5	3	0	.975	16	5	2	0
1944—	St. Louis N.L.	6	165	59	1	3	1	.996	20	8	7	0
	St. Louis A.L.	6	163	60	10	4	0	.957	22	7	13	1
1945—	Chicago N.L.	7	195	78	6	5	1	.978	25	8	14	3
	Detroit A.L.	7	197	85	5	4	2	.983	26	9	11	1
1946—	St. Louis N.L.	7	186	68	4	7	1	.984	19	7	5	0
	Boston A.L.	7	183	76	10	5	0	.963	26	11	10	3
1947—	Brooklyn N.L.	7	180	71	8	8	2	.969	24	8	19	5
	New York A.L.	7	185	70	4	4	2	.985	24	9	11	0
1948—	Boston N.L.	6	156	54	6	3	0	.972	20	6	8	4
	Cleveland A.L.	6	159	72	3	9	0	.987	23	8	3	0
1949—	Brooklyn N.L.	5	132	40	5	1	0	.972	25	9	11	0
	New York A.L.	5	135	44	3	5	0	.984	20	5	4	2
1950—	Philadelphia N.L.	4	107	35	4	1	0	.973	20	5	6	4
	New York A.L.	4	111	41	2	4	0	.987	18	5	2	2
1951—	New York N.L.	6	156	65	10	4	0	.957	24	9	10	2
	New York A.L.	6	159	67	4	10	1	.982	21	8	5	2
1952—	Brooklyn N.I.	7	192	71	4	4	0	.985	19	6	8	1
	New York A.L.	7	192	66	10	7	1	.963	19	8	6	1
1953—	Brooklyn N.L.	6	154	62	7	3	0	.969	23	10	8	0
	New York A.L.	6	156	60	1	5	0	.995	20	9	7	0
1954—	New York N.L.	4	111	40	7	2	0	.955	15	6	3	0
	Cleveland A.L.	4	106	40	4	2	0	.973	24	7	16	2

Year	Team, League	G	PO	A	E	DP	PB	Fielding Avg.	Players Used	Pitchers Used	PH	PR
1955—	Brooklyn N.L.	7	180	84	6	12	0	.978	22	10	6	1
	New York A.L.	7	180	72	2	7	0	.992	24	9	12	3
1956—	Brooklyn N.L.	7	183	69	2	8	0	.992	21	8	9	0
	New York A.L.	7	185	66	6	7	0	.977	22	8	6	0
1957—	Milwaukee N.L.	7	186	93	3	10	1	.989	23	8	9	2
	New York A.L.	7	187	72	6	5	0	.977	23	9	10	2
1958—	Milwaukee N.L.	7	189	78	7	5	0	.974	19	6	8	5
	New York A.L.	7	191	65	3	5	1	.988	22	9	9	0
1959—	Los Angeles N.L.	6	159	69	4	7	0	.983	24	9	13	4
	Chicago A.L.	6	156	62	4	2	1	.982	21	7	9	2
1960—	Pittsburgh N.L.	7	186	67	4	7	3	.984	25	10	9	2
	New York A.L.	7	183	93	8	9	0	.972	25	10	11	3
1961—	Cincinnati N.L.	5	132	42	4	7	1	.978	24	9	15	1
	New York A.L.	5	135	50	5	1	1	.974	18	6	4	1
1962—	San Francisco N.L.	7	183	67	8	9	1	.969	21	7	7	1
	New York A.L.	7	183	67	5	5	0	.980	18	6	4	0
1963—	Los Angeles N.L.	4	108	31	3	1	0	.979	13	4	1	0
	New York A.L.	4	102	49	1	7	0	.993	20	7	7	0
1964—	St. Louis N.L.	7	189	64	4	6	0	.984	21	8	12	3
	New York A.L.	7	186	82	9	6	3	.968	21	9	8	1
1965—	Los Angeles N.L.	7	180	72	6	7	0	.977	20	7	7	1
	Minnesota A.L.	7	180	58	5	3	0	.979	21	9	7	0
1966—	Los Angeles N.L.	4	102	44	6	4	0	.961	23	8	8	1
	Baltimore A.L.	4	108	33	0	4	0	1.000	13	4	0	0
1967—	St. Louis N.L.	7	183	66	4	3	0	.984	23	10	8	0
	Boston A.L.	7	183	66	4	4	1	.984	25	10	13	1
1968—	St. Louis N.L.	7	186	48	2	7	0	.992	25	10	8	1
	Detroit A.L.	7	186	72	11	4	0	.959	24	9	8	1
1969—	New York N.L.	5	135	42	2	0	0	.989	21	6	4	1
	Baltimore A.L.	5	129	51	4	4	0	.978	21	7	5	3
1970—	Cincinnati N.L.	5	129	50	3	4	0	.984	24	9	13	0
	Baltimore A.L.	5	135	43	5	3	0	.973	21	9	3	0
1971—	Pittsburgh N.L.	7	185	70	3	7	1	.988	25	10	8	1
	Baltimore A.L.	7	183	69	9	2	0	.966	21	10	6	1
1972—	Cincinnati N.L.	7	187	89	5	5	0	.982	22	8	16	2
	Oakland A.L.	7	186	65	9	4	0	.965	23	8	13	8
1973—	New York N.L.	7	195	72	10	3	1	.964	22	7	15	3
	Oakland A.L.	7	198	79	9	8	1	.969	24	8	20	4
1974—	Los Angeles N.L.	5	126	50	6	5	0	.967	19	6	9	2
	Oakland A.L.	5	132	51	5	6	0	.973	20	5	6	4
1975—	Cincinnati N.L.	7	195	76	2	8	0	.993	22	9	8	0
	Boston A.L.	7	196	72	6	6	0	.978	23	10	13	0
1976—	Cincinnati N.L.	4	108	36	5	4	0	.966	16	7	0	0
	New York A.L.	4	104	41	2	6	0	.986	21	7	9	0
1977—	Los Angeles N.L.	6	165	69	1	4	0	.996	25	9	10	1
	New York A.L.	6	168	68	3	2	1	.987	20	7	6	0
1978—	Los Angeles N.L.	6	158	64	7	4	0	.969	23	8	4	0
	New York A.L.	6	159	54	2	9	1	.991	24	8	5	2
1979—	Pittsburgh N.L.	7	186	79	9	11	0	.967	24	9	11	1
	Baltimore A.L.	7	186	85	9	5	0	.968	25	9	23	2
1980—	Philadelphia N.L.	6	161	68	2	8	0	.991	22	10	4	1
	Kansas City A.L.	6	156	72	7	8	0	.970	21	7	3	3
1981—	Los Angeles N.L.	6	156	65	9	6	0	.961	24	10	14	2
	New York A.L.	6	153	55	4	2	1	.981	24	9	10	5
1982—	St. Louis N.L.	7	183	74	7	9	0	.973	22	8	8	3
	Milwaukee A.L.	7	180	81	11	3	0	.960	21	9	2	1
1983—	Philadelphia N.L.	5	132	42	3	3	0	.983	23	8	12	3
	Baltimore A.L.	5	135	51	4	5	0	.979	23	7	13	2
1984—	San Diego N.L.	5	126	40	4	5	0	.976	24	10	4	3
	Detroit A.L.	5	132	52	4	2	0	.979	22	7	10	1
1985—	St. Louis N.L.	7	184	60	2	9	1	.992	24	9	8	2
	Kansas City A.L.	7	186	80	3	3	1	.989	22	6	13	3
1986—	New York N.L.	7	189	63	5	4	0	.981	22	8	11	2
	Boston A.L.	7	188	79	4	7	1	.985	21	8	6	3
1987—	St. Louis N.L.	7	177	69	6	2	1	.976	24	9	4	1
	Minnesota A.L.	7	180	74	3	4	0	.988	24	9	15	0
1988—	Los Angeles N.L.	5	133	36	3	3	1	.983	22	7	11	0
	Oakland A.L.	5	131	43	2	2	1	.989	24	10	4	3
1989—	San Francisco N.L.	4	102	40	4	3	0	.973	24	9	10	0
	Oakland A.L.	4	108	35	1	1	0	.993	19	6	4	0
1990—	Cincinnati N.L.	4	111	42	4	2	0	.975	21	8	6	0
	Oakland A.L.	4	106	46	5	5	0	.968	25	10	8	1
1991—	Atlanta N.L.	7	196	86	5	9	0	.983	25	10	16	1
	Minnesota A.L.	7	202	75	5	6	1	.982	25	9	21	2

Year	Team, League	G	PO	A	E	DP	PB	Fielding Avg.	Players Used	Pitchers Used	PH	PR
1992—	Atlanta N.L.	6	163	68	2	7	0	.991	22	8	7	3
	Toronto A.L.	6	165	47	4	5	0	.981	23	10	8	0
1993—	Philadelphia N.L.	6	157	54	2	5	1	.991	23	10	7	1
	Toronto A.L.	6	159	45	7	5	0	.967	23	10	3	3
1994—	No series played.											

MANAGERIAL RECORDS

AMERICAN LEAGUE

	Series W	Series L	Games W	Games L	T
Joe Altobelli, Baltimore	1	0	4	1	0
Sparky Anderson, Detroit	1	0	4	1	0
Del Baker, Detroit	0	1	3	4	0
Ed Barrow, Boston	1	0	4	2	0
Hank Bauer, Baltimore	1	0	4	0	0
Yogi Berra, New York	0	1	3	4	0
Lou Boudreau, Cleveland	1	0	4	2	0
Bill Carrigan, Boston	2	0	8	2	0
Mickey Cochrane, Detroit	1	1	7	6	0
Jimmy Collins, Boston	1	0	5	3	0
Joe Cronin, Washington, Boston	0	2	4	8	0
Alvin Dark, Oakland	1	0	4	1	0
Jim Frey, Kansas City	0	1	2	4	0
Cito Gaston, Toronto	2	0	8	4	0
Kid Gleason, Chicago	0	1	3	5	0
Bucky Harris, Washington, New York	2	1	11	10	0
Ralph Houk, New York	2	1	8	8	0
Dick Howser, Kansas City	1	0	4	3	0
Miller Huggins, New York	3	3	18	15	1
Hughey Jennings, Detroit	0	3	4	12	1
Darrell Johnson, Boston	0	1	3	4	0
Fielder Jones, Chicago	1	0	4	2	0
Tom Kelly, Minnesota	2	0	8	6	0
Harvey Kuenn, Milwaukee	0	1	3	4	0
Tony La Russa, Oakland	1	2	5	8	0
Bob Lemon, New York	1	1	6	6	0
Al Lopez, Cleveland, Chicago	0	2	2	8	0
Connie Mack, Philadelphia	5	3	24	19	0
Billy Martin, New York	1	1	4	6	0
Joe McCarthy, New York	7	1	29	9	0
John McNamara, Boston	0	1	3	4	0
Sam Mele, Minnesota	0	1	3	4	0
Steve O'Neill, Detroit	1	0	4	3	0
Pants Rowland, Chicago	1	0	4	2	0
Luke Sewell, St. Louis	0	1	2	4	0
Mayo Smith, Detroit	1	0	4	3	0
Tris Speaker, Cleveland	1	0	5	2	0
Jake Stahl, Boston	1	0	4	3	1
Casey Stengel, New York	7	3	37	26	0
Earl Weaver, Baltimore	1	3	11	13	0
Dick Williams, Boston, Oakland	2	1	11	10	0

Total number of managers: (41)

NATIONAL LEAGUE

	Series W	Series L	Games W	Games L	T
Walter Alston, Brooklyn, Los Angeles	4	3	20	20	0
Sparky Anderson, Cincinnati	2	2	12	11	0
Yogi Berra, New York	0	1	3	4	0
Donie Bush, Pittsburgh	0	1	0	4	0
Frank Chance, Chicago	2	2	11	9	1
Fred Clarke, Pittsburgh	1	1	7	8	0
Bobby Cox, Atlanta	0	2	5	8	0
Roger Craig, San Francisco	0	1	0	4	0
Alvin Dark, San Francisco	0	1	3	4	0
Chuck Dressen, Brooklyn	0	2	5	8	0
Leo Durocher, Brooklyn, New York	1	2	7	8	0
Eddie Dyer, St. Louis	1	0	4	3	0
Jim Fregosi, Philadelphia	0	1	2	4	0
Frank Frisch, St. Louis	1	0	4	3	0
Dallas Green, Philadelphia	1	0	4	2	0
Chuck Grimm, Chicago	0	3	5	12	0
Fred Haney, Milwaukee	1	1	7	7	0
Gabby Hartnett, Chicago	0	1	0	4	0
Whitey Herzog, St. Louis	1	2	10	11	0
Gil Hodges, New York	1	0	4	1	0
Rogers Hornsby, St. Louis	1	0	4	3	0
Fred Hutchinson, Cincinnati	0	1	1	4	0
Dave Johnson, New York	1	0	4	3	0
Johnny Keane, St. Louis	1	0	4	3	0
Tom Lasorda, Los Angeles	2	2	12	11	0
Joe McCarthy, Chicago	0	1	1	4	0
John McGraw, New York	3	6	26	28	2
Bill McKechnie, Pittsburgh, St. Louis, Cincinnati	2	2	8	14	0
Fred Mitchell, Chicago	0	1	2	4	0
Pat Moran, Philadelphia, Cincinnati	1	1	6	7	0
Danny Murtaugh, Pittsburgh	2	0	8	6	0
Paul Owens, Philadelphia	0	1	1	4	0
Lou Piniella, Cincinnati	1	0	4	0	0
Wilbert Robinson, Brooklyn	0	2	3	9	0
Eddie Sawyer, Philadelphia	0	1	0	4	0
Red Schoendienst, St. Louis	1	1	7	7	0
Burt Shotton, Brooklyn	0	2	4	8	0
Billy Southworth, St. Louis, Boston	2	2	11	11	0
George Stallings, Boston	1	0	4	0	0
Gabby Street, St. Louis	1	1	6	7	0
Chuck Tanner, Pittsburgh	1	0	4	3	0
Bill Terry, New York	1	2	7	9	0
Dick Williams, San Diego	0	1	1	4	0

Total number of managers: (43)

COMBINED RECORDS FOR BOTH LEAGUES

	Series W	Series L	Games W	Games L	T
Joe McCarthy, Chicago N.L., New York A.L.	7	2	30	13	0
Yogi Berra, New York A.L., New York N.L.	0	2	6	8	0
Alvin Dark, San Francisco N.L., Oakland A.L.	1	1	7	5	0
Sparky Anderson, Cincinnati N.L., Detroit A.L.	3	2	16	12	0
Dick Williams, Boston A.L., Oakland A.L., San Diego N.L.	2	2	12	14	0

Total number of managers: (5)

ALL-STAR GAME

Service

Batting (Individual, Club)

Baserunning

Pitching

Fielding (Individual, Club)

Miscellaneous

Non-Playing Personnel

General Reference

SERVICE

INDIVIDUAL

TWO-LEAGUE PLAYERS

Players participating for both leagues in All-Star Games (57)

Hank Aaron, Dick Allen, Roberto Alomar, Vida Blue, Bobby Bonds, Bob Boone, Jim Bunning, Will Clark, David Cone, Mike Cuellar, Ray Culp, Chili Davis, Bo Diaz, Ron Fairly, Tony Fernandez, Rollie Fingers, Ken Forsch, Phil Garner, Rich Gossage, George Hendrick, Dave Johnson, Doug Jones, Ruppert Jones, Bobby Kelly, Terry Kennedy, Jeffrey Leonard, Johnny Mize, Rick Monday, Bobby Murcer, Eddie Murray, Graig Nettles, Al Oliver, Paul O'Neill, Rafael Palmeiro, Lance Parrish, Larry Parrish, Gaylord Perry, Willie Randolph, Jeff Reardon, Frank Robinson, Cookie Rojas, John Roseboro, Schoolboy Rowe, Nolan Ryan, Steve Sax, Ted Simmons, Bill Singer, Lee Smith, Reggie Smith, Rusty Staub, Johnny Temple, Jason Thompson, Manny Trillo, Frank Viola, Claudell Washington, Bob Welch, Dave Winfield.

PLAYING ON WINNING AND LOSING CLUBS

Most times playing on winning club

17—Willie Mays, N.L., 1955, 1956, 1959 (first game), 1960, 1961 (first game), 1962 (first game), 1963, 1964, 1965, 1966, 1967, 1968, 1969, 1970, 1972, 1973 (one tie—1961, second game).

Hank Aaron, N.L., 1955, 1956, 1959 (first game), 1960, 1960, 1961 (first game), 1963, 1964, 1965, 1966, 1967, 1968, 1969, 1970, 1972, 1973, 1974 (one tie—1961, second game).

Most times playing on losing club

15—Brooks Robinson, A.L., 1960, 1960, 1961 (first game), 1962 (first game), 1963, 1964, 1965, 1966, 1967, 1968, 1969, 1970, 1972, 1973, 1974 (one tie—1961, second game).

YOUNGEST AND OLDEST PLAYERS

Youngest player

19 years, 7 months, 24 days—Dwight Gooden, N.L., 1984.

Oldest player

47 years, 7 days—Satchel Paige, A.L., 1953.

POSITIONS

Most fielding positions played, career

5—Pete Rose, N.L. (second base, left field, right field, third base, first base; 16 games).

Most fielding positions played, game

2—Held by many players.

CLUB

PLAYERS USED

Most players, game

29—N.L., August 9, 1981.

Most players by both clubs, game

56—N.L. (29), A.L. (27), August 9, 1981.

Fewest players, game

11—A.L., July 6, 1942.

Fewest players by both clubs, game

27—A.L. (15), N.L. (12), July 1, 1938.

PINCH-HITTERS

Most pinch-hitters, nine-inning game

8—N.L., July 9, 1957.

Most pinch-hitters by both clubs, game

11—N.L. (7), A.L. (4), July 24, 1973.
    N.L. (7), A.L. (4), August 9, 1981.
    N.L. (6), A.L. (5), July 11, 1967, 15 innings.

Fewest pinch-hitters, game

0—A.L., July 8, 1935.
   N.L., July 9, 1940.
   A.L., July 8, 1980.

Fewest pinch-hitters by both clubs, game

1—A.L. (1), N.L. (0), July 9, 1940.

INDIVIDUAL BATTING

GAMES

Most games played

24—Stan Musial, N.L., 1943, 1944, 1946, 1947, 1948, 1949, 1950, 1951, 1952, 1953, 1954, 1955, 1956, 1957, 1958, 1959, 1959, 1960, 1960, 1961, 1961, 1962, 1962, 1963 (consecutive).
Willie Mays, N.L., 1954, 1955, 1956, 1957, 1958, 1959, 1959, 1960, 1960, 1961, 1961, 1962, 1962, 1963, 1964, 1965, 1966, 1967, 1968, 1969, 1970, 1971, 1972, 1973 (consecutive).
Hank Aaron, N.L., 1955, 1956, 1957, 1958, 1959, 1959, 1960, 1960, 1961, 1961, 1962, 1963, 1964, 1965, 1966, 1967, 1968, 1969, 1970, 1971, 1972, 1973, 1974 (23 games); A.L., 1975 (one game).

Most games by pinch-hitter

10—Stan Musial, 1947 1955, 1959 (first game), 1960, 1960, 1961, 1961, 1962, 1962, 1963 (10 pinch-hit at-bats).

BATTING AVERAGE AND AT-BATS

Highest batting average, career (five or more games)

.500—Charlie Gehringer, A.L., 1933, 1934, 1935, 1936, 1937, 1938 (six games, 20 at-bats).

Most at-bats, career

75—Willie Mays, N.L., 1954, 1955, 1956, 1957, 1958, 1959, , 1959, 1960, 1960, 1961, 1961, 1962, 1962, 1963, 1964, 1965, 1966, 1967, 1968, 1969, 1970, 1971, 1972, 1973 (24 games).

Most at-bats, nine-inning game

5—Held by many players. Last players—Cal Ripken, A.L., July 12, 1994; Ivan Rodriguez, A.L., July 12, 1994; Tony Gwynn, N.L., July 12, 1994.

Most at-bats, extra-inning game

7—Willie Jones, N.L., July 11, 1950, 14 innings.

Most at-bats, inning

2—Jim Rice, A.L., July 6, 1983, third inning.

Most times faced pitcher, inning

2—Babe Ruth, A.L., July 10, 1934, fifth inning.
Lou Gehrig, A.L., July 10, 1934, fifth inning.
Jim Rice, A.L., July 6, 1983, third inning.

RUNS

Most runs, career

20—Willie Mays, N.L., 1954, 1955, 1956, 1957, 1958, 1959, 1959, 1960, 1960, 1961, 1961, 1962, 1962, 1963, 1964, 1965, 1966, 1967, 1968, 1969, 1970, 1971, 1972, 1973 (24 games).

Most runs, game

4—Ted Williams, A.L., July 9, 1946.

Most runs, inning

1—Held by many players.

HITS

Most hits, career

23—Willie Mays, N.L., 1954, 1955, 1956, 1957, 1958, 1959, 1960, 1960, 1961, 1961, 1962, 1962, 1963, 1964, 1965, 1966, 1967, 1968, 1969, 1970, 1971, 1972, 1973 (24 games).

Most hits by pinch-hitter, career

3—Stan Musial, N.L., 1943, 1944, 1946, 1947, 1948, 1949, 1950, 1951, 1952, 1953, 1954, 1955, 1956, 1957, 1958,

1959, 1959, 1960, 1960, 1961, 1961, 1962, 1962, 1963 (24 games).

Most consecutive games batted safely

7—Mickey Mantle, A.L., 1954, 1955, 1956, 1957, 1958, 1959 (second game), 1960, second game. (Pinch-ran in 1959, first game, and received two bases on balls in 1960, first game.)
Joe Morgan, N.L., 1970, 1972, 1973, 1974, 1975, 1976, 1977 (was not on team in 1971).
Dave Winfield, A.L., 1982, 1983, 1984, 1985, 1986, 1987, 1988.

Most at-bats without a hit, career

10—Terry Moore, N.L., 1939, 1940, 1941, 1942 (four games).

Most hits, game

4—Joe Medwick, N.L., July 7, 1937 (two singles, two doubles; consecutive).
Ted Williams, A.L., July 9, 1946 (two singles, two home runs, also one base on balls; consecutive).
Carl Yastrzemski, A.L., July 14, 1970, 12 innings (three singles, one double).

Most times reached first base safely, game

5—Charlie Gehringer, A.L., July 10, 1934 (three bases on balls, two singles).
Phil Cavarretta, N.L., July 11, 1944 (three bases on balls, one single, one triple).
Ted Williams, A.L., July 9, 1946 (two singles, two home runs, one base on balls).

Most hits, inning

1—Held by many players.

SINGLES

Most singles, game

3—Charlie Gehringer, A.L., July 7, 1937.
Billy Herman, N.L., July 9, 1940.
Stan Hack, N.L., July 13, 1943.
Bobby Avila, A.L., July 13, 1954.
Ken Boyer, N.L., July 10, 1956.
Harmon Killebrew, A.L., July 7, 1964.
Carl Yastrzemski, A.L., July 14, 1970, 12 innings.
Rickey Henderson, A.L., July 13, 1982.

Most singles, inning

1—Held by many players.

DOUBLES

Most doubles, career

7—Dave Winfield, N.L., 1977, 1978, 1979, 1980; A.L., 1981, 1982, 1983, 1984, 1985, 1986, 1987, 1988 (12 games).

Most doubles, game

2—Joe Medwick, N.L., July 7, 1937.
Al Simmons, A.L., July 10, 1934.
Ted Kluszewski, N.L., July 10, 1956.
Ernie Banks, N.L., July 7, 1959.
Barry Bonds, N.L., July 13, 1993.

Most doubles, inning

1—Held by many players.

Most doubles driving in three runs, inning

Never accomplished.

TRIPLES

Most triples, career

3—Willie Mays, N.L., 1954, 1955, 1956, 1957, 1958, 1959, 1959, 1960, 1960, 1961, 1961, 1962, 1962, 1963, 1964,

1965, 1966, 1967, 1968, 1969, 1970, 1971, 1972, 1973 (24 games).

Brooks Robinson, A.L., 1960, 1960, 1961, 1961, 1962, 1962, 1963, 1964, 1965, 1966, 1967, 1968, 1969, 1970, 1971, 1972, 1973, 1974 (18 games).

Most triples, game

2—Rod Carew, A.L., July 11, 1978.

Most triples, inning

1—Held by many players.

Most triples driving in three runs, inning

Never accomplished.

HOME RUNS

Most home runs, career

6—Stan Musial, N.L., 1943, 1944, 1946, 1947, 1948, 1949, 1950, 1951, 1952, 1953, 1954, 1955, 1956, 1957, 1958, 1959, 1959, 1960, 1960, 1961, 1961, 1962, 1962, 1963 (24 games).

Most home runs, game

2—Arky Vaughan, N.L., July 8, 1941 (consecutive).
Ted Williams, A.L., July 9, 1946.
Al Rosen, A.L., July 13, 1954 (consecutive).
Willie McCovey, N.L., July 23, 1969 (consecutive).
Gary Carter, N.L., August 9, 1981 (consecutive).

Most home runs by pinch-hitter, game (15)

1—Mickey Owen, N.L., July 6, 1942, eighth inning.
Gus Bell, N.L., July 13, 1954, eighth inning.
Larry Doby, A.L., July 14, 1954, eighth inning.
Willie Mays, N.L., July 10, 1956, fourth inning.
Stan Musial, N.L., July 13, 1960, seventh inning.
Harmon Killebrew, A.L., July 11, 1961, sixth inning.
George Altman, N.L., July 11, 1961, eighth inning.
Pete Runnels, A.L., July 30, 1962, third inning.
Reggie Jackson, A.L., July 13, 1971, third inning.
Cookie Rojas, A.L., July 25, 1972, eighth inning.
Willie Davis, N.L., July 24, 1973, sixth inning.
Carl Yastrzemski, A.L., July 15, 1975, sixth inning.
Lee Mazzilli, N.L., July 17, 1979, eighth inning.
Frank White, A.L., July 15, 1986, seventh inning.
Fred McGriff, N.L., July 12, 1994, ninth inning.

Most home runs as leadoff batter, start of game

1—Frankie Frisch, N.L., July 10, 1934.
Lou Boudreau, A.L., July 6, 1942.
Willie Mays, N.L., July 13, 1965.
Joe Morgan, N.L., July 19, 1977.
Bo Jackson, A.L., July 11, 1989.

Hitting home run in first at-bat (8)

Max West, N.L., July 9, 1940, first inning.
Hoot Evers, A.L., July 13, 1948, second inning.
Jim Gilliam, N.L., Aug. 3, 1959, seventh inning.
George Altman, N.L., July 11, 1961, eighth inning.
Johnny Bench, N.L., July 23, 1969, second inning.
Dick Dietz, N.L., July 14, 1970, ninth inning.
Lee Mazzilli, N.L., July 17, 1979, eighth inning.
Terry Steinbach, A.L., July 12, 1988, third inning.
Bo Jackson, A.L., July 11, 1989, first inning.

Most grand slams, game

1—Fred Lynn, A.L., July 6, 1983, third inning.

Most home runs, inning

1—Held by many players.

TOTAL BASES

Most total bases, career

40—Stan Musial, N.L., 1943, 1944, 1946, 1947, 1948, 1949, 1950, 1951, 1952, 1953, 1954, 1955, 1956, 1957, 1958, 1959, 1959, 1960, 1960, 1961, 1961, 1962, 1962, 1963 (24 games).
Willie Mays, N.L., 1954, 1955, 1956, 1957, 1958, 1959, 1959, 1960, 1960, 1961, 1961, 1962, 1962, 1963, 1964, 1965, 1966, 1967, 1968, 1969, 1970, 1971, 1972, 1973 (24 games).

Most total bases, game

10—Ted Williams, A.L., July 9, 1946.

Most total bases, inning

4—Held by many players.

LONG HITS

Most long hits, career

8—Stan Musial, N.L., 1943, 1944, 1946, 1947, 1948, 1949, 1950, 1951, 1952, 1953, 1954, 1955, 1956, 1957, 1958, 1959, 1959, 1960, 1960, 1961, 1961, 1962, 1962, 1963 (24 games; two doubles, six home runs).
Willie Mays, N.L., 1954, 1955, 1956, 1957, 1958, 1959, 1959, 1960, 1960, 1961, 1961, 1962, 1962, 1963, 1964, 1965, 1966, 1967, 1968, 1969, 1970, 1971, 1972, 1973 (24 games; two doubles, three triples, three home runs.)

Most long hits, game

2—Held by many players.

Most long hits, inning

1—Held by many players.

RUNS BATTED IN

Most runs batted in, career

12—Ted Williams, A.L., 1940, 1941, 1942, 1946, 1947, 1948, 1949, 1950, 1951, 1954, 1955, 1956, 1957, 1958, 1959, 1959, 1960, 1960 (18 games).

Most runs batted in, game

5—Ted Williams A.L., July 9, 1946.
Al Rosen, A.L., July 13, 1954.

Most runs batted in, inning

4—Fred Lynn, A.L., July 6, 1983, third inning.

BASES ON BALLS

Most bases on balls, career

11—Ted Williams, A.L., 1940, 1941, 1942, 1946, 1947, 1948, 1949, 1950, 1951, 1954, 1955, 1956, 1957, 1958, 1959, 1959, 1960, 1960 (18 games).

Most bases on balls, game

3—Charlie Gehringer, A.L., July 10, 1934.
Phil Cavarretta, N.L., July 11, 1944 (also one single, one triple).

Most bases on balls, inning

1—Held by many players.

STRIKEOUTS

Most strikeouts, career

17—Mickey Mantle, A.L., 1953, 1954, 1955, 1956, 1957, 1958, 1959, 1959, 1960, 1960, 1961, 1961, 1962, 1964, 1967, 1968 (16 games).

Most strikeouts, nine-inning game

3—Lou Gehrig, A.L., July 10, 1934.
Bob L. Johnson, A.L., July 8, 1935.
Stan Hack, N.L., July 11, 1939.
Joe Gordon, A.L., July 6, 1942.
Ken Keltner, A.L., July 13, 1943.
Jim Hegan, A.L., July 11, 1950.
Mickey Mantle, A.L., July 10, 1956.
Johnny Roseboro, N.L., July 31, 1961.
Willie McCovey, A.L., July 9, 1968.
Johnny Bench, N.L., July 14, 1970.

Most strikeouts, extra-inning game
4—Roberto Clemente, N.L., July 11, 1967 (consecutive).

Most strikeouts, inning
1—Held by many players.

SACRIFICE HITS AND FLIES

Most sacrifice hits, career
1—Held by many players.

Most sacrifice hits, game or inning
1—Held by many players.

Most sacrifice flies, career
3—George Brett, A.L., 1976, 1977, 1978, 1979, 1981, 1982, 1983, 1984, 1985, 1988 (10 games).

Most sacrifice flies, game or inning
1—Held by many players.

HIT BY PITCH, GROUNDING INTO DOUBLE PLAYS

Most hit by pitch, career
1—Held by many players.

Most grounding into double plays, career
3—Joe DiMaggio, A.L., 1936, 1937, 1938, 1939, 1940, 1941, 1942, 1947, 1948, 1949, 1950 (11 games).
Pete Rose N.L., 1965, 1967, 1969, 1970, 1971, 1973, 1974, 1975, 1976, 1977, 1978, 1979, 1980, 1981, 1982, 1985 (16 games).

Most grounding into double plays, game
2—Bobby Richardson, A.L., July 9, 1963.

REACHING ON ERRORS OR INTERFERENCE

Most times reaching base on catcher's interference, game
1—Paul Molitor, A.L., July 9, 1991.

CLUB BATTING

Highest batting average, game
.436—A.L., July 13, 1954 (39 at-bats, 17 hits).
Lowest batting average, game
.069—N.L., July 10, 1990 (29 at-bats, two hits).

AT-BATS AND PLATE APPEARANCES

Most at-bats, nine-inning game
44—A.L., July 14, 1992.
Most at-bats by both clubs, nine-inning game
83—A.L. 44, N.L. 39, July 14, 1992.
Fewest at-bats, nine-inning game
27—N.L., July 9, 1968 (batted eight innings).
29—N.L., July 9, 1940 (batted eight innings).
    A.L., July 9, 1940.
    A.L., July 13, 1943 (batted eight innings).
    A.L., July 13, 1948 (batted eight innings).
    A.L., July 10, 1962.
    A.L., July 13, 1976.
    N.L., July 13, 1982 (batted eight innings).
    N.L., July 10, 1990.
Fewest at-bats by both clubs, nine-inning game
57—A.L. 30, N.L. 27, July 9, 1968.
Most consecutive batters facing pitcher with none reaching base, game
20—A.L., July 9, 1968. (Jim Fregosi doubled to start game, then 20 consecutive batters were retired before Tony Oliva doubled in seventh inning.)
Most batters facing pitcher, inning
11—A.L., July 10, 1934, fifth inning.
Most batters facing pitcher by both clubs, inning
19—A.L. 11, N.L. 8, July 10, 1934, fifth inning.

RUNS

Most runs, game
13—A.L., July 6, 1983.
    A.L., July 14, 1992.
Most runs by both clubs, game
20—A.L. 11, N.L. 9, July 13, 1954.
Most runs, inning
7—A.L., July 6, 1983, third inning.
Most runs by both clubs, inning
9—A.L. 6, N.L. 3, July 10, 1934, fifth inning.
Most innings scored, game
5—A.L., July 9, 1946; N.L., July 10, 1951; A.L., July 13, 1954; N.L., July 10, 1956; A.L., July 30, 1962; N.L., July 23, 1974; A.L., July 6, 1983; A.L., July 14, 1992; A.L., July 13, 1993; N.L., July 12, 1994 (10 innings).
Most innings scored by both clubs, game
9—A.L. 5, N.L. 4, July 30, 1962.
Most consecutive scoreless innings by one league, total games
19—A.L.; last nine innings, 1967; all nine innings, 1968; first inning, 1969.

EARNED RUNS

Most earned runs, game
13—A.L., July 14, 1992.

Most earned runs by both clubs, game
20—A.L. 11, N.L. 9, July 13, 1954.
Fewest earned runs, game
0—N.L., July 11, 1939; A.L., July 9, 1940; N.L., July 9, 1946; A.L., July 13, 1960; A.L., July 9, 1968; N.L., July 9, 1968; A.L., July 16, 1985; A.L., July 14, 1987; N.L., July 10, 1990.
Fewest earned runs by both clubs, game
0—A.L. 0, N.L. 0, July 9, 1968.

HITS

Most hits, game
19—A.L., July 14, 1992.
Most hits by both clubs, game
31—A.L. 17, N.L. 14, July 13, 1954.
    A.L. 19, N.L. 12, July 14, 1992.
Fewest hits, game
2—N.L., July 10, 1990.
Fewest hits by both clubs, game
8—N.L. 5, A.L. 3, July 9, 1968.

SINGLES

Most singles, game
13—A.L. July 13, 1954.
    A.L., July 14, 1992.
Most singles by both clubs, game
22—A.L. 13, N.L. 9, July 13, 1954.
    A.L. 13, N.L., 9, July 14, 1992.
Fewest singles, game
0—A.L., July 9, 1968.
Fewest singles by both clubs, game
4—N.L. 4, A.L. 0, July 9, 1968.

DOUBLES

Most doubles, game
5—A.L., July 10, 1934.
    A.L., July 12, 1949.
Most doubles by both clubs, game
7—A.L. 5, N.L. 2, July 12, 1949.
    A.L. 4, N.L. 3, July 13, 1993.
Fewest doubles, game
0—Made in many games.
Fewest doubles by both clubs, game
0—July 6, 1942; July 9, 1946; July 13, 1948; July 8, 1958; July 13, 1976.

TRIPLES

Most triples, game
2—A.L., July 10, 1934.
    A.L., July 10, 1951.
    N.L., July 13, 1976.
    A.L., July 11, 1978.
    A.L., July 6, 1983.
Most triples by both clubs, game
3—A.L. 2, N.L. 1, July 11, 1978.
Fewest triples, game
0—Made in many games.

Fewest triples by both clubs, game

0—Made in many games.

HOME RUNS

Most home runs, game

4—N.L., July 10, 1951.
  A.L., July 13, 1954.
  N.L., July 13, 1960.
  N.L., August 9, 1981.

Most home runs by both clubs, game

6—N.L. 4, A.L. 2, July 10, 1951.
  A.L. 4, N.L. 2, July 13, 1954.
  A.L. 3, N.L. 3, July 13, 1971.

Most home runs accounting for all runs by both clubs, extra-inning game

3—N.L. 2, A.L. 1, July 11, 1967.

Fewest home runs, game

0—Made in many games.

Fewest home runs by both clubs, game

0—Made in many games.

Most consecutive games, one or more home runs

9—N.L., 1969, 1970, 1971, 1972, 1973, 1974, 1975, 1976, 1977.

Most consecutive home runs from start of game

2—A.L., July 11, 1989 (Jackson, Boggs).

Most home runs, inning (12 times; *consecutive)

2—A.L., July 6, 1942, first inning (Boudreau, York).
  N.L., July 10, 1951, fourth inning (Musial, Elliott).
  A.L., July 13, 1954, third inning* (Rosen, Boone).
  A.L., July 10, 1956, sixth inning* (Williams, Mantle).
  N.L., July 7, 1964, fourth inning (Williams, Boyer).
  N.L., July 13, 1965, first inning (Mays, Torre).
  A.L., July 13, 1965, fifth inning (McAuliffe, Killebrew).
  A.L., July 13, 1971, third inning (Jackson, F. Robinson).
  N.L., July 15, 1975, second inning* (Garvey, Wynn).
  N.L., July 19, 1977, first inning (Morgan, Luzinski).
  A.L., July 6, 1983, third inning (Rice, Lynn).
  A.L., July 11, 1989, first inning* (Jackson, Boggs).

Most home runs by both clubs, inning

3—N.L. 2 (Musial, Elliott), A.L. 1 (Wertz), July 10, 1951, fourth inning.
  A.L. 2 (Jackson, F. Robinson), N.L. 1 (Aaron), July 13, 1971, third inning.

TOTAL BASES

Most total bases, game

29—A.L., July 13, 1954.

Most total bases by both clubs, game

52—A.L. 29, N.L. 23, July 13, 1954.

Fewest total bases, game

2—N.L., July 10, 1990.

Fewest total bases by both clubs, game

12—A.L. 6, N.L. 6, 1968.

LONG HITS

Most long hits, game

7—A.L., July 10, 1934 (five doubles, two triples).
  A.L., July 6, 1983 (three doubles, two triples, two home runs).

Most long hits by both clubs, game

10—N.L. 5 (one double, four home runs); A.L. 5 (one double, two triples, two home runs), July 10, 1951.
  A.L. 6 (four doubles, two home runs); N.L. 4 (three doubles, one home run), July 13, 1993.

Fewest long hits, game

0—A.L., July 11, 1944; N.L., July 9, 1946; A.L., July 14, 1953; N.L., July 8, 1958; A.L., July 8, 1958; N.L., July 9, 1963; A.L., July 16, 1985; N.L., July 12, 1988; N.L., July 11, 1989; N.L., July 10, 1990.

Fewest long hits by both clubs, game

0—July 8, 1958.

EXTRA BASES ON LONG HITS

Most extra bases on long hits, game

14—N.L., August 9, 1981.

Most extra bases on long hits by both clubs, game

24—N.L. 13, A.L. 11, July 10, 1951.

Fewest extra bases on long hits, game

0—A.L., July 11, 1944; N.L., July 9, 1946; A.L., July 14, 1953; N.L., July 8, 1958; A.L., July 8, 1958; N.L., July 9, 1963; A.L., July 16, 1985; N.L., July 12, 1988; N.L., July 11, 1989; N.L., July 10, 1990.

Fewest extra bases on long hits by both clubs, game

0—July 8, 1958.

RUNS BATTED IN

Most runs batted in, game

13—A.L., July 6, 1983.
  A.L., July 14, 1992.

Most runs batted in by both clubs, game

20—A.L. 11, N.L. 9, July 13, 1954.

Fewest runs batted in, game

0—A.L., July 9, 1940; N.L., July 9, 1946; A.L., July 13, 1960; A.L., July 12, 1966; A.L., July 9, 1968; N.L., July 9, 1968; A.L., July 14, 1987; N.L., July 12, 1988; N.L., July 10, 1990.

Fewest runs batted in, game, both clubs

0—A.L. 0, N.L. 0, July 9, 1968.

BASES ON BALLS

Most bases on balls, game

9—A.L., July 10, 1934.

Most bases on balls by both clubs, game

13—N.L. 8, A.L. 5, July 12, 1949.

Fewest bases on balls, game

0—N.L., July 6, 1933; N.L., July 7, 1937; N.L., July 6, 1938; A.L., July 6, 1942; A.L., July 10, 1956; N.L., July 11, 1967, 15 innings; A.L., July 9, 1968; N.L., July 15, 1975.

Fewest bases on balls by both clubs, nine-inning game

1—A.L. 1, N.L. 0, July 15, 1975.

Fewest bases on balls by both clubs, extra-inning game

2—A.L. 2, N.L. 0, July 11, 1967, 15 innings.

STRIKEOUTS

Most strikeouts, nine-inning game

12—A.L., July 10, 1934.
  N.L., July 10, 1956.
  A.L., August 3, 1959.
  A.L., July 15, 1986.

Most strikeouts, extra-inning game

17—A.L., July 11, 1967, 15 innings.

Most strikeouts by both clubs, nine-inning game

21—A.L. 11, N.L. 10, July 10, 1984.

Most strikeouts by both clubs, extra-inning game

30—A.L. 17, N.L. 13, July 11, 1967, 15 innings.

Fewest strikeouts, game
0—N.L., July 7, 1937.
Fewest strikeouts by both clubs, game
6—A.L. 4, N.L. 2, July 8, 1958.

SACRIFICE HITS

Most sacrifice hits, nine-inning game
3—N.L., July 11, 1944.
Most sacrifice hits by both clubs, nine-inning game
3—N.L. 3, A.L. 0, July 11, 1944.
Fewest sacrifice hits, game
0—Made in many games.
Fewest sacrifice hits by both clubs, game
0—Made in many games.

HIT BY PITCH

Most hit by pitch, game
2—A.L., July 10, 1962.
Most hit by pitch by both clubs, game
2—A.L. 2, N.L. 0, July 10, 1962.
   A.L. 1, N.L. 1, July 15, 1975.
   A.L. 1, N.L. 1, July 19, 1977.
Fewest hit by pitch, game
0—Made in many games.
Fewest hit by pitch by both clubs, game
0—Made in many games.

BASERUNNING

Most stolen bases, career

6—Willie Mays, N.L., 1954, 1955, 1956, 1957, 1958, 1959, 1960, 1960, 1961, 1961, 1962, 1962, 1963, 1964, 1965, 1966, 1967, 1968, 1969, 1970, 1971, 1972, 1973 (24 games).

Most stolen bases, game

2—Willie Mays, N.L., July 9, 1963.
 Kelly Gruber, A.L., July 10, 1990.
 Roberto Alomar, A.L., July 14, 1992.

Stealing home, game

1—Pie Traynor, N.L., July 10, 1934, fifth inning (front end of a double steal with Mel Ott).

Most times caught stealing, nine-inning game

1—Held by many players.

Most times caught stealing, extra-inning game

2—Tony Oliva, A.L., July 11, 1967, 15 innings.

Most stolen bases, game

4—N.L., July 10, 1984.
 A.L., July 10, 1990.

Most stolen bases by both clubs, game

5—A.L. 3, N.L. 2, July 16, 1985.
 A.L. 4, N.L. 1, July 10, 1990.

Fewest stolen bases, game

0—Made in many games.

Fewest stolen bases by both clubs, game

0—Made in many games.

Most left on bases, game

12—A.L., July 10, 1934.
 N.L., July 12, 1949.
 A.L., July 13, 1960.

Most left on bases by both clubs, game

20—N.L. 12, A.L. 8, July 12, 1949.

Fewest left on bases, game

2—N.L., July 13, 1971.
 A.L., July 13, 1971 (batted eight innings).

Fewest left on bases by both clubs, game

4—N.L. 2, A.L. 2, July 13, 1971.

PITCHING

GAMES

Most games pitched

8—Jim Bunning, A.L., 1957, 1959 (first game), 1961, 1961, 1962 (first game), 1963; N.L., 1964, 1966.
  Don Drysdale, N.L., 1959, 1959, 1962 (first game), 1963, 1964, 1965, 1967, 1968.
  Juan Marichal, N.L., 1962, 1962, 1964, 1965, 1966, 1967, 1968, 1971.
  Tom Seaver, N.L., 1967, 1968, 1970, 1973, 1975, 1976, 1977, 1981.

Most consecutive games pitched

6—Ewell Blackwell, N.L., 1946, 1947, 1948, 1949, 1950, 1951.
  Early Wynn, A.L., 1955, 1956, 1957, 1958, 1959, 1959.

GAMES STARTED AND FINISHED

Most games started

5—Lefty Gomez, A.L., 1933, 1934, 1935, 1937, 1938.
  Robin Roberts, N.L., 1950, 1951, 1953, 1954, 1955.
  Don Drysdale, N.L. 1959 (2), 1962 (first game), 1964, 1968.

Most games finished

6—Rich Gossage, A.L., 1975, 1978, 1980; N.L., 1977, 1984, 1985.

INNINGS

Most innings pitched, career

19⅓—Don Drysdale, N.L., 1959 (2), 1962 (first game), 1963, 1964, 1965, 1967, 1968 (eight games).

Most innings, game

6—Lefty Gomez, A.L., July 8, 1935.

GAMES WON AND LOST

Most games won

3—Lefty Gomez, A.L., 1933, 1935, 1937.

Most games lost

2—Mort Cooper, N.L., 1942, 1943.
  Claude Passeau, N.L., 1941, 1946.
  Whitey Ford, A.L., 1959 (first game), 1960 (second game).
  Luis Tiant, A.L., 1968, 1974.
  Catfish Hunter, A.L., 1967, 1975.
  Dwight Gooden, N.L., 1986, 1988.

RUNS AND EARNED RUNS

Most runs allowed, career

13—Whitey Ford, A.L., 1954, 1955, 1956, 1959, 1960, 1961.

Most earned runs allowed, career

11—Whitey Ford, A.L., 1954, 1955, 1956, 1959, 1960, 1961.

Most runs allowed, game

7—Atlee Hammaker, N.L., July 6, 1983.

Most earned runs allowed, game

7—Atlee Hammaker, N.L., July 6, 1983.

Most runs allowed, inning

7—Atlee Hammaker, N.L., July 6, 1983, third inning.

Most earned runs allowed, inning

7—Atlee Hammaker, N.L., July 6, 1983, third inning.

HITS

Most hits allowed, total games

19—Whitey Ford, A.L., 1954, 1955, 1956, 1959, 1960, 1961.

Most hits allowed, game

9—Tom Glavine, N.L., July 14, 1992.

Most hits allowed, inning

7—Tom Glavine, N.L., July 14, 1992, first inning (consecutive).

HOME RUNS

Most home runs allowed, career

4—Vida Blue, A.L., 1971, 1975.
  Catfish Hunter, A.L., 1967, 1970, 1973, 1974, 1975, 1976.

Most home runs allowed, game

3—Jim Palmer, A.L., July 19, 1977.

Most home runs allowed, inning (12 times; *consecutive)

2—Mort Cooper, N.L., July 6, 1942, first inning.
  Eddie Lopat, A.L., July 10, 1951, fourth inning.
  Robin Roberts, N.L., July 13, 1954, third inning*.
  Warren Spahn, N.L., July 10, 1956, sixth inning*.
  John Wyatt, A.L., July 7, 1964, fourth inning.
  Milt Pappas, A.L., July 13, 1965, first inning.
  Jim Maloney, N.L., July 13, 1965, fifth inning.
  Dock Ellis, N.L., July 13, 1971, third inning.
  Vida Blue, A.L., July 15, 1975, second inning*.
  Jim Palmer, A.L., July 19, 1977, first inning.
  Atlee Hammaker, A.L., July 6, 1983, third inning.
  Rick Reuschel, N.L., July 11, 1989, first inning*.

BASES ON BALLS

Most bases on balls, career

7—Jim Palmer, A.L., 1970, 1971, 1972, 1977, 1978.

Most bases on balls, game

5—Bill Hallahan, N.L., July 6, 1933 (two innings).

STRIKEOUTS

Most strikeouts, career

19—Don Drysdale, N.L., 1959, 1959, 1962, 1963, 1964, 1965, 1967, 1968 (eight games).

Most strikeouts, game

6—Carl Hubbell, N.L., July 10, 1934 (three innings).
  Johnny Vander Meer, N.L., July 13, 1943 (2⅔ innings).
  Larry Jansen, N.L., July 11, 1950 (five innings).
  Ferguson Jenkins, N.L., July 11, 1967 (three innings).

Most consecutive strikeouts, game

5—Carl Hubbell, N.L., July 10, 1934; three in first inning, two in second inning (Ruth, Gehrig, Foxx, Simmons, Cronin).
  Fernando Valenzuela, N.L., July 15, 1986; three in fourth inning, two in fifth inning (Mattingly, Ripken, Barfield, Whitaker, Higuera).

HIT BATSMEN. WILD PITCHES AND BALKS

Most hit batsmen, inning or game

1—Held by many pitchers.

Most wild pitches, career

2—Ewell Blackwell, N.L., 1946, 1947, 1948, 1949, 1950, 1951.

Robin Roberts, N.L., 1950, 1951, 1953, 1954, 1955.
Tom Brewer, A.L., 1956.
Juan Marichal, N.L., 1962, 1962, 1964, 1965, 1966, 1967, 1968, 1971.
Dave Stieb, A.L., 1980, 1981.
Steve Rogers, N.L., 1978, 1979, 1982.
John Smoltz, N.L., 1989, 1992, 1993.

Most wild pitches, game

2—Tom Brewer, A.L., July 10, 1956, sixth and seventh innings.
Juan Marichal, N.L., July 30, 1962, ninth inning.
Dave Stieb, A.L., July 8, 1980, seventh inning.
John Smoltz, N.L., July 13, 1993, sixth inning.

Most wild pitches, inning

2—Juan Marichal, N.L., July 30, 1962, ninth inning.
Dave Stieb, A.L., July 8, 1980, seventh inning.
John Smoltz, N.L., July 13, 1993, sixth inning.

Most balks, career

2—Dwight Gooden, N.L., 1984, 1986, 1988.

Most balks, inning or game

1—Bob Friend, N.L., July 11, 1960.
Stu Miller, N.L., July 11, 1961.
Steve Busby, A.L., July 15, 1975.
Jim Kern, A.L., July 17, 1979.
Dwight Gooden, N.L., July 15, 1986; July 12, 1988.
Charlie Hough, A.L., July 15, 1986.

INDIVIDUAL FIELDING

FIRST BASEMEN

Most games played
10—Steve Garvey, N.L., 1974, 1975, 1976, 1977, 1978, 1979, 1980, 1981, 1984, 1985.

Most putouts, career
53—Lou Gehrig, A.L., 1933, 1934, 1935, 1936, 1937, 1938.

Most putouts, nine-inning game
14—George McQuinn, A.L., July 13, 1948.

Most putouts, extra-inning game
15—Harmon Killebrew, A.L., July 11, 1967.

Most assists, career
6—Steve Garvey, N.L., 1974, 1975, 1976, 1977, 1978, 1979, 1980, 1981, 1984, 1985.

Most assists, game
3—Rudy York, A.L., July 6, 1942.
Bill White, N.L., July 9, 1963.

Most chances accepted, career
55—Lou Gehrig, A.L., 1933, 1934, 1935, 1936, 1937, 1938.
Steve Garvey, N.L., 1974, 1975, 1976, 1977, 1978, 1979, 1980, 1981, 1984, 1985.

Most chances accepted, nine-inning game
14—Rudy York, A.L., July 6, 1942.
George McQuinn, A.L., July 13, 1948.

Most chances accepted, extra-inning game
16—Harmon Killebrew, A.L., July 11, 1967.

Most errors, career
2—Lou Gehrig, A.L., 1933, 1934, 1935, 1936, 1937, 1938.

Most errors, game
1—Held by many players.

Most double plays, career
6—Bill White, N.L., 1960, 1960, 1961, 1961, 1963.
Harmon Killebrew, A.L., 1965, 1967, 1968, 1971.

Most double plays, game
3—Stan Musial, N.L., July 8, 1958.

Most unassisted double plays, game
1—Pete Runnels, A.L., August 3, 1959, second inning.
Lee May, N.L., July 25, 1972, third inning.

SECOND BASEMEN

Most games played
13—Nellie Fox, A.L., 1951, 1953, 1954, 1955, 1956, 1957, 1958, 1959, 1959, 1960, 1960, 1961, 1963.

Most putouts, career
25—Nellie Fox, A.L., 1951, 1953, 1954, 1955, 1956, 1957, 1958, 1959, 1959, 1960, 1960, 1961, 1963.

Most putouts, nine-inning game
5—Frankie Frisch, N.L., July 6, 1933.

Most putouts, extra-inning game
7—Juan Samuel, N.L., July 14, 1987, 13 innings.

Most assists, career
23—Billy Herman, N.L., 1934, 1935, 1936, 1937, 1938, 1940, 1941, 1942, 1943.

Most assists, game
6—Willie Randolph, A.L., July 19, 1977.

Most chances accepted, career
39—Nellie Fox, A.L., 1951, 1953, 1954, 1955, 1956, 1957, 1958, 1959, 1959, 1960, 1960, 1961, 1963.

Most chances accepted, game
9—Bill Mazeroski, N.L., July 8, 1958.
Juan Samuel, N.L., July 14, 1987, 13 innings.

Most errors, career
2—Billy Herman, N.L., 1934, 1935, 1936, 1937, 1938, 1940, 1941, 1942, 1943.
Nellie Fox, A.L., 1951, 1953, 1954, 1955, 1956, 1957, 1958, 1959, 1959, 1960, 1960, 1961, 1963.
Willie Randolph, A.L., 1977, 1980, 1981.
Steve Sax, N.L., 1982, 1983.

Most errors, game
2—Billy Herman, N.L., July 13, 1943.
Willie Randolph, A.L., July 8, 1980.

Most double plays, career
4—Billy Herman, N.L., 1934, 1935, 1936, 1937, 1938, 1940, 1941, 1942, 1943.
Bill Mazeroski, N.L., 1958, 1959, 1960, 1960.

Most double plays, game
3—Billy Herman, N.L., July 13, 1943.
Bill Mazeroski, N.L., July 8, 1958.

Most unassisted double plays, game
Never accomplished.

THIRD BASEMEN

Most games played
18—Brooks Robinson, A.L., 1960, 1960, 1961, 1961, 1962, 1962, 1963, 1964, 1965, 1966, 1967, 1968, 1969, 1970, 1971, 1972, 1973, 1974 (consecutive).

Most putouts, career
11—Brooks Robinson, A.L., 1960, 1960, 1961, 1961, 1962, 1962, 1963, 1964, 1965, 1966, 1967, 1968, 1969, 1970, 1971, 1972, 1973, 1974.

Most putouts, game
4—George Kell, A.L., July 10, 1951.
Brooks Robinson, A.L., July 12, 1966, 9⅓ innings.

Most assists, career
32—Brooks Robinson, A.L., 1960, 1960, 1961, 1961, 1962, 1962, 1963, 1964, 1965, 1966, 1967, 1968, 1969, 1970, 1971, 1972, 1973, 1974.

Most assists, game
6—Ken Keltner, A.L., July 13, 1948.
Frank Malzone, A.L., August 3, 1959.

Most chances accepted, career
43—Brooks Robinson, A.L., 1960, 1960, 1961, 1961, 1962, 1962, 1963, 1964, 1965, 1966, 1967, 1968, 1969, 1970, 1971, 1972, 1973, 1974.

Most chances accepted, nine-inning game
7—Ken Keltner, A.L., July 13, 1948.
Frank Malzone, A.L., August 3, 1959.

Most chances accepted, extra-inning game
8—Brooks Robinson, A.L., July 12, 1966, 9⅓ innings.

Most errors, career
6—Eddie Mathews, N.L., 1953, 1955, 1957, 1959, 1960, 1960, 1961, 1961, 1962 (second game).

Most errors, game
2—Red Rolfe, A.L., July 7, 1937.
Eddie Mathews, N.L., July 11, 1960; July 30, 1962.
Ken Boyer, N.L., July 11, 1961, 10 innings.

Most errors, inning
2—Eddie Mathews, N.L., July 30, 1962, ninth inning.

Most double plays, career

3—Frank Malzone, A.L., 1957, 1958, 1959, 1959, 1960, 1960, 1963.
   Brooks Robinson, A.L., 1960, 1960, 1961, 1961, 1962, 1962, 1963, 1964, 1965, 1966, 1967, 1968, 1969, 1970, 1971, 1972, 1973, 1974.
   George Brett, A.L., 1976, 1977, 1978, 1979, 1981, 1982, 1983.

Most double plays, game

1—Held by many players.

Most unassisted double plays, game

Never accomplished.

Most games played

12—Ozzie Smith, N.L., 1981, 1982, 1983, 1984, 1985, 1986, 1987, 1988, 1989, 1990, 1991, 1992.

Most putouts, career

15—Luis Aparicio, A.L., 1958, 1959, 1959, 1960 (first game), 1961 (second game), 1962, 1962, 1963, 1970, 1971.
   Ozzie Smith, N.L., 1981, 1982, 1983, 1984, 1985, 1986, 1987, 1988, 1989, 1990, 1991, 1992.

Most putouts, nine-inning game

5—Chico Carrasquel, A.L., July 13, 1954.

Most assists, career

24—Joe Cronin, A.L., 1933, 1934, 1935, 1937, 1938, 1939, 1941.

Most assists, nine-inning game

8—Joe Cronin, A.L., July 10, 1934.

Most chances accepted, career

38—Joe Cronin, A.L., 1933, 1934, 1935, 1937, 1938, 1939, 1941.

Most chances accepted, nine-inning game

10—Joe Cronin, A.L., July 10, 1934.
   Marty Marion, N.L., July 9, 1946.

Most errors, career

2—Joe Cronin, A.L., 1933, 1934, 1935, 1937, 1938, 1939, 1941.
   Ernie Banks, N.L., 1955, 1957, 1958, 1959, 1959, 1960, 1960, 1961.

Most errors, game

1—Held by many players.

Most double plays, career

6—Ernie Banks, N.L., 1955, 1957, 1958, 1959, 1959, 1960, 1960, 1961.

Most double plays, game

2—Lou Boudreau, A.L., July 6, 1942.
   Marty Marion, N.L., July 9, 1946.
   Eddie Joost, A.L., July 12, 1949.
   Ernie Banks, N.L., July 8, 1958; July 13, 1960.
   Eddie Kasko, N.L., July 31, 1961.
   Luis Aparicio, A.L., July 30, 1962.
   Dick Groat, N.L., July 9, 1963.
   Tony Fernandez, A.L., July 11, 1989.

Most unassisted double plays, game

Never accomplished.

Most games played

22—Willie Mays, N.L., 1954, 1955, 1956, 1957, 1958, 1959, 1959, 1960, 1960, 1961, 1961, 1962, 1962, 1963, 1964, 1965, 1966, 1967, 1968, 1970, 1971, 1972.

Most putouts, career

55—Willie Mays, N.L., 1954, 1955, 1956, 1957, 1958, 1959, 1959, 1960, 1960, 1961, 1961, 1962, 1962, 1963, 1964, 1965, 1966, 1967, 1968, 1970, 1971, 1972.

Most putouts, center fielder, nine-inning game

7—Chet Laabs, A.L., July 13, 1943.
   Willie Mays, N.L., July 7, 1964.

Most putouts, center fielder, extra-inning game

9—Larry Doby, A.L., July 11, 1950, 14 innings.

Most putouts, left fielder, game

5—Sammy West, A.L., July 7, 1937.
   Frank Robinson, N.L., July 9, 1957.
   Joe Rudi, A.L., July 15, 1975.

Most putouts, right fielder, nine-inning game

4—Charlie Keller, A.L., July 9, 1940.
   Enos Slaughter, N.L., July 14, 1953.
   Darryl Strawberry, N.L., July 12, 1988.

Most putouts, right fielder, extra-inning game

6—Roberto Clemente, N.L., July 11, 1967, 15 innings.

Most assists, career

3—Stan Musial, N.L., 1943, 1944, 1946, 1948, 1949, 1951, 1952, 1953, 1954, 1955, 1956, 1962 (second game).

Most assists, center fielder, game

1—Held by many players.

Most assists, left fielder, game

1—Held by many players.

Most assists, right fielder, game

2—Dave Parker, N.L., July 17, 1979.
   Tony Gwynn, N.L., July 14, 1992.

Most chances accepted, career

55—Willie Mays, N.L., 1954, 1955, 1956, 1957, 1958, 1959, 1959, 1960, 1960, 1961, 1961, 1962, 1962, 1963, 1964, 1965, 1966, 1967, 1968, 1970, 1971, 1972.

Most chances accepted, center fielder, nine-inning game

7—Chet Laabs, A.L., July 13, 1943.
   Willie Mays, N.L., July 7, 1964.

Most chances accepted, center fielder, extra-inning game

9—Larry Doby, A.L., July 11, 1950, 14 innings.

Most chances accepted, left fielder, game

5—Samny West, A.L., July 7, 1937.
   Joe Rudi, A.L., July 15, 1975.

Most chances accepted, right fielder, game

4—Charlie Keller, A.L., July 9, 1940.
   Enos Slaughter, N.L., July 14, 1953.
   Darryl Strawberry, N.L., July 12, 1988.

Most errors, career

2—Pete Reiser, N.L., 1941, 1942.
   Joe DiMaggio, A.L., 1936, 1937, 1938, 1939, 1940, 1941, 1942, 1947, 1949, 1950.

Most errors, center fielder, game

2—Pete Reiser, N.L., July 8, 1941.

Most errors, left fielder, game

1—Held by many players.

Most errors, right fielder, game

1—Held by many players.

Most double plays, career

1—Stan Spence, A.L., 1944, 1946, 1947.
   Tommy Davis, N.L., 1962, 1962, 1963.

Most double plays, center fielder, game

Never accomplished.

Most double plays, left fielder, game

1—Tommy Davis, N.L., July 9, 1963.

Most double plays, right fielder, game

1—Stan Spence, A.L., July 11, 1944.
   Darryl Strawberry, N.L., July 10, 1990.

Most unassisted double plays

Never accomplished.

CATCHERS

Most games played

14—Yogi Berra, A.L., 1949, 1950, 1951, 1952, 1953, 1954, 1955, 1956, 1957, 1958, 1959, 1960, 1960, 1961.

Most innings caught, game

15—Bill Freehan, A.L., July 11, 1967 (complete game).

Most putouts, career

61—Yogi Berra, A.L., 1949, 1950, 1951, 1952, 1953, 1954, 1955, 1956, 1957, 1958, 1959, 1960, 1960, 1961.

Most putouts, nine-inning game

10—Bill Dickey, A.L., July 11, 1939.
Yogi Berra, A.L., July 10, 1956.
Del Crandall, N.L., July 7, 1959.
Johnny Bench, N.L., July 15, 1975.

Most putouts, extra-inning game

13—Roy Campanella, N.L., July 11, 1950, 14 innings.
Smoky Burgess, N.L., July 11, 1961, 10 innings.
Bill Freehan, A.L., July 11, 1967, 15 innings.

Most assists, career

7—Yogi Berra, A.L., 1949, 1950, 1951, 1952, 1953, 1954, 1955, 1956, 1957, 1958, 1959, 1960, 1960, 1961.

Most assists, game

3—Lance Parrish, A.L., July 13, 1982.

Most chances accepted, career

68—Yogi Berra, A.L., 1949, 1950, 1951, 1952, 1953, 1954, 1955, 1956, 1957, 1958, 1959, 1960, 1960, 1961.

Most chances accepted, nine-inning game

11—Yogi Berra, A.L., July 10, 1956.
Johnny Bench, N.L., July 15, 1975.

Most chances accepted, extra-inning game

15—Roy Campanella, N.L., July 11, 1950, 14 innings.

Most errors, career

2—Smoky Burgess, N.L., 1954, 1955, 1960, 1960, 1961, 1961.

Most errors, game

1—Held by many players.

Most passed balls, career and game

1—Held by many catchers.

Most double plays, career and game

1—Held by many catchers.

Most unassisted double plays, game

Never accomplished.

PITCHERS

Most games pitched

8—Jim Bunning, A.L., 1957, 1959 (first game), 1961, 1961, 1962 (first game), 1963; N.L., 1964, 1966.
Don Drysdale, N.L., 1959, 1959, 1962 (first game), 1963, 1964, 1965, 1967, 1968.
Juan Marichal, N.L., 1962, 1962, 1964, 1965, 1966, 1967, 1968, 1971.
Tom Seaver, N.L., 1967, 1968, 1970, 1973, 1975, 1976, 1977, 1981.

Most putouts, career

3—Spud Chandler, A.L., 1942.

Most putouts, game

3—Spud Chandler, A.L., July 6, 1942.

Most assists, career

5—Johnny Vander Meer, N.L., 1938, 1942, 1943.

Most assists, game

3—Johnny Vander Meer, N.L., July 6, 1938.
Don Drysdale, N.L., July 7, 1964.
Mickey Lolich, A.L., July 13, 1971.

Most chances accepted, career

5—Mel Harder, A.L., 1934, 1935, 1936, 1937.
Johnny Vander Meer, N.L., 1938, 1942, 1943.
Don Drysdale, N.L., 1959, 1959, 1962 (first game), 1963, 1964, 1965, 1967, 1968.

Most chances accepted, game

4—Spud Chandler, A.L., July 6, 1942.

Most errors, career and game

1—Held by many pitchers.

Most double plays, career and game

1—Held by many pitchers.

Most unassisted double plays, game

Never accomplished.

CLUB FIELDING

NUMBER OF PLAYERS AT POSITIONS

INFIELDERS

Most infielders, game

10—N.L., July 13, 1960 (second game).
N.L., July 14, 1970, 12 innings.
N.L., July 13, 1976.

Most infielders by both clubs, game

18—N.L. 10, A.L. 8, July 13, 1976.
A.L. 9, N.L. 9, July 14, 1992.

Most first basemen, nine-inning game

3—N.L., July 9, 1946.
N.L., July 13, 1960 (second game).
N.L., July 24, 1973.

Most first basemen by both clubs, nine-inning game

5—N.L. 3, A.L. 2, July 9, 1946.
N.L. 3, A.L. 2, July 13, 1960 (second game).

Most second basemen, nine-inning game

3—N.L., July 13, 1960 (second game).
N.L., August 9, 1981.
A.L., July 14, 1992.

Most second basemen by both clubs, nine-inning game

5—N.L. 3, A.L. 2, July 13, 1960 (second game).
N.L. 3, A.L. 2, August 9, 1981.
A.L. 3, N.L. 2, July 14, 1992.

Most third basemen, nine-inning game

3—Held by many clubs.

Most third basemen by both clubs, nine-inning game

5—Occurred many times.

Most shortstops, nine-inning game

3—Held by many clubs.

Most shortstops by both clubs, nine-inning game

6—A.L. 3, N.L. 3, July 13, 1976.

OUTFIELDERS

Most outfielders, nine-inning game

8—N.L., July 24, 1973.

Most outfielders by both clubs, game

14—N.L. 7, A.L. 7, July 8, 1980.

Most right fielders, nine-inning game

4—N.L., July 13, 1976.

Most right fielders by both clubs, nine-inning game

6—N.L. 4, A.L. 2, July 13, 1976.

Most center fielders, nine-inning game

3—Occurred many times.

Most center fielders by both clubs, nine-inning game

5—Occurred many times.

Most left fielders, nine-inning game

3—Occurred many times.

Most left fielders by both clubs, nine-inning game

5—Occurred many times.

Most left fielders by both clubs, nine-inning game

6—N.L. 3, A.L. 3, July 14, 1970, 12 innings.

BATTERY

Most catchers, nine-inning game

3—Occurred many times.

Most catchers by both clubs, nine-inning game

6—Occurred many times.

Most pitchers, game

10—A.L., July 14, 1992.

Most pitchers by both clubs, nine-inning game

18—A.L. 10, N.L. 8, July 14, 1992.

Fewest pitchers, game

2—A.L., July 8, 1935.
A.L., July 6, 1942.

Fewest pitchers by both clubs, game

6—Occurred many times.

Most players one or more putouts, nine-inning game

14—N.L., July 13, 1976; A.L., July 6, 1983; A.L., July 14, 1992.

Most players one or more putouts by both clubs, nine-inning game

25—N.L. 14, A.L. 11, July 13, 1976.
A.L. 13, N.L. 12, July 16, 1985.
A.L. 14, N.L. 11, July 14, 1992.

Most assists, nine-inning game

16—A.L., July 6, 1942.
A.L., August 9, 1981.

Most assists by both clubs, nine-inning game

26—A.L. 15, N.L. 11, July 12, 1949.
A.L. 16, N.L. 10, August 9, 1981.

Fewest assists, eight-inning game

4—A.L., July 9, 1940.
N.L., July 13, 1948.

Fewest assists, nine-inning game

5—N.L., July 10, 1934.
N.L., July 9, 1957.
N.L., July 23, 1969.

Fewest assists by both clubs, nine-inning game

11—N.L. 6, A.L. 5, July 7, 1959.

Most players one or more assists, nine-inning game

10—N.L., July 24, 1973.

Most players one or more assists by both clubs, nine-inning game

19—N.L. 10, A.L. 9, July 24, 1973.

Most errors, game

5—N.L., July 12, 1949.
N.L., July 11, 1961.

Most errors by both clubs, nine-inning game

6—N.L. 5, A.L. 1, July 12, 1949.

Most errors by both clubs, extra-inning game

7—N.L. 5, A.L. 2, July 11, 1961, 10 innings.

Fewest errors, game

0—Occurred many times.

Fewest errors by both clubs, game

0—Occurred many times.

Most consecutive errorless games

11— 1963 through 1973.

Most double plays, game

3—Occurred many times.

Most double plays by both clubs, game

4—Occurred many times.

Fewest double plays, game

0—Occurred many times.

Fewest double plays by both clubs, game

0—Occurred many times.

MISCELLANEOUS

EARLIEST AND LATEST GAME DATES

Earliest date for All-Star Game

July 6, 1933 at Comiskey Park, Chicago.
July 6, 1938 at Crosley Field, Cincinnati.
July 6, 1942 at Polo Grounds, New York.
July 6, 1983 at Comiskey Park, Chicago.

Latest date for All-Star Game

August 9, 1981 at Municipal Stadium, Cleveland.

NIGHT GAMES

First night game

July 13, 1943 at Shibe Park, Philadelphia.

LENGTH OF GAMES

Longest game, by innings

15 innings—at Anaheim Stadium, California, July 11, 1967.

Shortest game, by innings

5 innings—at Shibe Park, Philadelphia, July 8, 1952 (rain).

Longest nine-inning game, by time

3 hours, 10 minutes—at Municipal Stadium, Cleveland, July 13, 1954.

Shortest nine-inning game, by time

1 hour, 53 minutes—at Sportsman's Park, St. Louis, July 9, 1940.

Longest extra-inning game, by time

3 hours, 41 minutes—at Anaheim Stadium, California, July 11, 1967, 15 innings.

GAMES WON AND LOST

All-Star games won

38—National League (lost 26, tied one).
26—American League (lost 38, tied one).

Most consecutive All-Star games won

11—National League, 1972 through 1982.

Most consecutive All-Star games lost

11—American League, 1972 through 1982.

ATTENDANCE

Largest attendance, game

72,086—at Municipal Stadium, Cleveland, August 9, 1981.

Smallest attendance, game

25,556—at Braves Field, Boston, July 7, 1936.

NON-PLAYING PERSONNEL

Most All-Star games managed

10—Casey Stengel, A.L., 1950, 1951, 1952, 1953, 1954, 1956, 1957, 1958, 1959, 1959 (won four, lost six).

Most consecutive All-Star games managed

5—Casey Stengel, A.L., 1950, 1951, 1952, 1953, 1954; also 1956, 1957, 1958, 1959, 1959.

Most All-Star games won as manager

7—Walter Alston, N.L., 1956, 1960, 1960, 1964, 1966, 1967, 1975 (lost two).

Most All-Star games lost as manager

6—Casey Stengel, A.L., 1950, 1951, 1952, 1953, 1956, 1959, first game (won four).

Most consecutive defeats as All-Star manager

5—Al Lopez, A.L., 1955, 1960, 1960, 1964, 1965.

Most consecutive years managing All-Star losers

4—Casey Stengel, A.L., 1950, 1951, 1952, 1953.

UMPIRES

Most games umpired

7—Al Barlick, N.L., 1942, 1949, 1952, 1955, 1959, 1966, 1970.

Most consecutive games umpired

2—Held by many umpires.

GENERAL REFERENCE

RESULTS

Year	Date	Site	Winner	Loser	Score
1933	July 6	Comiskey Park, Chicago	A.L.	N.L.	4-2
1934	July 10	Polo Grounds, New York	A.L.	N.L.	9-7
1935	July 8	Cleveland Stadium, Cleveland	A.L.	N.L.	4-1
1936	July 7	Braves Field, Boston	N.L.	A.L.	4-3
1937	July 7	Griffith Stadium, Washington	A.L.	N.L.	8-3
1938	July 6	Crosley Field, Cincinnati	N.L.	A.L.	4-1
1939	July 11	Yankee Stadium, New York	A.L.	N.L.	3-1
1940	July 9	Sportsman's Park, St. Louis	N.L.	A.L.	4-0
1941	July 8	Briggs, Stadium, Detroit	A.L.	N.L.	7-5
1942	July 6	Polo Grounds, New York	A.L.	N.L.	3-1
1943	July 13	Shibe Park, Philadelphia	A.L.	N.L.	5-3
1944	July 11	Forbes Field, Pittsburgh	N.L.	A.L.	7-1
1945	— Game cancelled due to wartime travel restrictions.				
1946	July 9	Fenway Park, Boston	A.L.	N.L.	12-0
1947	July 8	Wrigley Field, Chicago	A.L.	N.L.	2-1
1948	July 13	Sportsman's Park, St. Louis	A.L.	N.L.	5-2
1949	July 12	Ebbets Field, Brooklyn	A.L.	N.L.	11-7
1950	July 11	Comiskey Park, Chicago	N.L.	A.L.	4-3, 14 innings
1951	July 10	Briggs Stadium, Detroit	N.L.	A.L.	8-3
1952	July 8	Shibe Park, Philadelphia	N.L.	A.L.	3-2, five innings (rain)
1953	July 14	Crosley Field, Cincinnati	N.L.	A.L.	5-1
1954	July 13	Cleveland Stadium, Cleveland	A.L.	N.L.	11-9
1955	July 12	County Stadium, Milwaukee	N.L.	A.L.	6-5, 12 innings
1956	July 10	Griffith Stadium, Washington	N.L.	A.L.	7-3
1957	July 9	Busch Stadium, St. Louis	A.L.	N.L.	6-5
1958	July 8	Memorial Stadium, Baltimore	A.L.	N.L.	4-3
1959	July 7	Forbes Field, Pittsburgh	N.L.	A.L.	5-4
	August 3	Memorial Coliseum, Los Angeles	A.L.	N.L.	5-3
1960	July 11	Municipal Stadium, Kansas City	N.L.	A.L.	5-3
	July 13	Yankee Stadium, New York	N.L.	A.L.	6-0
1961	July 11	Candlestick Park, San Francisco	N.L.	A.L.	5-4, 10 innings
	July 31	Fenway Park, Boston	N.L.	A.L.	1-1 (tie)
1962	July 10	District of Columbia Stadium, Washington	N.L.	A.L.	3-1
	July 30	Wrigley Field, Chicago	A.L.	N.L.	9-4
1963	July 9	Cleveland Stadium, Cleveland	N.L.	A.L.	5-3
1964	July 7	Shea Stadium, New York	N.L.	A.L.	7-4
1965	July 13	Metropolitan Stadium, Bloomington	N.L.	A.L.	6-5
1966	July 12	Busch Memorial Stadium, St. Louis	N.L.	A.L.	2-1, 10 innings
1967	July 11	Anaheim Stadium, Anaheim	N.L.	A.L.	2-1, 15 innings
1968	July 9	Astrodome, Houston	N.L.	A.L.	1-0
1969	July 23	Robert F. Kennedy Memorial Stadium, Washington	N.L.	A.L.	9-3
1970	July 14	Riverfront Stadium, Cincinnati	N.L.	A.L.	5-4, 12 innings
1971	July 13	Tiger Stadium, Detroit	A.L.	N.L.	6-4
1972	July 25	Atlanta Stadium, Atlanta	N.L.	A.L.	4-3, 10 innings
1973	July 24	Royals Stadium, Kansas City	N.L.	A.L.	7-1
1974	July 23	Three Rivers Stadium, Pittsburgh	N.L.	A.L.	7-2
1975	July 15	County Stadium, Milwaukee	N.L.	A.L.	6-3
1976	July 13	Veterans Stadium, Philadelphia	N.L.	A.L.	7-1
1977	July 19	Yankee Stadium, New York	N.L.	A.L.	7-5
1978	July 11	San Diego Stadium, San Diego	N.L.	A.L.	7-3
1979	July 17	Kingdome, Seattle	N.L.	A.L.	7-6
1980	July 8	Dodger Stadium, Los Angeles	N.L.	A.L.	4-2
1981	August 9	Cleveland Stadium, Cleveland	N.L.	A.L.	5-4
1982	July 13	Olympic Stadium, Montreal	N.L.	A.L.	4-1
1983	July 6	Comiskey Park, Chicago	A.L.	N.L.	13-3
1984	July 10	Candlestick Park, San Francisco	N.L.	A.L.	3-1
1985	July 16	Metrodome, Minneapolis	N.L.	A.L.	6-1
1986	July 15	Astrodome, Houston	A.L.	N.L.	3-2
1987	July 14	Oakland Coliseum, Oakland	N.L.	A.L.	2-0, 13 innings
1988	July 12	Riverfront Stadium, Cincinnati	A.L.	N.L.	2-1
1989	July 11	Anaheim Stadium, Anaheim	A.L.	N.L.	5-3
1990	July 10	Wrigley Field, Chicago	A.L.	N.L.	2-0
1991	July 9	SkyDome, Toronto	A.L.	N.L.	4-2
1992	July 14	Jack Murphy Stadium, San Diego	A.L.	N.L.	13-6
1993	July 13	Oriole Park at Camden Yards, Baltimore	A.L.	N.L.	9-3
1994	July 12	Three Rivers Stadium, Pittsburgh	N.L.	A.L.	8-7, 10 innings

Player	Date	Inning	On	Pitcher
Babe Ruth, A.L.	July 6, 1933	3	1	Bill Hallahan
Frankie Frisch, N.L.	July 6, 1933	6	0	Alvin Crowder
Frankie Frisch, N.L.	July 10, 1934	1	0	Lefty Gomez
Joe Medwick, N.L.	July 10, 1934	3	2	Lefty Gomez
Jimmie Foxx, A.L.	July 8, 1935	1	1	Bill Walker
Augie Galan, N.L.	July 7, 1936	5	0	Schoolboy Rowe
Lou Gehrig, A.L.	July 7, 1936	7	0	Curt Davis
Lou Gehrig, A.L.	July 7, 1937	3	1	Dizzy Dean
Joe DiMaggio, A.L.	July 11, 1939	5	0	Bill C. Lee
Max West, N.L.	July 9, 1940	1	2	Red Ruffing
Arky Vaughan, N.L.	July 8, 1941	7	1	Sid Hudson
Arky Vaughan, N.L.	July 8, 1941	8	1	Eddie Smith
Ted Williams, A.L.	July 8, 1941	9	2	Claude Passeau
Lou Boudreau, A.L.	July 6, 1942	1	0	Mort Cooper
Rudy York, A.L.	July 6, 1942	1	1	Mort Cooper
Mickey Owen, N.L.	July 6, 1942	8	0	Al Benton
Bobby Doerr, A.L.	July 13, 1943	2	2	Morton Cooper
Vince DiMaggio, N.L.	July 13, 1943	9	0	Cecil Hughson
Charlie Keller, A.L.	July 9, 1946	1	1	Claude Passeau
Ted Williams, A.L.	July 9, 1946	4	0	Kirby Higbe
Ted Williams, A.L.	July 9, 1946	8	2	Rip Sewell
Johnny Mize, N.L.	July 8, 1947	4	0	Spec Shea
Stan Musial, N.L.	July 13, 1948	1	1	Walt Masterson
Hoot Evers, A.L.	July 13, 1948	2	0	Ralph Branca
Stan Musial, N.L.	July 12, 1949	1	1	Mel Parnell
Ralph Kiner, N.L.	July 12, 1949	6	1	Lou Brissie
Ralph Kiner, N.L.	July 11, 1950	9	0	Art Houtteman
Red Schoendienst, N.L.	July 11, 1950	14	0	Ted Gray
Stan Musial, N.L.	July 10, 1951	4	0	Eddie Lopat
Bob Elliott, N.L.	July 10, 1951	4	1	Eddie Lopat
Vic Wertz, A.L.	July 10, 1951	4	0	Sal Maglie
George Kell, A.L.	July 10, 1951	5	0	Sal Maglie
Gil Hodges, N.L.	July 10, 1951	6	1	Fred Hutchinson
Ralph Kiner, N.L.	July 10, 1951	8	0	Mel Parnell
Jackie Robinson, N.L.	July 8, 1952	1	0	Vic Raschi
Hank Sauer, N.L.	July 8, 1952	4	1	Bob Lemon
Al Rosen, A.L.	July 13, 1954	3	2	Robin Roberts
Ray Boone, A.L.	July 13, 1954	3	0	Robin Roberts
Ted Kluszewski, N.L.	July 13, 1954	5	1	Bob Porterfield
Al Rosen, A.L.	July 13, 1954	5	1	Johnny Antonelli
Gus Bell, N.L.	July 13, 1954	8	1	Bob Keegan
Larry Doby, A.L.	July 13, 1954	8	0	Gene Conley
Mickey Mantle, A.L.	July 12, 1955	1	2	Robin Roberts
Stan Musial, N.L.	July 12, 1955	12	0	Frank Sullivan
Willie Mays, N.L.	July 10, 1956	4	1	Whitey Ford
Ted Williams, A.L.	July 10, 1956	6	1	Warren Spahn
Mickey Mantle, A.L.	July 10, 1956	6	0	Warren Spahn
Stan Musial, N.L.	July 10, 1956	7	0	Tom Brewer
Eddie Mathews, N.L.	July 7, 1959	1	0	Early Wynn
Al Kaline, A.L.	July 7, 1959	4	0	Lew Burdette
Frank Malzone, A.L.	Aug. 3, 1959	2	0	Don Drysdale
Yogi Berra, A.L.	Aug. 3, 1959	3	1	Don Drysdale
Frank Robinson, N.L.	Aug. 3, 1959	5	0	Early Wynn
Jim Gilliam, N.L.	Aug. 3, 1959	7	0	Billy O'Dell
Rocky Colavito, A.L.	Aug. 3, 1959	8	0	Roy Face
Ernie Banks, N.L.	July 11, 1960	1	1	Bill Monbouquette
Del Crandall, N.L.	July 11, 1960	2	0	Bill Monbouquette
Al Kaline, A.L.	July 11, 1960	8	0	Bob Buhl
Eddie Mathews, N.L.	July 13, 1960	2	1	Whitey Ford
Willie Mays, N.L.	July 13, 1960	3	0	Whitey Ford
Stan Musial, N.L.	July 13, 1960	7	0	Gerry Staley
Ken Boyer, N.L.	July 13, 1960	9	1	Gary Bell
Harmon Killebrew, A.L.	July 11, 1961	6	0	Mike McCormick
George Altman, N.L.	July 11, 1961	8	0	Mike Fornieles
Rocky Colavito, A.L.	July 31, 1961	1	0	Bob Purkey
Pete Runnels, A.L.	July 30, 1962	3	0	Art Mahaffey
Leon Wagner, A.L.	July 30, 1962	4	1	Art Mahaffey
Rocky Colavito, A.L.	July 30, 1962	7	2	Dick Farrell
Johnny Roseboro, N.L.	July 30, 1962	9	0	Milt Pappas
Billy Williams, N.L.	July 7, 1964	4	0	John Wyatt
Ken Boyer, N.L.	July 7, 1964	4	0	John Wyatt
Johnny Callison, N.L.	July 7, 1964	9	2	Dick Radatz
Willie Mays, N.L.	July 13, 1965	1	0	Milt Pappas

Player	Date	Inning	On	Pitcher
Joe Torre, N.L.	July 13, 1965	1	1	Milt Pappas
Willie Stargell, N.L.	July 13, 1965	2	1	Mudcat Grant
Dick McAuliffe, A.L.	July 13, 1965	5	1	Jim Maloney
Harmon Killebrew, A.L.	July 13, 1965	5	1	Jim Maloney
Dick Allen, N.L.	July 11, 1967	2	0	Dean Chance
Brooks Robinson, A.L.	July 11, 1967	6	0	Ferguson Jenkins
Tony Perez, N.L.	July 11, 1967	15	0	Catfish Hunter
Johnny Bench, N.L.	July 23, 1969	2	1	Mel Stottlemyre
Frank Howard, A.L.	July 23, 1969	2	0	Steve Carlton
Willie McCovey, N.L.	July 23, 1969	3	1	Blue Moon Odom
Bill Freehan, A.L.	July 23, 1969	3	0	Steve Carlton
Willie McCovey, N.L.	July 23, 1969	4	0	Denny McLain
Dick Dietz, N.L.	July 14, 1970	9	0	Catfish Hunter
Johnny Bench, N.L.	July 13, 1971	2	1	Vida Blue
Hank Aaron, N.L.	July 13, 1971	3	0	Vida Blue
Reggie Jackson, A.L.	July 13, 1971	3	1	Dock Ellis
Frank Robinson, A.L.	July 13, 1971	3	1	Dock Ellis
Harmon Killebrew, A.L.	July 13, 1971	6	1	Ferguson Jenkins
Roberto Clemente, N.L.	July 13, 1971	8	0	Mickey Lolich
Hank Aaron, N.L.	July 23, 1972	6	1	Gaylord Perry
Cookie Rojas, A.L.	July 25, 1972	8	1	Bill Stoneman
Johnny Bench, N.L.	July 24, 1973	4	0	Bill Singer
Bobby Bonds, N.L.	July 24, 1973	5	1	Bill Singer
Willie Davis, N.L.	July 24, 1973	6	1	Nolan Ryan
Reggie Smith, N.L.	July 23, 1974	7	0	Catfish Hunter
Steve Garvey, N.L.	July 15, 1975	2	0	Vida Blue
Jimmy Wynn, N.L.	July 15, 1975	2	0	Vida Blue
Carl Yastrzemski, A.L.	July 15, 1975	6	2	Tom Seaver
George Foster, N.L.	July 13, 1976	3	1	Catfish Hunter
Fred Lynn, A.L.	July 13, 1976	4	0	Tom Seaver
Cesar Cedeno, N.L.	July 13, 1976	8	1	Frank Tanana
Joe Morgan, N.L.	July 19, 1977	1	0	Jim Palmer
Greg Luzinski, N.L.	July 19, 1977	1	1	Jim Palmer
Steve Garvey, N.L.	July 19, 1977	3	0	Jim Palmer
George Scott, A.L.	July 19, 1977	9	1	Rich Gossage
Fred Lynn, A.L.	July 17, 1979	1	1	Steve Carlton
Lee Mazzilli, N.L.	July 17, 1979	8	0	Jim Kern
Fred Lynn, A.L.	July 8, 1980	5	1	Bob Welch
Ken Griffey Sr., N.L.	July 8, 1980	5	0	Tommy John
Ken Singleton, A.L.	Aug. 9, 1981	2	0	Tom Seaver
Gary Carter, N.L.	Aug. 9, 1981	5	0	Ken Forsch
Dave Parker, N.L.	Aug. 9, 1981	6	0	Mike Norris
Gary Carter, N.L.	Aug. 9, 1981	7	0	Ron Davis
Mike Schmidt, N.L.	Aug. 9, 1981	8	1	Rollie Fingers
Dave Concepcion, N.L.	July 13, 1982	2	1	Dennis Eckersley
Jim Rice, A.L.	July 6, 1983	3	0	Atlee Hammaker
Fred Lynn, A.L.	July 6, 1983	3	3	Atlee Hammaker
George Brett, A.L.	July 10, 1984	2	0	Charlie Lea
Gary Carter, N.L.	July 10, 1984	2	0	Dave Stieb
Dale Murphy, N.L.	July 10, 1984	8	0	Guillermo Hernandez
Lou Whitaker, A.L.	July 15, 1986	2	1	Dwight Gooden
Frank White, A.L.	July 15, 1986	7	0	Mike Scott
Terry Steinbach, A.L.	July 12, 1988	3	0	Dwight Gooden
Bo Jackson, A.L.	July 11, 1989	1	0	Rick Reuschel
Wade Boggs, A.L.	July 11, 1989	1	0	Rick Reuschel
Cal Ripken, A.L.	July 9, 1991	3	2	Dennis Martinez
Andre Dawson, N.L.	July 9, 1991	4	0	Roger Clemens
Ken Griffey Jr., A.L.	July 14, 1992	3	0	Greg Maddux
Ruben Sierra, A.L.	July 14, 1992	6	1	Bob Tewksbury
Will Clark, N.L.	July 14, 1992	8	2	Rick Aguilera
Gary Sheffield, N.L.	July 13, 1993	1	1	Mark Langston
Kirby Puckett, A.L.	July 13, 1993	2	0	Terry Mulholland
Roberto Alomar, A.L.	July 13, 1993	3	0	Andy Benes
Marquis Grissom, N.L.	July 12, 1994	6	0	Randy Johnson
Fred McGriff, N.L.	July 12, 1994	9	1	Lee Smith

INDEX

Category	Individual	Club	League
40 Homers, 40 Stolen Bases	182		
30 Homers, 30 Stolen Bases	182		
20 Homers, 50 Stolen Bases	182		
Ruth's 60 in 1927	186		
Maris' 61 in 1961	185		
Two Consecutive Seasons	26		
Month	26	53	
Week	26		
Game	27	53	
Four and Three in Game	28, 179		
Two in Game	28		
25 Multiple-Homer Games	170		
Consecutive and in Consecutive Games	30	55	
Doubleheader	27	55	
One Day			64
Inning	27	55	
Five and Four in Inning		190	
Three Consecutive in Inning		191	
GRAND SLAMS	31	56	65
Eight or More	170		
TOTAL BASES	32	57	65
Yearly Leaders	153		
400 in Season	182		
4,000 or More	171		
LONG HITS	33	58	65
800 or More	171		
EXTRA BASES ON LONG HITS	34	58	65
1,500 or More	171		
RUNS BATTED IN	35	58	65
Yearly Leaders	154		
1,200 or More	172		
Game-Winning RBIs	36	58	
BASES ON BALLS	36	59	66
Yearly Leaders	155		
1,000 or More	172		
Intentional	37	59	66
STRIKEOUTS	37	60	66
Yearly Leaders	157		
1,200 or More	172		
SACRIFICE HITS	39	61	66
SACRIFICE FLIES	40	61	66
HIT BY PITCH	40	62	66
GROUNDING INTO DOUBLE PLAYS	41	62	66
REACHING BASE ON ERRORS	42	62	
REACHING BASE ON INTERFERENCE	42		

BASERUNNING

Category	Individual	Club	League
STOLEN BASES	67	69	71
Yearly Leaders	158		
400 or More	173		
50 Steals, 20 Homers	182		
40 Steals, 40 Homers	182		
30 Steals, 30 Homers	182		
Steals of Home	67	69	
10 or More	173		
CAUGHT STEALING	68	69	71
Caught off Base	68	69	
LEFT ON BASE		69	71

PITCHING

Category	Individual	Club	League
GAMES PITCHED	72		
700 or More	173		
GAMES STARTED	72		
500 or More	173		
GAMES RELIEVED	72		
GAMES FINISHED	73		
COMPLETE GAMES	73	88	91
300 or More	173		
INNINGS	73	88	91
3,500 or More	174		
WINNING PERCENTAGE	74		
Yearly Leaders	159		

Category			Individual					Club	League
GAMES WON								88	91
Career							74		
200 or More							175		
Season							74		
20 and 30-Victory Seasons							75		
Complete List							200		
20 Wins, Five Times							175		
30 Wins, Two Times							176		
Month							74		
Doubleheader							75, 198		
Consecutive							75		
12 Consecutive in Season							199		
SAVES							76	88	
100 or More							176		
GAMES LOST							76	88	91
12 Consecutive in Season							200		
AT-BATS AND PLATE APPEARANCES							77	88	
RUNS							77	88	91
1,800 or More							174		
EARNED RUNS							77	88	91
EARNED-RUN AVERAGE							78	88	91
Yearly Leaders							161		
3.50 or Under, Career							174		
SHUTOUTS							78	88	91
Yearly Leaders							162		
40 or More							176		
CONSECUTIVE SCORELESS INNINGS							79		
1-0 GAMES							79	89	91
10 or More							176		
HITS							80	89	
4,000 or More							174		
No-Hit Games							81	89	91
Complete List							193		
One-Hit Games							81	89	91
Singles							81		
Home Runs							81	89	92
Seven or More Grand Slams							175		
Long Hits and Total Bases							82		
BASES ON BALLS							82	90	92
1,200 or More							176		
STRIKEOUTS								90	92
Career							83		
2,000 or More							177		
Season							83		
Yearly Leaders							164		
Game and Inning							84		
Consecutive							85		
HIT BATSMEN							85	90	92
WILD PITCHES							86	90	92
SACRIFICE HITS							86	90	
SACRIFICE FLIES							87	90	
BALKS							87	90	92

FIELDING

Category	1B	2B	3B	SS	OF	C	P	Club	League
GAMES AND INNINGS	93	96	99	102	105	109	113		
AVERAGE	93	96	99	102	105	109	113	116	121
PUTOUTS	93	96	100	103	106	109	113	116	121
ASSISTS	94	97	100	103	106	110	113	116	121
CHANCES ACCEPTED AND OFFERED	94	97	100	103	107	110	114	117	121
ERRORS	95	98	101	104	107	111	114	118	121
PASSED BALLS						111		119	121
DOUBLE PLAYS	95	99	101	105	108	112	114	119	121
TRIPLE PLAYS							115	120	122
Unassisted	210	210		210				210	210
BASERUNNERS VS. CATCHERS						112			
NO-HITTERS CAUGHT						112			
NUMBER OF PLAYERS AT POSITIONS								10	

MISCELLANEOUS

Category	Individual	Club	League
HISTORIC FIRSTS	123	125	
NIGHT GAMES		127	134

OTHER BOOKS AVAILABLE
FROM THE SPORTING NEWS LIBRARY